Two Steps to Your Best Job Options

300 Best Jobs Without a Four-Year Degree

Fourth Edition

Part of JIST's Best Jobs® Series

Laurence Shatkin, Ph.D.

Also in JIST's *Best Jobs* Series

- ◉ *Best Jobs for the 21st Century*
- ◉ *50 Best Jobs for Your Personality*
- ◉ *150 Best Jobs for a Secure Future*
- ◉ *200 Best Jobs for College Graduates*
- ◉ *150 Best Jobs for the Military-to-Civilian Transition*
- ◉ *50 Best College Majors for a Secure Future*
- ◉ *250 Best-Paying Jobs*

- ◉ *10 Best College Majors for Your Personality*
- ◉ *150 Best Jobs for Your Skills*
- ◉ *150 Best Federal Jobs*
- ◉ *250 Best Jobs Through Apprenticeships*
- ◉ *150 Best Jobs for a Better World*
- ◉ *200 Best Jobs for Renewing America*
- ◉ *200 Best Jobs for Introverts*
- ◉ *150 Best Low-Stress Jobs*

JIST Works
America's Career Publisher®

300 Best Jobs Without a Four-Year Degree, Fourth Edition

© 2013 by JIST Publishing

Published by JIST Works, an imprint of JIST Publishing
875 Montreal Way
St. Paul, MN 55102

E-mail: info@jist.com Website: www.jist.com

Some Other Books by the Author

Quick Guide to College Majors and Careers	*2011 Career Plan*
90-Minute College Major Matcher	*Your $100,000 Career Plan*
Panicked Student's Guide to Choosing a College Major	*The Sequel*

Visit www.jist.com for information on JIST, free job search information, tables of contents, sample pages, and ordering information on our many products.

Acquisitions Editor: Susan Pines

Development Editor: Jeanne Clark

Production Editor: Lori Michelle Ryan

Interior Layout: Jack Ross

Proofreader: Charles A. Hutchinson

Indexer: Cheryl Lenser

Print ISBN 978-1-59357-928-9

E-book ISBN 978-1-59357-937-1

This Is a Big Book, But It Is Easy to Use

This book is designed for people who want to move ahead in their careers and have—or are considering getting—on-the-job training, vocational training, or a two-year degree.

It helps you explore your career options in a variety of interesting ways. The nice thing about this book is that you don't have to read it all. Instead, I designed it to allow you to browse and find information that most interests you.

The Table of Contents will give you a good idea of what's inside and how to use the book, so I suggest you start there. The first part is made up of interesting lists that will help you explore jobs based on pay, interests, education or training level, personality type, and many other criteria. The second part provides descriptions for the 300 jobs that met my criteria for this book (high pay, fast growth, and large number of openings). Just find a job that interests you in one of the lists in Part I and look up its description in Part II. Simple.

How the Best Jobs Without a Four-Year Degree Were Selected

Deciding on the "best" job is a choice that only you can make, but objective criteria can help you identify jobs that are, for example, better paying than other jobs with similar duties. Here is an explanation of the process I used to determine which jobs to include in this book.

I identified 420 major jobs that require less education or training than a bachelor's degree and sorted them from highest to lowest in terms of earnings, growth rate through 2020, and number of annual openings. I then assigned a number to their relative position on each list. The job position numbers on the three lists were then summed, and jobs with the best total scores were put on top, followed by jobs in order of their total scores on down the list. I included the 300 jobs with the best total scores in the book. The first list in Part I is called "The 300 Best Jobs That Don't Require a Four-Year Degree," and it contains the 300 jobs with the best combined scores on all three measures (earnings, growth rate, and number of openings). You can find descriptions for all 300 best jobs in Part II.

I'm not suggesting that the 300 jobs with the best overall scores for earnings, growth, and number of openings are all good ones for you to consider—some will not be. But the 300 jobs that met my criteria cover such a wide range that you are likely to find one or more that will interest you. The jobs that met my "best jobs" criteria are also more likely than average to have higher pay, faster projected growth, and a larger number of openings than other jobs at similar levels of education and training.

Some Things You Can Do with This Book

- ⊙ Identify more-interesting or better-paying jobs that don't require additional training or education.
- ⊙ Develop long-term plans that may require additional training, education, or experience.
- ⊙ Explore and select a training or educational program that relates to a career objective.
- ⊙ Find reliable earnings information to negotiate pay.
- ⊙ Prepare for interviews and the job search.

These are a few of the many ways you can use this book. I hope you find it as interesting to browse as I did to put together. I have tried to make it easy to use and as interesting as occupational information can be.

When you are done with this book, pass it along or tell someone else about it. I wish you well in your career and in your life.

Credits and Acknowledgments: While the author created this book, it is based on the work of many others. The occupational information is based on data obtained from the U.S. Department of Labor and the U.S. Census Bureau. These sources provide the most authoritative occupational information available. The noneconomic job-related information is from the O*NET database, which was developed by researchers and developers under the direction of the U.S. Department of Labor. They, in turn, were assisted by thousands of employers who provided details on the nature of work in the many thousands of job samplings used in the database's development. I used the most recent version of the O*NET database, release 16. I appreciate and thank the staff of the U.S. Department of Labor for their efforts and expertise in providing such a rich source of data. The taxonomy of college majors (the Classification of Instructional Programs) is from the U.S. Department of Education.

Table of Contents

Summary of Major Sections

Introduction. A short overview to help you better understand and use the book. *Starts on page 1.*

Part I—The Best Jobs Lists: Jobs That Don't Require a Four-Year Degree. Very useful for exploring career options! Lists are arranged into easy-to-use groups. The first group of lists presents the 300 jobs that do not require a four-year degree and that have the highest rankings based on earnings, projected growth, and number of openings. More-specialized lists follow, presenting the best jobs by age, gender, level of education or training, personality type, interest area, and more. The column starting at right presents all the list titles. *Starts on page 15.*

Part II—The Job Descriptions. Provides complete descriptions of the jobs that met my criteria for a combination of high pay, fast growth, and large number of openings. Each description contains information on earnings, projected growth, job duties, skills, related job titles, education and training required, related knowledge and courses, and many other details. *Starts on page 127.*

Detailed Table of Contents

Table of Contents

Table of Contents

Table of Contents

300 Best Jobs Without a Four-Year Degree © JIST Works

Introduction

I kept this Introduction short to encourage you to actually read it. For this reason, I don't provide many details on the technical issues involved in creating the job lists or descriptions. Instead, I give you short explanations to help you understand and use the information the book provides for career exploration or planning. I think this brief and user-oriented approach makes sense for most people who will use this book.

Who This Book Is For and What It Covers

This book is designed to help students and adults who want to get ahead or change jobs, but who do not have a four-year college degree and are not planning to obtain one in the next few years.

To create it, I started with the hundreds of major jobs that people typically prepare for with one or more of these credentials: a high school diploma, an associate degree, a postsecondary training program, on-the-job training, or work experience. From these, I selected those with the highest earnings, projected growth rate, and number of job openings. Part I contains lists that rank the jobs according to many criteria, including earnings, growth, openings, education level, and personality type. Part II contains detailed descriptions of all of the jobs.

I think you will find many of the job lists in Part I interesting and useful for identifying career options to consider. The job descriptions are also packed with useful information.

Where the Information Comes From

The information I used in creating this book comes from three major government sources:

- **The U.S. Department of Labor:** I used several data sources from the U.S. Department of Labor, starting with the facts reported by two programs of the Bureau of Labor Statistics. The Occupational Employment Statistics (OES) survey provided the most reliable figures on earnings I could obtain, and the Employment Projections program provided the nation's best figures on job growth and openings. For detailed noneconomic information about the 300 occupations and the job specializations that they subsume,

I drew from a database called the O*NET (Occupational Information Network). The Labor Department updates the O*NET on a regular basis, and I used the most recent one available, release 16.

◉ **The U.S. Census Bureau:** The Current Population Survey (CPS), conducted by the U.S. Census Bureau, furnished most of the data on the demographic characteristics of workers: the proportion of workers in each job who are in various age brackets, are self-employed, or are men and women. The figures for proportions of urban and rural workers are based on OES data.

◉ **The U.S. Department of Education:** I used the Classification of Instructional Programs, a system developed by the U.S. Department of Education, for the names of the educational or training programs related to each job. I linked programs to jobs by following the crosswalk developed jointly by the BLS and the National Center for Education Statistics. Information about the career clusters and pathways linked to each occupation is based on materials developed for the U.S. Department of Education's Office of Vocational and Adult Education.

Of course, information in a database format can be boring and even confusing, so I did many things to help make the data useful and present it to you in a form that allows you to compare occupations easily.

How the 300 Best Jobs Were Selected

The "This Is a Big Book, But It Is Easy to Use" section at the beginning of this book gives a brief description of how I selected the jobs I include in this book. Here are a few more details:

1. I began by creating my own database of information from the government sources listed in the previous section. The government uses one occupational classification scheme across all government sources: the Standard Occupational Classification (SOC). This taxonomy covers about 850 job titles at all levels of education and training. Of these, 533 have outlook information and require up to but not more than a two-year associate degree—including those requiring on-the-job training, work experience in a related field, or postsecondary vocational training.

2. I eliminated four occupations—such as Actors—that have such highly variable earnings that no figures are reported for annual earnings. I eliminated another 32 occupations because no information is available about their work tasks. I removed 36 more occupations because they are expected to shrink in size and offer fewer than 500 job openings per year and therefore cannot be considered good jobs. Finally, I removed 41 jobs because they have annual earnings of less than $22,380, which means that 75 percent of workers earn more than the average worker in these jobs.

3. I ranked the remaining 420 jobs three times, based on these major criteria: median annual earnings, projected growth through 2020, and average number of job openings projected per year.

4. I then added the three numerical rankings for each job to calculate its overall score.

5. To emphasize jobs that tend to pay more, are likely to grow more rapidly, and have more job openings, I selected the 300 job titles with the best total overall scores.

For example, the job with the best combined score for earnings, growth, and number of job openings is Registered Nurses, so this job is listed first even though it is not the best-paying job (which is Air Traffic Controllers) or the fastest-growing job (which is Helpers—Brickmasons, Blockmasons, Stonemasons, and Tile and Marble Setters). Registered Nurses does rank first for the number of job openings.

Understand the Limits of the Data in This Book

In this book, I used the most reliable and up-to-date information available on earnings, projected growth, number of openings, and other topics. As you look at the figures, keep in mind that they are estimates. They give you a general idea about the number of workers employed, annual earnings, rate of job growth, and number of annual job openings.

Understand that a problem with such data is that it describes an average. Just as there is no precisely average person, there is no such thing as a statistically average example of a particular job. I say this because data, while helpful, can also be misleading.

Take, for example, the yearly earnings information in this book. This is based on highly reliable data obtained from a large U.S. working population sample by the BLS. It reports the average annual pay received as of May 2011 by people in various job titles. (Actually, it is the median annual pay, which means that half earned more and half less.)

This sounds great, except that half of all people in that occupation earned less than that amount. For example, people who are new to the occupation or with only a few years of work experience often earn much less than the median amount. People who live in rural areas or who work for smaller employers typically earn less than those who do similar work in cities (where the cost of living is higher) or for bigger employers. People in certain areas of the country earn less than those in others. Other factors also influence how much you are likely to earn in a given job in your area. For example, some industries cluster in certain metropolitan areas (think of Detroit's automobile industry), causing workers there to be more productive and more often unionized, thus earning more.

Also keep in mind that the figures for job growth and number of openings are projections by labor economists—their best estimates of what our nation can expect between now and 2020. Those projections are not guarantees. A catastrophic economic downturn, war, or technological breakthrough could change the actual outcome.

Finally, don't forget that the job market consists of both job openings and job *seekers*. The figures on job growth and openings don't tell you how many people will be competing with you to be hired. At best, in Part II, I can provide a general, non-numerical statement regarding competition in an information topic called "Considerations for Job Outlook." Like earnings, however, competition can vary greatly from one community to another, so you need to research this issue locally for any career goal you're considering. You should speak to people in your community who educate or train tomorrow's workers; they probably have a good idea of how many local people with a background like yours find rewarding employment and how quickly. People in the local workforce can provide insights into this issue as well. Use your critical thinking skills to evaluate what people tell you. For example, educators or trainers may be trying to recruit you, whereas people in the workforce may be trying to discourage you from competing. Get a variety of opinions to balance out possible biases.

So, in reviewing the information in this book, please understand the limitations of the data. You need to use common sense in career decision making as in most other things in life. I hope that, by using that approach, you find the information helpful and interesting.

Data Complexities

For those of you who like details, I present some of the complexities inherent in my sources of information and what I did to make sense of them here. You don't need to know these things to use the book, so jump to the next section of the Introduction if details bore you.

I selected the jobs on the basis of economic data, and I include information on earnings, projected growth, and number of job openings for each job throughout this book. I think this information is important to most people, but getting it for each job is not a simple task.

Education or Training Required

I chose the 300 jobs for this book partly on the basis of the amount of education or training that they typically require for entry. All 300 jobs require some minimum amount of education or training, but for all the jobs, this minimum requirement is never as much as four years of college. In fact, some of the jobs don't even require a high school diploma. I base the educational requirement on ratings supplied by the Bureau of Labor Statistics.

You should keep in mind that some people working in these jobs may have credentials that differ considerably from the level listed here. For example, although Air Traffic Controllers need to have completed only long-term on-the-job training, 29 percent of these workers have a bachelor's degree. More than half of Registered Nurses have a bachelor's or higher degree, and although it is possible to enter this occupation with an associate degree or a diploma from an approved nursing program, career opportunities without the bachelor's are considerably more limited.

Some workers who have more than the minimum required education for their job have earned a higher degree *after* being hired. But others entered the job with this educational credential, and the more-advanced degree may have given them an advantage over other job seekers with less education. Some workers with *less* than the normal minimum requirement may have been hired on the basis of their work experience in a similar job. So don't assume that the one-line statement of "Education Required" in the Part II job descriptions gives a complete picture of how best to prepare for the job. The statements about "Work Experience Needed," "On-the-Job Training Needed," and "Certification/Licensure" provide some additional information. If you're considering the job seriously, you need to investigate this topic in greater detail. Informative sources are listed in the last section of this Introduction.

Earnings

The employment security agency of each state gathers information on earnings for various jobs and forwards it to the BLS. This information is organized in standardized ways by a BLS program called Occupational Employment Statistics, or OES. To keep the earnings for the various jobs and regions comparable, the OES screens out certain types of earnings and includes others, so the OES earnings figures I use in this book represent straight-time gross pay exclusive of premium pay. More specifically, the OES earnings include each job's base rate; cost-of-living allowances; guaranteed pay; hazardous-duty pay; incentive pay, including commissions and production bonuses; on-call pay; and tips. The OES earnings do not include back pay, jury duty pay, overtime pay, severance pay, shift differentials, nonproduction bonuses, or tuition reimbursements. Also, earnings of self-employed workers are not included in the estimates, and they can be a significant segment in certain occupations. The wage estimates are more reliable for occupations with large workforces. When data on annual earnings for an occupation is highly unreliable, OES does not report a figure, which meant that I reluctantly had to exclude a few occupations, such as Actors, from this book.

For each job, you'll find two facts related to earnings, both based on the OES survey:

- ⊙ The Annual Earnings figure shows the median earnings (half earn more, half earn less).
- ⊙ The Earnings Growth Potential statement represents the gap between the 10th percentile and the median. This information answers the question, "If I compared the wages of the low earners to the median, how much of a pay difference (as a percentage of the median) would I find?" If the difference is large, the job has great potential for increasing your earnings as you gain experience and skills. If the difference is small, you probably will need to move on to another occupation to improve your earnings substantially. Because a percentage figure, by itself, might be hard to interpret, I put the figure in parentheses and precede it with an easy-to-understand verbal tag that expresses the Earnings Growth Potential: "very low" when the percentage is less than 25 percent, "low" for 25 percent–35 percent, "medium" for 35 percent–40 percent, "high" for 40 percent–50 percent, and "very high" for any figure higher than 50 percent.

The median earnings for all workers in all occupations were $34,460 in May 2011. The 300 jobs in this book were chosen partly on the basis of good earnings, so their average is somewhat better: $40,330. (This is a weighted average, which means that jobs with larger workforces are given greater weight in the computation.)

Projected Growth and Number of Job Openings

This information comes from the Office of Occupational Statistics and Employment Projections, a program within the BLS that develops information about projected trends in the nation's labor market for the next 10 years. The most recent projections available cover the years from 2010 to 2020. The projections are based on information about people moving into and out of occupations. The BLS uses data from various sources in projecting the growth and number of openings for each job title: Some data comes from the Census Bureau's Current Population Survey and some comes from an Occupational Employment Statistics (OES) survey. In making the projections, the BLS economists assumed that there will be no major war, depression, or other economic upheaval. They also assumed that recessions may occur during the decade covered by these projections, as would be consistent with the pattern of business cycles the United States has experienced for several decades. However, because their projections cover 10 years, the figures for job growth and openings are intended to provide an average of both the good times and the bad times.

While salary figures are fairly straightforward, you may not know what to make of job-growth figures. For example, is projected growth of 15 percent good or bad? Keep in mind that the average (mean) growth projected for all occupations by the BLS is 14.3 percent. One-quarter of the occupations has a growth projection of 5 percent or lower. Growth of 11.5 percent is the median, meaning that half of the occupations have more, half less. Only one-quarter of the occupations has growth projected at 19 percent or more.

Because the jobs in this book were selected as "best" partly on the basis of job growth, their mean growth is 14.6 percent, which is slightly better than the mean for all jobs. Among these 300 jobs, the job ranked 100th by projected growth has a figure of 18.5 percent, the job ranked 150th (the median) has a projected growth of 14.5 percent, and the job ranked 200th has a projected growth of 10 percent.

The average number of job openings for the 300 best jobs—8,925—is significantly lower than the national average of about 35,000 openings for all occupations. But you should not be surprised by this; most of the jobs with a very large number of openings are low-skill jobs with rapid turnover, such as fast-food workers. The jobs in this book tend to require higher skills and are subject to slower turnover. Among them, the job ranked 100th for job openings has a figure of about 6,000 annual openings, the job ranked 150th (the median) has about 3,300 openings projected, and the job ranked 200th has about 1,700 openings projected.

Perhaps you're wondering why I present figures on both job growth *and* number of openings. Aren't these two ways of saying the same thing? Actually, you need to know both. Consider the occupation Pile-Driver Operators, which is projected to grow at the impressive rate of 36.6 percent. There should be lots of opportunities in such a fast-growing job, right? Not exactly. This is a small occupation, with only about 4,000 people currently employed. So, even though it is growing rapidly, it will not create many new jobs (about 200 per year). Now consider Farmers, Ranchers, and Other Agricultural Managers. Because technology allows farms to produce ever-larger output with fewer workers, many farmers are going out of business. As a result, this occupation is not growing at all; in fact, BLS projects that it will shrink by 8.3 percent. Nevertheless, this is a huge occupation that employs more than 1 million workers. So, even though the workforce size will shrink, the occupation is expected to take on 23,450 new workers each year through job turnover: new workers replacing existing workers who move on to other jobs, retire, or die. That's why I base my selection of the best jobs on both of these economic indicators and why you should pay attention to both when you scan the lists of best jobs.

Other Job Characteristics

In some of the lists in this book, two or more occupations have identical figures for a certain characteristic. Usually these are unrelated occupations, and the tie is a coincidence. For example, Dental Assistants and Segmental Pavers both have projected growth of 30.8 percent. On the other hand, in lists based on figures derived from the Census Bureau, the ties sometimes occur between related occupations and are not coincidental. This happens when the Census Bureau lumps two or more occupations together, reporting them under a single title. For example, the Census Bureau reports data about the age of workers for a single occupation called Helpers—Construction Trades rather than separately for Helpers—Carpenters, Helpers—Electricians, and several related jobs. As a result, you'll find these separate occupations ordered alphabetically but otherwise tied in the list of jobs with the highest percentage of workers age 16–24. You may notice similar figure-sharing among related jobs where I list the percentages of male and female workers.

Information in the Job Descriptions

For the job descriptions in Part II, I used the same government sources as for the lists in Part I. I explain how I interpreted the data from these various sources later in this Introduction, in the section "Part II: The Job Descriptions."

Part I: The Best Jobs Lists

There are 71 separate lists in Part I of this book—look in the table of contents for a complete list of the lists. The lists are not difficult to understand because they have clear titles and are organized into groupings of related lists.

Depending on your situation, some of the job lists in Part I will interest you more than others. For example, if you are young, you may be interested to learn the highest-paying jobs that employ high percentages of workers age 16–24. Other lists organize jobs by personality type, by level of education, and in other ways that you might find helpful in exploring your career options.

Whatever your situation, I suggest you use the lists that make sense for you to help explore career options. Following are the names of each group of lists along with short comments on each group. You will find additional information in a brief introduction provided at the beginning of each group of lists in Part I.

Here is an overview of each major group of lists you will find in Part I.

Best Jobs Overall: Lists of Jobs with the Highest Pay, Fastest Growth, and Most Openings

Four lists are in this group, and they are the ones that most people want to see first. The first list presents all 300 job titles in order of their combined scores for earnings, growth, and number of job openings. Three more lists in this group present the 100 jobs with the highest earnings, the 100 jobs projected to grow most rapidly, and the 100 jobs with the most openings.

Best Jobs Lists by Demographic

This group of lists presents interesting information for a variety of types of people based on data from the Census Bureau and the OES survey. The lists are arranged into groups for workers age 16–24, workers age 55 and older, self-employed workers, women, men, urban workers, and rural workers. I created five lists for each group, basing the last four on the information in the first list:

- ⊙ Jobs having the highest percentage of people of each type
- ⊙ The 25 jobs with the best combined scores for earnings, growth, and number of openings
- ⊙ The 25 jobs with the highest earnings
- ⊙ The 25 jobs with the highest growth rates
- ⊙ The 25 jobs with the largest number of openings

Best Jobs Lists Based on Levels of Education and Experience

The information about entry requirements is derived from the Department of Labor's Office of Occupational Statistics and Employment Projections. I put each of the 300 job titles into one of six lists based on the education, training, or experience required for entry. Jobs within these lists are presented in order of their total combined scores for earnings, growth, and number of openings. The lists include jobs with these entry requirements:

- ⊙ Short-term on-the-job training
- ⊙ Moderate-term on-the-job training
- ⊙ Long-term on-the-job training
- ⊙ Work experience in a related job
- ⊙ Postsecondary vocational training
- ⊙ Associate degree

Understand that some jobs on the lists require additional preparation beyond the kind on which the list is based. For example, some of the jobs that require an associate degree expect new hires to get additional on-the-job training. Some jobs that provide on-the-job training require applicants to have some previous college course work or work experience in a related job. Footnotes identify these additional requirements. On all these lists, it is assumed that a high school diploma is required, but a few exceptions are identified in footnotes.

Best Jobs Lists Based on Career Clusters

These lists organize the 300 jobs into the 16 career clusters that were developed by the U.S. Department of Education in 1999 and that are used by many educational institutions and career information resources to divide up the world of work and the educational and training programs that prepare for careers. Because a single occupation may be open to people who come out of several different educational or training programs, you will find some jobs that appear on the lists for two or more clusters. Here are the 16 interest career clusters used in these lists: Agriculture, Food, and Natural Resources; Architecture and Construction; Arts, Audio/Visual Technology, and Communication; Business, Management, and Administration; Education and Training; Finance; Government and Public Administration; Health Science; Hospitality and Tourism; Human Services; Information Technology; Law, Public Safety, Corrections, and Security; Manufacturing; Marketing, Sales, and Service; Science, Technology, Engineering, and Mathematics; and Transportation, Distribution, and Logistics. Some career resources use slightly different names for some of these clusters; I used the same titles as the online O*NET database (www.onetonline.org/find/career). Within each cluster's list, the jobs are ranked by their combined scores for earnings, growth, and number of openings.

Best Jobs Lists Based on Personality Types

These lists organize the 300 jobs into six personality types: Realistic, Investigative, Artistic, Social, Enterprising, and Conventional. If those terms don't mean a lot to you, you can find their definitions in the introduction to the lists. The jobs within each list are presented in order of their total scores for earnings, growth, and number of openings.

Bonus Lists: Jobs Employing a High Percentage of People Without a Four-Year Degree

The Department of Labor uses data from the Census Bureau to estimate, for each occupation, the percentages of workers at various education levels. These two lists show jobs in which few workers hold a bachelor's degree. The first list includes all the jobs from the 300 in which more than 90 percent of the workers do not hold a four-year degree. The second list shows the best 50 jobs from this set, sorted by their total scores for earnings, growth, and number of openings.

Bonus Lists: Jobs with the Greatest Changes in Outlook Since the Previous Edition

These two lists show the jobs that have had the greatest revisions to their job-growth projections since the previous edition of this book. One identifies the 25 jobs with the greatest increase in job-growth projection, and the other identifies the 25 jobs with the greatest decrease.

Part II: The Job Descriptions

This part of the book provides brief but information-packed descriptions of the jobs that met my criteria for this book. The descriptions in Part II are presented in alphabetical order by job title. This makes it easy to look up any job you find in Part I that you want to learn more about.

I used the most current information from several government sources to create the descriptions. I designed the descriptions to be easy to understand, and the sample that follows—with an explanation of each of its component parts—will help you better understand and use the descriptions.

- ⊙ **Job Title:** This is the job title for the job as defined by the U.S. Department of Labor and used in its Standard Occupational Classification (SOC).

- ⊙ **Data Elements:** The information on earnings, earnings growth potential, growth, annual openings, and percentage of self-employed workers comes from various government databases, as explained earlier in this Introduction.

- ⊙ **Considerations for Job Outlook:** This information explains some factors that are expected to affect job opportunities and which kinds of job seekers are most likely to find work. In a few cases, this information was not available and the entry simply says how the job compares to others in terms of projected growth. The content is derived from the Employment Projections Office of the Bureau of Labor Statistics.

- ⊙ **Job Specializations:** Thirty-nine of the jobs described in Part II contain specializations within the larger job category being described. These 105 specialized titles are based on the classification scheme used in the O*NET database. When specializations exist, some information topics (such as personality types and skills) are available only for the specializations and not for the "parent" occupation.

- ⊙ **Summary Description and Tasks:** The bold sentence provides a summary description of the occupation. It is followed by a listing of tasks that are generally performed by people who work in this job. This information comes from the O*NET database but where necessary has been edited to avoid exceeding 2,200 characters.

- ⊙ **Education/Training Required:** This is the level of education normally required for entry to the occupation, as identified by the Department of Labor.

- ⊙ **Education and Training Program(s):** This part of the job description provides the name of the educational or training program or programs for the job. It will help you identify sources of formal or informal training for a job that interests you.

⊙ **Knowledge/Courses:** This entry can help you understand the most important knowledge areas that are required for a job and the types of courses or programs you will likely need to take to prepare for it. For each job, I identified the highest-rated knowledge area in the O*NET database, so every job has at least one listed. I identified any additional knowledge area with a rating that was higher than the average rating for that knowledge area for all jobs. I listed as many as six knowledge areas, with definitions, in descending order.

Job Title →

Library Technicians

Data Elements →

⊙ Annual Earnings: $30,430
⊙ Earnings Growth Potential: Medium (39.8%)
⊙ Growth: 8.8%
⊙ Annual Job Openings: 5,950
⊙ Self-Employed: 0.0%

Considerations for Job Outlook →

Considerations for Job Outlook: Electronic information systems have simplified some tasks, allowing them to be performed by technicians and assistants, rather than librarians. Library technicians and assistants earn less than librarians; so as more libraries face budget issues, technicians and assistants will be increasingly used as a lower-cost method of providing library services.

Summary Description and Tasks →

Assist librarians by helping readers in the use of library catalogs, databases, and indexes to locate books and other materials and by answering questions that require only brief consultation of standard reference. Help patrons find and use library resources, such as reference materials, audiovisual equipment, computers, and other electronic resources, and provide technical assistance when needed. Answer routine telephone or in-person reference inquiries, referring patrons to librarians for further assistance when necessary. Process print and nonprint library materials to prepare them for inclusion in library collections. Reserve, circulate, renew, and discharge books and other materials. Catalogue and sort books and other print and nonprint materials according to procedure, and return them to shelves, files, or other designated storage areas. Provide assistance to teachers and students by locating materials and helping to complete special projects. Organize and maintain periodicals and reference materials. Deliver and retrieve items throughout the library by hand or using pushcart. Maintain and troubleshoot problems with library equipment including computers, photocopiers, and audiovisual equipment. Train other staff, volunteers, or student assistants, and schedule and supervise their work. Order all print and nonprint library materials, checking prices, figuring costs, preparing order slips, and making payments. Process interlibrary loans for patrons. Enter and update patrons' records on computers. Retrieve information from central databases for storage in a library's computers. Prepare volumes for binding. Verify bibliographical data for materials, including author, title, publisher, publication date, and edition. Review subject matter of materials to be classified, and select classification numbers and headings according to classification systems. Issue identification cards to borrowers. Send out notices about lost or overdue books. Collect fines, and respond to complaints about fines. Compile and maintain records relating to circulation, materials, and equipment.

Education/Training Required, Education and Training Program(s), Knowledge/Courses, Work Experience Needed, On-the-Job Training Needed, Certification/Licensure →

Education/Training Required: Postsecondary vocational training. **Education and Training Program:** Library and Archives Assisting. **Knowledge/Courses—Clerical Practices:** Administrative and clerical procedures and systems such as word processing, managing files and records, stenography and transcription, designing forms, and other office procedures and terminology. **Computers and Electronics:** Circuit boards, processors, chips, electronic equipment, and computer hardware and software, including applications and programming. **Law and Government:** Laws, legal codes, court procedures, precedents, government regulations, executive orders, agency rules, and the democratic political process. **Economics and Accounting:** Economic and accounting principles and practices, the financial markets, banking, and the analysis and reporting of financial data. **English Language:** The structure and content of the English language including the meaning and spelling of words, rules of composition, and grammar. **Work Experience Needed:** None. **On-the-Job Training Needed:** None. **Certification/Licensure:** None.

Personality Type, Career Cluster(s), Career Pathway(s) →

Personality Type: Conventional-Social-Enterprising. **Career Cluster:** 05 Education and Training. **Career Pathway:** 05.2 Professional Support Services. **Other Jobs in This Pathway:** Educational, Guidance, School, and Vocational Counselors; Librarians; Library Assistants, Clerical; Library Science Teachers, Postsecondary; Postsecondary Teachers, All Other.

Skills →

Skills—Service Orientation: Actively looking for ways to help people. **Programming:** Writing computer programs for various purposes. **Equipment Maintenance:** Performing routine maintenance on equipment and determining when and what kind of maintenance is needed. **Management of Material Resources:** Obtaining and seeing to the appropriate use of equipment, facilities, and materials needed to do certain work. **Reading Comprehension:** Understanding written sentences and paragraphs in work-related documents. **Management of Personnel Resources:** Motivating, developing, and directing people as they work, identifying the best people for the job.

Work Environment →

Work Environment: Indoors; sitting; repetitive motions.

- **Work Experience Needed:** This is the amount of experience in a related job that is usually required to enter the occupation. For example, many supervisory positions require experience in the kind of work being supervised.

- **On-the-Job Training Needed:** This is the amount of training that new workers need to get before they attain competency in the occupation. Short-term on-the-job training takes one month or less. Moderate-term training takes between one month and one year. Long-term training takes more than a year. For some occupations, an apprenticeship is the normal route; these usually take several years.

- **Certification/Licensure:** This statement indicates whether a certificate or license is required or helpful for entry to the occupation (or perhaps a specialization) in most states. I don't bother to note when an ordinary driver's license is needed or when certification is the usual outcome of an apprenticeship. Keep in mind that this information is a generalization that describes the whole nation and the full range of specializations within the occupation. Sometimes licensure is required or waived in a few individual states or for a highly specialized niche within the occupation.

- **Personality Type:** Each job description includes the name of the personality types that the O*NET links to the job. You'll find a primary personality type and as many as two secondary types. You can find more information on the personality types as well as a brief definition of each type in the introduction to the lists of jobs based on personality types in Part I.

- **Career Cluster(s)** and **Career Pathway(s):** This information cross-references the 16 career clusters developed by the U.S. Department of Education and used in a variety of educational institutions and career information systems. I identify the cluster and pathway (sometimes more than one) that the job fits into. I also identify other jobs in the same pathway(s). This information will help you discover other job titles that have similar interests, require similar skills, or need similar secondary school preparation.

- **Skills:** The O*NET database provides data on 35 skills, but I decided to list only those that were most important for each job rather than list pages of unhelpful details. For each job, I identify any skill with a rating for level of mastery that is higher than the average rating for this skill for all jobs and a rating for importance that was higher than very low. I order the skills by the amount by which their ratings exceed the average rating for all occupations, from highest to lowest. If there are more than eight such skills, I include only those eight with the highest ratings. Each skill name is followed by a brief definition.

- **Work Environment:** I include any work condition with a rating that exceeds the midpoint of the rating scale. The order does not indicate any condition's frequency on the job. Consider whether you like these conditions and whether any of these conditions would make you uncomfortable. Keep in mind that when hazards are present (for example, contaminants), protective equipment and procedures are provided to keep you safe.

Getting all the information I used in the job descriptions was not a simple process, and it is not always perfect. For some information topics, data is not available. However, I used the best and most recent sources of data I could find, and I think that the results will be helpful to many people.

Sources of Additional Information

Hundreds of sources of career information exist, so here are a few I consider most helpful in getting additional information on the jobs listed in this book.

Print References

- *O*NET Dictionary of Occupational Titles:* Revised on a regular basis, this book provides good descriptions for all jobs listed in the U.S. Department of Labor's O*NET database. There are almost 950 job descriptions at all levels of education and training, plus lists of related job titles in other major career information sources, educational programs, and other information. Published by JIST.

- *Enhanced Occupational Outlook Handbook:* Updated regularly, this book provides thorough descriptions for about 350 major jobs in the current *Occupational Outlook Handbook*, brief descriptions for the O*NET jobs that are related to each, brief descriptions of thousands of more-specialized jobs from the *Dictionary of Occupational Titles*, and other information. Published by JIST.

Internet Resources

- **The Bureau of Labor Statistics website:** The Bureau of Labor Statistics website (www.bls.gov) provides a lot of career information, including links to other webpages that provide information on the jobs covered in this book. This website is a bit formal and, well, confusing, but it will take you to the major sources of government career information if you explore its options.

- **O*NET Online:** Go to http://online.onetcenter.org for direct access to information from the O*NET database. Two other O*NET sites—mySkills myFuture (www.myskillsmyfuture.org) and My Next Move (www.mynextmove.org)—use portions of this database in formats that you may find more friendly.

- **CareerOneStop:** This site (www.careeronestop.org) is operated by the Minnesota Department of Labor on behalf of the U.S. Department of Labor and provides access to state and local information about occupations. It also can identify a one-stop career center near you that can help you find local job openings and providers of education and training.

Thanks

Thanks for reading this Introduction. You are surely a more thorough person than those who jumped into the book without reading it, and you will probably get more out of the book as a result. I wish you a satisfying career and, more importantly, a good life.

PART I

The Best Jobs Lists: Jobs That Don't Require a Four-Year Degree

This part contains a lot of interesting lists, and it's a good place for you to start using the book. Here are some suggestions for using the lists to explore career options:

- ⊙ The table of contents at the beginning of this book presents a complete listing of the list titles in this section. You can browse the lists or use the table of contents to find those that interest you most.

- ⊙ I gave the lists clear titles, so most require little explanation. I provide comments for each group of lists.

- ⊙ As you review the lists of jobs, one or more of the jobs may appeal to you enough that you want to seek additional information. As this happens, mark that job (or, if someone else will be using this book, write it on a separate sheet of paper) so that you can look up the description of the job in Part II.

- ⊙ Keep in mind that all jobs in these lists meet my basic criteria for being included in this book, as explained in the Introduction. All lists, therefore, contain jobs that require less than a four-year degree and that have high pay, high growth, or a large number of openings. These economic measures are easily quantified and are often presented in lists of best jobs in the newspapers and other media. Although required education or training, earnings, growth, and openings are important, you also should consider other factors in your career planning, such as location, liking the people you work with, and having opportunities to be creative. Many other factors that may help define the ideal job for you are difficult or impossible to quantify and thus aren't used in this book, so you will need to weigh the importance of these issues yourself. Consider using some of the career exploration resources listed in the last part of the Introduction. Also do some networking with people who know the field that interests you.

⊙ All data used to create these lists comes from the U.S. Department of Labor and the Census Bureau. The earnings figures are based on the average annual pay received by full-time workers. Because the earnings represent the national averages, actual pay rates can vary greatly by location, amount of previous work experience, and other factors. Even lists that focus on a particular type of worker (for example, rural workers) use earnings figures based on the national averages.

Some Details on the Lists

The sources of the information I used in constructing these lists are presented in this book's Introduction. Here are some additional details on how I created the lists:

⊙ Some jobs have the same scores for one or more data elements. For example, in the category of best-paying, two jobs (Insurance Sales Agents and Lodging Managers) have the same average earnings, $47,450. Therefore, I ordered these two jobs alphabetically, and their order has no other significance.

⊙ In many cases, jobs are not tied, but their differences are too small to be important. For example, Telemarketers are projected to have 8,350 job openings per year, whereas 8,340 openings are projected for Paralegals and Legal Assistants. This is a difference of only 10 jobs spread over the entire United States, and of course it is only a projection. So keep in mind that small differences of position on a list aren't very significant.

Best Jobs Overall: Lists of Jobs with the Highest Pay, Fastest Growth, and Most Openings

The four lists that follow are this book's premier lists. They are the lists that are most often mentioned in the media and the ones that most readers want to see.

To create these lists, I ranked 420 major jobs according to a combination of their earnings, growth, and number of openings. I then selected the 300 jobs with the best total scores for use in this book. (The process for ranking the jobs is explained in more detail in the Introduction.)

The first list presents all 300 best jobs according to these combined rankings for pay, growth, and number of openings. Three additional lists present the 100 jobs with the top scores in each of three measures: annual earnings, projected percentage growth through 2020, and projected number of annual openings. Descriptions of all the jobs in these lists are included in Part II.

The 300 Best Jobs That Don't Require a Four-Year Degree

This list arranges all 300 jobs that were selected for this book in order of their overall scores for pay, growth, and number of openings, as explained in the Introduction. The job with the best overall score was Registered Nurses. Other jobs follow in order of their total scores for pay, growth, and openings. These 300 jobs are the ones I use throughout this book—in the other lists in Part I and in the descriptions found in Part II.

The list includes a wide variety of jobs. Among the top 20 are jobs in health care, sales, repair, and construction. The top 20 also include several management and supervisory jobs, proving that these kinds of jobs do exist for people without a college degree.

As you look over the list, remember that jobs near the top of the list are not necessarily "good" jobs—nor are jobs toward the end of the list necessarily "bad" ones for you to consider. Their position in the list is simply a result of their total scores based on pay, growth, and number of openings. This means, for example, that some jobs with low pay and modest growth but a high number of openings appear higher on the list, while some jobs with higher pay and modest growth but a low number of openings appear toward the end of the list. A "right" job for you could be anywhere on this list.

The 300 Best Jobs That Don't Require a Four-Year Degree

Job	Annual Earnings	Percent Growth	Annual Openings
1. Registered Nurses	$65,950	26.0%	120,740
2. Dental Hygienists	$69,280	37.7%	10,490
3. Supervisors of Construction and Extraction Workers	$59,150	23.5%	25,970
4. Radiologic Technologists and Technicians	$55,120	27.7%	9,510
5. Electricians	$49,320	23.2%	28,920
6. Plumbers, Pipefitters, and Steamfitters	$47,750	25.6%	22,880
7. Construction Managers	$84,240	16.6%	12,040
8. Diagnostic Medical Sonographers	$65,210	43.6%	3,170
9. Respiratory Therapists	$55,250	27.7%	5,270
10. Heating, Air Conditioning, and Refrigeration Mechanics and Installers	$43,380	33.7%	13,760
11. Sales Representatives, Wholesale and Manufacturing, Except Technical and Scientific Products	$53,540	15.6%	55,990
12. Insurance Sales Agents	$47,450	21.9%	18,440
13. Physical Therapist Assistants	$51,040	45.7%	4,120
14. Brickmasons and Blockmasons	$46,800	40.5%	5,450
15. Administrative Services Managers	$79,540	14.5%	9,980
16. Licensed Practical and Licensed Vocational Nurses	$41,150	22.4%	36,920

(continued)

(continued)

The 300 Best Jobs That Don't Require a Four-Year Degree

Job	Annual Earnings	Percent Growth	Annual Openings
17. Industrial Machinery Mechanics	$46,270	21.6%	11,710
18. Business Operations Specialists, All Other	$64,030	11.6%	32,720
19. First-Line Supervisors of Helpers, Laborers, and Material Movers, Hand	$44,580	27.2%	8,000
20. Operating Engineers and Other Construction Equipment Operators	$41,510	23.5%	16,280
21. First-Line Supervisors of Office and Administrative Support Workers	$48,810	14.3%	58,440
22. Loan Officers	$58,030	14.2%	11,520
23. First-Line Supervisors of Mechanics, Installers, and Repairers	$59,850	11.9%	16,490
24. Carpenters	$40,010	19.6%	40,830
25. Heavy and Tractor-Trailer Truck Drivers	$37,930	20.6%	64,940
26. Construction and Building Inspectors	$53,180	18.0%	4,860
27. Paralegals and Legal Assistants	$46,730	18.3%	8,340
28. Managers, All Other	$99,540	7.9%	24,940
29. Cardiovascular Technologists and Technicians	$51,020	29.4%	2,210
30. Commercial Pilots	$70,000	21.1%	1,930
31. Occupational Therapy Assistants	$52,040	43.2%	1,680
32. Telecommunications Equipment Installers and Repairers, Except Line Installers	$53,960	14.6%	5,930
33. Executive Secretaries and Executive Administrative Assistants	$45,580	12.6%	32,180
34. First-Line Supervisors of Transportation and Material-Moving Machine and Vehicle Operators	$52,950	14.3%	6,930
35. Electrical Power-Line Installers and Repairers	$60,190	13.3%	5,270
36. Police and Sheriff's Patrol Officers	$54,230	8.2%	24,940
37. Dental Assistants	$34,140	30.8%	15,400
38. Cement Masons and Concrete Finishers	$35,600	34.6%	7,290
39. Medical Equipment Repairers	$44,870	31.4%	2,230
40. Medical Secretaries	$31,060	41.3%	27,840
41. Security and Fire Alarm Systems Installers	$39,540	32.9%	3,670
42. General and Operations Managers	$95,150	4.6%	41,010
43. Cargo and Freight Agents	$38,210	29.3%	4,420
44. Drywall and Ceiling Tile Installers	$36,970	27.6%	5,870
45. Substance Abuse and Behavioral Disorder Counselors	$38,560	27.4%	4,170
46. Mobile Heavy Equipment Mechanics, Except Engines	$45,600	16.2%	5,250
47. Automotive Service Technicians and Mechanics	$36,180	17.3%	31,170
48. Telecommunications Line Installers and Repairers	$51,720	13.6%	5,140

The 300 Best Jobs That Don't Require a Four-Year Degree

Job	Annual Earnings	Percent Growth	Annual Openings
49. Glaziers	$37,350	42.2%	3,340
50. Structural Iron and Steel Workers	$45,690	21.9%	2,540
51. Sheet Metal Workers	$42,730	17.6%	4,700
52. Self-Enrichment Education Teachers	$36,100	20.9%	9,150
53. Painters, Construction and Maintenance	$35,430	18.5%	15,730
54. Transportation, Storage, and Distribution Managers	$80,860	10.0%	3,370
55. Bus and Truck Mechanics and Diesel Engine Specialists	$41,640	14.5%	8,780
56. Automotive Body and Related Repairers	$38,180	18.4%	6,520
57. Health Technologists and Technicians, All Other	$38,080	23.2%	4,040
58. Emergency Medical Technicians and Paramedics	$30,710	33.3%	12,080
59. First-Line Supervisors of Landscaping, Lawn Service, and Groundskeeping Workers	$42,050	15.1%	6,010
60. Tapers	$44,910	34.9%	1,430
61. Advertising Sales Agents	$45,250	13.0%	6,990
62. Boilermakers	$56,910	21.2%	1,180
63. Medical Assistants	$29,100	30.9%	24,380
64. First-Line Supervisors of Non-Retail Sales Workers	$70,520	4.0%	12,350
65. Environmental Science and Protection Technicians, Including Health	$42,270	23.6%	1,950
66. Pharmacy Technicians	$28,940	32.4%	16,630
67. Surgical Technologists	$40,950	18.9%	3,390
68. Insulation Workers, Mechanical	$37,990	31.8%	2,010
69. Billing and Posting Clerks	$32,880	19.7%	18,760
70. Real Estate Sales Agents	$39,070	12.2%	12,760
71. Welders, Cutters, Solderers, and Brazers	$35,920	15.0%	14,070
72. Tile and Marble Setters	$37,080	25.4%	2,770
73. Purchasing Agents, Except Wholesale, Retail, and Farm Products	$57,580	5.3%	9,120
74. Firefighters	$45,420	8.6%	11,230
75. Massage Therapists	$35,830	20.1%	5,590
76. Construction Laborers	$29,730	21.3%	29,240
77. Social and Human Service Assistants	$28,740	27.6%	18,910
78. Fitness Trainers and Aerobics Instructors	$31,030	24.0%	10,060
79. Radiation Therapists	$76,630	20.1%	670
80. Veterinary Technologists and Technicians	$30,140	52.0%	5,570
81. Bookkeeping, Accounting, and Auditing Clerks	$34,740	13.6%	46,780
82. First-Line Supervisors of Fire Fighting and Prevention Workers	$69,510	8.2%	3,310

(continued)

(continued)

The 300 Best Jobs That Don't Require a Four-Year Degree

Job	Annual Earnings	Percent Growth	Annual Openings
83. Nuclear Medicine Technologists	$69,450	18.7%	750
84. Coaches and Scouts	$28,470	29.4%	13,300
85. Property, Real Estate, and Community Association Managers	$52,510	6.1%	8,230
86. Dispatchers, Except Police, Fire, and Ambulance	$35,200	18.6%	6,950
87. Pipelayers	$35,900	25.2%	2,880
88. Payroll and Timekeeping Clerks	$37,160	14.6%	6,570
89. Wholesale and Retail Buyers, Except Farm Products	$50,490	9.0%	4,170
90. Medical Records and Health Information Technicians	$33,310	21.0%	7,370
91. Receptionists and Information Clerks	$25,690	23.7%	56,560
92. Reinforcing Iron and Rebar Workers	$37,990	48.7%	1,320
93. Airline Pilots, Copilots, and Flight Engineers	$105,580	6.4%	3,130
94. Customer Service Representatives	$30,610	15.5%	95,960
95. Computer-Controlled Machine Tool Operators, Metal and Plastic	$35,220	19.2%	4,780
96. Hazardous Materials Removal Workers	$38,120	23.1%	1,890
97. Medical and Clinical Laboratory Technicians	$36,950	14.8%	5,510
98. Preschool Teachers, Except Special Education	$26,620	24.9%	23,240
99. Transportation Inspectors	$62,230	14.6%	1,070
100. Roofers	$35,280	17.8%	5,250
101. Private Detectives and Investigators	$43,710	20.5%	1,490
102. Crane and Tower Operators	$46,460	15.7%	1,720
103. Aircraft Mechanics and Service Technicians	$54,590	6.3%	4,520
104. Claims Adjusters, Examiners, and Investigators	$59,320	3.0%	7,990
105. First-Line Supervisors of Retail Sales Workers	$36,480	8.4%	51,370
106. Real Estate Brokers	$59,340	7.6%	2,970
107. Maintenance and Repair Workers, General	$35,030	11.0%	37,910
108. Farmers, Ranchers, and Other Agricultural Managers	$64,660	–8.0%	23,450
109. Bus Drivers, Transit and Intercity	$35,720	14.8%	6,350
110. Sailors and Marine Oilers	$36,800	21.3%	2,150
111. Pest Control Workers	$30,220	26.2%	4,850
112. Refuse and Recyclable Material Collectors	$32,280	20.2%	6,970
113. Civil Engineering Technicians	$46,900	11.9%	2,460
114. Excavating and Loading Machine and Dragline Operators	$37,380	17.4%	2,890
115. Opticians, Dispensing	$33,100	28.9%	3,060
116. Environmental Engineering Technicians	$44,850	24.5%	820
117. Machinists	$39,220	8.5%	9,950

The 300 Best Jobs That Don't Require a Four-Year Degree

Job	Annual Earnings	Percent Growth	Annual Openings
118. Water and Wastewater Treatment Plant and System Operators	$41,780	11.7%	4,150
119. Life, Physical, and Social Science Technicians, All Other	$43,120	11.8%	3,350
120. First-Line Supervisors of Production and Operating Workers	$53,670	1.9%	8,790
121. Production, Planning, and Expediting Clerks	$43,100	6.6%	8,880
122. First-Line Supervisors of Personal Service Workers	$35,230	13.5%	8,260
123. Mechanical Drafters	$49,200	11.1%	2,050
124. Office Clerks, General	$27,190	16.6%	101,150
125. Paving, Surfacing, and Tamping Equipment Operators	$35,270	22.1%	2,200
126. Audio and Video Equipment Technicians	$41,630	13.4%	2,560
127. Human Resources Assistants, Except Payroll and Timekeeping	$37,250	11.2%	6,160
128. Surveying and Mapping Technicians	$39,350	15.8%	2,000
129. Landscaping and Groundskeeping Workers	$23,410	20.9%	44,440
130. First-Line Supervisors of Police and Detectives	$77,890	2.2%	3,870
131. Rail Car Repairers	$47,740	17.1%	930
132. Bill and Account Collectors	$31,920	14.2%	13,550
133. Helpers—Pipelayers, Plumbers, Pipefitters, and Steamfitters	$27,010	45.4%	4,170
134. Light Truck or Delivery Services Drivers	$29,080	14.7%	29,590
135. Security Guards	$23,900	18.8%	35,950
136. Stonemasons	$36,640	36.5%	890
137. Choreographers	$39,600	24.2%	830
138. Helpers—Electricians	$27,620	30.6%	4,200
139. Pile-Driver Operators	$45,500	36.6%	230
140. Elevator Installers and Repairers	$75,060	11.6%	820
141. Detectives and Criminal Investigators	$71,770	2.9%	3,010
142. Helpers—Carpenters	$26,400	55.7%	3,820
143. Parts Salespersons	$29,350	16.0%	10,720
144. Postal Service Mail Carriers	$55,160	−12.0%	10,340
145. Aircraft Structure, Surfaces, Rigging, and Systems Assemblers	$46,210	14.3%	1,220
146. Interviewers, Except Eligibility and Loan	$29,560	17.3%	7,960
147. Radio, Cellular, and Tower Equipment Installers and Repairers	$42,160	29.3%	450
148. Helpers—Brickmasons, Blockmasons, Stonemasons, and Tile and Marble Setters	$27,820	59.9%	2,540
149. Appraisers and Assessors of Real Estate	$48,870	7.5%	2,220
150. Laborers and Freight, Stock, and Material Movers, Hand	$23,750	15.4%	98,020
151. Correctional Officers and Jailers	$38,990	5.2%	10,810
152. Social Science Research Assistants	$38,800	14.8%	1,700
153. Insurance Claims and Policy Processing Clerks	$35,210	8.7%	9,600

(continued)

(continued)

The 300 Best Jobs That Don't Require a Four-Year Degree

Job	Annual Earnings	Percent Growth	Annual Openings
154. Structural Metal Fabricators and Fitters	$35,170	15.7%	2,830
155. Athletes and Sports Competitors	$39,670	21.8%	780
156. Lodging Managers	$47,450	8.4%	1,820
157. Industrial Truck and Tractor Operators	$30,010	11.8%	20,950
158. Electrical and Electronic Engineering Technicians	$56,900	1.9%	3,180
159. Geological and Petroleum Technicians	$49,690	14.6%	700
160. Teacher Assistants	$23,580	14.8%	48,160
161. Nuclear Technicians	$68,030	14.1%	330
162. Residential Advisors	$24,540	24.9%	4,570
163. Inspectors, Testers, Sorters, Samplers, and Weighers	$34,040	8.0%	12,390
164. Aircraft Cargo Handling Supervisors	$46,840	20.6%	260
165. Cabinetmakers and Bench Carpenters	$30,530	16.8%	4,020
166. First-Line Supervisors of Correctional Officers	$55,030	5.5%	1,650
167. Engineering Technicians, Except Drafters, All Other	$58,670	4.7%	1,680
168. First-Line Supervisors of Food Preparation and Serving Workers	$29,550	9.8%	24,830
169. Skincare Specialists	$29,190	24.6%	2,040
170. Physical Therapist Aides	$23,680	43.2%	2,760
171. Police, Fire, and Ambulance Dispatchers	$35,930	11.7%	3,070
172. Helpers—Installation, Maintenance, and Repair Workers	$24,060	18.4%	8,040
173. Court Reporters	$48,530	14.1%	640
174. Bus Drivers, School or Special Client	$28,110	12.0%	14,450
175. Food Service Managers	$48,110	–3.3%	5,910
176. Insulation Workers, Floor, Ceiling, and Wall	$32,420	23.3%	1,460
177. Hairdressers, Hairstylists, and Cosmetologists	$22,570	15.7%	21,810
178. Motorboat Mechanics and Service Technicians	$35,520	20.7%	960
179. Mechanical Door Repairers	$36,640	24.2%	550
180. Secretaries and Administrative Assistants, Except Legal, Medical, and Executive	$31,870	5.8%	39,100
181. Taxi Drivers and Chauffeurs	$22,760	19.6%	7,670
182. Plasterers and Stucco Masons	$36,830	17.2%	1,050
183. Commercial Divers	$52,550	15.8%	130
184. Automotive Glass Installers and Repairers	$33,720	24.9%	920
185. Highway Maintenance Workers	$35,220	8.2%	5,140
186. Coin, Vending, and Amusement Machine Servicers and Repairers	$30,820	22.0%	1,630
187. Locksmiths and Safe Repairers	$36,680	17.9%	930
188. Fence Erectors	$29,580	23.7%	1,640

The 300 Best Jobs That Don't Require a Four-Year Degree

Job	Annual Earnings	Percent Growth	Annual Openings
189. Legal Secretaries	$42,460	3.5%	3,940
190. Septic Tank Servicers and Sewer Pipe Cleaners	$33,740	20.6%	1,190
191. Computer, Automated Teller, and Office Machine Repairers	$36,360	6.5%	4,540
192. Tree Trimmers and Pruners	$31,320	18.0%	1,800
193. Railroad Conductors and Yardmasters	$53,880	4.7%	1,430
194. Gaming Managers	$67,230	12.1%	100
195. Stationary Engineers and Boiler Operators	$53,070	6.1%	1,060
196. Architectural and Civil Drafters	$47,250	3.2%	2,090
197. Court, Municipal, and License Clerks	$34,300	8.0%	4,670
198. Occupational Health and Safety Technicians	$46,030	13.2%	510
199. Procurement Clerks	$37,640	5.7%	3,550
200. Painters, Transportation Equipment	$39,600	9.5%	1,430
201. Brokerage Clerks	$41,760	5.9%	1,970
202. Tire Repairers and Changers	$23,440	18.5%	4,390
203. Locomotive Engineers	$49,380	4.4%	1,550
204. Subway and Streetcar Operators	$63,820	9.2%	280
205. Sawing Machine Setters, Operators, and Tenders, Wood	$26,220	24.6%	1,810
206. Eligibility Interviewers, Government Programs	$41,060	3.1%	3,740
207. Demonstrators and Product Promoters	$23,770	17.5%	4,210
208. Fire Inspectors and Investigators	$53,330	8.8%	470
209. Metal-Refining Furnace Operators and Tenders	$38,680	16.0%	550
210. Motorcycle Mechanics	$32,410	23.3%	890
211. Electrical and Electronics Repairers, Commercial and Industrial Equipment	$52,320	1.2%	1,770
212. Library Technicians	$30,430	8.8%	5,950
213. Meat, Poultry, and Fish Cutters and Trimmers	$22,720	15.5%	7,400
214. Gaming Supervisors	$48,820	6.9%	920
215. Counter and Rental Clerks	$22,740	12.2%	14,660
216. Carpet Installers	$36,750	10.3%	1,520
217. Industrial Engineering Technicians	$49,090	4.2%	1,460
218. Avionics Technicians	$54,720	7.0%	580
219. Earth Drillers, Except Oil and Gas	$40,200	14.0%	620
220. Electrical and Electronics Repairers, Powerhouse, Substation, and Relay	$67,450	4.7%	690
221. Cooks, Institution and Cafeteria	$22,710	12.3%	13,620
222. Power Plant Operators	$65,280	–2.5%	1,440
223. Medical Equipment Preparers	$30,050	17.5%	1,620

(continued)

(continued)

The 300 Best Jobs That Don't Require a Four-Year Degree

Job	Annual Earnings	Percent Growth	Annual Openings
224. Service Unit Operators, Oil, Gas, and Mining	$40,750	8.6%	1,210
225. Maintenance Workers, Machinery	$39,490	6.4%	1,740
226. Electrical and Electronics Drafters	$54,470	5.5%	720
227. Electronic Home Entertainment Equipment Installers and Repairers	$34,470	13.9%	1,410
228. Outdoor Power Equipment and Other Small Engine Mechanics	$30,200	18.9%	1,350
229. Computer Numerically Controlled Machine Tool Programmers, Metal and Plastic	$45,890	10.8%	490
230. Psychiatric Technicians	$28,470	15.5%	2,460
231. Rotary Drill Operators, Oil and Gas	$51,310	7.1%	640
232. Woodworking Machine Setters, Operators, and Tenders, Except Sawing	$27,090	20.1%	1,740
233. Mechanical Engineering Technicians	$51,350	4.0%	1,040
234. Air Traffic Controllers	$113,540	−3.0%	1,020
235. Derrick Operators, Oil and Gas	$45,220	9.5%	570
236. Recreational Vehicle Service Technicians	$34,000	22.2%	480
237. Chemical Technicians	$42,070	6.7%	1,290
238. Driver/Sales Workers	$22,770	10.3%	12,290
239. Tax Preparers	$32,320	9.8%	2,630
240. Terrazzo Workers and Finishers	$41,240	16.2%	110
241. Photographers	$28,860	12.5%	3,100
242. Team Assemblers	$27,490	5.5%	24,100
243. Farm Equipment Mechanics and Service Technicians	$34,230	13.4%	1,290
244. Order Clerks	$28,940	7.4%	7,520
245. Fine Artists, Including Painters, Sculptors, and Illustrators	$44,600	7.8%	810
246. Petroleum Pump System Operators, Refinery Operators, and Gaugers	$61,260	−14.0%	1,440
247. Broadcast Technicians	$36,570	9.0%	1,380
248. Travel Agents	$33,930	10.0%	1,720
249. Merchandise Displayers and Window Trimmers	$26,190	12.8%	4,000
250. Couriers and Messengers	$24,750	12.6%	4,300
251. Transportation Security Screeners	$36,910	9.6%	1,040
252. Riggers	$43,020	10.5%	440
253. Mail Clerks and Mail Machine Operators, Except Postal Service	$26,610	12.0%	3,960
254. Weighers, Measurers, Checkers, and Samplers, Recordkeeping	$27,390	12.0%	3,420
255. Tour Guides and Escorts	$23,620	18.1%	1,960
256. Airfield Operations Specialists	$47,180	8.7%	320

The 300 Best Jobs That Don't Require a Four-Year Degree

Job	Annual Earnings	Percent Growth	Annual Openings
257. Chemical Plant and System Operators	$55,940	−12.2%	1,410
258. Layout Workers, Metal and Plastic	$39,870	13.5%	290
259. Library Assistants, Clerical	$23,440	10.2%	6,410
260. Postal Service Clerks	$53,100	−48.2%	1,550
261. Buyers and Purchasing Agents, Farm Products	$55,860	5.4%	320
262. Ambulance Drivers and Attendants, Except Emergency Medical Technicians	$22,820	32.1%	1,010
263. Traffic Technicians	$42,300	11.6%	280
264. Extruding and Drawing Machine Setters, Operators, and Tenders, Metal and Plastic	$32,300	8.4%	2,090
265. Fashion Designers	$64,690	0.0%	670
266. Helpers—Production Workers	$22,520	8.7%	9,980
267. Reservation and Transportation Ticket Agents and Travel Clerks	$33,300	5.8%	3,080
268. Butchers and Meat Cutters	$28,460	8.0%	4,680
269. Segmental Pavers	$32,340	30.8%	90
270. Nuclear Power Reactor Operators	$76,590	3.8%	200
271. Motorboat Operators	$36,620	16.1%	160
272. Psychiatric Aides	$25,170	15.1%	1,900
273. Chefs and Head Cooks	$42,350	−0.8%	1,800
274. Occupational Therapy Aides	$28,200	33.3%	360
275. Floor Sanders and Finishers	$33,350	17.8%	420
276. Transit and Railroad Police	$56,390	5.6%	110
277. Travel Guides	$30,670	23.8%	260
278. Rolling Machine Setters, Operators, and Tenders, Metal and Plastic	$36,920	8.1%	880
279. Medical Transcriptionists	$33,480	5.9%	2,020
280. Roustabouts, Oil and Gas	$32,980	8.3%	1,550
281. Bicycle Repairers	$23,210	37.4%	630
282. First-Line Supervisors of Housekeeping and Janitorial Workers	$35,230	0.8%	3,320
283. Shipping, Receiving, and Traffic Clerks	$28,790	0.3%	17,740
284. Veterinary Assistants and Laboratory Animal Caretakers	$22,830	14.2%	2,160
285. Control and Valve Installers and Repairers, Except Mechanical Door	$49,600	0.0%	810
286. Telemarketers	$22,520	7.4%	8,350
287. Fish and Game Wardens	$50,070	5.3%	220
288. Conveyor Operators and Tenders	$29,320	11.6%	1,490
289. Refractory Materials Repairers, Except Brickmasons	$42,700	9.5%	60

(continued)

(continued)

The 300 Best Jobs That Don't Require a Four-Year Degree

Job	Annual Earnings	Percent Growth	Annual Openings
290. Home Appliance Repairers	$35,440	6.5%	1,190
291. Welding, Soldering, and Brazing Machine Setters, Operators, and Tenders	$34,770	6.5%	1,380
292. Tellers	$24,590	1.3%	23,750
293. First-Line Supervisors of Farming, Fishing, and Forestry Workers	$42,600	–1.5%	1,360
294. Painting, Coating, and Decorating Workers	$25,660	17.4%	980
295. Ophthalmic Laboratory Technicians	$28,750	12.8%	1,320
296. Printing Press Operators	$34,290	–1.4%	3,920
297. Flight Attendants	$38,020	–0.2%	1,730
298. Coating, Painting, and Spraying Machine Setters, Operators, and Tenders	$30,020	6.1%	2,310
299. Embalmers	$43,800	5.6%	370
300. Bailiffs	$38,950	7.9%	450

The 100 Best-Paying Jobs That Don't Require a Four-Year Degree

I sorted all 300 jobs based on their annual median earnings from highest to lowest. *Median earnings* means that half of all workers in these jobs earn more than that amount and half earn less. I then selected the 100 jobs with the highest earnings to create the list that follows.

This is a popular list for obvious reasons. It includes jobs at all levels of training, although many of the better-paying jobs do require technical training or work experience.

For example, the highest-paying job on the list is Air Traffic Controllers, a job that requires considerable training and on-the-job experience. Among the top 25, several require managerial, supervisory, or technical skills.

Keep in mind that the earnings reflect the national average for all workers in the occupation. This is an important consideration, because starting pay in the job is usually much less than the pay that workers can earn with several years of experience. (In the Part II job descriptions, you can see how much potential each job has for income growth.) Earnings also vary significantly by region of the country, so actual pay in your area could be substantially different.

The 100 Best-Paying Jobs That Don't Require a Four-Year Degree

Job	Annual Earnings
1. Air Traffic Controllers	$113,540
2. Airline Pilots, Copilots, and Flight Engineers	$105,580
3. Managers, All Other	$99,540
4. General and Operations Managers	$95,150
5. Construction Managers	$84,240
6. Transportation, Storage, and Distribution Managers	$80,860
7. Administrative Services Managers	$79,540
8. First-Line Supervisors of Police and Detectives	$77,890
9. Radiation Therapists	$76,630
10. Nuclear Power Reactor Operators	$76,590
11. Elevator Installers and Repairers	$75,060
12. Detectives and Criminal Investigators	$71,770
13. First-Line Supervisors of Non-Retail Sales Workers	$70,520
14. Commercial Pilots	$70,000
15. First-Line Supervisors of Fire Fighting and Prevention Workers	$69,510
16. Nuclear Medicine Technologists	$69,450
17. Dental Hygienists	$69,280
18. Nuclear Technicians	$68,030
19. Electrical and Electronics Repairers, Powerhouse, Substation, and Relay	$67,450
20. Gaming Managers	$67,230
21. Registered Nurses	$65,950
22. Power Plant Operators	$65,280
23. Diagnostic Medical Sonographers	$65,210
24. Fashion Designers	$64,690
25. Farmers, Ranchers, and Other Agricultural Managers	$64,660
26. Business Operations Specialists, All Other	$64,030
27. Subway and Streetcar Operators	$63,820
28. Transportation Inspectors	$62,230
29. Petroleum Pump System Operators, Refinery Operators, and Gaugers	$61,260
30. Electrical Power-Line Installers and Repairers	$60,190
31. First-Line Supervisors of Mechanics, Installers, and Repairers	$59,850
32. Real Estate Brokers	$59,340
33. Claims Adjusters, Examiners, and Investigators	$59,320
34. Supervisors of Construction and Extraction Workers	$59,150
35. Engineering Technicians, Except Drafters, All Other	$58,670
36. Loan Officers	$58,030
37. Purchasing Agents, Except Wholesale, Retail, and Farm Products	$57,580

(continued)

(continued)

The 100 Best-Paying Jobs That Don't Require a Four-Year Degree

Job	Annual Earnings
38. Boilermakers	$56,910
39. Electrical and Electronic Engineering Technicians	$56,900
40. Transit and Railroad Police	$56,390
41. Chemical Plant and System Operators	$55,940
42. Buyers and Purchasing Agents, Farm Products	$55,860
43. Respiratory Therapists	$55,250
44. Postal Service Mail Carriers	$55,160
45. Radiologic Technologists and Technicians	$55,120
46. First-Line Supervisors of Correctional Officers	$55,030
47. Avionics Technicians	$54,720
48. Aircraft Mechanics and Service Technicians	$54,590
49. Electrical and Electronics Drafters	$54,470
50. Police and Sheriff's Patrol Officers	$54,230
51. Telecommunications Equipment Installers and Repairers, Except Line Installers	$53,960
52. Railroad Conductors and Yardmasters	$53,880
53. First-Line Supervisors of Production and Operating Workers	$53,670
54. Sales Representatives, Wholesale and Manufacturing, Except Technical and Scientific Products	$53,540
55. Fire Inspectors and Investigators	$53,330
56. Construction and Building Inspectors	$53,180
57. Postal Service Clerks	$53,100
58. Stationary Engineers and Boiler Operators	$53,070
59. First-Line Supervisors of Transportation and Material-Moving Machine and Vehicle Operators	$52,950
60. Commercial Divers	$52,550
61. Property, Real Estate, and Community Association Managers	$52,510
62. Electrical and Electronics Repairers, Commercial and Industrial Equipment	$52,320
63. Occupational Therapy Assistants	$52,040
64. Telecommunications Line Installers and Repairers	$51,720
65. Mechanical Engineering Technicians	$51,350
66. Rotary Drill Operators, Oil and Gas	$51,310
67. Physical Therapist Assistants	$51,040
68. Cardiovascular Technologists and Technicians	$51,020
69. Wholesale and Retail Buyers, Except Farm Products	$50,490
70. Fish and Game Wardens	$50,070
71. Geological and Petroleum Technicians	$49,690

The 100 Best-Paying Jobs That Don't Require a Four-Year Degree

Job	Annual Earnings
72. Control and Valve Installers and Repairers, Except Mechanical Door	$49,600
73. Locomotive Engineers	$49,380
74. Electricians	$49,320
75. Mechanical Drafters	$49,200
76. Industrial Engineering Technicians	$49,090
77. Appraisers and Assessors of Real Estate	$48,870
78. Gaming Supervisors	$48,820
79. First-Line Supervisors of Office and Administrative Support Workers	$48,810
80. Court Reporters	$48,530
81. Food Service Managers	$48,110
82. Plumbers, Pipefitters, and Steamfitters	$47,750
83. Rail Car Repairers	$47,740
84. Insurance Sales Agents	$47,450
85. Lodging Managers	$47,450
86. Architectural and Civil Drafters	$47,250
87. Airfield Operations Specialists	$47,180
88. Civil Engineering Technicians	$46,900
89. Aircraft Cargo Handling Supervisors	$46,840
90. Brickmasons and Blockmasons	$46,800
91. Paralegals and Legal Assistants	$46,730
92. Crane and Tower Operators	$46,460
93. Industrial Machinery Mechanics	$46,270
94. Aircraft Structure, Surfaces, Rigging, and Systems Assemblers	$46,210
95. Occupational Health and Safety Technicians	$46,030
96. Computer Numerically Controlled Machine Tool Programmers, Metal and Plastic	$45,890
97. Structural Iron and Steel Workers	$45,690
98. Mobile Heavy Equipment Mechanics, Except Engines	$45,600
99. Executive Secretaries and Executive Administrative Assistants	$45,580
100. Pile-Driver Operators	$45,500

The 100 Fastest-Growing Jobs That Don't Require a Four-Year Degree

I created this list by sorting all 300 best jobs by their projected growth over the 10-year period from 2010 to 2020. Growth rates are one measure to consider in exploring career options, as jobs with higher growth rates tend to provide more job opportunities.

Jobs in health care and construction dominate the 20 fastest-growing jobs. Helpers—Brickmasons, Blockmasons, Stonemasons, and Tile and Marble Setters is the job with the highest growth rate; the number employed is projected to grow by more than half from 2010 to 2020. You can find a wide range of rapidly growing jobs in a variety of fields and at different levels of training and education among the jobs in this list.

The 100 Fastest-Growing Jobs That Don't Require a Four-Year Degree

Job	Percent Growth
1. Helpers—Brickmasons, Blockmasons, Stonemasons, and Tile and Marble Setters	59.9%
2. Helpers—Carpenters	55.7%
3. Veterinary Technologists and Technicians	52.0%
4. Reinforcing Iron and Rebar Workers	48.7%
5. Physical Therapist Assistants	45.7%
6. Helpers—Pipelayers, Plumbers, Pipefitters, and Steamfitters	45.4%
7. Diagnostic Medical Sonographers	43.6%
8. Occupational Therapy Assistants	43.2%
9. Physical Therapist Aides	43.2%
10. Glaziers	42.2%
11. Medical Secretaries	41.3%
12. Brickmasons and Blockmasons	40.5%
13. Dental Hygienists	37.7%
14. Bicycle Repairers	37.4%
15. Pile-Driver Operators	36.6%
16. Stonemasons	36.5%
17. Tapers	34.9%
18. Cement Masons and Concrete Finishers	34.6%
19. Heating, Air Conditioning, and Refrigeration Mechanics and Installers	33.7%
20. Emergency Medical Technicians and Paramedics	33.3%
21. Occupational Therapy Aides	33.3%
22. Security and Fire Alarm Systems Installers	32.9%
23. Pharmacy Technicians	32.4%
24. Ambulance Drivers and Attendants, Except Emergency Medical Technicians	32.1%
25. Insulation Workers, Mechanical	31.8%
26. Medical Equipment Repairers	31.4%
27. Medical Assistants	30.9%
28. Dental Assistants	30.8%
29. Segmental Pavers	30.8%
30. Helpers—Electricians	30.6%
31. Cardiovascular Technologists and Technicians	29.4%
32. Coaches and Scouts	29.4%

The 100 Fastest-Growing Jobs That Don't Require a Four-Year Degree

Job	Percent Growth
33. Cargo and Freight Agents	29.3%
34. Radio, Cellular, and Tower Equipment Installers and Repairers	29.3%
35. Opticians, Dispensing	28.9%
36. Radiologic Technologists and Technicians	27.7%
37. Respiratory Therapists	27.7%
38. Drywall and Ceiling Tile Installers	27.6%
39. Social and Human Service Assistants	27.6%
40. Substance Abuse and Behavioral Disorder Counselors	27.4%
41. First-Line Supervisors of Helpers, Laborers, and Material Movers, Hand	27.2%
42. Pest Control Workers	26.2%
43. Registered Nurses	26.0%
44. Plumbers, Pipefitters, and Steamfitters	25.6%
45. Tile and Marble Setters	25.4%
46. Pipelayers	25.2%
47. Automotive Glass Installers and Repairers	24.9%
48. Preschool Teachers, Except Special Education	24.9%
49. Residential Advisors	24.9%
50. Sawing Machine Setters, Operators, and Tenders, Wood	24.6%
51. Skincare Specialists	24.6%
52. Environmental Engineering Technicians	24.5%
53. Choreographers	24.2%
54. Mechanical Door Repairers	24.2%
55. Fitness Trainers and Aerobics Instructors	24.0%
56. Travel Guides	23.8%
57. Fence Erectors	23.7%
58. Receptionists and Information Clerks	23.7%
59. Environmental Science and Protection Technicians, Including Health	23.6%
60. Operating Engineers and Other Construction Equipment Operators	23.5%
61. Supervisors of Construction and Extraction Workers	23.5%
62. Insulation Workers, Floor, Ceiling, and Wall	23.3%
63. Motorcycle Mechanics	23.3%
64. Electricians	23.2%
65. Health Technologists and Technicians, All Other	23.2%
66. Hazardous Materials Removal Workers	23.1%
67. Licensed Practical and Licensed Vocational Nurses	22.4%
68. Recreational Vehicle Service Technicians	22.2%
69. Paving, Surfacing, and Tamping Equipment Operators	22.1%

(continued)

(continued)

The 100 Fastest-Growing Jobs That Don't Require a Four-Year Degree

Job	Percent Growth
70. Coin, Vending, and Amusement Machine Servicers and Repairers	22.0%
71. Insurance Sales Agents	21.9%
72. Structural Iron and Steel Workers	21.9%
73. Athletes and Sports Competitors	21.8%
74. Industrial Machinery Mechanics	21.6%
75. Construction Laborers	21.3%
76. Sailors and Marine Oilers	21.3%
77. Boilermakers	21.2%
78. Commercial Pilots	21.1%
79. Medical Records and Health Information Technicians	21.0%
80. Landscaping and Groundskeeping Workers	20.9%
81. Self-Enrichment Education Teachers	20.9%
82. Motorboat Mechanics and Service Technicians	20.7%
83. Aircraft Cargo Handling Supervisors	20.6%
84. Heavy and Tractor-Trailer Truck Drivers	20.6%
85. Septic Tank Servicers and Sewer Pipe Cleaners	20.6%
86. Private Detectives and Investigators	20.5%
87. Refuse and Recyclable Material Collectors	20.2%
88. Massage Therapists	20.1%
89. Radiation Therapists	20.1%
90. Woodworking Machine Setters, Operators, and Tenders, Except Sawing	20.1%
91. Billing and Posting Clerks	19.7%
92. Carpenters	19.6%
93. Taxi Drivers and Chauffeurs	19.6%
94. Computer-Controlled Machine Tool Operators, Metal and Plastic	19.2%
95. Outdoor Power Equipment and Other Small Engine Mechanics	18.9%
96. Surgical Technologists	18.9%
97. Security Guards	18.8%
98. Nuclear Medicine Technologists	18.7%
99. Dispatchers, Except Police, Fire, and Ambulance	18.6%
100. Tire Repairers and Changers	18.5%

The 100 Jobs with the Most Openings That Don't Require a Four-Year Degree

I created this list by sorting all 300 best jobs by the number of job openings that each is expected to have per year. Jobs that employ lots of people are also likely to have more job openings in a given year. Many of these occupations, such as Customer Service Representatives, are not among the highest-paying jobs. But jobs with large numbers of openings often provide easier entry for new workers, make it easier to move from one position to another, or are attractive for other reasons. Some of these jobs may also appeal to people re-entering the labor market, part-time workers, and workers who want to move from one employer to another. And some of these jobs pay quite well, offer good benefits, or have other advantages.

The 100 Jobs with the Most Openings That Don't Require a Four-Year Degree	
Job	Annual Openings
1. Registered Nurses	120,740
2. Office Clerks, General	101,150
3. Laborers and Freight, Stock, and Material Movers, Hand	98,020
4. Customer Service Representatives	95,960
5. Heavy and Tractor-Trailer Truck Drivers	64,940
6. First-Line Supervisors of Office and Administrative Support Workers	58,440
7. Receptionists and Information Clerks	56,560
8. Sales Representatives, Wholesale and Manufacturing, Except Technical and Scientific Products	55,990
9. First-Line Supervisors of Retail Sales Workers	51,370
10. Teacher Assistants	48,160
11. Bookkeeping, Accounting, and Auditing Clerks	46,780
12. Landscaping and Groundskeeping Workers	44,440
13. General and Operations Managers	41,010
14. Carpenters	40,830
15. Secretaries and Administrative Assistants, Except Legal, Medical, and Executive	39,100
16. Maintenance and Repair Workers, General	37,910
17. Licensed Practical and Licensed Vocational Nurses	36,920
18. Security Guards	35,950
19. Business Operations Specialists, All Other	32,720
20. Executive Secretaries and Executive Administrative Assistants	32,180
21. Automotive Service Technicians and Mechanics	31,170
22. Light Truck or Delivery Services Drivers	29,590

(continued)

(continued)

The 100 Jobs with the Most Openings
That Don't Require a Four-Year Degree

Job	Annual Openings
23. Construction Laborers	29,240
24. Electricians	28,920
25. Medical Secretaries	27,840
26. Supervisors of Construction and Extraction Workers	25,970
27. Managers, All Other	24,940
28. Police and Sheriff's Patrol Officers	24,940
29. First-Line Supervisors of Food Preparation and Serving Workers	24,830
30. Medical Assistants	24,380
31. Team Assemblers	24,100
32. Tellers	23,750
33. Farmers, Ranchers, and Other Agricultural Managers	23,450
34. Preschool Teachers, Except Special Education	23,240
35. Plumbers, Pipefitters, and Steamfitters	22,880
36. Hairdressers, Hairstylists, and Cosmetologists	21,810
37. Industrial Truck and Tractor Operators	20,950
38. Social and Human Service Assistants	18,910
39. Billing and Posting Clerks	18,760
40. Insurance Sales Agents	18,440
41. Shipping, Receiving, and Traffic Clerks	17,740
42. Pharmacy Technicians	16,630
43. First-Line Supervisors of Mechanics, Installers, and Repairers	16,490
44. Operating Engineers and Other Construction Equipment Operators	16,280
45. Painters, Construction and Maintenance	15,730
46. Dental Assistants	15,400
47. Counter and Rental Clerks	14,660
48. Bus Drivers, School or Special Client	14,450
49. Welders, Cutters, Solderers, and Brazers	14,070
50. Heating, Air Conditioning, and Refrigeration Mechanics and Installers	13,760
51. Cooks, Institution and Cafeteria	13,620
52. Bill and Account Collectors	13,550
53. Coaches and Scouts	13,300
54. Real Estate Sales Agents	12,760
55. Inspectors, Testers, Sorters, Samplers, and Weighers	12,390
56. First-Line Supervisors of Non-Retail Sales Workers	12,350
57. Driver/Sales Workers	12,290

The 100 Jobs with the Most Openings That Don't Require a Four-Year Degree

Job	Annual Openings
58. Emergency Medical Technicians and Paramedics	12,080
59. Construction Managers	12,040
60. Industrial Machinery Mechanics	11,710
61. Loan Officers	11,520
62. Firefighters	11,230
63. Correctional Officers and Jailers	10,810
64. Parts Salespersons	10,720
65. Dental Hygienists	10,490
66. Postal Service Mail Carriers	10,340
67. Fitness Trainers and Aerobics Instructors	10,060
68. Administrative Services Managers	9,980
69. Helpers—Production Workers	9,980
70. Machinists	9,950
71. Insurance Claims and Policy Processing Clerks	9,600
72. Radiologic Technologists and Technicians	9,510
73. Self-Enrichment Education Teachers	9,150
74. Purchasing Agents, Except Wholesale, Retail, and Farm Products	9,120
75. Production, Planning, and Expediting Clerks	8,880
76. First-Line Supervisors of Production and Operating Workers	8,790
77. Bus and Truck Mechanics and Diesel Engine Specialists	8,780
78. Telemarketers	8,350
79. Paralegals and Legal Assistants	8,340
80. First-Line Supervisors of Personal Service Workers	8,260
81. Property, Real Estate, and Community Association Managers	8,230
82. Helpers—Installation, Maintenance, and Repair Workers	8,040
83. First-Line Supervisors of Helpers, Laborers, and Material Movers, Hand	8,000
84. Claims Adjusters, Examiners, and Investigators	7,990
85. Interviewers, Except Eligibility and Loan	7,960
86. Taxi Drivers and Chauffeurs	7,670
87. Order Clerks	7,520
88. Meat, Poultry, and Fish Cutters and Trimmers	7,400
89. Medical Records and Health Information Technicians	7,370
90. Cement Masons and Concrete Finishers	7,290
91. Advertising Sales Agents	6,990
92. Refuse and Recyclable Material Collectors	6,970

(continued)

(continued)

The 100 Jobs with the Most Openings That Don't Require a Four-Year Degree	
Job	**Annual Openings**
93. Dispatchers, Except Police, Fire, and Ambulance	6,950
94. First-Line Supervisors of Transportation and Material-Moving Machine and Vehicle Operators	6,930
95. Payroll and Timekeeping Clerks	6,570
96. Automotive Body and Related Repairers	6,520
97. Library Assistants, Clerical	6,410
98. Bus Drivers, Transit and Intercity	6,350
99. Human Resources Assistants, Except Payroll and Timekeeping	6,160
100. First-Line Supervisors of Landscaping, Lawn Service, and Groundskeeping Workers	6,010

Best Jobs Lists by Demographic

I decided that it would be interesting to include lists in this section that show what sorts of jobs different types of people are most likely to have. For example, what jobs have the highest percentages of men or young workers? I'm not saying that men or young people should consider these jobs over others, but it is interesting information to know.

In some cases, the lists can give you ideas for jobs to consider that you might otherwise overlook. For example, perhaps women should consider some jobs that traditionally have high percentages of men in them. Or older workers might consider some jobs typically held by young people. Although these aren't obvious ways of using these lists, the lists may give you some good ideas of jobs to consider. The lists may also help you identify jobs that work well for others in your situation—for example, jobs with plentiful opportunities for rural workers, if that's the lifestyle you prefer.

All lists in this section were created through a similar process. I began with the 300 best jobs that don't require a four-year degree and sorted those jobs in order of the primary criterion for each set of lists. For example, I sorted the 300 jobs based on the percentage of workers age 16 to 24 from highest to lowest percentage and then selected the jobs with a high percentage (34 jobs with a percentage greater than 20). From this initial list of jobs with a high percentage of each type of worker, I created four more-specialized lists:

- ⊙ 25 Best Jobs Overall (the subset of jobs that have the highest combined scores for earnings, growth rate, and number of openings)
- ⊙ 25 Best-Paying Jobs
- ⊙ 25 Fastest-Growing Jobs
- ⊙ 25 Jobs with the Most Openings

Again, each of these four lists includes only jobs that have high percentages of the specific type of worker. The same basic process was used to create all the lists in this section. The lists are interesting, and I hope you find them helpful.

Best Jobs with the Highest Percentages of Workers Age 16–24

From my list of 300 jobs used in this book (or, to be precise, the 287 for which I had information about the age of workers), this list contains jobs with the highest percentages (more than 20 percent) of workers age 16 to 24, presented in order of the percentage of these young workers in each job. Younger workers are found in all jobs, but jobs with higher percentages of younger workers may present more opportunities for initial entry or upward mobility.

Best Jobs with the Highest Percentages of Workers Age 16–24	
Job	Percent Age 16–24
1. Choreographers	44.5%
2. Helpers—Installation, Maintenance, and Repair Workers	36.9%
3. Athletes and Sports Competitors	36.5%
4. Coaches and Scouts	36.5%
5. Bicycle Repairers	34.2%
6. Recreational Vehicle Service Technicians	34.2%
7. Tire Repairers and Changers	34.2%
8. Library Technicians	33.5%
9. Telemarketers	32.6%
10. Helpers—Production Workers	31.7%
11. Veterinary Assistants and Laboratory Animal Caretakers	30.9%
12. Helpers—Brickmasons, Blockmasons, Stonemasons, and Tile and Marble Setters	29.9%
13. Helpers—Carpenters	29.9%
14. Helpers—Electricians	29.9%
15. Helpers—Pipelayers, Plumbers, Pipefitters, and Steamfitters	29.9%
16. Library Assistants, Clerical	29.8%
17. Cooks, Institution and Cafeteria	29.6%
18. Roustabouts, Oil and Gas	29.5%
19. Counter and Rental Clerks	29.1%
20. Laborers and Freight, Stock, and Material Movers, Hand	28.8%
21. Fitness Trainers and Aerobics Instructors	28.6%
22. Residential Advisors	27.9%
23. Tour Guides and Escorts	27.8%

(continued)

(continued)

Best Jobs with the Highest Percentages of Workers Age 16–24

Job	Percent Age 16–24
24. Travel Guides	27.8%
25. Medical Equipment Preparers	26.7%
26. Tellers	26.3%
27. Environmental Science and Protection Technicians, Including Health	24.7%
28. Life, Physical, and Social Science Technicians, All Other	24.7%
29. Demonstrators and Product Promoters	22.5%
30. Receptionists and Information Clerks	22.0%
31. Landscaping and Groundskeeping Workers	21.4%
32. Tree Trimmers and Pruners	21.4%
33. Refuse and Recyclable Material Collectors	20.8%
34. Sawing Machine Setters, Operators, and Tenders, Wood	20.1%

The jobs in the following four lists are derived from the preceding list of the jobs with the highest percentages of workers age 16–24.

25 Best Jobs Overall with High Percentages of Workers Age 16–24

Job	Percent Age 16–24	Annual Earnings	Percent Growth	Annual Openings
1. Coaches and Scouts	36.5%	$28,470	29.4%	13,300
2. Fitness Trainers and Aerobics Instructors	28.6%	$31,030	24.0%	10,060
3. Receptionists and Information Clerks	22.0%	$25,690	23.7%	56,560
4. Refuse and Recyclable Material Collectors	20.8%	$32,280	20.2%	6,970
5. Helpers—Brickmasons, Blockmasons, Stonemasons, and Tile and Marble Setters	29.9%	$27,820	59.9%	2,540
6. Helpers—Electricians	29.9%	$27,620	30.6%	4,200
7. Helpers—Pipelayers, Plumbers, Pipefitters, and Steamfitters	29.9%	$27,010	45.4%	4,170
8. Helpers—Carpenters	29.9%	$26,400	55.7%	3,820
9. Environmental Science and Protection Technicians, Including Health	24.7%	$42,270	23.6%	1,950
10. Choreographers	44.5%	$39,600	24.2%	830
11. Residential Advisors	27.9%	$24,540	24.9%	4,570
12. Landscaping and Groundskeeping Workers	21.4%	$23,410	20.9%	44,440
13. Athletes and Sports Competitors	36.5%	$39,670	21.8%	780
14. Laborers and Freight, Stock, and Material Movers, Hand	28.8%	$23,750	15.4%	98,020

25 Best Jobs Overall with High Percentages of Workers Age 16–24

Job	Percent Age 16–24	Annual Earnings	Percent Growth	Annual Openings
15. Life, Physical, and Social Science Technicians, All Other	24.7%	$43,120	11.8%	3,350
16. Helpers—Installation, Maintenance, and Repair Workers	36.9%	$24,060	18.4%	8,040
17. Recreational Vehicle Service Technicians	34.2%	$34,000	22.2%	480
18. Sawing Machine Setters, Operators, and Tenders, Wood	20.1%	$26,220	24.6%	1,810
19. Library Technicians	33.5%	$30,430	8.8%	5,950
20. Travel Guides	27.8%	$30,670	23.8%	260
21. Tree Trimmers and Pruners	21.4%	$31,320	18.0%	1,800
22. Tellers	26.3%	$24,590	1.3%	23,750
23. Tire Repairers and Changers	34.2%	$23,440	18.5%	4,390
24. Demonstrators and Product Promoters	22.5%	$23,770	17.5%	4,210
25. Counter and Rental Clerks	29.1%	$22,740	12.2%	14,660

25 Best-Paying Jobs with High Percentages of Workers Age 16–24

Job	Percent Age 16–24	Annual Earnings
1. Life, Physical, and Social Science Technicians, All Other	24.7%	$43,120
2. Environmental Science and Protection Technicians, Including Health	24.7%	$42,270
3. Athletes and Sports Competitors	36.5%	$39,670
4. Choreographers	44.5%	$39,600
5. Recreational Vehicle Service Technicians	34.2%	$34,000
6. Roustabouts, Oil and Gas	29.5%	$32,980
7. Refuse and Recyclable Material Collectors	20.8%	$32,280
8. Tree Trimmers and Pruners	21.4%	$31,320
9. Fitness Trainers and Aerobics Instructors	28.6%	$31,030
10. Travel Guides	27.8%	$30,670
11. Library Technicians	33.5%	$30,430
12. Medical Equipment Preparers	26.7%	$30,050
13. Coaches and Scouts	36.5%	$28,470
14. Helpers—Brickmasons, Blockmasons, Stonemasons, and Tile and Marble Setters	29.9%	$27,820
15. Helpers—Electricians	29.9%	$27,620
16. Helpers—Pipelayers, Plumbers, Pipefitters, and Steamfitters	29.9%	$27,010
17. Helpers—Carpenters	29.9%	$26,400

(continued)

(continued)

25 Best-Paying Jobs with High Percentages of Workers Age 16–24

Job	Percent Age 16–24	Annual Earnings
18. Sawing Machine Setters, Operators, and Tenders, Wood	20.1%	$26,220
19. Receptionists and Information Clerks	22.0%	$25,690
20. Tellers	26.3%	$24,590
21. Residential Advisors	27.9%	$24,540
22. Helpers—Installation, Maintenance, and Repair Workers	36.9%	$24,060
23. Demonstrators and Product Promoters	22.5%	$23,770
24. Laborers and Freight, Stock, and Material Movers, Hand	28.8%	$23,750
25. Tour Guides and Escorts	27.8%	$23,620

25 Fastest-Growing Jobs with High Percentages of Workers Age 16–24

Job	Percent Age 16-24	Percent Growth
1. Helpers—Brickmasons, Blockmasons, Stonemasons, and Tile and Marble Setters	29.9%	59.9%
2. Helpers—Carpenters	29.9%	55.7%
3. Helpers—Pipelayers, Plumbers, Pipefitters, and Steamfitters	29.9%	45.4%
4. Bicycle Repairers	34.2%	37.4%
5. Helpers—Electricians	29.9%	30.6%
6. Coaches and Scouts	36.5%	29.4%
7. Residential Advisors	27.9%	24.9%
8. Sawing Machine Setters, Operators, and Tenders, Wood	20.1%	24.6%
9. Choreographers	44.5%	24.2%
10. Fitness Trainers and Aerobics Instructors	28.6%	24.0%
11. Travel Guides	27.8%	23.8%
12. Receptionists and Information Clerks	22.0%	23.7%
13. Environmental Science and Protection Technicians, Including Health	24.7%	23.6%
14. Recreational Vehicle Service Technicians	34.2%	22.2%
15. Athletes and Sports Competitors	36.5%	21.8%
16. Landscaping and Groundskeeping Workers	21.4%	20.9%
17. Refuse and Recyclable Material Collectors	20.8%	20.2%
18. Tire Repairers and Changers	34.2%	18.5%
19. Helpers—Installation, Maintenance, and Repair Workers	36.9%	18.4%
20. Tour Guides and Escorts	27.8%	18.1%
21. Tree Trimmers and Pruners	21.4%	18.0%
22. Demonstrators and Product Promoters	22.5%	17.5%

25 Fastest-Growing Jobs with High Percentages of Workers Age 16–24

Job	Percent Age 16-24	Percent Growth
23. Medical Equipment Preparers	26.7%	17.5%
24. Laborers and Freight, Stock, and Material Movers, Hand	28.8%	15.4%
25. Veterinary Assistants and Laboratory Animal Caretakers	30.9%	14.2%

25 Jobs with the Most Openings with High Percentages of Workers Age 16–24

Job	Percent Age 16–24	Annual Openings
1. Laborers and Freight, Stock, and Material Movers, Hand	28.8%	98,020
2. Receptionists and Information Clerks	22.0%	56,560
3. Landscaping and Groundskeeping Workers	21.4%	44,440
4. Tellers	26.3%	23,750
5. Counter and Rental Clerks	29.1%	14,660
6. Cooks, Institution and Cafeteria	29.6%	13,620
7. Coaches and Scouts	36.5%	13,300
8. Fitness Trainers and Aerobics Instructors	28.6%	10,060
9. Helpers—Production Workers	31.7%	9,980
10. Telemarketers	32.6%	8,350
11. Helpers—Installation, Maintenance, and Repair Workers	36.9%	8,040
12. Refuse and Recyclable Material Collectors	20.8%	6,970
13. Library Assistants, Clerical	29.8%	6,410
14. Library Technicians	33.5%	5,950
15. Residential Advisors	27.9%	4,570
16. Tire Repairers and Changers	34.2%	4,390
17. Demonstrators and Product Promoters	22.5%	4,210
18. Helpers—Electricians	29.9%	4,200
19. Helpers—Pipelayers, Plumbers, Pipefitters, and Steamfitters	29.9%	4,170
20. Helpers—Carpenters	29.9%	3,820
21. Life, Physical, and Social Science Technicians, All Other	24.7%	3,350
22. Helpers—Brickmasons, Blockmasons, Stonemasons, and Tile and Marble Setters	29.9%	2,540
23. Veterinary Assistants and Laboratory Animal Caretakers	30.9%	2,160
24. Tour Guides and Escorts	27.8%	1,960
25. Environmental Science and Protection Technicians, Including Health	24.7%	1,950

Best Jobs with High Percentages of Workers Age 55 and Over

Older workers don't change careers as often as younger ones do, and on average, they tend to have been in their jobs for quite some time. Many of the jobs with the highest percentages of workers age 55 and over—and those with the highest earnings—require considerable preparation, either through experience or through education and training. As a result, these are not the sorts of jobs most younger workers could easily get.

But older workers who are considering a job change may find some interesting possibilities on the list of jobs with the highest percentages (more than 25 percent) of older workers. Some would make good "retirement" jobs, particularly if they allowed for part-time work or self-employment.

Best Jobs with the Highest Percentages of Workers Age 55 and Over

Job	Percent Age 55 and Over
1. Buyers and Purchasing Agents, Farm Products	55.3%
2. Farmers, Ranchers, and Other Agricultural Managers	54.0%
3. Nuclear Technicians	50.0%
4. Bus Drivers, School or Special Client	45.4%
5. Bus Drivers, Transit and Intercity	45.4%
6. Postal Service Clerks	43.9%
7. Real Estate Brokers	40.1%
8. Real Estate Sales Agents	40.1%
9. Stationary Engineers and Boiler Operators	39.3%
10. Property, Real Estate, and Community Association Managers	38.5%
11. Construction and Building Inspectors	38.4%
12. Tax Preparers	37.9%
13. Taxi Drivers and Chauffeurs	37.7%
14. Motorboat Mechanics and Service Technicians	37.5%
15. Motorcycle Mechanics	37.5%
16. Outdoor Power Equipment and Other Small Engine Mechanics	37.5%
17. First-Line Supervisors of Farming, Fishing, and Forestry Workers	37.4%
18. Medical Transcriptionists	37.2%
19. Appraisers and Assessors of Real Estate	37.1%
20. Motorboat Operators	36.7%
21. Locksmiths and Safe Repairers	36.6%
22. Gaming Managers	36.3%
23. Procurement Clerks	36.1%
24. Lodging Managers	34.1%

Best Jobs with the Highest Percentages of Workers Age 55 and Over

Job	Percent Age 55 and Over
25. Water and Wastewater Treatment Plant and System Operators	33.8%
26. Travel Agents	33.6%
27. Bookkeeping, Accounting, and Auditing Clerks	33.5%
28. Fine Artists, Including Painters, Sculptors, and Illustrators	33.5%
29. Maintenance Workers, Machinery	33.5%
30. Medical Equipment Repairers	33.4%
31. Library Assistants, Clerical	33.2%
32. First-Line Supervisors of Mechanics, Installers, and Repairers	32.5%
33. Chemical Plant and System Operators	32.2%
34. Home Appliance Repairers	31.6%
35. Tour Guides and Escorts	31.4%
36. Travel Guides	31.4%
37. Administrative Services Managers	31.2%
38. Demonstrators and Product Promoters	30.9%
39. Executive Secretaries and Executive Administrative Assistants	30.8%
40. First-Line Supervisors of Housekeeping and Janitorial Workers	30.8%
41. Legal Secretaries	30.8%
42. Medical Secretaries	30.8%
43. Secretaries and Administrative Assistants, Except Legal, Medical, and Executive	30.8%
44. Airline Pilots, Copilots, and Flight Engineers	30.7%
45. Commercial Pilots	30.7%
46. Cabinetmakers and Bench Carpenters	30.2%
47. Court, Municipal, and License Clerks	29.8%
48. Opticians, Dispensing	29.2%
49. Insurance Sales Agents	28.8%
50. Locomotive Engineers	28.7%
51. Managers, All Other	28.2%
52. Postal Service Mail Carriers	28.2%
53. Self-Enrichment Education Teachers	28.2%
54. Weighers, Measurers, Checkers, and Samplers, Recordkeeping	27.9%
55. Aircraft Structure, Surfaces, Rigging, and Systems Assemblers	27.8%
56. Maintenance and Repair Workers, General	27.7%
57. Court Reporters	27.5%
58. First-Line Supervisors of Non-Retail Sales Workers	27.3%
59. Interviewers, Except Eligibility and Loan	27.0%
60. Machinists	26.8%

(continued)

(continued)

Best Jobs with the Highest Percentages of Workers Age 55 and Over

Job	Percent Age 55 and Over
61. Security Guards	26.8%
62. Substance Abuse and Behavioral Disorder Counselors	26.8%
63. Mail Clerks and Mail Machine Operators, Except Postal Service	26.4%
64. Driver/Sales Workers	26.3%
65. Heavy and Tractor-Trailer Truck Drivers	26.3%
66. Light Truck or Delivery Services Drivers	26.3%
67. Parts Salespersons	26.2%
68. Social and Human Service Assistants	26.2%
69. Construction Managers	26.1%
70. Couriers and Messengers	25.9%
71. Registered Nurses	25.8%
72. Geological and Petroleum Technicians	25.6%
73. Medical Records and Health Information Technicians	25.6%
74. First-Line Supervisors of Office and Administrative Support Workers	25.4%
75. Purchasing Agents, Except Wholesale, Retail, and Farm Products	25.4%
76. Coin, Vending, and Amusement Machine Servicers and Repairers	25.3%
77. Control and Valve Installers and Repairers, Except Mechanical Door	25.2%
78. Mechanical Door Repairers	25.2%
79. Wholesale and Retail Buyers, Except Farm Products	25.1%

The jobs in the following four lists are derived from the preceding list of the jobs with the highest percentages of workers age 55 and over.

25 Best Jobs Overall with High Percentages of Workers Age 55 and Over

Job	Percent Age 55 and Over	Annual Earnings	Percent Growth	Annual Openings
1. Registered Nurses	25.8%	$65,950	26.0%	120,740
2. Construction Managers	26.1%	$84,240	16.6%	12,040
3. Insurance Sales Agents	28.8%	$47,450	21.9%	18,440
4. Administrative Services Managers	31.2%	$79,540	14.5%	9,980
5. Heavy and Tractor-Trailer Truck Drivers	26.3%	$37,930	20.6%	64,940
6. First-Line Supervisors of Office and Administrative Support Workers	25.4%	$48,810	14.3%	58,440
7. Managers, All Other	28.2%	$99,540	7.9%	24,940

25 Best Jobs Overall with High Percentages of Workers Age 55 and Over

Job	Percent Age 55 and Over	Annual Earnings	Percent Growth	Annual Openings
8. Construction and Building Inspectors	38.4%	$53,180	18.0%	4,860
9. First-Line Supervisors of Mechanics, Installers, and Repairers	32.5%	$59,850	11.9%	16,490
10. Commercial Pilots	30.7%	$70,000	21.1%	1,930
11. Medical Secretaries	30.8%	$31,060	41.3%	27,840
12. Executive Secretaries and Executive Administrative Assistants	30.8%	$45,580	12.6%	32,180
13. Substance Abuse and Behavioral Disorder Counselors	26.8%	$38,560	27.4%	4,170
14. Medical Equipment Repairers	33.4%	$44,870	31.4%	2,230
15. Self-Enrichment Education Teachers	28.2%	$36,100	20.9%	9,150
16. Social and Human Service Assistants	26.2%	$28,740	27.6%	18,910
17. Bookkeeping, Accounting, and Auditing Clerks	33.5%	$34,740	13.6%	46,780
18. First-Line Supervisors of Non-Retail Sales Workers	27.3%	$70,520	4.0%	12,350
19. Real Estate Sales Agents	40.1%	$39,070	12.2%	12,760
20. Farmers, Ranchers, and Other Agricultural Managers	54.0%	$64,660	–8.0%	23,450
21. Medical Records and Health Information Technicians	25.6%	$33,310	21.0%	7,370
22. Security Guards	26.8%	$23,900	18.8%	35,950
23. Maintenance and Repair Workers, General	27.7%	$35,030	11.0%	37,910
24. Light Truck or Delivery Services Drivers	26.3%	$29,080	14.7%	29,590
25. Opticians, Dispensing	29.2%	$33,100	28.9%	3,060

25 Best-Paying Jobs with High Percentages of Workers Age 55 and Over

Job	Percent Age 55 and Over	Annual Earnings
1. Airline Pilots, Copilots, and Flight Engineers	30.7%	$105,580
2. Managers, All Other	28.2%	$99,540
3. Construction Managers	26.1%	$84,240
4. Administrative Services Managers	31.2%	$79,540
5. First-Line Supervisors of Non-Retail Sales Workers	27.3%	$70,520
6. Commercial Pilots	30.7%	$70,000
7. Nuclear Technicians	50.0%	$68,030
8. Gaming Managers	36.3%	$67,230
9. Registered Nurses	25.8%	$65,950

(continued)

(continued)

25 Best-Paying Jobs with High Percentages of Workers Age 55 and Over

Job	Percent Age 55 and Over	Annual Earnings
10. Farmers, Ranchers, and Other Agricultural Managers	54.0%	$64,660
11. First-Line Supervisors of Mechanics, Installers, and Repairers	32.5%	$59,850
12. Real Estate Brokers	40.1%	$59,340
13. Purchasing Agents, Except Wholesale, Retail, and Farm Products	25.4%	$57,580
14. Chemical Plant and System Operators	32.2%	$55,940
15. Buyers and Purchasing Agents, Farm Products	55.3%	$55,860
16. Postal Service Mail Carriers	28.2%	$55,160
17. Construction and Building Inspectors	38.4%	$53,180
18. Postal Service Clerks	43.9%	$53,100
19. Stationary Engineers and Boiler Operators	39.3%	$53,070
20. Property, Real Estate, and Community Association Managers	38.5%	$52,510
21. Wholesale and Retail Buyers, Except Farm Products	25.1%	$50,490
22. Geological and Petroleum Technicians	25.6%	$49,690
23. Control and Valve Installers and Repairers, Except Mechanical Door	25.2%	$49,600
24. Locomotive Engineers	28.7%	$49,380
25. Appraisers and Assessors of Real Estate	37.1%	$48,870

25 Fastest-Growing Jobs with High Percentages of Workers Age 55 and Over

Job	Percent Age 55 and Over	Percent Growth
1. Medical Secretaries	30.8%	41.3%
2. Medical Equipment Repairers	33.4%	31.4%
3. Opticians, Dispensing	29.2%	28.9%
4. Social and Human Service Assistants	26.2%	27.6%
5. Substance Abuse and Behavioral Disorder Counselors	26.8%	27.4%
6. Registered Nurses	25.8%	26.0%
7. Mechanical Door Repairers	25.2%	24.2%
8. Travel Guides	31.4%	23.8%
9. Motorcycle Mechanics	37.5%	23.3%
10. Coin, Vending, and Amusement Machine Servicers and Repairers	25.3%	22.0%
11. Insurance Sales Agents	28.8%	21.9%
12. Commercial Pilots	30.7%	21.1%

25 Fastest-Growing Jobs with High Percentages of Workers Age 55 and Over

Job	Percent Age 55 and Over	Percent Growth
13. Medical Records and Health Information Technicians	25.6%	21.0%
14. Self-Enrichment Education Teachers	28.2%	20.9%
15. Motorboat Mechanics and Service Technicians	37.5%	20.7%
16. Heavy and Tractor-Trailer Truck Drivers	26.3%	20.6%
17. Taxi Drivers and Chauffeurs	37.7%	19.6%
18. Outdoor Power Equipment and Other Small Engine Mechanics	37.5%	18.9%
19. Security Guards	26.8%	18.8%
20. Tour Guides and Escorts	31.4%	18.1%
21. Construction and Building Inspectors	38.4%	18.0%
22. Locksmiths and Safe Repairers	36.6%	17.9%
23. Demonstrators and Product Promoters	30.9%	17.5%
24. Interviewers, Except Eligibility and Loan	27.0%	17.3%
25. Cabinetmakers and Bench Carpenters	30.2%	16.8%

25 Jobs with the Most Openings with High Percentages of Workers Age 55 and Over

Job	Percent Age 55 and Over	Annual Openings
1. Registered Nurses	25.8%	120,740
2. Heavy and Tractor-Trailer Truck Drivers	26.3%	64,940
3. First-Line Supervisors of Office and Administrative Support Workers	25.4%	58,440
4. Bookkeeping, Accounting, and Auditing Clerks	33.5%	46,780
5. Secretaries and Administrative Assistants, Except Legal, Medical, and Executive	30.8%	39,100
6. Maintenance and Repair Workers, General	27.7%	37,910
7. Security Guards	26.8%	35,950
8. Executive Secretaries and Executive Administrative Assistants	30.8%	32,180
9. Light Truck or Delivery Services Drivers	26.3%	29,590
10. Medical Secretaries	30.8%	27,840
11. Managers, All Other	28.2%	24,940
12. Farmers, Ranchers, and Other Agricultural Managers	54.0%	23,450
13. Social and Human Service Assistants	26.2%	18,910
14. Insurance Sales Agents	28.8%	18,440

(continued)

(continued)

25 Jobs with the Most Openings with High Percentages of Workers Age 55 and Over		
Job	Percent Age 55 and Over	Annual Openings
15. First-Line Supervisors of Mechanics, Installers, and Repairers	32.5%	16,490
16. Bus Drivers, School or Special Client	45.4%	14,450
17. Real Estate Sales Agents	40.1%	12,760
18. First-Line Supervisors of Non-Retail Sales Workers	27.3%	12,350
19. Driver/Sales Workers	26.3%	12,290
20. Construction Managers	26.1%	12,040
21. Parts Salespersons	26.2%	10,720
22. Postal Service Mail Carriers	28.2%	10,340
23. Administrative Services Managers	31.2%	9,980
24. Machinists	26.8%	9,950
25. Self-Enrichment Education Teachers	28.2%	9,150

Best Jobs with High Percentages of Self-Employed Workers

About 8 percent of all working people are self-employed. Although you may think of the self-employed as having similar jobs, they actually work in an enormous range of situations, fields, and work environments that you may not have considered.

Among the self-employed are people who own small or large businesses, as many real estate brokers and funeral directors do; professionals who own their own practices, as many lawyers, psychologists, and medical doctors do; people working on a contract basis for one or more employers, as many interior designers do; people running home consulting or other businesses; and people in many other situations. They may go to the same worksite every day, as most tellers do; visit multiple employers during the course of a week, as many models do; or do most of their work from home, as many craft artists do. Some work part time, others full time, some as a way to have fun, some so they can spend time with their kids or go to school.

The point is that people are self-employed in many different ways, and one of these arrangements could make sense for you now or in the future.

The following list contains jobs in which more than 20 percent of the workers are self-employed.

Best Jobs with the Highest Percentages of Self-Employed Workers

	Percent Self-Employed Workers
1. Construction Managers	60.9%
2. Photographers	60.1%
3. Fine Artists, Including Painters, Sculptors, and Illustrators	59.9%
4. Real Estate Brokers	58.3%
5. Real Estate Sales Agents	58.3%
6. Massage Therapists	57.2%
7. Managers, All Other	57.1%
8. First-Line Supervisors of Landscaping, Lawn Service, and Groundskeeping Workers	50.4%
9. Property, Real Estate, and Community Association Managers	45.9%
10. First-Line Supervisors of Non-Retail Sales Workers	45.6%
11. Lodging Managers	45.2%
12. Painters, Construction and Maintenance	45.0%
13. Hairdressers, Hairstylists, and Cosmetologists	43.5%
14. Food Service Managers	42.0%
15. Gaming Managers	38.6%
16. First-Line Supervisors of Personal Service Workers	37.8%
17. Gaming Supervisors	36.6%
18. Floor Sanders and Finishers	35.1%
19. Tile and Marble Setters	35.1%
20. Carpet Installers	35.0%
21. Carpenters	32.0%
22. Skincare Specialists	31.9%
23. First-Line Supervisors of Retail Sales Workers	30.6%
24. Tax Preparers	28.9%
25. Brickmasons and Blockmasons	27.3%
26. Appraisers and Assessors of Real Estate	27.2%
27. Stonemasons	27.1%
28. Fashion Designers	26.8%
29. Home Appliance Repairers	26.8%
30. Fence Erectors	26.7%
31. Merchandise Displayers and Window Trimmers	26.7%
32. Taxi Drivers and Chauffeurs	26.3%
33. Electronic Home Entertainment Equipment Installers and Repairers	25.8%
34. First-Line Supervisors of Housekeeping and Janitorial Workers	23.3%
35. Tree Trimmers and Pruners	22.7%
36. Insurance Sales Agents	22.4%

(continued)

(continued)

Best Jobs with the Highest Percentages of Self-Employed Workers

	Percent Self-Employed Workers
37. Landscaping and Groundskeeping Workers	22.0%
38. Construction Laborers	21.3%
39. Roofers	21.1%
40. Private Detectives and Investigators	20.7%
41. First-Line Supervisors of Farming, Fishing, and Forestry Workers	20.4%

The jobs in the following four lists are derived from the preceding list of jobs with the highest percentages of self-employed workers. Where the following lists give earnings estimates, keep in mind that these figures are based on a survey that *doesn't include self-employed workers*. The median earnings for self-employed workers in these occupations may be significantly higher or lower. The figures on job growth and number of openings apply to all workers in the occupation and not just to self-employed workers, who create their own jobs.

25 Best Jobs Overall with High Percentages of Self-Employed Workers

Job	Percent Self-Employed Workers	Annual Earnings	Percent Growth	Annual Openings
1. Insurance Sales Agents	22.4%	$47,450	21.9%	18,440
2. Construction Managers	60.9%	$84,240	16.6%	12,040
3. Brickmasons and Blockmasons	27.3%	$46,800	40.5%	5,450
4. Carpenters	32.0%	$40,010	19.6%	40,830
5. Managers, All Other	57.1%	$99,540	7.9%	24,940
6. Construction Laborers	21.3%	$29,730	21.3%	29,240
7. Painters, Construction and Maintenance	45.0%	$35,430	18.5%	15,730
8. Tile and Marble Setters	35.1%	$37,080	25.4%	2,770
9. Landscaping and Groundskeeping Workers	22.0%	$23,410	20.9%	44,440
10. First-Line Supervisors of Non-Retail Sales Workers	45.6%	$70,520	4.0%	12,350
11. First-Line Supervisors of Landscaping, Lawn Service, and Groundskeeping Workers	50.4%	$42,050	15.1%	6,010
12. Massage Therapists	57.2%	$35,830	20.1%	5,590
13. First-Line Supervisors of Retail Sales Workers	30.6%	$36,480	8.4%	51,370
14. Real Estate Sales Agents	58.3%	$39,070	12.2%	12,760
15. Private Detectives and Investigators	20.7%	$43,710	20.5%	1,490
16. Property, Real Estate, and Community Association Managers	45.9%	$52,510	6.1%	8,230

25 Best Jobs Overall with High Percentages of Self-Employed Workers

Job	Percent Self-Employed Workers	Annual Earnings	Percent Growth	Annual Openings
17. First-Line Supervisors of Personal Service Workers	37.8%	$35,230	13.5%	8,260
18. Real Estate Brokers	58.3%	$59,340	7.6%	2,970
19. Roofers	21.1%	$35,280	17.8%	5,250
20. Stonemasons	27.1%	$36,640	36.5%	890
21. Hairdressers, Hairstylists, and Cosmetologists	43.5%	$22,570	15.7%	21,810
22. Taxi Drivers and Chauffeurs	26.3%	$22,760	19.6%	7,670
23. Appraisers and Assessors of Real Estate	27.2%	$48,870	7.5%	2,220
24. Food Service Managers	42.0%	$48,110	–3.3%	5,910
25. Skincare Specialists	31.9%	$29,190	24.6%	2,040

25 Best-Paying Jobs with High Percentages of Self-Employed Workers

Job	Percent Self-Employed Workers	Annual Earnings
1. Managers, All Other	57.1%	$99,540
2. Construction Managers	60.9%	$84,240
3. First-Line Supervisors of Non-Retail Sales Workers	45.6%	$70,520
4. Gaming Managers	38.6%	$67,230
5. Fashion Designers	26.8%	$64,690
6. Real Estate Brokers	58.3%	$59,340
7. Property, Real Estate, and Community Association Managers	45.9%	$52,510
8. Appraisers and Assessors of Real Estate	27.2%	$48,870
9. Gaming Supervisors	36.6%	$48,820
10. Food Service Managers	42.0%	$48,110
11. Insurance Sales Agents	22.4%	$47,450
12. Lodging Managers	45.2%	$47,450
13. Brickmasons and Blockmasons	27.3%	$46,800
14. Fine Artists, Including Painters, Sculptors, and Illustrators	59.9%	$44,600
15. Private Detectives and Investigators	20.7%	$43,710
16. First-Line Supervisors of Farming, Fishing, and Forestry Workers	20.4%	$42,600
17. First-Line Supervisors of Landscaping, Lawn Service, and Groundskeeping Workers	50.4%	$42,050
18. Carpenters	32.0%	$40,010
19. Real Estate Sales Agents	58.3%	$39,070
20. Tile and Marble Setters	35.1%	$37,080

(continued)

(continued)

25 Best-Paying Jobs with High Percentages of Self-Employed Workers

Job	Percent Self-Employed Workers	Annual Earnings
21. Carpet Installers	35.0%	$36,750
22. Stonemasons	27.1%	$36,640
23. First-Line Supervisors of Retail Sales Workers	30.6%	$36,480
24. Massage Therapists	57.2%	$35,830
25. Home Appliance Repairers	26.8%	$35,440

25 Fastest-Growing Jobs with High Percentages of Self-Employed Workers

Job	Percent Self-Employed Workers	Percent Growth
1. Brickmasons and Blockmasons	27.3%	40.5%
2. Stonemasons	27.1%	36.5%
3. Tile and Marble Setters	35.1%	25.4%
4. Skincare Specialists	31.9%	24.6%
5. Fence Erectors	26.7%	23.7%
6. Insurance Sales Agents	22.4%	21.9%
7. Construction Laborers	21.3%	21.3%
8. Landscaping and Groundskeeping Workers	22.0%	20.9%
9. Private Detectives and Investigators	20.7%	20.5%
10. Massage Therapists	57.2%	20.1%
11. Carpenters	32.0%	19.6%
12. Taxi Drivers and Chauffeurs	26.3%	19.6%
13. Painters, Construction and Maintenance	45.0%	18.5%
14. Tree Trimmers and Pruners	22.7%	18.0%
15. Floor Sanders and Finishers	35.1%	17.8%
16. Roofers	21.1%	17.8%
17. Construction Managers	60.9%	16.6%
18. Hairdressers, Hairstylists, and Cosmetologists	43.5%	15.7%
19. First-Line Supervisors of Landscaping, Lawn Service, and Groundskeeping Workers	50.4%	15.1%
20. Electronic Home Entertainment Equipment Installers and Repairers	25.8%	13.9%
21. First-Line Supervisors of Personal Service Workers	37.8%	13.5%
22. Merchandise Displayers and Window Trimmers	26.7%	12.8%

25 Fastest-Growing Jobs with High Percentages of Self-Employed Workers

Job	Percent Self-Employed Workers	Percent Growth
23. Photographers	60.1%	12.5%
24. Real Estate Sales Agents	58.3%	12.2%
25. Gaming Managers	38.6%	12.1%

25 Jobs with the Most Openings with High Percentages of Self-Employed Workers

Job	Percent Self-Employed Workers	Annual Openings
1. First-Line Supervisors of Retail Sales Workers	30.6%	51,370
2. Landscaping and Groundskeeping Workers	22.0%	44,440
3. Carpenters	32.0%	40,830
4. Construction Laborers	21.3%	29,240
5. Managers, All Other	57.1%	24,940
6. Hairdressers, Hairstylists, and Cosmetologists	43.5%	21,810
7. Insurance Sales Agents	22.4%	18,440
8. Painters, Construction and Maintenance	45.0%	15,730
9. Real Estate Sales Agents	58.3%	12,760
10. First-Line Supervisors of Non-Retail Sales Workers	45.6%	12,350
11. Construction Managers	60.9%	12,040
12. First-Line Supervisors of Personal Service Workers	37.8%	8,260
13. Property, Real Estate, and Community Association Managers	45.9%	8,230
14. Taxi Drivers and Chauffeurs	26.3%	7,670
15. First-Line Supervisors of Landscaping, Lawn Service, and Groundskeeping Workers	50.4%	6,010
16. Food Service Managers	42.0%	5,910
17. Massage Therapists	57.2%	5,590
18. Brickmasons and Blockmasons	27.3%	5,450
19. Roofers	21.1%	5,250
20. Merchandise Displayers and Window Trimmers	26.7%	4,000
21. First-Line Supervisors of Housekeeping and Janitorial Workers	23.3%	3,320
22. Photographers	60.1%	3,100
23. Real Estate Brokers	58.3%	2,970
24. Tile and Marble Setters	35.1%	2,770
25. Tax Preparers	28.9%	2,630

Best Jobs Employing High Percentages of Women

To create the lists that follow, I sorted the 300 best jobs according to the percentages of women and men in the workforce, setting the cutoff level at 80 percent. Understand that a job with a figure of 100 percent women (or men, in the next set of lists) does have a small number of workers of the opposite sex, but the sample was too small for them to show up in the percentages.

Similar lists of the best jobs with high percentages of men and women are included in all the books in the *Best Jobs* series. It's important to understand that these lists aren't meant to restrict women or men from considering job options. Actually, my reasoning for including them is exactly the opposite: I hope the lists help people see possibilities that they might not otherwise have considered.

The fact is that jobs with high percentages of women or high percentages of men offer good opportunities for both men and women if they want to do one of these jobs. So I suggest that women browse the lists of jobs that employ high percentages of men and that men browse the lists of jobs with high percentages of women. There are jobs in both sets of lists that pay well, and women or men who are interested in them and who have or can obtain the necessary education and training should consider them. In fact, economists have found a recent uptick of men moving into jobs traditionally dominated by women.

An interesting and unfortunate tidbit to bring up at your next party is that the average earnings for the jobs in this book with the highest percentage of women is $36,652, compared to average earnings of $40,317 for the jobs with the highest percentage of men. But earnings don't tell the whole story. I computed the average growth and job openings of the jobs with the highest percentage of women and found an average of 17.6% growth and 22,932 openings, compared to an average of 15.3% growth and 6,365 openings for the jobs with the highest percentage of men. This discrepancy reinforces the idea that men have had more problems than women in adapting to an economy dominated by service and information-based jobs. Many women may simply be better prepared, possessing more appropriate skills for the jobs that now are growing rapidly and have more job openings.

Best Jobs Employing the Highest Percentages of Women

Job	Percent Women
1. Brokerage Clerks	100.0%
2. Preschool Teachers, Except Special Education	98.4%
3. Executive Secretaries and Executive Administrative Assistants	96.8%
4. Legal Secretaries	96.8%
5. Medical Secretaries	96.8%
6. Secretaries and Administrative Assistants, Except Legal, Medical, and Executive	96.8%
7. Dental Assistants	96.7%
8. Dental Hygienists	96.1%
9. Receptionists and Information Clerks	92.4%
10. Teacher Assistants	91.5%

11. Licensed Practical and Licensed Vocational Nurses	91.4%
12. Registered Nurses	90.7%
13. Medical Assistants	90.4%
14. Medical Equipment Preparers	90.4%
15. Medical Transcriptionists	90.4%
16. Veterinary Assistants and Laboratory Animal Caretakers	90.4%
17. Bookkeeping, Accounting, and Auditing Clerks	90.0%
18. Billing and Posting Clerks	89.6%
19. Occupational Health and Safety Technicians	88.9%
20. Payroll and Timekeeping Clerks	88.5%
21. Medical Records and Health Information Technicians	88.4%
22. Psychiatric Aides	88.0%
23. Tellers	87.1%
24. Hairdressers, Hairstylists, and Cosmetologists	87.0%
25. Eligibility Interviewers, Government Programs	86.9%
26. Paralegals and Legal Assistants	86.7%
27. Interviewers, Except Eligibility and Loan	84.4%
28. Travel Agents	84.1%
29. Office Clerks, General	82.2%
30. Insurance Claims and Policy Processing Clerks	80.6%
31. Demonstrators and Product Promoters	80.0%

The jobs in the following four lists are derived from the preceding list of the jobs employing the highest percentages of women. Keep in mind that the earnings estimates in the following lists are based on a survey of *all* workers, not just women. In some occupations women earn much less than their male coworkers; for example, female Insurance Sales Agents earn 19 percent less. In a few occupations women earn more—for example, female Teacher Assistants earn 5 percent more. On average, women earn about 80 percent of the earnings of men in the same occupation. The earnings differences for the occupations in the following lists may be significantly higher or lower.

25 Best Jobs Overall Employing High Percentages of Women

Job	Percent Women	Annual Earnings	Percent Growth	Annual Openings
1. Registered Nurses	90.7%	$65,950	26.0%	120,740
2. Dental Hygienists	96.1%	$69,280	37.7%	10,490
3. Licensed Practical and Licensed Vocational Nurses	91.4%	$41,150	22.4%	36,920
4. Medical Secretaries	96.8%	$31,060	41.3%	27,840
5. Dental Assistants	96.7%	$34,140	30.8%	15,400
6. Paralegals and Legal Assistants	86.7%	$46,730	18.3%	8,340

(continued)

(continued)

25 Best Jobs Overall Employing High Percentages of Women

Job	Percent Women	Annual Earnings	Percent Growth	Annual Openings
7. Medical Assistants	90.4%	$29,100	30.9%	24,380
8. Receptionists and Information Clerks	92.4%	$25,690	23.7%	56,560
9. Executive Secretaries and Executive Administrative Assistants	96.8%	$45,580	12.6%	32,180
10. Bookkeeping, Accounting, and Auditing Clerks	90.0%	$34,740	13.6%	46,780
11. Office Clerks, General	82.2%	$27,190	16.6%	101,150
12. Billing and Posting Clerks	89.6%	$32,880	19.7%	18,760
13. Preschool Teachers, Except Special Education	98.4%	$26,620	24.9%	23,240
14. Medical Records and Health Information Technicians	88.4%	$33,310	21.0%	7,370
15. Payroll and Timekeeping Clerks	88.5%	$37,160	14.6%	6,570
16. Teacher Assistants	91.5%	$23,580	14.8%	48,160
17. Secretaries and Administrative Assistants, Except Legal, Medical, and Executive	96.8%	$31,870	5.8%	39,100
18. Insurance Claims and Policy Processing Clerks	80.6%	$35,210	8.7%	9,600
19. Interviewers, Except Eligibility and Loan	84.4%	$29,560	17.3%	7,960
20. Occupational Health and Safety Technicians	88.9%	$46,030	13.2%	510
21. Legal Secretaries	96.8%	$42,460	3.5%	3,940
22. Hairdressers, Hairstylists, and Cosmetologists	87.0%	$22,570	15.7%	21,810
23. Brokerage Clerks	100.0%	$41,760	5.9%	1,970
24. Demonstrators and Product Promoters	80.0%	$23,770	17.5%	4,210
25. Eligibility Interviewers, Government Programs	86.9%	$41,060	3.1%	3,740

25 Best-Paying Jobs Employing High Percentages of Women

Job	Percent Women	Annual Earnings
1. Dental Hygienists	96.1%	$69,280
2. Registered Nurses	90.7%	$65,950
3. Paralegals and Legal Assistants	86.7%	$46,730
4. Occupational Health and Safety Technicians	88.9%	$46,030
5. Executive Secretaries and Executive Administrative Assistants	96.8%	$45,580
6. Legal Secretaries	96.8%	$42,460
7. Brokerage Clerks	100.0%	$41,760
8. Licensed Practical and Licensed Vocational Nurses	91.4%	$41,150
9. Eligibility Interviewers, Government Programs	86.9%	$41,060
10. Payroll and Timekeeping Clerks	88.5%	$37,160
11. Insurance Claims and Policy Processing Clerks	80.6%	$35,210

25 Best-Paying Jobs Employing High Percentages of Women

Job	Percent Women	Annual Earnings
12. Bookkeeping, Accounting, and Auditing Clerks	90.0%	$34,740
13. Dental Assistants	96.7%	$34,140
14. Travel Agents	84.1%	$33,930
15. Medical Transcriptionists	90.4%	$33,480
16. Medical Records and Health Information Technicians	88.4%	$33,310
17. Billing and Posting Clerks	89.6%	$32,880
18. Secretaries and Administrative Assistants, Except Legal, Medical, and Executive	96.8%	$31,870
19. Medical Secretaries	96.8%	$31,060
20. Medical Equipment Preparers	90.4%	$30,050
21. Interviewers, Except Eligibility and Loan	84.4%	$29,560
22. Medical Assistants	90.4%	$29,100
23. Office Clerks, General	82.2%	$27,190
24. Preschool Teachers, Except Special Education	98.4%	$26,620
25. Receptionists and Information Clerks	92.4%	$25,690

25 Fastest-Growing Jobs Employing High Percentages of Women

Job	Percent Women	Percent Growth
1. Medical Secretaries	96.8%	41.3%
2. Dental Hygienists	96.1%	37.7%
3. Medical Assistants	90.4%	30.9%
4. Dental Assistants	96.7%	30.8%
5. Registered Nurses	90.7%	26.0%
6. Preschool Teachers, Except Special Education	98.4%	24.9%
7. Receptionists and Information Clerks	92.4%	23.7%
8. Licensed Practical and Licensed Vocational Nurses	91.4%	22.4%
9. Medical Records and Health Information Technicians	88.4%	21.0%
10. Billing and Posting Clerks	89.6%	19.7%
11. Paralegals and Legal Assistants	86.7%	18.3%
12. Demonstrators and Product Promoters	80.0%	17.5%
13. Medical Equipment Preparers	90.4%	17.5%
14. Interviewers, Except Eligibility and Loan	84.4%	17.3%
15. Office Clerks, General	82.2%	16.6%
16. Hairdressers, Hairstylists, and Cosmetologists	87.0%	15.7%

(continued)

(continued)

25 Fastest-Growing Jobs Employing High Percentages of Women

Job	Percent Women	Percent Growth
17. Psychiatric Aides	88.0%	15.1%
18. Teacher Assistants	91.5%	14.8%
19. Payroll and Timekeeping Clerks	88.5%	14.6%
20. Veterinary Assistants and Laboratory Animal Caretakers	90.4%	14.2%
21. Bookkeeping, Accounting, and Auditing Clerks	90.0%	13.6%
22. Occupational Health and Safety Technicians	88.9%	13.2%
23. Executive Secretaries and Executive Administrative Assistants	96.8%	12.6%
24. Travel Agents	84.1%	10.0%
25. Insurance Claims and Policy Processing Clerks	80.6%	8.7%

25 Jobs with the Most Openings Employing High Percentages of Women

Job	Percent Women	Annual Openings
1. Registered Nurses	90.7%	120,740
2. Office Clerks, General	82.2%	101,150
3. Receptionists and Information Clerks	92.4%	56,560
4. Teacher Assistants	91.5%	48,160
5. Bookkeeping, Accounting, and Auditing Clerks	90.0%	46,780
6. Secretaries and Administrative Assistants, Except Legal, Medical, and Executive	96.8%	39,100
7. Licensed Practical and Licensed Vocational Nurses	91.4%	36,920
8. Executive Secretaries and Executive Administrative Assistants	96.8%	32,180
9. Medical Secretaries	96.8%	27,840
10. Medical Assistants	90.4%	24,380
11. Tellers	87.1%	23,750
12. Preschool Teachers, Except Special Education	98.4%	23,240
13. Hairdressers, Hairstylists, and Cosmetologists	87.0%	21,810
14. Billing and Posting Clerks	89.6%	18,760
15. Dental Assistants	96.7%	15,400
16. Dental Hygienists	96.1%	10,490
17. Insurance Claims and Policy Processing Clerks	80.6%	9,600
18. Paralegals and Legal Assistants	86.7%	8,340
19. Interviewers, Except Eligibility and Loan	84.4%	7,960
20. Medical Records and Health Information Technicians	88.4%	7,370
21. Payroll and Timekeeping Clerks	88.5%	6,570

25 Jobs with the Most Openings Employing High Percentages of Women

Job	Percent Women	Annual Openings
22. Demonstrators and Product Promoters	80.0%	4,210
23. Legal Secretaries	96.8%	3,940
24. Eligibility Interviewers, Government Programs	86.9%	3,740
25. Veterinary Assistants and Laboratory Animal Caretakers	90.4%	2,160

Best Jobs Employing High Percentages of Men

If you haven't already read the intro to the previous group of lists, jobs with high percentages of women, consider doing so. Much of the content there applies to these lists as well.

I didn't include these groups of lists with the assumption that men should consider only jobs with high percentages of men or that women should consider only jobs with high percentages of women. Instead, these lists are here because I think they are interesting and perhaps helpful in considering nontraditional career options. For example, some men would do well in and enjoy some of the jobs with high percentages of women but may not have considered them seriously. Similarly, some women would enjoy and do well in some jobs that traditionally have been held by high percentages of men. I hope these lists help you consider options that you didn't seriously consider before simply because of gender stereotypes.

In the jobs on the following lists, more than 80 percent of the workers are men, but increasing numbers of women are entering many of these jobs.

Best Jobs Employing the Highest Percentages of Men

Job	Percent Men
1. Automotive Glass Installers and Repairers	100.0%
2. Brickmasons and Blockmasons	100.0%
3. Commercial Divers	100.0%
4. Crane and Tower Operators	100.0%
5. Earth Drillers, Except Oil and Gas	100.0%
6. Electrical and Electronics Repairers, Commercial and Industrial Equipment	100.0%
7. Electrical and Electronics Repairers, Powerhouse, Substation, and Relay	100.0%
8. Elevator Installers and Repairers	100.0%
9. Fence Erectors	100.0%
10. Fire Inspectors and Investigators	100.0%
11. Fish and Game Wardens	100.0%
12. Glaziers	100.0%

(continued)

(continued)

Best Jobs Employing the Highest Percentages of Men

Job	Percent Men
13. Layout Workers, Metal and Plastic	100.0%
14. Motorboat Operators	100.0%
15. Nuclear Technicians	100.0%
16. Paving, Surfacing, and Tamping Equipment Operators	100.0%
17. Pile-Driver Operators	100.0%
18. Plasterers and Stucco Masons	100.0%
19. Reinforcing Iron and Rebar Workers	100.0%
20. Riggers	100.0%
21. Roustabouts, Oil and Gas	100.0%
22. Sailors and Marine Oilers	100.0%
23. Septic Tank Servicers and Sewer Pipe Cleaners	100.0%
24. Structural Metal Fabricators and Fitters	100.0%
25. Subway and Streetcar Operators	100.0%
26. Terrazzo Workers and Finishers	100.0%
27. Traffic Technicians	100.0%
28. Transit and Railroad Police	100.0%
29. Bus and Truck Mechanics and Diesel Engine Specialists	99.7%
30. Cement Masons and Concrete Finishers	99.6%
31. Stonemasons	99.6%
32. Heating, Air Conditioning, and Refrigeration Mechanics and Installers	99.4%
33. Operating Engineers and Other Construction Equipment Operators	99.1%
34. Pipelayers	99.0%
35. Plumbers, Pipefitters, and Steamfitters	99.0%
36. Roofers	98.7%
37. Farm Equipment Mechanics and Service Technicians	98.6%
38. Mobile Heavy Equipment Mechanics, Except Engines	98.6%
39. Automotive Service Technicians and Mechanics	98.4%
40. Electrical Power-Line Installers and Repairers	98.4%
41. Security and Fire Alarm Systems Installers	98.4%
42. Drywall and Ceiling Tile Installers	98.2%
43. Tapers	98.2%
44. Carpenters	98.1%
45. Highway Maintenance Workers	98.1%
46. Locomotive Engineers	98.1%
47. Automotive Body and Related Repairers	97.9%
48. Stationary Engineers and Boiler Operators	97.9%
49. Construction Laborers	97.7%

Best Jobs Employing the Highest Percentages of Men

Job	Percent Men
50. Pest Control Workers	97.7%
51. Sheet Metal Workers	97.6%
52. Chemical Plant and System Operators	97.5%
53. Electricians	97.5%
54. Petroleum Pump System Operators, Refinery Operators, and Gaugers	97.5%
55. Airline Pilots, Copilots, and Flight Engineers	97.4%
56. Commercial Pilots	97.4%
57. Supervisors of Construction and Extraction Workers	97.4%
58. Maintenance and Repair Workers, General	97.3%
59. Bicycle Repairers	97.0%
60. Excavating and Loading Machine and Dragline Operators	97.0%
61. Industrial Machinery Mechanics	97.0%
62. Mechanical Door Repairers	97.0%
63. Motorboat Mechanics and Service Technicians	97.0%
64. Motorcycle Mechanics	97.0%
65. Outdoor Power Equipment and Other Small Engine Mechanics	97.0%
66. Painters, Construction and Maintenance	97.0%
67. Rail Car Repairers	97.0%
68. Recreational Vehicle Service Technicians	97.0%
69. Refractory Materials Repairers, Except Brickmasons	97.0%
70. Tire Repairers and Changers	97.0%
71. Cabinetmakers and Bench Carpenters	96.9%
72. Maintenance Workers, Machinery	96.9%
73. Home Appliance Repairers	96.8%
74. Carpet Installers	96.6%
75. Derrick Operators, Oil and Gas	96.6%
76. Floor Sanders and Finishers	96.6%
77. Rotary Drill Operators, Oil and Gas	96.6%
78. Segmental Pavers	96.6%
79. Service Unit Operators, Oil, Gas, and Mining	96.6%
80. Telecommunications Line Installers and Repairers	96.6%
81. Tile and Marble Setters	96.6%
82. Driver/Sales Workers	96.3%
83. Heavy and Tractor-Trailer Truck Drivers	96.3%
84. Insulation Workers, Floor, Ceiling, and Wall	96.3%
85. Insulation Workers, Mechanical	96.3%
86. Light Truck or Delivery Services Drivers	96.3%

(continued)

(continued)

Best Jobs Employing the Highest Percentages of Men

Job	Percent Men
87. Control and Valve Installers and Repairers, Except Mechanical Door	96.2%
88. Structural Iron and Steel Workers	96.2%
89. Aircraft Mechanics and Service Technicians	96.1%
90. Landscaping and Groundskeeping Workers	96.0%
91. Tree Trimmers and Pruners	96.0%
92. Railroad Conductors and Yardmasters	95.9%
93. Welders, Cutters, Solderers, and Brazers	95.9%
94. Welding, Soldering, and Brazing Machine Setters, Operators, and Tenders	95.9%
95. First-Line Supervisors of Landscaping, Lawn Service, and Groundskeeping Workers	95.8%
96. Boilermakers	95.7%
97. Firefighters	95.5%
98. Helpers—Brickmasons, Blockmasons, Stonemasons, and Tile and Marble Setters	95.2%
99. Helpers—Carpenters	95.2%
100. Helpers—Electricians	95.2%
101. Helpers—Pipelayers, Plumbers, Pipefitters, and Steamfitters	95.2%
102. Electronic Home Entertainment Equipment Installers and Repairers	94.8%
103. Helpers—Installation, Maintenance, and Repair Workers	94.7%
104. Nuclear Power Reactor Operators	94.7%
105. Power Plant Operators	94.7%
106. Construction and Building Inspectors	94.4%
107. Machinists	93.8%
108. Construction Managers	93.6%
109. Surveying and Mapping Technicians	93.5%
110. Refuse and Recyclable Material Collectors	93.2%
111. Water and Wastewater Treatment Plant and System Operators	93.0%
112. Hazardous Materials Removal Workers	92.9%
113. Industrial Truck and Tractor Operators	92.5%
114. Avionics Technicians	92.3%
115. First-Line Supervisors of Fire Fighting and Prevention Workers	92.3%
116. Computer Numerically Controlled Machine Tool Programmers, Metal and Plastic	92.2%
117. Computer-Controlled Machine Tool Operators, Metal and Plastic	92.2%
118. Radio, Cellular, and Tower Equipment Installers and Repairers	92.2%
119. Telecommunications Equipment Installers and Repairers, Except Line Installers	92.2%
120. Locksmiths and Safe Repairers	92.0%
121. First-Line Supervisors of Farming, Fishing, and Forestry Workers	91.9%
122. Audio and Video Equipment Technicians	91.8%
123. Broadcast Technicians	91.8%

Best Jobs Employing the Highest Percentages of Men

Job	Percent Men
124. Transportation Inspectors	91.5%
125. Woodworking Machine Setters, Operators, and Tenders, Except Sawing	91.3%
126. Coating, Painting, and Spraying Machine Setters, Operators, and Tenders	91.0%
127. Painters, Transportation Equipment	91.0%
128. Painting, Coating, and Decorating Workers	91.0%
129. Parts Salespersons	90.9%
130. First-Line Supervisors of Mechanics, Installers, and Repairers	90.6%
131. Medical Equipment Repairers	89.4%
132. First-Line Supervisors of Police and Detectives	88.0%
133. Farmers, Ranchers, and Other Agricultural Managers	87.1%
134. Laborers and Freight, Stock, and Material Movers, Hand	86.6%
135. Transportation, Storage, and Distribution Managers	85.8%
136. Police and Sheriff's Patrol Officers	85.4%
137. Couriers and Messengers	84.9%
138. Taxi Drivers and Chauffeurs	84.8%
139. Chefs and Head Cooks	84.4%
140. Computer, Automated Teller, and Office Machine Repairers	84.4%
141. Athletes and Sports Competitors	84.0%
142. Coaches and Scouts	84.0%
143. Sawing Machine Setters, Operators, and Tenders, Wood	84.0%
144. First-Line Supervisors of Production and Operating Workers	83.7%
145. Ambulance Drivers and Attendants, Except Emergency Medical Technicians	83.3%
146. Civil Engineering Technicians	83.0%
147. Electrical and Electronic Engineering Technicians	83.0%
148. Engineering Technicians, Except Drafters, All Other	83.0%
149. Environmental Engineering Technicians	83.0%
150. Industrial Engineering Technicians	83.0%
151. Mechanical Engineering Technicians	83.0%
152. Metal-Refining Furnace Operators and Tenders	82.4%
153. Coin, Vending, and Amusement Machine Servicers and Repairers	81.8%
154. Helpers—Production Workers	80.8%
155. Buyers and Purchasing Agents, Farm Products	80.0%

The jobs in the following four lists are derived from the preceding list of the jobs employing the highest percentages of men. Keep in mind that the earnings estimates in the following lists are based on a survey of *all* workers, not just men. On average, men earn about 125 percent of the earnings of women in the same occupation. The earnings differences for the occupations in the following lists may be significantly higher or lower.

25 Best Jobs Overall Employing High Percentages of Men

Job	Percent Men	Annual Earnings	Percent Growth	Annual Openings
1. Supervisors of Construction and Extraction Workers	97.4%	$59,150	23.5%	25,970
2. Plumbers, Pipefitters, and Steamfitters	99.0%	$47,750	25.6%	22,880
3. Electricians	97.5%	$49,320	23.2%	28,920
4. Heating, Air Conditioning, and Refrigeration Mechanics and Installers	99.4%	$43,380	33.7%	13,760
5. Brickmasons and Blockmasons	100.0%	$46,800	40.5%	5,450
6. Construction Managers	93.6%	$84,240	16.6%	12,040
7. Industrial Machinery Mechanics	97.0%	$46,270	21.6%	11,710
8. Operating Engineers and Other Construction Equipment Operators	99.1%	$41,510	23.5%	16,280
9. Commercial Pilots	97.4%	$70,000	21.1%	1,930
10. First-Line Supervisors of Mechanics, Installers, and Repairers	90.6%	$59,850	11.9%	16,490
11. Carpenters	98.1%	$40,010	19.6%	40,830
12. Construction and Building Inspectors	94.4%	$53,180	18.0%	4,860
13. Heavy and Tractor-Trailer Truck Drivers	96.3%	$37,930	20.6%	64,940
14. Medical Equipment Repairers	89.4%	$44,870	31.4%	2,230
15. Cement Masons and Concrete Finishers	99.6%	$35,600	34.6%	7,290
16. Drywall and Ceiling Tile Installers	98.2%	$36,970	27.6%	5,870
17. Security and Fire Alarm Systems Installers	98.4%	$39,540	32.9%	3,670
18. Electrical Power-Line Installers and Repairers	98.4%	$60,190	13.3%	5,270
19. Telecommunications Equipment Installers and Repairers, Except Line Installers	92.2%	$53,960	14.6%	5,930
20. Glaziers	100.0%	$37,350	42.2%	3,340
21. Police and Sheriff's Patrol Officers	85.4%	$54,230	8.2%	24,940
22. Structural Iron and Steel Workers	96.2%	$45,690	21.9%	2,540
23. Tapers	98.2%	$44,910	34.9%	1,430
24. Mobile Heavy Equipment Mechanics, Except Engines	98.6%	$45,600	16.2%	5,250
25. Telecommunications Line Installers and Repairers	96.6%	$51,720	13.6%	5,140

25 Best-Paying Jobs Employing High Percentages of Men

Job	Percent Men	Annual Earnings
1. Airline Pilots, Copilots, and Flight Engineers	97.4%	$105,580
2. Construction Managers	93.6%	$84,240
3. Transportation, Storage, and Distribution Managers	85.8%	$80,860

25 Best-Paying Jobs Employing High Percentages of Men

Job	Percent Men	Annual Earnings
4. First-Line Supervisors of Police and Detectives	88.0%	$77,890
5. Nuclear Power Reactor Operators	94.7%	$76,590
6. Elevator Installers and Repairers	100.0%	$75,060
7. Commercial Pilots	97.4%	$70,000
8. First-Line Supervisors of Fire Fighting and Prevention Workers	92.3%	$69,510
9. Nuclear Technicians	100.0%	$68,030
10. Electrical and Electronics Repairers, Powerhouse, Substation, and Relay	100.0%	$67,450
11. Power Plant Operators	94.7%	$65,280
12. Farmers, Ranchers, and Other Agricultural Managers	87.1%	$64,660
13. Subway and Streetcar Operators	100.0%	$63,820
14. Transportation Inspectors	91.5%	$62,230
15. Petroleum Pump System Operators, Refinery Operators, and Gaugers	97.5%	$61,260
16. Electrical Power-Line Installers and Repairers	98.4%	$60,190
17. First-Line Supervisors of Mechanics, Installers, and Repairers	90.6%	$59,850
18. Supervisors of Construction and Extraction Workers	97.4%	$59,150
19. Engineering Technicians, Except Drafters, All Other	83.0%	$58,670
20. Boilermakers	95.7%	$56,910
21. Electrical and Electronic Engineering Technicians	83.0%	$56,900
22. Transit and Railroad Police	100.0%	$56,390
23. Chemical Plant and System Operators	97.5%	$55,940
24. Buyers and Purchasing Agents, Farm Products	80.0%	$55,860
25. Avionics Technicians	92.3%	$54,720

25 Fastest-Growing Jobs Employing High Percentages of Men

Job	Percent Men	Percent Growth
1. Helpers—Brickmasons, Blockmasons, Stonemasons, and Tile and Marble Setters	95.2%	59.9%
2. Helpers—Carpenters	95.2%	55.7%
3. Reinforcing Iron and Rebar Workers	100.0%	48.7%
4. Helpers—Pipelayers, Plumbers, Pipefitters, and Steamfitters	95.2%	45.4%
5. Glaziers	100.0%	42.2%
6. Brickmasons and Blockmasons	100.0%	40.5%
7. Bicycle Repairers	97.0%	37.4%
8. Pile-Driver Operators	100.0%	36.6%
9. Stonemasons	99.6%	36.5%

(continued)

(continued)

25 Fastest-Growing Jobs Employing High Percentages of Men

Job	Percent Men	Percent Growth
10. Tapers	98.2%	34.9%
11. Cement Masons and Concrete Finishers	99.6%	34.6%
12. Heating, Air Conditioning, and Refrigeration Mechanics and Installers	99.4%	33.7%
13. Security and Fire Alarm Systems Installers	98.4%	32.9%
14. Ambulance Drivers and Attendants, Except Emergency Medical Technicians	83.3%	32.1%
15. Insulation Workers, Mechanical	96.3%	31.8%
16. Medical Equipment Repairers	89.4%	31.4%
17. Segmental Pavers	96.6%	30.8%
18. Helpers—Electricians	95.2%	30.6%
19. Coaches and Scouts	84.0%	29.4%
20. Radio, Cellular, and Tower Equipment Installers and Repairers	92.2%	29.3%
21. Drywall and Ceiling Tile Installers	98.2%	27.6%
22. Pest Control Workers	97.7%	26.2%
23. Plumbers, Pipefitters, and Steamfitters	99.0%	25.6%
24. Tile and Marble Setters	96.6%	25.4%
25. Pipelayers	99.0%	25.2%

25 Jobs with the Most Openings Employing High Percentages of Men

Job	Percent Men	Annual Openings
1. Laborers and Freight, Stock, and Material Movers, Hand	86.6%	98,020
2. Heavy and Tractor-Trailer Truck Drivers	96.3%	64,940
3. Landscaping and Groundskeeping Workers	96.0%	44,440
4. Carpenters	98.1%	40,830
5. Maintenance and Repair Workers, General	97.3%	37,910
6. Automotive Service Technicians and Mechanics	98.4%	31,170
7. Light Truck or Delivery Services Drivers	96.3%	29,590
8. Construction Laborers	97.7%	29,240
9. Electricians	97.5%	28,920
10. Supervisors of Construction and Extraction Workers	97.4%	25,970
11. Police and Sheriff's Patrol Officers	85.4%	24,940
12. Farmers, Ranchers, and Other Agricultural Managers	87.1%	23,450
13. Plumbers, Pipefitters, and Steamfitters	99.0%	22,880
14. Industrial Truck and Tractor Operators	92.5%	20,950
15. First-Line Supervisors of Mechanics, Installers, and Repairers	90.6%	16,490

25 Jobs with the Most Openings Employing High Percentages of Men

Job	Percent Men	Annual Openings
16. Operating Engineers and Other Construction Equipment Operators	99.1%	16,280
17. Painters, Construction and Maintenance	97.0%	15,730
18. Welders, Cutters, Solderers, and Brazers	95.9%	14,070
19. Heating, Air Conditioning, and Refrigeration Mechanics and Installers	99.4%	13,760
20. Coaches and Scouts	84.0%	13,300
21. Driver/Sales Workers	96.3%	12,290
22. Construction Managers	93.6%	12,040
23. Industrial Machinery Mechanics	97.0%	11,710
24. Firefighters	95.5%	11,230
25. Parts Salespersons	90.9%	10,720

Best Jobs with High Percentages of Urban Workers

Some people have a strong preference for an urban setting. They want to live and work where there's more energy and excitement, more access to the arts, more diversity, more restaurants, and better public transportation. On the other hand, some prefer the open spaces, closeness to nature, quiet, and inexpensive housing of rural locations. If you are strongly attracted to either setting, you'll be interested in the following lists.

I identified urban jobs as those for which 30 percent or more of the workforce is located in the 38 most populous metropolitan areas of the United States. These 38 metro areas—the most populous 10 percent of all U.S. metro areas, according to the Census Bureau—consist primarily of built-up communities, unlike smaller metro areas, which consist of a core city surrounded by a lot of countryside. In the following lists of urban jobs, you'll see a figure called the "urban ratio" for each job that represents the percentage of the total U.S. workforce for the job that is located in those 38 huge metro areas.

The Census Bureau also identifies 173 nonmetropolitan areas—areas that have no city of 50,000 people and a total population of less than 100,000. I identified rural jobs as those for which 15 percent or more of the total U.S. workforce is located in these nonmetropolitan areas. In the following lists of rural jobs, you'll see a figure called the "rural ratio" that represents the percentage of the total U.S. workforce for the job that is located in nonmetropolitan areas.

The "best-overall" list of urban jobs is ordered by the usual three economic measures: earnings, growth, and number of openings. Another three lists follow, showing the top 25 highly urban jobs ordered on each of these criteria.

Best Jobs with the Highest Percentage of Urban Workers

Job	Urban Ratio
1. Aircraft Cargo Handling Supervisors	59.9%
2. Health Technologists and Technicians, All Other	54.4%
3. Medical Equipment Repairers	50.5%
4. Registered Nurses	50.3%
5. Tapers	49.6%
6. Radiologic Technologists and Technicians	48.0%
7. Electrical and Electronics Drafters	47.3%
8. Environmental Engineering Technicians	46.5%
9. Computer Numerically Controlled Machine Tool Programmers, Metal and Plastic	45.2%
10. Locksmiths and Safe Repairers	45.2%
11. Nuclear Medicine Technologists	44.4%
12. Skincare Specialists	43.0%
13. Occupational Therapy Assistants	42.0%
14. Painting, Coating, and Decorating Workers	41.8%
15. Elevator Installers and Repairers	41.1%
16. Environmental Science and Protection Technicians, Including Health	40.1%
17. Athletes and Sports Competitors	40.0%
18. Stonemasons	38.9%
19. Radiation Therapists	38.8%
20. Lodging Managers	38.4%
21. Transportation Security Screeners	38.4%
22. Airfield Operations Specialists	38.0%
23. Transportation Inspectors	37.9%
24. Broadcast Technicians	37.6%
25. Carpet Installers	37.5%
26. Occupational Therapy Aides	36.9%
27. Tile and Marble Setters	36.7%
28. Air Traffic Controllers	36.2%
29. Choreographers	35.7%
30. Occupational Health and Safety Technicians	35.3%
31. Fire Inspectors and Investigators	34.7%
32. Medical Equipment Preparers	34.3%
33. Electronic Home Entertainment Equipment Installers and Repairers	34.0%
34. Buyers and Purchasing Agents, Farm Products	33.7%
35. Reinforcing Iron and Rebar Workers	33.3%
36. Coin, Vending, and Amusement Machine Servicers and Repairers	33.1%
37. Floor Sanders and Finishers	32.9%

Best Jobs with the Highest Percentage of Urban Workers

Job	Urban Ratio
38. Septic Tank Servicers and Sewer Pipe Cleaners	32.7%
39. Commercial Pilots	32.6%
40. Tour Guides and Escorts	32.5%
41. Hazardous Materials Removal Workers	32.1%
42. Ophthalmic Laboratory Technicians	31.8%
43. Fine Artists, Including Painters, Sculptors, and Illustrators	31.4%
44. Insulation Workers, Floor, Ceiling, and Wall	31.1%
45. Pipelayers	31.0%
46. Motorboat Mechanics and Service Technicians	30.9%
47. Diagnostic Medical Sonographers	30.7%
48. Outdoor Power Equipment and Other Small Engine Mechanics	30.3%
49. Embalmers	30.2%
50. Helpers—Brickmasons, Blockmasons, Stonemasons, and Tile and Marble Setters	30.2%
51. Private Detectives and Investigators	30.2%

25 Best Jobs Overall Employing High Percentages of Urban Workers

Job	Urban Ratio	Annual Earnings	Percent Growth	Annual Openings
1. Diagnostic Medical Sonographers	30.7%	$65,210	43.6%	3,170
2. Registered Nurses	50.3%	$65,950	26.0%	120,740
3. Radiologic Technologists and Technicians	48.0%	$55,120	27.7%	9,510
4. Occupational Therapy Assistants	42.0%	$52,040	43.2%	1,680
5. Medical Equipment Repairers	50.5%	$44,870	31.4%	2,230
6. Commercial Pilots	32.6%	$70,000	21.1%	1,930
7. Tapers	49.6%	$44,910	34.9%	1,430
8. Tile and Marble Setters	36.7%	$37,080	25.4%	2,770
9. Health Technologists and Technicians, All Other	54.4%	$38,080	23.2%	4,040
10. Environmental Science and Protection Technicians, Including Health	40.1%	$42,270	23.6%	1,950
11. Pipelayers	31.0%	$35,900	25.2%	2,880
12. Helpers—Brickmasons, Blockmasons, Stonemasons, and Tile and Marble Setters	30.2%	$27,820	59.9%	2,540
13. Reinforcing Iron and Rebar Workers	33.3%	$37,990	48.7%	1,320
14. Hazardous Materials Removal Workers	32.1%	$38,120	23.1%	1,890
15. Skincare Specialists	43.0%	$29,190	24.6%	2,040
16. Private Detectives and Investigators	30.2%	$43,710	20.5%	1,490

(continued)

(continued)

25 Best Jobs Overall Employing High Percentages of Urban Workers

Job	Urban Ratio	Annual Earnings	Percent Growth	Annual Openings
17. Environmental Engineering Technicians	46.5%	$44,850	24.5%	820
18. Radiation Therapists	38.8%	$76,630	20.1%	670
19. Transportation Inspectors	37.9%	$62,230	14.6%	1,070
20. Lodging Managers	38.4%	$47,450	8.4%	1,820
21. Nuclear Medicine Technologists	44.4%	$69,450	18.7%	750
22. Stonemasons	38.9%	$36,640	36.5%	890
23. Choreographers	35.7%	$39,600	24.2%	830
24. Elevator Installers and Repairers	41.1%	$75,060	11.6%	820
25. Coin, Vending, and Amusement Machine Servicers and Repairers	33.1%	$30,820	22.0%	1,630

25 Best-Paying Jobs Employing High Percentages of Urban Workers

Job	Urban Ratio	Annual Earnings
1. Air Traffic Controllers	36.2%	$113,540
2. Radiation Therapists	38.8%	$76,630
3. Elevator Installers and Repairers	41.1%	$75,060
4. Commercial Pilots	32.6%	$70,000
5. Nuclear Medicine Technologists	44.4%	$69,450
6. Registered Nurses	50.3%	$65,950
7. Diagnostic Medical Sonographers	30.7%	$65,210
8. Transportation Inspectors	37.9%	$62,230
9. Buyers and Purchasing Agents, Farm Products	33.7%	$55,860
10. Radiologic Technologists and Technicians	48.0%	$55,120
11. Electrical and Electronics Drafters	47.3%	$54,470
12. Fire Inspectors and Investigators	34.7%	$53,330
13. Occupational Therapy Assistants	42.0%	$52,040
14. Lodging Managers	38.4%	$47,450
15. Airfield Operations Specialists	38.0%	$47,180
16. Aircraft Cargo Handling Supervisors	59.9%	$46,840
17. Occupational Health and Safety Technicians	35.3%	$46,030
18. Computer Numerically Controlled Machine Tool Programmers, Metal and Plastic	45.2%	$45,890
19. Tapers	49.6%	$44,910
20. Medical Equipment Repairers	50.5%	$44,870

25 Best-Paying Jobs Employing High Percentages of Urban Workers

Job	Urban Ratio	Annual Earnings
21. Environmental Engineering Technicians	46.5%	$44,850
22. Fine Artists, Including Painters, Sculptors, and Illustrators	31.4%	$44,600
23. Embalmers	30.2%	$43,800
24. Private Detectives and Investigators	30.2%	$43,710
25. Environmental Science and Protection Technicians, Including Health	40.1%	$42,270

25 Fastest-Growing Jobs Employing High Percentages of Urban Workers

Job	Urban Ratio	Percent Growth
1. Helpers—Brickmasons, Blockmasons, Stonemasons, and Tile and Marble Setters	30.2%	59.9%
2. Reinforcing Iron and Rebar Workers	33.3%	48.7%
3. Diagnostic Medical Sonographers	30.7%	43.6%
4. Occupational Therapy Assistants	42.0%	43.2%
5. Stonemasons	38.9%	36.5%
6. Tapers	49.6%	34.9%
7. Occupational Therapy Aides	36.9%	33.3%
8. Medical Equipment Repairers	50.5%	31.4%
9. Radiologic Technologists and Technicians	48.0%	27.7%
10. Registered Nurses	50.3%	26.0%
11. Tile and Marble Setters	36.7%	25.4%
12. Pipelayers	31.0%	25.2%
13. Skincare Specialists	43.0%	24.6%
14. Environmental Engineering Technicians	46.5%	24.5%
15. Choreographers	35.7%	24.2%
16. Environmental Science and Protection Technicians, Including Health	40.1%	23.6%
17. Insulation Workers, Floor, Ceiling, and Wall	31.1%	23.3%
18. Health Technologists and Technicians, All Other	54.4%	23.2%
19. Hazardous Materials Removal Workers	32.1%	23.1%
20. Coin, Vending, and Amusement Machine Servicers and Repairers	33.1%	22.0%
21. Athletes and Sports Competitors	40.0%	21.8%
22. Commercial Pilots	32.6%	21.1%
23. Motorboat Mechanics and Service Technicians	30.9%	20.7%
24. Aircraft Cargo Handling Supervisors	59.9%	20.6%
25. Septic Tank Servicers and Sewer Pipe Cleaners	32.7%	20.6%

25 Jobs with the Most Openings Employing High Percentages of Urban Workers

Job	Urban Ratio	Annual Openings
1. Registered Nurses	50.3%	120,740
2. Radiologic Technologists and Technicians	48.0%	9,510
3. Health Technologists and Technicians, All Other	54.4%	4,040
4. Diagnostic Medical Sonographers	30.7%	3,170
5. Pipelayers	31.0%	2,880
6. Tile and Marble Setters	36.7%	2,770
7. Helpers—Brickmasons, Blockmasons, Stonemasons, and Tile and Marble Setters	30.2%	2,540
8. Medical Equipment Repairers	50.5%	2,230
9. Skincare Specialists	43.0%	2,040
10. Tour Guides and Escorts	32.5%	1,960
11. Environmental Science and Protection Technicians, Including Health	40.1%	1,950
12. Commercial Pilots	32.6%	1,930
13. Hazardous Materials Removal Workers	32.1%	1,890
14. Lodging Managers	38.4%	1,820
15. Occupational Therapy Assistants	42.0%	1,680
16. Coin, Vending, and Amusement Machine Servicers and Repairers	33.1%	1,630
17. Medical Equipment Preparers	34.3%	1,620
18. Carpet Installers	37.5%	1,520
19. Private Detectives and Investigators	30.2%	1,490
20. Insulation Workers, Floor, Ceiling, and Wall	31.1%	1,460
21. Tapers	49.6%	1,430
22. Electronic Home Entertainment Equipment Installers and Repairers	34.0%	1,410
23. Broadcast Technicians	37.6%	1,380
24. Outdoor Power Equipment and Other Small Engine Mechanics	30.3%	1,350
25. Ophthalmic Laboratory Technicians	31.8%	1,320

Best Jobs with High Percentages of Rural Workers

The Census Bureau identifies 173 nonmetropolitan areas—areas that have no city of 50,000 people and a total population of less than 100,000. I identified rural jobs as those for which 15 percent or more of the total U.S. workforce is located in these nonmetropolitan areas. In the following lists of rural jobs, you'll see a figure called the "rural ratio" that represents the percentage of the total U.S. workforce for the job that is located in nonmetropolitan areas.

Like other "best-overall" lists, the following list of rural jobs is ordered by the usual three economic measures: earnings, growth, and number of openings. Another three lists follow, showing the top 25 highly rural jobs ordered on each of these criteria.

Best Jobs with the Highest Percentage of Rural Workers

Job	Rural Ratio
1. Sawing Machine Setters, Operators, and Tenders, Wood	46.9%
2. Farm Equipment Mechanics and Service Technicians	46.8%
3. Roustabouts, Oil and Gas	41.9%
4. Service Unit Operators, Oil, Gas, and Mining	38.4%
5. Highway Maintenance Workers	38.3%
6. Woodworking Machine Setters, Operators, and Tenders, Except Sawing	37.0%
7. Water and Wastewater Treatment Plant and System Operators	28.8%
8. Correctional Officers and Jailers	28.6%
9. Meat, Poultry, and Fish Cutters and Trimmers	28.2%
10. Operating Engineers and Other Construction Equipment Operators	27.1%
11. Electrical Power-Line Installers and Repairers	26.9%
12. Rotary Drill Operators, Oil and Gas	26.7%
13. Welders, Cutters, Solderers, and Brazers	24.7%
14. Excavating and Loading Machine and Dragline Operators	24.7%
15. Coating, Painting, and Spraying Machine Setters, Operators, and Tenders	24.5%
16. Cooks, Institution and Cafeteria	24.5%
17. Conveyor Operators and Tenders	24.5%
18. First-Line Supervisors of Correctional Officers	23.8%
19. First-Line Supervisors of Farming, Fishing, and Forestry Workers	23.7%
20. Earth Drillers, Except Oil and Gas	23.3%
21. Maintenance Workers, Machinery	23.0%
22. Emergency Medical Technicians and Paramedics	22.7%
23. Derrick Operators, Oil and Gas	22.5%
24. Court, Municipal, and License Clerks	22.4%
25. Police, Fire, and Ambulance Dispatchers	22.2%
26. Industrial Machinery Mechanics	21.7%
27. Heavy and Tractor-Trailer Truck Drivers	21.7%
28. Team Assemblers	21.3%
29. Bus Drivers, School or Special Client	20.5%
30. First-Line Supervisors of Production and Operating Workers	20.4%
31. Helpers—Production Workers	20.3%
32. Licensed Practical and Licensed Vocational Nurses	19.4%
33. Parts Salespersons	19.1%
34. Welding, Soldering, and Brazing Machine Setters, Operators, and Tenders	19.1%
35. Mobile Heavy Equipment Mechanics, Except Engines	19.0%
36. Tellers	18.7%
37. Cabinetmakers and Bench Carpenters	18.6%

(continued)

(continued)

Best Jobs with the Highest Percentage of Rural Workers

Job	Rural Ratio
38. Refuse and Recyclable Material Collectors	18.5%
39. Teacher Assistants	18.0%
40. Postal Service Clerks	17.9%
41. Bus and Truck Mechanics and Diesel Engine Specialists	17.9%
42. Industrial Truck and Tractor Operators	17.8%
43. Computer-Controlled Machine Tool Operators, Metal and Plastic	17.5%
44. Postal Service Mail Carriers	17.2%
45. Inspectors, Testers, Sorters, Samplers, and Weighers	17.1%
46. Paving, Surfacing, and Tamping Equipment Operators	16.9%
47. Maintenance and Repair Workers, General	16.9%
48. Butchers and Meat Cutters	16.8%
49. Library Technicians	16.3%
50. Supervisors of Construction and Extraction Workers	16.1%
51. Machinists	16.0%
52. Carpenters	16.0%
53. First-Line Supervisors of Mechanics, Installers, and Repairers	15.9%
54. Social and Human Service Assistants	15.9%
55. Pharmacy Technicians	15.8%
56. First-Line Supervisors of Retail Sales Workers	15.7%
57. Extruding and Drawing Machine Setters, Operators, and Tenders, Metal and Plastic	15.6%
58. Surveying and Mapping Technicians	15.5%
59. Construction Laborers	15.5%
60. Power Plant Operators	15.3%
61. First-Line Supervisors of Transportation and Material-Moving Machine and Vehicle Operators	15.3%
62. Physical Therapist Assistants	15.2%
63. Helpers—Installation, Maintenance, and Repair Workers	15.2%
64. Automotive Service Technicians and Mechanics	15.1%

25 Best Jobs Overall Employing High Percentages of Rural Workers

Job	Rural Ratio	Annual Earnings	Percent Growth	Annual Openings
1. Supervisors of Construction and Extraction Workers	16.1%	$59,150	23.5%	25,970
2. Licensed Practical and Licensed Vocational Nurses	19.4%	$41,150	22.4%	36,920
3. Heavy and Tractor-Trailer Truck Drivers	21.7%	$37,930	20.6%	64,940

25 Best Jobs Overall Employing High Percentages of Rural Workers

Job	Rural Ratio	Annual Earnings	Percent Growth	Annual Openings
4. Operating Engineers and Other Construction Equipment Operators	27.1%	$41,510	23.5%	16,280
5. Carpenters	16.0%	$40,010	19.6%	40,830
6. Industrial Machinery Mechanics	21.7%	$46,270	21.6%	11,710
7. First-Line Supervisors of Mechanics, Installers, and Repairers	15.9%	$59,850	11.9%	16,490
8. Physical Therapist Assistants	15.2%	$51,040	45.7%	4,120
9. Automotive Service Technicians and Mechanics	15.1%	$36,180	17.3%	31,170
10. Emergency Medical Technicians and Paramedics	22.7%	$30,710	33.3%	12,080
11. Construction Laborers	15.5%	$29,730	21.3%	29,240
12. Electrical Power-Line Installers and Repairers	26.9%	$60,190	13.3%	5,270
13. Pharmacy Technicians	15.8%	$28,940	32.4%	16,630
14. First-Line Supervisors of Transportation and Material-Moving Machine and Vehicle Operators	15.3%	$52,950	14.3%	6,930
15. Mobile Heavy Equipment Mechanics, Except Engines	19.0%	$45,600	16.2%	5,250
16. Social and Human Service Assistants	15.9%	$28,740	27.6%	18,910
17. Bus and Truck Mechanics and Diesel Engine Specialists	17.9%	$41,640	14.5%	8,780
18. Welders, Cutters, Solderers, and Brazers	24.7%	$35,920	15.0%	14,070
19. First-Line Supervisors of Retail Sales Workers	15.7%	$36,480	8.4%	51,370
20. Maintenance and Repair Workers, General	16.9%	$35,030	11.0%	37,910
21. Computer-Controlled Machine Tool Operators, Metal and Plastic	17.5%	$35,220	19.2%	4,780
22. Refuse and Recyclable Material Collectors	18.5%	$32,280	20.2%	6,970
23. Paving, Surfacing, and Tamping Equipment Operators	16.9%	$35,270	22.1%	2,200
24. Teacher Assistants	18.0%	$23,580	14.8%	48,160
25. Excavating and Loading Machine and Dragline Operators	24.7%	$37,380	17.4%	2,890

25 Best-Paying Jobs Employing High Percentages of Rural Workers

Job	Rural Ratio	Annual Earnings
1. Power Plant Operators	15.3%	$65,280
2. Electrical Power-Line Installers and Repairers	26.9%	$60,190
3. First-Line Supervisors of Mechanics, Installers, and Repairers	15.9%	$59,850

(continued)

(continued)

25 Best-Paying Jobs Employing High Percentages of Rural Workers

Job	Rural Ratio	Annual Earnings
4. Supervisors of Construction and Extraction Workers	16.1%	$59,150
5. Postal Service Mail Carriers	17.2%	$55,160
6. First-Line Supervisors of Correctional Officers	23.8%	$55,030
7. First-Line Supervisors of Production and Operating Workers	20.4%	$53,670
8. Postal Service Clerks	17.9%	$53,100
9. First-Line Supervisors of Transportation and Material-Moving Machine and Vehicle Operators	15.3%	$52,950
10. Rotary Drill Operators, Oil and Gas	26.7%	$51,310
11. Physical Therapist Assistants	15.2%	$51,040
12. Industrial Machinery Mechanics	21.7%	$46,270
13. Mobile Heavy Equipment Mechanics, Except Engines	19.0%	$45,600
14. Derrick Operators, Oil and Gas	22.5%	$45,220
15. First-Line Supervisors of Farming, Fishing, and Forestry Workers	23.7%	$42,600
16. Water and Wastewater Treatment Plant and System Operators	28.8%	$41,780
17. Bus and Truck Mechanics and Diesel Engine Specialists	17.9%	$41,640
18. Operating Engineers and Other Construction Equipment Operators	27.1%	$41,510
19. Licensed Practical and Licensed Vocational Nurses	19.4%	$41,150
20. Service Unit Operators, Oil, Gas, and Mining	38.4%	$40,750
21. Earth Drillers, Except Oil and Gas	23.3%	$40,200
22. Carpenters	16.0%	$40,010
23. Maintenance Workers, Machinery	23.0%	$39,490
24. Surveying and Mapping Technicians	15.5%	$39,350
25. Machinists	16.0%	$39,220

25 Fastest-Growing Jobs Employing High Percentages of Rural Workers

Job	Rural Ratio	Percent Growth
1. Physical Therapist Assistants	15.2%	45.7%
2. Emergency Medical Technicians and Paramedics	22.7%	33.3%
3. Pharmacy Technicians	15.8%	32.4%
4. Social and Human Service Assistants	15.9%	27.6%
5. Sawing Machine Setters, Operators, and Tenders, Wood	46.9%	24.6%
6. Operating Engineers and Other Construction Equipment Operators	27.1%	23.5%
7. Supervisors of Construction and Extraction Workers	16.1%	23.5%
8. Licensed Practical and Licensed Vocational Nurses	19.4%	22.4%
9. Paving, Surfacing, and Tamping Equipment Operators	16.9%	22.1%

25 Fastest-Growing Jobs Employing High Percentages of Rural Workers

Job	Rural Ratio	Percent Growth
10. Industrial Machinery Mechanics	21.7%	21.6%
11. Construction Laborers	15.5%	21.3%
12. Heavy and Tractor-Trailer Truck Drivers	21.7%	20.6%
13. Refuse and Recyclable Material Collectors	18.5%	20.2%
14. Woodworking Machine Setters, Operators, and Tenders, Except Sawing	37.0%	20.1%
15. Carpenters	16.0%	19.6%
16. Computer-Controlled Machine Tool Operators, Metal and Plastic	17.5%	19.2%
17. Helpers—Installation, Maintenance, and Repair Workers	15.2%	18.4%
18. Excavating and Loading Machine and Dragline Operators	24.7%	17.4%
19. Automotive Service Technicians and Mechanics	15.1%	17.3%
20. Cabinetmakers and Bench Carpenters	18.6%	16.8%
21. Mobile Heavy Equipment Mechanics, Except Engines	19.0%	16.2%
22. Parts Salespersons	19.1%	16.0%
23. Surveying and Mapping Technicians	15.5%	15.8%
24. Meat, Poultry, and Fish Cutters and Trimmers	28.2%	15.5%
25. Welders, Cutters, Solderers, and Brazers	24.7%	15.0%

25 Jobs with the Most Openings Employing High Percentages of Rural Workers

Job	Rural Ratio	Annual Openings
1. Heavy and Tractor-Trailer Truck Drivers	21.7%	64,940
2. First-Line Supervisors of Retail Sales Workers	15.7%	51,370
3. Teacher Assistants	18.0%	48,160
4. Carpenters	16.0%	40,830
5. Maintenance and Repair Workers, General	16.9%	37,910
6. Licensed Practical and Licensed Vocational Nurses	19.4%	36,920
7. Automotive Service Technicians and Mechanics	15.1%	31,170
8. Construction Laborers	15.5%	29,240
9. Supervisors of Construction and Extraction Workers	16.1%	25,970
10. Team Assemblers	21.3%	24,100
11. Tellers	18.7%	23,750
12. Industrial Truck and Tractor Operators	17.8%	20,950
13. Social and Human Service Assistants	15.9%	18,910
14. Pharmacy Technicians	15.8%	16,630

(continued)

(continued)

25 Jobs with the Most Openings Employing High Percentages of Rural Workers		
Job	Rural Ratio	Annual Openings
15. First-Line Supervisors of Mechanics, Installers, and Repairers	15.9%	16,490
16. Operating Engineers and Other Construction Equipment Operators	27.1%	16,280
17. Bus Drivers, School or Special Client	20.5%	14,450
18. Welders, Cutters, Solderers, and Brazers	24.7%	14,070
19. Cooks, Institution and Cafeteria	24.5%	13,620
20. Inspectors, Testers, Sorters, Samplers, and Weighers	17.1%	12,390
21. Emergency Medical Technicians and Paramedics	22.7%	12,080
22. Industrial Machinery Mechanics	21.7%	11,710
23. Correctional Officers and Jailers	28.6%	10,810
24. Parts Salespersons	19.1%	10,720
25. Postal Service Mail Carriers	17.2%	10,340

Best Jobs Lists Based on Levels of Education and Experience

The lists in this section organize the 300 best jobs into groups based on the education or training typically required for entry. Unlike in the previous sections, here I don't include separate lists for highest pay, growth, or number of openings. Instead, for each of the education levels, I provide one list that includes all the occupations in my database that fit there and that ranks them by their total combined score for earnings, growth, and number of openings.

These lists can help you identify a job with higher earnings or upward mobility but with a similar level of education to the job you now hold. For example, you will find jobs within the same level of education that require similar skills, yet one pays significantly better than the other, is projected to grow more rapidly, or has significantly more job openings per year. This information can help you leverage your present skills and experience into jobs that might provide better long-term career opportunities.

You can also use these lists to explore job options that would be possible if you were to get additional training, education, or work experience. For example, you can use these lists to identify occupations that offer high potential and then look into the education or training required to get the jobs that interest you most.

The lists can also help you when you plan your education. For example, you might be thinking about a construction job, but you aren't sure what kind of work you want to do. The lists show that Floor Sanders and Finishers need moderate-term on-the-job training and earn $33,350, whereas Pipelayers need only short-term on-the-job training but earn an average of

$35,900. If you want higher earnings without lengthy training, this information might make a difference in your choice.

The Education Levels

On average, a clear relationship exists between education and earnings: The more education or training you have, the more you are likely to earn. The lists that follow arrange all the jobs that met my criteria for inclusion in this book (see the Introduction) by level of education, training, and work experience. These are the levels typically required for a new entrant to begin work in the occupation.

The following definitions are used by the federal government to classify jobs based on the minimum level of education or training typically required for entry into a job. I use these definitions to construct the lists in this section. Use the training and education level descriptions as guidelines that can help you understand what is generally required, but check the footnotes and understand that you will need to learn more about specific requirements before you make a decision on one career over another.

- **Short-term on-the-job training:** It is possible to work in these occupations and achieve an average level of performance within a few days or weeks through on-the-job training.

- **Moderate-term on-the-job training:** Occupations requiring this type of training can be performed adequately after a one- to 12-month period of combined on-the-job and informal training. Typically, untrained workers observe experienced workers performing tasks and are gradually moved into progressively more difficult assignments.

- **Long-term on-the-job training:** This training requires more than 12 months of on-the-job training or combined work experience and formal classroom instruction. This includes occupations that use formal apprenticeships for training workers that may take up to four years. It also includes intensive occupation-specific, employer-sponsored training, such as police academies. Furthermore, it includes occupations that require natural talent that must be developed over many years.

- **Work experience in a related occupation:** This type of job requires experience in a related occupation. For example, police detectives are selected based on their experience as police patrol officers.

- **Postsecondary vocational training:** This requirement usually involves a few months to less than one year of training. In a few instances, as many as four years of training may be required.

- **Associate degree:** This degree usually requires two years of full-time academic work beyond high school.

For the great majority of jobs in the following lists, you need to complete high school before getting any of these types of education, training, or work experience. For 34 of the jobs, however, a high school diploma is usually not needed; footnotes to the lists indicate which jobs these are. For example, Construction Laborers do not usually need a high school diploma before they are hired and given short-term on-the-job training.

Footnotes also indicate the jobs that require *additional* preparation for entry beyond what is indicated by the level on which the list is based. For example, some of the jobs that require an associate degree also require moderate-term on-the-job training after you've been hired. Some of the jobs that require on-the-job training also require several years of previous work experience in a related job. In the list of jobs that require long-term on-the-job training, some footnotes indicate jobs for which the training typically takes the form of an apprenticeship. That means (among other things) that the training program involves night classes in addition to the workplace-based training.

Another Warning About the Data

I warned you in the Introduction to use caution in interpreting the data in this book, and I want to do it again here. The occupational data I use is the most accurate available anywhere, but it has its limitations. The education or training requirements for entry into a job that I identify in this book are those typically required as a minimum, but some people working in those jobs may have considerably more or different credentials. For example, although an associate degree (together with at least five years of work experience in a related job) is considered the usual requirement for Construction Managers, more than one-third of the people working in this occupation have no formal education beyond high school. On the other hand, Fitness Trainers and Aerobics Instructors usually need to have completed only short-term on-the-job training (plus perhaps passing a certification exam), but more than half of these workers have college degrees.

You also need to be cautious about assuming that more education or training always leads to higher income. It is true that people with jobs that require long-term on-the-job training typically earn more than people with jobs that require short-term on-the-job training. (For the jobs in this book, the difference is an average of $39,341 versus $27,697.) However, some people with short-term on-the-job training do earn more than the average for the highest-paying occupations listed in this book; furthermore, some people with long-term on-the-job training earn much less than the average shown in this book—this is particularly true early in a person's career.

So as you browse the following lists, please use them as a way to be encouraged rather than discouraged. Education and training are important for success in the labor market of the future, but so are ability, drive, initiative, and—yes—luck.

Having said this, I encourage you to get as much education and training as you can. You used to be able to get your schooling and then close the schoolbooks forever, but this isn't a good attitude to have now. You will probably need to continue learning new things throughout your working life. This can be done by going to school, which is a good thing for many people to do. But further schooling is not necessary for many of the jobs in this book. (In fact, later in Part I you can see a bonus list of the jobs in which few workers hold a bachelor's degree.) Many workers continue their learning through workshops, adult education programs, certification programs, employer training, professional conferences, Web-based training, or reading related books and magazines. Upgrading your computer skills—and other technical skills—is particularly important in our rapidly changing workplace, and you avoid doing so at your peril.

Best Jobs Requiring Short-Term On-the-Job Training

Job	Annual Earnings	Percent Growth	Annual Openings
1. Cargo and Freight Agents	$38,210	29.3%	4,420
2. Billing and Posting Clerks	$32,880	19.7%	18,760
3. Construction Laborers	$29,730	21.3%	29,240
4. Social and Human Service Assistants	$28,740	27.6%	18,910
5. Fitness Trainers and Aerobics Instructors	$31,030	24.0%	10,060
6. Customer Service Representatives	$30,610	15.5%	95,960
7. Receptionists and Information Clerks	$25,690	23.7%	56,560
8. Pipelayers	$35,900	25.2%	2,880
9. Office Clerks, General	$27,190	16.6%	101,150
10. Refuse and Recyclable Material Collectors	$32,280	20.2%	6,970
11. Sailors and Marine Oilers	$36,800	21.3%	2,150
12. Light Truck or Delivery Services Drivers	$29,080	14.7%	29,590
13. Helpers—Electricians	$27,620	30.6%	4,200
14. Interviewers, Except Eligibility and Loan	$29,560	17.3%	7,960
15. Helpers—Brickmasons, Blockmasons, Stonemasons, and Tile and Marble Setters	$27,820	59.9%	2,540
16. Landscaping and Groundskeeping Workers	$23,410	20.9%	44,440
17. Helpers—Pipelayers, Plumbers, Pipefitters, and Steamfitters	$27,010	45.4%	4,170
18. Security Guards	$23,900	18.8%	35,950
19. Helpers—Carpenters	$26,400	55.7%	3,820
20. Laborers and Freight, Stock, and Material Movers, Hand	$23,750	15.4%	98,020
21. Postal Service Mail Carriers	$55,160	–12.0%	10,340
22. Secretaries and Administrative Assistants, Except Legal, Medical, and Executive	$31,870	5.8%	39,100
23. Insulation Workers, Floor, Ceiling, and Wall	$32,420	23.3%	1,460
24. Coin, Vending, and Amusement Machine Servicers and Repairers	$30,820	22.0%	1,630
25. Human Resources Assistants, Except Payroll and Timekeeping	$37,250	11.2%	6,160
26. Teacher Assistants	$23,580	14.8%	48,160
27. Transportation Inspectors	$62,230	14.6%	1,070
28. Tree Trimmers and Pruners	$31,320	18.0%	1,800
29. Occupational Therapy Aides	$28,200	33.3%	360
30. Court Reporters	$48,530	14.1%	640
31. Sawing Machine Setters, Operators, and Tenders, Wood	$26,220	24.6%	1,810
32. Taxi Drivers and Chauffeurs	$22,760	19.6%	7,670
33. Motorboat Operators	$36,620	16.1%	160
34. Woodworking Machine Setters, Operators, and Tenders, Except Sawing	$27,090	20.1%	1,740

(continued)

(continued)

Best Jobs Requiring Short-Term On-the-Job Training

Job	Annual Earnings	Percent Growth	Annual Openings
35. Demonstrators and Product Promoters	$23,770	17.5%	4,210
36. Shipping, Receiving, and Traffic Clerks	$28,790	0.3%	17,740
37. Order Clerks	$28,940	7.4%	7,520
38. Reservation and Transportation Ticket Agents and Travel Clerks	$33,300	5.8%	3,080
39. Riggers	$43,020	10.5%	440
40. Traffic Technicians	$42,300	11.6%	280
41. Carpet Installers	$36,750	10.3%	1,520
42. Counter and Rental Clerks	$22,740	12.2%	14,660
43. Derrick Operators, Oil and Gas	$45,220	9.5%	570
44. Meat, Poultry, and Fish Cutters and Trimmers	$22,720	15.5%	7,400
45. Cooks, Institution and Cafeteria	$22,710	12.3%	13,620
46. Couriers and Messengers	$24,750	12.6%	4,300
47. Postal Service Clerks	$53,100	–48.2%	1,550
48. Weighers, Measurers, Checkers, and Samplers, Recordkeeping	$27,390	12.0%	3,420
49. Mail Clerks and Mail Machine Operators, Except Postal Service	$26,610	12.0%	3,960
50. Tellers	$24,590	1.3%	23,750
51. Driver/Sales Workers	$22,770	10.3%	12,290
52. Psychiatric Aides	$25,170	15.1%	1,900
53. Transit and Railroad Police	$56,390	5.6%	110
54. Fish and Game Wardens	$50,070	5.3%	220
55. Conveyor Operators and Tenders	$29,320	11.6%	1,490
56. Library Assistants, Clerical	$23,440	10.2%	6,410
57. Veterinary Assistants and Laboratory Animal Caretakers	$22,830	14.2%	2,160
58. Helpers—Production Workers	$22,520	8.7%	9,980
59. Telemarketers	$22,520	7.4%	8,350

Before on-the job training, job 27 usually requires some college, but no degree. Jobs 3, 10, 11, 15, 16, 19, 20, 23, 32, 40, 41, 42, 43, 44, 45, 55, 58, and 59 do not usually require a high school diploma.

Best Jobs Requiring Moderate-Term On-the-Job Training

Job	Annual Earnings	Percent Growth	Annual Openings
1. Insurance Sales Agents	$47,450	21.9%	18,440
2. Operating Engineers and Other Construction Equipment Operators	$41,510	23.5%	16,280
3. Sales Representatives, Wholesale and Manufacturing, Except Technical and Scientific Products	$53,540	15.6%	55,990

Best Jobs Requiring Moderate-Term On-the-Job Training

Job	Annual Earnings	Percent Growth	Annual Openings
4. Loan Officers	$58,030	14.2%	11,520
5. Cement Masons and Concrete Finishers	$35,600	34.6%	7,290
6. Security and Fire Alarm Systems Installers	$39,540	32.9%	3,670
7. Medical Secretaries	$31,060	41.3%	27,840
8. Drywall and Ceiling Tile Installers	$36,970	27.6%	5,870
9. Police and Sheriff's Patrol Officers	$54,230	8.2%	24,940
10. Substance Abuse and Behavioral Disorder Counselors	$38,560	27.4%	4,170
11. Tapers	$44,910	34.9%	1,430
12. Painters, Construction and Maintenance	$35,430	18.5%	15,730
13. Automotive Body and Related Repairers	$38,180	18.4%	6,520
14. Advertising Sales Agents	$45,250	13.0%	6,990
15. Medical Assistants	$29,100	30.9%	24,380
16. Pharmacy Technicians	$28,940	32.4%	16,630
17. Private Detectives and Investigators	$43,710	20.5%	1,490
18. Dispatchers, Except Police, Fire, and Ambulance	$35,200	18.6%	6,950
19. Computer-Controlled Machine Tool Operators, Metal and Plastic	$35,220	19.2%	4,780
20. Hazardous Materials Removal Workers	$38,120	23.1%	1,890
21. Payroll and Timekeeping Clerks	$37,160	14.6%	6,570
22. Pile-Driver Operators	$45,500	36.6%	230
23. Bookkeeping, Accounting, and Auditing Clerks	$34,740	13.6%	46,780
24. Roofers	$35,280	17.8%	5,250
25. Bus Drivers, Transit and Intercity	$35,720	14.8%	6,350
26. Production, Planning, and Expediting Clerks	$43,100	6.6%	8,880
27. Maintenance and Repair Workers, General	$35,030	11.0%	37,910
28. Paving, Surfacing, and Tamping Equipment Operators	$35,270	22.1%	2,200
29. Pest Control Workers	$30,220	26.2%	4,850
30. Surveying and Mapping Technicians	$39,350	15.8%	2,000
31. Aircraft Structure, Surfaces, Rigging, and Systems Assemblers	$46,210	14.3%	1,220
32. Bill and Account Collectors	$31,920	14.2%	13,550
33. Correctional Officers and Jailers	$38,990	5.2%	10,810
34. Physical Therapist Aides	$23,680	43.2%	2,760
35. Insurance Claims and Policy Processing Clerks	$35,210	8.7%	9,600
36. Parts Salespersons	$29,350	16.0%	10,720
37. Mechanical Door Repairers	$36,640	24.2%	550
38. Helpers—Installation, Maintenance, and Repair Workers	$24,060	18.4%	8,040
39. Structural Metal Fabricators and Fitters	$35,170	15.7%	2,830

(continued)

(continued)

Best Jobs Requiring Moderate-Term On-the-Job Training

Job	Annual Earnings	Percent Growth	Annual Openings
40. Police, Fire, and Ambulance Dispatchers	$35,930	11.7%	3,070
41. Legal Secretaries	$42,460	3.5%	3,940
42. Cabinetmakers and Bench Carpenters	$30,530	16.8%	4,020
43. Occupational Health and Safety Technicians	$46,030	13.2%	510
44. Inspectors, Testers, Sorters, Samplers, and Weighers	$34,040	8.0%	12,390
45. Painters, Transportation Equipment	$39,600	9.5%	1,430
46. Highway Maintenance Workers	$35,220	8.2%	5,140
47. Metal-Refining Furnace Operators and Tenders	$38,680	16.0%	550
48. Bus Drivers, School or Special Client	$28,110	12.0%	14,450
49. Earth Drillers, Except Oil and Gas	$40,200	14.0%	620
50. Automotive Glass Installers and Repairers	$33,720	24.9%	920
51. Brokerage Clerks	$41,760	5.9%	1,970
52. Fence Erectors	$29,580	23.7%	1,640
53. Railroad Conductors and Yardmasters	$53,880	4.7%	1,430
54. Tire Repairers and Changers	$23,440	18.5%	4,390
55. Septic Tank Servicers and Sewer Pipe Cleaners	$33,740	20.6%	1,190
56. Subway and Streetcar Operators	$63,820	9.2%	280
57. Computer Numerically Controlled Machine Tool Programmers, Metal and Plastic	$45,890	10.8%	490
58. Service Unit Operators, Oil, Gas, and Mining	$40,750	8.6%	1,210
59. Maintenance Workers, Machinery	$39,490	6.4%	1,740
60. Procurement Clerks	$37,640	5.7%	3,550
61. Rotary Drill Operators, Oil and Gas	$51,310	7.1%	640
62. Layout Workers, Metal and Plastic	$39,870	13.5%	290
63. Court, Municipal, and License Clerks	$34,300	8.0%	4,670
64. Outdoor Power Equipment and Other Small Engine Mechanics	$30,200	18.9%	1,350
65. Segmental Pavers	$32,340	30.8%	90
66. Medical Equipment Preparers	$30,050	17.5%	1,620
67. Bicycle Repairers	$23,210	37.4%	630
68. Ambulance Drivers and Attendants, Except Emergency Medical Technicians	$22,820	32.1%	1,010
69. Control and Valve Installers and Repairers, Except Mechanical Door	$49,600	0.0%	810
70. Tour Guides and Escorts	$23,620	18.1%	1,960
71. Tax Preparers	$32,320	9.8%	2,630
72. Transportation Security Screeners	$36,910	9.6%	1,040
73. Team Assemblers	$27,490	5.5%	24,100

Best Jobs Requiring Moderate-Term On-the-Job Training

Job	Annual Earnings	Percent Growth	Annual Openings
74. Merchandise Displayers and Window Trimmers	$26,190	12.8%	4,000
75. Travel Agents	$33,930	10.0%	1,720
76. Travel Guides	$30,670	23.8%	260
77. Flight Attendants	$38,020	–0.2%	1,730
78. Extruding and Drawing Machine Setters, Operators, and Tenders, Metal and Plastic	$32,300	8.4%	2,090
79. Floor Sanders and Finishers	$33,350	17.8%	420
80. Rolling Machine Setters, Operators, and Tenders, Metal and Plastic	$36,920	8.1%	880
81. Printing Press Operators	$34,290	–1.4%	3,920
82. Bailiffs	$38,950	7.9%	450
83. Roustabouts, Oil and Gas	$32,980	8.3%	1,550
84. Home Appliance Repairers	$35,440	6.5%	1,190
85. Painting, Coating, and Decorating Workers	$25,660	17.4%	980
86. Welding, Soldering, and Brazing Machine Setters, Operators, and Tenders	$34,770	6.5%	1,380
87. Ophthalmic Laboratory Technicians	$28,750	12.8%	1,320
88. Coating, Painting, and Spraying Machine Setters, Operators, and Tenders	$30,020	6.1%	2,310

Before on-the-job training, job 17 usually requires some college and one to five years of work experience in a related job. Jobs 5, 8, 11, 12, 24, 36, 55, 58, 61, and 83 do not usually require a high school diploma.

Best Jobs Requiring Long-Term On-the-Job Training

Job	Annual Earnings	Percent Growth	Annual Openings
1. Electricians	$49,320	23.2%	28,920
2. Plumbers, Pipefitters, and Steamfitters	$47,750	25.6%	22,880
3. Brickmasons and Blockmasons	$46,800	40.5%	5,450
4. Industrial Machinery Mechanics	$46,270	21.6%	11,710
5. Commercial Pilots	$70,000	21.1%	1,930
6. Carpenters	$40,010	19.6%	40,830
7. Electrical Power-Line Installers and Repairers	$60,190	13.3%	5,270
8. Telecommunications Line Installers and Repairers	$51,720	13.6%	5,140
9. Glaziers	$37,350	42.2%	3,340
10. Boilermakers	$56,910	21.2%	1,180
11. Coaches and Scouts	$28,470	29.4%	13,300

(continued)

(continued)

Best Jobs Requiring Long-Term On-the-Job Training

Job	Annual Earnings	Percent Growth	Annual Openings
12. Structural Iron and Steel Workers	$45,690	21.9%	2,540
13. Purchasing Agents, Except Wholesale, Retail, and Farm Products	$57,580	5.3%	9,120
14. Sheet Metal Workers	$42,730	17.6%	4,700
15. Claims Adjusters, Examiners, and Investigators	$59,320	3.0%	7,990
16. Mobile Heavy Equipment Mechanics, Except Engines	$45,600	16.2%	5,250
17. Automotive Service Technicians and Mechanics	$36,180	17.3%	31,170
18. Bus and Truck Mechanics and Diesel Engine Specialists	$41,640	14.5%	8,780
19. Insulation Workers, Mechanical	$37,990	31.8%	2,010
20. Reinforcing Iron and Rebar Workers	$37,990	48.7%	1,320
21. Wholesale and Retail Buyers, Except Farm Products	$50,490	9.0%	4,170
22. Tile and Marble Setters	$37,080	25.4%	2,770
23. Real Estate Sales Agents	$39,070	12.2%	12,760
24. Opticians, Dispensing	$33,100	28.9%	3,060
25. Elevator Installers and Repairers	$75,060	11.6%	820
26. Machinists	$39,220	8.5%	9,950
27. Power Plant Operators	$65,280	−2.5%	1,440
28. Water and Wastewater Treatment Plant and System Operators	$41,780	11.7%	4,150
29. Rail Car Repairers	$47,740	17.1%	930
30. Appraisers and Assessors of Real Estate	$48,870	7.5%	2,220
31. Petroleum Pump System Operators, Refinery Operators, and Gaugers	$61,260	−14.0%	1,440
32. Stonemasons	$36,640	36.5%	890
33. Athletes and Sports Competitors	$39,670	21.8%	780
34. Stationary Engineers and Boiler Operators	$53,070	6.1%	1,060
35. Chemical Plant and System Operators	$55,940	−12.2%	1,410
36. Nuclear Power Reactor Operators	$76,590	3.8%	200
37. Fashion Designers	$64,690	0.0%	670
38. Motorcycle Mechanics	$32,410	23.3%	890
39. Locksmiths and Safe Repairers	$36,680	17.9%	930
40. Motorboat Mechanics and Service Technicians	$35,520	20.7%	960
41. Plasterers and Stucco Masons	$36,830	17.2%	1,050
42. Photographers	$28,860	12.5%	3,100
43. Buyers and Purchasing Agents, Farm Products	$55,860	5.4%	320
44. Recreational Vehicle Service Technicians	$34,000	22.2%	480
45. Airfield Operations Specialists	$47,180	8.7%	320

Best Jobs Requiring Long-Term On-the-Job Training

Job	Annual Earnings	Percent Growth	Annual Openings
46. Terrazzo Workers and Finishers	$41,240	16.2%	110
47. Butchers and Meat Cutters	$28,460	8.0%	4,680
48. Farm Equipment Mechanics and Service Technicians	$34,230	13.4%	1,290
49. Fine Artists, Including Painters, Sculptors, and Illustrators	$44,600	7.8%	810

For jobs 1, 2, 3, 6, 9, 10, 12, 14, 19, 20, 25, 30, 32, and 46, the on-the-job training usually is part of an apprenticeship. Jobs 22, 41, and 47 do not usually require a high school diploma.

Best Jobs Requiring Work Experience in a Related Job

Job	Annual Earnings	Percent Growth	Annual Openings
1. Supervisors of Construction and Extraction Workers	$59,150	23.5%	25,970
2. Administrative Services Managers	$79,540	14.5%	9,980
3. Business Operations Specialists, All Other	$64,030	11.6%	32,720
4. Managers, All Other	$99,540	7.9%	24,940
5. First-Line Supervisors of Office and Administrative Support Workers	$48,810	14.3%	58,440
6. Heavy and Tractor-Trailer Truck Drivers	$37,930	20.6%	64,940
7. First-Line Supervisors of Mechanics, Installers, and Repairers	$59,850	11.9%	16,490
8. Construction and Building Inspectors	$53,180	18.0%	4,860
9. First-Line Supervisors of Helpers, Laborers, and Material Movers, Hand	$44,580	27.2%	8,000
10. Executive Secretaries and Executive Administrative Assistants	$45,580	12.6%	32,180
11. First-Line Supervisors of Transportation and Material-Moving Machine and Vehicle Operators	$52,950	14.3%	6,930
12. Transportation, Storage, and Distribution Managers	$80,860	10.0%	3,370
13. First-Line Supervisors of Non-Retail Sales Workers	$70,520	4.0%	12,350
14. Self-Enrichment Education Teachers	$36,100	20.9%	9,150
15. Airline Pilots, Copilots, and Flight Engineers	$105,580	6.4%	3,130
16. Farmers, Ranchers, and Other Agricultural Managers	$64,660	–8.0%	23,450
17. Welders, Cutters, Solderers, and Brazers	$35,920	15.0%	14,070
18. First-Line Supervisors of Landscaping, Lawn Service, and Groundskeeping Workers	$42,050	15.1%	6,010
19. First-Line Supervisors of Retail Sales Workers	$36,480	8.4%	51,370
20. First-Line Supervisors of Police and Detectives	$77,890	2.2%	3,870
21. Property, Real Estate, and Community Association Managers	$52,510	6.1%	8,230
22. Residential Advisors	$24,540	24.9%	4,570

(continued)

(continued)

Best Jobs Requiring Work Experience in a Related Job

Job	Annual Earnings	Percent Growth	Annual Openings
23. Gaming Managers	$67,230	12.1%	100
24. Crane and Tower Operators	$46,460	15.7%	1,720
25. Detectives and Criminal Investigators	$71,770	2.9%	3,010
26. First-Line Supervisors of Personal Service Workers	$35,230	13.5%	8,260
27. Industrial Truck and Tractor Operators	$30,010	11.8%	20,950
28. Real Estate Brokers	$59,340	7.6%	2,970
29. Aircraft Cargo Handling Supervisors	$46,840	20.6%	260
30. First-Line Supervisors of Food Preparation and Serving Workers	$29,550	9.8%	24,830
31. Choreographers	$39,600	24.2%	830
32. Excavating and Loading Machine and Dragline Operators	$37,380	17.4%	2,890
33. Fire Inspectors and Investigators	$53,330	8.8%	470
34. First-Line Supervisors of Correctional Officers	$55,030	5.5%	1,650
35. Lodging Managers	$47,450	8.4%	1,820
36. Food Service Managers	$48,110	−3.3%	5,910
37. Gaming Supervisors	$48,820	6.9%	920
38. Locomotive Engineers	$49,380	4.4%	1,550
39. Chefs and Head Cooks	$42,350	−0.8%	1,800
40. First-Line Supervisors of Housekeeping and Janitorial Workers	$35,230	0.8%	3,320
41. First-Line Supervisors of Farming, Fishing, and Forestry Workers	$42,600	−1.5%	1,360

All of these jobs usually require one to five years of work experience, except for jobs 3, 17, 22, and 27, which usually require less than one year of experience, and jobs 1, 8, 12, 13, 16, 23, 31, and 33, which usually require more than five years of experience. In addition, jobs 6 and 27 usually require short-term on-the-job training; jobs 8, 17, 20, 25, 32, 33, 34, and 38 usually require moderate-term on-the-job training; jobs 3, 15, 24, and 31 usually require long-term on-the-job training; and jobs 22 and 23 usually require some college, but no degree. Jobs 24, 27, and 32 do not usually require a high school diploma.

Best Jobs Requiring Postsecondary Vocational Training

Job	Annual Earnings	Percent Growth	Annual Openings
1. Heating, Air Conditioning, and Refrigeration Mechanics and Installers	$43,380	33.7%	13,760
2. Licensed Practical and Licensed Vocational Nurses	$41,150	22.4%	36,920
3. Dental Assistants	$34,140	30.8%	15,400
4. Telecommunications Equipment Installers and Repairers, Except Line Installers	$53,960	14.6%	5,930
5. Emergency Medical Technicians and Paramedics	$30,710	33.3%	12,080

Best Jobs Requiring Postsecondary Vocational Training

Job	Annual Earnings	Percent Growth	Annual Openings
6. Firefighters	$45,420	8.6%	11,230
7. Health Technologists and Technicians, All Other	$38,080	23.2%	4,040
8. First-Line Supervisors of Fire Fighting and Prevention Workers	$69,510	8.2%	3,310
9. Massage Therapists	$35,830	20.1%	5,590
10. Medical Records and Health Information Technicians	$33,310	21.0%	7,370
11. Aircraft Mechanics and Service Technicians	$54,590	6.3%	4,520
12. First-Line Supervisors of Production and Operating Workers	$53,670	1.9%	8,790
13. Surgical Technologists	$40,950	18.9%	3,390
14. Hairdressers, Hairstylists, and Cosmetologists	$22,570	15.7%	21,810
15. Commercial Divers	$52,550	15.8%	130
16. Audio and Video Equipment Technicians	$41,630	13.4%	2,560
17. Avionics Technicians	$54,720	7.0%	580
18. Skincare Specialists	$29,190	24.6%	2,040
19. Computer, Automated Teller, and Office Machine Repairers	$36,360	6.5%	4,540
20. Electrical and Electronics Repairers, Powerhouse, Substation, and Relay	$67,450	4.7%	690
21. Library Technicians	$30,430	8.8%	5,950
22. Electronic Home Entertainment Equipment Installers and Repairers	$34,470	13.9%	1,410
23. Refractory Materials Repairers, Except Brickmasons	$42,700	9.5%	60
24. Electrical and Electronics Repairers, Commercial and Industrial Equipment	$52,320	1.2%	1,770
25. Psychiatric Technicians	$28,470	15.5%	2,460
26. Embalmers	$43,800	5.6%	370
27. Medical Transcriptionists	$33,480	5.9%	2,020

Jobs 8 and 12 usually require, in addition to the certificate, one to five years of work experience in a related job. Jobs 7, 25, and 26 usually also require short-term on-the-job training. Jobs 4, 15, 16, and 23 usually also require moderate-term on-the-job training. Jobs 1, 6, and 20 usually also require long-term on-the-job training.

Best Jobs Requiring an Associate Degree

Job	Annual Earnings	Percent Growth	Annual Openings
1. Dental Hygienists	$69,280	37.7%	10,490
2. Registered Nurses	$65,950	26.0%	120,740
3. Construction Managers	$84,240	16.6%	12,040
4. Diagnostic Medical Sonographers	$65,210	43.6%	3,170

(continued)

(continued)

Best Jobs Requiring an Associate Degree

Job	Annual Earnings	Percent Growth	Annual Openings
5. Radiologic Technologists and Technicians	$55,120	27.7%	9,510
6. Physical Therapist Assistants	$51,040	45.7%	4,120
7. Respiratory Therapists	$55,250	27.7%	5,270
8. General and Operations Managers	$95,150	4.6%	41,010
9. Occupational Therapy Assistants	$52,040	43.2%	1,680
10. Cardiovascular Technologists and Technicians	$51,020	29.4%	2,210
11. Veterinary Technologists and Technicians	$30,140	52.0%	5,570
12. Medical Equipment Repairers	$44,870	31.4%	2,230
13. Paralegals and Legal Assistants	$46,730	18.3%	8,340
14. Preschool Teachers, Except Special Education	$26,620	24.9%	23,240
15. Nuclear Medicine Technologists	$69,450	18.7%	750
16. Radiation Therapists	$76,630	20.1%	670
17. Electrical and Electronic Engineering Technicians	$56,900	1.9%	3,180
18. Civil Engineering Technicians	$46,900	11.9%	2,460
19. Engineering Technicians, Except Drafters, All Other	$58,670	4.7%	1,680
20. Medical and Clinical Laboratory Technicians	$36,950	14.8%	5,510
21. Environmental Science and Protection Technicians, Including Health	$42,270	23.6%	1,950
22. Life, Physical, and Social Science Technicians, All Other	$43,120	11.8%	3,350
23. Mechanical Drafters	$49,200	11.1%	2,050
24. Nuclear Technicians	$68,030	14.1%	330
25. Air Traffic Controllers	$113,540	–3.0%	1,020
26. Environmental Engineering Technicians	$44,850	24.5%	820
27. Radio, Cellular, and Tower Equipment Installers and Repairers	$42,160	29.3%	450
28. Geological and Petroleum Technicians	$49,690	14.6%	700
29. Social Science Research Assistants	$38,800	14.8%	1,700
30. Architectural and Civil Drafters	$47,250	3.2%	2,090
31. Electrical and Electronics Drafters	$54,470	5.5%	720
32. Mechanical Engineering Technicians	$51,350	4.0%	1,040
33. Eligibility Interviewers, Government Programs	$41,060	3.1%	3,740
34. Industrial Engineering Technicians	$49,090	4.2%	1,460
35. Chemical Technicians	$42,070	6.7%	1,290
36. Broadcast Technicians	$36,570	9.0%	1,380

Two of these jobs usually require related work experience in addition to the degree: For job 8, one to five years is sufficient; for job 3, more than five years is usually required. Job 36 usually also requires short-term on-the-job training. Jobs 12, 21, 22, 24, 27, 28, 33, and 35 usually also require moderate-term on-the-job training. Job 25 usually also requires long-term on-the-job training.

Best Jobs Lists Based on Career Clusters

This group of lists organizes the 300 best jobs into 16 career clusters. The U.S. Department of Education's Office of Vocational and Adult Education developed these career clusters in 1999, and many states now use them to organize their career-oriented programs and career information. You can use these lists to identify jobs quickly based on your interests. When you find jobs you want to explore in more detail, look up their descriptions in Part II. You can also review clusters that represent areas in which you've had past experience, education, or training to see whether other jobs in those areas would meet your current requirements.

In this set of lists, you may notice that some occupations appear on multiple lists. This happens when two or more industries commonly employ workers with the same occupational title. For example, Nuclear Technicians may operate nuclear power plants (and thus work in the Manufacturing cluster) or aid in scientific research (Science, Technology, Engineering, and Mathematics). If you decide to pursue one of these multiple-cluster occupations, you may have to choose your intended industry early in your education or training pathway, or it may be possible to specialize later or (more rarely) even jump between industries after you have worked for several years.

Within each cluster, jobs are listed by combined score for earnings, job growth, and number of job openings, from highest to lowest.

Descriptions of the 16 Career Clusters

Brief descriptions follow of the 16 career clusters, defining them in terms of interests. Some of them refer to jobs (as examples) that aren't included in this book.

- **Agriculture, Food, and Natural Resources:** *An interest in working with plants, animals, forests, or mineral resources for agriculture, horticulture, conservation, extraction, and other purposes.* You can satisfy this interest by working in farming, landscaping, forestry, fishing, mining, and related fields. You may like doing physical work outdoors, such as on a farm or ranch, in a forest, or on a drilling rig. If you have a scientific curiosity, you could study plants and animals or analyze biological or rock samples in a lab. If you have management ability, you could own, operate, or manage a fish hatchery, a landscaping business, or a greenhouse.

- **Architecture and Construction:** *An interest in designing, assembling, and maintaining components of buildings and other structures.* You may want to be part of the team of architects, drafters, and others who design buildings and render plans. If construction interests you, you might find fulfillment in the many building projects that are being undertaken at all times. If you like to organize and plan, you can find careers in managing these projects. Or you can play a more direct role in putting up and finishing buildings by doing jobs such as plumbing, carpentry, masonry, painting, or roofing, either as a skilled craftsworker or as a helper. You can prepare the building site by operating heavy equipment or installing, maintaining, and repairing vital building equipment and systems such as electricity and heating.

- **Arts, Audio/Visual Technology, and Communication:** *An interest in creatively expressing feelings or ideas, in communicating news or information, or in performing.* You can satisfy this interest in creative, verbal, or performing activities. For example, if you enjoy literature, perhaps writing or editing would appeal to you. Journalism and public relations are other fields for people who like to use their writing or speaking skills. Do you prefer to work in the performing arts? If so, you could direct or perform in drama, music, or dance. If you especially enjoy the visual arts, you could create paintings, sculpture, or ceramics, or design products or visual displays. A flair for technology might lead you to specialize in photography, broadcast production, or dispatching.

- **Business, Management, and Administration:** *An interest in making a business organization or function run smoothly.* You can satisfy this interest by working in a position of leadership or by specializing in a function that contributes to the overall effort in a business, a nonprofit organization, or a government agency. If you especially enjoy working with people, you may find fulfillment from working in human resources. An interest in numbers may lead you to consider accounting, finance, budgeting, billing, or financial record-keeping. A job as an administrative assistant may interest you if you like a variety of tasks in a busy environment. If you are good with details and word processing, you may enjoy a job as a secretary or data-entry clerk. Or perhaps you would do well as the manager of a business.

- **Education and Training:** *An interest in helping people learn.* You can satisfy this interest by teaching students, who may be preschoolers, retirees, or any age in between. You may specialize in a particular academic field or work with learners of a particular age, with a particular interest, or with a particular learning problem. Working in a library or museum may give you an opportunity to expand people's understanding of the world.

- **Finance:** *An interest in helping businesses and people be assured of a financially secure future.* You can satisfy this interest by working in a financial or insurance business in a leadership or support role. If you like gathering and analyzing information, you may find fulfillment as an insurance adjuster or financial analyst. Or you may deal with information at the clerical level as a banking or insurance clerk or in person-to-person situations providing customer service. Another way to interact with people is to sell financial or insurance services that will meet their needs.

- **Government and Public Administration:** *An interest in helping a government agency serve the needs of the public.* You can satisfy this interest by working in a position of leadership or by specializing in a function that contributes to the role of government. You may help protect the public by working as an inspector or examiner to enforce standards. If you enjoy using clerical skills, you could work as a clerk in a law court or government office. Or perhaps you prefer the top-down perspective of a government executive or urban planner.

- **Health Science:** *An interest in helping people and animals be healthy.* You can satisfy this interest by working on a health-care team as a doctor, therapist, or nurse. You might specialize in one of the many different parts of the body (such as the teeth or eyes) or in one of the many different types of care. Or you may want to be a generalist who deals with the whole patient. If you like technology, you might find satisfaction working with X-rays or new diagnostic methods. You might work with healthy people, helping them to eat better. If you enjoy working with animals, you might care for them and keep them healthy.

⦿ **Hospitality and Tourism:** *An interest in catering to the personal wishes and needs of others so that they can enjoy a clean environment, good food and drink, comfortable lodging away from home, and recreation.* You can satisfy this interest by providing services for the convenience, care, and pampering of others in hotels, restaurants, airplanes, beauty parlors, and so on. You may want to use your love of cooking as a chef. If you like working with people, you may want to provide personal services by being a travel guide, a flight attendant, a concierge, a hairdresser, or a waiter. You may want to work in cleaning and building services if you like a clean environment. If you enjoy sports or games, you could work for an athletic team or casino.

⦿ **Human Services:** *An interest in improving people's social, mental, emotional, or spiritual well-being.* You can satisfy this interest as a counselor, social worker, or religious worker who helps people sort out their complicated lives or solve personal problems. You may work as a caretaker for young people or the elderly. Or you may interview people to help identify the social services they need.

⦿ **Information Technology:** *An interest in designing, developing, managing, and supporting information systems.* You can satisfy this interest by working with hardware, software, multimedia, or integrated systems. If you like to use your organizational skills, you might work as a systems or database administrator. Or you can solve complex problems as a software engineer or systems analyst. If you enjoy getting your hands on hardware, you might find work servicing computers, peripherals, and information-intense machines such as cash registers and ATMs.

⦿ **Law, Public Safety, Corrections, and Security:** *An interest in upholding people's rights or in protecting people and property by using authority, inspecting, or investigating.* You can satisfy this interest by working in law, law enforcement, fire fighting, the military, and related fields. For example, if you enjoy mental challenge and intrigue, you could investigate crimes or fires for a living. If you enjoy working with verbal skills and research skills, you may want to defend citizens in court or research deeds, wills, and other legal documents. If you want to help people in critical situations, you may want to fight fires, work as a police officer, or become a paramedic. Or, if you want more routine work in public safety, perhaps a job in guarding, patrolling, or inspecting would appeal to you. If you have management ability, you could seek a leadership position in law enforcement and the protective services. Work in the military gives you a chance to use technical and leadership skills while serving your country.

⦿ **Manufacturing:** *An interest in processing materials into intermediate or final products or maintaining and repairing products by using machines or hand tools.* You can satisfy this interest by working in one of many industries that mass-produce goods or by working for a utility that distributes electric power or other resources. You might enjoy manual work, using your hands or hand tools in highly skilled jobs such as assembling engines or electronic equipment. If you enjoy making machines run efficiently or fixing them when they break down, you could seek a job installing or repairing such devices as copiers, aircraft engines, cars, or watches. Perhaps you prefer to set up or operate machines that are used to manufacture products made of food, glass, or paper. You could enjoy cutting and grinding metal and plastic parts to desired shapes and measurements. Or you may want to operate equipment in systems that provide water and process wastewater. You may like inspecting, sorting, counting, or weighing products. Another option is to work with your hands and machinery to move boxes and freight in a warehouse. If leadership appeals to you, you could manage people engaged in production and repair.

⊙ **Marketing, Sales, and Service:** *An interest in bringing others to a particular point of view by personal persuasion and by sales and promotional techniques.* You can satisfy this interest in various jobs that involve persuasion and selling. If you like using knowledge of science, you may enjoy selling pharmaceutical, medical, or electronic products or services. Real estate offers several kinds of sales jobs as well. If you like speaking on the phone, you could work as a telemarketer. Or you may enjoy selling apparel and other merchandise in a retail setting. If you prefer to help people, you may want a job in customer service.

⊙ **Science, Technology, Engineering, and Mathematics:** *An interest in discovering, collecting, and analyzing information about the natural world; in applying scientific research findings to problems in medicine, the life sciences, human behavior, and the natural sciences; in imagining and manipulating quantitative data; and in applying technology to manufacturing, transportation, and other economic activities.* You can satisfy this interest by working with the knowledge and processes of the sciences. You may enjoy researching and developing new knowledge in mathematics, or perhaps solving problems in the physical, life, or social sciences would appeal to you. You may want to study engineering and help create new machines, processes, and structures. If you want to work with scientific equipment and procedures, you could seek a job in a research or testing laboratory.

⊙ **Transportation, Distribution, and Logistics:** *An interest in operations that move people or materials.* You can satisfy this interest by managing a transportation service, by helping vehicles keep on their assigned schedules and routes, or by driving or piloting a vehicle. If you enjoy taking responsibility, perhaps managing a rail line would appeal to you. If you work well with details and can take pressure on the job, you might consider being an air traffic controller. Or would you rather get out on the highway, on the water, or up in the air? If so, you could drive a truck from state to state, be employed on a ship, or fly a crop duster over a cornfield. If you prefer to stay closer to home, you could drive a delivery van, taxi, or school bus. You can use your physical strength to load freight and arrange it so that it gets to its destination in one piece.

Best Jobs for People Interested in Agriculture, Food, and Natural Resources

Job	Annual Earnings	Percent Growth	Annual Openings
1. First-Line Supervisors of Office and Administrative Support Workers	$48,810	14.3%	58,440
2. Mobile Heavy Equipment Mechanics, Except Engines	$45,600	16.2%	5,250
3. Environmental Science and Protection Technicians, Including Health	$42,270	23.6%	1,950

Best Jobs for People Interested in Agriculture, Food, and Natural Resources

Job	Annual Earnings	Percent Growth	Annual Openings
4. Farmers, Ranchers, and Other Agricultural Managers	$64,660	–8.0%	23,450
5. First-Line Supervisors of Landscaping, Lawn Service, and Groundskeeping Workers	$42,050	15.1%	6,010
6. Pest Control Workers	$30,220	26.2%	4,850
7. Refuse and Recyclable Material Collectors	$32,280	20.2%	6,970
8. Environmental Engineering Technicians	$44,850	24.5%	820
9. Hazardous Materials Removal Workers	$38,120	23.1%	1,890
10. Landscaping and Groundskeeping Workers	$23,410	20.9%	44,440
11. Engineering Technicians, Except Drafters, All Other	$58,670	4.7%	1,680
12. First-Line Supervisors of Retail Sales Workers	$36,480	8.4%	51,370
13. Geological and Petroleum Technicians	$49,690	14.6%	700
14. Water and Wastewater Treatment Plant and System Operators	$41,780	11.7%	4,150
15. Industrial Truck and Tractor Operators	$30,010	11.8%	20,950
16. Tree Trimmers and Pruners	$31,320	18.0%	1,800
17. Rotary Drill Operators, Oil and Gas	$51,310	7.1%	640
18. Mechanical Engineering Technicians	$51,350	4.0%	1,040
19. Buyers and Purchasing Agents, Farm Products	$55,860	5.4%	320
20. Farm Equipment Mechanics and Service Technicians	$34,230	13.4%	1,290
21. Derrick Operators, Oil and Gas	$45,220	9.5%	570
22. Chemical Technicians	$42,070	6.7%	1,290
23. First-Line Supervisors of Farming, Fishing, and Forestry Workers	$42,600	–1.5%	1,360
24. Service Unit Operators, Oil, Gas, and Mining	$40,750	8.6%	1,210
25. Fish and Game Wardens	$50,070	5.3%	220
26. Conveyor Operators and Tenders	$29,320	11.6%	1,490

Best Jobs for People Interested in Architecture and Construction

Job	Annual Earnings	Percent Growth	Annual Openings
1. Supervisors of Construction and Extraction Workers	$59,150	23.5%	25,970
2. Brickmasons and Blockmasons	$46,800	40.5%	5,450
3. Electricians	$49,320	23.2%	28,920
4. Plumbers, Pipefitters, and Steamfitters	$47,750	25.6%	22,880
5. Heating, Air Conditioning, and Refrigeration Mechanics and Installers	$43,380	33.7%	13,760

(continued)

(continued)

Best Jobs for People Interested in Architecture and Construction

Job	Annual Earnings	Percent Growth	Annual Openings
6. Operating Engineers and Other Construction Equipment Operators	$41,510	23.5%	16,280
7. Construction Managers	$84,240	16.6%	12,040
8. Carpenters	$40,010	19.6%	40,830
9. Construction and Building Inspectors	$53,180	18.0%	4,860
10. Glaziers	$37,350	42.2%	3,340
11. Cement Masons and Concrete Finishers	$35,600	34.6%	7,290
12. Security and Fire Alarm Systems Installers	$39,540	32.9%	3,670
13. Electrical Power-Line Installers and Repairers	$60,190	13.3%	5,270
14. Drywall and Ceiling Tile Installers	$36,970	27.6%	5,870
15. Tapers	$44,910	34.9%	1,430
16. Structural Iron and Steel Workers	$45,690	21.9%	2,540
17. Reinforcing Iron and Rebar Workers	$37,990	48.7%	1,320
18. Insulation Workers, Mechanical	$37,990	31.8%	2,010
19. Pile-Driver Operators	$45,500	36.6%	230
20. Tile and Marble Setters	$37,080	25.4%	2,770
21. Helpers—Carpenters	$26,400	55.7%	3,820
22. Helpers—Pipelayers, Plumbers, Pipefitters, and Steamfitters	$27,010	45.4%	4,170
23. Boilermakers	$56,910	21.2%	1,180
24. Helpers—Brickmasons, Blockmasons, Stonemasons, and Tile and Marble Setters	$27,820	59.9%	2,540
25. Painters, Construction and Maintenance	$35,430	18.5%	15,730
26. Construction Laborers	$29,730	21.3%	29,240
27. Pipelayers	$35,900	25.2%	2,880
28. Civil Engineering Technicians	$46,900	11.9%	2,460
29. Helpers—Electricians	$27,620	30.6%	4,200
30. Mechanical Drafters	$49,200	11.1%	2,050
31. Excavating and Loading Machine and Dragline Operators	$37,380	17.4%	2,890
32. Roofers	$35,280	17.8%	5,250
33. Stonemasons	$36,640	36.5%	890
34. Crane and Tower Operators	$46,460	15.7%	1,720
35. Maintenance and Repair Workers, General	$35,030	11.0%	37,910
36. Engineering Technicians, Except Drafters, All Other	$58,670	4.7%	1,680
37. Architectural and Civil Drafters	$47,250	3.2%	2,090
38. Paving, Surfacing, and Tamping Equipment Operators	$35,270	22.1%	2,200
39. Surveying and Mapping Technicians	$39,350	15.8%	2,000

Best Jobs for People Interested in Architecture and Construction

Job	Annual Earnings	Percent Growth	Annual Openings
40. Electrical and Electronics Drafters	$54,470	5.5%	720
41. Highway Maintenance Workers	$35,220	8.2%	5,140
42. Insulation Workers, Floor, Ceiling, and Wall	$32,420	23.3%	1,460
43. Coin, Vending, and Amusement Machine Servicers and Repairers	$30,820	22.0%	1,630
44. Earth Drillers, Except Oil and Gas	$40,200	14.0%	620
45. Terrazzo Workers and Finishers	$41,240	16.2%	110
46. Plasterers and Stucco Masons	$36,830	17.2%	1,050
47. Segmental Pavers	$32,340	30.8%	90
48. Riggers	$43,020	10.5%	440
49. Septic Tank Servicers and Sewer Pipe Cleaners	$33,740	20.6%	1,190
50. Carpet Installers	$36,750	10.3%	1,520
51. Floor Sanders and Finishers	$33,350	17.8%	420
52. Home Appliance Repairers	$35,440	6.5%	1,190

Best Jobs for People Interested in Arts, Audio/Visual Technology, and Communication

Job	Annual Earnings	Percent Growth	Annual Openings
1. Telecommunications Equipment Installers and Repairers, Except Line Installers	$53,960	14.6%	5,930
2. Managers, All Other	$99,540	7.9%	24,940
3. Audio and Video Equipment Technicians	$41,630	13.4%	2,560
4. Choreographers	$39,600	24.2%	830
5. Radio, Cellular, and Tower Equipment Installers and Repairers	$42,160	29.3%	450
6. Electronic Home Entertainment Equipment Installers and Repairers	$34,470	13.9%	1,410
7. Photographers	$28,860	12.5%	3,100
8. Painting, Coating, and Decorating Workers	$25,660	17.4%	980
9. Broadcast Technicians	$36,570	9.0%	1,380
10. Fashion Designers	$64,690	0.0%	670
11. Fine Artists, Including Painters, Sculptors, and Illustrators	$44,600	7.8%	810

Best Jobs for People Interested in Business, Management, and Administration

Job	Annual Earnings	Percent Growth	Annual Openings
1. Construction Managers	$84,240	16.6%	12,040
2. First-Line Supervisors of Office and Administrative Support Workers	$48,810	14.3%	58,440
3. Administrative Services Managers	$79,540	14.5%	9,980
4. Business Operations Specialists, All Other	$64,030	11.6%	32,720
5. Executive Secretaries and Executive Administrative Assistants	$45,580	12.6%	32,180
6. Customer Service Representatives	$30,610	15.5%	95,960
7. Managers, All Other	$99,540	7.9%	24,940
8. Billing and Posting Clerks	$32,880	19.7%	18,760
9. Bookkeeping, Accounting, and Auditing Clerks	$34,740	13.6%	46,780
10. Office Clerks, General	$27,190	16.6%	101,150
11. General and Operations Managers	$95,150	4.6%	41,010
12. Receptionists and Information Clerks	$25,690	23.7%	56,560
13. Cargo and Freight Agents	$38,210	29.3%	4,420
14. Dispatchers, Except Police, Fire, and Ambulance	$35,200	18.6%	6,950
15. Advertising Sales Agents	$45,250	13.0%	6,990
16. First-Line Supervisors of Personal Service Workers	$35,230	13.5%	8,260
17. Payroll and Timekeeping Clerks	$37,160	14.6%	6,570
18. Interviewers, Except Eligibility and Loan	$29,560	17.3%	7,960
19. Postal Service Mail Carriers	$55,160	–12.0%	10,340
20. Transportation, Storage, and Distribution Managers	$80,860	10.0%	3,370
21. Insurance Claims and Policy Processing Clerks	$35,210	8.7%	9,600
22. Human Resources Assistants, Except Payroll and Timekeeping	$37,250	11.2%	6,160
23. Secretaries and Administrative Assistants, Except Legal, Medical, and Executive	$31,870	5.8%	39,100
24. Court, Municipal, and License Clerks	$34,300	8.0%	4,670
25. Gaming Supervisors	$48,820	6.9%	920
26. Brokerage Clerks	$41,760	5.9%	1,970
27. Order Clerks	$28,940	7.4%	7,520
28. Procurement Clerks	$37,640	5.7%	3,550
29. Shipping, Receiving, and Traffic Clerks	$28,790	0.3%	17,740
30. Postal Service Clerks	$53,100	–48.2%	1,550
31. Couriers and Messengers	$24,750	12.6%	4,300
32. Mail Clerks and Mail Machine Operators, Except Postal Service	$26,610	12.0%	3,960
33. Tax Preparers	$32,320	9.8%	2,630
34. Weighers, Measurers, Checkers, and Samplers, Recordkeeping	$27,390	12.0%	3,420

Best Jobs for People Interested in Education and Training

Job	Annual Earnings	Percent Growth	Annual Openings
1. Coaches and Scouts	$28,470	29.4%	13,300
2. Fitness Trainers and Aerobics Instructors	$31,030	24.0%	10,060
3. Preschool Teachers, Except Special Education	$26,620	24.9%	23,240
4. Self-Enrichment Education Teachers	$36,100	20.9%	9,150
5. Athletes and Sports Competitors	$39,670	21.8%	780
6. Teacher Assistants	$23,580	14.8%	48,160
7. Library Technicians	$30,430	8.8%	5,950
8. Library Assistants, Clerical	$23,440	10.2%	6,410

Best Jobs for People Interested in Finance

Job	Annual Earnings	Percent Growth	Annual Openings
1. Insurance Sales Agents	$47,450	21.9%	18,440
2. Bill and Account Collectors	$31,920	14.2%	13,550
3. Loan Officers	$58,030	14.2%	11,520
4. Claims Adjusters, Examiners, and Investigators	$59,320	3.0%	7,990
5. Tellers	$24,590	1.3%	23,750
6. Telemarketers	$22,520	7.4%	8,350

Best Jobs for People Interested in Government and Public Administration

Job	Annual Earnings	Percent Growth	Annual Openings
1. Managers, All Other	$99,540	7.9%	24,940
2. Administrative Services Managers	$79,540	14.5%	9,980
3. General and Operations Managers	$95,150	4.6%	41,010
4. Transportation, Storage, and Distribution Managers	$80,860	10.0%	3,370
5. Surveying and Mapping Technicians	$39,350	15.8%	2,000
6. Tax Preparers	$32,320	9.8%	2,630

Best Jobs for People Interested in Health Science

Job	Annual Earnings	Percent Growth	Annual Openings
1. Dental Hygienists	$69,280	37.7%	10,490
2. Registered Nurses	$65,950	26.0%	120,740
3. Physical Therapist Assistants	$51,040	45.7%	4,120
4. Diagnostic Medical Sonographers	$65,210	43.6%	3,170
5. Medical Secretaries	$31,060	41.3%	27,840
6. Radiologic Technologists and Technicians	$55,120	27.7%	9,510
7. Licensed Practical and Licensed Vocational Nurses	$41,150	22.4%	36,920
8. Respiratory Therapists	$55,250	27.7%	5,270
9. Dental Assistants	$34,140	30.8%	15,400
10. First-Line Supervisors of Office and Administrative Support Workers	$48,810	14.3%	58,440
11. Occupational Therapy Assistants	$52,040	43.2%	1,680
12. Veterinary Technologists and Technicians	$30,140	52.0%	5,570
13. Emergency Medical Technicians and Paramedics	$30,710	33.3%	12,080
14. Medical Assistants	$29,100	30.9%	24,380
15. Pharmacy Technicians	$28,940	32.4%	16,630
16. Cardiovascular Technologists and Technicians	$51,020	29.4%	2,210
17. Executive Secretaries and Executive Administrative Assistants	$45,580	12.6%	32,180
18. Substance Abuse and Behavioral Disorder Counselors	$38,560	27.4%	4,170
19. Receptionists and Information Clerks	$25,690	23.7%	56,560
20. Social and Human Service Assistants	$28,740	27.6%	18,910
21. Health Technologists and Technicians, All Other	$38,080	23.2%	4,040
22. Massage Therapists	$35,830	20.1%	5,590
23. Medical Records and Health Information Technicians	$33,310	21.0%	7,370
24. Radiation Therapists	$76,630	20.1%	670
25. Opticians, Dispensing	$33,100	28.9%	3,060
26. Nuclear Medicine Technologists	$69,450	18.7%	750
27. Surgical Technologists	$40,950	18.9%	3,390
28. Medical and Clinical Laboratory Technicians	$36,950	14.8%	5,510
29. Physical Therapist Aides	$23,680	43.2%	2,760
30. First-Line Supervisors of Food Preparation and Serving Workers	$29,550	9.8%	24,830
31. Life, Physical, and Social Science Technicians, All Other	$43,120	11.8%	3,350
32. Nuclear Technicians	$68,030	14.1%	330
33. Occupational Therapy Aides	$28,200	33.3%	360
34. Ambulance Drivers and Attendants, Except Emergency Medical Technicians	$22,820	32.1%	1,010
35. Occupational Health and Safety Technicians	$46,030	13.2%	510
36. Cooks, Institution and Cafeteria	$22,710	12.3%	13,620

Best Jobs for People Interested in Health Science

Job	Annual Earnings	Percent Growth	Annual Openings
37. Medical Equipment Preparers	$30,050	17.5%	1,620
38. Fine Artists, Including Painters, Sculptors, and Illustrators	$44,600	7.8%	810
39. Psychiatric Technicians	$28,470	15.5%	2,460
40. Medical Transcriptionists	$33,480	5.9%	2,020
41. Psychiatric Aides	$25,170	15.1%	1,900
42. Veterinary Assistants and Laboratory Animal Caretakers	$22,830	14.2%	2,160
43. Ophthalmic Laboratory Technicians	$28,750	12.8%	1,320

Best Jobs for People Interested in Hospitality and Tourism

Job	Annual Earnings	Percent Growth	Annual Openings
1. Managers, All Other	$99,540	7.9%	24,940
2. First-Line Supervisors of Food Preparation and Serving Workers	$29,550	9.8%	24,830
3. Residential Advisors	$24,540	24.9%	4,570
4. Meat, Poultry, and Fish Cutters and Trimmers	$22,720	15.5%	7,400
5. Cooks, Institution and Cafeteria	$22,710	12.3%	13,620
6. Food Service Managers	$48,110	−3.3%	5,910
7. Gaming Managers	$67,230	12.1%	100
8. Lodging Managers	$47,450	8.4%	1,820
9. Tour Guides and Escorts	$23,620	18.1%	1,960
10. Travel Guides	$30,670	23.8%	260
11. Butchers and Meat Cutters	$28,460	8.0%	4,680
12. First-Line Supervisors of Housekeeping and Janitorial Workers	$35,230	0.8%	3,320
13. Travel Agents	$33,930	10.0%	1,720
14. Reservation and Transportation Ticket Agents and Travel Clerks	$33,300	5.8%	3,080
15. Chefs and Head Cooks	$42,350	−0.8%	1,800
16. Flight Attendants	$38,020	−0.2%	1,730

Best Jobs for People Interested in Human Services

Job	Annual Earnings	Percent Growth	Annual Openings
1. Managers, All Other	$99,540	7.9%	24,940
2. Substance Abuse and Behavioral Disorder Counselors	$38,560	27.4%	4,170
3. First-Line Supervisors of Retail Sales Workers	$36,480	8.4%	51,370

(continued)

(continued)

Best Jobs for People Interested in Human Services

Job	Annual Earnings	Percent Growth	Annual Openings
4. Preschool Teachers, Except Special Education	$26,620	24.9%	23,240
5. Hairdressers, Hairstylists, and Cosmetologists	$22,570	15.7%	21,810
6. Skincare Specialists	$29,190	24.6%	2,040
7. Social Science Research Assistants	$38,800	14.8%	1,700
8. Eligibility Interviewers, Government Programs	$41,060	3.1%	3,740
9. Embalmers	$43,800	5.6%	370

Best Jobs for People Interested in Information Technology

Job	Annual Earnings	Percent Growth	Annual Openings
1. Computer Numerically Controlled Machine Tool Programmers, Metal and Plastic	$45,890	10.8%	490

Best Jobs for People Interested in Law, Public Safety, Corrections, and Security

Job	Annual Earnings	Percent Growth	Annual Openings
1. Paralegals and Legal Assistants	$46,730	18.3%	8,340
2. Police and Sheriff's Patrol Officers	$54,230	8.2%	24,940
3. Security Guards	$23,900	18.8%	35,950
4. Firefighters	$45,420	8.6%	11,230
5. First-Line Supervisors of Fire Fighting and Prevention Workers	$69,510	8.2%	3,310
6. Private Detectives and Investigators	$43,710	20.5%	1,490
7. First-Line Supervisors of Police and Detectives	$77,890	2.2%	3,870
8. Court Reporters	$48,530	14.1%	640
9. Detectives and Criminal Investigators	$71,770	2.9%	3,010
10. Fire Inspectors and Investigators	$53,330	8.8%	470
11. First-Line Supervisors of Correctional Officers	$55,030	5.5%	1,650
12. Police, Fire, and Ambulance Dispatchers	$35,930	11.7%	3,070
13. Correctional Officers and Jailers	$38,990	5.2%	10,810
14. Legal Secretaries	$42,460	3.5%	3,940
15. Transit and Railroad Police	$56,390	5.6%	110
16. Transportation Security Screeners	$36,910	9.6%	1,040
17. Bailiffs	$38,950	7.9%	450

Best Jobs for People Interested in Manufacturing

Job	Annual Earnings	Percent Growth	Annual Openings
1. First-Line Supervisors of Mechanics, Installers, and Repairers	$59,850	11.9%	16,490
2. Industrial Machinery Mechanics	$46,270	21.6%	11,710
3. Medical Equipment Repairers	$44,870	31.4%	2,230
4. Telecommunications Line Installers and Repairers	$51,720	13.6%	5,140
5. Mobile Heavy Equipment Mechanics, Except Engines	$45,600	16.2%	5,250
6. Sheet Metal Workers	$42,730	17.6%	4,700
7. Environmental Science and Protection Technicians, Including Health	$42,270	23.6%	1,950
8. Computer-Controlled Machine Tool Operators, Metal and Plastic	$35,220	19.2%	4,780
9. Welders, Cutters, Solderers, and Brazers	$35,920	15.0%	14,070
10. Aircraft Mechanics and Service Technicians	$54,590	6.3%	4,520
11. Civil Engineering Technicians	$46,900	11.9%	2,460
12. Hazardous Materials Removal Workers	$38,120	23.1%	1,890
13. Machinists	$39,220	8.5%	9,950
14. First-Line Supervisors of Production and Operating Workers	$53,670	1.9%	8,790
15. Life, Physical, and Social Science Technicians, All Other	$43,120	11.8%	3,350
16. Environmental Engineering Technicians	$44,850	24.5%	820
17. Elevator Installers and Repairers	$75,060	11.6%	820
18. Helpers—Installation, Maintenance, and Repair Workers	$24,060	18.4%	8,040
19. Electrical and Electronic Engineering Technicians	$56,900	1.9%	3,180
20. Nuclear Technicians	$68,030	14.1%	330
21. Rail Car Repairers	$47,740	17.1%	930
22. Cabinetmakers and Bench Carpenters	$30,530	16.8%	4,020
23. Structural Metal Fabricators and Fitters	$35,170	15.7%	2,830
24. Inspectors, Testers, Sorters, Samplers, and Weighers	$34,040	8.0%	12,390
25. Sawing Machine Setters, Operators, and Tenders, Wood	$26,220	24.6%	1,810
26. Tire Repairers and Changers	$23,440	18.5%	4,390
27. Engineering Technicians, Except Drafters, All Other	$58,670	4.7%	1,680
28. Fence Erectors	$29,580	23.7%	1,640
29. Computer, Automated Teller, and Office Machine Repairers	$36,360	6.5%	4,540
30. Helpers—Production Workers	$22,520	8.7%	9,980
31. Woodworking Machine Setters, Operators, and Tenders, Except Sawing	$27,090	20.1%	1,740
32. Locksmiths and Safe Repairers	$36,680	17.9%	930
33. Mechanical Door Repairers	$36,640	24.2%	550
34. Electrical and Electronics Repairers, Commercial and Industrial Equipment	$52,320	1.2%	1,770

(continued)

(continued)

Best Jobs for People Interested in Manufacturing

Job	Annual Earnings	Percent Growth	Annual Openings
35. Power Plant Operators	$65,280	−2.5%	1,440
36. Electrical and Electronics Repairers, Powerhouse, Substation, and Relay	$67,450	4.7%	690
37. Stationary Engineers and Boiler Operators	$53,070	6.1%	1,060
38. Team Assemblers	$27,490	5.5%	24,100
39. Avionics Technicians	$54,720	7.0%	580
40. Petroleum Pump System Operators, Refinery Operators, and Gaugers	$61,260	−14.0%	1,440
41. Industrial Engineering Technicians	$49,090	4.2%	1,460
42. Maintenance Workers, Machinery	$39,490	6.4%	1,740
43. Chemical Plant and System Operators	$55,940	−12.2%	1,410
44. Extruding and Drawing Machine Setters, Operators, and Tenders, Metal and Plastic	$32,300	8.4%	2,090
45. Metal-Refining Furnace Operators and Tenders	$38,680	16.0%	550
46. Nuclear Power Reactor Operators	$76,590	3.8%	200
47. Chemical Technicians	$42,070	6.7%	1,290
48. Mechanical Engineering Technicians	$51,350	4.0%	1,040
49. Fashion Designers	$64,690	0.0%	670
50. Recreational Vehicle Service Technicians	$34,000	22.2%	480
51. Layout Workers, Metal and Plastic	$39,870	13.5%	290
52. Roustabouts, Oil and Gas	$32,980	8.3%	1,550
53. Refractory Materials Repairers, Except Brickmasons	$42,700	9.5%	60
54. Rolling Machine Setters, Operators, and Tenders, Metal and Plastic	$36,920	8.1%	880
55. Coating, Painting, and Spraying Machine Setters, Operators, and Tenders	$30,020	6.1%	2,310
56. Printing Press Operators	$34,290	−1.4%	3,920
57. Control and Valve Installers and Repairers, Except Mechanical Door	$49,600	0.0%	810
58. Welding, Soldering, and Brazing Machine Setters, Operators, and Tenders	$34,770	6.5%	1,380

Best Jobs for People Interested in Marketing, Sales, and Service

Job	Annual Earnings	Percent Growth	Annual Openings
1. Sales Representatives, Wholesale and Manufacturing, Except Technical and Scientific Products	$53,540	15.6%	55,990

Best Jobs for People Interested in Marketing, Sales, and Service

Job	Annual Earnings	Percent Growth	Annual Openings
2. Real Estate Sales Agents	$39,070	12.2%	12,760
3. First-Line Supervisors of Retail Sales Workers	$36,480	8.4%	51,370
4. Parts Salespersons	$29,350	16.0%	10,720
5. First-Line Supervisors of Non-Retail Sales Workers	$70,520	4.0%	12,350
6. Counter and Rental Clerks	$22,740	12.2%	14,660
7. Demonstrators and Product Promoters	$23,770	17.5%	4,210
8. Wholesale and Retail Buyers, Except Farm Products	$50,490	9.0%	4,170
9. Purchasing Agents, Except Wholesale, Retail, and Farm Products	$57,580	5.3%	9,120
10. Driver/Sales Workers	$22,770	10.3%	12,290
11. Real Estate Brokers	$59,340	7.6%	2,970
12. Property, Real Estate, and Community Association Managers	$52,510	6.1%	8,230
13. Merchandise Displayers and Window Trimmers	$26,190	12.8%	4,000
14. Appraisers and Assessors of Real Estate	$48,870	7.5%	2,220
15. Lodging Managers	$47,450	8.4%	1,820
16. Travel Agents	$33,930	10.0%	1,720
17. Telemarketers	$22,520	7.4%	8,350
18. Reservation and Transportation Ticket Agents and Travel Clerks	$33,300	5.8%	3,080

Best Jobs for People Interested in Science, Technology, Engineering, and Mathematics

Job	Annual Earnings	Percent Growth	Annual Openings
1. Nuclear Technicians	$68,030	14.1%	330
2. Industrial Engineering Technicians	$49,090	4.2%	1,460

Best Jobs for People Interested in Transportation, Distribution, and Logistics

Job	Annual Earnings	Percent Growth	Annual Openings
1. First-Line Supervisors of Helpers, Laborers, and Material Movers, Hand	$44,580	27.2%	8,000
2. Commercial Pilots	$70,000	21.1%	1,930

(continued)

(continued)

Best Jobs for People Interested in Transportation, Distribution, and Logistics

Job	Annual Earnings	Percent Growth	Annual Openings
3. Operating Engineers and Other Construction Equipment Operators	$41,510	23.5%	16,280
4. Heavy and Tractor-Trailer Truck Drivers	$37,930	20.6%	64,940
5. Managers, All Other	$99,540	7.9%	24,940
6. Environmental Science and Protection Technicians, Including Health	$42,270	23.6%	1,950
7. Automotive Service Technicians and Mechanics	$36,180	17.3%	31,170
8. First-Line Supervisors of Transportation and Material-Moving Machine and Vehicle Operators	$52,950	14.3%	6,930
9. Transportation, Storage, and Distribution Managers	$80,860	10.0%	3,370
10. Automotive Body and Related Repairers	$38,180	18.4%	6,520
11. Sailors and Marine Oilers	$36,800	21.3%	2,150
12. Airline Pilots, Copilots, and Flight Engineers	$105,580	6.4%	3,130
13. Bus and Truck Mechanics and Diesel Engine Specialists	$41,640	14.5%	8,780
14. Crane and Tower Operators	$46,460	15.7%	1,720
15. Transportation Inspectors	$62,230	14.6%	1,070
16. Laborers and Freight, Stock, and Material Movers, Hand	$23,750	15.4%	98,020
17. Parts Salespersons	$29,350	16.0%	10,720
18. Light Truck or Delivery Services Drivers	$29,080	14.7%	29,590
19. Aircraft Mechanics and Service Technicians	$54,590	6.3%	4,520
20. Aircraft Cargo Handling Supervisors	$46,840	20.6%	260
21. Production, Planning, and Expediting Clerks	$43,100	6.6%	8,880
22. Taxi Drivers and Chauffeurs	$22,760	19.6%	7,670
23. Automotive Glass Installers and Repairers	$33,720	24.9%	920
24. Bus Drivers, Transit and Intercity	$35,720	14.8%	6,350
25. Aircraft Structure, Surfaces, Rigging, and Systems Assemblers	$46,210	14.3%	1,220
26. Commercial Divers	$52,550	15.8%	130
27. Motorboat Mechanics and Service Technicians	$35,520	20.7%	960
28. Air Traffic Controllers	$113,540	−3.0%	1,020
29. Motorcycle Mechanics	$32,410	23.3%	890
30. Bus Drivers, School or Special Client	$28,110	12.0%	14,450
31. Railroad Conductors and Yardmasters	$53,880	4.7%	1,430
32. Outdoor Power Equipment and Other Small Engine Mechanics	$30,200	18.9%	1,350
33. Subway and Streetcar Operators	$63,820	9.2%	280
34. Bicycle Repairers	$23,210	37.4%	630

Best Jobs for People Interested in Transportation, Distribution, and Logistics

Job	Annual Earnings	Percent Growth	Annual Openings
35. Locomotive Engineers	$49,380	4.4%	1,550
36. Avionics Technicians	$54,720	7.0%	580
37. Painters, Transportation Equipment	$39,600	9.5%	1,430
38. Airfield Operations Specialists	$47,180	8.7%	320
39. Shipping, Receiving, and Traffic Clerks	$28,790	0.3%	17,740
40. Motorboat Operators	$36,620	16.1%	160
41. Traffic Technicians	$42,300	11.6%	280

Best Jobs Lists Based on Personality Types

These lists organize the 300 best jobs into groups matching six personality types. Within each personality type, I ranked the jobs based on each one's total combined score for earnings, growth, and number of job openings.

The personality types are Realistic, Investigative, Artistic, Social, Enterprising, and Conventional. This system was developed by Dr. John L. Holland and is used in the *Self-Directed Search (SDS)* and other career assessment inventories and information systems. If you have used one of these career inventories or systems, the lists will help you identify jobs that most closely match these personality types. Even if you have not used one of these systems, the concept of personality types and the jobs that are related to them can help you identify jobs that suit the type of person you are.

I assigned some the jobs to more than one of the following lists to match the differing characteristics of job specializations. For example, you will find the job Architectural and Civil Drafters on two lists because it is linked to the specializations Architectural Drafters (Artistic) and Civil Drafters (Realistic). Some of the list assignments may surprise you. For example, Registered Nurses appears on the Enterprising list (as well as the Social list) because it is linked to Clinical Nurse Specialists, a job that is primarily managerial.

In addition, you should be aware that these lists are based on the primary personality type that describes the job, but most jobs also are linked to one or two secondary personality types. The job descriptions in Part II indicate all significant personality types. Consider reviewing the jobs for more than one personality type so you don't overlook possible jobs that would interest you.

Descriptions of the Six Personality Types

Following are brief descriptions for each of the six personality types used in the lists. Select the two or three descriptions that most closely describe you and then use the lists to identify jobs that best fit these personality types.

- **Realistic:** These occupations frequently involve work activities that include practical, hands-on problems and solutions. They often deal with plants; animals; and real-world materials such as wood, tools, and machinery. Many of the occupations require working outside and don't involve a lot of paperwork or working closely with others.

- **Investigative:** These occupations frequently involve working with ideas and require an extensive amount of thinking. These occupations can involve searching for facts and figuring out problems mentally.

- **Artistic:** These occupations frequently involve working with forms, designs, and patterns. They often require self-expression, and the work can be done without following a clear set of rules.

- **Social:** These occupations frequently involve working with, communicating with, and teaching people. These occupations often involve helping or providing service to others.

- **Enterprising:** These occupations frequently involve starting up and carrying out projects. These occupations can involve leading people and making many decisions. They sometimes require risk taking and often deal with business.

- **Conventional:** These occupations frequently involve following set procedures and routines. These occupations can include working with data and details more than with ideas. Usually there is a clear line of authority to follow.

Best Jobs for People with a Realistic Personality Type

Job	Annual Earnings	Percent Growth	Annual Openings
1. Radiologic Technologists and Technicians	$55,120	27.7%	9,510
2. Plumbers, Pipefitters, and Steamfitters	$47,750	25.6%	22,880
3. Electricians	$49,320	23.2%	28,920
4. Heating, Air Conditioning, and Refrigeration Mechanics and Installers	$43,380	33.7%	13,760
5. Brickmasons and Blockmasons	$46,800	40.5%	5,450
6. Industrial Machinery Mechanics	$46,270	21.6%	11,710
7. Operating Engineers and Other Construction Equipment Operators	$41,510	23.5%	16,280
8. Cardiovascular Technologists and Technicians	$51,020	29.4%	2,210
9. Business Operations Specialists, All Other	$64,030	11.6%	32,720
10. Carpenters	$40,010	19.6%	40,830
11. Construction and Building Inspectors	$53,180	18.0%	4,860

Best Jobs for People with a Realistic Personality Type

Job	Annual Earnings	Percent Growth	Annual Openings
12. Commercial Pilots	$70,000	21.1%	1,930
13. Heavy and Tractor-Trailer Truck Drivers	$37,930	20.6%	64,940
14. Medical Equipment Repairers	$44,870	31.4%	2,230
15. Drywall and Ceiling Tile Installers	$36,970	27.6%	5,870
16. Security and Fire Alarm Systems Installers	$39,540	32.9%	3,670
17. Cement Masons and Concrete Finishers	$35,600	34.6%	7,290
18. Telecommunications Equipment Installers and Repairers, Except Line Installers	$53,960	14.6%	5,930
19. Electrical Power-Line Installers and Repairers	$60,190	13.3%	5,270
20. Glaziers	$37,350	42.2%	3,340
21. Structural Iron and Steel Workers	$45,690	21.9%	2,540
22. Mobile Heavy Equipment Mechanics, Except Engines	$45,600	16.2%	5,250
23. Police and Sheriff's Patrol Officers	$54,230	8.2%	24,940
24. Tapers	$44,910	34.9%	1,430
25. Telecommunications Line Installers and Repairers	$51,720	13.6%	5,140
26. Sheet Metal Workers	$42,730	17.6%	4,700
27. Health Technologists and Technicians, All Other	$38,080	23.2%	4,040
28. Veterinary Technologists and Technicians	$30,140	52.0%	5,570
29. Automotive Body and Related Repairers	$38,180	18.4%	6,520
30. Boilermakers	$56,910	21.2%	1,180
31. Automotive Service Technicians and Mechanics	$36,180	17.3%	31,170
32. Insulation Workers, Mechanical	$37,990	31.8%	2,010
33. Bus and Truck Mechanics and Diesel Engine Specialists	$41,640	14.5%	8,780
34. Tile and Marble Setters	$37,080	25.4%	2,770
35. Painters, Construction and Maintenance	$35,430	18.5%	15,730
36. Surgical Technologists	$40,950	18.9%	3,390
37. Construction Laborers	$29,730	21.3%	29,240
38. Pipelayers	$35,900	25.2%	2,880
39. Firefighters	$45,420	8.6%	11,230
40. Reinforcing Iron and Rebar Workers	$37,990	48.7%	1,320
41. Pest Control Workers	$30,220	26.2%	4,850
42. Hazardous Materials Removal Workers	$38,120	23.1%	1,890
43. Welders, Cutters, Solderers, and Brazers	$35,920	15.0%	14,070
44. Landscaping and Groundskeeping Workers	$23,410	20.9%	44,440
45. Helpers—Pipelayers, Plumbers, Pipefitters, and Steamfitters	$27,010	45.4%	4,170
46. Airline Pilots, Copilots, and Flight Engineers	$105,580	6.4%	3,130
47. Helpers—Carpenters	$26,400	55.7%	3,820

(continued)

(continued)

Best Jobs for People with a Realistic Personality Type

Job	Annual Earnings	Percent Growth	Annual Openings
48. Pile-Driver Operators	$45,500	36.6%	230
49. Refuse and Recyclable Material Collectors	$32,280	20.2%	6,970
50. Aircraft Mechanics and Service Technicians	$54,590	6.3%	4,520
51. Computer-Controlled Machine Tool Operators, Metal and Plastic	$35,220	19.2%	4,780
52. Environmental Engineering Technicians	$44,850	24.5%	820
53. Medical and Clinical Laboratory Technicians	$36,950	14.8%	5,510
54. Crane and Tower Operators	$46,460	15.7%	1,720
55. Helpers—Brickmasons, Blockmasons, Stonemasons, and Tile and Marble Setters	$27,820	59.9%	2,540
56. Roofers	$35,280	17.8%	5,250
57. Helpers—Electricians	$27,620	30.6%	4,200
58. Sailors and Marine Oilers	$36,800	21.3%	2,150
59. Security Guards	$23,900	18.8%	35,950
60. Transportation Inspectors	$62,230	14.6%	1,070
61. Civil Engineering Technicians	$46,900	11.9%	2,460
62. Excavating and Loading Machine and Dragline Operators	$37,380	17.4%	2,890
63. Bus Drivers, Transit and Intercity	$35,720	14.8%	6,350
64. Life, Physical, and Social Science Technicians, All Other	$43,120	11.8%	3,350
65. Paving, Surfacing, and Tamping Equipment Operators	$35,270	22.1%	2,200
66. Water and Wastewater Treatment Plant and System Operators	$41,780	11.7%	4,150
67. Radio, Cellular, and Tower Equipment Installers and Repairers	$42,160	29.3%	450
68. Machinists	$39,220	8.5%	9,950
69. Mechanical Drafters	$49,200	11.1%	2,050
70. Audio and Video Equipment Technicians	$41,630	13.4%	2,560
71. Maintenance and Repair Workers, General	$35,030	11.0%	37,910
72. Stonemasons	$36,640	36.5%	890
73. Electrical and Electronic Engineering Technicians	$56,900	1.9%	3,180
74. Light Truck or Delivery Services Drivers	$29,080	14.7%	29,590
75. Rail Car Repairers	$47,740	17.1%	930
76. Surveying and Mapping Technicians	$39,350	15.8%	2,000
77. Laborers and Freight, Stock, and Material Movers, Hand	$23,750	15.4%	98,020
78. Helpers—Installation, Maintenance, and Repair Workers	$24,060	18.4%	8,040
79. Taxi Drivers and Chauffeurs	$22,760	19.6%	7,670
80. Athletes and Sports Competitors	$39,670	21.8%	780
81. Elevator Installers and Repairers	$75,060	11.6%	820
82. Aircraft Structure, Surfaces, Rigging, and Systems Assemblers	$46,210	14.3%	1,220

Best Jobs for People with a Realistic Personality Type

Job	Annual Earnings	Percent Growth	Annual Openings
83. Correctional Officers and Jailers	$38,990	5.2%	10,810
84. Nuclear Technicians	$68,030	14.1%	330
85. Engineering Technicians, Except Drafters, All Other	$58,670	4.7%	1,680
86. Industrial Truck and Tractor Operators	$30,010	11.8%	20,950
87. Insulation Workers, Floor, Ceiling, and Wall	$32,420	23.3%	1,460
88. Geological and Petroleum Technicians	$49,690	14.6%	700
89. Cabinetmakers and Bench Carpenters	$30,530	16.8%	4,020
90. Fence Erectors	$29,580	23.7%	1,640
91. Coin, Vending, and Amusement Machine Servicers and Repairers	$30,820	22.0%	1,630
92. Structural Metal Fabricators and Fitters	$35,170	15.7%	2,830
93. Sawing Machine Setters, Operators, and Tenders, Wood	$26,220	24.6%	1,810
94. Bus Drivers, School or Special Client	$28,110	12.0%	14,450
95. Commercial Divers	$52,550	15.8%	130
96. Tire Repairers and Changers	$23,440	18.5%	4,390
97. Mechanical Door Repairers	$36,640	24.2%	550
98. Power Plant Operators	$65,280	−2.5%	1,440
99. Electrical and Electronics Repairers, Commercial and Industrial Equipment	$52,320	1.2%	1,770
100. Architectural and Civil Drafters	$47,250	3.2%	2,090
101. Automotive Glass Installers and Repairers	$33,720	24.9%	920
102. Meat, Poultry, and Fish Cutters and Trimmers	$22,720	15.5%	7,400
103. Petroleum Pump System Operators, Refinery Operators, and Gaugers	$61,260	−14.0%	1,440
104. Tree Trimmers and Pruners	$31,320	18.0%	1,800
105. Motorboat Mechanics and Service Technicians	$35,520	20.7%	960
106. Locomotive Engineers	$49,380	4.4%	1,550
107. Chemical Plant and System Operators	$55,940	−12.2%	1,410
108. Highway Maintenance Workers	$35,220	8.2%	5,140
109. Plasterers and Stucco Masons	$36,830	17.2%	1,050
110. Septic Tank Servicers and Sewer Pipe Cleaners	$33,740	20.6%	1,190
111. Subway and Streetcar Operators	$63,820	9.2%	280
112. Locksmiths and Safe Repairers	$36,680	17.9%	930
113. Motorcycle Mechanics	$32,410	23.3%	890
114. Cooks, Institution and Cafeteria	$22,710	12.3%	13,620
115. Stationary Engineers and Boiler Operators	$53,070	6.1%	1,060
116. Woodworking Machine Setters, Operators, and Tenders, Except Sawing	$27,090	20.1%	1,740

(continued)

(continued)

Best Jobs for People with a Realistic Personality Type

Job	Annual Earnings	Percent Growth	Annual Openings
117. Computer, Automated Teller, and Office Machine Repairers	$36,360	6.5%	4,540
118. Electrical and Electronics Repairers, Powerhouse, Substation, and Relay	$67,450	4.7%	690
119. Painters, Transportation Equipment	$39,600	9.5%	1,430
120. Ambulance Drivers and Attendants, Except Emergency Medical Technicians	$22,820	32.1%	1,010
121. Avionics Technicians	$54,720	7.0%	580
122. Driver/Sales Workers	$22,770	10.3%	12,290
123. Medical Equipment Preparers	$30,050	17.5%	1,620
124. Outdoor Power Equipment and Other Small Engine Mechanics	$30,200	18.9%	1,350
125. Metal-Refining Furnace Operators and Tenders	$38,680	16.0%	550
126. Terrazzo Workers and Finishers	$41,240	16.2%	110
127. Recreational Vehicle Service Technicians	$34,000	22.2%	480
128. Maintenance Workers, Machinery	$39,490	6.4%	1,740
129. Mechanical Engineering Technicians	$51,350	4.0%	1,040
130. Rotary Drill Operators, Oil and Gas	$51,310	7.1%	640
131. Bicycle Repairers	$23,210	37.4%	630
132. Earth Drillers, Except Oil and Gas	$40,200	14.0%	620
133. Electrical and Electronics Drafters	$54,470	5.5%	720
134. Segmental Pavers	$32,340	30.8%	90
135. Team Assemblers	$27,490	5.5%	24,100
136. Couriers and Messengers	$24,750	12.6%	4,300
137. Service Unit Operators, Oil, Gas, and Mining	$40,750	8.6%	1,210
138. Carpet Installers	$36,750	10.3%	1,520
139. Derrick Operators, Oil and Gas	$45,220	9.5%	570
140. Helpers—Production Workers	$22,520	8.7%	9,980
141. Nuclear Power Reactor Operators	$76,590	3.8%	200
142. Electronic Home Entertainment Equipment Installers and Repairers	$34,470	13.9%	1,410
143. Riggers	$43,020	10.5%	440
144. Layout Workers, Metal and Plastic	$39,870	13.5%	290
145. Transit and Railroad Police	$56,390	5.6%	110
146. Traffic Technicians	$42,300	11.6%	280
147. Butchers and Meat Cutters	$28,460	8.0%	4,680
148. Control and Valve Installers and Repairers, Except Mechanical Door	$49,600	0.0%	810
149. First-Line Supervisors of Farming, Fishing, and Forestry Workers	$42,600	–1.5%	1,360

Best Jobs for People with a Realistic Personality Type

Job	Annual Earnings	Percent Growth	Annual Openings
150. Broadcast Technicians	$36,570	9.0%	1,380
151. Veterinary Assistants and Laboratory Animal Caretakers	$22,830	14.2%	2,160
152. Farm Equipment Mechanics and Service Technicians	$34,230	13.4%	1,290
153. Transportation Security Screeners	$36,910	9.6%	1,040
154. Motorboat Operators	$36,620	16.1%	160
155. Extruding and Drawing Machine Setters, Operators, and Tenders, Metal and Plastic	$32,300	8.4%	2,090
156. Printing Press Operators	$34,290	–1.4%	3,920
157. Fish and Game Wardens	$50,070	5.3%	220
158. Floor Sanders and Finishers	$33,350	17.8%	420
159. Refractory Materials Repairers, Except Brickmasons	$42,700	9.5%	60
160. Painting, Coating, and Decorating Workers	$25,660	17.4%	980
161. Embalmers	$43,800	5.6%	370
162. Roustabouts, Oil and Gas	$32,980	8.3%	1,550
163. Conveyor Operators and Tenders	$29,320	11.6%	1,490
164. Coating, Painting, and Spraying Machine Setters, Operators, and Tenders	$30,020	6.1%	2,310
165. Ophthalmic Laboratory Technicians	$28,750	12.8%	1,320
166. Rolling Machine Setters, Operators, and Tenders, Metal and Plastic	$36,920	8.1%	880
167. Bailiffs	$38,950	7.9%	450
168. Welding, Soldering, and Brazing Machine Setters, Operators, and Tenders	$34,770	6.5%	1,380
169. Home Appliance Repairers	$35,440	6.5%	1,190

Best Jobs for People with an Investigative Personality Type

Job	Annual Earnings	Percent Growth	Annual Openings
1. Diagnostic Medical Sonographers	$65,210	43.6%	3,170
2. Environmental Science and Protection Technicians, Including Health	$42,270	23.6%	1,950
3. Nuclear Medicine Technologists	$69,450	18.7%	750
4. Engineering Technicians, Except Drafters, All Other	$58,670	4.7%	1,680
5. Fire Inspectors and Investigators	$53,330	8.8%	470
6. Industrial Engineering Technicians	$49,090	4.2%	1,460
7. Chemical Technicians	$42,070	6.7%	1,290

Best Jobs for People with an Artistic Personality Type

Job	Annual Earnings	Percent Growth	Annual Openings
1. Choreographers	$39,600	24.2%	830
2. Hairdressers, Hairstylists, and Cosmetologists	$22,570	15.7%	21,810
3. Merchandise Displayers and Window Trimmers	$26,190	12.8%	4,000
4. Architectural and Civil Drafters	$47,250	3.2%	2,090
5. Photographers	$28,860	12.5%	3,100
6. Fine Artists, Including Painters, Sculptors, and Illustrators	$44,600	7.8%	810
7. Fashion Designers	$64,690	0.0%	670

Best Jobs for People with a Social Personality Type

Job	Annual Earnings	Percent Growth	Annual Openings
1. Dental Hygienists	$69,280	37.7%	10,490
2. Registered Nurses	$65,950	26.0%	120,740
3. Physical Therapist Assistants	$51,040	45.7%	4,120
4. Licensed Practical and Licensed Vocational Nurses	$41,150	22.4%	36,920
5. Respiratory Therapists	$55,250	27.7%	5,270
6. Emergency Medical Technicians and Paramedics	$30,710	33.3%	12,080
7. Medical Assistants	$29,100	30.9%	24,380
8. Occupational Therapy Assistants	$52,040	43.2%	1,680
9. Coaches and Scouts	$28,470	29.4%	13,300
10. Substance Abuse and Behavioral Disorder Counselors	$38,560	27.4%	4,170
11. Fitness Trainers and Aerobics Instructors	$31,030	24.0%	10,060
12. Customer Service Representatives	$30,610	15.5%	95,960
13. Self-Enrichment Education Teachers	$36,100	20.9%	9,150
14. Preschool Teachers, Except Special Education	$26,620	24.9%	23,240
15. Massage Therapists	$35,830	20.1%	5,590
16. Radiation Therapists	$76,630	20.1%	670
17. Physical Therapist Aides	$23,680	43.2%	2,760
18. Occupational Therapy Aides	$28,200	33.3%	360
19. Residential Advisors	$24,540	24.9%	4,570
20. Eligibility Interviewers, Government Programs	$41,060	3.1%	3,740
21. Teacher Assistants	$23,580	14.8%	48,160
22. Psychiatric Technicians	$28,470	15.5%	2,460
23. Tour Guides and Escorts	$23,620	18.1%	1,960
24. Psychiatric Aides	$25,170	15.1%	1,900

Best Jobs for People with an Enterprising Personality Type

Job	Annual Earnings	Percent Growth	Annual Openings
1. Registered Nurses	$65,950	26.0%	120,740
2. Supervisors of Construction and Extraction Workers	$59,150	23.5%	25,970
3. Construction Managers	$84,240	16.6%	12,040
4. Administrative Services Managers	$79,540	14.5%	9,980
5. Business Operations Specialists, All Other	$64,030	11.6%	32,720
6. Managers, All Other	$99,540	7.9%	24,940
7. First-Line Supervisors of Office and Administrative Support Workers	$48,810	14.3%	58,440
8. Insurance Sales Agents	$47,450	21.9%	18,440
9. First-Line Supervisors of Mechanics, Installers, and Repairers	$59,850	11.9%	16,490
10. General and Operations Managers	$95,150	4.6%	41,010
11. Police and Sheriff's Patrol Officers	$54,230	8.2%	24,940
12. First-Line Supervisors of Helpers, Laborers, and Material Movers, Hand	$44,580	27.2%	8,000
13. Transportation, Storage, and Distribution Managers	$80,860	10.0%	3,370
14. Customer Service Representatives	$30,610	15.5%	95,960
15. First-Line Supervisors of Transportation and Material-Moving Machine and Vehicle Operators	$52,950	14.3%	6,930
16. First-Line Supervisors of Non-Retail Sales Workers	$70,520	4.0%	12,350
17. Real Estate Sales Agents	$39,070	12.2%	12,760
18. First-Line Supervisors of Fire Fighting and Prevention Workers	$69,510	8.2%	3,310
19. First-Line Supervisors of Retail Sales Workers	$36,480	8.4%	51,370
20. Advertising Sales Agents	$45,250	13.0%	6,990
21. Farmers, Ranchers, and Other Agricultural Managers	$64,660	–8.0%	23,450
22. First-Line Supervisors of Landscaping, Lawn Service, and Groundskeeping Workers	$42,050	15.1%	6,010
23. Parts Salespersons	$29,350	16.0%	10,720
24. Opticians, Dispensing	$33,100	28.9%	3,060
25. Wholesale and Retail Buyers, Except Farm Products	$50,490	9.0%	4,170
26. First-Line Supervisors of Personal Service Workers	$35,230	13.5%	8,260
27. First-Line Supervisors of Police and Detectives	$77,890	2.2%	3,870
28. Property, Real Estate, and Community Association Managers	$52,510	6.1%	8,230
29. First-Line Supervisors of Food Preparation and Serving Workers	$29,550	9.8%	24,830
30. Gaming Managers	$67,230	12.1%	100
31. Real Estate Brokers	$59,340	7.6%	2,970
32. Detectives and Criminal Investigators	$71,770	2.9%	3,010
33. First-Line Supervisors of Production and Operating Workers	$53,670	1.9%	8,790
34. Private Detectives and Investigators	$43,710	20.5%	1,490

(continued)

(continued)

Best Jobs for People with an Enterprising Personality Type

Job	Annual Earnings	Percent Growth	Annual Openings
35. Demonstrators and Product Promoters	$23,770	17.5%	4,210
36. Aircraft Cargo Handling Supervisors	$46,840	20.6%	260
37. Skincare Specialists	$29,190	24.6%	2,040
38. Appraisers and Assessors of Real Estate	$48,870	7.5%	2,220
39. Air Traffic Controllers	$113,540	–3.0%	1,020
40. Lodging Managers	$47,450	8.4%	1,820
41. First-Line Supervisors of Correctional Officers	$55,030	5.5%	1,650
42. Travel Guides	$30,670	23.8%	260
43. Buyers and Purchasing Agents, Farm Products	$55,860	5.4%	320
44. Railroad Conductors and Yardmasters	$53,880	4.7%	1,430
45. Food Service Managers	$48,110	–3.3%	5,910
46. Airfield Operations Specialists	$47,180	8.7%	320
47. Telemarketers	$22,520	7.4%	8,350
48. Gaming Supervisors	$48,820	6.9%	920
49. Travel Agents	$33,930	10.0%	1,720
50. First-Line Supervisors of Housekeeping and Janitorial Workers	$35,230	0.8%	3,320
51. Chefs and Head Cooks	$42,350	–0.8%	1,800
52. Flight Attendants	$38,020	–0.2%	1,730
53. First-Line Supervisors of Farming, Fishing, and Forestry Workers	$42,600	–1.5%	1,360

Best Jobs for People with a Conventional Personality Type

Job	Annual Earnings	Percent Growth	Annual Openings
1. Sales Representatives, Wholesale and Manufacturing, Except Technical and Scientific Products	$53,540	15.6%	55,990
2. Business Operations Specialists, All Other	$64,030	11.6%	32,720
3. Loan Officers	$58,030	14.2%	11,520
4. Executive Secretaries and Executive Administrative Assistants	$45,580	12.6%	32,180
5. Managers, All Other	$99,540	7.9%	24,940
6. Paralegals and Legal Assistants	$46,730	18.3%	8,340
7. Dental Assistants	$34,140	30.8%	15,400
8. Medical Secretaries	$31,060	41.3%	27,840
9. Bookkeeping, Accounting, and Auditing Clerks	$34,740	13.6%	46,780
10. Billing and Posting Clerks	$32,880	19.7%	18,760
11. Receptionists and Information Clerks	$25,690	23.7%	56,560

Best Jobs for People with a Conventional Personality Type

Job	Annual Earnings	Percent Growth	Annual Openings
12. Pharmacy Technicians	$28,940	32.4%	16,630
13. Cargo and Freight Agents	$38,210	29.3%	4,420
14. Office Clerks, General	$27,190	16.6%	101,150
15. Social and Human Service Assistants	$28,740	27.6%	18,910
16. Dispatchers, Except Police, Fire, and Ambulance	$35,200	18.6%	6,950
17. Medical Records and Health Information Technicians	$33,310	21.0%	7,370
18. Payroll and Timekeeping Clerks	$37,160	14.6%	6,570
19. Bill and Account Collectors	$31,920	14.2%	13,550
20. Purchasing Agents, Except Wholesale, Retail, and Farm Products	$57,580	5.3%	9,120
21. Claims Adjusters, Examiners, and Investigators	$59,320	3.0%	7,990
22. Geological and Petroleum Technicians	$49,690	14.6%	700
23. Interviewers, Except Eligibility and Loan	$29,560	17.3%	7,960
24. Postal Service Mail Carriers	$55,160	–12.0%	10,340
25. Surveying and Mapping Technicians	$39,350	15.8%	2,000
26. Production, Planning, and Expediting Clerks	$43,100	6.6%	8,880
27. Life, Physical, and Social Science Technicians, All Other	$43,120	11.8%	3,350
28. Court Reporters	$48,530	14.1%	640
29. Insurance Claims and Policy Processing Clerks	$35,210	8.7%	9,600
30. Social Science Research Assistants	$38,800	14.8%	1,700
31. Human Resources Assistants, Except Payroll and Timekeeping	$37,250	11.2%	6,160
32. Inspectors, Testers, Sorters, Samplers, and Weighers	$34,040	8.0%	12,390
33. Occupational Health and Safety Technicians	$46,030	13.2%	510
34. Secretaries and Administrative Assistants, Except Legal, Medical, and Executive	$31,870	5.8%	39,100
35. Counter and Rental Clerks	$22,740	12.2%	14,660
36. Detectives and Criminal Investigators	$71,770	2.9%	3,010
37. Appraisers and Assessors of Real Estate	$48,870	7.5%	2,220
38. Police, Fire, and Ambulance Dispatchers	$35,930	11.7%	3,070
39. Fire Inspectors and Investigators	$53,330	8.8%	470
40. Computer Numerically Controlled Machine Tool Programmers, Metal and Plastic	$45,890	10.8%	490
41. Court, Municipal, and License Clerks	$34,300	8.0%	4,670
42. Electrical and Electronics Drafters	$54,470	5.5%	720
43. Legal Secretaries	$42,460	3.5%	3,940
44. Library Technicians	$30,430	8.8%	5,950
45. Procurement Clerks	$37,640	5.7%	3,550

(continued)

(continued)

Best Jobs for People with a Conventional Personality Type			
Job	Annual Earnings	Percent Growth	Annual Openings
46. Mail Clerks and Mail Machine Operators, Except Postal Service	$26,610	12.0%	3,960
47. Brokerage Clerks	$41,760	5.9%	1,970
48. Order Clerks	$28,940	7.4%	7,520
49. Shipping, Receiving, and Traffic Clerks	$28,790	0.3%	17,740
50. Weighers, Measurers, Checkers, and Samplers, Recordkeeping	$27,390	12.0%	3,420
51. Postal Service Clerks	$53,100	−48.2%	1,550
52. Tax Preparers	$32,320	9.8%	2,630
53. Tellers	$24,590	1.3%	23,750
54. Library Assistants, Clerical	$23,440	10.2%	6,410
55. Medical Transcriptionists	$33,480	5.9%	2,020
56. Reservation and Transportation Ticket Agents and Travel Clerks	$33,300	5.8%	3,080

Bonus Lists: Jobs Employing a High Percentage of People Without a Four-Year Degree

Although this book focuses on jobs that don't require four years of college, many workers in these jobs actually hold bachelor's (or higher) degrees. For example, among Registered Nurses, 42.5 percent hold a bachelor's degree, 10.1 percent have a master's, and 3.3 percent have a doctorate. These workers may not have held these degrees when they first entered the occupation, but they do now.

I thought you might be interested in a list of the jobs where *very few* workers have a bachelor's. In these jobs, a bachelor's probably provides little advantage for being hired or even for advancement.

The first list shows the 120 jobs in which more than 90 percent of the workers don't have a four-year degree. The second list shows the 50 best jobs from this set, based on the usual three economic criteria.

Jobs Employing the Highest Percentages of Workers Without a Four-Year Degree

Job	Percent Without a Four-Year Degree
1. Paving, Surfacing, and Tamping Equipment Operators	98.6%
2. Cement Masons and Concrete Finishers	98.1%
3. Terrazzo Workers and Finishers	98.1%
4. Drywall and Ceiling Tile Installers	97.9%
5. Tapers	97.9%
6. Crane and Tower Operators	97.8%
7. Automotive Body and Related Repairers	97.6%
8. Rolling Machine Setters, Operators, and Tenders, Metal and Plastic	97.6%
9. Welders, Cutters, Solderers, and Brazers	97.6%
10. Welding, Soldering, and Brazing Machine Setters, Operators, and Tenders	97.6%
11. Industrial Truck and Tractor Operators	97.5%
12. Sawing Machine Setters, Operators, and Tenders, Wood	97.5%
13. Operating Engineers and Other Construction Equipment Operators	97.3%
14. Plasterers and Stucco Masons	97.3%
15. Reinforcing Iron and Rebar Workers	97.3%
16. Roustabouts, Oil and Gas	97.3%
17. Bus and Truck Mechanics and Diesel Engine Specialists	97.2%
18. Butchers and Meat Cutters	97.1%
19. Meat, Poultry, and Fish Cutters and Trimmers	97.1%
20. Roofers	97.1%
21. Metal-Refining Furnace Operators and Tenders	96.8%
22. Boilermakers	96.6%
23. Machinists	96.5%
24. Woodworking Machine Setters, Operators, and Tenders, Except Sawing	96.5%
25. Brickmasons and Blockmasons	96.4%
26. Coating, Painting, and Spraying Machine Setters, Operators, and Tenders	96.4%
27. Glaziers	96.4%
28. Helpers—Brickmasons, Blockmasons, Stonemasons, and Tile and Marble Setters	96.4%
29. Helpers—Carpenters	96.4%
30. Helpers—Electricians	96.4%
31. Helpers—Pipelayers, Plumbers, Pipefitters, and Steamfitters	96.4%
32. Highway Maintenance Workers	96.4%
33. Painters, Transportation Equipment	96.4%
34. Painting, Coating, and Decorating Workers	96.4%

(continued)

(continued)

Jobs Employing the Highest Percentages of Workers Without a Four-Year Degree

Job	Percent Without a Four-Year Degree
35. Stonemasons	96.4%
36. Farm Equipment Mechanics and Service Technicians	96.2%
37. Mobile Heavy Equipment Mechanics, Except Engines	96.2%
38. Rail Car Repairers	96.2%
39. Structural Iron and Steel Workers	96.2%
40. Automotive Service Technicians and Mechanics	96.1%
41. Helpers—Installation, Maintenance, and Repair Workers	96.1%
42. Sheet Metal Workers	96.1%
43. Septic Tank Servicers and Sewer Pipe Cleaners	96.0%
44. Bicycle Repairers	95.9%
45. Recreational Vehicle Service Technicians	95.9%
46. Tire Repairers and Changers	95.9%
47. Carpet Installers	95.8%
48. Excavating and Loading Machine and Dragline Operators	95.8%
49. Floor Sanders and Finishers	95.8%
50. Insulation Workers, Floor, Ceiling, and Wall	95.8%
51. Insulation Workers, Mechanical	95.8%
52. Motorboat Mechanics and Service Technicians	95.8%
53. Motorcycle Mechanics	95.8%
54. Outdoor Power Equipment and Other Small Engine Mechanics	95.8%
55. Refuse and Recyclable Material Collectors	95.8%
56. Tile and Marble Setters	95.8%
57. Derrick Operators, Oil and Gas	95.6%
58. Layout Workers, Metal and Plastic	95.6%
59. Pipelayers	95.6%
60. Plumbers, Pipefitters, and Steamfitters	95.6%
61. Rotary Drill Operators, Oil and Gas	95.6%
62. Service Unit Operators, Oil, Gas, and Mining	95.6%
63. Extruding and Drawing Machine Setters, Operators, and Tenders, Metal and Plastic	95.5%
64. Pile-Driver Operators	95.5%
65. Earth Drillers, Except Oil and Gas	95.4%
66. Fence Erectors	95.4%
67. Automotive Glass Installers and Repairers	95.3%
68. Conveyor Operators and Tenders	95.3%

Jobs Employing the Highest Percentages of Workers Without a Four-Year Degree

Job	Percent Without a Four-Year Degree
69. Cooks, Institution and Cafeteria	95.3%
70. Driver/Sales Workers	95.0%
71. Electrical Power-Line Installers and Repairers	95.0%
72. Heating, Air Conditioning, and Refrigeration Mechanics and Installers	95.0%
73. Heavy and Tractor-Trailer Truck Drivers	95.0%
74. Light Truck or Delivery Services Drivers	95.0%
75. Laborers and Freight, Stock, and Material Movers, Hand	94.9%
76. Helpers—Production Workers	94.8%
77. Industrial Machinery Mechanics	94.8%
78. Refractory Materials Repairers, Except Brickmasons	94.8%
79. Team Assemblers	94.8%
80. Maintenance Workers, Machinery	94.6%
81. Control and Valve Installers and Repairers, Except Mechanical Door	94.5%
82. Mechanical Door Repairers	94.5%
83. Construction Laborers	94.4%
84. Segmental Pavers	94.2%
85. Hairdressers, Hairstylists, and Cosmetologists	94.1%
86. Structural Metal Fabricators and Fitters	93.9%
87. Aircraft Structure, Surfaces, Rigging, and Systems Assemblers	93.7%
88. Computer Numerically Controlled Machine Tool Programmers, Metal and Plastic	93.7%
89. Computer-Controlled Machine Tool Operators, Metal and Plastic	93.7%
90. Riggers	93.7%
91. Parts Salespersons	93.5%
92. Licensed Practical and Licensed Vocational Nurses	93.3%
93. Maintenance and Repair Workers, General	93.3%
94. Landscaping and Groundskeeping Workers	93.2%
95. Tree Trimmers and Pruners	93.2%
96. Home Appliance Repairers	93.1%
97. Printing Press Operators	92.9%
98. Carpenters	92.8%
99. Electricians	92.8%
100. Shipping, Receiving, and Traffic Clerks	92.8%
101. Surveying and Mapping Technicians	92.8%
102. Bus Drivers, School or Special Client	92.6%

(continued)

(continued)

Jobs Employing the Highest Percentages of Workers Without a Four-Year Degree

Job	Percent Without a Four-Year Degree
103. Bus Drivers, Transit and Intercity	92.6%
104. Painters, Construction and Maintenance	92.6%
105. Elevator Installers and Repairers	92.4%
106. Psychiatric Aides	91.9%
107. Cabinetmakers and Bench Carpenters	91.3%
108. Telecommunications Line Installers and Repairers	91.3%
109. Chemical Plant and System Operators	90.8%
110. Petroleum Pump System Operators, Refinery Operators, and Gaugers	90.8%
111. Coin, Vending, and Amusement Machine Servicers and Repairers	90.7%
112. Dental Assistants	90.7%
113. Water and Wastewater Treatment Plant and System Operators	90.7%
114. Security and Fire Alarm Systems Installers	90.4%
115. Mail Clerks and Mail Machine Operators, Except Postal Service	90.2%
116. Pest Control Workers	90.2%
117. Hazardous Materials Removal Workers	90.1%
118. Electrical and Electronics Repairers, Commercial and Industrial Equipment	90.0%
119. Electrical and Electronics Repairers, Powerhouse, Substation, and Relay	90.0%
120. Sailors and Marine Oilers	90.0%

50 Best Jobs Overall Employing High Percentages of Workers Without a Four-Year Degree

Job	Percent Without a Four-Year Degree	Annual Earnings	Percent Growth	Annual Openings
1. Plumbers, Pipefitters, and Steamfitters	95.6%	$47,750	25.6%	22,880
2. Electricians	92.8%	$49,320	23.2%	28,920
3. Brickmasons and Blockmasons	96.4%	$46,800	40.5%	5,450
4. Heating, Air Conditioning, and Refrigeration Mechanics and Installers	95.0%	$43,380	33.7%	13,760
5. Licensed Practical and Licensed Vocational Nurses	93.3%	$41,150	22.4%	36,920
6. Operating Engineers and Other Construction Equipment Operators	97.3%	$41,510	23.5%	16,280

50 Best Jobs Overall Employing High Percentages of Workers Without a Four-Year Degree

Job	Percent Without a Four-Year Degree	Annual Earnings	Percent Growth	Annual Openings
7. Industrial Machinery Mechanics	94.8%	$46,270	21.6%	11,710
8. Carpenters	92.8%	$40,010	19.6%	40,830
9. Heavy and Tractor-Trailer Truck Drivers	95.0%	$37,930	20.6%	64,940
10. Cement Masons and Concrete Finishers	98.1%	$35,600	34.6%	7,290
11. Drywall and Ceiling Tile Installers	97.9%	$36,970	27.6%	5,870
12. Security and Fire Alarm Systems Installers	90.4%	$39,540	32.9%	3,670
13. Dental Assistants	90.7%	$34,140	30.8%	15,400
14. Glaziers	96.4%	$37,350	42.2%	3,340
15. Structural Iron and Steel Workers	96.2%	$45,690	21.9%	2,540
16. Tapers	97.9%	$44,910	34.9%	1,430
17. Mobile Heavy Equipment Mechanics, Except Engines	96.2%	$45,600	16.2%	5,250
18. Automotive Service Technicians and Mechanics	96.1%	$36,180	17.3%	31,170
19. Electrical Power-Line Installers and Repairers	95.0%	$60,190	13.3%	5,270
20. Insulation Workers, Mechanical	95.8%	$37,990	31.8%	2,010
21. Sheet Metal Workers	96.1%	$42,730	17.6%	4,700
22. Automotive Body and Related Repairers	97.6%	$38,180	18.4%	6,520
23. Telecommunications Line Installers and Repairers	91.3%	$51,720	13.6%	5,140
24. Tile and Marble Setters	95.8%	$37,080	25.4%	2,770
25. Painters, Construction and Maintenance	92.6%	$35,430	18.5%	15,730
26. Bus and Truck Mechanics and Diesel Engine Specialists	97.2%	$41,640	14.5%	8,780
27. Reinforcing Iron and Rebar Workers	97.3%	$37,990	48.7%	1,320
28. Boilermakers	96.6%	$56,910	21.2%	1,180
29. Pipelayers	95.6%	$35,900	25.2%	2,880
30. Construction Laborers	94.4%	$29,730	21.3%	29,240
31. Hazardous Materials Removal Workers	90.1%	$38,120	23.1%	1,890
32. Pile-Driver Operators	95.5%	$45,500	36.6%	230
33. Pest Control Workers	90.2%	$30,220	26.2%	4,850
34. Welders, Cutters, Solderers, and Brazers	97.6%	$35,920	15.0%	14,070
35. Helpers—Pipelayers, Plumbers, Pipefitters, and Steamfitters	96.4%	$27,010	45.4%	4,170
36. Sailors and Marine Oilers	90.0%	$36,800	21.3%	2,150

(continued)

(continued)

50 Best Jobs Overall Employing High Percentages of Workers Without a Four-Year Degree

Job	Percent Without a Four-Year Degree	Annual Earnings	Percent Growth	Annual Openings
37. Landscaping and Groundskeeping Workers	93.2%	$23,410	20.9%	44,440
38. Computer-Controlled Machine Tool Operators, Metal and Plastic	93.7%	$35,220	19.2%	4,780
39. Crane and Tower Operators	97.8%	$46,460	15.7%	1,720
40. Roofers	97.1%	$35,280	17.8%	5,250
41. Excavating and Loading Machine and Dragline Operators	95.8%	$37,380	17.4%	2,890
42. Helpers—Brickmasons, Blockmasons, Stonemasons, and Tile and Marble Setters	96.4%	$27,820	59.9%	2,540
43. Helpers—Carpenters	96.4%	$26,400	55.7%	3,820
44. Refuse and Recyclable Material Collectors	95.8%	$32,280	20.2%	6,970
45. Paving, Surfacing, and Tamping Equipment Operators	98.6%	$35,270	22.1%	2,200
46. Stonemasons	96.4%	$36,640	36.5%	890
47. Helpers—Electricians	96.4%	$27,620	30.6%	4,200
48. Water and Wastewater Treatment Plant and System Operators	90.7%	$41,780	11.7%	4,150
49. Maintenance and Repair Workers, General	93.3%	$35,030	11.0%	37,910
50. Machinists	96.5%	$39,220	8.5%	9,950

Bonus Lists: Jobs with the Greatest Changes in Outlook Since the Previous Edition

The previous edition of this book, which came out in 2009, used job-growth figures from the Bureau of Labor Statistics (BLS) that were projected for the period from 2006 to 2016. Since that edition was prepared, BLS has updated its projections twice, based on the latest economic data and improvements to its forecasting models. Some jobs now are expected to have much better job growth than was previously projected; for other jobs, expectations for job growth have been scaled back.

I thought you might be interested in seeing which 25 jobs had the greatest *increases* and greatest *decreases* in job-growth projection, so I compiled the following two lists. I based the lists on the 213 jobs that were included among the best 300 jobs in both editions. Construction jobs dominate the list of jobs with the most improved outlook, and public-sector jobs are conspicuous among those with a gloomier outlook.

25 Jobs with the Greatest Increases in Job-Growth Projection

Job	Projected Job Growth 2006–2016	Projected Job Growth 2010–2020	Change in Forecast
1. Helpers—Brickmasons, Blockmasons, Stonemasons, and Tile and Marble Setters	16.4%	60.1%	43.7%
2. Reinforcing Iron and Rebar Workers	12.6%	48.6%	36.0%
3. Glaziers	7.7%	42.4%	34.7%
4. Helpers—Carpenters	23.3%	55.7%	32.4%
5. Brickmasons and Blockmasons	11.5%	40.5%	29.0%
6. Diagnostic Medical Sonographers	18.3%	43.5%	25.2%
7. Stonemasons	11.6%	36.5%	24.9%
8. Emergency Medical Technicians and Paramedics	9.0%	33.3%	24.3%
9. First-Line Supervisors of Helpers, Laborers, and Material Movers, Hand	3.6%	27.2%	23.6%
10. Automotive Glass Installers and Repairers	1.8%	25.0%	23.2%
11. Pile-Driver Operators	13.1%	36.0%	22.9%
12. Cement Masons and Concrete Finishers	12.9%	34.6%	21.7%
13. Tapers	13.0%	34.7%	21.7%
14. Dispatchers, Except Police, Fire, and Ambulance	−2.6%	18.6%	21.2%
15. Payroll and Timekeeping Clerks	−5.2%	14.6%	19.8%
16. Helpers—Pipelayers, Plumbers, Pipefitters, and Steamfitters	25.7%	45.4%	19.7%
17. First-Line Supervisors of Transportation and Material-Moving Machine and Vehicle Operators	−3.7%	14.3%	18.0%
18. Automotive Body and Related Repairers	0.5%	18.4%	17.9%
19. Tire Repairers and Changers	0.9%	18.5%	17.6%
20. Human Resources Assistants, Except Payroll and Timekeeping	−5.7%	11.2%	16.9%
21. Welders, Cutters, Solderers, and Brazers	−1.6%	15.0%	16.6%
22. Veterinary Technologists and Technicians	35.8%	52.0%	16.2%
23. Laborers and Freight, Stock, and Material Movers, Hand	−0.8%	15.4%	16.2%
24. Structural Metal Fabricators and Fitters	−0.4%	15.7%	16.1%
25. Residential Advisors	9.1%	25.0%	15.9%

25 Jobs with the Greatest Decreases in Job-Growth Projections

Job	Projected Job Growth 2006–2016	Projected Job Growth 2010–2020	Change in Forecast
1. Postal Service Clerks	–18.0%	–48.2%	–30.2%
2. Air Traffic Controllers	13.0%	–2.9%	–15.9%
3. Nuclear Power Reactor Operators	18.9%	3.6%	–15.3%
4. Legal Secretaries	18.4%	3.5%	–14.9%
5. Detectives and Criminal Investigators	16.6%	2.9%	–13.7%
6. Skincare Specialists	37.9%	24.6%	–13.3%
7. Self-Enrichment Education Teachers	32.0%	20.9%	–11.1%
8. Postal Service Mail Carriers	–1.1%	–12.0%	–10.9%
9. Firefighters	18.5%	8.6%	–9.9%
10. Paralegals and Legal Assistants	28.1%	18.3%	–9.8%
11. First-Line Supervisors of Farming, Fishing, and Forestry Workers	7.8%	–1.5%	–9.3%
12. Subway and Streetcar Operators	18.8%	9.8%	–9.0%
13. Purchasing Agents, Except Wholesale, Retail, and Farm Products	13.9%	5.3%	–8.6%
14. Food Service Managers	5.3%	–3.3%	–8.6%
15. Tree Trimmers and Pruners	26.3%	17.9%	–8.4%
16. Water and Wastewater Treatment Plant and System Operators	19.8%	11.6%	–8.2%
17. Radiation Therapists	27.1%	20.3%	–6.8%
18. Surgical Technologists	25.3%	18.9%	–6.4%
19. Police, Fire, and Ambulance Dispatchers	17.8%	11.7%	–6.1%
20. Eligibility Interviewers, Government Programs	9.2%	3.1%	–6.1%
21. First-Line Supervisors of Police and Detectives	8.1%	2.1%	–6.0%
22. Architectural and Civil Drafters	9.1%	3.2%	–5.9%
23. Environmental Engineering Technicians	30.1%	24.3%	–5.8%
24. Fitness Trainers and Aerobics Instructors	29.4%	24.0%	–5.4%
25. Environmental Science and Protection Technicians, Including Health	28.9%	23.6%	–5.3%

PART II

The Job Descriptions

This part of the book provides descriptions for all the jobs included in one or more of the lists in Part I. The Introduction gives more details on how to use and interpret the job descriptions, but here is some additional information:

- Job descriptions are arranged in alphabetical order by job title. This approach allows you to quickly find a description if you know its correct title from one of the lists in Part I.

- If you are using this section to browse for interesting options, we suggest you begin with the Table of Contents. Part I features many interesting lists that will help you identify job titles to explore in more detail. If you have not browsed the lists in Part I, consider spending some time there. The lists are interesting and will help you identify job titles you can find described in the material that follows. The job titles in Part II are also listed in the Table of Contents.

Administrative Services Managers

- ⊙ Annual Earnings: $79,540
- ⊙ Earnings Growth Potential: High (45.8%)
- ⊙ Growth: 14.5%
- ⊙ Annual Job Openings: 9,980
- ⊙ Self-Employed: 0.3%

Considerations for Job Outlook: Applicants will likely face strong competition for the limited number of higher-level administrative services management jobs. Competition should be less severe for lower-level management jobs. Job prospects also are expected to be better for those who can manage a wide range of responsibilities than for those who specialize in particular functions.

Plan, direct, or coordinate one or more administrative services of an organization. Monitor the facility to ensure that it remains safe, secure, and well-maintained. Direct or coordinate the supportive services department of a business, agency, or organization. Set goals and deadlines for the department. Prepare and review operational reports and schedules to ensure accuracy and efficiency. Analyze internal processes, recommending and implementing procedural or policy changes to improve operations such as supply changes or the disposal of records. Acquire, distribute, and store supplies. Plan, administer, and control budgets for contracts, equipment, and supplies. Oversee construction and renovation projects to improve efficiency and to ensure that facilities meet environmental, health, and security standards and comply with government regulations. Hire and terminate clerical and administrative personnel. Oversee the maintenance and repair of machinery, equipment, and electrical and mechanical systems. Manage leasing of facility space. Participate in architectural and engineering planning and design, including space and installation management. Conduct classes to teach procedures to staff. Dispose of, or oversee the disposal of, surplus or unclaimed property.

Education/Training Required: High school diploma or equivalent. **Education and Training Programs:** Business Administration and Management, General; Business/Commerce, General; Medical Staff Services Technology/Technician; Medical/Health Management and Clinical Assistant/Specialist Training; Public Administration; Purchasing, Procurement/Acquisitions and Contracts

Management; Transportation/Mobility Management. **Knowledge/Courses—Clerical Practices:** Administrative and clerical procedures and systems such as word processing, managing files and records, stenography and transcription, designing forms, and other office procedures and terminology. **Economics and Accounting:** Economic and accounting principles and practices, the financial markets, banking, and the analysis and reporting of financial data. **Personnel and Human Resources:** Principles and procedures for personnel recruitment, selection, training, compensation and benefits, labor relations and negotiation, and personnel information systems. **Customer and Personal Service:** Principles and processes for providing customer and personal services. This includes customer needs assessment, meeting quality standards for services, and evaluation of customer satisfaction. **Sales and Marketing:** Principles and methods for showing, promoting, and selling products or services. This includes marketing strategy and tactics, product demonstration, sales techniques, and sales control systems. **Administration and Management:** Business and management principles involved in strategic planning, resource allocation, human resources modeling, leadership technique, production methods, and coordination of people and resources. **Work Experience Needed:** 1 to 5 years. **On-the-Job Training Needed:** None. **Certification/Licensure:** Licensure for some specializations.

Personality Type: Enterprising-Conventional. **Career Clusters:** 04 Business, Management, and Administration; 07 Government and Public Administration. **Career Pathways:** 04.1 Management; 07.1 Governance. **Other Jobs in These Pathways:** Agents and Business Managers of Artists, Performers, and Athletes; Biofuels Production Managers; Biomass Power Plant Managers; Brownfield Redevelopment Specialists and Site Managers; Business Continuity Planners; Business Operations Specialists, All Other; Business Teachers, Postsecondary; Chief Executives; Chief Sustainability Officers; Communications Teachers, Postsecondary; Compliance Managers; Computer and Information Systems Managers; Construction Managers; Cost Estimators; Customs Brokers; Economics Teachers, Postsecondary; Economists; Energy Auditors; Environmental Economists; First-Line Supervisors of Office and Administrative Support Workers; First-Line Supervisors of Personal Service Workers; Gaming Supervisors; General and Operations Managers; Geothermal Production Managers; Hydroelectric Production Managers; Industrial Production Managers; Investment Fund Managers; Legislators;

Logisticians; Logistics Analysts; Logistics Engineers; Logistics Managers; others.

Skills—Management of Financial Resources: Determining how money will be spent to get the work done and accounting for these expenditures. **Management of Material Resources:** Obtaining and seeing to the appropriate use of equipment, facilities, and materials needed to do certain work. **Management of Personnel Resources:** Motivating, developing, and directing people as they work, identifying the best people for the job. **Negotiation:** Bringing others together and trying to reconcile differences. **Coordination:** Adjusting actions in relation to others' actions. **Time Management:** Managing one's own time and the time of others. **Social Perceptiveness:** Being aware of others' reactions and understanding why they react as they do. **Service Orientation:** Actively looking for ways to help people.

Work Environment: Indoors; sitting.

Advertising Sales Agents

- ⊙ Annual Earnings: $45,250
- ⊙ Earnings Growth Potential: High (50.4%)
- ⊙ Growth: 13.0%
- ⊙ Annual Job Openings: 6,990
- ⊙ Self-Employed: 9.3%

Considerations for Job Outlook: Competition is expected to be strong for advertising sales agents. Applicants with experience in sales or a bachelor's degree should have the best opportunities.

Sell or solicit advertising space, time, or media in publications, signage, TV, radio, or Internet establishments or public spaces. Maintain assigned account bases while developing new accounts. Explain to customers how specific types of advertising will help promote their products or services in the most effective way possible. Provide clients with estimates of the costs of advertising products or services. Locate and contact potential clients to offer advertising services. Process all correspondence and paperwork related to accounts. Inform customers of available options for advertisement artwork and provide samples. Prepare and deliver sales presentations to new and existing customers to sell new advertising programs and to protect and increase existing advertising. Deliver advertising or illustration proofs to customers for approval. Prepare promotional

plans, sales literature, media kits, and sales contracts, using computer. Recommend appropriate sizes and formats for advertising, depending on medium being used. Draw up contracts for advertising work and collect payments due.

Education/Training Required: High school diploma or equivalent. **Education and Training Program:** Advertising. **Knowledge/Courses—Sales and Marketing:** Principles and methods for showing, promoting, and selling products or services. This includes marketing strategy and tactics, product demonstration, sales techniques, and sales control systems. **Communications and Media:** Media production, communication, and dissemination techniques and methods. This includes alternative ways to inform and entertain via written, oral, and visual media. **Clerical Practices:** Administrative and clerical procedures and systems such as word processing, managing files and records, stenography and transcription, designing forms, and other office procedures and terminology. **Customer and Personal Service:** Principles and processes for providing customer and personal services. This includes customer needs assessment, meeting quality standards for services, and evaluation of customer satisfaction. **Economics and Accounting:** Economic and accounting principles and practices, the financial markets, banking, and the analysis and reporting of financial data. **Telecommunications:** Transmission, broadcasting, switching, control, and operation of telecommunications systems. **Work Experience Needed:** None. **On-the-Job Training Needed:** Moderate-term on-the-job training. **Certification/Licensure:** None.

Personality Type: Enterprising-Conventional-Artistic. **Career Cluster:** 04 Business, Management, and Administration. **Career Pathway:** 04.5 Marketing. **Other Jobs in This Pathway:** Business Teachers, Postsecondary; Communications Teachers, Postsecondary; Technical Writers.

Skills—Persuasion: Persuading others to change their minds or behavior. **Negotiation:** Bringing others together and trying to reconcile differences. **Service Orientation:** Actively looking for ways to help people. **Speaking:** Talking to others to convey information effectively. **Management of Financial Resources:** Determining how money will be spent to get the work done and accounting for these expenditures. **Social Perceptiveness:** Being aware of others' reactions and understanding why they react as they do. **Mathematics:** Using mathematics to solve problems. **Systems Evaluation:** Identifying measures or indicators of system performance and the actions needed to improve or correct performance relative to the goals of the system.

Work Environment: More often indoors than outdoors; sitting; noise.

Air Traffic Controllers

⊙ Annual Earnings: $113,540
⊙ Earnings Growth Potential: High (45.7%)
⊙ Growth: –3.0%
⊙ Annual Job Openings: 1,020
⊙ Self-Employed: 0.0%

Considerations for Job Outlook: Most new jobs will result as the majority of today's air traffic control workforce retires over the next decade. Despite the increasing number of job openings, competition to get into the FAA Academy will remain high because there are generally more test applicants than job openings. Job opportunities will be best for individuals in their early 20s who obtain an air traffic management degree from an FAA certified school.

Control air traffic on and within the vicinity of airports and the movement of air traffic between altitude sectors and control centers according to established procedures and policies. Issue landing and takeoff authorizations and instructions. Monitor and direct the movement of aircraft within an assigned air space and on the ground at airports to minimize delays and maximize safety. Monitor aircraft within a specific airspace, using radar, computer equipment, and visual references. Inform pilots about nearby planes as well as potentially hazardous conditions such as weather, speed and direction of wind, and visibility problems. Provide flight path changes or directions to emergency landing fields for pilots traveling in bad weather or in emergency situations. Alert airport emergency services in cases of emergency and when aircraft are experiencing difficulties. Direct pilots to runways when space is available, or direct them to maintain a traffic pattern until there is space for them to land. Transfer control of departing flights to traffic control centers and accept control of arriving flights. Direct ground traffic, including taxiing aircraft, maintenance and baggage vehicles, and airport workers. Determine the timing and procedures for flight vector changes. Maintain radio and telephone contact with adjacent control towers, terminal control units,

and other area control centers in order to coordinate aircraft movement. Contact pilots by radio to provide meteorological, navigational, and other information. Initiate and coordinate searches for missing aircraft. Check conditions and traffic at different altitudes in response to pilots' requests for altitude changes. Relay to control centers such air traffic information as courses, altitudes, and expected arrival times. Compile information about flights from flight plans, pilot reports, radar, and observations. Inspect, adjust, and control radio equipment and airport lights. Conduct pre-flight briefings on weather conditions, suggested routes, altitudes, indications of turbulence, and other flight safety information.

Education/Training Required: Associate degree. **Education and Training Program:** Air Traffic Controller Training. **Knowledge/Courses—Transportation:** Principles and methods for moving people or goods by air, rail, sea, or road, including the relative costs and benefits. **Geography:** Principles and methods for describing the features of land, sea, and air masses, including their physical characteristics, locations, interrelationships, and distribution of plant, animal, and human life. **Telecommunications:** Transmission, broadcasting, switching, control, and operation of telecommunications systems. **Public Safety and Security:** Relevant equipment, policies, procedures, and strategies to promote effective local, state, or national security operations for the protection of people, data, property, and institutions. **Physics:** Physical principles, laws, their interrelationships, and applications to understanding fluid, material, and atmospheric dynamics, and mechanical, electrical, atomic, and subatomic structures and processes. **Education and Training:** Principles and methods for curriculum and training design, teaching and instruction for individuals and groups, and the measurement of training effects. **Work Experience Needed:** None. **On-the-Job Training Needed:** Long-term on-the-job training. **Certification/Licensure:** Federal licensure.

Personality Type: Enterprising-Conventional. **Career Cluster:** 16 Transportation, Distribution, and Logistics. **Career Pathway:** 16.1 Transportation Operations. **Other Jobs in This Pathway:** Aerospace Engineering and Operations Technicians; Aircraft Cargo Handling Supervisors; Airfield Operations Specialists; Airline Pilots, Copilots, and Flight Engineers; Automotive and Watercraft Service Attendants; Automotive Master Mechanics; Aviation Inspectors; Bridge and Lock Tenders; Bus

Drivers, School or Special Client; Bus Drivers, Transit and Intercity; Commercial Divers; Commercial Pilots; Crane and Tower Operators; First-Line Supervisors of Helpers, Laborers, and Material Movers, Hand; First-Line Supervisors of Transportation and Material-Moving Machine and Vehicle Operators; Freight and Cargo Inspectors; Heavy and Tractor-Trailer Truck Drivers; Hoist and Winch Operators; Laborers and Freight, Stock, and Material Movers, Hand; Light Truck or Delivery Services Drivers; Mates—Ship, Boat, and Barge; Motor Vehicle Operators, All Other; Motorboat Operators; Operating Engineers and Other Construction Equipment Operators; Parking Lot Attendants; Pilots, Ship; others.

Skills—Complex Problem Solving: Identifying complex problems and reviewing related information to develop and evaluate options and implement solutions. **Operation Monitoring:** Watching gauges, dials, or other indicators to make sure a machine is working properly. **Operations Analysis:** Analyzing needs and product requirements to create a design. **Judgment and Decision Making:** Considering the relative costs and benefits of potential actions to choose the most appropriate one. **Monitoring:** Monitoring or assessing your performance or that of other individuals or organizations to make improvements or take corrective action. **Coordination:** Adjusting actions in relation to others' actions. **Systems Analysis:** Determining how a system should work and how changes in conditions, operations, and the environment will affect outcomes. **Active Learning:** Understanding the implications of new information for both current and future problem solving and decision making.

Work Environment: Indoors; sitting; using hands; repetitive motions; noise.

Aircraft Cargo Handling Supervisors

- ⊙ Annual Earnings: $46,840
- ⊙ Earnings Growth Potential: Medium (38.9%)
- ⊙ Growth: 20.6%
- ⊙ Annual Job Openings: 260
- ⊙ Self-Employed: 1.0%

Considerations for Job Outlook: Faster-than-average employment growth is projected.

Supervise and coordinate the activities of ground crew in the loading, unloading, securing, and staging of aircraft cargo or baggage. Calculate load weights for different aircraft compartments, using charts and computers. Determine the quantity and orientation of cargo, and compute an aircraft's center of gravity. Direct ground crews in the loading, unloading, securing, and staging of aircraft cargo or baggage. Distribute cargo in such a manner that space use is maximized. Accompany aircraft as a member of the flight crew in order to monitor and handle cargo in flight. Brief aircraft passengers on safety and emergency procedures.

Education/Training Required: High school diploma or equivalent. **Education and Training Program:** Aviation/Airway Management and Operations. **Knowledge/Courses—Transportation:** Principles and methods for moving people or goods by air, rail, sea, or road, including the relative costs and benefits. **Public Safety and Security:** Relevant equipment, policies, procedures, and strategies to promote effective local, state, or national security operations for the protection of people, data, property, and institutions. **Geography:** Principles and methods for describing the features of land, sea, and air masses, including their physical characteristics, locations, interrelationships, and distribution of plant, animal, and human life. **Personnel and Human Resources:** Principles and procedures for personnel recruitment, selection, training, compensation and benefits, labor relations and negotiation, and personnel information systems. **Psychology:** Human behavior and performance; individual differences in ability, personality, and interests; learning and motivation; psychological research methods; and the assessment and treatment of behavioral and affective disorders. **Customer and Personal Service:** Principles and processes for providing customer and personal services. This includes customer needs assessment, meeting quality standards for services, and evaluation of customer satisfaction. **Work Experience Needed:** 1 to 5 years. **On-the-Job Training Needed:** None. **Certification/Licensure:** None.

Personality Type: Enterprising-Realistic. **Career Cluster:** 16 Transportation, Distribution, and Logistics. **Career Pathway:** 16.1 Transportation Operations. **Other Jobs in This Pathway:** Aerospace Engineering and Operations Technicians; Air Traffic Controllers; Airfield Operations Specialists; Airline Pilots, Copilots, and Flight Engineers; Automotive and Watercraft Service Attendants; Automotive Master Mechanics; Aviation Inspectors; Bridge and

Lock Tenders; Bus Drivers, School or Special Client; Bus Drivers, Transit and Intercity; Commercial Divers; Commercial Pilots; Crane and Tower Operators; First-Line Supervisors of Helpers, Laborers, and Material Movers, Hand; First-Line Supervisors of Transportation and Material-Moving Machine and Vehicle Operators; Freight and Cargo Inspectors; Heavy and Tractor-Trailer Truck Drivers; Hoist and Winch Operators; Laborers and Freight, Stock, and Material Movers, Hand; Light Truck or Delivery Services Drivers; Mates—Ship, Boat, and Barge; Motor Vehicle Operators, All Other; Motorboat Operators; Operating Engineers and Other Construction Equipment Operators; Parking Lot Attendants; Pilots, Ship; others.

Skills—Management of Personnel Resources: Motivating, developing, and directing people as they work, identifying the best people for the job. **Repairing:** Repairing machines or systems using the needed tools. **Learning Strategies:** Selecting and using training/instructional methods and procedures appropriate for the situation when learning or teaching new things. **Equipment Maintenance:** Performing routine maintenance on equipment and determining when and what kind of maintenance is needed. **Operation and Control:** Controlling operations of equipment or systems. **Management of Material Resources:** Obtaining and seeing to the appropriate use of equipment, facilities, and materials needed to do certain work. **Equipment Selection:** Determining the kind of tools and equipment needed to do a job. **Troubleshooting:** Determining causes of operating errors and deciding what to do about them.

Work Environment: Outdoors; standing; walking and running; using hands; repetitive motions; noise; very hot or cold; bright or inadequate lighting; contaminants; hazardous equipment.

Aircraft Mechanics and Service Technicians

- ⊙ Annual Earnings: $54,590
- ⊙ Earnings Growth Potential: Medium (36.6%)
- ⊙ Growth: 6.3%
- ⊙ Annual Job Openings: 4,520
- ⊙ Self-Employed: 1.9%

Considerations for Job Outlook: Job prospects should be best for mechanics and technicians who hold an Airframe and Powerplant (A&P) certificate and a bachelor's degree in aircraft maintenance. Job prospects also will be better for those who keep up with technical advances in aircraft electronics and composite materials. Job opportunities may arise from the need to replace mechanics who leave the workforce. Over the next decade, many aircraft mechanics are expected to retire. As older mechanics retire and younger mechanics advance, entry-level positions may open up. However, if airlines continue to send maintenance work to other countries, competition for new jobs will remain strong.

Diagnose, adjust, repair, or overhaul aircraft engines and assemblies, such as hydraulic and pneumatic systems. Read and interpret maintenance manuals, service bulletins, and other specifications to determine the feasibility and method of repairing or replacing malfunctioning or damaged components. Inspect completed work to certify that maintenance meets standards and that aircraft are ready for operation. Maintain repair logs, documenting all preventive and corrective aircraft maintenance. Conduct routine and special inspections as required by regulations. Examine and inspect aircraft components, including landing gear, hydraulic systems, and de-icers to locate cracks, breaks, leaks, or other problems. Inspect airframes for wear or other defects. Maintain, repair, and rebuild aircraft structures, functional components, and parts such as wings and fuselage, rigging, hydraulic units, oxygen systems, fuel systems, electrical systems, gaskets, and seals. Measure the tension of control cables. Replace or repair worn, defective, or damaged components, using hand tools, gauges, and testing equipment. Measure parts for wear, using precision instruments. Assemble and install electrical, plumbing, mechanical, hydraulic, and structural components and accessories, using hand tools and power tools. Test operation of engines and other systems, using test equipment such as ignition analyzers, compression checkers, distributor timers, and ammeters. Obtain fuel and oil samples, and check them for contamination. Reassemble engines following repair or inspection, and re-install engines in aircraft. Read and interpret pilots' descriptions of problems in order to diagnose causes. Modify aircraft structures, space vehicles, systems, or components, following drawings, schematics, charts, engineering orders, and technical publications. Install and align repaired or replacement parts for subsequent riveting or welding, using clamps and wrenches. Locate and mark dimensions and reference lines on defective or replacement parts, using templates, scribes, compasses, and steel rules.

Education/Training Required: Postsecondary vocational training. **Education and Training Programs:** Agricultural Mechanics and Equipment/Machine Technology; Aircraft Powerplant Technology/Technician; Airframe Mechanics and Aircraft Maintenance Technology/Technician. **Knowledge/Courses—Mechanical Devices:** Machines and tools, including their designs, uses, repair, and maintenance. **Design:** Design techniques, tools, and principles involved in production of precision technical plans, blueprints, drawings, and models. **Physics:** Physical principles, laws, their interrelationships, and applications to understanding fluid, material, and atmospheric dynamics, and mechanical, electrical, atomic, and subatomic structures and processes. **Engineering and Technology:** The practical application of engineering science and technology. This includes applying principles, techniques, procedures, and equipment to the design and production of various goods and services. **Chemistry:** The chemical composition, structure, and properties of substances and of the chemical processes and transformations that they undergo. This includes uses of chemicals and their danger signs, production techniques, and disposal methods. **Transportation:** Principles and methods for moving people or goods by air, rail, sea, or road, including the relative costs and benefits. **Work Experience Needed:** None. **On-the-Job Training Needed:** None. **Certification/Licensure:** Licensure based on FAA certification.

Personality Type: Realistic-Conventional-Investigative. **Career Clusters:** 13 Manufacturing; 16 Transportation, Distribution, and Logistics. **Career Pathways:** 13.3 Maintenance, Installation, and Repair; 16.4 Facility and Mobile Equipment Maintenance. **Other Jobs in These Pathways:** Aircraft Structure, Surfaces, Rigging, and Systems Assemblers; Automotive Body and Related Repairers; Automotive Engineering Technicians; Automotive Glass Installers and Repairers; Automotive Master Mechanics; Automotive Specialty Technicians; Avionics Technicians; Bicycle Repairers; Biological Technicians; Bus and Truck Mechanics and Diesel Engine Specialists; Camera and Photographic Equipment Repairers; Chemical Equipment Operators and Tenders; Civil Engineering Technicians; Cleaners of Vehicles and Equipment; Coil Winders, Tapers, and Finishers; Computer, Automated

Teller, and Office Machine Repairers; Construction and Related Workers, All Other; Control and Valve Installers and Repairers, Except Mechanical Door; Electric Motor, Power Tool, and Related Repairers; Electrical and Electronic Equipment Assemblers; Electrical and Electronics Installers and Repairers, Transportation Equipment; Electrical and Electronics Repairers, Commercial and Industrial Equipment; others.

Skills—Equipment Maintenance: Performing routine maintenance on equipment and determining when and what kind of maintenance is needed. **Repairing:** Repairing machines or systems using the needed tools. **Troubleshooting:** Determining causes of operating errors and deciding what to do about them. **Equipment Selection:** Determining the kind of tools and equipment needed to do a job. **Quality Control Analysis:** Conducting tests and inspections of products, services, or processes to evaluate quality or performance. **Operation Monitoring:** Watching gauges, dials, or other indicators to make sure a machine is working properly. **Operation and Control:** Controlling operations of equipment or systems. **Installation:** Installing equipment, machines, wiring, or programs to meet specifications.

Work Environment: Indoors; standing; walking and running; using hands; bending or twisting the body; noise; contaminants; cramped work space; hazardous conditions; hazardous equipment.

Aircraft Structure, Surfaces, Rigging, and Systems Assemblers

- ⊙ Annual Earnings: $46,210
- ⊙ Earnings Growth Potential: Medium (38.1%)
- ⊙ Growth: 14.3%
- ⊙ Annual Job Openings: 1,220
- ⊙ Self-Employed: 0.8%

Considerations for Job Outlook: Qualified applicants, including those with technical vocational training and certification, should have the best job opportunities in the manufacturing sector, particularly in growing, high-technology industries, such as aerospace and electromedical devices. Some employers report difficulty finding qualified applicants looking for manufacturing employment.

Many job openings should result from the need to replace workers leaving or retiring from this large occupation.

Assemble, fit, fasten, and install parts of airplanes, space vehicles, or missiles. Form loops or splices in cables, using clamps and fittings, or reweave cable strands. Align and fit structural assemblies manually, or signal crane operators to position assemblies for joining. Align, fit, assemble, connect, and install system components, using jigs, fixtures, measuring instruments, hand tools, and power tools. Assemble and fit prefabricated parts to form subassemblies. Assemble, install, and connect parts, fittings, and assemblies on aircraft, using layout tools, hand tools, power tools, and fasteners such as bolts, screws, rivets, and clamps. Attach brackets, hinges, or clips to secure or support components and subassemblies, using bolts, screws, rivets, chemical bonding, or welding. Select and install accessories in swaging machines, using hand tools. Fit and fasten sheet metal coverings to surface areas and other sections of aircraft prior to welding or riveting. Lay out and mark reference points and locations for installation of parts and components, using jigs, templates, and measuring and marking instruments. Inspect and test installed units, parts, systems, and assemblies for fit, alignment, performance, defects, and compliance with standards, using measuring instruments and test equipment. Install mechanical linkages and actuators, and verify tension of cables, using tensiometers. Join structural assemblies such as wings, tails, and fuselage. Measure and cut cables and tubing, using master templates, measuring instruments, and cable cutters or saws. Read and interpret blueprints, illustrations, and specifications to determine layouts, sequences of operations, or identities and relationships of parts. Prepare and load live ammunition, missiles, and bombs onto aircraft, according to established procedures. Adjust, repair, rework, or replace parts and assemblies to eliminate malfunctions and to ensure proper operation.

Education/Training Required: High school diploma or equivalent. **Education and Training Programs:** Aircraft Powerplant Technology/Technician; Airframe Mechanics and Aircraft Maintenance Technology/Technician; Avionics Maintenance Technology/Technician. **Knowledge/Courses—Mechanical Devices:** Machines and tools, including their designs, uses, repair, and maintenance. **Design:** Design techniques, tools, and principles involved in production of precision technical plans, blueprints, drawings, and models. **Chemistry:** The chemical composition, structure, and properties of substances and of the chemical processes and transformations that they undergo. This includes uses of chemicals and their danger signs, production techniques, and disposal methods. **Public Safety and Security:** Relevant equipment, policies, procedures, and strategies to promote effective local, state, or national security operations for the protection of people, data, property, and institutions. **Work Experience Needed:** None. **On-the-Job Training Needed:** Moderate-term on-the-job training. **Certification/Licensure:** Voluntary certification for some specializations.

Personality Type: Realistic-Conventional. **Career Cluster:** 16 Transportation, Distribution, and Logistics. **Career Pathway:** 16.4 Facility and Mobile Equipment Maintenance. **Other Jobs in This Pathway:** Aircraft Mechanics and Service Technicians; Automotive Body and Related Repairers; Automotive Glass Installers and Repairers; Automotive Master Mechanics; Automotive Specialty Technicians; Bicycle Repairers; Bus and Truck Mechanics and Diesel Engine Specialists; Cleaners of Vehicles and Equipment; Electrical and Electronics Installers and Repairers, Transportation Equipment; Electronic Equipment Installers and Repairers, Motor Vehicles; Engine and Other Machine Assemblers; Gem and Diamond Workers; Installation, Maintenance, and Repair Workers, All Other; Motorboat Mechanics and Service Technicians; Motorcycle Mechanics; Outdoor Power Equipment and Other Small Engine Mechanics; Painters, Transportation Equipment.

Skills—Installation: Installing equipment, machines, wiring, or programs to meet specifications. **Troubleshooting:** Determining causes of operating errors and deciding what to do about them. **Equipment Selection:** Determining the kind of tools and equipment needed to do a job. **Repairing:** Repairing machines or systems using the needed tools. **Quality Control Analysis:** Conducting tests and inspections of products, services, or processes to evaluate quality or performance. **Equipment Maintenance:** Performing routine maintenance on equipment and determining when and what kind of maintenance is needed. **Operation and Control:** Controlling operations of equipment or systems. **Technology Design:** Generating or adapting equipment and technology to serve user needs.

Work Environment: Standing; walking and running; using hands; bending or twisting the body; repetitive motions; noise; very hot or cold; bright or inadequate lighting; contaminants; cramped work space; hazardous conditions; hazardous equipment; minor burns, cuts, bites, or stings.

Airfield Operations Specialists

- ⊙ Annual Earnings: $47,180
- ⊙ Earnings Growth Potential: High (46.6%)
- ⊙ Growth: 8.7%
- ⊙ Annual Job Openings: 320
- ⊙ Self-Employed: 0.0%

Considerations for Job Outlook: Slower-than-average employment growth is projected.

Ensure the safe takeoff and landing of commercial and military aircraft. Implement airfield safety procedures to ensure a safe operating environment for personnel and aircraft operation. Plan and coordinate airfield construction. Coordinate with agencies such as air traffic control, civil engineers, and command posts to ensure support of airfield management activities. Monitor the arrival, parking, refueling, loading, and departure of all aircraft. Maintain air-to-ground and point-to-point radio contact with aircraft commanders. Train operations staff. Relay departure, arrival, delay, aircraft and airfield status, and other pertinent information to upline controlling agencies. Procure, produce, and provide information on the safe operation of aircraft, such as flight planning publications, operations publications, charts and maps, and weather information. Coordinate communications between air-traffic control and maintenance personnel. Perform and supervise airfield management activities, which may include mobile airfield management functions. Receive, transmit, and control message traffic. Receive and post weather information and flight plan data such as air routes and arrival and departure times. Maintain flight and events logs, air crew flying records, and flight operations records of incoming and outgoing flights. Coordinate with agencies to meet aircrew requirements for billeting, messing, refueling, ground transportation, and transient aircraft maintenance. Collaborate with others to plan flight schedules and air crew assignments. Coordinate changes to flight itineraries with appropriate Air Traffic Control (ATC) agencies. Anticipate aircraft equipment needs for air evacuation and cargo flights. Provide aircrews with information and services needed for airfield management and flight planning.

Conduct departure and arrival briefings. Use airfield landing and navigational aids and digital data terminal communications equipment to perform duties. Post visual display boards and status boards.

Education/Training Required: High school diploma or equivalent. **Education and Training Program:** Air Traffic Controller Training. **Knowledge/Courses—Transportation:** Principles and methods for moving people or goods by air, rail, sea, or road, including the relative costs and benefits. **Geography:** Principles and methods for describing the features of land, sea, and air masses, including their physical characteristics, locations, interrelationships, and distribution of plant, animal, and human life. **Telecommunications:** Transmission, broadcasting, switching, control, and operation of telecommunications systems. **Customer and Personal Service:** Principles and processes for providing customer and personal services. This includes customer needs assessment, meeting quality standards for services, and evaluation of customer satisfaction. **Physics:** Physical principles, laws, their interrelationships, and applications to understanding fluid, material, and atmospheric dynamics, and mechanical, electrical, atomic, and subatomic structures and processes. **Computers and Electronics:** Circuit boards, processors, chips, electronic equipment, and computer hardware and software, including applications and programming. **Work Experience Needed:** None. **On-the-Job Training Needed:** Long-term on-the-job training. **Certification/Licensure:** Federal licensure.

Personality Type: Enterprising-Conventional-Realistic. **Career Cluster:** 16 Transportation, Distribution, and Logistics. **Career Pathway:** 16.1 Transportation Operations. **Other Jobs in This Pathway:** Aerospace Engineering and Operations Technicians; Air Traffic Controllers; Aircraft Cargo Handling Supervisors; Airline Pilots, Copilots, and Flight Engineers; Automotive and Watercraft Service Attendants; Automotive Master Mechanics; Aviation Inspectors; Bridge and Lock Tenders; Bus Drivers, School or Special Client; Bus Drivers, Transit and Intercity; Commercial Divers; Commercial Pilots; Crane and Tower Operators; First-Line Supervisors of Helpers, Laborers, and Material Movers, Hand; First-Line Supervisors of Transportation and Material-Moving Machine and Vehicle Operators; Freight and Cargo Inspectors; Heavy and Tractor-Trailer Truck Drivers; Hoist and Winch Operators; Laborers and Freight, Stock, and Material Movers, Hand; Light Truck or Delivery Services

Drivers; Mates—Ship, Boat, and Barge; Motor Vehicle Operators, All Other; Motorboat Operators; Operating Engineers and Other Construction Equipment Operators; Parking Lot Attendants; Pilots, Ship; others.

Skills—Operation and Control: Controlling operations of equipment or systems. **Operations Analysis:** Analyzing needs and product requirements to create a design. **Operation Monitoring:** Watching gauges, dials, or other indicators to make sure a machine is working properly. **Systems Evaluation:** Identifying measures or indicators of system performance and the actions needed to improve or correct performance relative to the goals of the system. **Service Orientation:** Actively looking for ways to help people. **Management of Personnel Resources:** Motivating, developing, and directing people as they work, identifying the best people for the job. **Coordination:** Adjusting actions in relation to others' actions. **Negotiation:** Bringing others together and trying to reconcile differences.

Work Environment: More often indoors than outdoors; sitting; using hands; repetitive motions; noise; very hot or cold; bright or inadequate lighting; contaminants.

Airline Pilots, Copilots, and Flight Engineers

- ⊙ Annual Earnings: $105,580
- ⊙ Earnings Growth Potential: High (45.6%)
- ⊙ Growth: 6.4%
- ⊙ Annual Job Openings: 3,130
- ⊙ Self-Employed: 0.0%

Considerations for Job Outlook: As older pilots retire and younger pilots advance, entry-level positions may open up. And the demand for flight instructors may increase as they are needed to train a greater number of student pilots. Job prospects should be best with regional airlines, on low-cost carriers, or in general aviation, because these segments are anticipated to grow faster than the major airlines. In addition, entry-level requirements are lower for regional and commercial jobs. However, pilots with fewer than 500 flight hours will probably need to accumulate hours as flight instructors or commercial pilots before qualifying for regional airline jobs. Pilots seeking jobs at the major airlines will face strong competition because those firms

tend to attract many more applicants than the number of job openings.

Pilot and navigate the flight of fixed-wing, multi-engine aircraft, usually on scheduled air carrier routes, for the transport of passengers and cargo. Use instrumentation to guide flights when visibility is poor. Respond to and report in-flight emergencies and malfunctions. Work as part of a flight team with other crew members, especially during takeoffs and landings. Contact control towers for takeoff clearances, arrival instructions, and other information, using radio equipment. Steer aircraft along planned routes with the assistance of autopilot and flight management computers. Monitor gauges, warning devices, and control panels to verify aircraft performance and to regulate engine speed. Start engines, operate controls, and pilot airplanes to transport passengers, mail, or freight, while adhering to flight plans, regulations, and procedures. Inspect aircraft for defects and malfunctions, according to preflight checklists. Check passenger and cargo distributions and fuel amounts, to ensure that weight and balance specifications are met. Monitor engine operation, fuel consumption, and functioning of aircraft systems during flights. Confer with flight dispatchers and weather forecasters to keep abreast of flight conditions. Coordinate flight activities with ground crews and air-traffic control, and inform crew members of flight and test procedures. Order changes in fuel supplies, loads, routes, or schedules to ensure safety of flights. Choose routes, altitudes, and speeds that will provide the fastest, safest, and smoothest flights. Direct activities of aircraft crews during flights. Brief crews about flight details such as destinations, duties, and responsibilities. Record in log books information such as flight times, distances flown, and fuel consumption. Make announcements regarding flights, using public address systems. File instrument flight plans with air traffic control to ensure that flights are coordinated with other air traffic. Perform minor maintenance work, or arrange for major maintenance. Instruct other pilots and student pilots in aircraft operations and the principles of flight.

Education/Training Required: High school diploma or equivalent. **Education and Training Programs:** Airline/Commercial/Professional Pilot and Flight Crew Training; Flight Instructor Training. **Knowledge/Courses—Transportation:** Principles and methods for moving people or goods by air, rail, sea, or road, including the relative costs and benefits. **Geography:** Principles and methods for describing the features of land, sea, and air masses, including their physical characteristics, locations, interrelationships, and distribution of plant, animal, and human life. **Physics:** Physical principles, laws, their interrelationships, and applications to understanding fluid, material, and atmospheric dynamics, and mechanical, electrical, atomic, and subatomic structures and processes. **Public Safety and Security:** Relevant equipment, policies, procedures, and strategies to promote effective local, state, or national security operations for the protection of people, data, property, and institutions. **Psychology:** Human behavior and performance; individual differences in ability, personality, and interests; learning and motivation; psychological research methods; and the assessment and treatment of behavioral and affective disorders. **Mechanical Devices:** Machines and tools, including their designs, uses, repair, and maintenance. **Work Experience Needed:** 1 to 5 years. **On-the-Job Training Needed:** Long-term on-the-job training. **Certification/Licensure:** Federal licensure.

Personality Type: Realistic-Conventional-Investigative. **Career Cluster:** 16 Transportation, Distribution, and Logistics. **Career Pathway:** 16.1 Transportation Operations. **Other Jobs in This Pathway:** Aerospace Engineering and Operations Technicians; Air Traffic Controllers; Aircraft Cargo Handling Supervisors; Airfield Operations Specialists; Automotive and Watercraft Service Attendants; Automotive Master Mechanics; Aviation Inspectors; Bridge and Lock Tenders; Bus Drivers, School or Special Client; Bus Drivers, Transit and Intercity; Commercial Divers; Commercial Pilots; Crane and Tower Operators; First-Line Supervisors of Helpers, Laborers, and Material Movers, Hand; First-Line Supervisors of Transportation and Material-Moving Machine and Vehicle Operators; Freight and Cargo Inspectors; Heavy and Tractor-Trailer Truck Drivers; Hoist and Winch Operators; Laborers and Freight, Stock, and Material Movers, Hand; Light Truck or Delivery Services Drivers; Mates—Ship, Boat, and Barge; Motor Vehicle Operators, All Other; Motorboat Operators; Operating Engineers and Other Construction Equipment Operators; Parking Lot Attendants; Pilots, Ship; others.

Skills—Operation and Control: Controlling operations of equipment or systems. **Operation Monitoring:** Watching gauges, dials, or other indicators to make sure a machine is working properly. **Science:** Using scientific rules and methods to solve problems. **Troubleshooting:** Determining causes of operating errors and deciding what

to do about them. **Instructing:** Teaching others how to do something. **Judgment and Decision Making:** Considering the relative costs and benefits of potential actions to choose the most appropriate one. **Quality Control Analysis:** Conducting tests and inspections of products, services, or processes to evaluate quality or performance. **Mathematics:** Using mathematics to solve problems.

Work Environment: More often indoors than outdoors; sitting; using hands; noise; very hot or cold; bright or inadequate lighting; contaminants; cramped work space; exposed to radiation.

Ambulance Drivers and Attendants, Except Emergency Medical Technicians

- ⊙ Annual Earnings: $22,820
- ⊙ Earnings Growth Potential: Low (26.0%)
- ⊙ Growth: 32.1%
- ⊙ Annual Job Openings: 1,010
- ⊙ Self-Employed: 0.0%

Considerations for Job Outlook: Rapid employment growth is projected.

Drive ambulance or assist ambulance driver in transporting sick, injured, or convalescent persons. Remove and replace soiled linens and equipment in order to maintain sanitary conditions. Place patients on stretchers, and load stretchers into ambulances, usually with assistance from other attendants. Accompany and assist emergency medical technicians on calls. Earn and maintain appropriate certifications. Replace supplies and disposable items on ambulances. Report facts concerning accidents or emergencies to hospital personnel or law enforcement officials. Administer first aid such as bandaging, splinting, and administering oxygen. Restrain or shackle violent patients.

Education/Training Required: High school diploma or equivalent. **Education and Training Program:** Emergency Medical Technology/Technician (EMT Paramedic). **Knowledge/Courses—Transportation:** Principles and methods for moving people or goods by air, rail, sea, or road, including the relative costs and benefits. **Psychology:** Human behavior and performance; individual differences in ability, personality, and interests; learning and motivation; psychological research methods; and the assessment and treatment of behavioral and affective disorders. **Medicine and Dentistry:** The information and techniques needed to diagnose and treat human injuries, diseases, and deformities. This includes symptoms, treatment alternatives, drug properties and interactions, and preventive health-care measures. **Customer and Personal Service:** Principles and processes for providing customer and personal services. This includes customer needs assessment, meeting quality standards for services, and evaluation of customer satisfaction. **Telecommunications:** Transmission, broadcasting, switching, control, and operation of telecommunications systems. **Public Safety and Security:** Relevant equipment, policies, procedures, and strategies to promote effective local, state, or national security operations for the protection of people, data, property, and institutions. **Work Experience Needed:** None. **On-the-Job Training Needed:** Moderate-term on-the-job training. **Certification/Licensure:** Licensure.

Personality Type: Realistic-Social. **Career Cluster:** 08 Health Science. **Career Pathway:** 08.2 Diagnostics Services. **Other Jobs in This Pathway:** Anesthesiologist Assistants; Athletic Trainers; Cardiovascular Technologists and Technicians; Cytogenetic Technologists; Cytotechnologists; Diagnostic Medical Sonographers; Emergency Medical Technicians and Paramedics; Endoscopy Technicians; Health Diagnosing and Treating Practitioners, All Other; Health Specialties Teachers, Postsecondary; Health Technologists and Technicians, All Other; Healthcare Practitioners and Technical Workers, All Other; Histotechnologists and Histologic Technicians; Medical and Clinical Laboratory Technicians; Medical and Clinical Laboratory Technologists; Medical and Health Services Managers; Medical Assistants; Medical Equipment Preparers; Neurodiagnostic Technologists; Nuclear Equipment Operation Technicians; Nuclear Medicine Technologists; Ophthalmic Laboratory Technicians; Pathologists; Physical Scientists, All Other; Physician Assistants; Radiation Therapists; Radiologic Technicians; Radiologic Technologists; Radiologists; others.

Skills—Operation and Control: Controlling operations of equipment or systems. **Service Orientation:** Actively looking for ways to help people. **Equipment Maintenance:** Performing routine maintenance on equipment and determining when and what kind of maintenance is needed. **Negotiation:** Bringing others together and trying to reconcile differences. **Operation Monitoring:** Watching gauges, dials, or other indicators to make sure a machine is working properly. **Repairing:** Repairing machines or systems using the needed tools. **Equipment Selection:** Determining the kind of tools and equipment needed to do a job.

Work Environment: Outdoors; sitting; using hands; noise; very hot or cold; exposed to disease or infections.

Appraisers and Assessors of Real Estate

- ⊙ Annual Earnings: $48,870
- ⊙ Earnings Growth Potential: High (48.4%)
- ⊙ Growth: 7.5%
- ⊙ Annual Job Openings: 2,220
- ⊙ Self-Employed: 18.2%

Considerations for Job Outlook: Overall job opportunities are expected to be highly competitive. Employment opportunities should be best in areas with active real estate markets. Although opportunities for established certified appraisers are expected to be available in these areas, the cyclical nature of the real estate market will directly affect the number of jobs for appraisers, especially those who appraise residential properties. In times of recession, fewer people buy or sell real estate, decreasing the demand for appraisers. As a result, job opportunities should be best for appraisers who are able to switch specialties and appraise different types of properties.

Appraise real property and estimate its fair value. For task data, see Job Specializations.

Education/Training Required: High school diploma or equivalent. **Work Experience Needed:** None. **On-the-Job Training Needed:** Apprenticeship. **Certification/Licensure:** Certification required for some specializations, voluntary for others.

Job Specialization: Appraisers, Real Estate

Appraise real property to determine its value for purchase, sales, investment, mortgage, or loan purposes. Prepare written reports that estimate property values, outline methods by which the estimations were made, and meet appraisal standards. Compute final estimation of property values, taking into account such factors as depreciation, replacement costs, value comparisons of similar properties, and income potential. Search public records for transactions such as sales, leases, and assessments. Inspect properties to evaluate construction, condition, special features, and functional design, and to take property measurements. Photograph interiors and exteriors of properties in order to assist in estimating property value, substantiate findings, and complete appraisal reports. Evaluate land and neighborhoods where properties are situated, considering locations and trends or impending changes that could influence future values. Obtain county land values and sales information about nearby properties in order to aid in establishment of property values. Verify legal descriptions of properties by comparing them to county records. Check building codes and zoning bylaws in order to determine any effects on the properties being appraised. Estimate building replacement costs using building valuation manuals and professional cost estimators. Examine income records and operating costs of income properties. Interview persons familiar with properties and immediate surroundings, such as contractors, home owners, and realtors, in order to obtain pertinent information. Examine the type and location of nearby services such as shopping centers, schools, parks, and other neighborhood features in order to evaluate their impact on property values. Draw land diagrams that will be used in appraisal reports to support findings. Testify in court as to the value of a piece of real estate property.

Education and Training Program: Real Estate. **Knowledge/Courses—Building and Construction:** Materials, methods, and the tools involved in the construction or repair of houses, buildings, or other structures such as highways and roads. **Economics and Accounting:** Economic and accounting principles and practices, the financial markets, banking, and the analysis and reporting of financial data. **Geography:** Principles and methods for describing the features of land, sea, and air masses, including their physical characteristics, locations, interrelationships, and distribution of plant, animal, and human life. **Clerical Practices:** Administrative and clerical procedures and systems such as word processing, managing files and records, stenography and transcription, designing forms, and other office procedures and terminology. **Law and Government:** Laws, legal codes, court procedures, precedents, government regulations, executive orders, agency rules, and the democratic political process. **Sales and Marketing:** Principles and methods for showing, promoting, and selling products or services. This includes marketing strategy and tactics, product demonstration, sales techniques, and sales control systems.

Personality Type: Enterprising-Conventional-Realistic. **Career Cluster:** 14 Marketing, Sales, and Service. **Career Pathway:** 14.2 Professional Sales and Marketing. **Other Jobs in This Pathway:** Assessors; Cashiers; Counter and Rental Clerks; Demonstrators and Product Promoters; Door-To-Door Sales Workers, News and Street Vendors, and Related Workers; Driver/Sales Workers; Energy Brokers; First-Line Supervisors of Non-Retail Sales Workers; First-Line Supervisors of Retail Sales Workers; Gaming Change Persons and Booth Cashiers; Hotel, Motel, and Resort Desk Clerks; Interior Designers; Lodging Managers; Marketing Managers; Marking Clerks; Meeting, Convention, and Event Planners; Merchandise Displayers and Window Trimmers; Models; Online Merchants; Order Fillers, Wholesale and Retail Sales; Parts Salespersons; Property, Real Estate, and Community Association Managers; Real Estate Brokers; Real Estate Sales Agents; Reservation and Transportation Ticket Agents and Travel Clerks; Retail Salespersons; Sales and Related Workers, All Other; Sales Engineers; Sales Representatives, Services, All Other; others.

Skills—Management of Financial Resources: Determining how money will be spent to get the work done and accounting for these expenditures. **Mathematics:** Using mathematics to solve problems. **Management of Material Resources:** Obtaining and seeing to the appropriate use of equipment, facilities, and materials needed to do certain work. **Active Listening:** Giving full attention to what other people are saying, taking time to understand the points being made, asking questions as appropriate, and not interrupting at inappropriate times. **Writing:** Communicating effectively in writing as appropriate for the needs of the audience. **Critical Thinking:** Using logic and reasoning to identify the strengths and weaknesses of alternative solutions, conclusions, or approaches to problems. **Judgment and Decision Making:** Considering the relative costs and benefits of potential actions to choose the most appropriate one. **Science:** Using scientific rules and methods to solve problems.

Work Environment: More often outdoors than indoors; sitting.

Job Specialization: Assessors

Appraise real and personal property to determine its fair value. May assess taxes in accordance with prescribed schedules. Determine taxability and value of properties, using methods such as field inspection, structural measurement, calculation, sales analysis, market trend studies, and income and expense analysis. Inspect new construction and major improvements to existing structures to determine values. Explain assessed values to property owners and defend appealed assessments at public hearings. Inspect properties, considering factors such as market value, location, and building or replacement costs to determine appraisal value. Prepare and maintain current data on each parcel assessed, including maps of boundaries, inventories of land and structures, property characteristics, and any applicable exemptions. Identify the ownership of each piece of taxable property. Conduct regular reviews of property within jurisdictions to determine changes in property due to construction or demolition. Complete and maintain assessment rolls that show the assessed values and status of all property in a municipality. Review information about transfers of property to ensure its accuracy, checking basic information on buyers, sellers, and sales prices and making corrections as necessary. Maintain familiarity with aspects of local real estate markets. Analyze trends in sales prices, construction costs, and rents, to assess property values or determine the accuracy of assessments. Establish uniform and equitable systems for assessing all classes and kinds of property. Write and submit appraisal and tax reports for public record. Issue notices of assessments and taxes. Approve applications for property tax exemptions or deductions. Serve on assessment review boards. Hire staff members. Provide sales analyses to be used for equalization of school aid. Calculate tax bills for properties by multiplying assessed values by jurisdiction tax rates. Supervise staff members.

Education and Training Program: Real Estate. **Knowledge/Courses—Geography:** Principles and methods for describing the features of land, sea, and air masses, including their physical characteristics, locations, interrelationships, and distribution of plant, animal, and human life. **Building and Construction:** Materials, methods, and the tools involved in the construction or repair of houses, buildings, or other structures such as highways and roads. **Economics and Accounting:** Economic and accounting principles and practices, the financial markets, banking, and the analysis and reporting of financial data. **Clerical Practices:** Administrative and clerical procedures and systems such as word processing, managing files and records, stenography and transcription, designing forms, and other office procedures and terminology. **Law and Government:** Laws, legal codes, court procedures, precedents, government regulations, executive orders, agency rules, and the democratic political process. **Customer and Personal Service:** Principles and processes for providing customer and personal services. This includes customer needs assessment, meeting quality standards for services, and evaluation of customer satisfaction.

Personality Type: Conventional-Enterprising-Investigative. **Career Cluster:** 14 Marketing, Sales, and Service. **Career Pathway:** 14.2 Professional Sales and Marketing. **Other Jobs in This Pathway:** Appraisers, Real Estate; Cashiers; Counter and Rental Clerks; Demonstrators and Product Promoters; Door-To-Door Sales Workers, News and Street Vendors, and Related Workers; Driver/Sales Workers; Energy Brokers; First-Line Supervisors of Non-Retail Sales Workers; First-Line Supervisors of Retail Sales Workers; Gaming Change Persons and Booth Cashiers; Hotel, Motel, and Resort Desk Clerks; Interior Designers; Lodging Managers; Marketing Managers; Marking Clerks; Meeting, Convention, and Event Planners; Merchandise Displayers and Window Trimmers; Models; Online Merchants; Order Fillers, Wholesale and Retail Sales; Parts Salespersons; Property, Real Estate, and Community Association Managers; Real Estate Brokers; Real Estate Sales Agents; Reservation and Transportation Ticket Agents and Travel Clerks; Retail Salespersons; Sales and Related Workers, All Other; Sales Engineers; Sales Representatives, Services, All Other; others.

Skills—Mathematics: Using mathematics to solve problems. **Writing:** Communicating effectively in writing as appropriate for the needs of the audience. **Judgment and**

Decision Making: Considering the relative costs and benefits of potential actions to choose the most appropriate one. **Active Listening:** Giving full attention to what other people are saying, taking time to understand the points being made, asking questions as appropriate, and not interrupting at inappropriate times. **Speaking:** Talking to others to convey information effectively. **Critical Thinking:** Using logic and reasoning to identify the strengths and weaknesses of alternative solutions, conclusions, or approaches to problems. **Quality Control Analysis:** Conducting tests and inspections of products, services, or processes to evaluate quality or performance. **Negotiation:** Bringing others together and trying to reconcile differences.

Work Environment: Indoors; sitting.

Architectural and Civil Drafters

- ⊙ Annual Earnings: $47,250
- ⊙ Earnings Growth Potential: Low (33.3%)
- ⊙ Growth: 3.2%
- ⊙ Annual Job Openings: 2,090
- ⊙ Self-Employed: 4.2%

Considerations for Job Outlook: New software, such as PDM and BIM, will require drafters to work in collaboration with other professionals on projects, whether constructing a new building or manufacturing a new product. This new software, however, requires that someone build and maintain large databases. Workers with knowledge of drafting and of the software will be needed to oversee these databases.

Prepare detailed drawings of architectural and structural features of buildings or drawings and topographical relief maps. For task data, see Job Specializations.

Education/Training Required: Associate degree. **Work Experience Needed:** None. **On-the-Job Training Needed:** None. **Certification/Licensure:** Voluntary certification by association.

Job Specialization: Architectural Drafters

Prepare detailed drawings of architectural designs and plans for buildings and structures according to specifications provided by architect. Analyze building codes, by-laws, space and site requirements, and other technical documents and reports to determine their effect on architectural designs. Operate computer-aided drafting (CAD) equipment or a conventional drafting station to produce designs, working drawings, charts, forms, and records. Coordinate structural, electrical, and mechanical designs and determine a method of presentation to graphically represent building plans. Obtain and assemble data to complete architectural designs, visiting job sites to compile measurements as necessary. Draw rough and detailed scale plans for foundations, buildings, and structures, based on preliminary concepts, sketches, engineering calculations, specification sheets, and other data. Lay out and plan interior room arrangements for commercial buildings using computer-assisted drafting (CAD) equipment and software. Supervise, coordinate, and inspect the work of draftspersons, technicians, and technologists on construction projects.

Education and Training Programs: Architectural Drafting and Architectural CAD/CADD; Architectural Technology/Technician; CAD/CADD Drafting and/or Design Technology/Technician; Civil Drafting and Civil Engineering CAD/CADD; Drafting and Design Technology/Technician, General. **Knowledge/Courses—Design:** Design techniques, tools, and principles involved in production of precision technical plans, blueprints, drawings, and models. **Building and Construction:** Materials, methods, and the tools involved in the construction or repair of houses, buildings, or other structures such as highways and roads. **Engineering and Technology:** The practical application of engineering science and technology. This includes applying principles, techniques, procedures, and equipment to the design and production of various goods and services. **Fine Arts:** The theory and techniques required to compose, produce, and perform works of music, dance, visual arts, drama, and sculpture. **Computers and Electronics:** Circuit boards, processors, chips, electronic equipment, and computer hardware and software, including applications and programming. **Law and Government:** Laws, legal codes, court procedures, precedents, government regulations, executive orders, agency rules, and the democratic political process.

Personality Type: Artistic-Realistic-Investigative. **Career Cluster:** 02 Architecture and Construction. **Career Pathway:** 02.1 Design/Pre-Construction. **Other Jobs in This Pathway:** Architects, Except Landscape and Naval; Architectural and Engineering Managers; Architecture Teachers,

Postsecondary; Cartographers and Photogrammetrists; Civil Drafters; Civil Engineering Technicians; Drafters, All Other; Electrical Drafters; Electronic Drafters; Engineering Teachers, Postsecondary; Engineering Technicians, Except Drafters, All Other; Engineers, All Other; Geodetic Surveyors; Interior Designers; Landscape Architects; Mechanical Drafters; Surveying Technicians; Surveyors.

Skills—Mathematics: Using mathematics to solve problems. **Programming:** Writing computer programs for various purposes. **Systems Analysis:** Determining how a system should work and how changes in conditions, operations, and the environment will affect outcomes. **Quality Control Analysis:** Conducting tests and inspections of products, services, or processes to evaluate quality or performance. **Operations Analysis:** Analyzing needs and product requirements to create a design. **Management of Financial Resources:** Determining how money will be spent to get the work done and accounting for these expenditures. **Management of Material Resources:** Obtaining and seeing to the appropriate use of equipment, facilities, and materials needed to do certain work. **Time Management:** Managing one's own time and the time of others.

Work Environment: Indoors; sitting; using hands; repetitive motions.

Job Specialization: Civil Drafters

Prepare drawings and topographical and relief maps used in civil engineering projects such as highways, bridges, pipelines, flood control projects, and water and sewerage control systems. Produce drawings using computer-assisted drafting systems (CAD) or drafting machines, or by hand using compasses, dividers, protractors, triangles, and other drafting devices. Draft plans and detailed drawings for structures, installations, and construction projects such as highways, sewage disposal systems, and dikes, working from sketches or notes. Draw maps, diagrams, and profiles, using cross-sections and surveys, to represent elevations, topographical contours, subsurface formations, and structures. Correlate, interpret, and modify data obtained from topographical surveys, well logs, and geophysical prospecting reports. Finish and duplicate drawings and documentation packages, according to required mediums and specifications for reproduction using blueprinting, photography, or other duplicating methods. Review rough sketches, drawings, specifications,

and other engineering data received from civil engineers to ensure that they conform to design concepts. Supervise and train other technologists, technicians, and drafters. Supervise or conduct field surveys, inspections, or technical investigations to obtain data required to revise construction drawings. Determine the order of work and method of presentation, such as orthographic or isometric drawing. Calculate excavation tonnage and prepare graphs and fill-hauling diagrams for use in earth-moving operations. Explain drawings to production or construction teams and provide adjustments as necessary. Locate and identify symbols located on topographical surveys to denote geological and geophysical formations or oil field installations. Calculate weights, volumes, and stress factors and their implications for technical aspects of designs. Determine quality, cost, strength, and quantity of required materials, and enter figures on materials lists. Plot characteristics of boreholes for oil and gas wells from photographic subsurface survey recordings and other data, representing depth, degree, and direction of inclination.

Education and Training Programs: Architectural Drafting and Architectural CAD/CADD; Architectural Technology/Technician; CAD/CADD Drafting and/or Design Technology/Technician; Civil Drafting and Civil Engineering CAD/CADD; Drafting and Design Technology/Technician, General. **Knowledge/Courses—Design:** Design techniques, tools, and principles involved in production of precision technical plans, blueprints, drawings, and models. **Engineering and Technology:** The practical application of engineering science and technology. This includes applying principles, techniques, procedures, and equipment to the design and production of various goods and services. **Building and Construction:** Materials, methods, and the tools involved in the construction or repair of houses, buildings, or other structures such as highways and roads. **Geography:** Principles and methods for describing the features of land, sea, and air masses, including their physical characteristics, locations, interrelationships, and distribution of plant, animal, and human life. **Mathematics:** Arithmetic, algebra, geometry, calculus, statistics, and their applications. **Physics:** Physical principles, laws, their interrelationships, and applications to understanding fluid, material, and atmospheric dynamics, and mechanical, electrical, atomic, and subatomic structures and processes.

Personality Type: Realistic-Conventional-Investigative. **Career Cluster:** 02 Architecture and Construction. **Career**

Pathway: 02.1 Design/Pre-Construction. **Other Jobs in This Pathway:** Architects, Except Landscape and Naval; Architectural and Engineering Managers; Architectural Drafters; Architecture Teachers, Postsecondary; Cartographers and Photogrammetrists; Civil Engineering Technicians; Drafters, All Other; Electrical Drafters; Electronic Drafters; Engineering Teachers, Postsecondary; Engineering Technicians, Except Drafters, All Other; Engineers, All Other; Geodetic Surveyors; Interior Designers; Landscape Architects; Mechanical Drafters; Surveying Technicians; Surveyors.

Skills—Mathematics: Using mathematics to solve problems. **Operations Analysis:** Analyzing needs and product requirements to create a design. **Quality Control Analysis:** Conducting tests and inspections of products, services, or processes to evaluate quality or performance. **Science:** Using scientific rules and methods to solve problems. **Systems Evaluation:** Identifying measures or indicators of system performance and the actions needed to improve or correct performance relative to the goals of the system. **Systems Analysis:** Determining how a system should work and how changes in conditions, operations, and the environment will affect outcomes. **Reading Comprehension:** Understanding written sentences and paragraphs in work-related documents. **Management of Personnel Resources:** Motivating, developing, and directing people as they work, identifying the best people for the job.

Work Environment: Indoors; sitting; using hands; repetitive motions.

Athletes and Sports Competitors

- ⊙ Annual Earnings: $39,670
- ⊙ Earnings Growth Potential: Very high (54.7%)
- ⊙ Growth: 21.8%
- ⊙ Annual Job Openings: 780
- ⊙ Self-Employed: 18.9%

Considerations for Job Outlook: Competition for professional athlete jobs will continue to be extremely intense, with progressively more favorable opportunities in lower levels of competition. In major sports, such as basketball and football, only about 1 in 5,000 high school athletes becomes professional. The expansion of nontraditional

sports may create some additional job opportunities. Most professional athletes' careers last only a few years because of debilitating injuries. Therefore, yearly replacement needs for these jobs is high, creating some job opportunities. However, the talented young men and women who dream of becoming sports superstars greatly outnumber the number of openings.

Compete in athletic events. Assess performance following athletic competition, identifying strengths and weaknesses, and making adjustments to improve future performance. Receive instructions from coaches and other sports staff prior to events, and discuss their performance afterward. Lead teams by serving as captains. Maintain equipment used in a particular sport. Represent teams or professional sports clubs, performing such activities as meeting with members of the media, making speeches, or participating in charity events. Participate in athletic events and competitive sports, according to established rules and regulations. Attend scheduled practice and training sessions. Exercise and practice under the direction of athletic trainers or professional coaches, in order to develop skills, improve physical condition, and prepare for competitions. Maintain optimum physical fitness levels by training regularly, following nutrition plans, and consulting with health professionals.

Education/Training Required: High school diploma or equivalent. **Education and Training Program:** Health and Physical Education, General. **Knowledge/Courses—Therapy and Counseling:** Principles, methods, and procedures for diagnosis, treatment, and rehabilitation of physical and mental dysfunctions, and for career counseling and guidance. **Communications and Media:** Media production, communication, and dissemination techniques and methods. This includes alternative ways to inform and entertain via written, oral, and visual media. **Psychology:** Human behavior and performance; individual differences in ability, personality, and interests; learning and motivation; psychological research methods; and the assessment and treatment of behavioral and affective disorders. **Sales and Marketing:** Principles and methods for showing, promoting, and selling products or services. This includes marketing strategy and tactics, product demonstration, sales techniques, and sales control systems. **Work Experience Needed:** None. **On-the-Job Training Needed:** Long-term on-the-job training. **Certification/Licensure:** Licensure for some specializations and in some localities.

Personality Type: Realistic-Enterprising. **Career Cluster:** 05 Education and Training. **Career Pathway:** 05.3 Teaching/Training. **Other Jobs in This Pathway:** Adult Basic and Secondary Education and Literacy Teachers and Instructors; Agricultural Sciences Teachers, Postsecondary; Anthropology and Archeology Teachers, Postsecondary; Architecture Teachers, Postsecondary; Area, Ethnic, and Cultural Studies Teachers, Postsecondary; Art, Drama, and Music Teachers, Postsecondary; Atmospheric, Earth, Marine, and Space Sciences Teachers, Postsecondary; Audio-Visual and Multimedia Collections Specialists; Biological Science Teachers, Postsecondary; Business Teachers, Postsecondary; Career/Technical Education Teachers, Middle School; Career/Technical Education Teachers, Secondary School; Chemists; Coaches and Scouts; Communications Teachers, Postsecondary; Computer Science Teachers, Postsecondary; Criminal Justice and Law Enforcement Teachers, Postsecondary; Dietitians and Nutritionists; Education Teachers, Postsecondary; Elementary School Teachers, Except Special Education; Engineering Teachers, Postsecondary; others.

Skills—Coordination: Adjusting actions in relation to others' actions. **Operations Analysis:** Analyzing needs and product requirements to create a design.

Work Environment: Indoors; standing; balancing; using hands; bending or twisting the body; repetitive motions; noise; very hot or cold.

Audio and Video Equipment Technicians

- Annual Earnings: $41,630
- Earnings Growth Potential: High (44.1%)
- Growth: 13.4%
- Annual Job Openings: 2,560
- Self-Employed: 13.6%

Considerations for Job Outlook: Competition for jobs will be strong. This occupation attracts many applicants who are interested in working with the latest technology and electronic equipment. Many applicants also are attracted to working in the radio and television industry. Those looking for work in this industry will have the most job opportunities in smaller markets or stations. Those with hands-on experience with electronics or with work experience at a radio or television station will have the best job prospects. In addition, technicians are expected to be versatile and contribute to the setup, operation, and maintenance of equipment, whereas previously technicians typically specialized in one area.

Set up, or set up and operate audio and video equipment. Notify supervisors when major equipment repairs are needed. Monitor incoming and outgoing pictures and sound feeds to ensure quality; notify directors of any possible problems. Mix and regulate sound inputs and feeds or coordinate audio feeds with television pictures. Install, adjust, and operate electronic equipment used to record, edit, and transmit radio and television programs, cable programs, and motion pictures. Design layouts of audio and video equipment and perform upgrades and maintenance. Perform minor repairs and routine cleaning of audio and video equipment. Diagnose and resolve media system problems in classrooms. Switch sources of video input from one camera or studio to another, from film to live programming, or from network to local programming. Meet with directors and senior members of camera crews to discuss assignments and determine filming sequences, camera movements, and picture composition. Construct and position properties, sets, lighting equipment, and other equipment. Compress, digitize, duplicate, and store audio and video data. Obtain, set up, and load videotapes for scheduled productions or broadcasts. Edit videotapes by erasing and removing portions of programs and adding video or sound as required. Direct and coordinate activities of assistants and other personnel during production. Plan and develop preproduction ideas into outlines, scripts, storyboards, and graphics, using own ideas or specifications of assignments.

Education/Training Required: Postsecondary vocational training. **Education and Training Programs:** Agricultural Communication/Journalism; Photographic and Film/Video Technology/Technician and Assistant; Recording Arts Technology/Technician. **Knowledge/Courses—Telecommunications:** Transmission, broadcasting, switching, control, and operation of telecommunications systems. **Communications and Media:** Media production, communication, and dissemination techniques and methods. This includes alternative ways to inform and entertain via written, oral, and visual media. **Fine Arts:** The theory and techniques required to compose, produce, and perform works of music, dance, visual arts, drama, and sculpture. **Computers and Electronics:** Circuit boards, processors, chips, electronic equipment, and computer hardware and software, including applications and programming. **Engineering and Technology:** The practical application of engineering science and technology. This includes applying principles, techniques, procedures, and equipment to the design and production of various goods and services. **Production and Processing:** Raw materials, production processes, quality control, costs, and other techniques for maximizing the effective manufacture and distribution of goods. **Work Experience Needed:** None. **On-the-Job Training Needed:** Moderate-term on-the-job training. **Certification/Licensure:** Voluntary certification for some specializations.

Personality Type: Realistic-Investigative-Conventional. **Career Cluster:** 03 Arts and Communications. **Career Pathways:** 03.3 Visual Arts; 03.5 Journalism and Broadcasting. **Other Jobs in These Pathways:** Art Directors; Art, Drama, and Music Teachers, Postsecondary; Artists and Related Workers, All Other; Broadcast News Analysts; Broadcast Technicians; Camera Operators, Television, Video, and Motion Picture; Commercial and Industrial Designers; Communications Teachers, Postsecondary; Copy Writers; Craft Artists; Designers, All Other; Directors—Stage, Motion Pictures, Television, and Radio; Editors; English Language and Literature Teachers, Postsecondary; Fashion Designers; Film and Video Editors; Fine Artists, Including Painters, Sculptors, and Illustrators; Graphic Designers; Interior Designers; Media and Communication Workers, All Other; Multimedia Artists and Animators; Painting, Coating, and Decorating Workers; Photographers; Postsecondary Teachers, All Other; Producers; Program Directors; Public Address System and Other Announcers; Public Relations Specialists; Radio and Television Announcers; Reporters and Correspondents; Set and Exhibit Designers; Sound Engineering Technicians; others.

Skills—Installation: Installing equipment, machines, wiring, or programs to meet specifications. **Troubleshooting:** Determining causes of operating errors and deciding what to do about them. **Equipment Selection:** Determining the kind of tools and equipment needed to do a job. **Operation and Control:** Controlling operations of equipment or systems. **Repairing:** Repairing machines or systems using the needed tools. **Operation Monitoring:** Watching gauges, dials, or other indicators to make sure a machine is working properly. **Equipment Maintenance:**

Performing routine maintenance on equipment and determining when and what kind of maintenance is needed. **Quality Control Analysis:** Conducting tests and inspections of products, services, or processes to evaluate quality or performance.

Work Environment: Indoors; sitting; using hands; repetitive motions.

Automotive Body and Related Repairers

- ⊙ Annual Earnings: $38,180
- ⊙ Earnings Growth Potential: High (41.0%)
- ⊙ Growth: 18.4%
- ⊙ Annual Job Openings: 6,520
- ⊙ Self-Employed: 15.0%

Considerations for Job Outlook: Job opportunities should be very good for job seekers with industry certification and formal training in automotive body repair and refinishing and in collision repair. Furthermore, demand for qualified workers with knowledge of specific technologies, materials, and makes and models of cars should create new job opportunities. Those without any training or experience will face strong competition for jobs. The need to replace experienced repair technicians who retire, change occupations, or stop working for other reasons also will provide some job opportunities.

Repair and refinish automotive vehicle bodies and straighten vehicle frames. Follow supervisors' instructions as to which parts to restore or replace and how much time the job should take. Review damage reports, prepare or review repair cost estimates, and plan work to be performed. Sand body areas to be painted and cover bumpers, windows, and trim with masking tape or paper to protect them from the paint. Fit and weld replacement parts into place, using wrenches and welding equipment, and grind down welds to smooth them, using power grinders and other tools. Prime and paint repaired surfaces, using paint sprayguns and motorized sanders. Remove damaged sections of vehicles using metal-cutting guns, air grinders, and wrenches, and install replacement parts using wrenches or welding equipment. Chain or clamp frames and sections to alignment machines that use hydraulic pressure to align damaged components. Fill small dents that cannot be worked out with plastic or solder. File, grind, sand, and smooth filled or repaired surfaces, using power tools and hand tools. Remove upholstery, accessories, electrical window-and-seat-operating equipment, and trim to gain access to vehicle bodies and fenders. Mix polyester resins and hardeners to be used in restoring damaged areas. Position dolly blocks against surfaces of dented areas and beat opposite surfaces to remove dents, using hammers. Adjust or align headlights, wheels, and brake systems. Cut and tape plastic separating film to outside repair areas to avoid damaging surrounding surfaces during repair procedure, and remove tape and wash surfaces after repairs are complete. Remove small pits and dimples in body metal using pick hammers and punches. Fit and secure windows, vinyl roofs, and metal trim to vehicle bodies, using caulking guns, adhesive brushes, and mallets. Remove damaged panels, and identify the family and properties of the plastic used on a vehicle. Clean work areas, using air hoses, to remove damaged material and discarded fiberglass strips used in repair procedures.

Education/Training Required: High school diploma or equivalent. **Education and Training Program:** Autobody/Collision and Repair Technology/Technician. **Knowledge/Courses—Mechanical Devices:** Machines and tools, including their designs, uses, repair, and maintenance. **Chemistry:** The chemical composition, structure, and properties of substances and of the chemical processes and transformations that they undergo. This includes uses of chemicals and their danger signs, production techniques, and disposal methods. **Production and Processing:** Raw materials, production processes, quality control, costs, and other techniques for maximizing the effective manufacture and distribution of goods. **Engineering and Technology:** The practical application of engineering science and technology. This includes applying principles, techniques, procedures, and equipment to the design and production of various goods and services. **Work Experience Needed:** None. **On-the-Job Training Needed:** Moderate-term on-the-job training. **Certification/Licensure:** Voluntary certification by association.

Personality Type: Realistic. **Career Cluster:** 16 Transportation, Distribution, and Logistics. **Career Pathway:** 16.4 Facility and Mobile Equipment Maintenance. **Other Jobs in This Pathway:** Aircraft Mechanics and Service Technicians; Aircraft Structure, Surfaces, Rigging, and Systems Assemblers; Automotive Glass Installers and Repairers; Automotive Master Mechanics; Automotive Specialty Technicians; Bicycle Repairers; Bus and Truck Mechanics and Diesel Engine Specialists; Cleaners of Vehicles and Equipment; Electrical and Electronics Installers and Repairers, Transportation Equipment; Electronic Equipment Installers and Repairers, Motor Vehicles; Engine and Other Machine Assemblers; Gem and Diamond Workers; Installation, Maintenance, and Repair Workers, All Other; Motorboat Mechanics and Service Technicians; Motorcycle Mechanics; Outdoor Power Equipment and Other Small Engine Mechanics; Painters, Transportation Equipment.

Skills—Repairing: Repairing machines or systems using the needed tools. **Equipment Selection:** Determining the kind of tools and equipment needed to do a job. **Installation:** Installing equipment, machines, wiring, or programs to meet specifications. **Equipment Maintenance:** Performing routine maintenance on equipment and determining when and what kind of maintenance is needed. **Operation and Control:** Controlling operations of equipment or systems. **Troubleshooting:** Determining causes of operating errors and deciding what to do about them. **Quality Control Analysis:** Conducting tests and inspections of products, services, or processes to evaluate quality or performance. **Operation Monitoring:** Watching gauges, dials, or other indicators to make sure a machine is working properly.

Work Environment: Standing; walking and running; kneeling, crouching, stooping, or crawling; using hands; bending or twisting the body; noise; contaminants; cramped work space; hazardous conditions; hazardous equipment; minor burns, cuts, bites, or stings.

Automotive Glass Installers and Repairers

- ⊙ Annual Earnings: $33,720
- ⊙ Earnings Growth Potential: Medium (38.6%)
- ⊙ Growth: 24.9%
- ⊙ Annual Job Openings: 920
- ⊙ Self-Employed: 22.5%

Considerations for Job Outlook: Job opportunities should be very good for job seekers with industry certification and formal training in automotive body repair and refinishing and in collision repair. Furthermore, demand for qualified workers with knowledge of specific technologies, materials, and makes and models of cars should create new job opportunities. Those without any training or experience will face strong competition for jobs. The need to replace experienced repair technicians who retire, change occupations, or stop working for other reasons also will provide some job opportunities.

Replace or repair broken windshields and window glass in motor vehicles. Remove all dirt, foreign matter, and loose glass from damaged areas; then apply primer along windshield or window edges and allow it to dry. Install replacement glass in vehicles after old glass has been removed and all necessary preparations have been made. Allow all glass parts installed with urethane ample time to cure, taking temperature and humidity into account. Prime all scratches on pinchwelds with primer, and allow primed scratches to dry. Obtain windshields or windows for specific automobile makes and models from stock, and examine them for defects prior to installation. Check for moisture or contamination in damaged areas, dry out any moisture prior to making repairs, and keep damaged areas dry until repairs are complete. Apply a bead of urethane around the perimeter of each pinchweld, and dress the remaining urethane on the pinchwelds so that it is of uniform level and thickness all the way around. Select appropriate tools, safety equipment, and parts according to job requirements. Remove broken or damaged glass windshields or window glass from motor vehicles, using hand tools to remove screws from frames holding glass. Replace all moldings, clips, windshield wipers, and any other parts that were removed prior to glass replacement or repair. Remove all moldings, clips, windshield wipers, screws, bolts, and inside A-pillar moldings; then lower headliners prior to beginning installation or repair work. Install, repair, and replace safety glass and related materials, such as backglass heating-elements, on vehicles and equipment. Install rubber-channeling strips around edges of glass or frames in order to weatherproof windows or to prevent rattling. Hold cut or uneven edges of glass against automated abrasive belts in order to shape or smooth edges. Cut flat safety glass according to specified patterns, or perform precision pattern making and glass cutting to custom-fit replacement windows. Replace or adjust motorized or manual window-raising mechanisms.

Education/Training Required: High school diploma or equivalent. **Education and Training Program:** Autobody/Collision and Repair Technology/Technician. **Knowledge/Courses—Mechanical Devices:** Machines and tools, including their designs, uses, repair, and maintenance. **Production and Processing:** Raw materials, production processes, quality control, costs, and other techniques for maximizing the effective manufacture and distribution of goods. **Customer and Personal Service:** Principles and processes for providing customer and personal services. This includes customer needs assessment, meeting quality standards for services, and evaluation of customer satisfaction. **Sales and Marketing:** Principles and methods for showing, promoting, and selling products or services. This includes marketing strategy and tactics, product demonstration, sales techniques, and sales control systems. **Administration and Management:** Business and management principles involved in strategic planning, resource allocation, human resources modeling, leadership technique, production methods, and coordination of people and resources. **Transportation:** Principles and methods for moving people or goods by air, rail, sea, or road, including the relative costs and benefits. **Work Experience Needed:** None. **On-the-Job Training Needed:** Moderate-term on-the-job training. **Certification/Licensure:** Voluntary certification by association.

Personality Type: Realistic-Conventional-Enterprising. **Career Cluster:** 16 Transportation, Distribution, and Logistics. **Career Pathway:** 16.4 Facility and Mobile Equipment Maintenance. **Other Jobs in This Pathway:** Aircraft Mechanics and Service Technicians; Aircraft Structure, Surfaces, Rigging, and Systems Assemblers; Automotive Body and Related Repairers; Automotive Master Mechanics; Automotive Specialty Technicians; Bicycle Repairers; Bus and Truck Mechanics and Diesel Engine Specialists; Cleaners of Vehicles and Equipment; Electrical and Electronics Installers and Repairers, Transportation Equipment; Electronic Equipment Installers and Repairers, Motor Vehicles; Engine and Other Machine Assemblers; Gem and Diamond Workers; Installation, Maintenance, and Repair Workers, All Other; Motorboat Mechanics and Service Technicians; Motorcycle Mechanics; Outdoor Power Equipment and Other Small Engine Mechanics; Painters, Transportation Equipment.

Skills—Installation: Installing equipment, machines, wiring, or programs to meet specifications. **Repairing:**

Repairing machines or systems using the needed tools. **Equipment Selection:** Determining the kind of tools and equipment needed to do a job. **Equipment Maintenance:** Performing routine maintenance on equipment and determining when and what kind of maintenance is needed. **Operation and Control:** Controlling operations of equipment or systems. **Troubleshooting:** Determining causes of operating errors and deciding what to do about them. **Quality Control Analysis:** Conducting tests and inspections of products, services, or processes to evaluate quality or performance. **Management of Material Resources:** Obtaining and seeing to the appropriate use of equipment, facilities, and materials needed to do certain work.

Work Environment: Outdoors; standing; using hands; bending or twisting the body; repetitive motions; noise; very hot or cold; bright or inadequate lighting; contaminants; cramped work space; hazardous equipment; minor burns, cuts, bites, or stings.

Automotive Service Technicians and Mechanics

- ⊙ Annual Earnings: $36,180
- ⊙ Earnings Growth Potential: High (43.0%)
- ⊙ Growth: 17.3%
- ⊙ Annual Job Openings: 31,170
- ⊙ Self-Employed: 18.3%

Considerations for Job Outlook: Job opportunities should be very good for job seekers with industry certification and formal training in automotive body repair and refinishing and in collision repair. Furthermore, demand for qualified workers with knowledge of specific technologies, materials, and makes and models of cars should create new job opportunities. Those without any training or experience will face strong competition for jobs. The need to replace experienced repair technicians who retire, change occupations, or stop working for other reasons also will provide some job opportunities.

Diagnose, adjust, repair, or overhaul automotive vehicles. For task data, see Job Specializations.

Education/Training Required: High school diploma or equivalent. **Work Experience Needed:** None. **On-the-Job Training Needed:** Long-term on-the-job training.

Certification/Licensure: Voluntary certification by association.

Job Specialization: Automotive Master Mechanics

Repair automobiles, trucks, buses, and other vehicles. Master mechanics repair virtually any part on the vehicle or specialize in the transmission system. Test drive vehicles, and test components and systems, using equipment such as infrared engine analyzers, compression gauges, and computerized diagnostic devices. Examine vehicles to determine extent of damage or malfunctions. Repair, reline, replace, and adjust brakes. Follow checklists to ensure all important parts are examined, including belts, hoses, steering systems, spark plugs, brake and fuel systems, wheel bearings, and other potentially troublesome areas. Confer with customers to obtain descriptions of vehicle problems and to discuss work to be performed and future repair requirements. Perform routine and scheduled maintenance services such as oil changes, lubrications, and tune-ups. Repair and service air conditioning, heating, engine-cooling, and electrical systems. Test and adjust repaired systems to meet manufacturers' performance specifications. Review work orders and discuss work with supervisors. Tear down, repair, and rebuild faulty assemblies such as power systems, steering systems, and linkages. Plan work procedures, using charts, technical manuals, and experience. Disassemble units and inspect parts for wear, using micrometers, calipers, and gauges. Repair or replace parts such as pistons, rods, gears, valves, and bearings. Rewire ignition systems, lights, and instrument panels. Repair manual and automatic transmissions. Install and repair accessories such as radios, heaters, mirrors, and windshield wipers. Maintain cleanliness of work area. Repair or replace shock absorbers. Replace and adjust headlights. Overhaul or replace carburetors, blowers, generators, distributors, starters, and pumps. Repair radiator leaks. Align vehicles' front ends. Rebuild parts such as crankshafts and cylinder blocks. Repair damaged automobile bodies.

Education and Training Programs: Alternative Fuel Vehicle Technology/Technician; Autobody/Collision and Repair Technology/Technician; Automobile/Automotive Mechanics Technology/Technician; Automotive Engineering Technology/Technician; Medium/Heavy Vehicle and Truck Technology/Technician; Vehicle Emissions

Inspection and Maintenance Technology/Technician. **Knowledge/Courses—Mechanical Devices:** Machines and tools, including their designs, uses, repair, and maintenance. **Engineering and Technology:** The practical application of engineering science and technology. This includes applying principles, techniques, procedures, and equipment to the design and production of various goods and services. **Physics:** Physical principles, laws, their interrelationships, and applications to understanding fluid, material, and atmospheric dynamics, and mechanical, electrical, atomic, and subatomic structures and processes. **Design:** Design techniques, tools, and principles involved in production of precision technical plans, blueprints, drawings, and models. **Chemistry:** The chemical composition, structure, and properties of substances and of the chemical processes and transformations that they undergo. This includes uses of chemicals and their danger signs, production techniques, and disposal methods. **Computers and Electronics:** Circuit boards, processors, chips, electronic equipment, and computer hardware and software, including applications and programming.

Personality Type: Realistic-Investigative. **Career Cluster:** 16 Transportation, Distribution, and Logistics. **Career Pathways:** 16.1 Transportation Operations; 16.4 Facility and Mobile Equipment Maintenance. **Other Jobs in These Pathways:** Aerospace Engineering and Operations Technicians; Air Traffic Controllers; Aircraft Cargo Handling Supervisors; Aircraft Mechanics and Service Technicians; Aircraft Structure, Surfaces, Rigging, and Systems Assemblers; Airfield Operations Specialists; Airline Pilots, Copilots, and Flight Engineers; Automotive and Watercraft Service Attendants; Automotive Body and Related Repairers; Automotive Glass Installers and Repairers; Automotive Specialty Technicians; Aviation Inspectors; Bicycle Repairers; Bridge and Lock Tenders; Bus and Truck Mechanics and Diesel Engine Specialists; Bus Drivers, School or Special Client; Bus Drivers, Transit and Intercity; Cleaners of Vehicles and Equipment; Commercial Divers; Commercial Pilots; Crane and Tower Operators; Electrical and Electronics Installers and Repairers, Transportation Equipment; Electronic Equipment Installers and Repairers, Motor Vehicles; Engine and Other Machine Assemblers; others.

Skills—Repairing: Repairing machines or systems using the needed tools. **Equipment Maintenance:** Performing routine maintenance on equipment and determining when and what kind of maintenance is needed. **Installation:** Installing equipment, machines, wiring, or programs to meet specifications. **Troubleshooting:** Determining causes of operating errors and deciding what to do about them. **Equipment Selection:** Determining the kind of tools and equipment needed to do a job. **Operation and Control:** Controlling operations of equipment or systems. **Quality Control Analysis:** Conducting tests and inspections of products, services, or processes to evaluate quality or performance. **Operation Monitoring:** Watching gauges, dials, or other indicators to make sure a machine is working properly.

Work Environment: Standing; using hands; bending or twisting the body; repetitive motions; noise; very hot or cold; bright or inadequate lighting; contaminants; cramped work space; hazardous conditions; hazardous equipment; minor burns, cuts, bites, or stings.

Job Specialization: Automotive Specialty Technicians

Repair only one system or component on a vehicle, such as brakes, suspension, or radiator. Examine vehicles, compile estimates of repair costs, and secure customers' approval to perform repairs. Repair, overhaul, and adjust automobile brake systems. Use electronic test equipment to locate and correct malfunctions in fuel, ignition, and emissions control systems. Repair and replace defective balljoint suspensions, brakeshoes, and wheelbearings. Inspect and test new vehicles for damage; then record findings so that necessary repairs can be made. Test electronic computer components in automobiles to ensure that they are working properly. Tune automobile engines to ensure proper and efficient functioning. Install and repair air conditioners, and service components such as compressors, condensers, and controls. Repair, replace, and adjust defective carburetor parts and gasoline filters. Remove and replace defective mufflers and tailpipes. Repair and replace automobile leaf springs. Rebuild, repair, and test automotive fuel injection units. Align and repair wheels, axles, frames, torsion bars, and steering mechanisms of automobiles, using special alignment equipment and wheel-balancing machines. Repair, install, and adjust hydraulic and electromagnetic automatic lift mechanisms used to raise and lower automobile windows, seats, and tops. Repair and rebuild clutch systems. Convert vehicle fuel systems from gasoline to butane gas operations, and repair and service operating butane fuel units.

Education and Training Programs: Alternative Fuel Vehicle Technology/Technician; Autobody/Collision and Repair Technology/Technician; Automobile/Automotive Mechanics Technology/Technician; Automotive Engineering Technology/Technician; Medium/Heavy Vehicle and Truck Technology/Technician; Vehicle Emissions Inspection and Maintenance Technology/Technician. **Knowledge/Courses—Mechanical Devices:** Machines and tools, including their designs, uses, repair, and maintenance. **Physics:** Physical principles, laws, their interrelationships, and applications to understanding fluid, material, and atmospheric dynamics, and mechanical, electrical, atomic, and subatomic structures and processes. **Engineering and Technology:** The practical application of engineering science and technology. This includes applying principles, techniques, procedures, and equipment to the design and production of various goods and services. **Customer and Personal Service:** Principles and processes for providing customer and personal services. This includes customer needs assessment, meeting quality standards for services, and evaluation of customer satisfaction. **Sales and Marketing:** Principles and methods for showing, promoting, and selling products or services. This includes marketing strategy and tactics, product demonstration, sales techniques, and sales control systems. **Administration and Management:** Business and management principles involved in strategic planning, resource allocation, human resources modeling, leadership technique, production methods, and coordination of people and resources.

Personality Type: Realistic-Investigative-Conventional. **Career Clusters:** 13 Manufacturing; 16 Transportation, Distribution, and Logistics. **Career Pathways:** 16.4 Facility and Mobile Equipment Maintenance; 13.3 Maintenance, Installation, and Repair. **Other Jobs in These Pathways:** Aircraft Mechanics and Service Technicians; Aircraft Structure, Surfaces, Rigging, and Systems Assemblers; Automotive Body and Related Repairers; Automotive Engineering Technicians; Automotive Glass Installers and Repairers; Automotive Master Mechanics; Avionics Technicians; Bicycle Repairers; Biological Technicians; Bus and Truck Mechanics and Diesel Engine Specialists; Camera and Photographic Equipment Repairers; Chemical Equipment Operators and Tenders; Civil Engineering Technicians; Cleaners of Vehicles and Equipment; Coil

Winders, Tapers, and Finishers; Computer, Automated Teller, and Office Machine Repairers; Construction and Related Workers, All Other; Control and Valve Installers and Repairers, Except Mechanical Door; Electric Motor, Power Tool, and Related Repairers; Electrical and Electronic Equipment Assemblers; Electrical and Electronics Installers and Repairers, Transportation Equipment; Electrical and Electronics Repairers, Commercial and Industrial Equipment; others.

Skills—Repairing: Repairing machines or systems using the needed tools. **Equipment Maintenance:** Performing routine maintenance on equipment and determining when and what kind of maintenance is needed. **Troubleshooting:** Determining causes of operating errors and deciding what to do about them. **Operation and Control:** Controlling operations of equipment or systems. **Equipment Selection:** Determining the kind of tools and equipment needed to do a job. **Installation:** Installing equipment, machines, wiring, or programs to meet specifications. **Quality Control Analysis:** Conducting tests and inspections of products, services, or processes to evaluate quality or performance. **Operation Monitoring:** Watching gauges, dials, or other indicators to make sure a machine is working properly.

Work Environment: Standing; walking and running; kneeling, crouching, stooping, or crawling; using hands; bending or twisting the body; repetitive motions; noise; very hot or cold; bright or inadequate lighting; contaminants; cramped work space; hazardous conditions; hazardous equipment; minor burns, cuts, bites, or stings.

Avionics Technicians

- Annual Earnings: $54,720
- Earnings Growth Potential: Low (31.1%)
- Growth: 7.0%
- Annual Job Openings: 580
- Self-Employed: 0.0%

Considerations for Job Outlook: Job prospects also will be better for those who keep up with technical advances in aircraft electronics and composite materials. Job opportunities may arise from the need to replace mechanics who leave the workforce. Over the next decade, many aircraft mechanics are expected to retire. As older mechanics retire and younger mechanics advance, entry-level positions may open up. However, if airlines continue to send maintenance work to other countries, competition for new jobs will remain strong.

Install, inspect, test, adjust, or repair avionics equipment, such as radar, radio, navigation, and missile control systems in aircraft or space vehicles. Set up and operate ground support and test equipment to perform functional flight tests of electrical and electronic systems. Test and troubleshoot instruments, components, and assemblies, using circuit testers, oscilloscopes, and voltmeters. Keep records of maintenance and repair work. Coordinate work with that of engineers, technicians, and other aircraft maintenance personnel. Interpret flight test data in order to diagnose malfunctions and systemic performance problems. Install electrical and electronic components, assemblies, and systems in aircraft, using hand tools, power tools, and/or soldering irons. Adjust, repair, or replace malfunctioning components or assemblies, using hand tools and/or soldering irons. Connect components to assemblies such as radio systems, instruments, magnetos, inverters, and in-flight refueling systems, using hand tools and soldering irons. Assemble components such as switches, electrical controls, and junction boxes, using hand tools and soldering irons. Fabricate parts and test aids as required. Lay out installation of aircraft assemblies and systems, following documentation such as blueprints, manuals, and wiring diagrams. Assemble prototypes or models of circuits, instruments, and systems so that they can be used for testing. Operate computer-aided drafting and design applications to design avionics system modifications.

Education/Training Required: Postsecondary vocational training. **Education and Training Programs:** Airframe Mechanics and Aircraft Maintenance Technology/Technician; Avionics Maintenance Technology/Technician. **Knowledge/Courses—Engineering and Technology:** The practical application of engineering science and technology. This includes applying principles, techniques, procedures, and equipment to the design and production of various goods and services. **Mechanical Devices:** Machines and tools, including their designs, uses, repair, and maintenance. **Computers and Electronics:** Circuit boards, processors, chips, electronic equipment, and computer hardware and software, including applications and programming. **Telecommunications:** Transmission, broadcasting, switching, control, and operation of

telecommunications systems. **Production and Processing:** Raw materials, production processes, quality control, costs, and other techniques for maximizing the effective manufacture and distribution of goods. **Design:** Design techniques, tools, and principles involved in production of precision technical plans, blueprints, drawings, and models. **Work Experience Needed:** None. **On-the-Job Training Needed:** None. **Certification/Licensure:** Federal certification for some specializations and for those without military or manufacturer experience.

Personality Type: Realistic-Investigative-Conventional. **Career Clusters:** 13 Manufacturing; 16 Transportation, Distribution, and Logistics. **Career Pathways:** 13.1 Production; 16.7 Sales and Service; 13.3 Maintenance, Installation, and Repair. **Other Jobs in These Pathways:** Adhesive Bonding Machine Operators and Tenders; Aircraft Mechanics and Service Technicians; Assemblers and Fabricators, All Other; Automotive Engineering Technicians; Automotive Specialty Technicians; Biological Technicians; Cabinetmakers and Bench Carpenters; Camera and Photographic Equipment Repairers; Chemical Equipment Operators and Tenders; Civil Engineering Technicians; Cleaning, Washing, and Metal Pickling Equipment Operators and Tenders; Coating, Painting, and Spraying Machine Setters, Operators, and Tenders; Coil Winders, Tapers, and Finishers; Computer, Automated Teller, and Office Machine Repairers; Computer-Controlled Machine Tool Operators, Metal and Plastic; Construction and Related Workers, All Other; Control and Valve Installers and Repairers, Except Mechanical Door; Cooling and Freezing Equipment Operators and Tenders; Cost Estimators; Crushing, Grinding, and Polishing Machine Setters, Operators, and Tenders; Cutters and Trimmers, Hand; others.

Skills—Repairing: Repairing machines or systems using the needed tools. **Equipment Maintenance:** Performing routine maintenance on equipment and determining when and what kind of maintenance is needed. **Troubleshooting:** Determining causes of operating errors and deciding what to do about them. **Equipment Selection:** Determining the kind of tools and equipment needed to do a job. **Installation:** Installing equipment, machines, wiring, or programs to meet specifications. **Quality Control Analysis:** Conducting tests and inspections of products, services, or processes to evaluate quality or performance. **Science:** Using scientific rules and methods to solve problems.

Operation Monitoring: Watching gauges, dials, or other indicators to make sure a machine is working properly.

Work Environment: Indoors; sitting; using hands; noise; contaminants; hazardous conditions.

Bailiffs

- ⊙ Annual Earnings: $38,950
- ⊙ Earnings Growth Potential: Very high (51.7%)
- ⊙ Growth: 7.9%
- ⊙ Annual Job Openings: 450
- ⊙ Self-Employed: 0.0%

Considerations for Job Outlook: Slower-than-average job growth is projected.

Maintain order in courts of law. Maintain order in the courtroom during trials and guard juries from outside contact. Enforce courtroom rules of behavior and warn persons not to smoke or disturb court procedure. Report needs for police or medical assistance to sheriff's office. Announce the entrance of judges. Stop people from entering the courtroom while judges charge juries. Screen persons entering the courthouse using magnetometers, X-ray machines, and other devices to collect and retain unauthorized firearms and other contraband. Provide security by patrolling the interior and exterior of the courthouse and escorting judges and other court employees. Check the courtroom for security and cleanliness and assure availability of sundry supplies, such as notepads, for use by judges, jurors, and attorneys. Screen, control, and handle evidence and exhibits during court proceedings. Guard the lodging of sequestered juries. Provide jury escort to restaurants and other areas outside the courtroom to prevent jury contact with the public. Escort prisoners to and from the courthouse and maintain custody of prisoners during court proceedings. Maintain court dockets.

Education/Training Required: High school diploma or equivalent. **Education and Training Program:** Criminal Justice/Police Science. **Knowledge/Courses—Public Safety and Security:** Relevant equipment, policies, procedures, and strategies to promote effective local, state, or national security operations for the protection of people, data, property, and institutions. **Law and Government:** Laws, legal codes, court procedures, precedents,

government regulations, executive orders, agency rules, and the democratic political process. **Psychology:** Human behavior and performance; individual differences in ability, personality, and interests; learning and motivation; psychological research methods; and the assessment and treatment of behavioral and affective disorders. **Telecommunications:** Transmission, broadcasting, switching, control, and operation of telecommunications systems. **Customer and Personal Service:** Principles and processes for providing customer and personal services. This includes customer needs assessment, meeting quality standards for services, and evaluation of customer satisfaction. **Work Experience Needed:** None. **On-the-Job Training Needed:** Moderate-term on-the-job training. **Certification/Licensure:** May be licensed where classified as peace officers.

Personality Type: Realistic-Conventional-Enterprising. **Career Cluster:** 12 Law, Public Safety, Corrections, and Security. **Career Pathway:** 12.4 Law Enforcement Services. **Other Jobs in This Pathway:** Anthropology and Archeology Teachers, Postsecondary; Correctional Officers and Jailers; Criminal Investigators and Special Agents; Criminal Justice and Law Enforcement Teachers, Postsecondary; First-Line Supervisors of Police and Detectives; Forensic Science Technicians; Immigration and Customs Inspectors; Intelligence Analysts; Police Detectives; Police Identification and Records Officers; Police Patrol Officers; Remote Sensing Scientists and Technologists; Sheriffs and Deputy Sheriffs.

Skills—Social Perceptiveness: Being aware of others' reactions and understanding why they react as they do. **Negotiation:** Bringing others together and trying to reconcile differences.

Work Environment: Indoors; sitting.

Bicycle Repairers

- ⊙ Annual Earnings: $23,210
- ⊙ Earnings Growth Potential: Low (25.8%)
- ⊙ Growth: 37.4%
- ⊙ Annual Job Openings: 630
- ⊙ Self-Employed: 4.4%

Considerations for Job Outlook: Rapid employment growth is projected, but the small size of this occupation should limit job openings.

Repair and service bicycles. Install and adjust speed and gear mechanisms. Assemble new bicycles. Install, repair, and replace equipment or accessories, such as handlebars, stands, lights, and seats. Align wheels. Disassemble axles in order to repair, adjust, and replace defective parts, using hand tools. Shape replacement parts, using bench grinders. Repair holes in tire tubes, using scrapers and patches. Weld broken or cracked frames together, using oxyacetylene torches and welding rods. Paint bicycle frames, using spray guns or brushes.

Education/Training Required: High school diploma or equivalent. **Education and Training Program:** Bicycle Mechanics and Repair Technology/Technician. **Knowledge/Courses—Mechanical Devices:** Machines and tools, including their designs, uses, repair, and maintenance. **Building and Construction:** Materials, methods, and the tools involved in the construction or repair of houses, buildings, or other structures such as highways and roads. **Design:** Design techniques, tools, and principles involved in production of precision technical plans, blueprints, drawings, and models. **Engineering and Technology:** The practical application of engineering science and technology. This includes applying principles, techniques, procedures, and equipment to the design and production of various goods and services. **Sales and Marketing:** Principles and methods for showing, promoting, and selling products or services. This includes marketing strategy and tactics, product demonstration, sales techniques, and sales control systems. **Customer and Personal Service:** Principles and processes for providing customer and personal services. This includes customer needs assessment, meeting quality standards for services, and evaluation of customer satisfaction. **Work Experience Needed:** None. **On-the-Job Training Needed:** Moderate-term on-the-job training. **Certification/Licensure:** None.

Personality Type: Realistic-Conventional-Investigative. **Career Cluster:** 16 Transportation, Distribution, and Logistics. **Career Pathway:** 16.4 Facility and Mobile Equipment Maintenance. **Other Jobs in This Pathway:** Aircraft Mechanics and Service Technicians; Aircraft Structure, Surfaces, Rigging, and Systems Assemblers; Automotive Body and Related Repairers; Automotive Glass Installers and Repairers; Automotive Master Mechanics; Automotive Specialty Technicians; Bus and Truck Mechanics and Diesel Engine Specialists; Cleaners of Vehicles and Equipment; Electrical and Electronics Installers and Repairers, Transportation Equipment; Electronic Equipment Installers and Repairers, Motor Vehicles; Engine and Other Machine Assemblers; Gem and Diamond Workers; Installation, Maintenance, and Repair Workers, All Other; Motorboat Mechanics and Service Technicians; Motorcycle Mechanics; Outdoor Power Equipment and Other Small Engine Mechanics; Painters, Transportation Equipment.

Skills—Repairing: Repairing machines or systems using the needed tools. **Equipment Maintenance:** Performing routine maintenance on equipment and determining when and what kind of maintenance is needed. **Troubleshooting:** Determining causes of operating errors and deciding what to do about them. **Equipment Selection:** Determining the kind of tools and equipment needed to do a job. **Quality Control Analysis:** Conducting tests and inspections of products, services, or processes to evaluate quality or performance. **Installation:** Installing equipment, machines, wiring, or programs to meet specifications. **Technology Design:** Generating or adapting equipment and technology to serve user needs. **Operation and Control:** Controlling operations of equipment or systems.

Work Environment: Indoors; standing; using hands; noise; contaminants; hazardous equipment; minor burns, cuts, bites, or stings.

Bill and Account Collectors

- Annual Earnings: $31,920
- Earnings Growth Potential: Low (32.5%)
- Growth: 14.2%
- Annual Job Openings: 13,550
- Self-Employed: 0.2%

Considerations for Job Outlook: Job prospects should be excellent for this occupation. Workers frequently leave the occupation, which leads to numerous job openings. Prospects should be best for applicants who have worked in a call center before because some companies prefer to hire collectors with this kind of experience. Unlike many other occupations, collections jobs usually remain stable during economic downturns. When the economy weakens, many consumers and businesses fall behind on their financial obligations, increasing the amount of debt to be collected.

However, the success rate of collectors decreases because fewer people can afford to pay their debts.

Locate and notify customers of delinquent accounts by mail, telephone, or personal visit to solicit payment. Receive payments, and post amounts paid to customer accounts. Locate and monitor overdue accounts, using computers and a variety of automated systems. Record information about financial status of customers and status of collection efforts. Confer with customers by telephone or in person to determine reasons for overdue payments and to review the terms of sales, service, or credit contracts. Advise customers of necessary actions and strategies for debt repayment. Persuade customers to pay amounts due on credit accounts, damage claims, or nonpayable checks or to return merchandise. Sort and file correspondence, and perform miscellaneous clerical duties such as answering correspondence and writing reports. Perform various administrative functions for assigned accounts, such as recording address changes and purging the records of deceased customers. Arrange for debt repayment, or establish repayment schedules based on customers' financial situations. Negotiate credit extensions when necessary. Trace delinquent customers to new addresses by inquiring at post offices, telephone companies, or credit bureaus or through the questioning of neighbors. Notify credit departments, order merchandise repossession or service disconnection, and turn over account records to attorneys when customers fail to respond to collection attempts.

Education/Training Required: High school diploma or equivalent. **Education and Training Program:** Banking and Financial Support Services. **Knowledge/Courses—Clerical Practices:** Administrative and clerical procedures and systems such as word processing, managing files and records, stenography and transcription, designing forms, and other office procedures and terminology. **Economics and Accounting:** Economic and accounting principles and practices, the financial markets, banking, and the analysis and reporting of financial data. **Customer and Personal Service:** Principles and processes for providing customer and personal services. This includes customer needs assessment, meeting quality standards for services, and evaluation of customer satisfaction. **Law and Government:** Laws, legal codes, court procedures, precedents, government regulations, executive orders, agency rules, and the democratic political process. **Computers and Electronics:** Circuit boards, processors, chips, electronic equipment, and computer hardware and software, including applications and programming. **Work Experience Needed:** None. **On-the-Job Training Needed:** Moderate-term on-the-job training. **Certification/Licensure:** None.

Personality Type: Conventional-Enterprising. **Career Cluster:** 06 Finance. **Career Pathway:** 06.3 Banking and Related Services. **Other Jobs in This Pathway:** Credit Analysts; Credit Authorizers; Credit Checkers; Loan Counselors; Loan Interviewers and Clerks; Loan Officers; New Accounts Clerks; Tellers; Title Examiners, Abstractors, and Searchers.

Skills—Persuasion: Persuading others to change their minds or behavior. **Negotiation:** Bringing others together and trying to reconcile differences. **Speaking:** Talking to others to convey information effectively. **Active Listening:** Giving full attention to what other people are saying, taking time to understand the points being made, asking questions as appropriate, and not interrupting at inappropriate times. **Social Perceptiveness:** Being aware of others' reactions and understanding why they react as they do. **Mathematics:** Using mathematics to solve problems. **Writing:** Communicating effectively in writing as appropriate for the needs of the audience. **Critical Thinking:** Using logic and reasoning to identify the strengths and weaknesses of alternative solutions, conclusions, or approaches to problems.

Work Environment: Indoors; sitting; using hands; repetitive motions; noise.

Billing and Posting Clerks

- ⊙ Annual Earnings: $32,880
- ⊙ Earnings Growth Potential: Low (31.0%)
- ⊙ Growth: 19.7%
- ⊙ Annual Job Openings: 18,760
- ⊙ Self-Employed: 2.3%

Considerations for Job Outlook: Job prospects for financial clerks should be favorable, because many workers are expected to leave this occupation. Employers will need to hire new workers to replace those leaving the occupation.

Compile, compute, and record billing, accounting, statistical, and other numerical data for billing purposes. For task data, see Job Specializations.

Education/Training Required: High school diploma or equivalent. **Work Experience Needed:** None. **On-the-Job Training Needed:** Short-term on-the-job training. **Certification/Licensure:** None.

Job Specialization: Billing, Cost, and Rate Clerks

Compile data, compute fees and charges, and prepare invoices for billing purposes. Duties include computing costs and calculating rates for goods, services, and shipment of goods; posting data; and keeping other relevant records. May involve use of computer or typewriter, calculator, and adding and bookkeeping machines. Verify accuracy of billing data, and revise any errors. Operate typing, adding, calculating, and billing machines. Prepare itemized statements, bills, or invoices, and record amounts due for items purchased or services rendered. Review documents such as purchase orders, sales tickets, charge slips, or hospital records to compute fees and charges due. Perform bookkeeping work, including posting data and keeping other records concerning costs of goods and services and the shipment of goods. Keep records of invoices and support documents. Resolve discrepancies in accounting records. Type billing documents, shipping labels, credit memoranda, and credit forms, using typewriters or computers. Contact customers to obtain or relay account information. Compute credit terms, discounts, shipment charges, and rates for goods and services to complete billing documents. Answer mail and telephone inquiries regarding rates, routing, and procedures. Track accumulated hours and dollar amounts charged to each client job to calculate client fees for professional services such as legal and accounting services. Review compiled data on operating costs and revenues to set rates. Compile reports of cost factors, such as labor, production, storage, and equipment. Consult sources such as rate books, manuals, and insurance company representatives to determine specific charges and information such as rules, regulations, and government tax and tariff information.

Education and Training Program: Accounting Technology/Technician and Bookkeeping. **Knowledge/Courses—Clerical Practices:** Administrative and clerical procedures and systems such as word processing, managing files and records, stenography and transcription, designing forms, and other office procedures and terminology. **Economics and Accounting:** Economic and accounting

principles and practices, the financial markets, banking, and the analysis and reporting of financial data. **Computers and Electronics:** Circuit boards, processors, chips, electronic equipment, and computer hardware and software, including applications and programming.

Personality Type: Conventional-Enterprising. **Career Cluster:** 04 Business, Management, and Administration. **Career Pathway:** 04.2 Business, Financial Management, and Accounting. **Other Jobs in This Pathway:** Accountants; Auditors; Bioinformatics Technicians; Bookkeeping, Accounting, and Auditing Clerks; Brokerage Clerks; Brownfield Redevelopment Specialists and Site Managers; Budget Analysts; Business Teachers, Postsecondary; Compliance Managers; Credit Analysts; Financial Analysts; Financial Examiners; Financial Managers, Branch or Department; Gaming Cage Workers; Investment Fund Managers; Logistics Managers; Loss Prevention Managers; Managers, All Other; Natural Sciences Managers; Payroll and Timekeeping Clerks; Regulatory Affairs Managers; Security Managers; Statement Clerks; Statistical Assistants; Statisticians; Supply Chain Managers; Tax Preparers; Treasurers and Controllers; Wind Energy Operations Managers; Wind Energy Project Managers.

Skills—Programming: Writing computer programs for various purposes. **Mathematics:** Using mathematics to solve problems. **Active Listening:** Giving full attention to what other people are saying, taking time to understand the points being made, asking questions as appropriate, and not interrupting at inappropriate times. **Service Orientation:** Actively looking for ways to help people.

Work Environment: Indoors; sitting.

Job Specialization: Statement Clerks

Prepare and distribute bank statements to customers, answer inquiries, and reconcile discrepancies in records and accounts. Encode and cancel checks, using bank machines. Take orders for imprinted checks. Compare previously prepared bank statements with canceled checks, and reconcile discrepancies. Verify signatures and required information on checks. Post stop-payment notices to prevent payment of protested checks. Maintain files of canceled checks and customers' signatures. Match statements with batches of canceled checks by account numbers. Weigh envelopes containing statements to determine correct postage, and affix postage using stamps or metering equipment. Load machines with statements, canceled checks, and envelopes to prepare statements for distribution to customers, or stuff envelopes by hand. Retrieve checks returned to customers in error, adjusting customer accounts and answering inquiries about errors as necessary. Route statements for mailing or over-the-counter delivery to customers. Monitor equipment to ensure proper operation. Fix minor problems, such as equipment jams, and notify repair personnel of major equipment problems.

Education and Training Program: Accounting Technology/Technician and Bookkeeping. **Knowledge/ Courses—Economics and Accounting:** Economic and accounting principles and practices, the financial markets, banking, and the analysis and reporting of financial data. **Clerical Practices:** Administrative and clerical procedures and systems such as word processing, managing files and records, stenography and transcription, designing forms, and other office procedures and terminology. **Administration and Management:** Business and management principles involved in strategic planning, resource allocation, human resources modeling, leadership technique, production methods, and coordination of people and resources.

Personality Type: Conventional-Enterprising-Social. **Career Cluster:** 04 Business, Management, and Administration. **Career Pathway:** 04.2 Business, Financial Management, and Accounting. **Other Jobs in This Pathway:** Accountants; Auditors; Billing, Cost, and Rate Clerks; Bioinformatics Technicians; Bookkeeping, Accounting, and Auditing Clerks; Brokerage Clerks; Brownfield Redevelopment Specialists and Site Managers; Budget Analysts; Business Teachers, Postsecondary; Compliance Managers; Credit Analysts; Financial Analysts; Financial Examiners; Financial Managers, Branch or Department; Gaming Cage Workers; Investment Fund Managers; Logistics Managers; Loss Prevention Managers; Managers, All Other; Natural Sciences Managers; Payroll and Timekeeping Clerks; Regulatory Affairs Managers; Security Managers; Statistical Assistants; Statisticians; Supply Chain Managers; Tax Preparers; Treasurers and Controllers; Wind Energy Operations Managers; Wind Energy Project Managers.

Skills—Programming: Writing computer programs for various purposes.

Work Environment: Indoors; sitting; repetitive motions.

Boilermakers

- ⊙ Annual Earnings: $56,910
- ⊙ Earnings Growth Potential: High (43.6%)
- ⊙ Growth: 21.2%
- ⊙ Annual Job Openings: 1,180
- ⊙ Self-Employed: 4.0%

Considerations for Job Outlook: Overall job prospects should be favorable because the work of a boilermaker remains hazardous and physically demanding, leading some qualified applicants to seek other types of work. Although employment growth will generate some job openings, the majority of positions will arise from the need to replace the large number of boilermakers expected to retire in the coming decade. People who have welding training or a welding certificate should have the best opportunities to be selected for boilermaker apprenticeship programs. As with many other construction workers, employment of boilermakers is sensitive to fluctuations of the economy. On the one hand, workers may experience periods of unemployment when the overall level of construction falls. On the other hand, shortages of workers may occur in some areas during peak periods of building activity. However, maintenance and repair of boilers must continue even during economic downturns, so boilermaker mechanics in manufacturing and other industries generally have more stable employment than those in construction.

Construct, assemble, maintain, and repair stationary steam boilers and boiler house auxiliaries. Examine boilers, pressure vessels, tanks, and vats to locate defects such as leaks, weak spots, and defective sections so that they can be repaired. Bolt or arc-weld pressure vessel structures and parts together, using wrenches and welding equipment. Inspect assembled vessels and individual components, such as tubes, fittings, valves, controls, and auxiliary mechanisms, to locate any defects. Repair or replace defective pressure vessel parts, such as safety valves and regulators, using torches, jacks, caulking hammers, power saws, threading dies, welding equipment, and metalworking machinery. Attach rigging and signal crane or hoist operators to lift heavy frame and plate sections and other parts into place. Bell, bead with power hammers, or weld pressure vessel tube ends in order to ensure leakproof joints. Lay out plate, sheet steel, or other heavy metal, and locate and mark bending and cutting lines, using protractors, compasses, and drawing instruments or templates. Install manholes, handholes, taps, tubes, valves, gauges, and feedwater connections in drums of water tube boilers, using hand tools. Study blueprints to determine locations, relationships, and dimensions of parts. Straighten or reshape bent pressure vessel plates and structure parts, using hammers, jacks, and torches.

Education/Training Required: High school diploma or equivalent. **Education and Training Program:** Boilermaking/Boilermaker. **Knowledge/Courses—Building and Construction:** Materials, methods, and the tools involved in the construction or repair of houses, buildings, or other structures such as highways and roads. **Mechanical Devices:** Machines and tools, including their designs, uses, repair, and maintenance. **Engineering and Technology:** The practical application of engineering science and technology. This includes applying principles, techniques, procedures, and equipment to the design and production of various goods and services. **Design:** Design techniques, tools, and principles involved in production of precision technical plans, blueprints, drawings, and models. **Physics:** Physical principles, laws, their interrelationships, and applications to understanding fluid, material, and atmospheric dynamics, and mechanical, electrical, atomic, and subatomic structures and processes. **Transportation:** Principles and methods for moving people or goods by air, rail, sea, or road, including the relative costs and benefits. **Work Experience Needed:** None. **On-the-Job Training Needed:** Apprenticeship. **Certification/Licensure:** Licensure in some states.

Personality Type: Realistic-Conventional. **Career Cluster:** 02 Architecture and Construction. **Career Pathway:** 02.2 Construction. **Other Jobs in This Pathway:** Brickmasons and Blockmasons; Carpet Installers; Cement Masons and Concrete Finishers; Construction and Building Inspectors; Construction and Related Workers, All Other; Construction Carpenters; Construction Laborers; Construction Managers; Continuous Mining Machine Operators; Cost Estimators; Crane and Tower Operators; Dredge Operators; Drywall and Ceiling Tile Installers; Earth Drillers, Except Oil and Gas; Electrical Power-Line Installers and Repairers; Electricians; Electromechanical Equipment Assemblers; Engineering Technicians, Except Drafters, All Other; Excavating and Loading Machine and Dragline Operators; Explosives Workers, Ordnance Handling Experts, and Blasters; Extraction Workers, All Other; First-Line Supervisors of Construction Trades and Extraction Workers; Floor Layers, Except Carpet, Wood, and Hard Tiles; Floor Sanders and Finishers; Glaziers; Heating and Air Conditioning Mechanics and Installers; Helpers, Construction Trades, All Other; others.

Skills—Repairing: Repairing machines or systems using the needed tools. **Equipment Maintenance:** Performing routine maintenance on equipment and determining when and what kind of maintenance is needed. **Operation and Control:** Controlling operations of equipment or systems. **Troubleshooting:** Determining causes of operating errors and deciding what to do about them. **Equipment Selection:** Determining the kind of tools and equipment needed to do a job. **Quality Control Analysis:** Conducting tests and inspections of products, services, or processes to evaluate quality or performance. **Operation Monitoring:** Watching gauges, dials, or other indicators to make sure a machine is working properly. **Installation:** Installing equipment, machines, wiring, or programs to meet specifications.

Work Environment: Outdoors; standing; using hands; noise; very hot or cold; bright or inadequate lighting; contaminants; cramped work space; high places; hazardous conditions; hazardous equipment; minor burns, cuts, bites, or stings.

Bookkeeping, Accounting, and Auditing Clerks

- ⊙ Annual Earnings: $34,740
- ⊙ Earnings Growth Potential: Medium (38.3%)
- ⊙ Growth: 13.6%
- ⊙ Annual Job Openings: 46,780
- ⊙ Self-Employed: 6.2%

Considerations for Job Outlook: Because this is a large occupation, there will be a large number of job openings from workers leaving the occupation. This means that opportunities to enter the occupation should be plentiful.

Compute, classify, and record numerical data to keep financial records complete. Operate computers programmed with accounting software to record, store, and analyze information. Check figures, postings, and documents for correct entry, mathematical accuracy, and proper codes. Comply with federal, state, and company policies, procedures, and regulations. Debit, credit, and total accounts on computer spreadsheets and databases, using specialized accounting software. Classify, record, and summarize numerical and financial data to compile and keep financial records, using journals and ledgers or computers. Calculate, prepare, and issue bills, invoices, account statements, and other financial statements according to established procedures. Code documents according to company procedures. Compile statistical, financial, accounting, or auditing reports and tables pertaining to such matters as cash receipts, expenditures, accounts payable and receivable, and profits and losses. Operate 10-key calculators, typewriters, and copy machines to perform calculations and produce documents. Access computerized financial information to answer general questions as well as those related to specific accounts. Reconcile or note and report discrepancies found in records. Perform financial calculations such as amounts due, interest charges, balances, discounts, equity, and principal. Perform general office duties such as filing, answering telephones, and handling routine correspondence.

Education/Training Required: High school diploma or equivalent. **Education and Training Programs:** Accounting and Related Services, Other; Accounting Technology/Technician and Bookkeeping. **Knowledge/Courses—Economics and Accounting:** Economic and accounting principles and practices, the financial markets, banking, and the analysis and reporting of financial data. **Clerical Practices:** Administrative and clerical procedures and systems such as word processing, managing files and records, stenography and transcription, designing forms, and other office procedures and terminology. **Mathematics:** Arithmetic, algebra, geometry, calculus, statistics, and their applications. **Computers and Electronics:** Circuit boards, processors, chips, electronic equipment, and computer hardware and software, including applications and programming. **Work Experience Needed:** None. **On-the-Job Training Needed:** Moderate-term on-the-job training. **Certification/Licensure:** None.

Personality Type: Conventional-Enterprising. **Career Cluster:** 04 Business, Management, and Administration. **Career Pathway:** 04.2 Business, Financial Management, and Accounting. **Other Jobs in This Pathway:** Accountants; Auditors; Billing, Cost, and Rate Clerks; Bioinformatics Technicians; Brokerage Clerks; Brownfield Redevelopment Specialists and Site Managers; Budget Analysts; Business Teachers, Postsecondary; Compliance Managers; Credit Analysts; Financial Analysts; Financial Examiners; Financial Managers, Branch or Department; Gaming Cage Workers; Investment Fund Managers; Logistics Managers; Loss Prevention Managers; Managers, All Other; Natural Sciences Managers; Payroll and Timekeeping Clerks; Regulatory Affairs Managers; Security Managers; Statement Clerks; Statistical Assistants; Statisticians; Supply Chain Managers; Tax Preparers; Treasurers and Controllers; Wind Energy Operations Managers; Wind Energy Project Managers.

Skills—Management of Financial Resources: Determining how money will be spent to get the work done and accounting for these expenditures. **Mathematics:** Using mathematics to solve problems. **Active Listening:** Giving full attention to what other people are saying, taking time to understand the points being made, asking questions as appropriate, and not interrupting at inappropriate times. **Reading Comprehension:** Understanding written sentences and paragraphs in work-related documents. **Time Management:** Managing one's own time and the time of others. **Writing:** Communicating effectively in writing as appropriate for the needs of the audience. **Speaking:** Talking to others to convey information effectively.

Work Environment: Indoors; sitting; using hands; repetitive motions.

Brickmasons and Blockmasons

- ⊙ Annual Earnings: $46,800
- ⊙ Earnings Growth Potential: Medium (38.1%)
- ⊙ Growth: 40.5%
- ⊙ Annual Job Openings: 5,450
- ⊙ Self-Employed: 28.6%

Considerations for Job Outlook: Overall job prospects should improve over the coming decade as construction activity rebounds from the recent recession. As with many other construction workers, employment is sensitive to the fluctuations of the economy. On the one hand, workers may experience periods of unemployment when the overall level of construction falls. On the other hand, shortages of workers may occur in some areas during peak periods of building activity. The masonry workforce is growing older, and a large number of masons are expected to retire over the next decade, which will create many job openings. Highly skilled masons with a good job history and work experience in construction should have the best job opportunities.

Lay and bind building materials, such as brick, structural tile, concrete block, cinder block, glass block, and terra-cotta block, with mortar and other substances. Construct corners by fastening in plumb position a corner pole or building a corner pyramid of bricks and filling in between the corners, using a line from corner to corner to guide each course, or layer, of brick. Measure the distance from reference points and mark guidelines to lay out work, using plumb bobs and levels. Fasten or fuse brick or other building materials to structures with wire clamps, anchor holes, torches, or cement. Calculate angles and courses, and determine vertical and horizontal alignment of courses. Break or cut bricks, tiles, or blocks to size, using trowel edges, hammers, or power saws. Remove excess mortar with trowels and hand tools and finish mortar joints with jointing tools for a sealed, uniform appearance. Interpret blueprints and drawings to determine specifications and to calculate the materials required. Apply and smooth mortar or other mixtures over work surface. Mix specified amounts of sand, clay, dirt, or mortar powder with water to form refractory mixtures. Examine brickwork or structures to determine needs for repair. Clean working surfaces to remove scale, dust, soot, or chips of brick and mortar, using brooms, wire brushes, or scrapers. Lay and align bricks, blocks, or tiles to build or repair structures or high-temperature equipment, such as cupolas, kilns, ovens, or furnaces. Remove burned or damaged brick or mortar, using sledgehammers, crowbars, chipping guns, or chisels.

Education/Training Required: High school diploma or equivalent. **Education and Training Program:** Masonry/Mason Training. **Knowledge/Courses—Building and Construction:** Materials, methods, and the tools involved in the construction or repair of houses, buildings, or other structures such as highways and roads. **Design:** Design techniques, tools, and principles involved in production of precision technical plans, blueprints, drawings, and models. **Engineering and Technology:** The practical application of engineering science and technology. This includes applying principles, techniques, procedures, and equipment to the design and production of various goods and services. **Production and Processing:** Raw materials, production processes, quality control, costs, and other techniques for maximizing the effective manufacture and distribution of goods. **Physics:** Physical principles, laws, their interrelationships, and applications to understanding fluid, material, and atmospheric dynamics, and mechanical, electrical, atomic, and subatomic structures and processes. **Public Safety and Security:** Relevant equipment, policies, procedures, and strategies to promote effective local, state, or national security operations for the protection of people, data, property, and institutions. **Work Experience Needed:** None. **On-the-Job Training Needed:** Apprenticeship. **Certification/Licensure:** None.

Personality Type: Realistic-Conventional-Investigative. **Career Cluster:** 02 Architecture and Construction. **Career Pathway:** 02.2 Construction. **Other Jobs in This Pathway:** Boilermakers; Carpet Installers; Cement Masons and Concrete Finishers; Construction and Building Inspectors; Construction and Related Workers, All Other; Construction Carpenters; Construction Laborers; Construction Managers; Continuous Mining Machine Operators; Cost Estimators; Crane and Tower Operators; Dredge Operators; Drywall and Ceiling Tile Installers; Earth Drillers, Except Oil and Gas; Electrical Power-Line Installers and Repairers; Electricians; Electromechanical Equipment Assemblers; Engineering Technicians, Except Drafters, All Other; Excavating and Loading Machine and Dragline Operators; Explosives Workers, Ordnance Handling Experts, and Blasters; Extraction Workers, All Other; First-Line Supervisors of Construction Trades and Extraction Workers; Floor Layers, Except Carpet, Wood, and Hard Tiles; Floor Sanders and Finishers; Glaziers; Heating and Air Conditioning Mechanics and Installers; Helpers, Construction Trades, All Other; others.

Skills—Repairing: Repairing machines or systems using the needed tools. **Mathematics:** Using mathematics to solve problems. **Equipment Maintenance:** Performing routine maintenance on equipment and determining when and what kind of maintenance is needed. **Equipment Selection:** Determining the kind of tools and equipment needed to do a job. **Quality Control Analysis:** Conducting tests and inspections of products, services, or processes to evaluate quality or performance. **Operation and Control:** Controlling operations of equipment or systems. **Management of Material Resources:** Obtaining and seeing to the appropriate use of equipment, facilities, and materials needed to do certain work. **Troubleshooting:**

Determining causes of operating errors and deciding what to do about them.

Work Environment: Outdoors; standing; walking and running; using hands; bending or twisting the body; repetitive motions; noise; very hot or cold; contaminants; cramped work space; high places; hazardous equipment; minor burns, cuts, bites, or stings.

Broadcast Technicians

- ⊙ Annual Earnings: $36,570
- ⊙ Earnings Growth Potential: High (49.6%)
- ⊙ Growth: 9.0%
- ⊙ Annual Job Openings: 1,380
- ⊙ Self-Employed: 14.5%

Considerations for Job Outlook: Competition for jobs will be strong. This occupation attracts many applicants who are interested in working with the latest technology and electronic equipment. Many applicants also are attracted to working in the radio and television industry. Those looking for work in this industry will have the most job opportunities in smaller markets or stations. Those with hands-on experience with electronics or with work experience at a radio or television station will have the best job prospects. In addition, technicians are expected to be versatile and contribute to the setup, operation, and maintenance of equipment, whereas previously technicians typically specialized in one area.

Set up, operate, and maintain the electronic equipment used to transmit radio and television programs. Control audio equipment to regulate the volume and sound quality during radio and television broadcasts. Monitor strength, clarity, and reliability of incoming and outgoing signals, and adjust equipment as necessary to maintain quality broadcasts. Observe monitors and converse with station personnel to determine audio and video levels and to ascertain that programs are airing. Report equipment problems, ensure that repairs are made, and make emergency repairs to equipment when necessary and possible. Align antennae with receiving dishes to obtain the clearest signal for transmission of broadcasts from field locations. Monitor and log transmitter readings. Play and record broadcast programs using automation systems.

Education/Training Required: Associate degree. **Education and Training Programs:** Audiovisual Communications Technologies/Technicians, Other; Communications Technology/Technician; Radio and Television Broadcasting Technology/Technician. **Knowledge/Courses—Telecommunications:** Transmission, broadcasting, switching, control, and operation of telecommunications systems. **Communications and Media:** Media production, communication, and dissemination techniques and methods. This includes alternative ways to inform and entertain via written, oral, and visual media. **Engineering and Technology:** The practical application of engineering science and technology. This includes applying principles, techniques, procedures, and equipment to the design and production of various goods and services. **Computers and Electronics:** Circuit boards, processors, chips, electronic equipment, and computer hardware and software, including applications and programming. **Mechanical Devices:** Machines and tools, including their designs, uses, repair, and maintenance. **Production and Processing:** Raw materials, production processes, quality control, costs, and other techniques for maximizing the effective manufacture and distribution of goods. **Work Experience Needed:** None. **On-the-Job Training Needed:** Short-term on-the-job training. **Certification/Licensure:** Voluntary certification by association.

Personality Type: Realistic-Conventional-Investigative. **Career Cluster:** 03 Arts and Communications. **Career Pathways:** 03.6 Telecommunications; 03.1 Audio and Video Technology and Film; 03.5 Journalism and Broadcasting. **Other Jobs in These Pathways:** Agents and Business Managers of Artists, Performers, and Athletes; Archivists; Art, Drama, and Music Teachers, Postsecondary; Artists and Related Workers, All Other; Audio and Video Equipment Technicians; Broadcast News Analysts; Camera Operators, Television, Video, and Motion Picture; Choreographers; Commercial and Industrial Designers; Communications Equipment Operators, All Other; Communications Teachers, Postsecondary; Copy Writers; Craft Artists; Curators; Dancers; Directors—Stage, Motion Pictures, Television, and Radio; Editors; Electronic Home Entertainment Equipment Installers and Repairers; English Language and Literature Teachers, Postsecondary; Film and Video Editors; Fine Artists, Including Painters, Sculptors, and Illustrators; Graphic Designers; Historians; Managers, All Other; Media and Communication Equipment Workers, All Other; Media and Communication

Workers, All Other; Multimedia Artists and Animators; Museum Technicians and Conservators; Photographers; others.

Skills—Equipment Selection: Determining the kind of tools and equipment needed to do a job. **Installation:** Installing equipment, machines, wiring, or programs to meet specifications. **Repairing:** Repairing machines or systems using the needed tools. **Equipment Maintenance:** Performing routine maintenance on equipment and determining when and what kind of maintenance is needed. **Troubleshooting:** Determining causes of operating errors and deciding what to do about them. **Operation Monitoring:** Watching gauges, dials, or other indicators to make sure a machine is working properly. **Quality Control Analysis:** Conducting tests and inspections of products, services, or processes to evaluate quality or performance. **Technology Design:** Generating or adapting equipment and technology to serve user needs.

Work Environment: Indoors; sitting; using hands.

Brokerage Clerks

- Annual Earnings: $41,760
- Earnings Growth Potential: Low (33.3%)
- Growth: 5.9%
- Annual Job Openings: 1,970
- Self-Employed: 0.0%

Considerations for Job Outlook: Job prospects for financial clerks should be favorable, because many workers are expected to leave this occupation. Employers will need to hire new workers to replace those leaving the occupation.

Perform duties related to the purchase, sale, or holding of securities. Correspond with customers and confer with coworkers in order to answer inquiries, discuss market fluctuations, and resolve account problems. Record and document security transactions, such as purchases, sales, conversions, redemptions, and payments, using computers, accounting ledgers, and certificate records. Schedule and coordinate transfer and delivery of security certificates between companies, departments, and customers. Prepare forms, such as receipts, withdrawal orders, transmittal papers, and transfer confirmations, based on transaction requests from stockholders. File, type, and operate standard office machines. Monitor daily stock prices, and compute fluctuations in order to determine the need for additional collateral to secure loans. Prepare reports summarizing daily transactions and earnings for individual customer accounts. Compute total holdings, dividends, interest, transfer taxes, brokerage fees, and commissions, and allocate appropriate payments to customers. Verify ownership and transaction information and dividend distribution instructions to ensure conformance with governmental regulations, using stock records and reports.

Education/Training Required: High school diploma or equivalent. **Education and Training Program:** Accounting Technology/Technician and Bookkeeping. **Knowledge/Courses—Economics and Accounting:** Economic and accounting principles and practices, the financial markets, banking, and the analysis and reporting of financial data. **Clerical Practices:** Administrative and clerical procedures and systems such as word processing, managing files and records, stenography and transcription, designing forms, and other office procedures and terminology. **Customer and Personal Service:** Principles and processes for providing customer and personal services. This includes customer needs assessment, meeting quality standards for services, and evaluation of customer satisfaction. **Sales and Marketing:** Principles and methods for showing, promoting, and selling products or services. This includes marketing strategy and tactics, product demonstration, sales techniques, and sales control systems. **Mathematics:** Arithmetic, algebra, geometry, calculus, statistics, and their applications. **Computers and Electronics:** Circuit boards, processors, chips, electronic equipment, and computer hardware and software, including applications and programming. **Work Experience Needed:** None. **On-the-Job Training Needed:** Moderate-term on-the-job training. **Certification/Licensure:** None.

Personality Type: Conventional-Enterprising. **Career Cluster:** 04 Business, Management, and Administration. **Career Pathway:** 04.2 Business, Financial Management, and Accounting. **Other Jobs in This Pathway:** Accountants; Auditors; Billing, Cost, and Rate Clerks; Bioinformatics Technicians; Bookkeeping, Accounting, and Auditing Clerks; Brownfield Redevelopment Specialists and Site Managers; Budget Analysts; Business Teachers, Postsecondary; Compliance Managers; Credit Analysts; Financial Analysts; Financial Examiners; Financial Managers, Branch or Department; Gaming Cage Workers; Investment Fund Managers; Logistics Managers; Loss

Prevention Managers; Managers, All Other; Natural Sciences Managers; Payroll and Timekeeping Clerks; Regulatory Affairs Managers; Security Managers; Statement Clerks; Statistical Assistants; Statisticians; Supply Chain Managers; Tax Preparers; Treasurers and Controllers; Wind Energy Operations Managers; Wind Energy Project Managers.

Skills—Mathematics: Using mathematics to solve problems. **Programming:** Writing computer programs for various purposes. **Active Listening:** Giving full attention to what other people are saying, taking time to understand the points being made, asking questions as appropriate, and not interrupting at inappropriate times. **Service Orientation:** Actively looking for ways to help people. **Reading Comprehension:** Understanding written sentences and paragraphs in work-related documents. **Writing:** Communicating effectively in writing as appropriate for the needs of the audience. **Speaking:** Talking to others to convey information effectively. **Active Learning:** Understanding the implications of new information for both current and future problem solving and decision making.

Work Environment: Indoors; sitting; repetitive motions.

Bus and Truck Mechanics and Diesel Engine Specialists

- ⊙ Annual Earnings: $41,640
- ⊙ Earnings Growth Potential: Medium (36.4%)
- ⊙ Growth: 14.5%
- ⊙ Annual Job Openings: 8,780
- ⊙ Self-Employed: 7.5%

Considerations for Job Outlook: Job opportunities should be good for those who have completed formal post-secondary education and have strong technical skills, as employers sometimes report difficulty finding qualified workers. Workers without formal training often require more supervision and on-the-job instruction than others—an expensive and time-consuming process for employers. Because of this, untrained candidates will face strong competition for jobs.

Diagnose, adjust, repair, or overhaul buses and trucks, or maintain and repair any type of diesel engines. Use hand tools such as screwdrivers, pliers, wrenches, pressure gauges, and precision instruments, as well as power tools such as pneumatic wrenches, lathes, welding equipment, and jacks and hoists. Inspect brake systems, steering mechanisms, wheel bearings, and other important parts to ensure that they are in proper operating condition. Adjust and reline brakes, align wheels, tighten bolts and screws, and reassemble equipment. Raise trucks, buses, and heavy parts or equipment using hydraulic jacks or hoists. Perform routine maintenance such as changing oil, checking batteries, and lubricating equipment and machinery. Test drive trucks and buses to diagnose malfunctions or to ensure that they are working properly. Examine and adjust protective guards, loose bolts, and specified safety devices. Attach test instruments to equipment, and read dials and gauges to diagnose malfunctions. Inspect, test, and listen to defective equipment to diagnose malfunctions, using test instruments such as handheld computers, motor analyzers, chassis charts, and pressure gauges. Inspect, repair, and maintain automotive and mechanical equipment and machinery such as pumps and compressors. Rewire ignition systems, lights, and instrument panels. Diagnose and repair vehicle heating and cooling systems. Recondition and replace parts, pistons, bearings, gears, and valves. Inspect and verify dimensions and clearances of parts to ensure conformance to factory specifications. Disassemble and overhaul internal combustion engines, pumps, generators, transmissions, clutches, and differential units. Specialize in repairing and maintaining parts of the engine, such as fuel injection systems. Repair and adjust seats, doors, and windows, and install and repair accessories. Rebuild gas or diesel engines. Align front ends and suspension systems. Operate valve-grinding machines to grind and reset valves.

Education/Training Required: High school diploma or equivalent. **Education and Training Programs:** Diesel Mechanics Technology/Technician; Medium/Heavy Vehicle and Truck Technology/Technician. **Knowledge/Courses—Mechanical Devices:** Machines and tools, including their designs, uses, repair, and maintenance. **Transportation:** Principles and methods for moving people or goods by air, rail, sea, or road, including the relative costs and benefits. **Physics:** Physical principles, laws, their interrelationships, and applications to understanding fluid, material, and atmospheric dynamics, and mechanical, electrical, atomic, and subatomic structures and processes. **Public Safety and Security:** Relevant equipment, policies, procedures, and strategies to promote effective local, state, or national security operations for the protection of people, data, property, and institutions. **Engineering and Technology:** The practical application of engineering science and technology. This includes applying principles, techniques, procedures, and equipment to the design and production of various goods and services. **Mathematics:** Arithmetic, algebra, geometry, calculus, statistics, and their applications. **Work Experience Needed:** None. **On-the-Job Training Needed:** Long-term on-the-job training. **Certification/ Licensure:** Voluntary certification by association.

Personality Type: Realistic-Conventional. **Career Cluster:** 16 Transportation, Distribution, and Logistics. **Career Pathway:** 16.4 Facility and Mobile Equipment Maintenance. **Other Jobs in This Pathway:** Aircraft Mechanics and Service Technicians; Aircraft Structure, Surfaces, Rigging, and Systems Assemblers; Automotive Body and Related Repairers; Automotive Glass Installers and Repairers; Automotive Master Mechanics; Automotive Specialty Technicians; Bicycle Repairers; Cleaners of Vehicles and Equipment; Electrical and Electronics Installers and Repairers, Transportation Equipment; Electronic Equipment Installers and Repairers, Motor Vehicles; Engine and Other Machine Assemblers; Gem and Diamond Workers; Installation, Maintenance, and Repair Workers, All Other; Motorboat Mechanics and Service Technicians; Motorcycle Mechanics; Outdoor Power Equipment and Other Small Engine Mechanics; Painters, Transportation Equipment.

Skills—Repairing: Repairing machines or systems using the needed tools. **Equipment Maintenance:** Performing routine maintenance on equipment and determining when and what kind of maintenance is needed. **Troubleshooting:** Determining causes of operating errors and deciding what to do about them. **Equipment Selection:** Determining the kind of tools and equipment needed to do a job. **Operation and Control:** Controlling operations of equipment or systems. **Quality Control Analysis:** Conducting tests and inspections of products, services, or processes to evaluate quality or performance. **Operation Monitoring:** Watching gauges, dials, or other indicators to make sure a machine is working properly. **Installation:** Installing equipment, machines, wiring, or programs to meet specifications.

Work Environment: Outdoors; standing; walking and running; kneeling, crouching, stooping, or crawling; using hands; bending or twisting the body; repetitive motions; noise; very hot or cold; bright or inadequate lighting; contaminants; cramped work space; hazardous conditions; hazardous equipment; minor burns, cuts, bites, or stings.

Bus Drivers, School or Special Client

- ⊙ Annual Earnings: $28,110
- ⊙ Earnings Growth Potential: Medium (37.4%)
- ⊙ Growth: 12.0%
- ⊙ Annual Job Openings: 14,450
- ⊙ Self-Employed: 1.2%

Considerations for Job Outlook: Job opportunities for bus drivers should be favorable, especially for school bus drivers, as many drivers leave the occupation. Those willing to work part time or irregular shifts should have the best prospects. Prospects for motor coach drivers will depend on tourism, which fluctuates with the economy.

Transport students or special clients, such as the elderly or persons with disabilities. Follow safety rules as students board and exit buses or cross streets near bus stops. Comply with traffic regulations to operate vehicles in a safe and courteous manner. Check the condition of a vehicle's tires, brakes, windshield wipers, lights, oil, fuel, water, and safety equipment to ensure that everything is in working order. Maintain order among pupils during trips to ensure safety. Pick up and drop off students at regularly scheduled neighborhood locations, following strict time schedules. Report any bus malfunctions or needed repairs. Drive gasoline, diesel, or electrically powered multipassenger vehicles to transport students between neighborhoods, schools, and school activities. Prepare and submit reports that may include the number of passengers or trips, hours worked, mileage, fuel consumption, or fares received. Maintain knowledge of first-aid procedures. Keep bus interiors clean for passengers. Read maps and follow written and verbal geographic directions. Report delays, accidents, or other traffic and transportation situations, using telephones or mobile two-way radios. Regulate heating, lighting, and ventilation systems for passenger comfort. Escort small children across roads and highways. Make minor repairs to vehicles.

Education/Training Required: High school diploma or equivalent. **Education and Training Program:** Truck and Bus Driver Training/Commercial Vehicle Operator and Instructor Training. **Knowledge/Courses—Transportation:** Principles and methods for moving people or goods by air, rail, sea, or road, including the relative costs and benefits. **Public Safety and Security:** Relevant equipment, policies, procedures, and strategies to promote effective local, state, or national security operations for the protection of people, data, property, and institutions. **Psychology:** Human behavior and performance; individual differences in ability, personality, and interests; learning and motivation; psychological research methods; and the assessment and treatment of behavioral and affective disorders. **Work Experience Needed:** None. **On-the-Job Training Needed:** Moderate-term on-the-job training. **Certification/Licensure:** Licensure.

Personality Type: Realistic-Conventional. **Career Cluster:** 16 Transportation, Distribution, and Logistics. **Career Pathway:** 16.1 Transportation Operations. **Other Jobs in This Pathway:** Aerospace Engineering and Operations Technicians; Air Traffic Controllers; Aircraft Cargo Handling Supervisors; Airfield Operations Specialists; Airline Pilots, Copilots, and Flight Engineers; Automotive and Watercraft Service Attendants; Automotive Master Mechanics; Aviation Inspectors; Bridge and Lock Tenders; Bus Drivers, Transit and Intercity; Commercial Divers; Commercial Pilots; Crane and Tower Operators; First-Line Supervisors of Helpers, Laborers, and Material Movers, Hand; First-Line Supervisors of Transportation and Material-Moving Machine and Vehicle Operators; Freight and Cargo Inspectors; Heavy and Tractor-Trailer Truck Drivers; Hoist and Winch Operators; Laborers and Freight, Stock, and Material Movers, Hand; Light Truck or Delivery Services Drivers; Mates—Ship, Boat, and Barge; Motor Vehicle Operators, All Other; Motorboat Operators; Operating Engineers and Other Construction Equipment Operators; Parking Lot Attendants; Pilots, Ship; others.

Skills—Repairing: Repairing machines or systems using the needed tools. **Equipment Maintenance:** Performing routine maintenance on equipment and determining when and what kind of maintenance is needed. **Operation and Control:** Controlling operations of equipment or systems. **Troubleshooting:** Determining causes of operating errors and deciding what to do about them. **Equipment Selection:** Determining the kind of tools and equipment needed to do a job. **Operation Monitoring:** Watching gauges, dials, or other indicators to make sure a machine is

working properly. **Quality Control Analysis:** Conducting tests and inspections of products, services, or processes to evaluate quality or performance.

Work Environment: Outdoors; sitting; using hands; noise; contaminants; exposed to disease or infections.

Bus Drivers, Transit and Intercity

- ⊙ Annual Earnings: $35,720
- ⊙ Earnings Growth Potential: High (41.0%)
- ⊙ Growth: 14.8%
- ⊙ Annual Job Openings: 6,350
- ⊙ Self-Employed: 1.2%

Considerations for Job Outlook: Job opportunities for bus drivers should be favorable, as many drivers leave the occupation. Those willing to work part time or irregular shifts should have the best prospects. Prospects for motor coach drivers will depend on tourism, which fluctuates with the economy.

Drive a bus or motor coach, including regular route operations, charters, and private carriage. Inspect vehicles, and check gas, oil, and water levels prior to departure. Park vehicles at loading areas so that passengers can board. Report delays or accidents. Advise passengers to be seated and orderly while on vehicles. Regulate heating, lighting, and ventilating systems for passenger comfort. Drive vehicles over specified routes or to specified destinations according to time schedules, complying with traffic regulations to ensure that passengers have a smooth and safe ride. Assist passengers, such as elderly or disabled individuals, on and off the bus, ensure they are seated properly, help carry baggage, and answer questions about bus schedules or routes. Handle passenger emergencies or disruptions. Record information, such as cash receipts and ticket fares, and maintain a log book. Collect tickets or cash fares from passengers. Maintain cleanliness of the bus or motor coach.

Education/Training Required: High school diploma or equivalent. **Education and Training Program:** Truck and Bus Driver Training/Commercial Vehicle Operator and Instructor Training. **Knowledge/Courses—Transportation:** Principles and methods for moving people or goods by air, rail, sea, or road, including the relative costs and benefits. **Public Safety and Security:** Relevant equipment, policies, procedures, and strategies to promote effective local, state, or national security operations for the protection of people, data, property, and institutions. **Geography:** Principles and methods for describing the features of land, sea, and air masses, including their physical characteristics, locations, interrelationships, and distribution of plant, animal, and human life. **Psychology:** Human behavior and performance; individual differences in ability, personality, and interests; learning and motivation; psychological research methods; and the assessment and treatment of behavioral and affective disorders. **Telecommunications:** Transmission, broadcasting, switching, control, and operation of telecommunications systems. **Customer and Personal Service:** Principles and processes for providing customer and personal services. This includes customer needs assessment, meeting quality standards for services, and evaluation of customer satisfaction. **Work Experience Needed:** None. **On-the-Job Training Needed:** Moderate-term on-the-job training. **Certification/Licensure:** Licensure.

Personality Type: Realistic-Social. **Career Cluster:** 16 Transportation, Distribution, and Logistics. **Career Pathway:** 16.1 Transportation Operations. **Other Jobs in This Pathway:** Aerospace Engineering and Operations Technicians; Air Traffic Controllers; Aircraft Cargo Handling Supervisors; Airfield Operations Specialists; Airline Pilots, Copilots, and Flight Engineers; Automotive and Watercraft Service Attendants; Automotive Master Mechanics; Aviation Inspectors; Bridge and Lock Tenders; Bus Drivers, School or Special Client; Commercial Divers; Commercial Pilots; Crane and Tower Operators; First-Line Supervisors of Helpers, Laborers, and Material Movers, Hand; First-Line Supervisors of Transportation and Material-Moving Machine and Vehicle Operators; Freight and Cargo Inspectors; Heavy and Tractor-Trailer Truck Drivers; Hoist and Winch Operators; Laborers and Freight, Stock, and Material Movers, Hand; Light Truck or Delivery Services Drivers; Mates—Ship, Boat, and Barge; Motor Vehicle Operators, All Other; Motorboat Operators; Operating Engineers and Other Construction Equipment Operators; Parking Lot Attendants; Pilots, Ship; others.

Skills—Operation and Control: Controlling operations of equipment or systems. **Operation Monitoring:** Watching gauges, dials, or other indicators to make sure a machine is working properly. **Troubleshooting:** Determining causes of operating errors and deciding what to do about them. **Equipment Maintenance:** Performing routine maintenance on equipment and determining when and what kind of maintenance is needed. **Repairing:** Repairing machines or systems using the needed tools.

Work Environment: Outdoors; sitting; using hands; repetitive motions; noise; very hot or cold; bright or inadequate lighting; contaminants; exposed to disease or infections.

Business Operations Specialists, All Other

- ⊙ Annual Earnings: $64,030
- ⊙ Earnings Growth Potential: High (46.5%)
- ⊙ Growth: 11.6%
- ⊙ Annual Job Openings: 32,720
- ⊙ Self-Employed: 0.4%

Considerations for Job Outlook: In federal government, a small increase is expected as positions with specialized titles in areas such as defense and energy increase.

All business operations specialists not listed separately. For task data, see Job Specializations.

Education/Training Required: High school diploma or equivalent. **Education and Training Program:** Business Administration and Management, General. **Work Experience Needed:** Less than 1 year. **On-the-Job Training Needed:** Long-term on-the-job training. **Certification/Licensure:** Licensure for some specializations; voluntary certification by association. **Career Cluster:** 04 Business, Management, and Administration. **Career Pathway:** 04.1 Management. **Other Jobs in This Pathway:** Administrative Services Managers; Agents and Business Managers of Artists, Performers, and Athletes; Biofuels Production Managers; Biomass Power Plant Managers; Brownfield Redevelopment Specialists and Site Managers; Business Continuity Planners; Business Teachers, Postsecondary; Chief Executives; Chief Sustainability Officers; Communications Teachers, Postsecondary; Compliance Managers; Computer and Information Systems Managers; Construction Managers; Cost Estimators; Customs Brokers; Economics Teachers, Postsecondary; Economists; Energy Auditors; Environmental Economists; First-Line Supervisors of Office and Administrative Support Workers; First-Line Supervisors of Personal Service Workers; Gaming Supervisors; General and Operations Managers;

Geothermal Production Managers; Hydroelectric Production Managers; Industrial Production Managers; Investment Fund Managers; Logisticians; Logistics Analysts; Logistics Engineers; Logistics Managers; Loss Prevention Managers; others.

Job Specialization: Business Continuity Planners

Develop, maintain, and implement business continuity and disaster recovery strategies and solutions. Perform risk analyses. Act as a coordinator for recovery efforts in emergency situations. Write reports to summarize testing activities, including descriptions of goals, planning, scheduling, execution, results, analysis, conclusions, and recommendations. Maintain and update organization information technology applications and network systems blueprints. Interpret government regulations and applicable codes to ensure compliance. Identify individual or transaction targets to direct intelligence collection. Establish, maintain, or test call trees to ensure appropriate communication during disaster. Design or implement products and services to mitigate risk, or facilitate use of technology-based tools and methods. Create business continuity and disaster recovery budgets. Create or administer training and awareness presentations or materials. Attend professional meetings, read literature, and participate in training or other educational offerings to keep abreast of new developments and technologies related to disaster recovery and business continuity. Test documented disaster recovery strategies and plans. Review existing disaster recovery, crisis management, or business continuity plans. Recommend or implement methods to monitor, evaluate, or enable resolution of safety, operations, or compliance interruptions. Prepare reports summarizing operational results, financial performance, or accomplishments of specified objectives, goals, or plans.

Education and Training Program: Business Administration and Management, General. **Knowledge/Courses— Public Safety and Security:** Relevant equipment, policies, procedures, and strategies to promote effective local, state, or national security operations for the protection of people, data, property, and institutions. **Telecommunications:** Transmission, broadcasting, switching, control, and operation of telecommunications systems. **Administration and Management:** Business and management principles involved in strategic planning, resource allocation,

human resources modeling, leadership technique, production methods, and coordination of people and resources. **Communications and Media:** Media production, communication, and dissemination techniques and methods. This includes alternative ways to inform and entertain via written, oral, and visual media. **Geography:** Principles and methods for describing the features of land, sea, and air masses, including their physical characteristics, locations, interrelationships, and distribution of plant, animal, and human life. **Economics and Accounting:** Economic and accounting principles and practices, the financial markets, banking, and the analysis and reporting of financial data.

Personality Type: No data available. **Career Cluster:** 04 Business, Management, and Administration. **Career Pathway:** 04.1 Management. **Other Jobs in This Pathway:** Administrative Services Managers; Agents and Business Managers of Artists, Performers, and Athletes; Biofuels Production Managers; Biomass Power Plant Managers; Brownfield Redevelopment Specialists and Site Managers; Business Operations Specialists, All Other; Business Teachers, Postsecondary; Chief Executives; Chief Sustainability Officers; Communications Teachers, Postsecondary; Compliance Managers; Computer and Information Systems Managers; Construction Managers; Cost Estimators; Customs Brokers; Economics Teachers, Postsecondary; Economists; Energy Auditors; Environmental Economists; First-Line Supervisors of Office and Administrative Support Workers; First-Line Supervisors of Personal Service Workers; Gaming Supervisors; General and Operations Managers; Geothermal Production Managers; Hydroelectric Production Managers; Industrial Production Managers; Investment Fund Managers; Logisticians; Logistics Analysts; Logistics Engineers; Logistics Managers; Loss Prevention Managers; others.

Skills—Management of Financial Resources: Determining how money will be spent to get the work done and accounting for these expenditures. **Management of Material Resources:** Obtaining and seeing to the appropriate use of equipment, facilities, and materials needed to do certain work. **Complex Problem Solving:** Identifying complex problems and reviewing related information to develop and evaluate options and implement solutions. **Systems Analysis:** Determining how a system should work and how changes in conditions, operations, and the environment will affect outcomes. **Systems Evaluation:** Identifying measures or indicators of system performance and the actions needed to improve or correct performance relative to the goals of the system. **Judgment and Decision Making:** Considering the relative costs and benefits of potential actions to choose the most appropriate one. **Operations Analysis:** Analyzing needs and product requirements to create a design. **Critical Thinking:** Using logic and reasoning to identify the strengths and weaknesses of alternative solutions, conclusions, or approaches to problems.

Work Environment: Indoors; sitting.

Job Specialization: Customs Brokers

Prepare customs documentation and ensure that shipments meet all applicable laws to facilitate the import and export of goods. Determine and track duties and taxes payable and process payments on behalf of client. Sign documents under a power of attorney. Represent clients in meetings with customs officials and apply for duty refunds and tariff reclassifications. Coordinate transportation and storage of imported goods. Sign documents on behalf of clients, using powers of attorney. Provide advice on transportation options, types of carriers, or shipping routes. Post bonds for the products being imported, or assist clients in obtaining bonds. Insure cargo against loss, damage, or pilferage. Obtain line releases for frequent shippers of low-risk commodities, high-volume entries, or multiple-container loads. Contract with freight forwarders for destination services. Arrange for transportation, warehousing, or product distribution of imported or exported products. Suggest best methods of packaging or labeling products. Request or compile necessary import documentation, such as customs invoices, certificates of origin, and cargo-control documents. Stay abreast of changes in import or export laws or regulations by reading current literature, attending meetings or conferences, or conferring with colleagues. Quote duty and tax rates on goods to be imported, based on federal tariffs and excise taxes. Prepare papers for shippers to appeal duty charges. Pay, or arrange for payment of, taxes and duties on shipments. Monitor or trace the location of goods. Maintain relationships with customs brokers in other ports to expedite the clearing of cargo. Inform importers and exporters of steps to reduce duties and taxes. Confer with officials in various agencies to facilitate the clearance of goods through customs and quarantine. Classify goods according to tariff coding system.

Education and Training Program: Traffic, Customs, and Transportation Clerk/Technician Training. **Knowledge/Courses—Clerical Practices:** Administrative and clerical procedures and systems such as word processing, managing files and records, stenography and transcription, designing forms, and other office procedures and terminology. **Geography:** Principles and methods for describing the features of land, sea, and air masses, including their physical characteristics, locations, interrelationships, and distribution of plant, animal, and human life. **Transportation:** Principles and methods for moving people or goods by air, rail, sea, or road, including the relative costs and benefits. **Sales and Marketing:** Principles and methods for showing, promoting, and selling products or services. This includes marketing strategy and tactics, product demonstration, sales techniques, and sales control systems. **Law and Government:** Laws, legal codes, court procedures, precedents, government regulations, executive orders, agency rules, and the democratic political process. **Economics and Accounting:** Economic and accounting principles and practices, the financial markets, banking, and the analysis and reporting of financial data.

Personality Type: Enterprising-Conventional. **Career Cluster:** 04 Business, Management, and Administration. **Career Pathway:** 04.1 Management. **Other Jobs in This Pathway:** Administrative Services Managers; Agents and Business Managers of Artists, Performers, and Athletes; Biofuels Production Managers; Biomass Power Plant Managers; Brownfield Redevelopment Specialists and Site Managers; Business Continuity Planners; Business Operations Specialists, All Other; Business Teachers, Postsecondary; Chief Executives; Chief Sustainability Officers; Communications Teachers, Postsecondary; Compliance Managers; Computer and Information Systems Managers; Construction Managers; Cost Estimators; Economics Teachers, Postsecondary; Economists; Energy Auditors; Environmental Economists; First-Line Supervisors of Office and Administrative Support Workers; First-Line Supervisors of Personal Service Workers; Gaming Supervisors; General and Operations Managers; Geothermal Production Managers; Hydroelectric Production Managers; Industrial Production Managers; Investment Fund Managers; Logisticians; Logistics Analysts; Logistics Engineers; Logistics Managers; others.

Skills—Management of Financial Resources: Determining how money will be spent to get the work done and accounting for these expenditures. **Management of Material Resources:** Obtaining and seeing to the appropriate use of equipment, facilities, and materials needed to do certain work. **Negotiation:** Bringing others together and trying to reconcile differences. **Programming:** Writing computer programs for various purposes. **Mathematics:** Using mathematics to solve problems. **Management of Personnel Resources:** Motivating, developing, and directing people as they work, identifying the best people for the job. **Writing:** Communicating effectively in writing as appropriate for the needs of the audience. **Systems Analysis:** Determining how a system should work and how changes in conditions, operations, and the environment will affect outcomes.

Work Environment: Indoors; sitting.

Job Specialization: Energy Auditors

Conduct energy audits of buildings, building systems, and process systems. May also conduct investment grade audits of buildings or systems. Identify and prioritize energy-saving measures. Prepare audit reports containing energy analysis results and recommendations for energy cost savings. Inspect or evaluate building envelopes, mechanical systems, electrical systems, or process systems to determine the energy consumption of each system. Collect and analyze field data related to energy usage. Perform tests such as blower-door tests to locate air leaks. Calculate potential for energy savings. Educate customers on energy efficiency, or answer questions on topics such as the costs of running household appliances and the selection of energy-efficient appliances. Recommend energy-efficient technologies or alternative energy sources. Prepare job specification sheets for home energy improvements such as attic insulation, window retrofits, and heating system upgrades. Quantify energy consumption to establish baselines for energy use and need. Identify opportunities to improve the operation, maintenance, or energy efficiency of building or process systems. Analyze technical feasibility of energy-saving measures using knowledge of engineering, energy production, energy use, construction, maintenance, system operation, or process systems. Analyze energy bills including utility rates or tariffs to gather historical energy-usage data.

Education and Training Program: Energy Management and Systems Technology/Technician. **Knowledge/Courses—Building and Construction:** Materials, methods, and the tools involved in the construction or repair of houses, buildings, or other structures such as highways and roads. **Physics:** Physical principles, laws, their interrelationships, and applications to understanding fluid, material, and atmospheric dynamics, and mechanical, electrical, atomic, and subatomic structures and processes. **Sales and Marketing:** Principles and methods for showing, promoting, and selling products or services. This includes marketing strategy and tactics, product demonstration, sales techniques, and sales control systems. **Design:** Design techniques, tools, and principles involved in production of precision technical plans, blueprints, drawings, and models. **Clerical Practices:** Administrative and clerical procedures and systems such as word processing, managing files and records, stenography and transcription, designing forms, and other office procedures and terminology. **Mechanical Devices:** Machines and tools, including their designs, uses, repair, and maintenance.

Personality Type: Conventional-Enterprising. **Career Cluster:** 04 Business, Management, and Administration. **Career Pathway:** 04.1 Management. **Other Jobs in This Pathway:** Administrative Services Managers; Agents and Business Managers of Artists, Performers, and Athletes; Biofuels Production Managers; Biomass Power Plant Managers; Brownfield Redevelopment Specialists and Site Managers; Business Continuity Planners; Business Operations Specialists, All Other; Business Teachers, Postsecondary; Chief Executives; Chief Sustainability Officers; Communications Teachers, Postsecondary; Compliance Managers; Computer and Information Systems Managers; Construction Managers; Cost Estimators; Customs Brokers; Economics Teachers, Postsecondary; Economists; Environmental Economists; First-Line Supervisors of Office and Administrative Support Workers; First-Line Supervisors of Personal Service Workers; Gaming Supervisors; General and Operations Managers; Geothermal Production Managers; Hydroelectric Production Managers; Industrial Production Managers; Investment Fund Managers; Logisticians; Logistics Analysts; Logistics Engineers; Logistics Managers; others.

Skills—Operations Analysis: Analyzing needs and product requirements to create a design. **Science:** Using scientific rules and methods to solve problems. **Systems**

Evaluation: Identifying measures or indicators of system performance and the actions needed to improve or correct performance relative to the goals of the system. **Systems Analysis:** Determining how a system should work and how changes in conditions, operations, and the environment will affect outcomes. **Mathematics:** Using mathematics to solve problems. **Management of Financial Resources:** Determining how money will be spent to get the work done and accounting for these expenditures. **Operation and Control:** Controlling operations of equipment or systems. **Writing:** Communicating effectively in writing as appropriate for the needs of the audience.

Work Environment: More often outdoors than indoors; standing; using hands; very hot or cold; bright or inadequate lighting; contaminants; cramped work space; high places.

Job Specialization: Online Merchants

Plan, direct, or coordinate retail activities of businesses operating online. May perform duties such as preparing business strategies, buying merchandise, managing inventory, implementing marketing activities, fulfilling and shipping online orders, and balancing financial records. Participate in online forums and conferences to stay abreast of online retailing trends, techniques, and security threats. Upload digital media, such as photos, video, or scanned images, to online storefront, auction sites, or other shopping websites. Order or purchase merchandise to maintain optimal inventory levels. Maintain inventory of shipping supplies, such as boxes, labels, tape, bubble wrap, loose packing materials, and tape guns. Integrate online retailing strategy with physical and catalogue retailing operations. Determine and set product prices. Disclose merchant information and terms and policies of transactions in online and offline materials. Deliver e-mail confirmation of completed transactions and shipment. Create, manage, and automate orders and invoices using order management and invoicing software. Create and maintain database of customer accounts. Create and distribute offline promotional material, such as brochures, pamphlets, business cards, stationery, and signage. Collaborate with search engine shopping specialists to place marketing content in desired online locations. Cancel orders based on customer requests or problems with inventory or delivery. Transfer digital media, such as music, video, and software, to customers via the Internet. Select and purchase

technical web services, such as web hosting services, online merchant accounts, shopping cart software, payment gateway software, and spyware.

Education and Training Program: E-Commerce/Electronic Commerce.

Personality Type: Enterprising-Conventional-Realistic. **Career Cluster:** 14 Marketing, Sales, and Service. **Career Pathway:** 14.2 Professional Sales and Marketing. **Other Jobs in This Pathway:** Appraisers, Real Estate; Assessors; Cashiers; Counter and Rental Clerks; Demonstrators and Product Promoters; Door-To-Door Sales Workers, News and Street Vendors, and Related Workers; Driver/Sales Workers; Energy Brokers; First-Line Supervisors of Non-Retail Sales Workers; First-Line Supervisors of Retail Sales Workers; Gaming Change Persons and Booth Cashiers; Hotel, Motel, and Resort Desk Clerks; Interior Designers; Lodging Managers; Marketing Managers; Marking Clerks; Meeting, Convention, and Event Planners; Merchandise Displayers and Window Trimmers; Models; Order Fillers, Wholesale and Retail Sales; Parts Salespersons; Property, Real Estate, and Community Association Managers; Real Estate Brokers; Real Estate Sales Agents; Reservation and Transportation Ticket Agents and Travel Clerks; Retail Salespersons; Sales and Related Workers, All Other; Sales Engineers; Sales Representatives, Services, All Other; others.

Work Environment: No data available.

Job Specialization: Security Management Specialists

Conduct security assessments for organizations, and design security systems and processes. May specialize in areas such as physical security, personnel security, or information security. May work in fields such as health care, banking, gaming, security engineering, or manufacturing. Prepare documentation for case reports or court proceedings. Review design drawings or technical documents for completeness, correctness, or appropriateness. Monitor tapes or digital recordings to identify the source of losses. Interview witnesses or suspects to identify persons responsible for security breaches, establish losses, pursue prosecutions, or obtain restitution. Budget and schedule security design work. Develop conceptual designs of security systems. Respond to emergency situations on an on-call basis. Train personnel in security procedures or use of security equipment. Prepare, maintain, or update security procedures, security system drawings, or related documentation. Monitor the work of contractors in the design, construction, and start-up phases of security systems. Inspect security design features, installations, or programs to ensure compliance with applicable standards or regulations. Inspect fire, intruder detection, or other security systems. Engineer, install, maintain, or repair security systems, programmable logic controls, or other security-related electronic systems. Recommend improvements in security systems or procedures. Develop or review specifications for design or construction of security systems. Design security policies, programs, or practices to ensure adequate security relating to issues such as protection of assets, alarm response, and access card use.

Education and Training Program: Security and Loss Prevention Services.

Personality Type: Realistic-Investigative-Conventional. **Career Cluster:** 04 Business, Management, and Administration. **Career Pathway:** 04.1 Management. **Other Jobs in This Pathway:** Administrative Services Managers; Agents and Business Managers of Artists, Performers, and Athletes; Biofuels Production Managers; Biomass Power Plant Managers; Brownfield Redevelopment Specialists and Site Managers; Business Continuity Planners; Business Operations Specialists, All Other; Business Teachers, Postsecondary; Chief Executives; Chief Sustainability Officers; Communications Teachers, Postsecondary; Compliance Managers; Computer and Information Systems Managers; Construction Managers; Cost Estimators; Customs Brokers; Economics Teachers, Postsecondary; Economists; Energy Auditors; Environmental Economists; First-Line Supervisors of Office and Administrative Support Workers; First-Line Supervisors of Personal Service Workers; Gaming Supervisors; General and Operations Managers; Geothermal Production Managers; Hydroelectric Production Managers; Industrial Production Managers; Investment Fund Managers; Logisticians; Logistics Analysts; Logistics Engineers; Logistics Managers; others.

Work Environment: No data available.

Job Specialization: Sustainability Specialists

Address organizational sustainability issues, such as waste stream management, green building practices,

and green procurement plans. Review and revise sustainability proposals or policies. Research or review regulatory, technical, or market issues related to sustainability. Identify or investigate violations of natural resources, waste management, recycling, or other environmental policies. Identify or create new sustainability indicators. Write grant applications, rebate applications, or project proposals to secure funding for sustainability projects. Provide technical or administrative support for sustainability programs or issues. Identify or procure needed resources to implement sustainability programs or projects. Create or maintain plans or other documents related to sustainability projects. Develop reports or presentations to communicate the effectiveness of sustainability initiatives. Create marketing or outreach media, such as brochures or websites, to communicate sustainability issues, procedures, or objectives. Collect information about waste stream management or green building practices to inform decision makers. Assess or propose sustainability initiatives, considering factors such as cost effectiveness, technical feasibility, and acceptance. Monitor or track sustainability indicators, such as energy usage, natural resource usage, waste generation, and recycling. Develop sustainability project goals, objectives, initiatives, or strategies in collaboration with other sustainability professionals.

Education and Training Program: Business Administration and Management, General.

Personality Type: No data available. **Career Cluster:** 04 Business, Management, and Administration. **Career Pathway:** 04.1 Management. **Other Jobs in This Pathway:** Administrative Services Managers; Agents and Business Managers of Artists, Performers, and Athletes; Biofuels Production Managers; Biomass Power Plant Managers; Brownfield Redevelopment Specialists and Site Managers; Business Continuity Planners; Business Operations Specialists, All Other; Business Teachers, Postsecondary; Chief Executives; Chief Sustainability Officers; Communications Teachers, Postsecondary; Compliance Managers; Computer and Information Systems Managers; Construction Managers; Cost Estimators; Customs Brokers; Economics Teachers, Postsecondary; Economists; Energy Auditors; Environmental Economists; First-Line Supervisors of Office and Administrative Support Workers; First-Line Supervisors of Personal Service Workers; Gaming Supervisors; General and Operations Managers; Geothermal Production Managers; Hydroelectric Production

Managers; Industrial Production Managers; Investment Fund Managers; Logisticians; Logistics Analysts; Logistics Engineers; Logistics Managers; others.

Work Environment: No data available.

Butchers and Meat Cutters

- ⊙ Annual Earnings: $28,460
- ⊙ Earnings Growth Potential: Medium (36.4%)
- ⊙ Growth: 8.0%
- ⊙ Annual Job Openings: 4,680
- ⊙ Self-Employed: 0.9%

Considerations for Job Outlook: More people around the world are demanding prepared and precut food. Also, more people are buying partially prepared and easy-to-cook products. Both of these trends are expected to drive demand for food processing workers. These trends will create growth.

Cut, trim, or prepare consumer-sized portions of meat for use or sale in retail establishments. Wrap, weigh, label, and price cuts of meat. Prepare and place meat cuts and products in display counter, so they will appear attractive and catch the shopper's eye. Prepare special cuts of meat ordered by customers. Cut, trim, bone, tie, and grind meats, such as beef, pork, poultry, and fish, to prepare meat in cooking form. Receive, inspect, and store meat upon delivery, to ensure meat quality. Shape, lace, and tie roasts, using boning knife, skewer, and twine. Estimate requirements and order or requisition meat supplies to maintain inventories. Supervise other butchers or meat cutters. Record quantity of meat received and issued to cooks and/or keep records of meat sales. Negotiate with representatives from supply companies to determine order details. Cure, smoke, tenderize, and preserve meat. Total sales, and collect money from customers.

Education/Training Required: Less than high school. **Education and Training Program:** Meat Cutting/Meat Cutter Training. **Knowledge/Courses—Food Production:** Techniques and equipment for planting, growing, and harvesting food products (both plant and animal) for consumption, including storage/handling techniques. **Production and Processing:** Raw materials, production processes, quality control, costs, and other techniques for maximizing the effective manufacture and distribution of goods. **Mechanical Devices:** Machines and tools,

including their designs, uses, repair, and maintenance. **Sales and Marketing:** Principles and methods for showing, promoting, and selling products or services. This includes marketing strategy and tactics, product demonstration, sales techniques, and sales control systems. **Work Experience Needed:** None. **On-the-Job Training Needed:** Long-term on-the-job training. **Certification/Licensure:** None.

Personality Type: Realistic-Conventional-Enterprising. **Career Cluster:** 09 Hospitality and Tourism. **Career Pathway:** 09.1 Restaurants and Food/Beverage Services. **Other Jobs in This Pathway:** Bakers; Baristas; Bartenders; Chefs and Head Cooks; Combined Food Preparation and Serving Workers, Including Fast Food; Cooks, All Other; Cooks, Fast Food; Cooks, Institution and Cafeteria; Cooks, Private Household; Cooks, Restaurant; Cooks, Short Order; Counter Attendants, Cafeteria, Food Concession, and Coffee Shop; Dining Room and Cafeteria Attendants and Bartender Helpers; Dishwashers; First-Line Supervisors of Food Preparation and Serving Workers; Food Preparation and Serving Related Workers, All Other; Food Preparation Workers; Food Servers, Nonrestaurant; Food Service Managers; Gaming Managers; Hosts and Hostesses, Restaurant, Lounge, and Coffee Shop; Meat, Poultry, and Fish Cutters and Trimmers; Slaughterers and Meat Packers; Waiters and Waitresses.

Skills—Negotiation: Bringing others together and trying to reconcile differences. **Management of Financial Resources:** Determining how money will be spent to get the work done and accounting for these expenditures. **Operation and Control:** Controlling operations of equipment or systems. **Troubleshooting:** Determining causes of operating errors and deciding what to do about them. **Quality Control Analysis:** Conducting tests and inspections of products, services, or processes to evaluate quality or performance. **Management of Personnel Resources:** Motivating, developing, and directing people as they work, identifying the best people for the job.

Work Environment: Indoors; standing; walking and running; using hands; bending or twisting the body; repetitive motions; noise; very hot or cold; hazardous equipment; minor burns, cuts, bites, or stings.

Buyers and Purchasing Agents, Farm Products

- ◉ Annual Earnings: $55,860
- ◉ Earnings Growth Potential: High (42.2%)
- ◉ Growth: 5.4%
- ◉ Annual Job Openings: 320
- ◉ Self-Employed: 16.1%

Considerations for Job Outlook: Growth will be driven largely by the performance of the wholesale and retail industries. Continued employment decreases in manufacturing, as well as decreases in federal government, which includes defense purchasing, are expected. However, growth is expected for this occupation in firms that provide health-care and computer systems design and related services.

Purchase farm products either for further processing or resale. Coordinate and direct activities of workers engaged in cutting, transporting, storing, or milling products and in maintaining records. Maintain records of business transactions and product inventories, reporting data to companies or government agencies as necessary. Sell supplies such as seed, feed, fertilizers, and insecticides, arranging for loans or financing as necessary. Estimate land production possibilities, surveying property and studying factors such as crop rotation history, soil fertility, and irrigation facilities. Negotiate contracts with farmers for the production or purchase of farm products. Review orders to determine product types and quantities required to meet demand. Examine and test crops and products to estimate their value, determine their grade, and locate any evidence of disease or insect damage. Arrange for transportation and/or storage of purchased products. Arrange for processing and/or resale of purchased products.

Education/Training Required: High school diploma or equivalent. **Education and Training Program:** Agricultural/Farm Supplies Retailing and Wholesaling. **Knowledge/Courses—Food Production:** Techniques and equipment for planting, growing, and harvesting food products (both plant and animal) for consumption, including storage/handling techniques. **Economics and Accounting:** Economic and accounting principles and practices, the financial markets, banking, and the analysis and reporting of financial data. **Production and**

Processing: Raw materials, production processes, quality control, costs, and other techniques for maximizing the effective manufacture and distribution of goods. **Sales and Marketing:** Principles and methods for showing, promoting, and selling products or services. This includes marketing strategy and tactics, product demonstration, sales techniques, and sales control systems. **Geography:** Principles and methods for describing the features of land, sea, and air masses, including their physical characteristics, locations, interrelationships, and distribution of plant, animal, and human life. **Transportation:** Principles and methods for moving people or goods by air, rail, sea, or road, including the relative costs and benefits. **Work Experience Needed:** None. **On-the-Job Training Needed:** Long-term on-the-job training. **Certification/Licensure:** Licensure for some specializations.

Personality Type: Enterprising-Conventional-Realistic. **Career Cluster:** 01 Agriculture, Food, and Natural Resources. **Career Pathway:** 01.1 Food Products and Processing Systems. **Other Jobs in This Pathway:** Agricultural Inspectors; Agricultural Sciences Teachers, Postsecondary; Agricultural Technicians; Chemical Technicians; First-Line Supervisors of Office and Administrative Support Workers; Food and Tobacco Roasting, Baking, and Drying Machine Operators and Tenders; Food Batchmakers; Food Cooking Machine Operators and Tenders; Food Science Technicians; Food Scientists and Technologists; Graders and Sorters, Agricultural Products; Nonfarm Animal Caretakers; Office Machine Operators, Except Computer; Pest Control Workers.

Skills—Management of Financial Resources: Determining how money will be spent to get the work done and accounting for these expenditures. **Management of Material Resources:** Obtaining and seeing to the appropriate use of equipment, facilities, and materials needed to do certain work. **Persuasion:** Persuading others to change their minds or behavior. **Negotiation:** Bringing others together and trying to reconcile differences. **Management of Personnel Resources:** Motivating, developing, and directing people as they work, identifying the best people for the job. **Mathematics:** Using mathematics to solve problems. **Operation and Control:** Controlling operations of equipment or systems. **Speaking:** Talking to others to convey information effectively.

Work Environment: Indoors; sitting.

Cabinetmakers and Bench Carpenters

- ⊙ Annual Earnings: $30,530
- ⊙ Earnings Growth Potential: Medium (35.2%)
- ⊙ Growth: 16.8%
- ⊙ Annual Job Openings: 4,020
- ⊙ Self-Employed: 15.2%

Considerations for Job Outlook: Those with advanced skills, including advanced math and the ability to read blueprints, should have the best job opportunities in manufacturing industries. Woodworkers who know how to create and carry out custom designs on a computer will likely be in strong demand. Some job openings will result from the need to replace those who retire or leave the occupation for other reasons. However, employment in all woodworking specialties is highly sensitive to economic cycles. During economic downturns, workers are subject to layoffs or reductions in hours.

Cut, shape, and assemble wooden articles or set up and operate a variety of woodworking machines. Produce and assemble components of articles such as store fixtures, office equipment, cabinets, and high-grade furniture. Verify dimensions, and check the quality and fit of pieces in order to ensure adherence to specifications. Set up and operate machines, including power saws, jointers, mortisers, tenoners, molders, and shapers, to cut, mold, and shape woodstock and wood substitutes. Measure and mark dimensions of parts on paper or lumber stock prior to cutting, following blueprints, to ensure a tight fit and quality product. Reinforce joints with nails or other fasteners to prepare articles for finishing. Attach parts and subassemblies together to form completed units, using glue, dowels, nails, screws, and/or clamps. Establish the specifications of articles to be constructed or repaired, and plan the methods and operations for shaping and assembling parts, based on blueprints, drawings, diagrams, or oral or written instructions. Cut timber to the right size and shape and trim parts of joints to ensure a snug fit, using hand tools such as planes, chisels, or wood files. Trim, sand, and scrape surfaces and joints to prepare articles for finishing. Match materials for color, grain, and texture, giving attention to knots and other features of the wood. Bore holes for insertion of screws or dowels, by hand or using boring machines. Program computers to operate machinery.

Estimate the amounts, types, and costs of needed materials. Perform final touch-ups with sandpaper and steel wool. Install hardware such as hinges, handles, catches, and drawer pulls, using hand tools. Discuss projects with customers, and draw up detailed specifications. Repair or alter wooden furniture, cabinetry, fixtures, paneling, and other pieces. Apply masonite, formica, and vinyl surfacing materials. Design furniture, using computer-aided drawing programs. Dip, brush, or spray assembled articles with protective or decorative finishes such as stain, varnish, paint, or lacquer.

Education/Training Required: High school diploma or equivalent. **Education and Training Program:** Cabinetmaking and Millwork. **Knowledge/Courses—Design:** Design techniques, tools, and principles involved in production of precision technical plans, blueprints, drawings, and models. **Production and Processing:** Raw materials, production processes, quality control, costs, and other techniques for maximizing the effective manufacture and distribution of goods. **Mechanical Devices:** Machines and tools, including their designs, uses, repair, and maintenance. **Building and Construction:** Materials, methods, and the tools involved in the construction or repair of houses, buildings, or other structures such as highways and roads. **Engineering and Technology:** The practical application of engineering science and technology. This includes applying principles, techniques, procedures, and equipment to the design and production of various goods and services. **Work Experience Needed:** None. **On-the-Job Training Needed:** Moderate-term on-the-job training. **Certification/Licensure:** None.

Personality Type: Realistic-Conventional. **Career Cluster:** 13 Manufacturing. **Career Pathway:** 13.1 Production. **Other Jobs in This Pathway:** Adhesive Bonding Machine Operators and Tenders; Assemblers and Fabricators, All Other; Avionics Technicians; Cleaning, Washing, and Metal Pickling Equipment Operators and Tenders; Coating, Painting, and Spraying Machine Setters, Operators, and Tenders; Computer-Controlled Machine Tool Operators, Metal and Plastic; Cooling and Freezing Equipment Operators and Tenders; Cost Estimators; Crushing, Grinding, and Polishing Machine Setters, Operators, and Tenders; Cutters and Trimmers, Hand; Cutting and Slicing Machine Setters, Operators, and Tenders; Cutting, Punching, and Press Machine Setters, Operators, and Tenders, Metal and Plastic; Drilling and Boring Machine

Tool Setters, Operators, and Tenders, Metal and Plastic; Extruding and Drawing Machine Setters, Operators, and Tenders, Metal and Plastic; Extruding and Forming Machine Setters, Operators, and Tenders, Synthetic and Glass Fibers; Extruding, Forming, Pressing, and Compacting Machine Setters, Operators, and Tenders; others.

Skills—Equipment Selection: Determining the kind of tools and equipment needed to do a job. **Equipment Maintenance:** Performing routine maintenance on equipment and determining when and what kind of maintenance is needed. **Repairing:** Repairing machines or systems using the needed tools. **Troubleshooting:** Determining causes of operating errors and deciding what to do about them. **Operation and Control:** Controlling operations of equipment or systems. **Quality Control Analysis:** Conducting tests and inspections of products, services, or processes to evaluate quality or performance. **Operations Analysis:** Analyzing needs and product requirements to create a design. **Technology Design:** Generating or adapting equipment and technology to serve user needs.

Work Environment: Standing; walking and running; using hands; bending or twisting the body; repetitive motions; noise; very hot or cold; contaminants; hazardous equipment; minor burns, cuts, bites, or stings.

Cardiovascular Technologists and Technicians

- ⊙ Annual Earnings: $51,020
- ⊙ Earnings Growth Potential: High (46.2%)
- ⊙ Growth: 29.4%
- ⊙ Annual Job Openings: 2,210
- ⊙ Self-Employed: 0.2%

Considerations for Job Outlook: Job prospects should be best for those who have multiple professional credentials and are trained to do a wide range of procedures. Technologists or technicians who are willing to move or to work irregular hours also should have better opportunities.

Conduct tests on pulmonary or cardiovascular systems of patients for diagnostic purposes. Monitor patients' blood pressure and heart rate using electrocardiogram (EKG) equipment during diagnostic and therapeutic procedures to notify the physician if something appears wrong. Monitor patients' comfort and safety during tests, alerting physicians to abnormalities or changes in patient responses. Explain testing procedures to patient to obtain cooperation and reduce anxiety. Prepare reports of diagnostic procedures for interpretation by physician. Observe gauges, recorder, and video screens of data analysis system during imaging of cardiovascular system. Conduct electrocardiogram (EKG), phonocardiogram, echocardiogram, stress testing, or other cardiovascular tests to record patients' cardiac activity, using specialized electronic test equipment, recording devices, and laboratory instruments. Prepare and position patients for testing. Obtain and record patient identification, medical history or test results. Attach electrodes to the patients' chests, arms, and legs, connect electrodes to leads from the electrocardiogram (EKG) machine, and operate the EKG machine to obtain a reading. Adjust equipment and controls according to physicians' orders or established protocol. Check, test, and maintain cardiology equipment, making minor repairs when necessary, to ensure proper operation. Supervise and train other cardiology technologists and students. Assist physicians in diagnosis and treatment of cardiac and peripheral vascular treatments, for example, assisting with balloon angioplasties to treat blood vessel blockages. Operate diagnostic imaging equipment to produce contrast enhanced radiographs of heart and cardiovascular system. Inject contrast medium into patients' blood vessels. Observe ultrasound display screen and listen to signals to record vascular information such as blood pressure, limb volume changes, oxygen saturation and cerebral circulation. Assess cardiac physiology and calculate valve areas from blood flow velocity measurements.

Education/Training Required: Associate degree. **Education and Training Programs:** Cardiopulmonary Technology/Technologist; Cardiovascular Technology/Technologist; Electrocardiograph Technology/Technician; Perfusion Technology/Perfusionist. **Knowledge/Courses—Medicine and Dentistry:** The information and techniques needed to diagnose and treat human injuries, diseases, and deformities. This includes symptoms, treatment alternatives, drug properties and interactions, and preventive health-care measures. **Biology:** Plant and animal organisms and their tissues, cells, functions, interdependencies, and interactions with each other and the environment. **Psychology:** Human behavior and performance; individual differences in ability, personality, and interests; learning and motivation; psychological research methods; and the assessment and treatment of behavioral and affective disorders. **Customer and Personal Service:** Principles and processes for providing customer and personal services. This includes customer needs assessment, meeting quality standards for services, and evaluation of customer satisfaction. **Sociology and Anthropology:** Group behavior and dynamics, societal trends and influences, human migrations, ethnicity, and cultures and their history and origins. **Chemistry:** The chemical composition, structure, and properties of substances and of the chemical processes and transformations that they undergo. This includes uses of chemicals and their danger signs, production techniques, and disposal methods. **Work Experience Needed:** None. **On-the-Job Training Needed:** None. **Certification/Licensure:** Voluntary certification by association.

Personality Type: Realistic-Investigative-Social. **Career Cluster:** 08 Health Science. **Career Pathway:** 08.2 Diagnostics Services. **Other Jobs in This Pathway:** Ambulance Drivers and Attendants, Except Emergency Medical Technicians; Anesthesiologist Assistants; Athletic Trainers; Cytogenetic Technologists; Cytotechnologists; Diagnostic Medical Sonographers; Emergency Medical Technicians and Paramedics; Endoscopy Technicians; Health Diagnosing and Treating Practitioners, All Other; Health Specialties Teachers, Postsecondary; Health Technologists and Technicians, All Other; Healthcare Practitioners and Technical Workers, All Other; Histotechnologists and Histologic Technicians; Medical and Clinical Laboratory Technicians; Medical and Clinical Laboratory Technologists; Medical and Health Services Managers; Medical Assistants; Medical Equipment Preparers; Neurodiagnostic Technologists; Nuclear Equipment Operation Technicians; Nuclear Medicine Technologists; Ophthalmic Laboratory Technicians; Pathologists; Physical Scientists, All Other; Physician Assistants; Radiation Therapists; Radiologic Technicians; Radiologic Technologists; Radiologists; others.

Skills—Science: Using scientific rules and methods to solve problems. **Equipment Maintenance:** Performing routine maintenance on equipment and determining when and what kind of maintenance is needed. **Operation and Control:** Controlling operations of equipment or systems. **Repairing:** Repairing machines or systems using the needed tools. **Operation Monitoring:** Watching gauges, dials, or other indicators to make sure a machine is working properly. **Service Orientation:** Actively looking for ways to help people. **Equipment Selection:** Determining the kind of tools and equipment needed to do a job. **Troubleshooting:** Determining causes of operating errors and deciding what to do about them.

Work Environment: Indoors; standing; walking and running; using hands; repetitive motions; exposed to radiation; exposed to disease or infections.

Cargo and Freight Agents

- ⊙ Annual Earnings: $38,210
- ⊙ Earnings Growth Potential: Medium (38.9%)
- ⊙ Growth: 29.3%
- ⊙ Annual Job Openings: 4,420
- ⊙ Self-Employed: 0.4%

Considerations for Job Outlook: Job prospects should be best for those with strong computer and customer-service skills. Some employers report difficulty finding workers who have these abilities. Although job opportunities are expected to be good, employment of cargo and freight agents is sensitive to fluctuations in the economy. Workers may experience higher-levels of unemployment when the overall level of economic activity falls.

Expedite and route movement of incoming and outgoing cargo and freight shipments in airline, train, and trucking terminals, and shipping docks. Negotiate and arrange transport of goods with shipping or freight companies. Notify consignees, passengers, or customers of the arrival of freight or baggage, and arrange for delivery. Advise clients on transportation and payment methods. Prepare manifests showing baggage, mail, and freight weights and number of passengers on airplanes, and transmit data to destinations. Determine method of shipment, and prepare bills of lading, invoices, and other shipping documents. Check import/export documentation to determine cargo contents, and classify goods into different fee or tariff groups using a tariff coding system. Estimate freight or postal rates, and record shipment costs and weights. Enter shipping information into a computer by hand or by using a handheld scanner that reads bar codes on goods. Retrieve stored items, and trace lost shipments as necessary. Pack goods for shipping, using tools such as staplers, strapping machines, and hammers. Direct delivery trucks to shipping doors or designated marshalling areas, and help load and unload goods safely. Inspect and count items received, and check them against invoices or other documents, recording shortages and rejecting damaged goods. Install straps, braces, and padding to loads to prevent shifting or damage during shipment. Keep records of all goods shipped, received, and stored. Coordinate and supervise activities of workers engaged in packing and shipping merchandise. Arrange insurance coverage for goods.

Education/Training Required: High school diploma or equivalent. **Education and Training Program:** General Office Occupations and Clerical Services. **Knowledge/ Courses—Transportation:** Principles and methods for moving people or goods by air, rail, sea, or road, including the relative costs and benefits. **Geography:** Principles and methods for describing the features of land, sea, and air masses, including their physical characteristics, locations, interrelationships, and distribution of plant, animal, and human life. **Customer and Personal Service:** Principles and processes for providing customer and personal services. This includes customer needs assessment, meeting quality standards for services, and evaluation of customer satisfaction. **Clerical Practices:** Administrative and clerical procedures and systems such as word processing, managing files and records, stenography and transcription, designing forms, and other office procedures and terminology. **Administration and Management:** Business and management principles involved in strategic planning, resource allocation, human resources modeling, leadership technique, production methods, and coordination of people and resources. **Work Experience Needed:** None. **On-the-Job Training Needed:** Short-term on-the-job training. **Certification/Licensure:** None.

Personality Type: Conventional-Enterprising-Realistic. **Career Cluster:** 04 Business, Management, and Administration. **Career Pathway:** 04.6 Administrative and Information Support. **Other Jobs in This Pathway:** Correspondence Clerks; Couriers and Messengers; Court Clerks; Customer Service Representatives; Data Entry Keyers; Dispatchers, Except Police, Fire, and Ambulance; Executive Secretaries and Executive Administrative Assistants; File Clerks; Freight Forwarders; Human Resources Assistants, Except Payroll and Timekeeping; Information and Record Clerks, All Other; Insurance Claims Clerks; Insurance Policy Processing Clerks; Interviewers, Except Eligibility and Loan; License Clerks; Mail Clerks and Mail Machine Operators, Except Postal Service; Meter Readers,

Utilities; Municipal Clerks; Office and Administrative Support Workers, All Other; Office Clerks, General; Office Machine Operators, Except Computer; Order Clerks; Patient Representatives; Postal Service Clerks; Postal Service Mail Carriers; Postal Service Mail Sorters, Processors, and Processing Machine Operators; Procurement Clerks; Receptionists and Information Clerks; others.

Skills—Negotiation: Bringing others together and trying to reconcile differences. **Service Orientation:** Actively looking for ways to help people. **Time Management:** Managing one's own time and the time of others. **Mathematics:** Using mathematics to solve problems. **Speaking:** Talking to others to convey information effectively. **Systems Evaluation:** Identifying measures or indicators of system performance and the actions needed to improve or correct performance relative to the goals of the system. **Persuasion:** Persuading others to change their minds or behavior. **Critical Thinking:** Using logic and reasoning to identify the strengths and weaknesses of alternative solutions, conclusions, or approaches to problems.

Work Environment: Indoors; sitting; repetitive motions.

Job Specialization: Freight Forwarders

Research rates, routings, or modes of transport for shipment of products. Maintain awareness of regulations affecting the international movement of cargo. Make arrangements for additional services such as storage and inland transportation. Select shipment routes, based on the nature of the goods shipped, transit times, or security needs. Determine efficient and cost-effective methods of moving goods from one location to another. Reserve necessary space on ships, aircraft, trains, or trucks. Arrange delivery or storage of goods at destinations. Arrange for special transport of sensitive cargoes, such as livestock, food, or medical supplies. Assist clients in obtaining insurance reimbursements. Calculate weight, volume, and cost of goods to be moved. Complete shipping documentation, such as including bills of lading, packing lists, dock receipts, and certificates of origin. Consolidate loads with a common destination to reduce costs to individual shippers. Inform clients of factors such as shipping options, timelines, transfers, and regulations affecting shipments. Keep records of goods dispatched and received. Maintain current knowledge of relevant legislation, political situations, or other factors that could affect freight shipping. Monitor and record locations of goods in transit. Negotiate shipping rates with freight carriers. Obtain or arrange cargo insurance. Pay, or arrange for payment of, freight and insurance fees, or other charges. Prepare invoices and cost quotations for freight transportation. Recommend or arrange appropriate merchandise packing methods, according to climate, terrain, weight, nature of goods, or costs. Verify proper packaging and labeling of exported goods.

Education and Training Program: General Office Occupations and Clerical Services.

Personality Type: Conventional-Enterprising. **Career Cluster:** 04 Business, Management, and Administration. **Career Pathway:** 04.6 Administrative and Information Support. **Other Jobs in This Pathway:** Cargo and Freight Agents; Correspondence Clerks; Couriers and Messengers; Court Clerks; Customer Service Representatives; Data Entry Keyers; Dispatchers, Except Police, Fire, and Ambulance; Executive Secretaries and Executive Administrative Assistants; File Clerks; Human Resources Assistants, Except Payroll and Timekeeping; Information and Record Clerks, All Other; Insurance Claims Clerks; Insurance Policy Processing Clerks; Interviewers, Except Eligibility and Loan; License Clerks; Mail Clerks and Mail Machine Operators, Except Postal Service; Meter Readers, Utilities; Municipal Clerks; Office and Administrative Support Workers, All Other; Office Clerks, General; Office Machine Operators, Except Computer; Order Clerks; Patient Representatives; Postal Service Clerks; Postal Service Mail Carriers; Postal Service Mail Sorters, Processors, and Processing Machine Operators; Procurement Clerks; Receptionists and Information Clerks; others.

Work Environment: No data available.

Carpenters

- ◉ Annual Earnings: $40,010
- ◉ Earnings Growth Potential: Medium (37.8%)
- ◉ Growth: 19.6%
- ◉ Annual Job Openings: 40,830
- ◉ Self-Employed: 39.0%

Considerations for Job Outlook: Overall job prospects for carpenters should improve over the coming decade as construction activity rebounds from the recent recession. The number of openings is expected to vary by geographic area. Because construction activity parallels the movement of people and businesses, areas of the country with the largest population increases will require the most carpenters. Employment of carpenters, like that of many other construction workers, is sensitive to fluctuations in the economy. On the one hand, workers in these trades may experience periods of unemployment when the overall level of construction falls. On the other hand, peak periods of building activity may produce shortages of carpenters. Experienced carpenters should have the best job opportunities.

Construct, erect, install, or repair structures and fixtures made of wood. For task data, see Job Specializations.

Education/Training Required: High school diploma or equivalent. **Work Experience Needed:** None. **On-the-Job Training Needed:** Apprenticeship. **Certification/Licensure:** None.

Job Specialization: Construction Carpenters

Construct, erect, install, and repair structures and fixtures of wood, plywood, and wallboard, using carpenter's hand tools and power tools. Measure and mark cutting lines on materials, using rulers, pencils, chalk, and marking gauges. Follow established safety rules and regulations, and maintain a safe and clean environment. Verify trueness of structures using plumb bobs and levels. Shape or cut materials to specified measurements using hand tools, machines, or power saws. Study specifications in blueprints, sketches, or building plans to prepare project layout and determine dimensions and materials required. Assemble and fasten materials to make frameworks or props using hand tools and wood screws, nails, dowel pins, or glue. Build or repair cabinets, doors, frameworks, floors, and other wooden fixtures included in buildings using woodworking machines, carpenter's hand tools, and power tools. Erect scaffolding and ladders for assembling structures above ground level. Remove damaged or defective parts or sections of structures, and repair or replace using hand tools. Install structures and fixtures, such as windows, frames, floorings, and trim, or hardware, using carpenter's hand and power tools. Select and order lumber and other required materials. Maintain records, document actions, and present written progress reports. Finish surfaces of woodwork or wallboard in houses and buildings using paint, hand tools, and paneling. Prepare cost estimates for clients or employers. Arrange for subcontractors to deal with special areas such as heating and electrical wiring work.

Education and Training Program: Carpentry/Carpenter. **Knowledge/Courses—Building and Construction:** Materials, methods, and the tools involved in the construction or repair of houses, buildings, or other structures such as highways and roads. **Design:** Design techniques, tools, and principles involved in production of precision technical plans, blueprints, drawings, and models. **Mechanical Devices:** Machines and tools, including their designs, uses, repair, and maintenance. **Engineering and Technology:** The practical application of engineering science and technology. This includes applying principles, techniques, procedures, and equipment to the design and production of various goods and services. **Production and Processing:** Raw materials, production processes, quality control, costs, and other techniques for maximizing the effective manufacture and distribution of goods. **Mathematics:** Arithmetic, algebra, geometry, calculus, statistics, and their applications.

Personality Type: Realistic-Conventional-Investigative. **Career Cluster:** 02 Architecture and Construction. **Career Pathway:** 02.2 Construction. **Other Jobs in This Pathway:** Boilermakers; Brickmasons and Blockmasons; Carpet Installers; Cement Masons and Concrete Finishers; Construction and Building Inspectors; Construction and Related Workers, All Other; Construction Laborers; Construction Managers; Continuous Mining Machine Operators; Cost Estimators; Crane and Tower Operators; Dredge Operators; Drywall and Ceiling Tile Installers; Earth Drillers, Except Oil and Gas; Electrical Power-Line Installers and Repairers; Electricians; Electromechanical Equipment Assemblers; Engineering Technicians, Except Drafters, All Other; Excavating and Loading Machine and Dragline Operators; Explosives Workers, Ordnance Handling Experts, and Blasters; Extraction Workers, All Other; First-Line Supervisors of Construction Trades and Extraction Workers; Floor Layers, Except Carpet, Wood, and Hard Tiles; Floor Sanders and Finishers; Glaziers; Heating and Air Conditioning Mechanics and Installers; Helpers, Construction Trades, All Other; others.

Skills—Repairing: Repairing machines or systems using the needed tools. **Equipment Selection:** Determining the kind of tools and equipment needed to do a job.

Installation: Installing equipment, machines, wiring, or programs to meet specifications. **Quality Control Analysis:** Conducting tests and inspections of products, services, or processes to evaluate quality or performance. **Equipment Maintenance:** Performing routine maintenance on equipment and determining when and what kind of maintenance is needed. **Operation and Control:** Controlling operations of equipment or systems. **Troubleshooting:** Determining causes of operating errors and deciding what to do about them. **Management of Material Resources:** Obtaining and seeing to the appropriate use of equipment, facilities, and materials needed to do certain work.

Work Environment: Outdoors; standing; walking and running; kneeling, crouching, stooping, or crawling; using hands; bending or twisting the body; repetitive motions; noise; very hot or cold; bright or inadequate lighting; contaminants; cramped work space; high places; hazardous equipment; minor burns, cuts, bites, or stings.

Job Specialization: Rough Carpenters

Build rough wooden structures, such as concrete forms; scaffolds; tunnel, bridge, or sewer supports; billboard signs; and temporary frame shelters, according to sketches, blueprints, or oral instructions. Study blueprints and diagrams to determine the dimensions of structures or forms to be constructed. Measure materials or distances, using squares, measuring tapes, or rules to lay out work. Cut or saw boards, timbers, or plywood to required sizes, using handsaws, power saws, or woodworking machines. Assemble and fasten materials together to construct wood or metal frameworks of structures, using bolts, nails, or screws. Anchor and brace forms and other structures in place, using nails, bolts, anchor rods, steel cables, planks, wedges, and timbers. Mark cutting lines on materials, using pencils and scribers. Erect forms, frameworks, scaffolds, hoists, roof supports, or chutes, using hand tools, plumb rules, and levels. Install rough door and window frames, subflooring, fixtures, or temporary supports in structures undergoing construction or repair. Examine structural timbers and supports to detect decay and replace timbers as required, using hand tools, nuts, and bolts. Bore boltholes in timber, masonry, or concrete walls, using power drills. Fabricate parts, using woodworking and metalworking machines. Dig or direct digging of post holes and set poles to support structures. Build sleds from logs and timbers for use in hauling camp buildings and machinery through wooded areas. Build chutes for pouring concrete.

Education and Training Program: Carpentry/Carpenter. **Knowledge/Courses—Building and Construction:** Materials, methods, and the tools involved in the construction or repair of houses, buildings, or other structures such as highways and roads. **Design:** Design techniques, tools, and principles involved in production of precision technical plans, blueprints, drawings, and models. **Mechanical Devices:** Machines and tools, including their designs, uses, repair, and maintenance. **Production and Processing:** Raw materials, production processes, quality control, costs, and other techniques for maximizing the effective manufacture and distribution of goods. **Public Safety and Security:** Relevant equipment, policies, procedures, and strategies to promote effective local, state, or national security operations for the protection of people, data, property, and institutions. **Mathematics:** Arithmetic, algebra, geometry, calculus, statistics, and their applications.

Personality Type: Realistic-Conventional-Investigative. **Career Cluster:** 02 Architecture and Construction. **Career Pathway:** 02.2 Construction. **Other Jobs in This Pathway:** Boilermakers; Brickmasons and Blockmasons; Carpet Installers; Cement Masons and Concrete Finishers; Construction and Building Inspectors; Construction and Related Workers, All Other; Construction Carpenters; Construction Laborers; Construction Managers; Continuous Mining Machine Operators; Cost Estimators; Crane and Tower Operators; Dredge Operators; Drywall and Ceiling Tile Installers; Earth Drillers, Except Oil and Gas; Electrical Power-Line Installers and Repairers; Electricians; Electromechanical Equipment Assemblers; Engineering Technicians, Except Drafters, All Other; Excavating and Loading Machine and Dragline Operators; Explosives Workers, Ordnance Handling Experts, and Blasters; Extraction Workers, All Other; First-Line Supervisors of Construction Trades and Extraction Workers; Floor Layers, Except Carpet, Wood, and Hard Tiles; Floor Sanders and Finishers; Glaziers; Heating and Air Conditioning Mechanics and Installers; Helpers, Construction Trades, All Other; others.

Skills—Repairing: Repairing machines or systems using the needed tools. **Equipment Maintenance:** Performing routine maintenance on equipment and determining when and what kind of maintenance is needed. **Troubleshooting:** Determining causes of operating errors and deciding

what to do about them. **Operation and Control:** Controlling operations of equipment or systems. **Installation:** Installing equipment, machines, wiring, or programs to meet specifications. **Mathematics:** Using mathematics to solve problems. **Operation Monitoring:** Watching gauges, dials, or other indicators to make sure a machine is working properly. **Coordination:** Adjusting actions in relation to others' actions.

Work Environment: Outdoors; standing; walking and running; kneeling, crouching, stooping, or crawling; balancing; using hands; bending or twisting the body; repetitive motions; noise; very hot or cold; contaminants; cramped work space; high places; hazardous equipment; minor burns, cuts, bites, or stings.

Carpet Installers

- ⊙ Annual Earnings: $36,750
- ⊙ Earnings Growth Potential: High (41.8%)
- ⊙ Growth: 10.3%
- ⊙ Annual Job Openings: 1,520
- ⊙ Self-Employed: 47.8%

Considerations for Job Outlook: Job prospects for carpet installers depend, in part, on the amount of new construction taking place in the economy. As construction activity rebounds over the projection decade, job opportunities for carpet installers should improve. In addition to job growth, many job openings will result from the need to replace workers who leave this occupation.

Lay and install carpet from rolls or blocks on floors. Install padding and trim flooring materials. Join edges of carpet and seam edges where necessary, by sewing or by using tape with glue and heated carpet iron. Cut and trim carpet to fit along wall edges, openings, and projections, finishing the edges with a wall trimmer. Inspect the surface to be covered to determine its condition, and correct any imperfections that might show through carpet or cause carpet to wear unevenly. Roll out, measure, mark, and cut carpeting to size with a carpet knife, following floor sketches and allowing extra carpet for final fitting. Plan the layout of the carpet, allowing for expected traffic patterns and placing seams for best appearance and longest wear. Stretch carpet to align with walls and ensure a smooth surface, and press carpet in place over tack strips or use staples, tape, tacks, or glue to hold carpet in place. Take measurements and study floor sketches to calculate the area to be carpeted and the amount of material needed. Cut carpet padding to size and install padding, following prescribed methods. Install carpet on some floors using adhesive, following prescribed methods. Nail tack strips around areas to be carpeted or use old strips to attach edges of new carpet. Fasten metal treads across door openings or where carpet meets flooring to hold carpet in place. Measure, cut, and install tackless strips along the baseboard or wall. Draw building diagrams and record dimensions. Move furniture from areas to be carpeted and remove old carpet and padding. Cut and bind material. Clean up before and after installation, including vacuuming carpet and discarding remnant pieces.

Education/Training Required: Less than high school. **Education and Training Program:** Construction Trades, Other. **Knowledge/Courses—Building and Construction:** Materials, methods, and the tools involved in the construction or repair of houses, buildings, or other structures such as highways and roads. **Design:** Design techniques, tools, and principles involved in production of precision technical plans, blueprints, drawings, and models. **Mechanical Devices:** Machines and tools, including their designs, uses, repair, and maintenance. **Production and Processing:** Raw materials, production processes, quality control, costs, and other techniques for maximizing the effective manufacture and distribution of goods. **Transportation:** Principles and methods for moving people or goods by air, rail, sea, or road, including the relative costs and benefits. **Customer and Personal Service:** Principles and processes for providing customer and personal services. This includes customer needs assessment, meeting quality standards for services, and evaluation of customer satisfaction. **Work Experience Needed:** None. **On-the-Job Training Needed:** Short-term on-the-job training. **Certification/Licensure:** None.

Personality Type: Realistic-Enterprising. **Career Cluster:** 02 Architecture and Construction. **Career Pathway:** 02.2 Construction. **Other Jobs in This Pathway:** Boilermakers; Brickmasons and Blockmasons; Cement Masons and Concrete Finishers; Construction and Building Inspectors; Construction and Related Workers, All Other; Construction Carpenters; Construction Laborers; Construction Managers; Continuous Mining Machine Operators; Cost Estimators; Crane and Tower Operators;

Dredge Operators; Drywall and Ceiling Tile Installers; Earth Drillers, Except Oil and Gas; Electrical Power-Line Installers and Repairers; Electricians; Electromechanical Equipment Assemblers; Engineering Technicians, Except Drafters, All Other; Excavating and Loading Machine and Dragline Operators; Explosives Workers, Ordnance Handling Experts, and Blasters; Extraction Workers, All Other; First-Line Supervisors of Construction Trades and Extraction Workers; Floor Layers, Except Carpet, Wood, and Hard Tiles; Floor Sanders and Finishers; Glaziers; Heating and Air Conditioning Mechanics and Installers; Helpers, Construction Trades, All Other; others.

Skills—Mathematics: Using mathematics to solve problems. **Equipment Selection:** Determining the kind of tools and equipment needed to do a job. **Repairing:** Repairing machines or systems using the needed tools. **Equipment Maintenance:** Performing routine maintenance on equipment and determining when and what kind of maintenance is needed. **Quality Control Analysis:** Conducting tests and inspections of products, services, or processes to evaluate quality or performance. **Troubleshooting:** Determining causes of operating errors and deciding what to do about them. **Operation and Control:** Controlling operations of equipment or systems. **Installation:** Installing equipment, machines, wiring, or programs to meet specifications.

Work Environment: Indoors; kneeling, crouching, stooping, or crawling; using hands; bending or twisting the body; repetitive motions; noise; contaminants; cramped work space; minor burns, cuts, bites, or stings.

Cement Masons and Concrete Finishers

- ⊙ Annual Earnings: $35,600
- ⊙ Earnings Growth Potential: Low (34.9%)
- ⊙ Growth: 34.6%
- ⊙ Annual Job Openings: 7,290
- ⊙ Self-Employed: 6.1%

Considerations for Job Outlook: Job opportunities for cement masons and terrazzo workers are expected to be good, particularly for those with more experience and skills. During peak construction periods, employers report difficulty in finding workers with the right skills, because many qualified job seekers often prefer work that is less strenuous and has more comfortable working conditions. Applicants who take masonry-related courses at technical schools will have the best job opportunities. As with many other construction workers, employment of cement masons and terrazzo workers is sensitive to the fluctuations of the economy. On the one hand, workers may experience periods of unemployment when the overall level of construction falls. On the other hand, shortages of workers may occur in some areas during peak periods of building activity.

Smooth and finish surfaces of poured concrete, such as floors, walks, sidewalks, roads, or curbs using a variety of hand and power tools. Check the forms that hold concrete to see that they are properly constructed. Set the forms that hold concrete to the desired pitch and depth, and align them. Spread, level, and smooth concrete, using rakes, shovels, hand or power trowels, hand or power screeds, and floats. Mold expansion joints and edges using edging tools, jointers, and straightedges. Monitor how the wind, heat, or cold affect the curing of the concrete throughout the entire process. Signal truck drivers to position trucks to facilitate pouring concrete and move chutes to direct concrete on forms. Produce rough concrete surfaces, using brooms. Operate power vibrators to compact concrete. Direct the casting of concrete and supervise laborers who use shovels or special tools to spread it. Mix cement, sand, and water to produce concrete, grout, or slurry, using hoes, trowels, tampers, scrapers, or concrete-mixing machines. Cut out damaged areas, drill holes for reinforcing rods, and position reinforcing rods to repair concrete using power saws and drills. Wet surface to prepare for bonding, fill holes and cracks with grout or slurry, and smooth using trowels. Wet concrete surface and rub with stone to smooth surface and obtain specified finish. Clean chipped areas using wire brushes, and feel and observe surface to determine if it is rough or uneven. Apply hardening and sealing compounds to cure surface of concrete and waterproof or restore surface.

Education/Training Required: Less than high school. **Education and Training Program:** Concrete Finishing/Concrete Finisher. **Knowledge/Courses—Building and Construction:** Materials, methods, and the tools involved in the construction or repair of houses, buildings, or other structures such as highways and roads. **Mechanical Devices:** Machines and tools, including their designs, uses, repair, and maintenance. **Engineering and Technology:** The practical application of engineering science and technology. This includes applying principles, techniques, procedures, and equipment to the design and production of various goods and services. **Design:** Design techniques, tools, and principles involved in production of precision technical plans, blueprints, drawings, and models. **Chemistry:** The chemical composition, structure, and properties of substances and of the chemical processes and transformations that they undergo. This includes uses of chemicals and their danger signs, production techniques, and disposal methods. **Physics:** Physical principles, laws, their interrelationships, and applications to understanding fluid, material, and atmospheric dynamics, and mechanical, electrical, atomic, and subatomic structures and processes. **Work Experience Needed:** None. **On-the-Job Training Needed:** Moderate-term on-the-job training. **Certification/Licensure:** None.

Personality Type: Realistic-Enterprising. **Career Cluster:** 02 Architecture and Construction. **Career Pathway:** 02.2 Construction. **Other Jobs in This Pathway:** Boilermakers; Brickmasons and Blockmasons; Carpet Installers; Construction and Building Inspectors; Construction and Related Workers, All Other; Construction Carpenters; Construction Laborers; Construction Managers; Continuous Mining Machine Operators; Cost Estimators; Crane and Tower Operators; Dredge Operators; Drywall and Ceiling Tile Installers; Earth Drillers, Except Oil and Gas; Electrical Power-Line Installers and Repairers; Electricians; Electromechanical Equipment Assemblers; Engineering Technicians, Except Drafters, All Other; Excavating and Loading Machine and Dragline Operators; Explosives Workers, Ordnance Handling Experts, and Blasters; Extraction Workers, All Other; First-Line Supervisors of Construction Trades and Extraction Workers; Floor Layers, Except Carpet, Wood, and Hard Tiles; Floor Sanders and Finishers; Glaziers; Heating and Air Conditioning Mechanics and Installers; Helpers, Construction Trades, All Other; others.

Skills—Operation and Control: Controlling operations of equipment or systems. **Mathematics:** Using mathematics to solve problems. **Quality Control Analysis:** Conducting tests and inspections of products, services, or processes to evaluate quality or performance. **Equipment Selection:** Determining the kind of tools and equipment needed to do a job. **Installation:** Installing equipment, machines, wiring, or programs to meet specifications. **Coordination:** Adjusting actions in relation to others' actions.

Work Environment: Outdoors; standing; walking and running; kneeling, crouching, stooping, or crawling; using hands; bending or twisting the body; repetitive motions; noise; very hot or cold; bright or inadequate lighting; contaminants; whole-body vibration; hazardous equipment; minor burns, cuts, bites, or stings.

Chefs and Head Cooks

- ⊙ Annual Earnings: $42,350
- ⊙ Earnings Growth Potential: High (41.5%)
- ⊙ Growth: −0.8%
- ⊙ Annual Job Openings: 1,800
- ⊙ Self-Employed: 7.4%

Considerations for Job Outlook: Job opportunities will be best for chefs and head cooks with several years of work experience. The majority of job openings will stem from the need to replace workers who leave the occupation. The fast pace, long hours, and high energy levels required for these jobs often lead to a high rate of turnover. There will be strong competition for jobs at upscale restaurants, hotels, and casinos, which tend to pay more. Workers with a combination of business skills, previous work experience, and creativity will have the best job prospects.

Direct and may participate in the preparation, seasoning, and cooking of salads, soups, fish, meats, vegetables, desserts, or other foods. Check the quality of raw and cooked food products to ensure that standards are met. Monitor sanitation practices to ensure that employees follow standards and regulations. Check the quantity and quality of received products. Order or requisition food and other supplies needed to ensure efficient operation. Supervise and coordinate activities of cooks and workers engaged in food preparation. Inspect supplies, equipment, and work areas to ensure conformance to established standards. Determine how food should be presented, and create decorative food displays. Instruct cooks and other workers in the preparation, cooking, garnishing, and presentation of food. Estimate amounts and costs of required supplies, such as food and ingredients. Collaborate with other personnel to plan and develop recipes and menus, taking into account such factors as seasonal availability of ingredients and the likely number of customers. Analyze recipes to assign prices to menu items, based on food, labor, and overhead costs. Prepare and cook foods of all types, either on a

regular basis or for special guests or functions. Determine production schedules and staff requirements necessary to ensure timely delivery of services. Recruit and hire staff, including cooks and other kitchen workers. Meet with customers to discuss menus for special occasions such as weddings, parties, and banquets. Demonstrate new cooking techniques and equipment to staff. Meet with sales representatives to negotiate prices and order supplies. Arrange for equipment purchases and repairs. Record production and operational data on specified forms. Plan, direct, and supervise the food preparation and cooking activities of multiple kitchens or restaurants in establishments such as restaurant chains, hospitals, or hotels. Coordinate planning, budgeting, and purchasing for all the food operations within establishments such as clubs, hotels, or restaurant chains.

Education/Training Required: High school diploma or equivalent. **Education and Training Programs:** Baking and Pastry Arts/Baker/Pastry Chef Training; Culinary Arts/Chef Training. **Knowledge/Courses—Food Production:** Techniques and equipment for planting, growing, and harvesting food products (both plant and animal) for consumption, including storage/handling techniques. **Production and Processing:** Raw materials, production processes, quality control, costs, and other techniques for maximizing the effective manufacture and distribution of goods. **Administration and Management:** Business and management principles involved in strategic planning, resource allocation, human resources modeling, leadership technique, production methods, and coordination of people and resources. **Chemistry:** The chemical composition, structure, and properties of substances and of the chemical processes and transformations that they undergo. This includes uses of chemicals and their danger signs, production techniques, and disposal methods. **Education and Training:** Principles and methods for curriculum and training design, teaching and instruction for individuals and groups, and the measurement of training effects. **Personnel and Human Resources:** Principles and procedures for personnel recruitment, selection, training, compensation and benefits, labor relations and negotiation, and personnel information systems. **Work Experience Needed:** 1 to 5 years. **On-the-Job Training Needed:** None. **Certification/Licensure:** Voluntary certification by association.

Personality Type: Enterprising-Realistic-Artistic. **Career Cluster:** 09 Hospitality and Tourism. **Career Pathway:**

09.1 Restaurants and Food/Beverage Services. **Other Jobs in This Pathway:** Bakers; Baristas; Bartenders; Butchers and Meat Cutters; Combined Food Preparation and Serving Workers, Including Fast Food; Cooks, All Other; Cooks, Fast Food; Cooks, Institution and Cafeteria; Cooks, Private Household; Cooks, Restaurant; Cooks, Short Order; Counter Attendants, Cafeteria, Food Concession, and Coffee Shop; Dining Room and Cafeteria Attendants and Bartender Helpers; Dishwashers; First-Line Supervisors of Food Preparation and Serving Workers; Food Preparation and Serving Related Workers, All Other; Food Preparation Workers; Food Servers, Nonrestaurant; Food Service Managers; Gaming Managers; Hosts and Hostesses, Restaurant, Lounge, and Coffee Shop; Meat, Poultry, and Fish Cutters and Trimmers; Slaughterers and Meat Packers; Waiters and Waitresses.

Skills—Management of Financial Resources: Determining how money will be spent to get the work done and accounting for these expenditures. **Management of Material Resources:** Obtaining and seeing to the appropriate use of equipment, facilities, and materials needed to do certain work. **Management of Personnel Resources:** Motivating, developing, and directing people as they work, identifying the best people for the job. **Negotiation:** Bringing others together and trying to reconcile differences. **Operations Analysis:** Analyzing needs and product requirements to create a design. **Time Management:** Managing one's own time and the time of others. **Active Learning:** Understanding the implications of new information for both current and future problem solving and decision making. **Instructing:** Teaching others how to do something.

Work Environment: Indoors; standing; walking and running; using hands; bending or twisting the body; repetitive motions; minor burns, cuts, bites, or stings.

Chemical Plant and System Operators

- ⊙ Annual Earnings: $55,940
- ⊙ Earnings Growth Potential: Medium (38.5%)
- ⊙ Growth: −12.2%
- ⊙ Annual Job Openings: 1,410
- ⊙ Self-Employed: 1.0%

Considerations for Job Outlook: In petroleum and coal products manufacturing, a small increase is expected as a result of growth in petroleum refineries relative to other manufacturing activities.

Control or operate entire chemical processes or system of machines. Move control settings to make necessary adjustments on equipment units affecting speeds of chemical reactions, quality, and yields. Monitor recording instruments, flowmeters, panel lights, and other indicators, and listen for warning signals, in order to verify conformity of process conditions. Control or operate chemical processes or systems of machines, using panelboards, control boards, or semi-automatic equipment. Record operating data such as process conditions, test results, and instrument readings. Confer with technical and supervisory personnel to report or resolve conditions affecting safety, efficiency, and product quality. Draw samples of products, and conduct quality control tests in order to monitor processing, and to ensure that standards are met. Regulate or shut down equipment during emergency situations, as directed by supervisory personnel. Start pumps to wash and rinse reactor vessels, to exhaust gases and vapors, to regulate the flow of oil, steam, air, and perfume to towers, and to add products to converter or blending vessels. Interpret chemical reactions visible through sight glasses or on television monitors, and review laboratory test reports for process adjustments. Patrol work areas to ensure that solutions in tanks and troughs are not in danger of overflowing. Notify maintenance, stationary-engineering, and other auxiliary personnel to correct equipment malfunctions and to adjust power, steam, water, or air supplies. Inspect operating units such as towers, soap-spray storage tanks, scrubbers, collectors, and driers to ensure that all are functioning, and to maintain maximum efficiency. Direct workers engaged in operating machinery that regulates the flow of materials and products. Turn valves to regulate flow of products or byproducts through agitator tanks, storage drums, or neutralizer tanks. Calculate material requirements or yields according to formulas. Gauge tank levels, using calibrated rods. Repair and replace damaged equipment.

Education/Training Required: High school diploma or equivalent. **Education and Training Program:** Chemical Technology/Technician. **Knowledge/Courses—Production and Processing:** Raw materials, production processes, quality control, costs, and other techniques for maximizing the effective manufacture and distribution of goods.

Mechanical Devices: Machines and tools, including their designs, uses, repair, and maintenance. **Chemistry:** The chemical composition, structure, and properties of substances and of the chemical processes and transformations that they undergo. This includes uses of chemicals and their danger signs, production techniques, and disposal methods. **Physics:** Physical principles, laws, their interrelationships, and applications to understanding fluid, material, and atmospheric dynamics, and mechanical, electrical, atomic, and subatomic structures and processes. **Engineering and Technology:** The practical application of engineering science and technology. This includes applying principles, techniques, procedures, and equipment to the design and production of various goods and services. **Public Safety and Security:** Relevant equipment, policies, procedures, and strategies to promote effective local, state, or national security operations for the protection of people, data, property, and institutions. **Work Experience Needed:** None. **On-the-Job Training Needed:** Long-term on-the-job training. **Certification/Licensure:** No data available.

Personality Type: Realistic-Conventional. **Career Cluster:** 13 Manufacturing. **Career Pathway:** 13.2 Manufacturing Production Process Development. **Other Jobs in This Pathway:** Biofuels Processing Technicians; Biomass Plant Technicians; Chemical Technicians; Electrical Engineering Technicians; Electromechanical Equipment Assemblers; Environmental Science and Protection Technicians, Including Health; Fabric and Apparel Patternmakers; Farm and Home Management Advisors; Fashion Designers; Hydroelectric Plant Technicians; Life, Physical, and Social Science Technicians, All Other; Methane/Landfill Gas Generation System Technicians; Nuclear Monitoring Technicians; Quality Control Analysts; Textile, Apparel, and Furnishings Workers, All Other.

Skills—Operation Monitoring: Watching gauges, dials, or other indicators to make sure a machine is working properly. **Operation and Control:** Controlling operations of equipment or systems. **Repairing:** Repairing machines or systems using the needed tools. **Equipment Maintenance:** Performing routine maintenance on equipment and determining when and what kind of maintenance is needed. **Quality Control Analysis:** Conducting tests and inspections of products, services, or processes to evaluate quality or performance. **Mathematics:** Using mathematics to solve problems. **Science:** Using scientific rules and methods to solve problems. **Troubleshooting:** Determining causes of operating errors and deciding what to do about them.

Work Environment: More often indoors than outdoors; standing; using hands; noise; very hot or cold; contaminants; high places; hazardous conditions.

Chemical Technicians

- ⊙ Annual Earnings: $42,070
- ⊙ Earnings Growth Potential: Medium (38.2%)
- ⊙ Growth: 6.7%
- ⊙ Annual Job Openings: 1,290
- ⊙ Self-Employed: 0.0%

Considerations for Job Outlook: As the instrumentation and techniques used in research, development, and production become more complex, employers will seek job candidates with highly developed technical skills. Job opportunities are expected to be best for graduates of applied science technology programs who are well trained on equipment used in laboratories or production facilities. In addition to job openings created by growth, many openings should arise from the need to replace technicians who retire or leave the labor force for other reasons.

Conduct chemical and physical laboratory tests to assist scientists in making qualitative and quantitative analyses. Monitor product quality to ensure compliance to standards and specifications. Compile and interpret results of tests and analyses. Set up and conduct chemical experiments, tests, and analyses using techniques such as chromatography, spectroscopy, physical and chemical separation techniques, and microscopy. Conduct chemical and physical laboratory tests to assist scientists in making qualitative and quantitative analyses of solids, liquids, and gaseous materials. Provide and maintain a safe work environment by participating in safety programs, committees, or teams, and by conducting laboratory and plant safety audits. Prepare chemical solutions for products and processes following standardized formulas, or create experimental formulas. Maintain, clean, and sterilize laboratory instruments and equipment. Write technical reports or prepare graphs and charts to document experimental results. Provide technical support and assistance to chemists and engineers. Order and inventory materials to maintain supplies. Develop and conduct programs of sampling and analysis to maintain quality standards of raw materials, chemical intermediates, and products. Operate experimental pilot plants, assisting with experimental design. Design and fabricate experimental apparatus to develop new products and processes. Develop new chemical engineering processes or production techniques. Direct or monitor other workers producing chemical products.

Education/Training Required: Associate degree. **Education and Training Programs:** Chemical Technology/Technician; Food Science. **Knowledge/Courses—Chemistry:** The chemical composition, structure, and properties of substances and of the chemical processes and transformations that they undergo. This includes uses of chemicals and their danger signs, production techniques, and disposal methods. **Physics:** Physical principles, laws, their interrelationships, and applications to understanding fluid, material, and atmospheric dynamics, and mechanical, electrical, atomic, and subatomic structures and processes. **Biology:** Plant and animal organisms and their tissues, cells, functions, interdependencies, and interactions with each other and the environment. **Computers and Electronics:** Circuit boards, processors, chips, electronic equipment, and computer hardware and software, including applications and programming. **Engineering and Technology:** The practical application of engineering science and technology. This includes applying principles, techniques, procedures, and equipment to the design and production of various goods and services. **Mathematics:** Arithmetic, algebra, geometry, calculus, statistics, and their applications. **Work Experience Needed:** None. **On-the-Job Training Needed:** Moderate-term on-the-job training. **Certification/Licensure:** None.

Personality Type: Investigative-Realistic-Conventional. **Career Clusters:** 01 Agriculture, Food, and Natural Resources; 13 Manufacturing. **Career Pathways:** 13.2 Manufacturing Production Process Development; 01.1 Food Products and Processing Systems. **Other Jobs in These Pathways:** Agricultural Inspectors; Agricultural Sciences Teachers, Postsecondary; Agricultural Technicians; Biofuels Processing Technicians; Biomass Plant Technicians; Buyers and Purchasing Agents, Farm Products; Chemical Plant and System Operators; Electrical Engineering Technicians; Electromechanical Equipment Assemblers; Environmental Science and Protection Technicians, Including Health; Fabric and Apparel Patternmakers; Farm and Home Management Advisors; Fashion Designers; First-Line Supervisors of Office and Administrative Support Workers; Food and Tobacco Roasting, Baking, and Drying Machine Operators and Tenders; Food Batchmakers; Food Cooking Machine Operators and Tenders; Food Science Technicians; Food Scientists and Technologists; Graders and Sorters, Agricultural Products; Hydroelectric Plant Technicians; Life, Physical, and Social Science Technicians, All Other; Methane/Landfill Gas Generation System Technicians; Nonfarm Animal Caretakers; Nuclear Monitoring Technicians; others.

Skills—Science: Using scientific rules and methods to solve problems. **Repairing:** Repairing machines or systems using the needed tools. **Equipment Maintenance:** Performing routine maintenance on equipment and determining when and what kind of maintenance is needed. **Equipment Selection:** Determining the kind of tools and equipment needed to do a job. **Troubleshooting:** Determining causes of operating errors and deciding what to do about them. **Quality Control Analysis:** Conducting tests and inspections of products, services, or processes to evaluate quality or performance. **Operations Analysis:** Analyzing needs and product requirements to create a design. **Mathematics:** Using mathematics to solve problems.

Work Environment: Indoors; standing; using hands; repetitive motions; contaminants; hazardous conditions.

Choreographers

- ⊙ Annual Earnings: $39,600
- ⊙ Earnings Growth Potential: Very high (51.5%)
- ⊙ Growth: 24.2%
- ⊙ Annual Job Openings: 830
- ⊙ Self-Employed: 9.7%

Considerations for Job Outlook: Dancers and choreographers face intense competition, and the number of applicants is expected to vastly exceed the number of job openings. Dancers who attend schools or conservatories associated with a dance company may have a better chance of finding work at that company. In addition, many choreographers recruit dancers from nationally accredited college programs.

Create new dance routines. Rehearse performance of routines. Direct rehearsals to instruct dancers in how to use dance steps and in techniques to achieve desired effects. Read and study story lines and musical scores to determine how to translate ideas and moods into dance movements. Design dances for individual dancers, dance companies, musical theater, opera, fashion shows, film, television productions, and special events, and for dancers ranging from beginners to professionals. Choose the music, sound effects, or spoken narrative to accompany a dance. Advise dancers on how to stand and move properly, teaching correct dance techniques to help prevent injuries. Coordinate production music with music directors. Audition performers for one or more dance parts. Direct and stage dance presentations for various forms of entertainment. Develop ideas for creating dances, keeping notes and sketches to record influences. Train, exercise, and attend dance classes to maintain high levels of technical proficiency, physical ability, and physical fitness. Teach students, dancers, and other performers about rhythm and interpretive movement. Assess students' dancing abilities to determine where improvement or change is needed. Experiment with different types of dancers, steps, dances, and placements, testing ideas informally to get feedback from dancers. Seek influences from other art forms such as theater, the visual arts, and architecture. Design sets, lighting, costumes, and other artistic elements of productions, in collaboration with cast members. Record dance movements and their technical aspects, using a technical understanding of the patterns and formations of choreography. Restage traditional dances and works in dance companies' repertoires, developing new interpretations. Manage dance schools or assist in their management.

Education/Training Required: High school diploma or equivalent. **Education and Training Programs:** Dance, General; Dance, Other. **Knowledge/Courses—Fine Arts:** The theory and techniques required to compose, produce, and perform works of music, dance, visual arts, drama, and sculpture. **History and Archeology:** Historical events and their causes, indicators, and effects on civilizations and cultures. **Philosophy and Theology:** Different philosophical systems and religions. This includes their basic principles, values, ethics, ways of thinking, customs, practices, and their impact on human culture. **Sociology and Anthropology:** Group behavior and dynamics, societal trends and influences, human migrations, ethnicity, and cultures and their history and origins. **Communications and Media:** Media production, communication, and dissemination techniques and methods. This includes alternative ways to inform and entertain via written, oral, and visual media. **Psychology:** Human behavior and performance; individual differences in ability, personality, and interests; learning and motivation; psychological research methods; and the assessment and treatment of behavioral and affective disorders. **Work Experience Needed:** More than 5 years. **On-the-Job Training Needed:** Long-term on-the-job training. **Certification/Licensure:** None.

Personality Type: Artistic-Social-Enterprising. **Career Cluster:** 03 Arts and Communications. **Career Pathways:** 03.1 Audio and Video Technology and Film; 03.4 Performing Arts. **Other Jobs in These Pathways:** Actors; Agents and Business Managers of Artists, Performers, and Athletes; Archivists; Art, Drama, and Music Teachers, Postsecondary; Artists and Related Workers, All Other; Broadcast Technicians; Camera Operators, Television, Video, and Motion Picture; Commercial and Industrial Designers; Craft Artists; Curators; Dancers; Designers, All Other; Directors—Stage, Motion Pictures, Television, and Radio; Entertainers and Performers, Sports and Related Workers, All Other; Film and Video Editors; Fine Artists, Including Painters, Sculptors, and Illustrators; Graphic Designers; Historians; Managers, All Other; Media and Communication Equipment Workers, All Other; Media and Communication Workers, All Other; Multimedia Artists and Animators; Museum Technicians and Conservators; Music Composers and Arrangers; Music Directors; Musicians, Instrumental; Photographers; Poets, Lyricists and Creative Writers; Producers; Program Directors; Set and Exhibit Designers; Singers; Talent Directors; others.

Skills—Instructing: Teaching others how to do something. **Management of Personnel Resources:** Motivating, developing, and directing people as they work, identifying the best people for the job. **Operations Analysis:** Analyzing needs and product requirements to create a design. **Coordination:** Adjusting actions in relation to others' actions. **Social Perceptiveness:** Being aware of others' reactions and understanding why they react as they do. **Learning Strategies:** Selecting and using training/instructional methods and procedures appropriate for the situation when learning or teaching new things. **Negotiation:** Bringing others together and trying to reconcile differences. **Time Management:** Managing one's own time and the time of others.

Work Environment: Indoors; standing; walking and running; kneeling, crouching, stooping, or crawling; balancing; bending or twisting the body; repetitive motions.

Civil Engineering Technicians

- ⊙ Annual Earnings: $46,900
- ⊙ Earnings Growth Potential: Medium (38.3%)
- ⊙ Growth: 11.9%
- ⊙ Annual Job Openings: 2,460
- ⊙ Self-Employed: 0.5%

Considerations for Job Outlook: Civil engineering technicians learn to use design software that civil engineers typically do not. Thus, those who master it, keep their skills current, and stay abreast of the latest software will likely improve their chances for employment.

Apply theory and principles of civil engineering under the direction of engineering staff or physical scientists. Calculate dimensions, square footage, profile and component specifications, and material quantities using calculators or computers. Draft detailed dimensional drawings, and design layouts for projects and to ensure conformance to specifications. Analyze proposed site factors, and design maps, graphs, tracings, and diagrams to illustrate findings. Read and review project blueprints and structural specifications to determine dimensions of structures or system and material requirements. Prepare reports, and document project activities and data. Confer with supervisor to determine project details such as plan preparation, acceptance testing, and evaluation of field conditions. Inspect project sites, and evaluate contractor work to detect design malfunctions and ensure conformance to design specifications and applicable codes. Plan and conduct field surveys to locate new sites, and analyze details of project sites. Develop plans and estimate costs for installation of systems, utilization of facilities, or construction of structures. Report maintenance problems occurring at project sites to supervisor, and negotiate changes to resolve system conflicts. Conduct materials tests and analyses using tools and equipment and applying engineering knowledge. Respond to public suggestions and complaints. Evaluate facilities to determine suitability for occupancy and square footage availability.

Education/Training Required: Associate degree. **Education and Training Programs:** Civil Engineering Technology/Technician; Construction Engineering Technology/Technician. **Knowledge/Courses—Building and Construction:** Materials, methods, and the tools involved in the construction or repair of houses, buildings, or other structures such as highways and roads. **Engineering and Technology:** The practical application of engineering science and technology. This includes applying principles, techniques, procedures, and equipment to the design and production of various goods and services. **Design:** Design techniques, tools, and principles involved in production of precision technical plans, blueprints, drawings, and models. **Geography:** Principles and methods for describing the features of land, sea, and air masses, including their physical characteristics, locations, interrelationships, and distribution of plant, animal, and human life. **Transportation:** Principles and methods for moving people or goods by air, rail, sea, or road, including the relative costs and benefits. **Physics:** Physical principles, laws, their interrelationships, and applications to understanding fluid, material, and atmospheric dynamics, and mechanical, electrical, atomic, and subatomic structures and processes. **Work Experience Needed:** None. **On-the-Job Training Needed:** None. **Certification/Licensure:** Voluntary certification by association.

Personality Type: Realistic-Conventional-Investigative. **Career Clusters:** 02 Architecture and Construction; 13 Manufacturing. **Career Pathways:** 13.3 Maintenance, Installation, and Repair; 02.1 Design/Pre-Construction. **Other Jobs in These Pathways:** Aircraft Mechanics and Service Technicians; Architects, Except Landscape and Naval; Architectural and Engineering Managers; Architectural Drafters; Architecture Teachers, Postsecondary; Automotive Engineering Technicians; Automotive Specialty Technicians; Avionics Technicians; Biological Technicians; Camera and Photographic Equipment Repairers; Cartographers and Photogrammetrists; Chemical Equipment Operators and Tenders; Civil Drafters; Coil Winders, Tapers, and Finishers; Computer, Automated Teller, and Office Machine Repairers; Construction and Related Workers, All Other; Control and Valve Installers and Repairers, Except Mechanical Door; Drafters, All Other; Electric Motor, Power Tool, and Related Repairers; Electrical and Electronic Equipment Assemblers; Electrical and Electronics Repairers, Commercial and Industrial Equipment; Electrical and Electronics Repairers, Powerhouse,

Substation, and Relay; Electrical Drafters; Electrical Engineering Technicians; others.

Skills—Operations Analysis: Analyzing needs and product requirements to create a design. **Operation Monitoring:** Watching gauges, dials, or other indicators to make sure a machine is working properly. **Operation and Control:** Controlling operations of equipment or systems. **Mathematics:** Using mathematics to solve problems. **Science:** Using scientific rules and methods to solve problems. **Management of Financial Resources:** Determining how money will be spent to get the work done and accounting for these expenditures. **Management of Material Resources:** Obtaining and seeing to the appropriate use of equipment, facilities, and materials needed to do certain work. **Active Listening:** Giving full attention to what other people are saying, taking time to understand the points being made, asking questions as appropriate, and not interrupting at inappropriate times.

Work Environment: More often indoors than outdoors; sitting; using hands; repetitive motions.

Claims Adjusters, Examiners, and Investigators

- ⊙ Annual Earnings: $59,320
- ⊙ Earnings Growth Potential: Medium (38.8%)
- ⊙ Growth: 3.0%
- ⊙ Annual Job Openings: 7,990
- ⊙ Self-Employed: 0.9%

Considerations for Job Outlook: Job opportunities for claims adjusters and examiners should be best in the health insurance industry as the number of health insurance customers expands. Additionally, prospects for claims adjusters in property and casualty insurance will likely be best in areas susceptible to natural disasters.

Review settled claims to determine that payments and settlements are made in accordance with company practices and procedures. For task data, see Job Specializations.

Education/Training Required: High school diploma or equivalent. **Work Experience Needed:** None. **On-the-Job Training Needed:** Long-term on-the-job training.

Certification/Licensure: Licensure in some states for some specializations.

Job Specialization: Claims Examiners, Property and Casualty Insurance

Review settled insurance claims to determine that payments and settlements have been made in accordance with company practices and procedures. Report overpayments, underpayments, and other irregularities. Confer with legal counsel on claims requiring litigation. Investigate, evaluate, and settle claims, applying technical knowledge and human relations skills to effect fair and prompt disposal of cases and to contribute to a reduced loss ratio. Pay and process claims within designated authority level. Adjust reserves or provide reserve recommendations to ensure that reserve activities are consistent with corporate policies. Enter claim payments, reserves, and new claims on computer system, inputting concise yet sufficient file documentation. Resolve complex severe exposure claims, using high-service-oriented file handling. Maintain claim files such as records of settled claims and an inventory of claims requiring detailed analysis. Verify and analyze data used in settling claims to ensure that claims are valid and that settlements are made according to company practices and procedures. Examine claims investigated by insurance adjusters, further investigating questionable claims to determine whether to authorize payments. Present cases, and participate in their discussion at claim committee meetings. Contact or interview claimants, doctors, medical specialists, or employers to get additional information. Confer with legal counsel on claims requiring litigation. Report overpayments, underpayments, and other irregularities. Communicate with reinsurance brokers to obtain information necessary for processing claims. Supervise claims adjusters to ensure that adjusters have followed proper methods.

Education and Training Programs: Health/Medical Claims Examiner Training; Insurance. **Knowledge/Courses—Customer and Personal Service:** Principles and processes for providing customer and personal services. This includes customer needs assessment, meeting quality standards for services, and evaluation of customer satisfaction. **Law and Government:** Laws, legal codes, court procedures, precedents, government regulations, executive orders, agency rules, and the democratic political process. **Building and Construction:** Materials, methods, and the tools involved in the construction or repair of houses, buildings, or other structures such as highways and roads. **Administration and Management:** Business and management principles involved in strategic planning, resource allocation, human resources modeling, leadership technique, production methods, and coordination of people and resources. **English Language:** The structure and content of the English language including the meaning and spelling of words, rules of composition, and grammar. **Clerical Practices:** Administrative and clerical procedures and systems such as word processing, managing files and records, stenography and transcription, designing forms, and other office procedures and terminology.

Personality Type: Conventional-Enterprising. **Career Cluster:** 06 Finance. **Career Pathway:** 06.4 Insurance Services. **Other Jobs in This Pathway:** Actuaries; Business Teachers, Postsecondary; Insurance Adjusters, Examiners, and Investigators; Insurance Appraisers, Auto Damage; Insurance Sales Agents; Insurance Underwriters; Telemarketers.

Skills—Negotiation: Bringing others together and trying to reconcile differences. **Persuasion:** Persuading others to change their minds or behavior. **Service Orientation:** Actively looking for ways to help people. **Reading Comprehension:** Understanding written sentences and paragraphs in work-related documents. **Writing:** Communicating effectively in writing as appropriate for the needs of the audience. **Critical Thinking:** Using logic and reasoning to identify the strengths and weaknesses of alternative solutions, conclusions, or approaches to problems. **Management of Financial Resources:** Determining how money will be spent to get the work done and accounting for these expenditures. **Mathematics:** Using mathematics to solve problems.

Work Environment: Indoors; sitting; repetitive motions; noise.

Job Specialization: Insurance Adjusters, Examiners, and Investigators

Investigate, analyze, and determine the extent of insurance company's liability concerning personal, casualty, or property loss or damages and attempt to effect settlement with claimants. Correspond with or interview medical specialists, agents, witnesses, or claimants to compile information. Calculate benefit payments and approve payment of claims within a certain monetary limit. Interview or correspond with claimants and witnesses, consult police and hospital records, and inspect property damage to determine extent of liability. Investigate and assess damage to property. Examine claims forms and other records to determine insurance coverage. Analyze information gathered by investigation, and report findings and recommendations. Negotiate claim settlements, and recommend litigation when settlement cannot be negotiated. Collect evidence to support contested claims in court. Prepare reports of findings of investigation. Interview or correspond with agents and claimants to correct errors or omissions and to investigate questionable claims. Refer questionable claims to investigators or claims adjusters for investigation or settlement. Examine titles to property to determine validity, and act as company agent in transactions with property owners. Obtain credit information from banks and other credit services. Communicate with former associates to verify employment records and to obtain background information regarding persons or businesses applying for credit.

Education and Training Programs: Health/Medical Claims Examiner Training; Insurance. **Knowledge/Courses—Customer and Personal Service:** Principles and processes for providing customer and personal services. This includes customer needs assessment, meeting quality standards for services, and evaluation of customer satisfaction. **Clerical Practices:** Administrative and clerical procedures and systems such as word processing, managing files and records, stenography and transcription, designing forms, and other office procedures and terminology. **Building and Construction:** Materials, methods, and the tools involved in the construction or repair of houses, buildings, or other structures such as highways and roads. **English Language:** The structure and content of the English language including the meaning and spelling of words, rules of composition, and grammar. **Law and Government:** Laws, legal codes, court procedures, precedents, government regulations, executive orders, agency rules, and the democratic political process. **Mathematics:** Arithmetic, algebra, geometry, calculus, statistics, and their applications.

Personality Type: Conventional-Enterprising. **Career Cluster:** 06 Finance. **Career Pathway:** 06.4 Insurance Services. **Other Jobs in This Pathway:** Actuaries; Business Teachers, Postsecondary; Claims Examiners, Property and Casualty Insurance; Insurance Appraisers, Auto Damage; Insurance Sales Agents; Insurance Underwriters; Telemarketers.

Skills—Management of Financial Resources: Determining how money will be spent to get the work done and accounting for these expenditures. **Negotiation:** Bringing others together and trying to reconcile differences. **Mathematics:** Using mathematics to solve problems. **Critical Thinking:** Using logic and reasoning to identify the strengths and weaknesses of alternative solutions, conclusions, or approaches to problems. **Active Listening:** Giving full attention to what other people are saying, taking time to understand the points being made, asking questions as appropriate, and not interrupting at inappropriate times. **Speaking:** Talking to others to convey information effectively. **Reading Comprehension:** Understanding written sentences and paragraphs in work-related documents. **Writing:** Communicating effectively in writing as appropriate for the needs of the audience.

Work Environment: Indoors; sitting; repetitive motions.

Coaches and Scouts

- ⊙ Annual Earnings: $28,470
- ⊙ Earnings Growth Potential: Medium (39.9%)
- ⊙ Growth: 29.4%
- ⊙ Annual Job Openings: 13,300
- ⊙ Self-Employed: 18.7%

Considerations for Job Outlook: Those who have a degree or are state-certified to teach academic subjects should have the best prospects for getting coaching and instructor jobs at high schools. The need to replace the many high school coaches who change occupations or leave the labor force also will provide some jobs. Coaches in girls' and women's sports may have better job opportunities and face less competition for positions. Strong competition is expected for higher-paying jobs at the college level and will be even greater for jobs in professional sports. Competition should also be strong for paying jobs as scouts, particularly for professional teams, because there are few available jobs.

Instruct or coach groups or individuals in the fundamentals of sports. Plan, organize, and conduct practice sessions. Provide training direction, encouragement, and motivation to prepare athletes for games, competitive events, or tours. Identify and recruit potential athletes, arranging and offering incentives such as athletic scholarships. Plan strategies and choose team members for individual games or sports seasons. Plan and direct physical conditioning programs that will enable athletes to achieve maximum performance. Adjust coaching techniques based on the strengths and weaknesses of athletes. File scouting reports that detail player assessments, provide recommendations on athlete recruitment, and identify locations and individuals to be targeted for future recruitment efforts. Keep records of athlete, team, and opposing team performance. Instruct individuals or groups in sports rules, game strategies, and performance principles such as specific ways of moving the body, hands, and feet in order to achieve desired results. Analyze the strengths and weaknesses of opposing teams to develop game strategies. Evaluate athletes' skills and review performance records to determine their fitness and potential in a particular area of athletics. Keep abreast of changing rules, techniques, technologies, and philosophies relevant to their sport. Monitor athletes' use of equipment to ensure safe and proper use. Explain and enforce safety rules and regulations. Develop and arrange competition schedules and programs.

Education/Training Required: High school diploma or equivalent. **Education and Training Programs:** Health and Physical Education, General; Physical Education Teaching and Coaching; Sport and Fitness Administration/Management. **Knowledge/Courses—Education and Training:** Principles and methods for curriculum and training design, teaching and instruction for individuals and groups, and the measurement of training effects. **Therapy and Counseling:** Principles, methods, and procedures for diagnosis, treatment, and rehabilitation of physical and mental dysfunctions, and for career counseling and guidance. **Sales and Marketing:** Principles and methods for showing, promoting, and selling products or services. This includes marketing strategy and tactics, product demonstration, sales techniques, and sales control systems. **Personnel and Human Resources:** Principles and procedures for personnel recruitment, selection, training, compensation and benefits, labor relations and negotiation, and personnel information systems. **Psychology:** Human behavior and performance; individual differences in ability, personality, and interests; learning and motivation; psychological research methods; and the assessment and treatment of behavioral and affective disorders. **English Language:** The structure and content of the English language including the meaning and spelling of words, rules of composition, and grammar. **Work Experience Needed:** None. **On-the-Job Training Needed:** Long-term on-the-job training. **Certification/Licensure:** Licensure in some states for some specializations.

Personality Type: Social-Realistic-Enterprising. **Career Cluster:** 05 Education and Training. **Career Pathways:** 05.3 Teaching/Training; 05.1 Administration and Administrative Support. **Other Jobs in These Pathways:** Adult Basic and Secondary Education and Literacy Teachers and Instructors; Agricultural Sciences Teachers, Postsecondary; Anthropology and Archeology Teachers, Postsecondary; Architecture Teachers, Postsecondary; Area, Ethnic, and Cultural Studies Teachers, Postsecondary; Art, Drama, and Music Teachers, Postsecondary; Athletes and Sports Competitors; Atmospheric, Earth, Marine, and Space Sciences Teachers, Postsecondary; Audio-Visual and Multimedia Collections Specialists; Biological Science Teachers, Postsecondary; Business Teachers, Postsecondary; Career/Technical Education Teachers, Middle School; Career/Technical Education Teachers, Secondary School; Chemists; Communications Teachers, Postsecondary; Computer Science Teachers, Postsecondary; Criminal Justice and Law Enforcement Teachers, Postsecondary; Dietitians and Nutritionists; Distance Learning Coordinators; Education Administrators, All Other; Education Administrators, Elementary and Secondary School; others.

Skills—Management of Personnel Resources: Motivating, developing, and directing people as they work, identifying the best people for the job. **Instructing:** Teaching others how to do something. **Systems Evaluation:** Identifying measures or indicators of system performance and the actions needed to improve or correct performance relative to the goals of the system. **Monitoring:** Monitoring or assessing your performance or that of other individuals or organizations to make improvements or take corrective action. **Management of Material Resources:** Obtaining and seeing to the appropriate use of equipment, facilities, and materials needed to do certain work. **Negotiation:** Bringing others together and trying to reconcile differences. **Learning Strategies:** Selecting and using training/instructional methods and procedures appropriate for the situation when learning or teaching new things. **Persuasion:** Persuading others to change their minds or behavior.

Work Environment: Indoors; standing; noise; very hot or cold.

Coating, Painting, and Spraying Machine Setters, Operators, and Tenders

- ⊙ Annual Earnings: $30,020
- ⊙ Earnings Growth Potential: Low (32.5%)
- ⊙ Growth: 6.1%
- ⊙ Annual Job Openings: 2,310
- ⊙ Self-Employed: 5.5%

Considerations for Job Outlook: As with many skilled manufacturing jobs, employers often report difficulty finding qualified workers. Therefore, job opportunities should be very good for those with painting experience. Job openings also should result from the need to replace workers who leave the occupation and from increased specialization in manufacturing. Although higher educational requirements would normally reduce competition for automotive painters in repair shops, the large number of people who enjoy working on cars should offset that reduction.

Set up, operate, or tend machines to coat or paint any of a wide variety of products. Observe machine gauges and equipment operation to detect defects or deviations from standards, and make adjustments as necessary. Determine paint flow, viscosity, and coating quality by performing visual inspections or by using viscometers. Weigh or measure chemicals, coatings, or paints before adding them to machines. Select appropriate coatings, paints, or sprays, or prepare them by mixing substances according to formulas, using automated paint mixing equipment. Set up and operate machines to paint or coat products with such materials as silver and copper solution, rubber, paint, glaze, oil, or rustproofing materials. Turn dials, handwheels, valves, or switches to regulate conveyor speeds, machine temperature, air pressure and circulation, and the flow or spray of coatings or paints. Start and stop the operation of machines, using levers or buttons. Record operational data on specified forms. Start pumps to mix solutions and fill tanks. Fill hoppers, reservoirs, troughs, or pans with material used to coat, paint, or spray, using conveyors or pails. Operate auxiliary machines or equipment used in coating or painting processes. Perform test runs to ensure that equipment is set up properly. Clean machines, related equipment, and work areas, using water, solvents, and other cleaning aids. Thread or feed items or products through or around machine rollers and dryers. Attach hoses or nozzles to machines, using wrenches and pliers, and make adjustments to obtain the proper dispersion of spray. Remove materials, parts, or workpieces from painting or coating machines, using hand tools. Transfer completed items or products from machines to drying or storage areas, using handcarts, handtrucks, or cranes. Attach and align machine parts such as rollers, guides, brushes, and blades, using hand tools. Examine, measure, weigh, or test sample products to ensure conformance to specifications. Hold or position spray guns to direct spray onto articles.

Education/Training Required: High school diploma or equivalent. **Education and Training Programs:** No related CIP programs; this job is learned through informal moderate-term on-the-job training. **Knowledge/Courses—Production and Processing:** Raw materials, production processes, quality control, costs, and other techniques for maximizing the effective manufacture and distribution of goods. **Mechanical Devices:** Machines and tools, including their designs, uses, repair, and maintenance. **Work Experience Needed:** None. **On-the-Job Training Needed:** Moderate-term on-the-job training. **Certification/Licensure:** Voluntary certification for some specializations.

Personality Type: Realistic-Conventional-Investigative. **Career Cluster:** 13 Manufacturing. **Career Pathway:** 13.1 Production. **Other Jobs in This Pathway:** Adhesive Bonding Machine Operators and Tenders; Assemblers and Fabricators, All Other; Avionics Technicians; Cabinetmakers and Bench Carpenters; Cleaning, Washing, and Metal Pickling Equipment Operators and Tenders; Computer-Controlled Machine Tool Operators, Metal and Plastic; Cooling and Freezing Equipment Operators and Tenders; Cost Estimators; Crushing, Grinding, and Polishing Machine Setters, Operators, and Tenders; Cutters and Trimmers, Hand; Cutting and Slicing Machine Setters, Operators, and Tenders; Cutting, Punching, and Press Machine Setters, Operators, and Tenders, Metal and Plastic; Drilling and Boring Machine Tool Setters, Operators, and Tenders, Metal and Plastic; Extruding and Drawing Machine Setters, Operators, and Tenders, Metal and Plastic; Extruding and Forming Machine Setters, Operators, and Tenders, Synthetic and Glass Fibers; Extruding, Forming, Pressing, and Compacting Machine Setters, Operators, and Tenders; Fiberglass Laminators and Fabricators; others.

Skills—Equipment Maintenance: Performing routine maintenance on equipment and determining when and what kind of maintenance is needed. **Repairing:** Repairing machines or systems using the needed tools. **Equipment Selection:** Determining the kind of tools and equipment needed to do a job. **Operation and Control:** Controlling operations of equipment or systems. **Operation Monitoring:** Watching gauges, dials, or other indicators to make sure a machine is working properly. **Quality Control Analysis:** Conducting tests and inspections of products, services, or processes to evaluate quality or performance. **Troubleshooting:** Determining causes of operating errors and deciding what to do about them. **Installation:** Installing equipment, machines, wiring, or programs to meet specifications.

Work Environment: Standing; walking and running; using hands; repetitive motions; noise; bright or inadequate lighting; contaminants; hazardous conditions; hazardous equipment.

Coin, Vending, and Amusement Machine Servicers and Repairers

- ⊙ Annual Earnings: $30,820
- ⊙ Earnings Growth Potential: Medium (36.2%)
- ⊙ Growth: 22.0%
- ⊙ Annual Job Openings: 1,630
- ⊙ Self-Employed: 7.2%

Considerations for Job Outlook: Although the number of vending and slot machines is expected to rise, these machines are becoming easier to maintain and repair. There will be fewer video arcade machines as people play more of these games at home. Job opportunities should be excellent for repairers with training in electronics who are willing to travel and to work irregular hours.

Install, service, adjust, or repair coin, vending, or amusement machines including video games, juke boxes, pinball machines, or slot machines. Clean and oil machine parts. Replace malfunctioning parts, such as worn magnetic heads on automatic teller machine (ATM) card readers. Adjust and repair coin, vending, or amusement machines and meters and replace defective mechanical and electrical parts, using hand tools, soldering irons, and diagrams. Collect coins and bills from machines, prepare invoices, and settle accounts with concessionaires. Disassemble and assemble machines, according to specifications and using hand and power tools. Fill machines with products, ingredients, money, and other supplies. Inspect machines and meters to determine causes of malfunctions and fix minor problems such as jammed bills or stuck products. Install machines, making the necessary water and electrical connections in compliance with codes. Make service calls to maintain and repair machines. Adjust machine pressure gauges and thermostats. Test machines to determine proper functioning. Refer to manuals and wiring diagrams to gather information needed to repair machines. Contact other repair personnel or make arrangements for the removal of machines in cases where major repairs are required. Count cash and items deposited at automatic teller machines (ATMs) by customers, and compare numbers to transactions indicated on transaction tapes. Install automatic teller machine (ATM) hardware, software, and peripheral equipment, and check that all components are configured correctly and connected to power sources and communications lines. Keep records of merchandise distributed and money collected. Maintain records of machine maintenance and repair. Order parts needed for machine repairs. Prepare repair cost estimates. Record transaction information on forms or logs, and notify designated personnel of discrepancies. Transport machines to installation sites. Shellac or paint dial markings or mechanism exteriors, using brushes or spray guns.

Education/Training Required: High school diploma or equivalent. **Education and Training Programs:** Business Machine Repair; Computer Installation and Repair Technology/Technician; Electrical/Electronics Maintenance and Repair Technology, Other. **Knowledge/Courses— Food Production:** Techniques and equipment for planting, growing, and harvesting food products (both plant and animal) for consumption, including storage/handling techniques. **Mechanical Devices:** Machines and tools, including their designs, uses, repair, and maintenance. **Mathematics:** Arithmetic, algebra, geometry, calculus, statistics, and their applications. **Public Safety and Security:** Relevant equipment, policies, procedures, and strategies to promote effective local, state, or national security operations for the protection of people, data, property, and institutions. **Customer and Personal Service:** Principles and processes for providing customer and personal services. This includes customer needs assessment, meeting quality standards for services, and evaluation of

customer satisfaction. **Building and Construction:** Materials, methods, and the tools involved in the construction or repair of houses, buildings, or other structures such as highways and roads. **Work Experience Needed:** None. **On-the-Job Training Needed:** Short-term on-the-job training. **Certification/Licensure:** None.

Personality Type: Realistic-Conventional. **Career Cluster:** 02 Architecture and Construction. **Career Pathway:** 02.3 Maintenance/Operations. **Other Jobs in This Pathway:** Heating and Air Conditioning Mechanics and Installers; Home Appliance Repairers; Refrigeration Mechanics and Installers; Security and Fire Alarm Systems Installers.

Skills—Repairing: Repairing machines or systems using the needed tools. **Equipment Maintenance:** Performing routine maintenance on equipment and determining when and what kind of maintenance is needed. **Installation:** Installing equipment, machines, wiring, or programs to meet specifications. **Troubleshooting:** Determining causes of operating errors and deciding what to do about them. **Operation and Control:** Controlling operations of equipment or systems. **Equipment Selection:** Determining the kind of tools and equipment needed to do a job. **Operation Monitoring:** Watching gauges, dials, or other indicators to make sure a machine is working properly. **Quality Control Analysis:** Conducting tests and inspections of products, services, or processes to evaluate quality or performance.

Work Environment: More often indoors than outdoors; standing; walking and running; using hands; bending or twisting the body; repetitive motions; noise; very hot or cold; bright or inadequate lighting; minor burns, cuts, bites, or stings.

Commercial Divers

- ⊙ Annual Earnings: $52,550
- ⊙ Earnings Growth Potential: High (40.0%)
- ⊙ Growth: 15.8%
- ⊙ Annual Job Openings: 130
- ⊙ Self-Employed: 0.0%

Considerations for Job Outlook: About-average employment growth is projected.

Work below surface of water, using scuba gear to inspect, repair, remove, or install equipment and structures. Perform activities related to underwater search and rescue, salvage, recovery, and cleanup operations. Take appropriate safety precautions, such as monitoring dive lengths and depths, and registering with authorities before diving expeditions begin. Set or guide placement of pilings and sandbags to provide support for structures such as docks, bridges, cofferdams, and platforms. Salvage wrecked ships and/or their cargo, using pneumatic power velocity and hydraulic tools, and explosive charges when necessary. Repair ships, bridge foundations, and other structures below the water line, using caulk, bolts, and hand tools. Remove obstructions from strainers and marine railway or launching ways, using pneumatic and power hand tools. Inspect and test docks, ships, bouyage systems, plant intakes and outflows, and underwater pipelines, cables, and sewers, using closed circuit television, still photography, and testing equipment. Perform offshore oil and gas exploration and extraction duties such as conducting underwater surveys and repairing and maintaining drilling rigs and platforms. Install, inspect, clean, and repair piping and valves. Carry out non-destructive testing such as tests for cracks on the legs of oil rigs at sea. Check and maintain diving equipment such as helmets, masks, air tanks, harnesses and gauges. Communicate with workers on the surface while underwater, using signal lines or telephones. Cut and weld steel, using underwater welding equipment, jigs, and supports. Descend into water with the aid of diver helpers, using scuba gear or diving suits. Recover objects by placing rigging around sunken objects, hooking rigging to crane lines, and operating winches, derricks, or cranes to raise objects. Install pilings or footings for piers and bridges. Supervise and train other divers, including hobby divers. Obtain information about diving tasks and environmental conditions. Remove rubbish and pollution from the sea.

Education/Training Required: Postsecondary vocational training. **Education and Training Program:** Diver Training, Professional and Instructor. **Knowledge/Courses— Building and Construction:** Materials, methods, and the tools involved in the construction or repair of houses, buildings, or other structures such as highways and roads. **Mechanical Devices:** Machines and tools, including their designs, uses, repair, and maintenance. **Physics:** Physical principles, laws, their interrelationships, and applications to understanding fluid, material, and atmospheric dynamics, and mechanical, electrical, atomic, and subatomic structures and processes. **Engineering and Technology:** The practical application of engineering science and technology. This includes applying principles, techniques, procedures, and equipment to the design and production of various goods and services. **Design:** Design techniques, tools, and principles involved in production of precision technical plans, blueprints, drawings, and models. **Biology:** Plant and animal organisms and their tissues, cells, functions, interdependencies, and interactions with each other and the environment. **Work Experience Needed:** None. **On-the-Job Training Needed:** Moderate-term on-the-job training. **Certification/Licensure:** Voluntary certification by association.

Personality Type: Realistic. **Career Cluster:** 16 Transportation, Distribution, and Logistics. **Career Pathway:** 16.1 Transportation Operations. **Other Jobs in This Pathway:** Aerospace Engineering and Operations Technicians; Air Traffic Controllers; Aircraft Cargo Handling Supervisors; Airfield Operations Specialists; Airline Pilots, Copilots, and Flight Engineers; Automotive and Watercraft Service Attendants; Automotive Master Mechanics; Aviation Inspectors; Bridge and Lock Tenders; Bus Drivers, School or Special Client; Bus Drivers, Transit and Intercity; Commercial Pilots; Crane and Tower Operators; First-Line Supervisors of Helpers, Laborers, and Material Movers, Hand; First-Line Supervisors of Transportation and Material-Moving Machine and Vehicle Operators; Freight and Cargo Inspectors; Heavy and Tractor-Trailer Truck Drivers; Hoist and Winch Operators; Laborers and Freight, Stock, and Material Movers, Hand; Light Truck or Delivery Services Drivers; Mates—Ship, Boat, and Barge; Motor Vehicle Operators, All Other; Motorboat Operators; Operating Engineers and Other Construction Equipment Operators; Parking Lot Attendants; others.

Skills—Repairing: Repairing machines or systems using the needed tools. **Equipment Maintenance:** Performing routine maintenance on equipment and determining when and what kind of maintenance is needed. **Equipment Selection:** Determining the kind of tools and equipment needed to do a job. **Installation:** Installing equipment, machines, wiring, or programs to meet specifications. **Troubleshooting:** Determining causes of operating errors and deciding what to do about them. **Operation and Control:** Controlling operations of equipment or systems. **Operation Monitoring:** Watching gauges, dials, or other

C

indicators to make sure a machine is working properly. **Quality Control Analysis:** Conducting tests and inspections of products, services, or processes to evaluate quality or performance.

Work Environment: Outdoors; standing; using hands; bending or twisting the body; repetitive motions; noise; very hot or cold; bright or inadequate lighting; contaminants; cramped work space; whole-body vibration; hazardous conditions; hazardous equipment; minor burns, cuts, bites, or stings.

Commercial Pilots

- ☉ Annual Earnings: $70,000
- ☉ Earnings Growth Potential: High (48.2%)
- ☉ Growth: 21.1%
- ☉ Annual Job Openings: 1,930
- ☉ Self-Employed: 9.0%

Considerations for Job Outlook: As older pilots retire and younger pilots advance, entry-level positions may open up. And the demand for flight instructors may increase as they are needed to train a greater number of student pilots. Job prospects should be best with regional airlines, on low-cost carriers, or in general aviation, because these segments are anticipated to grow faster than the major airlines. In addition, entry-level requirements are lower for regional and commercial jobs. However, pilots with fewer than 500 flight hours will probably need to accumulate hours as flight instructors or commercial pilots before qualifying for regional airline jobs.

Pilot and navigate the flight of fixed-wing aircraft on nonscheduled air carrier routes, or helicopters. Check aircraft prior to flights to ensure that the engines, controls, instruments, and other systems are functioning properly. Start engines, operate controls, and pilot airplanes to transport passengers, mail, or freight while adhering to flight plans, regulations, and procedures. Contact control towers for takeoff clearances, arrival instructions, and other information, using radio equipment. Monitor engine operation, fuel consumption, and functioning of aircraft systems during flights. Consider airport altitudes, outside temperatures, plane weights, and wind speeds and directions to calculate the speed needed to become airborne. Order changes in fuel supplies, loads, routes, or schedules

to ensure safety of flights. Obtain and review data such as load weights, fuel supplies, weather conditions, and flight schedules to determine flight plans and to see if changes might be necessary. Plan flights, following government and company regulations, using aeronautical charts and navigation instruments. Use instrumentation to pilot aircraft when visibility is poor. Check baggage or cargo to ensure that it has been loaded correctly. Request changes in altitudes or routes as circumstances dictate. Choose routes, altitudes, and speeds that will provide the fastest, safest, and smoothest flights. Coordinate flight activities with ground crews and air-traffic control, and inform crew members of flight and test procedures.

Education/Training Required: High school diploma or equivalent. **Education and Training Programs:** Airline/Commercial/Professional Pilot and Flight Crew Training; Flight Instructor Training. **Knowledge/Courses—Transportation:** Principles and methods for moving people or goods by air, rail, sea, or road, including the relative costs and benefits. **Geography:** Principles and methods for describing the features of land, sea, and air masses, including their physical characteristics, locations, interrelationships, and distribution of plant, animal, and human life. **Mechanical Devices:** Machines and tools, including their designs, uses, repair, and maintenance. **Physics:** Physical principles, laws, their interrelationships, and applications to understanding fluid, material, and atmospheric dynamics, and mechanical, electrical, atomic, and subatomic structures and processes. **Telecommunications:** Transmission, broadcasting, switching, control, and operation of telecommunications systems. **Psychology:** Human behavior and performance; individual differences in ability, personality, and interests; learning and motivation; psychological research methods; and the assessment and treatment of behavioral and affective disorders. **Work Experience Needed:** None. **On-the-Job Training Needed:** Long-term on-the-job training. **Certification/Licensure:** Licensure.

Personality Type: Realistic-Investigative-Enterprising. **Career Cluster:** 16 Transportation, Distribution, and Logistics. **Career Pathway:** 16.1 Transportation Operations. **Other Jobs in This Pathway:** Aerospace Engineering and Operations Technicians; Air Traffic Controllers; Aircraft Cargo Handling Supervisors; Airfield Operations Specialists; Airline Pilots, Copilots, and Flight Engineers; Automotive and Watercraft Service Attendants; Automotive Master Mechanics; Aviation Inspectors; Bridge and

Lock Tenders; Bus Drivers, School or Special Client; Bus Drivers, Transit and Intercity; Commercial Divers; Crane and Tower Operators; First-Line Supervisors of Helpers, Laborers, and Material Movers, Hand; First-Line Supervisors of Transportation and Material-Moving Machine and Vehicle Operators; Freight and Cargo Inspectors; Heavy and Tractor-Trailer Truck Drivers; Hoist and Winch Operators; Laborers and Freight, Stock, and Material Movers, Hand; Light Truck or Delivery Services Drivers; Mates—Ship, Boat, and Barge; Motor Vehicle Operators, All Other; Motorboat Operators; Operating Engineers and Other Construction Equipment Operators; Parking Lot Attendants; others.

Skills—Operation and Control: Controlling operations of equipment or systems. **Operation Monitoring:** Watching gauges, dials, or other indicators to make sure a machine is working properly. **Science:** Using scientific rules and methods to solve problems. **Instructing:** Teaching others how to do something. **Troubleshooting:** Determining causes of operating errors and deciding what to do about them. **Operations Analysis:** Analyzing needs and product requirements to create a design. **Judgment and Decision Making:** Considering the relative costs and benefits of potential actions to choose the most appropriate one. **Complex Problem Solving:** Identifying complex problems and reviewing related information to develop and evaluate options and implement solutions.

Work Environment: Outdoors; sitting; using hands; noise; very hot or cold; contaminants; cramped work space.

Computer Numerically Controlled Machine Tool Programmers, Metal and Plastic

- ⊙ Annual Earnings: $45,890
- ⊙ Earnings Growth Potential: Low (33.4%)
- ⊙ Growth: 10.8%
- ⊙ Annual Job Openings: 490
- ⊙ Self-Employed: 0.0%

Considerations for Job Outlook: Despite slower-than-average employment growth, a number of these jobs are expected to become available for highly skilled workers because of an expected increase in retirements, primarily of baby boomers, in the coming years. In addition, workers who have a thorough background in machine operations, certifications from industry associations, and a good working knowledge of the properties of metals and plastics should have the best job opportunities.

Develop programs to control machining or processing of metal or plastic parts by automatic machine tools, equipment, or systems. Determine the sequence of machine operations, and select the proper cutting tools needed to machine workpieces into the desired shapes. Revise programs and/or tapes to eliminate errors, and retest programs to check that problems have been solved. Analyze job orders, drawings, blueprints, specifications, printed circuit board pattern films, and design data in order to calculate dimensions, tool selection, machine speeds, and feed rates. Determine reference points, machine cutting paths, or hole locations, and compute angular and linear dimensions, radii, and curvatures. Observe machines on trial runs or conduct computer simulations to ensure that programs and machinery will function properly and produce items that meet specifications. Compare encoded tapes or computer printouts with original part specifications and blueprints to verify accuracy of instructions. Enter coordinates of hole locations into program memories by depressing pedals or buttons of programmers. Write programs in the language of a machine's controller and store programs on media such as punch tapes, magnetic tapes, or disks. Modify existing programs to enhance efficiency. Enter computer commands to store or retrieve parts patterns, graphic displays, or programs that transfer data to other media. Prepare geometric layouts from graphic displays, using computer-assisted drafting software or drafting instruments and graph paper. Write instruction sheets and cutter lists for a machine's controller in order to guide setup and encode numerical control tapes. Sort shop orders into groups to maximize materials utilization and minimize machine setup time. Draw machine tool paths on pattern film, using colored markers and following guidelines for tool speed and efficiency. Align and secure pattern film on reference tables of optical programmers, and observe enlarger scope views of printed circuit boards.

Education/Training Required: High school diploma or equivalent. **Education and Training Programs:** Computer Programming/Programmer, General; Data Processing and Data Processing Technology/Technician. **Knowledge/Courses—Design:** Design techniques, tools, and principles involved in production of precision technical plans, blueprints, drawings, and models. **Mechanical Devices:** Machines and tools, including their designs, uses, repair, and maintenance. **Engineering and Technology:** The practical application of engineering science and technology. This includes applying principles, techniques, procedures, and equipment to the design and production of various goods and services. **Mathematics:** Arithmetic, algebra, geometry, calculus, statistics, and their applications. **Physics:** Physical principles, laws, their interrelationships, and applications to understanding fluid, material, and atmospheric dynamics, and mechanical, electrical, atomic, and subatomic structures and processes. **Production and Processing:** Raw materials, production processes, quality control, costs, and other techniques for maximizing the effective manufacture and distribution of goods. **Work Experience Needed:** None. **On-the-Job Training Needed:** Moderate-term on-the-job training. **Certification/Licensure:** Voluntary certification by association.

Personality Type: Conventional-Investigative-Realistic. **Career Cluster:** 11 Information Technology. **Career Pathways:** 11.2 Information Support Services; 11.4 Programming and Software Development. **Other Jobs in These Pathways:** Architectural and Engineering Managers; Bioinformatics Scientists; Computer and Information Systems Managers; Computer Hardware Engineers; Computer Operators; Computer Science Teachers, Postsecondary; Engineering Teachers, Postsecondary; Remote Sensing Scientists and Technologists; Remote Sensing Technicians.

Skills—Programming: Writing computer programs for various purposes. **Equipment Selection:** Determining the kind of tools and equipment needed to do a job. **Repairing:** Repairing machines or systems using the needed tools. **Technology Design:** Generating or adapting equipment and technology to serve user needs. **Equipment Maintenance:** Performing routine maintenance on equipment and determining when and what kind of maintenance is needed. **Troubleshooting:** Determining causes of operating errors and deciding what to do about them. **Operation Monitoring:** Watching gauges, dials, or other indicators to make sure a machine is working properly. **Operation and Control:** Controlling operations of equipment or systems.

Work Environment: Indoors; standing; using hands; repetitive motions; noise; contaminants; hazardous equipment; minor burns, cuts, bites, or stings.

Computer, Automated Teller, and Office Machine Repairers

- ⊙ Annual Earnings: $36,360
- ⊙ Earnings Growth Potential: Medium (38.6%)
- ⊙ Growth: 6.5%
- ⊙ Annual Job Openings: 4,540
- ⊙ Self-Employed: 24.4%

Considerations for Job Outlook: Workers with experience, education from a trade school, and some certification often will have the best opportunities. Employers also prefer to hire workers whose military service has provided them with relevant training and experience. ATM repairers with training in the security of ATM networks have the best job prospects. Job opportunities should be good for those who have completed formal postsecondary education and have strong technical skills, as employers sometimes report difficulty finding qualified workers. Workers without formal training often require more supervision and on-the-job instruction than others—an expensive and time-consuming process for employers. Because of this, untrained candidates will face strong competition for jobs.

Repair, maintain, or install computers, word processing systems, automated teller machines, and electronic office machines such as duplicating and fax machines. Converse with customers to determine details of equipment problems. Reassemble machines after making repairs or replacing parts. Travel to customers' stores or offices to service machines or to provide emergency repair service. Reinstall software programs or adjust settings on existing software to fix machine malfunctions. Advise customers concerning equipment operation, maintenance, and programming. Test new systems to ensure that they are in working order. Assemble machines according to specifications, using hand tools, power tools, and measuring devices. Operate machines to test functioning of parts and mechanisms. Maintain records of equipment maintenance work and repairs. Install and configure new equipment, including operating software and peripheral equipment. Maintain parts inventories, and order any additional parts needed for repairs. Update existing equipment, performing tasks such as installing updated circuit boards or additional memory. Test components and circuits of faulty equipment to locate defects, using oscilloscopes, signal generators, ammeters, voltmeters, or special diagnostic software programs. Align, adjust, and calibrate equipment according to specifications. Repair, adjust, or replace electrical and mechanical components and parts, using hand tools, power tools, and soldering or welding equipment. Complete repair bills, shop records, time cards, and expense reports. Disassemble machine to examine parts such as wires, gears, and bearings for wear and defects, using hand tools, power tools, and measuring devices. Clean, oil, and adjust mechanical parts to maintain machines' operating efficiency and to prevent breakdowns. Read specifications such as blueprints, charts, and schematics to determine machine settings and adjustments. Enter information into computers to copy programs from one electronic component to another, or to draw, modify, or store schematics.

Education/Training Required: Postsecondary vocational training. **Education and Training Programs:** Business Machine Repair; Computer Installation and Repair Technology/Technician. **Knowledge/Courses—Computers and Electronics:** Circuit boards, processors, chips, electronic equipment, and computer hardware and software, including applications and programming. **Telecommunications:** Transmission, broadcasting, switching, control, and operation of telecommunications systems. **Mechanical Devices:** Machines and tools, including their designs, uses, repair, and maintenance. **Customer and Personal Service:** Principles and processes for providing customer and personal services. This includes customer needs assessment, meeting quality standards for services, and evaluation of customer satisfaction. **Engineering and Technology:** The practical application of engineering science and technology. This includes applying principles, techniques, procedures, and equipment to the design and production of various goods and services. **Sales and Marketing:** Principles and methods for showing, promoting, and selling products or services. This includes marketing strategy and tactics, product demonstration, sales techniques, and sales control systems. **Work Experience Needed:** None. **On-the-Job Training Needed:** None. **Certification/Licensure:** Voluntary certification for some specializations.

Personality Type: Realistic-Conventional-Investigative. **Career Cluster:** 13 Manufacturing. **Career Pathway:** 13.3 Maintenance, Installation, and Repair. **Other Jobs in This Pathway:** Aircraft Mechanics and Service Technicians; Automotive Engineering Technicians; Automotive Specialty Technicians; Avionics Technicians; Biological Technicians; Camera and Photographic Equipment Repairers;

Chemical Equipment Operators and Tenders; Civil Engineering Technicians; Coil Winders, Tapers, and Finishers; Construction and Related Workers, All Other; Control and Valve Installers and Repairers, Except Mechanical Door; Electric Motor, Power Tool, and Related Repairers; Electrical and Electronic Equipment Assemblers; Electrical and Electronics Repairers, Commercial and Industrial Equipment; Electrical and Electronics Repairers, Powerhouse, Substation, and Relay; Electrical Engineering Technicians; Electrical Engineering Technologists; Electromechanical Engineering Technologists; Electromechanical Equipment Assemblers; Electronics Engineering Technicians; Electronics Engineering Technologists; Elevator Installers and Repairers; Engine and Other Machine Assemblers; others.

Skills—Repairing: Repairing machines or systems using the needed tools. **Installation:** Installing equipment, machines, wiring, or programs to meet specifications. **Equipment Maintenance:** Performing routine maintenance on equipment and determining when and what kind of maintenance is needed. **Troubleshooting:** Determining causes of operating errors and deciding what to do about them. **Equipment Selection:** Determining the kind of tools and equipment needed to do a job. **Operation and Control:** Controlling operations of equipment or systems. **Technology Design:** Generating or adapting equipment and technology to serve user needs. **Operation Monitoring:** Watching gauges, dials, or other indicators to make sure a machine is working properly.

Work Environment: Indoors; sitting; using hands; repetitive motions.

Computer-Controlled Machine Tool Operators, Metal and Plastic

- Annual Earnings: $35,220
- Earnings Growth Potential: Low (34.0%)
- Growth: 19.2%
- Annual Job Openings: 4,780
- Self-Employed: 0.0%

Considerations for Job Outlook: A number of these jobs are expected to become available for highly skilled workers because of an expected increase in retirements, primarily of baby boomers, in the coming years. In addition, workers who have a thorough background in machine operations, certifications from industry associations, and a good working knowledge of the properties of metals and plastics should have the best job opportunities.

Operate computer-controlled machines or robots to perform one or more machine functions on metal or plastic workpieces. Measure dimensions of finished workpieces to ensure conformance to specifications, using precision measuring instruments, templates, and fixtures. Remove and replace dull cutting tools. Mount, install, align, and secure tools, attachments, fixtures, and workpieces on machines, using hand tools and precision measuring instruments. Listen to machines during operation to detect sounds such as those made by dull cutting tools or excessive vibration, and adjust machines to compensate for problems. Adjust machine feed and speed, change cutting tools, or adjust machine controls when automatic programming is faulty or if machines malfunction. Stop machines to remove finished workpieces or to change tooling, setup, or workpiece placement, according to required machining sequences. Lift workpieces to machines manually or with hoists or cranes. Modify cutting programs to account for problems encountered during operation and save modified programs. Calculate machine speed and feed ratios and the size and position of cuts. Insert control instructions into machine control units to start operation. Check to ensure that workpieces are properly lubricated and cooled during machine operation. Input initial part dimensions into machine control panels. Set up and operate computer-controlled machines or robots to perform one or more machine functions on metal or plastic workpieces. Confer with supervisors or programmers to resolve machine malfunctions and production errors and to obtain approval to continue production. Review program specifications or blueprints to determine and set machine operations and sequencing, finished workpiece dimensions, or numerical control sequences. Monitor machine operation and control panel displays, and compare readings to specifications in order to detect malfunctions. Control coolant systems. Maintain machines, and remove and replace broken or worn machine tools, using hand tools.

Education/Training Required: High school diploma or equivalent. **Education and Training Program:** Machine Shop Technology/Assistant. **Knowledge/Courses—Mechanical Devices:** Machines and tools, including their designs, uses, repair, and maintenance. **Production and Processing:** Raw materials, production processes, quality control, costs, and other techniques for maximizing the effective manufacture and distribution of goods. **Engineering and Technology:** The practical application of engineering science and technology. This includes applying principles, techniques, procedures, and equipment to the design and production of various goods and services. **Design:** Design techniques, tools, and principles involved in production of precision technical plans, blueprints, drawings, and models. **Mathematics:** Arithmetic, algebra, geometry, calculus, statistics, and their applications. **Work Experience Needed:** None. **On-the-Job Training Needed:** Moderate-term on-the-job training. **Certification/Licensure:** Voluntary certification by some training or educational institutions.

Personality Type: Realistic-Conventional. **Career Cluster:** 13 Manufacturing. **Career Pathway:** 13.1 Production. **Other Jobs in This Pathway:** Adhesive Bonding Machine Operators and Tenders; Assemblers and Fabricators, All Other; Avionics Technicians; Cabinetmakers and Bench Carpenters; Cleaning, Washing, and Metal Pickling Equipment Operators and Tenders; Coating, Painting, and Spraying Machine Setters, Operators, and Tenders; Cooling and Freezing Equipment Operators and Tenders; Cost Estimators; Crushing, Grinding, and Polishing Machine Setters, Operators, and Tenders; Cutters and Trimmers, Hand; Cutting and Slicing Machine Setters, Operators, and Tenders; Cutting, Punching, and Press Machine Setters, Operators, and Tenders, Metal and Plastic; Drilling and Boring Machine Tool Setters, Operators, and Tenders, Metal and Plastic; Extruding and Drawing Machine Setters, Operators, and Tenders, Metal and Plastic; Extruding and Forming Machine Setters, Operators, and Tenders, Synthetic and Glass Fibers; Extruding, Forming, Pressing, and Compacting Machine Setters, Operators, and Tenders; Fiberglass Laminators and Fabricators; others.

Skills—Equipment Maintenance: Performing routine maintenance on equipment and determining when and what kind of maintenance is needed. **Operation and Control:** Controlling operations of equipment or systems. **Programming:** Writing computer programs for various purposes. **Repairing:** Repairing machines or systems using the needed tools. **Operation Monitoring:** Watching gauges, dials, or other indicators to make sure a machine is working properly. **Troubleshooting:** Determining causes of operating errors and deciding what to do about them. **Quality Control Analysis:** Conducting tests and inspections of products, services, or processes to evaluate quality or performance. **Equipment Selection:** Determining the kind of tools and equipment needed to do a job.

Work Environment: Indoors; standing; walking and running; using hands; bending or twisting the body; repetitive motions; noise; contaminants; hazardous equipment; minor burns, cuts, bites, or stings.

Construction and Building Inspectors

- ⊙ Annual Earnings: $53,180
- ⊙ Earnings Growth Potential: Medium (39.7%)
- ⊙ Growth: 18.0%
- ⊙ Annual Job Openings: 4,860
- ⊙ Self-Employed: 11.4%

Considerations for Job Outlook: Construction and building inspectors who are certified and can do a variety of inspections should have the best job opportunities. Inspectors with construction-related work experience or training in engineering, architecture, construction technology, or related fields will likely also have better job prospects. In addition, inspectors with thorough knowledge of construction practices and skills, such as reading and evaluating blueprints and plans, should have better job opportunities.

Inspect structures using engineering skills to determine structural soundness and compliance with specifications, building codes, and other regulations. Issue violation notices and stop-work orders, conferring with owners, violators, and authorities to explain regulations and recommend rectifications. Inspect bridges, dams, highways, buildings, wiring, plumbing, electrical circuits, sewers, heating systems, and foundations during and after construction for structural quality, general safety, and conformance to specifications and codes. Approve and sign plans that meet required specifications. Review and interpret plans, blueprints, site layouts, specifications, and construction methods to ensure compliance to legal requirements and safety regulations. Monitor installation of plumbing, wiring, equipment, and appliances to ensure that installation is performed properly and is in compliance with applicable regulations. Inspect and monitor construction sites to ensure adherence to safety standards, building codes, and specifications. Measure dimensions and verify level, alignment, and elevation of structures and fixtures to ensure compliance to building plans and codes. Maintain daily logs, and supplement inspection records with photographs. Use survey instruments, metering devices, tape measures, and test equipment such as concrete strength measurers to perform inspections. Train, direct, and supervise other construction inspectors. Issue permits for construction, relocation, demolition, and occupancy.

Education/Training Required: High school diploma or equivalent. **Education and Training Program:** Building/Home/Construction Inspection/Inspector. **Knowledge/Courses—Building and Construction:** Materials, methods, and the tools involved in the construction or repair of houses, buildings, or other structures such as highways and roads. **Engineering and Technology:** The practical application of engineering science and technology. This includes applying principles, techniques, procedures, and equipment to the design and production of various goods and services. **Design:** Design techniques, tools, and principles involved in production of precision technical plans, blueprints, drawings, and models. **Physics:** Physical principles, laws, their interrelationships, and applications to understanding fluid, material, and atmospheric dynamics, and mechanical, electrical, atomic, and subatomic structures and processes. **Public Safety and Security:** Relevant equipment, policies, procedures, and strategies to promote effective local, state, or national security operations for the protection of people, data, property, and institutions. **Mechanical Devices:** Machines and tools, including their designs, uses, repair, and maintenance. **Work Experience Needed:** More than 5 years. **On-the-Job Training Needed:** Moderate-term on-the-job training. **Certification/Licensure:** Licensure in most states.

Personality Type: Realistic-Conventional-Investigative. **Career Cluster:** 02 Architecture and Construction. **Career Pathway:** 02.2 Construction. **Other Jobs in This Pathway:** Boilermakers; Brickmasons and Blockmasons; Carpet Installers; Cement Masons and Concrete Finishers; Construction and Related Workers, All Other; Construction Carpenters; Construction Laborers; Construction Managers; Continuous Mining Machine Operators; Cost Estimators; Crane and Tower Operators; Dredge Operators; Drywall and Ceiling Tile Installers; Earth Drillers, Except Oil and Gas; Electrical Power-Line Installers and Repairers; Electricians; Electromechanical Equipment Assemblers; Engineering Technicians, Except Drafters,

C

All Other; Excavating and Loading Machine and Drag-line Operators; Explosives Workers, Ordnance Handling Experts, and Blasters; Extraction Workers, All Other; First-Line Supervisors of Construction Trades and Extraction Workers; Floor Layers, Except Carpet, Wood, and Hard Tiles; Floor Sanders and Finishers; Glaziers; Heating and Air Conditioning Mechanics and Installers; Helpers, Construction Trades, All Other; others.

Skills—Science: Using scientific rules and methods to solve problems. **Quality Control Analysis:** Conducting tests and inspections of products, services, or processes to evaluate quality or performance. **Operation and Control:** Controlling operations of equipment or systems. **Systems Evaluation:** Identifying measures or indicators of system performance and the actions needed to improve or correct performance relative to the goals of the system. **Mathematics:** Using mathematics to solve problems. **Systems Analysis:** Determining how a system should work and how changes in conditions, operations, and the environment will affect outcomes. **Operation Monitoring:** Watching gauges, dials, or other indicators to make sure a machine is working properly. **Troubleshooting:** Determining causes of operating errors and deciding what to do about them.

Work Environment: More often outdoors than indoors; standing; noise; very hot or cold; bright or inadequate lighting; contaminants; cramped work space; high places.

Construction Laborers

- ⊙ Annual Earnings: $29,730
- ⊙ Earnings Growth Potential: Medium (36.7%)
- ⊙ Growth: 21.3%
- ⊙ Annual Job Openings: 29,240
- ⊙ Self-Employed: 23.5%

Considerations for Job Outlook: Construction laborers with the most skills should have the best job opportunities. Opportunities also will vary by occupation; for example, carpenters' helpers should have the best job prospects, while painters', paperhangers', plasterers', and stucco masons' helpers will likely find fewer job openings. Prospective employees with military service often have better opportunities when applying for a job. Employment of construction laborers and helpers is especially sensitive to the fluctuations of the economy. On the one hand, workers

in these trades may experience periods of unemployment when the overall level of construction falls. On the other hand, shortages of these workers may occur in some areas during peak periods of building activity.

Perform tasks involving physical labor at construction sites. Clean and prepare construction sites to eliminate possible hazards. Read and interpret plans, instructions, and specifications to determine work activities. Control traffic passing near, in, and around work zones. Signal equipment operators to facilitate alignment, movement, and adjustment of machinery, equipment, and materials. Dig ditches or trenches, backfill excavations, and compact and level earth to grade specifications, using picks, shovels, pneumatic tampers, and rakes. Measure, mark, and record openings and distances to lay out areas where construction work will be performed. Position, join, align, and seal structural components such as concrete wall sections and pipes. Load, unload, and identify building materials, machinery, and tools, and distribute them to the appropriate locations according to project plans and specifications. Erect and disassemble scaffolding, shoring, braces, traffic barricades, ramps, and other temporary structures. Build and position forms for pouring concrete, and dismantle forms after use, using saws, hammers, nails, or bolts. Lubricate, clean, and repair machinery, equipment, and tools. Operate jackhammers and drills to break up concrete or pavement. Smooth and finish freshly poured cement or concrete using floats, trowels, screeds, or powered cement-finishing tools. Operate, read, and maintain air-monitoring and other sampling devices in confined or hazardous environments.

Education/Training Required: Less than high school. **Education and Training Program:** Construction Trades, Other. **Knowledge/Courses—Building and Construction:** Materials, methods, and the tools involved in the construction or repair of houses, buildings, or other structures such as highways and roads. **Design:** Design techniques, tools, and principles involved in production of precision technical plans, blueprints, drawings, and models. **Mechanical Devices:** Machines and tools, including their designs, uses, repair, and maintenance. **Transportation:** Principles and methods for moving people or goods by air, rail, sea, or road, including the relative costs and benefits. **Public Safety and Security:** Relevant equipment, policies, procedures, and strategies to promote effective local, state, or national security operations for the protection of people, data, property, and institutions.

Engineering and Technology: The practical application of engineering science and technology. This includes applying principles, techniques, procedures, and equipment to the design and production of various goods and services. **Work Experience Needed:** None. **On-the-Job Training Needed:** Short-term on-the-job training. **Certification/Licensure:** None.

Personality Type: Realistic-Conventional. **Career Cluster:** 02 Architecture and Construction. **Career Pathway:** 02.2 Construction. **Other Jobs in This Pathway:** Boilermakers; Brickmasons and Blockmasons; Carpet Installers; Cement Masons and Concrete Finishers; Construction and Building Inspectors; Construction and Related Workers, All Other; Construction Carpenters; Construction Managers; Continuous Mining Machine Operators; Cost Estimators; Crane and Tower Operators; Dredge Operators; Drywall and Ceiling Tile Installers; Earth Drillers, Except Oil and Gas; Electrical Power-Line Installers and Repairers; Electricians; Electromechanical Equipment Assemblers; Engineering Technicians, Except Drafters, All Other; Excavating and Loading Machine and Dragline Operators; Explosives Workers, Ordnance Handling Experts, and Blasters; Extraction Workers, All Other; First-Line Supervisors of Construction Trades and Extraction Workers; Floor Layers, Except Carpet, Wood, and Hard Tiles; Floor Sanders and Finishers; Glaziers; Heating and Air Conditioning Mechanics and Installers; Helpers, Construction Trades, All Other; others.

Skills—Operation and Control: Controlling operations of equipment or systems. **Equipment Selection:** Determining the kind of tools and equipment needed to do a job. **Installation:** Installing equipment, machines, wiring, or programs to meet specifications. **Equipment Maintenance:** Performing routine maintenance on equipment and determining when and what kind of maintenance is needed. **Operation Monitoring:** Watching gauges, dials, or other indicators to make sure a machine is working properly. **Troubleshooting:** Determining causes of operating errors and deciding what to do about them. **Repairing:** Repairing machines or systems using the needed tools. **Quality Control Analysis:** Conducting tests and inspections of products, services, or processes to evaluate quality or performance.

Work Environment: Outdoors; standing; using hands; bending or twisting the body; repetitive motions; noise; very hot or cold; bright or inadequate lighting; contaminants; whole-body vibration; hazardous equipment; minor burns, cuts, bites, or stings.

Construction Managers

- Annual Earnings: $84,240
- Earnings Growth Potential: Medium (39.9%)
- Growth: 16.6%
- Annual Job Openings: 12,040
- Self-Employed: 63.8%

Considerations for Job Outlook: Job opportunities for qualified job seekers are expected to be good. Those with a bachelor's degree in construction science, construction management, or civil engineering, coupled with construction experience, will have the best job prospects. Employment growth will provide many new job openings. A substantial number of construction managers are expected to retire over the next decade, resulting in additional job opportunities. Employment of construction managers, like that of many other construction workers, is sensitive to fluctuations in the economy.

Plan, direct, or coordinate activities concerned with the construction and maintenance of structures, facilities, and systems. Schedule the project in logical steps, and budget time required to meet deadlines. Confer with supervisory personnel, owners, contractors, and design professionals to discuss and resolve matters such as work procedures, complaints, and construction problems. Prepare contracts, and negotiate revisions, changes, and additions to contractual agreements with architects, consultants, clients, suppliers, and subcontractors. Prepare and submit budget estimates and progress and cost-tracking reports. Interpret and explain plans and contract terms to administrative staff, workers, and clients, representing the owner or developer. Plan, organize, and direct activities concerned with the construction and maintenance of structures, facilities, and systems. Take actions to deal with the results of delays, bad weather, or emergencies at construction sites. Inspect and review projects to monitor compliance with building and safety codes and other regulations. Study job specifications to determine appropriate construction methods. Select, contract, and oversee workers who complete specific pieces of the project, such as painting or plumbing. Obtain all necessary permits and licenses. Direct and supervise workers. Develop and implement quality control programs. Investigate damage, accidents, or delays at construction sites to ensure that proper procedures are being carried out. Determine labor requirements, and dispatch workers to construction sites.

Education/Training Required: Associate degree. **Education and Training Programs:** Business Administration and Management, General; Business/Commerce, General; Construction Engineering Technology/Technician; Operations Management and Supervision. **Knowledge/ Courses—Building and Construction:** Materials, methods, and the tools involved in the construction or repair of houses, buildings, or other structures such as highways and roads. **Design:** Design techniques, tools, and principles involved in production of precision technical plans, blueprints, drawings, and models. **Engineering and Technology:** The practical application of engineering science and technology. This includes applying principles, techniques, procedures, and equipment to the design and production of various goods and services. **Mechanical Devices:** Machines and tools, including their designs, uses, repair, and maintenance. **Administration and Management:** Business and management principles involved in strategic planning, resource allocation, human resources modeling, leadership technique, production methods, and coordination of people and resources. **Personnel and Human Resources:** Principles and procedures for personnel recruitment, selection, training, compensation and benefits, labor relations and negotiation, and personnel information systems. **Work Experience Needed:** More than 5 years. **On-the-Job Training Needed:** None. **Certification/Licensure:** Licensure for some specializations; voluntary certification by association.

Personality Type: Enterprising-Realistic-Conventional. **Career Clusters:** 02 Architecture and Construction; 04 Business, Management, and Administration. **Career Pathways:** 04.1 Management; 02.2 Construction. **Other Jobs in These Pathways:** Administrative Services Managers; Agents and Business Managers of Artists, Performers, and Athletes; Biofuels Production Managers; Biomass Power Plant Managers; Boilermakers; Brickmasons and Blockmasons; Brownfield Redevelopment Specialists and Site Managers; Business Continuity Planners; Business Operations Specialists, All Other; Business Teachers, Postsecondary; Carpet Installers; Cement Masons and Concrete Finishers; Chief Executives; Chief Sustainability Officers; Communications Teachers, Postsecondary; Compliance Managers; Computer and Information Systems Managers; Construction and Building Inspectors; Construction and Related Workers, All Other; Construction Carpenters; Construction Laborers; Continuous Mining Machine Operators; Cost Estimators; Crane and Tower Operators; Customs Brokers; Dredge Operators; Drywall and Ceiling Tile Installers; Earth Drillers, Except Oil and Gas; Economics Teachers, Postsecondary; Economists; Electrical Power-Line Installers and Repairers; others.

Skills—Management of Financial Resources: Determining how money will be spent to get the work done and accounting for these expenditures. **Management of Material Resources:** Obtaining and seeing to the appropriate use of equipment, facilities, and materials needed to do certain work. **Operations Analysis:** Analyzing needs and product requirements to create a design. **Management of Personnel Resources:** Motivating, developing, and directing people as they work, identifying the best people for the job. **Negotiation:** Bringing others together and trying to reconcile differences. **Mathematics:** Using mathematics to solve problems. **Persuasion:** Persuading others to change their minds or behavior. **Systems Evaluation:** Identifying measures or indicators of system performance and the actions needed to improve or correct performance relative to the goals of the system.

Work Environment: More often outdoors than indoors; sitting; noise; contaminants; hazardous equipment.

Control and Valve Installers and Repairers, Except Mechanical Door

- ⊙ Annual Earnings: $49,600
- ⊙ Earnings Growth Potential: High (43.0%)
- ⊙ Growth: 0.0%
- ⊙ Annual Job Openings: 810
- ⊙ Self-Employed: 0.0%

Considerations for Job Outlook: Little or no change in employment is projected.

Install, repair, and maintain mechanical regulating and controlling devices, such as electric meters, gas regulators, thermostats, safety and flow valves, and other mechanical governors. Turn meters on or off to establish or close service. Turn valves to allow measured amounts of air or gas to pass through meters at specified flow rates. Report hazardous field situations and damaged or missing meters. Record meter readings and installation data on meter cards, work orders, or field service orders, or enter data into handheld computers. Connect regulators to test stands, and turn screw adjustments until gauges indicate that inlet and outlet pressures meet specifications. Disassemble and repair mechanical control devices or valves, such as regulators, thermostats, or hydrants, using power tools, hand tools, and cutting torches. Record maintenance information, including test results, material usage, and repairs made. Disconnect and/or remove defective or unauthorized meters, using hand tools. Lubricate wearing surfaces of mechanical parts, using oils or other lubricants. Test valves and regulators for leaks and accurate temperature and pressure settings, using precision testing equipment. Install regulators and related equipment such as gas meters, odorization units, and gas pressure telemetering equipment. Shut off service and notify repair crews when major repairs are required, such as the replacement of underground pipes or wiring. Examine valves or mechanical control device parts for defects, dents, or loose attachments, and mark malfunctioning areas of defective units. Attach air hoses to meter inlets and then plug outlets and observe gauges for pressure losses in order to test internal seams for leaks. Dismantle meters, and replace or adjust defective parts such as cases, shafts, gears, disks, and recording mechanisms, using soldering irons and hand tools. Advise customers on proper installation of valves or regulators and related equipment. Connect hoses from provers to meter inlets and outlets, and raise prover bells until prover gauges register zero.

Education/Training Required: High school diploma or equivalent. **Education and Training Program:** Industrial Mechanics and Maintenance Technology. **Knowledge/ Courses—Mechanical Devices:** Machines and tools, including their designs, uses, repair, and maintenance. **Transportation:** Principles and methods for moving people or goods by air, rail, sea, or road, including the relative costs and benefits. **Physics:** Physical principles, laws, their interrelationships, and applications to understanding fluid, material, and atmospheric dynamics, and mechanical, electrical, atomic, and subatomic structures and processes. **Public Safety and Security:** Relevant equipment, policies, procedures, and strategies to promote effective local, state, or national security operations for the protection of people, data, property, and institutions. **Design:** Design

techniques, tools, and principles involved in production of precision technical plans, blueprints, drawings, and models. **Chemistry:** The chemical composition, structure, and properties of substances and of the chemical processes and transformations that they undergo. This includes uses of chemicals and their danger signs, production techniques, and disposal methods. **Work Experience Needed:** None. **On-the-Job Training Needed:** Moderate-term on-the-job training. **Certification/Licensure:** None.

Personality Type: Realistic-Conventional-Investigative. **Career Cluster:** 13 Manufacturing. **Career Pathway:** 13.3 Maintenance, Installation, and Repair. **Other Jobs in This Pathway:** Aircraft Mechanics and Service Technicians; Automotive Engineering Technicians; Automotive Specialty Technicians; Avionics Technicians; Biological Technicians; Camera and Photographic Equipment Repairers; Chemical Equipment Operators and Tenders; Civil Engineering Technicians; Coil Winders, Tapers, and Finishers; Computer, Automated Teller, and Office Machine Repairers; Construction and Related Workers, All Other; Electric Motor, Power Tool, and Related Repairers; Electrical and Electronic Equipment Assemblers; Electrical and Electronics Repairers, Commercial and Industrial Equipment; Electrical and Electronics Repairers, Powerhouse, Substation, and Relay; Electrical Engineering Technicians; Electrical Engineering Technologists; Electromechanical Engineering Technologists; Electromechanical Equipment Assemblers; Electronics Engineering Technicians; Electronics Engineering Technologists; Elevator Installers and Repairers; Engine and Other Machine Assemblers; others.

Skills—Repairing: Repairing machines or systems using the needed tools. **Equipment Maintenance:** Performing routine maintenance on equipment and determining when and what kind of maintenance is needed. **Troubleshooting:** Determining causes of operating errors and deciding what to do about them. **Quality Control Analysis:** Conducting tests and inspections of products, services, or processes to evaluate quality or performance. **Equipment Selection:** Determining the kind of tools and equipment needed to do a job. **Installation:** Installing equipment, machines, wiring, or programs to meet specifications. **Operation Monitoring:** Watching gauges, dials, or other indicators to make sure a machine is working properly. **Operation and Control:** Controlling operations of equipment or systems.

Work Environment: Outdoors; standing; using hands; noise; very hot or cold; bright or inadequate lighting; contaminants; cramped work space; high places; hazardous conditions; hazardous equipment.

Conveyor Operators and Tenders

- ⊙ Annual Earnings: $29,320
- ⊙ Earnings Growth Potential: Low (31.2%)
- ⊙ Growth: 11.6%
- ⊙ Annual Job Openings: 1,490
- ⊙ Self-Employed: 0.0%

Considerations for Job Outlook: Job prospects should be favorable. A high number of job openings should be created by the need to replace workers who leave this occupation. As automation increases, the technology used by this occupation will become more complex.

Control or tend conveyors or conveyor systems that move materials or products to and from stockpiles, processing stations, departments, or vehicles. Position deflector bars, gates, chutes, or spouts to divert flow of materials from one conveyor onto another conveyor. Weigh or measure materials and products, using scales or other measuring instruments, or read scales on conveyors that continually weigh products, in order to verify specified tonnages and prevent overloads. Manipulate controls, levers, and valves to start pumps, auxiliary equipment, or conveyors, and to adjust equipment positions, speeds, timing, and material flows. Record production data such as weights, types, quantities, and storage locations of materials, as well as equipment performance problems and downtime. Inform supervisors of equipment malfunctions that need to be addressed. Clean, sterilize, and maintain equipment, machinery, and work stations, using hand tools, shovels, brooms, chemicals, hoses, and lubricants. Observe conveyor operations and monitor lights, dials, and gauges, in order to maintain specified operating levels and to detect equipment malfunctions. Operate elevator systems in conjunction with conveyor systems. Read production and delivery schedules, and confer with supervisors, to determine sorting and transfer procedures, arrangement of packages on pallets, and destinations of loaded pallets. Repair or replace equipment components or parts such as blades, rolls, and pumps. Contact workers in work stations or other departments to request movement of materials, products, or machinery, or to notify them of incoming shipments and their estimated delivery times. Stop equipment or machinery and clear jams, using poles, bars, and hand tools, or remove damaged materials from conveyors. Collect samples of materials or products, checking them to ensure conformance to specifications or sending them to laboratories for analysis. Load, unload, or adjust materials or products on conveyors by hand, by using lifts, hoists, and scoops, or by opening gates, chutes, or hoppers. Operate consoles to control automatic palletizing equipment.

Education/Training Required: Less than high school. **Education and Training Program:** Ground Transportation, Other. **Knowledge/Courses—Mechanical Devices:** Machines and tools, including their designs, uses, repair, and maintenance. **Chemistry:** The chemical composition, structure, and properties of substances and of the chemical processes and transformations that they undergo. This includes uses of chemicals and their danger signs, production techniques, and disposal methods. **Physics:** Physical principles, laws, their interrelationships, and applications to understanding fluid, material, and atmospheric dynamics, and mechanical, electrical, atomic, and subatomic structures and processes. **Engineering and Technology:** The practical application of engineering science and technology. This includes applying principles, techniques, procedures, and equipment to the design and production of various goods and services. **Production and Processing:** Raw materials, production processes, quality control, costs, and other techniques for maximizing the effective manufacture and distribution of goods. **Education and Training:** Principles and methods for curriculum and training design, teaching and instruction for individuals and groups, and the measurement of training effects. **Work Experience Needed:** None. **On-the-Job Training Needed:** Short-term on-the-job training. **Certification/Licensure:** None.

Personality Type: Realistic-Conventional. **Career Cluster:** 01 Agriculture, Food, and Natural Resources. **Career Pathway:** 01.5 Natural Resources Systems. **Other Jobs in This Pathway:** Biological Science Teachers, Postsecondary; Climate Change Analysts; Derrick Operators, Oil and Gas; Engineering Technicians, Except Drafters, All Other; Environmental Economists; Environmental Restoration Planners; Environmental Science and Protection Technicians, Including Health; Environmental Science Teachers, Postsecondary; Environmental Scientists and Specialists,

Including Health; Fallers; Fish and Game Wardens; Fishers and Related Fishing Workers; Forest and Conservation Technicians; Forest and Conservation Workers; Foresters; Forestry and Conservation Science Teachers, Postsecondary; Gas Compressor and Gas Pumping Station Operators; Geological Sample Test Technicians; Geophysical Data Technicians; Helpers—Extraction Workers; Industrial Ecologists; Industrial Truck and Tractor Operators; Loading Machine Operators, Underground Mining; Log Graders and Scalers; Logging Equipment Operators; Logging Workers, All Other; Mechanical Engineering Technicians; Mine Shuttle Car Operators; others.

Skills—Operation and Control: Controlling operations of equipment or systems. **Equipment Maintenance:** Performing routine maintenance on equipment and determining when and what kind of maintenance is needed. **Repairing:** Repairing machines or systems using the needed tools. **Operation Monitoring:** Watching gauges, dials, or other indicators to make sure a machine is working properly. **Troubleshooting:** Determining causes of operating errors and deciding what to do about them. **Equipment Selection:** Determining the kind of tools and equipment needed to do a job. **Quality Control Analysis:** Conducting tests and inspections of products, services, or processes to evaluate quality or performance. **Science:** Using scientific rules and methods to solve problems.

Work Environment: Outdoors; standing; walking and running; using hands; noise; very hot or cold; bright or inadequate lighting; contaminants; cramped work space; high places; hazardous conditions; minor burns, cuts, bites, or stings.

Cooks, Institution and Cafeteria

- ⊙ Annual Earnings: $22,710
- ⊙ Earnings Growth Potential: Low (26.1%)
- ⊙ Growth: 12.3%
- ⊙ Annual Job Openings: 13,620
- ⊙ Self-Employed: 1.1%

Considerations for Job Outlook: The majority of job openings will stem from the need to replace workers who leave the occupation. The fast pace, long hours, and high energy levels required for these jobs often lead to a high rate of turnover. There will be strong competition for jobs at upscale restaurants, hotels, and casinos, which tend to pay more. Workers with a combination of business skills, previous work experience, and creativity will have the best job prospects.

Prepare and cook large quantities of food for institutions such as schools, hospitals, or cafeterias. Clean and inspect galley equipment, kitchen appliances, and work areas in order to ensure cleanliness and functional operation. Apportion and serve food to facility residents, employees, or patrons. Cook foodstuffs according to menus, special dietary or nutritional restrictions, and numbers of portions to be served. Clean, cut, and cook meat, fish, and poultry. Monitor use of government food commodities to ensure that proper procedures are followed. Wash pots, pans, dishes, utensils, and other cooking equipment. Compile and maintain records of food use and expenditures. Direct activities of one or more workers who assist in preparing and serving meals. Bake breads, rolls, and other pastries. Train new employees. Take inventory of supplies and equipment. Monitor menus and spending in order to ensure that meals are prepared economically. Plan menus that are varied, nutritionally balanced, and appetizing, taking advantage of foods in season and local availability. Requisition food supplies, kitchen equipment, and appliances, based on estimates of future needs. Determine meal prices based on calculations of ingredient prices.

Education/Training Required: Less than high school. **Education and Training Programs:** Culinary Arts and Related Services, Other; Food Preparation/Professional Cooking/Kitchen Assistant Training; Foodservice Systems Administration/Management; Institutional Food Worker Training. **Knowledge/Courses—Food Production:** Techniques and equipment for planting, growing, and harvesting food products (both plant and animal) for consumption, including storage/handling techniques. **Work Experience Needed:** None. **On-the-Job Training Needed:** Short-term on-the-job training. **Certification/Licensure:** None.

Personality Type: Realistic-Conventional. **Career Clusters:** 08 Health Science; 09 Hospitality and Tourism. **Career Pathways:** 08.4 Support Services; 09.1 Restaurants and Food/Beverage Services. **Other Jobs in These Pathways:** Bakers; Baristas; Bartenders; Butchers and Meat Cutters; Chefs and Head Cooks; Combined Food Preparation and Serving Workers, Including Fast Food; Cooks, All Other; Cooks, Fast Food; Cooks, Private Household;

Cooks, Restaurant; Cooks, Short Order; Counter Attendants, Cafeteria, Food Concession, and Coffee Shop; Dietetic Technicians; Dietitians and Nutritionists; Dining Room and Cafeteria Attendants and Bartender Helpers; Dishwashers; Farm and Home Management Advisors; First-Line Supervisors of Food Preparation and Serving Workers; Food Batchmakers; Food Preparation and Serving Related Workers, All Other; Food Preparation Workers; Food Servers, Nonrestaurant; Food Service Managers; Gaming Managers; Home Economics Teachers, Postsecondary; Hosts and Hostesses, Restaurant, Lounge, and Coffee Shop; Meat, Poultry, and Fish Cutters and Trimmers; Slaughterers and Meat Packers; Waiters and Waitresses.

Skills—Management of Financial Resources: Determining how money will be spent to get the work done and accounting for these expenditures. **Management of Material Resources:** Obtaining and seeing to the appropriate use of equipment, facilities, and materials needed to do certain work. **Operation and Control:** Controlling operations of equipment or systems. **Management of Personnel Resources:** Motivating, developing, and directing people as they work, identifying the best people for the job. **Quality Control Analysis:** Conducting tests and inspections of products, services, or processes to evaluate quality or performance. **Time Management:** Managing one's own time and the time of others. **Operation Monitoring:** Watching gauges, dials, or other indicators to make sure a machine is working properly. **Service Orientation:** Actively looking for ways to help people.

Work Environment: Indoors; standing; walking and running; using hands; bending or twisting the body; repetitive motions; noise; very hot or cold; minor burns, cuts, bites, or stings.

Correctional Officers and Jailers

- ⊙ Annual Earnings: $38,990
- ⊙ Earnings Growth Potential: Low (31.5%)
- ⊙ Growth: 5.2%
- ⊙ Annual Job Openings: 10,810
- ⊙ Self-Employed: 0.0%

Considerations for Job Outlook: Some local and state corrections agencies experience high job turnover because of low salaries and shift work, as well as the stress that many correctional officers feel. The need to replace correctional officers who transfer to other occupations, retire, or leave the labor force, coupled with rising employment demand, should generate job openings. Some employment opportunities also will come in the private sector as public authorities contract with private companies to provide and staff corrections facilities. Some state and federal corrections agencies use private prison services.

Guard inmates in penal or rehabilitative institutions in accordance with established regulations and procedures. Conduct head counts to ensure that each prisoner is present. Monitor conduct of prisoners in housing unit or during work or recreational activities according to established policies, regulations, and procedures to prevent escape or violence. Inspect conditions of locks, window bars, grills, doors, and gates at correctional facilities to ensure security and help prevent escapes. Record information such as prisoner identification, charges, and incidences of inmate disturbance, and keep daily logs of prisoner activities. Search prisoners and vehicles and conduct shakedowns of cells for valuables and contraband such as weapons or drugs. Use weapons, handcuffs, and physical force to maintain discipline and order among prisoners. Guard facility entrances to screen visitors. Inspect mail for the presence of contraband. Maintain records of prisoners' identification and charges. Process or book convicted individuals into prison. Settle disputes between inmates. Conduct fire, safety, and sanitation inspections. Provide to supervisors oral and written reports of the quality and quantity of work performed by inmates, inmate disturbances and rule violations, and unusual occurrences. Participate in required job training. Take prisoners into custody, and escort them to locations within and outside the facility, such as visiting room, courtroom, or airport. Serve meals, distribute commissary items, and dispense prescribed medications to prisoners.

Education/Training Required: High school diploma or equivalent. **Education and Training Programs:** Corrections; Corrections and Criminal Justice, Other; Juvenile Corrections. **Knowledge/Courses—Public Safety and Security:** Relevant equipment, policies, procedures, and strategies to promote effective local, state, or national security operations for the protection of people, data, property, and institutions. **Psychology:** Human behavior and performance; individual differences in ability, personality, and interests; learning and motivation; psychological research methods; and the assessment and treatment of behavioral and affective disorders. **Therapy and Counseling:** Principles, methods, and procedures for diagnosis, treatment, and rehabilitation of physical and mental dysfunctions, and for career counseling and guidance. **Law and Government:** Laws, legal codes, court procedures, precedents, government regulations, executive orders, agency rules, and the democratic political process. **Medicine and Dentistry:** The information and techniques needed to diagnose and treat human injuries, diseases, and deformities. This includes symptoms, treatment alternatives, drug properties and interactions, and preventive health-care measures. **Sociology and Anthropology:** Group behavior and dynamics, societal trends and influences, human migrations, ethnicity, and cultures and their history and origins. **Work Experience Needed:** None. **On-the-Job Training Needed:** Moderate-term on-the-job training. **Certification/Licensure:** Voluntary certification by association.

Personality Type: Realistic-Enterprising-Conventional. **Career Cluster:** 12 Law, Public Safety, Corrections, and Security. **Career Pathways:** 12.4 Law Enforcement Services; 12.2 Emergency and Fire Management Services. **Other Jobs in These Pathways:** Anthropology and Archeology Teachers, Postsecondary; Bailiffs; Criminal Investigators and Special Agents; Criminal Justice and Law Enforcement Teachers, Postsecondary; Fire Inspectors; Fire Investigators; First-Line Supervisors of Police and Detectives; Forensic Science Technicians; Forest Fire Fighting and Prevention Supervisors; Forest Fire Inspectors and Prevention Specialists; Forest Firefighters; Immigration and Customs Inspectors; Intelligence Analysts; Municipal Fire Fighting and Prevention Supervisors; Municipal Firefighters; Police Detectives; Police Identification and Records Officers; Police Patrol Officers; Remote Sensing Scientists and Technologists; Sheriffs and Deputy Sheriffs.

Skills—Negotiation: Bringing others together and trying to reconcile differences. **Persuasion:** Persuading others to change their minds or behavior. **Social Perceptiveness:** Being aware of others' reactions and understanding why they react as they do. **Service Orientation:** Actively looking for ways to help people. **Monitoring:** Monitoring or assessing your performance or that of other individuals or organizations to make improvements or take corrective action. **Instructing:** Teaching others how to do something. **Coordination:** Adjusting actions in relation to

others' actions. **Operation Monitoring:** Watching gauges, dials, or other indicators to make sure a machine is working properly.

Work Environment: Indoors; more often sitting than standing; walking and running; using hands; repetitive motions; noise; bright or inadequate lighting; contaminants; exposed to disease or infections.

Counter and Rental Clerks

- ⊙ Annual Earnings: $22,740
- ⊙ Earnings Growth Potential: Low (25.4%)
- ⊙ Growth: 12.2%
- ⊙ Annual Job Openings: 14,660
- ⊙ Self-Employed: 1.4%

Considerations for Job Outlook: Trends such as online shopping may impede employment growth for these workers. But because these occupations usually require personal contact, they are difficult to automate. Opportunities are expected to be favorable.

Receive orders, generally in person, for repairs, rentals, and services. Compute charges for merchandise or services and receive payments. Prepare merchandise for display or for purchase or rental. Recommend and provide advice on a wide variety of products and services. Answer telephones to provide information and receive orders. Greet customers and discuss the type, quality, and quantity of merchandise sought for rental. Keep records of transactions and of the number of customers entering an establishment. Prepare rental forms, obtaining customer signatures and other information, such as required licenses. Receive, examine, and tag articles to be altered, cleaned, stored, or repaired. Inspect and adjust rental items to meet the needs of customers. Explain rental fees, policies, and procedures. Reserve items for requested times and keep records of items rented. Receive orders for services such as rentals, repairs, dry cleaning, and storage. Rent items, arrange for provision of services to customers, and accept returns.

Education/Training Required: Less than high school. **Education and Training Program:** Selling Skills and Sales Operations. **Knowledge/Courses—Sales and Marketing:** Principles and methods for showing, promoting, and selling products or services. This includes marketing strategy and tactics, product demonstration, sales techniques, and sales control systems. **Computers and Electronics:** Circuit boards, processors, chips, electronic equipment, and computer hardware and software, including applications and programming. **Production and Processing:** Raw materials, production processes, quality control, costs, and other techniques for maximizing the effective manufacture and distribution of goods. **Clerical Practices:** Administrative and clerical procedures and systems such as word processing, managing files and records, stenography and transcription, designing forms, and other office procedures and terminology. **Work Experience Needed:** None. **On-the-Job Training Needed:** Short-term on-the-job training. **Certification/Licensure:** None.

Personality Type: Conventional-Enterprising. **Career Cluster:** 14 Marketing, Sales, and Service. **Career Pathway:** 14.2 Professional Sales and Marketing. **Other Jobs in This Pathway:** Appraisers, Real Estate; Assessors; Cashiers; Demonstrators and Product Promoters; Door-To-Door Sales Workers, News and Street Vendors, and Related Workers; Driver/Sales Workers; Energy Brokers; First-Line Supervisors of Non-Retail Sales Workers; First-Line Supervisors of Retail Sales Workers; Gaming Change Persons and Booth Cashiers; Hotel, Motel, and Resort Desk Clerks; Interior Designers; Lodging Managers; Marketing Managers; Marking Clerks; Meeting, Convention, and Event Planners; Merchandise Displayers and Window Trimmers; Models; Online Merchants; Order Fillers, Wholesale and Retail Sales; Parts Salespersons; Property, Real Estate, and Community Association Managers; Real Estate Brokers; Real Estate Sales Agents; Reservation and Transportation Ticket Agents and Travel Clerks; Retail Salespersons; Sales and Related Workers, All Other; Sales Engineers; Sales Representatives, Services, All Other; others.

Skills—Service Orientation: Actively looking for ways to help people. **Management of Financial Resources:** Determining how money will be spent to get the work done and accounting for these expenditures. **Operation and Control:** Controlling operations of equipment or systems. **Management of Material Resources:** Obtaining and seeing to the appropriate use of equipment, facilities, and materials needed to do certain work. **Negotiation:** Bringing others together and trying to reconcile differences.

Work Environment: Indoors; standing; walking and running; repetitive motions; noise.

Couriers and Messengers

- ⊙ Annual Earnings: $24,750
- ⊙ Earnings Growth Potential: Low (29.5%)
- ⊙ Growth: 12.6%
- ⊙ Annual Job Openings: 4,300
- ⊙ Self-Employed: 23.6%

Considerations for Job Outlook: Job opportunities are expected to be best for those who deliver sensitive items, particularly medical samples and specimens that cannot be sent electronically. Those who specialize in document delivery, however, will face limited job opportunities. Applicants with strong customer service skills are likely to have better job opportunities.

Pick up and deliver messages, documents, packages, and other items between offices or departments within an establishment or directly to other business concerns. Walk, ride bicycles, drive vehicles, or use public conveyances in order to reach destinations to deliver messages or materials. Load vehicles with listed goods, ensuring goods are loaded correctly and taking precautions with hazardous goods. Unload and sort items collected along delivery routes. Receive messages or materials to be delivered, and information on recipients, such as names, addresses, telephone numbers, and delivery instructions, communicated via telephone, two-way radio, or in person. Plan and follow the most efficient routes for delivering goods. Deliver messages and items, such as newspapers, documents, and packages, between establishment departments, and to other establishments and private homes. Sort items to be delivered according to the delivery route. Obtain signatures and payments, or arrange for recipients to make payments. Record information, such as items received and delivered and recipients' responses to messages. Check with home offices after completed deliveries, in order to confirm deliveries and collections and to receive instructions for other deliveries. Perform routine maintenance on delivery vehicles, such as monitoring fluid levels and replenishing fuel. Call by telephone in order to deliver verbal messages. Open, sort, and distribute incoming mail. Perform general office or clerical work such as filing materials, operating duplicating machines, or running errands. Collect, seal, and stamp outgoing mail, using postage meters and envelope sealers. Unload goods from large trucks, and load them onto smaller delivery vehicles.

Education/Training Required: High school diploma or equivalent. **Education and Training Programs:** No related CIP programs; this job is learned through informal short-term on-the-job training. **Knowledge/Courses—Transportation:** Principles and methods for moving people or goods by air, rail, sea, or road, including the relative costs and benefits. **Work Experience Needed:** None. **On-the-Job Training Needed:** Short-term on-the-job training. **Certification/Licensure:** None.

Personality Type: Realistic-Conventional-Enterprising. **Career Cluster:** 04 Business, Management, and Administration. **Career Pathway:** 04.6 Administrative and Information Support. **Other Jobs in This Pathway:** Cargo and Freight Agents; Correspondence Clerks; Court Clerks; Customer Service Representatives; Data Entry Keyers; Dispatchers, Except Police, Fire, and Ambulance; Executive Secretaries and Executive Administrative Assistants; File Clerks; Freight Forwarders; Human Resources Assistants, Except Payroll and Timekeeping; Information and Record Clerks, All Other; Insurance Claims Clerks; Insurance Policy Processing Clerks; Interviewers, Except Eligibility and Loan; License Clerks; Mail Clerks and Mail Machine Operators, Except Postal Service; Meter Readers, Utilities; Municipal Clerks; Office and Administrative Support Workers, All Other; Office Clerks, General; Office Machine Operators, Except Computer; Order Clerks; Patient Representatives; Postal Service Clerks; Postal Service Mail Carriers; Postal Service Mail Sorters, Processors, and Processing Machine Operators; Procurement Clerks; Receptionists and Information Clerks; others.

Skills—Operation and Control: Controlling operations of equipment or systems. **Troubleshooting:** Determining causes of operating errors and deciding what to do about them.

Work Environment: More often outdoors than indoors; standing; walking and running; using hands; bending or twisting the body; repetitive motions; noise; very hot or cold; contaminants.

Court Reporters

- ⊙ Annual Earnings: $48,530
- ⊙ Earnings Growth Potential: High (46.2%)
- ⊙ Growth: 14.1%
- ⊙ Annual Job Openings: 640
- ⊙ Self-Employed: 14.1%

Considerations for Job Outlook: Job prospects for graduates of court reporting programs are expected to be very good. Many training programs report that nearly all graduates are able to find jobs. Those with experience and training in CART and real-time captioning will have the best job prospects.

Use verbatim methods and equipment to capture, store, retrieve, and transcribe pretrial and trial proceedings or other information. Take notes in shorthand, or use a stenotype or shorthand machine that prints letters on a paper tape. Provide transcripts of proceedings upon request of judges, lawyers, or the public. Record verbatim proceedings of courts, legislative assemblies, committee meetings, and other proceedings, using computerized recording equipment, electronic stenograph machines, or stenomasks. Transcribe recorded proceedings in accordance with established formats. Ask speakers to clarify inaudible statements. File a legible transcript of records of a court case with the court clerk's office. File and store shorthand notes of court sessions. Respond to requests during court sessions to read portions of the proceedings already recorded. Record depositions and other proceedings for attorneys. Verify accuracy of transcripts by checking copies against original records of proceedings and accuracy of rulings by checking with judges. Record symbols on computer discs or CD-ROMs and then translate and display them as text in a computer-aided transcription process.

Education/Training Required: High school diploma or equivalent. **Education and Training Program:** Court Reporting/Court Reporter. **Knowledge/Courses—Clerical Practices:** Administrative and clerical procedures and systems such as word processing, managing files and records, stenography and transcription, designing forms, and other office procedures and terminology. **English Language:** The structure and content of the English language including the meaning and spelling of words, rules of composition, and grammar. **Computers and Electronics:** Circuit boards, processors, chips, electronic equipment, and computer hardware and software, including applications and programming. **Law and Government:** Laws, legal codes, court procedures, precedents, government regulations, executive orders, agency rules, and the democratic political process. **Work Experience Needed:** None. **On-the-Job Training Needed:** Short-term on-the-job training. **Certification/Licensure:** Licensure in many states; voluntary certification by association in others.

Personality Type: Conventional-Enterprising. **Career Cluster:** 12 Law, Public Safety, Corrections, and Security. **Career Pathway:** 12.5 Legal Services. **Other Jobs in This Pathway:** Administrative Law Judges, Adjudicators, and Hearing Officers; Arbitrators, Mediators, and Conciliators; Farm and Home Management Advisors; Judges, Magistrate Judges, and Magistrates; Law Teachers, Postsecondary; Lawyers; Legal Secretaries; Legal Support Workers, All Other; Paralegals and Legal Assistants; Title Examiners, Abstractors, and Searchers.

Skills—Active Listening: Giving full attention to what other people are saying, taking time to understand the points being made, asking questions as appropriate, and not interrupting at inappropriate times. **Writing:** Communicating effectively in writing as appropriate for the needs of the audience.

Work Environment: Indoors; sitting; using hands; repetitive motions.

Court, Municipal, and License Clerks

- ◉ Annual Earnings: $34,300
- ◉ Earnings Growth Potential: Low (34.3%)
- ◉ Growth: 8.0%
- ◉ Annual Job Openings: 4,670
- ◉ Self-Employed: 1.8%

Considerations for Job Outlook: Employment growth will vary by specialty. Projected employment change is most rapid for interviewers and correspondence clerks.

Perform clerical duties for courts of law, municipalities, or governmental licensing agencies and bureaus. For task data, see Job Specializations.

Education/Training Required: High school diploma or equivalent. **Work Experience Needed:** None. **On-the-Job Training Needed:** Moderate-term on-the-job training. **Certification/Licensure:** None.

Job Specialization: Court Clerks

Perform clerical duties in court of law; prepare docket of cases to be called; secure information for judges; and contact witnesses, attorneys, and litigants to obtain information for court. Prepare dockets or calendars of cases to be called, using typewriters or computers. Record case dispositions, court orders, and arrangements made for payment of court fees. Answer inquiries from the general public regarding judicial procedures, court appearances, trial dates, adjournments, outstanding warrants, summonses, subpoenas, witness fees, and payment of fines. Prepare and issue orders of the court, including probation orders, release documentation, sentencing information, and summonses. Prepare documents recording the outcomes of court proceedings. Instruct parties about timing of court appearances. Explain procedures or forms to parties in cases or to the general public. Search files and contact witnesses, attorneys, and litigants to obtain information for the court. Follow procedures to secure courtrooms and exhibits such as money, drugs, and weapons. Amend indictments when necessary, and endorse indictments with pertinent information. Read charges and related information to the court, and, if necessary, record defendants' pleas. Swear in jury members, interpreters, witnesses, and defendants. Collect court fees or fines, and record amounts collected. Direct support staff in handling of paperwork processed by clerks' offices. Examine legal documents submitted to courts for adherence to laws or court procedures. Prepare and mark all applicable court exhibits and evidence.

Education and Training Program: General Office Occupations and Clerical Services. **Knowledge/Courses—Clerical Practices:** Administrative and clerical procedures and systems such as word processing, managing files and records, stenography and transcription, designing forms, and other office procedures and terminology. **Law and Government:** Laws, legal codes, court procedures, precedents, government regulations, executive orders, agency rules, and the democratic political process. **Computers and Electronics:** Circuit boards, processors, chips, electronic equipment, and computer hardware and software, including applications and programming.

Personality Type: Conventional-Enterprising-Realistic. **Career Cluster:** 04 Business, Management, and Administration. **Career Pathway:** 04.6 Administrative and Information Support. **Other Jobs in This Pathway:** Cargo and Freight Agents; Correspondence Clerks; Couriers and Messengers; Customer Service Representatives; Data Entry Keyers; Dispatchers, Except Police, Fire, and Ambulance; Executive Secretaries and Executive Administrative Assistants; File Clerks; Freight Forwarders; Human Resources

Assistants, Except Payroll and Timekeeping; Information and Record Clerks, All Other; Insurance Claims Clerks; Insurance Policy Processing Clerks; Interviewers, Except Eligibility and Loan; License Clerks; Mail Clerks and Mail Machine Operators, Except Postal Service; Meter Readers, Utilities; Municipal Clerks; Office and Administrative Support Workers, All Other; Office Clerks, General; Office Machine Operators, Except Computer; Order Clerks; Patient Representatives; Postal Service Clerks; Postal Service Mail Carriers; Postal Service Mail Sorters, Processors, and Processing Machine Operators; Procurement Clerks; Receptionists and Information Clerks; others.

Skills—Reading Comprehension: Understanding written sentences and paragraphs in work-related documents. **Writing:** Communicating effectively in writing as appropriate for the needs of the audience. **Negotiation:** Bringing others together and trying to reconcile differences. **Active Listening:** Giving full attention to what other people are saying, taking time to understand the points being made, asking questions as appropriate, and not interrupting at inappropriate times. **Time Management:** Managing one's own time and the time of others. **Speaking:** Talking to others to convey information effectively. **Service Orientation:** Actively looking for ways to help people.

Work Environment: Indoors; sitting; using hands; repetitive motions; noise.

Job Specialization: License Clerks

Issue licenses or permits to qualified applicants. Obtain necessary information, record data, advise applicants on requirements, collect fees, and issue licenses. May conduct oral, written, visual, or performance testing. Collect prescribed fees for licenses. Code information on license applications for entry into computers. Evaluate information on applications to verify completeness and accuracy and to determine whether applicants are qualified to obtain desired licenses. Answer questions and provide advice to the public regarding licensing policies, procedures, and regulations. Maintain records of applications made and licensing fees collected. Question applicants to obtain required information, such as name, address, and age, and record data on prescribed forms. Update operational records and licensing information, using computer terminals. Inform customers by mail or telephone of additional steps they need to take to obtain licenses. Perform routine data entry and other office support activities, including creating, sorting, photocopying, distributing, and filing documents. Stock counters with adequate supplies of forms, film, licenses, and other required materials. Enforce canine licensing regulations, contacting noncompliant owners in person or by mail to inform them of the required regulations and potential enforcement actions. Assemble photographs with printed license information to produce completed documents. Prepare bank deposits, and take them to banks. Operate specialized photographic equipment to obtain photographs for drivers' licenses and photo identification cards.

Education and Training Program: General Office Occupations and Clerical Services. **Knowledge/Courses—Clerical Practices:** Administrative and clerical procedures and systems such as word processing, managing files and records, stenography and transcription, designing forms, and other office procedures and terminology. **Customer and Personal Service:** Principles and processes for providing customer and personal services. This includes customer needs assessment, meeting quality standards for services, and evaluation of customer satisfaction. **Law and Government:** Laws, legal codes, court procedures, precedents, government regulations, executive orders, agency rules, and the democratic political process. **Computers and Electronics:** Circuit boards, processors, chips, electronic equipment, and computer hardware and software, including applications and programming.

Personality Type: Conventional-Enterprising. **Career Cluster:** 04 Business, Management, and Administration. **Career Pathway:** 04.6 Administrative and Information Support. **Other Jobs in This Pathway:** Cargo and Freight Agents; Correspondence Clerks; Couriers and Messengers; Court Clerks; Customer Service Representatives; Data Entry Keyers; Dispatchers, Except Police, Fire, and Ambulance; Executive Secretaries and Executive Administrative Assistants; File Clerks; Freight Forwarders; Human Resources Assistants, Except Payroll and Timekeeping; Information and Record Clerks, All Other; Insurance Claims Clerks; Insurance Policy Processing Clerks; Interviewers, Except Eligibility and Loan; Mail Clerks and Mail Machine Operators, Except Postal Service; Meter Readers, Utilities; Municipal Clerks; Office and Administrative Support Workers, All Other; Office Clerks, General; Office Machine Operators, Except Computer; Order Clerks; Patient Representatives; Postal Service Clerks;

Postal Service Mail Carriers; Postal Service Mail Sorters, Processors, and Processing Machine Operators; Procurement Clerks; Receptionists and Information Clerks; others.

Skills—Service Orientation: Actively looking for ways to help people.

Work Environment: Indoors; sitting; using hands; repetitive motions; noise.

Job Specialization: Municipal Clerks

Draft agendas and bylaws for town or city council, record minutes of council meetings, answer official correspondence, keep fiscal records and accounts, and prepare reports on civic needs. Participate in the administration of municipal elections, including preparation and distribution of ballots, appointment and training of election officers, and tabulation and certification of results. Record and edit the minutes of meetings; then distribute them to appropriate officials and staff members. Plan and direct the maintenance, filing, safekeeping, and computerization of all municipal documents. Issue public notification of all official activities and meetings. Maintain and update documents such as municipal codes and city charters. Prepare meeting agendas and packets of related information. Prepare ordinances, resolutions, and proclamations so that they can be executed, recorded, archived, and distributed. Respond to requests for information from the public, other municipalities, state officials, and state and federal legislative offices. Maintain fiscal records and accounts. Perform budgeting duties, including assisting in budget preparation, expenditure review, and budget administration. Perform general office duties such as taking and transcribing dictation, typing and proofreading correspondence, distributing and filing official forms, and scheduling appointments. Coordinate and maintain office-tracking systems for correspondence and follow-up actions. Research information in the municipal archives upon request of public officials and private citizens. Perform contract administration duties, assisting with bid openings and the awarding of contracts.

Education and Training Program: General Office Occupations and Clerical Services. **Knowledge/Courses— Clerical Practices:** Administrative and clerical procedures and systems such as word processing, managing files and records, stenography and transcription, designing forms, and other office procedures and terminology. **Law and**

Government: Laws, legal codes, court procedures, precedents, government regulations, executive orders, agency rules, and the democratic political process. **Economics and Accounting:** Economic and accounting principles and practices, the financial markets, banking, and the analysis and reporting of financial data. **English Language:** The structure and content of the English language including the meaning and spelling of words, rules of composition, and grammar. **Personnel and Human Resources:** Principles and procedures for personnel recruitment, selection, training, compensation and benefits, labor relations and negotiation, and personnel information systems. **Administration and Management:** Business and management principles involved in strategic planning, resource allocation, human resources modeling, leadership technique, production methods, and coordination of people and resources.

Personality Type: Conventional-Enterprising. **Career Cluster:** 04 Business, Management, and Administration. **Career Pathway:** 04.6 Administrative and Information Support. **Other Jobs in This Pathway:** Cargo and Freight Agents; Correspondence Clerks; Couriers and Messengers; Court Clerks; Customer Service Representatives; Data Entry Keyers; Dispatchers, Except Police, Fire, and Ambulance; Executive Secretaries and Executive Administrative Assistants; File Clerks; Freight Forwarders; Human Resources Assistants, Except Payroll and Timekeeping; Information and Record Clerks, All Other; Insurance Claims Clerks; Insurance Policy Processing Clerks; Interviewers, Except Eligibility and Loan; License Clerks; Mail Clerks and Mail Machine Operators, Except Postal Service; Meter Readers, Utilities; Office and Administrative Support Workers, All Other; Office Clerks, General; Office Machine Operators, Except Computer; Order Clerks; Patient Representatives; Postal Service Clerks; Postal Service Mail Carriers; Postal Service Mail Sorters, Processors, and Processing Machine Operators; Procurement Clerks; Receptionists and Information Clerks; others.

Skills—Management of Financial Resources: Determining how money will be spent to get the work done and accounting for these expenditures. **Writing:** Communicating effectively in writing as appropriate for the needs of the audience. **Reading Comprehension:** Understanding written sentences and paragraphs in work-related documents. **Speaking:** Talking to others to convey information effectively. **Active Listening:** Giving full attention to what other people are saying, taking time to understand the points being made, asking questions as appropriate, and not interrupting at inappropriate times. **Critical Thinking:** Using logic and reasoning to identify the strengths and weaknesses of alternative solutions, conclusions, or approaches to problems. **Service Orientation:** Actively looking for ways to help people. **Coordination:** Adjusting actions in relation to others' actions.

Work Environment: Indoors; sitting.

Crane and Tower Operators

- ◉ Annual Earnings: $46,460
- ◉ Earnings Growth Potential: Medium (38.3%)
- ◉ Growth: 15.7%
- ◉ Annual Job Openings: 1,720
- ◉ Self-Employed: 0.6%

Considerations for Job Outlook: Job prospects should be favorable. A high number of job openings should be created by the need to replace workers who leave this occupation. As automation increases, the technology used by this occupation will become more complex.

Operate mechanical boom and cable or tower and cable equipment to lift and move materials, machines, or products in many directions. Determine load weights and check them against lifting capacities in order to prevent overload. Move levers, depress foot pedals, and turn dials to operate cranes, cherry pickers, electromagnets, or other moving equipment for lifting, moving, and placing loads. Inspect cables and grappling devices for wear, and install or replace cables as needed. Clean, lubricate, and maintain mechanisms such as cables, pulleys, and grappling devices, making repairs as necessary. Inspect and adjust crane mechanisms and lifting accessories in order to prevent malfunctions and damage. Direct helpers engaged in placing blocking and outrigging under cranes. Load and unload bundles from trucks, and move containers to storage bins, using moving equipment. Weigh bundles, using floor scales, and record weights for company records. Review daily work and delivery schedules to determine orders, sequences of deliveries, and special loading instructions. Direct truck drivers backing vehicles into loading bays, and cover, uncover, and secure loads for delivery. Inspect bundle packaging for conformance to regulations

and customer requirements, and remove and batch packaging tickets.

Education/Training Required: Less than high school. **Education and Training Programs:** Construction/Heavy Equipment/Earthmoving Equipment Operation; Mobile Crane Operation/Operator. **Knowledge/Courses— Building and Construction:** Materials, methods, and the tools involved in the construction or repair of houses, buildings, or other structures such as highways and roads. **Mechanical Devices:** Machines and tools, including their designs, uses, repair, and maintenance. **Transportation:** Principles and methods for moving people or goods by air, rail, sea, or road, including the relative costs and benefits. **Engineering and Technology:** The practical application of engineering science and technology. This includes applying principles, techniques, procedures, and equipment to the design and production of various goods and services. **Public Safety and Security:** Relevant equipment, policies, procedures, and strategies to promote effective local, state, or national security operations for the protection of people, data, property, and institutions. **Design:** Design techniques, tools, and principles involved in production of precision technical plans, blueprints, drawings, and models. **Work Experience Needed:** 1 to 5 years. **On-the-Job Training Needed:** Long-term on-the-job training. **Certification/Licensure:** Licensure in many states; voluntary certification by association in others.

Personality Type: Realistic-Conventional-Investigative. **Career Clusters:** 02 Architecture and Construction; 16 Transportation, Distribution, and Logistics. **Career Pathways:** 02.2 Construction; 16.1 Transportation Operations. **Other Jobs in These Pathways:** Aerospace Engineering and Operations Technicians; Air Traffic Controllers; Aircraft Cargo Handling Supervisors; Airfield Operations Specialists; Airline Pilots, Copilots, and Flight Engineers; Automotive and Watercraft Service Attendants; Automotive Master Mechanics; Aviation Inspectors; Boilermakers; Brickmasons and Blockmasons; Bridge and Lock Tenders; Bus Drivers, School or Special Client; Bus Drivers, Transit and Intercity; Carpet Installers; Cement Masons and Concrete Finishers; Commercial Divers; Commercial Pilots; Construction and Building Inspectors; Construction and Related Workers, All Other; Construction Carpenters; Construction Laborers; Construction Managers; Continuous Mining Machine Operators; Cost Estimators; Dredge Operators; Drywall and Ceiling Tile Installers;

Earth Drillers, Except Oil and Gas; Electrical Power-Line Installers and Repairers; Electricians; Electromechanical Equipment Assemblers; others.

Skills—Equipment Maintenance: Performing routine maintenance on equipment and determining when and what kind of maintenance is needed. **Operation and Control:** Controlling operations of equipment or systems. **Repairing:** Repairing machines or systems using the needed tools. **Troubleshooting:** Determining causes of operating errors and deciding what to do about them. **Equipment Selection:** Determining the kind of tools and equipment needed to do a job. **Quality Control Analysis:** Conducting tests and inspections of products, services, or processes to evaluate quality or performance. **Operation Monitoring:** Watching gauges, dials, or other indicators to make sure a machine is working properly. **Installation:** Installing equipment, machines, wiring, or programs to meet specifications.

Work Environment: Outdoors; sitting; using hands; repetitive motions; noise; very hot or cold; bright or inadequate lighting; contaminants; whole-body vibration; high places; hazardous equipment.

Customer Service Representatives

- ⊙ Annual Earnings: $30,610
- ⊙ Earnings Growth Potential: Medium (35.9%)
- ⊙ Growth: 15.5%
- ⊙ Annual Job Openings: 95,960
- ⊙ Self-Employed: 0.4%

Considerations for Job Outlook: Job prospects for customer service representatives are expected to be good. Many job openings will arise from the need to replace workers who leave the occupation. There will be greater competition for in-house customer service jobs—which often have higher pay and greater advancement potential—than for those jobs in the call center industry.

Interact with customers to provide information in response to inquiries about products and services and to handle and resolve complaints. Confer with customers by telephone or in person to provide information about products and services, to take orders or cancel accounts, or to obtain details of complaints. Keep records of customer interactions and transactions, recording details of inquiries, complaints, and comments, as well as actions taken. Resolve customers' service or billing complaints by performing activities such as exchanging merchandise, refunding money, and adjusting bills. Check to ensure that appropriate changes were made to resolve customers' problems. Contact customers to respond to inquiries or to notify them of claim-investigation results and any planned adjustments. Refer unresolved customer grievances to designated departments for further investigation. Determine charges for services requested, collect deposits or payments, or arrange for billing. Complete contract forms, prepare change of address records, and issue service-discontinuance orders, using computers. Obtain and examine all relevant information to assess validity of complaints and to determine possible causes, such as extreme weather conditions, that could increase utility bills. Solicit sale of new or additional services or products. Review insurance policy terms to determine whether a particular loss is covered by insurance. Review claims adjustments with dealers, examining parts claimed to be defective and approving or disapproving dealers' claims.

Education/Training Required: High school diploma or equivalent. **Education and Training Programs:** Customer Service Support/Call Center/Teleservice Operation; Receptionist Training. **Knowledge/Courses—Clerical Practices:** Administrative and clerical procedures and systems such as word processing, managing files and records, stenography and transcription, designing forms, and other office procedures and terminology. **Customer and Personal Service:** Principles and processes for providing customer and personal services. This includes customer needs assessment, meeting quality standards for services, and evaluation of customer satisfaction. **English Language:** The structure and content of the English language including the meaning and spelling of words, rules of composition, and grammar. **Work Experience Needed:** None. **On-the-Job Training Needed:** Short-term on-the-job training. **Certification/Licensure:** Licensure for some specializations.

Personality Type: Enterprising-Social-Conventional. **Career Cluster:** 04 Business, Management, and Administration. **Career Pathway:** 04.6 Administrative and Information Support. **Other Jobs in This Pathway:** Cargo and Freight Agents; Correspondence Clerks; Couriers and Messengers; Court Clerks; Data Entry Keyers; Dispatchers, Except Police, Fire, and Ambulance; Executive

Secretaries and Executive Administrative Assistants; File Clerks; Freight Forwarders; Human Resources Assistants, Except Payroll and Timekeeping; Information and Record Clerks, All Other; Insurance Claims Clerks; Insurance Policy Processing Clerks; Interviewers, Except Eligibility and Loan; License Clerks; Mail Clerks and Mail Machine Operators, Except Postal Service; Meter Readers, Utilities; Municipal Clerks; Office and Administrative Support Workers, All Other; Office Clerks, General; Office Machine Operators, Except Computer; Order Clerks; Patient Representatives; Postal Service Clerks; Postal Service Mail Carriers; Postal Service Mail Sorters, Processors, and Processing Machine Operators; Procurement Clerks; Receptionists and Information Clerks; others.

Skills—Service Orientation: Actively looking for ways to help people. **Persuasion:** Persuading others to change their minds or behavior. **Negotiation:** Bringing others together and trying to reconcile differences. **Active Listening:** Giving full attention to what other people are saying, taking time to understand the points being made, asking questions as appropriate, and not interrupting at inappropriate times. **Speaking:** Talking to others to convey information effectively. **Reading Comprehension:** Understanding written sentences and paragraphs in work-related documents.

Work Environment: Indoors; sitting; using hands; repetitive motions; noise.

Job Specialization: Patient Representatives

Assist patients in obtaining services, understanding policies and making health-care decisions. Explain policies, procedures, or services to patients using medical or administrative knowledge. Coordinate communication between patients, family members, medical staff, administrative staff, or regulatory agencies. Investigate and direct patient inquiries or complaints to appropriate medical staff members, and follow up to ensure satisfactory resolution. Interview patients or their representatives to identify problems relating to care. Refer patients to appropriate health-care services or resources. Analyze patients' abilities to pay to determine charges on a sliding scale. Collect and report data on topics such as patient encounters and inter-institutional problems, making recommendations for change when appropriate. Develop and distribute news-letters, brochures, or other printed materials to share

information with patients or medical staff. Teach patients to use home health-care equipment. Identify and share research, recommendations, or other information regarding legal liabilities, risk management, or quality of care. Read current literature, talk with colleagues, continue education, or participate in professional organizations or conferences to keep abreast of developments in the field. Maintain knowledge of community services and resources available to patients. Provide consultation or training to volunteers or staff on topics such as guest relations, patients' rights, and medical issues.

Education and Training Programs: Customer Service Support/Call Center/Teleservice Operation; Receptionist Training. **Knowledge/Courses—Therapy and Counseling:** Principles, methods, and procedures for diagnosis, treatment, and rehabilitation of physical and mental dysfunctions, and for career counseling and guidance. **Psychology:** Human behavior and performance; individual differences in ability, personality, and interests; learning and motivation; psychological research methods; and the assessment and treatment of behavioral and affective disorders. **Customer and Personal Service:** Principles and processes for providing customer and personal services. This includes customer needs assessment, meeting quality standards for services, and evaluation of customer satisfaction. **Sociology and Anthropology:** Group behavior and dynamics, societal trends and influences, human migrations, ethnicity, and cultures and their history and origins. **Philosophy and Theology:** Different philosophical systems and religions. This includes their basic principles, values, ethics, ways of thinking, customs, practices, and their impact on human culture. **Medicine and Dentistry:** The information and techniques needed to diagnose and treat human injuries, diseases, and deformities. This includes symptoms, treatment alternatives, drug properties and interactions, and preventive health-care measures.

Personality Type: Social-Enterprising. **Career Cluster:** 04 Business, Management, and Administration. **Career Pathway:** 04.6 Administrative and Information Support. **Other Jobs in This Pathway:** Cargo and Freight Agents; Correspondence Clerks; Couriers and Messengers; Court Clerks; Customer Service Representatives; Data Entry Keyers; Dispatchers, Except Police, Fire, and Ambulance; Executive Secretaries and Executive Administrative Assistants; File Clerks; Freight Forwarders; Human Resources Assistants, Except Payroll and Timekeeping; Information and Record Clerks, All Other; Insurance Claims Clerks; Insurance Policy Processing Clerks; Interviewers, Except Eligibility and Loan; License Clerks; Mail Clerks and Mail Machine Operators, Except Postal Service; Meter Readers, Utilities; Municipal Clerks; Office and Administrative Support Workers, All Other; Office Clerks, General; Office Machine Operators, Except Computer; Order Clerks; Postal Service Clerks; Postal Service Mail Carriers; Postal Service Mail Sorters, Processors, and Processing Machine Operators; Procurement Clerks; Receptionists and Information Clerks; others.

Skills—Service Orientation: Actively looking for ways to help people. **Persuasion:** Persuading others to change their minds or behavior. **Social Perceptiveness:** Being aware of others' reactions and understanding why they react as they do. **Negotiation:** Bringing others together and trying to reconcile differences. **Systems Evaluation:** Identifying measures or indicators of system performance and the actions needed to improve or correct performance relative to the goals of the system. **Instructing:** Teaching others how to do something. **Critical Thinking:** Using logic and reasoning to identify the strengths and weaknesses of alternative solutions, conclusions, or approaches to problems. **Systems Analysis:** Determining how a system should work and how changes in conditions, operations, and the environment will affect outcomes.

Work Environment: Indoors; sitting; noise; exposed to disease or infections.

Demonstrators and Product Promoters

- ⊙ Annual Earnings: $23,770
- ⊙ Earnings Growth Potential: Low (25.0%)
- ⊙ Growth: 17.5%
- ⊙ Annual Job Openings: 4,210
- ⊙ Self-Employed: 16.2%

Considerations for Job Outlook: Job prospects for demonstrators and product promoters should be favorable. Many people enter this occupation and then leave to take jobs in other occupations, creating openings for new workers. Employers look for candidates who are energetic and outgoing.

Demonstrate merchandise and answer questions for the purpose of creating public interest in buying the product. Demonstrate and explain products, methods, or services in order to persuade customers to purchase products or utilize services. Learn about competitors' products and consumers' interests and concerns in order to answer questions and provide more complete information. Recommend product or service improvements to employers. Train demonstrators to present a company's products or services. Give tours of plants where specific products are made. Develop lists of prospective clients from sources such as newspaper items, company records, local merchants, and customers. Contact businesses and civic establishments to arrange to exhibit and sell merchandise. Visit trade shows, stores, community organizations, and other venues to demonstrate products or services, and to answer questions from potential customers. Write articles and pamphlets about products. Transport, assemble, and disassemble materials used in presentations. Instruct customers in alteration of products. Collect fees or accept donations. Identify interested and qualified customers in order to provide them with additional information. Work as part of a team of demonstrators to accommodate large crowds. Wear costumes or sign boards and walk in public to promote merchandise, services, or events. Provide product information, using lectures, films, charts, and/or slide shows. Prepare and alter presentation contents to target specific audiences. Keep areas neat while working, and return items to correct locations following demonstrations. Record and report demonstration-related information such as the number of questions asked by the audience and the number of coupons distributed. Research and investigate products to be presented to prepare for demonstrations. Sell products being promoted, and keep records of sales. Set up and arrange displays and demonstration areas to attract the attention of prospective customers. Stock shelves with products. Suggest specific product purchases to meet customers' needs.

Education/Training Required: High school diploma or equivalent. **Education and Training Program:** Retailing and Retail Operations. **Knowledge/Courses—Sales and Marketing:** Principles and methods for showing, promoting, and selling products or services. This includes marketing strategy and tactics, product demonstration, sales techniques, and sales control systems. **Customer and Personal Service:** Principles and processes for providing customer and personal services. This includes customer needs assessment, meeting quality standards for services, and evaluation of customer satisfaction. **Work Experience Needed:** None. **On-the-Job Training Needed:** Short-term on-the-job training. **Certification/Licensure:** None.

Personality Type: Enterprising-Conventional-Realistic. **Career Cluster:** 14 Marketing, Sales, and Service. **Career Pathway:** 14.2 Professional Sales and Marketing. **Other Jobs in This Pathway:** Appraisers, Real Estate; Assessors; Cashiers; Counter and Rental Clerks; Door-To-Door Sales Workers, News and Street Vendors, and Related Workers; Driver/Sales Workers; Energy Brokers; First-Line Supervisors of Non-Retail Sales Workers; First-Line Supervisors of Retail Sales Workers; Gaming Change Persons and Booth Cashiers; Hotel, Motel, and Resort Desk Clerks; Interior Designers; Lodging Managers; Marketing Managers; Marking Clerks; Meeting, Convention, and Event Planners; Merchandise Displayers and Window Trimmers; Models; Online Merchants; Order Fillers, Wholesale and Retail Sales; Parts Salespersons; Property, Real Estate, and Community Association Managers; Real Estate Brokers; Real Estate Sales Agents; Reservation and Transportation Ticket Agents and Travel Clerks; Retail Salespersons; Sales and Related Workers, All Other; Sales Engineers; Sales Representatives, Services, All Other; Sales Representatives, Wholesale and Manufacturing, Except Technical and Scientific Products; others.

Skills—Persuasion: Persuading others to change their minds or behavior. **Operations Analysis:** Analyzing needs and product requirements to create a design. **Speaking:** Talking to others to convey information effectively. **Service Orientation:** Actively looking for ways to help people. **Troubleshooting:** Determining causes of operating errors and deciding what to do about them. **Active Listening:** Giving full attention to what other people are saying, taking time to understand the points being made, asking questions as appropriate, and not interrupting at inappropriate times. **Learning Strategies:** Selecting and using training/instructional methods and procedures appropriate for the situation when learning or teaching new things. **Coordination:** Adjusting actions in relation to others' actions.

Work Environment: Standing.

Dental Assistants

- ⊙ Annual Earnings: $34,140
- ⊙ Earnings Growth Potential: Low (32.4%)
- ⊙ Growth: 30.8%
- ⊙ Annual Job Openings: 15,400
- ⊙ Self-Employed: 0.0%

Considerations for Job Outlook: Ongoing research linking oral health and general health will likely continue to increase the demand for preventive dental services. Dentists will continue to hire more dental assistants to complete routine tasks, allowing the dentists to see more patients in their practice and spend their time on more complex procedures. As dental practices grow, more dental assistants will be needed. As the large baby-boom population ages, and as people keep more of their original teeth than did previous generations, the need to maintain and treat teeth will continue to increase the need for dental assistants.

Assist dentist, set up equipment, prepare patients for treatment, and keep records. Prepare patients, sterilize and disinfect instruments, set up instrument trays, prepare materials, and assist dentist during dental procedures. Expose dental diagnostic X-rays. Record treatment information in patient records. Take and record medical and dental histories and vital signs of patients. Provide postoperative instructions prescribed by dentist. Assist dentist in management of medical and dental emergencies. Pour, trim, and polish study casts. Instruct patients in oral hygiene and plaque-control programs. Make preliminary impressions for study casts and occlusal registrations for mounting study casts. Clean and polish removable appliances. Clean teeth, using dental instruments. Apply protective coating of fluoride to teeth. Fabricate temporary restorations and custom impressions from preliminary impressions. Schedule appointments, prepare bills, and receive payment for dental services; complete insurance forms; and maintain records, manually or using computer.

Education/Training Required: Postsecondary vocational training. **Education and Training Program:** Dental Assisting/Assistant. **Knowledge/Courses—Medicine and Dentistry:** The information and techniques needed to diagnose and treat human injuries, diseases, and deformities. This includes symptoms, treatment alternatives, drug properties and interactions, and preventive health-care

D

measures. **Customer and Personal Service:** Principles and processes for providing customer and personal services. This includes customer needs assessment, meeting quality standards for services, and evaluation of customer satisfaction. **Psychology:** Human behavior and performance; individual differences in ability, personality, and interests; learning and motivation; psychological research methods; and the assessment and treatment of behavioral and affective disorders. **Sales and Marketing:** Principles and methods for showing, promoting, and selling products or services. This includes marketing strategy and tactics, product demonstration, sales techniques, and sales control systems. **Work Experience Needed:** None. **On-the-Job Training Needed:** None. **Certification/Licensure:** Licensure for some specializations; voluntary certification by association.

Personality Type: Conventional-Realistic-Social. **Career Cluster:** 08 Health Science. **Career Pathway:** 08.1 Therapeutic Services. **Other Jobs in This Pathway:** Acupuncturists; Allergists and Immunologists; Anesthesiologists; Art Therapists; Chiropractors; Clinical Psychologists; Community and Social Service Specialists, All Other; Counseling Psychologists; Counselors, All Other; Dental Hygienists; Dentists, All Other Specialists; Dentists, General; Dermatologists; Diagnostic Medical Sonographers; Dietetic Technicians; Dietitians and Nutritionists; Family and General Practitioners; Health Diagnosing and Treating Practitioners, All Other; Health Specialties Teachers, Postsecondary; Health Technologists and Technicians, All Other; Healthcare Practitioners and Technical Workers, All Other; Healthcare Support Workers, All Other; Home Health Aides; Hospitalists; Industrial-Organizational Psychologists; Internists, General; Licensed Practical and Licensed Vocational Nurses; Life, Physical, and Social Science Technicians, All Other; Low Vision Therapists, Orientation and Mobility Specialists, and Vision Rehabilitation Therapists; Massage Therapists; others.

Skills—Repairing: Repairing machines or systems using the needed tools. **Equipment Maintenance:** Performing routine maintenance on equipment and determining when and what kind of maintenance is needed. **Operation Monitoring:** Watching gauges, dials, or other indicators to make sure a machine is working properly. **Equipment Selection:** Determining the kind of tools and equipment needed to do a job. **Science:** Using scientific rules and methods to solve problems. **Service Orientation:** Actively looking for ways

to help people. **Operation and Control:** Controlling operations of equipment or systems. **Quality Control Analysis:** Conducting tests and inspections of products, services, or processes to evaluate quality or performance.

Work Environment: Indoors; standing; walking and running; using hands; bending or twisting the body; repetitive motions; contaminants; exposed to radiation; exposed to disease or infections; hazardous conditions.

Dental Hygienists

- ⊙ Annual Earnings: $69,280
- ⊙ Earnings Growth Potential: Low (33.6%)
- ⊙ Growth: 37.7%
- ⊙ Annual Job Openings: 10,490
- ⊙ Self-Employed: 1.6%

Considerations for Job Outlook: Demand for dental services follows the trends in the economy because patients or private insurance companies pay for these services. As a result, during slow times in the economy, demand for dental services may decrease. During such times, dental hygienists may have difficulty finding employment or, if they are currently employed, they might work fewer hours.

Clean teeth and examine oral areas, head, and neck for signs of oral disease. Clean calcareous deposits, accretions, and stains from teeth and beneath margins of gums, using dental instruments. Feel and visually examine gums for sores and signs of disease. Chart conditions of decay and disease for diagnosis and treatment by dentist. Feel lymph nodes under patient's chin to detect swelling or tenderness that could indicate presence of oral cancer. Apply fluorides and other cavity-preventing agents to arrest dental decay. Examine gums, using probes, to locate periodontal recessed gums and signs of gum disease. Expose and develop X-ray film. Provide clinical services and health education to improve and maintain oral health of schoolchildren. Remove excess cement from coronal surfaces of teeth. Make impressions for study casts. Place, carve, and finish amalgam restorations. Administer local anesthetic agents. Conduct dental health clinics for community groups to augment services of dentist. Remove sutures and dressings. Place and remove rubber dams, matrices, and temporary restorations.

Education/Training Required: Associate degree. **Education and Training Program:** Dental Hygiene/Hygienist.

Knowledge/Courses—Medicine and Dentistry: The information and techniques needed to diagnose and treat human injuries, diseases, and deformities. This includes symptoms, treatment alternatives, drug properties and interactions, and preventive health-care measures. **Psychology:** Human behavior and performance; individual differences in ability, personality, and interests; learning and motivation; psychological research methods; and the assessment and treatment of behavioral and affective disorders. **Therapy and Counseling:** Principles, methods, and procedures for diagnosis, treatment, and rehabilitation of physical and mental dysfunctions, and for career counseling and guidance. **Chemistry:** The chemical composition, structure, and properties of substances and of the chemical processes and transformations that they undergo. This includes uses of chemicals and their danger signs, production techniques, and disposal methods. **Biology:** Plant and animal organisms and their tissues, cells, functions, interdependencies, and interactions with each other and the environment. **Sales and Marketing:** Principles and methods for showing, promoting, and selling products or services. This includes marketing strategy and tactics, product demonstration, sales techniques, and sales control systems. **Work Experience Needed:** None. **On-the-Job Training Needed:** None. **Certification/Licensure:** Licensure.

Personality Type: Social-Realistic-Conventional. **Career Cluster:** 08 Health Science. **Career Pathway:** 08.1 Therapeutic Services. **Other Jobs in This Pathway:** Acupuncturists; Allergists and Immunologists; Anesthesiologists; Art Therapists; Chiropractors; Clinical Psychologists; Community and Social Service Specialists, All Other; Counseling Psychologists; Counselors, All Other; Dental Assistants; Dentists, All Other Specialists; Dentists, General; Dermatologists; Diagnostic Medical Sonographers; Dietetic Technicians; Dietitians and Nutritionists; Family and General Practitioners; Health Diagnosing and Treating Practitioners, All Other; Health Specialties Teachers, Postsecondary; Health Technologists and Technicians, All Other; Healthcare Practitioners and Technical Workers, All Other; Healthcare Support Workers, All Other; Home Health Aides; Hospitalists; Industrial-Organizational Psychologists; Internists, General; Licensed Practical and Licensed Vocational Nurses; Life, Physical, and Social Science Technicians, All Other; Low Vision Therapists, Orientation and Mobility Specialists, and Vision Rehabilitation Therapists; Massage Therapists; others.

Skills—Science: Using scientific rules and methods to solve problems. **Troubleshooting:** Determining causes of operating errors and deciding what to do about them. **Service Orientation:** Actively looking for ways to help people. **Writing:** Communicating effectively in writing as appropriate for the needs of the audience. **Instructing:** Teaching others how to do something. **Coordination:** Adjusting actions in relation to others' actions. **Operation Monitoring:** Watching gauges, dials, or other indicators to make sure a machine is working properly. **Active Learning:** Understanding the implications of new information for both current and future problem solving and decision making.

Work Environment: Indoors; sitting; using hands; bending or twisting the body; repetitive motions; noise; contaminants; exposed to radiation; exposed to disease or infections.

Derrick Operators, Oil and Gas

- ⊙ Annual Earnings: $45,220
- ⊙ Earnings Growth Potential: Low (29.5%)
- ⊙ Growth: 9.5%
- ⊙ Annual Job Openings: 570
- ⊙ Self-Employed: 2.2%

Considerations for Job Outlook: Demand for oil and gas workers will depend on the demand for the products and services of two industries in particular: oil and gas extraction and support for mining activities. Because of higher prices for resources, oil and gas companies are more likely to drill in deeper waters and harsher environments than in the past. These complex operations require more workers. Higher prices will also encourage oil and gas companies to return to existing wells to try new extraction methods, thereby increasing demand for oil and gas workers. Also, changes in policy could expand exploration and drilling for oil and natural gas in currently protected areas, potentially boosting employment. However, new production technologies are expected to dampen overall demand for oil and gas workers.

Rig derrick equipment and operate pumps to circulate mud through drill hole. Inspect derricks, or order their inspection, prior to being raised or lowered. Inspect derricks for flaws, and clean and oil derricks in order to maintain proper working conditions. Control the viscosity and weight of the drilling fluid. Repair pumps, mud tanks, and related equipment. Set and bolt crown blocks to posts at tops of derricks. Listen to mud pumps and check regularly for vibration and other problems, in order to ensure that rig pumps and drilling mud systems are working properly. Start pumps that circulate mud through drill pipes and boreholes to cool drill bits and flush out drill-cuttings. Position and align derrick elements, using harnesses and platform climbing devices. Supervise crew members, and provide assistance in training them. Guide lengths of pipe into and out of elevators. Prepare mud reports, and instruct crews about the handling of any chemical additives. Clamp holding fixtures on ends of hoisting cables. Weigh clay, and mix with water and chemicals in order to make drilling mud, using portable mixers. String cables through pulleys and blocks. Steady pipes during connection to or disconnection from drill or casing strings.

Education/Training Required: Less than high school. **Education and Training Program:** Well Drilling/Driller. **Knowledge/Courses—Mechanical Devices:** Machines and tools, including their designs, uses, repair, and maintenance. **Building and Construction:** Materials, methods, and the tools involved in the construction or repair of houses, buildings, or other structures such as highways and roads. **Physics:** Physical principles, laws, their interrelationships, and applications to understanding fluid, material, and atmospheric dynamics, and mechanical, electrical, atomic, and subatomic structures and processes. **Transportation:** Principles and methods for moving people or goods by air, rail, sea, or road, including the relative costs and benefits. **Chemistry:** The chemical composition, structure, and properties of substances and of the chemical processes and transformations that they undergo. This includes uses of chemicals and their danger signs, production techniques, and disposal methods. **Public Safety and Security:** Relevant equipment, policies, procedures, and strategies to promote effective local, state, or national security operations for the protection of people, data, property, and institutions. **Work Experience Needed:** None. **On-the-Job Training Needed:** Short-term on-the-job training. **Certification/Licensure:** None.

Personality Type: Realistic-Conventional-Investigative. **Career Cluster:** 01 Agriculture, Food, and Natural Resources. **Career Pathway:** 01.5 Natural Resources Systems. **Other Jobs in This Pathway:** Biological Science Teachers, Postsecondary; Climate Change Analysts; Conveyor Operators and Tenders; Engineering Technicians, Except Drafters, All Other; Environmental Economists; Environmental Restoration Planners; Environmental Science and Protection Technicians, Including Health; Environmental Science Teachers, Postsecondary; Environmental Scientists and Specialists, Including Health; Fallers; Fish and Game Wardens; Fishers and Related Fishing Workers; Forest and Conservation Technicians; Forest and Conservation Workers; Foresters; Forestry and Conservation Science Teachers, Postsecondary; Gas Compressor and Gas Pumping Station Operators; Geological Sample Test Technicians; Geophysical Data Technicians; Helpers—Extraction Workers; Industrial Ecologists; Industrial Truck and Tractor Operators; Loading Machine Operators, Underground Mining; Log Graders and Scalers; Logging Equipment Operators; Logging Workers, All Other; Mechanical Engineering Technicians; Mine Shuttle Car Operators; others.

Skills—Repairing: Repairing machines or systems using the needed tools. **Equipment Maintenance:** Performing routine maintenance on equipment and determining when and what kind of maintenance is needed. **Operation and Control:** Controlling operations of equipment or systems. **Troubleshooting:** Determining causes of operating errors and deciding what to do about them. **Operation Monitoring:** Watching gauges, dials, or other indicators to make sure a machine is working properly. **Quality Control Analysis:** Conducting tests and inspections of products, services, or processes to evaluate quality or performance. **Equipment Selection:** Determining the kind of tools and equipment needed to do a job. **Management of Personnel Resources:** Motivating, developing, and directing people as they work, identifying the best people for the job.

Work Environment: Outdoors; standing; climbing; walking and running; using hands; bending or twisting the body; repetitive motions; noise; very hot or cold; bright or inadequate lighting; contaminants; cramped work space; whole-body vibration; high places; hazardous conditions; hazardous equipment; minor burns, cuts, bites, or stings.

Detectives and Criminal Investigators

- ⊙ Annual Earnings: $71,770
- ⊙ Earnings Growth Potential: High (44.7%)
- ⊙ Growth: 2.9%
- ⊙ Annual Job Openings: 3,010
- ⊙ Self-Employed: 0.8%

Considerations for Job Outlook: Continued demand for public safety will lead to new openings for officers in local departments; however, both state and federal jobs may be more competitive. Because they typically offer low salaries, many local departments face high turnover rates, making opportunities more plentiful for qualified applicants. However, some smaller departments may have fewer opportunities as budgets limit the ability to hire additional officers. Jobs in state and federal agencies will remain more competitive as they often offer high pay and more opportunities for both promotions and interagency transfers. Bilingual applicants with a bachelor's degree and law enforcement or military experience, especially investigative experience, should have the best opportunities in federal agencies.

Conduct investigations related to suspected violations of federal, state, or local laws to prevent or solve crimes. For task data, see Job Specializations.

Education/Training Required: High school diploma or equivalent. **Work Experience Needed:** 1 to 5 years. **On-the-Job Training Needed:** Moderate-term on-the-job training. **Certification/Licensure:** Licensure in some states.

Job Specialization: Criminal Investigators and Special Agents

Investigate alleged or suspected criminal violations of federal, state, or local laws to determine if evidence is sufficient to recommend prosecution. Record evidence and documents, using equipment such as cameras and photocopy machines. Obtain and verify evidence by interviewing and observing suspects and witnesses or by analyzing records. Examine records to locate links in chains of evidence or information. Prepare reports that detail investigation findings. Determine scope, timing, and direction of investigations. Collaborate with other offices and agencies to exchange information and coordinate activities. Testify before grand juries concerning criminal activity investigations. Analyze evidence in laboratories or in the field. Investigate organized crime, public corruption, financial crime, copyright infringement, civil rights violations, bank robbery, extortion, kidnapping, and other violations of federal or state statutes. Identify case issues and evidence needed, based on analysis of charges, complaints, or allegations of law violations. Obtain and use search and arrest warrants. Serve subpoenas or other official papers. Collaborate with

other authorities on activities such as surveillance, transcription, and research. Develop relationships with informants to obtain information related to cases. Search for and collect evidence such as fingerprints, using investigative equipment. Collect and record physical information about arrested suspects, including fingerprints, height and weight measurements, and photographs.

Education and Training Programs: Criminal Justice/Police Science; Criminalistics and Criminal Science. **Knowledge/Courses—Public Safety and Security:** Relevant equipment, policies, procedures, and strategies to promote effective local, state, or national security operations for the protection of people, data, property, and institutions. **Psychology:** Human behavior and performance; individual differences in ability, personality, and interests; learning and motivation; psychological research methods; and the assessment and treatment of behavioral and affective disorders. **Law and Government:** Laws, legal codes, court procedures, precedents, government regulations, executive orders, agency rules, and the democratic political process. **Customer and Personal Service:** Principles and processes for providing customer and personal services. This includes customer needs assessment, meeting quality standards for services, and evaluation of customer satisfaction. **Sociology and Anthropology:** Group behavior and dynamics, societal trends and influences, human migrations, ethnicity, and cultures and their history and origins. **Therapy and Counseling:** Principles, methods, and procedures for diagnosis, treatment, and rehabilitation of physical and mental dysfunctions, and for career counseling and guidance.

Personality Type: Enterprising-Investigative. **Career Cluster:** 12 Law, Public Safety, Corrections, and Security. **Career Pathway:** 12.4 Law Enforcement Services. **Other Jobs in This Pathway:** Anthropology and Archeology Teachers, Postsecondary; Bailiffs; Correctional Officers and Jailers; Criminal Justice and Law Enforcement Teachers, Postsecondary; First-Line Supervisors of Police and Detectives; Forensic Science Technicians; Immigration and Customs Inspectors; Intelligence Analysts; Police Detectives; Police Identification and Records Officers; Police Patrol Officers; Remote Sensing Scientists and Technologists; Sheriffs and Deputy Sheriffs.

Skills—Negotiation: Bringing others together and trying to reconcile differences. **Science:** Using scientific rules and methods to solve problems. **Complex Problem Solving:**

Identifying complex problems and reviewing related information to develop and evaluate options and implement solutions. **Persuasion:** Persuading others to change their minds or behavior. **Judgment and Decision Making:** Considering the relative costs and benefits of potential actions to choose the most appropriate one. **Speaking:** Talking to others to convey information effectively. **Critical Thinking:** Using logic and reasoning to identify the strengths and weaknesses of alternative solutions, conclusions, or approaches to problems. **Social Perceptiveness:** Being aware of others' reactions and understanding why they react as they do.

Work Environment: Indoors; sitting; noise; very hot or cold; contaminants; exposed to disease or infections.

Job Specialization: Immigration and Customs Inspectors

Investigate and inspect persons, common carriers, goods, and merchandise arriving in or departing from the United States or moving between states to detect violations of immigration and customs laws and regulations. Examine immigration applications, visas, and passports and interview persons to determine eligibility for admission, residence, and travel in the United States. Detain persons found to be in violation of customs or immigration laws, and arrange for legal action such as deportation. Locate and seize contraband or undeclared merchandise and vehicles, aircraft, or boats that contain such merchandise. Interpret and explain laws and regulations to travelers, prospective immigrants, shippers, and manufacturers. Inspect cargo, baggage, and personal articles entering or leaving the U.S. for compliance with revenue laws and U.S. Customs Service regulations. Record and report job-related activities, findings, transactions, violations, discrepancies, and decisions. Institute civil and criminal prosecutions, and cooperate with other law enforcement agencies in the investigation and prosecution of those in violation of immigration or customs laws. Testify regarding decisions at immigration appeals or in federal court. Determine duty and taxes to be paid on goods. Collect samples of merchandise for examination, appraisal, or testing. Investigate applications for duty refunds, and petition for remission or mitigation of penalties when warranted.

Education and Training Programs: Criminal Justice/Police Science; Criminalistics and Criminal Science. **Knowledge/Courses—Public Safety and Security:** Relevant equipment, policies, procedures, and strategies to promote effective local, state, or national security operations for the protection of people, data, property, and institutions. **Law and Government:** Laws, legal codes, court procedures, precedents, government regulations, executive orders, agency rules, and the democratic political process. **Foreign Language:** The structure and content of a foreign (non-English) language including the meaning and spelling of words, rules of composition and grammar, and pronunciation. **Geography:** Principles and methods for describing the features of land, sea, and air masses, including their physical characteristics, locations, interrelationships, and distribution of plant, animal, and human life. **Customer and Personal Service:** Principles and processes for providing customer and personal services. This includes customer needs assessment, meeting quality standards for services, and evaluation of customer satisfaction. **Philosophy and Theology:** Different philosophical systems and religions. This includes their basic principles, values, ethics, ways of thinking, customs, practices, and their impact on human culture.

Personality Type: Conventional-Enterprising-Realistic. **Career Cluster:** 12 Law, Public Safety, Corrections, and Security. **Career Pathway:** 12.4 Law Enforcement Services. **Other Jobs in This Pathway:** Anthropology and Archeology Teachers, Postsecondary; Bailiffs; Correctional Officers and Jailers; Criminal Investigators and Special Agents; Criminal Justice and Law Enforcement Teachers, Postsecondary; First-Line Supervisors of Police and Detectives; Forensic Science Technicians; Intelligence Analysts; Police Detectives; Police Identification and Records Officers; Police Patrol Officers; Remote Sensing Scientists and Technologists; Sheriffs and Deputy Sheriffs.

Skills—Active Listening: Giving full attention to what other people are saying, taking time to understand the points being made, asking questions as appropriate, and not interrupting at inappropriate times. **Persuasion:** Persuading others to change their minds or behavior. **Negotiation:** Bringing others together and trying to reconcile differences. **Operation and Control:** Controlling operations of equipment or systems. **Speaking:** Talking to others to convey information effectively. **Social Perceptiveness:** Being aware of others' reactions and understanding why they react as they do. **Time Management:** Managing one's own time and the time of others. **Judgment and Decision Making:** Considering the relative costs and benefits of potential actions to choose the most appropriate one.

Work Environment: More often outdoors than indoors; more often sitting than standing; using hands; repetitive motions; noise; very hot or cold; bright or inadequate lighting; contaminants; cramped work space; exposed to radiation; hazardous equipment.

Job Specialization: Intelligence Analysts

Gather, analyze, and evaluate information from a variety of sources, such as law enforcement databases, surveillance, intelligence networks, and geographic information systems. Use data to anticipate and prevent organized crime activities, such as terrorism. Predict future gang, organized crime, or terrorist activity, using analyses of intelligence data. Study activities relating to narcotics, money laundering, gangs, auto theft rings, terrorism, or other national security threats. Design, use, or maintain databases and software applications, such as geographic information systems (GIS) mapping and artificial intelligence tools. Establish criminal profiles to aid in connecting criminal organizations with their members. Evaluate records of communications, such as telephone calls, to plot activity and determine the size and location of criminal groups and members. Gather and evaluate information, using tools such as aerial photographs, radar equipment, or sensitive radio equipment. Gather intelligence information by field observation, confidential information sources, or public records. Gather, analyze, correlate, or evaluate information from a variety of resources, such as law enforcement databases. Link or chart suspects to criminal organizations or events to determine activities and interrelationships. Operate cameras, radios, or other surveillance equipment to intercept communications or document activities. Prepare comprehensive written reports, presentations, maps, or charts based on research, collection, and analysis of intelligence data. Prepare plans to intercept foreign communications transmissions. Study the assets of criminal suspects to determine the flow of money from or to targeted groups.

Education and Training Programs: Criminal Justice/Police Science; Criminalistics and Criminal Science.

Personality Type: No data available. **Career Cluster:** 12 Law, Public Safety, Corrections, and Security. **Career Pathway:** 12.4 Law Enforcement Services. **Other Jobs in This Pathway:** Anthropology and Archeology Teachers, Postsecondary; Bailiffs; Correctional Officers and Jailers; Criminal Investigators and Special Agents; Criminal Justice and Law Enforcement Teachers, Postsecondary; First-Line Supervisors of Police and Detectives; Forensic Science Technicians; Immigration and Customs Inspectors; Police Detectives; Police Identification and Records Officers; Police Patrol Officers; Remote Sensing Scientists and Technologists; Sheriffs and Deputy Sheriffs.

Work Environment: No data available.

Job Specialization: Police Detectives

Conduct investigations to prevent crimes or solve criminal cases. Examine crime scenes to obtain clues and evidence, such as loose hairs, fibers, clothing, or weapons. Secure deceased body and obtain evidence from it, preventing bystanders from tampering with it prior to medical examiner's arrival. Obtain evidence from suspects. Provide testimony as a witness in court. Analyze completed police reports to determine what additional information and investigative work is needed. Prepare charges or responses to charges, or information for court cases, according to formalized procedures. Note, mark, and photograph location of objects found, such as footprints, tire tracks, bullets and bloodstains, and take measurements of the scene. Obtain facts or statements from complainants, witnesses, and accused persons and record interviews, using recording device. Obtain summary of incident from officer in charge at crime scene, taking care to avoid disturbing evidence. Examine records and governmental agency files to find identifying data about suspects. Prepare and serve search and arrest warrants. Block or rope off scene and check perimeter to ensure that entire scene is secured. Summon medical help for injured individuals and alert medical personnel to take statements from them. Provide information to lab personnel concerning the source of an item of evidence and tests to be performed. Monitor conditions of victims who are unconscious so that arrangements can be made to take statements if consciousness is regained. Secure persons at scene, keeping witnesses from conversing or leaving the scene before investigators arrive. Preserve, process, and analyze items of evidence obtained from crime scenes and suspects, placing them in proper containers and destroying evidence no longer needed. Record progress of investigation, maintain informational files on suspects, and submit reports to commanding officer or magistrate to authorize warrants.

Education and Training Programs: Criminal Justice/Police Science; Criminalistics and Criminal Science. **Knowledge/Courses—Public Safety and Security:** Relevant equipment, policies, procedures, and strategies to promote effective local, state, or national security operations for the protection of people, data, property, and institutions. **Law and Government:** Laws, legal codes, court procedures, precedents, government regulations, executive orders, agency rules, and the democratic political process. **Psychology:** Human behavior and performance; individual differences in ability, personality, and interests; learning and motivation; psychological research methods; and the assessment and treatment of behavioral and affective disorders. **Therapy and Counseling:** Principles, methods, and procedures for diagnosis, treatment, and rehabilitation of physical and mental dysfunctions, and for career counseling and guidance. **Customer and Personal Service:** Principles and processes for providing customer and personal services. This includes customer needs assessment, meeting quality standards for services, and evaluation of customer satisfaction. **Philosophy and Theology:** Different philosophical systems and religions. This includes their basic principles, values, ethics, ways of thinking, customs, practices, and their impact on human culture.

Personality Type: Enterprising-Investigative. **Career Cluster:** 12 Law, Public Safety, Corrections, and Security. **Career Pathway:** 12.4 Law Enforcement Services. **Other Jobs in This Pathway:** Anthropology and Archeology Teachers, Postsecondary; Bailiffs; Correctional Officers and Jailers; Criminal Investigators and Special Agents; Criminal Justice and Law Enforcement Teachers, Postsecondary; First-Line Supervisors of Police and Detectives; Forensic Science Technicians; Immigration and Customs Inspectors; Intelligence Analysts; Police Identification and Records Officers; Police Patrol Officers; Remote Sensing Scientists and Technologists; Sheriffs and Deputy Sheriffs.

Skills—Science: Using scientific rules and methods to solve problems. **Negotiation:** Bringing others together and trying to reconcile differences. **Operation and Control:** Controlling operations of equipment or systems. **Social Perceptiveness:** Being aware of others' reactions and understanding why they react as they do. **Operation**

Monitoring: Watching gauges, dials, or other indicators to make sure a machine is working properly. **Service Orientation:** Actively looking for ways to help people. **Active Learning:** Understanding the implications of new information for both current and future problem solving and decision making. **Critical Thinking:** Using logic and reasoning to identify the strengths and weaknesses of alternative solutions, conclusions, or approaches to problems.

Work Environment: More often outdoors than indoors; sitting; noise; very hot or cold; contaminants; exposed to disease or infections.

Job Specialization: Police Identification and Records Officers

Collect evidence at crime scenes, classify and identify fingerprints, and photograph evidence for use in criminal and civil cases. Photograph crime or accident scenes for evidence records. Analyze and process evidence at crime scenes and in the laboratory, wearing protective equipment and using powders and chemicals. Look for trace evidence, such as fingerprints, hairs, fibers, or shoe impressions, using alternative light sources when necessary. Dust selected areas of crime scenes and lift latent fingerprints, adhering to proper preservation procedures. Testify in court, and present evidence. Package, store, and retrieve evidence. Serve as technical advisor and coordinate with other law enforcement workers to exchange information on crime-scene collection activities. Perform emergency work during off-hours. Submit evidence to supervisors. Process film and prints from crime or accident scenes. Identify, classify, and file fingerprints, using systems such as the Henry Classification system.

Education and Training Programs: Criminal Justice/Police Science; Criminalistics and Criminal Science. **Knowledge/Courses—Public Safety and Security:** Relevant equipment, policies, procedures, and strategies to promote effective local, state, or national security operations for the protection of people, data, property, and institutions. **Law and Government:** Laws, legal codes, court procedures, precedents, government regulations, executive orders, agency rules, and the democratic political process. **Chemistry:** The chemical composition, structure, and properties of substances and of the chemical processes and transformations that they undergo. This includes uses of chemicals and their danger signs, production techniques, and disposal methods. **Customer and Personal Service:** Principles and processes for providing customer and personal services. This includes customer needs assessment, meeting quality standards for services, and evaluation of customer satisfaction. **Clerical Practices:** Administrative and clerical procedures and systems such as word processing, managing files and records, stenography and transcription, designing forms, and other office procedures and terminology. **Telecommunications:** Transmission, broadcasting, switching, control, and operation of telecommunications systems.

Personality Type: Conventional-Realistic-Investigative. **Career Cluster:** 12 Law, Public Safety, Corrections, and Security. **Career Pathway:** 12.4 Law Enforcement Services. **Other Jobs in This Pathway:** Anthropology and Archeology Teachers, Postsecondary; Bailiffs; Correctional Officers and Jailers; Criminal Investigators and Special Agents; Criminal Justice and Law Enforcement Teachers, Postsecondary; First-Line Supervisors of Police and Detectives; Forensic Science Technicians; Immigration and Customs Inspectors; Intelligence Analysts; Police Detectives; Police Patrol Officers; Remote Sensing Scientists and Technologists; Sheriffs and Deputy Sheriffs.

Skills—Operation and Control: Controlling operations of equipment or systems. **Speaking:** Talking to others to convey information effectively. **Negotiation:** Bringing others together and trying to reconcile differences. **Operation Monitoring:** Watching gauges, dials, or other indicators to make sure a machine is working properly. **Critical Thinking:** Using logic and reasoning to identify the strengths and weaknesses of alternative solutions, conclusions, or approaches to problems. **Active Listening:** Giving full attention to what other people are saying, taking time to understand the points being made, asking questions as appropriate, and not interrupting at inappropriate times. **Persuasion:** Persuading others to change their minds or behavior. **Technology Design:** Generating or adapting equipment and technology to serve user needs.

Work Environment: Indoors; sitting; using hands; noise; contaminants; exposed to disease or infections; hazardous conditions.

Diagnostic Medical Sonographers

- ⊙ Annual Earnings: $65,210
- ⊙ Earnings Growth Potential: Low (31.1%)
- ⊙ Growth: 43.6%
- ⊙ Annual Job Openings: 3,170
- ⊙ Self-Employed: 0.2%

Considerations for Job Outlook: Sonographers who are certified in more than one specialty are expected to have better job opportunities.

Produce ultrasonic recordings of internal organs for use by physicians. Decide which images to include, looking for differences between healthy and pathological areas. Observe screen during scan to ensure that image produced is satisfactory for diagnostic purposes, making adjustments to equipment as required. Observe and care for patients throughout examinations to ensure their safety and comfort. Provide sonogram and oral or written summary of technical findings to physician for use in medical diagnosis. Operate ultrasound equipment to produce and record images of the motion, shape and composition of blood, organs, tissues and bodily masses such as fluid accumulations. Select appropriate equipment settings and adjust patient positions to obtain the best sites and angles. Determine whether scope of exam should be extended, based on findings. Process and code film from procedures and complete appropriate documentation. Obtain and record accurate patient history, including prior test results and information from physical examinations. Record and store suitable images, using camera unit connected to the ultrasound equipment. Prepare patients for exam by explaining procedure, transferring them to ultrasound table, scrubbing skin and applying gel, and positioning them properly. Coordinate work with physicians and other health-care team members, including providing assistance during invasive procedures. Maintain records that include patient information, sonographs and interpretations, files of correspondence, publications and regulations, or quality assurance records such as pathology, biopsy, or postoperative reports. Perform legal and ethical duties including preparing safety and accident reports, obtaining written consent from patient to perform invasive procedures, and reporting symptoms of abuse and neglect. Supervise and train students and other medical sonographers. Maintain stock and

D

supplies, preparing supplies for special examinations and ordering supplies when necessary.

Education/Training Required: Associate degree. **Education and Training Programs:** Allied Health Diagnostic, Intervention, and Treatment Professions, Other; Diagnostic Medical Sonography/Sonographer and Ultrasound Technician Training. **Knowledge/Courses—Medicine and Dentistry:** The information and techniques needed to diagnose and treat human injuries, diseases, and deformities. This includes symptoms, treatment alternatives, drug properties and interactions, and preventive health-care measures. **Physics:** Physical principles, laws, their interrelationships, and applications to understanding fluid, material, and atmospheric dynamics, and mechanical, electrical, atomic, and subatomic structures and processes. **Biology:** Plant and animal organisms and their tissues, cells, functions, interdependencies, and interactions with each other and the environment. **Customer and Personal Service:** Principles and processes for providing customer and personal services. This includes customer needs assessment, meeting quality standards for services, and evaluation of customer satisfaction. **Psychology:** Human behavior and performance; individual differences in ability, personality, and interests; learning and motivation; psychological research methods; and the assessment and treatment of behavioral and affective disorders. **Clerical Practices:** Administrative and clerical procedures and systems such as word processing, managing files and records, stenography and transcription, designing forms, and other office procedures and terminology. **Work Experience Needed:** None. **On-the-Job Training Needed:** None. **Certification/Licensure:** Voluntary certification by association.

Personality Type: Investigative-Social-Realistic. **Career Cluster:** 08 Health Science. **Career Pathways:** 08.1 Therapeutic Services; 08.2 Diagnostics Services. **Other Jobs in These Pathways:** Acupuncturists; Allergists and Immunologists; Ambulance Drivers and Attendants, Except Emergency Medical Technicians; Anesthesiologist Assistants; Anesthesiologists; Art Therapists; Athletic Trainers; Cardiovascular Technologists and Technicians; Chiropractors; Clinical Psychologists; Community and Social Service Specialists, All Other; Counseling Psychologists; Counselors, All Other; Cytogenetic Technologists; Cytotechnologists; Dental Assistants; Dental Hygienists; Dentists, All Other Specialists; Dentists, General; Dermatologists; Dietetic Technicians; Dietitians and Nutritionists; Emergency Medical Technicians and Paramedics; Endoscopy Technicians; Family and General Practitioners; Health Diagnosing and Treating Practitioners, All Other; Health Specialties Teachers, Postsecondary; Health Technologists and Technicians, All Other; Healthcare Practitioners and Technical Workers, All Other; Healthcare Support Workers, All Other; Histotechnologists and Histologic Technicians; others.

Skills—Science: Using scientific rules and methods to solve problems. **Equipment Maintenance:** Performing routine maintenance on equipment and determining when and what kind of maintenance is needed. **Equipment Selection:** Determining the kind of tools and equipment needed to do a job. **Repairing:** Repairing machines or systems using the needed tools. **Operation and Control:** Controlling operations of equipment or systems. **Troubleshooting:** Determining causes of operating errors and deciding what to do about them. **Operation Monitoring:** Watching gauges, dials, or other indicators to make sure a machine is working properly. **Quality Control Analysis:** Conducting tests and inspections of products, services, or processes to evaluate quality or performance.

Work Environment: Indoors; more often sitting than standing; using hands; bending or twisting the body; repetitive motions; contaminants; exposed to disease or infections.

Dispatchers, Except Police, Fire, and Ambulance

- ⊙ Annual Earnings: $35,200
- ⊙ Earnings Growth Potential: High (40.0%)
- ⊙ Growth: 18.6%
- ⊙ Annual Job Openings: 6,950
- ⊙ Self-Employed: 1.5%

Considerations for Job Outlook: About-average employment growth is expected.

Schedule and dispatch workers, work crews, equipment, or service vehicles to appropriate locations according to customer requests, specifications, or needs, using radios or telephones. Confer with customers or supervising personnel to address questions, problems, and requests for service or equipment. Monitor personnel or equipment locations and utilization to coordinate service and schedules. Receive or prepare work orders. Relay work orders, messages, and information to or from work crews, supervisors, and field inspectors using telephones or two-way radios. Record and maintain files and records of customer requests, work or services performed, charges, expenses, inventory, and other dispatch information. Prepare daily work and run schedules. Determine types or amounts of equipment, vehicles, materials, or personnel required according to work orders or specifications. Advise personnel about traffic problems such as construction areas, accidents, congestion, weather conditions, and other hazards. Arrange for necessary repairs to restore service and schedules. Oversee all communications within specifically assigned territories. Ensure timely and efficient movement of trains according to train orders and schedules. Order supplies and equipment, and issue them to personnel.

Education/Training Required: High school diploma or equivalent. **Education and Training Programs:** No related CIP programs; this job is learned through moderate-term on-the-job training. **Knowledge/Courses— Transportation:** Principles and methods for moving people or goods by air, rail, sea, or road, including the relative costs and benefits. **Geography:** Principles and methods for describing the features of land, sea, and air masses, including their physical characteristics, locations, interrelationships, and distribution of plant, animal, and human life. **Customer and Personal Service:** Principles and processes for providing customer and personal services. This includes customer needs assessment, meeting quality standards for services, and evaluation of customer satisfaction. **Sales and Marketing:** Principles and methods for showing, promoting, and selling products or services. This includes marketing strategy and tactics, product demonstration, sales techniques, and sales control systems. **Administration and Management:** Business and management principles involved in strategic planning, resource allocation, human resources modeling, leadership technique, production methods, and coordination of people and resources. **Public Safety and Security:** Relevant equipment, policies, procedures, and strategies to promote effective local, state, or national security operations for the protection of people, data, property, and institutions. **Work Experience Needed:** None. **On-the-Job Training Needed:** Moderate-term on-the-job training. **Certification/Licensure:** None.

Personality Type: Conventional-Realistic-Enterprising. **Career Cluster:** 04 Business, Management, and Administration. **Career Pathway:** 04.6 Administrative and Information Support. **Other Jobs in This Pathway:** Cargo and Freight Agents; Correspondence Clerks; Couriers and Messengers; Court Clerks; Customer Service Representatives; Data Entry Keyers; Executive Secretaries and Executive Administrative Assistants; File Clerks; Freight Forwarders; Human Resources Assistants, Except Payroll and Timekeeping; Information and Record Clerks, All Other; Insurance Claims Clerks; Insurance Policy Processing Clerks; Interviewers, Except Eligibility and Loan; License Clerks; Mail Clerks and Mail Machine Operators, Except Postal Service; Meter Readers, Utilities; Municipal Clerks; Office and Administrative Support Workers, All Other; Office Clerks, General; Office Machine Operators, Except Computer; Order Clerks; Patient Representatives; Postal Service Clerks; Postal Service Mail Carriers; Postal Service Mail Sorters, Processors, and Processing Machine Operators; Procurement Clerks; Receptionists and Information Clerks; Secretaries and Administrative Assistants, Except Legal, Medical, and Executive; others.

Skills—Negotiation: Bringing others together and trying to reconcile differences. **Persuasion:** Persuading others to change their minds or behavior. **Coordination:** Adjusting actions in relation to others' actions. **Active Listening:** Giving full attention to what other people are saying, taking time to understand the points being made, asking questions as appropriate, and not interrupting at inappropriate times. **Speaking:** Talking to others to convey information effectively. **Time Management:** Managing one's own time and the time of others. **Service Orientation:** Actively looking for ways to help people. **Social Perceptiveness:** Being aware of others' reactions and understanding why they react as they do.

Work Environment: Indoors; sitting; repetitive motions; contaminants.

Driver/Sales Workers

- ⊙ Annual Earnings: $22,770
- ⊙ Earnings Growth Potential: Low (26.9%)
- ⊙ Growth: 10.3%
- ⊙ Annual Job Openings: 12,290
- ⊙ Self-Employed: 7.9%

Considerations for Job Outlook: Delivery truck driver and driver/sales worker jobs are expected to be competitive.

Because these drivers do not have to spend long periods away from home, these local jobs are more desirable than long-haul trucking jobs. Those with experience, or who work for the company in another occupation, should have the best job prospects.

Drive truck or other vehicle over established routes or within an established territory and sell or deliver goods or pick up or deliver items. Collect money from customers, make change, and record transactions on customer receipts. Listen to and resolve customers' complaints regarding products or services. Inform regular customers of new products or services and price changes. Write customer orders and sales contracts according to company guidelines. Drive trucks in order to deliver such items as food, medical supplies, or newspapers. Collect coins from vending machines, refill machines, and remove aged merchandise. Call on prospective customers in order to explain company services and to solicit new business. Record sales or delivery information on daily sales or delivery record. Review lists of dealers, customers, or station drops and load trucks. Arrange merchandise and sales promotion displays, or issue sales promotion materials to customers. Maintain trucks and food-dispensing equipment and clean inside of machines that dispense food or beverages. Sell food specialties, such as sandwiches and beverages, to office workers and patrons of sports events.

Education/Training Required: High school diploma or equivalent. **Education and Training Program:** Retailing and Retail Operations. **Knowledge/Courses—Transportation:** Principles and methods for moving people or goods by air, rail, sea, or road, including the relative costs and benefits. **Sales and Marketing:** Principles and methods for showing, promoting, and selling products or services. This includes marketing strategy and tactics, product demonstration, sales techniques, and sales control systems. **Work Experience Needed:** None. **On-the-Job Training Needed:** Short-term on-the-job training. **Certification/Licensure:** Licensure in some states.

Personality Type: Realistic-Enterprising. **Career Cluster:** 14 Marketing, Sales, and Service. **Career Pathway:** 14.2 Professional Sales and Marketing. **Other Jobs in This Pathway:** Appraisers, Real Estate; Assessors; Cashiers; Counter and Rental Clerks; Demonstrators and Product Promoters; Door-To-Door Sales Workers, News and Street Vendors, and Related Workers; Energy Brokers; First-Line Supervisors of Non-Retail Sales Workers; First-Line

Supervisors of Retail Sales Workers; Gaming Change Persons and Booth Cashiers; Hotel, Motel, and Resort Desk Clerks; Interior Designers; Lodging Managers; Marketing Managers; Marking Clerks; Meeting, Convention, and Event Planners; Merchandise Displayers and Window Trimmers; Models; Online Merchants; Order Fillers, Wholesale and Retail Sales; Parts Salespersons; Property, Real Estate, and Community Association Managers; Real Estate Brokers; Real Estate Sales Agents; Reservation and Transportation Ticket Agents and Travel Clerks; Retail Salespersons; Sales and Related Workers, All Other; Sales Engineers; Sales Representatives, Services, All Other; others.

Skills—Equipment Maintenance: Performing routine maintenance on equipment and determining when and what kind of maintenance is needed. **Critical Thinking:** Using logic and reasoning to identify the strengths and weaknesses of alternative solutions, conclusions, or approaches to problems. **Negotiation:** Bringing others together and trying to reconcile differences. **Service Orientation:** Actively looking for ways to help people. **Operation and Control:** Controlling operations of equipment or systems. **Operation Monitoring:** Watching gauges, dials, or other indicators to make sure a machine is working properly. **Quality Control Analysis:** Conducting tests and inspections of products, services, or processes to evaluate quality or performance. **Persuasion:** Persuading others to change their minds or behavior.

Work Environment: More often outdoors than indoors; sitting; using hands; repetitive motions; very hot or cold.

Drywall and Ceiling Tile Installers

- ⊙ Annual Earnings: $36,970
- ⊙ Earnings Growth Potential: Low (33.2%)
- ⊙ Growth: 27.6%
- ⊙ Annual Job Openings: 5,870
- ⊙ Self-Employed: 27.2%

Considerations for Job Outlook: Job prospects for drywall and ceiling tile installers and tapers should improve over the coming decade as construction activity rebounds from the recent recession. As with many other construction workers, employment of these workers is sensitive to the fluctuations of the economy. On the one hand, they may experience periods of unemployment when the overall level of construction falls. On the other hand, shortages of workers may occur in some areas during peak periods of building activity. Skilled drywall and ceiling tile installers and tapers with good work history and experience in the construction industry should have the best job opportunities.

Apply plasterboard or other wallboard to ceilings or interior walls of buildings. Inspect furrings, mechanical mountings, and masonry surface for plumbness and level, using spirit or water levels. Install metal lath where plaster applications will be exposed to weather or water or for curved or irregular surfaces. Install blanket insulation between studs, and tack plastic moisture barriers over insulation. Coordinate work with drywall finishers who cover the seams between drywall panels. Trim rough edges from wallboard to maintain even joints using knives. Seal joints between ceiling tiles and walls. Scribe and cut edges of tile to fit walls where wall molding is not specified. Read blueprints and other specifications to determine methods of installation, work procedures, and material and tool requirements. Nail channels or wood furring strips to surfaces to provide mounting for tile. Mount tile by using adhesives or by nailing, screwing, stapling, or wire-tying lath directly to structural frameworks. Measure and mark surfaces to lay out work according to blueprints and drawings using tape measures, straightedges or squares, and marking devices. Hang drywall panels on metal frameworks of walls and ceilings in offices, schools, and other large buildings using lifts or hoists to adjust panel heights when necessary. Install horizontal and vertical metal or wooden studs to frames so that wallboard can be attached to interior walls.

Education/Training Required: Less than high school. **Education and Training Program:** Drywall Installation/ Drywaller. **Knowledge/Courses—Building and Construction:** Materials, methods, and the tools involved in the construction or repair of houses, buildings, or other structures such as highways and roads. **Design:** Design techniques, tools, and principles involved in production of precision technical plans, blueprints, drawings, and models. **Mechanical Devices:** Machines and tools, including their designs, uses, repair, and maintenance. **Mathematics:** Arithmetic, algebra, geometry, calculus, statistics, and their applications. **Production and Processing:** Raw materials, production processes, quality control, costs, and other techniques for maximizing the effective manufacture

and distribution of goods. **Public Safety and Security:** Relevant equipment, policies, procedures, and strategies to promote effective local, state, or national security operations for the protection of people, data, property, and institutions. **Work Experience Needed:** None. **On-the-Job Training Needed:** Moderate-term on-the-job training. **Certification/Licensure:** None.

Personality Type: Realistic-Conventional. **Career Cluster:** 02 Architecture and Construction. **Career Pathway:** 02.2 Construction. **Other Jobs in This Pathway:** Boilermakers; Brickmasons and Blockmasons; Carpet Installers; Cement Masons and Concrete Finishers; Construction and Building Inspectors; Construction and Related Workers, All Other; Construction Carpenters; Construction Laborers; Construction Managers; Continuous Mining Machine Operators; Cost Estimators; Crane and Tower Operators; Dredge Operators; Earth Drillers, Except Oil and Gas; Electrical Power-Line Installers and Repairers; Electricians; Electromechanical Equipment Assemblers; Engineering Technicians, Except Drafters, All Other; Excavating and Loading Machine and Dragline Operators; Explosives Workers, Ordnance Handling Experts, and Blasters; Extraction Workers, All Other; First-Line Supervisors of Construction Trades and Extraction Workers; Floor Layers, Except Carpet, Wood, and Hard Tiles; Floor Sanders and Finishers; Glaziers; Heating and Air Conditioning Mechanics and Installers; Helpers, Construction Trades, All Other; others.

Skills—Repairing: Repairing machines or systems using the needed tools. **Equipment Maintenance:** Performing routine maintenance on equipment and determining when and what kind of maintenance is needed. **Installation:** Installing equipment, machines, wiring, or programs to meet specifications. **Operation and Control:** Controlling operations of equipment or systems. **Troubleshooting:** Determining causes of operating errors and deciding what to do about them. **Equipment Selection:** Determining the kind of tools and equipment needed to do a job. **Quality Control Analysis:** Conducting tests and inspections of products, services, or processes to evaluate quality or performance. **Operation Monitoring:** Watching gauges, dials, or other indicators to make sure a machine is working properly.

Work Environment: More often outdoors than indoors; standing; climbing; walking and running; kneeling, crouching, stooping, or crawling; balancing; using hands;

bending or twisting the body; repetitive motions; noise; very hot or cold; bright or inadequate lighting; contaminants; cramped work space; high places; hazardous equipment; minor burns, cuts, bites, or stings.

Earth Drillers, Except Oil and Gas

- ⊙ Annual Earnings: $40,200
- ⊙ Earnings Growth Potential: Low (32.4%)
- ⊙ Growth: 14.0%
- ⊙ Annual Job Openings: 620
- ⊙ Self-Employed: 8.0%

Considerations for Job Outlook: About average growth is expected as the mining industry replaces traditional drilling methods with new methods.

Operate a variety of drills to tap sub-surface water and salt deposits, to remove core samples during mineral exploration or soil testing, and to facilitate the use of explosives. Drive or guide truck-mounted equipment into position, level and stabilize rigs, and extend telescoping derricks. Withdraw drill rods from holes, and extract core samples. Operate hoists to lift power line poles into position. Fabricate well casings. Disinfect, reconstruct, and redevelop contaminated wells and water pumping systems, and clean and disinfect new wells in preparation for use. Design well pumping systems. Assemble and position machines, augers, casing pipes, and other equipment, using hand and power tools. Signal crane operators to move equipment. Record drilling progress and geological data. Retrieve lost equipment from bore holes, using retrieval tools and equipment. Review client requirements and proposed locations for drilling operations to determine feasibility, and to determine cost estimates. Perform routine maintenance and upgrade work on machines and equipment, such as replacing parts, building up drill bits, and lubricating machinery. Perform pumping tests to assess well performance. Drive trucks, tractors, or truck-mounted drills to and from work sites. Verify depths and alignments of boring positions. Operate water-well drilling rigs and other equipment to drill, bore, and dig for water wells or for environmental assessment purposes. Drill or bore holes in rock for blasting, grouting, anchoring, or building foundations. Inspect core samples to determine nature of strata, or take samples to laboratories for analysis. Monitor drilling operations, checking gauges and listening to equipment to assess drilling conditions and to determine the need to adjust drilling or alter equipment. Observe electronic graph recorders and flow meters that monitor the water used to flush debris from holes. Document geological formations encountered during work. Operate machines to flush earth cuttings or to blow dust from holes. Start, stop, and control drilling speed of machines and insertion of casings into holes.

Education/Training Required: High school diploma or equivalent. **Education and Training Programs:** Construction/Heavy Equipment/Earthmoving Equipment Operation; Well Drilling/Driller. **Knowledge/Courses—Mechanical Devices:** Machines and tools, including their designs, uses, repair, and maintenance. **Building and Construction:** Materials, methods, and the tools involved in the construction or repair of houses, buildings, or other structures such as highways and roads. **Chemistry:** The chemical composition, structure, and properties of substances and of the chemical processes and transformations that they undergo. This includes uses of chemicals and their danger signs, production techniques, and disposal methods. **Engineering and Technology:** The practical application of engineering science and technology. This includes applying principles, techniques, procedures, and equipment to the design and production of various goods and services. **Public Safety and Security:** Relevant equipment, policies, procedures, and strategies to promote effective local, state, or national security operations for the protection of people, data, property, and institutions. **Work Experience Needed:** None. **On-the-Job Training Needed:** Moderate-term on-the-job training. **Certification/Licensure:** Licensure in many states.

Personality Type: Realistic-Investigative-Conventional. **Career Cluster:** 02 Architecture and Construction. **Career Pathway:** 02.2 Construction. **Other Jobs in This Pathway:** Boilermakers; Brickmasons and Blockmasons; Carpet Installers; Cement Masons and Concrete Finishers; Construction and Building Inspectors; Construction and Related Workers, All Other; Construction Carpenters; Construction Laborers; Construction Managers; Continuous Mining Machine Operators; Cost Estimators; Crane and Tower Operators; Dredge Operators; Drywall and Ceiling Tile Installers; Electrical Power-Line Installers and Repairers; Electricians; Electromechanical Equipment Assemblers; Engineering Technicians, Except Drafters, All Other; Excavating and Loading Machine

and Dragline Operators; Explosives Workers, Ordnance Handling Experts, and Blasters; Extraction Workers, All Other; First-Line Supervisors of Construction Trades and Extraction Workers; Floor Layers, Except Carpet, Wood, and Hard Tiles; Floor Sanders and Finishers; Glaziers; Heating and Air Conditioning Mechanics and Installers; Helpers, Construction Trades, All Other; others.

Skills—Equipment Maintenance: Performing routine maintenance on equipment and determining when and what kind of maintenance is needed. **Repairing:** Repairing machines or systems using the needed tools. **Operation and Control:** Controlling operations of equipment or systems. **Operation Monitoring:** Watching gauges, dials, or other indicators to make sure a machine is working properly. **Equipment Selection:** Determining the kind of tools and equipment needed to do a job. **Troubleshooting:** Determining causes of operating errors and deciding what to do about them. **Quality Control Analysis:** Conducting tests and inspections of products, services, or processes to evaluate quality or performance. **Installation:** Installing equipment, machines, wiring, or programs to meet specifications.

Work Environment: Outdoors; standing; using hands; repetitive motions; noise; very hot or cold; bright or inadequate lighting; contaminants; cramped work space; whole-body vibration; high places; hazardous conditions; hazardous equipment; minor burns, cuts, bites, or stings.

Electrical and Electronic Engineering Technicians

- ⊙ Annual Earnings: $56,900
- ⊙ Earnings Growth Potential: High (40.2%)
- ⊙ Growth: 1.9%
- ⊙ Annual Job Openings: 3,180
- ⊙ Self-Employed: 0.5%

Considerations for Job Outlook: Some technicians work in traditional manufacturing industries, many of which are growing slowly or declining. However, employment growth for electrical and electronic engineering technicians will likely occur in engineering services firms as companies seek to contract out these services as a way to lower costs. They also work closely with electrical and electronics and computer hardware engineers in the computer systems

design services industry. Demand is expected to be high for technicians in this industry as computer and electronics systems become more integrated. For example, computer, cellular phone, and global positioning systems (GPS) technologies are being included in automobiles and various portable and household electronics systems.

Apply electrical and electronic theory and related knowledge under the direction of engineering staff. For task data, see Job Specializations.

Education/Training Required: Associate degree. **Work Experience Needed:** None. **On-the-Job Training Needed:** None. **Certification/Licensure:** None.

Job Specialization: Electrical Engineering Technicians

Apply electrical theory and related knowledge to test and modify developmental or operational electrical machinery and electrical control equipment and circuitry in industrial or commercial plants and laboratories. Usually work under the direction of engineering staff. Provide technical assistance and resolution when electrical or engineering problems are encountered before, during, and after construction. Assemble electrical and electronic systems and prototypes according to engineering data and knowledge of electrical principles, using hand tools and measuring instruments. Modify electrical prototypes, parts, assemblies, and systems to correct functional deviations. Set up and operate test equipment to evaluate the performance of developmental parts, assemblies, or systems under simulated operating conditions, and record results. Collaborate with electrical engineers and other personnel to identify, define, and solve developmental problems. Build, calibrate, maintain, troubleshoot, and repair electrical instruments or testing equipment. Analyze and interpret test information to resolve design-related problems. Draw or modify diagrams and write engineering specifications to clarify design details and functional criteria of experimental electronics units.

Education and Training Programs: Computer Engineering Technology/Technician; Computer Technology/Computer Systems Technology; Electrical and Electronic Engineering Technologies/Technicians, Other; Electrical, Electronic, and Communications Engineering Technology/Technician; Telecommunications Technology/Technician. **Knowledge/Courses—Computers and**

E

Electronics: Circuit boards, processors, chips, electronic equipment, and computer hardware and software, including applications and programming. **Design:** Design techniques, tools, and principles involved in production of precision technical plans, blueprints, drawings, and models. **Engineering and Technology:** The practical application of engineering science and technology. This includes applying principles, techniques, procedures, and equipment to the design and production of various goods and services. **Mechanical Devices:** Machines and tools, including their designs, uses, repair, and maintenance. **Production and Processing:** Raw materials, production processes, quality control, costs, and other techniques for maximizing the effective manufacture and distribution of goods. **Physics:** Physical principles, laws, their interrelationships, and applications to understanding fluid, material, and atmospheric dynamics, and mechanical, electrical, atomic, and subatomic structures and processes.

Personality Type: Realistic-Investigative-Conventional. **Career Cluster:** 13 Manufacturing. **Career Pathways:** 13.2 Manufacturing Production Process Development; 13.3 Maintenance, Installation, and Repair. **Other Jobs in These Pathways:** Aircraft Mechanics and Service Technicians; Automotive Engineering Technicians; Automotive Specialty Technicians; Avionics Technicians; Biofuels Processing Technicians; Biological Technicians; Biomass Plant Technicians; Camera and Photographic Equipment Repairers; Chemical Equipment Operators and Tenders; Chemical Plant and System Operators; Chemical Technicians; Civil Engineering Technicians; Coil Winders, Tapers, and Finishers; Computer, Automated Teller, and Office Machine Repairers; Construction and Related Workers, All Other; Control and Valve Installers and Repairers, Except Mechanical Door; Electric Motor, Power Tool, and Related Repairers; Electrical and Electronic Equipment Assemblers; Electrical and Electronics Repairers, Commercial and Industrial Equipment; Electrical and Electronics Repairers, Powerhouse, Substation, and Relay; Electrical Engineering Technologists; Electromechanical Engineering Technologists; Electromechanical Equipment Assemblers; others.

Skills—Installation: Installing equipment, machines, wiring, or programs to meet specifications. **Technology Design:** Generating or adapting equipment and technology to serve user needs. **Repairing:** Repairing machines or systems using the needed tools. **Equipment Maintenance:** Performing routine maintenance on equipment and determining when and what kind of maintenance is needed. **Equipment Selection:** Determining the kind of tools and equipment needed to do a job. **Troubleshooting:** Determining causes of operating errors and deciding what to do about them. **Quality Control Analysis:** Conducting tests and inspections of products, services, or processes to evaluate quality or performance. **Operation Monitoring:** Watching gauges, dials, or other indicators to make sure a machine is working properly.

Work Environment: Indoors; sitting; using hands; noise.

Job Specialization: Electronics Engineering Technicians

Lay out, build, test, troubleshoot, repair, and modify developmental and production electronic components, parts, equipment, and systems, such as computer equipment, missile control instrumentation, electron tubes, test equipment, and machine tool numerical controls, applying principles and theories of electronics, electrical circuitry, engineering mathematics, electronic and electrical testing, and physics. Usually work under the direction of engineering staff. Test electronics units, using standard test equipment, and analyze results to evaluate performance and determine the need for adjustment. Perform preventive maintenance and calibration of equipment and systems. Read blueprints, wiring diagrams, schematic drawings, and engineering instructions for assembling electronics units, applying knowledge of electronic theory and components. Maintain system logs and manuals to document testing and operation of equipment. Identify and resolve equipment malfunctions, working with manufacturers and field representatives as necessary to procure replacement parts. Assemble, test, and maintain circuitry or electronic components according to engineering instructions, technical manuals, and knowledge of electronics, using hand and power tools. Adjust and replace defective or improperly functioning circuitry and electronics components, using hand tools and soldering iron. Procure parts and maintain inventory and related documentation. Maintain working knowledge of state-of-the-art tools or software by reading or attending conferences, workshops or other training. Provide user applications and engineering support and recommendations for new and existing equipment with regard to installation, upgrades, and enhancement. Write reports and record data on testing techniques, laboratory equipment, and specifications to assist engineers. Provide customer support and education, working with users to identify needs, determine sources of problems, and provide information on product use. Design basic circuitry and draft sketches for clarification of details and design documentation under engineers' direction, using drafting instruments and computer-aided design (CAD) equipment. Build prototypes from rough sketches or plans. Develop and upgrade preventive maintenance procedures for components, equipment, parts, and systems. Fabricate parts, such as coils, terminal boards, and chassis, using bench lathes, drills, or other machine tools.

Education and Training Programs: Computer Engineering Technology/Technician; Computer Technology/Computer Systems Technology; Electrical and Electronic Engineering Technologies/Technicians, Other; Electrical, Electronic, and Communications Engineering Technology/Technician; Telecommunications Technology/Technician. **Knowledge/Courses—Telecommunications:** Transmission, broadcasting, switching, control, and operation of telecommunications systems. **Engineering and Technology:** The practical application of engineering science and technology. This includes applying principles, techniques, procedures, and equipment to the design and production of various goods and services. **Design:** Design techniques, tools, and principles involved in production of precision technical plans, blueprints, drawings, and models. **Mechanical Devices:** Machines and tools, including their designs, uses, repair, and maintenance. **Computers and Electronics:** Circuit boards, processors, chips, electronic equipment, and computer hardware and software, including applications and programming. **Physics:** Physical principles, laws, their interrelationships, and applications to understanding fluid, material, and atmospheric dynamics, and mechanical, electrical, atomic, and subatomic structures and processes.

Personality Type: Realistic-Investigative. **Career Cluster:** 13 Manufacturing. **Career Pathway:** 13.3 Maintenance, Installation, and Repair. **Other Jobs in This Pathway:** Aircraft Mechanics and Service Technicians; Automotive Engineering Technicians; Automotive Specialty Technicians; Avionics Technicians; Biological Technicians; Camera and Photographic Equipment Repairers; Chemical Equipment Operators and Tenders; Civil Engineering Technicians; Coil Winders, Tapers, and Finishers; Computer, Automated Teller, and Office Machine Repairers;

Construction and Related Workers, All Other; Control and Valve Installers and Repairers, Except Mechanical Door; Electric Motor, Power Tool, and Related Repairers; Electrical and Electronic Equipment Assemblers; Electrical and Electronics Repairers, Commercial and Industrial Equipment; Electrical and Electronics Repairers, Powerhouse, Substation, and Relay; Electrical Engineering Technicians; Electrical Engineering Technologists; Electromechanical Engineering Technologists; Electromechanical Equipment Assemblers; Electronics Engineering Technologists; Elevator Installers and Repairers; others.

Skills—Repairing: Repairing machines or systems using the needed tools. **Equipment Maintenance:** Performing routine maintenance on equipment and determining when and what kind of maintenance is needed. **Troubleshooting:** Determining causes of operating errors and deciding what to do about them. **Equipment Selection:** Determining the kind of tools and equipment needed to do a job. **Operations Analysis:** Analyzing needs and product requirements to create a design. **Science:** Using scientific rules and methods to solve problems. **Programming:** Writing computer programs for various purposes. **Quality Control Analysis:** Conducting tests and inspections of products, services, or processes to evaluate quality or performance.

Work Environment: Indoors; sitting; using hands; noise.

Electrical and Electronics Drafters

⊙ Annual Earnings: $54,470
⊙ Earnings Growth Potential: Medium (37.4%)
⊙ Growth: 5.5%
⊙ Annual Job Openings: 720
⊙ Self-Employed: 4.1%

Considerations for Job Outlook: New software, such as PDM and BIM, will require drafters to work in collaboration with other professionals on projects, whether constructing a new building or manufacturing a new product. This new software, however, requires that someone build and maintain large databases. Workers with knowledge of drafting and of the software will be needed to oversee these databases. Many drafting jobs are in construction and manufacturing, so they are subject to the ups and downs of those industries. Demand for particular drafting specialties

E

varies across the country because jobs depend on the needs of local industries.

Prepare wiring diagrams, circuit board assembly diagrams, and layout drawings used for the manufacture, installation, or repair of electrical equipment. For task data, see Job Specializations.

Education/Training Required: Associate degree. **Work Experience Needed:** None. **On-the-Job Training Needed:** None. **Certification/Licensure:** Voluntary certification by association.

Job Specialization: Electrical Drafters

Develop specifications and instructions for installation of voltage transformers, overhead or underground cables, and related electrical equipment used to conduct electrical energy from transmission lines or high-voltage distribution lines to consumers. Use computer-aided drafting equipment and/or conventional drafting stations, technical handbooks, tables, calculators, and traditional drafting tools such as boards, pencils, protractors, and T-squares. Draft working drawings, wiring diagrams, wiring connection specifications or cross-sections of underground cables, as required for instructions to installation crew. Confer with engineering staff and other personnel to resolve problems. Draw master sketches to scale showing relation of proposed installations to existing facilities and exact specifications and dimensions. Measure factors that affect installation and arrangement of equipment, such as distances to be spanned by wire and cable. Assemble documentation packages and produce drawing sets which are then checked by an engineer or an architect. Review completed construction drawings and cost estimates for accuracy and conformity to standards and regulations. Prepare and interpret specifications, calculating weights, volumes, and stress factors. Explain drawings to production or construction teams and provide adjustments as necessary. Supervise and train other technologists, technicians, and drafters. Study work order requests to determine type of service, such as lighting or power, demanded by installation. Visit proposed installation sites and draw rough sketches of location. Determine the order of work and the method of presentation, such as orthographic or isometric drawing. Reproduce working drawings on copy machines or trace drawings in ink. Write technical reports and draw charts that display statistics and data.

Education and Training Program: Electrical/Electronics Drafting and Electrical/Electronics CAD/CADD. **Knowledge/Courses—Design:** Design techniques, tools, and principles involved in production of precision technical plans, blueprints, drawings, and models. **Engineering and Technology:** The practical application of engineering science and technology. This includes applying principles, techniques, procedures, and equipment to the design and production of various goods and services. **Building and Construction:** Materials, methods, and the tools involved in the construction or repair of houses, buildings, or other structures such as highways and roads. **Telecommunications:** Transmission, broadcasting, switching, control, and operation of telecommunications systems. **Computers and Electronics:** Circuit boards, processors, chips, electronic equipment, and computer hardware and software, including applications and programming. **Clerical Practices:** Administrative and clerical procedures and systems such as word processing, managing files and records, stenography and transcription, designing forms, and other office procedures and terminology.

Personality Type: Realistic-Investigative-Conventional. **Career Cluster:** 02 Architecture and Construction. **Career Pathway:** 02.1 Design/Pre-Construction. **Other Jobs in This Pathway:** Architects, Except Landscape and Naval; Architectural and Engineering Managers; Architectural Drafters; Architecture Teachers, Postsecondary; Cartographers and Photogrammetrists; Civil Drafters; Civil Engineering Technicians; Drafters, All Other; Electronic Drafters; Engineering Teachers, Postsecondary; Engineering Technicians, Except Drafters, All Other; Engineers, All Other; Geodetic Surveyors; Interior Designers; Landscape Architects; Mechanical Drafters; Surveying Technicians; Surveyors.

Skills—Operations Analysis: Analyzing needs and product requirements to create a design. **Systems Analysis:** Determining how a system should work and how changes in conditions, operations, and the environment will affect outcomes. **Systems Evaluation:** Identifying measures or indicators of system performance and the actions needed to improve or correct performance relative to the goals of the system. **Mathematics:** Using mathematics to solve problems. **Complex Problem Solving:** Identifying complex problems and reviewing related information to develop and evaluate options and implement solutions. **Reading Comprehension:** Understanding written sentences and paragraphs in work-related documents. **Writing:** Communicating effectively in writing as appropriate for the needs of the audience. **Active Learning:** Understanding the implications of new information for both current and future problem solving and decision making.

Work Environment: Indoors; sitting.

Job Specialization: Electronic Drafters

Draw wiring diagrams, circuit board assembly diagrams, schematics, and layout drawings used for manufacture, installation, and repair of electronic equipment. Draft detail and assembly drawings of design components, circuitry, and printed circuit boards, using computer-assisted equipment or standard drafting techniques and devices. Consult with engineers to discuss and interpret design concepts, and determine requirements of detailed working drawings. Locate files relating to specified design project in database library, load program into computer, and record completed job data. Examine electronic schematics and supporting documents to develop, compute, and verify specifications for drafting data, such as configuration of parts, dimensions, and tolerances. Supervise and coordinate work activities of workers engaged in drafting, designing layouts, assembling, and testing printed circuit boards. Compare logic element configuration on display screen with engineering schematics and calculate figures to convert, redesign, and modify element. Review work orders and procedural manuals and confer with vendors and design staff to resolve problems and modify design. Review blueprints to determine customer requirements and consult with assembler regarding schematics, wiring procedures, and conductor paths. Train students to use drafting machines and to prepare schematic diagrams, block diagrams, control drawings, logic diagrams, integrated circuit drawings, and interconnection diagrams. Generate computer tapes of final layout design to produce layered photo masks and photo plotting design onto film. Select drill size to drill test head, according to test design and specifications, and submit guide layout to designated department. Key and program specified commands and engineering specifications into computer system to change functions and test final layout. Copy drawings of printed circuit board fabrication, using print machine or blueprinting procedure. Plot electrical test points on layout sheets, and draw schematics for wiring test fixture heads to frames.

Education and Training Program: Electrical/Electronics Drafting and Electrical/Electronics CAD/CADD. **Knowledge/Courses—Design:** Design techniques, tools, and principles involved in production of precision technical plans, blueprints, drawings, and models. **Engineering and Technology:** The practical application of engineering science and technology. This includes applying principles, techniques, procedures, and equipment to the design and production of various goods and services. **Mechanical Devices:** Machines and tools, including their designs, uses, repair, and maintenance. **Physics:** Physical principles, laws, their interrelationships, and applications to understanding fluid, material, and atmospheric dynamics, and mechanical, electrical, atomic, and subatomic structures and processes. **Telecommunications:** Transmission, broadcasting, switching, control, and operation of telecommunications systems. **Mathematics:** Arithmetic, algebra, geometry, calculus, statistics, and their applications.

Personality Type: Conventional-Realistic-Investigative. **Career Cluster:** 02 Architecture and Construction. **Career Pathway:** 02.1 Design/Pre-Construction. **Other Jobs in This Pathway:** Architects, Except Landscape and Naval; Architectural and Engineering Managers; Architectural Drafters; Architecture Teachers, Postsecondary; Cartographers and Photogrammetrists; Civil Drafters; Civil Engineering Technicians; Drafters, All Other; Electrical Drafters; Engineering Teachers, Postsecondary; Engineering Technicians, Except Drafters, All Other; Engineers, All Other; Geodetic Surveyors; Interior Designers; Landscape Architects; Mechanical Drafters; Surveying Technicians; Surveyors.

Skills—Operations Analysis: Analyzing needs and product requirements to create a design. **Science:** Using scientific rules and methods to solve problems. **Programming:** Writing computer programs for various purposes. **Systems Analysis:** Determining how a system should work and how changes in conditions, operations, and the environment will affect outcomes. **Systems Evaluation:** Identifying measures or indicators of system performance and the actions needed to improve or correct performance relative to the goals of the system. **Reading Comprehension:** Understanding written sentences and paragraphs in work-related documents. **Mathematics:** Using mathematics to solve problems. **Active Listening:** Giving full attention to what other people are saying, taking time to understand the points being made, asking questions as appropriate, and not interrupting at inappropriate times.

Work Environment: Indoors; sitting; using hands; repetitive motions; noise.

Electrical and Electronics Repairers, Commercial and Industrial Equipment

- ◉ Annual Earnings: $52,320
- ◉ Earnings Growth Potential: Medium (37.7%)
- ◉ Growth: 1.2%
- ◉ Annual Job Openings: 1,770
- ◉ Self-Employed: 0.0%

Considerations for Job Outlook: Overall job opportunities should be best for applicants who have an associate degree in electronics, certification, or related experience. In addition to employment growth, the need to replace workers who transfer to other occupations or leave the labor force will result in some job openings.

Repair, test, adjust, or install electronic equipment, such as industrial controls, transmitters, and antennas. Test faulty equipment to diagnose malfunctions, using test equipment and software and applying knowledge of the functional operation of electronic units and systems. Inspect components of industrial equipment for accurate assembly and installation and for defects such as loose connections and frayed wires. Install repaired equipment in various settings, such as industrial or military establishments. Examine work orders and converse with equipment operators to detect equipment problems and to ascertain whether mechanical or human errors contributed to the problems. Perform scheduled preventive maintenance tasks, such as checking, cleaning, and repairing equipment, to detect and prevent problems. Set up and test industrial equipment to ensure that it functions properly. Study blueprints, schematics, manuals, and other specifications to determine installation procedures. Repair and adjust equipment, machines, and defective components, replacing worn parts such as gaskets and seals in watertight electrical equipment. Calibrate testing instruments and installed or repaired equipment to prescribed specifications. Maintain equipment logs that record performance problems, repairs, calibrations, and tests. Develop or modify industrial electronic devices, circuits, and equipment according to available specifications. Coordinate efforts with other workers involved in installing and maintaining equipment or components. Operate equipment to demonstrate proper use and to analyze malfunctions. Consult with customers, supervisors, and engineers to plan layout of equipment and to resolve problems in system operation and maintenance. Enter information into computers to copy programs or to draw, modify, or store schematics, applying knowledge of software packages used. Advise management regarding customer satisfaction, product performance, and suggestions for product improvements.

Education/Training Required: Postsecondary vocational training. **Education and Training Programs:** Computer Installation and Repair Technology/Technician; Industrial Electronics Technology/Technician. **Knowledge/Courses—Mechanical Devices:** Machines and tools, including their designs, uses, repair, and maintenance. **Computers and Electronics:** Circuit boards, processors, chips, electronic equipment, and computer hardware and software, including applications and programming. **Engineering and Technology:** The practical application of engineering science and technology. This includes applying principles, techniques, procedures, and equipment to the design and production of various goods and services. **Design:** Design techniques, tools, and principles involved in production of precision technical plans, blueprints, drawings, and models. **Telecommunications:** Transmission, broadcasting, switching, control, and operation of telecommunications systems. **Physics:** Physical principles, laws, their interrelationships, and applications to understanding fluid, material, and atmospheric dynamics, and mechanical, electrical, atomic, and subatomic structures and processes. **Work Experience Needed:** None. **On-the-Job Training Needed:** Long-term on-the-job training. **Certification/Licensure:** Voluntary certification by association.

Personality Type: Realistic-Investigative-Conventional. **Career Cluster:** 13 Manufacturing. **Career Pathway:** 13.3 Maintenance, Installation, and Repair. **Other Jobs in This Pathway:** Aircraft Mechanics and Service Technicians; Automotive Engineering Technicians; Automotive Specialty Technicians; Avionics Technicians; Biological Technicians; Camera and Photographic Equipment Repairers; Chemical Equipment Operators and Tenders; Civil Engineering Technicians; Coil Winders, Tapers, and Finishers;

Computer, Automated Teller, and Office Machine Repairers; Construction and Related Workers, All Other; Control and Valve Installers and Repairers, Except Mechanical Door; Electric Motor, Power Tool, and Related Repairers; Electrical and Electronic Equipment Assemblers; Electrical and Electronics Repairers, Powerhouse, Substation, and Relay; Electrical Engineering Technicians; Electrical Engineering Technologists; Electromechanical Engineering Technologists; Electromechanical Equipment Assemblers; Electronics Engineering Technicians; Electronics Engineering Technologists; Elevator Installers and Repairers; Engine and Other Machine Assemblers; others.

Skills—Installation: Installing equipment, machines, wiring, or programs to meet specifications. **Repairing:** Repairing machines or systems using the needed tools. **Equipment Maintenance:** Performing routine maintenance on equipment and determining when and what kind of maintenance is needed. **Equipment Selection:** Determining the kind of tools and equipment needed to do a job. **Troubleshooting:** Determining causes of operating errors and deciding what to do about them. **Quality Control Analysis:** Conducting tests and inspections of products, services, or processes to evaluate quality or performance. **Technology Design:** Generating or adapting equipment and technology to serve user needs. **Operation Monitoring:** Watching gauges, dials, or other indicators to make sure a machine is working properly.

Work Environment: More often indoors than outdoors; standing; using hands; noise; very hot or cold; contaminants; cramped work space; hazardous conditions; hazardous equipment; minor burns, cuts, bites, or stings.

Electrical and Electronics Repairers, Powerhouse, Substation, and Relay

- ⊙ Annual Earnings: $67,450
- ⊙ Earnings Growth Potential: Low (30.5%)
- ⊙ Growth: 4.7%
- ⊙ Annual Job Openings: 690
- ⊙ Self-Employed: 0.0%

Considerations for Job Outlook: Overall job opportunities should be best for applicants who have an associate degree in electronics, certification, or related experience. In addition to employment growth, the need to replace workers who transfer to other occupations or leave the labor force will result in some job openings.

Inspect, test, repair, or maintain electrical equipment in generating stations, substations, and in-service relays. Construct, test, maintain, and repair substation relay and control systems. Inspect and test equipment and circuits to identify malfunctions or defects, using wiring diagrams and testing devices such as ohmmeters, voltmeters, or ammeters. Consult manuals, schematics, wiring diagrams, and engineering personnel in order to troubleshoot and solve equipment problems and to determine optimum equipment functioning. Notify facility personnel of equipment shutdowns. Open and close switches to isolate defective relays and then perform adjustments or repairs. Prepare and maintain records detailing tests, repairs, and maintenance. Analyze test data in order to diagnose malfunctions, to determine performance characteristics of systems, and to evaluate effects of system modifications. Repair, replace, and clean equipment and components such as circuit breakers, brushes, and commutators. Test insulators and bushings of equipment by inducing voltage across insulation, testing current, and calculating insulation loss. Disconnect voltage regulators, bolts, and screws, and connect replacement regulators to high-voltage lines. Schedule and supervise the construction and testing of special devices and the implementation of unique monitoring or control systems. Run signal quality and connectivity tests for individual cables, and record results. Schedule and supervise splicing or termination of cables in color-code order. Test oil in circuit breakers and transformers for dielectric strength, refilling oil periodically. Maintain inventories of spare parts for all equipment, requisitioning parts as necessary. Set forms and pour concrete footings for installation of heavy equipment.

Education/Training Required: Postsecondary vocational training. **Education and Training Programs:** Electrical and Power Transmission Installers, Other; Mechanic and Repair Technologies/Technicians, Other. **Knowledge/Courses—Mechanical Devices:** Machines and tools, including their designs, uses, repair, and maintenance. **Design:** Design techniques, tools, and principles involved in production of precision technical plans, blueprints, drawings, and models. **Telecommunications:** Transmission, broadcasting, switching, control, and operation of telecommunications systems. **Building and**

E

Construction: Materials, methods, and the tools involved in the construction or repair of houses, buildings, or other structures such as highways and roads. **Physics:** Physical principles, laws, their interrelationships, and applications to understanding fluid, material, and atmospheric dynamics, and mechanical, electrical, atomic, and subatomic structures and processes. **Public Safety and Security:** Relevant equipment, policies, procedures, and strategies to promote effective local, state, or national security operations for the protection of people, data, property, and institutions. **Work Experience Needed:** None. **On-the-Job Training Needed:** Long-term on-the-job training. **Certification/Licensure:** Voluntary certification by association.

Personality Type: Realistic-Conventional. **Career Cluster:** 13 Manufacturing. **Career Pathway:** 13.3 Maintenance, Installation, and Repair. **Other Jobs in This Pathway:** Aircraft Mechanics and Service Technicians; Automotive Engineering Technicians; Automotive Specialty Technicians; Avionics Technicians; Biological Technicians; Camera and Photographic Equipment Repairers; Chemical Equipment Operators and Tenders; Civil Engineering Technicians; Coil Winders, Tapers, and Finishers; Computer, Automated Teller, and Office Machine Repairers; Construction and Related Workers, All Other; Control and Valve Installers and Repairers, Except Mechanical Door; Electric Motor, Power Tool, and Related Repairers; Electrical and Electronic Equipment Assemblers; Electrical and Electronics Repairers, Commercial and Industrial Equipment; Electrical Engineering Technicians; Electrical Engineering Technologists; Electromechanical Engineering Technologists; Electromechanical Equipment Assemblers; Electronics Engineering Technicians; Electronics Engineering Technologists; Elevator Installers and Repairers; Engine and Other Machine Assemblers; others.

Skills—Equipment Maintenance: Performing routine maintenance on equipment and determining when and what kind of maintenance is needed. **Repairing:** Repairing machines or systems using the needed tools. **Troubleshooting:** Determining causes of operating errors and deciding what to do about them. **Operation and Control:** Controlling operations of equipment or systems. **Quality Control Analysis:** Conducting tests and inspections of products, services, or processes to evaluate quality or performance. **Science:** Using scientific rules and methods to solve problems. **Operation Monitoring:** Watching gauges, dials, or other indicators to make sure a machine is working properly. **Equipment Selection:** Determining the kind of tools and equipment needed to do a job.

Work Environment: More often outdoors than indoors; standing; using hands; noise; very hot or cold; bright or inadequate lighting; contaminants; hazardous conditions; hazardous equipment; minor burns, cuts, bites, or stings.

Electrical Power-Line Installers and Repairers

- ⊙ Annual Earnings: $60,190
- ⊙ Earnings Growth Potential: High (42.5%)
- ⊙ Growth: 13.3%
- ⊙ Annual Job Openings: 5,270
- ⊙ Self-Employed: 1.1%

Considerations for Job Outlook: Good job opportunities are expected overall. Highly skilled workers with apprenticeship training or a two-year associate degree in telecommunications, electronics, or electricity should have the best job opportunities. Employment opportunities should be particularly good for electrical power-line installers and repairers, as many workers in this field are expected to retire. Because of layoffs in the 1990s, more of the electrical power industry is near retirement age than in most industries. This is of special concern for electrical line workers who must be in good physical shape and cannot necessarily put off retirement.

Install or repair cables or wires used in electrical power or distribution systems. Adhere to safety practices and procedures, such as checking equipment regularly and erecting barriers around work areas. Open switches or attach grounding devices to remove electrical hazards from disturbed or fallen lines or to facilitate repairs. Climb poles or use truck-mounted buckets to access equipment. Place insulating or fireproofing materials over conductors and joints. Install, maintain, and repair electrical distribution and transmission systems, including conduits; cables; wires; and related equipment such as transformers, circuit breakers, and switches. Identify defective sectionalizing devices, circuit breakers, fuses, voltage regulators, transformers, switches, relays, or wiring, using wiring diagrams and electrical-testing instruments. Drive vehicles equipped with tools and materials to job sites. Coordinate work-assignment preparation and completion with other workers. String wire conductors and cables between poles, towers, trenches, pylons, and buildings, setting lines in place and using winches to adjust tension. Inspect and test power lines and auxiliary equipment to locate and identify problems, using reading and testing instruments. Test conductors according to electrical diagrams and specifications to identify corresponding conductors and to prevent incorrect connections. Replace damaged poles with new poles, and straighten the poles. Install watt-hour meters, and connect service drops between power lines and consumers' facilities.

Education/Training Required: High school diploma or equivalent. **Education and Training Programs:** Electrical and Power Transmission Installation/Installer, General; Electrical and Power Transmission Installers, Other; Lineworker. **Knowledge/Courses—Building and Construction:** Materials, methods, and the tools involved in the construction or repair of houses, buildings, or other structures such as highways and roads. **Mechanical Devices:** Machines and tools, including their designs, uses, repair, and maintenance. **Customer and Personal Service:** Principles and processes for providing customer and personal services. This includes customer needs assessment, meeting quality standards for services, and evaluation of customer satisfaction. **Engineering and Technology:** The practical application of engineering science and technology. This includes applying principles, techniques, procedures, and equipment to the design and production of various goods and services. **Transportation:** Principles and methods for moving people or goods by air, rail, sea, or road, including the relative costs and benefits. **Design:** Design techniques, tools, and principles involved in production of precision technical plans, blueprints, drawings, and models. **Work Experience Needed:** None. **On-the-Job Training Needed:** Long-term on-the-job training. **Certification/Licensure:** Voluntary certification by association.

Personality Type: Realistic-Investigative-Conventional. **Career Cluster:** 02 Architecture and Construction. **Career Pathway:** 02.2 Construction. **Other Jobs in This Pathway:** Boilermakers; Brickmasons and Blockmasons; Carpet Installers; Cement Masons and Concrete Finishers; Construction and Building Inspectors; Construction and Related Workers, All Other; Construction Carpenters; Construction Laborers; Construction Managers; Continuous Mining Machine Operators; Cost Estimators; Crane and Tower Operators; Dredge Operators; Drywall and Ceiling Tile Installers; Earth Drillers, Except Oil and Gas; Electricians; Electromechanical Equipment Assemblers; Engineering Technicians, Except Drafters, All Other; Excavating and Loading Machine and Dragline Operators; Explosives Workers, Ordnance Handling Experts, and Blasters; Extraction Workers, All Other; First-Line Supervisors of Construction Trades and Extraction Workers; Floor Layers, Except Carpet, Wood, and Hard Tiles; Floor Sanders and Finishers; Glaziers; Heating and Air Conditioning Mechanics and Installers; Helpers, Construction Trades, All Other; others.

Skills—Repairing: Repairing machines or systems using the needed tools. **Troubleshooting:** Determining causes of operating errors and deciding what to do about them. **Equipment Maintenance:** Performing routine maintenance on equipment and determining when and what kind of maintenance is needed. **Operation and Control:** Controlling operations of equipment or systems. **Quality Control Analysis:** Conducting tests and inspections of products, services, or processes to evaluate quality or performance. **Operation Monitoring:** Watching gauges, dials, or other indicators to make sure a machine is working properly. **Installation:** Installing equipment, machines, wiring, or programs to meet specifications. **Equipment Selection:** Determining the kind of tools and equipment needed to do a job.

Work Environment: Outdoors; standing; walking and running; using hands; bending or twisting the body; repetitive motions; noise; very hot or cold; bright or inadequate lighting; contaminants; cramped work space; high places; hazardous conditions; hazardous equipment; minor burns, cuts, bites, or stings.

Electricians

- ⊙ Annual Earnings: $49,320
- ⊙ Earnings Growth Potential: Medium (38.4%)
- ⊙ Growth: 23.2%
- ⊙ Annual Job Openings: 28,920
- ⊙ Self-Employed: 10.3%

Considerations for Job Outlook: Employment of electricians fluctuates with the overall economy. On the one hand, there is great demand for electricians during peak periods of building and manufacturing. On the other hand, workers may experience periods of unemployment when the overall level of construction falls. Inside electricians in factories tend to have the most stable employment.

Install, maintain, and repair electrical wiring, equipment, and fixtures. Maintain current electrician's license or identification card to meet governmental regulations. Connect wires to circuit breakers, transformers, or other components. Repair or replace wiring, equipment, and fixtures, using hand tools and power tools. Assemble, install, test, and maintain electrical or electronic wiring, equipment, appliances, apparatus, and fixtures, using hand tools and power tools. Test electrical systems and continuity of circuits in electrical wiring, equipment, and fixtures, using testing devices such as ohmmeters, voltmeters, and oscilloscopes, to ensure compatibility and safety of system. Use a variety of tools and equipment such as power construction equipment, measuring devices, power tools, and testing equipment, including oscilloscopes, ammeters, and test lamps. Plan layout and installation of electrical wiring, equipment, and fixtures based on job specifications and local codes. Inspect electrical systems, equipment, and components to identify hazards, defects, and the need for adjustment or repair and to ensure compliance with codes. Direct and train workers to install, maintain, or repair electrical wiring, equipment, and fixtures. Diagnose malfunctioning systems, apparatus, and components, using test equipment and hand tools, to locate the cause of a breakdown and correct the problem. Prepare sketches or follow blueprints to determine the location of wiring and equipment and to ensure conformance to building and safety codes.

Education/Training Required: High school diploma or equivalent. **Education and Training Program:** Electrician. **Knowledge/Courses—Building and Construction:** Materials, methods, and the tools involved in the construction or repair of houses, buildings, or other structures such as highways and roads. **Mechanical Devices:** Machines and tools, including their designs, uses, repair, and maintenance. **Design:** Design techniques, tools, and principles involved in production of precision technical plans, blueprints, drawings, and models. **Physics:** Physical principles, laws, their interrelationships, and applications to understanding fluid, material, and atmospheric dynamics, and mechanical, electrical, atomic, and subatomic structures and processes. **Telecommunications:** Transmission, broadcasting, switching, control, and operation of

telecommunications systems. **Engineering and Technology:** The practical application of engineering science and technology. This includes applying principles, techniques, procedures, and equipment to the design and production of various goods and services. **Work Experience Needed:** None. **On-the-Job Training Needed:** Apprenticeship. **Certification/Licensure:** Licensure.

Personality Type: Realistic-Investigative-Conventional. **Career Cluster:** 02 Architecture and Construction. **Career Pathway:** 02.2 Construction. **Other Jobs in This Pathway:** Boilermakers; Brickmasons and Blockmasons; Carpet Installers; Cement Masons and Concrete Finishers; Construction and Building Inspectors; Construction and Related Workers, All Other; Construction Carpenters; Construction Laborers; Construction Managers; Continuous Mining Machine Operators; Cost Estimators; Crane and Tower Operators; Dredge Operators; Drywall and Ceiling Tile Installers; Earth Drillers, Except Oil and Gas; Electrical Power-Line Installers and Repairers; Electromechanical Equipment Assemblers; Engineering Technicians, Except Drafters, All Other; Excavating and Loading Machine and Dragline Operators; Explosives Workers, Ordnance Handling Experts, and Blasters; Extraction Workers, All Other; First-Line Supervisors of Construction Trades and Extraction Workers; Floor Layers, Except Carpet, Wood, and Hard Tiles; Floor Sanders and Finishers; Glaziers; Heating and Air Conditioning Mechanics and Installers; Helpers, Construction Trades, All Other; others.

Skills—Installation: Installing equipment, machines, wiring, or programs to meet specifications. **Repairing:** Repairing machines or systems using the needed tools. **Equipment Maintenance:** Performing routine maintenance on equipment and determining when and what kind of maintenance is needed. **Troubleshooting:** Determining causes of operating errors and deciding what to do about them. **Equipment Selection:** Determining the kind of tools and equipment needed to do a job. **Quality Control Analysis:** Conducting tests and inspections of products, services, or processes to evaluate quality or performance. **Operation and Control:** Controlling operations of equipment or systems. **Management of Financial Resources:** Determining how money will be spent to get the work done and accounting for these expenditures.

Work Environment: More often outdoors than indoors; standing; climbing; walking and running; using hands; bending or twisting the body; repetitive motions; noise; very hot or cold; bright or inadequate lighting; contaminants; cramped work space; high places; hazardous conditions; hazardous equipment; minor burns, cuts, bites, or stings.

Electronic Home Entertainment Equipment Installers and Repairers

- ☉ Annual Earnings: $34,470
- ☉ Earnings Growth Potential: Medium (38.4%)
- ☉ Growth: 13.9%
- ☉ Annual Job Openings: 1,410
- ☉ Self-Employed: 17.0%

Considerations for Job Outlook: Certified applicants with good customer service skills and a background in electronics repair should have the best job opportunities. Noncertified applicants will likely face competition for jobs. The majority of job openings will come from the need to replace workers who retire or leave the occupation. It is also likely that a majority of job openings will occur in electronics and appliance stores and repair shops, because these types of stores employ about one-third of all service technicians.

Repair, adjust, or install audio or television receivers, stereo systems, camcorders, video systems, or other electronic home entertainment equipment. Tune or adjust equipment and instruments to obtain optimum visual or auditory reception, according to specifications, manuals, and drawings. Compute cost estimates for labor and materials. Instruct customers on the safe and proper use of equipment. Keep records of work orders and test and maintenance reports. Make service calls to repair units in customers' homes, or return units to shops for major repairs. Position or mount speakers, and wire speakers to consoles. Install, service, and repair electronic equipment or instruments such as televisions, radios, and videocassette recorders. Disassemble entertainment equipment and repair or replace loose, worn, or defective components and wiring, using hand tools and soldering irons. Confer with customers to determine the nature of problems or to explain repairs. Calibrate and test equipment, and locate circuit and component faults, using hand and power tools and measuring and testing instruments such as resistance meters and oscilloscopes. Read and interpret electronic circuit diagrams, function block diagrams, specifications, engineering drawings, and service manuals.

Education/Training Required: Postsecondary vocational training. **Education and Training Program:** Communications Systems Installation and Repair Technology. **Knowledge/Courses—Telecommunications:** Transmission, broadcasting, switching, control, and operation of telecommunications systems. **Engineering and Technology:** The practical application of engineering science and technology. This includes applying principles, techniques, procedures, and equipment to the design and production of various goods and services. **Computers and Electronics:** Circuit boards, processors, chips, electronic equipment, and computer hardware and software, including applications and programming. **Mechanical Devices:** Machines and tools, including their designs, uses, repair, and maintenance. **Physics:** Physical principles, laws, their interrelationships, and applications to understanding fluid, material, and atmospheric dynamics, and mechanical, electrical, atomic, and subatomic structures and processes. **Design:** Design techniques, tools, and principles involved in production of precision technical plans, blueprints, drawings, and models. **Work Experience Needed:** None. **On-the-Job Training Needed:** None. **Certification/Licensure:** Voluntary certification by association.

Personality Type: Realistic-Conventional. **Career Cluster:** 03 Arts and Communications. **Career Pathway:** 03.6 Telecommunications. **Other Jobs in This Pathway:** Broadcast Technicians; Communications Equipment Operators, All Other; Film and Video Editors; Media and Communication Workers, All Other; Radio Mechanics; Radio Operators; Sound Engineering Technicians; Telecommunications Equipment Installers and Repairers, Except Line Installers.

Skills—Installation: Installing equipment, machines, wiring, or programs to meet specifications. **Repairing:** Repairing machines or systems using the needed tools. **Troubleshooting:** Determining causes of operating errors and deciding what to do about them. **Equipment Maintenance:** Performing routine maintenance on equipment and determining when and what kind of maintenance is needed. **Equipment Selection:** Determining the kind of tools and equipment needed to do a job. **Quality Control Analysis:** Conducting tests and inspections of products, services, or processes to evaluate quality or performance. **Programming:** Writing computer programs for various purposes. **Management of Financial Resources:** Determining how money will be spent to get the work done and accounting for these expenditures.

Work Environment: Indoors; standing; using hands; hazardous conditions.

Elevator Installers and Repairers

- ⊙ Annual Earnings: $75,060
- ⊙ Earnings Growth Potential: High (46.1%)
- ⊙ Growth: 11.6%
- ⊙ Annual Job Openings: 820
- ⊙ Self-Employed: 0.0%

Considerations for Job Outlook: Overall job opportunities should be excellent because the dangerous and physically challenging aspects of the work reduce the number of qualified applicants. Job prospects for entry-level workers should be best for those who have postsecondary education in electronics or who have experience in the military. Elevators, escalators, lifts, moving walkways, and related equipment need to keep working year-round, so employment of elevator repairers is less affected by economic downturns and seasonality than employment in other construction occupations.

Assemble, install, repair, or maintain electric or hydraulic freight or passenger elevators, escalators, or dumbwaiters. Assemble, install, repair, and maintain elevators, escalators, moving sidewalks, and dumbwaiters, using hand and power tools, and testing devices such as test lamps, ammeters, and voltmeters. Test newly installed equipment to ensure that it meets specifications such as stopping at floors for set amounts of time. Locate malfunctions in brakes, motors, switches, and signal and control systems, using test equipment. Check that safety regulations and building codes are met, and complete service reports verifying conformance to standards. Connect electrical wiring to control panels and electric motors. Read and interpret blueprints to determine the layout of system components, frameworks, and foundations, and to select installation equipment. Adjust safety controls; counterweights; door mechanisms; and components such as valves, ratchets, seals, and brake linings. Inspect wiring connections, control panel hookups, door installations, and alignments and clearances of cars and hoistways to ensure that equipment will operate properly. Disassemble defective units,

and repair or replace parts such as locks, gears, cables, and electric wiring. Maintain log books that detail all repairs and checks performed. Participate in additional training to keep skills up-to-date. Attach guide shoes and rollers to minimize the lateral motion of cars as they travel through shafts. Connect car frames to counterweights, using steel cables. Bolt or weld steel rails to the walls of shafts to guide elevators, working from scaffolding or platforms. Assemble elevator cars, installing each car's platform, walls, and doors. Install outer doors and door frames at elevator entrances on each floor of a structure. Install electrical wires and controls by attaching conduit along shaft walls from floor to floor and then pulling plastic-covered wires through the conduit. Cut prefabricated sections of framework, rails, and other components to specified dimensions.

Education/Training Required: High school diploma or equivalent. **Education and Training Program:** Industrial Mechanics and Maintenance Technology. **Knowledge/ Courses—Building and Construction:** Materials, methods, and the tools involved in the construction or repair of houses, buildings, or other structures such as highways and roads. **Mechanical Devices:** Machines and tools, including their designs, uses, repair, and maintenance. **Physics:** Physical principles, laws, their interrelationships, and applications to understanding fluid, material, and atmospheric dynamics, and mechanical, electrical, atomic, and subatomic structures and processes. **Design:** Design techniques, tools, and principles involved in production of precision technical plans, blueprints, drawings, and models. **Engineering and Technology:** The practical application of engineering science and technology. This includes applying principles, techniques, procedures, and equipment to the design and production of various goods and services. **Public Safety and Security:** Relevant equipment, policies, procedures, and strategies to promote effective local, state, or national security operations for the protection of people, data, property, and institutions. **Work Experience Needed:** None. **On-the-Job Training Needed:** Apprenticeship. **Certification/Licensure:** Licensure; voluntary certification by association.

Personality Type: Realistic-Investigative-Conventional. **Career Cluster:** 13 Manufacturing. **Career Pathway:** 13.3 Maintenance, Installation, and Repair. **Other Jobs in This Pathway:** Aircraft Mechanics and Service Technicians; Automotive Engineering Technicians; Automotive Specialty Technicians; Avionics Technicians; Biological Technicians;

Camera and Photographic Equipment Repairers; Chemical Equipment Operators and Tenders; Civil Engineering Technicians; Coil Winders, Tapers, and Finishers; Computer, Automated Teller, and Office Machine Repairers; Construction and Related Workers, All Other; Control and Valve Installers and Repairers, Except Mechanical Door; Electric Motor, Power Tool, and Related Repairers; Electrical and Electronic Equipment Assemblers; Electrical and Electronics Repairers, Commercial and Industrial Equipment; Electrical and Electronics Repairers, Powerhouse, Substation, and Relay; Electrical Engineering Technicians; Electrical Engineering Technologists; Electromechanical Engineering Technologists; Electromechanical Equipment Assemblers; Electronics Engineering Technicians; Electronics Engineering Technologists; others.

Skills—Repairing: Repairing machines or systems using the needed tools. **Equipment Maintenance:** Performing routine maintenance on equipment and determining when and what kind of maintenance is needed. **Installation:** Installing equipment, machines, wiring, or programs to meet specifications. **Troubleshooting:** Determining causes of operating errors and deciding what to do about them. **Equipment Selection:** Determining the kind of tools and equipment needed to do a job. **Operation and Control:** Controlling operations of equipment or systems. **Quality Control Analysis:** Conducting tests and inspections of products, services, or processes to evaluate quality or performance. **Operation Monitoring:** Watching gauges, dials, or other indicators to make sure a machine is working properly.

Work Environment: More often indoors than outdoors; standing; walking and running; using hands; bending or twisting the body; noise; very hot or cold; bright or inadequate lighting; contaminants; cramped work space; high places; hazardous conditions; hazardous equipment; minor burns, cuts, bites, or stings.

Eligibility Interviewers, Government Programs

- ⊙ Annual Earnings: $41,060
- ⊙ Earnings Growth Potential: Low (31.7%)
- ⊙ Growth: 3.1%
- ⊙ Annual Job Openings: 3,740
- ⊙ Self-Employed: 0.0%

Considerations for Job Outlook: Employment growth will vary by specialty. Projected employment change is most rapid for interviewers and correspondence clerks.

Determine eligibility of persons applying to receive assistance from government programs and agency resources, such as welfare, unemployment benefits, social security, and public housing. Answer applicants' questions about benefits and claim procedures. Interview benefits recipients at specified intervals to certify their eligibility for continuing benefits. Interpret and explain information such as eligibility requirements, application details, payment methods, and applicants' legal rights. Initiate procedures to grant, modify, deny, or terminate assistance, or refer applicants to other agencies for assistance. Compile, record, and evaluate personal and financial data in order to verify completeness and accuracy, and to determine eligibility status. Interview and investigate applicants for public assistance to gather information pertinent to their applications. Check with employers or other references to verify answers and obtain further information. Schedule benefits claimants for adjudication interviews to address questions of eligibility. Keep records of assigned cases, and prepare required reports. Prepare applications and forms for applicants for such purposes as school enrollment, employment, and medical services. Refer applicants to job openings or to interviews with other staff, in accordance with administrative guidelines or office procedures. Provide social workers with pertinent information gathered during applicant interviews. Compute and authorize amounts of assistance for programs such as grants, monetary payments, and food stamps. Monitor the payments of benefits throughout the duration of a claim. Provide applicants with assistance in completing application forms such as those for job referrals or unemployment compensation claims. Investigate claimants for the possibility of fraud or abuse. Conduct annual, interim, and special housing reviews and home visits to ensure conformance to regulations.

Education/Training Required: Associate degree. **Education and Training Program:** Community Organization and Advocacy. **Knowledge/Courses—Clerical Practices:** Administrative and clerical procedures and systems such as word processing, managing files and records, stenography and transcription, designing forms, and other office procedures and terminology. **Customer and Personal Service:** Principles and processes for providing customer and personal services. This includes customer needs assessment, meeting quality standards for services, and evaluation of customer satisfaction. **Law and Government:** Laws, legal codes, court procedures, precedents, government regulations, executive orders, agency rules, and the democratic political process. **Psychology:** Human behavior and performance; individual differences in ability, personality, and interests; learning and motivation; psychological research methods; and the assessment and treatment of behavioral and affective disorders. **Sociology and Anthropology:** Group behavior and dynamics, societal trends and influences, human migrations, ethnicity, and cultures and their history and origins. **Computers and Electronics:** Circuit boards, processors, chips, electronic equipment, and computer hardware and software, including applications and programming. **Work Experience Needed:** None. **On-the-Job Training Needed:** Moderate-term on-the-job training. **Certification/Licensure:** None.

Personality Type: Social-Conventional-Enterprising. **Career Cluster:** 10 Human Services. **Career Pathway:** 10.3 Family and Community Services. **Other Jobs in This Pathway:** Chief Executives; Child, Family, and School Social Workers; Childcare Workers; City and Regional Planning Aides; Counselors, All Other; Farm and Home Management Advisors; Home Economics Teachers, Postsecondary; Legislators; Managers, All Other; Marriage and Family Therapists; Nannies; Personal Care Aides; Probation Officers and Correctional Treatment Specialists; Protective Service Workers, All Other; Social and Community Service Managers; Social Science Research Assistants; Social Scientists and Related Workers, All Other; Social Work Teachers, Postsecondary; Social Workers, All Other; Sociologists; Supply Chain Managers.

Skills—Service Orientation: Actively looking for ways to help people. **Speaking:** Talking to others to convey information effectively. **Active Listening:** Giving full attention to what other people are saying, taking time to understand the points being made, asking questions as appropriate, and not interrupting at inappropriate times. **Social Perceptiveness:** Being aware of others' reactions and understanding why they react as they do. **Negotiation:** Bringing others together and trying to reconcile differences. **Reading Comprehension:** Understanding written sentences and paragraphs in work-related documents. **Writing:** Communicating effectively in writing as appropriate for the needs of the audience. **Critical Thinking:** Using logic and reasoning to identify the strengths and weaknesses

of alternative solutions, conclusions, or approaches to problems.

Work Environment: Indoors; sitting; using hands; repetitive motions; contaminants.

Embalmers

- ⊙ Annual Earnings: $43,800
- ⊙ Earnings Growth Potential: Medium (38.3%)
- ⊙ Growth: 5.6%
- ⊙ Annual Job Openings: 370
- ⊙ Self-Employed: 3.8%

Considerations for Job Outlook: Slower-than-average employment growth is projected.

Prepare bodies for interment in conformity with legal requirements. Conform to laws of health and sanitation, and ensure that legal requirements concerning embalming are met. Apply cosmetics to impart lifelike appearance to the deceased. Incise stomach and abdominal walls and probe internal organs, using trocar, to withdraw blood and waste matter from organs. Close incisions, using needles and sutures. Reshape or reconstruct disfigured or maimed bodies when necessary, using derma-surgery techniques and materials such as clay, cotton, plaster of paris, and wax. Dress bodies and place them in caskets. Make incisions in arms or thighs and drain blood from circulatory system and replace it with embalming fluid, using pump. Join lips, using needles and thread or wire. Conduct interviews to arrange for the preparation of obituary notices, to assist with the selection of caskets or urns, and to determine the location and time of burials or cremations. Perform the duties of funeral directors, including coordinating funeral activities. Attach trocar to pump-tube, start pump, and repeat probing to force embalming fluid into organs. Perform special procedures necessary for remains that are to be transported to other states or overseas, or where death was caused by infectious disease. Maintain records such as itemized lists of clothing or valuables delivered with body and names of persons embalmed. Insert convex celluloid or cotton between eyeballs and eyelids to prevent slipping and sinking of eyelids. Wash and dry bodies, using germicidal soap and towels or hot air dryers. Arrange for transporting the deceased to another state for interment. Supervise funeral attendants and other funeral home staff. Pack body orifices with cotton saturated with embalming fluid to prevent escape of gases or waste matter. Assist with placing caskets in hearses, and organize cemetery processions. Serve as pallbearers, attend visiting rooms, and provide other assistance to the bereaved. Direct casket and floral display placement and arrange guest seating.

Education/Training Required: Postsecondary vocational training. **Education and Training Programs:** Funeral Service and Mortuary Science, General; Mortuary Science and Embalming/Embalmer. **Knowledge/Courses— Chemistry:** The chemical composition, structure, and properties of substances and of the chemical processes and transformations that they undergo. This includes uses of chemicals and their danger signs, production techniques, and disposal methods. **Biology:** Plant and animal organisms and their tissues, cells, functions, interdependencies, and interactions with each other and the environment. **Philosophy and Theology:** Different philosophical systems and religions. This includes their basic principles, values, ethics, ways of thinking, customs, practices, and their impact on human culture. **Customer and Personal Service:** Principles and processes for providing customer and personal services. This includes customer needs assessment, meeting quality standards for services, and evaluation of customer satisfaction. **Therapy and Counseling:** Principles, methods, and procedures for diagnosis, treatment, and rehabilitation of physical and mental dysfunctions, and for career counseling and guidance. **Medicine and Dentistry:** The information and techniques needed to diagnose and treat human injuries, diseases, and deformities. This includes symptoms, treatment alternatives, drug properties and interactions, and preventive health-care measures. **Work Experience Needed:** None. **On-the-Job Training Needed:** Short-term on-the-job training. **Certification/Licensure:** Licensure.

Personality Type: Realistic-Conventional-Investigative. **Career Cluster:** 10 Human Services. **Career Pathway:** 10.4 Personal Care Services. **Other Jobs in This Pathway:** Barbers; Funeral Attendants; Funeral Service Managers; Hairdressers, Hairstylists, and Cosmetologists; Laundry and Dry-Cleaning Workers; Makeup Artists, Theatrical and Performance; Manicurists and Pedicurists; Pressers, Textile, Garment, and Related Materials; Sewers, Hand; Sewing Machine Operators; Shampooers; Skincare Specialists; Tailors, Dressmakers, and Custom Sewers; Textile Bleaching and Dyeing Machine Operators and Tenders.

Skills—Science: Using scientific rules and methods to solve problems. **Social Perceptiveness:** Being aware of others' reactions and understanding why they react as they do. **Service Orientation:** Actively looking for ways to help people. **Operation and Control:** Controlling operations of equipment or systems. **Negotiation:** Bringing others together and trying to reconcile differences. **Equipment Maintenance:** Performing routine maintenance on equipment and determining when and what kind of maintenance is needed. **Instructing:** Teaching others how to do something. **Time Management:** Managing one's own time and the time of others.

Work Environment: More often indoors than outdoors; standing; using hands; contaminants; exposed to disease or infections; hazardous conditions.

Emergency Medical Technicians and Paramedics

- Annual Earnings: $30,710
- Earnings Growth Potential: Medium (35.3%)
- Growth: 33.3%
- Annual Job Openings: 12,080
- Self-Employed: 0.8%

Considerations for Job Outlook: Emergencies such as car crashes, natural disasters, and violence will continue to create demand for EMTs and paramedics. There will also continue to be demand for part-time, volunteer EMTs and paramedics in rural areas and smaller metropolitan areas. Growth in the middle-aged and elderly population will lead to an increase in the number of age-related health emergencies, such as heart attacks or strokes.

Assess injuries, administer emergency medical care, and extricate trapped individuals. Transport injured or sick persons to medical facilities. Administer first-aid treatment and life-support care to sick or injured persons in prehospital setting. Operate equipment such as electrocardiograms (EKGs), external defibrillators, and bag-valve mask resuscitators in advanced life-support environments. Assess nature and extent of illness or injury to establish and prioritize medical procedures. Maintain vehicles and medical and communication equipment, and replenish first-aid equipment and supplies. Observe, record, and report to physician the patient's condition or injury, the treatment

E

provided, and reactions to drugs and treatment. Perform emergency diagnostic and treatment procedures, such as stomach suction, airway management, or heart monitoring, during ambulance ride. Administer drugs, orally or by injection, and perform intravenous procedures under a physician's direction. Comfort and reassure patients. Communicate with dispatchers and treatment center personnel to provide information about situation, to arrange reception of victims, and to receive instructions for further treatment. Immobilize patient for placement on stretcher and ambulance transport, using backboard or other spinal immobilization device. Coordinate work with other emergency medical team members and police and fire department personnel. Decontaminate ambulance interior following treatment of patient with infectious disease and report case to proper authorities. Drive mobile intensive care unit to specified location, following instructions from emergency medical dispatcher. Coordinate with treatment center personnel to obtain patients' vital statistics and medical history, to determine the circumstances of the emergency, and to administer emergency treatment.

Education/Training Required: Postsecondary vocational training. **Education and Training Programs:** Emergency Care Attendant (EMT Ambulance) Training; Emergency Medical Technology/Technician (EMT Paramedic). **Knowledge/Courses—Medicine and Dentistry:** The information and techniques needed to diagnose and treat human injuries, diseases, and deformities. This includes symptoms, treatment alternatives, drug properties and interactions, and preventive health-care measures. **Customer and Personal Service:** Principles and processes for providing customer and personal services. This includes customer needs assessment, meeting quality standards for services, and evaluation of customer satisfaction. **Therapy and Counseling:** Principles, methods, and procedures for diagnosis, treatment, and rehabilitation of physical and mental dysfunctions, and for career counseling and guidance. **Psychology:** Human behavior and performance; individual differences in ability, personality, and interests; learning and motivation; psychological research methods; and the assessment and treatment of behavioral and affective disorders. **Transportation:** Principles and methods for moving people or goods by air, rail, sea, or road, including the relative costs and benefits. **Education and Training:** Principles and methods for curriculum and training design, teaching and instruction for individuals and groups, and the measurement of training effects.

Work Experience Needed: None. **On-the-Job Training Needed:** None. **Certification/Licensure:** Licensure.

Personality Type: Social-Investigative-Realistic. **Career Cluster:** 08 Health Science. **Career Pathway:** 08.2 Diagnostics Services. **Other Jobs in This Pathway:** Ambulance Drivers and Attendants, Except Emergency Medical Technicians; Anesthesiologist Assistants; Athletic Trainers; Cardiovascular Technologists and Technicians; Cytogenetic Technologists; Cytotechnologists; Diagnostic Medical Sonographers; Endoscopy Technicians; Health Diagnosing and Treating Practitioners, All Other; Health Specialties Teachers, Postsecondary; Health Technologists and Technicians, All Other; Healthcare Practitioners and Technical Workers, All Other; Histotechnologists and Histologic Technicians; Medical and Clinical Laboratory Technicians; Medical and Clinical Laboratory Technologists; Medical and Health Services Managers; Medical Assistants; Medical Equipment Preparers; Neurodiagnostic Technologists; Nuclear Equipment Operation Technicians; Nuclear Medicine Technologists; Ophthalmic Laboratory Technicians; Pathologists; Physical Scientists, All Other; Physician Assistants; Radiation Therapists; Radiologic Technicians; Radiologic Technologists; Radiologists; others.

Skills—Science: Using scientific rules and methods to solve problems. **Operation and Control:** Controlling operations of equipment or systems. **Service Orientation:** Actively looking for ways to help people. **Coordination:** Adjusting actions in relation to others' actions. **Operation Monitoring:** Watching gauges, dials, or other indicators to make sure a machine is working properly. **Active Learning:** Understanding the implications of new information for both current and future problem solving and decision making. **Troubleshooting:** Determining causes of operating errors and deciding what to do about them. **Equipment Selection:** Determining the kind of tools and equipment needed to do a job.

Work Environment: More often outdoors than indoors; standing; using hands; bending or twisting the body; repetitive motions; noise; very hot or cold; bright or inadequate lighting; contaminants; cramped work space; exposed to disease or infections; hazardous conditions; hazardous equipment; minor burns, cuts, bites, or stings.

Engineering Technicians, Except Drafters, All Other

- ⊙ Annual Earnings: $58,670
- ⊙ Earnings Growth Potential: High (46.5%)
- ⊙ Growth: 4.7%
- ⊙ Annual Job Openings: 1,680
- ⊙ Self-Employed: 0.5%

Considerations for Job Outlook: As network technology becomes more complex and has wider applications, these workers will be needed to resolve problems. Prospects should be good; job seekers with a bachelor's degree and relevant work experience should have the best opportunities.

All engineering technicians, except drafters, not listed separately. For task data, see Job Specializations.

Education/Training Required: Associate degree. **Work Experience Needed:** None. **On-the-Job Training Needed:** None. **Certification/Licensure:** None.

Job Specialization: Electrical Engineering Technologists

Apply engineering theory and technical skills to support electrical engineering activities such as process control, electrical power distribution, and instrumentation design. Prepare layouts of machinery and equipment, plan the flow of work, conduct statistical studies, and analyze production costs. Participate in training and continuing education activities to stay abreast of engineering and industry advances. Assist engineers and scientists in conducting applied research in electrical engineering. Diagnose, test, or analyze the performance of electrical components, assemblies, and systems. Set up and operate standard and specialized testing equipment. Review installation and quality assurance documentation. Review, develop, and prepare maintenance standards. Compile and maintain records documenting engineering schematics, installed equipment, installation and operational problems, resources used, and repairs or corrective action performed. Supervise the construction and testing of electrical prototypes according to general instructions and established standards. Review electrical engineering plans to ensure adherence to design specifications and compliance with applicable electrical codes and standards. Install

or maintain electrical control systems; industrial automation systems; and electrical equipment including control circuits, variable speed drives, or programmable logic controllers. Design or modify engineering schematics for electrical transmission and distribution systems or for electrical installation in residential, commercial, or industrial buildings, using computer-aided design (CAD) software. Calculate design specifications or cost, material, and resource estimates, and prepare project schedules and budgets.

Education and Training Program: Electrical, Electronic, and Communications Engineering Technology/Technician.

Personality Type: Realistic-Investigative-Conventional. **Career Cluster:** 13 Manufacturing. **Career Pathway:** 13.3 Maintenance, Installation, and Repair. **Other Jobs in This Pathway:** Aircraft Mechanics and Service Technicians; Automotive Engineering Technicians; Automotive Specialty Technicians; Avionics Technicians; Biological Technicians; Camera and Photographic Equipment Repairers; Chemical Equipment Operators and Tenders; Civil Engineering Technicians; Coil Winders, Tapers, and Finishers; Computer, Automated Teller, and Office Machine Repairers; Construction and Related Workers, All Other; Control and Valve Installers and Repairers, Except Mechanical Door; Electric Motor, Power Tool, and Related Repairers; Electrical and Electronic Equipment Assemblers; Electrical and Electronics Repairers, Commercial and Industrial Equipment; Electrical and Electronics Repairers, Powerhouse, Substation, and Relay; Electrical Engineering Technicians; Electromechanical Engineering Technologists; Electromechanical Equipment Assemblers; Electronics Engineering Technicians; Electronics Engineering Technologists; Elevator Installers and Repairers; others.

Work Environment: No data available.

Job Specialization: Electromechanical Engineering Technologists

Apply engineering theory and technical skills to support electromechanical engineering activities such as computer-based process control, instrumentation, and machine design. Prepare layouts of machinery and equipment, plan the flow of work, conduct statistical studies, and analyze production costs. Modify, maintain, or repair electrical, electronic, and mechanical components, equipment, and systems to ensure proper functioning.

Specify, coordinate, and conduct quality-control and quality-assurance programs and procedures. Establish and maintain inventory, records, and documentation systems. Fabricate or assemble mechanical, electrical, and electronic components and assemblies. Select electromechanical equipment, materials, components, and systems to meet functional specifications. Select and use laboratory, operational, and diagnostic techniques and test equipment to assess electromechanical circuits, equipment, processes, systems, and subsystems. Produce electrical, electronic, and mechanical drawings and other related documents or graphics necessary for electromechanical design using computer-aided design (CAD) software. Install and program computer hardware and machine and instrumentation software in microprocessor-based systems. Consult with machinists and technicians to ensure that electromechanical equipment and systems meet design specifications. Translate electromechanical drawings into design specifications, applying principles of engineering, thermal and fluid sciences, mathematics, and statistics. Collaborate with engineers to implement electromechanical designs in industrial or other settings. Analyze engineering designs of logic and digital circuitry, motor controls, instrumentation, and data acquisition for implementation into new or existing automated, servomechanical, or other electromechanical systems.

Education and Training Program: Electrical, Electronic, and Communications Engineering Technology/Technician.

Personality Type: Realistic-Investigative-Conventional. **Career Cluster:** 13 Manufacturing. **Career Pathway:** 13.3 Maintenance, Installation, and Repair. **Other Jobs in This Pathway:** Aircraft Mechanics and Service Technicians; Automotive Engineering Technicians; Automotive Specialty Technicians; Avionics Technicians; Biological Technicians; Camera and Photographic Equipment Repairers; Chemical Equipment Operators and Tenders; Civil Engineering Technicians; Coil Winders, Tapers, and Finishers; Computer, Automated Teller, and Office Machine Repairers; Construction and Related Workers, All Other; Control and Valve Installers and Repairers, Except Mechanical Door; Electric Motor, Power Tool, and Related Repairers; Electrical and Electronic Equipment Assemblers; Electrical and Electronics Repairers, Commercial and Industrial Equipment; Electrical and Electronics Repairers, Powerhouse, Substation, and Relay; Electrical Engineering Technicians; Electrical Engineering Technologists;

Electromechanical Equipment Assemblers; Electronics Engineering Technicians; Electronics Engineering Technologists; Elevator Installers and Repairers; Engine and Other Machine Assemblers; others.

Work Environment: No data available.

Job Specialization: Electronics Engineering Technologists

Apply engineering theory and technical skills to support electronics engineering activities such as electronics systems and instrumentation design and digital signal processing. Provide support to technical sales staff regarding product characteristics. Educate equipment operators on the proper use of equipment. Modify, maintain, and repair electronics equipment and systems to ensure that they function properly. Assemble circuitry for electronic systems according to engineering instructions, production specifications, and technical manuals. Specify, coordinate, or conduct quality control and quality assurance programs and procedures. Prepare and maintain design, testing, or operational records and documentation. Troubleshoot microprocessors and electronic instruments, equipment, and systems using electronic test equipment such as logic analyzers. Set up and operate specialized and standard test equipment to diagnose, test, and analyze the performance of electronic components, assemblies, and systems. Select electronics equipment, components, and systems to meet functional specifications.

Education and Training Program: Electrical, Electronic, and Communications Engineering Technology/Technician. **Knowledge/Courses—Engineering and Technology:** The practical application of engineering science and technology. This includes applying principles, techniques, procedures, and equipment to the design and production of various goods and services. **Telecommunications:** Transmission, broadcasting, switching, control, and operation of telecommunications systems. **Physics:** Physical principles, laws, their interrelationships, and applications to understanding fluid, material, and atmospheric dynamics, and mechanical, electrical, atomic, and subatomic structures and processes. **Computers and Electronics:** Circuit boards, processors, chips, electronic equipment, and computer hardware and software, including applications and programming. **Design:** Design techniques, tools, and principles involved in production of precision technical plans, blueprints, drawings, and models. **Mathematics:** Arithmetic, algebra, geometry, calculus, statistics, and their applications.

Personality Type: Realistic-Investigative-Conventional. **Career Cluster:** 13 Manufacturing. **Career Pathway:** 13.3 Maintenance, Installation, and Repair. **Other Jobs in This Pathway:** Aircraft Mechanics and Service Technicians; Automotive Engineering Technicians; Automotive Specialty Technicians; Avionics Technicians; Biological Technicians; Camera and Photographic Equipment Repairers; Chemical Equipment Operators and Tenders; Civil Engineering Technicians; Coil Winders, Tapers, and Finishers; Computer, Automated Teller, and Office Machine Repairers; Construction and Related Workers, All Other; Control and Valve Installers and Repairers, Except Mechanical Door; Electric Motor, Power Tool, and Related Repairers; Electrical and Electronic Equipment Assemblers; Electrical and Electronics Repairers, Commercial and Industrial Equipment; Electrical and Electronics Repairers, Powerhouse, Substation, and Relay; Electrical Engineering Technicians; Electrical Engineering Technologists; Electromechanical Engineering Technologists; Electromechanical Equipment Assemblers; Electronics Engineering Technicians; Elevator Installers and Repairers; Engine and Other Machine Assemblers; others.

Skills—Repairing: Repairing machines or systems using the needed tools. **Equipment Maintenance:** Performing routine maintenance on equipment and determining when and what kind of maintenance is needed. **Equipment Selection:** Determining the kind of tools and equipment needed to do a job. **Troubleshooting:** Determining causes of operating errors and deciding what to do about them. **Technology Design:** Generating or adapting equipment and technology to serve user needs. **Installation:** Installing equipment, machines, wiring, or programs to meet specifications. **Science:** Using scientific rules and methods to solve problems. **Programming:** Writing computer programs for various purposes.

Work Environment: Indoors; sitting; using hands; noise; hazardous conditions.

Job Specialization: Fuel Cell Technicians

Install, operate, and maintain integrated fuel cell systems in transportation, stationary, or portable applications. Troubleshoot test equipment. Recommend improvements to fuel cell design and performance. Perform routine vehicle maintenance procedures such as part replacements and tune-ups. Build or test power plant systems, including pumps, blowers, heat exchangers, or sensors. Order testing materials. Build or test electrical systems, making electrical calculations as needed. Report results of fuel cell test results. Perform routine and preventive maintenance on test equipment. Document or analyze fuel cell test data using spreadsheets or other computer software. Collect and maintain fuel cell test data. Calibrate equipment used for fuel cell testing. Build prototypes, following engineering specifications. Test fuel cells or fuel cell stacks, using complex electronic equipment. Assemble fuel cells or fuel cell stacks according to mechanical or electrical assembly documents or schematics.

Education and Training Program: Manufacturing Engineering Technology/Technician.

Personality Type: No data available. **Career Cluster:** 13 Manufacturing. **Career Pathway:** 13.3 Maintenance, Installation, and Repair. **Other Jobs in This Pathway:** Aircraft Mechanics and Service Technicians; Automotive Engineering Technicians; Automotive Specialty Technicians; Avionics Technicians; Biological Technicians; Camera and Photographic Equipment Repairers; Chemical Equipment Operators and Tenders; Civil Engineering Technicians; Coil Winders, Tapers, and Finishers; Computer, Automated Teller, and Office Machine Repairers; Construction and Related Workers, All Other; Control and Valve Installers and Repairers, Except Mechanical Door; Electric Motor, Power Tool, and Related Repairers; Electrical and Electronic Equipment Assemblers; Electrical and Electronics Repairers, Commercial and Industrial Equipment; Electrical and Electronics Repairers, Powerhouse, Substation, and Relay; Electrical Engineering Technicians; Electrical Engineering Technologists; Electromechanical Engineering Technologists; Electromechanical Equipment Assemblers; Electronics Engineering Technicians; Electronics Engineering Technologists; others.

Work Environment: No data available.

Job Specialization: Industrial Engineering Technologists

Apply engineering theory and technical skills to support industrial engineering activities such as quality control, inventory control, and material flow methods.

May conduct statistical studies and analyze production costs. Interpret engineering drawings, sketches, or diagrams. Prepare schedules for equipment use or routine maintenance. Request equipment upgrades or purchases. Supervise production workers. Create computer applications for manufacturing processes or operations using computer-aided design (CAD) or computer-assisted manufacturing (CAM) tools. Oversee and inspect production processes. Prepare reports regarding inventories of raw materials and finished products. Modify equipment or processes to improve resource or cost efficiency. Develop and conduct quality control tests to ensure consistent production quality. Compile operational data to develop cost or time estimates, schedules, or specifications. Collect and analyze data related to quality or industrial health and safety programs. Analyze operational, production, economic, or other data using statistical procedures. Prepare layouts of machinery and equipment using drafting equipment or computer-aided design (CAD) software. Plan the flow of work or materials to maximize efficiency. Monitor and control inventory. Conduct time and motion studies to identify opportunities to improve worker efficiency. Design plant or production facility layouts. Develop and implement programs to address problems related to production, materials, safety, or quality. Analyze, estimate, or report production costs.

Education and Training Program: Quality Control Technology/Technician.

Personality Type: Investigative-Realistic-Conventional. **Career Cluster:** 13 Manufacturing. **Career Pathway:** 13.3 Maintenance, Installation, and Repair. **Other Jobs in This Pathway:** Aircraft Mechanics and Service Technicians; Automotive Engineering Technicians; Automotive Specialty Technicians; Avionics Technicians; Biological Technicians; Camera and Photographic Equipment Repairers; Chemical Equipment Operators and Tenders; Civil Engineering Technicians; Coil Winders, Tapers, and Finishers; Computer, Automated Teller, and Office Machine Repairers; Construction and Related Workers, All Other; Control and Valve Installers and Repairers, Except Mechanical Door; Electric Motor, Power Tool, and Related Repairers; Electrical and Electronic Equipment Assemblers; Electrical and Electronics Repairers, Commercial and Industrial Equipment; Electrical and Electronics Repairers, Powerhouse, Substation, and Relay; Electrical Engineering Technicians; Electrical Engineering Technologists;

Electromechanical Engineering Technologists; Electromechanical Equipment Assemblers; Electronics Engineering Technicians; Electronics Engineering Technologists; others.

Work Environment: No data available.

Job Specialization: Manufacturing Production Technicians

Apply knowledge of manufacturing engineering systems and tools to set up, test, and adjust manufacturing machinery and equipment, using any combination of electrical, electronic, mechanical, hydraulic, pneumatic, and computer technologies. Adhere to all applicable regulations, policies, and procedures for health, safety, and environmental compliance. Inspect finished products for quality and adherence to customer specifications. Set up and operate production equipment in accordance with current good manufacturing practices and standard operating procedures. Calibrate or adjust equipment to ensure quality production using tools such as calipers, micrometers, height gauges, protractors, and ring gauges. Set up and verify the functionality of safety equipment. Troubleshoot problems with equipment, devices, or products. Monitor and adjust production processes or equipment for quality and productivity. Test products or subassemblies for functionality or quality. Plan and lay out work to meet production and schedule requirements. Start up and shut down processing equipment. Prepare and assemble materials. Provide advice or training to other technicians. Measure and record data associated with operating equipment. Assist engineers in developing, building, or testing prototypes and new products, processes, or procedures. Prepare production documents such as standard operating procedures, manufacturing batch records, inventory reports, and productivity reports. Install new equipment. Keep production logs. Clean production equipment and work areas. Provide production, progress, or changeover reports to shift supervisors. Collect hazardous or nonhazardous waste in correctly labeled barrels or other containers and transfer them to collection areas. Select cleaning materials, tools, and equipment. Build product subassemblies or final assemblies. Ship packages following carrier specifications. Maintain inventory of job materials. Build packaging for finished products. Package finished products.

Education and Training Program: Manufacturing Engineering Technology/Technician. **Knowledge/Courses— Mechanical Devices:** Machines and tools, including their designs, uses, repair, and maintenance. **Design:** Design techniques, tools, and principles involved in production of precision technical plans, blueprints, drawings, and models. **Engineering and Technology:** The practical application of engineering science and technology. This includes applying principles, techniques, procedures, and equipment to the design and production of various goods and services. **Production and Processing:** Raw materials, production processes, quality control, costs, and other techniques for maximizing the effective manufacture and distribution of goods. **Physics:** Physical principles, laws, their interrelationships, and applications to understanding fluid, material, and atmospheric dynamics, and mechanical, electrical, atomic, and subatomic structures and processes. **Chemistry:** The chemical composition, structure, and properties of substances and of the chemical processes and transformations that they undergo. This includes uses of chemicals and their danger signs, production techniques, and disposal methods.

Personality Type: Realistic-Investigative. **Career Cluster:** 13 Manufacturing. **Career Pathway:** 13.3 Maintenance, Installation, and Repair. **Other Jobs in This Pathway:** Aircraft Mechanics and Service Technicians; Automotive Engineering Technicians; Automotive Specialty Technicians; Avionics Technicians; Biological Technicians; Camera and Photographic Equipment Repairers; Chemical Equipment Operators and Tenders; Civil Engineering Technicians; Coil Winders, Tapers, and Finishers; Computer, Automated Teller, and Office Machine Repairers; Construction and Related Workers, All Other; Control and Valve Installers and Repairers, Except Mechanical Door; Electric Motor, Power Tool, and Related Repairers; Electrical and Electronic Equipment Assemblers; Electrical and Electronics Repairers, Commercial and Industrial Equipment; Electrical and Electronics Repairers, Powerhouse, Substation, and Relay; Electrical Engineering Technicians; Electrical Engineering Technologists; Electromechanical Engineering Technologists; Electromechanical Equipment Assemblers; Electronics Engineering Technicians; Electronics Engineering Technologists; others.

Skills—Equipment Maintenance: Performing routine maintenance on equipment and determining when and what kind of maintenance is needed. **Repairing:** Repairing machines or systems using the needed tools. **Troubleshooting:** Determining causes of operating errors and deciding what to do about them. **Installation:** Installing equipment, machines, wiring, or programs to meet specifications. **Operation and Control:** Controlling operations of equipment or systems. **Quality Control Analysis:** Conducting tests and inspections of products, services, or processes to evaluate quality or performance. **Operation Monitoring:** Watching gauges, dials, or other indicators to make sure a machine is working properly. **Equipment Selection:** Determining the kind of tools and equipment needed to do a job.

Work Environment: Indoors; standing; using hands; noise; contaminants; hazardous equipment.

Job Specialization: Manufacturing Engineering Technologists

Apply engineering theory and technical skills to support manufacturing engineering activities. Develop tools; implement designs; and integrate machinery, equipment, and computer technologies to ensure effective manufacturing processes. Recommend corrective or preventive actions to assure or improve product quality or reliability. Prepare layouts, drawings, or sketches of machinery and equipment such as shop tooling, scale layouts, and new equipment design using drafting equipment or computer-aided design software. Identify and implement new manufacturing technologies, processes, or equipment. Identify opportunities for improvements in quality, cost, or efficiency of automation equipment. Monitor or measure manufacturing processes to identify ways to reduce losses, decrease time requirements, or improve quality. Ensure adherence to safety rules and practices. Coordinate equipment purchases, installations, or transfers. Plan, estimate, or schedule production work. Select material quantities and processing methods needed to achieve efficient production. Develop or maintain programs associated with automated production equipment. Estimate manufacturing costs. Install and evaluate manufacturing equipment, materials, or components. Oversee equipment start-up, characterization, qualification, or release. Develop production, inventory, or quality assurance programs. Create computer applications for manufacturing processes or operations using computer-aided design (CAD) or computer-assisted manufacturing (CAM) tools. Develop manufacturing infrastructure to integrate or deploy new manufacturing processes. Verify weights, measurements, counts, or calculations and record results on batch records. Design plant layouts and production facilities. Operate complex processing equipment. Train manufacturing technicians on topics such as safety, health, fire prevention, and quality. Erect manufacturing engineering equipment. Perform routine equipment maintenance.

Education and Training Program: Manufacturing Engineering Technology/Technician. **Knowledge/Courses— Engineering and Technology:** The practical application of engineering science and technology. This includes applying principles, techniques, procedures, and equipment to the design and production of various goods and services. **Design:** Design techniques, tools, and principles involved in production of precision technical plans, blueprints, drawings, and models. **Mechanical Devices:** Machines and tools, including their designs, uses, repair, and maintenance. **Physics:** Physical principles, laws, their interrelationships, and applications to understanding fluid, material, and atmospheric dynamics, and mechanical, electrical, atomic, and subatomic structures and processes. **Production and Processing:** Raw materials, production processes, quality control, costs, and other techniques for maximizing the effective manufacture and distribution of goods. **Mathematics:** Arithmetic, algebra, geometry, calculus, statistics, and their applications.

Personality Type: Realistic-Investigative-Conventional. **Career Cluster:** 13 Manufacturing. **Career Pathway:** 13.3 Maintenance, Installation, and Repair. **Other Jobs in This Pathway:** Aircraft Mechanics and Service Technicians; Automotive Engineering Technicians; Automotive Specialty Technicians; Avionics Technicians; Biological Technicians; Camera and Photographic Equipment Repairers; Chemical Equipment Operators and Tenders; Civil Engineering Technicians; Coil Winders, Tapers, and Finishers; Computer, Automated Teller, and Office Machine Repairers; Construction and Related Workers, All Other; Control and Valve Installers and Repairers, Except Mechanical Door; Electric Motor, Power Tool, and Related Repairers; Electrical and Electronic Equipment Assemblers; Electrical and Electronics Repairers, Commercial and Industrial Equipment; Electrical and Electronics Repairers, Powerhouse, Substation, and Relay; Electrical Engineering Technicians; Electrical Engineering Technologists; Electromechanical Engineering Technologists; Electromechanical Equipment Assemblers; Electronics Engineering Technicians; Electronics Engineering Technologists; others.

Skills—Equipment Selection: Determining the kind of tools and equipment needed to do a job. **Installation:** Installing equipment, machines, wiring, or programs to meet specifications. **Technology Design:** Generating or adapting equipment and technology to serve user needs. **Equipment Maintenance:** Performing routine maintenance on equipment and determining when and what kind of maintenance is needed. **Programming:** Writing computer programs for various purposes. **Management of Financial Resources:** Determining how money will be spent to get the work done and accounting for these expenditures. **Troubleshooting:** Determining causes of operating errors and deciding what to do about them. **Mathematics:** Using mathematics to solve problems.

Work Environment: Indoors; sitting; noise; contaminants.

Job Specialization: Mechanical Engineering Technologists

Apply engineering theory and technical skills to support mechanical engineering activities such as generation, transmission, and use of mechanical and fluid energy. Prepare layouts of machinery and equipment and plan the flow of work. May conduct statistical studies and analyze production costs. Prepare equipment inspection schedules, reliability schedules, work plans, and other records. Prepare cost and materials estimates and project schedules. Provide technical support to other employees regarding mechanical design, fabrication, testing, or documentation. Interpret engineering sketches, specifications, and drawings. Perform routine maintenance on equipment such as leak detectors, glove boxes, and mechanical pumps. Design specialized or customized equipment, machines, or structures. Design molds, tools, dies, jigs, or fixtures for use in manufacturing processes. Conduct failure analyses, document results, and recommend corrective actions. Assist engineers to design, develop, test, or manufacture industrial machinery, consumer products, or other equipment. Analyze or estimate production costs such as labor, equipment, and plant space. Apply testing or monitoring apparatus to operating equipment. Test machines, components, materials, or products to determine characteristics such as performance, strength, and response to stress. Prepare specifications, designs, or sketches for machines, components, and systems related to the generation, transmission, or use of mechanical and fluid energy. Prepare layouts of machinery, tools, plants, and equipment. Inspect and test mechanical equipment. Oversee, monitor, or inspect mechanical installations or construction projects. Assist mechanical engineers in product testing through activities such as setting up instrumentation for automobile crash tests. Assemble or disassemble complex mechanical systems.

Education and Training Program: Mechanical Engineering/Mechanical Technology/Technician.

Personality Type: Realistic-Investigative-Conventional. **Career Cluster:** 13 Manufacturing. **Career Pathway:** 13.3 Maintenance, Installation, and Repair. **Other Jobs in This Pathway:** Aircraft Mechanics and Service Technicians; Automotive Engineering Technicians; Automotive Specialty Technicians; Avionics Technicians; Biological Technicians; Camera and Photographic Equipment Repairers; Chemical Equipment Operators and Tenders; Civil Engineering Technicians; Coil Winders, Tapers, and Finishers; Computer, Automated Teller, and Office Machine Repairers; Construction and Related Workers, All Other; Control and Valve Installers and Repairers, Except Mechanical Door; Electric Motor, Power Tool, and Related Repairers; Electrical and Electronic Equipment Assemblers; Electrical and Electronics Repairers, Commercial and Industrial Equipment; Electrical and Electronics Repairers, Powerhouse, Substation, and Relay; Electrical Engineering Technicians; Electrical Engineering Technologists; Electromechanical Engineering Technologists; Electromechanical Equipment Assemblers; Electronics Engineering Technicians; Electronics Engineering Technologists; others.

Work Environment: No data available.

Job Specialization: Nanotechnology Engineering Technologists

Implement production processes for nanoscale designs to produce and modify materials, devices, and systems of unique molecular or macromolecular composition. Operate advanced microscopy equipment to manipulate nanoscale objects. Work under the supervision of engineering staff. Supervise or provide technical direction to technicians engaged in nanotechnology research or production. Install nanotechnology production equipment at customer or manufacturing sites. Contribute written material or data for grant or patent applications. Produce images and measurements, using tools and techniques such as atomic force microscopy, scanning electron microscopy,

optical microscopy, particle size analysis, and zeta potential analysis. Prepare detailed verbal or written presentations for scientists, engineers, project managers, or upper management. Prepare capability data, training materials, or other documentation for transfer of processes to production. Develop or modify wet chemical or industrial laboratory experimental techniques for nanoscale use. Collect and compile nanotechnology research and engineering data. Inspect or measure thin films of carbon nanotubes, polymers, or inorganic coatings, using a variety of techniques and analytical tools. Implement new or enhanced methods and processes for the processing, testing, or manufacture of nanotechnology materials or products. Design or conduct experiments in collaboration with scientists or engineers supportive of the development of nanotechnology materials, components, devices, or systems.

Education and Training Program: Nanotechnology.

Personality Type: No data available. **Career Cluster:** 13 Manufacturing. **Career Pathway:** 13.3 Maintenance, Installation, and Repair. **Other Jobs in This Pathway:** Aircraft Mechanics and Service Technicians; Automotive Engineering Technicians; Automotive Specialty Technicians; Avionics Technicians; Biological Technicians; Camera and Photographic Equipment Repairers; Chemical Equipment Operators and Tenders; Civil Engineering Technicians; Coil Winders, Tapers, and Finishers; Computer, Automated Teller, and Office Machine Repairers; Construction and Related Workers, All Other; Control and Valve Installers and Repairers, Except Mechanical Door; Electric Motor, Power Tool, and Related Repairers; Electrical and Electronic Equipment Assemblers; Electrical and Electronics Repairers, Commercial and Industrial Equipment; Electrical and Electronics Repairers, Powerhouse, Substation, and Relay; Electrical Engineering Technicians; Electrical Engineering Technologists; Electromechanical Engineering Technologists; Electromechanical Equipment Assemblers; Electronics Engineering Technicians; Electronics Engineering Technologists; others.

Work Environment: No data available.

Job Specialization: Nanotechnology Engineering Technicians

Operate commercial-scale production equipment to produce, test, and modify materials, devices, and systems of molecular or macromolecular composition.

Work under the supervision of engineering staff. Track inventory and order new supplies, as needed. Repair nanotechnology processing or testing equipment, or submit work orders for equipment repair. Maintain work area according to clean-room and other processing standards. Set up and execute experiments according to detailed instructions. Compile information and prepare reports. Record test results in logs, laboratory notebooks, or spreadsheet software. Produce detailed images and measurement of objects, using tools such as scanning tunneling microscopes and oscilloscopes. Perform functional tests of nano-enhanced assemblies, components, or systems, using equipment such as torque gauges and conductivity meters. Operate computer-controlled machine tools. Monitor equipment during operation to ensure adherence to specifications for characteristics such as pressure, temperature, and flow. Measure or mix chemicals or compounds in accordance with detailed instructions or formulas. Calibrate nanotechnology equipment such as weighing, testing, and production equipment. Inspect work products to ensure quality and adherence to specifications. Maintain accurate production record or batch record documentation. Assist scientists, engineers, or technologists in writing process specifications or documentation. Assist scientists, engineers, or technologists in processing or characterizing materials according to physical and chemical properties. Assemble components, using techniques such as interference fitting, solvent bonding, adhesive bonding, heat sealing, and ultrasonic welding. Operate nanotechnology compounding, testing, processing, or production equipment, following appropriate standard operating procedures, good manufacturing practices, hazardous material restrictions, or health and safety requirements.

Education and Training Program: Nanotechnology.

Personality Type: No data available. **Career Cluster:** 13 Manufacturing. **Career Pathway:** 13.3 Maintenance, Installation, and Repair. **Other Jobs in This Pathway:** Aircraft Mechanics and Service Technicians; Automotive Engineering Technicians; Automotive Specialty Technicians; Avionics Technicians; Biological Technicians; Camera and Photographic Equipment Repairers; Chemical Equipment Operators and Tenders; Civil Engineering Technicians; Coil Winders, Tapers, and Finishers; Computer, Automated Teller, and Office Machine Repairers; Construction and Related Workers, All Other; Control and Valve Installers and Repairers, Except Mechanical Door;

Electric Motor, Power Tool, and Related Repairers; Electrical and Electronic Equipment Assemblers; Electrical and Electronics Repairers, Commercial and Industrial Equipment; Electrical and Electronics Repairers, Powerhouse, Substation, and Relay; Electrical Engineering Technicians; Electrical Engineering Technologists; Electromechanical Engineering Technologists; Electromechanical Equipment Assemblers; Electronics Engineering Technicians; Electronics Engineering Technologists; others.

Work Environment: No data available.

Job Specialization: Non-Destructive Testing Specialists

Test the safety of structures, vehicles, or vessels using X-ray, ultrasound, fiber-optic, or related equipment. Supervise or direct the work of non-destructive testing (NDT) trainees or staff. Produce images of objects on film using radiographic techniques. Develop or use new non-destructive testing methods such as acoustic emission testing, leak testing, and thermal or infrared testing. Document non-destructive testing methods, processes, or results. Map the presence of imperfections within objects using sonic measurements. Make radiographic images to detect flaws in objects while leaving objects intact. Visually examine materials, structures, or components using tools and equipment such as endoscopes, closed circuit television systems, and fiber optics for signs of corrosion, metal fatigue, cracks, or other flaws. Interpret or evaluate test results in accordance with applicable codes, standards, specifications, or procedures. Identify defects in solid materials using ultrasonic testing techniques. Select, calibrate, or operate equipment used in the non-destructive testing of products or materials. Conduct liquid penetrant tests to locate surface cracks by coating objects with fluorescent dyes, cleaning excess penetrant, and applying developer. Prepare reports on non-destructive testing results. Interpret the results of all methods of non-destructive testing, such as acoustic emission, electromagnetic, leak, liquid penetrant, magnetic particle, neutron radiographic, radiographic, thermal or infrared, ultrasonic, vibration analysis, and visual testing. Examine structures or vehicles such as aircraft, trains, nuclear reactors, bridges, dams, and pipelines using non-destructive testing techniques. Evaluate material properties using radio astronomy, voltage and amperage measurement, or rheometric flow measurement.

Identify defects in concrete or other building materials using thermal or infrared testing.

Education and Training Program: Industrial Radiologic Technology/Technician. **Knowledge/Courses—Engineering and Technology:** The practical application of engineering science and technology. This includes applying principles, techniques, procedures, and equipment to the design and production of various goods and services. **Physics:** Physical principles, laws, their interrelationships, and applications to understanding fluid, material, and atmospheric dynamics, and mechanical, electrical, atomic, and subatomic structures and processes. **Chemistry:** The chemical composition, structure, and properties of substances and of the chemical processes and transformations that they undergo. This includes uses of chemicals and their danger signs, production techniques, and disposal methods. **Production and Processing:** Raw materials, production processes, quality control, costs, and other techniques for maximizing the effective manufacture and distribution of goods. **Mechanical Devices:** Machines and tools, including their designs, uses, repair, and maintenance. **Design:** Design techniques, tools, and principles involved in production of precision technical plans, blueprints, drawings, and models.

Personality Type: Realistic-Investigative-Conventional. **Career Cluster:** 13 Manufacturing. **Career Pathway:** 13.3 Maintenance, Installation, and Repair. **Other Jobs in This Pathway:** Aircraft Mechanics and Service Technicians; Automotive Engineering Technicians; Automotive Specialty Technicians; Avionics Technicians; Biological Technicians; Camera and Photographic Equipment Repairers; Chemical Equipment Operators and Tenders; Civil Engineering Technicians; Coil Winders, Tapers, and Finishers; Computer, Automated Teller, and Office Machine Repairers; Construction and Related Workers, All Other; Control and Valve Installers and Repairers, Except Mechanical Door; Electric Motor, Power Tool, and Related Repairers; Electrical and Electronic Equipment Assemblers; Electrical and Electronics Repairers, Commercial and Industrial Equipment; Electrical and Electronics Repairers, Powerhouse, Substation, and Relay; Electrical Engineering Technicians; Electrical Engineering Technologists; Electromechanical Engineering Technologists; Electromechanical Equipment Assemblers; Electronics Engineering Technicians; Electronics Engineering Technologists; others.

Skills—Equipment Maintenance: Performing routine maintenance on equipment and determining when and what kind of maintenance is needed. **Troubleshooting:** Determining causes of operating errors and deciding what to do about them. **Equipment Selection:** Determining the kind of tools and equipment needed to do a job. **Repairing:** Repairing machines or systems using the needed tools. **Quality Control Analysis:** Conducting tests and inspections of products, services, or processes to evaluate quality or performance. **Operation Monitoring:** Watching gauges, dials, or other indicators to make sure a machine is working properly. **Operation and Control:** Controlling operations of equipment or systems. **Programming:** Writing computer programs for various purposes.

Work Environment: More often outdoors than indoors; standing; using hands; noise; very hot or cold; bright or inadequate lighting; contaminants; cramped work space; exposed to radiation.

Job Specialization: Photonics Technicians

Build, install, test, and maintain optical and fiber-optic equipment such as lasers, lenses, and mirrors using spectrometers, interferometers, or related equipment. Recommend design or material changes to reduce costs or processing times. Monitor inventory levels and order supplies as necessary. Maintain clean working environments according to clean room standards. Document procedures such as calibration. Maintain activity logs. Record test results and compute test data. Test and perform failure analysis for optomechanical or optoelectrical products according to test plans. Assist scientists or engineers in the conduct of photonic experiments. Perform diagnostic analyses of processing steps using analytical or metrological tools such as microscopy, profilometry, and ellipsometry devices. Optimize process parameters by making prototype and production devices. Mix, pour, and use processing chemicals or gases according to safety standards and established operating procedures. Design, build, or modify fixtures used to assemble parts. Lay out cutting lines for machining using drafting tools. Assist engineers in the development of new products, fixtures, tools, or processes. Assemble and adjust parts or related electrical units of prototypes to prepare for testing. Splice fibers using fusion splicing or other techniques. Terminate, cure, polish, or test fiber cables with mechanical connectors. Set up or operate prototype or test apparatus such as control consoles, collimators, recording equipment, and cables. Set up or operate assembly or processing equipment such as lasers, cameras, die bonders, wire bonders, dispensers, reflow ovens, soldering irons, die shears, wire pull testers, temperature or humidity chambers, and optical spectrum analyzers. Repair or calibrate products such as surgical lasers. Perform laser seam welding, heat treatment, or hard facing operations. Fabricate devices such as optoelectronic and semiconductor devices. Build prototype optomechanical devices for use in equipment such as aerial cameras, gun sights, and telescopes.

Education and Training Program: Engineering-Related Technologies, Other.

Personality Type: Realistic-Investigative-Conventional. **Career Cluster:** 13 Manufacturing. **Career Pathway:** 13.3 Maintenance, Installation, and Repair. **Other Jobs in This Pathway:** Aircraft Mechanics and Service Technicians; Automotive Engineering Technicians; Automotive Specialty Technicians; Avionics Technicians; Biological Technicians; Camera and Photographic Equipment Repairers; Chemical Equipment Operators and Tenders; Civil Engineering Technicians; Coil Winders, Tapers, and Finishers; Computer, Automated Teller, and Office Machine Repairers; Construction and Related Workers, All Other; Control and Valve Installers and Repairers, Except Mechanical Door; Electric Motor, Power Tool, and Related Repairers; Electrical and Electronic Equipment Assemblers; Electrical and Electronics Repairers, Commercial and Industrial Equipment; Electrical and Electronics Repairers, Powerhouse, Substation, and Relay; Electrical Engineering Technicians; Electrical Engineering Technologists; Electromechanical Engineering Technologists; Electromechanical Equipment Assemblers; Electronics Engineering Technicians; Electronics Engineering Technologists; others.

Work Environment: No data available.

Environmental Engineering Technicians

- ⊙ Annual Earnings: $44,850
- ⊙ Earnings Growth Potential: Medium (36.8%)
- ⊙ Growth: 24.5%
- ⊙ Annual Job Openings: 820
- ⊙ Self-Employed: 0.5%

Considerations for Job Outlook: Employment in this occupation is typically tied to projects created by environmental engineers. State and local governments are expected to focus efforts and resources on efficient water use and wastewater treatment, which will support the demand for environmental engineering technicians.

Apply theory and principles of environmental engineering to modify, test, and operate equipment and devices used in the prevention, control, and remediation of environmental problems. Receive, set up, test, and decontaminate equipment. Maintain project logbook records and computer program files. Perform environmental quality work in field and office settings. Conduct pollution surveys, collecting and analyzing samples such as air and groundwater. Review technical documents to ensure completeness and conformance to requirements. Perform laboratory work such as logging numerical and visual observations, preparing and packaging samples, recording test results, and performing photo documentation. Review work plans to schedule activities. Obtain product information, identify vendors and suppliers, and order materials and equipment to maintain inventory. Arrange for the disposal of lead, asbestos, and other hazardous materials. Inspect facilities to monitor compliance with regulations governing substances such as asbestos, lead, and wastewater. Provide technical engineering support in the planning of projects such as wastewater treatment plants to ensure compliance with environmental regulations and policies. Improve chemical processes to reduce toxic emissions. Oversee support staff. Assist in the cleanup of hazardous material spills. Produce environmental assessment reports, tabulating data and preparing charts, graphs, and sketches. Maintain process parameters, and evaluate process anomalies. Work with customers to assess the environmental impact of proposed construction and to develop pollution prevention programs.

Education/Training Required: Associate degree. **Education and Training Programs:** Environmental Engineering Technology/Environmental Technology; Hazardous Materials Information Systems Technology/Technician. **Knowledge/Courses—Biology:** Plant and animal organisms and their tissues, cells, functions, interdependencies, and interactions with each other and the environment. **Building and Construction:** Materials, methods, and the tools involved in the construction or repair of houses, buildings, or other structures such as highways and roads.

Physics: Physical principles, laws, their interrelationships, and applications to understanding fluid, material, and atmospheric dynamics, and mechanical, electrical, atomic, and subatomic structures and processes. **Chemistry:** The chemical composition, structure, and properties of substances and of the chemical processes and transformations that they undergo. This includes uses of chemicals and their danger signs, production techniques, and disposal methods. **Engineering and Technology:** The practical application of engineering science and technology. This includes applying principles, techniques, procedures, and equipment to the design and production of various goods and services. **Design:** Design techniques, tools, and principles involved in production of precision technical plans, blueprints, drawings, and models. **Work Experience Needed:** None. **On-the-Job Training Needed:** None. **Certification/Licensure:** None.

Personality Type: Realistic-Investigative-Conventional. **Career Clusters:** 01 Agriculture, Food, and Natural Resources; 13 Manufacturing. **Career Pathways:** 01.6 Environmental Service Systems; 13.4 Quality Assurance. **Other Jobs in These Pathways:** Hazardous Materials Removal Workers; Inspectors, Testers, Sorters, Samplers, and Weighers; Occupational Health and Safety Specialists; Water and Wastewater Treatment Plant and System Operators.

Skills—Science: Using scientific rules and methods to solve problems. **Mathematics:** Using mathematics to solve problems. **Equipment Maintenance:** Performing routine maintenance on equipment and determining when and what kind of maintenance is needed. **Quality Control Analysis:** Conducting tests and inspections of products, services, or processes to evaluate quality or performance. **Management of Material Resources:** Obtaining and seeing to the appropriate use of equipment, facilities, and materials needed to do certain work. **Equipment Selection:** Determining the kind of tools and equipment needed to do a job. **Troubleshooting:** Determining causes of operating errors and deciding what to do about them. **Repairing:** Repairing machines or systems using the needed tools.

Work Environment: Indoors.

Environmental Science and Protection Technicians, Including Health

⊙ Annual Earnings: $42,270
⊙ Earnings Growth Potential: Medium (36.8%)
⊙ Growth: 23.6%
⊙ Annual Job Openings: 1,950
⊙ Self-Employed: 0.5%

Considerations for Job Outlook: Environmental science and protection technicians should have good opportunities for employment. In addition to openings due to growth, many job openings are expected to be created by those who retire or leave the occupation for other reasons. Job candidates with an associate degree or experience should have the best opportunities. Job opportunities available in state and local governments will vary from year to year with the budgets of state and local environmental protection agencies.

Perform laboratory and field tests to monitor the environment and investigate sources of pollution under the direction of an environmental scientist, engineer, or other specialist. Collect samples of gases, soils, water, industrial wastewater, and asbestos products to conduct tests on pollutant levels and identify sources of pollution. Record test data, and prepare reports, summaries, and charts that interpret test results. Develop and implement programs for monitoring of environmental pollution and radiation. Discuss test results and analyses with customers. Set up equipment or stations to monitor and collect pollutants from sites such as smokestacks, manufacturing plants, or mechanical equipment. Maintain files, such as hazardous waste databases, chemical usage data, personnel exposure information, and diagrams showing equipment locations. Develop testing procedures or direct activities of workers in laboratory. Prepare samples or photomicrographs for testing and analysis. Calibrate microscopes, and test instruments. Examine and analyze material for presence and concentration of contaminants such as asbestos, using variety of microscopes. Calculate amount of pollutant in samples or compute air pollution or gas flow in industrial processes, using chemical and mathematical formulas. Make recommendations to control or eliminate unsafe conditions at workplaces or public facilities. Weigh, analyze, and measure collected sample particles such as lead, coal dust, or rock to determine concentration of pollutants.

Education/Training Required: Associate degree. **Education and Training Programs:** Environmental Science; Environmental Studies; Physical Science Technologies/Technicians, Other; Science Technologies/Technicians, Other. **Knowledge/Courses—Biology:** Plant and animal organisms and their tissues, cells, functions, interdependencies, and interactions with each other and the environment. **Chemistry:** The chemical composition, structure, and properties of substances and of the chemical processes and transformations that they undergo. This includes uses of chemicals and their danger signs, production techniques, and disposal methods. **Geography:** Principles and methods for describing the features of land, sea, and air masses, including their physical characteristics, locations, interrelationships, and distribution of plant, animal, and human life. **Physics:** Physical principles, laws, their interrelationships, and applications to understanding fluid, material, and atmospheric dynamics, and mechanical, electrical, atomic, and subatomic structures and processes. **Computers and Electronics:** Circuit boards, processors, chips, electronic equipment, and computer hardware and software, including applications and programming. **Building and Construction:** Materials, methods, and the tools involved in the construction or repair of houses, buildings, or other structures such as highways and roads. **Work Experience Needed:** None. **On-the-Job Training Needed:** Moderate-term on-the-job training. **Certification/Licensure:** Licensure for some specializations.

Personality Type: Investigative-Realistic-Conventional. **Career Clusters:** 01 Agriculture, Food, and Natural Resources; 13 Manufacturing; 16 Transportation, Distribution, and Logistics. **Career Pathways:** 16.6 Health, Safety, and Environmental Management; 13.2 Manufacturing Production Process Development; 01.5 Natural Resources Systems. **Other Jobs in These Pathways:** Biofuels Processing Technicians; Biological Science Teachers, Postsecondary; Biomass Plant Technicians; Chemical Plant and System Operators; Chemical Technicians; Climate Change Analysts; Conveyor Operators and Tenders; Derrick Operators, Oil and Gas; Electrical Engineering Technicians; Electromechanical Equipment Assemblers; Engineering Technicians, Except Drafters, All Other; Environmental Compliance Inspectors; Environmental Economists; Environmental Engineers; Environmental Restoration Planners; Environmental Science Teachers, Postsecondary; Environmental Scientists and Specialists, Including Health; Fabric and Apparel Patternmakers; Fallers; Farm and Home Management Advisors; Fashion Designers; Fish and Game Wardens; Fishers and Related Fishing Workers; Forest and Conservation Technicians; Forest and Conservation Workers; Foresters; Forestry and Conservation Science Teachers, Postsecondary; Gas Compressor and Gas Pumping Station Operators; Geological Sample Test Technicians; others.

Skills—Science: Using scientific rules and methods to solve problems. **Equipment Maintenance:** Performing routine maintenance on equipment and determining when and what kind of maintenance is needed. **Troubleshooting:** Determining causes of operating errors and deciding what to do about them. **Operation and Control:** Controlling operations of equipment or systems. **Operations Analysis:** Analyzing needs and product requirements to create a design. **Repairing:** Repairing machines or systems using the needed tools. **Equipment Selection:** Determining the kind of tools and equipment needed to do a job. **Mathematics:** Using mathematics to solve problems.

Work Environment: More often outdoors than indoors; standing; using hands; noise; very hot or cold; bright or inadequate lighting; contaminants; hazardous conditions; hazardous equipment; minor burns, cuts, bites, or stings.

Excavating and Loading Machine and Dragline Operators

⊙ Annual Earnings: $37,380
⊙ Earnings Growth Potential: Low (32.5%)
⊙ Growth: 17.4%
⊙ Annual Job Openings: 2,890
⊙ Self-Employed: 21.3%

Considerations for Job Outlook: Job prospects should be favorable. A high number of job openings should be created by the need to replace workers who leave this occupation. As automation increases, the technology used by this occupation will become more complex.

Operate or tend machinery equipped with scoops, shovels, or buckets to excavate and load loose materials. Move levers, depress foot pedals, and turn dials to operate power machinery such as power shovels, stripping-shovels, scraper loaders, or backhoes. Set up and inspect equipment prior to operation. Observe hand signals, grade stakes, and other markings when operating machines so that work can be performed to specifications. Become familiar with digging plans, machine capabilities and limitations, and efficient and safe digging procedures in a given application. Operate machinery to perform activities such as backfilling excavations, vibrating or breaking rock or concrete, and making winter roads. Create and maintain inclines and ramps, and handle slides, mud, and pit cleanings and maintenance. Lubricate, adjust, and repair machinery, and replace parts such as gears, bearings, and bucket teeth. Move materials over short distances such as around a construction site, factory, or warehouse. Measure and verify levels of rock or gravel, bases, and other excavated material. Receive written or oral instructions regarding material movement or excavation. Adjust dig face angles for varying overburden depths and set lengths. Drive machines to work sites. Perform manual labor to prepare or finish sites, such as shoveling materials by hand. Direct ground workers engaged in activities such as moving stakes or markers, or changing positions of towers. Direct workers engaged in placing blocks and outriggers in order to prevent capsizing of machines when lifting heavy loads.

Education/Training Required: Less than high school. **Education and Training Program:** Construction/Heavy Equipment/Earthmoving Equipment Operation. **Knowledge/Courses—Building and Construction:** Materials, methods, and the tools involved in the construction or repair of houses, buildings, or other structures such as highways and roads. **Mechanical Devices:** Machines and tools, including their designs, uses, repair, and maintenance. **Transportation:** Principles and methods for moving people or goods by air, rail, sea, or road, including the relative costs and benefits. **Production and Processing:** Raw materials, production processes, quality control, costs, and other techniques for maximizing the effective manufacture and distribution of goods. **Public Safety and Security:** Relevant equipment, policies, procedures, and strategies to promote effective local, state, or national security operations for the protection of people, data, property, and institutions. **Engineering and Technology:** The practical application of engineering science and technology. This includes applying principles, techniques, procedures, and equipment to the design and production of

various goods and services. **Work Experience Needed:** 1 to 5 years. **On-the-Job Training Needed:** Moderate-term on-the-job training. **Certification/Licensure:** Licensure for some specializations.

Personality Type: Realistic. **Career Cluster:** 02 Architecture and Construction. **Career Pathway:** 02.2 Construction. **Other Jobs in This Pathway:** Boilermakers; Brickmasons and Blockmasons; Carpet Installers; Cement Masons and Concrete Finishers; Construction and Building Inspectors; Construction and Related Workers, All Other; Construction Carpenters; Construction Laborers; Construction Managers; Continuous Mining Machine Operators; Cost Estimators; Crane and Tower Operators; Dredge Operators; Drywall and Ceiling Tile Installers; Earth Drillers, Except Oil and Gas; Electrical Power-Line Installers and Repairers; Electricians; Electromechanical Equipment Assemblers; Engineering Technicians, Except Drafters, All Other; Explosives Workers, Ordnance Handling Experts, and Blasters; Extraction Workers, All Other; First-Line Supervisors of Construction Trades and Extraction Workers; Floor Layers, Except Carpet, Wood, and Hard Tiles; Floor Sanders and Finishers; Glaziers; Heating and Air Conditioning Mechanics and Installers; Helpers, Construction Trades, All Other; others.

Skills—Repairing: Repairing machines or systems using the needed tools. **Equipment Maintenance:** Performing routine maintenance on equipment and determining when and what kind of maintenance is needed. **Operation and Control:** Controlling operations of equipment or systems. **Equipment Selection:** Determining the kind of tools and equipment needed to do a job. **Troubleshooting:** Determining causes of operating errors and deciding what to do about them. **Operation Monitoring:** Watching gauges, dials, or other indicators to make sure a machine is working properly. **Quality Control Analysis:** Conducting tests and inspections of products, services, or processes to evaluate quality or performance. **Coordination:** Adjusting actions in relation to others' actions.

Work Environment: Outdoors; sitting; using hands; repetitive motions; noise; very hot or cold; contaminants; whole-body vibration; hazardous equipment.

E

Executive Secretaries and Executive Administrative Assistants

- ⊙ Annual Earnings: $45,580
- ⊙ Earnings Growth Potential: Low (33.5%)
- ⊙ Growth: 12.6%
- ⊙ Annual Job Openings: 32,180
- ⊙ Self-Employed: 1.1%

Considerations for Job Outlook: In addition to jobs coming from employment growth, numerous job openings will arise from the need to replace secretaries and administrative assistants who transfer to other occupations or retire. Job opportunities should be best for applicants with extensive knowledge of computer software applications. Applicants with a bachelor's degree are expected to be in great demand and will act as managerial assistants who perform more complex tasks.

Provide high-level administrative support by conducting research, preparing statistical reports, handling information requests, and performing clerical functions. Manage and maintain executives' schedules. Prepare invoices, reports, memos, letters, financial statements, and other documents, using word-processing, spreadsheet, database, or presentation software. Open, sort, and distribute incoming correspondence, including faxes and e-mail. Read and analyze incoming memos, submissions, and reports to determine their significance and plan their distribution. File and retrieve corporate documents, records, and reports. Greet visitors, and determine whether they should be given access to specific individuals. Prepare responses to correspondence containing routine inquiries. Perform general office duties such as ordering supplies, maintaining records-management systems, and performing basic bookkeeping work. Prepare agendas and make arrangements for committee, board, and other meetings. Make travel arrangements for executives. Conduct research, compile data, and prepare papers for consideration and presentation by executives, committees, and boards of directors. Compile, transcribe, and distribute minutes of meetings. Attend meetings to record minutes. Coordinate and direct office services, such as records and budget preparation, personnel, and housekeeping, to aid executives. Meet with individuals, special-interest groups, and others on behalf of executives, committees, and boards of directors. Set up and oversee administrative policies and procedures for offices or organizations. Supervise and train other clerical staff.

Education/Training Required: High school diploma or equivalent. **Education and Training Programs:** Administrative Assistant and Secretarial Science, General; Executive Assistant/Executive Secretary Training; Medical Administrative/Executive Assistant and Medical Secretary Training. **Knowledge/Courses—Clerical Practices:** Administrative and clerical procedures and systems such as word processing, managing files and records, stenography and transcription, designing forms, and other office procedures and terminology. **Personnel and Human Resources:** Principles and procedures for personnel recruitment, selection, training, compensation and benefits, labor relations and negotiation, and personnel information systems. **Work Experience Needed:** 1 to 5 years. **On-the-Job Training Needed:** None. **Certification/Licensure:** Voluntary certification by association.

Personality Type: Conventional-Enterprising. **Career Clusters:** 04 Business, Management, and Administration; 08 Health Science. **Career Pathways:** 04.6 Administrative and Information Support; 08.3 Health Informatics. **Other Jobs in These Pathways:** Cargo and Freight Agents; Clinical Psychologists; Communications Teachers, Postsecondary; Correspondence Clerks; Couriers and Messengers; Court Clerks; Customer Service Representatives; Data Entry Keyers; Dental Laboratory Technicians; Dispatchers, Except Police, Fire, and Ambulance; Editors; Engineers, All Other; File Clerks; Fine Artists, Including Painters, Sculptors, and Illustrators; First-Line Supervisors of Office and Administrative Support Workers; Freight Forwarders; Health Educators; Health Specialties Teachers, Postsecondary; Human Resources Assistants, Except Payroll and Timekeeping; Information and Record Clerks, All Other; Insurance Claims Clerks; Insurance Policy Processing Clerks; Interviewers, Except Eligibility and Loan; License Clerks; Mail Clerks and Mail Machine Operators, Except Postal Service; Medical and Health Services Managers; Medical Appliance Technicians; Medical Assistants; Medical Records and Health Information Technicians; Medical Secretaries; others.

Skills—Service Orientation: Actively looking for ways to help people. **Programming:** Writing computer programs for various purposes. **Active Listening:** Giving full attention to what other people are saying, taking time to understand the points being made, asking questions as appropriate, and not interrupting at inappropriate times. **Writing:** Communicating effectively in writing as appropriate for the needs of the audience. **Speaking:** Talking to others to convey information effectively. **Time Management:** Managing one's own time and the time of others. **Reading Comprehension:** Understanding written sentences and paragraphs in work-related documents. **Monitoring:** Monitoring or assessing your performance or that of other individuals or organizations to make improvements or take corrective action.

Work Environment: Indoors; sitting; repetitive motions; noise.

Extruding and Drawing Machine Setters, Operators, and Tenders, Metal and Plastic

- ⊙ Annual Earnings: $32,300
- ⊙ Earnings Growth Potential: Medium (35.3%)
- ⊙ Growth: 8.4%
- ⊙ Annual Job Openings: 2,090
- ⊙ Self-Employed: 0.0%

Considerations for Job Outlook: Despite slower-than-average employment growth, a number of these jobs are expected to become available for highly skilled workers because of an expected increase in retirements, primarily of baby boomers, in the coming years. In addition, workers who have a thorough background in machine operations, certifications from industry associations, and a good working knowledge of the properties of metals and plastics should have the best job opportunities.

Set up, operate, or tend machines to extrude or draw thermoplastic or metal materials into tubes, rods, hoses, wire, bars, or structural shapes. Measure and examine extruded products in order to locate defects, and to check for conformance to specifications; adjust controls as necessary to alter products. Determine setup procedures and select machine dies and parts, according to specifications. Install dies, machine screws, and sizing rings on machines that extrude thermoplastic or metal materials. Change dies on extruding machines according to production line changes. Start machines and set controls to regulate vacuum, air pressure, sizing rings, and temperature, and to synchronize speed

of extrusion. Replace worn dies when products vary from specifications. Reel extruded products into rolls of specified lengths and weights. Troubleshoot, maintain, and make minor repairs to equipment. Clean work areas. Adjust controls to draw or press metal into specified shapes and diameters. Operate shearing mechanisms to cut rods to specified lengths. Select nozzles, spacers, and wire guides, according to diameters and lengths of rods. Weigh and mix pelletized, granular, or powdered thermoplastic materials and coloring pigments. Load machine hoppers with mixed materials, using augers, or stuff rolls of plastic dough into machine cylinders. Test physical properties of products with testing devices such as acid-bath testers, burst testers, and impact testers. Maintain an inventory of materials.

Education/Training Required: High school diploma or equivalent. **Education and Training Program:** Machine Tool Technology/Machinist. **Knowledge/Courses—Mechanical Devices:** Machines and tools, including their designs, uses, repair, and maintenance. **Medicine and Dentistry:** The information and techniques needed to diagnose and treat human injuries, diseases, and deformities. This includes symptoms, treatment alternatives, drug properties and interactions, and preventive health-care measures. **Chemistry:** The chemical composition, structure, and properties of substances and of the chemical processes and transformations that they undergo. This includes uses of chemicals and their danger signs, production techniques, and disposal methods. **Sociology and Anthropology:** Group behavior and dynamics, societal trends and influences, human migrations, ethnicity, and cultures and their history and origins. **Engineering and Technology:** The practical application of engineering science and technology. This includes applying principles, techniques, procedures, and equipment to the design and production of various goods and services. **Education and Training:** Principles and methods for curriculum and training design, teaching and instruction for individuals and groups, and the measurement of training effects. **Work Experience Needed:** None. **On-the-Job Training Needed:** Moderate-term on-the-job training. **Certification/Licensure:** None.

Personality Type: Realistic-Conventional. **Career Cluster:** 13 Manufacturing. **Career Pathway:** 13.1 Production. **Other Jobs in This Pathway:** Adhesive Bonding Machine Operators and Tenders; Assemblers and Fabricators, All Other; Avionics Technicians; Cabinetmakers and Bench Carpenters; Cleaning, Washing, and Metal Pickling

Equipment Operators and Tenders; Coating, Painting, and Spraying Machine Setters, Operators, and Tenders; Computer-Controlled Machine Tool Operators, Metal and Plastic; Cooling and Freezing Equipment Operators and Tenders; Cost Estimators; Crushing, Grinding, and Polishing Machine Setters, Operators, and Tenders; Cutters and Trimmers, Hand; Cutting and Slicing Machine Setters, Operators, and Tenders; Cutting, Punching, and Press Machine Setters, Operators, and Tenders, Metal and Plastic; Drilling and Boring Machine Tool Setters, Operators, and Tenders, Metal and Plastic; Extruding and Forming Machine Setters, Operators, and Tenders, Synthetic and Glass Fibers; Extruding, Forming, Pressing, and Compacting Machine Setters, Operators, and Tenders; Fiberglass Laminators and Fabricators; others.

Skills—Repairing: Repairing machines or systems using the needed tools. **Equipment Maintenance:** Performing routine maintenance on equipment and determining when and what kind of maintenance is needed. **Operation and Control:** Controlling operations of equipment or systems. **Equipment Selection:** Determining the kind of tools and equipment needed to do a job. **Installation:** Installing equipment, machines, wiring, or programs to meet specifications. **Operation Monitoring:** Watching gauges, dials, or other indicators to make sure a machine is working properly. **Quality Control Analysis:** Conducting tests and inspections of products, services, or processes to evaluate quality or performance. **Troubleshooting:** Determining causes of operating errors and deciding what to do about them.

Work Environment: Standing; walking and running; using hands; bending or twisting the body; repetitive motions; noise; very hot or cold; bright or inadequate lighting; contaminants; hazardous equipment; minor burns, cuts, bites, or stings.

Farm Equipment Mechanics and Service Technicians

- ⊙ Annual Earnings: $34,230
- ⊙ Earnings Growth Potential: Medium (35.2%)
- ⊙ Growth: 13.4%
- ⊙ Annual Job Openings: 1,290
- ⊙ Self-Employed: 5.5%

Considerations for Job Outlook: Most job opportunities will come from the need to replace workers who retire or leave the occupation. Those with certificates from vocational schools or two-year degrees from community colleges should have very good job opportunities as employers strongly prefer these candidates. Those without formal training will have difficulty finding jobs. The majority of job openings are expected to be in sectors that sell, rent, or lease heavy vehicles and mobile equipment, where a large proportion of service technicians are employed. The construction and mining industries, which use large numbers of heavy equipment, are sensitive to fluctuations in the economy. As a result, job opportunities for service technicians in these sectors will vary with overall economic conditions. Job opportunities for farm equipment mechanics are seasonal and are generally best during warmer months.

Diagnose, adjust, repair, or overhaul farm machinery and vehicles, such as tractors, harvesters, dairy equipment, and irrigation systems. Examine and listen to equipment, read inspection reports, and confer with customers to locate and diagnose malfunctions. Repair bent or torn sheet metal. Calculate bills according to record of repairs made, labor time, and parts used. Record details of repairs made and parts used. Fabricate new metal parts, using drill presses, engine lathes, and other machine tools. Dismantle defective machines for repair, using hand tools. Install and repair agricultural irrigation, plumbing, and sprinkler systems. Drive trucks to haul tools and equipment for on-site repair of large machinery. Test and replace electrical components and wiring, using test meters, soldering equipment, and hand tools. Repair or replace defective parts, using hand tools, milling and woodworking machines, lathes, welding equipment, grinders, or saws. Reassemble machines and equipment following repair; test operation; and make adjustments as necessary. Maintain, repair, and overhaul farm machinery and vehicles, such as tractors, harvesters, and irrigation systems. Clean and lubricate parts. Tune or overhaul engines.

Education/Training Required: High school diploma or equivalent. **Education and Training Programs:** Agricultural Mechanics and Equipment/Machine Technology; Agricultural Mechanization, General; Agricultural Mechanization, Other; Agricultural Power Machinery Operation. **Knowledge/Courses—Mechanical Devices:** Machines and tools, including their designs, uses, repair, and maintenance. **Physics:** Physical principles, laws, their interrelationships, and applications to understanding fluid, material, and atmospheric dynamics, and mechanical, electrical, atomic, and subatomic structures and processes. **Transportation:** Principles and methods for moving people or goods by air, rail, sea, or road, including the relative costs and benefits. **Engineering and Technology:** The practical application of engineering science and technology. This includes applying principles, techniques, procedures, and equipment to the design and production of various goods and services. **Sales and Marketing:** Principles and methods for showing, promoting, and selling products or services. This includes marketing strategy and tactics, product demonstration, sales techniques, and sales control systems. **Chemistry:** The chemical composition, structure, and properties of substances and of the chemical processes and transformations that they undergo. This includes uses of chemicals and their danger signs, production techniques, and disposal methods. **Work Experience Needed:** None. **On-the-Job Training Needed:** Long-term on-the-job training. **Certification/Licensure:** Voluntary certification by manufacturer.

Personality Type: Realistic-Conventional-Investigative. **Career Cluster:** 01 Agriculture, Food, and Natural Resources. **Career Pathway:** 01.4 Power Structure and Technical Systems. **Other Jobs in This Pathway:** Agricultural Sciences Teachers, Postsecondary; Mobile Heavy Equipment Mechanics, Except Engines.

Skills—Repairing: Repairing machines or systems using the needed tools. **Equipment Maintenance:** Performing routine maintenance on equipment and determining when and what kind of maintenance is needed. **Troubleshooting:** Determining causes of operating errors and deciding what to do about them. **Equipment Selection:** Determining the kind of tools and equipment needed to do a job. **Installation:** Installing equipment, machines, wiring, or programs to meet specifications. **Operation and Control:** Controlling operations of equipment or systems. **Quality Control Analysis:** Conducting tests and inspections of products, services, or processes to evaluate quality or performance. **Operation Monitoring:** Watching gauges, dials, or other indicators to make sure a machine is working properly.

Work Environment: Outdoors; standing; kneeling, crouching, stooping, or crawling; using hands; bending or twisting the body; noise; very hot or cold; bright or inadequate lighting; contaminants; cramped work space; hazardous conditions; hazardous equipment; minor burns, cuts, bites, or stings.

Farmers, Ranchers, and Other Agricultural Managers

- ⊙ Annual Earnings: $64,660
- ⊙ Earnings Growth Potential: High (50.5%)
- ⊙ Growth: –8.0%
- ⊙ Annual Job Openings: 23,450
- ⊙ Self-Employed: 78.9%

Considerations for Job Outlook: The continuing ability of the agricultural sector to produce more with fewer workers will cause some farmers to go out of business. As land, machinery, seed, and chemicals become more expensive, only well-capitalized farmers and corporations will be able to buy many of the farms that become available. These larger, more productive farms are better able to withstand the adverse effects of climate and price fluctuations on farm output and income. Still, several new programs in the Farm Bill, ones designed to help beginning farmers and ranchers acquire land and operating capital, may offset these market pressures. In contrast, agricultural managers should have more opportunities.

Plan, direct, or coordinate the management or operation of farms, ranches, greenhouses, aquacultural operations, nurseries, timber tracts, or other agricultural establishments. For task data, see Job Specializations.

Education/Training Required: High school diploma or equivalent. **Work Experience Needed:** More than 5 years. **On-the-Job Training Needed:** None. **Certification/Licensure:** Licensure in some states for some specializations.

Job Specialization: Aquacultural Managers

Direct and coordinate, through subordinate supervisory personnel, activities of workers engaged in fish hatchery production for corporations, cooperatives, or other owners. Grow fish and shellfish as cash crops or for release into freshwater or saltwater. Supervise and train aquaculture and fish hatchery support workers. Collect and record growth, production, and environmental data. Conduct and supervise stock examinations in order to identify diseases or parasites. Account for and disburse funds. Devise and participate in activities to improve fish hatching and growth rates, and to prevent disease in hatcheries. Monitor environments to ensure maintenance of optimum conditions for aquatic life. Direct and monitor trapping and spawning of fish, egg incubation, and fry rearing, applying knowledge of management and fish culturing techniques. Coordinate the selection and maintenance of brood stock. Direct and monitor the transfer of mature fish to lakes, ponds, streams, or commercial tanks. Determine, administer, and execute policies relating to operations administration and standards, and facility maintenance. Collect information regarding techniques for fish collection and fertilization, spawn incubation, and treatment of spawn and fry. Determine how to allocate resources and how to respond to unanticipated problems such as insect infestation, drought, and fire. Operate and maintain cultivating and harvesting equipment. Confer with biologists, fish pathologists, and other fishery personnel to obtain data concerning fish habits, diseases, food, and environmental requirements. Prepare reports required by state and federal laws. Identify environmental requirements of a particular species, and select and oversee the preparation of sites for species cultivation. Scuba dive in order to inspect sea farm operations. Design and construct pens, floating stations, and collector strings or fences for sea farms.

Education and Training Program: Aquaculture. **Knowledge/Courses—Food Production:** Techniques and equipment for planting, growing, and harvesting food products (both plant and animal) for consumption, including storage/handling techniques. **Biology:** Plant and animal organisms and their tissues, cells, functions, interdependencies, and interactions with each other and the environment. **Engineering and Technology:** The practical application of engineering science and technology. This includes applying principles, techniques, procedures, and equipment to the design and production of various goods and services. **Building and Construction:** Materials, methods, and the tools involved in the construction or repair of houses, buildings, or other structures such as highways and roads. **Chemistry:** The chemical composition, structure, and properties of substances and of the chemical processes and transformations that they undergo. This includes uses of chemicals and their danger signs, production techniques, and disposal methods. **Mechanical**

Devices: Machines and tools, including their designs, uses, repair, and maintenance.

Personality Type: Enterprising-Realistic-Conventional. **Career Cluster:** 01 Agriculture, Food, and Natural Resources. **Career Pathways:** 01.3 Animal Systems; 01.1 Food Products and Processing Systems; 01.2 Plant Systems. **Other Jobs in These Pathways:** Agricultural Inspectors; Agricultural Sciences Teachers, Postsecondary; Agricultural Technicians; Animal Breeders; Animal Scientists; Animal Trainers; Biochemists and Biophysicists; Biologists; Buyers and Purchasing Agents, Farm Products; Chemical Technicians; Economists; Environmental Economists; Farm and Home Management Advisors; First-Line Supervisors of Landscaping, Lawn Service, and Groundskeeping Workers; First-Line Supervisors of Office and Administrative Support Workers; First-Line Supervisors of Retail Sales Workers; Floral Designers; Food and Tobacco Roasting, Baking, and Drying Machine Operators and Tenders; Food Batchmakers; Food Cooking Machine Operators and Tenders; Food Science Technicians; Food Scientists and Technologists; Geneticists; Graders and Sorters, Agricultural Products; Grounds Maintenance Workers, All Other; Landscaping and Groundskeeping Workers; Nonfarm Animal Caretakers; Office Machine Operators, Except Computer; Pest Control Workers; others.

Skills—Science: Using scientific rules and methods to solve problems. **Management of Financial Resources:** Determining how money will be spent to get the work done and accounting for these expenditures. **Equipment Maintenance:** Performing routine maintenance on equipment and determining when and what kind of maintenance is needed. **Operations Analysis:** Analyzing needs and product requirements to create a design. **Repairing:** Repairing machines or systems using the needed tools. **Systems Analysis:** Determining how a system should work and how changes in conditions, operations, and the environment will affect outcomes. **Quality Control Analysis:** Conducting tests and inspections of products, services, or processes to evaluate quality or performance. **Management of Material Resources:** Obtaining and seeing to the appropriate use of equipment, facilities, and materials needed to do certain work.

Work Environment: More often outdoors than indoors; standing; using hands; noise; very hot or cold; contaminants.

Job Specialization: Farm and Ranch Managers

Plan, direct, or coordinate the management or operation of farms, ranches, greenhouses, aquacultural operations, nurseries, timber tracts, or other agricultural establishments. May hire, train, or supervise farm workers or contract for services to carry out the day-to-day activities of the managed operation. May engage in or supervise planting, cultivating, harvesting, financial, or marketing activities. Change processes such as drying, grading, storing, or shipping to improve efficiency or profitability. Determine types or quantities of crops or livestock to be raised, according to factors such as market conditions, federal programs or incentives, or soil conditions. Direct crop production operations such as planning, tilling, planting, fertilizing, cultivating, spraying, or harvesting. Direct the breeding or raising of stock, such as cattle, poultry, or honeybees, using recognized breeding practices to ensure stock improvement. Evaluate marketing or sales alternatives for farm or ranch products. Hire, train, or supervise workers engaged in planting, cultivating, irrigating, harvesting, or marketing crops, or in raising livestock. Inspect farm or ranch structures, such as buildings, fences, or roads, ordering repair or maintenance activities as needed. Maintain financial, operational, production, or employment records for farms or ranches. Monitor activities such as irrigation, chemical application, harvesting, milking, breeding, or grading to ensure adherence to safety regulations or standards. Monitor pasture or grazing land use to ensure that livestock are properly fed or that conservation methods, such as rotational grazing, are used. Negotiate with buyers for the sale, storage, or shipment of crops or livestock. Obtain financing necessary for purchases of machinery, land, supplies, or livestock. Operate or oversee the operations of dairy farms that produce bulk milk.

Education and Training Program: Farm/Farm and Ranch Management.

Personality Type: No data available. **Career Cluster:** 01 Agriculture, Food, and Natural Resources. **Career Pathways:** 01.3 Animal Systems; 01.2 Plant Systems. **Other Jobs in These Pathways:** Agricultural Sciences Teachers, Postsecondary; Agricultural Technicians; Animal Breeders; Animal Scientists; Animal Trainers; Biochemists and Biophysicists; Biologists; Economists; Environmental Economists; Farm and Home Management Advisors; First-Line Supervisors of Landscaping, Lawn Service, and Groundskeeping Workers; First-Line Supervisors of Retail Sales Workers; Floral Designers; Food Science Technicians; Food Scientists and Technologists; Geneticists; Grounds Maintenance Workers, All Other; Landscaping and Groundskeeping Workers; Nonfarm Animal Caretakers; Pesticide Handlers, Sprayers, and Applicators, Vegetation; Precision Agriculture Technicians; Retail Salespersons; Soil and Plant Scientists; Tree Trimmers and Pruners; Veterinarians.

Work Environment: No data available.

Job Specialization: Nursery and Greenhouse Managers

Plan, organize, direct, control, and coordinate activities of workers engaged in propagating, cultivating, and harvesting horticultural specialties such as trees, shrubs, flowers, mushrooms, and other plants. Manage nurseries that grow horticultural plants for sale to trade or retail customers, for display or exhibition, or for research. Identify plants as well as problems such as diseases, weeds, and insect pests. Tour work areas to observe work being done, to inspect crops, and to evaluate plant and soil conditions. Assign work schedules and duties to nursery or greenhouse staff, and supervise their work. Determine plant growing conditions, such as greenhouses, hydroponics, or natural settings, and set planting and care schedules. Apply pesticides and fertilizers to plants. Hire employees and train them in gardening techniques. Select and purchase seeds, plant nutrients, disease control chemicals, and garden and lawn care equipment. Determine types and quantities of horticultural plants to be grown, based on budgets, projected sales volumes, and/or executive directives. Explain and enforce safety regulations and policies. Position and regulate plant irrigation systems, and program environmental and irrigation control computers. Inspect facilities and equipment for signs of disrepair, and perform necessary maintenance work. Coordinate clerical, record-keeping, inventory, requisitioning, and marketing activities. Prepare soil for planting, and plant or transplant seeds, bulbs, and cuttings. Confer with horticultural personnel in order to plan facility renovations or additions. Cut and prune trees, shrubs, flowers, and plants.

Education and Training Programs: Greenhouse Operations and Management; Landscaping and Groundskeeping; Ornamental Horticulture; Plant Nursery Operations and Management. **Knowledge/Courses—Biology:** Plant and animal organisms and their tissues, cells, functions, interdependencies, and interactions with each other and the environment. **Production and Processing:** Raw materials, production processes, quality control, costs, and other techniques for maximizing the effective manufacture and distribution of goods. **Sales and Marketing:** Principles and methods for showing, promoting, and selling products or services. This includes marketing strategy and tactics, product demonstration, sales techniques, and sales control systems. **Chemistry:** The chemical composition, structure, and properties of substances and of the chemical processes and transformations that they undergo. This includes uses of chemicals and their danger signs, production techniques, and disposal methods. **Personnel and Human Resources:** Principles and procedures for personnel recruitment, selection, training, compensation and benefits, labor relations and negotiation, and personnel information systems. **Design:** Design techniques, tools, and principles involved in production of precision technical plans, blueprints, drawings, and models.

Personality Type: Enterprising-Realistic-Conventional. **Career Cluster:** 01 Agriculture, Food, and Natural Resources. **Career Pathway:** 01.2 Plant Systems. **Other Jobs in This Pathway:** Agricultural Sciences Teachers, Postsecondary; Agricultural Technicians; Animal Scientists; Biochemists and Biophysicists; Biologists; Economists; Environmental Economists; Farm and Home Management Advisors; First-Line Supervisors of Landscaping, Lawn Service, and Groundskeeping Workers; First-Line Supervisors of Retail Sales Workers; Floral Designers; Food Science Technicians; Food Scientists and Technologists; Geneticists; Grounds Maintenance Workers, All Other; Landscaping and Groundskeeping Workers; Pesticide Handlers, Sprayers, and Applicators, Vegetation; Precision Agriculture Technicians; Retail Salespersons; Soil and Plant Scientists; Tree Trimmers and Pruners.

Skills—Management of Material Resources: Obtaining and seeing to the appropriate use of equipment, facilities, and materials needed to do certain work. **Management of Financial Resources:** Determining how money will be spent to get the work done and accounting for these expenditures. **Science:** Using scientific rules and methods to solve problems. **Management of Personnel Resources:** Motivating, developing, and directing people as they work, identifying the best people for the job. **Instructing:**

Teaching others how to do something. **Negotiation:** Bringing others together and trying to reconcile differences. **Operation and Control:** Controlling operations of equipment or systems. **Persuasion:** Persuading others to change their minds or behavior.

Work Environment: More often outdoors than indoors; standing; walking and running; kneeling, crouching, stooping, or crawling; noise; very hot or cold; contaminants; hazardous conditions; minor burns, cuts, bites, or stings.

Fashion Designers

- ◉ Annual Earnings: $64,690
- ◉ Earnings Growth Potential: High (49.5%)
- ◉ Growth: 0.0%
- ◉ Annual Job Openings: 670
- ◉ Self-Employed: 29.9%

Considerations for Job Outlook: Strong competition for jobs is expected because of the large number of people who seek employment as fashion designers and the relatively few positions available. Those with formal education in fashion design, with excellent portfolios, and with industry experience will have the best job prospects. In addition, it may be necessary for some fashion designers to relocate. Employment opportunities for fashion designers are highly concentrated in New York and California. In May 2010, almost 75 percent of all salaried fashion designers worked in these two states.

Design clothing and accessories. Create original designs or adapt fashion trends. Examine sample garments on and off models; then modify designs to achieve desired effects. Determine prices for styles. Select materials and production techniques to be used for products. Draw patterns for articles designed; then cut patterns and cut material according to patterns, using measuring instruments and scissors. Design custom clothing and accessories for individuals; retailers; or theatrical, television, or film productions. Attend fashion shows and review garment magazines and manuals to gather information about fashion trends and consumer preferences. Develop a group of products and/or accessories, and market them through venues such as boutiques or mail-order catalogs. Test fabrics or oversee testing so that garment-care labels can be created.

Visit textile showrooms to keep up to date on the latest fabrics. Sew together sections of material to form mock-ups or samples of garments or articles, using sewing equipment. Research the styles and periods of clothing needed for film or theatrical productions. Direct and coordinate workers involved in drawing and cutting patterns and constructing samples or finished garments. Purchase new or used clothing and accessory items as needed to complete designs. Provide sample garments to agents and sales representatives, and arrange for showings of sample garments at sales meetings or fashion shows. Identify target markets for designs, looking at factors such as age, gender, and socioeconomic status.

Education/Training Required: High school diploma or equivalent. **Education and Training Programs:** Apparel and Textile Manufacture; Fashion and Fabric Consultant Training; Fashion/Apparel Design; Textile Science. **Knowledge/Courses—Fine Arts:** The theory and techniques required to compose, produce, and perform works of music, dance, visual arts, drama, and sculpture. **Design:** Design techniques, tools, and principles involved in production of precision technical plans, blueprints, drawings, and models. **Sales and Marketing:** Principles and methods for showing, promoting, and selling products or services. This includes marketing strategy and tactics, product demonstration, sales techniques, and sales control systems. **Production and Processing:** Raw materials, production processes, quality control, costs, and other techniques for maximizing the effective manufacture and distribution of goods. **Communications and Media:** Media production, communication, and dissemination techniques and methods. This includes alternative ways to inform and entertain via written, oral, and visual media. **Administration and Management:** Business and management principles involved in strategic planning, resource allocation, human resources modeling, leadership technique, production methods, and coordination of people and resources. **Work Experience Needed:** None. **On-the-Job Training Needed:** Long-term on-the-job training. **Certification/Licensure:** None.

Personality Type: Artistic-Enterprising-Realistic. **Career Clusters:** 03 Arts and Communications; 13 Manufacturing. **Career Pathways:** 03.3 Visual Arts; 13.2 Manufacturing Production Process Development. **Other Jobs in These Pathways:** Art Directors; Art, Drama, and Music Teachers, Postsecondary; Artists and Related Workers, All Other; Audio and Video Equipment Technicians; Biofuels Processing Technicians; Biomass Plant Technicians; Chemical Plant and System Operators; Chemical Technicians; Commercial and Industrial Designers; Craft Artists; Designers, All Other; Electrical Engineering Technicians; Electromechanical Equipment Assemblers; Environmental Science and Protection Technicians, Including Health; Fabric and Apparel Patternmakers; Farm and Home Management Advisors; Fine Artists, Including Painters, Sculptors, and Illustrators; Graphic Designers; Hydroelectric Plant Technicians; Interior Designers; Life, Physical, and Social Science Technicians, All Other; Methane/Landfill Gas Generation System Technicians; Multimedia Artists and Animators; Nuclear Monitoring Technicians; Painting, Coating, and Decorating Workers; Photographers; Quality Control Analysts; Set and Exhibit Designers; others.

Skills—Operations Analysis: Analyzing needs and product requirements to create a design. **Management of Financial Resources:** Determining how money will be spent to get the work done and accounting for these expenditures. **Management of Material Resources:** Obtaining and seeing to the appropriate use of equipment, facilities, and materials needed to do certain work. **Systems Evaluation:** Identifying measures or indicators of system performance and the actions needed to improve or correct performance relative to the goals of the system. **Time Management:** Managing one's own time and the time of others. **Negotiation:** Bringing others together and trying to reconcile differences. **Persuasion:** Persuading others to change their minds or behavior. **Social Perceptiveness:** Being aware of others' reactions and understanding why they react as they do.

Work Environment: Indoors; sitting; using hands; repetitive motions; noise; contaminants; cramped work space.

Fence Erectors

- Annual Earnings: $29,580
- Earnings Growth Potential: Low (34.2%)
- Growth: 23.7%
- Annual Job Openings: 1,640
- Self-Employed: 37.4%

Considerations for Job Outlook: Rapid employment growth is projected.

Erect and repair fences and fence gates, using hand and power tools. Mix and pour concrete around bases of posts, or tamp soil into postholes to embed posts. Measure and lay out fence lines and mark posthole positions, following instructions, drawings, or specifications. Stretch wire, wire mesh, or chain link fencing between posts, and attach fencing to frames. Insert metal tubing through rail supports. Blast rock formations and rocky areas with dynamite to facilitate posthole digging. Set metal or wooden posts in upright positions in postholes. Nail top and bottom rails to fence posts, or insert them in slots on posts. Discuss fencing needs with customers, and estimate and quote prices. Nail pointed slats to rails to construct picket fences. Align posts, using lines or by sighting, and verify vertical alignment of posts, using plumb bobs or spirit levels. Weld metal parts together, using portable gas welding equipment. Make rails for fences, by sawing lumber or by cutting metal tubing to required lengths. Establish the location for a fence, and gather information needed to ensure that there are no electric cables or water lines in the area. Erect alternate panel, basket weave, and louvered fences. Dig postholes, using spades, posthole diggers, or power-driven augers. Construct and repair barriers, retaining walls, trellises, and other types of fences, walls, and gates. Complete top fence rails of metal fences by connecting tube sections, using metal sleeves. Attach rails or tension wire along bottoms of posts to form fencing frames. Attach fence rail supports to posts, using hammers and pliers. Assemble gates, and fasten gates into position, using hand tools.

Education/Training Required: High school diploma or equivalent. **Education and Training Program:** Construction Trades, Other. **Knowledge/Courses—Building and Construction:** Materials, methods, and the tools involved in the construction or repair of houses, buildings, or other structures such as highways and roads. **Work Experience Needed:** None. **On-the-Job Training Needed:** Moderate-term on-the-job training. **Certification/Licensure:** None.

Personality Type: Realistic-Conventional. **Career Cluster:** 13 Manufacturing. **Career Pathway:** 13.3 Maintenance, Installation, and Repair. **Other Jobs in This Pathway:** Aircraft Mechanics and Service Technicians; Automotive Engineering Technicians; Automotive Specialty Technicians; Avionics Technicians; Biological Technicians; Camera and Photographic Equipment Repairers; Chemical Equipment Operators and Tenders; Civil Engineering Technicians; Coil Winders, Tapers, and Finishers; Computer, Automated Teller, and Office Machine Repairers; Construction and Related Workers, All Other; Control and Valve Installers and Repairers, Except Mechanical Door; Electric Motor, Power Tool, and Related Repairers; Electrical and Electronic Equipment Assemblers; Electrical and Electronics Repairers, Commercial and Industrial Equipment; Electrical and Electronics Repairers, Powerhouse, Substation, and Relay; Electrical Engineering Technicians; Electrical Engineering Technologists; Electromechanical Engineering Technologists; Electromechanical Equipment Assemblers; Electronics Engineering Technicians; Electronics Engineering Technologists; others.

Skills—Equipment Maintenance: Performing routine maintenance on equipment and determining when and what kind of maintenance is needed. **Equipment Selection:** Determining the kind of tools and equipment needed to do a job. **Repairing:** Repairing machines or systems using the needed tools. **Operation and Control:** Controlling operations of equipment or systems. **Troubleshooting:** Determining causes of operating errors and deciding what to do about them. **Quality Control Analysis:** Conducting tests and inspections of products, services, or processes to evaluate quality or performance. **Operation Monitoring:** Watching gauges, dials, or other indicators to make sure a machine is working properly. **Mathematics:** Using mathematics to solve problems.

Work Environment: Outdoors; standing; walking and running; kneeling, crouching, stooping, or crawling; using hands; bending or twisting the body; repetitive motions; noise; very hot or cold; contaminants; hazardous equipment; minor burns, cuts, bites, or stings.

Fine Artists, Including Painters, Sculptors, and Illustrators

- Annual Earnings: $44,600
- Earnings Growth Potential: Very high (57.1%)
- Growth: 7.8%
- Annual Job Openings: 810
- Self-Employed: 59.0%

Considerations for Job Outlook: Competition for jobs as craft and fine artists is expected to be strong because there are more qualified candidates than available jobs. Only the most successful craft and fine artists receive major commissions for their work. Despite the competition, studios, galleries, and individual clients are always on the lookout for artists who display outstanding talent, creativity, and style. Talented individuals who have developed a mastery of artistic techniques and skills will have the best job prospects. Competition among artists for the privilege of being shown in galleries is expected to remain intense, as is competition for grants from funders such as private foundations, state and local arts councils, and the National Endowment for the Arts. Because of their reliance on grants, and because the demand for artwork is dependent on consumers having extra income to spend, many of these artists will find that their income changes with the overall economy.

Create original artwork using any of a wide variety of media and techniques. Use materials such as pens and ink, watercolors, charcoal, oil, or computer software to create artwork. Integrate and develop visual elements, such as line, space, mass, color, and perspective, in order to produce desired effects such as the illustration of ideas, emotions, or moods. Confer with clients, editors, writers, art directors, and other interested parties regarding the nature and content of artwork to be produced. Submit preliminary or finished artwork or project plans to clients for approval, incorporating changes as necessary. Maintain portfolios of artistic work to demonstrate styles, interests, and abilities. Create finished art work as decoration, or to elucidate or substitute for spoken or written messages. Cut, bend, laminate, arrange, and fasten individual or mixed raw and manufactured materials and products to form works of art. Monitor events, trends, and other circumstances; research specific subject areas; attend art exhibitions; and read art publications in order to develop ideas and keep current on art world activities. Study different techniques to learn how to apply them to artistic endeavors. Render drawings, illustrations, and sketches of buildings, manufactured products, or models, working from sketches, blueprints, memory, models, or reference materials. Create sculptures, statues, and other three-dimensional artwork by using abrasives and tools to shape, carve, and fabricate materials such as clay, stone, wood, or metal. Create sketches, profiles, or likenesses of posed subjects or photographs, using any combination of freehand drawing, mechanical assembly kits, and computer imaging.

Study styles, techniques, colors, textures, and materials used in works undergoing restoration to ensure consistency during the restoration process. Develop project budgets for approval, estimating time lines and material costs.

Education/Training Required: High school diploma or equivalent. **Education and Training Programs:** Art/Art Studies, General; Ceramic Arts and Ceramics; Drawing; Fine Arts and Art Studies, Other; Fine/Studio Arts, General; Intermedia/Multimedia; Medical Illustration/Medical Illustrator; Painting; Printmaking; Sculpture; Visual and Performing Arts, General. **Knowledge/Courses—Fine Arts:** The theory and techniques required to compose, produce, and perform works of music, dance, visual arts, drama, and sculpture. **Design:** Design techniques, tools, and principles involved in production of precision technical plans, blueprints, drawings, and models. **Sales and Marketing:** Principles and methods for showing, promoting, and selling products or services. This includes marketing strategy and tactics, product demonstration, sales techniques, and sales control systems. **Production and Processing:** Raw materials, production processes, quality control, costs, and other techniques for maximizing the effective manufacture and distribution of goods. **Economics and Accounting:** Economic and accounting principles and practices, the financial markets, banking, and the analysis and reporting of financial data. **Communications and Media:** Media production, communication, and dissemination techniques and methods. This includes alternative ways to inform and entertain via written, oral, and visual media. **Work Experience Needed:** None. **On-the-Job Training Needed:** Long-term on-the-job training. **Certification/Licensure:** None.

Personality Type: Artistic-Realistic. **Career Clusters:** 03 Arts and Communications; 08 Health Science. **Career Pathways:** 03.1 Audio and Video Technology and Film; 03.2 Printing Technology; 03.3 Visual Arts; 08.3 Health Informatics. **Other Jobs in These Pathways:** Agents and Business Managers of Artists, Performers, and Athletes; Archivists; Art Directors; Art, Drama, and Music Teachers, Postsecondary; Artists and Related Workers, All Other; Audio and Video Equipment Technicians; Broadcast Technicians; Camera Operators, Television, Video, and Motion Picture; Choreographers; Clinical Psychologists; Commercial and Industrial Designers; Communications Teachers, Postsecondary; Craft Artists; Curators; Dancers; Data Entry Keyers; Dental Laboratory Technicians; Designers,

All Other; Desktop Publishers; Editors; Engineers, All Other; Etchers and Engravers; Executive Secretaries and Executive Administrative Assistants; Fashion Designers; Film and Video Editors; First-Line Supervisors of Office and Administrative Support Workers; Graphic Designers; Health Educators; Health Specialties Teachers, Postsecondary; Historians; Interior Designers; Managers, All Other; Media and Communication Equipment Workers, All Other; others.

Skills—Management of Financial Resources: Determining how money will be spent to get the work done and accounting for these expenditures. **Technology Design:** Generating or adapting equipment and technology to serve user needs. **Operations Analysis:** Analyzing needs and product requirements to create a design. **Equipment Selection:** Determining the kind of tools and equipment needed to do a job. **Management of Material Resources:** Obtaining and seeing to the appropriate use of equipment, facilities, and materials needed to do certain work. **Quality Control Analysis:** Conducting tests and inspections of products, services, or processes to evaluate quality or performance. **Operation and Control:** Controlling operations of equipment or systems. **Active Learning:** Understanding the implications of new information for both current and future problem solving and decision making.

Work Environment: Indoors; standing; using hands; repetitive motions; contaminants.

Fire Inspectors and Investigators

- ⊙ Annual Earnings: $53,330
- ⊙ Earnings Growth Potential: Medium (35.2%)
- ⊙ Growth: 8.8%
- ⊙ Annual Job Openings: 470
- ⊙ Self-Employed: 1.5%

Considerations for Job Outlook: Job seekers should expect limited opportunities due to competition for limited positions. Those who have experience in fire suppression, have completed some fire suppression education at a community college, or have experience and training related to criminal investigation should have an advantage.

Inspect buildings to detect fire hazards and enforce local ordinances and state laws, or investigate and gather facts to determine cause of fires and explosions. For task data, see Job Specializations.

Education/Training Required: High school diploma or equivalent. **Work Experience Needed:** More than 5 years. **On-the-Job Training Needed:** Moderate-term on-the-job training. **Certification/Licensure:** Licensure.

Job Specialization: Fire Inspectors

Inspect buildings and equipment to detect fire hazards and enforce state and local regulations. Inspect buildings to locate hazardous conditions and fire code violations such as accumulations of combustible material, electrical wiring problems, and inadequate or nonfunctional fire exits. Present and explain fire code requirements and fire prevention information to architects, contractors, attorneys, engineers, developers, fire service personnel, and the general public. Identify corrective actions necessary to bring properties into compliance with applicable fire codes, laws, regulations, and standards, and explain these measures to property owners or their representatives. Attend training classes to maintain current knowledge of fire prevention, safety, and firefighting procedures. Conduct fire code compliance follow-ups to ensure that corrective actions have been taken in cases where violations were found. Write detailed reports of fire inspections performed, fire code violations observed, and corrective recommendations offered. Inspect properties that store, handle, and use hazardous materials to ensure compliance with laws, codes, and regulations, and issue hazardous materials permits to facilities found in compliance. Develop or review fire exit plans. Inspect and test fire protection or fire detection systems to verify that such systems are installed in accordance with appropriate laws, codes, ordinances, regulations, and standards. Conduct inspections and acceptance testing of newly installed fire protection systems. Review blueprints and plans for new or remodeled buildings to ensure the structures meet fire safety codes. Inspect liquefied petroleum installations, storage containers, and transportation and delivery systems for compliance with fire laws. Develop and coordinate fire prevention programs such as false alarm billing, fire inspection reporting, and hazardous materials management. Conduct fire exit drills to monitor and evaluate evacuation procedures. Teach public education programs on fire safety and prevention.

Education and Training Programs: Fire Prevention and Safety Technology/Technician; Fire Science/Firefighting. **Knowledge/Courses—Building and Construction:** Materials, methods, and the tools involved in the construction or repair of houses, buildings, or other structures such as highways and roads. **Public Safety and Security:** Relevant equipment, policies, procedures, and strategies to promote effective local, state, or national security operations for the protection of people, data, property, and institutions. **Chemistry:** The chemical composition, structure, and properties of substances and of the chemical processes and transformations that they undergo. This includes uses of chemicals and their danger signs, production techniques, and disposal methods. **Law and Government:** Laws, legal codes, court procedures, precedents, government regulations, executive orders, agency rules, and the democratic political process. **Physics:** Physical principles, laws, their interrelationships, and applications to understanding fluid, material, and atmospheric dynamics, and mechanical, electrical, atomic, and subatomic structures and processes. **Customer and Personal Service:** Principles and processes for providing customer and personal services. This includes customer needs assessment, meeting quality standards for services, and evaluation of customer satisfaction.

Personality Type: Conventional-Realistic. **Career Cluster:** 12 Law, Public Safety, Corrections, and Security. **Career Pathway:** 12.2 Emergency and Fire Management Services. **Other Jobs in This Pathway:** Correctional Officers and Jailers; Fire Investigators; Forest Fire Fighting and Prevention Supervisors; Forest Fire Inspectors and Prevention Specialists; Forest Firefighters; Municipal Fire Fighting and Prevention Supervisors; Municipal Firefighters.

Skills—Quality Control Analysis: Conducting tests and inspections of products, services, or processes to evaluate quality or performance. **Science:** Using scientific rules and methods to solve problems. **Operation Monitoring:** Watching gauges, dials, or other indicators to make sure a machine is working properly. **Troubleshooting:** Determining causes of operating errors and deciding what to do about them. **Systems Evaluation:** Identifying measures or indicators of system performance and the actions needed to improve or correct performance relative to the goals of the system. **Operation and Control:** Controlling operations of equipment or systems. **Systems Analysis:** Determining how a system should work and how changes in conditions, operations, and the environment will affect

outcomes. **Operations Analysis:** Analyzing needs and product requirements to create a design.

Work Environment: More often outdoors than indoors; more often sitting than standing; noise; very hot or cold; bright or inadequate lighting; contaminants.

Job Specialization: Fire Investigators

Conduct investigations to determine causes of fires and explosions. Package collected pieces of evidence in securely closed containers such as bags, crates, or boxes, to protect them. Examine fire sites and collect evidence such as glass, metal fragments, charred wood, and accelerant residue for use in determining the causes of fires. Instruct children about the dangers of fire. Analyze evidence and other information to determine probable causes of fires or explosions. Photograph damage and evidence related to causes of fires or explosions to document investigation findings. Subpoena and interview witnesses, property owners, and building occupants to obtain information and sworn testimony. Swear out warrants, and arrest and process suspected arsonists. Testify in court cases involving fires, suspected arson, and false alarms. Prepare and maintain reports of investigation results and records of convicted arsonists and arson suspects. Test sites and materials to establish facts, such as burn patterns and flash points of materials, using test equipment.

Education and Training Programs: Fire Prevention and Safety Technology/Technician; Fire Science/Firefighting. **Knowledge/Courses—Public Safety and Security:** Relevant equipment, policies, procedures, and strategies to promote effective local, state, or national security operations for the protection of people, data, property, and institutions. **Law and Government:** Laws, legal codes, court procedures, precedents, government regulations, executive orders, agency rules, and the democratic political process. **Chemistry:** The chemical composition, structure, and properties of substances and of the chemical processes and transformations that they undergo. This includes uses of chemicals and their danger signs, production techniques, and disposal methods. **Psychology:** Human behavior and performance; individual differences in ability, personality, and interests; learning and motivation; psychological research methods; and the assessment and treatment of behavioral and affective disorders. **Building and Construction:** Materials, methods, and the tools involved in the construction or repair of houses, buildings, or other structures such as highways and roads. **Customer and Personal Service:** Principles and processes for providing customer and personal services. This includes customer needs assessment, meeting quality standards for services, and evaluation of customer satisfaction.

Personality Type: Investigative-Realistic-Conventional. **Career Cluster:** 12 Law, Public Safety, Corrections, and Security. **Career Pathway:** 12.2 Emergency and Fire Management Services. **Other Jobs in This Pathway:** Correctional Officers and Jailers; Fire Inspectors; Forest Fire Fighting and Prevention Supervisors; Forest Fire Inspectors and Prevention Specialists; Forest Firefighters; Municipal Fire Fighting and Prevention Supervisors; Municipal Firefighters.

Skills—Science: Using scientific rules and methods to solve problems. **Active Listening:** Giving full attention to what other people are saying, taking time to understand the points being made, asking questions as appropriate, and not interrupting at inappropriate times. **Speaking:** Talking to others to convey information effectively. **Troubleshooting:** Determining causes of operating errors and deciding what to do about them. **Critical Thinking:** Using logic and reasoning to identify the strengths and weaknesses of alternative solutions, conclusions, or approaches to problems. **Mathematics:** Using mathematics to solve problems. **Writing:** Communicating effectively in writing as appropriate for the needs of the audience. **Learning Strategies:** Selecting and using training/instructional methods and procedures appropriate for the situation when learning or teaching new things.

Work Environment: More often outdoors than indoors; standing; using hands; noise; very hot or cold; bright or inadequate lighting; contaminants; cramped work space; hazardous conditions; hazardous equipment.

Firefighters

- ⊙ Annual Earnings: $45,420
- ⊙ Earnings Growth Potential: High (50.5%)
- ⊙ Growth: 8.6%
- ⊙ Annual Job Openings: 11,230
- ⊙ Self-Employed: 0.0%

Considerations for Job Outlook: Prospective firefighters will face tough competition for positions. Many people are attracted to the job's challenge, opportunity for public service, relatively low formal educational requirements, and pensions that are usually guaranteed after 25 years of service. As a result, a department often receives hundreds or thousands of applicants for a single position. Physically fit applicants with high test scores, some postsecondary firefighter education, and paramedic training have the best prospects.

Control and extinguish fires or respond to emergency situations where life, property, or the environment is at risk. For task data, see Job Specializations.

Education/Training Required: Postsecondary vocational training. **Work Experience Needed:** None. **On-the-Job Training Needed:** Long-term on-the-job training. **Certification/Licensure:** Licensure in some states; certification by association; municipal examination.

Job Specialization: Forest Firefighters

Control and suppress fires in forests or vacant public land. Maintain contact with fire dispatchers at all times to notify them of the need for additional firefighters and supplies or to detail any difficulties encountered. Rescue fire victims, and administer emergency medical aid. Collaborate with other firefighters as a member of a firefighting crew. Patrol burned areas after fires to locate and eliminate hot spots that may restart fires. Extinguish flames and embers to suppress fires using shovels or engine- or hand-driven water or chemical pumps. Fell trees, cut and clear brush, and dig trenches to create firelines using axes, chain saws, or shovels. Maintain knowledge of current firefighting practices by participating in drills and by attending seminars, conventions, and conferences. Operate pumps connected to high-pressure hoses. Participate in physical training to maintain high levels of physical fitness. Establish water supplies, connect hoses, and direct water onto fires. Maintain fire equipment and firehouse living quarters. Inform and educate the public about fire prevention. Take action to contain any hazardous chemicals that could catch fire, leak, or spill. Organize fire caches, positioning equipment for the most effective response. Transport personnel and cargo to and from fire areas. Participate in fire-prevention and inspection programs. Perform forest-maintenance and improvement tasks such as cutting brush, planting trees, building trails, and marking timber.

Education and Training Programs: Fire Protection, Other; Fire Science/Firefighting. **Knowledge/Courses—Geography:** Principles and methods for describing the features of land, sea, and air masses, including their physical characteristics, locations, interrelationships, and distribution of plant, animal, and human life. **Building and Construction:** Materials, methods, and the tools involved in the construction or repair of houses, buildings, or other structures such as highways and roads. **Telecommunications:** Transmission, broadcasting, switching, control, and operation of telecommunications systems. **Mechanical Devices:** Machines and tools, including their designs, uses, repair, and maintenance. **Public Safety and Security:** Relevant equipment, policies, procedures, and strategies to promote effective local, state, or national security operations for the protection of people, data, property, and institutions. **Customer and Personal Service:** Principles and processes for providing customer and personal services. This includes customer needs assessment, meeting quality standards for services, and evaluation of customer satisfaction.

Personality Type: Realistic-Social. **Career Cluster:** 12 Law, Public Safety, Corrections, and Security. **Career Pathways:** 12.3 Security and Protective Services; 12.2 Emergency and Fire Management Services. **Other Jobs in These Pathways:** Animal Control Workers; Correctional Officers and Jailers; Criminal Justice and Law Enforcement Teachers, Postsecondary; Crossing Guards; Fire Inspectors; Fire Investigators; First-Line Supervisors of Protective Service Workers, All Other; Forest Fire Fighting and Prevention Supervisors; Forest Fire Inspectors and Prevention Specialists; Gaming Surveillance Officers and Gaming Investigators; Lifeguards, Ski Patrol, and Other Recreational Protective Service Workers; Municipal Fire Fighting and Prevention Supervisors; Municipal Firefighters; Parking Enforcement Workers; Police, Fire, and Ambulance Dispatchers; Private Detectives and Investigators; Retail Loss Prevention Specialists; Security Guards; Sheriffs and Deputy Sheriffs; Transit and Railroad Police.

Skills—Repairing: Repairing machines or systems using the needed tools. **Equipment Maintenance:** Performing routine maintenance on equipment and determining when and what kind of maintenance is needed. **Equipment Selection:** Determining the kind of tools and equipment needed to do a job. **Operation and Control:** Controlling operations of equipment or systems. **Troubleshooting:** Determining causes of operating errors and deciding what to do about them. **Quality Control Analysis:** Conducting tests and inspections of products, services, or processes to evaluate quality or performance. **Operation Monitoring:** Watching gauges, dials, or other indicators to make sure a machine is working properly. **Coordination:** Adjusting actions in relation to others' actions.

Work Environment: Outdoors; standing; walking and running; using hands; bending or twisting the body; repetitive motions; noise; very hot or cold; bright or inadequate lighting; contaminants; hazardous conditions; hazardous equipment; minor burns, cuts, bites, or stings.

Job Specialization: Municipal Firefighters

Control and extinguish municipal fires, protect life and property, and conduct rescue efforts. Administer first aid and cardiopulmonary resuscitation to injured persons. Rescue victims from burning buildings and accident sites. Search burning buildings to locate fire victims. Drive and operate firefighting vehicles and equipment. Move toward the source of a fire, using knowledge of types of fires, construction design, building materials, and physical layout of properties. Dress with equipment such as fire-resistant clothing and breathing apparatus. Position and climb ladders to gain access to upper levels of buildings or to rescue individuals from burning structures. Take action to contain hazardous chemicals that might catch fire, leak, or spill. Assess fires and situations, and report conditions to superiors to receive instructions using two-way radios. Respond to fire alarms and other calls for assistance, such as automobile and industrial accidents. Operate pumps connected to high-pressure hoses. Select and attach hose nozzles, depending on fire type, and direct streams of water or chemicals onto fires. Create openings in buildings for ventilation or entrance, using axes, chisels, crowbars, electric saws, or core cutters. Inspect fire sites after flames have been extinguished to ensure that there is no further danger. Lay hose lines, and connect them to water supplies. Protect property from water and smoke using waterproof salvage covers, smoke ejectors, and deodorants. Participate in physical training activities to maintain a high level of physical fitness.

Education and Training Programs: Fire Protection, Other; Fire Science/Firefighting. **Knowledge/Courses—Building and Construction:** Materials, methods, and the tools involved in the construction or repair of houses, buildings, or other structures such as highways and roads. **Public Safety and Security:** Relevant equipment, policies, procedures, and strategies to promote effective local, state, or national security operations for the protection of people, data, property, and institutions. **Mechanical Devices:** Machines and tools, including their designs, uses, repair, and maintenance. **Customer and Personal Service:** Principles and processes for providing customer and personal services. This includes customer needs assessment, meeting quality standards for services, and evaluation of customer satisfaction. **Physics:** Physical principles, laws, their interrelationships, and applications to understanding fluid, material, and atmospheric dynamics, and mechanical, electrical, atomic, and subatomic structures and processes. **Geography:** Principles and methods for describing the features of land, sea, and air masses, including their physical characteristics, locations, interrelationships, and distribution of plant, animal, and human life.

Personality Type: Realistic-Social-Enterprising. **Career Cluster:** 12 Law, Public Safety, Corrections, and Security. **Career Pathway:** 12.2 Emergency and Fire Management Services. **Other Jobs in This Pathway:** Correctional Officers and Jailers; Fire Inspectors; Fire Investigators; Forest Fire Fighting and Prevention Supervisors; Forest Fire Inspectors and Prevention Specialists; Forest Firefighters; Municipal Fire Fighting and Prevention Supervisors.

Skills—Equipment Maintenance: Performing routine maintenance on equipment and determining when and what kind of maintenance is needed. **Repairing:** Repairing machines or systems using the needed tools. **Troubleshooting:** Determining causes of operating errors and deciding what to do about them. **Operation and Control:** Controlling operations of equipment or systems. **Equipment Selection:** Determining the kind of tools and equipment needed to do a job. **Science:** Using scientific rules and methods to solve problems. **Operation Monitoring:** Watching gauges, dials, or other indicators to make sure a machine is working properly. **Quality Control Analysis:** Conducting tests and inspections of products, services, or processes to evaluate quality or performance.

Work Environment: More often outdoors than indoors; standing; using hands; noise; very hot or cold; bright or inadequate lighting; contaminants; cramped work space; exposed to disease or infections; hazardous conditions; hazardous equipment; minor burns, cuts, bites, or stings.

First-Line Supervisors of Correctional Officers

- ⊙ Annual Earnings: $55,030
- ⊙ Earnings Growth Potential: Low (32.1%)
- ⊙ Growth: 5.5%
- ⊙ Annual Job Openings: 1,650
- ⊙ Self-Employed: 0.0%

Considerations for Job Outlook: Slower-than-average employment growth is expected as slow growth of prisons reduces the ratio of corrections managers.

Directly supervise and coordinate activities of correctional officers and jailers. Take, receive, and check periodic inmate counts. Maintain order, discipline, and security within assigned areas in accordance with relevant rules, regulations, policies, and laws. Respond to emergencies such as escapes. Maintain knowledge of, comply with, and enforce all institutional policies, rules, procedures, and regulations. Supervise and direct the work of correctional officers to ensure the safe custody, discipline, and welfare of inmates. Restrain, secure, and control offenders, using chemical agents, firearms, and other weapons of force as necessary. Supervise and perform searches of inmates and their quarters to locate contraband items. Monitor behavior of subordinates to ensure alert, courteous, and professional behavior toward inmates, parolees, fellow employees, visitors, and the public. Complete administrative paperwork, and supervise the preparation and maintenance of records, forms, and reports. Instruct employees, and provide on-the-job training. Supervise activities such as searches, shakedowns, riot control, and institutional tours. Conduct roll calls of correctional officers. Carry injured offenders or employees to safety, and provide emergency first aid when necessary. Supervise and provide security for offenders performing tasks such as construction, maintenance, laundry, food service, and other industrial or agricultural operations. Develop work and security procedures. Set up employee work schedules. Resolve problems between inmates. Read and review offender information to identify issues that require special attention. Rate behavior of inmates, promoting acceptable attitudes and behaviors to those with low ratings. Transfer and transport offenders on foot, or by driving vehicles such as trailers, vans, and buses. Examine incoming and outgoing mail to ensure conformance with regulations. Convey correctional officers' and inmates' complaints to superiors.

Education/Training Required: High school diploma or equivalent. **Education and Training Programs:** Corrections; Corrections Administration. **Knowledge/Courses—Public Safety and Security:** Relevant equipment, policies, procedures, and strategies to promote effective local, state, or national security operations for the protection of people, data, property, and institutions. **Psychology:** Human behavior and performance; individual differences in ability, personality, and interests; learning and motivation; psychological research methods; and the assessment and treatment of behavioral and affective disorders. **Therapy and Counseling:** Principles, methods, and procedures for diagnosis, treatment, and rehabilitation of physical and mental dysfunctions, and for career counseling and guidance. **Personnel and Human Resources:** Principles and procedures for personnel recruitment, selection, training, compensation and benefits, labor relations and negotiation, and personnel information systems. **Clerical Practices:** Administrative and clerical procedures and systems such as word processing, managing files and records, stenography and transcription, designing forms, and other office procedures and terminology. **Law and Government:** Laws, legal codes, court procedures, precedents, government regulations, executive orders, agency rules, and the democratic political process. **Work Experience Needed:** 1 to 5 years. **On-the-Job Training Needed:** Moderate-term on-the-job training. **Certification/Licensure:** None.

Personality Type: Enterprising-Conventional-Realistic. **Career Cluster:** 12 Law, Public Safety, Corrections, and Security. **Career Pathway:** 12.1 Correction Services. **Other Jobs in This Pathway:** Child, Family, and School Social Workers; Criminal Justice and Law Enforcement Teachers, Postsecondary; First-Line Supervisors of Police and Detectives; Protective Service Workers, All Other; Psychology Teachers, Postsecondary; Security Guards.

Skills—Management of Personnel Resources: Motivating, developing, and directing people as they work, identifying the best people for the job. **Negotiation:** Bringing others together and trying to reconcile differences.

Persuasion: Persuading others to change their minds or behavior. **Time Management:** Managing one's own time and the time of others. **Social Perceptiveness:** Being aware of others' reactions and understanding why they react as they do. **Coordination:** Adjusting actions in relation to others' actions. **Learning Strategies:** Selecting and using training/instructional methods and procedures appropriate for the situation when learning or teaching new things. **Systems Evaluation:** Identifying measures or indicators of system performance and the actions needed to improve or correct performance relative to the goals of the system.

Work Environment: More often indoors than outdoors; more often sitting than standing; walking and running; using hands; noise; very hot or cold; bright or inadequate lighting; contaminants; exposed to disease or infections.

First-Line Supervisors of Farming, Fishing, and Forestry Workers

- ⊚ Annual Earnings: $42,600
- ⊚ Earnings Growth Potential: High (43.0%)
- ⊚ Growth: –1.5%
- ⊚ Annual Job Openings: 1,360
- ⊚ Self-Employed: 16.3%

Considerations for Job Outlook: Slow decline in employment is projected.

Directly supervise and coordinate the activities of agricultural, forestry, aquacultural, and related workers. For task data, see Job Specializations.

Education/Training Required: High school diploma or equivalent. **Work Experience Needed:** 1 to 5 years. **On-the-Job Training Needed:** None. **Certification/Licensure:** None.

Job Specialization: First-Line Supervisors of Logging Workers

Directly supervise and coordinate activities of logging workers. Monitor workers to ensure that safety regulations are followed, warning or disciplining those who violate safety regulations. Plan and schedule logging operations such as felling and bucking trees and grading, sorting, yarding, or loading logs. Change logging operations or methods to eliminate unsafe conditions. Monitor logging operations to identify and solve problems; improve work methods; and ensure compliance with safety, company, and government regulations. Train workers in tree felling and bucking, operation of tractors and loading machines, yarding and loading techniques, and safety regulations. Determine logging operation methods, crew sizes, and equipment requirements, conferring with mill, company, and forestry officials as necessary. Assign to workers duties such as trees to be cut; cutting sequences and specifications; and loading of trucks, railcars, or rafts. Supervise and coordinate the activities of workers engaged in logging operations and silvicultural operations.

Education and Training Programs: Agricultural Animal Breeding; Agricultural Business and Management, Other; Agricultural Production Operations, General; Agricultural Production Operations, Other; Agriculture, Agriculture Operations, and Related Sciences, Other; Animal Nutrition; Animal/Livestock Husbandry and Production; Aquaculture; Crop Production; Dairy Husbandry and Production; Dairy Science; Farm/Farm and Ranch Management; Fishing and Fisheries Sciences and Management; Horse Husbandry/Equine Science and Management; Livestock Management; Plant Sciences, General; Poultry Science; Range Science and Management. **Knowledge/Courses— Mechanical Devices:** Machines and tools, including their designs, uses, repair, and maintenance. **Production and Processing:** Raw materials, production processes, quality control, costs, and other techniques for maximizing the effective manufacture and distribution of goods. **Economics and Accounting:** Economic and accounting principles and practices, the financial markets, banking, and the analysis and reporting of financial data. **Administration and Management:** Business and management principles involved in strategic planning, resource allocation, human resources modeling, leadership technique, production methods, and coordination of people and resources. **Building and Construction:** Materials, methods, and the tools involved in the construction or repair of houses, buildings, or other structures such as highways and roads. **Transportation:** Principles and methods for moving people or goods by air, rail, sea, or road, including the relative costs and benefits.

Personality Type: Enterprising-Realistic-Conventional. **Career Cluster:** 01 Agriculture, Food, and Natural Resources. **Career Pathways:** 01.2 Plant Systems; 01.1 Food Products and Processing Systems. **Other Jobs in These Pathways:** Agricultural Inspectors; Agricultural

Sciences Teachers, Postsecondary; Agricultural Technicians; Animal Scientists; Biochemists and Biophysicists; Biologists; Buyers and Purchasing Agents, Farm Products; Chemical Technicians; Economists; Environmental Economists; Farm and Home Management Advisors; First-Line Supervisors of Landscaping, Lawn Service, and Groundskeeping Workers; First-Line Supervisors of Office and Administrative Support Workers; First-Line Supervisors of Retail Sales Workers; Floral Designers; Food and Tobacco Roasting, Baking, and Drying Machine Operators and Tenders; Food Batchmakers; Food Cooking Machine Operators and Tenders; Food Science Technicians; Food Scientists and Technologists; Geneticists; Graders and Sorters, Agricultural Products; Grounds Maintenance Workers, All Other; Landscaping and Groundskeeping Workers; Nonfarm Animal Caretakers; Office Machine Operators, Except Computer; Pest Control Workers; others.

Skills—Operation and Control: Controlling operations of equipment or systems. **Equipment Selection:** Determining the kind of tools and equipment needed to do a job. **Repairing:** Repairing machines or systems using the needed tools. **Equipment Maintenance:** Performing routine maintenance on equipment and determining when and what kind of maintenance is needed. **Management of Material Resources:** Obtaining and seeing to the appropriate use of equipment, facilities, and materials needed to do certain work. **Operation Monitoring:** Watching gauges, dials, or other indicators to make sure a machine is working properly. **Troubleshooting:** Determining causes of operating errors and deciding what to do about them. **Management of Personnel Resources:** Motivating, developing, and directing people as they work, identifying the best people for the job.

Work Environment: Outdoors; sitting; using hands; noise; very hot or cold; contaminants; hazardous equipment; minor burns, cuts, bites, or stings.

Job Specialization: First-Line Supervisors of Animal Husbandry and Animal Care Workers

Directly supervise and coordinate activities of animal husbandry or animal care workers. Study feed, weight, health, genetic, or milk production records in order to determine feed formulas and rations and breeding schedules. Inspect buildings, fences, fields or ranges, supplies, and equipment in order to determine work to be performed. Monitor animal care, maintenance, or breeding; or packing and transfer activities to ensure work is done correctly. Train workers in animal care procedures, maintenance duties, and safety precautions. Perform the same animal care duties as subordinates. Observe animals for signs of illness, injury, or unusual behavior; notifying veterinarians or managers as warranted. Plan budgets and arrange for purchase of animals, feed, or supplies. Direct and assist workers in maintenance and repair of facilities. Recruit, hire, and pay workers. Confer with managers to determine production requirements, conditions of equipment and supplies, and work schedules. Transport or arrange for transport of animals, equipment, food, animal feed, and other supplies to and from worksites. Treat animal illnesses or injuries, following experience or instructions of veterinarians. Inseminate livestock artificially to produce desired offspring. Investigate complaints of animal neglect or cruelty, and follow up on complaints appearing to require prosecution. Monitor eggs and adjust incubator thermometers and gauges to facilitate hatching progress and to maintain specified conditions. Operate euthanasia equipment to destroy animals. Prepare reports concerning facility activities, employees' time records, and animal treatment. Assign tasks such as feeding and treatment of animals, and cleaning and maintenance of animal quarters. Establish work schedules and procedures.

Education and Training Programs: Agricultural Animal Breeding; Agricultural Business and Management, Other; Agricultural Production Operations, General; Agricultural Production Operations, Other; Agriculture, Agriculture Operations, and Related Sciences, Other; Animal Nutrition; Animal/Livestock Husbandry and Production; Aquaculture; Crop Production; Dairy Husbandry and Production; Dairy Science; Farm/Farm and Ranch Management; Fishing and Fisheries Sciences and Management; Horse Husbandry/Equine Science and Management; Livestock Management; Plant Sciences, General; Poultry Science; Range Science and Management. **Knowledge/Courses—Food Production:** Techniques and equipment for planting, growing, and harvesting food products (both plant and animal) for consumption, including storage/handling techniques. **Biology:** Plant and animal organisms and their tissues, cells, functions, interdependencies, and interactions with each other and the environment. **Chemistry:** The chemical composition, structure, and properties of substances and of the chemical processes

and transformations that they undergo. This includes uses of chemicals and their danger signs, production techniques, and disposal methods. **Mechanical Devices:** Machines and tools, including their designs, uses, repair, and maintenance. **Transportation:** Principles and methods for moving people or goods by air, rail, sea, or road, including the relative costs and benefits. **Personnel and Human Resources:** Principles and procedures for personnel recruitment, selection, training, compensation and benefits, labor relations and negotiation, and personnel information systems.

Personality Type: Enterprising-Realistic. **Career Cluster:** 01 Agriculture, Food, and Natural Resources. **Career Pathways:** 01.1 Food Products and Processing Systems; 01.3 Animal Systems. **Other Jobs in These Pathways:** Agricultural Inspectors; Agricultural Sciences Teachers, Postsecondary; Agricultural Technicians; Animal Breeders; Animal Scientists; Animal Trainers; Biologists; Buyers and Purchasing Agents, Farm Products; Chemical Technicians; Farm and Home Management Advisors; First-Line Supervisors of Office and Administrative Support Workers; Food and Tobacco Roasting, Baking, and Drying Machine Operators and Tenders; Food Batchmakers; Food Cooking Machine Operators and Tenders; Food Science Technicians; Food Scientists and Technologists; Geneticists; Graders and Sorters, Agricultural Products; Nonfarm Animal Caretakers; Office Machine Operators, Except Computer; Pest Control Workers; Precision Agriculture Technicians; Veterinarians.

Skills—Management of Financial Resources: Determining how money will be spent to get the work done and accounting for these expenditures. **Management of Material Resources:** Obtaining and seeing to the appropriate use of equipment, facilities, and materials needed to do certain work. **Science:** Using scientific rules and methods to solve problems. **Equipment Selection:** Determining the kind of tools and equipment needed to do a job. **Repairing:** Repairing machines or systems using the needed tools. **Equipment Maintenance:** Performing routine maintenance on equipment and determining when and what kind of maintenance is needed. **Management of Personnel Resources:** Motivating, developing, and directing people as they work, identifying the best people for the job. **Quality Control Analysis:** Conducting tests and inspections of products, services, or processes to evaluate quality or performance.

Work Environment: Outdoors; standing; walking and running; using hands; noise; very hot or cold; contaminants; hazardous conditions; hazardous equipment; minor burns, cuts, bites, or stings.

Job Specialization: First-Line Supervisors of Aquacultural Workers

Directly supervise and coordinate activities of aquacultural workers. Engage in the same fishery work as workers supervised. Requisition supplies. Assign to workers duties such as fertilizing and incubating spawn; feeding and transferring fish; and planting, cultivating, and harvesting shellfish beds. Perform both supervisory and management functions such as accounting, marketing, and personnel work. Confer with managers to determine times and places of seed planting, and cultivating, feeding, or harvesting of fish or shellfish. Maintain workers' time records. Record the numbers and types of fish or shellfish reared, harvested, released, sold, and shipped. Interview and select new employees. Train workers in spawning, rearing, cultivating, and harvesting methods, and in the use of equipment. Supervise the artificial spawning of various salmon and trout species. Prepare or direct the preparation of fish food, and specify medications to be added to food and water to treat fish for diseases. Plan work schedules according to personnel and equipment availability, tidal levels, feeding schedules, or transfer and harvest needs. Observe fish and beds or ponds to detect diseases, monitor fish growth, determine quality of fish, or determine completeness of harvesting. Direct workers to correct problems such as disease, quality of seed distribution, or adequacy of cultivation. Direct and monitor worker activities such as treatment and rearing of fingerlings, maintenance of equipment, and harvesting of fish or shellfish. Select and ship eggs to other hatcheries.

Education and Training Programs: Agricultural Animal Breeding; Agricultural Business and Management, Other; Agricultural Production Operations, General; Agricultural Production Operations, Other; Agriculture, Agriculture Operations, and Related Sciences, Other; Animal Nutrition; Animal/Livestock Husbandry and Production; Aquaculture; Crop Production; Dairy Husbandry and Production; Dairy Science; Farm/Farm and Ranch Management; Fishing and Fisheries Sciences and Management; Horse Husbandry/Equine Science and Management; Livestock Management; Plant Sciences, General; Poultry Science; Range Science and Management. **Knowledge/Courses—Biology:** Plant and animal organisms and their tissues, cells, functions, interdependencies, and interactions with each other and the environment. **Building and Construction:** Materials, methods, and the tools involved in the construction or repair of houses, buildings, or other structures such as highways and roads. **Food Production:** Techniques and equipment for planting, growing, and harvesting food products (both plant and animal) for consumption, including storage/handling techniques. **Chemistry:** The chemical composition, structure, and properties of substances and of the chemical processes and transformations that they undergo. This includes uses of chemicals and their danger signs, production techniques, and disposal methods. **Mechanical Devices:** Machines and tools, including their designs, uses, repair, and maintenance. **Engineering and Technology:** The practical application of engineering science and technology. This includes applying principles, techniques, procedures, and equipment to the design and production of various goods and services.

Personality Type: Enterprising-Realistic-Conventional. **Career Cluster:** 01 Agriculture, Food, and Natural Resources. **Career Pathways:** 01.2 Plant Systems; 01.5 Natural Resources Systems; 01.1 Food Products and Processing Systems. **Other Jobs in These Pathways:** Agricultural Inspectors; Agricultural Sciences Teachers, Postsecondary; Agricultural Technicians; Animal Scientists; Biochemists and Biophysicists; Biological Science Teachers, Postsecondary; Biologists; Buyers and Purchasing Agents, Farm Products; Chemical Technicians; Climate Change Analysts; Conveyor Operators and Tenders; Derrick Operators, Oil and Gas; Economists; Engineering Technicians, Except Drafters, All Other; Environmental Economists; Environmental Restoration Planners; Environmental Science and Protection Technicians, Including Health; Environmental Science Teachers, Postsecondary; Environmental Scientists and Specialists, Including Health; Fallers; Farm and Home Management Advisors; First-Line Supervisors of Landscaping, Lawn Service, and Groundskeeping Workers; First-Line Supervisors of Office and Administrative Support Workers; First-Line Supervisors of Retail Sales Workers; Fish and Game Wardens; Fishers and Related Fishing Workers; Floral Designers; others.

Skills—Management of Financial Resources: Determining how money will be spent to get the work done and accounting for these expenditures. **Management of**

Material Resources: Obtaining and seeing to the appropriate use of equipment, facilities, and materials needed to do certain work. **Management of Personnel Resources:** Motivating, developing, and directing people as they work, identifying the best people for the job. **Equipment Maintenance:** Performing routine maintenance on equipment and determining when and what kind of maintenance is needed. **Quality Control Analysis:** Conducting tests and inspections of products, services, or processes to evaluate quality or performance. **Science:** Using scientific rules and methods to solve problems. **Operation and Control:** Controlling operations of equipment or systems. **Equipment Selection:** Determining the kind of tools and equipment needed to do a job.

Work Environment: More often outdoors than indoors; standing; noise; very hot or cold; bright or inadequate lighting; contaminants; hazardous equipment; minor burns, cuts, bites, or stings.

Job Specialization: First-Line Supervisors of Agricultural Crop and Horticultural Workers

Directly supervise and coordinate activities of agricultural crop or horticultural workers. Prepare and maintain time and payroll reports, as well as details of personnel actions such as performance evaluations, hires, promotions, and disciplinary actions. Monitor and oversee construction projects such as horticultural buildings and irrigation systems. Calculate and monitor budgets for maintenance and development of collections, grounds, and infrastructure. Perform hardscape activities including installation and repair of irrigation systems, resurfacing and grading of paths, rockwork, or erosion control. Prepare reports regarding farm conditions, crop yields, machinery breakdowns, or labor problems. Requisition and purchase supplies such as insecticides, machine parts or lubricants, and tools. Investigate grievances and settle disputes to maintain harmony among workers. Issue equipment such as farm implements, machinery, ladders, or containers to workers, and collect equipment when work is complete. Confer with managers to evaluate weather and soil conditions, to develop plans and procedures, and to discuss issues such as changes in fertilizers, herbicides, or cultivating techniques. Estimate labor requirements for jobs, and plan work schedules accordingly. Inspect crops, fields, and plant stock to determine conditions and need for cultivating, spraying, weeding, or harvesting. Observe workers to detect inefficient and unsafe work procedures or to identify problems, initiating corrective action as necessary. Assign duties such as cultivation, irrigation and harvesting of crops or plants, product packaging and grading, and equipment maintenance. Recruit, hire, and discharge workers. Read inventory records, customer orders, and shipping schedules to determine required activities. Review employees' work to evaluate quality and quantity. Train workers in techniques such as planting, harvesting, weeding, and insect identification, and in the use of safety measures. Arrange for transportation, equipment, and living quarters for seasonal workers.

Education and Training Programs: Agricultural Animal Breeding; Agricultural Business and Management, Other; Agricultural Production Operations, General; Agricultural Production Operations, Other; Agriculture, Agriculture Operations, and Related Sciences, Other; Animal Nutrition; Animal/Livestock Husbandry and Production; Aquaculture; Crop Production; Dairy Husbandry and Production; Dairy Science; Farm/Farm and Ranch Management; Fishing and Fisheries Sciences and Management; Horse Husbandry/Equine Science and Management; Livestock Management; Plant Sciences, General; Poultry Science; Range Science and Management. **Knowledge/Courses—Food Production:** Techniques and equipment for planting, growing, and harvesting food products (both plant and animal) for consumption, including storage/handling techniques. **Mechanical Devices:** Machines and tools, including their designs, uses, repair, and maintenance. **Foreign Language:** The structure and content of a foreign (non-English) language including the meaning and spelling of words, rules of composition and grammar, and pronunciation. **Production and Processing:** Raw materials, production processes, quality control, costs, and other techniques for maximizing the effective manufacture and distribution of goods. **Personnel and Human Resources:** Principles and procedures for personnel recruitment, selection, training, compensation and benefits, labor relations and negotiation, and personnel information systems.

Personality Type: Realistic-Enterprising-Conventional. **Career Cluster:** 01 Agriculture, Food, and Natural Resources. **Career Pathways:** 01.1 Food Products and Processing Systems; 01.2 Plant Systems. **Other Jobs in These Pathways:** Agricultural Inspectors; Agricultural Sciences Teachers, Postsecondary; Agricultural Technicians;

Animal Scientists; Biochemists and Biophysicists; Biologists; Buyers and Purchasing Agents, Farm Products; Chemical Technicians; Economists; Environmental Economists; Farm and Home Management Advisors; First-Line Supervisors of Landscaping, Lawn Service, and Groundskeeping Workers; First-Line Supervisors of Office and Administrative Support Workers; First-Line Supervisors of Retail Sales Workers; Floral Designers; Food and Tobacco Roasting, Baking, and Drying Machine Operators and Tenders; Food Batchmakers; Food Cooking Machine Operators and Tenders; Food Science Technicians; Food Scientists and Technologists; Geneticists; Graders and Sorters, Agricultural Products; Grounds Maintenance Workers, All Other; Landscaping and Groundskeeping Workers; Nonfarm Animal Caretakers; Office Machine Operators, Except Computer; Pest Control Workers; others.

Skills—Management of Financial Resources: Determining how money will be spent to get the work done and accounting for these expenditures. **Management of Material Resources:** Obtaining and seeing to the appropriate use of equipment, facilities, and materials needed to do certain work. **Repairing:** Repairing machines or systems using the needed tools. **Equipment Maintenance:** Performing routine maintenance on equipment and determining when and what kind of maintenance is needed. **Operation and Control:** Controlling operations of equipment or systems. **Troubleshooting:** Determining causes of operating errors and deciding what to do about them. **Equipment Selection:** Determining the kind of tools and equipment needed to do a job. **Management of Personnel Resources:** Motivating, developing, and directing people as they work, identifying the best people for the job.

Work Environment: More often outdoors than indoors; standing; using hands; noise; very hot or cold; contaminants; hazardous equipment.

First-Line Supervisors of Fire Fighting and Prevention Workers

- ⊙ Annual Earnings: $69,510
- ⊙ Earnings Growth Potential: High (41.7%)
- ⊙ Growth: 8.2%
- ⊙ Annual Job Openings: 3,310
- ⊙ Self-Employed: 0.0%

Considerations for Job Outlook: Most job growth will stem from the conversion of volunteer firefighting positions into paid positions. Job seekers are expected to face keen competition. Those who have completed some firefighter education at a community college and have EMT or paramedic certification should have the best prospects.

Directly supervise and coordinate activities of workers engaged in firefighting and fire prevention and control. For task data, see Job Specializations.

Education/Training Required: Postsecondary vocational training. **Work Experience Needed:** 1 to 5 years. **On-the-Job Training Needed:** None. **Certification/Licensure:** Licensure in some states; certification by association; municipal examination.

Job Specialization: Forest Fire Fighting and Prevention Supervisors

Supervise firefighters who control and suppress fires in forests or vacant public land. Communicate fire details to superiors, subordinates, and interagency dispatch centers, using two-way radios. Serve as working leader of an engine, hand, helicopter, or prescribed fire crew of three or more firefighters. Maintain fire suppression equipment in good condition, checking equipment periodically to ensure that it is ready for use. Evaluate size, location, and condition of forest fires in order to request and dispatch crews and position equipment so fires can be contained safely and effectively. Operate wildland fire engines and hoselays. Direct and supervise prescribed burn projects, and prepare post-burn reports analyzing burn conditions and results. Monitor prescribed burns to ensure that they are conducted safely and effectively. Identify staff training and development needs to ensure that appropriate training can be arranged. Maintain knowledge of forest fire laws and fire prevention techniques and tactics. Recommend equipment modifications or new equipment purchases. Perform administrative duties such as compiling and maintaining records, completing forms, preparing reports, and composing correspondence. Recruit and hire forest firefighting personnel. Train workers in such skills as parachute jumping, fire suppression, aerial observation, and radio communication, both in the classroom and on the job. Review and evaluate employee performance.

Education and Training Programs: Fire Prevention and Safety Technology/Technician; Fire Services

Administration. **Knowledge/Courses—Public Safety and Security:** Relevant equipment, policies, procedures, and strategies to promote effective local, state, or national security operations for the protection of people, data, property, and institutions. **Building and Construction:** Materials, methods, and the tools involved in the construction or repair of houses, buildings, or other structures such as highways and roads. **Mechanical Devices:** Machines and tools, including their designs, uses, repair, and maintenance. **Customer and Personal Service:** Principles and processes for providing customer and personal services. This includes customer needs assessment, meeting quality standards for services, and evaluation of customer satisfaction. **Personnel and Human Resources:** Principles and procedures for personnel recruitment, selection, training, compensation and benefits, labor relations and negotiation, and personnel information systems. **Transportation:** Principles and methods for moving people or goods by air, rail, sea, or road, including the relative costs and benefits.

Personality Type: Enterprising-Realistic-Conventional. **Career Cluster:** 12 Law, Public Safety, Corrections, and Security. **Career Pathway:** 12.2 Emergency and Fire Management Services. **Other Jobs in This Pathway:** Correctional Officers and Jailers; Fire Inspectors; Fire Investigators; Forest Fire Inspectors and Prevention Specialists; Forest Firefighters; Municipal Fire Fighting and Prevention Supervisors; Municipal Firefighters.

Skills—Operations Analysis: Analyzing needs and product requirements to create a design. **Equipment Maintenance:** Performing routine maintenance on equipment and determining when and what kind of maintenance is needed. **Operation and Control:** Controlling operations of equipment or systems. **Management of Personnel Resources:** Motivating, developing, and directing people as they work, identifying the best people for the job. **Coordination:** Adjusting actions in relation to others' actions. **Operation Monitoring:** Watching gauges, dials, or other indicators to make sure a machine is working properly. **Monitoring:** Monitoring or assessing your performance or that of other individuals or organizations to make improvements or take corrective action. **Equipment Selection:** Determining the kind of tools and equipment needed to do a job.

Work Environment: Outdoors; standing; walking and running; using hands; noise; very hot or cold; bright or inadequate lighting; contaminants; cramped work space; hazardous equipment; minor burns, cuts, bites, or stings.

Job Specialization: Municipal Fire Fighting and Prevention Supervisors

Supervise firefighters who control and extinguish municipal fires, protect life and property, and conduct rescue efforts. Assign firefighters to jobs at strategic locations to facilitate rescue of persons and maximize application of extinguishing agents. Provide emergency medical services as required, and perform light to heavy rescue functions at emergencies. Assess nature and extent of fires, condition of buildings, danger to adjacent buildings, and water supply status to determine crew or company requirements. Instruct and drill fire department personnel in assigned duties, including firefighting, medical care, hazardous materials response, fire prevention, and related subjects. Inspect and test new and existing fire protection systems, fire detection systems, and fire safety equipment to ensure that they are operating properly. Compile and maintain records on personnel, accidents, equipment, and supplies. Perform maintenance and minor repairs on firefighting equipment, including vehicles, and write and submit proposals to modify, replace, and repair equipment. Prepare activity reports listing fire call locations, actions taken, fire types and probable causes, damage estimates, and situation dispositions. Evaluate the performance of assigned firefighting personnel. Direct the training of firefighters, assigning of instructors to training classes, and providing of supervisors with reports on training progress and status. Maintain required maps and records. Present and interpret fire prevention and fire code information to citizens' groups, organizations, contractors, engineers, and developers. Recommend personnel actions related to disciplinary procedures, performance, leaves of absence, and grievances. Direct firefighters in station maintenance duties, and participate in these duties. Attend in-service training classes to remain current in knowledge of codes, laws, ordinances, and regulations. Evaluate fire station procedures to ensure efficiency and enforcement of departmental regulations. Coordinate the distribution of fire prevention promotional materials.

Education and Training Programs: Fire Prevention and Safety Technology/Technician; Fire Services Administration. **Knowledge/Courses—Building and Construction:** Materials, methods, and the tools involved in the construction or repair of houses, buildings, or other structures such as highways and roads. **Public Safety and Security:** Relevant equipment, policies, procedures, and strategies to promote effective local, state, or national security operations for the protection of people, data, property, and institutions. **Medicine and Dentistry:** The information and techniques needed to diagnose and treat human injuries, diseases, and deformities. This includes symptoms, treatment alternatives, drug properties and interactions, and preventive health-care measures. **Mechanical Devices:** Machines and tools, including their designs, uses, repair, and maintenance. **Chemistry:** The chemical composition, structure, and properties of substances and of the chemical processes and transformations that they undergo. This includes uses of chemicals and their danger signs, production techniques, and disposal methods. **Personnel and Human Resources:** Principles and procedures for personnel recruitment, selection, training, compensation and benefits, labor relations and negotiation, and personnel information systems.

Personality Type: Enterprising-Realistic-Social. **Career Cluster:** 12 Law, Public Safety, Corrections, and Security. **Career Pathway:** 12.2 Emergency and Fire Management Services. **Other Jobs in This Pathway:** Correctional Officers and Jailers; Fire Inspectors; Fire Investigators; Forest Fire Fighting and Prevention Supervisors; Forest Fire Inspectors and Prevention Specialists; Forest Firefighters; Municipal Firefighters.

Skills—Operation and Control: Controlling operations of equipment or systems. **Science:** Using scientific rules and methods to solve problems. **Equipment Selection:** Determining the kind of tools and equipment needed to do a job. **Repairing:** Repairing machines or systems using the needed tools. **Equipment Maintenance:** Performing routine maintenance on equipment and determining when and what kind of maintenance is needed. **Quality Control Analysis:** Conducting tests and inspections of products, services, or processes to evaluate quality or performance. **Management of Personnel Resources:** Motivating, developing, and directing people as they work, identifying the best people for the job. **Systems Analysis:** Determining how a system should work and how changes in conditions, operations, and the environment will affect outcomes.

Work Environment: More often outdoors than indoors; standing; using hands; noise; very hot or cold; bright or inadequate lighting; contaminants; cramped work space; exposed to disease or infections; high places; hazardous conditions; hazardous equipment; minor burns, cuts, bites, or stings.

First-Line Supervisors of Food Preparation and Serving Workers

- ⊙ Annual Earnings: $29,550
- ⊙ Earnings Growth Potential: Low (33.1%)
- ⊙ Growth: 9.8%
- ⊙ Annual Job Openings: 24,830
- ⊙ Self-Employed: 3.1%

Considerations for Job Outlook: Consumer demand for convenience and a growing variety of dining venues are expected to create some jobs, but most openings are expected to arise from the need to replace workers who leave the occupation. Competition should be keen for jobs at upscale restaurants.

Directly supervise and coordinate activities of workers engaged in preparing and serving food. Compile and balance cash receipts at the end of the day or shift. Resolve customer complaints regarding food service. Train workers in food preparation and in service, sanitation, and safety procedures. Inspect supplies, equipment, and work areas to ensure efficient service and conformance to standards. Control inventories of food, equipment, smallware, and liquor and report shortages to designated personnel. Assign duties, responsibilities, and work stations to employees in accordance with work requirements. Estimate ingredients and supplies required to prepare a recipe. Analyze operational problems, such as theft and wastage, and establish procedures to alleviate these problems. Specify food portions and courses, production and time sequences, and work station and equipment arrangements. Recommend measures for improving work procedures and worker performance to increase service quality and enhance job safety. Forecast staff, equipment, and supply requirements based on a master menu.

Education/Training Required: High school diploma or equivalent. **Education and Training Programs:** Foodservice Systems Administration/Management; Restaurant, Culinary, and Catering Management/Manager. **Knowledge/Courses—Food Production:** Techniques and equipment for planting, growing, and harvesting food products (both plant and animal) for consumption, including storage/handling techniques. **Economics and Accounting:** Economic and accounting principles and practices, the financial markets, banking, and the analysis and reporting of financial data. **Administration and Management:** Business and management principles involved in strategic planning, resource allocation, human resources modeling, leadership technique, production methods, and coordination of people and resources. **Production and Processing:** Raw materials, production processes, quality control, costs, and other techniques for maximizing the effective manufacture and distribution of goods. **Personnel and Human Resources:** Principles and procedures for personnel recruitment, selection, training, compensation and benefits, labor relations and negotiation, and personnel information systems. **Sales and Marketing:** Principles and methods for showing, promoting, and selling products or services. This includes marketing strategy and tactics, product demonstration, sales techniques, and sales control systems. **Work Experience Needed:** 1 to 5 years. **On-the-Job Training Needed:** None. **Certification/Licensure:** None.

Personality Type: Enterprising-Conventional-Realistic. **Career Clusters:** 08 Health Science; 09 Hospitality and Tourism. **Career Pathways:** 08.4 Support Services; 09.1 Restaurants and Food/Beverage Services. **Other Jobs in These Pathways:** Bakers; Baristas; Bartenders; Butchers and Meat Cutters; Chefs and Head Cooks; Combined Food Preparation and Serving Workers, Including Fast Food; Cooks, All Other; Cooks, Fast Food; Cooks, Institution and Cafeteria; Cooks, Private Household; Cooks, Restaurant; Cooks, Short Order; Counter Attendants, Cafeteria, Food Concession, and Coffee Shop; Dietetic Technicians; Dietitians and Nutritionists; Dining Room and Cafeteria Attendants and Bartender Helpers; Dishwashers; Farm and Home Management Advisors; Food Batchmakers; Food Preparation and Serving Related Workers, All Other; Food Preparation Workers; Food Servers, Nonrestaurant; Food Service Managers; Gaming Managers; Home Economics Teachers, Postsecondary; Hosts and Hostesses, Restaurant, Lounge, and Coffee Shop; Meat, Poultry, and Fish Cutters and Trimmers; Slaughterers and Meat Packers; Waiters and Waitresses.

Skills—Management of Financial Resources: Determining how money will be spent to get the work done and accounting for these expenditures. **Management of Material Resources:** Obtaining and seeing to the appropriate use of equipment, facilities, and materials needed to do certain work. **Systems Evaluation:** Identifying measures or indicators of system performance and the actions needed to improve or correct performance relative to the goals of the

system. **Management of Personnel Resources:** Motivating, developing, and directing people as they work, identifying the best people for the job. **Coordination:** Adjusting actions in relation to others' actions. **Service Orientation:** Actively looking for ways to help people. **Time Management:** Managing one's own time and the time of others. **Social Perceptiveness:** Being aware of others' reactions and understanding why they react as they do.

Work Environment: Indoors; standing; walking and running; using hands; bending or twisting the body; repetitive motions; noise; very hot or cold; contaminants; minor burns, cuts, bites, or stings.

First-Line Supervisors of Helpers, Laborers, and Material Movers, Hand

- ⊙ Annual Earnings: $44,580
- ⊙ Earnings Growth Potential: Medium (37.3%)
- ⊙ Growth: 27.2%
- ⊙ Annual Job Openings: 8,000
- ⊙ Self-Employed: 1.1%

Considerations for Job Outlook: Slower-than-average employment growth is projected.

Directly supervise and coordinate the activities of helpers, laborers, or material movers. Plan work schedules and assign duties to maintain adequate staffing levels, to ensure that activities are performed effectively, and to respond to fluctuating workloads. Collaborate with workers and managers to solve work-related problems. Review work throughout the work process and at completion, in order to ensure that it has been performed properly. Transmit and explain work orders to laborers. Check specifications of materials loaded or unloaded against information contained in work orders. Examine freight to determine loading sequences. Inform designated employees or departments of items loaded, and problems encountered. Evaluate employee performance, and prepare performance appraisals. Perform the same work duties as those whom they supervise, and/or perform more difficult or skilled tasks or assist in their performance. Prepare and maintain work records and reports that include information such as employee time and wages, daily receipts, and inspection results. Conduct staff meetings to relay general information or to address specific topics such as safety. Counsel employees in work-related activities, personal growth, and career development. Inspect equipment for wear and for conformance to specifications. Resolve personnel problems, complaints, and formal grievances when possible, or refer them to higher-level supervisors for resolution. Recommend or initiate personnel actions such as promotions, transfers, and disciplinary measures. Assess training needs of staff, and then arrange for or provide appropriate instruction. Schedule times of shipment and modes of transportation for materials. Quote prices to customers. Estimate material, time, and staffing requirements for a given project, based on work orders, job specifications, and experience. Provide assistance in balancing books, tracking, monitoring, and projecting a unit's budget needs, and in developing unit policies and procedures.

Education/Training Required: High school diploma or equivalent. **Education and Training Programs:** No related CIP programs; this job is learned through work experience in a related occupation. **Knowledge/Courses—Production and Processing:** Raw materials, production processes, quality control, costs, and other techniques for maximizing the effective manufacture and distribution of goods. **Transportation:** Principles and methods for moving people or goods by air, rail, sea, or road, including the relative costs and benefits. **Personnel and Human Resources:** Principles and procedures for personnel recruitment, selection, training, compensation and benefits, labor relations and negotiation, and personnel information systems. **Administration and Management:** Business and management principles involved in strategic planning, resource allocation, human resources modeling, leadership technique, production methods, and coordination of people and resources. **Public Safety and Security:** Relevant equipment, policies, procedures, and strategies to promote effective local, state, or national security operations for the protection of people, data, property, and institutions. **Psychology:** Human behavior and performance; individual differences in ability, personality, and interests; learning and motivation; psychological research methods; and the assessment and treatment of behavioral and affective disorders. **Work Experience Needed:** 1 to 5 years. **On-the-Job Training Needed:** None. **Certification/Licensure:** None.

Personality Type: Enterprising-Realistic-Conventional. **Career Cluster:** 16 Transportation, Distribution, and Logistics. **Career Pathway:** 16.1 Transportation Operations. **Other Jobs in This Pathway:** Aerospace Engineering and Operations Technicians; Air Traffic Controllers; Aircraft Cargo Handling Supervisors; Airfield Operations Specialists; Airline Pilots, Copilots, and Flight Engineers; Automotive and Watercraft Service Attendants; Automotive Master Mechanics; Aviation Inspectors; Bridge and Lock Tenders; Bus Drivers, School or Special Client; Bus Drivers, Transit and Intercity; Commercial Divers; Commercial Pilots; Crane and Tower Operators; First-Line Supervisors of Transportation and Material-Moving Machine and Vehicle Operators; Freight and Cargo Inspectors; Heavy and Tractor-Trailer Truck Drivers; Hoist and Winch Operators; Laborers and Freight, Stock, and Material Movers, Hand; Light Truck or Delivery Services Drivers; Mates—Ship, Boat, and Barge; Motor Vehicle Operators, All Other; Motorboat Operators; Operating Engineers and Other Construction Equipment Operators; Parking Lot Attendants; Pilots, Ship; Rail Transportation Workers, All Other; others.

Skills—Management of Material Resources: Obtaining and seeing to the appropriate use of equipment, facilities, and materials needed to do certain work. **Management of Financial Resources:** Determining how money will be spent to get the work done and accounting for these expenditures. **Management of Personnel Resources:** Motivating, developing, and directing people as they work, identifying the best people for the job. **Negotiation:** Bringing others together and trying to reconcile differences. **Persuasion:** Persuading others to change their minds or behavior. **Operations Analysis:** Analyzing needs and product requirements to create a design. **Time Management:** Managing one's own time and the time of others. **Systems Evaluation:** Identifying measures or indicators of system performance and the actions needed to improve or correct performance relative to the goals of the system.

Work Environment: Indoors; standing; walking and running; noise; very hot or cold; contaminants.

Job Specialization: Recycling Coordinators

Supervise curbside and drop-off recycling programs for municipal governments or private firms. Oversee recycling pick-up or drop-off programs to ensure compliance with community ordinances. Supervise recycling technicians, community service workers, or other recycling operations employees or volunteers. Assign truck drivers or recycling technicians to routes. Coordinate recycling collection schedules to optimize service and efficiency. Coordinate shipments of recycling materials with shipping brokers or processing companies. Create or manage recycling operations budgets. Design community solid and hazardous waste management programs. Develop community or corporate recycling plans and goals to minimize waste and conform to resource constraints. Implement grant-funded projects, monitoring and reporting progress in accordance with sponsoring agency requirements. Investigate violations of solid waste or recycling ordinances. Make presentations to educate the public on how to recycle or on the environmental advantages of recycling. Negotiate contracts with waste management or other firms. Operate fork lifts, skid loaders, or trucks to move or store recyclable materials. Operate recycling processing equipment, such as sorters, balers, crushers, and granulators, to sort and process materials. Oversee campaigns to promote recycling or waste reduction programs in communities or private companies. Prepare grant applications to fund recycling programs or program enhancements. Schedule movement of recycling materials into and out of storage areas. Identify or investigate new opportunities for materials to be collected and recycled. Inspect physical condition of recycling or hazardous waste facilities for compliance with safety, quality, and service standards. Maintain logs of recycling materials received or shipped to processing companies. Prepare bills of lading, statements of shipping records, or customer receipts related to recycling or hazardous material services.

Education and Training Programs: No related CIP programs; this job is learned through work experience in a related occupation.

Personality Type: No data available. **Career Cluster:** 13 Manufacturing. **Career Pathway:** 13.1 Production. **Other Jobs in This Pathway:** Adhesive Bonding Machine Operators and Tenders; Assemblers and Fabricators, All Other; Avionics Technicians; Cabinetmakers and Bench Carpenters; Cleaning, Washing, and Metal Pickling Equipment Operators and Tenders; Coating, Painting, and Spraying Machine Setters, Operators, and Tenders; Computer-Controlled Machine Tool Operators, Metal and Plastic; Cooling and Freezing Equipment Operators and Tenders; Cost Estimators; Crushing, Grinding, and Polishing Machine Setters, Operators, and Tenders; Cutters

and Trimmers, Hand; Cutting and Slicing Machine Setters, Operators, and Tenders; Cutting, Punching, and Press Machine Setters, Operators, and Tenders, Metal and Plastic; Drilling and Boring Machine Tool Setters, Operators, and Tenders, Metal and Plastic; Extruding and Drawing Machine Setters, Operators, and Tenders, Metal and Plastic; Extruding and Forming Machine Setters, Operators, and Tenders, Synthetic and Glass Fibers; others.

Work Environment: No data available.

First-Line Supervisors of Housekeeping and Janitorial Workers

- ⊙ Annual Earnings: $35,230
- ⊙ Earnings Growth Potential: Medium (37.4%)
- ⊙ Growth: 0.8%
- ⊙ Annual Job Openings: 3,320
- ⊙ Self-Employed: 20.1%

Considerations for Job Outlook: Employment of building cleaning workers should grow, although slowly, as the number of buildings in operation increases. The need to replace workers who leave the occupation should create good job prospects.

Directly supervise and coordinate work activities of cleaning personnel in hotels, hospitals, offices, and other establishments. Inspect work performed to ensure that it meets specifications and established standards. Plan and prepare employee work schedules. Perform or assist with cleaning duties as necessary. Investigate complaints about service and equipment, and take corrective action. Coordinate activities with other departments to ensure that services are provided in an efficient and timely manner. Inspect and evaluate the physical condition of facilities to determine the type of work required. Select the most suitable cleaning materials for different types of linens, furniture, flooring, and surfaces. Instruct staff in work policies and procedures, and the use and maintenance of equipment. Issue supplies and equipment to workers. Forecast necessary levels of staffing and stock at different times to facilitate effective scheduling and ordering. Inventory stock to ensure that supplies and equipment are available in adequate amounts. Evaluate employee performance and recommend personnel actions such as promotions, transfers, and dismissals. Confer with staff to resolve performance and personnel problems and to discuss company policies. Establish and implement operational standards and procedures for the departments supervised. Recommend or arrange for additional services such as painting, repair work, renovations, and the replacement of furnishings and equipment. Select and order or purchase new equipment, supplies, or furnishings. Recommend changes that could improve service and increase operational efficiency. Maintain required records of work hours, budgets, payrolls, and other information. Screen job applicants, and hire new employees. Prepare reports on activity; personnel; and information such as occupancy, hours worked, facility usage, work performed, and departmental expenses. Check and maintain equipment to ensure that it is in working order. Direct activities for stopping the spread of infections in facilities such as hospitals.

Education/Training Required: High school diploma or equivalent. **Education and Training Programs:** No related CIP programs; this job is learned through work experience in a related occupation. **Knowledge/Courses—Personnel and Human Resources:** Principles and procedures for personnel recruitment, selection, training, compensation and benefits, labor relations and negotiation, and personnel information systems. **Chemistry:** The chemical composition, structure, and properties of substances and of the chemical processes and transformations that they undergo. This includes uses of chemicals and their danger signs, production techniques, and disposal methods. **Customer and Personal Service:** Principles and processes for providing customer and personal services. This includes customer needs assessment, meeting quality standards for services, and evaluation of customer satisfaction. **Administration and Management:** Business and management principles involved in strategic planning, resource allocation, human resources modeling, leadership technique, production methods, and coordination of people and resources. **Education and Training:** Principles and methods for curriculum and training design, teaching and instruction for individuals and groups, and the measurement of training effects. **Mechanical Devices:** Machines and tools, including their designs, uses, repair, and maintenance. **Work Experience Needed:** 1 to 5 years. **On-the-Job Training Needed:** None. **Certification/Licensure:** None.

Personality Type: Enterprising-Conventional-Realistic. **Career Cluster:** 09 Hospitality and Tourism. **Career**

Pathway: 09.2 Lodging. **Other Jobs in This Pathway:** Building Cleaning Workers, All Other; Food Service Managers; Janitors and Cleaners, Except Maids and Housekeeping Cleaners; Lodging Managers; Maids and Housekeeping Cleaners; Residential Advisors.

Skills—Management of Material Resources: Obtaining and seeing to the appropriate use of equipment, facilities, and materials needed to do certain work. **Management of Financial Resources:** Determining how money will be spent to get the work done and accounting for these expenditures. **Management of Personnel Resources:** Motivating, developing, and directing people as they work, identifying the best people for the job. **Time Management:** Managing one's own time and the time of others. **Negotiation:** Bringing others together and trying to reconcile differences. **Social Perceptiveness:** Being aware of others' reactions and understanding why they react as they do. **Quality Control Analysis:** Conducting tests and inspections of products, services, or processes to evaluate quality or performance. **Troubleshooting:** Determining causes of operating errors and deciding what to do about them.

Work Environment: Indoors; standing; walking and running; using hands; bending or twisting the body; repetitive motions; contaminants.

First-Line Supervisors of Landscaping, Lawn Service, and Groundskeeping Workers

- ⊙ Annual Earnings: $42,050
- ⊙ Earnings Growth Potential: Medium (36.4%)
- ⊙ Growth: 15.1%
- ⊙ Annual Job Openings: 6,010
- ⊙ Self-Employed: 49.3%

Considerations for Job Outlook: Demand for lawn care and landscaping services is expected to grow, resulting in employment growth for these workers. Job prospects are expected to be good. Opportunities for year-round work should be best in regions with temperate climates.

Directly supervise and coordinate activities of workers engaged in landscaping or groundskeeping activities. Establish and enforce operating procedures and work standards that will ensure adequate performance and personnel safety. Inspect completed work to ensure conformance to specifications, standards, and contract requirements. Direct activities of workers who perform duties such as landscaping, cultivating lawns, or pruning trees and shrubs. Schedule work for crews depending on work priorities, crew and equipment availability, and weather conditions. Plant and maintain vegetation through activities such as mulching, fertilizing, watering, mowing, and pruning. Monitor project activities to ensure that instructions are followed, deadlines are met, and schedules are maintained. Train workers in tasks such as transplanting and pruning trees and shrubs, finishing cement, using equipment, and caring for turf. Inventory supplies of tools, equipment, and materials to ensure that sufficient supplies are available and items are in usable condition. Provide workers with assistance in performing duties as necessary to meet deadlines. Confer with other supervisors to coordinate work activities with those of other departments or units. Perform personnel-related activities such as hiring workers, evaluating staff performance, and taking disciplinary actions when performance problems occur. Direct or perform mixing and application of fertilizers, insecticides, herbicides, and fungicides. Review contracts or work assignments to determine service, machine, and workforce requirements for jobs. Maintain required records such as personnel information and project records. Prepare and maintain required records such as work activity and personnel reports. Order the performance of corrective work when problems occur, and recommend procedural changes to avoid such problems. Identify diseases and pests affecting landscaping, and order appropriate treatments. Investigate work-related complaints in order to verify problems, and to determine responses.

Education/Training Required: High school diploma or equivalent. **Education and Training Programs:** Landscaping and Groundskeeping; Ornamental Horticulture; Turf and Turfgrass Management. **Knowledge/Courses—Mechanical Devices:** Machines and tools, including their designs, uses, repair, and maintenance. **Building and Construction:** Materials, methods, and the tools involved in the construction or repair of houses, buildings, or other structures such as highways and roads. **Design:** Design techniques, tools, and principles involved in production of precision technical plans, blueprints, drawings, and models. **Biology:** Plant and animal organisms and their tissues, cells, functions, interdependencies, and interactions with each other and the environment. **Chemistry:** The chemical composition, structure, and properties of substances and of the chemical processes and transformations that they undergo. This includes uses of chemicals and their danger signs, production techniques, and disposal methods. **Education and Training:** Principles and methods for curriculum and training design, teaching and instruction for individuals and groups, and the measurement of training effects. **Work Experience Needed:** 1 to 5 years. **On-the-Job Training Needed:** None. **Certification/Licensure:** None.

Personality Type: Enterprising-Realistic-Conventional. **Career Cluster:** 01 Agriculture, Food, and Natural Resources. **Career Pathway:** 01.2 Plant Systems. **Other Jobs in This Pathway:** Agricultural Sciences Teachers, Postsecondary; Agricultural Technicians; Animal Scientists; Biochemists and Biophysicists; Biologists; Economists; Environmental Economists; Farm and Home Management Advisors; First-Line Supervisors of Retail Sales Workers; Floral Designers; Food Science Technicians; Food Scientists and Technologists; Geneticists; Grounds Maintenance Workers, All Other; Landscaping and Groundskeeping Workers; Pesticide Handlers, Sprayers, and Applicators, Vegetation; Precision Agriculture Technicians; Retail Salespersons; Soil and Plant Scientists; Tree Trimmers and Pruners.

Skills—Operation and Control: Controlling operations of equipment or systems. **Repairing:** Repairing machines or systems using the needed tools. **Equipment Maintenance:** Performing routine maintenance on equipment and determining when and what kind of maintenance is needed. **Operation Monitoring:** Watching gauges, dials, or other indicators to make sure a machine is working properly. **Management of Financial Resources:** Determining how money will be spent to get the work done and accounting for these expenditures. **Management of Material Resources:** Obtaining and seeing to the appropriate use of equipment, facilities, and materials needed to do certain work. **Troubleshooting:** Determining causes of operating errors and deciding what to do about them. **Quality Control Analysis:** Conducting tests and inspections of products, services, or processes to evaluate quality or performance.

Work Environment: More often outdoors than indoors; standing; walking and running; using hands; noise; very hot or cold; bright or inadequate lighting; contaminants; hazardous equipment; minor burns, cuts, bites, or stings.

First-Line Supervisors of Mechanics, Installers, and Repairers

- ⊙ Annual Earnings: $59,850
- ⊙ Earnings Growth Potential: Medium (39.6%)
- ⊙ Growth: 11.9%
- ⊙ Annual Job Openings: 16,490
- ⊙ Self-Employed: 1.2%

Considerations for Job Outlook: Slower-than-average employment growth is projected.

Directly supervise and coordinate the activities of mechanics, installers, and repairers. Determine schedules, sequences, and assignments for work activities, based on work priority, quantity of equipment, and skill of personnel. Monitor employees' work levels, and review work performance. Monitor tool and part inventories and the condition and maintenance of shops to ensure adequate working conditions. Recommend or initiate personnel actions such as hires, promotions, transfers, discharges, and disciplinary measures. Investigate accidents and injuries, and prepare reports of findings. Compile operational and personnel records such as time and production records, inventory data, repair and maintenance statistics, and test results. Develop, implement, and evaluate maintenance policies and procedures. Counsel employees about work-related issues, and assist employees to correct job-skill deficiencies. Examine objects, systems, or facilities, and analyze information to determine needed installations, services, or repairs. Conduct or arrange for worker training in safety, repair, and maintenance techniques; operational procedures; or equipment use. Inspect and monitor work areas, examine tools and equipment, and provide employee safety training to prevent, detect, and correct unsafe conditions or violations of procedures and safety rules. Inspect, test, and measure completed work, using devices such as hand tools and gauges to verify conformance to standards and repair requirements. Requisition materials and supplies such as tools, equipment, and replacement parts.

Education/Training Required: High school diploma or equivalent. **Education and Training Program:**

Operations Management and Supervision. **Knowledge/Courses—Mechanical Devices:** Machines and tools, including their designs, uses, repair, and maintenance. **Personnel and Human Resources:** Principles and procedures for personnel recruitment, selection, training, compensation and benefits, labor relations and negotiation, and personnel information systems. **Production and Processing:** Raw materials, production processes, quality control, costs, and other techniques for maximizing the effective manufacture and distribution of goods. **Building and Construction:** Materials, methods, and the tools involved in the construction or repair of houses, buildings, or other structures such as highways and roads. **Engineering and Technology:** The practical application of engineering science and technology. This includes applying principles, techniques, procedures, and equipment to the design and production of various goods and services. **Economics and Accounting:** Economic and accounting principles and practices, the financial markets, banking, and the analysis and reporting of financial data. **Work Experience Needed:** 1 to 5 years. **On-the-Job Training Needed:** None. **Certification/Licensure:** None.

Personality Type: Enterprising-Conventional-Realistic. **Career Cluster:** 13 Manufacturing. **Career Pathway:** 13.1 Production. **Other Jobs in This Pathway:** Adhesive Bonding Machine Operators and Tenders; Assemblers and Fabricators, All Other; Avionics Technicians; Cabinetmakers and Bench Carpenters; Cleaning, Washing, and Metal Pickling Equipment Operators and Tenders; Coating, Painting, and Spraying Machine Setters, Operators, and Tenders; Computer-Controlled Machine Tool Operators, Metal and Plastic; Cooling and Freezing Equipment Operators and Tenders; Cost Estimators; Crushing, Grinding, and Polishing Machine Setters, Operators, and Tenders; Cutters and Trimmers, Hand; Cutting and Slicing Machine Setters, Operators, and Tenders; Cutting, Punching, and Press Machine Setters, Operators, and Tenders, Metal and Plastic; Drilling and Boring Machine Tool Setters, Operators, and Tenders, Metal and Plastic; Extruding and Drawing Machine Setters, Operators, and Tenders, Metal and Plastic; Extruding and Forming Machine Setters, Operators, and Tenders, Synthetic and Glass Fibers; others.

Skills—Repairing: Repairing machines or systems using the needed tools. **Management of Financial Resources:** Determining how money will be spent to get the work done and accounting for these expenditures. **Equipment Maintenance:** Performing routine maintenance on equipment and determining when and what kind of maintenance is needed. **Troubleshooting:** Determining causes of operating errors and deciding what to do about them. **Management of Material Resources:** Obtaining and seeing to the appropriate use of equipment, facilities, and materials needed to do certain work. **Equipment Selection:** Determining the kind of tools and equipment needed to do a job. **Quality Control Analysis:** Conducting tests and inspections of products, services, or processes to evaluate quality or performance. **Operation and Control:** Controlling operations of equipment or systems.

Work Environment: More often indoors than outdoors; standing; noise; contaminants; hazardous conditions.

First-Line Supervisors of Non-Retail Sales Workers

- ⊙ Annual Earnings: $70,520
- ⊙ Earnings Growth Potential: High (47.4%)
- ⊙ Growth: 4.0%
- ⊙ Annual Job Openings: 12,350
- ⊙ Self-Employed: 41.8%

Considerations for Job Outlook: In the Postal Service, a very large decrease is expected because sales staff will be cut as post offices attempt to cut costs.

Directly supervise and coordinate activities of sales workers other than retail sales workers. Listen to and resolve customer complaints regarding services, products, or personnel. Monitor sales staff performance to ensure that goals are met. Hire, train, and evaluate personnel. Confer with company officials to develop methods and procedures to increase sales, expand markets, and promote business. Direct and supervise employees engaged in sales, inventory taking, reconciling cash receipts, or performing specific services such as pumping gasoline for customers. Provide staff members with assistance in performing difficult or complicated duties. Plan and prepare work schedules, and assign employees to specific duties. Attend company meetings to exchange product information and coordinate work activities with other departments. Prepare sales and inventory reports for management and budget departments. Formulate pricing policies on merchandise according to

profitability requirements. Examine merchandise to ensure correct pricing and display, and ensure that it functions as advertised. Analyze details of sales territories to assess their growth potential and to set quotas. Visit retailers and sales representatives to promote products and gather information. Keep records pertaining to purchases, sales, and requisitions. Coordinate sales promotion activities, and prepare merchandise displays and advertising copy. Prepare rental or lease agreements, specifying charges and payment procedures for use of machinery, tools, or other items.

Education/Training Required: High school diploma or equivalent. **Education and Training Programs:** Business, Management, Marketing, and Related Support Services, Other; General Merchandising, Sales, and Related Marketing Operations, Other; Special Products Marketing Operations; Specialized Merchandising, Sales, and Marketing Operations, Other. **Knowledge/Courses— Sales and Marketing:** Principles and methods for showing, promoting, and selling products or services. This includes marketing strategy and tactics, product demonstration, sales techniques, and sales control systems. **Economics and Accounting:** Economic and accounting principles and practices, the financial markets, banking, and the analysis and reporting of financial data. **Personnel and Human Resources:** Principles and procedures for personnel recruitment, selection, training, compensation and benefits, labor relations and negotiation, and personnel information systems. **Administration and Management:** Business and management principles involved in strategic planning, resource allocation, human resources modeling, leadership technique, production methods, and coordination of people and resources. **Mathematics:** Arithmetic, algebra, geometry, calculus, statistics, and their applications. **Clerical Practices:** Administrative and clerical procedures and systems such as word processing, managing files and records, stenography and transcription, designing forms, and other office procedures and terminology. **Work Experience Needed:** More than 5 years. **On-the-Job Training Needed:** None. **Certification/Licensure:** None.

Personality Type: Enterprising-Conventional-Social. **Career Cluster:** 14 Marketing, Sales, and Service. **Career Pathway:** 14.2 Professional Sales and Marketing. **Other Jobs in This Pathway:** Appraisers, Real Estate; Assessors; Cashiers; Counter and Rental Clerks; Demonstrators and Product Promoters; Door-To-Door Sales Workers, News and Street Vendors, and Related Workers; Driver/

Sales Workers; Energy Brokers; First-Line Supervisors of Retail Sales Workers; Gaming Change Persons and Booth Cashiers; Hotel, Motel, and Resort Desk Clerks; Interior Designers; Lodging Managers; Marketing Managers; Marking Clerks; Meeting, Convention, and Event Planners; Merchandise Displayers and Window Trimmers; Models; Online Merchants; Order Fillers, Wholesale and Retail Sales; Parts Salespersons; Property, Real Estate, and Community Association Managers; Real Estate Brokers; Real Estate Sales Agents; Reservation and Transportation Ticket Agents and Travel Clerks; Retail Salespersons; Sales and Related Workers, All Other; Sales Engineers; Sales Representatives, Services, All Other; Sales Representatives, Wholesale and Manufacturing, Except Technical and Scientific Products; others.

Skills—Management of Financial Resources: Determining how money will be spent to get the work done and accounting for these expenditures. **Management of Material Resources:** Obtaining and seeing to the appropriate use of equipment, facilities, and materials needed to do certain work. **Systems Evaluation:** Identifying measures or indicators of system performance and the actions needed to improve or correct performance relative to the goals of the system. **Instructing:** Teaching others how to do something. **Negotiation:** Bringing others together and trying to reconcile differences. **Management of Personnel Resources:** Motivating, developing, and directing people as they work, identifying the best people for the job. **Persuasion:** Persuading others to change their minds or behavior. **Monitoring:** Monitoring or assessing your performance or that of other individuals or organizations to make improvements or take corrective action.

Work Environment: Indoors; noise.

First-Line Supervisors of Office and Administrative Support Workers

- Annual Earnings: $48,810
- Earnings Growth Potential: Medium (37.9%)
- Growth: 14.3%
- Annual Job Openings: 58,440
- Self-Employed: 1.2%

Considerations for Job Outlook: Employment growth is expected to be tempered by technological advances that increase the productivity of—and thus decrease the need for—these workers and the workers they supervise. Keen competition is expected.

Directly supervise and coordinate the activities of clerical and administrative support workers. Resolve customer complaints, and answer customers' questions regarding policies and procedures. Supervise the work of office, administrative, or customer service employees to ensure adherence to quality standards, deadlines, and proper procedures, correcting errors or problems. Provide employees with guidance in handling difficult or complex problems and in resolving escalated complaints or disputes. Implement corporate and departmental policies, procedures, and service standards in conjunction with management. Discuss job performance problems with employees to identify causes and issues and to work on resolving problems. Train and instruct employees in job duties and company policies, or arrange for training to be provided. Evaluate employees' job performance and conformance to regulations, and recommend appropriate personnel action. Recruit, interview, and select employees. Review records and reports pertaining to activities such as production, payroll, and shipping to verify details, monitor work activities, and evaluate performance. Interpret and communicate work procedures and company policies to staff. Prepare and issue work schedules, deadlines, and duty assignments of office or administrative staff. Maintain records pertaining to inventory, personnel, orders, supplies, and machine maintenance. Compute figures such as balances, totals, and commissions.

Education/Training Required: High school diploma or equivalent. **Education and Training Programs:** Agricultural Business Technology; Customer Service Management; Medical Staff Services Technology/Technician; Medical/Health Management and Clinical Assistant/Specialist Training; Office Management and Supervision. **Knowledge/Courses—Clerical Practices:** Administrative and clerical procedures and systems such as word processing, managing files and records, stenography and transcription, designing forms, and other office procedures and terminology. **Economics and Accounting:** Economic and accounting principles and practices, the financial markets, banking, and the analysis and reporting of financial data. **Administration and Management:** Business and management principles involved in strategic planning, resource allocation, human resources modeling, leadership technique, production methods, and coordination of people and resources. **Personnel and Human Resources:** Principles and procedures for personnel recruitment, selection, training, compensation and benefits, labor relations and negotiation, and personnel information systems. **Customer and Personal Service:** Principles and processes for providing customer and personal services. This includes customer needs assessment, meeting quality standards for services, and evaluation of customer satisfaction. **Education and Training:** Principles and methods for curriculum and training design, teaching and instruction for individuals and groups, and the measurement of training effects. **Work Experience Needed:** 1 to 5 years. **On-the-Job Training Needed:** None. **Certification/Licensure:** None.

Personality Type: Enterprising-Conventional-Social. **Career Clusters:** 01 Agriculture, Food, and Natural Resources; 04 Business, Management, and Administration; 08 Health Science. **Career Pathways:** 01.1 Food Products and Processing Systems; 08.3 Health Informatics; 04.1 Management. **Other Jobs in These Pathways:** Administrative Services Managers; Agents and Business Managers of Artists, Performers, and Athletes; Agricultural Inspectors; Agricultural Sciences Teachers, Postsecondary; Agricultural Technicians; Biofuels Production Managers; Biomass Power Plant Managers; Brownfield Redevelopment Specialists and Site Managers; Business Continuity Planners; Business Operations Specialists, All Other; Business Teachers, Postsecondary; Buyers and Purchasing Agents, Farm Products; Chemical Technicians; Chief Executives; Chief Sustainability Officers; Clinical Psychologists; Communications Teachers, Postsecondary; Compliance Managers; Computer and Information Systems Managers; Construction Managers; Cost Estimators; Customs Brokers; Dental Laboratory Technicians; Economics Teachers, Postsecondary; Economists; Editors; Energy Auditors; Engineers, All Other; Environmental Economists; Executive Secretaries and Executive Administrative Assistants; others.

Skills—Management of Financial Resources: Determining how money will be spent to get the work done and accounting for these expenditures. **Management of Material Resources:** Obtaining and seeing to the appropriate use of equipment, facilities, and materials needed to do certain work. **Negotiation:** Bringing others together and trying to reconcile differences. **Monitoring:** Monitoring or assessing your performance or that of other individuals

or organizations to make improvements or take corrective action. **Management of Personnel Resources:** Motivating, developing, and directing people as they work, identifying the best people for the job. **Learning Strategies:** Selecting and using training/instructional methods and procedures appropriate for the situation when learning or teaching new things. **Persuasion:** Persuading others to change their minds or behavior. **Time Management:** Managing one's own time and the time of others.

Work Environment: Indoors; sitting; noise.

First-Line Supervisors of Personal Service Workers

- ⊙ Annual Earnings: $35,230
- ⊙ Earnings Growth Potential: Medium (37.5%)
- ⊙ Growth: 13.5%
- ⊙ Annual Job Openings: 8,260
- ⊙ Self-Employed: 37.6%

Considerations for Job Outlook: About-average employment growth is projected.

Directly supervise and coordinate activities of personal service workers, such as flight attendants, hairdressers, or caddies. Requisition necessary supplies, equipment, and services. Inform workers about interests and special needs of specific groups. Participate in continuing education to stay abreast of industry trends and developments. Meet with managers and other supervisors to stay informed of changes affecting operations. Collaborate with staff members to plan and develop programs of events, schedules of activities, or menus. Train workers in proper operational procedures and functions, and explain company policies. Furnish customers with information on events and activities. Resolve customer complaints regarding worker performance and services rendered. Analyze and record personnel and operational data, and write related activity reports. Observe and evaluate workers' appearance and performance to ensure quality service and compliance with specifications. Inspect work areas and operating equipment to ensure conformance to established standards in areas such as cleanliness and maintenance. Direct and coordinate the activities of workers such as flight attendants, hotel staff, or hair stylists. Assign work schedules, following work requirements, to ensure quality and timely delivery of service.

Apply customer/guest feedback to service improvement efforts. Direct marketing, advertising, and other customer recruitment efforts. Take disciplinary action to address performance problems. Recruit and hire staff members.

Education/Training Required: High school diploma or equivalent. **Education and Training Program:** Business, Management, Marketing, and Related Support Services, Other. **Knowledge/Courses—Psychology:** Human behavior and performance; individual differences in ability, personality, and interests; learning and motivation; psychological research methods; and the assessment and treatment of behavioral and affective disorders. **Therapy and Counseling:** Principles, methods, and procedures for diagnosis, treatment, and rehabilitation of physical and mental dysfunctions, and for career counseling and guidance. **Education and Training:** Principles and methods for curriculum and training design, teaching and instruction for individuals and groups, and the measurement of training effects. **Philosophy and Theology:** Different philosophical systems and religions. This includes their basic principles, values, ethics, ways of thinking, customs, practices, and their impact on human culture. **Public Safety and Security:** Relevant equipment, policies, procedures, and strategies to promote effective local, state, or national security operations for the protection of people, data, property, and institutions. **Medicine and Dentistry:** The information and techniques needed to diagnose and treat human injuries, diseases, and deformities. This includes symptoms, treatment alternatives, drug properties and interactions, and preventive health-care measures. **Work Experience Needed:** 1 to 5 years. **On-the-Job Training Needed:** None. **Certification/Licensure:** None.

Personality Type: Enterprising-Conventional-Social. **Career Cluster:** 04 Business, Management, and Administration. **Career Pathway:** 04.1 Management. **Other Jobs in This Pathway:** Administrative Services Managers; Agents and Business Managers of Artists, Performers, and Athletes; Biofuels Production Managers; Biomass Power Plant Managers; Brownfield Redevelopment Specialists and Site Managers; Business Continuity Planners; Business Operations Specialists, All Other; Business Teachers, Postsecondary; Chief Executives; Chief Sustainability Officers; Communications Teachers, Postsecondary; Compliance Managers; Computer and Information Systems Managers; Construction Managers; Cost Estimators; Customs Brokers; Economics Teachers, Postsecondary; Economists;

Energy Auditors; Environmental Economists; First-Line Supervisors of Office and Administrative Support Workers; Gaming Supervisors; General and Operations Managers; Geothermal Production Managers; Hydroelectric Production Managers; Industrial Production Managers; Investment Fund Managers; Logisticians; Logistics Analysts; Logistics Engineers; Logistics Managers; Loss Prevention Managers; Management Analysts; others.

Skills—Management of Personnel Resources: Motivating, developing, and directing people as they work, identifying the best people for the job. **Time Management:** Managing one's own time and the time of others. **Management of Financial Resources:** Determining how money will be spent to get the work done and accounting for these expenditures. **Operation Monitoring:** Watching gauges, dials, or other indicators to make sure a machine is working properly. **Negotiation:** Bringing others together and trying to reconcile differences. **Management of Material Resources:** Obtaining and seeing to the appropriate use of equipment, facilities, and materials needed to do certain work. **Service Orientation:** Actively looking for ways to help people. **Systems Evaluation:** Identifying measures or indicators of system performance and the actions needed to improve or correct performance relative to the goals of the system.

Work Environment: Indoors; standing; walking and running; using hands; noise; contaminants.

Job Specialization: Spa Managers

Plan, direct, or coordinate activities of a spa facility. Coordinate programs, schedule and direct staff, and oversee financial activities. Inform staff of job responsibilities, performance expectations, client service standards, or corporate policies and guidelines. Plan or direct spa services and programs. Train staff in the use or sale of products, programs, or activities. Assess employee performance, and suggest ways to improve work. Check spa equipment to ensure proper functioning. Coordinate facility schedules to maximize usage and efficiency. Develop staff service or retail goals, and guide staff in goal achievement. Establish spa budgets and financial goals. Inventory products, and order new supplies. Monitor operations to ensure compliance with applicable health, safety, or hygiene standards. Perform accounting duties, such as recording daily cash flow, preparing bank deposits, or generating financial statements. Recruit, interview, or hire employees. Respond to customer inquiries or complaints. Schedule staff, or supervise scheduling. Verify staff credentials, such as educational and certification requirements. Develop or implement marketing strategies. Direct facility maintenance or repair. Maintain client databases. Participate in continuing education classes to maintain current knowledge of industry. Schedule guest appointments. Sell products, services, or memberships.

Education and Training Program: Resort Management.

Personality Type: Enterprising-Conventional-Social. **Career Cluster:** 04 Business, Management, and Administration. **Career Pathway:** 04.1 Management. **Other Jobs in This Pathway:** Administrative Services Managers; Agents and Business Managers of Artists, Performers, and Athletes; Biofuels Production Managers; Biomass Power Plant Managers; Brownfield Redevelopment Specialists and Site Managers; Business Continuity Planners; Business Operations Specialists, All Other; Business Teachers, Postsecondary; Chief Executives; Chief Sustainability Officers; Communications Teachers, Postsecondary; Compliance Managers; Computer and Information Systems Managers; Construction Managers; Cost Estimators; Customs Brokers; Economics Teachers, Postsecondary; Economists; Energy Auditors; Environmental Economists; First-Line Supervisors of Office and Administrative Support Workers; First-Line Supervisors of Personal Service Workers; Gaming Supervisors; General and Operations Managers; Geothermal Production Managers; Hydroelectric Production Managers; Industrial Production Managers; Investment Fund Managers; Logisticians; Logistics Analysts; Logistics Engineers; Logistics Managers; others.

Work Environment: No data available.

First-Line Supervisors of Police and Detectives

- ⊙ Annual Earnings: $77,890
- ⊙ Earnings Growth Potential: High (40.0%)
- ⊙ Growth: 2.2%
- ⊙ Annual Job Openings: 3,870
- ⊙ Self-Employed: 0.0%

Considerations for Job Outlook: Population growth is the main source of demand for police services. Overall, opportunities in local police departments should be favorable for qualified applicants.

Directly supervise and coordinate activities of members of police force. Supervise and coordinate the investigation of criminal cases, offering guidance and expertise to investigators, and ensuring that procedures are conducted in accordance with laws and regulations. Maintain logs, prepare reports, and direct the preparation, handling, and maintenance of departmental records. Explain police operations to subordinates to assist them in performing their job duties. Cooperate with court personnel and officials from other law enforcement agencies, and testify in court as necessary. Review contents of written orders to ensure adherence to legal requirements. Investigate and resolve personnel problems within organization and charges of misconduct against staff. Direct collection, preparation, and handling of evidence and personal property of prisoners. Inform personnel of changes in regulations and policies, implications of new or amended laws, and new techniques of police work. Train staff in proper police work procedures. Monitor and evaluate the job performance of subordinates, and authorize promotions and transfers. Prepare work schedules, and assign duties to subordinates. Conduct raids, and order detention of witnesses and suspects for questioning. Discipline staff members for violation of departmental rules and regulations. Develop, implement, and revise departmental policies and procedures. Inspect facilities, supplies, vehicles, and equipment to ensure conformance to standards. Requisition and issue equipment and supplies.

Education/Training Required: High school diploma or equivalent. **Education and Training Programs:** Corrections; Criminal Justice/Law Enforcement Administration; Criminal Justice/Safety Studies. **Knowledge/Courses— Public Safety and Security:** Relevant equipment, policies, procedures, and strategies to promote effective local, state, or national security operations for the protection of people, data, property, and institutions. **Law and Government:** Laws, legal codes, court procedures, precedents, government regulations, executive orders, agency rules, and the democratic political process. **Psychology:** Human behavior and performance; individual differences in ability, personality, and interests; learning and motivation; psychological research methods; and the assessment and treatment of behavioral and affective disorders. **Sociology and Anthropology:** Group behavior and dynamics, societal trends and influences, human migrations, ethnicity, and cultures and their history and origins. **Therapy and Counseling:** Principles, methods, and procedures for diagnosis, treatment, and rehabilitation of physical and mental dysfunctions, and for career counseling and guidance. **Personnel and Human Resources:** Principles and procedures for personnel recruitment, selection, training, compensation and benefits, labor relations and negotiation, and personnel information systems. **Work Experience Needed:** 1 to 5 years. **On-the-Job Training Needed:** Moderate-term on-the-job training. **Certification/Licensure:** Licensure in some states.

Personality Type: Enterprising-Social-Conventional. **Career Cluster:** 12 Law, Public Safety, Corrections, and Security. **Career Pathways:** 12.4 Law Enforcement Services; 12.1 Correction Services. **Other Jobs in These Pathways:** Anthropology and Archeology Teachers, Postsecondary; Bailiffs; Child, Family, and School Social Workers; Correctional Officers and Jailers; Criminal Investigators and Special Agents; Criminal Justice and Law Enforcement Teachers, Postsecondary; First-Line Supervisors of Correctional Officers; Forensic Science Technicians; Immigration and Customs Inspectors; Intelligence Analysts; Police Detectives; Police Identification and Records Officers; Police Patrol Officers; Protective Service Workers, All Other; Psychology Teachers, Postsecondary; Remote Sensing Scientists and Technologists; Security Guards; Sheriffs and Deputy Sheriffs.

Skills—Management of Financial Resources: Determining how money will be spent to get the work done and accounting for these expenditures. **Management of Personnel Resources:** Motivating, developing, and directing people as they work, identifying the best people for the job. **Persuasion:** Persuading others to change their minds or behavior. **Management of Material Resources:** Obtaining and seeing to the appropriate use of equipment, facilities, and materials needed to do certain work. **Monitoring:** Monitoring or assessing your performance or that of other individuals or organizations to make improvements or take corrective action. **Learning Strategies:** Selecting and using training/instructional methods and procedures appropriate for the situation when learning or teaching new things. **Time Management:** Managing one's own time and the time of others. **Instructing:** Teaching others how to do something.

Work Environment: More often indoors than outdoors; sitting; noise; very hot or cold; bright or inadequate lighting; contaminants; hazardous equipment.

First-Line Supervisors of Production and Operating Workers

- ⊙ Annual Earnings: $53,670
- ⊙ Earnings Growth Potential: Medium (39.6%)
- ⊙ Growth: 1.9%
- ⊙ Annual Job Openings: 8,790
- ⊙ Self-Employed: 4.7%

Considerations for Job Outlook: Little change in employment is projected.

Directly supervise and coordinate the activities of production and operating workers. Enforce safety and sanitation regulations. Direct and coordinate the activities of employees engaged in the production or processing of goods, such as inspectors, machine setters, and fabricators. Read and analyze charts, work orders, production schedules, and other records and reports to determine production requirements and to evaluate current production estimates and outputs. Confer with other supervisors to coordinate operations and activities within or between departments. Plan and establish work schedules, assignments, and production sequences to meet production goals. Inspect materials, products, or equipment to detect defects or malfunctions. Observe work and monitor gauges, dials, and other indicators to ensure that operators conform to production or processing standards. Confer with management or subordinates to resolve worker problems, complaints, or grievances. Interpret specifications, blueprints, job orders, and company policies and procedures for workers. Maintain operations data, such as time, production, and cost records, and prepare management reports of production results. Recommend or implement measures to motivate employees and to improve production methods, equipment performance, product quality, or efficiency. Determine standards, budgets, production goals, and rates, based on company policies, equipment and labor availability, and workloads. Requisition materials, supplies, equipment parts, or repair services. Set up and adjust machines and equipment. Conduct employee training in equipment operations or work and safety procedures, or assign employee training to experienced workers. Keep records of employees' attendance and hours worked. Recommend or execute personnel actions, such as hirings, evaluations, and promotions. Calculate labor and equipment requirements and production specifications, using standard formulas. Plan and develop new products and production processes.

Education/Training Required: Postsecondary vocational training. **Education and Training Program:** Operations Management and Supervision. **Knowledge/Courses— Mechanical Devices:** Machines and tools, including their designs, uses, repair, and maintenance. **Production and Processing:** Raw materials, production processes, quality control, costs, and other techniques for maximizing the effective manufacture and distribution of goods. **Engineering and Technology:** The practical application of engineering science and technology. This includes applying principles, techniques, procedures, and equipment to the design and production of various goods and services. **Design:** Design techniques, tools, and principles involved in production of precision technical plans, blueprints, drawings, and models. **Personnel and Human Resources:** Principles and procedures for personnel recruitment, selection, training, compensation and benefits, labor relations and negotiation, and personnel information systems. **Administration and Management:** Business and management principles involved in strategic planning, resource allocation, human resources modeling, leadership technique, production methods, and coordination of people and resources. **Work Experience Needed:** 1 to 5 years. **On-the-Job Training Needed:** None. **Certification/Licensure:** None.

Personality Type: Enterprising-Realistic-Conventional. **Career Cluster:** 13 Manufacturing. **Career Pathway:** 13.1 Production. **Other Jobs in This Pathway:** Adhesive Bonding Machine Operators and Tenders; Assemblers and Fabricators, All Other; Avionics Technicians; Cabinetmakers and Bench Carpenters; Cleaning, Washing, and Metal Pickling Equipment Operators and Tenders; Coating, Painting, and Spraying Machine Setters, Operators, and Tenders; Computer-Controlled Machine Tool Operators, Metal and Plastic; Cooling and Freezing Equipment Operators and Tenders; Cost Estimators; Crushing, Grinding, and Polishing Machine Setters, Operators, and Tenders; Cutters and Trimmers, Hand; Cutting and Slicing Machine Setters, Operators, and Tenders; Cutting, Punching, and Press Machine Setters, Operators, and

Tenders, Metal and Plastic; Drilling and Boring Machine Tool Setters, Operators, and Tenders, Metal and Plastic; Extruding and Drawing Machine Setters, Operators, and Tenders, Metal and Plastic; Extruding and Forming Machine Setters, Operators, and Tenders, Synthetic and Glass Fibers; others.

Skills—Management of Financial Resources: Determining how money will be spent to get the work done and accounting for these expenditures. **Repairing:** Repairing machines or systems using the needed tools. **Management of Personnel Resources:** Motivating, developing, and directing people as they work, identifying the best people for the job. **Equipment Maintenance:** Performing routine maintenance on equipment and determining when and what kind of maintenance is needed. **Management of Material Resources:** Obtaining and seeing to the appropriate use of equipment, facilities, and materials needed to do certain work. **Operations Analysis:** Analyzing needs and product requirements to create a design. **Equipment Selection:** Determining the kind of tools and equipment needed to do a job. **Quality Control Analysis:** Conducting tests and inspections of products, services, or processes to evaluate quality or performance.

Work Environment: Standing; walking and running; noise; very hot or cold; contaminants; hazardous equipment; minor burns, cuts, bites, or stings.

First-Line Supervisors of Retail Sales Workers

- ⊙ Annual Earnings: $36,480
- ⊙ Earnings Growth Potential: Medium (36.1%)
- ⊙ Growth: 8.4%
- ⊙ Annual Job Openings: 51,370
- ⊙ Self-Employed: 28.4%

Considerations for Job Outlook: Limited job growth is expected as retailers increase the responsibilities of existing sales worker supervisors and as the retail industry grows slowly overall. Competition is expected. Job seekers with college degrees and retail experience should have the best prospects.

Directly supervise and coordinate activities of retail sales workers in an establishment or department.

Provide customer service by greeting and assisting customers and responding to customer inquiries and complaints. Direct and supervise employees engaged in sales, inventory-taking, reconciling cash receipts, or performing services for customers. Monitor sales activities to ensure that customers receive satisfactory service and quality goods. Inventory stock and reorder when inventory drops to a specified level. Instruct staff on how to handle difficult and complicated sales. Hire, train, and evaluate personnel in sales or marketing establishments, promoting or firing workers when appropriate. Assign employees to specific duties. Enforce safety, health, and security rules. Examine merchandise to ensure that it is correctly priced and displayed and that it functions as advertised. Plan budgets and authorize payments and merchandise returns. Perform work activities of subordinates, such as cleaning and organizing shelves and displays and selling merchandise.

Education/Training Required: High school diploma or equivalent. **Education and Training Programs:** Business, Management, Marketing, and Related Support Services, Other; Consumer Merchandising/Retailing Management; E-Commerce/Electronic Commerce; Floriculture/Floristry Operations and Management; Retailing and Retail Operations; Selling Skills and Sales Operations; Special Products Marketing Operations; Specialized Merchandising, Sales, and Marketing Operations, Other. **Knowledge/Courses—Sales and Marketing:** Principles and methods for showing, promoting, and selling products or services. This includes marketing strategy and tactics, product demonstration, sales techniques, and sales control systems. **Customer and Personal Service:** Principles and processes for providing customer and personal services. This includes customer needs assessment, meeting quality standards for services, and evaluation of customer satisfaction. **Personnel and Human Resources:** Principles and procedures for personnel recruitment, selection, training, compensation and benefits, labor relations and negotiation, and personnel information systems. **Administration and Management:** Business and management principles involved in strategic planning, resource allocation, human resources modeling, leadership technique, production methods, and coordination of people and resources. **Economics and Accounting:** Economic and accounting principles and practices, the financial markets, banking, and the analysis and reporting of financial data. **Education and Training:** Principles and methods for curriculum and training design, teaching

and instruction for individuals and groups, and the measurement of training effects. **Work Experience Needed:** 1 to 5 years. **On-the-Job Training Needed:** None. **Certification/Licensure:** None.

Personality Type: Enterprising-Conventional-Social. **Career Clusters:** 01 Agriculture, Food, and Natural Resources; 10 Human Services; 14 Marketing, Sales, and Service. **Career Pathways:** 10.5 Consumer Services Career; 01.2 Plant Systems; 14.5 Marketing Information Management and Research; 14.2 Professional Sales and Marketing. **Other Jobs in These Pathways:** Agricultural Sciences Teachers, Postsecondary; Agricultural Technicians; Animal Scientists; Appraisers, Real Estate; Assessors; Biochemists and Biophysicists; Biologists; Business Teachers, Postsecondary; Cashiers; Counter and Rental Clerks; Demonstrators and Product Promoters; Door-To-Door Sales Workers, News and Street Vendors, and Related Workers; Driver/Sales Workers; Economists; Energy Brokers; Environmental Economists; Farm and Home Management Advisors; First-Line Supervisors of Landscaping, Lawn Service, and Groundskeeping Workers; First-Line Supervisors of Non-Retail Sales Workers; Floral Designers; Food Science Technicians; Food Scientists and Technologists; Gaming Change Persons and Booth Cashiers; Geneticists; Grounds Maintenance Workers, All Other; Home Economics Teachers, Postsecondary; Hotel, Motel, and Resort Desk Clerks; Interior Designers; Interpreters and Translators; Landscaping and Groundskeeping Workers; Lodging Managers; Marketing Managers; Marking Clerks; others.

Skills—Management of Financial Resources: Determining how money will be spent to get the work done and accounting for these expenditures. **Management of Material Resources:** Obtaining and seeing to the appropriate use of equipment, facilities, and materials needed to do certain work. **Negotiation:** Bringing others together and trying to reconcile differences. **Management of Personnel Resources:** Motivating, developing, and directing people as they work, identifying the best people for the job. **Persuasion:** Persuading others to change their minds or behavior. **Systems Evaluation:** Identifying measures or indicators of system performance and the actions needed to improve or correct performance relative to the goals of the system. **Learning Strategies:** Selecting and using training/instructional methods and procedures appropriate for the situation when learning or teaching new things. **Instructing:** Teaching others how to do something.

Work Environment: Indoors; standing; walking and running; using hands; repetitive motions; noise.

First-Line Supervisors of Transportation and Material-Moving Machine and Vehicle Operators

- ⊙ Annual Earnings: $52,950
- ⊙ Earnings Growth Potential: High (40.1%)
- ⊙ Growth: 14.3%
- ⊙ Annual Job Openings: 6,930
- ⊙ Self-Employed: 1.1%

Considerations for Job Outlook: About-average increase in employment is projected.

Directly supervise and coordinate activities of transportation and material-moving machine and vehicle operators and helpers. Enforce safety rules and regulations. Plan work assignments and equipment allocations in order to meet transportation, operations, or production goals. Confer with customers, supervisors, contractors, and other personnel to exchange information and to resolve problems. Direct workers in transportation or related services, such as pumping, moving, storing, and loading/unloading of materials or people. Resolve worker problems, or collaborate with employees to assist in problem resolution. Review orders, production schedules, blueprints, and shipping/receiving notices to determine work sequences and material shipping dates, types, volumes, and destinations. Monitor field work to ensure that it is being performed properly and that materials are being used as they should be. Recommend and implement measures to improve worker motivation, equipment performance, work methods, and customer services. Maintain or verify records of time, materials, expenditures, and crew activities. Interpret transportation and tariff regulations, shipping orders, safety regulations, and company policies and procedures for workers. Explain and demonstrate work tasks to new workers, or assign workers to more experienced workers for further training. Prepare, compile, and submit reports on work activities, operations, production, and work-related

accidents. Recommend or implement personnel actions such as employee selection, evaluation, and rewards or disciplinary actions. Requisition needed personnel, supplies, equipment, parts, or repair services. Plan and establish transportation routes. Inspect or test materials, stock, vehicles, equipment, and facilities to ensure that they are safe, free of defects, and meet specifications. Compute and estimate cash, payroll, transportation, personnel, and storage requirements. Dispatch personnel and vehicles in response to telephone or radio reports of emergencies. Perform or schedule repairs and preventive maintenance of vehicles and other equipment.

Education/Training Required: High school diploma or equivalent. **Education and Training Programs:** No related CIP programs; this job is learned through work experience in a related occupation. **Knowledge/Courses—Transportation:** Principles and methods for moving people or goods by air, rail, sea, or road, including the relative costs and benefits. **Production and Processing:** Raw materials, production processes, quality control, costs, and other techniques for maximizing the effective manufacture and distribution of goods. **Personnel and Human Resources:** Principles and procedures for personnel recruitment, selection, training, compensation and benefits, labor relations and negotiation, and personnel information systems. **Customer and Personal Service:** Principles and processes for providing customer and personal services. This includes customer needs assessment, meeting quality standards for services, and evaluation of customer satisfaction. **Public Safety and Security:** Relevant equipment, policies, procedures, and strategies to promote effective local, state, or national security operations for the protection of people, data, property, and institutions. **Administration and Management:** Business and management principles involved in strategic planning, resource allocation, human resources modeling, leadership technique, production methods, and coordination of people and resources. **Work Experience Needed:** 1 to 5 years. **On-the-Job Training Needed:** None. **Certification/Licensure:** None.

Personality Type: Enterprising-Conventional-Realistic. **Career Cluster:** 16 Transportation, Distribution, and Logistics. **Career Pathway:** 16.1 Transportation Operations. **Other Jobs in This Pathway:** Aerospace Engineering and Operations Technicians; Air Traffic Controllers; Aircraft Cargo Handling Supervisors; Airfield Operations Specialists; Airline Pilots, Copilots, and Flight Engineers;

Automotive and Watercraft Service Attendants; Automotive Master Mechanics; Aviation Inspectors; Bridge and Lock Tenders; Bus Drivers, School or Special Client; Bus Drivers, Transit and Intercity; Commercial Divers; Commercial Pilots; Crane and Tower Operators; First-Line Supervisors of Helpers, Laborers, and Material Movers, Hand; Freight and Cargo Inspectors; Heavy and Tractor-Trailer Truck Drivers; Hoist and Winch Operators; Laborers and Freight, Stock, and Material Movers, Hand; Light Truck or Delivery Services Drivers; Mates—Ship, Boat, and Barge; Motor Vehicle Operators, All Other; Motorboat Operators; Operating Engineers and Other Construction Equipment Operators; Parking Lot Attendants; Pilots, Ship; Rail Transportation Workers, All Other; others.

Skills—Management of Material Resources: Obtaining and seeing to the appropriate use of equipment, facilities, and materials needed to do certain work. **Management of Financial Resources:** Determining how money will be spent to get the work done and accounting for these expenditures. **Management of Personnel Resources:** Motivating, developing, and directing people as they work, identifying the best people for the job. **Systems Evaluation:** Identifying measures or indicators of system performance and the actions needed to improve or correct performance relative to the goals of the system. **Systems Analysis:** Determining how a system should work and how changes in conditions, operations, and the environment will affect outcomes. **Operations Analysis:** Analyzing needs and product requirements to create a design. **Time Management:** Managing one's own time and the time of others. **Negotiation:** Bringing others together and trying to reconcile differences.

Work Environment: Indoors; sitting; noise; contaminants.

Fish and Game Wardens

- ⊙ Annual Earnings: $50,070
- ⊙ Earnings Growth Potential: Medium (36.7%)
- ⊙ Growth: 5.3%
- ⊙ Annual Job Openings: 220
- ⊙ Self-Employed: 0.0%

Considerations for Job Outlook: Continued demand for public safety will lead to new openings for officers in local departments; however, both state and federal jobs may be more competitive. Because they typically offer low salaries, many local departments face high turnover rates, making opportunities more plentiful for qualified applicants. However, some smaller departments may have fewer opportunities as budgets limit the ability to hire additional officers. Jobs in state and federal agencies will remain more competitive as they often offer high pay and more opportunities for both promotions and interagency transfers. Bilingual applicants with a bachelor's degree and law enforcement or military experience, especially investigative experience, should have the best opportunities in federal agencies.

Patrol assigned area to prevent fish and game law violations. Investigate reports of damage to crops or property by wildlife. Compile biological data. Patrol assigned areas by car, boat, airplane, horse, or on foot, to enforce game, fish, or boating laws and to manage wildlife programs, lakes, or land. Investigate hunting accidents and reports of fish and game law violations, and issue warnings or citations and file reports as necessary. Serve warrants, make arrests, and compile and present evidence for court actions. Protect and preserve native wildlife, plants, and ecosystems. Promote and provide hunter and trapper safety training. Seize equipment used in fish and game law violations, and arrange for disposition of fish or game illegally taken or possessed. Provide assistance to other local law enforcement agencies as required. Address schools, civic groups, sporting clubs, and the media to disseminate information concerning wildlife conservation and regulations. Recommend revisions or changes in hunting and trapping regulations or seasons and in animal management programs so that wildlife balances and habitats can be maintained. Inspect commercial operations relating to fish and wildlife, recreation, and protected areas. Collect and report information on populations and conditions of fish and wildlife in their habitats, availability of game food and cover, and suspected pollution. Survey areas and compile figures of bag counts of hunters in order to determine the effectiveness of control measures. Participate in search-and-rescue operations and in firefighting efforts. Investigate crop, property, or habitat damage or destruction, or instances of water pollution, in order to determine causes and to advise property owners of preventive measures. Design and implement control measures to prevent or counteract damage caused by wildlife or people. Document and detail the extent of crop, property, or habitat damage, and make financial loss estimates and compensation recommendations. Supervise the activities of seasonal workers. Issue licenses, permits, and other documentation.

Education/Training Required: High school diploma or equivalent. **Education and Training Programs:** Fishing and Fisheries Sciences and Management; Natural Resource Economics; Wildlife, Fish, and Wildlands Science and Management. **Knowledge/Courses—Biology:** Plant and animal organisms and their tissues, cells, functions, interdependencies, and interactions with each other and the environment. **Law and Government:** Laws, legal codes, court procedures, precedents, government regulations, executive orders, agency rules, and the democratic political process. **Geography:** Principles and methods for describing the features of land, sea, and air masses, including their physical characteristics, locations, interrelationships, and distribution of plant, animal, and human life. **Public Safety and Security:** Relevant equipment, policies, procedures, and strategies to promote effective local, state, or national security operations for the protection of people, data, property, and institutions. **Psychology:** Human behavior and performance; individual differences in ability, personality, and interests; learning and motivation; psychological research methods; and the assessment and treatment of behavioral and affective disorders. **Sociology and Anthropology:** Group behavior and dynamics, societal trends and influences, human migrations, ethnicity, and cultures and their history and origins. **Work Experience Needed:** None. **On-the-Job Training Needed:** Short-term on-the-job training. **Certification/Licensure:** None.

Personality Type: Realistic-Investigative. **Career Cluster:** 01 Agriculture, Food, and Natural Resources. **Career Pathway:** 01.5 Natural Resources Systems. **Other Jobs in This Pathway:** Biological Science Teachers, Postsecondary; Climate Change Analysts; Conveyor Operators and Tenders; Derrick Operators, Oil and Gas; Engineering Technicians, Except Drafters, All Other; Environmental Economists; Environmental Restoration Planners; Environmental Science and Protection Technicians, Including Health; Environmental Science Teachers, Postsecondary; Environmental Scientists and Specialists, Including Health; Fallers; Fishers and Related Fishing Workers; Forest and Conservation Technicians; Forest and Conservation Workers; Foresters; Forestry and Conservation Science Teachers, Postsecondary; Gas Compressor and Gas Pumping Station Operators; Geological Sample Test Technicians; Geophysical Data Technicians; Helpers—Extraction Workers; Industrial Ecologists; Industrial Truck and Tractor Operators; Loading Machine Operators, Underground Mining; Log Graders and Scalers; Logging Equipment Operators; Logging Workers, All Other; Mechanical Engineering Technicians; others.

Skills—Repairing: Repairing machines or systems using the needed tools. **Science:** Using scientific rules and methods to solve problems. **Operation and Control:** Controlling operations of equipment or systems. **Operations Analysis:** Analyzing needs and product requirements to create a design. **Systems Analysis:** Determining how a system should work and how changes in conditions, operations, and the environment will affect outcomes. **Persuasion:** Persuading others to change their minds or behavior. **Systems Evaluation:** Identifying measures or indicators of system performance and the actions needed to improve or correct performance relative to the goals of the system. **Quality Control Analysis:** Conducting tests and inspections of products, services, or processes to evaluate quality or performance.

Work Environment: Outdoors; sitting; using hands; noise; very hot or cold; bright or inadequate lighting; contaminants; hazardous equipment; minor burns, cuts, bites, or stings.

Fitness Trainers and Aerobics Instructors

- ⊙ Annual Earnings: $31,030
- ⊙ Earnings Growth Potential: High (44.1%)
- ⊙ Growth: 24.0%
- ⊙ Annual Job Openings: 10,060
- ⊙ Self-Employed: 7.9%

Considerations for Job Outlook: Job prospects should be best for workers with professional certification or increased levels of formal education in health or fitness.

Instruct or coach groups or individuals in exercise activities. Explain and enforce safety rules and regulations governing sports, recreational activities, and the use of exercise equipment. Offer alternatives during classes to accommodate different levels of fitness. Plan routines, choose appropriate music, and choose different movements for each set of muscles, depending on participants' capabilities and limitations. Observe participants, and inform them of corrective measures necessary for skill improvement. Teach proper breathing techniques used during physical exertion. Teach and demonstrate the use of gymnastic and training equipment such as trampolines and weights. Instruct participants in maintaining exertion levels to maximize the benefits from exercise routines. Maintain fitness equipment. Conduct therapeutic, recreational, or athletic activities. Monitor participants' progress, and adapt programs as needed. Evaluate individuals' abilities, needs, and physical conditions, and develop suitable training programs to meet any special requirements. Plan physical education programs to promote development of participants' physical attributes and social skills. Provide students with information and resources regarding nutrition, weight control, and lifestyle issues. Administer emergency first aid, wrap injuries, treat minor chronic disabilities, or refer injured persons to physicians. Advise clients about proper clothing and shoes.

Education/Training Required: High school diploma or equivalent. **Education and Training Programs:** Health and Physical Education, General; Physical Education Teaching and Coaching; Sport and Fitness Administration/ Management. **Knowledge/Courses—Education and Training:** Principles and methods for curriculum and training design, teaching and instruction for individuals and groups, and the measurement of training effects. **Therapy and Counseling:** Principles, methods, and procedures for diagnosis, treatment, and rehabilitation of physical and mental dysfunctions, and for career counseling and guidance. **Psychology:** Human behavior and performance; individual differences in ability, personality, and interests; learning and motivation; psychological research methods; and the assessment and treatment of behavioral and affective disorders. **Customer and Personal Service:** Principles and processes for providing customer and personal services. This includes customer needs assessment, meeting quality standards for services, and evaluation of customer satisfaction. **Medicine and Dentistry:** The information and techniques needed to diagnose and treat human injuries, diseases, and deformities. This includes symptoms, treatment alternatives, drug properties and interactions, and preventive health-care measures. **Biology:** Plant and animal organisms and their tissues, cells, functions, interdependencies, and interactions with each other and the environment. **Work Experience Needed:** None. **On-the-Job Training Needed:** Short-term on-the-job training. **Certification/Licensure:** Voluntary certification by association.

Personality Type: Social-Realistic-Enterprising. **Career Cluster:** 05 Education and Training. **Career Pathways:** 05.3 Teaching/Training; 05.1 Administration and Administrative Support. **Other Jobs in These Pathways:** Adult Basic and Secondary Education and Literacy Teachers and Instructors; Agricultural Sciences Teachers, Postsecondary; Anthropology and Archeology Teachers, Postsecondary; Architecture Teachers, Postsecondary; Area, Ethnic, and Cultural Studies Teachers, Postsecondary; Art, Drama, and Music Teachers, Postsecondary; Athletes and Sports Competitors; Atmospheric, Earth, Marine, and Space Sciences Teachers, Postsecondary; Audio-Visual and Multimedia Collections Specialists; Biological Science Teachers, Postsecondary; Business Teachers, Postsecondary; Career/Technical Education Teachers, Middle School; Career/Technical Education Teachers, Secondary School; Chemists; Coaches and Scouts; Communications Teachers, Postsecondary; Computer Science Teachers, Postsecondary; Criminal Justice and Law Enforcement Teachers, Postsecondary; Dietitians and Nutritionists; Distance Learning Coordinators; Education Administrators, All Other; Education Administrators, Elementary and Secondary School; others.

Skills—Learning Strategies: Selecting and using training/instructional methods and procedures appropriate for the situation when learning or teaching new things. **Service Orientation:** Actively looking for ways to help people. **Operations Analysis:** Analyzing needs and product requirements to create a design. **Instructing:** Teaching others how to do something. **Social Perceptiveness:** Being aware of others' reactions and understanding why they react as they do. **Technology Design:** Generating or adapting equipment and technology to serve user needs. **Systems Evaluation:** Identifying measures or indicators of system performance and the actions needed to improve or correct performance relative to the goals of the system. **Persuasion:** Persuading others to change their minds or behavior.

Work Environment: Indoors; standing; walking and running; bending or twisting the body; repetitive motions.

Flight Attendants

- Annual Earnings: $38,020
- Earnings Growth Potential: Low (34.3%)
- Growth: –0.2%
- Annual Job Openings: 1,730
- Self-Employed: 0.0%

Considerations for Job Outlook: Competition for jobs will remain strong because the occupation is expected to attract more applicants than there are job openings. When entry-level positions do become available, job prospects should be best for applicants with a college degree and one to two years of customer service experience. Job opportunities may be slightly better at regional or low-cost airlines.

Provide personal services to ensure the safety, security, and comfort of airline passengers during flight. Direct and assist passengers in emergency procedures, such as evacuating a plane following an emergency landing. Announce and demonstrate safety and emergency procedures, such as the use of oxygen masks, seat belts, and life jackets. Walk aisles of planes to verify that passengers have complied with federal regulations prior to takeoffs and landings. Verify that first aid kits and other emergency equipment, including fire extinguishers and oxygen bottles, are in working order. Administer first aid to passengers in distress. Attend preflight briefings concerning weather, altitudes, routes, emergency procedures, crew coordination, lengths of flights, food and beverage services offered, and numbers of passengers. Prepare passengers and aircraft for landing, following procedures. Determine special assistance needs of passengers such as small children, the elderly, or disabled persons. Check to ensure that food, beverages, blankets, reading material, emergency equipment, and other supplies are aboard and are in adequate supply. Reassure passengers when situations such as turbulence are encountered. Announce flight delays and descent preparations. Inspect passenger tickets to verify information and to obtain destination information. Answer passengers' questions about flights, aircraft, weather, travel routes and services, arrival times, or schedules. Assist passengers entering or disembarking the aircraft. Inspect and clean cabins, checking for any problems and making sure that cabins are in order. Greet passengers boarding aircraft and direct them to assigned seats. Conduct periodic trips through the cabin to ensure passenger comfort and to distribute reading material, headphones, pillows, playing cards, and blankets. Take inventory of headsets, alcoholic beverages, and money collected. Operate audio and video systems. Assist passengers in placing carry-on luggage in overhead, garment, or under-seat storage.

Education/Training Required: High school diploma or equivalent. **Education and Training Program:** Airline Flight Attendant Training. **Knowledge/Courses—Customer and Personal Service:** Principles and processes for providing customer and personal services. This includes customer needs assessment, meeting quality standards for services, and evaluation of customer satisfaction. **Psychology:** Human behavior and performance; individual differences in ability, personality, and interests; learning and motivation; psychological research methods; and the assessment and treatment of behavioral and affective disorders. **Geography:** Principles and methods for describing the features of land, sea, and air masses, including their physical characteristics, locations, interrelationships, and distribution of plant, animal, and human life. **Transportation:** Principles and methods for moving people or goods by air, rail, sea, or road, including the relative costs and benefits. **Philosophy and Theology:** Different philosophical systems and religions. This includes their basic principles, values, ethics, ways of thinking, customs, practices, and their impact on human culture. **Public Safety and Security:** Relevant equipment, policies, procedures, and strategies to promote effective local, state, or national security operations for the protection of people, data, property, and institutions. **Work Experience Needed:** None. **On-the-Job Training Needed:** Moderate-term on-the-job training. **Certification/Licensure:** Federal certification.

Personality Type: Enterprising-Social-Conventional. **Career Cluster:** 09 Hospitality and Tourism. **Career Pathway:** 02.2 Construction. **Other Jobs in This Pathway:** Boilermakers; Brickmasons and Blockmasons; Carpet Installers; Cement Masons and Concrete Finishers; Construction and Building Inspectors; Construction and Related Workers, All Other; Construction Carpenters; Construction Laborers; Construction Managers; Continuous Mining Machine Operators; Cost Estimators; Crane and Tower Operators; Dredge Operators; Drywall and Ceiling Tile Installers; Earth Drillers, Except Oil and Gas; Electrical Power-Line Installers and Repairers; Electricians; Electromechanical Equipment Assemblers; Engineering Technicians, Except Drafters, All Other; Excavating and Loading Machine and Dragline Operators; Explosives Workers, Ordnance Handling Experts, and Blasters; Extraction Workers, All Other; First-Line Supervisors of Construction Trades and Extraction Workers; Floor Layers, Except Carpet, Wood, and Hard Tiles; Floor Sanders and Finishers; Glaziers; Heating and Air Conditioning Mechanics and Installers; Helpers, Construction Trades, All Other; others.

Skills—Service Orientation: Actively looking for ways to help people. **Negotiation:** Bringing others together and trying to reconcile differences. **Critical Thinking:** Using logic and reasoning to identify the strengths and weaknesses of alternative solutions, conclusions, or approaches to problems. **Coordination:** Adjusting actions in relation to others' actions. **Quality Control Analysis:** Conducting tests and inspections of products, services, or processes to evaluate quality or performance. **Troubleshooting:** Determining causes of operating errors and deciding what to do about them. **Persuasion:** Persuading others to change their minds or behavior. **Technology Design:** Generating or adapting equipment and technology to serve user needs.

Work Environment: Indoors; standing; walking and running; balancing; using hands; bending or twisting the body; repetitive motions; noise; contaminants; cramped work space; exposed to disease or infections; high places.

Floor Sanders and Finishers

- ⊙ Annual Earnings: $33,350
- ⊙ Earnings Growth Potential: Medium (35.7%)
- ⊙ Growth: 17.8%
- ⊙ Annual Job Openings: 420
- ⊙ Self-Employed: 47.9%

Considerations for Job Outlook: Expected employment gains for these workers will arise from growing population and resulting increases in building and renovating structures. Job openings are also expected from the need to replace workers who leave the occupations permanently.

Scrape and sand wooden floors to smooth surfaces using floor scraper and floor sanding machine, and apply coats of finish. Scrape and sand floor edges and areas inaccessible to floor sanders, using scrapers, disk-type sanders, and sandpaper. Remove excess glue from joints, using knives, scrapers, or wood chisels. Apply filler compound

and coats of finish to floors in order to seal wood. Attach sandpaper to rollers of sanding machines. Guide sanding machines over surfaces of floors until surfaces are smooth. Inspect floors for smoothness.

Education/Training Required: High school diploma or equivalent. **Education and Training Program:** Construction Trades, Other. **Knowledge/Courses—Building and Construction:** Materials, methods, and the tools involved in the construction or repair of houses, buildings, or other structures such as highways and roads. **Mechanical Devices:** Machines and tools, including their designs, uses, repair, and maintenance. **Customer and Personal Service:** Principles and processes for providing customer and personal services. This includes customer needs assessment, meeting quality standards for services, and evaluation of customer satisfaction. **Transportation:** Principles and methods for moving people or goods by air, rail, sea, or road, including the relative costs and benefits. **Production and Processing:** Raw materials, production processes, quality control, costs, and other techniques for maximizing the effective manufacture and distribution of goods. **Work Experience Needed:** None. **On-the-Job Training Needed:** Moderate-term on-the-job training. **Certification/Licensure:** None.

Personality Type: Realistic. **Career Cluster:** 02 Architecture and Construction. **Career Pathway:** 02.2 Construction. **Other Jobs in This Pathway:** Boilermakers; Brickmasons and Blockmasons; Carpet Installers; Cement Masons and Concrete Finishers; Construction and Building Inspectors; Construction and Related Workers, All Other; Construction Carpenters; Construction Laborers; Construction Managers; Continuous Mining Machine Operators; Cost Estimators; Crane and Tower Operators; Dredge Operators; Drywall and Ceiling Tile Installers; Earth Drillers, Except Oil and Gas; Electrical Power-Line Installers and Repairers; Electricians; Electromechanical Equipment Assemblers; Engineering Technicians, Except Drafters, All Other; Excavating and Loading Machine and Dragline Operators; Explosives Workers, Ordnance Handling Experts, and Blasters; Extraction Workers, All Other; First-Line Supervisors of Construction Trades and Extraction Workers; Floor Layers, Except Carpet, Wood, and Hard Tiles; Glaziers; Heating and Air Conditioning Mechanics and Installers; Helpers, Construction Trades, All Other; others.

Skills—Equipment Maintenance: Performing routine maintenance on equipment and determining when and what kind of maintenance is needed. **Operation and Control:** Controlling operations of equipment or systems. **Repairing:** Repairing machines or systems using the needed tools. **Troubleshooting:** Determining causes of operating errors and deciding what to do about them. **Equipment Selection:** Determining the kind of tools and equipment needed to do a job. **Operation Monitoring:** Watching gauges, dials, or other indicators to make sure a machine is working properly. **Quality Control Analysis:** Conducting tests and inspections of products, services, or processes to evaluate quality or performance.

Work Environment: Indoors; standing; walking and running; kneeling, crouching, stooping, or crawling; using hands; bending or twisting the body; repetitive motions; noise; contaminants; cramped work space; hazardous conditions; hazardous equipment; minor burns, cuts, bites, or stings.

Food Service Managers

- ⊙ Annual Earnings: $48,110
- ⊙ Earnings Growth Potential: Medium (36.5%)
- ⊙ Growth: –3.3%
- ⊙ Annual Job Openings: 5,910
- ⊙ Self-Employed: 41.7%

Considerations for Job Outlook: Job opportunities for food service managers are expected to be highly competitive. Most openings will result from the need to replace managers who retire or transfer to other occupations. Although practical experience is an integral part of becoming a food service manager, applicants with a degree in hospitality or restaurant or institutional food service management should have an edge when competing for jobs at upscale restaurants.

Plan, direct, or coordinate activities of an organization or department that serves food and beverages. Test cooked food by tasting and smelling it to ensure palatability and flavor conformity. Investigate and resolve complaints regarding food quality, service, or accommodations. Schedule and receive food and beverage deliveries, checking delivery contents to verify product quality and quantity. Monitor food preparation methods, portion sizes, and garnishing and presentation of food to ensure that food is prepared and presented in an acceptable manner. Monitor budgets and payroll records, and review financial transactions to ensure that expenditures are authorized and budgeted. Schedule staff hours and assign duties. Monitor compliance with health and fire regulations regarding food preparation and serving, and building maintenance in lodging and dining facilities. Coordinate assignments of cooking personnel to ensure economical use of food and timely preparation. Keep records required by government agencies regarding sanitation, and food subsidies when appropriate. Establish standards for personnel performance and customer service. Estimate food, liquor, wine, and other beverage consumption to anticipate amounts to be purchased or requisitioned. Review work procedures and operational problems to determine ways to improve service, performance, or safety. Perform some food preparation or service tasks such as cooking, clearing tables, and serving food and drinks when necessary. Maintain food and equipment inventories, and keep inventory records. Organize and direct worker training programs, resolve personnel problems, hire new staff, and evaluate employee performance in dining and lodging facilities. Order and purchase equipment and supplies. Review menus and analyze recipes to determine labor and overhead costs, and assign prices to menu items. Record the number, type, and cost of items sold to determine which items may be unpopular or less profitable. Assess staffing needs, and recruit staff using methods such as newspaper advertisements or attendance at job fairs.

Education/Training Required: High school diploma or equivalent. **Education and Training Programs:** Hospitality Administration/Management, General; Hotel/Motel Administration/Management; Restaurant, Culinary, and Catering Management/Manager; Restaurant/Food Services Management. **Knowledge/Courses—Food Production:** Techniques and equipment for planting, growing, and harvesting food products (both plant and animal) for consumption, including storage/handling techniques. **Sales and Marketing:** Principles and methods for showing, promoting, and selling products or services. This includes marketing strategy and tactics, product demonstration, sales techniques, and sales control systems. **Personnel and Human Resources:** Principles and procedures for personnel recruitment, selection, training, compensation and benefits, labor relations and negotiation, and personnel information systems. **Production and Processing:**

Raw materials, production processes, quality control, costs, and other techniques for maximizing the effective manufacture and distribution of goods. **Education and Training:** Principles and methods for curriculum and training design, teaching and instruction for individuals and groups, and the measurement of training effects. **Administration and Management:** Business and management principles involved in strategic planning, resource allocation, human resources modeling, leadership technique, production methods, and coordination of people and resources. **Work Experience Needed:** 1 to 5 years. **On-the-Job Training Needed:** None. **Certification/Licensure:** Licensure in some states.

Personality Type: Enterprising-Conventional-Realistic. **Career Cluster:** 09 Hospitality and Tourism. **Career Pathways:** 09.2 Lodging; 09.1 Restaurants and Food/Beverage Services; 09.3 Travel and Tourism. **Other Jobs in These Pathways:** Bakers; Baristas; Bartenders; Building Cleaning Workers, All Other; Butchers and Meat Cutters; Chefs and Head Cooks; Combined Food Preparation and Serving Workers, Including Fast Food; Cooks, All Other; Cooks, Fast Food; Cooks, Institution and Cafeteria; Cooks, Private Household; Cooks, Restaurant; Cooks, Short Order; Counter Attendants, Cafeteria, Food Concession, and Coffee Shop; Dining Room and Cafeteria Attendants and Bartender Helpers; Dishwashers; First-Line Supervisors of Food Preparation and Serving Workers; First-Line Supervisors of Housekeeping and Janitorial Workers; Food Preparation and Serving Related Workers, All Other; Food Preparation Workers; Food Servers, Nonrestaurant; Gaming Managers; Hosts and Hostesses, Restaurant, Lounge, and Coffee Shop; Janitors and Cleaners, Except Maids and Housekeeping Cleaners; Lodging Managers; Maids and Housekeeping Cleaners; Managers, All Other; Meat, Poultry, and Fish Cutters and Trimmers; others.

Skills—Management of Financial Resources: Determining how money will be spent to get the work done and accounting for these expenditures. **Management of Material Resources:** Obtaining and seeing to the appropriate use of equipment, facilities, and materials needed to do certain work. **Operations Analysis:** Analyzing needs and product requirements to create a design. **Management of Personnel Resources:** Motivating, developing, and directing people as they work, identifying the best people for the job. **Negotiation:** Bringing others together and trying to reconcile differences. **Equipment Maintenance:**

Performing routine maintenance on equipment and determining when and what kind of maintenance is needed. **Service Orientation:** Actively looking for ways to help people. **Repairing:** Repairing machines or systems using the needed tools.

Work Environment: Indoors; standing; walking and running; using hands; repetitive motions; noise; contaminants; minor burns, cuts, bites, or stings.

Gaming Managers

- Annual Earnings: $67,230
- Earnings Growth Potential: Medium (36.4%)
- Growth: 12.1%
- Annual Job Openings: 100
- Self-Employed: 0.0%

Considerations for Job Outlook: Although job openings will occur due to workers leaving the occupation, strong competition is expected for jobs at casinos. Those with work experience in customer service at a hotel or resort should have better job prospects because of the importance of customer service in casinos.

Plan, direct, or coordinate gaming operations in a casino. Resolve customer complaints regarding problems such as payout errors. Remove suspected cheaters, such as card counters and other players who may have systems that shift the odds of winning to their favor. Maintain familiarity with all games used at a facility, as well as strategies and tricks employed in those games. Train new workers and evaluate their performance. Circulate among gaming tables to ensure that operations are conducted properly, that dealers follow house rules, and that players are not cheating. Explain and interpret house rules, such as game rules and betting limits. Monitor staffing levels to ensure that games and tables are adequately staffed for each shift, arranging for staff rotations and breaks, and locating substitute employees as necessary. Interview and hire workers. Prepare work schedules and station assignments, and keep attendance records. Direct the distribution of complimentary hotel rooms, meals, and other discounts or free items given to players based on their length of play and betting totals. Establish policies on issues such as the type of gambling offered and the odds, the extension of credit, and the serving of food and beverages. Track supplies of money to tables, and perform any required paperwork. Set and maintain a bank and table limit for each game. Monitor credit extended to players. Review operational expenses, budget estimates, betting accounts, and collection reports for accuracy. Record, collect, and pay off bets, issuing receipts as necessary. Direct workers compiling summary sheets that show wager amounts and payoffs for races and events. Notify board attendants of table vacancies so that waiting patrons can play.

Education/Training Required: Some college, no degree. **Education and Training Program:** Casino Management. **Knowledge/Courses—Sales and Marketing:** Principles and methods for showing, promoting, and selling products or services. This includes marketing strategy and tactics, product demonstration, sales techniques, and sales control systems. **Personnel and Human Resources:** Principles and procedures for personnel recruitment, selection, training, compensation and benefits, labor relations and negotiation, and personnel information systems. **Customer and Personal Service:** Principles and processes for providing customer and personal services. This includes customer needs assessment, meeting quality standards for services, and evaluation of customer satisfaction. **Administration and Management:** Business and management principles involved in strategic planning, resource allocation, human resources modeling, leadership technique, production methods, and coordination of people and resources. **Economics and Accounting:** Economic and accounting principles and practices, the financial markets, banking, and the analysis and reporting of financial data. **Mathematics:** Arithmetic, algebra, geometry, calculus, statistics, and their applications. **Work Experience Needed:** More than 5 years. **On-the-Job Training Needed:** None. **Certification/Licensure:** Licensure in some states.

Personality Type: Enterprising-Conventional. **Career Cluster:** 09 Hospitality and Tourism. **Career Pathway:** 09.1 Restaurants and Food/Beverage Services. **Other Jobs in This Pathway:** Bakers; Baristas; Bartenders; Butchers and Meat Cutters; Chefs and Head Cooks; Combined Food Preparation and Serving Workers, Including Fast Food; Cooks, All Other; Cooks, Fast Food; Cooks, Institution and Cafeteria; Cooks, Private Household; Cooks, Restaurant; Cooks, Short Order; Counter Attendants, Cafeteria, Food Concession, and Coffee Shop; Dining Room and Cafeteria Attendants and Bartender Helpers; Dishwashers; First-Line Supervisors of Food Preparation and Serving

Workers; Food Preparation and Serving Related Workers, All Other; Food Preparation Workers; Food Servers, Non-restaurant; Food Service Managers; Hosts and Hostesses, Restaurant, Lounge, and Coffee Shop; Meat, Poultry, and Fish Cutters and Trimmers; Slaughterers and Meat Packers; Waiters and Waitresses.

Skills—Management of Financial Resources: Determining how money will be spent to get the work done and accounting for these expenditures. **Persuasion:** Persuading others to change their minds or behavior. **Negotiation:** Bringing others together and trying to reconcile differences. **Service Orientation:** Actively looking for ways to help people. **Management of Personnel Resources:** Motivating, developing, and directing people as they work, identifying the best people for the job. **Monitoring:** Monitoring or assessing your performance or that of other individuals or organizations to make improvements or take corrective action. **Systems Evaluation:** Identifying measures or indicators of system performance and the actions needed to improve or correct performance relative to the goals of the system. **Time Management:** Managing one's own time and the time of others.

Work Environment: Indoors; standing; walking and running; noise; contaminants.

Gaming Supervisors

- ⊙ Annual Earnings: $48,820
- ⊙ Earnings Growth Potential: Medium (36.3%)
- ⊙ Growth: 6.9%
- ⊙ Annual Job Openings: 920
- ⊙ Self-Employed: 35.7%

Considerations for Job Outlook: Although job openings will occur due to workers leaving the occupation, strong competition is expected for jobs at casinos. Those with work experience in customer service at a hotel or resort should have better job prospects because of the importance of customer service in casinos.

Supervise and coordinate activities of workers in assigned gaming areas. Monitor game operations to ensure that house rules are followed, that tribal, state, and federal regulations are adhered to, and that employees provide prompt and courteous service. Observe gamblers' behavior for signs of cheating such as marking, switching, or counting cards; notify security staff of suspected cheating. Maintain familiarity with the games at a facility, and with strategies and tricks used by cheaters at such games. Perform paperwork required for monetary transactions. Resolve customer and employee complaints. Greet customers and ask about the quality of service they are receiving. Establish and maintain banks and table limits for each game. Report customer-related incidents occurring in gaming areas to supervisors. Monitor stations and games, and move dealers from game to game to ensure adequate staffing. Explain and interpret house rules, such as game rules and betting limits, for patrons. Supervise the distribution of complimentary meals, hotel rooms, discounts, and other items given to players based on length of play and amount bet. Evaluate workers' performance and prepare written performance evaluations. Monitor patrons for signs of compulsive gambling, offering assistance if necessary. Record, issue receipts for, and pay off bets. Monitor and verify the counting, wrapping, weighing, and distribution of currency and coins. Direct workers compiling summary sheets for each race or event to record amounts wagered and amounts to be paid to winners. Determine how many gaming tables to open each day and schedule staff accordingly. Establish policies on types of gambling offered, odds, and extension of credit. Interview, hire, and train workers. Provide fire protection and first-aid assistance when necessary. Review operational expenses, budget estimates, betting accounts, and collection reports for accuracy.

Education/Training Required: High school diploma or equivalent. **Education and Training Program:** Casino Management. **Knowledge/Courses—Customer and Personal Service:** Principles and processes for providing customer and personal services. This includes customer needs assessment, meeting quality standards for services, and evaluation of customer satisfaction. **Psychology:** Human behavior and performance; individual differences in ability, personality, and interests; learning and motivation; psychological research methods; and the assessment and treatment of behavioral and affective disorders. **Mathematics:** Arithmetic, algebra, geometry, calculus, statistics, and their applications. **Law and Government:** Laws, legal codes, court procedures, precedents, government regulations, executive orders, agency rules, and the democratic political process. **Sales and Marketing:** Principles and methods for showing, promoting, and selling products or services. This includes marketing strategy and tactics, product demonstration, sales techniques, and sales control systems.

Personnel and Human Resources: Principles and procedures for personnel recruitment, selection, training, compensation and benefits, labor relations and negotiation, and personnel information systems. **Work Experience Needed:** 1 to 5 years. **On-the-Job Training Needed:** None. **Certification/Licensure:** Licensure in some states.

Personality Type: Enterprising-Conventional. **Career Cluster:** 04 Business, Management, and Administration. **Career Pathway:** 04.1 Management. **Other Jobs in This Pathway:** Administrative Services Managers; Agents and Business Managers of Artists, Performers, and Athletes; Biofuels Production Managers; Biomass Power Plant Managers; Brownfield Redevelopment Specialists and Site Managers; Business Continuity Planners; Business Operations Specialists, All Other; Business Teachers, Postsecondary; Chief Executives; Chief Sustainability Officers; Communications Teachers, Postsecondary; Compliance Managers; Computer and Information Systems Managers; Construction Managers; Cost Estimators; Customs Brokers; Economics Teachers, Postsecondary; Economists; Energy Auditors; Environmental Economists; First-Line Supervisors of Office and Administrative Support Workers; First-Line Supervisors of Personal Service Workers; General and Operations Managers; Geothermal Production Managers; Hydroelectric Production Managers; Industrial Production Managers; Investment Fund Managers; Logisticians; Logistics Analysts; Logistics Engineers; Logistics Managers; others.

Skills—Management of Financial Resources: Determining how money will be spent to get the work done and accounting for these expenditures. **Management of Personnel Resources:** Motivating, developing, and directing people as they work, identifying the best people for the job. **Social Perceptiveness:** Being aware of others' reactions and understanding why they react as they do. **Negotiation:** Bringing others together and trying to reconcile differences. **Time Management:** Managing one's own time and the time of others. **Service Orientation:** Actively looking for ways to help people. **Systems Evaluation:** Identifying measures or indicators of system performance and the actions needed to improve or correct performance relative to the goals of the system. **Monitoring:** Monitoring or assessing your performance or that of other individuals or organizations to make improvements or take corrective action.

Work Environment: Indoors; standing; walking and running; noise; contaminants.

General and Operations Managers

- Annual Earnings: $95,150
- Earnings Growth Potential: High (50.0%)
- Growth: 4.6%
- Annual Job Openings: 41,010
- Self-Employed: 1.2%

Considerations for Job Outlook: Educational requirements vary by industry, but candidates who can demonstrate strong leadership abilities and experience getting positive results will have better job opportunities.

Plan, direct, or coordinate the operations of public or private sector organizations. Oversee activities directly related to making products or providing services. Direct and coordinate activities of businesses or departments concerned with the production, pricing, sales, or distribution of products. Review financial statements, sales and activity reports, and other performance data to measure productivity and goal achievement and to determine areas needing cost reduction and program improvement. Manage staff, preparing work schedules and assigning specific duties. Direct and coordinate organization's financial and budget activities to fund operations, maximize investments, and increase efficiency. Establish and implement departmental policies, goals, objectives, and procedures, conferring with board members, organization officials, and staff members as necessary. Determine staffing requirements, and interview, hire, and train new employees, or oversee those personnel processes. Plan and direct activities such as sales promotions, coordinating with other department heads as required. Determine goods and services to be sold, and set prices and credit terms based on forecasts of customer demand. Monitor businesses and agencies to ensure that they efficiently and effectively provide needed services while staying within budgetary limits. Locate, select, and procure merchandise for resale, representing management in purchase negotiations. Perform sales floor work such as greeting and assisting customers, stocking shelves, and taking inventory.

Education/Training Required: Associate degree. **Education and Training Programs:** Business Administration and Management, General; Entrepreneurship/Entrepreneurial Studies; International Business/Trade/Commerce; Public Administration. **Knowledge/Courses—Economics and Accounting:** Economic and accounting principles and practices, the financial markets, banking, and the analysis and reporting of financial data. **Personnel and Human Resources:** Principles and procedures for personnel recruitment, selection, training, compensation and benefits, labor relations and negotiation, and personnel information systems. **Administration and Management:** Business and management principles involved in strategic planning, resource allocation, human resources modeling, leadership technique, production methods, and coordination of people and resources. **Sales and Marketing:** Principles and methods for showing, promoting, and selling products or services. This includes marketing strategy and tactics, product demonstration, sales techniques, and sales control systems. **Building and Construction:** Materials, methods, and the tools involved in the construction or repair of houses, buildings, or other structures such as highways and roads. **Clerical Practices:** Administrative and clerical procedures and systems such as word processing, managing files and records, stenography and transcription, designing forms, and other office procedures and terminology. **Work Experience Needed:** 1 to 5 years. **On-the-Job Training Needed:** None. **Certification/Licensure:** Licensure for some specializations.

Personality Type: Enterprising-Conventional-Social. **Career Clusters:** 04 Business, Management, and Administration; 07 Government and Public Administration. **Career Pathways:** 04.1 Management; 07.1 Governance. **Other Jobs in These Pathways:** Administrative Services Managers; Agents and Business Managers of Artists, Performers, and Athletes; Biofuels Production Managers; Biomass Power Plant Managers; Brownfield Redevelopment Specialists and Site Managers; Business Continuity Planners; Business Operations Specialists, All Other; Business Teachers, Postsecondary; Chief Executives; Chief Sustainability Officers; Communications Teachers, Postsecondary; Compliance Managers; Computer and Information Systems Managers; Construction Managers; Cost Estimators; Customs Brokers; Economics Teachers, Postsecondary; Economists; Energy Auditors; Environmental Economists; First-Line Supervisors of Office and Administrative Support Workers; First-Line Supervisors of Personal Service Workers; Gaming Supervisors; Geothermal Production Managers; Hydroelectric Production Managers; Industrial Production Managers; Investment Fund Managers; Legislators; Logisticians; Logistics Analysts; Logistics Engineers; Logistics Managers; others.

Skills—Management of Material Resources: Obtaining and seeing to the appropriate use of equipment, facilities, and materials needed to do certain work. **Management of Financial Resources:** Determining how money will be spent to get the work done and accounting for these expenditures. **Operations Analysis:** Analyzing needs and product requirements to create a design. **Management of Personnel Resources:** Motivating, developing, and directing people as they work, identifying the best people for the job. **Negotiation:** Bringing others together and trying to reconcile differences. **Systems Analysis:** Determining how a system should work and how changes in conditions, operations, and the environment will affect outcomes. **Coordination:** Adjusting actions in relation to others' actions. **Systems Evaluation:** Identifying measures or indicators of system performance and the actions needed to improve or correct performance relative to the goals of the system.

Work Environment: Indoors; more often sitting than standing; noise.

Geological and Petroleum Technicians

- ⊙ Annual Earnings: $49,690
- ⊙ Earnings Growth Potential: High (42.4%)
- ⊙ Growth: 14.6%
- ⊙ Annual Job Openings: 700
- ⊙ Self-Employed: 0.0%

Considerations for Job Outlook: High prices and growing demand for natural resources—especially oil and natural gas—are expected to increase demand for geological exploration and extraction in the future. Historically, when oil and natural gas prices are low, companies limit exploration and hire fewer technicians. When prices are high, however, companies explore and extract more. If oil prices remain high over the long run, the demand for geological and petroleum technicians will remain high as well.

Assist scientists or engineers in the use of electronic, sonic, or nuclear measuring instruments in both laboratory and production activities to obtain data indicating potential resources. For task data, see Job Specializations.

Education/Training Required: Associate degree. **Work Experience Needed:** None. **On-the-Job Training Needed:** Moderate-term on-the-job training. **Certification/Licensure:** None.

Job Specialization: Geological Sample Test Technicians

Test and analyze geological samples, crude oil, or petroleum products to detect presence of petroleum, gas, or mineral deposits indicating potential for exploration and production or to determine physical and chemical properties to ensure that products meet quality standards. Test and analyze samples in order to determine their content and characteristics, using laboratory apparatus and testing equipment. Collect and prepare solid and fluid samples for analysis. Assemble, operate, and maintain field and laboratory testing, measuring, and mechanical equipment, working as part of a crew when required. Compile and record testing and operational data for review and further analysis. Adjust and repair testing, electrical, and mechanical equipment and devices. Supervise well exploration and drilling activities, and well completions. Inspect engines for wear and defective parts, using equipment and measuring devices. Prepare notes, sketches, geological maps, and cross-sections. Participate in geological, geophysical, geochemical, hydrographic, or oceanographic surveys; prospecting field trips; exploratory drilling; well logging; or underground mine survey programs. Plot information from aerial photographs, well logs, section descriptions, and other databases. Assess the environmental impacts of development projects on subsurface materials. Collaborate with hydrogeologists in order to evaluate groundwater and well circulation. Prepare, transcribe, and/or analyze seismic, gravimetric, well log, or other geophysical and survey data. Participate in the evaluation of possible mining locations.

Education and Training Program: Petroleum Technology/Technician. **Knowledge/Courses—Chemistry:** The chemical composition, structure, and properties of substances and of the chemical processes and transformations that they undergo. This includes uses of chemicals and their danger signs, production techniques, and disposal methods. **Geography:** Principles and methods for describing the features of land, sea, and air masses, including their physical characteristics, locations, interrelationships, and distribution of plant, animal, and human life. **Mechanical Devices:** Machines and tools, including their designs, uses, repair, and maintenance. **Physics:** Physical principles, laws, their interrelationships, and applications to understanding fluid, material, and atmospheric dynamics, and mechanical, electrical, atomic, and subatomic structures and processes. **Mathematics:** Arithmetic, algebra, geometry, calculus, statistics, and their applications. **Clerical Practices:** Administrative and clerical procedures and systems such as word processing, managing files and records, stenography and transcription, designing forms, and other office procedures and terminology.

Personality Type: Realistic-Investigative-Conventional. **Career Cluster:** 01 Agriculture, Food, and Natural Resources. **Career Pathway:** 01.5 Natural Resources Systems. **Other Jobs in This Pathway:** Biological Science Teachers, Postsecondary; Climate Change Analysts; Conveyor Operators and Tenders; Derrick Operators, Oil and Gas; Engineering Technicians, Except Drafters, All Other; Environmental Economists; Environmental Restoration Planners; Environmental Science and Protection Technicians, Including Health; Environmental Science Teachers, Postsecondary; Environmental Scientists and Specialists, Including Health; Fallers; Fish and Game Wardens; Fishers and Related Fishing Workers; Forest and Conservation Technicians; Forest and Conservation Workers; Foresters; Forestry and Conservation Science Teachers, Postsecondary; Gas Compressor and Gas Pumping Station Operators; Geophysical Data Technicians; Helpers—Extraction Workers; Industrial Ecologists; Industrial Truck and Tractor Operators; Loading Machine Operators, Underground Mining; Log Graders and Scalers; Logging Equipment Operators; Logging Workers, All Other; Mechanical Engineering Technicians; Mine Shuttle Car Operators; others.

Skills—Repairing: Repairing machines or systems using the needed tools. **Science:** Using scientific rules and methods to solve problems. **Equipment Selection:** Determining the kind of tools and equipment needed to do a job. **Equipment Maintenance:** Performing routine maintenance on equipment and determining when and what kind of maintenance is needed. **Troubleshooting:** Determining causes of operating errors and deciding what to do about them. **Mathematics:** Using mathematics to solve problems. **Operation and Control:** Controlling operations of equipment or systems. **Quality Control Analysis:** Conducting tests and inspections of products, services, or processes to evaluate quality or performance.

Work Environment: Indoors; more often sitting than standing; using hands; noise; contaminants; hazardous equipment.

Job Specialization: Geophysical Data Technicians

Measure, record, and evaluate geological data by using sonic, electronic, electrical, seismic, or gravity-measuring instruments to prospect for oil or gas. May collect and evaluate core samples and cuttings. Prepare notes, sketches, geological maps, and cross-sections. Read and study reports to compile information and data for geological and geophysical prospecting. Interview individuals and research public databases to obtain information. Assemble, maintain, and distribute information for library or record systems. Operate and adjust equipment and apparatus used to obtain geological data. Plan and direct activities of workers who operate equipment to collect data. Set up, or direct setup of, instruments used to collect geological data. Record readings to compile data used in prospecting for oil or gas. Supervise oil, water, and gas well drilling activities. Collect samples and cuttings, using equipment and hand tools. Develop and print photographic recordings of information, using equipment. Measure geological characteristics used in prospecting for oil or gas, using measuring instruments. Evaluate and interpret core samples and cuttings, and other geological data used in prospecting for oil or gas. Diagnose and repair malfunctioning instruments and equipment, using manufacturers' manuals and hand tools. Prepare and attach packing instructions to shipping containers. Develop and design packing materials and handling procedures for shipping of objects.

Education and Training Program: Petroleum Technology/Technician. **Knowledge/Courses—Geography:** Principles and methods for describing the features of land, sea, and air masses, including their physical characteristics, locations, interrelationships, and distribution of plant, animal, and human life. **Engineering and Technology:** The practical application of engineering science and technology. This includes applying principles, techniques, procedures, and equipment to the design and production of various goods and services. **Physics:** Physical principles, laws, their interrelationships, and applications to understanding fluid, material, and atmospheric dynamics, and mechanical, electrical, atomic, and subatomic structures and processes. **Computers and Electronics:** Circuit boards, processors, chips, electronic equipment, and computer hardware and software, including applications and programming. **Mathematics:** Arithmetic, algebra, geometry, calculus, statistics, and their applications. **Chemistry:** The chemical composition, structure, and properties of substances and of the chemical processes and transformations that they undergo. This includes uses of chemicals and their danger signs, production techniques, and disposal methods.

Personality Type: Conventional-Realistic-Investigative. **Career Cluster:** 01 Agriculture, Food, and Natural Resources. **Career Pathway:** 01.5 Natural Resources Systems. **Other Jobs in This Pathway:** Biological Science Teachers, Postsecondary; Climate Change Analysts; Conveyor Operators and Tenders; Derrick Operators, Oil and Gas; Engineering Technicians, Except Drafters, All Other; Environmental Economists; Environmental Restoration Planners; Environmental Science and Protection Technicians, Including Health; Environmental Science Teachers, Postsecondary; Environmental Scientists and Specialists, Including Health; Fallers; Fish and Game Wardens; Fishers and Related Fishing Workers; Forest and Conservation Technicians; Forest and Conservation Workers; Foresters; Forestry and Conservation Science Teachers, Postsecondary; Gas Compressor and Gas Pumping Station Operators; Geological Sample Test Technicians; Helpers—Extraction Workers; Industrial Ecologists; Industrial Truck and Tractor Operators; Loading Machine Operators, Underground Mining; Log Graders and Scalers; Logging Equipment Operators; Logging Workers, All Other; Mechanical Engineering Technicians; others.

Skills—Science: Using scientific rules and methods to solve problems. **Operation and Control:** Controlling operations of equipment or systems. **Operation Monitoring:** Watching gauges, dials, or other indicators to make sure a machine is working properly. **Reading Comprehension:** Understanding written sentences and paragraphs in work-related documents. **Operations Analysis:** Analyzing needs and product requirements to create a design. **Writing:** Communicating effectively in writing as appropriate for the needs of the audience. **Technology Design:** Generating or adapting equipment and technology to serve user needs. **Troubleshooting:** Determining causes of operating errors and deciding what to do about them.

Work Environment: Indoors; sitting.

Glaziers

- ⊙ Annual Earnings: $37,350
- ⊙ Earnings Growth Potential: Medium (36.8%)
- ⊙ Growth: 42.2%
- ⊙ Annual Job Openings: 3,340
- ⊙ Self-Employed: 4.8%

Considerations for Job Outlook: Good job opportunities are expected as many openings should arise from the need to replace glaziers who leave the occupation. Because employers prefer workers who do many different tasks, glaziers with a wide range of skills will have the best job opportunities. In addition, workers with military service are viewed favorably during initial hiring. As with many other construction workers, employment of glaziers is sensitive to the fluctuations of the economy. On the one hand, glaziers may experience periods of unemployment when the overall level of construction falls. On the other hand, shortages of workers may occur in some areas during peak periods of building activity. Employment opportunities should be best in the South and in metropolitan areas, where most glazing contractors and glass shops are located.

Install glass in windows, skylights, store fronts, and display cases, or on surfaces such as building fronts, interior walls, ceilings, and tabletops. Read and interpret blueprints and specifications to determine size, shape, color, type, and thickness of glass; location of framing; installation procedures; and staging and scaffolding materials required. Determine plumb of walls or ceilings, using plumb-lines and levels. Measure mirrors and dimensions of areas to be covered in order to determine work procedures. Fabricate and install metal sashes and moldings for glass installation, using aluminum or steel framing. Fasten glass panes into wood sashes or frames with clips, points, or moldings, adding weather seals or putty around pane edges to seal joints. Secure mirrors in position, using mastic cement, putty, bolts, or screws. Cut, fit, install, repair, and replace glass and glass substitutes, such as plastic and aluminum, in building interiors or exteriors and in furniture or other products. Cut and remove broken glass prior to installing replacement glass. Set glass doors into frames, and bolt metal hinges, handles, locks, and other hardware to attach doors to frames and walls. Score glass with cutters' wheels, breaking off excess glass by hand or with notched tools. Cut, assemble, fit, and attach metal-framed glass enclosures for showers, bathtubs, display cases, skylights, solariums, and other structures. Drive trucks to installation sites, and unload mirrors, glass equipment, and tools. Load and arrange glass and mirrors onto delivery trucks, using suction cups or cranes to lift glass. Install pre-assembled metal or wood frameworks for windows or doors to be fitted with glass panels, using hand tools. Assemble, erect, and dismantle scaffolds, rigging, and hoisting equipment. Cut and attach mounting strips, metal or wood moldings, rubber gaskets, or metal clips to surfaces in preparation for mirror installation. Grind and polish glass, and smooth edges when necessary. Measure and mark outlines or patterns on glass to indicate cutting lines.

Education/Training Required: High school diploma or equivalent. **Education and Training Program:** Glazier Training. **Knowledge/Courses—Building and Construction:** Materials, methods, and the tools involved in the construction or repair of houses, buildings, or other structures such as highways and roads. **Mechanical Devices:** Machines and tools, including their designs, uses, repair, and maintenance. **Design:** Design techniques, tools, and principles involved in production of precision technical plans, blueprints, drawings, and models. **Engineering and Technology:** The practical application of engineering science and technology. This includes applying principles, techniques, procedures, and equipment to the design and production of various goods and services. **Mathematics:** Arithmetic, algebra, geometry, calculus, statistics, and their applications. **Work Experience Needed:** None. **On-the-Job Training Needed:** Apprenticeship. **Certification/Licensure:** Voluntary certification by association.

Personality Type: Realistic-Conventional. **Career Cluster:** 02 Architecture and Construction. **Career Pathway:** 02.2 Construction. **Other Jobs in This Pathway:** Boilermakers; Brickmasons and Blockmasons; Carpet Installers; Cement Masons and Concrete Finishers; Construction and Building Inspectors; Construction and Related Workers, All Other; Construction Carpenters; Construction Laborers; Construction Managers; Continuous Mining Machine Operators; Cost Estimators; Crane and Tower Operators; Dredge Operators; Drywall and Ceiling Tile Installers; Earth Drillers, Except Oil and Gas; Electrical Power-Line Installers and Repairers; Electricians; Electromechanical Equipment Assemblers; Engineering Technicians, Except Drafters, All Other; Excavating and Loading Machine and Dragline Operators; Explosives Workers, Ordnance Handling Experts, and Blasters; Extraction Workers, All Other; First-Line Supervisors of Construction Trades and Extraction Workers; Floor Layers, Except Carpet, Wood, and Hard Tiles; Floor Sanders and Finishers; Heating and Air Conditioning Mechanics and Installers; Helpers, Construction Trades, All Other; others.

Skills—Operation and Control: Controlling operations of equipment or systems. **Installation:** Installing equipment, machines, wiring, or programs to meet specifications. **Quality Control Analysis:** Conducting tests and inspections of products, services, or processes to evaluate quality or performance. **Operation Monitoring:** Watching gauges, dials, or other indicators to make sure a machine is working properly. **Troubleshooting:** Determining causes of operating errors and deciding what to do about them.

Work Environment: Outdoors; standing; climbing; walking and running; using hands; bending or twisting the body; repetitive motions; noise; very hot or cold; contaminants; high places; hazardous equipment; minor burns, cuts, bites, or stings.

Hairdressers, Hairstylists, and Cosmetologists

- ⊙ Annual Earnings: $22,570
- ⊙ Earnings Growth Potential: Low (26.0%)
- ⊙ Growth: 15.7%
- ⊙ Annual Job Openings: 21,810
- ⊙ Self-Employed: 44.9%

Considerations for Job Outlook: Overall job opportunities for barbers, hairdressers, and cosmetologists are expected to be good. A large number of job openings will stem from the need to replace workers who transfer to other occupations, retire, or leave the occupations for other reasons. However, workers should expect stiff competition for jobs and clients at higher-paying salons, of which there are relatively few and for which applicants must compete with a large pool of experienced hairdressers and cosmetologists. Because employment of shampooers is expected to decline, job opportunities should be somewhat limited, available only from the need to replace those who leave the occupation.

Provide beauty services, such as shampooing, cutting, coloring, and styling hair, and massaging and treating scalp. Keep work stations clean, and sanitize tools such as scissors and combs. Cut, trim, and shape hair or hairpieces based on customers' instructions, hair type, and facial features, using clippers, scissors, trimmers, and razors. Analyze patrons' hair and other physical features to determine and recommend beauty treatment or suggest hairstyles. Schedule client appointments. Bleach, dye, or tint hair, using applicator or brush. Update and maintain customer-information records, such as beauty services provided. Shampoo, rinse, condition, and dry hair and scalp or hairpieces with water, liquid soap, or other solutions. Operate cash registers to receive payments from patrons. Demonstrate and sell hair-care products and cosmetics. Apply water, setting, straightening, or waving solutions to hair, and use curlers, rollers, hot combs, and curling irons to press and curl hair. Develop new styles and techniques. Comb, brush, and spray hair or wigs to set style. Shape eyebrows and remove facial hair, using depilatory cream, tweezers, electrolysis, or wax. Administer therapeutic medication, and advise patron to seek medical treatment for chronic or contagious scalp conditions. Massage and treat scalp for hygienic and remedial purposes, using hands, fingers, or vibrating equipment. Shave, trim, and shape beards and moustaches. Train or supervise other hairstylists, hairdressers, and assistants.

Education/Training Required: Postsecondary vocational training. **Education and Training Programs:** Cosmetology and Related Personal Grooming Arts, Other; Cosmetology, Barber/Styling, and Nail Instructor; Cosmetology/Cosmetologist Training, General; Electrolysis/Electrology and Electrolysis Technician Training; Hair Styling/Stylist and Hair Design; Make-Up Artist/Specialist Training; Permanent Cosmetics/Makeup and Tattooing; Salon/Beauty Salon Management/Manager Training. **Knowledge/Courses—Chemistry:** The chemical composition, structure, and properties of substances and of the chemical processes and transformations that they undergo. This includes uses of chemicals and their danger signs, production techniques, and disposal methods. **Sales and Marketing:** Principles and methods for showing, promoting, and selling products or services. This includes marketing strategy and tactics, product demonstration, sales techniques, and sales control systems. **Work Experience Needed:** None. **On-the-Job Training Needed:** None. **Certification/Licensure:** Licensure.

Personality Type: Artistic-Enterprising-Social. **Career Cluster:** 10 Human Services. **Career Pathway:** 10.4 Personal Care Services. **Other Jobs in This Pathway:** Barbers; Embalmers; Funeral Attendants; Funeral Service Managers; Laundry and Dry-Cleaning Workers; Makeup Artists, Theatrical and Performance; Manicurists and Pedicurists; Pressers, Textile, Garment, and Related Materials; Sewers, Hand; Sewing Machine Operators; Shampooers; Skincare Specialists; Tailors, Dressmakers, and Custom Sewers; Textile Bleaching and Dyeing Machine Operators and Tenders.

Skills—Service Orientation: Actively looking for ways to help people. **Learning Strategies:** Selecting and using training/instructional methods and procedures appropriate for the situation when learning or teaching new things. **Instructing:** Teaching others how to do something. **Equipment Selection:** Determining the kind of tools and equipment needed to do a job. **Operations Analysis:** Analyzing needs and product requirements to create a design.

Work Environment: Indoors; standing; using hands; bending or twisting the body; repetitive motions; contaminants; hazardous conditions; minor burns, cuts, bites, or stings.

Hazardous Materials Removal Workers

- Annual Earnings: $38,120
- Earnings Growth Potential: Low (33.7%)
- Growth: 23.1%
- Annual Job Openings: 1,890
- Self-Employed: 2.5%

Considerations for Job Outlook: Many job openings are expected for hazmat removal workers because of the need to replace workers who leave the occupation. Job opportunities for radiation safety technicians and decontamination workers should be good as new workers replace those who retire or leave the occupation for other reasons. Additional job openings may result for remediation workers as new facilities open in the coming decade. Lead and asbestos workers will likely have limited job opportunities at specialty remediation companies as the restoration of federal buildings and historic structures continues at a slower pace than in the past. Also, hazmat removal workers should continue to face competition from construction laborers and insulation workers to do these cleanups. The best employment opportunities for mold remediation workers should be in the Southeast and parts of the Northeast and Northwest, where mold tends to thrive. Applicants who have experience working with reactors in the U.S. Navy have better opportunities when they apply for hazmat removal work at nuclear facilities.

Identify, remove, pack, transport, or dispose of hazardous materials. Follow prescribed safety procedures, and comply with federal laws regulating waste disposal methods. Record numbers of containers stored at disposal sites, and specify amounts and types of equipment and waste disposed. Drive trucks or other heavy equipment to convey contaminated waste to designated sea or ground locations. Operate machines and equipment to remove, package, store, or transport loads of waste materials. Load and unload materials into containers and onto trucks, using hoists or forklifts. Clean contaminated equipment or areas for re-use, using detergents and solvents, sandblasters, filter pumps, and steam cleaners. Construct scaffolding or build containment areas prior to beginning abatement or decontamination work. Remove asbestos and/or lead from surfaces, using hand and power tools such as scrapers, vacuums, and high-pressure sprayers. Unload baskets of irradiated elements onto packaging machines that automatically insert fuel elements into canisters and secure lids. Apply chemical compounds to lead-based paint, allow compounds to dry, and then scrape the hazardous material into containers for removal or storage. Identify asbestos, lead, or other hazardous materials that need to be removed, using monitoring devices. Pull tram cars along underwater tracks, and position cars to receive irradiated fuel elements; then pull loaded cars to mechanisms that automatically unload elements onto underwater tables. Package, store, and move irradiated fuel elements in the underwater storage basin of a nuclear reactor plant, using machines and equipment. Organize and track the locations of hazardous items in landfills. Operate cranes to move and load baskets, casks, and canisters. Manipulate handgrips of mechanical arms to place irradiated fuel elements into baskets. Mix and pour concrete into forms to encase waste material for disposal.

Education/Training Required: High school diploma or equivalent. **Education and Training Programs:** Construction Trades, Other; Hazardous Materials Management

and Waste Technology/Technician; Mechanic and Repair Technologies/Technicians, Other. **Knowledge/Courses— Chemistry:** The chemical composition, structure, and properties of substances and of the chemical processes and transformations that they undergo. This includes uses of chemicals and their danger signs, production techniques, and disposal methods. **Mechanical Devices:** Machines and tools, including their designs, uses, repair, and maintenance. **Building and Construction:** Materials, methods, and the tools involved in the construction or repair of houses, buildings, or other structures such as highways and roads. **Transportation:** Principles and methods for moving people or goods by air, rail, sea, or road, including the relative costs and benefits. **Physics:** Physical principles, laws, their interrelationships, and applications to understanding fluid, material, and atmospheric dynamics, and mechanical, electrical, atomic, and subatomic structures and processes. **Public Safety and Security:** Relevant equipment, policies, procedures, and strategies to promote effective local, state, or national security operations for the protection of people, data, property, and institutions. **Work Experience Needed:** None. **On-the-Job Training Needed:** Moderate-term on-the-job training. **Certification/Licensure:** Licensure specific to materials worked with.

Personality Type: Realistic-Conventional. **Career Clusters:** 01 Agriculture, Food, and Natural Resources; 13 Manufacturing. **Career Pathways:** 01.6 Environmental Service Systems; 13.1 Production; 13.3 Maintenance, Installation, and Repair. **Other Jobs in These Pathways:** Adhesive Bonding Machine Operators and Tenders; Aircraft Mechanics and Service Technicians; Assemblers and Fabricators, All Other; Automotive Engineering Technicians; Automotive Specialty Technicians; Avionics Technicians; Biological Technicians; Cabinetmakers and Bench Carpenters; Camera and Photographic Equipment Repairers; Chemical Equipment Operators and Tenders; Civil Engineering Technicians; Cleaning, Washing, and Metal Pickling Equipment Operators and Tenders; Coating, Painting, and Spraying Machine Setters, Operators, and Tenders; Coil Winders, Tapers, and Finishers; Computer, Automated Teller, and Office Machine Repairers; Computer-Controlled Machine Tool Operators, Metal and Plastic; Construction and Related Workers, All Other; Control and Valve Installers and Repairers, Except Mechanical Door; Cooling and Freezing Equipment Operators and Tenders; Cost Estimators; Crushing,

Grinding, and Polishing Machine Setters, Operators, and Tenders; Cutters and Trimmers, Hand; others.

Skills—Equipment Maintenance: Performing routine maintenance on equipment and determining when and what kind of maintenance is needed. **Operation and Control:** Controlling operations of equipment or systems. **Repairing:** Repairing machines or systems using the needed tools. **Troubleshooting:** Determining causes of operating errors and deciding what to do about them. **Equipment Selection:** Determining the kind of tools and equipment needed to do a job. **Operation Monitoring:** Watching gauges, dials, or other indicators to make sure a machine is working properly. **Quality Control Analysis:** Conducting tests and inspections of products, services, or processes to evaluate quality or performance. **Installation:** Installing equipment, machines, wiring, or programs to meet specifications.

Work Environment: More often outdoors than indoors; standing; using hands; bending or twisting the body; repetitive motions; noise; very hot or cold; contaminants; high places; hazardous conditions; hazardous equipment.

Health Technologists and Technicians, All Other

- ⊙ Annual Earnings: $38,080
- ⊙ Earnings Growth Potential: Low (32.9%)
- ⊙ Growth: 23.2%
- ⊙ Annual Job Openings: 4,040
- ⊙ Self-Employed: 3.5%

Considerations for Job Outlook: Rapid employment growth is projected.

All health technologists and technicians not listed separately. For task data, see Job Specializations.

Education/Training Required: Postsecondary vocational training. **Education and Training Program:** Allied Health Diagnostic, Intervention, and Treatment Professions, Other. **Work Experience Needed:** None. **On-the-Job Training Needed:** Short-term on-the-job training. **Certification/Licensure:** Licensure for some specializations.

Job Specialization: Neurodiagnostic Technologists

Conduct electroneurodiagnostic (END) tests such as electroencephalograms, evoked potentials, polysomnograms, or electronystagmograms. May perform nerve conduction studies. Attach electrodes to patients using adhesives. Summarize technical data to assist physicians to diagnose brain, sleep, or nervous system disorders. Conduct tests or studies such as electroencephalography (EEG), polysomnography (PSG), nerve conduction studies (NCS), electromyography (EMG), and intraoperative monitoring (IOM). Calibrate, troubleshoot, or repair equipment, and correct malfunctions as needed. Conduct tests to determine cerebral death, the absence of brain activity, or the probability of recovery from a coma. Measure visual, auditory, or somatosensory evoked potentials (EPs) to determine responses to stimuli. Indicate artifacts or interferences derived from sources outside the brain, such as poor electrode contact or patient movement, on electroneurodiagnostic recordings. Measure patients' body parts and mark locations where electrodes are to be placed. Monitor patients during tests or surgeries, using electroencephalographs (EEG), evoked potential (EP) instruments, or video recording equipment. Set up, program, or record montages or electrical combinations when testing peripheral nerve, spinal cord, subcortical, or cortical responses. Adjust equipment to optimize viewing of the nervous system. Collect patients' medical information needed to customize tests. Submit reports to physicians summarizing test results. Assist in training technicians, medical students, residents, or other staff members.

Education and Training Program: Electroneurodiagnostic/Electroencephalographic Technology/Technologist. **Knowledge/Courses—Medicine and Dentistry:** The information and techniques needed to diagnose and treat human injuries, diseases, and deformities. This includes symptoms, treatment alternatives, drug properties and interactions, and preventive health-care measures. **Biology:** Plant and animal organisms and their tissues, cells, functions, interdependencies, and interactions with each other and the environment. **Psychology:** Human behavior and performance; individual differences in ability, personality, and interests; learning and motivation; psychological research methods; and the assessment and treatment of behavioral and affective disorders. **Computers and Electronics:** Circuit boards, processors, chips, electronic equipment, and computer hardware and software, including applications and programming. **Customer and Personal Service:** Principles and processes for providing customer and personal services. This includes customer needs assessment, meeting quality standards for services, and evaluation of customer satisfaction. **Clerical Practices:** Administrative and clerical procedures and systems such as word processing, managing files and records, stenography and transcription, designing forms, and other office procedures and terminology.

Personality Type: Realistic-Investigative. **Career Cluster:** 08 Health Science. **Career Pathway:** 08.2 Diagnostics Services. **Other Jobs in This Pathway:** Ambulance Drivers and Attendants, Except Emergency Medical Technicians; Anesthesiologist Assistants; Athletic Trainers; Cardiovascular Technologists and Technicians; Cytogenetic Technologists; Cytotechnologists; Diagnostic Medical Sonographers; Emergency Medical Technicians and Paramedics; Endoscopy Technicians; Health Diagnosing and Treating Practitioners, All Other; Health Specialties Teachers, Postsecondary; Health Technologists and Technicians, All Other; Healthcare Practitioners and Technical Workers, All Other; Histotechnologists and Histologic Technicians; Medical and Clinical Laboratory Technicians; Medical and Clinical Laboratory Technologists; Medical and Health Services Managers; Medical Assistants; Medical Equipment Preparers; Nuclear Equipment Operation Technicians; Nuclear Medicine Technologists; Ophthalmic Laboratory Technicians; Pathologists; Physical Scientists, All Other; Physician Assistants; Radiation Therapists; Radiologic Technicians; Radiologic Technologists; others.

Skills—Repairing: Repairing machines or systems using the needed tools. **Troubleshooting:** Determining causes of operating errors and deciding what to do about them. **Equipment Maintenance:** Performing routine maintenance on equipment and determining when and what kind of maintenance is needed. **Operation and Control:** Controlling operations of equipment or systems. **Quality Control Analysis:** Conducting tests and inspections of products, services, or processes to evaluate quality or performance. **Operation Monitoring:** Watching gauges, dials, or other indicators to make sure a machine is working properly. **Science:** Using scientific rules and methods to solve problems. **Learning Strategies:** Selecting and using

training/instructional methods and procedures appropriate for the situation when learning or teaching new things.

Work Environment: Indoors; sitting; using hands; contaminants; exposed to disease or infections.

Job Specialization: Ophthalmic Medical Technologists

Assist ophthalmologists by performing ophthalmic clinical functions and ophthalmic photography. Provide instruction and supervision to other ophthalmic personnel. Assist with minor surgical procedures, applying aseptic techniques and preparing instruments. May perform eye exams, administer eye medications, and instruct patients in the care and use of corrective lenses. Administer topical ophthalmic or oral medications. Assess abnormalities of color vision, such as amblyopia. Assess refractive condition of eyes, using retinoscope. Assist physicians in performing ophthalmic procedures, including surgery. Calculate corrections for refractive errors. Collect ophthalmic measurements or other diagnostic information, using ultrasound equipment such as A-scan ultrasound biometry or B-scan ultrasonography equipment. Conduct binocular disparity tests to assess depth perception. Conduct ocular motility tests to measure function of eye muscles. Conduct tests, such as the Amsler Grid test, to measure central visual field used in the early diagnosis of macular degeneration, glaucoma, or diseases of the eye. Conduct tonometry or tonography tests to measure intraocular pressure. Conduct visual field tests to measure field of vision. Create three-dimensional images of the eye, using computed tomography (CT). Measure and record lens power, using lensometers. Measure corneal curvature with keratometers or ophthalmometers to aid in the diagnosis of conditions such as astigmatism. Measure corneal thickness, using pachymeter or contact ultrasound methods. Measure the thickness of the retinal nerve, using scanning laser polarimetry techniques to aid in diagnosis of glaucoma. Measure visual acuity, including near, distance, pinhole, or dynamic visual acuity, using appropriate tests. Perform advanced ophthalmic procedures, including electrophysiological, electrophysical, or microbial procedures. Perform fluorescein angiography of the eye. Perform slit lamp biomicroscopy procedures to diagnose disorders of the eye, such as retinitis, presbyopia, cataracts, or retinal detachment. Photograph patients' eye areas, using clinical photography techniques, to document retinal or corneal defects. Supervise or instruct ophthalmic staff. Take anatomical or functional ocular measurements of the eye or surrounding tissue, such as axial length measurements.

Education and Training Program: Ophthalmic Technician/Technologist Training.

Personality Type: No data available. **Career Cluster:** 08 Health Science. **Career Pathway:** 08.1 Therapeutic Services. **Other Jobs in This Pathway:** Acupuncturists; Allergists and Immunologists; Anesthesiologists; Art Therapists; Chiropractors; Clinical Psychologists; Community and Social Service Specialists, All Other; Counseling Psychologists; Counselors, All Other; Dental Assistants; Dental Hygienists; Dentists, All Other Specialists; Dentists, General; Dermatologists; Diagnostic Medical Sonographers; Dietetic Technicians; Dietitians and Nutritionists; Family and General Practitioners; Health Diagnosing and Treating Practitioners, All Other; Health Specialties Teachers, Postsecondary; Health Technologists and Technicians, All Other; Healthcare Practitioners and Technical Workers, All Other; Healthcare Support Workers, All Other; Home Health Aides; Hospitalists; Industrial-Organizational Psychologists; Internists, General; Licensed Practical and Licensed Vocational Nurses; Life, Physical, and Social Science Technicians, All Other; Low Vision Therapists, Orientation and Mobility Specialists, and Vision Rehabilitation Therapists; others.

Work Environment: No data available.

Job Specialization: Radiologic Technicians

Maintain and use equipment and supplies necessary to demonstrate portions of the human body on X-ray film or fluoroscopic screen for diagnostic purposes. Use beam-restrictive devices and patient-shielding techniques to minimize radiation exposure to patients and staff. Position X-ray equipment and adjust controls to set exposure factors such as time and distance. Position patients on examining tables, and set up and adjust equipment to obtain optimum view of specific body areas as requested by physicians. Determine patients' X-ray needs by reading requests or instructions from physicians. Make exposures necessary for the requested procedures, rejecting and repeating work that does not meet established standards. Process exposed radiographs using film processors or computer-generated methods. Explain procedures to patients to reduce anxieties and obtain cooperation. Perform procedures such as linear tomography, mammography, sonograms, joint and cyst aspirations, routine contrast studies, routine fluoroscopy, and examinations of the head, trunk, and extremities under supervision of physician. Prepare and set up X-ray rooms for patients. Provide assistance to physicians or other technologists in the performance of more complex procedures. Provide students and other technologists with suggestions of additional views, alternative positioning, or improved techniques to ensure the images produced are of the highest quality. Coordinate work of other technicians or technologists when procedures require more than one person.

Education and Training Program: Medical Radiologic Technology/Science—Radiation Therapist. **Knowledge/Courses—Physics:** Physical principles, laws, their interrelationships, and applications to understanding fluid, material, and atmospheric dynamics, and mechanical, electrical, atomic, and subatomic structures and processes. **Medicine and Dentistry:** The information and techniques needed to diagnose and treat human injuries, diseases, and deformities. This includes symptoms, treatment alternatives, drug properties and interactions, and preventive healthcare measures. **Psychology:** Human behavior and performance; individual differences in ability, personality, and interests; learning and motivation; psychological research methods; and the assessment and treatment of behavioral and affective disorders. **Biology:** Plant and animal organisms and their tissues, cells, functions, interdependencies, and interactions with each other and the environment. **Chemistry:** The chemical composition, structure, and properties of substances and of the chemical processes and transformations that they undergo. This includes uses of chemicals and their danger signs, production techniques, and disposal methods. **Customer and Personal Service:** Principles and processes for providing customer and personal services. This includes customer needs assessment, meeting quality standards for services, and evaluation of customer satisfaction.

Personality Type: Realistic-Conventional-Social. **Career Cluster:** 08 Health Science. **Career Pathways:** 08.2 Diagnostics Services; 08.1 Therapeutic Services. **Other Jobs in These Pathways:** Acupuncturists; Allergists and Immunologists; Ambulance Drivers and Attendants, Except Emergency Medical Technicians; Anesthesiologist Assistants; Anesthesiologists; Art Therapists; Athletic Trainers;

Cardiovascular Technologists and Technicians; Chiropractors; Clinical Psychologists; Community and Social Service Specialists, All Other; Counseling Psychologists; Counselors, All Other; Cytogenetic Technologists; Cytotechnologists; Dental Assistants; Dental Hygienists; Dentists, All Other Specialists; Dentists, General; Dermatologists; Diagnostic Medical Sonographers; Dietetic Technicians; Dietitians and Nutritionists; Emergency Medical Technicians and Paramedics; Endoscopy Technicians; Family and General Practitioners; Health Diagnosing and Treating Practitioners, All Other; Health Specialties Teachers, Postsecondary; Health Technologists and Technicians, All Other; Healthcare Practitioners and Technical Workers, All Other; Healthcare Support Workers, All Other; others.

Skills—Operation and Control: Controlling operations of equipment or systems. **Science:** Using scientific rules and methods to solve problems. **Operation Monitoring:** Watching gauges, dials, or other indicators to make sure a machine is working properly. **Service Orientation:** Actively looking for ways to help people. **Troubleshooting:** Determining causes of operating errors and deciding what to do about them. **Technology Design:** Generating or adapting equipment and technology to serve user needs. **Coordination:** Adjusting actions in relation to others' actions. **Quality Control Analysis:** Conducting tests and inspections of products, services, or processes to evaluate quality or performance.

Work Environment: Indoors; standing; walking and running; using hands; bending or twisting the body; repetitive motions; contaminants; exposed to radiation; exposed to disease or infections.

Job Specialization: Surgical Assistants

Assist surgeons during surgery by performing duties such as tissue retraction, insertion of tubes and intravenous lines, or closure of surgical wounds. Perform preoperative and postoperative duties to facilitate patient care. Adjust and maintain operating room temperature, humidity, or lighting, according to surgeons' specifications. Apply sutures, staples, clips, or other materials to close skin, fascia, or subcutaneous wound layers. Assess skin integrity or other body conditions upon completion of procedures to determine if damage has occurred from body positioning. Assist in the insertion, positioning, or suturing of closed-wound drainage systems. Assist members of surgical teams with gowning or gloving. Clamp, ligate, or cauterize blood vessels to control bleeding during surgical entry using hemostatic clamps, suture ligatures, or electrocautery equipment. Coordinate or participate in the positioning of patients using body-stabilizing equipment or protective padding to provide appropriate exposure for procedures or to protect against nerve damage or circulation impairment. Coordinate with anesthesia personnel to maintain patient temperature. Discuss with surgeons the nature of surgical procedures, including operative consent, methods of operative exposure, diagnostic or laboratory data, or patient-advanced directives or other needs. Incise tissue layers in lower extremities to harvest veins. Maintain unobstructed operative fields using surgical retractors, sponges, or suctioning and irrigating equipment. Monitor and maintain aseptic technique throughout procedures. Monitor patients' intra-operative status, including patient position, vital signs, or volume or color of blood.

Education and Training Program: Surgical Technology/Technologist.

Personality Type: No data available. **Career Cluster:** 08 Health Science. **Career Pathway:** 08.1 Therapeutic Services. **Other Jobs in This Pathway:** Acupuncturists; Allergists and Immunologists; Anesthesiologists; Art Therapists; Chiropractors; Clinical Psychologists; Community and Social Service Specialists, All Other; Counseling Psychologists; Counselors, All Other; Dental Assistants; Dental Hygienists; Dentists, All Other Specialists; Dentists, General; Dermatologists; Diagnostic Medical Sonographers; Dietetic Technicians; Dietitians and Nutritionists; Family and General Practitioners; Health Diagnosing and Treating Practitioners, All Other; Health Specialties Teachers, Postsecondary; Health Technologists and Technicians, All Other; Healthcare Practitioners and Technical Workers, All Other; Healthcare Support Workers, All Other; Home Health Aides; Hospitalists; Industrial-Organizational Psychologists; Internists, General; Licensed Practical and Licensed Vocational Nurses; Life, Physical, and Social Science Technicians, All Other; Low Vision Therapists, Orientation and Mobility Specialists, and Vision Rehabilitation Therapists; others.

Work Environment: No data available.

Heating, Air Conditioning, and Refrigeration Mechanics and Installers

- ⊙ Annual Earnings: $43,380
- ⊙ Earnings Growth Potential: Medium (38.2%)
- ⊙ Growth: 33.7%
- ⊙ Annual Job Openings: 13,760
- ⊙ Self-Employed: 16.2%

Considerations for Job Outlook: Job opportunities for HVACR technicians are expected to be excellent, particularly for those who have completed training at an accredited technical school or through a formal apprenticeship. Candidates familiar with computers and electronics will have the best job opportunities as employers continue to have trouble finding qualified technicians to work on complex new systems. Technicians who specialize in installation work may experience periods of unemployment when the level of new construction activity declines. Maintenance and repair work, however, usually remains relatively stable. Businesses and homeowners depend on their climate-control or refrigeration systems and must keep them in good working order, regardless of economic conditions.

Install or repair heating, central air conditioning, or refrigeration systems, including oil burners, hot-air furnaces, and heating stoves. For task data, see Job Specializations.

Education/Training Required: Postsecondary vocational training. **Work Experience Needed:** None. **On-the-Job Training Needed:** Long-term on-the-job training. **Certification/Licensure:** Licensure.

Job Specialization: Heating and Air Conditioning Mechanics and Installers

Install, service, and repair heating and air conditioning systems in residences and commercial establishments. Obtain and maintain required certifications. Comply with all applicable standards, policies, and procedures, including safety procedures and the maintenance of a clean work area. Repair or replace defective equipment, components, or wiring. Test electrical circuits and components for continuity, using electrical test equipment. Reassemble and

test equipment following repairs. Inspect and test systems to verify system compliance with plans and specifications and to detect and locate malfunctions. Discuss heating-cooling system malfunctions with users to isolate problems or to verify that malfunctions have been corrected. Test pipe or tubing joints and connections for leaks, using pressure gauges or soap-and-water solutions. Record and report all faults, deficiencies, and other unusual occurrences, as well as the time and materials expended on work orders. Adjust system controls to settings recommended by manufacturers to balance systems, using hand tools. Recommend, develop, and perform preventive and general-maintenance procedures such as cleaning, power-washing, and vacuuming equipment; oiling parts; and changing filters. Lay out and connect electrical wiring between controls and equipment according to wiring diagrams, using electrician's hand tools. Install auxiliary components to heating-cooling equipment, such as expansion and discharge valves, air ducts, pipes, blowers, dampers, flues, and stokers, following blueprints.

Education and Training Programs: Heating, Air Conditioning, Ventilation, and Refrigeration Maintenance Technology/Technician (HAC, HACR, HVAC, HVACR); Heating, Ventilation, Air Conditioning, and Refrigeration Engineering Technology/Technician; Solar Energy Technology/Technician. **Knowledge/Courses—Mechanical Devices:** Machines and tools, including their designs, uses, repair, and maintenance. **Building and Construction:** Materials, methods, and the tools involved in the construction or repair of houses, buildings, or other structures such as highways and roads. **Physics:** Physical principles, laws, their interrelationships, and applications to understanding fluid, material, and atmospheric dynamics, and mechanical, electrical, atomic, and subatomic structures and processes. **Chemistry:** The chemical composition, structure, and properties of substances and of the chemical processes and transformations that they undergo. This includes uses of chemicals and their danger signs, production techniques, and disposal methods. **Design:** Design techniques, tools, and principles involved in production of precision technical plans, blueprints, drawings, and models. **Engineering and Technology:** The practical application of engineering science and technology. This includes applying principles, techniques, procedures, and equipment to the design and production of various goods and services.

Personality Type: Realistic-Conventional-Investigative.
Career Cluster: 02 Architecture and Construction.
Career Pathways: 02.3 Maintenance/Operations; 02.2 Construction. **Other Jobs in These Pathways:** Boilermakers; Brickmasons and Blockmasons; Carpet Installers; Cement Masons and Concrete Finishers; Coin, Vending, and Amusement Machine Servicers and Repairers; Construction and Building Inspectors; Construction and Related Workers, All Other; Construction Carpenters; Construction Laborers; Construction Managers; Continuous Mining Machine Operators; Cost Estimators; Crane and Tower Operators; Dredge Operators; Drywall and Ceiling Tile Installers; Earth Drillers, Except Oil and Gas; Electrical Power-Line Installers and Repairers; Electricians; Electromechanical Equipment Assemblers; Engineering Technicians, Except Drafters, All Other; Excavating and Loading Machine and Dragline Operators; Explosives Workers, Ordnance Handling Experts, and Blasters; Extraction Workers, All Other; First-Line Supervisors of Construction Trades and Extraction Workers; Floor Layers, Except Carpet, Wood, and Hard Tiles; Floor Sanders and Finishers; Glaziers; Helpers, Construction Trades, All Other; others.

Skills—Installation: Installing equipment, machines, wiring, or programs to meet specifications. **Repairing:** Repairing machines or systems using the needed tools. **Equipment Maintenance:** Performing routine maintenance on equipment and determining when and what kind of maintenance is needed. **Troubleshooting:** Determining causes of operating errors and deciding what to do about them. **Equipment Selection:** Determining the kind of tools and equipment needed to do a job. **Operation and Control:** Controlling operations of equipment or systems. **Quality Control Analysis:** Conducting tests and inspections of products, services, or processes to evaluate quality or performance. **Mathematics:** Using mathematics to solve problems.

Work Environment: More often outdoors than indoors; standing; walking and running; kneeling, crouching, stooping, or crawling; using hands; bending or twisting the body; noise; very hot or cold; bright or inadequate lighting; contaminants; cramped work space; high places; hazardous conditions; hazardous equipment; minor burns, cuts, bites, or stings.

Job Specialization: Refrigeration Mechanics and Installers

Install and repair industrial and commercial refrigerating systems. Braze or solder parts to repair defective joints and leaks. Observe and test system operation, using gauges and instruments. Test lines, components, and connections for leaks. Dismantle malfunctioning systems, and test components using electrical, mechanical, and pneumatic testing equipment. Adjust or replace worn or defective mechanisms and parts, and reassemble repaired systems. Read blueprints to determine location, size, capacity, and types of components needed to build refrigeration systems. Supervise and instruct assistants. Perform mechanical overhauls and refrigerant reclaiming. Install wiring to connect components to electric power sources. Cut, bend, thread, and connect pipe to functional components and water, power, or refrigeration systems. Adjust valves according to specifications, and charge systems with proper type of refrigerant by pumping the specified gas or fluid into the system. Estimate, order, pick up, deliver, and install materials and supplies needed to maintain equipment in good working condition. Install expansion and control valves using acetylene torches and wrenches. Mount compressor, condenser, and other components in specified locations on frames using hand tools and acetylene welding equipment. Keep records of repairs and replacements made and causes of malfunctions. Schedule work with customers, and initiate work orders, house requisitions, and orders from stock.

Education and Training Programs: Heating, Air Conditioning, Ventilation, and Refrigeration Maintenance Technology/Technician (HAC, HACR, HVAC, HVACR); Heating, Ventilation, Air Conditioning, and Refrigeration Engineering Technology/Technician. **Knowledge/Courses—Mechanical Devices:** Machines and tools, including their designs, uses, repair, and maintenance. **Physics:** Physical principles, laws, their interrelationships, and applications to understanding fluid, material, and atmospheric dynamics, and mechanical, electrical, atomic, and subatomic structures and processes. **Building and Construction:** Materials, methods, and the tools involved in the construction or repair of houses, buildings, or other structures such as highways and roads. **Engineering and Technology:** The practical application of engineering science and technology. This includes applying principles, techniques, procedures, and equipment to the design and production of various goods and services. **Design:** Design techniques, tools, and principles involved in production of precision technical plans, blueprints, drawings, and models. **Chemistry:** The chemical composition, structure, and properties of substances and of the chemical processes and transformations that they undergo. This includes uses of chemicals and their danger signs, production techniques, and disposal methods.

Personality Type: Realistic-Conventional-Enterprising. **Career Cluster:** 02 Architecture and Construction. **Career Pathways:** 02.2 Construction; 02.3 Maintenance/ Operations. **Other Jobs in These Pathways:** Boilermakers; Brickmasons and Blockmasons; Carpet Installers; Cement Masons and Concrete Finishers; Coin, Vending, and Amusement Machine Servicers and Repairers; Construction and Building Inspectors; Construction and Related Workers, All Other; Construction Carpenters; Construction Laborers; Construction Managers; Continuous Mining Machine Operators; Cost Estimators; Crane and Tower Operators; Dredge Operators; Drywall and Ceiling Tile Installers; Earth Drillers, Except Oil and Gas; Electrical Power-Line Installers and Repairers; Electricians; Electromechanical Equipment Assemblers; Engineering Technicians, Except Drafters, All Other; Excavating and Loading Machine and Dragline Operators; Explosives Workers, Ordnance Handling Experts, and Blasters; Extraction Workers, All Other; First-Line Supervisors of Construction Trades and Extraction Workers; Floor Layers, Except Carpet, Wood, and Hard Tiles; Floor Sanders and Finishers; Glaziers; others.

Skills—Installation: Installing equipment, machines, wiring, or programs to meet specifications. **Repairing:** Repairing machines or systems using the needed tools. **Equipment Maintenance:** Performing routine maintenance on equipment and determining when and what kind of maintenance is needed. **Troubleshooting:** Determining causes of operating errors and deciding what to do about them. **Equipment Selection:** Determining the kind of tools and equipment needed to do a job. **Operation and Control:** Controlling operations of equipment or systems. **Quality Control Analysis:** Conducting tests and inspections of products, services, or processes to evaluate quality or performance. **Management of Material Resources:** Obtaining and seeing to the appropriate use of equipment, facilities, and materials needed to do certain work.

Work Environment: More often outdoors than indoors; standing; walking and running; kneeling, crouching, stooping, or crawling; using hands; bending or twisting the body; repetitive motions; noise; very hot or cold; bright or inadequate lighting; contaminants; cramped work space; high places; hazardous conditions; hazardous equipment; minor burns, cuts, bites, or stings.

Heavy and Tractor-Trailer Truck Drivers

- ⊙ Annual Earnings: $37,930
- ⊙ Earnings Growth Potential: Low (34.4%)
- ⊙ Growth: 20.6%
- ⊙ Annual Job Openings: 64,940
- ⊙ Self-Employed: 7.9%

Considerations for Job Outlook: Job prospects for heavy and tractor-trailer truck drivers are expected to be favorable. Due to the somewhat difficult lifestyle and time spent away from home, many companies have trouble finding qualified long-haul drivers. Those who have the necessary experience and other qualifications should be able to find jobs.

Drive a tractor-trailer combination or a truck with a capacity of at least 26,000 pounds gross vehicle weight (GVW). Follow appropriate safety procedures when transporting dangerous goods. Check vehicles before driving them to ensure that mechanical, safety, and emergency equipment is in good working order. Maintain logs of working hours and of vehicle service and repair status, following applicable state and federal regulations. Obtain receipts or signatures when loads are delivered, and collect payment for services when required. Check all load-related documentation to ensure that it is complete and accurate. Maneuver trucks into loading or unloading positions, following signals from loading crew as needed; check that vehicle position is correct and any special loading equipment is properly positioned. Drive trucks with capacities greater than three tons, including tractor-trailer combinations, to transport and deliver products, livestock, or other materials. Secure cargo for transport, using ropes, blocks, chains, binders, or covers. Read bills of lading to determine assignment details. Report vehicle defects, accidents, traffic violations, or damage to the vehicles. Read and interpret maps to determine vehicle routes. Couple and uncouple trailers by changing trailer jack positions, connecting or disconnecting air and electrical lines, and manipulating fifth-wheel locks. Collect delivery instructions from appropriate sources, verifying instructions and routes. Drive trucks to weigh stations before and after loading and along routes to document weights and to comply with state regulations.

Education/Training Required: High school diploma or equivalent. **Education and Training Program:** Truck and Bus Driver Training/Commercial Vehicle Operator and Instructor Training. **Knowledge/Courses—Transportation:** Principles and methods for moving people or goods by air, rail, sea, or road, including the relative costs and benefits. **Food Production:** Techniques and equipment for planting, growing, and harvesting food products (both plant and animal) for consumption, including storage/handling techniques. **Mechanical Devices:** Machines and tools, including their designs, uses, repair, and maintenance. **Building and Construction:** Materials, methods, and the tools involved in the construction or repair of houses, buildings, or other structures such as highways and roads. **Design:** Design techniques, tools, and principles involved in production of precision technical plans, blueprints, drawings, and models. **Personnel and Human Resources:** Principles and procedures for personnel recruitment, selection, training, compensation and benefits, labor relations and negotiation, and personnel information systems. **Work Experience Needed:** 1 to 5 years. **On-the-Job Training Needed:** Short-term on-the-job training. **Certification/Licensure:** Licensure.

Personality Type: Realistic-Conventional. **Career Cluster:** 16 Transportation, Distribution, and Logistics. **Career Pathway:** 16.1 Transportation Operations. **Other Jobs in This Pathway:** Aerospace Engineering and Operations Technicians; Air Traffic Controllers; Aircraft Cargo Handling Supervisors; Airfield Operations Specialists; Airline Pilots, Copilots, and Flight Engineers; Automotive and Watercraft Service Attendants; Automotive Master Mechanics; Aviation Inspectors; Bridge and Lock Tenders; Bus Drivers, School or Special Client; Bus Drivers, Transit and Intercity; Commercial Divers; Commercial Pilots; Crane and Tower Operators; First-Line Supervisors of Helpers, Laborers, and Material Movers, Hand; First-Line Supervisors of Transportation and Material-Moving Machine and Vehicle Operators; Freight and Cargo Inspectors; Hoist and Winch Operators; Laborers and Freight, Stock, and Material Movers, Hand; Light Truck or Delivery Services Drivers; Mates—Ship, Boat, and Barge; Motor Vehicle Operators, All Other; Motorboat Operators; Operating Engineers and Other Construction Equipment Operators; Parking Lot Attendants; Pilots, Ship; others.

Skills—Repairing: Repairing machines or systems using the needed tools. **Operation and Control:** Controlling operations of equipment or systems. **Equipment Maintenance:** Performing routine maintenance on equipment and determining when and what kind of maintenance is needed. **Troubleshooting:** Determining causes of operating errors and deciding what to do about them. **Operation Monitoring:** Watching gauges, dials, or other indicators to make sure a machine is working properly. **Equipment Selection:** Determining the kind of tools and equipment needed to do a job. **Quality Control Analysis:** Conducting tests and inspections of products, services, or processes to evaluate quality or performance. **Installation:** Installing equipment, machines, wiring, or programs to meet specifications.

Work Environment: Outdoors; sitting; using hands; repetitive motions; noise; very hot or cold; bright or inadequate lighting; contaminants; cramped work space; hazardous equipment.

Helpers—Brickmasons, Blockmasons, Stonemasons, and Tile and Marble Setters

- ☉ Annual Earnings: $27,820
- ☉ Earnings Growth Potential: Low (29.8%)
- ☉ Growth: 59.9%
- ☉ Annual Job Openings: 2,540
- ☉ Self-Employed: 1.8%

Considerations for Job Outlook: Construction laborers with the most skills should have the best job opportunities. Opportunities also will vary by occupation; for example, carpenters' helpers should have the best job prospects, while painters', paperhangers', plasterers', and stucco masons' helpers will likely find fewer job openings. Prospective employees with military service often have better opportunities when applying for a job. Employment of construction laborers and helpers is especially sensitive to the fluctuations of the economy.

Help brickmasons, blockmasons, stonemasons, or tile and marble setters by performing duties requiring less skill. Transport materials, tools, and machines to installation sites, manually or using conveyance equipment. Move or position materials such as marble slabs, using cranes, hoists, or dollies. Modify material moving, mixing, grouting, grinding, polishing, or cleaning procedures according to installation or material requirements. Correct surface imperfections or fill chipped, cracked or broken bricks or tiles, using fillers, adhesives, and grouting materials. Arrange and store materials, machines, tools, and equipment. Apply caulk, sealants, or other agents to installed surfaces. Select or locate and supply materials to masons for installation, following drawings or numbered sequences. Remove excess grout and residue from tile or brick joints, using sponges or trowels. Remove damaged tile, brick, or mortar, and clean and prepare surfaces, using pliers, hammers, chisels, drills, wire brushes, and metal wire anchors. Provide assistance in the preparation, installation, repair, and/or rebuilding of tile, brick, or stone surfaces. Mix mortar, plaster, and grout, manually or using machines, according to standard formulas. Erect scaffolding or other installation structures. Cut materials to specified sizes for installation, using power saws or tile cutters. Clean installation surfaces, equipment, tools, work sites, and storage areas, using water, chemical solutions, oxygen lances, or polishing machines. Apply grout between joints of bricks or tiles, using grouting trowels.

Education/Training Required: Less than high school. **Education and Training Program:** Masonry/Mason Training. **Knowledge/Courses—Building and Construction:** Materials, methods, and the tools involved in the construction or repair of houses, buildings, or other structures such as highways and roads. **Chemistry:** The chemical composition, structure, and properties of substances and of the chemical processes and transformations that they undergo. This includes uses of chemicals and their danger signs, production techniques, and disposal methods. **Transportation:** Principles and methods for moving people or goods by air, rail, sea, or road, including the relative costs and benefits. **Production and Processing:** Raw materials, production processes, quality control, costs, and other techniques for maximizing the effective manufacture and distribution of goods. **Mechanical Devices:** Machines and tools, including their designs, uses, repair, and maintenance. **Design:** Design techniques, tools, and principles involved in production of precision technical plans, blueprints, drawings, and models. **Work Experience Needed:** None. **On-the-Job Training Needed:** Short-term on-the-job training. **Certification/Licensure:** None.

Personality Type: Realistic. **Career Cluster:** 02 Architecture and Construction. **Career Pathway:** 02.2 Construction. **Other Jobs in This Pathway:** Boilermakers; Brickmasons and Blockmasons; Carpet Installers; Cement Masons and Concrete Finishers; Construction and Building Inspectors; Construction and Related Workers, All Other; Construction Carpenters; Construction Laborers; Construction Managers; Continuous Mining Machine Operators; Cost Estimators; Crane and Tower Operators; Dredge Operators; Drywall and Ceiling Tile Installers; Earth Drillers, Except Oil and Gas; Electrical Power-Line Installers and Repairers; Electricians; Electromechanical Equipment Assemblers; Engineering Technicians, Except Drafters, All Other; Excavating and Loading Machine and Dragline Operators; Explosives Workers, Ordnance Handling Experts, and Blasters; Extraction Workers, All Other; First-Line Supervisors of Construction Trades and Extraction Workers; Floor Layers, Except Carpet, Wood, and Hard Tiles; Floor Sanders and Finishers; Glaziers; Heating and Air Conditioning Mechanics and Installers; Helpers, Construction Trades, All Other; others.

Skills—Equipment Maintenance: Performing routine maintenance on equipment and determining when and what kind of maintenance is needed. **Repairing:** Repairing machines or systems using the needed tools. **Equipment Selection:** Determining the kind of tools and equipment needed to do a job. **Troubleshooting:** Determining causes of operating errors and deciding what to do about them. **Operation and Control:** Controlling operations of equipment or systems. **Technology Design:** Generating or adapting equipment and technology to serve user needs. **Operation Monitoring:** Watching gauges, dials, or other indicators to make sure a machine is working properly. **Quality Control Analysis:** Conducting tests and inspections of products, services, or processes to evaluate quality or performance.

Work Environment: Outdoors; standing; climbing; walking and running; using hands; bending or twisting the body; repetitive motions; noise; very hot or cold; contaminants; high places; hazardous equipment; minor burns, cuts, bites, or stings.

Helpers—Carpenters

- Annual Earnings: $26,400
- Earnings Growth Potential: Low (32.4%)
- Growth: 55.7%
- Annual Job Openings: 3,820
- Self-Employed: 1.7%

Considerations for Job Outlook: Construction laborers with the most skills should have the best job opportunities. Opportunities also will vary by occupation; for example, carpenters' helpers should have the best job prospects, while painters', paperhangers', plasterers', and stucco masons' helpers will likely find fewer job openings. Prospective employees with military service often have better opportunities when applying for a job. Employment of construction laborers and helpers is especially sensitive to the fluctuations of the economy.

Help carpenters by performing duties requiring less skill. Position and hold timbers, lumber, and paneling in place for fastening or cutting. Erect scaffolding, shoring, and braces. Select tools, equipment, and materials from storage and transport items to work site. Fasten timbers and lumber with glue, screws, pegs, or nails, and install hardware. Clean work areas, machines, and equipment, to maintain a clean and safe jobsite. Hold plumb bobs, sighting rods, and other equipment, to aid in establishing reference points and lines. Align, straighten, plumb, and square forms for installation. Cut timbers, lumber, and paneling to specified dimensions, and drill holes in timbers or lumber. Smooth and sand surfaces to remove ridges, tool marks, glue, or caulking. Perform tie spacing layout, and then measure, mark, drill, and cut. Secure stakes to grids for constructions of footings, nail scabs to footing forms, and vibrate and float concrete. Construct forms, and then assist in raising them to the required elevation. Install handrails under the direction of a carpenter. Glue and clamp edges or joints of assembled parts. Cut and install insulating or sound-absorbing material. Cut tile or linoleum to fit, and spread adhesives on flooring to install tile or linoleum. Cover surfaces with laminated plastic covering material.

Education/Training Required: Less than high school. **Education and Training Program:** Carpentry/Carpenter. **Knowledge/Courses—Building and Construction:** Materials, methods, and the tools involved in the construction or repair of houses, buildings, or other structures such as highways and roads. **Design:** Design techniques, tools, and principles involved in production of precision technical plans, blueprints, drawings, and models. **Engineering and Technology:** The practical application of engineering science and technology. This includes applying principles, techniques, procedures, and equipment to the design and production of various goods and services. **Work Experience Needed:** None. **On-the-Job Training Needed:** Short-term on-the-job training. **Certification/Licensure:** None.

Personality Type: Realistic-Conventional. **Career Cluster:** 02 Architecture and Construction. **Career Pathway:** 02.2 Construction. **Other Jobs in This Pathway:** Boilermakers; Brickmasons and Blockmasons; Carpet Installers; Cement Masons and Concrete Finishers; Construction and Building Inspectors; Construction and Related Workers, All Other; Construction Carpenters; Construction Laborers; Construction Managers; Continuous Mining Machine Operators; Cost Estimators; Crane and Tower Operators; Dredge Operators; Drywall and Ceiling Tile Installers; Earth Drillers, Except Oil and Gas; Electrical Power-Line Installers and Repairers; Electricians; Electromechanical Equipment Assemblers; Engineering Technicians, Except Drafters, All Other; Excavating and Loading Machine and Dragline Operators; Explosives Workers, Ordnance Handling Experts, and Blasters; Extraction Workers, All Other; First-Line Supervisors of Construction Trades and Extraction Workers; Floor Layers, Except Carpet, Wood, and Hard Tiles; Floor Sanders and Finishers; Glaziers; Heating and Air Conditioning Mechanics and Installers; Helpers, Construction Trades, All Other; others.

Skills—Equipment Selection: Determining the kind of tools and equipment needed to do a job. **Installation:** Installing equipment, machines, wiring, or programs to meet specifications. **Repairing:** Repairing machines or systems using the needed tools. **Equipment Maintenance:** Performing routine maintenance on equipment and determining when and what kind of maintenance is needed. **Operation and Control:** Controlling operations of equipment or systems. **Quality Control Analysis:** Conducting tests and inspections of products, services, or processes to evaluate quality or performance. **Troubleshooting:** Determining causes of operating errors and deciding what to do about them. **Technology Design:** Generating or adapting equipment and technology to serve user needs.

Work Environment: Outdoors; standing; walking and running; kneeling, crouching, stooping, or crawling; using hands; bending or twisting the body; repetitive motions; noise; very hot or cold; bright or inadequate lighting; contaminants; cramped work space; hazardous equipment; minor burns, cuts, bites, or stings.

Helpers—Electricians

- ⊚ Annual Earnings: $27,620
- ⊚ Earnings Growth Potential: Low (29.4%)
- ⊚ Growth: 30.6%
- ⊚ Annual Job Openings: 4,200
- ⊚ Self-Employed: 1.7%

Considerations for Job Outlook: Construction laborers with the most skills should have the best job opportunities. Opportunities also will vary by occupation; for example, carpenters' helpers should have the best job prospects, while painters', paperhangers', plasterers', and stucco masons' helpers will likely find fewer job openings. Prospective employees with military service often have better opportunities when applying for a job. Employment of construction laborers and helpers is especially sensitive to the fluctuations of the economy.

Help electricians by performing duties requiring less skill. Trace out short circuits in wiring, using test meter. Measure, cut, and bend wire and conduit, using measuring instruments and hand tools. Maintain tools, vehicles, and equipment and keep parts and supplies in order. Drill holes and pull or push wiring through openings, using hand and power tools. Perform semi-skilled and unskilled laboring duties related to the installation, maintenance, and repair of a wide variety of electrical systems and equipment. Disassemble defective electrical equipment, replace defective or worn parts, and reassemble equipment, using hand tools. Transport tools, materials, equipment, and supplies to work site by hand, handtruck, or heavy, motorized truck. Examine electrical units for loose connections and broken insulation and tighten connections, using hand tools. Strip insulation from wire ends, using wire stripping pliers, and attach wires to terminals for subsequent soldering. Thread conduit ends, connect couplings, and fabricate and secure

conduit support brackets, using hand tools. Construct controllers and panels, using power drills, drill presses, taps, saws, and punches. Clean work area and wash parts. Erect electrical system components and barricades, and rig scaffolds, hoists, and shoring. Install copper-clad ground rods, using manual post drivers. Raise, lower, or position equipment, tools, and materials, using hoists, hand lines, or block and tackle. Dig trenches or holes for installation of conduit or supports. Break up concrete, using airhammers, to facilitate installation, construction, or repair of equipment. String transmission lines or cables through ducts or conduits, under the ground, through equipment, or to towers. Requisition materials, using warehouse requisition or release forms. Bolt component parts together to form tower assemblies, using hand tools. Paint a variety of objects related to electrical functions.

Education/Training Required: High school diploma or equivalent. **Education and Training Program:** Electrician. **Knowledge/Courses—Mechanical Devices:** Machines and tools, including their designs, uses, repair, and maintenance. **Building and Construction:** Materials, methods, and the tools involved in the construction or repair of houses, buildings, or other structures such as highways and roads. **Design:** Design techniques, tools, and principles involved in production of precision technical plans, blueprints, drawings, and models. **Transportation:** Principles and methods for moving people or goods by air, rail, sea, or road, including the relative costs and benefits. **Physics:** Physical principles, laws, their interrelationships, and applications to understanding fluid, material, and atmospheric dynamics, and mechanical, electrical, atomic, and subatomic structures and processes. **English Language:** The structure and content of the English language including the meaning and spelling of words, rules of composition, and grammar. **Work Experience Needed:** None. **On-the-Job Training Needed:** Short-term on-the-job training. **Certification/Licensure:** None.

Personality Type: Realistic-Conventional. **Career Cluster:** 02 Architecture and Construction. **Career Pathway:** 02.2 Construction. **Other Jobs in This Pathway:** Boilermakers; Brickmasons and Blockmasons; Carpet Installers; Cement Masons and Concrete Finishers; Construction and Building Inspectors; Construction and Related Workers, All Other; Construction Carpenters; Construction Laborers; Construction Managers; Continuous Mining Machine Operators; Cost Estimators; Crane and Tower Operators;

Dredge Operators; Drywall and Ceiling Tile Installers; Earth Drillers, Except Oil and Gas; Electrical Power-Line Installers and Repairers; Electricians; Electromechanical Equipment Assemblers; Engineering Technicians, Except Drafters, All Other; Excavating and Loading Machine and Dragline Operators; Explosives Workers, Ordnance Handling Experts, and Blasters; Extraction Workers, All Other; First-Line Supervisors of Construction Trades and Extraction Workers; Floor Layers, Except Carpet, Wood, and Hard Tiles; Floor Sanders and Finishers; Glaziers; Heating and Air Conditioning Mechanics and Installers; Helpers, Construction Trades, All Other; others.

Skills—Installation: Installing equipment, machines, wiring, or programs to meet specifications. **Repairing:** Repairing machines or systems using the needed tools. **Equipment Maintenance:** Performing routine maintenance on equipment and determining when and what kind of maintenance is needed. **Troubleshooting:** Determining causes of operating errors and deciding what to do about them. **Equipment Selection:** Determining the kind of tools and equipment needed to do a job. **Operation and Control:** Controlling operations of equipment or systems. **Quality Control Analysis:** Conducting tests and inspections of products, services, or processes to evaluate quality or performance. **Operation Monitoring:** Watching gauges, dials, or other indicators to make sure a machine is working properly.

Work Environment: Outdoors; standing; climbing; walking and running; kneeling, crouching, stooping, or crawling; using hands; bending or twisting the body; repetitive motions; noise; very hot or cold; bright or inadequate lighting; contaminants; cramped work space; high places; hazardous conditions; hazardous equipment; minor burns, cuts, bites, or stings.

Helpers—Installation, Maintenance, and Repair Workers

- ⊙ Annual Earnings: $24,060
- ⊙ Earnings Growth Potential: Low (28.6%)
- ⊙ Growth: 18.4%
- ⊙ Annual Job Openings: 8,040
- ⊙ Self-Employed: 0.0%

Considerations for Job Outlook: About-average employment growth is projected.

Help installation, maintenance, and repair workers in maintenance, parts replacement, and repair of vehicles, industrial machinery, and electrical and electronic equipment. Tend and observe equipment and machinery to verify efficient and safe operation. Examine and test machinery, equipment, components, and parts for defects to ensure proper functioning. Adjust, connect, or disconnect wiring, piping, tubing, and other parts, using hand or power tools. Install or replace machinery, equipment, and new or replacement parts and instruments, using hand or power tools. Clean or lubricate vehicles, machinery, equipment, instruments, tools, work areas, and other objects, using hand tools, power tools, and cleaning equipment. Apply protective materials to equipment, components, and parts to prevent defects and corrosion. Transfer tools, parts, equipment, and supplies to and from work stations and other areas. Disassemble broken or defective equipment to facilitate repair and reassemble equipment when repairs are complete. Assemble and maintain physical structures, using hand or power tools. Position vehicles, machinery, equipment, physical structures, and other objects for assembly or installation, using hand tools, power tools, and moving equipment. Hold or supply tools, parts, equipment, and supplies for other workers. Adjust, maintain, and repair tools, equipment, and machines, and assist more skilled workers with similar tasks. Prepare work stations for use by mechanics and repairers. Order new parts to maintain inventory. Diagnose electrical problems and install and rewire electrical components. Design, weld, and fabricate parts, using blueprints or other mechanical plans.

Education/Training Required: High school diploma or equivalent. **Education and Training Program:** Industrial Mechanics and Maintenance Technology. **Knowledge/ Courses—Mechanical Devices:** Machines and tools, including their designs, uses, repair, and maintenance. **Building and Construction:** Materials, methods, and the tools involved in the construction or repair of houses, buildings, or other structures such as highways and roads. **Physics:** Physical principles, laws, their interrelationships, and applications to understanding fluid, material, and atmospheric dynamics, and mechanical, electrical, atomic, and subatomic structures and processes. **Work Experience Needed:** None. **On-the-Job Training Needed:**

Moderate-term on-the-job training. **Certification/Licensure:** Licensure for some specializations.

Personality Type: Realistic-Conventional-Investigative. **Career Cluster:** 13 Manufacturing. **Career Pathway:** 13.3 Maintenance, Installation, and Repair. **Other Jobs in This Pathway:** Aircraft Mechanics and Service Technicians; Automotive Engineering Technicians; Automotive Specialty Technicians; Avionics Technicians; Biological Technicians; Camera and Photographic Equipment Repairers; Chemical Equipment Operators and Tenders; Civil Engineering Technicians; Coil Winders, Tapers, and Finishers; Computer, Automated Teller, and Office Machine Repairers; Construction and Related Workers, All Other; Control and Valve Installers and Repairers, Except Mechanical Door; Electric Motor, Power Tool, and Related Repairers; Electrical and Electronic Equipment Assemblers; Electrical and Electronics Repairers, Commercial and Industrial Equipment; Electrical and Electronics Repairers, Powerhouse, Substation, and Relay; Electrical Engineering Technicians; Electrical Engineering Technologists; Electromechanical Engineering Technologists; Electromechanical Equipment Assemblers; Electronics Engineering Technicians; Electronics Engineering Technologists; others.

Skills—Equipment Maintenance: Performing routine maintenance on equipment and determining when and what kind of maintenance is needed. **Repairing:** Repairing machines or systems using the needed tools. **Installation:** Installing equipment, machines, wiring, or programs to meet specifications. **Troubleshooting:** Determining causes of operating errors and deciding what to do about them. **Operation and Control:** Controlling operations of equipment or systems. **Equipment Selection:** Determining the kind of tools and equipment needed to do a job. **Quality Control Analysis:** Conducting tests and inspections of products, services, or processes to evaluate quality or performance. **Operation Monitoring:** Watching gauges, dials, or other indicators to make sure a machine is working properly.

Work Environment: Outdoors; standing; walking and running; using hands; bending or twisting the body; very hot or cold; cramped work space; hazardous equipment; minor burns, cuts, bites, or stings.

Helpers—Pipelayers, Plumbers, Pipefitters, and Steamfitters

- ⊙ Annual Earnings: $27,010
- ⊙ Earnings Growth Potential: Low (31.7%)
- ⊙ Growth: 45.4%
- ⊙ Annual Job Openings: 4,170
- ⊙ Self-Employed: 1.7%

Considerations for Job Outlook: Construction laborers with the most skills should have the best job opportunities. Opportunities also will vary by occupation; for example, carpenters' helpers should have the best job prospects, while painters', paperhangers', plasterers', and stucco masons' helpers will likely find fewer job openings. Prospective employees with military service often have better opportunities when applying for a job. Employment of construction laborers and helpers is especially sensitive to the fluctuations of the economy.

Help plumbers, pipefitters, steamfitters, or pipelayers by performing duties requiring less skill. Cut or drill holes in walls or floors to accommodate the passage of pipes. Measure, cut, thread, and assemble new pipe, placing the assembled pipe in hangers or other supports. Mount brackets and hangers on walls and ceilings to hold pipes, and set sleeves or inserts to provide support for pipes. Requisition tools and equipment, select type and size of pipe, and collect and transport materials and equipment to work site. Fit or assist in fitting valves, couplings, or assemblies to tanks, pumps, or systems, using hand tools. Assist pipe fitters in the layout, assembly, and installation of piping for air, ammonia, gas, and water systems. Excavate and grade ditches, and lay and join pipe for water and sewer service. Cut pipe and lift up to fitters. Disassemble and remove damaged or worn pipe. Clean shop, work area, and machines, using solvent and rags. Perform rough-ins; repair and replace fixtures and water heaters; and locate, repair, or remove leaking or broken pipes. Install gas burners to convert furnaces from wood, coal, or oil. Immerse pipe in chemical solution to remove dirt, oil, and scale. Clean and renew steam traps. Fill pipes with sand or resin to prevent distortion, and hold pipes during bending and installation.

Education/Training Required: High school diploma or equivalent. **Education and Training Program:** Plumbing

Technology/Plumber. **Knowledge/Courses—Building and Construction:** Materials, methods, and the tools involved in the construction or repair of houses, buildings, or other structures such as highways and roads. **Mechanical Devices:** Machines and tools, including their designs, uses, repair, and maintenance. **Design:** Design techniques, tools, and principles involved in production of precision technical plans, blueprints, drawings, and models. **Transportation:** Principles and methods for moving people or goods by air, rail, sea, or road, including the relative costs and benefits. **Engineering and Technology:** The practical application of engineering science and technology. This includes applying principles, techniques, procedures, and equipment to the design and production of various goods and services. **Customer and Personal Service:** Principles and processes for providing customer and personal services. This includes customer needs assessment, meeting quality standards for services, and evaluation of customer satisfaction. **Work Experience Needed:** None. **On-the-Job Training Needed:** Short-term on-the-job training. **Certification/Licensure:** None.

Personality Type: Realistic. **Career Cluster:** 02 Architecture and Construction. **Career Pathway:** 02.2 Construction. **Other Jobs in This Pathway:** Boilermakers; Brickmasons and Blockmasons; Carpet Installers; Cement Masons and Concrete Finishers; Construction and Building Inspectors; Construction and Related Workers, All Other; Construction Carpenters; Construction Laborers; Construction Managers; Continuous Mining Machine Operators; Cost Estimators; Crane and Tower Operators; Dredge Operators; Drywall and Ceiling Tile Installers; Earth Drillers, Except Oil and Gas; Electrical Power-Line Installers and Repairers; Electricians; Electromechanical Equipment Assemblers; Engineering Technicians, Except Drafters, All Other; Excavating and Loading Machine and Dragline Operators; Explosives Workers, Ordnance Handling Experts, and Blasters; Extraction Workers, All Other; First-Line Supervisors of Construction Trades and Extraction Workers; Floor Layers, Except Carpet, Wood, and Hard Tiles; Floor Sanders and Finishers; Glaziers; Heating and Air Conditioning Mechanics and Installers; Helpers, Construction Trades, All Other; others.

Skills—Repairing: Repairing machines or systems using the needed tools. **Installation:** Installing equipment, machines, wiring, or programs to meet specifications. **Equipment Selection:** Determining the kind of tools and equipment needed to do a job. **Equipment Maintenance:** Performing routine maintenance on equipment and determining when and what kind of maintenance is needed. **Troubleshooting:** Determining causes of operating errors and deciding what to do about them. **Operation and Control:** Controlling operations of equipment or systems.

Work Environment: More outdoors than indoors; standing; walking and running; kneeling, crouching, stooping, or crawling; using hands; bending or twisting the body; repetitive motions; noise; very hot or cold; bright or inadequate lighting; contaminants; cramped work space; hazardous equipment; minor burns, cuts, bites, or stings.

Helpers—Production Workers

- ⊙ Annual Earnings: $22,520
- ⊙ Earnings Growth Potential: Very low (24.6%)
- ⊙ Growth: 8.7%
- ⊙ Annual Job Openings: 9,980
- ⊙ Self-Employed: 0.2%

Considerations for Job Outlook: Slower-than-average growth in employment is projected.

Help production workers by performing duties requiring less skill. Operate machinery used in the production process, or assist machine operators. Examine products to verify conformance to quality standards. Observe equipment operations so that malfunctions can be detected, and notify operators of any malfunctions. Lift raw materials, finished products, and packed items, manually or using hoists. Count finished products to determine if product orders are complete. Mark or tag identification on parts. Load and unload items from machines, conveyors, and conveyances. Help production workers by performing duties of lesser skill, such as supplying or holding materials or tools, and cleaning work areas and equipment. Clean and lubricate equipment. Record information such as the number of products tested, meter readings, and dates and times of product production. Start machines or equipment in order to begin production processes. Separate products according to weight, grade, size, and composition of materials used to produce them. Turn valves to regulate flow of liquids or air, to reverse machines, to start pumps, or to regulate equipment. Place products in equipment or on work surfaces for further processing, inspecting, or wrapping. Pack and store materials and products. Remove products, machine attachments, and waste material from machines. Tie products in bundles for further processing or shipment, following prescribed procedures. Transfer finished products, raw materials, tools, or equipment between storage and work areas of plants and warehouses, by hand or using hand trucks or powered lift trucks. Signal coworkers to direct them to move products during the production process. Prepare raw materials for processing. Measure amounts of products, lengths of extruded articles, or weights of filled containers to ensure conformance to specifications. Thread ends of items such as thread, cloth, and lace through needles and rollers, and around take-up tubes. Read gauges and charts, and record data obtained.

Education/Training Required: Less than high school. **Education and Training Programs:** No related CIP programs; this job is learned through informal short-term on-the-job training. **Work Experience Needed:** None. **On-the-Job Training Needed:** Short-term on-the-job training. **Certification/Licensure:** None.

Personality Type: Realistic-Conventional. **Career Cluster:** 13 Manufacturing. **Career Pathway:** 13.1 Production. **Other Jobs in This Pathway:** Adhesive Bonding Machine Operators and Tenders; Assemblers and Fabricators, All Other; Avionics Technicians; Cabinetmakers and Bench Carpenters; Cleaning, Washing, and Metal Pickling Equipment Operators and Tenders; Coating, Painting, and Spraying Machine Setters, Operators, and Tenders; Computer-Controlled Machine Tool Operators, Metal and Plastic; Cooling and Freezing Equipment Operators and Tenders; Cost Estimators; Crushing, Grinding, and Polishing Machine Setters, Operators, and Tenders; Cutters and Trimmers, Hand; Cutting and Slicing Machine Setters, Operators, and Tenders; Cutting, Punching, and Press Machine Setters, Operators, and Tenders, Metal and Plastic; Drilling and Boring Machine Tool Setters, Operators, and Tenders, Metal and Plastic; Extruding and Drawing Machine Setters, Operators, and Tenders, Metal and Plastic; Extruding and Forming Machine Setters, Operators, and Tenders, Synthetic and Glass Fibers; others.

Skills—Repairing: Repairing machines or systems using the needed tools. **Operation and Control:** Controlling operations of equipment or systems. **Equipment Maintenance:** Performing routine maintenance on equipment and determining when and what kind of maintenance is needed. **Troubleshooting:** Determining causes of operating errors

and deciding what to do about them. **Operation Monitoring:** Watching gauges, dials, or other indicators to make sure a machine is working properly. **Equipment Selection:** Determining the kind of tools and equipment needed to do a job.

Work Environment: Standing; walking and running; using hands; bending or twisting the body; repetitive motions; noise; very hot or cold; contaminants; hazardous equipment; minor burns, cuts, bites, or stings.

Highway Maintenance Workers

- ⊙ Annual Earnings: $35,220
- ⊙ Earnings Growth Potential: Medium (37.6%)
- ⊙ Growth: 8.2%
- ⊙ Annual Job Openings: 5,140
- ⊙ Self-Employed: 1.5%

Considerations for Job Outlook: Slower-than-average employment growth is projected.

Maintain highways, municipal and rural roads, airport runways, and rights-of-way. Flag motorists to warn them of obstacles or repair work ahead. Set out signs and cones around work areas to divert traffic. Dump, spread, and tamp asphalt, using pneumatic tampers, to repair joints and patch broken pavement. Drive trucks to transport crews and equipment to work sites. Inspect, clean, and repair drainage systems, bridges, tunnels, and other structures. Haul and spread sand, gravel, and clay to fill washouts and repair road shoulders. Erect, install, or repair guardrails, road shoulders, berms, highway markers, warning signals, and highway lighting, using hand tools and power tools. Remove litter and debris from roadways, including debris from rock and mud slides. Clean and clear debris from culverts, catch basins, drop inlets, ditches, and other drain structures. Perform roadside landscaping work, such as clearing weeds and brush, and planting and trimming trees. Perform preventive maintenance on vehicles and heavy equipment.

Education/Training Required: High school diploma or equivalent. **Education and Training Program:** Construction/Heavy Equipment/Earthmoving Equipment Operation. **Knowledge/Courses—Building and Construction:** Materials, methods, and the tools involved in the construction or repair of houses, buildings, or other structures such as highways and roads. **Transportation:** Principles and methods for moving people or goods by air, rail, sea, or road, including the relative costs and benefits. **Public Safety and Security:** Relevant equipment, policies, procedures, and strategies to promote effective local, state, or national security operations for the protection of people, data, property, and institutions. **Mechanical Devices:** Machines and tools, including their designs, uses, repair, and maintenance. **Law and Government:** Laws, legal codes, court procedures, precedents, government regulations, executive orders, agency rules, and the democratic political process. **Telecommunications:** Transmission, broadcasting, switching, control, and operation of telecommunications systems. **Work Experience Needed:** None. **On-the-Job Training Needed:** Moderate-term on-the-job training. **Certification/Licensure:** None.

Personality Type: Realistic-Conventional. **Career Cluster:** 02 Architecture and Construction. **Career Pathway:** 02.2 Construction. **Other Jobs in This Pathway:** Boilermakers; Brickmasons and Blockmasons; Carpet Installers; Cement Masons and Concrete Finishers; Construction and Building Inspectors; Construction and Related Workers, All Other; Construction Carpenters; Construction Laborers; Construction Managers; Continuous Mining Machine Operators; Cost Estimators; Crane and Tower Operators; Dredge Operators; Drywall and Ceiling Tile Installers; Earth Drillers, Except Oil and Gas; Electrical Power-Line Installers and Repairers; Electricians; Electromechanical Equipment Assemblers; Engineering Technicians, Except Drafters, All Other; Excavating and Loading Machine and Dragline Operators; Explosives Workers, Ordnance Handling Experts, and Blasters; Extraction Workers, All Other; First-Line Supervisors of Construction Trades and Extraction Workers; Floor Layers, Except Carpet, Wood, and Hard Tiles; Floor Sanders and Finishers; Glaziers; Heating and Air Conditioning Mechanics and Installers; Helpers, Construction Trades, All Other; others.

Skills—Repairing: Repairing machines or systems using the needed tools. **Equipment Maintenance:** Performing routine maintenance on equipment and determining when and what kind of maintenance is needed. **Operation and Control:** Controlling operations of equipment or systems. **Troubleshooting:** Determining causes of operating errors and deciding what to do about them. **Operation Monitoring:** Watching gauges, dials, or other indicators to make sure a machine is working properly. **Quality Control**

Analysis: Conducting tests and inspections of products, services, or processes to evaluate quality or performance. **Equipment Selection:** Determining the kind of tools and equipment needed to do a job. **Coordination:** Adjusting actions in relation to others' actions.

Work Environment: Outdoors; standing; using hands; bending or twisting the body; repetitive motions; noise; very hot or cold; contaminants; cramped work space; whole-body vibration; hazardous equipment; minor burns, cuts, bites, or stings.

Home Appliance Repairers

- ⊙ Annual Earnings: $35,440
- ⊙ Earnings Growth Potential: High (43.5%)
- ⊙ Growth: 6.5%
- ⊙ Annual Job Openings: 1,190
- ⊙ Self-Employed: 29.9%

Considerations for Job Outlook: Despite slower-than-average employment growth, job opportunities for home appliance repairers should be very good because of job openings created by workers who retire or leave the occupation for other reasons. A lack of qualified workers in the field will also lead to good job prospects. Technicians with vocational training in appliance and electronics repair will have better job prospects than those who do not. Job opportunities at personal and household goods and repair shops should be very good as large electronics retail stores continue to outsource their repair work.

Repair, adjust, or install all types of electric or gas household appliances, such as refrigerators, washers, dryers, and ovens. Clean, lubricate, and touch up minor defects on newly installed or repaired appliances. Observe and test operation of appliances following installation, and make any initial installation adjustments that are necessary. Maintain stocks of parts used in on-site installation, maintenance, and repair of appliances. Level washing machines and connect hoses to water pipes, using hand tools. Disassemble appliances so that problems can be diagnosed and repairs can be made. Level refrigerators, adjust doors, and connect water lines to water pipes for ice makers and water dispensers, using hand tools. Clean and reinstall parts. Instruct customers regarding operation and care of appliances, and provide information such as emergency service numbers. Provide repair cost estimates, and recommend whether appliance repair or replacement is a better choice. Conserve, recover, and recycle refrigerants used in cooling systems. Contact supervisors or offices to receive repair assignments. Install appliances such as refrigerators, washing machines, and stoves. Install gas pipes and water lines to connect appliances to existing gas lines or plumbing. Record maintenance and repair work performed on appliances. Light and adjust pilot lights on gas stoves, and examine valves and burners for gas leakage and specified flame. Refer to schematic drawings, product manuals, and troubleshooting guides in order to diagnose and repair problems. Respond to emergency calls for problems such as gas leaks. Assemble new or reconditioned appliances. Disassemble and reinstall existing kitchen cabinets, or assemble and install prefabricated kitchen cabinets and trim in conjunction with appliance installation. Hang steel supports from beams or joists to hold hoses, vents, and gas pipes in place. Take measurements to determine if appliances will fit in installation locations; perform minor carpentry work when necessary to ensure proper installation.

Education/Training Required: High school diploma or equivalent. **Education and Training Programs:** Appliance Installation and Repair Technology/Technician; Electrical/Electronics Equipment Installation and Repair, General; Home Furnishings and Equipment Installer Training. **Knowledge/Courses—Sales and Marketing:** Principles and methods for showing, promoting, and selling products or services. This includes marketing strategy and tactics, product demonstration, sales techniques, and sales control systems. **Mechanical Devices:** Machines and tools, including their designs, uses, repair, and maintenance. **Customer and Personal Service:** Principles and processes for providing customer and personal services. This includes customer needs assessment, meeting quality standards for services, and evaluation of customer satisfaction. **Physics:** Physical principles, laws, their interrelationships, and applications to understanding fluid, material, and atmospheric dynamics, and mechanical, electrical, atomic, and subatomic structures and processes. **Economics and Accounting:** Economic and accounting principles and practices, the financial markets, banking, and the analysis and reporting of financial data. **Engineering and Technology:** The practical application of engineering science and technology. This includes applying principles, techniques, procedures, and equipment to the design and production of various goods and services.

Work Experience Needed: None. **On-the-Job Training Needed:** Moderate-term on-the-job training. **Certification/Licensure:** Licensure for some specializations; voluntary certification by association.

Personality Type: Realistic-Conventional-Investigative. **Career Cluster:** 02 Architecture and Construction. **Career Pathway:** 02.3 Maintenance/Operations. **Other Jobs in This Pathway:** Coin, Vending, and Amusement Machine Servicers and Repairers; Heating and Air Conditioning Mechanics and Installers; Refrigeration Mechanics and Installers; Security and Fire Alarm Systems Installers.

Skills—Repairing: Repairing machines or systems using the needed tools. **Equipment Maintenance:** Performing routine maintenance on equipment and determining when and what kind of maintenance is needed. **Troubleshooting:** Determining causes of operating errors and deciding what to do about them. **Installation:** Installing equipment, machines, wiring, or programs to meet specifications. **Quality Control Analysis:** Conducting tests and inspections of products, services, or processes to evaluate quality or performance. **Equipment Selection:** Determining the kind of tools and equipment needed to do a job. **Operation and Control:** Controlling operations of equipment or systems. **Operation Monitoring:** Watching gauges, dials, or other indicators to make sure a machine is working properly.

Work Environment: Indoors; standing; kneeling, crouching, stooping, or crawling; using hands; bending or twisting the body; contaminants; cramped work space; minor burns, cuts, bites, or stings.

Human Resources Assistants, Except Payroll and Timekeeping

- ⊙ Annual Earnings: $37,250
- ⊙ Earnings Growth Potential: Low (33.1%)
- ⊙ Growth: 11.2%
- ⊙ Annual Job Openings: 6,160
- ⊙ Self-Employed: 0.0%

Considerations for Job Outlook: Employment growth will vary by specialty. Projected employment change is most rapid for interviewers and correspondence clerks.

Compile and keep personnel records. Process, verify, and maintain personnel-related documentation, including staffing, recruitment, training, grievances, performance evaluations, classifications, and employee leaves of absence. Explain company personnel policies, benefits, and procedures to employees or job applicants. Record data for each employee, including such information as addresses, weekly earnings, absences, amount of sales or production, supervisory reports on performance, and dates of and reasons for terminations. Gather personnel records from other departments or employees. Examine employee files to answer inquiries and provide information for personnel actions. Answer questions regarding examinations, eligibility, salaries, benefits, and other pertinent information. Compile and prepare reports and documents pertaining to personnel activities. Request information from law enforcement officials, previous employers, and other references to determine applicants' employment acceptability. Process and review employment applications to evaluate qualifications or eligibility of applicants. Arrange for advertising or posting of job vacancies, and notify eligible workers of position availability. Provide assistance in administering employee benefit programs and worker's compensation plans. Select applicants, meeting specified job requirements, and refer them to hiring personnel. Inform job applicants of their acceptance or rejection of employment. Interview job applicants to obtain and verify information used to screen and evaluate them. Search employee files to obtain information for authorized persons and organizations, such as credit bureaus and finance companies. Administer and score applicant and employee aptitude, personality, and interest assessment instruments. Prepare badges, passes, and identification cards, and perform other security-related duties. Arrange for in-house and external training activities.

Education/Training Required: High school diploma or equivalent. **Education and Training Program:** General Office Occupations and Clerical Services. **Knowledge/Courses—Clerical Practices:** Administrative and clerical procedures and systems such as word processing, managing files and records, stenography and transcription, designing forms, and other office procedures and terminology. **Personnel and Human Resources:** Principles and procedures for personnel recruitment, selection, training, compensation and benefits, labor relations and negotiation, and personnel information systems. **Customer and Personal Service:** Principles and processes for providing customer and personal services. This includes customer needs assessment, meeting quality standards for services, and evaluation of customer satisfaction. **Economics and Accounting:** Economic and accounting principles and practices, the financial markets, banking, and the analysis and reporting of financial data. **Computers and Electronics:** Circuit boards, processors, chips, electronic equipment, and computer hardware and software, including applications and programming. **Law and Government:** Laws, legal codes, court procedures, precedents, government regulations, executive orders, agency rules, and the democratic political process. **Work Experience Needed:** None. **On-the-Job Training Needed:** Short-term on-the-job training. **Certification/Licensure:** None.

Personality Type: Conventional-Enterprising-Social. **Career Cluster:** 04 Business, Management, and Administration. **Career Pathway:** 04.6 Administrative and Information Support. **Other Jobs in This Pathway:** Cargo and Freight Agents; Correspondence Clerks; Couriers and Messengers; Court Clerks; Customer Service Representatives; Data Entry Keyers; Dispatchers, Except Police, Fire, and Ambulance; Executive Secretaries and Executive Administrative Assistants; File Clerks; Freight Forwarders; Information and Record Clerks, All Other; Insurance Claims Clerks; Insurance Policy Processing Clerks; Interviewers, Except Eligibility and Loan; License Clerks; Mail Clerks and Mail Machine Operators, Except Postal Service; Meter Readers, Utilities; Municipal Clerks; Office and Administrative Support Workers, All Other; Office Clerks, General; Office Machine Operators, Except Computer; Order Clerks; Patient Representatives; Postal Service Clerks; Postal Service Mail Carriers; Postal Service Mail Sorters, Processors, and Processing Machine Operators; Procurement Clerks; Receptionists and Information Clerks; Secretaries and Administrative Assistants, Except Legal, Medical, and Executive; others.

Skills—Active Listening: Giving full attention to what other people are saying, taking time to understand the points being made, asking questions as appropriate, and not interrupting at inappropriate times. **Reading Comprehension:** Understanding written sentences and paragraphs in work-related documents. **Service Orientation:** Actively looking for ways to help people. **Writing:** Communicating effectively in writing as appropriate for the needs of the audience. **Speaking:** Talking to others to convey information effectively. **Social Perceptiveness:** Being aware of others' reactions and understanding why they react as they do.

Management of Personnel Resources: Motivating, developing, and directing people as they work, identifying the best people for the job.

Work Environment: Indoors; sitting; repetitive motions.

Industrial Engineering Technicians

- Annual Earnings: $49,090
- Earnings Growth Potential: Low (34.1%)
- Growth: 4.2%
- Annual Job Openings: 1,460
- Self-Employed: 0.5%

Considerations for Job Outlook: Industrial engineering is versatile because of its wide applicability in many industries. The growing emphasis on cost control through increasing efficiency is expected to sustain demand for industrial engineering technicians' services in most industries, including nonprofits.

Apply engineering theory and principles to problems of industrial layout or manufacturing production, usually under the direction of engineering staff. Study time, motion, methods, or speed involved in maintenance, production, or other operations to establish standard production rate or improve efficiency. Interpret engineering drawings, schematic diagrams, or formulas and confer with management or engineering staff to determine quality and reliability standards. Recommend modifications to existing quality or production standards to achieve optimum quality within limits of equipment capability. Aid in planning work assignments in accordance with worker performance, machine capacity, production schedules, or anticipated delays. Observe workers using equipment to verify that equipment is being operated and maintained according to quality assurance standards. Prepare charts, graphs, or diagrams to illustrate workflow, routing, floor layouts, material handling, or machine utilization. Evaluate data and write reports to validate or indicate deviations from existing standards. Read worker logs, product processing sheets, or specification sheets to verify that records adhere to quality assurance specifications. Prepare graphs or charts of data or enter data into computers for analysis. Record test data, applying statistical quality control procedures. Select products for tests at specified stages in their production process, and test products for performance characteristics and adherence to specifications. Compile and evaluate statistical data to determine and maintain quality and reliability of products. Design new equipment and materials or recommend revision to methods of operation, material handling, equipment layout, or other changes to increase production or improve standards. Observe workers operating equipment or performing tasks to determine time involved and fatigue rate using timing devices.

Education/Training Required: Associate degree. **Education and Training Programs:** Engineering/Industrial Management; Industrial Production Technologies/Technicians, Other; Industrial Technology/Technician; Manufacturing Engineering Technology/Technician. **Knowledge/Courses—Engineering and Technology:** The practical application of engineering science and technology. This includes applying principles, techniques, procedures, and equipment to the design and production of various goods and services. **Design:** Design techniques, tools, and principles involved in production of precision technical plans, blueprints, drawings, and models. **Mechanical Devices:** Machines and tools, including their designs, uses, repair, and maintenance. **Physics:** Physical principles, laws, their interrelationships, and applications to understanding fluid, material, and atmospheric dynamics, and mechanical, electrical, atomic, and subatomic structures and processes. **Production and Processing:** Raw materials, production processes, quality control, costs, and other techniques for maximizing the effective manufacture and distribution of goods. **Chemistry:** The chemical composition, structure, and properties of substances and of the chemical processes and transformations that they undergo. This includes uses of chemicals and their danger signs, production techniques, and disposal methods. **Work Experience Needed:** None. **On-the-Job Training Needed:** None. **Certification/Licensure:** No data available.

Personality Type: Investigative-Realistic-Conventional. **Career Clusters:** 13 Manufacturing; 15 Science, Technology, Engineering, and Mathematics. **Career Pathways:** 15.1 Engineering and Technology; 13.3 Maintenance, Installation, and Repair. **Other Jobs in These Pathways:** Aerospace Engineers; Agricultural Engineers; Aircraft Mechanics and Service Technicians; Architectural and Engineering Managers; Architecture Teachers, Postsecondary; Automotive Engineering Technicians; Automotive Engineers; Automotive Specialty Technicians; Avionics Technicians; Biochemical Engineers; Biofuels/

Biodiesel Technology and Product Development Managers; Biological Technicians; Biomedical Engineers; Camera and Photographic Equipment Repairers; Chemical Engineers; Chemical Equipment Operators and Tenders; Civil Engineering Technicians; Civil Engineers; Coil Winders, Tapers, and Finishers; Computer Hardware Engineers; Computer, Automated Teller, and Office Machine Repairers; Construction and Related Workers, All Other; Control and Valve Installers and Repairers, Except Mechanical Door; Cost Estimators; Drafters, All Other; Education, Training, and Library Workers, All Other; Electric Motor, Power Tool, and Related Repairers; Electrical and Electronic Equipment Assemblers; others.

Skills—Technology Design: Generating or adapting equipment and technology to serve user needs. **Mathematics:** Using mathematics to solve problems. **Systems Evaluation:** Identifying measures or indicators of system performance and the actions needed to improve or correct performance relative to the goals of the system. **Systems Analysis:** Determining how a system should work and how changes in conditions, operations, and the environment will affect outcomes. **Operations Analysis:** Analyzing needs and product requirements to create a design. **Science:** Using scientific rules and methods to solve problems. **Programming:** Writing computer programs for various purposes. **Monitoring:** Monitoring or assessing your performance or that of other individuals or organizations to make improvements or take corrective action.

Work Environment: More often indoors than outdoors; sitting; noise; contaminants; hazardous equipment.

Industrial Machinery Mechanics

- ⊙ Annual Earnings: $46,270
- ⊙ Earnings Growth Potential: Low (33.5%)
- ⊙ Growth: 21.6%
- ⊙ Annual Job Openings: 11,710
- ⊙ Self-Employed: 1.7%

Considerations for Job Outlook: Applicants with a broad range of skills in machine repair should have good job prospects overall. The need to replace the many older workers who are expected to retire, as well as those who leave the occupation for other reasons, should result in numerous job openings. Some employers have reported difficulty

in recruiting young workers with the necessary skills. Mechanics are not as affected by changes in production levels as are other manufacturing workers because mechanics often are kept during production downtime to complete overhauls to major equipment and to keep expensive machinery in working order.

Repair, install, adjust, or maintain industrial production and processing machinery or refinery and pipeline distribution systems. Disassemble machinery and equipment to remove parts and make repairs. Repair and replace broken or malfunctioning components of machinery and equipment. Repair and maintain the operating condition of industrial production and processing machinery and equipment. Examine parts for defects such as breakage and excessive wear. Reassemble equipment after completion of inspections, testing, or repairs. Observe and test the operation of machinery and equipment to diagnose malfunctions, using voltmeters and other testing devices. Operate newly repaired machinery and equipment to verify the adequacy of repairs. Clean, lubricate, and adjust parts, equipment, and machinery. Analyze test results, machine error messages, and information obtained from operators to diagnose equipment problems. Record repairs and maintenance performed. Study blueprints and manufacturers' manuals to determine correct installation and operation of machinery. Record parts and materials used, ordering or requisitioning new parts and materials as necessary. Cut and weld metal to repair broken metal parts, fabricate new parts, and assemble new equipment. Demonstrate equipment functions and features to machine operators. Enter codes and instructions to program computer-controlled machinery.

Education/Training Required: High school diploma or equivalent. **Education and Training Programs:** Heavy/Industrial Equipment Maintenance Technologies, Other; Industrial Mechanics and Maintenance Technology. **Knowledge/Courses—Mechanical Devices:** Machines and tools, including their designs, uses, repair, and maintenance. **Engineering and Technology:** The practical application of engineering science and technology. This includes applying principles, techniques, procedures, and equipment to the design and production of various goods and services. **Building and Construction:** Materials, methods, and the tools involved in the construction or repair of houses, buildings, or other structures such as highways and roads. **Design:** Design techniques, tools, and principles involved in production of precision technical plans, blueprints, drawings, and models. **Chemistry:** The chemical composition, structure, and properties of substances and of the chemical processes and transformations that they undergo. This includes uses of chemicals and their danger signs, production techniques, and disposal methods. **Physics:** Physical principles, laws, their interrelationships, and applications to understanding fluid, material, and atmospheric dynamics, and mechanical, electrical, atomic, and subatomic structures and processes. **Work Experience Needed:** None. **On-the-Job Training Needed:** Long-term on-the-job training. **Certification/Licensure:** None.

Personality Type: Realistic-Investigative-Conventional. **Career Cluster:** 13 Manufacturing. **Career Pathway:** 13.3 Maintenance, Installation, and Repair. **Other Jobs in This Pathway:** Aircraft Mechanics and Service Technicians; Automotive Engineering Technicians; Automotive Specialty Technicians; Avionics Technicians; Biological Technicians; Camera and Photographic Equipment Repairers; Chemical Equipment Operators and Tenders; Civil Engineering Technicians; Coil Winders, Tapers, and Finishers; Computer, Automated Teller, and Office Machine Repairers; Construction and Related Workers, All Other; Control and Valve Installers and Repairers, Except Mechanical Door; Electric Motor, Power Tool, and Related Repairers; Electrical and Electronic Equipment Assemblers; Electrical and Electronics Repairers, Commercial and Industrial Equipment; Electrical and Electronics Repairers, Powerhouse, Substation, and Relay; Electrical Engineering Technicians; Electrical Engineering Technologists; Electromechanical Engineering Technologists; Electromechanical Equipment Assemblers; Electronics Engineering Technicians; Electronics Engineering Technologists; others.

Skills—Repairing: Repairing machines or systems using the needed tools. **Equipment Maintenance:** Performing routine maintenance on equipment and determining when and what kind of maintenance is needed. **Troubleshooting:** Determining causes of operating errors and deciding what to do about them. **Installation:** Installing equipment, machines, wiring, or programs to meet specifications. **Operation Monitoring:** Watching gauges, dials, or other indicators to make sure a machine is working properly. **Equipment Selection:** Determining the kind of tools and equipment needed to do a job. **Operation and Control:** Controlling operations of equipment or systems. **Quality Control Analysis:** Conducting tests and inspections of products, services, or processes to evaluate quality or performance.

Work Environment: Standing; walking and running; kneeling, crouching, stooping, or crawling; using hands; bending or twisting the body; repetitive motions; noise; very hot or cold; contaminants; cramped work space; high places; hazardous conditions; hazardous equipment; minor burns, cuts, bites, or stings.

Industrial Truck and Tractor Operators

- ☉ Annual Earnings: $30,010
- ☉ Earnings Growth Potential: Low (32.3%)
- ☉ Growth: 11.8%
- ☉ Annual Job Openings: 20,950
- ☉ Self-Employed: 0.1%

Considerations for Job Outlook: Job prospects should be favorable. A high number of job openings should be created by the need to replace workers who leave this occupation. As automation increases, the technology used by this occupation will become more complex.

Operate industrial trucks or tractors equipped to move materials around a warehouse, storage yard, factory, construction site, or similar location. Move controls to drive gasoline- or electric-powered trucks, cars, or tractors and transport materials between loading, processing, and storage areas. Move levers and controls that operate lifting devices, such as forklifts, lift beams and swivel-hooks, hoists, and elevating platforms, to load, unload, transport, and stack material. Position lifting devices under, over, or around loaded pallets, skids, and boxes, and secure material or products for transport to designated areas. Manually load or unload materials onto or off pallets, skids, platforms, cars, or lifting devices. Perform routine maintenance on vehicles and auxiliary equipment, such as cleaning, lubricating, recharging batteries, fueling, or replacing liquefied-gas tank. Weigh materials or products, and record weight and other production data on tags or labels. Operate or tend automatic stacking, loading, packaging, or cutting machines. Signal workers to discharge, dump, or level materials. Hook tow trucks to trailer hitches and fasten attachments, such as graders, plows, rollers, and winch cables to tractors, using hitchpins. Turn valves and open chutes to dump, spray, or release materials from dump cars or storage bins into hoppers.

Education/Training Required: Less than high school. **Education and Training Program:** Ground Transportation, Other. **Knowledge/Courses—Production and Processing:** Raw materials, production processes, quality control, costs, and other techniques for maximizing the effective manufacture and distribution of goods. **Work Experience Needed:** Less than 1 year. **On-the-Job Training Needed:** Short-term on-the-job training. **Certification/Licensure:** None.

Personality Type: Realistic-Conventional. **Career Cluster:** 01 Agriculture, Food, and Natural Resources. **Career Pathway:** 01.5 Natural Resources Systems. **Other Jobs in This Pathway:** Biological Science Teachers, Postsecondary; Climate Change Analysts; Conveyor Operators and Tenders; Derrick Operators, Oil and Gas; Engineering Technicians, Except Drafters, All Other; Environmental Economists; Environmental Restoration Planners; Environmental Science and Protection Technicians, Including Health; Environmental Science Teachers, Postsecondary; Environmental Scientists and Specialists, Including Health; Fallers; Fish and Game Wardens; Fishers and Related Fishing Workers; Forest and Conservation Technicians; Forest and Conservation Workers; Foresters; Forestry and Conservation Science Teachers, Postsecondary; Gas Compressor and Gas Pumping Station Operators; Geological Sample Test Technicians; Geophysical Data Technicians; Helpers—Extraction Workers; Industrial Ecologists; Loading Machine Operators, Underground Mining; Log Graders and Scalers; Logging Equipment Operators; Logging Workers, All Other; Mechanical Engineering Technicians; Mine Shuttle Car Operators; others.

Skills—Equipment Maintenance: Performing routine maintenance on equipment and determining when and what kind of maintenance is needed. **Operation and Control:** Controlling operations of equipment or systems. **Operation Monitoring:** Watching gauges, dials, or other indicators to make sure a machine is working properly. **Troubleshooting:** Determining causes of operating errors and deciding what to do about them. **Repairing:** Repairing machines or systems using the needed tools.

Work Environment: Indoors; sitting; using hands; bending or twisting the body; repetitive motions; noise; very hot or cold; contaminants; hazardous equipment.

Inspectors, Testers, Sorters, Samplers, and Weighers

- ⊙ Annual Earnings: $34,040
- ⊙ Earnings Growth Potential: High (40.1%)
- ⊙ Growth: 8.0%
- ⊙ Annual Job Openings: 12,390
- ⊙ Self-Employed: 0.8%

Considerations for Job Outlook: Numerous jobs in the manufacturing industry are expected to arise over the coming decade as workers retire or leave the occupation for other reasons. Those with advanced skills and experience should qualify for many of these positions. The best job opportunities are expected to be in the employment services industry and in plastic product manufacturing.

Inspect, test, sort, sample, or weigh nonagricultural raw materials or processed, machined, fabricated, or assembled parts or products for defects, wear, and deviations from specifications. Discard or reject products, materials, and equipment not meeting specifications. Analyze and interpret blueprints, data, manuals, and other materials to determine specifications, inspection and testing procedures, adjustment and certification methods, formulas, and measuring instruments required. Inspect, test, or measure materials, products, installations, and work for conformance to specifications. Notify supervisors and other personnel of production problems, and assist in identifying and correcting these problems. Discuss inspection results with those responsible for products, and recommend necessary corrective actions. Record inspection or test data, such as weights, temperatures, grades, or moisture content, and quantities inspected or graded. Mark items with details such as grade and acceptance or rejection status. Observe and monitor production operations and equipment to ensure conformance to specifications and make or order necessary process or assembly adjustments. Measure dimensions of products to verify conformance to specifications, using measuring instruments such as rulers, calipers, gauges, or micrometers. Analyze test data and make computations as necessary to determine test results. Collect or select samples for testing or for use as models. Check arriving materials to ensure that they match purchase orders and submit discrepancy reports when problems are found. Compare colors, shapes, textures, or grades of products or materials with color charts, templates, or samples to verify conformance to standards. Write test and inspection reports describing results, recommendations, and needed repairs. Read dials and meters to verify that equipment is functioning at specified levels. Remove defects, such as chips and burrs, and lap corroded or pitted surfaces. Clean, maintain, repair, and calibrate measuring instruments and test equipment such as dial indicators, fixed gauges, and height gauges.

Education/Training Required: High school diploma or equivalent. **Education and Training Program:** Quality Control Technology/Technician. **Knowledge/Courses— Production and Processing:** Raw materials, production processes, quality control, costs, and other techniques for maximizing the effective manufacture and distribution of goods. **Work Experience Needed:** None. **On-the-Job Training Needed:** Moderate-term on-the-job training. **Certification/Licensure:** Licensure for some specializations; voluntary certification by association.

Personality Type: Conventional-Realistic. **Career Cluster:** 13 Manufacturing. **Career Pathway:** 13.4 Quality Assurance. **Other Jobs in This Pathway:** Environmental Engineering Technicians; Occupational Health and Safety Specialists.

Skills—Quality Control Analysis: Conducting tests and inspections of products, services, or processes to evaluate quality or performance. **Operation and Control:** Controlling operations of equipment or systems. **Operation Monitoring:** Watching gauges, dials, or other indicators to make sure a machine is working properly. **Troubleshooting:** Determining causes of operating errors and deciding what to do about them. **Operations Analysis:** Analyzing needs and product requirements to create a design. **Science:** Using scientific rules and methods to solve problems.

Work Environment: Standing; using hands; repetitive motions; noise.

Insulation Workers, Floor, Ceiling, and Wall

- ☉ Annual Earnings: $32,420
- ☉ Earnings Growth Potential: Medium (36.0%)
- ☉ Growth: 23.3%
- ☉ Annual Job Openings: 1,460
- ☉ Self-Employed: 3.9%

Considerations for Job Outlook: Floor, ceiling, and wall insulators are expected to face competition for openings as they often compete for jobs with other construction workers. Openings will, nonetheless, continue to arise because the irritating nature of many insulation materials, combined with the often difficult working conditions, causes many residential insulation workers to leave the occupation each year. Insulation workers in the construction industry may experience periods of unemployment because of the short duration of many construction projects and the cyclical nature of construction activity. Workers employed to do industrial plant maintenance generally have more stable employment because maintenance and repair must be done continually.

Line and cover structures with insulating materials. Move controls, buttons, or levers to start blowers and regulate flow of materials through nozzles. Cover and line structures with blown or rolled forms of materials to insulate against cold, heat, or moisture, using saws, knives, rasps, trowels, blowers, and other tools and implements. Cover, seal, or finish insulated surfaces or access holes with plastic covers, canvas strips, sealants, tape, cement or asphalt mastic. Distribute insulating materials evenly into small spaces within floors, ceilings, or walls, using blowers and hose attachments, or cement mortars. Fill blower hoppers with insulating materials. Fit, wrap, staple, or glue insulating materials to structures or surfaces, using hand tools or wires. Read blueprints and select appropriate insulation, based on space characteristics and the heat retaining or excluding characteristics of the material. Remove old insulation such as asbestos, following safety procedures. Measure and cut insulation for covering surfaces, using tape measures, handsaws, power saws, knives, or scissors. Prepare surfaces for insulation application by brushing or spreading on adhesives, cement, or asphalt, or by attaching metal pins to surfaces.

Education/Training Required: Less than high school. **Education and Training Program:** Construction Trades, Other. **Knowledge/Courses—Building and Construction:** Materials, methods, and the tools involved in the construction or repair of houses, buildings, or other structures such as highways and roads. **Production and Processing:** Raw materials, production processes, quality control, costs, and other techniques for maximizing the effective manufacture and distribution of goods. **Transportation:** Principles and methods for moving people or goods by air, rail, sea, or road, including the relative costs and benefits. **Personnel and Human Resources:** Principles and procedures for personnel recruitment, selection, training, compensation and benefits, labor relations and negotiation, and personnel information systems. **Design:** Design techniques, tools, and principles involved in production of precision technical plans, blueprints, drawings, and models. **Economics and Accounting:** Economic and accounting principles and practices, the financial markets, banking, and the analysis and reporting of financial data. **Work Experience Needed:** None. **On-the-Job Training Needed:** Short-term on-the-job training. **Certification/Licensure:** Certification for some specializations.

Personality Type: Realistic. **Career Cluster:** 02 Architecture and Construction. **Career Pathway:** 02.2 Construction. **Other Jobs in This Pathway:** Boilermakers; Brickmasons and Blockmasons; Carpet Installers; Cement Masons and Concrete Finishers; Construction and Building Inspectors; Construction and Related Workers, All Other; Construction Carpenters; Construction Laborers; Construction Managers; Continuous Mining Machine Operators; Cost Estimators; Crane and Tower Operators; Dredge Operators; Drywall and Ceiling Tile Installers; Earth Drillers, Except Oil and Gas; Electrical Power-Line Installers and Repairers; Electricians; Electromechanical Equipment Assemblers; Engineering Technicians, Except Drafters, All Other; Excavating and Loading Machine and Dragline Operators; Explosives Workers, Ordnance Handling Experts, and Blasters; Extraction Workers, All Other; First-Line Supervisors of Construction Trades and Extraction Workers; Floor Layers, Except Carpet, Wood, and Hard Tiles; Floor Sanders and Finishers; Glaziers; Heating and Air Conditioning Mechanics and Installers; Helpers, Construction Trades, All Other; others.

Skills—Repairing: Repairing machines or systems using the needed tools. **Equipment Maintenance:** Performing routine maintenance on equipment and determining when and what kind of maintenance is needed. **Operation and Control:** Controlling operations of equipment or systems. **Equipment Selection:** Determining the kind of tools and equipment needed to do a job. **Troubleshooting:** Determining causes of operating errors and deciding what to do about them. **Quality Control Analysis:** Conducting tests and inspections of products, services, or processes to evaluate quality or performance. **Operation Monitoring:**

Watching gauges, dials, or other indicators to make sure a machine is working properly.

Work Environment: Outdoors; standing; climbing; walking and running; kneeling, crouching, stooping, or crawling; balancing; using hands; bending or twisting the body; repetitive motions; noise; very hot or cold; contaminants; cramped work space; high places; minor burns, cuts, bites, or stings.

Insulation Workers, Mechanical

- ⊙ Annual Earnings: $37,990
- ⊙ Earnings Growth Potential: Low (33.8%)
- ⊙ Growth: 31.8%
- ⊙ Annual Job Openings: 2,010
- ⊙ Self-Employed: 3.8%

Considerations for Job Outlook: Mechanical insulation workers with formal training should have the best job opportunities. Insulation workers in the construction industry may experience periods of unemployment because of the short duration of many construction projects and the cyclical nature of construction activity. Workers employed to do industrial plant maintenance generally have more stable employment because maintenance and repair must be done continually.

Apply insulating materials to pipes or ductwork, or other mechanical systems in order to help control and maintain temperature. Cover, seal, or finish insulated surfaces or access holes with plastic covers, canvas strips, sealants, tape, cement, or asphalt mastic. Measure and cut insulation for covering surfaces, using tape measures, handsaws, knives, and scissors. Prepare surfaces for insulation application by brushing or spreading on adhesives, cement, or asphalt, or by attaching metal pins to surfaces. Select appropriate insulation such as fiberglass, Styrofoam, or cork, based on the heat retaining or excluding characteristics of the material. Read blueprints and specifications to determine job requirements. Install sheet metal around insulated pipes with screws in order to protect the insulation from weather conditions or physical damage. Determine the amounts and types of insulation needed, and methods of installation, based on factors such as location, surface shape, and equipment use. Apply, remove, and repair insulation on industrial equipment, pipes, ductwork, or other mechanical systems such as heat exchangers, tanks, and vessels, to help control noise and maintain temperatures. Remove or seal off old asbestos insulation, following safety procedures. Move controls, buttons, or levers to start blowers, and to regulate flow of materials through nozzles. Fill blower hoppers with insulating materials. Distribute insulating materials evenly into small spaces within floors, ceilings, or walls, using blowers and hose attachments or cement mortar. Fit insulation around obstructions, and shape insulating materials and protective coverings as required.

Education/Training Required: High school diploma or equivalent. **Education and Training Program:** Construction Trades, Other. **Knowledge/Courses—Building and Construction:** Materials, methods, and the tools involved in the construction or repair of houses, buildings, or other structures such as highways and roads. **Design:** Design techniques, tools, and principles involved in production of precision technical plans, blueprints, drawings, and models. **Mechanical Devices:** Machines and tools, including their designs, uses, repair, and maintenance. **Transportation:** Principles and methods for moving people or goods by air, rail, sea, or road, including the relative costs and benefits. **Education and Training:** Principles and methods for curriculum and training design, teaching and instruction for individuals and groups, and the measurement of training effects. **Public Safety and Security:** Relevant equipment, policies, procedures, and strategies to promote effective local, state, or national security operations for the protection of people, data, property, and institutions. **Work Experience Needed:** None. **On-the-Job Training Needed:** Apprenticeship. **Certification/Licensure:** Certification for some specializations.

Personality Type: Realistic-Conventional-Investigative. **Career Cluster:** 02 Architecture and Construction. **Career Pathway:** 02.2 Construction. **Other Jobs in This Pathway:** Boilermakers; Brickmasons and Blockmasons; Carpet Installers; Cement Masons and Concrete Finishers; Construction and Building Inspectors; Construction and Related Workers, All Other; Construction Carpenters; Construction Laborers; Construction Managers; Continuous Mining Machine Operators; Cost Estimators; Crane and Tower Operators; Dredge Operators; Drywall and Ceiling Tile Installers; Earth Drillers, Except Oil and Gas; Electrical Power-Line Installers and Repairers; Electricians; Electromechanical Equipment Assemblers; Engineering

Technicians, Except Drafters, All Other; Excavating and Loading Machine and Dragline Operators; Explosives Workers, Ordnance Handling Experts, and Blasters; Extraction Workers, All Other; First-Line Supervisors of Construction Trades and Extraction Workers; Floor Layers, Except Carpet, Wood, and Hard Tiles; Floor Sanders and Finishers; Glaziers; Heating and Air Conditioning Mechanics and Installers; Helpers, Construction Trades, All Other; others.

Skills—Operation and Control: Controlling operations of equipment or systems. **Installation:** Installing equipment, machines, wiring, or programs to meet specifications. **Troubleshooting:** Determining causes of operating errors and deciding what to do about them. **Operation Monitoring:** Watching gauges, dials, or other indicators to make sure a machine is working properly. **Management of Material Resources:** Obtaining and seeing to the appropriate use of equipment, facilities, and materials needed to do certain work.

Work Environment: Outdoors; standing; climbing; walking and running; kneeling, crouching, stooping, or crawling; using hands; bending or twisting the body; repetitive motions; noise; very hot or cold; bright or inadequate lighting; contaminants; cramped work space; high places; hazardous conditions; hazardous equipment; minor burns, cuts, bites, or stings.

Insurance Claims and Policy Processing Clerks

- ⊙ Annual Earnings: $35,210
- ⊙ Earnings Growth Potential: Low (28.7%)
- ⊙ Growth: 8.7%
- ⊙ Annual Job Openings: 9,600
- ⊙ Self-Employed: 0.2%

Considerations for Job Outlook: Job prospects for financial clerks should be favorable, because many workers are expected to leave this occupation. Employers will need to hire new workers to replace those leaving the occupation.

Process new insurance policies, modifications to existing policies, and claims forms. For task data, see Job Specializations.

Education/Training Required: High school diploma or equivalent. **Work Experience Needed:** None. **On-the-Job Training Needed:** Moderate-term on-the-job training. **Certification/Licensure:** None.

Job Specialization: Insurance Claims Clerks

Obtain information from insured or designated persons for purpose of settling claim with insurance carrier. Review insurance policy to determine coverage. Prepare and review insurance-claim forms and related documents for completeness. Provide customer service, such as giving limited instructions on how to proceed with claims or providing referrals to auto repair facilities or local contractors. Organize and work with detailed office or warehouse records, using computers to enter, access, search, and retrieve data. Post or attach information to claim file. Pay small claims. Transmit claims for payment or further investigation. Contact insured or other involved persons to obtain missing information. Calculate amount of claim. Apply insurance rating systems.

Education and Training Program: General Office Occupations and Clerical Services. **Knowledge/Courses—Clerical Practices:** Administrative and clerical procedures and systems such as word processing, managing files and records, stenography and transcription, designing forms, and other office procedures and terminology. **Customer and Personal Service:** Principles and processes for providing customer and personal services. This includes customer needs assessment, meeting quality standards for services, and evaluation of customer satisfaction. **Computers and Electronics:** Circuit boards, processors, chips, electronic equipment, and computer hardware and software, including applications and programming. **Economics and Accounting:** Economic and accounting principles and practices, the financial markets, banking, and the analysis and reporting of financial data.

Personality Type: Conventional-Enterprising. **Career Cluster:** 04 Business, Management, and Administration. **Career Pathway:** 04.6 Administrative and Information Support. **Other Jobs in This Pathway:** Cargo and Freight Agents; Correspondence Clerks; Couriers and Messengers; Court Clerks; Customer Service Representatives; Data Entry Keyers; Dispatchers, Except Police, Fire, and Ambulance; Executive Secretaries and Executive Administrative Assistants; File Clerks; Freight Forwarders; Human Resources Assistants, Except Payroll and Timekeeping; Information and Record Clerks, All Other; Insurance Policy Processing Clerks; Interviewers, Except Eligibility and Loan; License Clerks; Mail Clerks and Mail Machine Operators, Except Postal Service; Meter Readers, Utilities; Municipal Clerks; Office and Administrative Support Workers, All Other; Office Clerks, General; Office Machine Operators, Except Computer; Order Clerks; Patient Representatives; Postal Service Clerks; Postal Service Mail Carriers; Postal Service Mail Sorters, Processors, and Processing Machine Operators; Procurement Clerks; Receptionists and Information Clerks; others.

Skills—Active Listening: Giving full attention to what other people are saying, taking time to understand the points being made, asking questions as appropriate, and not interrupting at inappropriate times. **Speaking:** Talking to others to convey information effectively. **Programming:** Writing computer programs for various purposes. **Reading Comprehension:** Understanding written sentences and paragraphs in work-related documents. **Mathematics:** Using mathematics to solve problems. **Service Orientation:** Actively looking for ways to help people.

Work Environment: Indoors; sitting; repetitive motions.

Job Specialization: Insurance Policy Processing Clerks

Process applications for, changes to, reinstatement of, and cancellation of insurance policies. Interview clients and take their calls to provide customer service and obtain information on claims. Process, prepare, and submit business or government forms, such as submitting applications for coverage to insurance carriers. Process and record new insurance policies and claims. Correspond with insured or agents to obtain information or inform them of account status or changes. Organize and work with detailed office or warehouse records, maintaining files for each policyholder, including policies that are to be reinstated or canceled. Review and verify data, such as age, name, address, and principal sum and value of property, on insurance applications and policies. Collect initial premiums and issue receipts. Modify, update, and process existing policies and claims to reflect any change in beneficiary, amount of coverage, or type of insurance. Transcribe data to worksheets and enter data into computers for use in preparing documents and adjusting accounts. Notify insurance agents and accounting departments of policy cancellation. Calculate premiums, refunds, commissions, adjustments, and new reserve requirements, using insurance rate standards. Examine letters from policyholders or agents, original insurance applications, and other company documents to determine if changes are needed and effects of changes. Compose business correspondence for supervisors, managers, and professionals. Compare information from applications to criteria for policy reinstatement and approve reinstatement when criteria are met. Obtain computer printout of policy cancellations or retrieve cancellation cards from file. Check computations of interest accrued, premiums due, and settlement surrender on loan values.

Education and Training Program: General Office Occupations and Clerical Services. **Knowledge/Courses—Clerical Practices:** Administrative and clerical procedures and systems such as word processing, managing files and records, stenography and transcription, designing forms, and other office procedures and terminology. **Sales and Marketing:** Principles and methods for showing, promoting, and selling products or services. This includes marketing strategy and tactics, product demonstration, sales techniques, and sales control systems. **Customer and Personal Service:** Principles and processes for providing customer and personal services. This includes customer needs assessment, meeting quality standards for services, and evaluation of customer satisfaction. **Communications and Media:** Media production, communication, and dissemination techniques and methods. This includes alternative ways to inform and entertain via written, oral, and visual media. **Computers and Electronics:** Circuit boards, processors, chips, electronic equipment, and computer hardware and software, including applications and programming. **Administration and Management:** Business and management principles involved in strategic planning, resource allocation, human resources modeling, leadership technique, production methods, and coordination of people and resources.

Personality Type: Conventional-Enterprising. **Career Cluster:** 04 Business, Management, and Administration. **Career Pathway:** 04.6 Administrative and Information Support. **Other Jobs in This Pathway:** Cargo and Freight Agents; Correspondence Clerks; Couriers and Messengers; Court Clerks; Customer Service Representatives; Data Entry Keyers; Dispatchers, Except Police, Fire, and Ambulance; Executive Secretaries and Executive Administrative Assistants; File Clerks; Freight Forwarders; Human Resources Assistants,

Except Payroll and Timekeeping; Information and Record Clerks, All Other; Insurance Claims Clerks; Interviewers, Except Eligibility and Loan; License Clerks; Mail Clerks and Mail Machine Operators, Except Postal Service; Meter Readers, Utilities; Municipal Clerks; Office and Administrative Support Workers, All Other; Office Clerks, General; Office Machine Operators, Except Computer; Order Clerks; Patient Representatives; Postal Service Clerks; Postal Service Mail Carriers; Postal Service Mail Sorters, Processors, and Processing Machine Operators; Procurement Clerks; Receptionists and Information Clerks; others.

Skills—Management of Financial Resources: Determining how money will be spent to get the work done and accounting for these expenditures. **Mathematics:** Using mathematics to solve problems. **Active Listening:** Giving full attention to what other people are saying, taking time to understand the points being made, asking questions as appropriate, and not interrupting at inappropriate times. **Service Orientation:** Actively looking for ways to help people. **Programming:** Writing computer programs for various purposes. **Speaking:** Talking to others to convey information effectively. **Judgment and Decision Making:** Considering the relative costs and benefits of potential actions to choose the most appropriate one. **Management of Material Resources:** Obtaining and seeing to the appropriate use of equipment, facilities, and materials needed to do certain work.

Work Environment: Indoors; sitting; repetitive motions.

Insurance Sales Agents

- ⊙ Annual Earnings: $47,450
- ⊙ Earnings Growth Potential: High (45.4%)
- ⊙ Growth: 21.9%
- ⊙ Annual Job Openings: 18,440
- ⊙ Self-Employed: 19.6%

Considerations for Job Outlook: College graduates who have sales ability, excellent customer-service skills, and expertise in a range of insurance and financial services products should enjoy the best prospects. Multilingual agents should have an advantage, because they can serve a wider customer base. Additionally, insurance language is often technical, so agents who have a firm understanding of the relevant technical and legal terms should also be desirable to employers.

Sell life, property, casualty, health, automotive, or other types of insurance. Call on policyholders to deliver and explain policy, to analyze insurance program and suggest additions or changes, or to change beneficiaries. Calculate premiums, and establish payment method. Customize insurance programs to suit individual customers, often covering a variety of risks. Sell various types of insurance policies to businesses and individuals on behalf of insurance companies, including automobile, fire, life, property, medical, and dental insurance or specialized policies such as marine, farm/crop, and medical malpractice. Interview prospective clients to obtain data about their financial resources and needs and the physical condition of the person or property to be insured and to discuss any existing coverage. Seek out new clients and develop clientele by networking to find new customers and generate lists of prospective clients. Explain features, advantages, and disadvantages of various policies to promote sale of insurance plans. Contact underwriter, and submit forms to obtain binder coverage. Ensure that policy requirements are fulfilled, including any necessary medical examinations and the completion of appropriate forms. Confer with clients to obtain and provide information when claims are made on a policy. Perform administrative tasks, such as maintaining records and handling policy renewals. Select company that offers type of coverage requested by client to underwrite policy.

Education/Training Required: High school diploma or equivalent. **Education and Training Program:** Insurance. **Knowledge/Courses—Sales and Marketing:** Principles and methods for showing, promoting, and selling products or services. This includes marketing strategy and tactics, product demonstration, sales techniques, and sales control systems. **Economics and Accounting:** Economic and accounting principles and practices, the financial markets, banking, and the analysis and reporting of financial data. **Customer and Personal Service:** Principles and processes for providing customer and personal services. This includes customer needs assessment, meeting quality standards for services, and evaluation of customer satisfaction. **Clerical Practices:** Administrative and clerical procedures and systems such as word processing, managing files and records, stenography and transcription, designing forms, and other office procedures and terminology. **Law and Government:** Laws, legal codes, court procedures, precedents, government regulations, executive orders, agency rules, and the democratic political process. **Computers**

and Electronics: Circuit boards, processors, chips, electronic equipment, and computer hardware and software, including applications and programming. **Work Experience Needed:** None. **On-the-Job Training Needed:** Moderate-term on-the-job training. **Certification/Licensure:** Licensure; voluntary certification by association.

Personality Type: Enterprising-Conventional-Social. **Career Cluster:** 06 Finance. **Career Pathway:** 06.4 Insurance Services. **Other Jobs in This Pathway:** Actuaries; Business Teachers, Postsecondary; Claims Examiners, Property and Casualty Insurance; Insurance Adjusters, Examiners, and Investigators; Insurance Appraisers, Auto Damage; Insurance Underwriters; Telemarketers.

Skills—Negotiation: Bringing others together and trying to reconcile differences. **Persuasion:** Persuading others to change their minds or behavior. **Service Orientation:** Actively looking for ways to help people. **Active Listening:** Giving full attention to what other people are saying, taking time to understand the points being made, asking questions as appropriate, and not interrupting at inappropriate times. **Speaking:** Talking to others to convey information effectively. **Systems Analysis:** Determining how a system should work and how changes in conditions, operations, and the environment will affect outcomes. **Active Learning:** Understanding the implications of new information for both current and future problem solving and decision making. **Systems Evaluation:** Identifying measures or indicators of system performance and the actions needed to improve or correct performance relative to the goals of the system.

Work Environment: Indoors; sitting.

Interviewers, Except Eligibility and Loan

- ⊙ Annual Earnings: $29,560
- ⊙ Earnings Growth Potential: Low (34.0%)
- ⊙ Growth: 17.3%
- ⊙ Annual Job Openings: 7,960
- ⊙ Self-Employed: 0.5%

Considerations for Job Outlook: Employment growth will vary by specialty. Projected employment change is most rapid for interviewers and correspondence clerks.

Interview persons by telephone, by mail, in person, or by other means for the purpose of completing forms, applications, or questionnaires. Ask questions in accordance with instructions to obtain various specified information such as each person's name, address, age, religious preference, and state of residency. Identify and resolve inconsistencies in interviewees' responses by means of appropriate questioning or explanation. Compile, record, and code results and data from interviews or surveys, using computers or specified forms. Review data obtained from interviews for completeness and accuracy. Contact individuals to be interviewed at home, places of business, or field locations by telephone, by mail, or in person. Assist individuals in filling out applications or questionnaires. Ensure payment for services by verifying benefits with individuals' insurance providers or working out financing options. Identify and report problems in obtaining valid data. Explain survey objectives and procedures to interviewees, and interpret survey questions to help interviewees' comprehension. Perform patient services such as answering the telephone and assisting patients with financial and medical questions. Prepare reports to provide answers in response to specific problems. Locate and list addresses and households. Perform other office duties as needed, such as telemarketing and customer-service inquiries, billing patients, and receiving payments. Meet with supervisor daily to submit completed assignments and discuss progress.

Education/Training Required: High school diploma or equivalent. **Education and Training Program:** Receptionist Training. **Knowledge/Courses—Clerical Practices:** Administrative and clerical procedures and systems such as word processing, managing files and records, stenography and transcription, designing forms, and other office procedures and terminology. **Customer and Personal Service:** Principles and processes for providing customer and personal services. This includes customer needs assessment, meeting quality standards for services, and evaluation of customer satisfaction. **Communications and Media:** Media production, communication, and dissemination techniques and methods. This includes alternative ways to inform and entertain via written, oral, and visual media. **Work Experience Needed:** None. **On-the-Job Training Needed:** Short-term on-the-job training. **Certification/Licensure:** None.

Personality Type: Conventional-Enterprising-Social. **Career Cluster:** 04 Business, Management, and Administration. **Career Pathway:** 04.6 Administrative and Information Support. **Other Jobs in This Pathway:** Cargo and Freight Agents; Correspondence Clerks; Couriers and Messengers; Court Clerks; Customer Service Representatives; Data Entry Keyers; Dispatchers, Except Police, Fire, and Ambulance; Executive Secretaries and Executive Administrative Assistants; File Clerks; Freight Forwarders; Human Resources Assistants, Except Payroll and Timekeeping; Information and Record Clerks, All Other; Insurance Claims Clerks; Insurance Policy Processing Clerks; License Clerks; Mail Clerks and Mail Machine Operators, Except Postal Service; Meter Readers, Utilities; Municipal Clerks; Office and Administrative Support Workers, All Other; Office Clerks, General; Office Machine Operators, Except Computer; Order Clerks; Patient Representatives; Postal Service Clerks; Postal Service Mail Carriers; Postal Service Mail Sorters, Processors, and Processing Machine Operators; Procurement Clerks; Receptionists and Information Clerks; Secretaries and Administrative Assistants, Except Legal, Medical, and Executive; others.

Skills—Active Listening: Giving full attention to what other people are saying, taking time to understand the points being made, asking questions as appropriate, and not interrupting at inappropriate times. **Speaking:** Talking to others to convey information effectively. **Programming:** Writing computer programs for various purposes. **Writing:** Communicating effectively in writing as appropriate for the needs of the audience. **Persuasion:** Persuading others to change their minds or behavior. **Instructing:** Teaching others how to do something. **Social Perceptiveness:** Being aware of others' reactions and understanding why they react as they do. **Negotiation:** Bringing others together and trying to reconcile differences.

Work Environment: Indoors; sitting; using hands; repetitive motions; noise.

Laborers and Freight, Stock, and Material Movers, Hand

- ⊙ Annual Earnings: $23,750
- ⊙ Earnings Growth Potential: Low (27.6%)
- ⊙ Growth: 15.4%
- ⊙ Annual Job Openings: 98,020
- ⊙ Self-Employed: 1.3%

Considerations for Job Outlook: Job prospects for hand laborers and material movers should be favorable. Despite slower growth in this occupation, the need to replace workers who leave the occupation should create a large number of job openings. As automation increases, the technology used by workers in this occupation will become more complex. Employers will likely prefer workers who are comfortable using technology such as tablet computers and handheld scanners.

Manually move freight, stock, or other materials or perform other general labor. Attach identifying tags to containers, or mark them with identifying information. Read work orders or receive oral instructions to determine work assignments and material and equipment needs. Record numbers of units handled and moved, using daily production sheets or work tickets. Move freight, stock, and other materials to and from storage and production areas, loading docks, delivery vehicles, ships, and containers, by hand or using trucks, tractors, and other equipment. Sort cargo before loading and unloading. Assemble product containers and crates, using hand tools and precut lumber. Load and unload ship cargo, using winches and other hoisting devices. Connect hoses and operate equipment to move liquid materials into and out of storage tanks on vessels. Pack containers and repack damaged containers. Carry needed tools and supplies from storage or trucks, and return them after use. Install protective devices, such as bracing, padding, or strapping, to prevent shifting or damage to items being transported. Maintain equipment storage areas to ensure that inventory is protected. Attach slings, hooks, and other devices to lift cargo and guide loads. Carry out general yard duties such as performing shunting on railway lines. Adjust controls to guide, position, and move equipment such as cranes, booms, and cameras. Guide loads being lifted in order to prevent swinging. Adjust or replace equipment parts such as rollers, belts, plugs, and caps, using hand tools. Stack cargo in locations such as transit sheds or in holds of ships as directed, using pallets or cargo boards. Connect electrical equipment to power sources so that it can be tested before use. Set up the equipment needed to produce special lighting and sound effects during performances. Bundle and band material such as fodder and tobacco leaves, using banding machines. Rig and dismantle props and equipment such as frames, scaffolding, platforms, or backdrops, using hand tools.

Education/Training Required: Less than high school. **Education and Training Programs:** No related CIP programs; this job is learned through informal short-term on-the-job training. **Knowledge/Courses—Transportation:** Principles and methods for moving people or goods by air, rail, sea, or road, including the relative costs and benefits. **Public Safety and Security:** Relevant equipment, policies, procedures, and strategies to promote effective local, state, or national security operations for the protection of people, data, property, and institutions. **Production and Processing:** Raw materials, production processes, quality control, costs, and other techniques for maximizing the effective manufacture and distribution of goods. **Work Experience Needed:** None. **On-the-Job Training Needed:** Short-term on-the-job training. **Certification/Licensure:** None.

Personality Type: Realistic. **Career Cluster:** 16 Transportation, Distribution, and Logistics. **Career Pathway:** 16.1 Transportation Operations. **Other Jobs in This Pathway:** Aerospace Engineering and Operations Technicians; Air Traffic Controllers; Aircraft Cargo Handling Supervisors; Airfield Operations Specialists; Airline Pilots, Copilots, and Flight Engineers; Automotive and Watercraft Service Attendants; Automotive Master Mechanics; Aviation Inspectors; Bridge and Lock Tenders; Bus Drivers, School or Special Client; Bus Drivers, Transit and Intercity; Commercial Divers; Commercial Pilots; Crane and Tower Operators; First-Line Supervisors of Helpers, Laborers, and Material Movers, Hand; First-Line Supervisors of Transportation and Material-Moving Machine and Vehicle Operators; Freight and Cargo Inspectors; Heavy and Tractor-Trailer Truck Drivers; Hoist and Winch Operators; Light Truck or Delivery Services Drivers; Mates—Ship, Boat, and Barge; Motor Vehicle Operators, All Other; Motorboat Operators; Operating Engineers and Other Construction Equipment Operators; Parking Lot Attendants; Pilots, Ship; others.

Skills—Repairing: Repairing machines or systems using the needed tools. **Equipment Maintenance:** Performing routine maintenance on equipment and determining when and what kind of maintenance is needed. **Troubleshooting:** Determining causes of operating errors and deciding what to do about them. **Operation and Control:** Controlling operations of equipment or systems. **Equipment Selection:** Determining the kind of tools and equipment needed to do a job. **Quality Control Analysis:** Conducting tests and inspections of products, services, or processes to evaluate quality or performance. **Operation Monitoring:** Watching gauges, dials, or other indicators to make sure a machine is working properly. **Installation:** Installing equipment, machines, wiring, or programs to meet specifications.

Work Environment: Outdoors; standing; walking and running; using hands; bending or twisting the body; repetitive motions; noise; very hot or cold; contaminants; cramped work space; hazardous equipment.

Landscaping and Groundskeeping Workers

- ⊙ Annual Earnings: $23,410
- ⊙ Earnings Growth Potential: Low (26.8%)
- ⊙ Growth: 20.9%
- ⊙ Annual Job Openings: 44,440
- ⊙ Self-Employed: 25.1%

Considerations for Job Outlook: Job prospects are expected to be favorable. Those with experience should have the best job opportunities. Most job openings will come from the need to replace many workers who leave or retire from this very large occupation.

Landscape or maintain grounds of property using hand or power tools or equipment. Operate powered equipment such as mowers, tractors, twin-axle vehicles, snow blowers, chain-saws, electric clippers, sod cutters, and pruning saws. Mow and edge lawns, using power mowers and edgers. Care for established lawns by mulching, aerating, weeding, grubbing and removing thatch, and trimming and edging around flower beds, walks, and walls. Shovel snow from walks, driveways, and parking lots, and spread salt in those areas. Use hand tools such as shovels, rakes, pruning saws, saws, hedge and brush trimmers, and axes. Prune and trim trees, shrubs, and hedges, using shears, pruners, or chain saws. Maintain and repair tools, equipment, and structures such as buildings, greenhouses, fences, and benches, using hand and power tools. Gather and remove litter. Mix and spray or spread fertilizers, herbicides, or insecticides onto grass, shrubs, and trees, using hand or automatic sprayers or spreaders. Provide proper upkeep of sidewalks, driveways, parking lots, fountains, planters, burial sites, and other grounds features. Water lawns, trees, and plants, using portable sprinkler systems, hoses, or watering cans. Trim and pick flowers, and clean flower beds. Rake, mulch, and compost leaves. Plant seeds, bulbs, foliage, flowering plants, grass, ground covers, trees, and shrubs, and apply mulch for protection, using gardening tools. Follow planned landscaping designs to determine where to lay sod, sow grass, or plant flowers and foliage. Decorate gardens with stones and plants. Maintain irrigation systems, including winterizing the systems and starting them up in spring. Care for natural turf fields, making sure the underlying soil has the required composition to allow proper drainage and to support the grasses used on the fields. Use irrigation methods to adjust the amount of water consumption and to prevent waste. Haul or spread topsoil, and spread straw over seeded soil to hold soil in place. Advise customers on plant selection and care.

Education/Training Required: Less than high school. **Education and Training Programs:** Landscaping and Groundskeeping; Turf and Turfgrass Management. **Knowledge/Courses—Mechanical Devices:** Machines and tools, including their designs, uses, repair, and maintenance. **Work Experience Needed:** None. **On-the-Job Training Needed:** Short-term on-the-job training. **Certification/Licensure:** Licensure for some specializations; voluntary certification by association.

Personality Type: Realistic-Conventional. **Career Cluster:** 01 Agriculture, Food, and Natural Resources. **Career Pathway:** 01.2 Plant Systems. **Other Jobs in This Pathway:** Agricultural Sciences Teachers, Postsecondary; Agricultural Technicians; Animal Scientists; Biochemists and Biophysicists; Biologists; Economists; Environmental Economists; Farm and Home Management Advisors; First-Line Supervisors of Landscaping, Lawn Service, and Groundskeeping Workers; First-Line Supervisors of Retail Sales Workers; Floral Designers; Food Science Technicians; Food Scientists and Technologists; Geneticists; Grounds Maintenance Workers, All Other; Pesticide Handlers, Sprayers, and Applicators, Vegetation; Precision Agriculture Technicians; Retail Salespersons; Soil and Plant Scientists; Tree Trimmers and Pruners.

Skills—Operation and Control: Controlling operations of equipment or systems. **Repairing:** Repairing machines or systems using the needed tools. **Equipment Maintenance:** Performing routine maintenance on equipment and determining when and what kind of maintenance is needed. **Troubleshooting:** Determining causes of operating errors and deciding what to do about them. **Operation**

Monitoring: Watching gauges, dials, or other indicators to make sure a machine is working properly. **Equipment Selection:** Determining the kind of tools and equipment needed to do a job. **Quality Control Analysis:** Conducting tests and inspections of products, services, or processes to evaluate quality or performance.

Work Environment: Outdoors; standing; walking and running; using hands; bending or twisting the body; repetitive motions; noise; very hot or cold; bright or inadequate lighting; contaminants; hazardous equipment; minor burns, cuts, bites, or stings.

Layout Workers, Metal and Plastic

- ⊙ Annual Earnings: $39,870
- ⊙ Earnings Growth Potential: High (41.0%)
- ⊙ Growth: 13.5%
- ⊙ Annual Job Openings: 290
- ⊙ Self-Employed: 0.0%

Considerations for Job Outlook: About-average employment growth is projected.

Lay out reference points and dimensions on metal or plastic stock or workpieces, such as sheets, plates, tubes, structural shapes, castings, or machine parts, for further processing. Fit and align fabricated parts to be welded or assembled. Plan and develop layouts from blueprints and templates, applying knowledge of trigonometry, design, effects of heat, and properties of metals. Lay out and fabricate metal structural parts such as plates, bulkheads, and frames. Mark curves, lines, holes, dimensions, and welding symbols onto workpieces, using scribes, soapstones, punches, and hand drills. Compute layout dimensions, and determine and mark reference points on metal stock or workpieces for further processing, such as welding and assembly. Locate center lines and verify template positions, using measuring instruments such as gauge blocks, height gauges, and dial indicators. Lift and position workpieces in relation to surface plates, manually or with hoists, and using parallel blocks and angle plates. Plan locations and sequences of cutting, drilling, bending, rolling, punching, and welding operations, using compasses, protractors, dividers, and rules. Inspect machined parts to verify conformance to specifications. Design and prepare templates of wood, paper, or metal. Brace parts in position

within hulls or ships for riveting or welding. Add dimensional details to blueprints or drawings made by other workers. Install doors, hatches, brackets, and clips. Apply pigment to layout surfaces, using paint brushes.

Education/Training Required: High school diploma or equivalent. **Education and Training Programs:** Machine Shop Technology/Assistant; Machine Tool Technology/Machinist. **Knowledge/Courses—Building and Construction:** Materials, methods, and the tools involved in the construction or repair of houses, buildings, or other structures such as highways and roads. **Mechanical Devices:** Machines and tools, including their designs, uses, repair, and maintenance. **Design:** Design techniques, tools, and principles involved in production of precision technical plans, blueprints, drawings, and models. **Production and Processing:** Raw materials, production processes, quality control, costs, and other techniques for maximizing the effective manufacture and distribution of goods. **Mathematics:** Arithmetic, algebra, geometry, calculus, statistics, and their applications. **Engineering and Technology:** The practical application of engineering science and technology. This includes applying principles, techniques, procedures, and equipment to the design and production of various goods and services. **Work Experience Needed:** None. **On-the-Job Training Needed:** Moderate-term on-the-job training. **Certification/Licensure:** None.

Personality Type: Realistic-Conventional-Investigative. **Career Cluster:** 13 Manufacturing. **Career Pathway:** 13.1 Production. **Other Jobs in This Pathway:** Adhesive Bonding Machine Operators and Tenders; Assemblers and Fabricators, All Other; Avionics Technicians; Cabinetmakers and Bench Carpenters; Cleaning, Washing, and Metal Pickling Equipment Operators and Tenders; Coating, Painting, and Spraying Machine Setters, Operators, and Tenders; Computer-Controlled Machine Tool Operators, Metal and Plastic; Cooling and Freezing Equipment Operators and Tenders; Cost Estimators; Crushing, Grinding, and Polishing Machine Setters, Operators, and Tenders; Cutters and Trimmers, Hand; Cutting and Slicing Machine Setters, Operators, and Tenders; Cutting, Punching, and Press Machine Setters, Operators, and Tenders, Metal and Plastic; Drilling and Boring Machine Tool Setters, Operators, and Tenders, Metal and Plastic; Extruding and Drawing Machine Setters, Operators, and Tenders, Metal and Plastic; Extruding and Forming

Machine Setters, Operators, and Tenders, Synthetic and Glass Fibers; others.

Skills—Equipment Maintenance: Performing routine maintenance on equipment and determining when and what kind of maintenance is needed. **Equipment Selection:** Determining the kind of tools and equipment needed to do a job. **Repairing:** Repairing machines or systems using the needed tools. **Operation and Control:** Controlling operations of equipment or systems. **Troubleshooting:** Determining causes of operating errors and deciding what to do about them. **Quality Control Analysis:** Conducting tests and inspections of products, services, or processes to evaluate quality or performance. **Operation Monitoring:** Watching gauges, dials, or other indicators to make sure a machine is working properly. **Mathematics:** Using mathematics to solve problems.

Work Environment: Outdoors; standing; walking and running; using hands; bending or twisting the body; repetitive motions; noise; very hot or cold; bright or inadequate lighting; contaminants; cramped work space; hazardous equipment; minor burns, cuts, bites, or stings.

Legal Secretaries

- Annual Earnings: $42,460
- Earnings Growth Potential: Medium (37.9%)
- Growth: 3.5%
- Annual Job Openings: 3,940
- Self-Employed: 1.2%

Considerations for Job Outlook: In addition to jobs coming from employment growth, numerous job openings will arise from the need to replace secretaries and administrative assistants who transfer to other occupations or retire. Job opportunities should be best for applicants with extensive knowledge of computer software applications. Applicants with a bachelor's degree are expected to be in great demand and will act as managerial assistants who perform more complex tasks.

Perform secretarial duties using legal terminology, procedures, and documents. Prepare legal papers and correspondence, such as summonses, complaints, motions, and subpoenas. Prepare and process legal documents and papers, such as summonses, subpoenas, complaints, appeals, motions, and pretrial agreements. Mail, fax, or arrange for delivery of legal correspondence to clients, witnesses, and court officials. Receive and place telephone calls. Schedule and make appointments. Make photocopies of correspondence, documents, and other printed matter. Organize and maintain law libraries, documents, and case files. Assist attorneys in collecting information such as employment, medical, and other records. Attend legal meetings, such as client interviews, hearings, or depositions, and take notes. Draft and type office memos. Review legal publications and perform database searches to identify laws and court decisions relevant to pending cases. Submit articles and information from searches to attorneys for review and approval for use. Complete various forms such as accident reports, trial and courtroom requests, and applications for clients.

Education/Training Required: High school diploma or equivalent. **Education and Training Program:** Legal Administrative Assistant/Secretary Training. **Knowledge/Courses—Clerical Practices:** Administrative and clerical procedures and systems such as word processing, managing files and records, stenography and transcription, designing forms, and other office procedures and terminology. **Law and Government:** Laws, legal codes, court procedures, precedents, government regulations, executive orders, agency rules, and the democratic political process. **Computers and Electronics:** Circuit boards, processors, chips, electronic equipment, and computer hardware and software, including applications and programming. **English Language:** The structure and content of the English language including the meaning and spelling of words, rules of composition, and grammar. **Customer and Personal Service:** Principles and processes for providing customer and personal services. This includes customer needs assessment, meeting quality standards for services, and evaluation of customer satisfaction. **Work Experience Needed:** None. **On-the-Job Training Needed:** Moderate-term on-the-job training. **Certification/Licensure:** Voluntary certification by association.

Personality Type: Conventional-Enterprising. **Career Cluster:** 12 Law, Public Safety, Corrections, and Security. **Career Pathway:** 12.5 Legal Services. **Other Jobs in This Pathway:** Administrative Law Judges, Adjudicators, and Hearing Officers; Arbitrators, Mediators, and Conciliators; Court Reporters; Farm and Home Management Advisors; Judges, Magistrate Judges, and Magistrates; Law Teachers, Postsecondary; Lawyers; Legal Support Workers, All

Other; Paralegals and Legal Assistants; Title Examiners, Abstractors, and Searchers.

Skills—Writing: Communicating effectively in writing as appropriate for the needs of the audience. **Reading Comprehension:** Understanding written sentences and paragraphs in work-related documents. **Active Listening:** Giving full attention to what other people are saying, taking time to understand the points being made, asking questions as appropriate, and not interrupting at inappropriate times. **Programming:** Writing computer programs for various purposes. **Service Orientation:** Actively looking for ways to help people. **Speaking:** Talking to others to convey information effectively.

Work Environment: Indoors; sitting; using hands; repetitive motions.

Library Assistants, Clerical

- ⊙ Annual Earnings: $23,440
- ⊙ Earnings Growth Potential: Low (27.5%)
- ⊙ Growth: 10.2%
- ⊙ Annual Job Openings: 6,410
- ⊙ Self-Employed: 0.0%

Considerations for Job Outlook: Electronic information systems have simplified some tasks, allowing them to be performed by technicians and assistants, rather than librarians. Library technicians and assistants earn less than librarians; so as more libraries face budget issues, technicians and assistants will be increasingly used as a lower-cost method of providing library services.

Compile records, sort, shelve, issue, and receive library materials. Process new materials including books, audiovisual materials, and computer software. Sort books, publications, and other items according to established procedures and return them to shelves, files, or other designated storage areas. Locate library materials for patrons, including books, periodicals, tape cassettes, Braille volumes, and pictures. Instruct patrons on how to use reference sources, card catalogs, and automated information systems. Answer routine inquiries, and refer patrons in need of professional assistance to librarians. Maintain records of items received, stored, issued, and returned, and file catalog cards according to system used. Provide assistance to librarians in the maintenance of collections of books, periodicals,

magazines, newspapers, and audiovisual and other materials. Take action to deal with disruptive or problem patrons. Open and close library during specified hours and secure library equipment such as computers and audiovisual (AV) equipment.

Education/Training Required: High school diploma or equivalent. **Education and Training Program:** Library and Archives Assisting. **Knowledge/Courses—Clerical Practices:** Administrative and clerical procedures and systems such as word processing, managing files and records, stenography and transcription, designing forms, and other office procedures and terminology. **Computers and Electronics:** Circuit boards, processors, chips, electronic equipment, and computer hardware and software, including applications and programming. **Customer and Personal Service:** Principles and processes for providing customer and personal services. This includes customer needs assessment, meeting quality standards for services, and evaluation of customer satisfaction. **English Language:** The structure and content of the English language including the meaning and spelling of words, rules of composition, and grammar. **Communications and Media:** Media production, communication, and dissemination techniques and methods. This includes alternative ways to inform and entertain via written, oral, and visual media. **Work Experience Needed:** None. **On-the-Job Training Needed:** Short-term on-the-job training. **Certification/Licensure:** None.

Personality Type: Conventional-Realistic-Social. **Career Cluster:** 05 Education and Training. **Career Pathway:** 05.2 Professional Support Services. **Other Jobs in This Pathway:** Educational, Guidance, School, and Vocational Counselors; Librarians; Library Science Teachers, Postsecondary; Library Technicians; Postsecondary Teachers, All Other.

Skills—Service Orientation: Actively looking for ways to help people. **Management of Material Resources:** Obtaining and seeing to the appropriate use of equipment, facilities, and materials needed to do certain work. **Technology Design:** Generating or adapting equipment and technology to serve user needs.

Work Environment: Indoors; sitting; using hands; repetitive motions; contaminants.

Library Technicians

- ⊙ Annual Earnings: $30,430
- ⊙ Earnings Growth Potential: Medium (39.8%)
- ⊙ Growth: 8.8%
- ⊙ Annual Job Openings: 5,950
- ⊙ Self-Employed: 0.0%

Considerations for Job Outlook: Electronic information systems have simplified some tasks, allowing them to be performed by technicians and assistants, rather than librarians. Library technicians and assistants earn less than librarians; so as more libraries face budget issues, technicians and assistants will be increasingly used as a lower-cost method of providing library services.

Assist librarians by helping readers in the use of library catalogs, databases, and indexes to locate books and other materials and by answering questions that require only brief consultation of standard reference. Help patrons find and use library resources, such as reference materials, audiovisual equipment, computers, and other electronic resources, and provide technical assistance when needed. Answer routine telephone or in-person reference inquiries, referring patrons to librarians for further assistance when necessary. Process print and nonprint library materials to prepare them for inclusion in library collections. Reserve, circulate, renew, and discharge books and other materials. Catalogue and sort books and other print and nonprint materials according to procedure, and return them to shelves, files, or other designated storage areas. Provide assistance to teachers and students by locating materials and helping to complete special projects. Organize and maintain periodicals and reference materials. Deliver and retrieve items throughout the library by hand or using pushcart. Maintain and troubleshoot problems with library equipment including computers, photocopiers, and audiovisual equipment. Train other staff, volunteers, or student assistants, and schedule and supervise their work. Order all print and nonprint library materials, checking prices, figuring costs, preparing order slips, and making payments. Process interlibrary loans for patrons. Enter and update patrons' records on computers. Retrieve information from central databases for storage in a library's computers. Prepare volumes for binding. Verify bibliographical data for materials, including author, title, publisher, publication date, and edition. Review subject matter of materials to be classified, and select classification numbers and headings according to classification systems. Issue identification cards to borrowers. Send out notices about lost or overdue books. Collect fines, and respond to complaints about fines. Compile and maintain records relating to circulation, materials, and equipment.

Education/Training Required: Postsecondary vocational training. **Education and Training Program:** Library and Archives Assisting. **Knowledge/Courses—Clerical Practices:** Administrative and clerical procedures and systems such as word processing, managing files and records, stenography and transcription, designing forms, and other office procedures and terminology. **Computers and Electronics:** Circuit boards, processors, chips, electronic equipment, and computer hardware and software, including applications and programming. **Law and Government:** Laws, legal codes, court procedures, precedents, government regulations, executive orders, agency rules, and the democratic political process. **Economics and Accounting:** Economic and accounting principles and practices, the financial markets, banking, and the analysis and reporting of financial data. **English Language:** The structure and content of the English language including the meaning and spelling of words, rules of composition, and grammar. **Work Experience Needed:** None. **On-the-Job Training Needed:** None. **Certification/Licensure:** None.

Personality Type: Conventional-Social-Enterprising. **Career Cluster:** 05 Education and Training. **Career Pathway:** 05.2 Professional Support Services. **Other Jobs in This Pathway:** Educational, Guidance, School, and Vocational Counselors; Librarians; Library Assistants, Clerical; Library Science Teachers, Postsecondary; Postsecondary Teachers, All Other.

Skills—Service Orientation: Actively looking for ways to help people. **Programming:** Writing computer programs for various purposes. **Equipment Maintenance:** Performing routine maintenance on equipment and determining when and what kind of maintenance is needed. **Management of Material Resources:** Obtaining and seeing to the appropriate use of equipment, facilities, and materials needed to do certain work. **Reading Comprehension:** Understanding written sentences and paragraphs in work-related documents. **Management of Personnel Resources:** Motivating, developing, and directing people as they work, identifying the best people for the job.

Work Environment: Indoors; sitting; repetitive motions.

Licensed Practical and Licensed Vocational Nurses

- ⊙ Annual Earnings: $41,150
- ⊙ Earnings Growth Potential: Low (25.5%)
- ⊙ Growth: 22.4%
- ⊙ Annual Job Openings: 36,920
- ⊙ Self-Employed: 1.2%

Considerations for Job Outlook: A large number of licensed practical and licensed vocational nurses are expected to retire over the coming decade. Job prospects should, therefore, be excellent for licensed and experienced LPNs and LVNs.

Care for ill, injured, or convalescing patients or persons with disabilities in hospitals, nursing homes, clinics, private homes, group homes, and similar institutions. Administer prescribed medications or start intravenous fluids, recording times and amounts on patients' charts. Observe patients, charting and reporting changes in patients' conditions, such as adverse reactions to medication or treatment, and taking any necessary actions. Provide basic patient care and treatments such as taking temperatures or blood pressures, dressing wounds, treating bedsores, giving enemas or douches, rubbing with alcohol, massaging, or performing catheterizations. Sterilize equipment and supplies, using germicides, sterilizer, or autoclave. Answer patients' calls, and determine how to assist them. Work as part of a health-care team to assess patient needs, plan and modify care, and implement interventions. Measure and record patients' vital signs, such as height, weight, temperature, blood pressure, pulse, and respiration. Collect samples such as blood, urine, and sputum from patients, and perform routine laboratory tests on samples. Prepare patients for examinations, tests, or treatments, and explain procedures. Assemble and use equipment such as catheters, tracheotomy tubes, and oxygen suppliers. Evaluate nursing intervention outcomes, conferring with other health-care team members as necessary. Record food and fluid intake and output. Help patients with bathing, dressing, maintaining personal hygiene, moving in bed, or standing and walking. Apply compresses, ice bags, and hot water bottles. Inventory and requisition supplies and instruments.

Education/Training Required: Postsecondary vocational training. **Education and Training Program:** Licensed Practical/Vocational Nurse Training. **Knowledge/Courses—Psychology:** Human behavior and performance; individual differences in ability, personality, and interests; learning and motivation; psychological research methods; and the assessment and treatment of behavioral and affective disorders. **Medicine and Dentistry:** The information and techniques needed to diagnose and treat human injuries, diseases, and deformities. This includes symptoms, treatment alternatives, drug properties and interactions, and preventive health-care measures. **Therapy and Counseling:** Principles, methods, and procedures for diagnosis, treatment, and rehabilitation of physical and mental dysfunctions, and for career counseling and guidance. **Biology:** Plant and animal organisms and their tissues, cells, functions, interdependencies, and interactions with each other and the environment. **Philosophy and Theology:** Different philosophical systems and religions. This includes their basic principles, values, ethics, ways of thinking, customs, practices, and their impact on human culture. **Customer and Personal Service:** Principles and processes for providing customer and personal services. This includes customer needs assessment, meeting quality standards for services, and evaluation of customer satisfaction. **Work Experience Needed:** None. **On-the-Job Training Needed:** None. **Certification/Licensure:** Licensure.

Personality Type: Social-Realistic. **Career Cluster:** 08 Health Science. **Career Pathway:** 08.1 Therapeutic Services. **Other Jobs in This Pathway:** Acupuncturists; Allergists and Immunologists; Anesthesiologists; Art Therapists; Chiropractors; Clinical Psychologists; Community and Social Service Specialists, All Other; Counseling Psychologists; Counselors, All Other; Dental Assistants; Dental Hygienists; Dentists, All Other Specialists; Dentists, General; Dermatologists; Diagnostic Medical Sonographers; Dietetic Technicians; Dietitians and Nutritionists; Family and General Practitioners; Health Diagnosing and Treating Practitioners, All Other; Health Specialties Teachers, Postsecondary; Health Technologists and Technicians, All Other; Healthcare Practitioners and Technical Workers, All Other; Healthcare Support Workers, All Other; Home Health Aides; Hospitalists; Industrial-Organizational Psychologists; Internists, General; Life, Physical, and Social Science Technicians, All Other; Low Vision Therapists, Orientation and Mobility Specialists, and Vision Rehabilitation Therapists; Massage Therapists; others.

Skills—Science: Using scientific rules and methods to solve problems. **Social Perceptiveness:** Being aware of others' reactions and understanding why they react as they do. **Service Orientation:** Actively looking for ways to help people. **Operation and Control:** Controlling operations of equipment or systems. **Persuasion:** Persuading others to change their minds or behavior. **Negotiation:** Bringing others together and trying to reconcile differences. **Speaking:** Talking to others to convey information effectively. **Operations Analysis:** Analyzing needs and product requirements to create a design.

Work Environment: Indoors; standing; walking and running; using hands; repetitive motions; noise; contaminants; cramped work space; exposed to disease or infections.

Life, Physical, and Social Science Technicians, All Other

- ⊙ Annual Earnings: $43,120
- ⊙ Earnings Growth Potential: High (42.3%)
- ⊙ Growth: 11.8%
- ⊙ Annual Job Openings: 3,350
- ⊙ Self-Employed: 0.4%

Considerations for Job Outlook: Slower-than-average employment growth is projected.

All life, physical, and social science technicians not listed separately. For task data, see Job Specializations.

Education/Training Required: Associate degree. **Education and Training Program:** Science Technologies/Technicians, Other. **Work Experience Needed:** None. **On-the-Job Training Needed:** Moderate-term on-the-job training. **Certification/Licensure:** None.

Job Specialization: Precision Agriculture Technicians

Apply geospatial technologies, including geographic information systems (GIS) and Global Positioning System (GPS), to agricultural production and management activities, such as pest scouting, site-specific pesticide application, yield mapping, and variable-rate irrigation. May use computers to develop and analyze maps and remote sensing images to compare physical topography with data on soils, fertilizer, pests, or weather. Collect information about soil and field attributes, yield data, or field boundaries, using field data recorders and basic geographic information systems (GIS). Create, layer, and analyze maps showing precision agricultural data such as crop yields, soil characteristics, input applications, terrain, drainage patterns, and field management history. Document and maintain records of precision agriculture information. Compile and analyze geospatial data to determine agricultural implications of factors such as soil quality, terrain, field productivity, fertilizers, and weather conditions. Divide agricultural fields into georeferenced zones based on soil characteristics and production potentials. Develop soil-sampling grids or identify sampling sites, using geospatial technology, for soil testing on characteristics such as nitrogen, phosphorus, and potassium content; pH; and micronutrients. Compare crop-yield maps with maps of soil-test data, chemical-application patterns, or other information to develop site-specific crop-management plans. Apply knowledge of government regulations when making agricultural recommendations. Recommend best crop varieties and seeding rates for specific field areas, based on analysis of geospatial data. Draw and read maps such as soil, contour, and plat maps. Process and analyze data from harvester monitors to develop yield maps.

Education and Training Program: Agricultural Mechanics and Equipment/Machine Technology. **Knowledge/Courses—Food Production:** Techniques and equipment for planting, growing, and harvesting food products (both plant and animal) for consumption, including storage/handling techniques. **Geography:** Principles and methods for describing the features of land, sea, and air masses, including their physical characteristics, locations, interrelationships, and distribution of plant, animal, and human life. **Biology:** Plant and animal organisms and their tissues, cells, functions, interdependencies, and interactions with each other and the environment. **Chemistry:** The chemical composition, structure, and properties of substances and of the chemical processes and transformations that they undergo. This includes uses of chemicals and their danger signs, production techniques, and disposal methods. **Sales and Marketing:** Principles and methods for showing, promoting, and selling products or services. This includes marketing strategy and tactics, product demonstration, sales techniques, and sales control systems. **Mechanical Devices:** Machines and tools, including their designs, uses, repair, and maintenance.

Personality Type: Realistic-Investigative-Conventional. **Career Cluster:** 01 Agriculture, Food, and Natural Resources. **Career Pathways:** 01.3 Animal Systems; 01.2 Plant Systems. **Other Jobs in These Pathways:** Agricultural Sciences Teachers, Postsecondary; Agricultural Technicians; Animal Breeders; Animal Scientists; Animal Trainers; Biochemists and Biophysicists; Biologists; Economists; Environmental Economists; Farm and Home Management Advisors; First-Line Supervisors of Landscaping, Lawn Service, and Groundskeeping Workers; First-Line Supervisors of Retail Sales Workers; Floral Designers; Food Science Technicians; Food Scientists and Technologists; Geneticists; Grounds Maintenance Workers, All Other; Landscaping and Groundskeeping Workers; Nonfarm Animal Caretakers; Pesticide Handlers, Sprayers, and Applicators, Vegetation; Retail Salespersons; Soil and Plant Scientists; Tree Trimmers and Pruners; Veterinarians.

Skills—Equipment Maintenance: Performing routine maintenance on equipment and determining when and what kind of maintenance is needed. **Repairing:** Repairing machines or systems using the needed tools. **Science:** Using scientific rules and methods to solve problems. **Troubleshooting:** Determining causes of operating errors and deciding what to do about them. **Equipment Selection:** Determining the kind of tools and equipment needed to do a job. **Operations Analysis:** Analyzing needs and product requirements to create a design. **Quality Control Analysis:** Conducting tests and inspections of products, services, or processes to evaluate quality or performance. **Operation and Control:** Controlling operations of equipment or systems.

Work Environment: Outdoors; very hot or cold.

Job Specialization: Quality Control Analysts

Conduct tests to determine quality of raw materials, bulk intermediate, and finished products. May conduct stability sample tests. Train other analysts to perform laboratory procedures and assays. Perform visual inspections of finished products. Serve as a technical liaison between quality control and other departments, vendors, or contractors. Participate in internal assessments and audits as required. Identify and troubleshoot equipment problems. Evaluate new technologies and methods to make recommendations regarding their use. Ensure that lab cleanliness

and safety standards are maintained. Develop and qualify new testing methods. Coordinate testing with contract laboratories and vendors. Write technical reports or documentation such as deviation reports, testing protocols, and trend analyses. Write or revise standard quality control operating procedures. Supply quality control data necessary for regulatory submissions. Receive and inspect raw materials. Review data from contract laboratories to ensure accuracy and regulatory compliance. Prepare or review required method transfer documentation, including technical transfer protocols or reports. Perform validations or transfers of analytical methods in accordance with applicable policies or guidelines. Participate in out-of-specification and failure investigations, and recommend corrective actions. Monitor testing procedures to ensure that all tests are performed according to established item specifications, standard test methods, or protocols. Investigate or report questionable test results.

Education and Training Program: Quality Control Technology/Technician.

Personality Type: Conventional-Investigative-Realistic. **Career Cluster:** 13 Manufacturing. **Career Pathway:** 13.2 Manufacturing Production Process Development. **Other Jobs in This Pathway:** Biofuels Processing Technicians; Biomass Plant Technicians; Chemical Plant and System Operators; Chemical Technicians; Electrical Engineering Technicians; Electromechanical Equipment Assemblers; Environmental Science and Protection Technicians, Including Health; Fabric and Apparel Patternmakers; Farm and Home Management Advisors; Fashion Designers; Hydroelectric Plant Technicians; Life, Physical, and Social Science Technicians, All Other; Methane/Landfill Gas Generation System Technicians; Nuclear Monitoring Technicians; Textile, Apparel, and Furnishings Workers, All Other.

Work Environment: No data available.

Job Specialization: Remote Sensing Technicians

Apply remote sensing technologies to assist scientists in areas such as natural resources, urban planning, and homeland security. May prepare flight plans and sensor configurations for flight trips. Participate in the planning and development of mapping projects. Maintain records of survey data. Document methods used, and write technical reports containing information collected. Develop specialized computer software routines to customize and integrate image analysis. Collect verification data on the ground using equipment such as global positioning receivers, digital cameras, and notebook computers. Verify integrity and accuracy of data contained in remote sensing image analysis systems. Prepare documentation and presentations including charts, photos, or graphs. Operate airborne remote sensing equipment such as survey cameras, sensors, and scanners. Monitor raw data quality during collection, and make equipment corrections as necessary. Merge scanned images or build photo mosaics of large areas using image processing software. Integrate remotely sensed data with other geospatial data. Evaluate remote sensing project requirements to determine the types of equipment or computer software necessary to meet project requirements such as specific image types and output resolutions. Develop and maintain geospatial information databases. Correct raw data for errors due to factors such as skew and atmospheric variation. Calibrate data collection equipment. Consult with remote sensing scientists, surveyors, cartographers, or engineers to determine project needs.

Education and Training Programs: Geographic Information Science and Cartography; Signal/Geospatial Intelligence.

Personality Type: Realistic-Investigative-Conventional. **Career Cluster:** 11 Information Technology. **Career Pathway:** 11.2 Information Support Services. **Other Jobs in This Pathway:** Computer and Information Systems Managers; Computer Numerically Controlled Machine Tool Programmers, Metal and Plastic; Computer Operators; Computer Science Teachers, Postsecondary; Remote Sensing Scientists and Technologists.

Work Environment: No data available.

Light Truck or Delivery Services Drivers

- Annual Earnings: $29,080
- Earnings Growth Potential: Medium (38.0%)
- Growth: 14.7%
- Annual Job Openings: 29,590
- Self-Employed: 7.8%

Considerations for Job Outlook: Delivery truck driver and driver/sales worker jobs are expected to be competitive. Because these drivers do not have to spend long periods away from home, these local jobs are more desirable than long-haul trucking jobs. Those with experience, or who work for the company in another occupation, should have the best job prospects.

Drive a light vehicle, such as a truck or van, with a capacity of less than 26,000 pounds gross vehicle weight (GVW), primarily to deliver or pick up merchandise or to deliver packages. Obey traffic laws, and follow established traffic and transportation procedures. Inspect and maintain vehicle supplies and equipment, such as gas, oil, water, tires, lights, and brakes in order to ensure that vehicles are in proper working condition. Report any mechanical problems encountered with vehicles. Present bills and receipts, and collect payments for goods delivered or loaded. Load and unload trucks, vans, or automobiles. Verify the contents of inventory loads against shipping papers. Turn in receipts and money received from deliveries. Maintain records such as vehicle logs, records of cargo, or billing statements in accordance with regulations. Read maps, and follow written and verbal geographic directions. Report delays, accidents, or other traffic and transportation situations to bases or other vehicles, using telephones or mobile two-way radios. Sell and keep records of sales for products from truck inventory. Drive vehicles with capacities under three tons in order to transport materials to and from specified destinations such as railroad stations, plants, residences and offices, or within industrial yards. Drive trucks equipped with public address systems through city streets in order to broadcast announcements for advertising or publicity purposes. Use and maintain the tools and equipment found on commercial vehicles, such as weighing and measuring devices. Perform emergency repairs such as changing tires or installing light bulbs, fuses, tire chains, and spark plugs.

Education/Training Required: High school diploma or equivalent. **Education and Training Program:** Truck and Bus Driver Training/Commercial Vehicle Operator and Instructor Training. **Knowledge/Courses—Transportation:** Principles and methods for moving people or goods by air, rail, sea, or road, including the relative costs and benefits. **Work Experience Needed:** None. **On-the-Job Training Needed:** Short-term on-the-job training. **Certification/Licensure:** Licensure in some states.

Personality Type: Realistic-Conventional. **Career Cluster:** 16 Transportation, Distribution, and Logistics. **Career Pathway:** 16.1 Transportation Operations. **Other Jobs in This Pathway:** Aerospace Engineering and Operations Technicians; Air Traffic Controllers; Aircraft Cargo Handling Supervisors; Airfield Operations Specialists; Airline Pilots, Copilots, and Flight Engineers; Automotive and Watercraft Service Attendants; Automotive Master Mechanics; Aviation Inspectors; Bridge and Lock Tenders; Bus Drivers, School or Special Client; Bus Drivers, Transit and Intercity; Commercial Divers; Commercial Pilots; Crane and Tower Operators; First-Line Supervisors of Helpers, Laborers, and Material Movers, Hand; First-Line Supervisors of Transportation and Material-Moving Machine and Vehicle Operators; Freight and Cargo Inspectors; Heavy and Tractor-Trailer Truck Drivers; Hoist and Winch Operators; Laborers and Freight, Stock, and Material Movers, Hand; Mates—Ship, Boat, and Barge; Motor Vehicle Operators, All Other; Motorboat Operators; Operating Engineers and Other Construction Equipment Operators; Parking Lot Attendants; Pilots, Ship; others.

Skills—Repairing: Repairing machines or systems using the needed tools. **Equipment Maintenance:** Performing routine maintenance on equipment and determining when and what kind of maintenance is needed. **Operation and Control:** Controlling operations of equipment or systems. **Equipment Selection:** Determining the kind of tools and equipment needed to do a job. **Quality Control Analysis:** Conducting tests and inspections of products, services, or processes to evaluate quality or performance. **Troubleshooting:** Determining causes of operating errors and deciding what to do about them. **Operation Monitoring:** Watching gauges, dials, or other indicators to make sure a machine is working properly. **Installation:** Installing equipment, machines, wiring, or programs to meet specifications.

Work Environment: More often outdoors than indoors; using hands; bending or twisting the body; repetitive motions; noise; very hot or cold; bright or inadequate lighting; contaminants; cramped work space; whole-body vibration; minor burns, cuts, bites, or stings.

Loan Officers

- ⊙ Annual Earnings: $58,030
- ⊙ Earnings Growth Potential: High (44.7%)
- ⊙ Growth: 14.2%
- ⊙ Annual Job Openings: 11,520
- ⊙ Self-Employed: 2.3%

Considerations for Job Outlook: Prospects for loan officers should improve over the coming decade as lending activity rebounds from the recent recession. Job opportunities should be good for those with a college degree and lending, banking, or sales experience. In addition, some firms require loan officers to find their own clients, so candidates with established contacts and a referral network should have the best job opportunities.

Evaluate, authorize, or recommend approval of commercial, real estate, or credit loans. Meet with applicants to obtain information for loan applications and to answer questions about the process. Approve loans within specified limits, and refer loan applications outside those limits to management for approval. Analyze applicants' financial status, credit, and property evaluations to determine feasibility of granting loans. Explain to customers the different types of loans and credit options that are available, as well as the terms of those services. Obtain and compile copies of loan applicants' credit histories, corporate financial statements, and other financial information. Review and update credit and loan files. Review loan agreements to ensure that they are complete and accurate according to policy. Compute payment schedules. Stay abreast of new types of loans and other financial services and products to better meet customers' needs. Submit applications to credit analysts for verification and recommendation. Handle customer complaints, and take appropriate action to resolve them. Work with clients to identify their financial goals and to find ways of reaching those goals. Confer with underwriters to aid in resolving mortgage application problems. Negotiate payment arrangements with customers who have delinquent loans. Market bank products to individuals and firms, promoting bank services that may meet customers' needs. Supervise loan personnel. Set credit policies, credit lines, procedures, and standards in conjunction with senior managers.

Education/Training Required: High school diploma or equivalent. Education and Training Programs: Credit Management; Finance, General. Knowledge/Courses—Sales and Marketing: Principles and methods for showing, promoting, and selling products or services. This includes marketing strategy and tactics, product demonstration, sales techniques, and sales control systems. Economics and Accounting: Economic and accounting principles and practices, the financial markets, banking, and the analysis and reporting of financial data. Customer and Personal Service: Principles and processes for providing customer and personal services. This includes customer needs assessment, meeting quality standards for services, and evaluation of customer satisfaction. Law and Government: Laws, legal codes, court procedures, precedents, government regulations, executive orders, agency rules, and the democratic political process. Clerical Practices: Administrative and clerical procedures and systems such as word processing, managing files and records, stenography and transcription, designing forms, and other office procedures and terminology. Mathematics: Arithmetic, algebra, geometry, calculus, statistics, and their applications. Work Experience Needed: None. On-the-Job Training Needed: Moderate-term on-the-job training. Certification/Licensure: Voluntary certification by association.

Personality Type: Conventional-Enterprising-Social. Career Cluster: 06 Finance. Career Pathways: 06.3 Banking and Related Services; 06.1 Financial and Investment Planning. Other Jobs in These Pathways: Bill and Account Collectors; Budget Analysts; Business Teachers, Postsecondary; Credit Analysts; Credit Authorizers; Credit Checkers; Financial Analysts; Financial Managers, Branch or Department; Financial Quantitative Analysts; Financial Specialists, All Other; Fraud Examiners, Investigators and Analysts; Investment Underwriters; Loan Counselors; Loan Interviewers and Clerks; New Accounts Clerks; Personal Financial Advisors; Risk Management Specialists; Sales Agents, Financial Services; Sales Agents, Securities and Commodities; Securities and Commodities Traders; Tellers; Title Examiners, Abstractors, and Searchers; Treasurers and Controllers.

Skills—Service Orientation: Actively looking for ways to help people. Mathematics: Using mathematics to solve problems. Judgment and Decision Making: Considering the relative costs and benefits of potential actions to choose the most appropriate one. Speaking: Talking to others to convey information effectively. Negotiation: Bringing others together and trying to reconcile differences. Active Listening: Giving full attention to what other people are saying, taking time to understand the points being made, asking questions as appropriate, and not interrupting at inappropriate times. Critical Thinking: Using logic and reasoning to identify the strengths and weaknesses of alternative solutions, conclusions, or approaches to problems. Reading Comprehension: Understanding written sentences and paragraphs in work-related documents.

Work Environment: More often indoors than outdoors; sitting.

Locksmiths and Safe Repairers

- ⊙ Annual Earnings: $36,680
- ⊙ Earnings Growth Potential: High (42.6%)
- ⊙ Growth: 17.9%
- ⊙ Annual Job Openings: 930
- ⊙ Self-Employed: 36.1%

Considerations for Job Outlook: About-average employment growth is projected.

Repair and open locks; make keys; change locks and safe combinations; and install and repair safes. Cut new or duplicate keys, using keycutting machines. Keep records of company locks and keys. Insert new or repaired tumblers into locks to change combinations. Move picklocks in cylinders to open door locks without keys. Disassemble mechanical or electrical locking devices, and repair or replace worn tumblers, springs, and other parts, using hand tools. Repair and adjust safes, vault doors, and vault components, using hand tools, lathes, drill presses, and welding and acetylene cutting apparatus. Open safe locks by drilling. Cut new or duplicate keys using impressions or code key machines. Set up and maintain master key systems. Install door hardware such as locks and closers. Install alarm and electronic access systems. Unlock cars and other vehicles.

Education/Training Required: High school diploma or equivalent. Education and Training Program: Locksmithing and Safe Repair. Knowledge/Courses—Mechanical Devices: Machines and tools, including their designs, uses, repair, and maintenance. Public Safety and Security: Relevant equipment, policies, procedures, and strategies to promote effective local, state, or national security operations for the protection of people, data, property, and institutions. **Building and Construction:** Materials, methods, and the tools involved in the construction or repair of houses, buildings, or other structures such as highways and roads. **Sales and Marketing:** Principles and methods for showing, promoting, and selling products or services. This includes marketing strategy and tactics, product demonstration, sales techniques, and sales control systems. **Law and Government:** Laws, legal codes, court procedures, precedents, government regulations, executive orders, agency rules, and the democratic political process. **Design:** Design techniques, tools, and principles involved in production of precision technical plans, blueprints, drawings, and models. **Work Experience Needed:** None. **On-the-Job Training Needed:** Long-term on-the-job training. **Certification/Licensure:** None.

Personality Type: Realistic-Conventional. **Career Cluster:** 13 Manufacturing. **Career Pathway:** 13.3 Maintenance, Installation, and Repair. **Other Jobs in This Pathway:** Aircraft Mechanics and Service Technicians; Automotive Engineering Technicians; Automotive Specialty Technicians; Avionics Technicians; Biological Technicians; Camera and Photographic Equipment Repairers; Chemical Equipment Operators and Tenders; Civil Engineering Technicians; Coil Winders, Tapers, and Finishers; Computer, Automated Teller, and Office Machine Repairers; Construction and Related Workers, All Other; Control and Valve Installers and Repairers, Except Mechanical Door; Electric Motor, Power Tool, and Related Repairers; Electrical and Electronic Equipment Assemblers; Electrical and Electronics Repairers, Commercial and Industrial Equipment; Electrical and Electronics Repairers, Powerhouse, Substation, and Relay; Electrical Engineering Technicians; Electrical Engineering Technologists; Electromechanical Engineering Technologists; Electromechanical Equipment Assemblers; Electronics Engineering Technicians; Electronics Engineering Technologists; others.

Skills—Repairing: Repairing machines or systems using the needed tools. **Equipment Maintenance:** Performing routine maintenance on equipment and determining when and what kind of maintenance is needed. **Installation:** Installing equipment, machines, wiring, or programs to meet specifications. **Troubleshooting:** Determining causes of operating errors and deciding what to do about them. **Equipment Selection:** Determining the kind of tools and equipment needed to do a job. **Quality Control Analysis:** Conducting tests and inspections of products, services, or processes to evaluate quality or performance. **Operation and Control:** Controlling operations of equipment or systems. **Technology Design:** Generating or adapting equipment and technology to serve user needs.

Work Environment: More often outdoors than indoors; standing; using hands; noise; very hot or cold; bright or inadequate lighting; cramped work space; hazardous equipment.

Locomotive Engineers

- ◉ Annual Earnings: $49,380
- ◉ Earnings Growth Potential: Low (27.6%)
- ◉ Growth: 4.4%
- ◉ Annual Job Openings: 1,550
- ◉ Self-Employed: 0.0%

Considerations for Job Outlook: Job opportunities should be favorable for this occupation. Although many workers stay in this occupation for a long time, currently more workers are nearing retirement than is the case in most occupations. When these workers begin to retire, many jobs should become available.

Drive electric, diesel-electric, steam, or gas-turbine-electric locomotives to transport passengers or freight. Monitor gauges and meters that measure speed, amperage, battery charge, and air pressure in brakelines and in main reservoirs. Observe tracks to detect obstructions. Interpret train orders, signals, and railroad rules and regulations that govern the operation of locomotives. Receive starting signals from conductors, and then move controls such as throttles and air brakes to drive electric, diesel-electric, steam, or gas-turbine-electric locomotives. Confer with conductors or traffic control center personnel via radiophones to issue or receive information concerning stops, delays, or oncoming trains. Operate locomotives to transport freight or passengers between stations and to assemble and disassemble trains within rail yards. Respond to emergency conditions or breakdowns, following applicable safety procedures and rules. Check to ensure that brake examination tests are conducted at shunting stations. Call out train signals to assistants in order to verify meanings. Inspect locomotives to verify adequate fuel, sand, water, and other supplies before each run and to check for mechanical problems. Prepare reports regarding any problems encountered, such as accidents, signaling problems, unscheduled stops, or delays. Check to ensure that documentation, including procedure manuals and logbooks, is in the driver's cab and available for staff use. Inspect locomotives after runs to detect damaged or defective equipment. Drive diesel-electric rail-detector cars to transport rail-flaw-detecting machines over tracks. Monitor train loading procedures to ensure that freight and rolling stock are loaded or unloaded without damage.

Education/Training Required: High school diploma or equivalent. **Education and Training Program:** Transportation and Materials Moving, Other. **Knowledge/Courses—Transportation:** Principles and methods for moving people or goods by air, rail, sea, or road, including the relative costs and benefits. **Mechanical Devices:** Machines and tools, including their designs, uses, repair, and maintenance. **Public Safety and Security:** Relevant equipment, policies, procedures, and strategies to promote effective local, state, or national security operations for the protection of people, data, property, and institutions. **Work Experience Needed:** 1 to 5 years. **On-the-Job Training Needed:** Moderate-term on-the-job training. **Certification/Licensure:** Federal certification.

Personality Type: Realistic-Conventional. **Career Cluster:** 16 Transportation, Distribution, and Logistics. **Career Pathway:** 16.1 Transportation Operations. **Other Jobs in This Pathway:** Aerospace Engineering and Operations Technicians; Air Traffic Controllers; Aircraft Cargo Handling Supervisors; Airfield Operations Specialists; Airline Pilots, Copilots, and Flight Engineers; Automotive and Watercraft Service Attendants; Automotive Master Mechanics; Aviation Inspectors; Bridge and Lock Tenders; Bus Drivers, School or Special Client; Bus Drivers, Transit and Intercity; Commercial Divers; Commercial Pilots; Crane and Tower Operators; First-Line Supervisors of Helpers, Laborers, and Material Movers, Hand; First-Line Supervisors of Transportation and Material-Moving Machine and Vehicle Operators; Freight and Cargo Inspectors; Heavy and Tractor-Trailer Truck Drivers; Hoist and Winch Operators; Laborers and Freight, Stock, and Material Movers, Hand; Light Truck or Delivery Services Drivers; Mates—Ship, Boat, and Barge; Motor Vehicle Operators, All Other; Motorboat Operators; Operating Engineers and Other Construction Equipment Operators; others.

Skills—Operation and Control: Controlling operations of equipment or systems. **Operation Monitoring:** Watching gauges, dials, or other indicators to make sure a machine is working properly. **Troubleshooting:** Determining causes of operating errors and deciding what to do about them. **Quality Control Analysis:** Conducting tests and inspections of products, services, or processes to evaluate quality or performance. **Mathematics:** Using mathematics to solve problems. **Monitoring:** Monitoring or assessing your performance or that of other individuals or organizations to make improvements or take corrective action. **Management of Personnel Resources:** Motivating, developing, and directing people as they work, identifying the best people for the job. **Management of Financial Resources:** Determining how money will be spent to get the work done and accounting for these expenditures.

Work Environment: Outdoors; sitting; using hands; repetitive motions; noise; very hot or cold; bright or inadequate lighting; contaminants; whole-body vibration; hazardous conditions; hazardous equipment; minor burns, cuts, bites, or stings.

Lodging Managers

⊙ Annual Earnings: $47,450
⊙ Earnings Growth Potential: Medium (37.7%)
⊙ Growth: 8.4%
⊙ Annual Job Openings: 1,820
⊙ Self-Employed: 40.1%

Considerations for Job Outlook: Those seeking jobs at hotels with the highest level of guest services are expected to face strong competition as these jobs are highly sought after by people trained in hospitality management or administration. Job opportunities at smaller hotels should be better. Those with a college degree in hotel or hospitality management are expected to have the best job opportunities, particularly at upscale and luxury hotels.

Plan, direct, or coordinate activities of an organization or department that provides lodging and other accommodations. Greet and register guests. Answer inquiries pertaining to hotel policies and services, and resolve occupants' complaints. Assign duties to workers, and schedule shifts. Coordinate front-office activities of hotels or motels, and resolve problems. Participate in financial activities such as the setting of room rates, the establishment of budgets, and the allocation of funds to departments. Confer and cooperate with other managers to ensure coordination of hotel activities. Manage and maintain temporary or permanent lodging facilities. Observe and monitor staff performance to ensure efficient operations and adherence to facility's policies and procedures. Train staff members. Show, rent, or assign accommodations. Develop and implement policies and procedures for the operation of a department or establishment. Inspect guest rooms, public areas, and grounds for cleanliness and appearance. Prepare required paperwork pertaining to departmental functions. Interview and hire applicants.

Education/Training Required: High school diploma or equivalent. **Education and Training Programs:** Hospitality Administration/Management, General; Hospitality and Recreation Marketing Operations; Hotel/Motel Administration/Management; Resort Management; Selling Skills and Sales Operations. **Knowledge/Courses—Sales and Marketing:** Principles and methods for showing, promoting, and selling products or services. This includes marketing strategy and tactics, product demonstration, sales techniques, and sales control systems. **Geography:** Principles and methods for describing the features of land, sea, and air masses, including their physical characteristics, locations, interrelationships, and distribution of plant, animal, and human life. **Clerical Practices:** Administrative and clerical procedures and systems such as word processing, managing files and records, stenography and transcription, designing forms, and other office procedures and terminology. **Personnel and Human Resources:** Principles and procedures for personnel recruitment, selection, training, compensation and benefits, labor relations and negotiation, and personnel information systems. **Economics and Accounting:** Economic and accounting principles and practices, the financial markets, banking, and the analysis and reporting of financial data. **Administration and Management:** Business and management principles involved in strategic planning, resource allocation, human resources modeling, leadership technique, production methods, and coordination of people and resources. **Work Experience Needed:** 1 to 5 years. **On-the-Job Training Needed:** None. **Certification/Licensure:** None.

Personality Type: Enterprising-Conventional-Social. **Career Clusters:** 09 Hospitality and Tourism; 14 Marketing, Sales, and Service. **Career Pathways:** 09.3 Travel and Tourism; 09.4 Recreation, Amusements, and Attractions; 14.2 Professional Sales and Marketing; 09.2 Lodging. **Other Jobs in These Pathways:** Amusement and Recreation Attendants; Appraisers, Real Estate; Assessors; Baggage Porters and Bellhops; Building Cleaning Workers, All Other; Cashiers; Concierges; Costume Attendants; Counter and Rental Clerks; Demonstrators and Product Promoters; Door-To-Door Sales Workers, News and Street Vendors, and Related Workers; Driver/Sales Workers; Energy Brokers; Entertainment Attendants and Related Workers, All Other; Farm and Home Management Advisors; First-Line Supervisors of Housekeeping and Janitorial Workers; First-Line Supervisors of Non-Retail Sales Workers; First-Line Supervisors of Retail Sales Workers; Food Service Managers; Gaming and Sports Book Writers and Runners; Gaming Change Persons and Booth Cashiers; Gaming Dealers; Gaming Service Workers, All Other; Hotel, Motel, and Resort Desk Clerks; Interior Designers; Janitors and Cleaners, Except Maids and Housekeeping Cleaners; Locker Room, Coatroom, and Dressing Room Attendants; Maids and Housekeeping Cleaners; others.

Skills—Management of Financial Resources: Determining how money will be spent to get the work done and accounting for these expenditures. **Management of Material Resources:** Obtaining and seeing to the appropriate use of equipment, facilities, and materials needed to do certain work. **Management of Personnel Resources:** Motivating, developing, and directing people as they work, identifying the best people for the job. **Systems Evaluation:** Identifying measures or indicators of system performance and the actions needed to improve or correct performance relative to the goals of the system. **Negotiation:** Bringing others together and trying to reconcile differences. **Service Orientation:** Actively looking for ways to help people. **Persuasion:** Persuading others to change their minds or behavior. **Monitoring:** Monitoring or assessing your performance or that of other individuals or organizations to make improvements or take corrective action.

Work Environment: Indoors.

Machinists

- Annual Earnings: $39,220
- Earnings Growth Potential: Medium (37.8%)
- Growth: 8.5%
- Annual Job Openings: 9,950
- Self-Employed: 3.4%

Considerations for Job Outlook: Job opportunities for machinists and tool and die makers should be excellent as employers continue to value the wide-ranging skills of these workers. Also, many young people with the educational and personal qualifications needed to become machinists or tool and die makers prefer to attend college or may not wish to enter production occupations. In fact, employers in certain parts of the country report difficulty attracting skilled workers and apprenticeship candidates with the abilities necessary to fill job openings. Therefore, the number of workers learning to be machinists or tool and die makers is expected to be smaller than the number of job openings arising each year from the need to replace experienced machinists who retire or leave the occupation for other reasons.

Set up and operate a variety of machine tools to produce precision parts and instruments. Calculate dimensions and tolerances using knowledge of mathematics and instruments such as micrometers and vernier calipers. Machine parts to specifications using machine tools such as lathes, milling machines, shapers, or grinders. Measure, examine, and test completed units to detect defects and ensure conformance to specifications, using precision instruments such as micrometers. Set up, adjust, and operate all of the basic machine tools and many specialized or advanced variation tools to perform precision machining operations. Align and secure holding fixtures, cutting tools, attachments, accessories, and materials onto machines. Monitor the feed and speed of machines during the machining process. Study sample parts, blueprints, drawings, and engineering information to determine methods and sequences of operations needed to fabricate products, and determine product dimensions and tolerances. Select the appropriate tools, machines, and materials to be used in preparation of machinery work. Lay out, measure, and mark metal stock to display placement of cuts. Observe and listen to operating machines or equipment to diagnose machine malfunctions and to determine need for adjustments or repairs.

Check workpieces to ensure that they are properly lubricated and cooled. Maintain industrial machines, applying knowledge of mechanics, shop mathematics, metal properties, layout, and machining procedures. Position and fasten workpieces. Operate equipment to verify operational efficiency. Install repaired parts into equipment, or install new equipment. Clean and lubricate machines, tools, and equipment to remove grease, rust, stains, and foreign matter. Advise clients about the materials being used for finished products. Set controls to regulate machining, or enter commands to retrieve, input, or edit computerized machine control media. Program computers and electronic instruments such as numerically controlled machine tools.

Education/Training Required: High school diploma or equivalent. **Education and Training Programs:** Machine Shop Technology/Assistant; Machine Tool Technology/Machinist. **Knowledge/Courses—Mechanical Devices:** Machines and tools, including their designs, uses, repair, and maintenance. **Design:** Design techniques, tools, and principles involved in production of precision technical plans, blueprints, drawings, and models. **Engineering and Technology:** The practical application of engineering science and technology. This includes applying principles, techniques, procedures, and equipment to the design and production of various goods and services. **Production and Processing:** Raw materials, production processes, quality control, costs, and other techniques for maximizing the effective manufacture and distribution of goods. **Mathematics:** Arithmetic, algebra, geometry, calculus, statistics, and their applications. **Work Experience Needed:** None. **On-the-Job Training Needed:** Long-term on-the-job training. **Certification/Licensure:** Voluntary certification by association.

Personality Type: Realistic-Conventional-Investigative. **Career Cluster:** 13 Manufacturing. **Career Pathway:** 13.1 Production. **Other Jobs in This Pathway:** Adhesive Bonding Machine Operators and Tenders; Assemblers and Fabricators, All Other; Avionics Technicians; Cabinetmakers and Bench Carpenters; Cleaning, Washing, and Metal Pickling Equipment Operators and Tenders; Coating, Painting, and Spraying Machine Setters, Operators, and Tenders; Computer-Controlled Machine Tool Operators, Metal and Plastic; Cooling and Freezing Equipment Operators and Tenders; Cost Estimators; Crushing, Grinding, and Polishing Machine Setters, Operators, and Tenders; Cutters and Trimmers, Hand; Cutting and Slicing

Machine Setters, Operators, and Tenders; Cutting, Punching, and Press Machine Setters, Operators, and Tenders, Metal and Plastic; Drilling and Boring Machine Tool Setters, Operators, and Tenders, Metal and Plastic; Extruding and Drawing Machine Setters, Operators, and Tenders, Metal and Plastic; Extruding and Forming Machine Setters, Operators, and Tenders, Synthetic and Glass Fibers; others.

Skills—Equipment Maintenance: Performing routine maintenance on equipment and determining when and what kind of maintenance is needed. **Installation:** Installing equipment, machines, wiring, or programs to meet specifications. **Repairing:** Repairing machines or systems using the needed tools. **Equipment Selection:** Determining the kind of tools and equipment needed to do a job. **Quality Control Analysis:** Conducting tests and inspections of products, services, or processes to evaluate quality or performance. **Technology Design:** Generating or adapting equipment and technology to serve user needs. **Troubleshooting:** Determining causes of operating errors and deciding what to do about them. **Operation and Control:** Controlling operations of equipment or systems.

Work Environment: Standing; walking and running; using hands; repetitive motions; noise; contaminants; hazardous equipment; minor burns, cuts, bites, or stings.

Mail Clerks and Mail Machine Operators, Except Postal Service

- ⊙ Annual Earnings: $26,610
- ⊙ Earnings Growth Potential: Low (31.8%)
- ⊙ Growth: 12.0%
- ⊙ Annual Job Openings: 3,960
- ⊙ Self-Employed: 0.0%

Considerations for Job Outlook: About-average growth in employment is projected.

Prepare incoming and outgoing mail for distribution. Release packages or letters to customers upon presentation of written notices or other identification. Sell mail products, and accept payment for products and mailing charges. Place incoming or outgoing letters or packages into sacks or bins based on destination or type, and place identifying tags on sacks or bins. Lift and unload containers of mail or parcels onto equipment for transportation to sortation stations. Inspect mail machine output for defects; determine how to eliminate causes of any defects. Use equipment such as forklifts and automated "trains" to move containers of mail. Remove containers of sorted mail/parcels, and transfer them to designated areas according to established procedures. Operate computer-controlled keyboards or voice recognition equipment in order to direct items according to established routing schemes. Wrap packages or bundles by hand, or by using tying machines. Fold letters or circulars and insert them in envelopes. Stamp dates and times of receipt of incoming mail. Operate embossing machines or typewriters to make corrections, additions, and changes to address plates. Remove from machines printed materials such as labeled articles, postmarked envelopes or tape, and folded sheets. Seal or open envelopes, by hand or by using machines. Mail merchandise samples or promotional literature in response to requests. Determine manner in which mail is to be sent, and prepare it for delivery to mailing facilities. Affix postage to packages or letters by hand, or stamp materials, using postage meters. Insert material for printing or addressing into loading racks on machines, select type or die sizes, and position plates, stencils, or tapes in machine magazines. Sort and route incoming mail, and collect outgoing mail, using carts as necessary. Start machines that automatically feed plates, stencils, or tapes through mechanisms, and observe machine operations in order to detect any malfunctions.

Education/Training Required: High school diploma or equivalent. **Education and Training Program:** General Office Occupations and Clerical Services. **Work Experience Needed:** None. **On-the-Job Training Needed:** Short-term on-the-job training. **Certification/Licensure:** None.

Personality Type: Conventional-Realistic. **Career Cluster:** 04 Business, Management, and Administration. **Career Pathway:** 04.6 Administrative and Information Support. **Other Jobs in This Pathway:** Cargo and Freight Agents; Correspondence Clerks; Couriers and Messengers; Court Clerks; Customer Service Representatives; Data Entry Keyers; Dispatchers, Except Police, Fire, and Ambulance; Executive Secretaries and Executive Administrative Assistants; File Clerks; Freight Forwarders; Human Resources Assistants, Except Payroll and Timekeeping; Information and Record Clerks, All Other; Insurance Claims Clerks; Insurance Policy Processing

Clerks; Interviewers, Except Eligibility and Loan; License Clerks; Meter Readers, Utilities; Municipal Clerks; Office and Administrative Support Workers, All Other; Office Clerks, General; Office Machine Operators, Except Computer; Order Clerks; Patient Representatives; Postal Service Clerks; Postal Service Mail Carriers; Postal Service Mail Sorters, Processors, and Processing Machine Operators; Procurement Clerks; Receptionists and Information Clerks; Secretaries and Administrative Assistants, Except Legal, Medical, and Executive; others.

Skills—Operation and Control: Controlling operations of equipment or systems. **Operation Monitoring:** Watching gauges, dials, or other indicators to make sure a machine is working properly.

Work Environment: Indoors; standing; using hands; repetitive motions.

Maintenance and Repair Workers, General

- ⊚ Annual Earnings: $35,030
- ⊚ Earnings Growth Potential: High (40.6%)
- ⊚ Growth: 11.0%
- ⊚ Annual Job Openings: 37,910
- ⊚ Self-Employed: 0.7%

Considerations for Job Outlook: There should be many job openings for general maintenance and repair workers, due to growth and the need to replace workers who leave the occupation. Many job openings are expected as experienced workers retire. Those with experience in repair- or maintenance-related fields should continue to have the best job prospects.

Perform work involving the skills of two or more maintenance or craft occupations to keep machines, mechanical equipment, or the structure of an establishment in repair. Repair or replace defective equipment parts, using hand tools and power tools, and reassemble equipment. Perform routine preventive maintenance to ensure that machines continue to run smoothly, building systems operate efficiently, or the physical condition of buildings does not deteriorate. Inspect drives, motors, and belts; check fluid levels; replace filters; or perform other maintenance actions, following checklists. Use tools ranging from common hand and power tools, such as hammers, hoists, saws, drills, and wrenches, to precision measuring instruments and electrical and electronic testing devices. Assemble, install, or repair wiring, electrical or electronic components, pipe systems, plumbing, machinery, or equipment. Diagnose mechanical problems and determine how to correct them, checking blueprints, repair manuals, or parts catalogs, as necessary. Inspect, operate, or test machinery or equipment to diagnose machine malfunctions. Record type and cost of maintenance or repair work. Clean or lubricate shafts, bearings, gears, or other parts of machinery. Dismantle devices to access and remove defective parts, using hoists, cranes, hand tools, and power tools. Plan and lay out repair work, using diagrams, drawings, blueprints, maintenance manuals, or schematic diagrams. Order parts, supplies, and equipment from catalogs and suppliers, or obtain them from storerooms. Adjust functional parts of devices or control instruments, using hand tools, levels, plumb bobs, or straightedges. Paint or repair roofs, windows, doors, floors, woodwork, plaster, drywall, or other parts of building structures. Operate cutting torches or welding equipment to cut or join metal parts. Maintain and repair specialized equipment and machinery found in cafeterias, laundries, hospitals, stores, offices, or factories. Provide groundskeeping services such as landscaping and snow removal. Perform general cleaning of buildings or properties.

Education/Training Required: High school diploma or equivalent. **Education and Training Program:** Industrial Mechanics and Maintenance Technology. **Knowledge/Courses—Building and Construction:** Materials, methods, and the tools involved in the construction or repair of houses, buildings, or other structures such as highways and roads. **Mechanical Devices:** Machines and tools, including their designs, uses, repair, and maintenance. **Design:** Design techniques, tools, and principles involved in production of precision technical plans, blueprints, drawings, and models. **Public Safety and Security:** Relevant equipment, policies, procedures, and strategies to promote effective local, state, or national security operations for the protection of people, data, property, and institutions. **Physics:** Physical principles, laws, their interrelationships, and applications to understanding fluid, material, and atmospheric dynamics, and mechanical, electrical, atomic, and subatomic structures and processes. **Engineering and Technology:** The practical application of engineering science and technology. This includes applying principles, techniques, procedures, and equipment to the design and production of various goods and services. **Work Experience Needed:** None. **On-the-Job Training Needed:** Moderate-term on-the-job training. **Certification/Licensure:** Voluntary certification for some specializations.

Personality Type: Realistic-Conventional-Investigative. **Career Cluster:** 02 Architecture and Construction. **Career Pathway:** 02.2 Construction. **Other Jobs in This Pathway:** Boilermakers; Brickmasons and Blockmasons; Carpet Installers; Cement Masons and Concrete Finishers; Construction and Building Inspectors; Construction and Related Workers, All Other; Construction Carpenters; Construction Laborers; Construction Managers; Continuous Mining Machine Operators; Cost Estimators; Crane and Tower Operators; Dredge Operators; Drywall and Ceiling Tile Installers; Earth Drillers, Except Oil and Gas; Electrical Power-Line Installers and Repairers; Electricians; Electromechanical Equipment Assemblers; Engineering Technicians, Except Drafters, All Other; Excavating and Loading Machine and Dragline Operators; Explosives Workers, Ordnance Handling Experts, and Blasters; Extraction Workers, All Other; First-Line Supervisors of Construction Trades and Extraction Workers; Floor Layers, Except Carpet, Wood, and Hard Tiles; Floor Sanders and Finishers; Glaziers; Heating and Air Conditioning Mechanics and Installers; Helpers, Construction Trades, All Other; others.

Skills—Repairing: Repairing machines or systems using the needed tools. **Equipment Maintenance:** Performing routine maintenance on equipment and determining when and what kind of maintenance is needed. **Installation:** Installing equipment, machines, wiring, or programs to meet specifications. **Equipment Selection:** Determining the kind of tools and equipment needed to do a job. **Troubleshooting:** Determining causes of operating errors and deciding what to do about them. **Operation and Control:** Controlling operations of equipment or systems. **Quality Control Analysis:** Conducting tests and inspections of products, services, or processes to evaluate quality or performance. **Operation Monitoring:** Watching gauges, dials, or other indicators to make sure a machine is working properly.

Work Environment: Outdoors; standing; walking and running; kneeling, crouching, stooping, or crawling; using hands; bending or twisting the body; noise; very hot or cold; contaminants; cramped work space; hazardous equipment; minor burns, cuts, bites, or stings.

Maintenance Workers, Machinery

- Annual Earnings: $39,490
- Earnings Growth Potential: Medium (38.5%)
- Growth: 6.4%
- Annual Job Openings: 1,740
- Self-Employed: 0.0%

Considerations for Job Outlook: Applicants with a broad range of skills in machine repair should have good job prospects overall. The need to replace the many older workers who are expected to retire, as well as those who leave the occupation for other reasons, should result in numerous job openings. Some employers have reported difficulty in recruiting young workers with the necessary skills. Mechanics are not as affected by changes in production levels as are other manufacturing workers because mechanics often are kept during production downtime to complete overhauls to major equipment and to keep expensive machinery in working order.

Lubricate machinery, change parts, or perform other routine machinery maintenance. Reassemble machines after the completion of repair or maintenance work. Start machines and observe mechanical operation to determine efficiency and to detect problems. Inspect or test damaged machine parts, and mark defective areas or advise supervisors of repair needs. Lubricate or apply adhesives or other materials to machines, machine parts, or other equipment, according to specified procedures. Install, replace, or change machine parts and attachments, according to production specifications. Dismantle machines and remove parts for repair, using hand tools, chain falls, jacks, cranes, or hoists. Record production, repair, and machine maintenance information. Read work orders and specifications to determine machines and equipment requiring repair or maintenance. Set up and operate machines, and adjust controls to regulate operations. Collaborate with other workers to repair or move machines, machine parts, or equipment. Inventory and requisition machine parts, equipment, and other supplies so that stock can be maintained and replenished. Transport machine parts, tools, equipment, and other material between work areas and storage, using cranes, hoists, or dollies. Collect and discard worn machine parts and other refuse in order to maintain machinery and work areas. Clean machines and machine parts, using cleaning solvents, cloths, air guns, hoses, vacuums, or other equipment. Replace or repair metal, wood, leather, glass, or other lining in machines or in equipment compartments or containers. Remove hardened material from machines or machine parts, using abrasives, power and hand tools, jackhammers, sledgehammers, or other equipment. Measure, mix, prepare, and test chemical solutions used to clean or repair machinery and equipment. Replace, empty, or replenish machine and equipment containers such as gas tanks or boxes.

Education/Training Required: High school diploma or equivalent. **Education and Training Programs:** Heavy/Industrial Equipment Maintenance Technologies, Other; Industrial Mechanics and Maintenance Technology. **Knowledge/Courses—Mechanical Devices:** Machines and tools, including their designs, uses, repair, and maintenance. **Building and Construction:** Materials, methods, and the tools involved in the construction or repair of houses, buildings, or other structures such as highways and roads. **Engineering and Technology:** The practical application of engineering science and technology. This includes applying principles, techniques, procedures, and equipment to the design and production of various goods and services. **Physics:** Physical principles, laws, their interrelationships, and applications to understanding fluid, material, and atmospheric dynamics, and mechanical, electrical, atomic, and subatomic structures and processes. **Chemistry:** The chemical composition, structure, and properties of substances and of the chemical processes and transformations that they undergo. This includes uses of chemicals and their danger signs, production techniques, and disposal methods. **Design:** Design techniques, tools, and principles involved in production of precision technical plans, blueprints, drawings, and models. **Work Experience Needed:** None. **On-the-Job Training Needed:** Moderate-term on-the-job training. **Certification/Licensure:** None.

Personality Type: Realistic-Conventional-Investigative. **Career Cluster:** 13 Manufacturing. **Career Pathway:** 13.3 Maintenance, Installation, and Repair. **Other Jobs in This Pathway:** Aircraft Mechanics and Service Technicians; Automotive Engineering Technicians; Automotive Specialty Technicians; Avionics Technicians; Biological Technicians; Camera and Photographic Equipment Repairers; Chemical Equipment Operators and Tenders; Civil Engineering Technicians; Coil Winders, Tapers, and Finishers; Computer, Automated Teller, and Office Machine Repairers; Construction and Related Workers, All Other; Control and Valve Installers and Repairers, Except Mechanical Door; Electric Motor, Power Tool, and Related Repairers; Electrical and Electronic Equipment Assemblers; Electrical and Electronics Repairers, Commercial and Industrial Equipment; Electrical and Electronics Repairers, Powerhouse, Substation, and Relay; Electrical Engineering Technicians; Electrical Engineering Technologists; Electromechanical Engineering Technologists; Electromechanical Equipment Assemblers; Electronics Engineering Technicians; Electronics Engineering Technologists; others.

Skills—Repairing: Repairing machines or systems using the needed tools. **Equipment Maintenance:** Performing routine maintenance on equipment and determining when and what kind of maintenance is needed. **Troubleshooting:** Determining causes of operating errors and deciding what to do about them. **Equipment Selection:** Determining the kind of tools and equipment needed to do a job. **Operation and Control:** Controlling operations of equipment or systems. **Operation Monitoring:** Watching gauges, dials, or other indicators to make sure a machine is working properly. **Installation:** Installing equipment, machines, wiring, or programs to meet specifications. **Quality Control Analysis:** Conducting tests and inspections of products, services, or processes to evaluate quality or performance.

Work Environment: Outdoors; standing; walking and running; using hands; bending or twisting the body; noise; very hot or cold; bright or inadequate lighting; contaminants; cramped work space; hazardous conditions; hazardous equipment; minor burns, cuts, bites, or stings.

Managers, All Other

- ⊙ Annual Earnings: $99,540
- ⊙ Earnings Growth Potential: High (48.4%)
- ⊙ Growth: 7.9%
- ⊙ Annual Job Openings: 24,940
- ⊙ Self-Employed: 55.8%

Considerations for Job Outlook: Slower-than-average employment growth is projected.

All managers not listed separately. For task data, see Job Specializations.

Education/Training Required: High school diploma or equivalent. **Education and Training Program:** Business/Commerce, General. **Work Experience Needed:** 1 to 5 years. **On-the-Job Training Needed:** None. **Certification/Licensure:** Licensure for some specializations.

Job Specialization: Brownfield Redevelopment Specialists and Site Managers

Participate in planning and directing cleanup and redevelopment of contaminated properties for reuse. Does not include properties sufficiently contaminated to qualify as Superfund sites. Review or evaluate environmental-remediation project proposals. Review or evaluate designs for contaminant treatment or disposal facilities. Provide training on hazardous-material or waste-cleanup procedures and technologies. Provide expert witness testimony on issues such as soil, air, or water contamination and associated cleanup measures. Prepare reports or presentations to communicate brownfield redevelopment needs, status, or progress. Negotiate contracts for services or materials needed for environmental remediation. Prepare and submit permit applications for demolition, cleanup, remediation, or construction projects. Maintain records of decisions, actions, and progress related to environmental-redevelopment projects. Inspect sites to assess environmental damage or monitor cleanup progress. Plan or implement brownfield redevelopment projects to ensure safety, quality, and compliance with applicable standards or requirements. Identify environmental-contamination sources. Estimate costs for environmental cleanup and remediation of land-redevelopment projects. Develop or implement plans for revegetation of brownfield sites. Design or implement plans for surface- or ground-water remediation. Design or implement plans for structural demolition and debris removal. Design or implement measures to improve the water, air, and soil quality of military test sites, abandoned mine land, or other contaminated sites. Design or conduct environmental-restoration studies.

Education and Training Program: Hazardous Materials Management and Waste Technology/Technician.

Personality Type: No data available. **Career Cluster:** 04 Business, Management, and Administration. **Career Pathways:** 04.2 Business, Financial Management, and Accounting; 04.1 Management. **Other Jobs in These**

Pathways: Accountants; Administrative Services Managers; Agents and Business Managers of Artists, Performers, and Athletes; Auditors; Billing, Cost, and Rate Clerks; Biofuels Production Managers; Bioinformatics Technicians; Biomass Power Plant Managers; Bookkeeping, Accounting, and Auditing Clerks; Brokerage Clerks; Budget Analysts; Business Continuity Planners; Business Operations Specialists, All Other; Business Teachers, Postsecondary; Chief Executives; Chief Sustainability Officers; Communications Teachers, Postsecondary; Compliance Managers; Computer and Information Systems Managers; Construction Managers; Cost Estimators; Credit Analysts; Customs Brokers; Economics Teachers, Postsecondary; Economists; Energy Auditors; Environmental Economists; Financial Analysts; Financial Examiners; Financial Managers, Branch or Department; First-Line Supervisors of Office and Administrative Support Workers; First-Line Supervisors of Personal Service Workers; Gaming Cage Workers; Gaming Supervisors; others.

Work Environment: No data available.

Job Specialization: Compliance Managers

Plan, direct, or coordinate activities of an organization to ensure compliance with ethical or regulatory standards. Verify that software technology is in place to adequately provide oversight and monitoring in all required areas. Serve as a confidential point of contact for employees to communicate with management, seek clarification on issues or dilemmas, or report irregularities. Maintain documentation of compliance activities such as complaints received and investigation outcomes. Consult with corporate attorneys as necessary to address difficult legal-compliance issues. Discuss emerging compliance issues with management or employees. Collaborate with human resources departments to ensure the implementation of consistent disciplinary action strategies in cases of compliance standard violations. Advise internal management or business partners on the implementation and operation of compliance programs. Review communications such as securities sales advertising to ensure there are no violations of standards or regulations. Provide employee training on compliance-related topics, policies, or procedures. Report violations of compliance or regulatory standards to duly authorized enforcement agencies as appropriate or required. Provide assistance to internal and external auditors in compliance reviews. Prepare management reports regarding compliance operations and progress. Oversee internal reporting systems such as corporate compliance hotlines, and inform employees about these systems. Monitor compliance systems to ensure their effectiveness.

Education and Training Program: Business Administration and Management, General.

Personality Type: Conventional-Enterprising-Realistic. **Career Clusters:** 04 Business, Management, and Administration; 07 Government and Public Administration. **Career Pathways:** 04.2 Business, Financial Management, and Accounting; 04.1 Management; 07.1 Governance. **Other Jobs in These Pathways:** Accountants; Administrative Services Managers; Agents and Business Managers of Artists, Performers, and Athletes; Auditors; Billing, Cost, and Rate Clerks; Biofuels Production Managers; Bioinformatics Technicians; Biomass Power Plant Managers; Bookkeeping, Accounting, and Auditing Clerks; Brokerage Clerks; Brownfield Redevelopment Specialists and Site Managers; Budget Analysts; Business Continuity Planners; Business Operations Specialists, All Other; Business Teachers, Postsecondary; Chief Executives; Chief Sustainability Officers; Communications Teachers, Postsecondary; Computer and Information Systems Managers; Construction Managers; Cost Estimators; Credit Analysts; Customs Brokers; Economics Teachers, Postsecondary; Economists; Energy Auditors; Environmental Economists; Financial Analysts; Financial Examiners; Financial Managers, Branch or Department; First-Line Supervisors of Office and Administrative Support Workers; First-Line Supervisors of Personal Service Workers; others.

Work Environment: No data available.

Job Specialization: Investment Fund Managers

Plan, direct, or coordinate investment strategy or operations for a large pool of liquid assets supplied by institutional investors or individual investors. Prepare for and respond to regulatory inquiries. Verify regulatory compliance of transaction reporting. Hire and evaluate staff. Direct activities of accounting or operations departments. Develop, implement, or monitor security valuation policies. Attend investment briefings or consult financial media to stay abreast of relevant investment markets. Review offering documents or marketing materials to ensure regulatory compliance. Perform or evaluate research, such as detailed company and industry analyses, to inform financial forecasting, decision making, or valuation. Present investment information, such as product risks, fees, and fund performance statistics. Monitor financial or operational performance of individual investments to ensure that portfolios meet risk goals. Monitor regulatory or tax law changes to ensure fund compliance or to capitalize on development opportunities. Meet with investors to determine investment goals or to discuss investment strategies. Identify group and individual target investors for a specific fund. Develop, or direct development of, offering documents or marketing materials. Evaluate the potential of new product developments or market opportunities according to factors such as business plans, technologies, and market potential. Develop and implement fund investment policies and strategies. Select and direct the execution of trades. Analyze acquisitions to ensure conformance with strategic goals or regulatory requirements.

Education and Training Program: Investments and Securities.

Personality Type: Enterprising-Conventional. **Career Cluster:** 04 Business, Management, and Administration. **Career Pathways:** 04.1 Management; 04.2 Business, Financial Management, and Accounting. **Other Jobs in These Pathways:** Accountants; Administrative Services Managers; Agents and Business Managers of Artists, Performers, and Athletes; Auditors; Billing, Cost, and Rate Clerks; Biofuels Production Managers; Bioinformatics Technicians; Biomass Power Plant Managers; Bookkeeping, Accounting, and Auditing Clerks; Brokerage Clerks; Brownfield Redevelopment Specialists and Site Managers; Budget Analysts; Business Continuity Planners; Business Operations Specialists, All Other; Business Teachers, Postsecondary; Chief Executives; Chief Sustainability Officers; Communications Teachers, Postsecondary; Compliance Managers; Computer and Information Systems Managers; Construction Managers; Cost Estimators; Credit Analysts; Customs Brokers; Economics Teachers, Postsecondary; Economists; Energy Auditors; Environmental Economists; Financial Analysts; Financial Examiners; Financial Managers, Branch or Department; First-Line Supervisors of Office and Administrative Support Workers; others.

Work Environment: No data available.

Job Specialization: Loss Prevention Managers

Plan and direct policies, procedures, or systems to prevent the loss of assets. Determine risk exposure or potential liability, and develop risk control measures. Review loss-prevention exception reports and cash discrepancies to ensure adherence to guidelines. Perform cash audits and deposit investigations to fully account for store cash. Provide recommendations and solutions in crisis situations such as workplace violence, protests, and demonstrations. Monitor and review paperwork procedures and systems to prevent error-related shortages. Maintain databases such as bad check logs, reports on multiple offenders, and alarm activation lists. Investigate or interview individuals suspected of shoplifting or internal theft. Direct installation of covert surveillance equipment such as security cameras. Advise retail establishments on development of loss-investigation procedures. Visit stores to ensure compliance with company policies and procedures. Verify correct use and maintenance of physical security systems such as closed-circuit television, merchandise tags, and burglar alarms. Train loss-prevention staff, retail managers, or store employees on loss control and prevention measures. Supervise surveillance, detection, or criminal processing related to theft and criminal cases. Recommend improvements in loss-prevention programs, staffing, scheduling, or training. Perform or direct inventory investigations in response to shrink results outside of acceptable ranges. Hire or supervise loss-prevention staff. Maintain documentation of all loss-prevention activity.

Education and Training Program: Security and Loss Prevention Services.

Personality Type: Enterprising-Conventional. **Career Cluster:** 04 Business, Management, and Administration. **Career Pathways:** 04.2 Business, Financial Management, and Accounting; 04.1 Management. **Other Jobs in These Pathways:** Accountants; Administrative Services Managers; Agents and Business Managers of Artists, Performers, and Athletes; Auditors; Billing, Cost, and Rate Clerks; Biofuels Production Managers; Bioinformatics Technicians; Biomass Power Plant Managers; Bookkeeping, Accounting, and Auditing Clerks; Brokerage Clerks; Brownfield Redevelopment Specialists and Site Managers; Budget Analysts; Business Continuity Planners; Business Operations Specialists, All Other; Business Teachers, Postsecondary; Chief Executives; Chief Sustainability Officers; Communications Teachers, Postsecondary; Compliance Managers; Computer and Information Systems Managers; Construction Managers; Cost Estimators; Credit Analysts; Customs Brokers; Economics Teachers, Postsecondary; Economists; Energy Auditors; Environmental Economists; Financial Analysts; Financial Examiners; Financial Managers, Branch or Department; First-Line Supervisors of Office and Administrative Support Workers; others.

Work Environment: No data available.

Job Specialization: Regulatory Affairs Managers

Plan, direct, or coordinate production activities of an organization to ensure compliance with regulations and standard operating procedures. Direct the preparation and submission of regulatory agency applications, reports, or correspondence. Review all regulatory agency submission materials to ensure timeliness, accuracy, comprehensiveness, and compliance with regulatory standards. Provide regulatory guidance to departments or development project teams regarding design, development, evaluation, or marketing of products. Formulate or implement regulatory affairs policies and procedures to ensure that regulatory compliance is maintained or enhanced. Manage activities such as audits, regulatory agency inspections, and product recalls. Communicate regulatory information to multiple departments, and ensure that information is interpreted correctly. Develop regulatory strategies and implementation plans for the preparation and submission of new products. Provide responses to regulatory agencies regarding product information or issues. Maintain current knowledge of relevant regulations including proposed and final rules. Investigate product complaints, and prepare documentation and submissions to appropriate regulatory agencies as necessary. Review materials such as marketing literature and user manuals to ensure that regulatory agency requirements are met. Implement or monitor complaint processing systems to ensure effective and timely resolution of all complaint investigations. Represent organizations before domestic or international regulatory agencies on major policy matters or decisions regarding company products.

Education and Training Program: Business Administration and Management, General. **Knowledge/Courses—Biology:** Plant and animal organisms and their tissues, cells, functions, interdependencies, and interactions with each other and the environment. **Medicine and Dentistry:** The information and techniques needed to diagnose and treat human injuries, diseases, and deformities. This includes symptoms, treatment alternatives, drug properties and interactions, and preventive health-care measures. **Law and Government:** Laws, legal codes, court procedures, precedents, government regulations, executive orders, agency rules, and the democratic political process. **Chemistry:** The chemical composition, structure, and properties of substances and of the chemical processes and transformations that they undergo. This includes uses of chemicals and their danger signs, production techniques, and disposal methods. **Clerical Practices:** Administrative and clerical procedures and systems such as word processing, managing files and records, stenography and transcription, designing forms, and other office procedures and terminology. **Personnel and Human Resources:** Principles and procedures for personnel recruitment, selection, training, compensation and benefits, labor relations and negotiation, and personnel information systems.

Personality Type: Enterprising-Conventional. **Career Clusters:** 04 Business, Management, and Administration; 07 Government and Public Administration. **Career Pathways:** 07.1 Governance; 07.6 Regulation; 04.2 Business, Financial Management, and Accounting; 04.1 Management. **Other Jobs in These Pathways:** Accountants; Administrative Services Managers; Agents and Business Managers of Artists, Performers, and Athletes; Auditors; Billing, Cost, and Rate Clerks; Biofuels Production Managers; Bioinformatics Technicians; Biomass Power Plant Managers; Bookkeeping, Accounting, and Auditing Clerks; Brokerage Clerks; Brownfield Redevelopment Specialists and Site Managers; Budget Analysts; Business Continuity Planners; Business Operations Specialists, All Other; Business Teachers, Postsecondary; Chief Executives; Chief Sustainability Officers; Communications Teachers, Postsecondary; Compliance Managers; Computer and Information Systems Managers; Construction Managers; Cost Estimators; Credit Analysts; Customs Brokers; Economics Teachers, Postsecondary; Economists; Energy Auditors; Environmental Compliance Inspectors; Environmental Economists; Financial Analysts; Financial Examiners; Financial Managers, Branch or Department; First-Line Supervisors of Office and Administrative Support Workers; others.

Skills—Operations Analysis: Analyzing needs and product requirements to create a design. **Management of Personnel Resources:** Motivating, developing, and directing people as they work, identifying the best people for the job. **Systems Evaluation:** Identifying measures or indicators of system performance and the actions needed to improve or correct performance relative to the goals of the system. **Systems Analysis:** Determining how a system should work and how changes in conditions, operations, and the environment will affect outcomes. **Negotiation:** Bringing others together and trying to reconcile differences. **Coordination:** Adjusting actions in relation to others' actions. **Science:** Using scientific rules and methods to solve problems. **Writing:** Communicating effectively in writing as appropriate for the needs of the audience.

Work Environment: Indoors; sitting.

Job Specialization: Security Managers

Direct an organization's security functions, including physical security and safety of employees, facilities, and assets. Write or review security-related documents, such as incident reports, proposals, and tactical or strategic initiatives. Train subordinate security professionals or other organization members in security rules and procedures. Plan security for special and high-risk events. Review financial reports to ensure efficiency and quality of security operations. Develop budgets for security operations. Order security-related supplies and equipment as needed. Coordinate security operations or activities with public law enforcement, fire, and other agencies. Attend meetings, professional seminars, or conferences to keep abreast of changes in executive legislative directives or new technologies impacting security operations. Assist in emergency management and contingency planning. Arrange for or perform executive protection activities. Respond to medical emergencies, bomb threats, fire alarms, or intrusion alarms, following emergency response procedures. Recommend security procedures for security call centers, operations centers, domains, asset classification systems, system acquisition, system development, system maintenance, access control, program models, or reporting tools. Prepare reports or make presentations on internal investigations; losses; or violations of regulations, policies, and procedures. Identify, investigate, or resolve security breaches.

Education and Training Program: Security and Loss Prevention Services.

Personality Type: No data available. **Career Cluster:** 04 Business, Management, and Administration. **Career Pathways:** 04.2 Business, Financial Management, and Accounting; 04.1 Management. **Other Jobs in These Pathways:** Accountants; Administrative Services Managers; Agents and Business Managers of Artists, Performers, and Athletes; Auditors; Billing, Cost, and Rate Clerks; Biofuels Production Managers; Bioinformatics Technicians; Biomass Power Plant Managers; Bookkeeping, Accounting, and Auditing Clerks; Brokerage Clerks; Brownfield Redevelopment Specialists and Site Managers; Budget Analysts; Business Continuity Planners; Business Operations Specialists, All Other; Business Teachers, Postsecondary; Chief Executives; Chief Sustainability Officers; Communications Teachers, Postsecondary; Compliance Managers; Computer and Information Systems Managers; Construction Managers; Cost Estimators; Credit Analysts; Customs Brokers; Economics Teachers, Postsecondary; Economists; Energy Auditors; Environmental Economists; Financial Analysts; Financial Examiners; Financial Managers, Branch or Department; First-Line Supervisors of Office and Administrative Support Workers; others.

Work Environment: No data available.

Job Specialization: Supply Chain Managers

Direct or coordinate production, purchasing, warehousing, distribution, or financial forecasting services and activities to limit costs and improve accuracy, customer service, and safety. Examine existing procedures and opportunities for streamlining activities to meet product distribution needs. Direct the movement, storage, and processing of inventory. Select transportation routes to maximize economy by combining shipments and consolidating warehousing and distribution. Diagram supply chain models to help facilitate discussions with customers. Develop material costs forecasts or standard cost lists. Assess appropriate material-handling equipment needs and staffing levels to load, unload, move, or store materials. Appraise vendor manufacturing ability through on-site visits and measurements. Negotiate prices and terms with suppliers, vendors, or freight forwarders. Monitor supplier performance to assess ability to meet quality and delivery requirements. Monitor forecasts and quotas to identify changes or to determine their effect on supply chain activities. Meet with suppliers to discuss performance metrics, to provide performance feedback, or to discuss production forecasts or changes. Implement new or improved supply chain processes. Collaborate with other departments, such as procurement, engineering, and quality assurance, to identify or qualify new suppliers. Document physical supply chain processes such as workflows, cycle times, position responsibilities, and system flows. Develop and implement procedures or systems to evaluate and select suppliers. Design and implement plant warehousing strategies for production materials or finished products. Confer with supply chain planners to forecast demand or create supply plans that ensure availability of materials and products.

Education and Training Program: Logistics, Materials, and Supply Chain Management. **Knowledge/Courses—Production and Processing:** Raw materials, production processes, quality control, costs, and other techniques for maximizing the effective manufacture and distribution of goods. **Transportation:** Principles and methods for moving people or goods by air, rail, sea, or road, including the relative costs and benefits. **Economics and Accounting:** Economic and accounting principles and practices, the financial markets, banking, and the analysis and reporting of financial data. **Administration and Management:** Business and management principles involved in strategic planning, resource allocation, human resources modeling, leadership technique, production methods, and coordination of people and resources. **Geography:** Principles and methods for describing the features of land, sea, and air masses, including their physical characteristics, locations, interrelationships, and distribution of plant, animal, and human life. **Sales and Marketing:** Principles and methods for showing, promoting, and selling products or services. This includes marketing strategy and tactics, product demonstration, sales techniques, and sales control systems.

Personality Type: Enterprising-Conventional. **Career Clusters:** 04 Business, Management, and Administration; 09 Hospitality and Tourism; 10 Human Services; 16 Transportation, Distribution, and Logistics. **Career Pathways:** 04.1 Management; 04.2 Business, Financial Management, and Accounting; 09.3 Travel and Tourism; 10.3 Family and Community Services; 16.2 Logistics, Planning, and Management Services. **Other Jobs in These Pathways:** Accountants; Administrative Services

Managers; Agents and Business Managers of Artists, Performers, and Athletes; Auditors; Billing, Cost, and Rate Clerks; Biofuels Production Managers; Bioinformatics Technicians; Biomass Power Plant Managers; Bookkeeping, Accounting, and Auditing Clerks; Brokerage Clerks; Brownfield Redevelopment Specialists and Site Managers; Budget Analysts; Business Continuity Planners; Business Operations Specialists, All Other; Business Teachers, Postsecondary; Chief Executives; Chief Sustainability Officers; Child, Family, and School Social Workers; Childcare Workers; City and Regional Planning Aides; Communications Teachers, Postsecondary; Compliance Managers; Computer and Information Systems Managers; Construction Managers; Cost Estimators; Counselors, All Other; Credit Analysts; Customs Brokers; Economics Teachers, Postsecondary; Economists; Eligibility Interviewers, Government Programs; Energy Auditors; Environmental Economists; others.

Skills—Management of Material Resources: Obtaining and seeing to the appropriate use of equipment, facilities, and materials needed to do certain work. **Management of Financial Resources:** Determining how money will be spent to get the work done and accounting for these expenditures. **Systems Evaluation:** Identifying measures or indicators of system performance and the actions needed to improve or correct performance relative to the goals of the system. **Negotiation:** Bringing others together and trying to reconcile differences. **Monitoring:** Monitoring or assessing your performance or that of other individuals or organizations to make improvements or take corrective action. **Management of Personnel Resources:** Motivating, developing, and directing people as they work, identifying the best people for the job. **Systems Analysis:** Determining how a system should work and how changes in conditions, operations, and the environment will affect outcomes. **Complex Problem Solving:** Identifying complex problems and reviewing related information to develop and evaluate options and implement solutions.

Work Environment: Indoors; sitting.

Job Specialization: Wind Energy Operations Managers

Manage wind field operations, including personnel, maintenance activities, financial activities, and planning. Train, or coordinate the training of, employees in operations, safety, environmental issues, or technical issues. Track and maintain records for wind operations, such as site performance, downtime events, parts usage, and substation events. Provide technical support to wind field customers, employees, or subcontractors. Manage warranty repair or replacement services. Order parts, tools, or equipment needed to maintain, restore, or improve wind field operations. Maintain operations records such as work orders, site inspection forms, or other documentation. Negotiate or review and approve wind farm contracts. Recruit or select wind operations employees, contractors, or subcontractors. Monitor and maintain records of daily facility operations. Estimate costs associated with operations, including repairs and preventive maintenance. Establish goals, objectives, or priorities for wind field operations. Develop relationships and communicate with customers, site managers, developers, land owners, authorities, utility representatives, or residents. Develop processes and procedures for wind operations, including transitioning from construction to commercial operations. Prepare wind field operational budgets. Supervise employees or subcontractors to ensure quality of work or adherence to safety regulations or policies. Oversee the maintenance of wind field equipment or structures, such as towers, transformers, electrical collector systems, roadways, and other site assets.

Education and Training Program: Energy Management and Systems Technology/Technician.

Personality Type: No data available. **Career Cluster:** 04 Business, Management, and Administration. **Career Pathways:** 04.1 Management; 04.2 Business, Financial Management, and Accounting. **Other Jobs in These Pathways:** Accountants; Administrative Services Managers; Agents and Business Managers of Artists, Performers, and Athletes; Auditors; Billing, Cost, and Rate Clerks; Biofuels Production Managers; Bioinformatics Technicians; Biomass Power Plant Managers; Bookkeeping, Accounting, and Auditing Clerks; Brokerage Clerks; Brownfield Redevelopment Specialists and Site Managers; Budget Analysts; Business Continuity Planners; Business Operations Specialists, All Other; Business Teachers, Postsecondary; Chief Executives; Chief Sustainability Officers; Communications Teachers, Postsecondary; Compliance Managers; Computer and Information Systems Managers; Construction Managers; Cost Estimators; Credit Analysts; Customs Brokers; Economics Teachers, Postsecondary; Economists; Energy Auditors; Environmental Economists; Financial

Analysts; Financial Examiners; Financial Managers, Branch or Department; First-Line Supervisors of Office and Administrative Support Workers; others.

Work Environment: No data available.

Job Specialization: Wind Energy Project Managers

Lead or manage the development and evaluation of potential wind energy business opportunities, including environmental studies, permitting, and proposals. May also manage construction of projects. Supervise the work of subcontractors or consultants to ensure quality and conformance to specifications or budgets. Prepare requests for proposals (RFPs) for wind project construction or equipment acquisition. Manage site assessments or environmental studies for wind fields. Lead or support negotiations involving tax agreements or abatements, power purchase agreements, land use, or interconnection agreements. Update schedules, estimates, forecasts, or budgets for wind projects. Review or evaluate proposals or bids to make recommendations regarding the awarding of contracts. Provide verbal or written project status reports to project teams, management, subcontractors, customers, or owners. Review civil design, engineering, or construction technical documentation to ensure compliance with applicable government or industrial codes, standards, requirements, or regulations. Provide technical support for the design, construction, or commissioning of wind farm projects. Prepare wind project documentation, including diagrams or layouts. Manage wind project costs to stay within budget limits. Develop scope of work for wind project functions, such as design, site assessment, environmental studies, surveying, and field support services. Coordinate or direct development, energy assessment, engineering, or construction activities to ensure that wind project needs and objectives are met.

Education and Training Program: Energy Management and Systems Technology/Technician.

Personality Type: No data available. **Career Cluster:** 04 Business, Management, and Administration. **Career Pathways:** 04.1 Management; 04.2 Business, Financial Management, and Accounting. **Other Jobs in These Pathways:** Accountants; Administrative Services Managers; Agents and Business Managers of Artists, Performers, and Athletes; Auditors; Billing, Cost, and Rate Clerks; Biofuels

Production Managers; Bioinformatics Technicians; Biomass Power Plant Managers; Bookkeeping, Accounting, and Auditing Clerks; Brokerage Clerks; Brownfield Redevelopment Specialists and Site Managers; Budget Analysts; Business Continuity Planners; Business Operations Specialists, All Other; Business Teachers, Postsecondary; Chief Executives; Chief Sustainability Officers; Communications Teachers, Postsecondary; Compliance Managers; Computer and Information Systems Managers; Construction Managers; Cost Estimators; Credit Analysts; Customs Brokers; Economics Teachers, Postsecondary; Economists; Energy Auditors; Environmental Economists; Financial Analysts; Financial Examiners; Financial Managers, Branch or Department; First-Line Supervisors of Office and Administrative Support Workers; others.

Work Environment: No data available.

Massage Therapists

- ⊙ Annual Earnings: $35,830
- ⊙ Earnings Growth Potential: High (48.9%)
- ⊙ Growth: 20.1%
- ⊙ Annual Job Openings: 5,590
- ⊙ Self-Employed: 60.5%

Considerations for Job Outlook: In states that regulate massage therapy, opportunities should be available to those who complete formal training programs and pass a professionally recognized exam. However, new massage therapists should expect to work only part time in spas, hotels, hospitals, physical therapy centers, and other businesses until they can build their own client base. Because referrals are a very important source of work for massage therapists, networking will increase the number of job opportunities. Joining a professional association also can help build strong contacts and further increase the likelihood of steady work.

Perform therapeutic massages of soft tissues and joints. Confer with clients about their medical histories and problems with stress or pain to determine how massage will be most helpful. Apply finger and hand pressure to specific points of the body. Massage and knead muscles and soft tissues of the body to provide treatment for medical conditions, injuries, or wellness maintenance. Maintain treatment records. Provide clients with guidance and information about techniques for postural improvement and stretching, strengthening, relaxation, and rehabilitative exercises. Assess clients' soft tissue condition, joint quality and function, muscle strength, and range of motion. Develop and propose client treatment plans that specify which types of massage are to be used. Refer clients to other types of therapists when necessary. Use complementary aids, such as infrared lamps, wet compresses, ice, and whirlpool baths, to promote clients' recovery, relaxation, and well-being. Treat clients in professional settings or travel to clients' offices and homes. Consult with other health-care professionals, such as physiotherapists, chiropractors, physicians, and psychologists, to develop treatment plans for clients. Prepare and blend oils and apply the blends to clients' skin.

Education/Training Required: Postsecondary vocational training. **Education and Training Programs:** Asian Bodywork Therapy; Massage Therapy/Therapeutic Massage; Somatic Bodywork; Somatic Bodywork and Related Therapeutic Services, Other. **Knowledge/Courses—Sales and Marketing:** Principles and methods for showing, promoting, and selling products or services. This includes marketing strategy and tactics, product demonstration, sales techniques, and sales control systems. **Medicine and Dentistry:** The information and techniques needed to diagnose and treat human injuries, diseases, and deformities. This includes symptoms, treatment alternatives, drug properties and interactions, and preventive health-care measures. **Biology:** Plant and animal organisms and their tissues, cells, functions, interdependencies, and interactions with each other and the environment. **Therapy and Counseling:** Principles, methods, and procedures for diagnosis, treatment, and rehabilitation of physical and mental dysfunctions, and for career counseling and guidance. **Psychology:** Human behavior and performance; individual differences in ability, personality, and interests; learning and motivation; psychological research methods; and the assessment and treatment of behavioral and affective disorders. **Customer and Personal Service:** Principles and processes for providing customer and personal services. This includes customer needs assessment, meeting quality standards for services, and evaluation of customer satisfaction. **Work Experience Needed:** None. **On-the-Job Training Needed:** None. **Certification/Licensure:** Licensure.

Personality Type: Social-Realistic. **Career Cluster:** 08 Health Science. **Career Pathway:** 08.1 Therapeutic Services. **Other Jobs in This Pathway:** Acupuncturists;

Allergists and Immunologists; Anesthesiologists; Art Therapists; Chiropractors; Clinical Psychologists; Community and Social Service Specialists, All Other; Counseling Psychologists; Counselors, All Other; Dental Assistants; Dental Hygienists; Dentists, All Other Specialists; Dentists, General; Dermatologists; Diagnostic Medical Sonographers; Dietetic Technicians; Dietitians and Nutritionists; Family and General Practitioners; Health Diagnosing and Treating Practitioners, All Other; Health Specialties Teachers, Postsecondary; Health Technologists and Technicians, All Other; Healthcare Practitioners and Technical Workers, All Other; Healthcare Support Workers, All Other; Home Health Aides; Hospitalists; Industrial-Organizational Psychologists; Internists, General; Licensed Practical and Licensed Vocational Nurses; Life, Physical, and Social Science Technicians, All Other; Low Vision Therapists, Orientation and Mobility Specialists, and Vision Rehabilitation Therapists; others.

Skills—Service Orientation: Actively looking for ways to help people. **Speaking:** Talking to others to convey information effectively. **Social Perceptiveness:** Being aware of others' reactions and understanding why they react as they do.

Work Environment: Indoors; standing; using hands; repetitive motions.

Meat, Poultry, and Fish Cutters and Trimmers

- ⊙ Annual Earnings: $22,720
- ⊙ Earnings Growth Potential: Very low (23.3%)
- ⊙ Growth: 15.5%
- ⊙ Annual Job Openings: 7,400
- ⊙ Self-Employed: 0.9%

Considerations for Job Outlook: More people around the world are demanding prepared and precut food. Also, more people are buying partially prepared and easy-to-cook products. Both of these trends are expected to drive demand for food processing workers. These trends will create growth.

Use hand or hand tools to perform routine cutting and trimming of meat, poultry, and seafood. Use knives, cleavers, meat saws, bandsaws, or other equipment to perform meat cutting and trimming. Clean, trim, slice, and section carcasses for future processing. Cut and trim meat to prepare for packing. Remove parts, such as skin, feathers, scales, or bones, from carcass. Inspect meat products for defects, bruises, or blemishes and remove them along with any excess fat. Produce hamburger meat and meat trimmings. Process primal parts into cuts that are ready for retail use. Obtain and distribute specified meat or carcass. Separate meats and byproducts into specified containers and seal containers. Weigh meats and tag containers for weight and contents. Clean and salt hides. Prepare sausages, luncheon meats, hot dogs, and other fabricated meat products, using meat trimmings and hamburger meat. Prepare ready-to-heat foods by filleting meat or fish or cutting it into bite-sized pieces, preparing and adding vegetables, or applying sauces or breading.

Education/Training Required: Less than high school. **Education and Training Program:** Meat Cutting/Meat Cutter Training. **Knowledge/Courses—Food Production:** Techniques and equipment for planting, growing, and harvesting food products (both plant and animal) for consumption, including storage/handling techniques. **Production and Processing:** Raw materials, production processes, quality control, costs, and other techniques for maximizing the effective manufacture and distribution of goods. **Mechanical Devices:** Machines and tools, including their designs, uses, repair, and maintenance. **Work Experience Needed:** None. **On-the-Job Training Needed:** Short-term on-the-job training. **Certification/Licensure:** Voluntary certification for some specializations.

Personality Type: Realistic. **Career Cluster:** 09 Hospitality and Tourism. **Career Pathway:** 09.1 Restaurants and Food/Beverage Services. **Other Jobs in This Pathway:** Bakers; Baristas; Bartenders; Butchers and Meat Cutters; Chefs and Head Cooks; Combined Food Preparation and Serving Workers, Including Fast Food; Cooks, All Other; Cooks, Fast Food; Cooks, Institution and Cafeteria; Cooks, Private Household; Cooks, Restaurant; Cooks, Short Order; Counter Attendants, Cafeteria, Food Concession, and Coffee Shop; Dining Room and Cafeteria Attendants and Bartender Helpers; Dishwashers; First-Line Supervisors of Food Preparation and Serving Workers; Food Preparation and Serving Related Workers, All Other; Food Preparation Workers; Food Servers, Nonrestaurant; Food Service Managers; Gaming Managers; Hosts

and Hostesses, Restaurant, Lounge, and Coffee Shop; Slaughterers and Meat Packers; Waiters and Waitresses.

Skills—Troubleshooting: Determining causes of operating errors and deciding what to do about them. **Operation and Control:** Controlling operations of equipment or systems.

Work Environment: Indoors; standing; walking and running; using hands; repetitive motions; noise; very hot or cold; hazardous equipment.

Mechanical Door Repairers

- ⊙ Annual Earnings: $36,640
- ⊙ Earnings Growth Potential: Medium (35.6%)
- ⊙ Growth: 24.2%
- ⊙ Annual Job Openings: 550
- ⊙ Self-Employed: 0.0%

Considerations for Job Outlook: Rapid employment growth is projected.

Install, service, or repair automatic door mechanisms and hydraulic doors. Adjust doors to open or close with the correct amount of effort, and make simple adjustments to electric openers. Wind large springs with upward motion of arm. Inspect job sites, assessing headroom, side room, and other conditions in order to determine appropriateness of door for a given location. Collect payment upon job completion. Complete required paperwork, such as work orders, according to services performed or required. Fasten angle iron back-hangers to ceilings and tracks, using fasteners or welding equipment. Repair or replace worn or broken door parts, using hand tools. Carry springs to tops of doors, using ladders or scaffolding, and attach springs to tracks in order to install spring systems. Set doors into place or stack hardware sections into openings after rail or track installation. Install door frames, rails, steel rolling curtains, electronic-eye mechanisms, and electric door openers and closers, using power tools, hand tools, and electronic test equipment. Remove or disassemble defective automatic mechanical door closers, using hand tools. Apply hardware to door sections, such as drilling holes to install locks. Assemble and fasten tracks to structures or bucks, using impact wrenches or welding equipment. Run low-voltage wiring on ceiling surfaces, using insulated staples. Cut door stops and angle irons to fit openings. Study blueprints and schematic diagrams in order to determine appropriate methods of installing and repairing automated door openers. Operate lifts, winches, or chain falls in order to move heavy curtain doors. Order replacement springs, sections, and slats. Bore and cut holes in flooring as required for installation, using hand tools and power tools. Set in and secure floor treadles for door activating mechanisms; then connect power packs and electrical panelboards to treadles. Lubricate door closer oil chambers and pack spindles with leather washers. Install dock seals, bumpers, and shelters.

Education/Training Required: High school diploma or equivalent. **Education and Training Program:** Industrial Mechanics and Maintenance Technology. **Knowledge/ Courses—Building and Construction:** Materials, methods, and the tools involved in the construction or repair of houses, buildings, or other structures such as highways and roads. **Mechanical Devices:** Machines and tools, including their designs, uses, repair, and maintenance. **Engineering and Technology:** The practical application of engineering science and technology. This includes applying principles, techniques, procedures, and equipment to the design and production of various goods and services. **Sales and Marketing:** Principles and methods for showing, promoting, and selling products or services. This includes marketing strategy and tactics, product demonstration, sales techniques, and sales control systems. **Design:** Design techniques, tools, and principles involved in production of precision technical plans, blueprints, drawings, and models. **Work Experience Needed:** None. **On-the-Job Training Needed:** Moderate-term on-the-job training. **Certification/Licensure:** None.

Personality Type: Realistic. **Career Cluster:** 13 Manufacturing. **Career Pathway:** 13.3 Maintenance, Installation, and Repair. **Other Jobs in This Pathway:** Aircraft Mechanics and Service Technicians; Automotive Engineering Technicians; Automotive Specialty Technicians; Avionics Technicians; Biological Technicians; Camera and Photographic Equipment Repairers; Chemical Equipment Operators and Tenders; Civil Engineering Technicians; Coil Winders, Tapers, and Finishers; Computer, Automated Teller, and Office Machine Repairers; Construction and Related Workers, All Other; Control and Valve Installers and Repairers, Except Mechanical Door; Electric Motor, Power Tool, and Related Repairers; Electrical and Electronic Equipment Assemblers; Electrical and Electronics Repairers, Commercial and Industrial Equipment; Electrical and Electronics Repairers, Powerhouse, Substation, and Relay; Electrical Engineering Technicians; Electrical Engineering Technologists; Electromechanical Engineering Technologists; Electromechanical Equipment Assemblers; Electronics Engineering Technicians; Electronics Engineering Technologists; others.

Skills—Installation: Installing equipment, machines, wiring, or programs to meet specifications. **Repairing:** Repairing machines or systems using the needed tools. **Equipment Maintenance:** Performing routine maintenance on equipment and determining when and what kind of maintenance is needed. **Troubleshooting:** Determining causes of operating errors and deciding what to do about them. **Equipment Selection:** Determining the kind of tools and equipment needed to do a job. **Quality Control Analysis:** Conducting tests and inspections of products, services, or processes to evaluate quality or performance. **Operation and Control:** Controlling operations of equipment or systems. **Technology Design:** Generating or adapting equipment and technology to serve user needs.

Work Environment: Outdoors; standing; climbing; walking and running; using hands; bending or twisting the body; repetitive motions; noise; very hot or cold; bright or inadequate lighting; contaminants; high places; hazardous equipment; minor burns, cuts, bites, or stings.

Mechanical Drafters

- ⊙ Annual Earnings: $49,200
- ⊙ Earnings Growth Potential: Low (34.4%)
- ⊙ Growth: 11.1%
- ⊙ Annual Job Openings: 2,050
- ⊙ Self-Employed: 4.1%

Considerations for Job Outlook: New software, such as PDM and BIM, will require drafters to work in collaboration with other professionals on projects, whether constructing a new building or manufacturing a new product. This new software, however, requires that someone build and maintain large databases. Workers with knowledge of drafting and of the software will be needed to oversee these databases. Many drafting jobs are in construction and manufacturing, so they are subject to the ups and downs of those industries. Demand for particular drafting specialties varies across the country because jobs depend on the needs of local industries.

Prepare detailed working diagrams of machinery and mechanical devices, including dimensions, fastening methods, and other engineering information. Develop detailed design drawings and specifications for mechanical equipment, dies, tools, and controls, using computer-assisted drafting (CAD) equipment. Lay out and draw schematic, orthographic, or angle views to depict functional relationships of components, assemblies, systems, and machines. Coordinate with and consult other workers to design, lay out, or detail components and systems and to resolve design or other problems. Check dimensions of materials to be used and assign numbers to the materials. Review and analyze specifications, sketches, drawings, ideas, and related data to assess factors affecting component designs and the procedures and instructions to be followed. Modify and revise designs to correct operating deficiencies or to reduce production problems. Compute mathematical formulas to develop and design detailed specifications for components or machinery using computer-assisted equipment. Position instructions and comments onto drawings. Lay out, draw, and reproduce illustrations for reference manuals and technical publications to describe operation and maintenance of mechanical systems. Design scale or full-size blueprints of specialty items such as furniture and automobile body or chassis components. Confer with customer representatives to review schematics and answer questions pertaining to installation of systems. Supervise and train other drafters, technologists, and technicians. Draw freehand sketches of designs, trace finished drawings onto designated paper for the reproduction of blueprints, and reproduce working drawings on copy machines. Shade or color drawings to clarify and emphasize details and dimensions or eliminate background using ink, crayon, airbrush, and overlays.

Education/Training Required: Associate degree. **Education and Training Program:** Mechanical Drafting and Mechanical Drafting CAD/CADD. **Knowledge/Courses—Design:** Design techniques, tools, and principles involved in production of precision technical plans, blueprints, drawings, and models. **Engineering and Technology:** The practical application of engineering science and technology. This includes applying principles, techniques, procedures, and equipment to the design and production of various goods and services. **Mechanical**

Devices: Machines and tools, including their designs, uses, repair, and maintenance. **Physics:** Physical principles, laws, their interrelationships, and applications to understanding fluid, material, and atmospheric dynamics, and mechanical, electrical, atomic, and subatomic structures and processes. **Mathematics:** Arithmetic, algebra, geometry, calculus, statistics, and their applications. **Production and Processing:** Raw materials, production processes, quality control, costs, and other techniques for maximizing the effective manufacture and distribution of goods. **Work Experience Needed:** None. **On-the-Job Training Needed:** None. **Certification/Licensure:** Voluntary certification by association.

Personality Type: Realistic-Conventional-Investigative. **Career Cluster:** 02 Architecture and Construction. **Career Pathway:** 02.1 Design/Pre-Construction. **Other Jobs in This Pathway:** Architects, Except Landscape and Naval; Architectural and Engineering Managers; Architectural Drafters; Architecture Teachers, Postsecondary; Cartographers and Photogrammetrists; Civil Drafters; Civil Engineering Technicians; Drafters, All Other; Electrical Drafters; Electronic Drafters; Engineering Teachers, Postsecondary; Engineering Technicians, Except Drafters, All Other; Engineers, All Other; Geodetic Surveyors; Interior Designers; Landscape Architects; Surveying Technicians; Surveyors.

Skills—Programming: Writing computer programs for various purposes. **Technology Design:** Generating or adapting equipment and technology to serve user needs. **Mathematics:** Using mathematics to solve problems. **Operations Analysis:** Analyzing needs and product requirements to create a design. **Quality Control Analysis:** Conducting tests and inspections of products, services, or processes to evaluate quality or performance. **Active Learning:** Understanding the implications of new information for both current and future problem solving and decision making. **Systems Evaluation:** Identifying measures or indicators of system performance and the actions needed to improve or correct performance relative to the goals of the system. **Systems Analysis:** Determining how a system should work and how changes in conditions, operations, and the environment will affect outcomes.

Work Environment: Indoors; sitting; using hands; repetitive motions.

Mechanical Engineering Technicians

- ⊙ Annual Earnings: $51,350
- ⊙ Earnings Growth Potential: Medium (35.9%)
- ⊙ Growth: 4.0%
- ⊙ Annual Job Openings: 1,040
- ⊙ Self-Employed: 0.5%

Considerations for Job Outlook: Mastering new technology and software will likely become more important for this occupation. Those who stay aware of the latest developments should have the best job prospects.

Apply theory and principles of mechanical engineering under direction of engineering staff or physical scientists. Read dials and meters to determine amperage, voltage, and electrical output and input at specific operating temperatures to analyze parts performance. Analyze test results in relation to design or rated specifications and test objectives, and modify or adjust equipment to meet specifications. Evaluate tool drawing designs by measuring drawing dimensions and comparing with original specifications for form and function using engineering skills. Devise, fabricate, and assemble new or modified mechanical components for products such as industrial machinery or equipment, and measuring instruments. Discuss changes in design, method of manufacture and assembly, and drafting techniques and procedures with staff and coordinate corrections. Operate drill presses, grinders, engine lathes, or other machines to modify parts tested or to fabricate experimental parts for testing. Review project instructions and blueprints to ascertain test specifications, procedures, and objectives, and test nature of technical problems such as redesign. Set up and conduct tests of complete units and components under operational conditions to investigate proposals for improving equipment performance. Record test procedures and results, numerical and graphical data, and recommendations for changes in product or test methods. Review project instructions and specifications to identify, modify, and plan requirements fabrication, assembly, and testing. Confer with technicians, submit reports of test results to engineering department, and recommend design or material changes. Prepare parts sketches and write work orders and purchase requests to be furnished by outside contractors. Calculate required capacities for equipment of proposed systems to obtain specified performance and submit data to engineering personnel for approval. Draft detail drawings or sketches for drafting room completion or to request parts fabrication by machine, sheet, or wood shops.

Education/Training Required: Associate degree. **Education and Training Programs:** Mechanical Engineering Related Technologies/Technicians, Other; Mechanical Engineering/Mechanical Technology/Technician. **Knowledge/Courses—Mechanical Devices:** Machines and tools, including their designs, uses, repair, and maintenance. **Design:** Design techniques, tools, and principles involved in production of precision technical plans, blueprints, drawings, and models. **Engineering and Technology:** The practical application of engineering science and technology. This includes applying principles, techniques, procedures, and equipment to the design and production of various goods and services. **Physics:** Physical principles, laws, their interrelationships, and applications to understanding fluid, material, and atmospheric dynamics, and mechanical, electrical, atomic, and subatomic structures and processes. **Production and Processing:** Raw materials, production processes, quality control, costs, and other techniques for maximizing the effective manufacture and distribution of goods. **Chemistry:** The chemical composition, structure, and properties of substances and of the chemical processes and transformations that they undergo. This includes uses of chemicals and their danger signs, production techniques, and disposal methods. **Work Experience Needed:** None. **On-the-Job Training Needed:** None. **Certification/Licensure:** None.

Personality Type: Realistic-Investigative. **Career Clusters:** 01 Agriculture, Food, and Natural Resources; 13 Manufacturing. **Career Pathways:** 13.3 Maintenance, Installation, and Repair; 01.5 Natural Resources Systems. **Other Jobs in These Pathways:** Aircraft Mechanics and Service Technicians; Automotive Engineering Technicians; Automotive Specialty Technicians; Avionics Technicians; Biological Science Teachers, Postsecondary; Biological Technicians; Camera and Photographic Equipment Repairers; Chemical Equipment Operators and Tenders; Civil Engineering Technicians; Climate Change Analysts; Coil Winders, Tapers, and Finishers; Computer, Automated Teller, and Office Machine Repairers; Construction and Related Workers, All Other; Control and Valve Installers and Repairers, Except Mechanical Door; Conveyor Operators and Tenders; Derrick Operators, Oil and Gas; Electric Motor, Power Tool, and Related Repairers;

Electrical and Electronic Equipment Assemblers; Electrical and Electronics Repairers, Commercial and Industrial Equipment; Electrical and Electronics Repairers, Powerhouse, Substation, and Relay; Electrical Engineering Technicians; Electrical Engineering Technologists; Electromechanical Engineering Technologists; others.

Skills—Equipment Maintenance: Performing routine maintenance on equipment and determining when and what kind of maintenance is needed. **Repairing:** Repairing machines or systems using the needed tools. **Troubleshooting:** Determining causes of operating errors and deciding what to do about them. **Science:** Using scientific rules and methods to solve problems. **Operation and Control:** Controlling operations of equipment or systems. **Quality Control Analysis:** Conducting tests and inspections of products, services, or processes to evaluate quality or performance. **Equipment Selection:** Determining the kind of tools and equipment needed to do a job. **Operations Analysis:** Analyzing needs and product requirements to create a design.

Work Environment: Indoors; standing; using hands; noise; contaminants; hazardous equipment.

Job Specialization: Automotive Engineering Technicians

Assist engineers in determining the practicality of proposed product design changes, and plan and carry out tests on experimental test devices and equipment for performance, durability, and efficiency. Develop instrumentation and laboratory test equipment for special purposes. Order new test equipment, supplies, or replacement parts. Set up mechanical, hydraulic, or electric test equipment in accordance with engineering specifications, standards, or test procedures. Recommend tests or testing conditions in accordance with designs, customer requirements, or industry standards to ensure test validity. Monitor computer-controlled test equipment according to written or verbal instructions. Read and interpret blueprints, schematics, work specifications, drawings, or charts. Maintain test equipment in operational condition by performing routine maintenance or making minor repairs or adjustments as needed. Install equipment such as instrumentation, test equipment, engines, and aftermarket products to ensure proper interfaces. Inspect and test parts to determine nature or cause of defects and malfunctions. Document test results

using cameras, spreadsheets, documents, or other tools. Fabricate prototype components or fixtures, or modify existing prototypes. Analyze test data for automotive systems, subsystems, or component parts. Calibrate test equipment. Recommend product or component design improvements based on data and observations. Perform or execute manual and automated tests of automotive system or component performance, efficiency, and durability.

Education and Training Programs: Mechanical Engineering Related Technologies/Technicians, Other; Mechanical Engineering/Mechanical Technology/Technician.

Personality Type: No data available. **Career Cluster:** 13 Manufacturing. **Career Pathway:** 13.3 Maintenance, Installation, and Repair. **Other Jobs in This Pathway:** Aircraft Mechanics and Service Technicians; Automotive Specialty Technicians; Avionics Technicians; Biological Technicians; Camera and Photographic Equipment Repairers; Chemical Equipment Operators and Tenders; Civil Engineering Technicians; Coil Winders, Tapers, and Finishers; Computer, Automated Teller, and Office Machine Repairers; Construction and Related Workers, All Other; Control and Valve Installers and Repairers, Except Mechanical Door; Electric Motor, Power Tool, and Related Repairers; Electrical and Electronic Equipment Assemblers; Electrical and Electronics Repairers, Commercial and Industrial Equipment; Electrical and Electronics Repairers, Powerhouse, Substation, and Relay; Electrical Engineering Technicians; Electrical Engineering Technologists; Electromechanical Engineering Technologists; Electromechanical Equipment Assemblers; Electronics Engineering Technicians; Electronics Engineering Technologists; Elevator Installers and Repairers; others.

Work Environment: No data available.

Medical and Clinical Laboratory Technicians

- ⊙ Annual Earnings: $36,950
- ⊙ Earnings Growth Potential: Low (33.5%)
- ⊙ Growth: 14.8%
- ⊙ Annual Job Openings: 5,510
- ⊙ Self-Employed: 0.8%

Considerations for Job Outlook: An increase in the aging population will lead to a greater need to diagnose medical conditions, such as cancer or type 2 diabetes, through laboratory procedures. Medical laboratory technologists and technicians will be needed to use and maintain the equipment needed for diagnosis and treatment.

Perform routine medical laboratory tests for the diagnosis, treatment, and prevention of disease. May work under the supervision of a medical technologist. Conduct chemical analyses of bodily fluids, such as blood and urine, using microscope or automatic analyzer to detect abnormalities or diseases, and enter findings into computer. Set up, adjust, maintain, and clean medical laboratory equipment. Analyze the results of tests and experiments to ensure conformity to specifications, using special mechanical and electrical devices. Analyze and record test data to issue reports that use charts, graphs, and narratives. Conduct blood tests for transfusion purposes, and perform blood counts. Perform medical research to further control and cure disease. Obtain specimens, cultivating, isolating, and identifying microorganisms for analysis. Examine cells stained with dye to locate abnormalities. Collect blood or tissue samples from patients, observing principles of asepsis to obtain blood sample. Consult with pathologists to determine final diagnoses when abnormal cells are found. Inoculate fertilized eggs, broths, or other bacteriological media with organisms. Cut, stain, and mount tissue samples for examination by pathologists. Supervise and instruct other technicians and laboratory assistants. Prepare standard volumetric solutions and reagents to be combined with samples, following standardized formulas or experimental procedures. Prepare vaccines and serums by standard laboratory methods, testing for virus inactivity and sterility.

Education/Training Required: Associate degree. **Education and Training Programs:** Blood Bank Technology Specialist Training; Clinical/Medical Laboratory Assistant Training; Clinical/Medical Laboratory Technician; Hematology Technology/Technician; Histologic Technician Training. **Knowledge/Courses—Chemistry:** The chemical composition, structure, and properties of substances and of the chemical processes and transformations that they undergo. This includes uses of chemicals and their danger signs, production techniques, and disposal methods. **Medicine and Dentistry:** The information and techniques needed to diagnose and treat human injuries, diseases, and deformities. This includes symptoms,

treatment alternatives, drug properties and interactions, and preventive health-care measures. **Biology:** Plant and animal organisms and their tissues, cells, functions, interdependencies, and interactions with each other and the environment. **Mechanical Devices:** Machines and tools, including their designs, uses, repair, and maintenance. **Computers and Electronics:** Circuit boards, processors, chips, electronic equipment, and computer hardware and software, including applications and programming. **Production and Processing:** Raw materials, production processes, quality control, costs, and other techniques for maximizing the effective manufacture and distribution of goods. **Work Experience Needed:** None. **On-the-Job Training Needed:** None. **Certification/Licensure:** Voluntary certification by association.

Personality Type: Realistic-Investigative-Conventional. **Career Cluster:** 08 Health Science. **Career Pathways:** 08.1 Therapeutic Services; 08.2 Diagnostics Services. **Other Jobs in These Pathways:** Acupuncturists; Allergists and Immunologists; Ambulance Drivers and Attendants, Except Emergency Medical Technicians; Anesthesiologist Assistants; Anesthesiologists; Art Therapists; Athletic Trainers; Cardiovascular Technologists and Technicians; Chiropractors; Clinical Psychologists; Community and Social Service Specialists, All Other; Counseling Psychologists; Counselors, All Other; Cytogenetic Technologists; Cytotechnologists; Dental Assistants; Dental Hygienists; Dentists, All Other Specialists; Dentists, General; Dermatologists; Diagnostic Medical Sonographers; Dietetic Technicians; Dietitians and Nutritionists; Emergency Medical Technicians and Paramedics; Endoscopy Technicians; Family and General Practitioners; Health Diagnosing and Treating Practitioners, All Other; Health Specialties Teachers, Postsecondary; Health Technologists and Technicians, All Other; Healthcare Practitioners and Technical Workers, All Other; Healthcare Support Workers, All Other; others.

Skills—Science: Using scientific rules and methods to solve problems. **Equipment Maintenance:** Performing routine maintenance on equipment and determining when and what kind of maintenance is needed. **Equipment Selection:** Determining the kind of tools and equipment needed to do a job. **Troubleshooting:** Determining causes of operating errors and deciding what to do about them. **Repairing:** Repairing machines or systems using the needed tools. **Operation and Control:** Controlling operations of equipment or systems. **Quality Control Analysis:** Conducting tests and inspections of products, services, or processes to evaluate quality or performance. **Operation Monitoring:** Watching gauges, dials, or other indicators to make sure a machine is working properly.

Work Environment: Indoors; standing; walking and running; using hands; repetitive motions; noise; contaminants; exposed to disease or infections; hazardous conditions.

Medical Assistants

- ⊙ Annual Earnings: $29,100
- ⊙ Earnings Growth Potential: Low (28.2%)
- ⊙ Growth: 30.9%
- ⊙ Annual Job Openings: 24,380
- ⊙ Self-Employed: 0.0%

Considerations for Job Outlook: The growth of the aging baby-boom population will continue to spur demand for preventive medical services, which are often provided by physicians. As their practices expand, physicians will hire more assistants to perform routine administrative and clinical duties, allowing the physicians to see more patients. Assistants will likely continue to be used in place of more expensive workers, such as nurses, to reduce costs. In addition, an increasing number of group practices, clinics, and other health-care facilities need support workers, particularly medical assistants, to do both administrative and clinical duties.

Perform administrative and certain clinical duties under the direction of a physician. Record patients' medical history, vital statistics, and information such as test results in medical records. Prepare treatment rooms for patient examinations, keeping the rooms neat and clean. Interview patients to obtain medical information, and measure their vital signs, weights, and heights. Authorize drug refills, and provide prescription information to pharmacies. Clean and sterilize instruments, and dispose of contaminated supplies. Prepare and administer medications as directed by a physician. Show patients to examination rooms, and prepare them for the physician. Explain treatment procedures, medications, diets, and physicians' instructions to patients. Help physicians examine and treat patients, handing them instruments and materials or performing such tasks as giving injections or removing sutures.

Collect blood, tissue, or other laboratory specimens, log the specimens, and prepare them for testing. Perform routine laboratory tests and sample analyses. Contact medical facilities or departments to schedule patients for tests or admission. Operate X-ray, electrocardiogram (EKG), and other equipment to administer routine diagnostic tests. Change dressings on wounds. Set up medical laboratory equipment. Perform general office duties such as answering telephones, taking dictation, or completing insurance forms. Greet and log in patients arriving at office or clinic. Schedule appointments for patients. Inventory and order medical, lab, or office supplies and equipment.

Education/Training Required: High school diploma or equivalent. **Education and Training Programs:** Allied Health and Medical Assisting Services, Other; Anesthesiologist Assistant Training; Chiropractic Assistant/Technician Training; Medical Administrative/Executive Assistant and Medical Secretary Training; Medical Insurance Coding Specialist/Coder Training; Medical Office Assistant/Specialist Training; Medical Office Management/Administration; Medical Reception/Receptionist; Medical/Clinical Assistant Training; Ophthalmic Technician/Technologist Training; Optometric Technician/Assistant Training; Orthoptics/Orthoptist. **Knowledge/Courses—Medicine and Dentistry:** The information and techniques needed to diagnose and treat human injuries, diseases, and deformities. This includes symptoms, treatment alternatives, drug properties and interactions, and preventive health-care measures. **Clerical Practices:** Administrative and clerical procedures and systems such as word processing, managing files and records, stenography and transcription, designing forms, and other office procedures and terminology. **Psychology:** Human behavior and performance; individual differences in ability, personality, and interests; learning and motivation; psychological research methods; and the assessment and treatment of behavioral and affective disorders. **Therapy and Counseling:** Principles, methods, and procedures for diagnosis, treatment, and rehabilitation of physical and mental dysfunctions, and for career counseling and guidance. **Customer and Personal Service:** Principles and processes for providing customer and personal services. This includes customer needs assessment, meeting quality standards for services, and evaluation of customer satisfaction. **Public Safety and Security:** Relevant equipment, policies, procedures, and strategies to promote effective local, state, or national security operations for the protection of people, data, property, and institutions.

Work Experience Needed: None. **On-the-Job Training Needed:** Moderate-term on-the-job training. **Certification/Licensure:** Voluntary certification by association.

Personality Type: Social-Conventional-Realistic. **Career Cluster:** 08 Health Science. **Career Pathways:** 08.2 Diagnostics Services; 08.3 Health Informatics. **Other Jobs in These Pathways:** Ambulance Drivers and Attendants, Except Emergency Medical Technicians; Anesthesiologist Assistants; Athletic Trainers; Cardiovascular Technologists and Technicians; Clinical Psychologists; Communications Teachers, Postsecondary; Cytogenetic Technologists; Cytotechnologists; Dental Laboratory Technicians; Diagnostic Medical Sonographers; Editors; Emergency Medical Technicians and Paramedics; Endoscopy Technicians; Engineers, All Other; Executive Secretaries and Executive Administrative Assistants; Fine Artists, Including Painters, Sculptors, and Illustrators; First-Line Supervisors of Office and Administrative Support Workers; Health Diagnosing and Treating Practitioners, All Other; Health Educators; Health Specialties Teachers, Postsecondary; Health Technologists and Technicians, All Other; Healthcare Practitioners and Technical Workers, All Other; Histotechnologists and Histologic Technicians; Medical and Clinical Laboratory Technicians; Medical and Clinical Laboratory Technologists; others.

Skills—Service Orientation: Actively looking for ways to help people. **Active Listening:** Giving full attention to what other people are saying, taking time to understand the points being made, asking questions as appropriate, and not interrupting at inappropriate times. **Science:** Using scientific rules and methods to solve problems. **Speaking:** Talking to others to convey information effectively. **Social Perceptiveness:** Being aware of others' reactions and understanding why they react as they do. **Negotiation:** Bringing others together and trying to reconcile differences. **Operation Monitoring:** Watching gauges, dials, or other indicators to make sure a machine is working properly. **Monitoring:** Monitoring or assessing your performance or that of other individuals or organizations to make improvements or take corrective action.

Work Environment: Indoors; standing; walking and running; using hands; repetitive motions; exposed to disease or infections.

Medical Equipment Preparers

- Annual Earnings: $30,050
- Earnings Growth Potential: Low (31.8%)
- Growth: 17.5%
- Annual Job Openings: 1,620
- Self-Employed: 2.3%

Considerations for Job Outlook: About-average employment growth is projected.

Prepare, sterilize, install, or clean laboratory or healthcare equipment. Organize and assemble routine and specialty surgical instrument trays and other sterilized supplies, filling special requests as needed. Clean instruments to prepare them for sterilization. Operate and maintain steam autoclaves, keeping records of loads completed, items in loads, and maintenance procedures performed. Record sterilizer test results. Start equipment and observe gauges and equipment operation to detect malfunctions and to ensure equipment is operating to prescribed standards. Examine equipment to detect leaks, worn or loose parts, or other indications of disrepair. Report defective equipment to appropriate supervisors or staff. Check sterile supplies to ensure that they are not outdated. Attend hospital in-service programs related to areas of work specialization. Purge wastes from equipment by connecting equipment to water sources and flushing water through systems. Stock crash carts or other medical supplies.

Education/Training Required: High school diploma or equivalent. **Education and Training Programs:** Allied Health and Medical Assisting Services, Other; Medical/Clinical Assistant Training. **Knowledge/Courses—Production and Processing:** Raw materials, production processes, quality control, costs, and other techniques for maximizing the effective manufacture and distribution of goods. **Chemistry:** The chemical composition, structure, and properties of substances and of the chemical processes and transformations that they undergo. This includes uses of chemicals and their danger signs, production techniques, and disposal methods. **Customer and Personal Service:** Principles and processes for providing customer and personal services. This includes customer needs assessment, meeting quality standards for services, and evaluation of customer satisfaction. **Biology:** Plant and animal organisms and their tissues, cells, functions, interdependencies, and interactions with each other and the environment. **Medicine and Dentistry:** The information and techniques needed to diagnose and treat human injuries, diseases, and deformities. This includes symptoms, treatment alternatives, drug properties and interactions, and preventive health-care measures. **Public Safety and Security:** Relevant equipment, policies, procedures, and strategies to promote effective local, state, or national security operations for the protection of people, data, property, and institutions. **Work Experience Needed:** None. **On-the-Job Training Needed:** Moderate-term on-the-job training. **Certification/Licensure:** Voluntary certification by association for some specializations.

Personality Type: Realistic-Conventional-Investigative. **Career Cluster:** 08 Health Science. **Career Pathways:** 08.1 Therapeutic Services; 08.2 Diagnostics Services. **Other Jobs in These Pathways:** Acupuncturists; Allergists and Immunologists; Ambulance Drivers and Attendants, Except Emergency Medical Technicians; Anesthesiologist Assistants; Anesthesiologists; Art Therapists; Athletic Trainers; Cardiovascular Technologists and Technicians; Chiropractors; Clinical Psychologists; Community and Social Service Specialists, All Other; Counseling Psychologists; Counselors, All Other; Cytogenetic Technologists; Cytotechnologists; Dental Assistants; Dental Hygienists; Dentists, All Other Specialists; Dentists, General; Dermatologists; Diagnostic Medical Sonographers; Dietetic Technicians; Dietitians and Nutritionists; Emergency Medical Technicians and Paramedics; Endoscopy Technicians; Family and General Practitioners; Health Diagnosing and Treating Practitioners, All Other; Health Specialties Teachers, Postsecondary; Health Technologists and Technicians, All Other; Healthcare Practitioners and Technical Workers, All Other; Healthcare Support Workers, All Other; others.

Skills—Installation: Installing equipment, machines, wiring, or programs to meet specifications. **Equipment Maintenance:** Performing routine maintenance on equipment and determining when and what kind of maintenance is needed. **Repairing:** Repairing machines or systems using the needed tools. **Equipment Selection:** Determining the kind of tools and equipment needed to do a job. **Troubleshooting:** Determining causes of operating errors and deciding what to do about them. **Operation and Control:** Controlling operations of equipment or systems. **Quality Control Analysis:** Conducting tests and inspections of products, services, or processes to evaluate quality or performance. **Operation Monitoring:** Watching gauges, dials, or other indicators to make sure a machine is working properly.

Work Environment: Indoors; standing; walking and running; using hands; bending or twisting the body; repetitive motions; noise; contaminants; exposed to disease or infections; hazardous conditions.

Medical Equipment Repairers

- ⊙ Annual Earnings: $44,870
- ⊙ Earnings Growth Potential: High (41.5%)
- ⊙ Growth: 31.4%
- ⊙ Annual Job Openings: 2,230
- ⊙ Self-Employed: 13.0%

Considerations for Job Outlook: A combination of rapid employment growth and the need to replace workers leaving the occupation will likely result in excellent job opportunities from 2010 to 2020. Candidates who have an associate degree in biomedical equipment technology or engineering should have the best job prospects. Job opportunities should be even better for those who are willing to relocate, because often there are relatively few qualified applicants in rural areas.

Test, adjust, or repair biomedical or electromedical equipment. Inspect and test malfunctioning medical and related equipment following manufacturers' specifications, using test and analysis instruments. Examine medical equipment and facility's structural environment, and check for proper use of equipment to protect patients and staff from electrical or mechanical hazards and to ensure compliance with safety regulations. Disassemble malfunctioning equipment, and remove, repair, and replace defective parts such as motors, clutches, or transformers. Keep records of maintenance, repair, and required updates of equipment. Perform preventive maintenance or service such as cleaning, lubricating, and adjusting equipment. Test and calibrate components and equipment, following manufacturers' manuals and troubleshooting techniques and using hand tools, power tools, and measuring devices. Explain and demonstrate correct operation and preventive maintenance of medical equipment to personnel. Study technical manuals and attend training sessions provided by equipment manufacturers to maintain current knowledge. Plan and carry out work assignments, using blueprints, schematic drawings, technical manuals, wiring diagrams, and liquid and air flow sheets, following prescribed regulations, directives, and other instructions as required. Solder loose connections, using soldering irons. Test, evaluate, and classify excess or in-use medical equipment, and determine serviceability, condition, and disposition in accordance with regulations.

Education/Training Required: Associate degree. **Education and Training Program:** Biomedical Technology/Technician. **Knowledge/Courses—Mechanical Devices:** Machines and tools, including their designs, uses, repair, and maintenance. **Engineering and Technology:** The practical application of engineering science and technology. This includes applying principles, techniques, procedures, and equipment to the design and production of various goods and services. **Physics:** Physical principles, laws, their interrelationships, and applications to understanding fluid, material, and atmospheric dynamics, and mechanical, electrical, atomic, and subatomic structures and processes. **Telecommunications:** Transmission, broadcasting, switching, control, and operation of telecommunications systems. **Computers and Electronics:** Circuit boards, processors, chips, electronic equipment, and computer hardware and software, including applications and programming. **Chemistry:** The chemical composition, structure, and properties of substances and of the chemical processes and transformations that they undergo. This includes uses of chemicals and their danger signs, production techniques, and disposal methods. **Work Experience Needed:** None. **On-the-Job Training Needed:** Moderate-term on-the-job training. **Certification/Licensure:** Voluntary certification by association.

Personality Type: Realistic-Investigative-Conventional. **Career Cluster:** 13 Manufacturing. **Career Pathway:** 13.3 Maintenance, Installation, and Repair. **Other Jobs in This Pathway:** Aircraft Mechanics and Service Technicians; Automotive Engineering Technicians; Automotive Specialty Technicians; Avionics Technicians; Biological Technicians; Camera and Photographic Equipment Repairers; Chemical Equipment Operators and Tenders; Civil Engineering Technicians; Coil Winders, Tapers, and Finishers; Computer, Automated Teller, and Office Machine Repairers; Construction and Related Workers, All Other; Control and Valve Installers and Repairers, Except Mechanical

Door; Electric Motor, Power Tool, and Related Repairers; Electrical and Electronic Equipment Assemblers; Electrical and Electronics Repairers, Commercial and Industrial Equipment; Electrical and Electronics Repairers, Powerhouse, Substation, and Relay; Electrical Engineering Technicians; Electrical Engineering Technologists; Electromechanical Engineering Technologists; Electromechanical Equipment Assemblers; Electronics Engineering Technicians; Electronics Engineering Technologists; others.

Skills—Equipment Maintenance: Performing routine maintenance on equipment and determining when and what kind of maintenance is needed. **Repairing:** Repairing machines or systems using the needed tools. **Troubleshooting:** Determining causes of operating errors and deciding what to do about them. **Equipment Selection:** Determining the kind of tools and equipment needed to do a job. **Quality Control Analysis:** Conducting tests and inspections of products, services, or processes to evaluate quality or performance. **Operation and Control:** Controlling operations of equipment or systems. **Installation:** Installing equipment, machines, wiring, or programs to meet specifications. **Operation Monitoring:** Watching gauges, dials, or other indicators to make sure a machine is working properly.

Work Environment: Indoors; standing; using hands; noise; bright or inadequate lighting; contaminants; cramped work space; exposed to disease or infections; hazardous conditions; hazardous equipment; minor burns, cuts, bites, or stings.

Medical Records and Health Information Technicians

- ⊙ Annual Earnings: $33,310
- ⊙ Earnings Growth Potential: Low (34.9%)
- ⊙ Growth: 21.0%
- ⊙ Annual Job Openings: 7,370
- ⊙ Self-Employed: 0.1%

Considerations for Job Outlook: Prospects will be best for those with a certification in health information. As EHR systems continue to become more common, technicians with computer skills will be needed to use them.

Compile, process, and maintain medical records of hospital and clinic patients in a manner consistent with requirements of the health-care system. Protect the security of medical records to ensure that confidentiality is maintained. Review records for completeness, accuracy, and compliance with regulations. Retrieve patient medical records for physicians, technicians, or other medical personnel. Release information to persons and agencies according to regulations. Plan, develop, maintain, and operate a variety of health record indexes and storage and retrieval systems to collect, classify, store, and analyze information. Enter data such as demographic characteristics, history and extent of disease, diagnostic procedures, and treatment into computer. Process and prepare business and government forms. Compile and maintain patients' medical records to document condition and treatment and to provide data for research or cost-control and care-improvement efforts. Process patient admission and discharge documents. Assign the patient to diagnosis-related groups (DRGs), using appropriate computer software. Transcribe medical reports. Identify, compile, abstract, and code patient data, using standard classification systems. Resolve or clarify codes and diagnoses with conflicting, missing, or unclear information by consulting with doctors or others or by participating in the coding team's regular meetings. Compile medical-care and census data for statistical reports on diseases treated, surgeries performed, or use of hospital beds. Post medical insurance billings. Train medical records staff.

Education/Training Required: Postsecondary vocational training. **Education and Training Programs:** Health Information/Medical Records Technology/Technician; Medical Insurance Coding Specialist/Coder Training. **Knowledge/Courses—Clerical Practices:** Administrative and clerical procedures and systems such as word processing, managing files and records, stenography and transcription, designing forms, and other office procedures and terminology. **Law and Government:** Laws, legal codes, court procedures, precedents, government regulations, executive orders, agency rules, and the democratic political process. **Work Experience Needed:** None. **On-the-Job Training Needed:** None. **Certification/Licensure:** Voluntary certification by association.

Personality Type: Conventional-Enterprising. **Career Cluster:** 08 Health Science. **Career Pathway:** 08.3 Health Informatics. **Other Jobs in This Pathway:** Clinical Psychologists; Communications Teachers, Postsecondary; Dental Laboratory Technicians; Editors; Engineers, All Other; Executive Secretaries and Executive Administrative Assistants; Fine Artists, Including Painters, Sculptors, and Illustrators; First-Line Supervisors of Office and Administrative Support Workers; Health Educators; Health Specialties Teachers, Postsecondary; Medical and Health Services Managers; Medical Appliance Technicians; Medical Assistants; Medical Secretaries; Medical Transcriptionists; Mental Health Counselors; Occupational Health and Safety Specialists; Occupational Health and Safety Technicians; Orthotists and Prosthetists; Physical Therapists; Psychiatric Aides; Psychiatric Technicians; Public Relations Specialists; Receptionists and Information Clerks; Recreational Therapists; Rehabilitation Counselors; Substance Abuse and Behavioral Disorder Counselors; Therapists, All Other.

Work Environment: Indoors; sitting; using hands; repetitive motions; exposed to disease or infections.

Medical Secretaries

- ⊙ Annual Earnings: $31,060
- ⊙ Earnings Growth Potential: Low (31.1%)
- ⊙ Growth: 41.3%
- ⊙ Annual Job Openings: 27,840
- ⊙ Self-Employed: 1.2%

Considerations for Job Outlook: In addition to jobs coming from employment growth, numerous job openings will arise from the need to replace secretaries and administrative assistants who transfer to other occupations or retire. Job opportunities should be best for applicants with extensive knowledge of computer software applications. Applicants with a bachelor's degree are expected to be in great demand and will act as managerial assistants who perform more complex tasks.

Perform secretarial duties using specific knowledge of medical terminology and hospital, clinic, or laboratory procedures. Answer telephones, and direct calls to appropriate staff. Schedule and confirm patient diagnostic appointments, surgeries, and medical consultations. Greet visitors, ascertain purpose of visit, and direct them to appropriate staff. Operate office equipment, such as voice mail messaging systems, and use word processing, spreadsheet, and other software applications to prepare reports, invoices, financial statements, letters, case histories, and medical records. Complete insurance and other claim forms. Interview patients to complete documents, case histories, and forms such as intake and insurance forms. Receive and route messages and documents such as laboratory results to appropriate staff. Compile and record medical charts, reports, and correspondence, using typewriter or personal computer. Transmit correspondence and medical records by mail, e-mail, or fax. Maintain medical records, technical library documents, and correspondence files. Perform various clerical and administrative functions, such as ordering and maintaining an inventory of supplies. Perform bookkeeping duties, such as credits and collections, preparing and sending financial statements and bills, and keeping financial records. Transcribe recorded messages and practitioners' diagnoses and recommendations into patients' medical records. Arrange hospital admissions for patients.

Education/Training Required: High school diploma or equivalent. **Education and Training Programs:** Medical Administrative/Executive Assistant and Medical Secretary Training; Medical Insurance Specialist/Medical Biller Training; Medical Office Assistant/Specialist Training. **Knowledge/Courses—Clerical Practices:** Administrative and clerical procedures and systems such as word processing, managing files and records, stenography and transcription, designing forms, and other office procedures and terminology. **Medicine and Dentistry:** The information and techniques needed to diagnose and treat human injuries, diseases, and deformities. This includes symptoms, treatment alternatives, drug properties and interactions, and preventive health-care measures. **Customer and Personal Service:** Principles and processes for providing customer and personal services. This includes customer needs assessment, meeting quality standards for services, and evaluation of customer satisfaction. **Computers and Electronics:** Circuit boards, processors, chips, electronic equipment, and computer hardware and software, including applications and programming. **Economics and Accounting:** Economic and accounting principles and practices, the financial markets, banking, and the analysis and reporting of financial data. **Work Experience Needed:** None. **On-the-Job Training Needed:** Moderate-term on-the-job training. **Certification/Licensure:** Voluntary certification by association.

Personality Type: Conventional-Social. **Career Cluster:** 08 Health Science. **Career Pathways:** 08.3 Health Informatics; 08.1 Therapeutic Services. **Other Jobs in These Pathways:** Acupuncturists; Allergists and Immunologists; Anesthesiologists; Art Therapists; Chiropractors; Clinical Psychologists; Communications Teachers, Postsecondary; Community and Social Service Specialists, All Other; Counseling Psychologists; Counselors, All Other; Dental Assistants; Dental Hygienists; Dental Laboratory Technicians; Dentists, All Other Specialists; Dentists, General; Dermatologists; Diagnostic Medical Sonographers; Dietetic Technicians; Dietitians and Nutritionists; Editors; Engineers, All Other; Executive Secretaries and Executive Administrative Assistants; Family and General Practitioners; Fine Artists, Including Painters, Sculptors, and Illustrators; First-Line Supervisors of Office and Administrative Support Workers; Health Diagnosing and Treating Practitioners, All Other; Health Educators; Health Specialties Teachers, Postsecondary; Health Technologists and Technicians, All Other; Healthcare Practitioners and Technical Workers, All Other; others.

Skills—Service Orientation: Actively looking for ways to help people. **Active Listening:** Giving full attention to what other people are saying, taking time to understand the points being made, asking questions as appropriate, and not interrupting at inappropriate times. **Speaking:** Talking to others to convey information effectively.

Work Environment: Indoors; sitting; repetitive motions; exposed to disease or infections.

Medical Transcriptionists

- ⊙ Annual Earnings: $33,480
- ⊙ Earnings Growth Potential: Low (34.3%)
- ⊙ Growth: 5.9%
- ⊙ Annual Job Openings: 2,020
- ⊙ Self-Employed: 15.1%

Considerations for Job Outlook: The volume of health-care services is expected to continue to increase, resulting in a growing number of medical tests and procedures, all of which will require transcription. At the same time, technological advances in recent years have changed the way medical transcription is done. As health-care providers seek to cut costs, some have hired transcription services in other countries. However, concerns about patient confidentiality and data security suggest a continued need for transcriptionists within the United States.

Transcribe medical reports recorded by physicians and other health-care practitioners. Transcribe dictation for a variety of medical reports such as patient histories, physical examinations, emergency room visits, operations, chart reviews, consultation, and discharge summaries. Review and edit transcribed reports or dictated material for spelling, grammar, clarity, consistency, and proper medical terminology. Distinguish between homonyms and recognize inconsistencies and mistakes in medical terms, referring to dictionaries, drug references, and other sources on anatomy, physiology, and medicine. Return dictated reports in printed or electronic form for physicians' review, signature, and corrections, and for inclusion in patients' medical records. Translate medical jargon and abbreviations into their expanded forms to ensure the accuracy of patient and health-care facility records. Take dictation using either shorthand or a stenotype machine, or using headsets and transcribing machines; then convert dictated materials or rough notes to written form. Identify mistakes in reports, and check with doctors to obtain the correct information. Perform data entry and data retrieval services, providing data for inclusion in medical records and for transmission to physicians. Produce medical reports, correspondence, records, patient-care information, statistics, medical research, and administrative material. Answer inquiries concerning the progress of medical cases, within the limits of confidentiality laws. Set up and maintain medical files and databases, including records such as X-ray, lab, and procedure reports; medical histories; diagnostic workups; admission and discharge summaries; and clinical resumes. Perform a variety of clerical and office tasks, such as handling incoming and outgoing mail, completing and submitting insurance claims, typing, filing, and operating office machines. Decide which information should be included or excluded in reports. Receive patients, schedule appointments, and maintain patient records.

Education/Training Required: Postsecondary vocational training. **Education and Training Program:** Medical Transcription/Transcriptionist. **Knowledge/Courses— Clerical Practices:** Administrative and clerical procedures and systems such as word processing, managing files and records, stenography and transcription, designing forms, and other office procedures and terminology. **English Language:** The structure and content of the English language including the meaning and spelling of words, rules of composition, and grammar. **Medicine and Dentistry:** The information and techniques needed to diagnose and treat human injuries, diseases, and deformities. This includes symptoms, treatment alternatives, drug properties and interactions, and preventive health-care measures. **Computers and Electronics:** Circuit boards, processors, chips, electronic equipment, and computer hardware and software, including applications and programming. **Work Experience Needed:** None. **On-the-Job Training Needed:** None. **Certification/Licensure:** Voluntary certification by association.

Personality Type: Conventional-Realistic. **Career Cluster:** 08 Health Science. **Career Pathway:** 08.3 Health Informatics. **Other Jobs in This Pathway:** Clinical Psychologists; Communications Teachers, Postsecondary; Dental Laboratory Technicians; Editors; Engineers, All Other; Executive Secretaries and Executive Administrative Assistants; Fine Artists, Including Painters, Sculptors, and Illustrators; First-Line Supervisors of Office and Administrative Support Workers; Health Educators; Health Specialties Teachers, Postsecondary; Medical and Health Services Managers; Medical Appliance Technicians; Medical Assistants; Medical Records and Health Information Technicians; Medical Secretaries; Mental Health Counselors; Occupational Health and Safety Specialists; Occupational Health and Safety Technicians; Orthotists and Prosthetists; Physical Therapists; Psychiatric Aides; Psychiatric Technicians; Public Relations Specialists; Receptionists and Information Clerks; Recreational Therapists; Rehabilitation Counselors; Substance Abuse and Behavioral Disorder Counselors; Therapists, All Other.

Skills—Reading Comprehension: Understanding written sentences and paragraphs in work-related documents.

Work Environment: Indoors; sitting; using hands; repetitive motions.

Merchandise Displayers and Window Trimmers

- ⊙ Annual Earnings: $26,190
- ⊙ Earnings Growth Potential: Low (33.1%)
- ⊙ Growth: 12.8%
- ⊙ Annual Job Openings: 4,000
- ⊙ Self-Employed: 30.1%

Considerations for Job Outlook: About-average employment growth is projected.

Plan and erect commercial displays, such as those in windows and interiors of retail stores and at trade exhibitions. Take photographs of displays and signage. Plan and erect commercial displays to entice and appeal to customers. Place prices and descriptive signs on backdrops, fixtures, merchandise, or floor. Change or rotate window displays, interior display areas, and signage to reflect changes in inventory or promotion. Obtain plans from display designers or display managers, and discuss their implementation with clients or supervisors. Develop ideas or plans for merchandise displays or window decorations. Consult with advertising and sales staff to determine type of merchandise to be featured and time and place for each display. Arrange properties, furniture, merchandise, backdrops, and other accessories as shown in prepared sketches. Construct or assemble displays and display components from fabric, glass, paper, and plastic according to specifications, using hand tools and woodworking power tools. Collaborate with others to obtain products and other display items. Use computers to produce signage. Dress mannequins for displays. Maintain props and mannequins, inspecting them for imperfections and applying preservative coatings as necessary. Select themes, lighting, colors, and props to be used. Attend training sessions and corporate planning meetings to obtain new ideas for product launches. Instruct sales staff in color-coordination of clothing racks and counter displays. Store, pack, and maintain records of props and display items.

Education/Training Required: High school diploma or equivalent. **Education and Training Program:** Commercial and Advertising Art. **Knowledge/Courses—Sales and Marketing:** Principles and methods for showing, promoting, and selling products or services. This includes marketing strategy and tactics, product demonstration, sales techniques, and sales control systems. **Design:** Design techniques, tools, and principles involved in production of precision technical plans, blueprints, drawings, and models. **Administration and Management:** Business and management principles involved in strategic planning, resource allocation, human resources modeling, leadership technique, production methods, and coordination of people and resources. **Work Experience Needed:** None. **On-the-Job Training Needed:** Moderate-term on-the-job training. **Certification/Licensure:** None.

Personality Type: Artistic-Enterprising-Realistic. **Career Cluster:** 14 Marketing, Sales, and Service. **Career**

Pathway: 14.2 Professional Sales and Marketing. **Other Jobs in This Pathway:** Appraisers, Real Estate; Assessors; Cashiers; Counter and Rental Clerks; Demonstrators and Product Promoters; Door-To-Door Sales Workers, News and Street Vendors, and Related Workers; Driver/Sales Workers; Energy Brokers; First-Line Supervisors of Non-Retail Sales Workers; First-Line Supervisors of Retail Sales Workers; Gaming Change Persons and Booth Cashiers; Hotel, Motel, and Resort Desk Clerks; Interior Designers; Lodging Managers; Marketing Managers; Marking Clerks; Meeting, Convention, and Event Planners; Models; Online Merchants; Order Fillers, Wholesale and Retail Sales; Parts Salespersons; Property, Real Estate, and Community Association Managers; Real Estate Brokers; Real Estate Sales Agents; Reservation and Transportation Ticket Agents and Travel Clerks; Retail Salespersons; Sales and Related Workers, All Other; Sales Engineers; Sales Representatives, Services, All Other; Sales Representatives, Wholesale and Manufacturing, Except Technical and Scientific Products; others.

Work Environment: More often indoors than outdoors; standing; climbing; walking and running; kneeling, crouching, stooping, or crawling; using hands; bending or twisting the body; repetitive motions; contaminants; cramped work space; high places.

Metal-Refining Furnace Operators and Tenders

- Annual Earnings: $38,680
- Earnings Growth Potential: Medium (35.8%)
- Growth: 16.0%
- Annual Job Openings: 550
- Self-Employed: 0.9%

Considerations for Job Outlook: A number of these jobs are expected to become available for highly skilled workers because of an expected increase in retirements, primarily of baby boomers, in the coming years. In addition, workers who have a thorough background in machine operations, certifications from industry associations, and a good working knowledge of the properties of metals and plastics should have the best job opportunities.

Operate or tend furnaces, such as gas, oil, coal, electric-arc or electric induction, open-hearth, or oxygen

furnaces, to melt and refine metal before casting or to produce specified types of steel. Draw smelted metal samples from furnaces or kettles for analysis, and calculate types and amounts of materials needed to ensure that materials meet specifications. Drain, transfer, or remove molten metal from furnaces, and place it into molds, using hoists, pumps, or ladles. Record production data, and maintain production logs. Operate controls to move or discharge metal workpieces from furnaces. Weigh materials to be charged into furnaces, using scales. Regulate supplies of fuel and air, or control flow of electric current and water coolant to heat furnaces and adjust temperatures. Observe air and temperature gauges or metal color and fluidity, and turn fuel valves or adjust controls to maintain required temperatures. Inspect furnaces and equipment to locate defects and wear. Observe operations inside furnaces, using television screens, to ensure that problems do not occur. Remove impurities from the surface of molten metal, using strainers. Kindle fires, and shovel fuel and other materials into furnaces or onto conveyors by hand, with hoists, or by directing crane operators. Sprinkle chemicals over molten metal to bring impurities to the surface. Direct work crews in the cleaning and repair of furnace walls and flooring. Prepare material to load into furnaces, including cleaning, crushing, or applying chemicals, by using crushing-machines, shovels, rakes, or sprayers. Scrape accumulations of metal oxides from floors, molds, and crucibles, and sift and store them for reclamation.

Education/Training Required: High school diploma or equivalent. **Education and Training Programs:** No related CIP programs; this job is learned through informal moderate-term on-the-job training. **Knowledge/Courses—Production and Processing:** Raw materials, production processes, quality control, costs, and other techniques for maximizing the effective manufacture and distribution of goods. **Chemistry:** The chemical composition, structure, and properties of substances and of the chemical processes and transformations that they undergo. This includes uses of chemicals and their danger signs, production techniques, and disposal methods. **Mechanical Devices:** Machines and tools, including their designs, uses, repair, and maintenance. **Engineering and Technology:** The practical application of engineering science and technology. This includes applying principles, techniques, procedures, and equipment to the design and production of various goods and services. **Work Experience Needed:**

None. **On-the-Job Training Needed:** Moderate-term on-the-job training. **Certification/Licensure:** None.

Personality Type: Realistic-Investigative-Conventional. **Career Cluster:** 13 Manufacturing. **Career Pathway:** 13.1 Production. **Other Jobs in This Pathway:** Adhesive Bonding Machine Operators and Tenders; Assemblers and Fabricators, All Other; Avionics Technicians; Cabinetmakers and Bench Carpenters; Cleaning, Washing, and Metal Pickling Equipment Operators and Tenders; Coating, Painting, and Spraying Machine Setters, Operators, and Tenders; Computer-Controlled Machine Tool Operators, Metal and Plastic; Cooling and Freezing Equipment Operators and Tenders; Cost Estimators; Crushing, Grinding, and Polishing Machine Setters, Operators, and Tenders; Cutters and Trimmers, Hand; Cutting and Slicing Machine Setters, Operators, and Tenders; Cutting, Punching, and Press Machine Setters, Operators, and Tenders, Metal and Plastic; Drilling and Boring Machine Tool Setters, Operators, and Tenders, Metal and Plastic; Extruding and Drawing Machine Setters, Operators, and Tenders, Metal and Plastic; Extruding and Forming Machine Setters, Operators, and Tenders, Synthetic and Glass Fibers; others.

Skills—Operation and Control: Controlling operations of equipment or systems. **Equipment Maintenance:** Performing routine maintenance on equipment and determining when and what kind of maintenance is needed. **Operation Monitoring:** Watching gauges, dials, or other indicators to make sure a machine is working properly. **Repairing:** Repairing machines or systems using the needed tools. **Equipment Selection:** Determining the kind of tools and equipment needed to do a job. **Quality Control Analysis:** Conducting tests and inspections of products, services, or processes to evaluate quality or performance. **Troubleshooting:** Determining causes of operating errors and deciding what to do about them. **Mathematics:** Using mathematics to solve problems.

Work Environment: Standing; walking and running; using hands; bending or twisting the body; repetitive motions; noise; very hot or cold; bright or inadequate lighting; contaminants; hazardous conditions; hazardous equipment; minor burns, cuts, bites, or stings.

Mobile Heavy Equipment Mechanics, Except Engines

- Annual Earnings: $45,600
- Earnings Growth Potential: Low (33.3%)
- Growth: 16.2%
- Annual Job Openings: 5,250
- Self-Employed: 5.5%

Considerations for Job Outlook: Most job opportunities will come from the need to replace workers who retire or leave the occupation. Those with certificates from vocational schools or two-year degrees from community colleges should have very good job opportunities as employers strongly prefer these candidates. Those without formal training will have difficulty finding jobs. The majority of job openings are expected to be in sectors that sell, rent, or lease heavy vehicles and mobile equipment, where a large proportion of service technicians are employed. The construction and mining industries, which use large numbers of heavy equipment, are sensitive to fluctuations in the economy. As a result, job opportunities for service technicians in these sectors will vary with overall economic conditions. Job opportunities for farm equipment mechanics are seasonal and are generally best during warmer months.

Diagnose, adjust, repair, or overhaul mobile mechanical, hydraulic, and pneumatic equipment. Test mechanical products and equipment after repair or assembly to ensure proper performance and compliance with manufacturers' specifications. Repair and replace damaged or worn parts. Diagnose faults or malfunctions to determine required repairs, using engine diagnostic equipment such as computerized test equipment and calibration devices. Operate and inspect machines or heavy equipment to diagnose defects. Dismantle and reassemble heavy equipment, using hoists and hand tools. Clean, lubricate, and perform other routine maintenance work on equipment and vehicles. Examine parts for damage or excessive wear, using micrometers and gauges. Read and understand operating manuals, blueprints, and technical drawings. Schedule maintenance for industrial machines and equipment, and keep equipment service records. Overhaul and test machines or equipment to ensure operating efficiency. Assemble gear systems, and align frames and gears. Fit bearings to adjust, repair, or overhaul mobile mechanical, hydraulic, and pneumatic equipment. Weld or solder broken parts and structural members, using electric or gas welders and soldering tools. Clean parts by spraying them with grease solvent or immersing them in tanks of solvent. Adjust, maintain, and repair or replace subassemblies, such as transmissions and crawler heads, using hand tools, jacks, and cranes. Adjust and maintain industrial machinery, using control and regulating devices. Fabricate needed parts or items from sheet metal.

Education/Training Required: High school diploma or equivalent. **Education and Training Programs:** Agricultural Mechanics and Equipment/Machine Technology; Heavy Equipment Maintenance Technology/Technician. **Knowledge/Courses—Mechanical Devices:** Machines and tools, including their designs, uses, repair, and maintenance. **Physics:** Physical principles, laws, their interrelationships, and applications to understanding fluid, material, and atmospheric dynamics, and mechanical, electrical, atomic, and subatomic structures and processes. **Building and Construction:** Materials, methods, and the tools involved in the construction or repair of houses, buildings, or other structures such as highways and roads. **Engineering and Technology:** The practical application of engineering science and technology. This includes applying principles, techniques, procedures, and equipment to the design and production of various goods and services. **Design:** Design techniques, tools, and principles involved in production of precision technical plans, blueprints, drawings, and models. **Transportation:** Principles and methods for moving people or goods by air, rail, sea, or road, including the relative costs and benefits. **Work Experience Needed:** None. **On-the-Job Training Needed:** Long-term on-the-job training. **Certification/Licensure:** Voluntary certification by manufacturer.

Personality Type: Realistic-Conventional. **Career Clusters:** 01 Agriculture, Food, and Natural Resources; 13 Manufacturing. **Career Pathways:** 01.4 Power Structure and Technical Systems; 13.3 Maintenance, Installation, and Repair. **Other Jobs in These Pathways:** Agricultural Sciences Teachers, Postsecondary; Aircraft Mechanics and Service Technicians; Automotive Engineering Technicians; Automotive Specialty Technicians; Avionics Technicians; Biological Technicians; Camera and Photographic Equipment Repairers; Chemical Equipment Operators and Tenders; Civil Engineering Technicians; Coil Winders, Tapers, and Finishers; Computer, Automated Teller, and Office Machine Repairers; Construction and Related Workers,

All Other; Control and Valve Installers and Repairers, Except Mechanical Door; Electric Motor, Power Tool, and Related Repairers; Electrical and Electronic Equipment Assemblers; Electrical and Electronics Repairers, Commercial and Industrial Equipment; Electrical and Electronics Repairers, Powerhouse, Substation, and Relay; Electrical Engineering Technicians; Electrical Engineering Technologists; Electromechanical Engineering Technologists; Electromechanical Equipment Assemblers; Electronics Engineering Technicians; others.

Skills—Repairing: Repairing machines or systems using the needed tools. **Equipment Maintenance:** Performing routine maintenance on equipment and determining when and what kind of maintenance is needed. **Troubleshooting:** Determining causes of operating errors and deciding what to do about them. **Installation:** Installing equipment, machines, wiring, or programs to meet specifications. **Equipment Selection:** Determining the kind of tools and equipment needed to do a job. **Quality Control Analysis:** Conducting tests and inspections of products, services, or processes to evaluate quality or performance. **Operation and Control:** Controlling operations of equipment or systems. **Operation Monitoring:** Watching gauges, dials, or other indicators to make sure a machine is working properly.

Work Environment: Outdoors; standing; walking and running; kneeling, crouching, stooping, or crawling; using hands; bending or twisting the body; repetitive motions; noise; very hot or cold; bright or inadequate lighting; contaminants; cramped work space; whole-body vibration; high places; hazardous conditions; hazardous equipment; minor burns, cuts, bites, or stings.

Motorboat Mechanics and Service Technicians

- ⊙ Annual Earnings: $35,520
- ⊙ Earnings Growth Potential: Medium (39.0%)
- ⊙ Growth: 20.7%
- ⊙ Annual Job Openings: 960
- ⊙ Self-Employed: 19.2%

Considerations for Job Outlook: Job opportunities are expected to be very good for candidates with formal training. Those without formal training can expect to face strong competition for jobs.

Repair and adjust electrical and mechanical equipment of inboard or inboard-outboard boat engines. Disassemble and inspect motors to locate defective parts, using mechanic's hand tools and gauges. Adjust generators and replace faulty wiring, using hand tools and soldering irons. Start motors, and monitor performance for signs of malfunctioning such as smoke, excessive vibration, and misfiring. Adjust carburetor mixtures, electrical point settings, and timing while motors are running in water-filled test tanks. Idle motors and observe thermometers to determine the effectiveness of cooling systems. Inspect and repair or adjust propellers and propeller shafts. Mount motors to boats and operate boats at various speeds on waterways to conduct operational tests. Replace parts such as gears, magneto points, piston rings, and spark plugs, and reassemble engines. Repair or rework parts, using machine tools such as lathes, mills, drills, and grinders. Repair engine mechanical equipment such as power-tilts, bilge pumps, or power takeoffs. Set starter locks, and align and repair steering or throttle controls, using gauges, screwdrivers, and wrenches. Document inspection and test results, and work performed or to be performed.

Education/Training Required: High school diploma or equivalent. **Education and Training Programs:** Marine Maintenance/Fitter and Ship Repair Technology/Technician; Small Engine Mechanics and Repair Technology/Technician. **Knowledge/Courses—Mechanical Devices:** Machines and tools, including their designs, uses, repair, and maintenance. **Engineering and Technology:** The practical application of engineering science and technology. This includes applying principles, techniques, procedures, and equipment to the design and production of various goods and services. **Design:** Design techniques, tools, and principles involved in production of precision technical plans, blueprints, drawings, and models. **Physics:** Physical principles, laws, their interrelationships, and applications to understanding fluid, material, and atmospheric dynamics, and mechanical, electrical, atomic, and subatomic structures and processes. **Chemistry:** The chemical composition, structure, and properties of substances and of the chemical processes and transformations that they undergo. This includes uses of chemicals and their danger signs, production techniques, and disposal methods. **Transportation:** Principles and methods for moving people or goods by air, rail, sea, or road, including the relative costs and benefits. **Work Experience Needed:** None. **On-the-Job Training Needed:** Long-term on-the-job training. **Certification/Licensure:** None.

Personality Type: Realistic-Conventional-Investigative. **Career Cluster:** 16 Transportation, Distribution, and Logistics. **Career Pathway:** 16.4 Facility and Mobile Equipment Maintenance. **Other Jobs in This Pathway:** Aircraft Mechanics and Service Technicians; Aircraft Structure, Surfaces, Rigging, and Systems Assemblers; Automotive Body and Related Repairers; Automotive Glass Installers and Repairers; Automotive Master Mechanics; Automotive Specialty Technicians; Bicycle Repairers; Bus and Truck Mechanics and Diesel Engine Specialists; Cleaners of Vehicles and Equipment; Electrical and Electronics Installers and Repairers, Transportation Equipment; Electronic Equipment Installers and Repairers, Motor Vehicles; Engine and Other Machine Assemblers; Gem and Diamond Workers; Installation, Maintenance, and Repair Workers, All Other; Motorcycle Mechanics; Outdoor Power Equipment and Other Small Engine Mechanics; Painters, Transportation Equipment.

Skills—Equipment Maintenance: Performing routine maintenance on equipment and determining when and what kind of maintenance is needed. **Repairing:** Repairing machines or systems using the needed tools. **Troubleshooting:** Determining causes of operating errors and deciding what to do about them. **Operation and Control:** Controlling operations of equipment or systems. **Equipment Selection:** Determining the kind of tools and equipment needed to do a job. **Operation Monitoring:** Watching gauges, dials, or other indicators to make sure a machine is working properly. **Quality Control Analysis:** Conducting tests and inspections of products, services, or processes to evaluate quality or performance. **Installation:** Installing equipment, machines, wiring, or programs to meet specifications.

Work Environment: Outdoors; standing; walking and running; using hands; bending or twisting the body; repetitive motions; noise; very hot or cold; bright or inadequate lighting; contaminants; cramped work space; hazardous conditions; hazardous equipment; minor burns, cuts, bites, or stings.

Motorboat Operators

- ⊙ Annual Earnings: $36,620
- ⊙ Earnings Growth Potential: High (48.1%)
- ⊙ Growth: 16.1%
- ⊙ Annual Job Openings: 160
- ⊙ Self-Employed: 12.3%

Considerations for Job Outlook: Job prospects should be favorable. Many workers leave water transportation occupations, especially sailors and marine oilers, because recently hired workers often decide they do not enjoy spending a lot of time away at sea. In addition, a number of officers and engineers are approaching retirement, creating job openings. The number of applicants for all types of jobs may be limited by high regulatory and security requirements.

Operate small motor-driven boats. Maintain desired courses, using compasses or electronic navigational aids. Clean boats and repair hulls and superstructures, using hand tools, paint, and brushes. Perform general labor duties such as repairing booms. Tow, push, or guide other boats, barges, logs, or rafts. Service motors by performing tasks such as changing oil and lubricating parts. Report any observed navigational hazards to authorities. Organize and direct the activities of crew members. Follow safety procedures in order to ensure the protection of passengers, cargo, and vessels. Direct safety operations in emergency situations. Issue directions for loading, unloading, and seating in boats. Arrange repairs, fuel, and supplies for vessels. Position booms around docked ships. Take depth soundings in turning basins. Secure boats to docks with mooring lines, and cast off lines to enable departure. Oversee operation of vessels used for carrying passengers, motor vehicles, or goods across rivers, harbors, lakes, and coastal waters. Operate engine throttles and steering mechanisms in order to guide boats on desired courses. Maintain equipment such as range markers, fire extinguishers, boat fenders, lines, pumps, and fittings.

Education/Training Required: High school diploma or equivalent. **Education and Training Program:** Marine Transportation Services, Other. **Knowledge/Courses—Geography:** Principles and methods for describing the features of land, sea, and air masses, including their physical characteristics, locations, interrelationships, and distribution of plant, animal, and human life. **Mechanical Devices:** Machines and tools, including their designs, uses, repair, and maintenance. **Biology:** Plant and animal organisms and their tissues, cells, functions, interdependencies, and interactions with each other and the environment. **Transportation:** Principles and methods for moving people or goods by air, rail, sea, or road, including the relative costs and benefits. **History and Archeology:** Historical events and their causes, indicators, and effects on civilizations and cultures. **Telecommunications:** Transmission, broadcasting, switching, control, and operation of telecommunications systems. **Work Experience Needed:** None. **On-the-Job Training Needed:** Short-term on-the-job training. **Certification/Licensure:** None.

Personality Type: Realistic-Conventional-Enterprising. **Career Cluster:** 16 Transportation, Distribution, and Logistics. **Career Pathway:** 16.1 Transportation Operations. **Other Jobs in This Pathway:** Aerospace Engineering and Operations Technicians; Air Traffic Controllers; Aircraft Cargo Handling Supervisors; Airfield Operations Specialists; Airline Pilots, Copilots, and Flight Engineers; Automotive and Watercraft Service Attendants; Automotive Master Mechanics; Aviation Inspectors; Bridge and Lock Tenders; Bus Drivers, School or Special Client; Bus Drivers, Transit and Intercity; Commercial Divers; Commercial Pilots; Crane and Tower Operators; First-Line Supervisors of Helpers, Laborers, and Material Movers, Hand; First-Line Supervisors of Transportation and Material-Moving Machine and Vehicle Operators; Freight and Cargo Inspectors; Heavy and Tractor-Trailer Truck Drivers; Hoist and Winch Operators; Laborers and Freight, Stock, and Material Movers, Hand; Light Truck or Delivery Services Drivers; Mates—Ship, Boat, and Barge; Motor Vehicle Operators, All Other; Operating Engineers and Other Construction Equipment Operators; Parking Lot Attendants; others.

Skills—Operation and Control: Controlling operations of equipment or systems. **Repairing:** Repairing machines or systems using the needed tools. **Equipment Maintenance:** Performing routine maintenance on equipment and determining when and what kind of maintenance is needed. **Equipment Selection:** Determining the kind of tools and equipment needed to do a job. **Operation Monitoring:** Watching gauges, dials, or other indicators to make sure a machine is working properly. **Troubleshooting:** Determining causes of operating errors and deciding what to do about them. **Quality Control Analysis:** Conducting tests and inspections of products, services, or processes to evaluate quality or performance. **Management of Personnel**

Resources: Motivating, developing, and directing people as they work, identifying the best people for the job.

Work Environment: More often outdoors than indoors; sitting; using hands; noise; bright or inadequate lighting; contaminants.

Motorcycle Mechanics

- ⊙ Annual Earnings: $32,410
- ⊙ Earnings Growth Potential: Medium (35.9%)
- ⊙ Growth: 23.3%
- ⊙ Annual Job Openings: 890
- ⊙ Self-Employed: 19.4%

Considerations for Job Outlook: Job opportunities are expected to be very good for candidates with formal training. Those without formal training can expect to face strong competition for jobs.

Diagnose, adjust, repair, or overhaul motorcycles, scooters, mopeds, dirt bikes, or similar motorized vehicles. Repair and adjust motorcycle subassemblies such as forks, transmissions, brakes, and drive chains, according to specifications. Replace defective parts, using hand tools, arbor presses, flexible power presses, or power tools. Connect test panels to engines and measure generator output, ignition timing, and other engine performance indicators. Listen to engines, examine vehicle frames, and confer with customers in order to determine nature and extent of malfunction or damage. Reassemble and test subassembly units. Remove cylinder heads, grind valves, and scrape off carbon, and replace defective valves, pistons, cylinders, and rings, using hand tools and power tools. Dismantle engines and repair or replace defective parts, such as magnetos, carburetors, and generators. Repair or replace other parts, such as headlights, horns, handlebar controls, gasoline and oil tanks, starters, and mufflers. Disassemble subassembly units and examine condition, movement or alignment of parts visually or using gauges. Hammer out dents and bends in frames, weld tears and breaks; then reassemble frames and reinstall engines.

Education/Training Required: High school diploma or equivalent. **Education and Training Program:** Motorcycle Maintenance and Repair Technology/Technician. **Knowledge/Courses—Mechanical Devices:** Machines and tools, including their designs, uses, repair, and maintenance. **Design:** Design techniques, tools, and principles involved in production of precision technical plans, blueprints, drawings, and models. **Engineering and Technology:** The practical application of engineering science and technology. This includes applying principles, techniques, procedures, and equipment to the design and production of various goods and services. **Physics:** Physical principles, laws, their interrelationships, and applications to understanding fluid, material, and atmospheric dynamics, and mechanical, electrical, atomic, and subatomic structures and processes. **Transportation:** Principles and methods for moving people or goods by air, rail, sea, or road, including the relative costs and benefits. **Sales and Marketing:** Principles and methods for showing, promoting, and selling products or services. This includes marketing strategy and tactics, product demonstration, sales techniques, and sales control systems. **Work Experience Needed:** None. **On-the-Job Training Needed:** Long-term on-the-job training. **Certification/Licensure:** None.

Personality Type: Realistic. **Career Cluster:** 16 Transportation, Distribution, and Logistics. **Career Pathway:** 16.4 Facility and Mobile Equipment Maintenance. **Other Jobs in This Pathway:** Aircraft Mechanics and Service Technicians; Aircraft Structure, Surfaces, Rigging, and Systems Assemblers; Automotive Body and Related Repairers; Automotive Glass Installers and Repairers; Automotive Master Mechanics; Automotive Specialty Technicians; Bicycle Repairers; Bus and Truck Mechanics and Diesel Engine Specialists; Cleaners of Vehicles and Equipment; Electrical and Electronics Installers and Repairers, Transportation Equipment; Electronic Equipment Installers and Repairers, Motor Vehicles; Engine and Other Machine Assemblers; Gem and Diamond Workers; Installation, Maintenance, and Repair Workers, All Other; Motorboat Mechanics and Service Technicians; Outdoor Power Equipment and Other Small Engine Mechanics; Painters, Transportation Equipment.

Skills—Repairing: Repairing machines or systems using the needed tools. **Equipment Maintenance:** Performing routine maintenance on equipment and determining when and what kind of maintenance is needed. **Troubleshooting:** Determining causes of operating errors and deciding what to do about them. **Equipment Selection:** Determining the kind of tools and equipment needed to do a job. **Quality Control Analysis:** Conducting tests and inspections of products, services, or processes to evaluate quality

or performance. **Operation and Control:** Controlling operations of equipment or systems. **Installation:** Installing equipment, machines, wiring, or programs to meet specifications. **Operation Monitoring:** Watching gauges, dials, or other indicators to make sure a machine is working properly.

Work Environment: Indoors; standing; using hands; bending or twisting the body; repetitive motions; noise; contaminants; hazardous conditions; minor burns, cuts, bites, or stings.

Nuclear Medicine Technologists

- ⊙ Annual Earnings: $69,450
- ⊙ Earnings Growth Potential: Low (28.5%)
- ⊙ Growth: 18.7%
- ⊙ Annual Job Openings: 750
- ⊙ Self-Employed: 0.0%

Considerations for Job Outlook: Nuclear medicine technologists can improve their job prospects by getting a specialty certification. A technologist can earn a certification in positron emission tomography (PET), nuclear cardiology (NCT), magnetic resonance imaging (MRI), or computed tomography (CT). The Nuclear Medicine Technology Certification Board (NMTCB) offers NCT and PET certification exams. The American Registry of Radiologic Technologists (ARRT) offers the CT and MRI certification exams.

Prepare, administer, and measure radioactive isotopes in therapeutic, diagnostic, and tracer studies using a variety of radioisotope equipment. Calculate, measure, and record radiation dosage or radiopharmaceuticals received, used, and disposed, using computer and following physicians' prescriptions. Detect and map radiopharmaceuticals in patients' bodies, using cameras to produce photographic or computer images. Administer radiopharmaceuticals or radiation to patients to detect or treat diseases, using radioisotope equipment, under direction of physician. Explain test procedures and safety precautions to patients and provide them with assistance during test procedures. Produce computer-generated or film images for interpretation by physicians. Process cardiac function studies, using computer. Dispose of radioactive materials and store radiopharmaceuticals, following radiation safety procedures. Record and process results of procedures. Prepare stock radiopharmaceuticals, adhering to safety standards that minimize radiation exposure to workers and patients. Maintain and calibrate radioisotope and laboratory equipment. Gather information on patients' illnesses and medical history to guide the choice of diagnostic procedures for therapy. Measure glandular activity, blood volume, red cell survival, and radioactivity of patients, using scanners, Geiger counters, scintillometers, and other laboratory equipment. Train and supervise student or subordinate nuclear medicine technologists. Position radiation fields, radiation beams, and patients to allow for the most effective treatment of patients' disease, using computers. Add radioactive substances to biological specimens, such as blood, urine, and feces, to determine therapeutic drug or hormone levels. Develop treatment procedures for nuclear medicine treatment programs.

Education/Training Required: Associate degree. **Education and Training Programs:** Nuclear Medical Technology/Technologist; Radiation Protection/Health Physics Technician Training. **Knowledge/Courses—Medicine and Dentistry:** The information and techniques needed to diagnose and treat human injuries, diseases, and deformities. This includes symptoms, treatment alternatives, drug properties and interactions, and preventive healthcare measures. **Biology:** Plant and animal organisms and their tissues, cells, functions, interdependencies, and interactions with each other and the environment. **Chemistry:** The chemical composition, structure, and properties of substances and of the chemical processes and transformations that they undergo. This includes uses of chemicals and their danger signs, production techniques, and disposal methods. **Physics:** Physical principles, laws, their interrelationships, and applications to understanding fluid, material, and atmospheric dynamics, and mechanical, electrical, atomic, and subatomic structures and processes. **Customer and Personal Service:** Principles and processes for providing customer and personal services. This includes customer needs assessment, meeting quality standards for services, and evaluation of customer satisfaction. **Therapy and Counseling:** Principles, methods, and procedures for diagnosis, treatment, and rehabilitation of physical and mental dysfunctions, and for career counseling and guidance. **Work Experience Needed:** None. **On-the-Job Training Needed:** None. **Certification/Licensure:** Voluntary certification by association.

Personality Type: Investigative-Realistic-Social. **Career Cluster:** 08 Health Science. **Career Pathways:** 08.1

Therapeutic Services; 08.2 Diagnostics Services. **Other Jobs in These Pathways:** Acupuncturists; Allergists and Immunologists; Ambulance Drivers and Attendants, Except Emergency Medical Technicians; Anesthesiologist Assistants; Anesthesiologists; Art Therapists; Athletic Trainers; Cardiovascular Technologists and Technicians; Chiropractors; Clinical Psychologists; Community and Social Service Specialists, All Other; Counseling Psychologists; Counselors, All Other; Cytogenetic Technologists; Cytotechnologists; Dental Assistants; Dental Hygienists; Dentists, All Other Specialists; Dentists, General; Dermatologists; Diagnostic Medical Sonographers; Dietetic Technicians; Dietitians and Nutritionists; Emergency Medical Technicians and Paramedics; Endoscopy Technicians; Family and General Practitioners; Health Diagnosing and Treating Practitioners, All Other; Health Specialties Teachers, Postsecondary; Health Technologists and Technicians, All Other; Healthcare Practitioners and Technical Workers, All Other; Healthcare Support Workers, All Other; others.

Skills—Science: Using scientific rules and methods to solve problems. **Equipment Maintenance:** Performing routine maintenance on equipment and determining when and what kind of maintenance is needed. **Quality Control Analysis:** Conducting tests and inspections of products, services, or processes to evaluate quality or performance. **Operation Monitoring:** Watching gauges, dials, or other indicators to make sure a machine is working properly. **Repairing:** Repairing machines or systems using the needed tools. **Operation and Control:** Controlling operations of equipment or systems. **Troubleshooting:** Determining causes of operating errors and deciding what to do about them. **Service Orientation:** Actively looking for ways to help people.

Work Environment: Indoors; standing; walking and running; using hands; contaminants; exposed to radiation; exposed to disease or infections; hazardous conditions.

Nuclear Power Reactor Operators

- ⊙ Annual Earnings: $76,590
- ⊙ Earnings Growth Potential: Low (26.9%)
- ⊙ Growth: 3.8%
- ⊙ Annual Job Openings: 200
- ⊙ Self-Employed: 0.0%

Considerations for Job Outlook: Job prospects should be good for those with related training and good mechanical skills. As many power plant operators, distributors, and dispatchers near retirement age, companies will need workers to replace operators and dispatchers who retire. Many individuals may show interest in these high-paying jobs, and job prospects will be best for those with strong technical and mechanical skills.

Operate or control nuclear reactors. Adjust controls to position rods and to regulate flux levels, reactor periods, coolant temperatures, and rates of power flow, following standard procedures. Respond to system or unit abnormalities, diagnosing the cause, and recommending or taking corrective action. Monitor all systems for normal running conditions, performing activities such as checking gauges to assess output or assess the effects of generator loading on other equipment. Implement operational procedures such as those controlling start-up and shut-down activities. Note malfunctions of equipment, instruments, or controls, and report these conditions to supervisors. Monitor and operate boilers, turbines, wells, and auxiliary power plant equipment. Dispatch orders and instructions to personnel through radiotelephone or intercommunication systems to coordinate auxiliary equipment operation. Record operating data, such as the results of surveillance tests.

Education/Training Required: High school diploma or equivalent. **Education and Training Program:** Nuclear/Nuclear Power Technology/Technician. **Knowledge/Courses—Physics:** Physical principles, laws, their interrelationships, and applications to understanding fluid, material, and atmospheric dynamics, and mechanical, electrical, atomic, and subatomic structures and processes. **Chemistry:** The chemical composition, structure, and properties of substances and of the chemical processes and transformations that they undergo. This includes uses of chemicals and their danger signs, production techniques, and disposal methods. **Engineering and Technology:** The practical application of engineering science and technology. This includes applying principles, techniques, procedures, and equipment to the design and production of various goods and services. **Mechanical Devices:** Machines and tools, including their designs, uses, repair, and maintenance. **Design:** Design techniques, tools, and principles involved in production of precision technical plans, blueprints, drawings, and models. **Mathematics:** Arithmetic, algebra, geometry, calculus, statistics, and

their applications. **Work Experience Needed:** None. **On-the-Job Training Needed:** Long-term on-the-job training. **Certification/Licensure:** Federal licensure.

Personality Type: Realistic-Conventional-Enterprising. **Career Cluster:** 13 Manufacturing. **Career Pathways:** 13.3 Maintenance, Installation, and Repair; 13.1 Production. **Other Jobs in These Pathways:** Adhesive Bonding Machine Operators and Tenders; Aircraft Mechanics and Service Technicians; Assemblers and Fabricators, All Other; Automotive Engineering Technicians; Automotive Specialty Technicians; Avionics Technicians; Biological Technicians; Cabinetmakers and Bench Carpenters; Camera and Photographic Equipment Repairers; Chemical Equipment Operators and Tenders; Civil Engineering Technicians; Cleaning, Washing, and Metal Pickling Equipment Operators and Tenders; Coating, Painting, and Spraying Machine Setters, Operators, and Tenders; Coil Winders, Tapers, and Finishers; Computer, Automated Teller, and Office Machine Repairers; Computer-Controlled Machine Tool Operators, Metal and Plastic; Construction and Related Workers, All Other; Control and Valve Installers and Repairers, Except Mechanical Door; Cooling and Freezing Equipment Operators and Tenders; Cost Estimators; Crushing, Grinding, and Polishing Machine Setters, Operators, and Tenders; Cutters and Trimmers, Hand; others.

Skills—Operation and Control: Controlling operations of equipment or systems. **Troubleshooting:** Determining causes of operating errors and deciding what to do about them. **Operation Monitoring:** Watching gauges, dials, or other indicators to make sure a machine is working properly. **Science:** Using scientific rules and methods to solve problems. **Quality Control Analysis:** Conducting tests and inspections of products, services, or processes to evaluate quality or performance. **Monitoring:** Monitoring or assessing your performance or that of other individuals or organizations to make improvements or take corrective action. **Instructing:** Teaching others how to do something. **Mathematics:** Using mathematics to solve problems.

Work Environment: Indoors; sitting; using hands; noise; exposed to radiation.

Nuclear Technicians

- ⊙ Annual Earnings: $68,030
- ⊙ Earnings Growth Potential: Medium (39.8%)
- ⊙ Growth: 14.1%
- ⊙ Annual Job Openings: 330
- ⊙ Self-Employed: 0.0%

Considerations for Job Outlook: Nuclear technicians should have good job opportunities over the next decade. In the nuclear power industry, many openings should arise from technicians who retire or leave the occupation for other reasons.

Assist nuclear physicists, nuclear engineers, or other scientists in laboratory or production activities. For task data, see Job Specializations.

Education/Training Required: Associate degree. **Work Experience Needed:** None. **On-the-Job Training Needed:** Moderate-term on-the-job training. **Certification/Licensure:** Security clearance in some positions.

Job Specialization: Nuclear Equipment Operation Technicians

Operate equipment used for the release, control, and utilization of nuclear energy to assist scientists in laboratory and production activities. Follow policies and procedures for radiation workers to ensure personnel safety.

Education and Training Programs: Industrial Radiologic Technology/Technician; Nuclear and Industrial Radiologic Technologies/Technicians, Other; Nuclear Engineering Technology/Technician; Nuclear/Nuclear Power Technology/Technician; Radiation Protection/Health Physics Technician Training. **Knowledge/Courses—Physics:** Physical principles, laws, their interrelationships, and applications to understanding fluid, material, and atmospheric dynamics, and mechanical, electrical, atomic, and subatomic structures and processes. **Chemistry:** The chemical composition, structure, and properties of substances and of the chemical processes and transformations that they undergo. This includes uses of chemicals and their danger signs, production techniques, and disposal methods. **Mechanical Devices:** Machines and tools, including their designs, uses, repair, and maintenance. **Public Safety and Security:** Relevant equipment, policies, procedures, and strategies to promote effective local, state, or national security operations for the protection of people, data, property, and institutions. **Engineering and Technology:** The practical application of engineering science and technology. This includes applying principles, techniques, procedures, and equipment to the design and production of various goods and services. **Mathematics:** Arithmetic, algebra, geometry, calculus, statistics, and their applications.

Personality Type: Realistic-Conventional-Investigative. **Career Clusters:** 08 Health Science; 13 Manufacturing; 15 Science, Technology, Engineering, and Mathematics. **Career Pathways:** 08.2 Diagnostics Services; 13.3 Maintenance, Installation, and Repair; 15.1 Engineering and Technology. **Other Jobs in These Pathways:** Aerospace Engineers; Agricultural Engineers; Aircraft Mechanics and Service Technicians; Ambulance Drivers and Attendants, Except Emergency Medical Technicians; Anesthesiologist Assistants; Architectural and Engineering Managers; Architecture Teachers, Postsecondary; Athletic Trainers; Automotive Engineering Technicians; Automotive Engineers; Automotive Specialty Technicians; Avionics Technicians; Biochemical Engineers; Biofuels/Biodiesel Technology and Product Development Managers; Biological Technicians; Biomedical Engineers; Camera and Photographic Equipment Repairers; Cardiovascular Technologists and Technicians; Chemical Engineers; Chemical Equipment Operators and Tenders; Civil Engineering Technicians; Civil Engineers; Coil Winders, Tapers, and Finishers; Computer Hardware Engineers; Computer, Automated Teller, and Office Machine Repairers; Construction and Related Workers, All Other; Control and Valve Installers and Repairers, Except Mechanical Door; Cost Estimators; others.

Skills—Repairing: Repairing machines or systems using the needed tools. **Equipment Maintenance:** Performing routine maintenance on equipment and determining when and what kind of maintenance is needed. **Operation and Control:** Controlling operations of equipment or systems. **Troubleshooting:** Determining causes of operating errors and deciding what to do about them. **Operation Monitoring:** Watching gauges, dials, or other indicators to make sure a machine is working properly. **Quality Control Analysis:** Conducting tests and inspections of products, services, or processes to evaluate quality or performance. **Mathematics:** Using mathematics to solve problems. **Science:** Using scientific rules and methods to solve problems.

Work Environment: More often indoors than outdoors; standing; walking and running; using hands; noise; very hot or cold; bright or inadequate lighting; contaminants; cramped work space; exposed to radiation; high places; hazardous conditions; hazardous equipment.

Job Specialization: Nuclear Monitoring Technicians

Collect and test samples to monitor results of nuclear experiments and contamination of humans, facilities, and environment. Calculate safe radiation exposure times for personnel using plant contamination readings and prescribed safe levels of radiation. Provide initial response to abnormal events and to alarms from radiation monitoring equipment. Monitor personnel to determine the amounts and intensities of radiation exposure. Inform supervisors when individual exposures or area radiation levels approach maximum permissible limits. Instruct personnel in radiation safety procedures and demonstrate use of protective clothing and equipment. Determine intensities and types of radiation in work areas, equipment, and materials, using radiation detectors and other instruments. Collect samples of air, water, gases, and solids to determine radioactivity levels of contamination. Set up equipment that automatically detects area radiation deviations and test detection equipment to ensure its accuracy.

Education and Training Programs: Industrial Radiologic Technology/Technician; Nuclear and Industrial Radiologic Technologies/Technicians, Other; Nuclear Engineering Technology/Technician; Nuclear/Nuclear Power Technology/Technician; Radiation Protection/Health Physics Technician Training. **Knowledge/Courses—Physics:** Physical principles, laws, their interrelationships, and applications to understanding fluid, material, and atmospheric dynamics, and mechanical, electrical, atomic, and subatomic structures and processes. **Chemistry:** The chemical composition, structure, and properties of substances and of the chemical processes and transformations that they undergo. This includes uses of chemicals and their danger signs, production techniques, and disposal methods. **Biology:** Plant and animal organisms and their tissues, cells, functions, interdependencies, and interactions with each other and the environment. **Mathematics:** Arithmetic,

algebra, geometry, calculus, statistics, and their applications. **Engineering and Technology:** The practical application of engineering science and technology. This includes applying principles, techniques, procedures, and equipment to the design and production of various goods and services. **Public Safety and Security:** Relevant equipment, policies, procedures, and strategies to promote effective local, state, or national security operations for the protection of people, data, property, and institutions.

Personality Type: Realistic-Conventional-Investigative. **Career Clusters:** 08 Health Science; 13 Manufacturing; 15 Science, Technology, Engineering, and Mathematics. **Career Pathways:** 13.2 Manufacturing Production Process Development; 15.1 Engineering and Technology; 08.1 Therapeutic Services; 13.3 Maintenance, Installation, and Repair. **Other Jobs in These Pathways:** Acupuncturists; Aerospace Engineers; Agricultural Engineers; Aircraft Mechanics and Service Technicians; Allergists and Immunologists; Anesthesiologists; Architectural and Engineering Managers; Architecture Teachers, Postsecondary; Art Therapists; Automotive Engineering Technicians; Automotive Engineers; Automotive Specialty Technicians; Avionics Technicians; Biochemical Engineers; Biofuels Processing Technicians; Biofuels/Biodiesel Technology and Product Development Managers; Biological Technicians; Biomass Plant Technicians; Biomedical Engineers; Camera and Photographic Equipment Repairers; Chemical Engineers; Chemical Equipment Operators and Tenders; Chemical Plant and System Operators; Chemical Technicians; Chiropractors; Civil Engineering Technicians; Civil Engineers; Clinical Psychologists; Coil Winders, Tapers, and Finishers; Community and Social Service Specialists, All Other; Computer Hardware Engineers; Computer, Automated Teller, and Office Machine Repairers; others.

Skills—Operation Monitoring: Watching gauges, dials, or other indicators to make sure a machine is working properly. **Troubleshooting:** Determining causes of operating errors and deciding what to do about them. **Science:** Using scientific rules and methods to solve problems. **Quality Control Analysis:** Conducting tests and inspections of products, services, or processes to evaluate quality or performance. **Operation and Control:** Controlling operations of equipment or systems. **Monitoring:** Monitoring or assessing your performance or that of other individuals or organizations to make improvements or take corrective action. **Systems Analysis:** Determining how a system should work and how changes in conditions, operations, and the environment will affect outcomes. **Mathematics:** Using mathematics to solve problems.

Work Environment: More often indoors than outdoors; sitting; using hands; noise; very hot or cold; bright or inadequate lighting; contaminants; exposed to radiation; high places; hazardous conditions; hazardous equipment.

Occupational Health and Safety Technicians

- ⊙ Annual Earnings: $46,030
- ⊙ Earnings Growth Potential: High (40.2%)
- ⊙ Growth: 13.2%
- ⊙ Annual Job Openings: 510
- ⊙ Self-Employed: 3.1%

Considerations for Job Outlook: New environmental regulations and laws will require new or revised procedures in the workplace. The increased adoption of nuclear power as a source of energy is expected to be a major factor for job growth in that field as new regulations and precautions need to be enforced. These technicians will be needed to collect and test the data to maintain the safety of both the workers and the environment. Insurance and workers' compensation costs have become a concern for many employers and insurance companies, especially with an aging population remaining in the workforce longer.

Collect data on work environments for analysis by occupational health and safety specialists. Maintain all required records and documentation. Supply, operate, and maintain personal protective equipment. Verify that safety equipment such as hearing protection and respirators is available to employees, and monitor employees' use of such equipment to ensure proper fit and use. Evaluate situations where a worker has refused to work on the grounds that danger or potential harm exists, and determine how such situations should be handled. Prepare and calibrate equipment used to collect and analyze samples. Test workplaces for environmental hazards such as exposure to radiation, chemical and biological hazards, and excessive noise. Prepare and review specifications and orders for the purchase of safety equipment, ensuring that proper features are present and that items conform to health and safety standards. Report the results of environmental contaminant analyses,

and recommend corrective measures to be applied. Review physicians' reports, and conduct worker studies in order to determine whether specific instances of disease or illness are job-related. Examine credentials, licenses, or permits to ensure compliance with licensing requirements. Conduct fire drills, and inspect fire-suppression systems and portable fire systems to ensure that they are in working order. Educate the public about health issues, and enforce health legislation in order to prevent diseases, to promote health, and to help people understand health protection procedures and regulations.

Education/Training Required: High school diploma or equivalent. **Education and Training Programs:** Environmental Health; Occupational Health and Industrial Hygiene; Radiation Protection/Health Physics Technician Training. **Knowledge/Courses—Building and Construction:** Materials, methods, and the tools involved in the construction or repair of houses, buildings, or other structures such as highways and roads. **Chemistry:** The chemical composition, structure, and properties of substances and of the chemical processes and transformations that they undergo. This includes uses of chemicals and their danger signs, production techniques, and disposal methods. **Public Safety and Security:** Relevant equipment, policies, procedures, and strategies to promote effective local, state, or national security operations for the protection of people, data, property, and institutions. **Engineering and Technology:** The practical application of engineering science and technology. This includes applying principles, techniques, procedures, and equipment to the design and production of various goods and services. **Physics:** Physical principles, laws, their interrelationships, and applications to understanding fluid, material, and atmospheric dynamics, and mechanical, electrical, atomic, and subatomic structures and processes. **Education and Training:** Principles and methods for curriculum and training design, teaching and instruction for individuals and groups, and the measurement of training effects. **Work Experience Needed:** None. **On-the-Job Training Needed:** Moderate-term on-the-job training. **Certification/Licensure:** Voluntary certification by association.

Personality Type: Conventional-Realistic. **Career Cluster:** 08 Health Science. **Career Pathways:** 08.1 Therapeutic Services; 08.3 Health Informatics. **Other Jobs in These Pathways:** Acupuncturists; Allergists and Immunologists; Anesthesiologists; Art Therapists; Chiropractors; Clinical

Psychologists; Communications Teachers, Postsecondary; Community and Social Service Specialists, All Other; Counseling Psychologists; Counselors, All Other; Dental Assistants; Dental Hygienists; Dental Laboratory Technicians; Dentists, All Other Specialists; Dentists, General; Dermatologists; Diagnostic Medical Sonographers; Dietetic Technicians; Dietitians and Nutritionists; Editors; Engineers, All Other; Executive Secretaries and Executive Administrative Assistants; Family and General Practitioners; Fine Artists, Including Painters, Sculptors, and Illustrators; First-Line Supervisors of Office and Administrative Support Workers; Health Diagnosing and Treating Practitioners, All Other; Health Educators; Health Specialties Teachers, Postsecondary; Health Technologists and Technicians, All Other; Healthcare Practitioners and Technical Workers, All Other; others.

Skills—Science: Using scientific rules and methods to solve problems. **Operation and Control:** Controlling operations of equipment or systems. **Operation Monitoring:** Watching gauges, dials, or other indicators to make sure a machine is working properly. **Reading Comprehension:** Understanding written sentences and paragraphs in work-related documents. **Writing:** Communicating effectively in writing as appropriate for the needs of the audience. **Active Listening:** Giving full attention to what other people are saying, taking time to understand the points being made, asking questions as appropriate, and not interrupting at inappropriate times. **Monitoring:** Monitoring or assessing your performance or that of other individuals or organizations to make improvements or take corrective action. **Systems Evaluation:** Identifying measures or indicators of system performance and the actions needed to improve or correct performance relative to the goals of the system.

Work Environment: More often outdoors than indoors; standing; noise; contaminants; high places; hazardous conditions; hazardous equipment.

Occupational Therapy Aides

- ⊙ Annual Earnings: $28,200
- ⊙ Earnings Growth Potential: Low (33.7%)
- ⊙ Growth: 33.3%
- ⊙ Annual Job Openings: 360
- ⊙ Self-Employed: 0.9%

Considerations for Job Outlook: Occupational therapy assistants and aides with experience working in an occupational therapy office or other health-care setting should have the best job opportunities. In addition to overall employment growth, job openings will also result from the need to replace occupational therapy assistants and aides who leave the occupation.

Under close supervision of an occupational therapist or occupational therapy assistant, perform only delegated, selected, or routine tasks in specific situations. Encourage patients and attend to their physical needs to facilitate the attainment of therapeutic goals. Report to supervisors or therapists, verbally or in writing, on patients' progress, attitudes, attendance, and accomplishments. Observe patients' attendance, progress, attitudes, and accomplishments, and record and maintain information in client records. Manage intradepartmental infection control and equipment security. Evaluate the living skills and capacities of physically, developmentally, or emotionally disabled clients. Prepare and maintain work area, materials, and equipment, and maintain inventory of treatment and educational supplies. Instruct patients and families in work, social, and living skills; the care and use of adaptive equipment; and other skills to facilitate home and work adjustment to disability. Supervise patients in choosing and completing work details or arts and crafts projects. Assist occupational therapists in planning, implementing, and administering therapy programs to restore, reinforce, and enhance performance, using selected activities and special equipment. Perform clerical, administrative, and secretarial duties such as answering phones, restocking and ordering supplies, filling out paperwork, and scheduling appointments. Demonstrate therapy techniques, such as manual and creative arts, and games. Transport patients to and from the occupational therapy work area. Adjust and repair assistive devices and make adaptive changes to other equipment and to environments. Assist educational specialists or clinical psychologists in administering situational or diagnostic tests to measure client's abilities or progress. Accompany patients on outings, providing transportation when necessary.

Education/Training Required: High school diploma or equivalent. **Education and Training Program:** Occupational Therapist Assistant Training. **Knowledge/Courses—Therapy and Counseling:** Principles, methods, and procedures for diagnosis, treatment, and rehabilitation of physical and mental dysfunctions, and for career counseling and guidance. **Medicine and Dentistry:** The information and techniques needed to diagnose and treat human injuries, diseases, and deformities. This includes symptoms, treatment alternatives, drug properties and interactions, and preventive health-care measures. **Psychology:** Human behavior and performance; individual differences in ability, personality, and interests; learning and motivation; psychological research methods; and the assessment and treatment of behavioral and affective disorders. **Biology:** Plant and animal organisms and their tissues, cells, functions, interdependencies, and interactions with each other and the environment. **Education and Training:** Principles and methods for curriculum and training design, teaching and instruction for individuals and groups, and the measurement of training effects. **Sociology and Anthropology:** Group behavior and dynamics, societal trends and influences, human migrations, ethnicity, and cultures and their history and origins. **Work Experience Needed:** None. **On-the-Job Training Needed:** Short-term on-the-job training. **Certification/Licensure:** None.

Personality Type: Social-Realistic. **Career Cluster:** 08 Health Science. **Career Pathway:** 08.1 Therapeutic Services. **Other Jobs in This Pathway:** Acupuncturists; Allergists and Immunologists; Anesthesiologists; Art Therapists; Chiropractors; Clinical Psychologists; Community and Social Service Specialists, All Other; Counseling Psychologists; Counselors, All Other; Dental Assistants; Dental Hygienists; Dentists, All Other Specialists; Dentists, General; Dermatologists; Diagnostic Medical Sonographers; Dietetic Technicians; Dietitians and Nutritionists; Family and General Practitioners; Health Diagnosing and Treating Practitioners, All Other; Health Specialties Teachers, Postsecondary; Health Technologists and Technicians, All Other; Healthcare Practitioners and Technical Workers, All Other; Healthcare Support Workers, All Other; Home Health Aides; Hospitalists; Industrial-Organizational Psychologists; Internists, General; Licensed Practical and Licensed Vocational Nurses; Life, Physical, and Social Science Technicians, All Other; Low Vision Therapists, Orientation and Mobility Specialists, and Vision Rehabilitation Therapists; others.

Skills—Service Orientation: Actively looking for ways to help people. **Social Perceptiveness:** Being aware of others' reactions and understanding why they react as they do.

Persuasion: Persuading others to change their minds or behavior. **Speaking:** Talking to others to convey information effectively. **Active Listening:** Giving full attention to what other people are saying, taking time to understand the points being made, asking questions as appropriate, and not interrupting at inappropriate times. **Instructing:** Teaching others how to do something. **Writing:** Communicating effectively in writing as appropriate for the needs of the audience.

Work Environment: Indoors; standing; walking and running; kneeling, crouching, stooping, or crawling; using hands; bending or twisting the body; repetitive motions; noise; contaminants; cramped work space; exposed to disease or infections.

Occupational Therapy Assistants

- ⊙ Annual Earnings: $52,040
- ⊙ Earnings Growth Potential: Medium (35.1%)
- ⊙ Growth: 43.2%
- ⊙ Annual Job Openings: 1,680
- ⊙ Self-Employed: 0.9%

Considerations for Job Outlook: Occupational therapy assistants and aides with experience working in an occupational therapy office or other health-care setting should have the best job opportunities. In addition to overall employment growth, job openings will also result from the need to replace occupational therapy assistants and aides who leave the occupation.

Assist occupational therapists in providing occupational therapy treatments and procedures. Observe and record patients' progress, attitudes, and behavior, and maintain this information in client records. Maintain and promote a positive attitude toward clients and their treatment programs. Monitor patients' performance in therapy activities, providing encouragement. Select therapy activities to fit patients' needs and capabilities. Instruct, or assist in instructing, patients and families in home programs, basic living skills, and the care and use of adaptive equipment. Evaluate the daily living skills and capacities of physically, developmentally, or emotionally disabled clients. Aid patients in dressing and grooming themselves. Implement, or assist occupational therapists with implementing, treatment plans designed to help clients function independently. Report to supervisors, verbally or in writing, on patients' progress, attitudes, and behavior. Alter treatment programs to obtain better results if treatment is not having the intended effect. Work under the direction of occupational therapists to plan, implement, and administer educational, vocational, and recreational programs that restore and enhance performance in individuals with functional impairments. Design, fabricate, and repair assistive devices, and make adaptive changes to equipment and environments. Assemble, clean, and maintain equipment and materials for patient use. Teach patients how to deal constructively with their emotions.

Education/Training Required: Associate degree. **Education and Training Program:** Occupational Therapist Assistant Training. **Knowledge/Courses—Psychology:** Human behavior and performance; individual differences in ability, personality, and interests; learning and motivation; psychological research methods; and the assessment and treatment of behavioral and affective disorders. **Therapy and Counseling:** Principles, methods, and procedures for diagnosis, treatment, and rehabilitation of physical and mental dysfunctions, and for career counseling and guidance. **Philosophy and Theology:** Different philosophical systems and religions. This includes their basic principles, values, ethics, ways of thinking, customs, practices, and their impact on human culture. **Medicine and Dentistry:** The information and techniques needed to diagnose and treat human injuries, diseases, and deformities. This includes symptoms, treatment alternatives, drug properties and interactions, and preventive health-care measures. **Sociology and Anthropology:** Group behavior and dynamics, societal trends and influences, human migrations, ethnicity, and cultures and their history and origins. **Education and Training:** Principles and methods for curriculum and training design, teaching and instruction for individuals and groups, and the measurement of training effects. **Work Experience Needed:** None. **On-the-Job Training Needed:** None. **Certification/Licensure:** Licensure, registration, or certification.

Personality Type: Social-Realistic. **Career Cluster:** 08 Health Science. **Career Pathway:** 08.1 Therapeutic Services. **Other Jobs in This Pathway:** Acupuncturists; Allergists and Immunologists; Anesthesiologists; Art Therapists; Chiropractors; Clinical Psychologists; Community and Social Service Specialists, All Other; Counseling Psychologists; Counselors, All Other; Dental Assistants; Dental Hygienists; Dentists, All Other Specialists; Dentists, General; Dermatologists; Diagnostic Medical Sonographers; Dietetic Technicians; Dietitians and Nutritionists; Family and General Practitioners; Health Diagnosing and Treating Practitioners, All Other; Health Specialties Teachers, Postsecondary; Health Technologists and Technicians, All Other; Healthcare Practitioners and Technical Workers, All Other; Healthcare Support Workers, All Other; Home Health Aides; Hospitalists; Industrial-Organizational Psychologists; Internists, General; Licensed Practical and Licensed Vocational Nurses; Life, Physical, and Social Science Technicians, All Other; Low Vision Therapists, Orientation and Mobility Specialists, and Vision Rehabilitation Therapists; others.

Skills—Learning Strategies: Selecting and using training/instructional methods and procedures appropriate for the situation when learning or teaching new things. **Social Perceptiveness:** Being aware of others' reactions and understanding why they react as they do. **Negotiation:** Bringing others together and trying to reconcile differences. **Service Orientation:** Actively looking for ways to help people. **Instructing:** Teaching others how to do something. **Persuasion:** Persuading others to change their minds or behavior. **Operation Monitoring:** Watching gauges, dials, or other indicators to make sure a machine is working properly. **Writing:** Communicating effectively in writing as appropriate for the needs of the audience.

Work Environment: Indoors; standing; using hands; noise; exposed to disease or infections.

Office Clerks, General

- ⊙ Annual Earnings: $27,190
- ⊙ Earnings Growth Potential: Low (34.8%)
- ⊙ Growth: 16.6%
- ⊙ Annual Job Openings: 101,150
- ⊙ Self-Employed: 0.3%

Considerations for Job Outlook: Job prospects are expected to be good in this large occupation. Workers will be needed to fill new jobs and replace those who leave the occupation. General office clerks who can learn new skills and adapt to changing technologies will have the best prospects.

Perform duties too varied and diverse to be classified in any specific office clerical occupation, requiring

knowledge of office systems and procedures. Collect, count, and disburse money; do basic bookkeeping; and complete banking transactions. Communicate with customers, employees, and other individuals to answer questions, disseminate or explain information, take orders, and address complaints. Answer telephones, direct calls, and take messages. Compile, copy, sort, and file records of office activities, business transactions, and other activities. Complete and mail bills, contracts, policies, invoices, or checks. Operate office machines such as photocopiers and scanners, facsimile machines, voice mail systems, and personal computers. Compute, record, and proofread data and other information, such as records or reports. Maintain and update filing, inventory, mailing, and database systems, either manually or using a computer. Open, sort, and route incoming mail; answer correspondence; and prepare outgoing mail. Review files, records, and other documents to obtain information to respond to requests. Deliver messages, and run errands. Inventory and order materials, supplies, and services. Complete work schedules, manage calendars, and arrange appointments. Process and prepare documents such as business or government forms and expense reports. Monitor and direct the work of lower-level clerks. Type, format, proofread, and edit correspondence and other documents from notes or dictating machines, using computers or typewriters. Count, weigh, measure, or organize materials.

Education/Training Required: High school diploma or equivalent. **Education and Training Program:** General Office Occupations and Clerical Services. **Knowledge/Courses—Clerical Practices:** Administrative and clerical procedures and systems such as word processing, managing files and records, stenography and transcription, designing forms, and other office procedures and terminology. **Customer and Personal Service:** Principles and processes for providing customer and personal services. This includes customer needs assessment, meeting quality standards for services, and evaluation of customer satisfaction. **Computers and Electronics:** Circuit boards, processors, chips, electronic equipment, and computer hardware and software, including applications and programming. **Work Experience Needed:** None. **On-the-Job Training Needed:** Short-term on-the-job training. **Certification/Licensure:** None.

Personality Type: Conventional-Enterprising-Realistic. **Career Cluster:** 04 Business, Management, and Administration. **Career Pathway:** 04.6 Administrative and

Information Support. **Other Jobs in This Pathway:** Cargo and Freight Agents; Correspondence Clerks; Couriers and Messengers; Court Clerks; Customer Service Representatives; Data Entry Keyers; Dispatchers, Except Police, Fire, and Ambulance; Executive Secretaries and Executive Administrative Assistants; File Clerks; Freight Forwarders; Human Resources Assistants, Except Payroll and Timekeeping; Information and Record Clerks, All Other; Insurance Claims Clerks; Insurance Policy Processing Clerks; Interviewers, Except Eligibility and Loan; License Clerks; Mail Clerks and Mail Machine Operators, Except Postal Service; Meter Readers, Utilities; Municipal Clerks; Office and Administrative Support Workers, All Other; Office Machine Operators, Except Computer; Order Clerks; Patient Representatives; Postal Service Clerks; Postal Service Mail Carriers; Postal Service Mail Sorters, Processors, and Processing Machine Operators; Procurement Clerks; Receptionists and Information Clerks; others.

Skills—Management of Material Resources: Obtaining and seeing to the appropriate use of equipment, facilities, and materials needed to do certain work. **Service Orientation:** Actively looking for ways to help people. **Active Listening:** Giving full attention to what other people are saying, taking time to understand the points being made, asking questions as appropriate, and not interrupting at inappropriate times. **Management of Financial Resources:** Determining how money will be spent to get the work done and accounting for these expenditures. **Reading Comprehension:** Understanding written sentences and paragraphs in work-related documents. **Speaking:** Talking to others to convey information effectively.

Work Environment: Indoors; sitting; repetitive motions.

Operating Engineers and Other Construction Equipment Operators

- ⊙ Annual Earnings: $41,510
- ⊙ Earnings Growth Potential: Medium (35.6%)
- ⊙ Growth: 23.5%
- ⊙ Annual Job Openings: 16,280
- ⊙ Self-Employed: 4.9%

Considerations for Job Outlook: Workers with the ability to operate multiple types of equipment should have the best job opportunities. As with many other construction workers, employment of construction equipment operators is sensitive to fluctuations of the economy. Workers may experience periods of unemployment when the overall level of construction falls. However, shortages of workers may occur in some areas during peak periods of building activity. Employment opportunities should be best in metropolitan areas, where most large commercial and multifamily buildings are constructed, and in states that are undertaking large transportation-related projects. In addition, the need to replace workers who leave the occupation should result in some job opportunities.

Operate one or several types of power construction equipment. Learn and follow safety regulations. Take actions to avoid potential hazards and obstructions such as utility lines, other equipment, other workers, and falling objects. Adjust handwheels and depress pedals to control attachments such as blades, buckets, scrapers, and swing booms. Start engines; move throttles, switches, and levers; and depress pedals to operate machines such as bulldozers, trench excavators, road graders, and backhoes. Locate underground services, such as pipes and wires, prior to beginning work. Monitor operations to ensure that health and safety standards are met. Align machines, cutterheads, or depth gauge makers with reference stakes and guidelines, or ground or position equipment by following hand signals of other workers. Load and move dirt, rocks, equipment, and materials, using trucks, crawler tractors, power cranes, shovels, graders, and related equipment. Drive and maneuver equipment outfitted with blades in successive passes over working areas to remove topsoil, vegetation, and rocks and to distribute and level earth or terrain. Coordinate machine actions with other activities, positioning or moving loads in response to hand or audio signals from crew members. Operate tractors and bulldozers to perform such tasks as clearing land, mixing sludge, trimming backfills, and building roadways and parking lots. Repair and maintain equipment, making emergency adjustments or assisting with major repairs as necessary.

Education/Training Required: High school diploma or equivalent. **Education and Training Programs:** Construction/Heavy Equipment/Earthmoving Equipment Operation; Mobile Crane Operation/Operator. **Knowledge/Courses—Building and Construction:** Materials, methods, and the tools involved in the construction or repair of houses, buildings, or other structures such as highways and roads. **Mechanical Devices:** Machines and

tools, including their designs, uses, repair, and maintenance. **Engineering and Technology:** The practical application of engineering science and technology. This includes applying principles, techniques, procedures, and equipment to the design and production of various goods and services. **Design:** Design techniques, tools, and principles involved in production of precision technical plans, blueprints, drawings, and models. **Production and Processing:** Raw materials, production processes, quality control, costs, and other techniques for maximizing the effective manufacture and distribution of goods. **Public Safety and Security:** Relevant equipment, policies, procedures, and strategies to promote effective local, state, or national security operations for the protection of people, data, property, and institutions. **Work Experience Needed:** None. **On-the-Job Training Needed:** Moderate-term on-the-job training. **Certification/Licensure:** Licensure for some specializations.

Personality Type: Realistic-Conventional-Investigative. **Career Clusters:** 02 Architecture and Construction; 16 Transportation, Distribution, and Logistics. **Career Pathways:** 16.1 Transportation Operations; 02.2 Construction. **Other Jobs in These Pathways:** Aerospace Engineering and Operations Technicians; Air Traffic Controllers; Aircraft Cargo Handling Supervisors; Airfield Operations Specialists; Airline Pilots, Copilots, and Flight Engineers; Automotive and Watercraft Service Attendants; Automotive Master Mechanics; Aviation Inspectors; Boilermakers; Brickmasons and Blockmasons; Bridge and Lock Tenders; Bus Drivers, School or Special Client; Bus Drivers, Transit and Intercity; Carpet Installers; Cement Masons and Concrete Finishers; Commercial Divers; Commercial Pilots; Construction and Building Inspectors; Construction and Related Workers, All Other; Construction Carpenters; Construction Laborers; Construction Managers; Continuous Mining Machine Operators; Cost Estimators; Crane and Tower Operators; Dredge Operators; Drywall and Ceiling Tile Installers; Earth Drillers, Except Oil and Gas; Electrical Power-Line Installers and Repairers; Electricians; Electromechanical Equipment Assemblers; others.

Skills—Operation and Control: Controlling operations of equipment or systems. **Repairing:** Repairing machines or systems using the needed tools. **Equipment Maintenance:** Performing routine maintenance on equipment and determining when and what kind of maintenance is needed. **Troubleshooting:** Determining causes of operating errors and deciding what to do about them. **Operation Monitoring:** Watching gauges, dials, or other indicators to make sure a machine is working properly. **Quality Control Analysis:** Conducting tests and inspections of products, services, or processes to evaluate quality or performance. **Equipment Selection:** Determining the kind of tools and equipment needed to do a job. **Installation:** Installing equipment, machines, wiring, or programs to meet specifications.

Work Environment: Outdoors; sitting; using hands; repetitive motions; noise; very hot or cold; bright or inadequate lighting; contaminants; whole-body vibration; hazardous equipment; minor burns, cuts, bites, or stings.

Ophthalmic Laboratory Technicians

- ⊙ Annual Earnings: $28,750
- ⊙ Earnings Growth Potential: Medium (35.2%)
- ⊙ Growth: 12.8%
- ⊙ Annual Job Openings: 1,320
- ⊙ Self-Employed: 6.1%

Considerations for Job Outlook: Most people need vision correction at some point in their lives. As the total population continues to grow, people will need more vision aids, such as glasses and contacts. Middle age is a time when many people use corrective lenses for the first time, and the need for vision care continues to increase with age. As the large baby-boom generation and their children get older, the need for vision correction will create a demand for ophthalmic laboratory services. As laser vision correction becomes less expensive, there will be an increase in the demand for that service and a decrease in the demand for eyeglasses. However, even with laser correction, almost all adults need reading glasses or corrective eyewear later in their lives. The cause is retinal hardening, which happens naturally as people age, making it harder for the eye to focus.

Cut, grind, and polish eyeglasses, contact lenses, or other precision optical elements. Adjust lenses and frames in order to correct alignment. Mount, secure, and align finished lenses in frames or optical assemblies, using precision hand tools. Mount and secure lens blanks or optical lenses in holding tools or chucks of cutting, polishing, grinding, or coating machines. Shape lenses appropriately so that they can be inserted into frames. Assemble eyeglass frames and attach shields, nose pads, and temple pieces, using pliers, screwdrivers, and drills. Inspect lens blanks in order to detect flaws, verify smoothness of surface, and ensure thickness of coating on lenses. Clean finished lenses and eyeglasses, using cloths and solvents. Select lens blanks, molds, tools, and polishing or grinding wheels, according to production specifications. Examine prescriptions, work orders, or broken or used eyeglasses in order to determine specifications for lenses, contact lenses, and other optical elements. Set dials and start machines to polish lenses, or hold lenses against rotating wheels in order to polish them manually. Set up machines to polish, bevel, edge, and grind lenses, flats, blanks, and other precision optical elements. Repair broken parts, using precision hand tools and soldering irons. Position and adjust cutting tools to specified curvature, dimensions, and depth of cut. Inspect, weigh, and measure mounted or unmounted lenses after completion in order to verify alignment and conformance to specifications, using precision instruments. Remove lenses from molds, and separate lenses in containers for further processing or storage. Lay out lenses and trace lens outlines on glass, using templates. Immerse eyeglass frames in solutions in order to harden, soften, or dye frames. Control equipment that coats lenses to alter their reflective qualities.

Education/Training Required: High school diploma or equivalent. **Education and Training Program:** Ophthalmic Laboratory Technology/Technician. **Knowledge/ Courses—Computers and Electronics:** Circuit boards, processors, chips, electronic equipment, and computer hardware and software, including applications and programming. **Work Experience Needed:** None. **On-the-Job Training Needed:** Moderate-term on-the-job training. **Certification/Licensure:** None.

Personality Type: Realistic-Conventional. **Career Cluster:** 08 Health Science. **Career Pathway:** 08.2 Diagnostics Services. **Other Jobs in This Pathway:** Ambulance Drivers and Attendants, Except Emergency Medical Technicians; Anesthesiologist Assistants; Athletic Trainers; Cardiovascular Technologists and Technicians; Cytogenetic Technologists; Cytotechnologists; Diagnostic Medical Sonographers; Emergency Medical Technicians and Paramedics; Endoscopy Technicians; Health Diagnosing and Treating Practitioners, All Other; Health Specialties Teachers, Postsecondary; Health Technologists and Technicians,

All Other; Healthcare Practitioners and Technical Workers, All Other; Histotechnologists and Histologic Technicians; Medical and Clinical Laboratory Technicians; Medical and Clinical Laboratory Technologists; Medical and Health Services Managers; Medical Assistants; Medical Equipment Preparers; Neurodiagnostic Technologists; Nuclear Equipment Operation Technicians; Nuclear Medicine Technologists; Pathologists; Physical Scientists, All Other; Physician Assistants; Radiation Therapists; Radiologic Technicians; Radiologic Technologists; others.

Skills—Equipment Selection: Determining the kind of tools and equipment needed to do a job. **Quality Control Analysis:** Conducting tests and inspections of products, services, or processes to evaluate quality or performance. **Repairing:** Repairing machines or systems using the needed tools. **Operation and Control:** Controlling operations of equipment or systems. **Equipment Maintenance:** Performing routine maintenance on equipment and determining when and what kind of maintenance is needed. **Troubleshooting:** Determining causes of operating errors and deciding what to do about them. **Technology Design:** Generating or adapting equipment and technology to serve user needs. **Operation Monitoring:** Watching gauges, dials, or other indicators to make sure a machine is working properly.

Work Environment: Indoors; standing; walking and running; using hands; repetitive motions; noise; contaminants.

Opticians, Dispensing

- ⊙ Annual Earnings: $33,100
- ⊙ Earnings Growth Potential: Medium (36.8%)
- ⊙ Growth: 28.9%
- ⊙ Annual Job Openings: 3,060
- ⊙ Self-Employed: 0.8%

Considerations for Job Outlook: An aging population is anticipated to lead to greater demand for eye care services. People usually have eye problems in greater frequency when they reach middle age, so the need for opticians is expected to grow with the increase in the number of older people. Awareness of the importance of eye exams is increasing across all age groups. Also, fashion influences demand for frames and contact lenses. In addition, more opticians are finding employment in group medical practices.

Design, measure, fit, and adapt lenses and frames for clients according to written optical prescriptions or specifications. Verify that finished lenses are ground to specifications. Prepare work orders and instructions for grinding lenses and fabricating eyeglasses. Measure clients' bridge and eye size, temple length, vertex distance, pupillary distance, and optical centers of eyes, using measuring devices. Heat, shape, or bend plastic or metal frames to adjust eyeglasses to fit clients, using pliers and hands. Assist clients in selecting frames according to style and color, and ensure that frames are coordinated with facial and eye measurements and optical prescriptions. Evaluate prescriptions in conjunction with clients' vocational and avocational visual requirements. Fabricate lenses to meet prescription specifications. Maintain records of customer prescriptions, work orders, and payments. Recommend specific lenses, lens coatings, and frames to suit client needs. Instruct clients in how to wear and care for eyeglasses. Sell goods such as contact lenses, spectacles, sunglasses, and other goods related to eyes in general. Determine clients' current lens prescriptions, when necessary, using lensometers or lens analyzers and clients' eyeglasses. Show customers how to insert, remove, and care for their contact lenses. Assemble eyeglasses by cutting and edging lenses, and fitting the lenses into frames. Obtain customers' previous records, or verify prescriptions with the examining optometrists or ophthalmologists. Supervise the training of student opticians. Order and purchase frames and lenses. Grind lens edges, or apply coatings to lenses. Perform administrative duties such as tracking inventory and sales, submitting patient insurance information, and performing simple bookkeeping. Repair damaged frames. Arrange and maintain displays of optical merchandise.

Education/Training Required: High school diploma or equivalent. **Education and Training Program:** Opticianry/Ophthalmic Dispensing Optician. **Knowledge/Courses—Sales and Marketing:** Principles and methods for showing, promoting, and selling products or services. This includes marketing strategy and tactics, product demonstration, sales techniques, and sales control systems. **Clerical Practices:** Administrative and clerical procedures and systems such as word processing, managing files and records, stenography and transcription, designing forms, and other office procedures and terminology. **Customer and Personal Service:** Principles and processes for providing customer and personal services. This includes customer needs assessment, meeting quality standards for services, and evaluation of customer satisfaction. **Production and Processing:** Raw materials, production processes, quality control, costs, and other techniques for maximizing the effective manufacture and distribution of goods. **Economics and Accounting:** Economic and accounting principles and practices, the financial markets, banking, and the analysis and reporting of financial data. **Psychology:** Human behavior and performance; individual differences in ability, personality, and interests; learning and motivation; psychological research methods; and the assessment and treatment of behavioral and affective disorders. **Work Experience Needed:** None. **On-the-Job Training Needed:** Long-term on-the-job training. **Certification/ Licensure:** Voluntary certification by manufacturer, licensure in many states.

Personality Type: Enterprising-Conventional-Realistic. **Career Cluster:** 08 Health Science. **Career Pathway:** 08.1 Therapeutic Services. **Other Jobs in This Pathway:** Acupuncturists; Allergists and Immunologists; Anesthesiologists; Art Therapists; Chiropractors; Clinical Psychologists; Community and Social Service Specialists, All Other; Counseling Psychologists; Counselors, All Other; Dental Assistants; Dental Hygienists; Dentists, All Other Specialists; Dentists, General; Dermatologists; Diagnostic Medical Sonographers; Dietetic Technicians; Dietitians and Nutritionists; Family and General Practitioners; Health Diagnosing and Treating Practitioners, All Other; Health Specialties Teachers, Postsecondary; Health Technologists and Technicians, All Other; Healthcare Practitioners and Technical Workers, All Other; Healthcare Support Workers, All Other; Home Health Aides; Hospitalists; Industrial-Organizational Psychologists; Internists, General; Licensed Practical and Licensed Vocational Nurses; Life, Physical, and Social Science Technicians, All Other; Low Vision Therapists, Orientation and Mobility Specialists, and Vision Rehabilitation Therapists; others.

Skills—Service Orientation: Actively looking for ways to help people. **Technology Design:** Generating or adapting equipment and technology to serve user needs. **Negotiation:** Bringing others together and trying to reconcile differences. **Operations Analysis:** Analyzing needs and product requirements to create a design. **Persuasion:** Persuading others to change their minds or behavior. **Instructing:** Teaching others how to do something. **Quality Control Analysis:** Conducting tests and inspections of products, services, or processes to evaluate quality or

performance. **Operation Monitoring:** Watching gauges, dials, or other indicators to make sure a machine is working properly.

Work Environment: Indoors; standing; using hands.

Order Clerks

- ⊙ Annual Earnings: $28,940
- ⊙ Earnings Growth Potential: Medium (36.7%)
- ⊙ Growth: 7.4%
- ⊙ Annual Job Openings: 7,520
- ⊙ Self-Employed: 0.8%

Considerations for Job Outlook: Employment growth will vary by specialty. Projected employment change is most rapid for interviewers and correspondence clerks.

Receive and process incoming orders for materials, merchandise, classified ads, or services such as repairs, installations, or rental of facilities. Obtain customers' names, addresses, and billing information, product numbers, and specifications of items to be purchased, and enter this information on order forms. Prepare invoices, shipping documents, and contracts. Inform customers by mail or telephone of order information, such as unit prices, shipping dates, and any anticipated delays. Receive and respond to customer complaints. Verify customer and order information for correctness, checking it against previously obtained information as necessary. Direct specified departments or units to prepare and ship orders to designated locations. Review orders for completeness according to reporting procedures and forward incomplete orders for further processing. Check inventory records to determine availability of requested merchandise. Attempt to sell additional merchandise or services to prospective or current customers by telephone or through visits. File copies of orders received, or post orders on records. Compute total charges for merchandise or services and shipping charges. Confer with production, sales, shipping, warehouse, or common carrier personnel in order to expedite or trace shipments. Recommend merchandise or services that will meet customers' needs. Adjust inventory records to reflect product movement. Collect payment for merchandise, record transactions, and send items such as checks or money orders for further processing. Inspect outgoing work for compliance with customers' specifications. Notify departments when supplies of specific items are low, or when orders would deplete available supplies. Recommend type of packing or labeling needed on order. Calculate and compile order-related statistics, and prepare reports for management.

Education/Training Required: High school diploma or equivalent. **Education and Training Program:** General Office Occupations and Clerical Services. **Knowledge/Courses—Customer and Personal Service:** Principles and processes for providing customer and personal services. This includes customer needs assessment, meeting quality standards for services, and evaluation of customer satisfaction. **Clerical Practices:** Administrative and clerical procedures and systems such as word processing, managing files and records, stenography and transcription, designing forms, and other office procedures and terminology. **Sales and Marketing:** Principles and methods for showing, promoting, and selling products or services. This includes marketing strategy and tactics, product demonstration, sales techniques, and sales control systems. **Building and Construction:** Materials, methods, and the tools involved in the construction or repair of houses, buildings, or other structures such as highways and roads. **Economics and Accounting:** Economic and accounting principles and practices, the financial markets, banking, and the analysis and reporting of financial data. **Production and Processing:** Raw materials, production processes, quality control, costs, and other techniques for maximizing the effective manufacture and distribution of goods. **Work Experience Needed:** None. **On-the-Job Training Needed:** Short-term on-the-job training. **Certification/Licensure:** None.

Personality Type: Conventional-Enterprising-Social. **Career Cluster:** 04 Business, Management, and Administration. **Career Pathway:** 04.6 Administrative and Information Support. **Other Jobs in This Pathway:** Cargo and Freight Agents; Correspondence Clerks; Couriers and Messengers; Court Clerks; Customer Service Representatives; Data Entry Keyers; Dispatchers, Except Police, Fire, and Ambulance; Executive Secretaries and Executive Administrative Assistants; File Clerks; Freight Forwarders; Human Resources Assistants, Except Payroll and Time-keeping; Information and Record Clerks, All Other; Insurance Claims Clerks; Insurance Policy Processing Clerks; Interviewers, Except Eligibility and Loan; License Clerks; Mail Clerks and Mail Machine Operators, Except Postal Service; Meter Readers, Utilities; Municipal Clerks; Office and Administrative Support Workers, All Other; Office

Clerks, General; Office Machine Operators, Except Computer; Patient Representatives; Postal Service Clerks; Postal Service Mail Carriers; Postal Service Mail Sorters, Processors, and Processing Machine Operators; Procurement Clerks; Receptionists and Information Clerks; others.

Skills—Negotiation: Bringing others together and trying to reconcile differences. **Critical Thinking:** Using logic and reasoning to identify the strengths and weaknesses of alternative solutions, conclusions, or approaches to problems. **Management of Material Resources:** Obtaining and seeing to the appropriate use of equipment, facilities, and materials needed to do certain work. **Service Orientation:** Actively looking for ways to help people. **Mathematics:** Using mathematics to solve problems. **Persuasion:** Persuading others to change their minds or behavior. **Active Learning:** Understanding the implications of new information for both current and future problem solving and decision making. **Speaking:** Talking to others to convey information effectively.

Work Environment: Indoors; sitting; very hot or cold; contaminants.

Outdoor Power Equipment and Other Small Engine Mechanics

- ⊙ Annual Earnings: $30,200
- ⊙ Earnings Growth Potential: Medium (35.4%)
- ⊙ Growth: 18.9%
- ⊙ Annual Job Openings: 1,350
- ⊙ Self-Employed: 19.7%

Considerations for Job Outlook: Job opportunities are expected to be very good for candidates with formal training. Those without formal training can expect to face strong competition for jobs.

Diagnose, adjust, repair, or overhaul small engines used to power lawn mowers, chain saws, recreational sporting equipment, and related equipment. Replace motors. Repair or replace defective parts such as magnetos, water pumps, gears, pistons, and carburetors, using hand tools. Dismantle engines, using hand tools, and examine parts for defects. Test and inspect engines to determine malfunctions, to locate missing and broken parts, and to verify repairs, using diagnostic instruments. Grind, ream, rebore, and retap parts to obtain specified clearances, using grinders, lathes, taps, reamers, boring machines, and micrometers. Remove engines from equipment, and position and bolt engines to repair stands. Reassemble engines after repair or maintenance work is complete. Obtain problem descriptions from customers, and prepare cost estimates for repairs. Adjust points, valves, carburetors, distributors, and spark plug gaps, using feeler gauges. Record repairs made, time spent, and parts used. Show customers how to maintain equipment. Sell parts and equipment. Repair and maintain gasoline engines used to power equipment such as portable saws, lawn mowers, generators, and compressors. Perform routine maintenance such as cleaning and oiling parts, honing cylinders, and tuning ignition systems.

Education/Training Required: High school diploma or equivalent. **Education and Training Program:** Small Engine Mechanics and Repair Technology/Technician. **Knowledge/Courses—Mechanical Devices:** Machines and tools, including their designs, uses, repair, and maintenance. **Engineering and Technology:** The practical application of engineering science and technology. This includes applying principles, techniques, procedures, and equipment to the design and production of various goods and services. **Sales and Marketing:** Principles and methods for showing, promoting, and selling products or services. This includes marketing strategy and tactics, product demonstration, sales techniques, and sales control systems. **Physics:** Physical principles, laws, their interrelationships, and applications to understanding fluid, material, and atmospheric dynamics, and mechanical, electrical, atomic, and subatomic structures and processes. **Economics and Accounting:** Economic and accounting principles and practices, the financial markets, banking, and the analysis and reporting of financial data. **Chemistry:** The chemical composition, structure, and properties of substances and of the chemical processes and transformations that they undergo. This includes uses of chemicals and their danger signs, production techniques, and disposal methods. **Work Experience Needed:** None. **On-the-Job Training Needed:** Moderate-term on-the-job training. **Certification/Licensure:** None.

Personality Type: Realistic-Conventional. **Career Cluster:** 16 Transportation, Distribution, and Logistics. **Career Pathway:** 16.4 Facility and Mobile Equipment Maintenance. **Other Jobs in This Pathway:** Aircraft Mechanics and Service Technicians; Aircraft Structure, Surfaces, Rigging, and Systems Assemblers; Automotive Body and Related Repairers; Automotive Glass Installers and Repairers; Automotive Master Mechanics; Automotive Specialty Technicians; Bicycle Repairers; Bus and Truck Mechanics and Diesel Engine Specialists; Cleaners of Vehicles and Equipment; Electrical and Electronics Installers and Repairers, Transportation Equipment; Electronic Equipment Installers and Repairers, Motor Vehicles; Engine and Other Machine Assemblers; Gem and Diamond Workers; Installation, Maintenance, and Repair Workers, All Other; Motorboat Mechanics and Service Technicians; Motorcycle Mechanics; Painters, Transportation Equipment.

Skills—Repairing: Repairing machines or systems using the needed tools. **Equipment Maintenance:** Performing routine maintenance on equipment and determining when and what kind of maintenance is needed. **Troubleshooting:** Determining causes of operating errors and deciding what to do about them. **Equipment Selection:** Determining the kind of tools and equipment needed to do a job. **Quality Control Analysis:** Conducting tests and inspections of products, services, or processes to evaluate quality or performance. **Operation and Control:** Controlling operations of equipment or systems. **Operation Monitoring:** Watching gauges, dials, or other indicators to make sure a machine is working properly. **Installation:** Installing equipment, machines, wiring, or programs to meet specifications.

Work Environment: Indoors; standing; using hands; bending or twisting the body; repetitive motions; noise; contaminants; hazardous conditions; hazardous equipment; minor burns, cuts, bites, or stings.

Painters, Construction and Maintenance

- ⊙ Annual Earnings: $35,430
- ⊙ Earnings Growth Potential: Low (34.6%)
- ⊙ Growth: 18.5%
- ⊙ Annual Job Openings: 15,730
- ⊙ Self-Employed: 52.6%

Considerations for Job Outlook: Overall job prospects should be good because of the need to replace workers who leave the occupation. There are no formal training requirements for entry into these jobs, so many people with limited skills work as painters for a relatively short time and then move on to other types of work with higher pay or better working conditions. Job opportunities for industrial painters should be excellent as the positions available should be greater than the pool of qualified individuals to fill them. Although industrial structures that require painting are located throughout the nation, the best employment opportunities should be in the Gulf Coast region, where strong demand and the largest concentration of workers exist. New painters and those with little experience should expect some periods of unemployment. In addition, many construction painting projects last only a short time. Employment of painters, like that of many other construction workers, is also sensitive to fluctuations in the economy.

Paint walls, equipment, buildings, bridges, and other structural surfaces, using brushes, rollers, and spray guns. Cover surfaces with dropcloths or masking tape and paper to protect surfaces during painting. Fill cracks, holes, and joints with caulk, putty, plaster, or other fillers, using caulking guns or putty knives. Apply primers or sealers to prepare new surfaces, such as bare wood or metal, for finish coats. Apply paint, stain, varnish, enamel, and other finishes to equipment, buildings, bridges, or other structures, using brushes, spray guns, or rollers. Calculate amounts of required materials and estimate costs, based on surface measurements or work orders. Read work orders or receive instructions from supervisors or homeowners in order to determine work requirements. Erect scaffolding and swing gates, or set up ladders, to work above ground level. Remove fixtures such as pictures, door knobs, lamps, and electric switch covers prior to painting. Wash and treat surfaces with oil, turpentine, mildew remover, or other preparations, and sand rough spots to ensure that finishes will adhere properly. Mix and match colors of paint, stain, or varnish with oil and thinning and drying additives in order to obtain desired colors and consistencies. Remove old finishes by stripping, sanding, wire brushing, burning, or using water or abrasive blasting. Select and purchase tools and finishes for surfaces to be covered, considering durability, ease of handling, methods of application, and customers' wishes. Smooth surfaces, using sandpaper, scrapers, brushes, steel wool, and sanding machines. Polish final coats to specified finishes. Use special finishing techniques such as sponging, ragging, layering, or faux finishing. Waterproof buildings, using waterproofers and caulking. Cut stencils, and brush and spray lettering and

decorations on surfaces. Spray or brush hot plastics or pitch onto surfaces. Bake finishes on painted and enameled articles, using baking ovens.

Education/Training Required: Less than high school. **Education and Training Program:** Painting/Painter and Wall Coverer Training. **Knowledge/Courses—Building and Construction:** Materials, methods, and the tools involved in the construction or repair of houses, buildings, or other structures such as highways and roads. **Transportation:** Principles and methods for moving people or goods by air, rail, sea, or road, including the relative costs and benefits. **Design:** Design techniques, tools, and principles involved in production of precision technical plans, blueprints, drawings, and models. **Customer and Personal Service:** Principles and processes for providing customer and personal services. This includes customer needs assessment, meeting quality standards for services, and evaluation of customer satisfaction. **Production and Processing:** Raw materials, production processes, quality control, costs, and other techniques for maximizing the effective manufacture and distribution of goods. **Administration and Management:** Business and management principles involved in strategic planning, resource allocation, human resources modeling, leadership technique, production methods, and coordination of people and resources. **Work Experience Needed:** None. **On-the-Job Training Needed:** Moderate-term on-the-job training. **Certification/Licensure:** None.

Personality Type: Realistic-Conventional. **Career Cluster:** 02 Architecture and Construction. **Career Pathway:** 02.2 Construction. **Other Jobs in This Pathway:** Boilermakers; Brickmasons and Blockmasons; Carpet Installers; Cement Masons and Concrete Finishers; Construction and Building Inspectors; Construction and Related Workers, All Other; Construction Carpenters; Construction Laborers; Construction Managers; Continuous Mining Machine Operators; Cost Estimators; Crane and Tower Operators; Dredge Operators; Drywall and Ceiling Tile Installers; Earth Drillers, Except Oil and Gas; Electrical Power-Line Installers and Repairers; Electricians; Electromechanical Equipment Assemblers; Engineering Technicians, Except Drafters, All Other; Excavating and Loading Machine and Dragline Operators; Explosives Workers, Ordnance Handling Experts, and Blasters; Extraction Workers, All Other; First-Line Supervisors of Construction Trades and Extraction Workers; Floor Layers, Except Carpet, Wood, and Hard Tiles; Floor Sanders and Finishers; Glaziers;

Heating and Air Conditioning Mechanics and Installers; Helpers, Construction Trades, All Other; others.

Skills—Operation and Control: Controlling operations of equipment or systems.

Work Environment: More often outdoors than indoors; standing; climbing; kneeling, crouching, stooping, or crawling; balancing; using hands; bending or twisting the body; repetitive motions; noise; contaminants; cramped work space; high places; hazardous conditions; minor burns, cuts, bites, or stings.

Painters, Transportation Equipment

- Annual Earnings: $39,600
- Earnings Growth Potential: Medium (36.7%)
- Growth: 9.5%
- Annual Job Openings: 1,430
- Self-Employed: 5.5%

Considerations for Job Outlook: As with many skilled manufacturing jobs, employers often report difficulty finding qualified workers. Therefore, job opportunities should be very good for those with painting experience. Job openings also should result from the need to replace workers who leave the occupation and from increased specialization in manufacturing. Although higher educational requirements would normally reduce competition for automotive painters in repair shops, the large number of people who enjoy working on cars should offset that reduction.

Operate or tend painting machines to paint surfaces of transportation equipment, such as automobiles, buses, trucks, trains, boats, and airplanes. Dispose of hazardous waste in an appropriate manner. Select paint according to company requirements, and match colors of paint following specified color charts. Mix paints to match color specifications or vehicles' original colors; then stir and thin the paints, using spatulas or power mixing equipment. Remove grease, dirt, paint, and rust from vehicle surfaces in preparation for paint application, using abrasives, solvents, brushes, blowtorches, washing tanks, or sandblasters. Pour paint into spray guns, and adjust nozzles and paint mixes in order to get the proper paint flow and coating thickness. Monitor painting operations in order to identify flaws such as blisters and streaks so that their causes can be corrected. Sand vehicle surfaces between coats of paint and/or primer

in order to remove flaws and enhance adhesion for subsequent coats. Disassemble, clean, and reassemble sprayers and power equipment, using solvents, wire brushes, and cloths for cleaning duties. Spray prepared surfaces with specified amounts of primers and decorative or finish coatings. Remove accessories from vehicles, such as chrome or mirrors, and mask other surfaces with tape or paper in order to protect them from paint. Allow the sprayed product to dry, and then touch up any spots that may have been missed. Apply rust-resistant undercoats, and caulk and seal seams. Select the correct spray gun system for the material being applied. Apply primer over any repairs made to vehicle surfaces. Adjust controls on infrared ovens, heat lamps, portable ventilators, and exhaust units in order to speed the drying of vehicles between coats. Fill small dents and scratches with body fillers, and smooth surfaces in order to prepare vehicles for painting. Apply designs, lettering, or other identifying or decorative items to finished products, using paint brushes or paint sprayers. Paint by hand areas that cannot be reached with a spray gun, or those that need retouching, using brushes.

Education/Training Required: High school diploma or equivalent. **Education and Training Program:** Autobody/Collision and Repair Technology/Technician. **Knowledge/Courses—Chemistry:** The chemical composition, structure, and properties of substances and of the chemical processes and transformations that they undergo. This includes uses of chemicals and their danger signs, production techniques, and disposal methods. **Mechanical Devices:** Machines and tools, including their designs, uses, repair, and maintenance. **Production and Processing:** Raw materials, production processes, quality control, costs, and other techniques for maximizing the effective manufacture and distribution of goods. **Work Experience Needed:** None. **On-the-Job Training Needed:** Moderate-term on-the-job training. **Certification/Licensure:** Voluntary certification by association.

Personality Type: Realistic-Conventional. **Career Cluster:** 16 Transportation, Distribution, and Logistics. **Career Pathway:** 16.4 Facility and Mobile Equipment Maintenance. **Other Jobs in This Pathway:** Aircraft Mechanics and Service Technicians; Aircraft Structure, Surfaces, Rigging, and Systems Assemblers; Automotive Body and Related Repairers; Automotive Glass Installers and Repairers; Automotive Master Mechanics; Automotive Specialty Technicians; Bicycle Repairers; Bus and

Truck Mechanics and Diesel Engine Specialists; Cleaners of Vehicles and Equipment; Electrical and Electronics Installers and Repairers, Transportation Equipment; Electronic Equipment Installers and Repairers, Motor Vehicles; Engine and Other Machine Assemblers; Gem and Diamond Workers; Installation, Maintenance, and Repair Workers, All Other; Motorboat Mechanics and Service Technicians; Motorcycle Mechanics; Outdoor Power Equipment and Other Small Engine Mechanics.

Skills—Equipment Selection: Determining the kind of tools and equipment needed to do a job. **Equipment Maintenance:** Performing routine maintenance on equipment and determining when and what kind of maintenance is needed. **Operation and Control:** Controlling operations of equipment or systems. **Quality Control Analysis:** Conducting tests and inspections of products, services, or processes to evaluate quality or performance. **Repairing:** Repairing machines or systems using the needed tools. **Troubleshooting:** Determining causes of operating errors and deciding what to do about them. **Operation Monitoring:** Watching gauges, dials, or other indicators to make sure a machine is working properly.

Work Environment: Indoors; standing; kneeling, crouching, stooping, or crawling; using hands; bending or twisting the body; repetitive motions; noise; very hot or cold; contaminants; cramped work space; high places; hazardous conditions; hazardous equipment; minor burns, cuts, bites, or stings.

Painting, Coating, and Decorating Workers

- ⊙ Annual Earnings: $25,660
- ⊙ Earnings Growth Potential: Low (30.0%)
- ⊙ Growth: 17.4%
- ⊙ Annual Job Openings: 980
- ⊙ Self-Employed: 5.6%

Considerations for Job Outlook: As with many skilled manufacturing jobs, employers often report difficulty finding qualified workers. Therefore, job opportunities should be very good for those with painting experience. Job openings also should result from the need to replace workers who leave the occupation and from increased specialization in manufacturing. Although higher educational

requirements would normally reduce competition for automotive painters in repair shops, the large number of people who enjoy working on cars should offset that reduction.

Paint, coat, or decorate articles such as furniture, glass, plateware, pottery, jewelry, toys, books, or leather. Apply coatings, such as paint, ink, or lacquer, to protect or decorate workpiece surfaces, using spray guns, pens, or brushes. Examine finished surfaces of workpieces to verify conformance to specifications and then retouch any defective areas. Clean and maintain tools and equipment, using solvents, brushes, and rags. Read job orders and inspect workpieces to determine work procedures and materials required. Clean surfaces of workpieces in preparation for coating, using cleaning fluids, solvents, brushes, scrapers, steam, sandpaper, or cloth. Rinse, drain, or wipe coated workpieces to remove excess coating material or to facilitate setting of finish coats on workpieces. Place coated workpieces in ovens or dryers for specified times in order to dry or harden finishes. Select and mix ingredients to prepare coating substances according to specifications, using paddles or mechanical mixers. Melt or heat coating materials to specified temperatures. Conceal blemishes in workpieces, such as nicks and dents, using fillers such as putty. Immerse workpieces into coating materials for specified times. Cut out sections in surfaces of materials to be inlaid with decorative pieces, using patterns and knives or scissors. Position and glue decorative pieces in cutout sections of workpieces, following patterns.

Education/Training Required: High school diploma or equivalent. **Education and Training Program:** Graphic Design. **Knowledge/Courses—Fine Arts:** The theory and techniques required to compose, produce, and perform works of music, dance, visual arts, drama, and sculpture. **Production and Processing:** Raw materials, production processes, quality control, costs, and other techniques for maximizing the effective manufacture and distribution of goods. **Design:** Design techniques, tools, and principles involved in production of precision technical plans, blueprints, drawings, and models. **Sales and Marketing:** Principles and methods for showing, promoting, and selling products or services. This includes marketing strategy and tactics, product demonstration, sales techniques, and sales control systems. **Transportation:** Principles and methods for moving people or goods by air, rail, sea, or road, including the relative costs and benefits. **Work Experience Needed:** None. **On-the-Job Training Needed:**

Moderate-term on-the-job training. **Certification/Licensure:** None.

Personality Type: Realistic. **Career Cluster:** 03 Arts and Communications. **Career Pathway:** 03.3 Visual Arts. **Other Jobs in This Pathway:** Art Directors; Art, Drama, and Music Teachers, Postsecondary; Artists and Related Workers, All Other; Audio and Video Equipment Technicians; Commercial and Industrial Designers; Craft Artists; Designers, All Other; Fashion Designers; Fine Artists, Including Painters, Sculptors, and Illustrators; Graphic Designers; Interior Designers; Multimedia Artists and Animators; Photographers; Set and Exhibit Designers.

Skills—Equipment Selection: Determining the kind of tools and equipment needed to do a job. **Equipment Maintenance:** Performing routine maintenance on equipment and determining when and what kind of maintenance is needed. **Operation and Control:** Controlling operations of equipment or systems. **Repairing:** Repairing machines or systems using the needed tools. **Operation Monitoring:** Watching gauges, dials, or other indicators to make sure a machine is working properly. **Troubleshooting:** Determining causes of operating errors and deciding what to do about them.

Work Environment: Standing; walking and running; using hands; bending or twisting the body; repetitive motions; noise; very hot or cold; contaminants; hazardous conditions.

Paralegals and Legal Assistants

- ⊙ Annual Earnings: $46,730
- ⊙ Earnings Growth Potential: Medium (37.1%)
- ⊙ Growth: 18.3%
- ⊙ Annual Job Openings: 8,340
- ⊙ Self-Employed: 2.0%

Considerations for Job Outlook: This occupation attracts many applicants, and competition for jobs will be strong. Experienced, formally trained paralegals should have the best job prospects. In addition, many firms will prefer paralegals with experience and specialization in high-demand practice areas.

Assist lawyers by investigating facts, preparing legal documents, or researching legal precedent. Conduct research to support a legal proceeding, to formulate a defense, or to initiate legal action. Prepare legal documents, including briefs, pleadings, appeals, wills, contracts, and real estate closing statements. Prepare affidavits or other documents, maintain document file, and file pleadings with court clerk. Gather and analyze research data, such as statutes; decisions; and legal articles, codes, and documents. Investigate facts and law of cases to determine causes of action and to prepare cases. Call upon witnesses to testify at hearing. Direct and coordinate law office activity, including delivery of subpoenas. Arbitrate disputes between parties, and assist in real estate closing process. Keep and monitor legal volumes to ensure that law library is up to date. Appraise and inventory real and personal property for estate planning.

Education/Training Required: Associate degree. **Education and Training Program:** Legal Assistant/Paralegal Training. **Knowledge/Courses—Clerical Practices:** Administrative and clerical procedures and systems such as word processing, managing files and records, stenography and transcription, designing forms, and other office procedures and terminology. **Law and Government:** Laws, legal codes, court procedures, precedents, government regulations, executive orders, agency rules, and the democratic political process. **English Language:** The structure and content of the English language including the meaning and spelling of words, rules of composition, and grammar. **Computers and Electronics:** Circuit boards, processors, chips, electronic equipment, and computer hardware and software, including applications and programming. **Communications and Media:** Media production, communication, and dissemination techniques and methods. This includes alternative ways to inform and entertain via written, oral, and visual media. **Work Experience Needed:** None. **On-the-Job Training Needed:** None. **Certification/Licensure:** Voluntary certification by association.

Personality Type: Conventional-Investigative-Enterprising. **Career Cluster:** 12 Law, Public Safety, Corrections, and Security. **Career Pathway:** 12.5 Legal Services. **Other Jobs in This Pathway:** Administrative Law Judges, Adjudicators, and Hearing Officers; Arbitrators, Mediators, and Conciliators; Court Reporters; Farm and Home Management Advisors; Judges, Magistrate Judges, and Magistrates; Law Teachers, Postsecondary; Lawyers; Legal Secretaries; Legal Support Workers, All Other; Title Examiners, Abstractors, and Searchers.

Skills—Writing: Communicating effectively in writing as appropriate for the needs of the audience. **Active Listening:** Giving full attention to what other people are saying, taking time to understand the points being made, asking questions as appropriate, and not interrupting at inappropriate times. **Speaking:** Talking to others to convey information effectively. **Service Orientation:** Actively looking for ways to help people.

Work Environment: Indoors; sitting; repetitive motions.

Parts Salespersons

- ⊙ Annual Earnings: $29,350
- ⊙ Earnings Growth Potential: Medium (37.1%)
- ⊙ Growth: 16.0%
- ⊙ Annual Job Openings: 10,720
- ⊙ Self-Employed: 1.1%

Considerations for Job Outlook: Many workers leave this occupation, which means there will be a large number of job openings. This large number of job openings combined with the large size of the occupation should result in many employment opportunities.

Sell spare and replacement parts and equipment in repair shop or parts store. Read catalogs, microfiche viewers, or computer displays in order to determine replacement part stock numbers and prices. Receive and fill telephone orders for parts. Determine replacement parts required, according to inspections of old parts, customer requests, or customers' descriptions of malfunctions. Fill customer orders from stock. Prepare sales slips or sales contracts. Receive payment or obtain credit authorization. Take inventory of stock. Advise customers on substitution or modification of parts when identical replacements are not available. Examine returned parts for defects, and exchange defective parts or refund money. Mark and store parts in stockrooms according to prearranged systems. Discuss use and features of various parts, based on knowledge of machines or equipment. Demonstrate equipment to customers and explain functioning of equipment. Place new merchandise on display. Measure parts, using precision measuring instruments, in order to determine whether similar parts may be machined to required sizes. Repair parts or equipment.

Education/Training Required: Less than high school. **Education and Training Programs:** Selling Skills and Sales Operations; Vehicle and Vehicle Parts and Accessories Marketing Operations. **Knowledge/Courses—Sales and Marketing:** Principles and methods for showing, promoting, and selling products or services. This includes marketing strategy and tactics, product demonstration, sales techniques, and sales control systems. **Customer and Personal Service:** Principles and processes for providing customer and personal services. This includes customer needs assessment, meeting quality standards for services, and evaluation of customer satisfaction. **Mechanical Devices:** Machines and tools, including their designs, uses, repair, and maintenance. **Production and Processing:** Raw materials, production processes, quality control, costs, and other techniques for maximizing the effective manufacture and distribution of goods. **Computers and Electronics:** Circuit boards, processors, chips, electronic equipment, and computer hardware and software, including applications and programming. **Mathematics:** Arithmetic, algebra, geometry, calculus, statistics, and their applications. **Work Experience Needed:** None. **On-the-Job Training Needed:** Moderate-term on-the-job training. **Certification/Licensure:** None.

Personality Type: Enterprising-Conventional-Realistic. **Career Clusters:** 14 Marketing, Sales, and Service; 16 Transportation, Distribution, and Logistics. **Career Pathways:** 16.7 Sales and Service; 14.2 Professional Sales and Marketing. **Other Jobs in These Pathways:** Appraisers, Real Estate; Assessors; Avionics Technicians; Cashiers; Counter and Rental Clerks; Demonstrators and Product Promoters; Door-To-Door Sales Workers, News and Street Vendors, and Related Workers; Driver/Sales Workers; Energy Brokers; First-Line Supervisors of Non-Retail Sales Workers; First-Line Supervisors of Retail Sales Workers; Gaming Change Persons and Booth Cashiers; Hotel, Motel, and Resort Desk Clerks; Interior Designers; Lodging Managers; Marketing Managers; Marking Clerks; Meeting, Convention, and Event Planners; Merchandise Displayers and Window Trimmers; Models; Online Merchants; Order Fillers, Wholesale and Retail Sales; Property, Real Estate, and Community Association Managers; Real Estate Brokers; Real Estate Sales Agents; Reservation and Transportation Ticket Agents and Travel Clerks; Retail Salespersons; Sales and Related Workers, All Other; Sales Engineers; Sales Representatives, Services, All Other; others.

Skills—Repairing: Repairing machines or systems using the needed tools. **Equipment Selection:** Determining the kind of tools and equipment needed to do a job. **Negotiation:** Bringing others together and trying to reconcile differences. **Service Orientation:** Actively looking for ways to help people. **Active Listening:** Giving full attention to what other people are saying, taking time to understand the points being made, asking questions as appropriate, and not interrupting at inappropriate times. **Persuasion:** Persuading others to change their minds or behavior. **Mathematics:** Using mathematics to solve problems. **Troubleshooting:** Determining causes of operating errors and deciding what to do about them.

Work Environment: Indoors; standing; repetitive motions; noise; contaminants.

Paving, Surfacing, and Tamping Equipment Operators

- ◉ Annual Earnings: $35,270
- ◉ Earnings Growth Potential: Low (32.7%)
- ◉ Growth: 22.1%
- ◉ Annual Job Openings: 2,200
- ◉ Self-Employed: 1.9%

Considerations for Job Outlook: Workers with the ability to operate multiple types of equipment should have the best job opportunities. As with many other construction workers, employment of construction equipment operators is sensitive to fluctuations of the economy. Workers may experience periods of unemployment when the overall level of construction falls. However, shortages of workers may occur in some areas during peak periods of building activity. Employment opportunities should be best in metropolitan areas, where most large commercial and multifamily buildings are constructed, and in states that are undertaking large transportation-related projects. In addition, the need to replace workers who leave the occupation should result in some job opportunities.

Operate equipment used for applying concrete, asphalt, or other materials or for tamping gravel, dirt, or other materials. Start machine, engage clutch, and push and move levers to guide machines along forms or guidelines and to control the operation of machine attachments. Inspect, clean, maintain, and repair equipment, using mechanics'

hand tools, or report malfunctions to supervisors. Operate machines to spread, smooth, level, or steel-reinforce stone, concrete, or asphalt on road beds. Coordinate truck dumping. Set up and tear down equipment. Operate tamping machines or manually roll surfaces to compact earth fills, foundation forms, and finished road materials, according to grade specifications. Shovel blacktop. Drive machines onto truck trailers, and drive trucks to transport machines and material to and from job sites. Observe distribution of paving material to adjust machine settings or material flow, and indicate low spots for workers to add material. Light burners or start heating units of machines, and regulate screed temperatures and asphalt flow rates. Fill tanks, hoppers, or machines with paving materials. Control traffic. Operate oil distributors, loaders, chip spreaders, dump trucks, and snow plows. Control paving machines to push dump trucks and to maintain a constant flow of asphalt or other material into hoppers or screeds. Set up forms and lay out guidelines for curbs, according to written specifications, using string, spray paint, and concrete/water mixes. Drive and operate curbing machines to extrude concrete or asphalt curbing. Cut or break up pavement and drive guardrail posts, using machines equipped with interchangeable hammers. Install dies, cutters, and extensions to screeds onto machines, using hand tools. Operate machines that clean or cut expansion joints in concrete or asphalt and that rout out cracks in pavement. Place strips of material such as cork, asphalt, or steel into joints, or place rolls of expansion-joint material on machines that automatically insert material.

Education/Training Required: High school diploma or equivalent. **Education and Training Program:** Construction/Heavy Equipment/Earthmoving Equipment Operation. **Knowledge/Courses—Building and Construction:** Materials, methods, and the tools involved in the construction or repair of houses, buildings, or other structures such as highways and roads. **Transportation:** Principles and methods for moving people or goods by air, rail, sea, or road, including the relative costs and benefits. **Mechanical Devices:** Machines and tools, including their designs, uses, repair, and maintenance. **Engineering and Technology:** The practical application of engineering science and technology. This includes applying principles, techniques, procedures, and equipment to the design and production of various goods and services. **Public Safety and Security:** Relevant equipment, policies, procedures, and strategies to promote effective local, state, or national security operations for the protection of people, data, property, and institutions. **Production and Processing:** Raw materials, production processes, quality control, costs, and other techniques for maximizing the effective manufacture and distribution of goods. **Work Experience Needed:** None. **On-the-Job Training Needed:** Moderate-term on-the-job training. **Certification/Licensure:** None.

Personality Type: Realistic-Conventional. **Career Cluster:** 02 Architecture and Construction. **Career Pathway:** 02.2 Construction. **Other Jobs in This Pathway:** Boilermakers; Brickmasons and Blockmasons; Carpet Installers; Cement Masons and Concrete Finishers; Construction and Building Inspectors; Construction and Related Workers, All Other; Construction Carpenters; Construction Laborers; Construction Managers; Continuous Mining Machine Operators; Cost Estimators; Crane and Tower Operators; Dredge Operators; Drywall and Ceiling Tile Installers; Earth Drillers, Except Oil and Gas; Electrical Power-Line Installers and Repairers; Electricians; Electromechanical Equipment Assemblers; Engineering Technicians, Except Drafters, All Other; Excavating and Loading Machine and Dragline Operators; Explosives Workers, Ordnance Handling Experts, and Blasters; Extraction Workers, All Other; First-Line Supervisors of Construction Trades and Extraction Workers; Floor Layers, Except Carpet, Wood, and Hard Tiles; Floor Sanders and Finishers; Glaziers; Heating and Air Conditioning Mechanics and Installers; Helpers, Construction Trades, All Other; others.

Skills—Repairing: Repairing machines or systems using the needed tools. **Equipment Maintenance:** Performing routine maintenance on equipment and determining when and what kind of maintenance is needed. **Operation and Control:** Controlling operations of equipment or systems. **Equipment Selection:** Determining the kind of tools and equipment needed to do a job. **Troubleshooting:** Determining causes of operating errors and deciding what to do about them. **Operation Monitoring:** Watching gauges, dials, or other indicators to make sure a machine is working properly. **Quality Control Analysis:** Conducting tests and inspections of products, services, or processes to evaluate quality or performance. **Coordination:** Adjusting actions in relation to others' actions.

Work Environment: Outdoors; standing; using hands; bending or twisting the body; repetitive motions; noise; very hot or cold; bright or inadequate lighting; contaminants; whole-body vibration; hazardous equipment; minor burns, cuts, bites, or stings.

Payroll and Timekeeping Clerks

- ⊙ Annual Earnings: $37,160
- ⊙ Earnings Growth Potential: Medium (35.3%)
- ⊙ Growth: 14.6%
- ⊙ Annual Job Openings: 6,570
- ⊙ Self-Employed: 1.1%

Considerations for Job Outlook: Job prospects for financial clerks should be favorable, because many workers are expected to leave this occupation. Employers will need to hire new workers to replace those leaving the occupation.

Compile and record employee time and payroll data. Review time sheets, work charts, wage computation, and other information to detect and reconcile payroll discrepancies. Process paperwork for new employees and enter employee information into the payroll system. Verify attendance, hours worked, and pay adjustments, and post information onto designated records. Compute wages and deductions, and enter data into computers. Record employee information, such as exemptions, transfers, and resignations, to maintain and update payroll records. Process and issue employee paychecks and statements of earnings and deductions. Keep track of leave time, such as vacation, personal, and sick leave, for employees. Compile employee time, production, and payroll data from time sheets and other records. Distribute and collect timecards each pay period. Issue and record adjustments to pay related to previous errors or retroactive increases. Provide information to employees and managers on payroll matters, tax issues, benefit plans, and collective agreement provisions. Keep informed about changes in tax and deduction laws that apply to the payroll process. Compile statistical reports, statements, and summaries related to pay and benefits accounts, and submit them to appropriate departments. Conduct verifications of employment. Complete time sheets showing employees' arrival and departure times. Prepare and balance period-end reports, and reconcile issued payrolls to bank statements. Complete, verify, and process forms and documentation for administration of benefits such as pension plans, unemployment, and medical insurance. Post relevant work hours to client files to bill clients properly. Coordinate special programs, such as United Way campaigns, that involve payroll deductions.

Education/Training Required: High school diploma or equivalent. **Education and Training Program:** Accounting Technology/Technician and Bookkeeping. **Knowledge/Courses—Clerical Practices:** Administrative and clerical procedures and systems such as word processing, managing files and records, stenography and transcription, designing forms, and other office procedures and terminology. **Economics and Accounting:** Economic and accounting principles and practices, the financial markets, banking, and the analysis and reporting of financial data. **Personnel and Human Resources:** Principles and procedures for personnel recruitment, selection, training, compensation and benefits, labor relations and negotiation, and personnel information systems. **Computers and Electronics:** Circuit boards, processors, chips, electronic equipment, and computer hardware and software, including applications and programming. **Work Experience Needed:** None. **On-the-Job Training Needed:** Moderate-term on-the-job training. **Certification/Licensure:** Voluntary certification by association.

Personality Type: Conventional-Enterprising. **Career Cluster:** 04 Business, Management, and Administration. **Career Pathway:** 04.2 Business, Financial Management, and Accounting. **Other Jobs in This Pathway:** Accountants; Auditors; Billing, Cost, and Rate Clerks; Bioinformatics Technicians; Bookkeeping, Accounting, and Auditing Clerks; Brokerage Clerks; Brownfield Redevelopment Specialists and Site Managers; Budget Analysts; Business Teachers, Postsecondary; Compliance Managers; Credit Analysts; Financial Analysts; Financial Examiners; Financial Managers, Branch or Department; Gaming Cage Workers; Investment Fund Managers; Logistics Managers; Loss Prevention Managers; Managers, All Other; Natural Sciences Managers; Regulatory Affairs Managers; Security Managers; Statement Clerks; Statistical Assistants; Statisticians; Supply Chain Managers; Tax Preparers; Treasurers and Controllers; Wind Energy Operations Managers; Wind Energy Project Managers.

Skills—Mathematics: Using mathematics to solve problems. **Reading Comprehension:** Understanding written sentences and paragraphs in work-related documents. **Writing:** Communicating effectively in writing as appropriate for the needs of the audience. **Management of Personnel Resources:** Motivating, developing, and directing people as they work, identifying the best people for the job.

Work Environment: Indoors; sitting.

Pest Control Workers

- Annual Earnings: $30,220
- Earnings Growth Potential: Low (34.0%)
- Growth: 26.2%
- Annual Job Openings: 4,850
- Self-Employed: 7.2%

Considerations for Job Outlook: Job opportunities are expected to be very good. The limited number of people seeking work in pest control, expected job growth, and the need to replace workers who leave this occupation should result in many job openings.

Apply or release chemical solutions or toxic gases and set traps to kill or remove pests and vermin that infest buildings and surrounding areas. Record work activities performed. Inspect premises to identify infestation sources and extent of damage to property, wall and roof porosity, and access to infested locations. Spray or dust chemical solutions, powders, or gases into rooms; onto clothing, furnishings, or wood; and over marshlands, ditches, and catch-basins. Clean work sites after completion of jobs. Direct or assist other workers in treatment and extermination processes to eliminate and control rodents, insects, and weeds. Drive trucks equipped with power spraying equipment. Measure area dimensions requiring treatment, using rules; calculate fumigant requirements; and estimate cost for services. Post warning signs and lock building doors to secure areas to be fumigated. Cut or bore openings in buildings or surrounding concrete, access infested areas, insert nozzles, and inject pesticide to impregnate ground. Study preliminary reports and diagrams of infested areas and determine treatment types required to eliminate and prevent recurrence of infestations. Dig up and burn weeds, or spray weeds with herbicides. Set mechanical traps and place poisonous paste or bait in sewers, burrows, and ditches. Clean and remove blockages from infested areas to facilitate spraying procedure and provide drainage, using brooms, mops, shovels, and rakes. Position and fasten edges of tarpaulins over building and tape vents to ensure air-tight environment and check for leaks.

Education/Training Required: High school diploma or equivalent. **Education and Training Program:** Agricultural/Farm Supplies Retailing and Wholesaling. **Knowledge/Courses—Sales and Marketing:** Principles and methods for showing, promoting, and selling products or services. This includes marketing strategy and tactics, product demonstration, sales techniques, and sales control systems. **Chemistry:** The chemical composition, structure, and properties of substances and of the chemical processes and transformations that they undergo. This includes uses of chemicals and their danger signs, production techniques, and disposal methods. **Biology:** Plant and animal organisms and their tissues, cells, functions, interdependencies, and interactions with each other and the environment. **Building and Construction:** Materials, methods, and the tools involved in the construction or repair of houses, buildings, or other structures such as highways and roads. **Customer and Personal Service:** Principles and processes for providing customer and personal services. This includes customer needs assessment, meeting quality standards for services, and evaluation of customer satisfaction. **Law and Government:** Laws, legal codes, court procedures, precedents, government regulations, executive orders, agency rules, and the democratic political process. **Work Experience Needed:** None. **On-the-Job Training Needed:** Moderate-term on-the-job training. **Certification/Licensure:** Licensure.

Personality Type: Realistic-Conventional. **Career Cluster:** 01 Agriculture, Food, and Natural Resources. **Career Pathway:** 01.1 Food Products and Processing Systems. **Other Jobs in This Pathway:** Agricultural Inspectors; Agricultural Sciences Teachers, Postsecondary; Agricultural Technicians; Buyers and Purchasing Agents, Farm Products; Chemical Technicians; First-Line Supervisors of Office and Administrative Support Workers; Food and Tobacco Roasting, Baking, and Drying Machine Operators and Tenders; Food Batchmakers; Food Cooking Machine Operators and Tenders; Food Science Technicians; Food Scientists and Technologists; Graders and Sorters, Agricultural Products; Nonfarm Animal Caretakers; Office Machine Operators, Except Computer.

Skills—Equipment Selection: Determining the kind of tools and equipment needed to do a job. **Repairing:** Repairing machines or systems using the needed tools. **Equipment Maintenance:** Performing routine maintenance on equipment and determining when and what kind of maintenance is needed. **Operation and Control:** Controlling operations of equipment or systems. **Troubleshooting:** Determining causes of operating errors and deciding what to do about them. **Mathematics:** Using mathematics to solve problems. **Persuasion:** Persuading others to change their minds or behavior. **Systems Analysis:** Determining how a system should work and how changes in conditions, operations, and the environment will affect outcomes.

Work Environment: More often outdoors than indoors; standing; walking and running; using hands; repetitive motions; very hot or cold; contaminants; cramped work space; hazardous conditions; minor burns, cuts, bites, or stings.

Petroleum Pump System Operators, Refinery Operators, and Gaugers

- ⊙ Annual Earnings: $61,260
- ⊙ Earnings Growth Potential: Medium (37.2%)
- ⊙ Growth: –14.0%
- ⊙ Annual Job Openings: 1,440
- ⊙ Self-Employed: 0.9%

Considerations for Job Outlook: Rapid decline in employment is projected.

Operate or control petroleum refining or processing units. Monitor process indicators, instruments, gauges, and meters in order to detect and report any possible problems. Control or operate manifold and pumping systems to circulate liquids through a petroleum refinery. Operate control panels to coordinate and regulate process variables such as temperature and pressure, and to direct product flow rate, according to process schedules. Lower thermometers into tanks to obtain temperature readings. Perform tests to check the qualities and grades of products, such as assessing levels of bottom sediment, water, and foreign materials in oil samples, using centrifugal testers. Inspect pipelines, tightening connections and lubricating valves as necessary. Calculate test result values, using standard formulas. Coordinate shutdowns and major projects. Conduct general housekeeping of units, including wiping up oil spills and performing general cleaning duties. Clean interiors of processing units by circulating chemicals and solvents within units. Clamp seals around valves to secure tanks. Verify that incoming and outgoing products are moving through the correct meters and that meters are working properly. Synchronize activities with other pumphouses to ensure a continuous flow of products and a minimum of contamination between products. Start pumps and open valves or use automated equipment to regulate the flow of oil in pipelines and into and out of tanks.

Maintain and repair equipment, or report malfunctioning equipment to supervisors so that repairs can be scheduled. Plan movement of products through lines to processing, storage, and shipping units, utilizing knowledge of system interconnections and capacities. Read and analyze specifications, schedules, logs, test results, and laboratory recommendations to determine how to set equipment controls to produce the required qualities and quantities of products.

Education/Training Required: High school diploma or equivalent. **Education and Training Program:** Mechanic and Repair Technologies/Technicians, Other. **Knowledge/Courses—Mechanical Devices:** Machines and tools, including their designs, uses, repair, and maintenance. **Chemistry:** The chemical composition, structure, and properties of substances and of the chemical processes and transformations that they undergo. This includes uses of chemicals and their danger signs, production techniques, and disposal methods. **Engineering and Technology:** The practical application of engineering science and technology. This includes applying principles, techniques, procedures, and equipment to the design and production of various goods and services. **Public Safety and Security:** Relevant equipment, policies, procedures, and strategies to promote effective local, state, or national security operations for the protection of people, data, property, and institutions. **Production and Processing:** Raw materials, production processes, quality control, costs, and other techniques for maximizing the effective manufacture and distribution of goods. **Work Experience Needed:** None. **On-the-Job Training Needed:** Long-term on-the-job training. **Certification/Licensure:** None.

Personality Type: Realistic-Conventional. **Career Cluster:** 13 Manufacturing. **Career Pathway:** 13.1 Production. **Other Jobs in This Pathway:** Adhesive Bonding Machine Operators and Tenders; Assemblers and Fabricators, All Other; Avionics Technicians; Cabinetmakers and Bench Carpenters; Cleaning, Washing, and Metal Pickling Equipment Operators and Tenders; Coating, Painting, and Spraying Machine Setters, Operators, and Tenders; Computer-Controlled Machine Tool Operators, Metal and Plastic; Cooling and Freezing Equipment Operators and Tenders; Cost Estimators; Crushing, Grinding, and Polishing Machine Setters, Operators, and Tenders; Cutters and Trimmers, Hand; Cutting and Slicing Machine Setters, Operators, and Tenders; Cutting, Punching, and Press Machine Setters, Operators, and Tenders, Metal and Plastic; Drilling and Boring Machine Tool Setters, Operators,

and Tenders, Metal and Plastic; Extruding and Drawing Machine Setters, Operators, and Tenders, Metal and Plastic; Extruding and Forming Machine Setters, Operators, and Tenders, Synthetic and Glass Fibers; others.

Skills—Operation Monitoring: Watching gauges, dials, or other indicators to make sure a machine is working properly. **Operation and Control:** Controlling operations of equipment or systems. **Equipment Maintenance:** Performing routine maintenance on equipment and determining when and what kind of maintenance is needed. **Repairing:** Repairing machines or systems using the needed tools. **Quality Control Analysis:** Conducting tests and inspections of products, services, or processes to evaluate quality or performance. **Troubleshooting:** Determining causes of operating errors and deciding what to do about them. **Equipment Selection:** Determining the kind of tools and equipment needed to do a job. **Mathematics:** Using mathematics to solve problems.

Work Environment: More often outdoors than indoors; standing; using hands; noise; very hot or cold; bright or inadequate lighting; contaminants; cramped work space; high places; hazardous conditions; hazardous equipment; minor burns, cuts, bites, or stings.

Pharmacy Technicians

- Annual Earnings: $28,940
- Earnings Growth Potential: Low (29.8%)
- Growth: 32.4%
- Annual Job Openings: 16,630
- Self-Employed: 0.2%

Considerations for Job Outlook: Job prospects should be excellent for pharmacy technicians, particularly those with formal training and those with experience in retail settings.

Prepare medications under the direction of a pharmacist. Receive written prescription or refill requests, and verify that information is complete and accurate. Maintain proper storage and security conditions for drugs. Answer telephones, responding to questions or requests. Fill bottles with prescribed medications, and type and affix labels. Assist customers by answering simple questions, locating items, or referring them to the pharmacist for medication information. Price and file prescriptions that have been filled. Clean and help maintain equipment and work areas, and sterilize glassware according to prescribed methods. Establish and maintain patient profiles, including lists of medications taken by individual patients. Order, label, and count stock of medications, chemicals, and supplies, and enter inventory data into computers. Receive and store incoming supplies, verify quantities against invoices, and inform supervisors of stock needs and shortages. Transfer medication from vials to the appropriate number of sterile disposable syringes, using aseptic techniques. Under pharmacist supervision, add measured drugs or nutrients to intravenous solutions under sterile conditions to prepare intravenous (IV) packs. Supply and monitor robotic machines that dispense medicine into containers, and label the containers. Prepare and process medical insurance claim forms and records. Mix pharmaceutical preparations according to written prescriptions. Operate cash registers to accept payment from customers.

Education/Training Required: High school diploma or equivalent. **Education and Training Program:** Pharmacy Technician/Assistant Training. **Knowledge/Courses— Medicine and Dentistry:** The information and techniques needed to diagnose and treat human injuries, diseases, and deformities. This includes symptoms, treatment alternatives, drug properties and interactions, and preventive health-care measures. **Clerical Practices:** Administrative and clerical procedures and systems such as word processing, managing files and records, stenography and transcription, designing forms, and other office procedures and terminology. **Computers and Electronics:** Circuit boards, processors, chips, electronic equipment, and computer hardware and software, including applications and programming. **Customer and Personal Service:** Principles and processes for providing customer and personal services. This includes customer needs assessment, meeting quality standards for services, and evaluation of customer satisfaction. **Chemistry:** The chemical composition, structure, and properties of substances and of the chemical processes and transformations that they undergo. This includes uses of chemicals and their danger signs, production techniques, and disposal methods. **Mathematics:** Arithmetic, algebra, geometry, calculus, statistics, and their applications. **Work Experience Needed:** None. **On-the-Job Training Needed:** Moderate-term on-the-job training. **Certification/Licensure:** Registration in most states; voluntary certification by association in others.

Personality Type: Conventional-Realistic. **Career Cluster:** 08 Health Science. **Career Pathway:** 08.1 Therapeutic

Services. **Other Jobs in This Pathway:** Acupuncturists; Allergists and Immunologists; Anesthesiologists; Art Therapists; Chiropractors; Clinical Psychologists; Community and Social Service Specialists, All Other; Counseling Psychologists; Counselors, All Other; Dental Assistants; Dental Hygienists; Dentists, All Other Specialists; Dentists, General; Dermatologists; Diagnostic Medical Sonographers; Dietetic Technicians; Dietitians and Nutritionists; Family and General Practitioners; Health Diagnosing and Treating Practitioners, All Other; Health Specialties Teachers, Postsecondary; Health Technologists and Technicians, All Other; Healthcare Practitioners and Technical Workers, All Other; Healthcare Support Workers, All Other; Home Health Aides; Hospitalists; Industrial-Organizational Psychologists; Internists, General; Licensed Practical and Licensed Vocational Nurses; Life, Physical, and Social Science Technicians, All Other; Low Vision Therapists, Orientation and Mobility Specialists, and Vision Rehabilitation Therapists; others.

Skills—Management of Financial Resources: Determining how money will be spent to get the work done and accounting for these expenditures. **Service Orientation:** Actively looking for ways to help people. **Science:** Using scientific rules and methods to solve problems. **Mathematics:** Using mathematics to solve problems. **Programming:** Writing computer programs for various purposes. **Active Listening:** Giving full attention to what other people are saying, taking time to understand the points being made, asking questions as appropriate, and not interrupting at inappropriate times.

Work Environment: Indoors; standing; walking and running; using hands; repetitive motions; exposed to disease or infections.

Photographers

- ⊙ Annual Earnings: $28,860
- ⊙ Earnings Growth Potential: Medium (39.5%)
- ⊙ Growth: 12.5%
- ⊙ Annual Job Openings: 3,100
- ⊙ Self-Employed: 62.8%

Considerations for Job Outlook: Photographers will face strong competition for most jobs. Because of reduced barriers to entry, there will be many qualified candidates for relatively few positions. In addition, salaried jobs may be more difficult to obtain as companies increasingly contract with freelancers rather than hire their own photographers. Job prospects will be best for candidates who are multitalented and possess related skills such as picture editing and capturing digital video.

Photograph people, landscapes, merchandise, or other subjects, using digital or film cameras and equipment. Take pictures of individuals, families, and small groups, either in studio or on location. Adjust apertures, shutter speeds, and camera focus based on a combination of factors such as lighting, field depth, subject motion, film type, and film speed. Use traditional or digital cameras, along with a variety of equipment such as tripods, filters, and flash attachments. Determine desired images and picture composition; and select and adjust subjects, equipment, and lighting to achieve desired effects. Create artificial light, using flashes and reflectors. Scan photographs into computers for editing, storage, and electronic transmission. Test equipment prior to use to ensure that it is in good working order. Review sets of photographs to select the best work. Estimate or measure light levels, distances, and numbers of exposures needed, using measuring devices and formulas. Manipulate and enhance scanned or digital images to create desired effects, using computers and specialized software. Perform maintenance tasks necessary to keep equipment working properly. Perform general office duties such as scheduling appointments, keeping books, and ordering supplies. Consult with clients or advertising staff, and study assignments to determine project goals, locations, and equipment needs. Select and assemble equipment and required background properties, according to subjects, materials, and conditions. Enhance, retouch, and resize photographs and negatives, using airbrushing and other techniques. Set up, mount, or install photographic equipment and cameras. Produce computer-readable, digital images from film, using flatbed scanners and photofinishing laboratories. Develop and print exposed film, using chemicals, touchup tools, and developing and printing equipment, or send film to photofinishing laboratories for processing. Direct activities of workers who are setting up photographic equipment.

Education/Training Required: High school diploma or equivalent. **Education and Training Programs:** Commercial Photography; Film/Video and Photographic Arts, Other; Photography; Photojournalism; Visual and Performing Arts, General. **Knowledge/Courses—Sales and Marketing:** Principles and methods for showing, promoting, and selling products or services. This includes marketing strategy and tactics, product demonstration, sales techniques, and sales control systems. **Fine Arts:** The theory and techniques required to compose, produce, and perform works of music, dance, visual arts, drama, and sculpture. **Clerical Practices:** Administrative and clerical procedures and systems such as word processing, managing files and records, stenography and transcription, designing forms, and other office procedures and terminology. **Customer and Personal Service:** Principles and processes for providing customer and personal services. This includes customer needs assessment, meeting quality standards for services, and evaluation of customer satisfaction. **Communications and Media:** Media production, communication, and dissemination techniques and methods. This includes alternative ways to inform and entertain via written, oral, and visual media. **Production and Processing:** Raw materials, production processes, quality control, costs, and other techniques for maximizing the effective manufacture and distribution of goods. **Work Experience Needed:** None. **On-the-Job Training Needed:** Long-term on-the-job training. **Certification/Licensure:** None.

Personality Type: Artistic-Realistic. **Career Cluster:** 03 Arts and Communications. **Career Pathways:** 03.1 Audio and Video Technology and Film; 03.3 Visual Arts; 03.5 Journalism and Broadcasting. **Other Jobs in These Pathways:** Agents and Business Managers of Artists, Performers, and Athletes; Archivists; Art Directors; Art, Drama, and Music Teachers, Postsecondary; Artists and Related Workers, All Other; Audio and Video Equipment Technicians; Broadcast News Analysts; Broadcast Technicians; Camera Operators, Television, Video, and Motion Picture; Choreographers; Commercial and Industrial Designers; Communications Teachers, Postsecondary; Copy Writers; Craft Artists; Curators; Dancers; Designers, All Other; Directors—Stage, Motion Pictures, Television, and Radio; Editors; English Language and Literature Teachers, Postsecondary; Fashion Designers; Film and Video Editors; Fine Artists, Including Painters, Sculptors, and Illustrators; Graphic Designers; Historians; Interior Designers; Managers, All Other; Media and Communication Equipment Workers, All Other; Media and Communication Workers, All Other; Multimedia Artists and Animators; Museum Technicians and Conservators; Painting, Coating, and Decorating Workers; others.

Skills—Operations Analysis: Analyzing needs and product requirements to create a design. **Science:** Using scientific rules and methods to solve problems. **Management of Personnel Resources:** Motivating, developing, and directing people as they work, identifying the best people for the job. **Technology Design:** Generating or adapting equipment and technology to serve user needs. **Operation and Control:** Controlling operations of equipment or systems. **Social Perceptiveness:** Being aware of others' reactions and understanding why they react as they do. **Operation Monitoring:** Watching gauges, dials, or other indicators to make sure a machine is working properly. **Negotiation:** Bringing others together and trying to reconcile differences.

Work Environment: More often indoors than outdoors; sitting; using hands.

Physical Therapist Aides

- ⊙ Annual Earnings: $23,680
- ⊙ Earnings Growth Potential: Low (27.4%)
- ⊙ Growth: 43.2%
- ⊙ Annual Job Openings: 2,760
- ⊙ Self-Employed: 0.0%

Considerations for Job Outlook: Opportunities for physical therapist assistants are expected to be very good. With help from physical therapist assistants, physical therapists can manage more patients. However, physical therapy aides may face keen competition from the large pool of qualified people. Job opportunities should be particularly good in acute hospital, skilled nursing, and orthopedic settings, where the elderly are most often treated. Job prospects should be especially favorable in rural areas, as many physical therapists cluster in highly populated urban and suburban areas.

Under close supervision of a physical therapist or physical therapy assistant, perform only delegated, selected, or routine tasks in specific situations. Clean and organize work area and disinfect equipment after treatment. Observe patients during treatment to compile and evaluate data on patients' responses and progress, and report to physical therapist. Instruct, motivate, safeguard, and assist patients practicing exercises and functional activities, under direction of medical staff. Secure patients into or onto therapy equipment. Transport patients to and from treatment areas, using wheelchairs or providing standing support. Confer with physical therapy staff or others to discuss and evaluate patient information for planning, modifying, and coordinating treatment. Record treatment given and equipment used. Perform clerical duties, such as taking inventory, ordering supplies, answering telephone, taking messages, and filling out forms. Maintain equipment and furniture to keep it in good working condition, including performing the assembly and disassembly of equipment and accessories. Change linens, such as bed sheets and pillow cases. Administer active and passive manual therapeutic exercises, therapeutic massage, and heat, light, sound, water, or electrical modality treatments, such as ultrasound. Arrange treatment supplies to keep them in order. Assist patients to dress, undress, and put on and remove supportive devices, such as braces, splints, and slings. Measure patients' range-of-joint motion, body parts, and vital signs to determine effects of treatments or for patient evaluations. Train patients to use orthopedic braces, prostheses, or supportive devices. Fit patients for orthopedic braces, prostheses, or supportive devices, adjusting fit as needed. Participate in patient care tasks, such as assisting with passing food trays, feeding residents, or bathing residents on bed rest. Administer traction to relieve neck and back pain, using intermittent and static traction equipment.

Education/Training Required: High school diploma or equivalent. **Education and Training Program:** Physical Therapy Technician/Assistant Training. **Knowledge/Courses—Medicine and Dentistry:** The information and techniques needed to diagnose and treat human injuries, diseases, and deformities. This includes symptoms, treatment alternatives, drug properties and interactions, and preventive health-care measures. **Therapy and Counseling:** Principles, methods, and procedures for diagnosis, treatment, and rehabilitation of physical and mental dysfunctions, and for career counseling and guidance. **Customer and Personal Service:** Principles and processes for providing customer and personal services. This includes customer needs assessment, meeting quality standards for services, and evaluation of customer satisfaction. **Psychology:** Human behavior and performance; individual differences in ability, personality, and interests; learning and motivation; psychological research methods; and the assessment and treatment of behavioral and affective disorders. **Public Safety and Security:** Relevant equipment, policies, procedures, and strategies to promote effective local, state, or national security operations for the protection of people, data, property, and institutions. **Work Experience Needed:** None. **On-the-Job Training Needed:** Moderate-term on-the-job training. **Certification/Licensure:** None.

Personality Type: Social-Realistic. **Career Cluster:** 08 Health Science. **Career Pathway:** 08.1 Therapeutic Services. **Other Jobs in This Pathway:** Acupuncturists; Allergists and Immunologists; Anesthesiologists; Art Therapists; Chiropractors; Clinical Psychologists; Community and Social Service Specialists, All Other; Counseling Psychologists; Counselors, All Other; Dental Assistants; Dental Hygienists; Dentists, All Other Specialists; Dentists, General; Dermatologists; Diagnostic Medical Sonographers; Dietetic Technicians; Dietitians and Nutritionists; Family and General Practitioners; Health Diagnosing and Treating Practitioners, All Other; Health Specialties Teachers, Postsecondary; Health Technologists and Technicians, All Other; Healthcare Practitioners and Technical Workers, All Other; Healthcare Support Workers, All Other; Home Health Aides; Hospitalists; Industrial-Organizational Psychologists; Internists, General; Licensed Practical and Licensed Vocational Nurses; Life, Physical, and Social Science Technicians, All Other; Low Vision Therapists, Orientation and Mobility Specialists, and Vision Rehabilitation Therapists; others.

Skills—Technology Design: Generating or adapting equipment and technology to serve user needs. **Operation and Control:** Controlling operations of equipment or systems. **Social Perceptiveness:** Being aware of others' reactions and understanding why they react as they do. **Troubleshooting:** Determining causes of operating errors and deciding what to do about them. **Service Orientation:** Actively looking for ways to help people. **Operation Monitoring:** Watching gauges, dials, or other indicators to make sure a machine is working properly. **Science:** Using scientific rules and methods to solve problems. **Installation:** Installing equipment, machines, wiring, or programs to meet specifications.

Work Environment: Indoors; standing; walking and running; using hands; bending or twisting the body; repetitive motions; exposed to disease or infections.

Physical Therapist Assistants

- ⊙ Annual Earnings: $51,040
- ⊙ Earnings Growth Potential: Medium (37.2%)
- ⊙ Growth: 45.7%
- ⊙ Annual Job Openings: 4,120
- ⊙ Self-Employed: 0.0%

Considerations for Job Outlook: Opportunities for physical therapist assistants are expected to be very good. With help from physical therapist assistants, physical therapists can manage more patients. However, physical therapy aides may face keen competition from the large pool of qualified people. Job opportunities should be particularly good in acute hospital, skilled nursing, and orthopedic settings, where the elderly are most often treated. Job prospects should be especially favorable in rural areas, as many physical therapists cluster in highly populated urban and suburban areas.

Assist physical therapists in providing physical therapy treatments and procedures. Instruct, motivate, safeguard, and assist patients as they practice exercises and functional activities. Observe patients during treatments to compile and evaluate data on their responses and progress, and provide results to physical therapists in person or through progress notes. Confer with physical therapy staffs or others to discuss and evaluate patient information for planning, modifying, and coordinating treatment. Transport patients to and from treatment areas, lifting and transferring them according to positioning requirements. Secure patients into or onto therapy equipment. Administer active and passive manual therapeutic exercises; therapeutic massages; aquatic physical therapy; and heat, light, sound, and electrical modality treatments such as ultrasound. Communicate with or instruct caregivers and family members on patient therapeutic activities and treatment plans. Measure patients' ranges-of-joint motion, body parts, and vital signs to determine effects of treatments or for patient evaluations. Monitor operation of equipment, and record use of equipment and administration of treatment. Fit patients for orthopedic braces, prostheses, and supportive devices such as crutches. Train patients in the use of orthopedic braces, prostheses, or supportive devices. Clean work areas, and check and store equipment after treatments. Assist patients to dress; undress; or put on and remove supportive devices such as braces, splints, and slings.

P

Education/Training Required: Associate degree. **Education and Training Program:** Physical Therapy Technician/Assistant Training. **Knowledge/Courses—Therapy and Counseling:** Principles, methods, and procedures for diagnosis, treatment, and rehabilitation of physical and mental dysfunctions, and for career counseling and guidance. **Medicine and Dentistry:** The information and techniques needed to diagnose and treat human injuries, diseases, and deformities. This includes symptoms, treatment alternatives, drug properties and interactions, and preventive health-care measures. **Psychology:** Human behavior and performance; individual differences in ability, personality, and interests; learning and motivation; psychological research methods; and the assessment and treatment of behavioral and affective disorders. **Biology:** Plant and animal organisms and their tissues, cells, functions, interdependencies, and interactions with each other and the environment. **Customer and Personal Service:** Principles and processes for providing customer and personal services. This includes customer needs assessment, meeting quality standards for services, and evaluation of customer satisfaction. **Education and Training:** Principles and methods for curriculum and training design, teaching and instruction for individuals and groups, and the measurement of training effects. **Work Experience Needed:** None. **On-the-Job Training Needed:** None. **Certification/Licensure:** Licensure, registration, or certification.

Personality Type: Social-Realistic-Investigative. **Career Cluster:** 08 Health Science. **Career Pathway:** 08.1 Therapeutic Services. **Other Jobs in This Pathway:** Acupuncturists; Allergists and Immunologists; Anesthesiologists; Art Therapists; Chiropractors; Clinical Psychologists; Community and Social Service Specialists, All Other; Counseling Psychologists; Counselors, All Other; Dental Assistants; Dental Hygienists; Dentists, All Other Specialists; Dentists, General; Dermatologists; Diagnostic Medical Sonographers; Dietetic Technicians; Dietitians and Nutritionists; Family and General Practitioners; Health Diagnosing and Treating Practitioners, All Other; Health Specialties Teachers, Postsecondary; Health Technologists and Technicians, All Other; Healthcare Practitioners and Technical Workers, All Other; Healthcare Support Workers, All Other; Home Health Aides; Hospitalists; Industrial-Organizational Psychologists; Internists, General; Licensed Practical and Licensed Vocational Nurses; Life, Physical, and Social Science Technicians, All Other; Low

Vision Therapists, Orientation and Mobility Specialists, and Vision Rehabilitation Therapists; others.

Skills—Service Orientation: Actively looking for ways to help people. **Quality Control Analysis:** Conducting tests and inspections of products, services, or processes to evaluate quality or performance. **Social Perceptiveness:** Being aware of others' reactions and understanding why they react as they do. **Science:** Using scientific rules and methods to solve problems. **Speaking:** Talking to others to convey information effectively. **Learning Strategies:** Selecting and using training/instructional methods and procedures appropriate for the situation when learning or teaching new things. **Reading Comprehension:** Understanding written sentences and paragraphs in work-related documents. **Systems Evaluation:** Identifying measures or indicators of system performance and the actions needed to improve or correct performance relative to the goals of the system.

Work Environment: Indoors; standing; walking and running; exposed to disease or infections.

Pile-Driver Operators

- ⊙ Annual Earnings: $45,500
- ⊙ Earnings Growth Potential: High (41.3%)
- ⊙ Growth: 36.6%
- ⊙ Annual Job Openings: 230
- ⊙ Self-Employed: 0.0%

Considerations for Job Outlook: Workers with the ability to operate multiple types of equipment should have the best job opportunities. As with many other construction workers, employment of construction equipment operators is sensitive to fluctuations of the economy. Workers may experience periods of unemployment when the overall level of construction falls. However, shortages of workers may occur in some areas during peak periods of building activity. Employment opportunities should be best in metropolitan areas, where most large commercial and multifamily buildings are constructed, and in states that are undertaking large transportation-related projects. In addition, the need to replace workers who leave the occupation should result in some job opportunities.

Operate pile drivers mounted on skids, barges, crawler treads, or locomotive cranes to drive pilings for retaining walls, bulkheads, and foundations of structures.

Move levers and turn valves to activate power hammers, or to raise and lower drophammers that drive piles to required depths. Clean, lubricate, and refill equipment. Conduct pre-operational checks on equipment to ensure proper functioning. Drive pilings to provide support for buildings or other structures, using heavy equipment with a pile driver head. Move hand and foot levers of hoisting equipment to position piling leads, hoist piling into leads, and position hammers over pilings.

Education/Training Required: High school diploma or equivalent. **Education and Training Program:** Construction/Heavy Equipment/Earthmoving Equipment Operation. **Knowledge/Courses—Building and Construction:** Materials, methods, and the tools involved in the construction or repair of houses, buildings, or other structures such as highways and roads. **Mechanical Devices:** Machines and tools, including their designs, uses, repair, and maintenance. **Transportation:** Principles and methods for moving people or goods by air, rail, sea, or road, including the relative costs and benefits. **Physics:** Physical principles, laws, their interrelationships, and applications to understanding fluid, material, and atmospheric dynamics, and mechanical, electrical, atomic, and subatomic structures and processes. **Design:** Design techniques, tools, and principles involved in production of precision technical plans, blueprints, drawings, and models. **Engineering and Technology:** The practical application of engineering science and technology. This includes applying principles, techniques, procedures, and equipment to the design and production of various goods and services. **Work Experience Needed:** None. **On-the-Job Training Needed:** Moderate-term on-the-job training. **Certification/Licensure:** Licensure in some states.

Personality Type: Realistic-Conventional-Investigative. **Career Cluster:** 02 Architecture and Construction. **Career Pathway:** 02.2 Construction. **Other Jobs in This Pathway:** Boilermakers; Brickmasons and Blockmasons; Carpet Installers; Cement Masons and Concrete Finishers; Construction and Building Inspectors; Construction and Related Workers, All Other; Construction Carpenters; Construction Laborers; Construction Managers; Continuous Mining Machine Operators; Cost Estimators; Crane and Tower Operators; Dredge Operators; Drywall and Ceiling Tile Installers; Earth Drillers, Except Oil and Gas; Electrical Power-Line Installers and Repairers; Electricians; Electromechanical Equipment Assemblers; Engineering Technicians, Except Drafters, All Other; Excavating and Loading Machine and Dragline Operators; Explosives Workers, Ordnance Handling Experts, and Blasters; Extraction Workers, All Other; First-Line Supervisors of Construction Trades and Extraction Workers; Floor Layers, Except Carpet, Wood, and Hard Tiles; Floor Sanders and Finishers; Glaziers; Heating and Air Conditioning Mechanics and Installers; Helpers, Construction Trades, All Other; others.

Skills—Equipment Maintenance: Performing routine maintenance on equipment and determining when and what kind of maintenance is needed. **Operation and Control:** Controlling operations of equipment or systems. **Repairing:** Repairing machines or systems using the needed tools. **Operation Monitoring:** Watching gauges, dials, or other indicators to make sure a machine is working properly. **Troubleshooting:** Determining causes of operating errors and deciding what to do about them. **Quality Control Analysis:** Conducting tests and inspections of products, services, or processes to evaluate quality or performance. **Equipment Selection:** Determining the kind of tools and equipment needed to do a job.

Work Environment: Outdoors; standing; using hands; bending or twisting the body; repetitive motions; noise; very hot or cold; bright or inadequate lighting; contaminants; cramped work space; whole-body vibration; high places; hazardous conditions; hazardous equipment; minor burns, cuts, bites, or stings.

Pipelayers

- ⊙ Annual Earnings: $35,900
- ⊙ Earnings Growth Potential: Medium (35.5%)
- ⊙ Growth: 25.2%
- ⊙ Annual Job Openings: 2,880
- ⊙ Self-Employed: 14.0%

Considerations for Job Outlook: A moderate increase is expected as demand for public utility construction fell significantly during the recent recession, employment of pipelayers experienced much larger declines than the construction industry as a whole. As the public utility construction industry recovers and large-scale pipeline projects progress, employment of these workers will rebound faster than the overall industry in the next decade.

Lay pipe for storm or sanitation sewers, drains, and water mains. Check slopes for conformance to requirements, using levels or lasers. Cover pipes with earth or other materials. Cut pipes to required lengths. Connect pipe pieces and seal joints, using welding equipment, cement, or glue. Install and repair sanitary and stormwater sewer structures and pipe systems. Install and use instruments such as lasers, grade rods, and transit levels. Grade and level trench bases, using tamping machines and hand tools. Lay out pipe routes, following written instructions or blueprints, and coordinating layouts with supervisors. Dig trenches to desired or required depths, by hand or using trenching tools. Align and position pipes to prepare them for welding or sealing. Operate mechanized equipment such as pickup trucks, rollers, tandem dump trucks, front-end loaders, and backhoes. Train others in pipe-laying, and provide supervision. Tap and drill holes into pipes to introduce auxiliary lines or devices. Locate existing pipes needing repair or replacement, using magnetic or radio indicators.

Education/Training Required: High school diploma or equivalent. **Education and Training Programs:** Pipefitting/Pipefitter and Sprinkler Fitter; Plumbing Technology/Plumber. **Knowledge/Courses—Building and Construction:** Materials, methods, and the tools involved in the construction or repair of houses, buildings, or other structures such as highways and roads. **Mechanical Devices:** Machines and tools, including their designs, uses, repair, and maintenance. **Work Experience Needed:** None. **On-the-Job Training Needed:** Short-term on-the-job training. **Certification/Licensure:** None.

Personality Type: Realistic. **Career Cluster:** 02 Architecture and Construction. **Career Pathway:** 02.2 Construction. **Other Jobs in This Pathway:** Boilermakers; Brickmasons and Blockmasons; Carpet Installers; Cement Masons and Concrete Finishers; Construction and Building Inspectors; Construction and Related Workers, All Other; Construction Carpenters; Construction Laborers; Construction Managers; Continuous Mining Machine Operators; Cost Estimators; Crane and Tower Operators; Dredge Operators; Drywall and Ceiling Tile Installers; Earth Drillers, Except Oil and Gas; Electrical Power-Line Installers and Repairers; Electricians; Electromechanical Equipment Assemblers; Engineering Technicians, Except Drafters, All Other; Excavating and Loading Machine and Dragline Operators; Explosives Workers, Ordnance Handling Experts, and Blasters; Extraction Workers, All Other; First-Line Supervisors of Construction Trades and Extraction Workers; Floor Layers, Except Carpet, Wood, and Hard Tiles; Floor Sanders and Finishers; Glaziers; Heating and Air Conditioning Mechanics and Installers; Helpers, Construction Trades, All Other; others.

Skills—Repairing: Repairing machines or systems using the needed tools. **Operation and Control:** Controlling operations of equipment or systems. **Equipment Maintenance:** Performing routine maintenance on equipment and determining when and what kind of maintenance is needed. **Troubleshooting:** Determining causes of operating errors and deciding what to do about them. **Equipment Selection:** Determining the kind of tools and equipment needed to do a job. **Installation:** Installing equipment, machines, wiring, or programs to meet specifications. **Quality Control Analysis:** Conducting tests and inspections of products, services, or processes to evaluate quality or performance. **Operation Monitoring:** Watching gauges, dials, or other indicators to make sure a machine is working properly.

Work Environment: Outdoors; standing; walking and running; using hands; bending or twisting the body; repetitive motions; noise; very hot or cold; bright or inadequate lighting; contaminants; cramped work space; whole-body vibration; hazardous equipment; minor burns, cuts, bites, or stings.

Plasterers and Stucco Masons

- ⊙ Annual Earnings: $36,830
- ⊙ Earnings Growth Potential: Low (32.6%)
- ⊙ Growth: 17.2%
- ⊙ Annual Job Openings: 1,050
- ⊙ Self-Employed: 11.0%

Considerations for Job Outlook: Overall job prospects should improve over the coming decade as construction activity rebounds from the recent recession. As with many other construction workers, employment of plasterers and stucco masons is particularly sensitive to fluctuations in the economy, and workers in this trade can expect periods of unemployment when the overall level of construction falls. However, shortages of workers may occur in some areas during peak periods of building activity. Highly skilled workers with good job histories and work experience in construction should have the best opportunities. Stucco masons will have the best job opportunities in parts of the country where stucco homes and other buildings are popular, such as the South and some Southwestern states. Plasterers will have better job opportunities in areas where power plants and oil refineries are being built or refurbished.

Apply interior or exterior plaster, cement, stucco, or similar materials. Apply coats of plaster or stucco to walls, ceilings, or partitions of buildings, using trowels, brushes, or spray guns. Mix mortar and plaster to desired consistency or direct workers who perform mixing. Create decorative textures in finish coat, using brushes or trowels, sand, pebbles, or stones. Apply insulation to building exteriors by installing prefabricated insulation systems over existing walls or by covering the outer wall with insulation board, reinforcing mesh, and a base coat. Cure freshly plastered surfaces. Clean and prepare surfaces for applications of plaster, cement, stucco, or similar materials, such as by drywall taping. Rough the undercoat surface with a scratcher so the finish coat will adhere. Apply weatherproof, decorative coverings to exterior surfaces of buildings, such as troweling or spraying on coats of stucco. Install guidewires on exterior surfaces of buildings to indicate thickness of plaster or stucco, and nail wire mesh, lath, or similar materials to the outside surface to hold stucco in place. Spray acoustic materials or texture finish over walls and ceilings. Mold and install ornamental plaster pieces, panels, and trim.

Education/Training Required: Less than high school. **Education and Training Program:** Construction Trades, Other. **Knowledge/Courses—Building and Construction:** Materials, methods, and the tools involved in the construction or repair of houses, buildings, or other structures such as highways and roads. **Public Safety and Security:** Relevant equipment, policies, procedures, and strategies to promote effective local, state, or national security operations for the protection of people, data, property, and institutions. **Work Experience Needed:** None. **On-the-Job Training Needed:** Long-term on-the-job training. **Certification/Licensure:** None.

Personality Type: Realistic. **Career Cluster:** 02 Architecture and Construction. **Career Pathway:** 02.2 Construction. **Other Jobs in This Pathway:** Boilermakers; Brickmasons and Blockmasons; Carpet Installers; Cement Masons and Concrete Finishers; Construction and Building Inspectors; Construction and Related Workers, All Other; Construction Carpenters; Construction Laborers; Construction Managers; Continuous Mining Machine Operators; Cost Estimators; Crane and Tower Operators; Dredge Operators; Drywall and Ceiling Tile Installers; Earth Drillers, Except Oil and Gas; Electrical Power-Line Installers and Repairers; Electricians; Electromechanical Equipment Assemblers; Engineering Technicians, Except Drafters, All Other; Excavating and Loading Machine and Dragline Operators; Explosives Workers, Ordnance Handling Experts, and Blasters; Extraction Workers, All Other; First-Line Supervisors of Construction Trades and Extraction Workers; Floor Layers, Except Carpet, Wood, and Hard Tiles; Floor Sanders and Finishers; Glaziers; Heating and Air Conditioning Mechanics and Installers; Helpers, Construction Trades, All Other; others.

Skills—Installation: Installing equipment, machines, wiring, or programs to meet specifications. **Quality Control Analysis:** Conducting tests and inspections of products, services, or processes to evaluate quality or performance. **Operation and Control:** Controlling operations of equipment or systems. **Equipment Selection:** Determining the kind of tools and equipment needed to do a job. **Technology Design:** Generating or adapting equipment and technology to serve user needs. **Troubleshooting:** Determining causes of operating errors and deciding what to do about them. **Operation Monitoring:** Watching gauges, dials, or other indicators to make sure a machine is working properly.

Work Environment: Outdoors; standing; climbing; walking and running; kneeling, crouching, stooping, or crawling; using hands; bending or twisting the body; repetitive motions; noise; very hot or cold; bright or inadequate lighting; contaminants; cramped work space; high places; minor burns, cuts, bites, or stings.

Plumbers, Pipefitters, and Steamfitters

- ⊙ Annual Earnings: $47,750
- ⊙ Earnings Growth Potential: High (40.7%)
- ⊙ Growth: 25.6%
- ⊙ Annual Job Openings: 22,880
- ⊙ Self-Employed: 14.0%

Considerations for Job Outlook: Job opportunities are expected to be good as some employers continue to report difficulty finding qualified professionals. In addition, many workers are expected to retire over the next 10 years, which will result in more job openings. Workers with welding experience may have the best opportunities. Like that of many other types of construction work, employment of plumbers, pipefitters, and steamfitters is sensitive to fluctuations of the economy. On the one hand, workers may experience periods of unemployment when the overall level of construction falls. On the other hand, shortages of workers may occur in some areas during peak periods of building activity. However, maintenance and repair of plumbing and pipe systems must continue even during economic downturns, so plumbers and fitters outside construction, especially those in manufacturing, tend to have more stable employment.

Assemble, install, alter, and repair pipelines or pipe systems that carry water, steam, air, or other liquids or gases. For task data, see Job Specializations.

Education/Training Required: High school diploma or equivalent. **Work Experience Needed:** None. **On-the-Job Training Needed:** Apprenticeship. **Certification/Licensure:** Licensure.

Job Specialization: Pipe Fitters and Steamfitters

Lay out, assemble, install, and maintain pipe systems, pipe supports, and related hydraulic and pneumatic equipment for steam, hot water, heating, cooling, lubricating, sprinkling, and industrial production and processing systems. Cut, thread, and hammer pipe to specifications, using tools such as saws, cutting torches, and pipe threaders and benders. Assemble and secure pipes, tubes, fittings, and related equipment according to specifications by welding, brazing, cementing, soldering, and threading joints. Attach pipes to walls, structures, and fixtures, such as radiators or tanks, using brackets, clamps, tools, or welding equipment. Inspect, examine, and test installed systems and pipelines, using pressure gauges, hydrostatic testing, observation, or other methods. Measure and mark pipes for cutting and threading. Lay out full-scale drawings of pipe systems, supports, and related equipment, following blueprints. Plan pipe-system layout, installation, or repair according to specifications. Select pipe sizes and types and related materials, such as supports, hangers, and hydraulic cylinders, according to specifications. Cut and bore holes in structures such as bulkheads,

decks, walls, and mains prior to pipe installation, using hand and power tools. Modify, clean, and maintain pipe systems, units, fittings, and related machines and equipment, following specifications and using hand and power tools. Install automatic controls used to regulate pipe systems. Turn valves to shut off steam, water, or other gases or liquids from pipe sections, using valve keys or wrenches. Remove and replace worn components. Prepare cost estimates for clients.

Education and Training Programs: Pipefitting/Pipefitter and Sprinkler Fitter; Plumbing and Related Water Supply Services, Other; Plumbing Technology/Plumber. **Knowledge/Courses—Building and Construction:** Materials, methods, and the tools involved in the construction or repair of houses, buildings, or other structures such as highways and roads. **Mechanical Devices:** Machines and tools, including their designs, uses, repair, and maintenance. **Physics:** Physical principles, laws, their interrelationships, and applications to understanding fluid, material, and atmospheric dynamics, and mechanical, electrical, atomic, and subatomic structures and processes. **Design:** Design techniques, tools, and principles involved in production of precision technical plans, blueprints, drawings, and models. **Engineering and Technology:** The practical application of engineering science and technology. This includes applying principles, techniques, procedures, and equipment to the design and production of various goods and services. **Chemistry:** The chemical composition, structure, and properties of substances and of the chemical processes and transformations that they undergo. This includes uses of chemicals and their danger signs, production techniques, and disposal methods.

Personality Type: Realistic-Conventional. **Career Cluster:** 02 Architecture and Construction. **Career Pathway:** 02.2 Construction. **Other Jobs in This Pathway:** Boilermakers; Brickmasons and Blockmasons; Carpet Installers; Cement Masons and Concrete Finishers; Construction and Building Inspectors; Construction and Related Workers, All Other; Construction Carpenters; Construction Laborers; Construction Managers; Continuous Mining Machine Operators; Cost Estimators; Crane and Tower Operators; Dredge Operators; Drywall and Ceiling Tile Installers; Earth Drillers, Except Oil and Gas; Electrical Power-Line Installers and Repairers; Electricians; Electromechanical Equipment Assemblers; Engineering Technicians, Except Drafters, All Other; Excavating and Loading Machine

and Dragline Operators; Explosives Workers, Ordnance Handling Experts, and Blasters; Extraction Workers, All Other; First-Line Supervisors of Construction Trades and Extraction Workers; Floor Layers, Except Carpet, Wood, and Hard Tiles; Floor Sanders and Finishers; Glaziers; Heating and Air Conditioning Mechanics and Installers; Helpers, Construction Trades, All Other; others.

Skills—Repairing: Repairing machines or systems using the needed tools. **Equipment Maintenance:** Performing routine maintenance on equipment and determining when and what kind of maintenance is needed. **Installation:** Installing equipment, machines, wiring, or programs to meet specifications. **Troubleshooting:** Determining causes of operating errors and deciding what to do about them. **Operation and Control:** Controlling operations of equipment or systems. **Quality Control Analysis:** Conducting tests and inspections of products, services, or processes to evaluate quality or performance. **Operation Monitoring:** Watching gauges, dials, or other indicators to make sure a machine is working properly. **Equipment Selection:** Determining the kind of tools and equipment needed to do a job.

Work Environment: More often outdoors than indoors; standing; using hands; bending or twisting the body; repetitive motions; noise; very hot or cold; bright or inadequate lighting; contaminants; cramped work space; high places; hazardous conditions; hazardous equipment; minor burns, cuts, bites, or stings.

Job Specialization: Plumbers

Assemble, install, and repair pipes, fittings, and fixtures of heating, water, and drainage systems according to specifications and plumbing codes. Measure, cut, thread, and bend pipe to required angles, using hand and power tools or machines such as pipe cutters, pipe-threading machines, and pipe-bending machines. Study building plans and inspect structures to assess material and equipment needs to establish the sequence of pipe installations and to plan installation around obstructions such as electrical wiring. Locate and mark the position of pipe installations, connections, passage holes, and fixtures in structures, using measuring instruments such as rulers and levels. Assemble pipe sections, tubing, and fittings, using couplings, clamps, screws, bolts, cement, plastic solvent, caulking, or soldering, brazing, and welding equipment. Fill pipes

or plumbing fixtures with water or air and observe pressure gauges to detect and locate leaks. Install pipe assemblies, fittings, valves, appliances such as dishwashers and water heaters, and fixtures such as sinks and toilets, using hand and power tools. Direct workers engaged in pipe cutting and preassembly and installation of plumbing systems and components. Cut openings in structures to accommodate pipes and pipe fittings, using hand and power tools. Review blueprints as well as building codes and specifications to determine work details and procedures. Install underground storm, sanitary, and water piping systems, and extend piping to connect fixtures and plumbing to these systems.

Education and Training Programs: Pipefitting/Pipefitter and Sprinkler Fitter; Plumbing and Related Water Supply Services, Other; Plumbing Technology/Plumber. **Knowledge/Courses—Building and Construction:** Materials, methods, and the tools involved in the construction or repair of houses, buildings, or other structures such as highways and roads. **Mechanical Devices:** Machines and tools, including their designs, uses, repair, and maintenance. **Physics:** Physical principles, laws, their interrelationships, and applications to understanding fluid, material, and atmospheric dynamics, and mechanical, electrical, atomic, and subatomic structures and processes. **Design:** Design techniques, tools, and principles involved in production of precision technical plans, blueprints, drawings, and models. **Engineering and Technology:** The practical application of engineering science and technology. This includes applying principles, techniques, procedures, and equipment to the design and production of various goods and services. **Customer and Personal Service:** Principles and processes for providing customer and personal services. This includes customer needs assessment, meeting quality standards for services, and evaluation of customer satisfaction.

Personality Type: Realistic-Conventional-Investigative. **Career Cluster:** 02 Architecture and Construction. **Career Pathway:** 02.2 Construction. **Other Jobs in This Pathway:** Boilermakers; Brickmasons and Blockmasons; Carpet Installers; Cement Masons and Concrete Finishers; Construction and Building Inspectors; Construction and Related Workers, All Other; Construction Carpenters; Construction Laborers; Construction Managers; Continuous Mining Machine Operators; Cost Estimators; Crane and Tower Operators; Dredge Operators; Drywall and Ceiling Tile Installers; Earth Drillers, Except Oil and Gas; Electrical

Power-Line Installers and Repairers; Electricians; Electromechanical Equipment Assemblers; Engineering Technicians, Except Drafters, All Other; Excavating and Loading Machine and Dragline Operators; Explosives Workers, Ordnance Handling Experts, and Blasters; Extraction Workers, All Other; First-Line Supervisors of Construction Trades and Extraction Workers; Floor Layers, Except Carpet, Wood, and Hard Tiles; Floor Sanders and Finishers; Glaziers; Heating and Air Conditioning Mechanics and Installers; Helpers, Construction Trades, All Other; others.

Skills—Repairing: Repairing machines or systems using the needed tools. **Equipment Maintenance:** Performing routine maintenance on equipment and determining when and what kind of maintenance is needed. **Installation:** Installing equipment, machines, wiring, or programs to meet specifications. **Troubleshooting:** Determining causes of operating errors and deciding what to do about them. **Equipment Selection:** Determining the kind of tools and equipment needed to do a job. **Operation and Control:** Controlling operations of equipment or systems. **Operation Monitoring:** Watching gauges, dials, or other indicators to make sure a machine is working properly. **Quality Control Analysis:** Conducting tests and inspections of products, services, or processes to evaluate quality or performance.

Work Environment: More often outdoors than indoors; standing; walking and running; kneeling, crouching, stooping, or crawling; using hands; bending or twisting the body; repetitive motions; noise; very hot or cold; bright or inadequate lighting; contaminants; cramped work space; whole-body vibration; hazardous equipment; minor burns, cuts, bites, or stings.

Police and Sheriff's Patrol Officers

- ⊙ Annual Earnings: $54,230
- ⊙ Earnings Growth Potential: High (40.8%)
- ⊙ Growth: 8.2%
- ⊙ Annual Job Openings: 24,940
- ⊙ Self-Employed: 0.0%

Considerations for Job Outlook: Continued demand for public safety will lead to new openings for officers in local departments; however, both state and federal jobs may be more competitive. Because they typically offer low salaries,

many local departments face high turnover rates, making opportunities more plentiful for qualified applicants. However, some smaller departments may have fewer opportunities as budgets limit the ability to hire additional officers. Jobs in state and federal agencies will remain more competitive as they often offer high pay and more opportunities for both promotions and interagency transfers. Bilingual applicants with a bachelor's degree and law enforcement or military experience, especially investigative experience, should have the best opportunities in federal agencies.

Maintain order and protect life and property by enforcing local, tribal, state, or federal laws and ordinances. For task data, see Job Specializations.

Education/Training Required: High school diploma or equivalent. **Work Experience Needed:** None. **On-the-Job Training Needed:** Moderate-term on-the-job training. **Certification/Licensure:** Licensure in some states.

Job Specialization: Police Patrol Officers

Patrol assigned areas to enforce laws and ordinances, regulate traffic, control crowds, prevent crime, and arrest violators. Provide for public safety by maintaining order, responding to emergencies, protecting people and property, enforcing motor vehicle and criminal laws, and promoting good community relations. Monitor, note, report, and investigate suspicious persons and situations, safety hazards, and unusual or illegal activity in patrol area. Record facts to prepare reports that document incidents and activities. Identify, pursue, and arrest suspects and perpetrators of criminal acts. Patrol specific areas on foot, horseback, or motorized conveyance, responding promptly to calls for assistance. Review facts of incidents to determine whether criminal acts or statute violations were involved. Investigate traffic accidents and other accidents to determine causes and to determine whether crimes have been committed. Render aid to accident victims and other persons requiring first aid for physical injuries. Testify in court to present evidence or act as witness in traffic and criminal cases. Photograph or draw diagrams of crime or accident scenes, and interview principals and eyewitnesses. Relay complaint and emergency-request information to appropriate agency dispatchers. Evaluate complaint and emergency-request information to determine response requirements. Process prisoners, and prepare and maintain records of prisoner bookings and prisoner statuses during booking and pretrial processes. Monitor traffic to ensure motorists observe traffic regulations and exhibit safe driving procedures.

Education and Training Programs: Criminal Justice/Police Science; Criminalistics and Criminal Science. **Knowledge/Courses—Psychology:** Human behavior and performance; individual differences in ability, personality, and interests; learning and motivation; psychological research methods; and the assessment and treatment of behavioral and affective disorders. **Public Safety and Security:** Relevant equipment, policies, procedures, and strategies to promote effective local, state, or national security operations for the protection of people, data, property, and institutions. **Law and Government:** Laws, legal codes, court procedures, precedents, government regulations, executive orders, agency rules, and the democratic political process. **Customer and Personal Service:** Principles and processes for providing customer and personal services. This includes customer needs assessment, meeting quality standards for services, and evaluation of customer satisfaction. **Therapy and Counseling:** Principles, methods, and procedures for diagnosis, treatment, and rehabilitation of physical and mental dysfunctions, and for career counseling and guidance. **Sociology and Anthropology:** Group behavior and dynamics, societal trends and influences, human migrations, ethnicity, and cultures and their history and origins.

Personality Type: Realistic-Enterprising-Conventional. **Career Cluster:** 12 Law, Public Safety, Corrections, and Security. **Career Pathway:** 12.4 Law Enforcement Services. **Other Jobs in This Pathway:** Anthropology and Archeology Teachers, Postsecondary; Bailiffs; Correctional Officers and Jailers; Criminal Investigators and Special Agents; Criminal Justice and Law Enforcement Teachers, Postsecondary; First-Line Supervisors of Police and Detectives; Forensic Science Technicians; Immigration and Customs Inspectors; Intelligence Analysts; Police Detectives; Police Identification and Records Officers; Remote Sensing Scientists and Technologists; Sheriffs and Deputy Sheriffs.

Skills—Negotiation: Bringing others together and trying to reconcile differences. **Persuasion:** Persuading others to change their minds or behavior. **Service Orientation:** Actively looking for ways to help people. **Operation and Control:** Controlling operations of equipment or systems. **Social Perceptiveness:** Being aware of others' reactions and understanding why they react as they do.

Active Listening: Giving full attention to what other people are saying, taking time to understand the points being made, asking questions as appropriate, and not interrupting at inappropriate times. **Critical Thinking:** Using logic and reasoning to identify the strengths and weaknesses of alternative solutions, conclusions, or approaches to problems. **Coordination:** Adjusting actions in relation to others' actions.

Work Environment: More often outdoors than indoors; sitting; using hands; noise; very hot or cold; bright or inadequate lighting; contaminants; exposed to disease or infections; hazardous equipment; minor burns, cuts, bites, or stings.

Job Specialization: Sheriffs and Deputy Sheriffs

Enforce law and order in rural or unincorporated districts, or serve legal processes of courts. May patrol courthouse, guard court or grand jury, or escort defendants. Drive vehicles or patrol specific areas to detect law violators, issue citations, and make arrests. Investigate illegal or suspicious activities. Verify that the proper legal charges have been made against law offenders. Execute arrest warrants, locating and taking persons into custody. Record daily activities, and submit logs and other related reports and paperwork to appropriate authorities. Patrol and guard courthouses, grand jury rooms, or assigned areas to provide security, enforce laws, maintain order, and arrest violators. Notify patrol units to take violators into custody or to provide needed assistance or medical aid. Place people in protective custody. Serve statements of claims, subpoenas, summonses, jury summonses, orders to pay alimony, and other court orders. Take control of accident scenes to maintain traffic flow, to assist accident victims, and to investigate causes. Question individuals entering secured areas to determine their business, directing and rerouting individuals as necessary. Transport or escort prisoners and defendants en route to courtrooms, prisons or jails, attorneys' offices, or medical facilities. Locate and confiscate real or personal property, as directed by court order. Manage jail operations, and tend to jail inmates.

Education and Training Programs: Criminal Justice/Police Science; Criminalistics and Criminal Science. **Knowledge/Courses—Public Safety and Security:** Relevant equipment, policies, procedures, and strategies to promote effective local, state, or national security operations for the protection of people, data, property, and institutions. **Law and Government:** Laws, legal codes, court procedures, precedents, government regulations, executive orders, agency rules, and the democratic political process. **Telecommunications:** Transmission, broadcasting, switching, control, and operation of telecommunications systems. **Psychology:** Human behavior and performance; individual differences in ability, personality, and interests; learning and motivation; psychological research methods; and the assessment and treatment of behavioral and affective disorders. **Therapy and Counseling:** Principles, methods, and procedures for diagnosis, treatment, and rehabilitation of physical and mental dysfunctions, and for career counseling and guidance. **Philosophy and Theology:** Different philosophical systems and religions. This includes their basic principles, values, ethics, ways of thinking, customs, practices, and their impact on human culture.

Personality Type: Enterprising-Realistic-Social. **Career Cluster:** 12 Law, Public Safety, Corrections, and Security. **Career Pathways:** 12.4 Law Enforcement Services; 12.3 Security and Protective Services. **Other Jobs in These Pathways:** Animal Control Workers; Anthropology and Archeology Teachers, Postsecondary; Bailiffs; Correctional Officers and Jailers; Criminal Investigators and Special Agents; Criminal Justice and Law Enforcement Teachers, Postsecondary; Crossing Guards; First-Line Supervisors of Police and Detectives; First-Line Supervisors of Protective Service Workers, All Other; Forensic Science Technicians; Forest Firefighters; Gaming Surveillance Officers and Gaming Investigators; Immigration and Customs Inspectors; Intelligence Analysts; Lifeguards, Ski Patrol, and Other Recreational Protective Service Workers; Parking Enforcement Workers; Police Detectives; Police Identification and Records Officers; Police Patrol Officers; Police, Fire, and Ambulance Dispatchers; Private Detectives and Investigators; Remote Sensing Scientists and Technologists; Retail Loss Prevention Specialists; Security Guards; Transit and Railroad Police.

Skills—Negotiation: Bringing others together and trying to reconcile differences. **Social Perceptiveness:** Being aware of others' reactions and understanding why they react as they do. **Persuasion:** Persuading others to change their minds or behavior. **Service Orientation:** Actively looking for ways to help people. **Management of Personnel Resources:** Motivating, developing, and directing people as they work, identifying the best people for the job. **Critical Thinking:** Using logic and reasoning to identify the strengths and weaknesses of alternative solutions, conclusions, or approaches to problems. **Time Management:** Managing one's own time and the time of others. **Reading Comprehension:** Understanding written sentences and paragraphs in work-related documents.

Work Environment: More often outdoors than indoors; sitting; using hands; repetitive motions; noise; very hot or cold; bright or inadequate lighting; contaminants; cramped work space; exposed to disease or infections; hazardous equipment.

Police, Fire, and Ambulance Dispatchers

- ⊙ Annual Earnings: $35,930
- ⊙ Earnings Growth Potential: Medium (36.8%)
- ⊙ Growth: 11.7%
- ⊙ Annual Job Openings: 3,070
- ⊙ Self-Employed: 0.0%

Considerations for Job Outlook: Favorable opportunities are expected, largely due to job openings arising from the need to replace workers who transfer to other occupations or who leave the occupation. The technology and equipment dispatchers use continue to evolve, creating a demand for workers with related technical skills. Job prospects will be best for those with customer service and computer skills.

Operate radio, telephone, or computer equipment at emergency response centers. Question callers about their locations and the nature of their problems to determine types of response needed. Receive incoming telephone or alarm system calls regarding emergency and nonemergency police and fire service, emergency ambulance service, information, and after-hours calls for departments within a city. Determine response requirements and relative priorities of situations, and dispatch units in accordance with established procedures. Record details of calls, dispatches, and messages. Enter, update, and retrieve information from teletype networks and computerized data systems regarding such things as wanted persons, stolen property, vehicle registration, and stolen vehicles. Maintain access to and security of highly sensitive materials.

Relay information and messages to and from emergency sites, to law enforcement agencies, and to all other individuals or groups requiring notification. Scan status charts and computer screens, and contact emergency response field units to determine emergency units available for dispatch. Observe alarm registers and scan maps to determine whether a specific emergency is in the dispatch service area. Maintain files of information relating to emergency calls such as personnel rosters and emergency call-out and pager files. Monitor various radio frequencies such as those used by public works departments, school security, and civil defense to keep apprised of developing situations. Learn material, and pass required tests for certification.

Education/Training Required: High school diploma or equivalent. **Education and Training Programs:** No related CIP programs; this job is learned through moderate-term on-the-job training. **Knowledge/Courses—Telecommunications:** Transmission, broadcasting, switching, control, and operation of telecommunications systems. **Customer and Personal Service:** Principles and processes for providing customer and personal services. This includes customer needs assessment, meeting quality standards for services, and evaluation of customer satisfaction. **Clerical Practices:** Administrative and clerical procedures and systems such as word processing, managing files and records, stenography and transcription, designing forms, and other office procedures and terminology. **Law and Government:** Laws, legal codes, court procedures, precedents, government regulations, executive orders, agency rules, and the democratic political process. **Public Safety and Security:** Relevant equipment, policies, procedures, and strategies to promote effective local, state, or national security operations for the protection of people, data, property, and institutions. **Psychology:** Human behavior and performance; individual differences in ability, personality, and interests; learning and motivation; psychological research methods; and the assessment and treatment of behavioral and affective disorders. **Work Experience Needed:** None. **On-the-Job Training Needed:** Moderate-term on-the-job training. **Certification/Licensure:** Licensure in some states.

Personality Type: Conventional-Realistic-Enterprising. **Career Cluster:** 12 Law, Public Safety, Corrections, and Security. **Career Pathway:** 12.3 Security and Protective Services. **Other Jobs in This Pathway:** Animal Control Workers; Criminal Justice and Law Enforcement Teachers, Postsecondary; Crossing Guards; First-Line Supervisors of Protective Service Workers, All Other; Forest Firefighters; Gaming Surveillance Officers and Gaming Investigators; Lifeguards, Ski Patrol, and Other Recreational Protective Service Workers; Parking Enforcement Workers; Private Detectives and Investigators; Retail Loss Prevention Specialists; Security Guards; Sheriffs and Deputy Sheriffs; Transit and Railroad Police.

Skills—Active Listening: Giving full attention to what other people are saying, taking time to understand the points being made, asking questions as appropriate, and not interrupting at inappropriate times. **Critical Thinking:** Using logic and reasoning to identify the strengths and weaknesses of alternative solutions, conclusions, or approaches to problems. **Persuasion:** Persuading others to change their minds or behavior. **Social Perceptiveness:** Being aware of others' reactions and understanding why they react as they do. **Service Orientation:** Actively looking for ways to help people. **Operation and Control:** Controlling operations of equipment or systems. **Programming:** Writing computer programs for various purposes. **Operations Analysis:** Analyzing needs and product requirements to create a design.

Work Environment: Indoors; sitting; using hands; repetitive motions; noise; contaminants.

Postal Service Clerks

- Annual Earnings: $53,100
- Earnings Growth Potential: Very low (6.5%)
- Growth: −48.2%
- Annual Job Openings: 1,550
- Self-Employed: 0.0%

Considerations for Job Outlook: Very strong competition is expected for all jobs, as the number of applicants typically is greater than the number of available positions.

Perform any combination of tasks in a post office. Keep money drawers in order, and record and balance daily transactions. Weigh letters and parcels; compute mailing costs based on type, weight, and destination; and affix correct postage. Obtain signatures from recipients of registered or special delivery mail. Register, certify, and insure letters and parcels. Sell and collect payment for products such as stamps, prepaid mail envelopes, and money orders. Check mail in order to ensure correct postage and that packages and letters are in proper condition for mailing. Answer questions regarding mail regulations and procedures, postage rates, and post office boxes. Complete forms regarding changes of address, about theft or loss of mail, or for special services such as registered or priority mail. Provide assistance to the public in complying with federal regulations of Postal Service and other federal agencies. Sort incoming and outgoing mail, according to type and destination, by hand or by operating electronic mail-sorting and scanning devices. Cash money orders. Rent post office boxes to customers. Put undelivered parcels away, retrieve them when customers come to claim them, and complete any related documentation. Provide customers with assistance in filing claims for mail theft or lost or damaged mail. Respond to complaints regarding mail theft, delivery problems, and lost or damaged mail, filling out forms and making appropriate referrals for investigation. Receive letters and parcels, and place mail into bags. Feed mail into postage-canceling devices or hand stamp mail to cancel postage. Transport mail from one work station to another. Set postage meters, and calibrate them to ensure correct operation. Post announcements or government information on public bulletin boards.

Education/Training Required: High school diploma or equivalent. **Education and Training Program:** General Office Occupations and Clerical Services. **Knowledge/ Courses—Sales and Marketing:** Principles and methods for showing, promoting, and selling products or services. This includes marketing strategy and tactics, product demonstration, sales techniques, and sales control systems. **Transportation:** Principles and methods for moving people or goods by air, rail, sea, or road, including the relative costs and benefits. **Clerical Practices:** Administrative and clerical procedures and systems such as word processing, managing files and records, stenography and transcription, designing forms, and other office procedures and terminology. **Public Safety and Security:** Relevant equipment, policies, procedures, and strategies to promote effective local, state, or national security operations for the protection of people, data, property, and institutions. **Work Experience Needed:** None. **On-the-Job Training Needed:** Short-term on-the-job training. **Certification/ Licensure:** None.

Personality Type: Conventional-Realistic. **Career Cluster:** 04 Business, Management, and Administration. **Career Pathway:** 04.6 Administrative and Information

Support. **Other Jobs in This Pathway:** Cargo and Freight Agents; Correspondence Clerks; Couriers and Messengers; Court Clerks; Customer Service Representatives; Data Entry Keyers; Dispatchers, Except Police, Fire, and Ambulance; Executive Secretaries and Executive Administrative Assistants; File Clerks; Freight Forwarders; Human Resources Assistants, Except Payroll and Timekeeping; Information and Record Clerks, All Other; Insurance Claims Clerks; Insurance Policy Processing Clerks; Interviewers, Except Eligibility and Loan; License Clerks; Mail Clerks and Mail Machine Operators, Except Postal Service; Meter Readers, Utilities; Municipal Clerks; Office and Administrative Support Workers, All Other; Office Clerks, General; Office Machine Operators, Except Computer; Order Clerks; Patient Representatives; Postal Service Mail Carriers; Postal Service Mail Sorters, Processors, and Processing Machine Operators; Procurement Clerks; Receptionists and Information Clerks; others.

Skills—Management of Financial Resources: Determining how money will be spent to get the work done and accounting for these expenditures. **Service Orientation:** Actively looking for ways to help people. **Quality Control Analysis:** Conducting tests and inspections of products, services, or processes to evaluate quality or performance. **Troubleshooting:** Determining causes of operating errors and deciding what to do about them. **Mathematics:** Using mathematics to solve problems.

Work Environment: Indoors; standing; using hands; bending or twisting the body; repetitive motions; noise; contaminants.

Postal Service Mail Carriers

- ⊙ Annual Earnings: $55,160
- ⊙ Earnings Growth Potential: Low (26.6%)
- ⊙ Growth: –12.0%
- ⊙ Annual Job Openings: 10,340
- ⊙ Self-Employed: 0.0%

Considerations for Job Outlook: Very strong competition is expected for all jobs, as the number of applicants typically is greater than the number of available positions.

Sort mail for delivery. Deliver mail on established routes by vehicle or on foot. Obtain signed receipts for registered, certified, and insured mail; collect associated charges; and complete any necessary paperwork. Sort mail for delivery, arranging it in delivery sequence. Deliver mail to residences and business establishments along specified routes by walking or driving, using a combination of satchels, carts, cars, and small trucks. Return to post offices with mail collected from homes, businesses, and public mailboxes. Turn in money and receipts collected along mail routes. Sign for cash-on-delivery and registered mail before leaving post offices. Record address changes, and redirect mail for those addresses. Hold mail for customers who are away from delivery locations. Bundle mail in preparation for delivery or transportation to relay boxes. Leave notices telling patrons where to collect mail that could not be delivered. Meet schedules for the collection and return of mail. Return incorrectly addressed mail to senders. Maintain accurate records of deliveries. Answer customers' questions about postal services and regulations. Provide customers with change-of-address cards and other forms. Report any unusual circumstances concerning mail delivery, including the condition of street letter boxes. Register, certify, and insure parcels and letters. Travel to post offices to pick up the mail for routes or pick up mail from postal relay boxes. Enter change-of-address orders into computers that process forwarding-address stickers.

Education/Training Required: High school diploma or equivalent. **Education and Training Program:** General Office Occupations and Clerical Services. **Knowledge/ Courses—Transportation:** Principles and methods for moving people or goods by air, rail, sea, or road, including the relative costs and benefits. **Public Safety and Security:** Relevant equipment, policies, procedures, and strategies to promote effective local, state, or national security operations for the protection of people, data, property, and institutions. **Work Experience Needed:** None. **On-the-Job Training Needed:** Short-term on-the-job training. **Certification/Licensure:** None.

Personality Type: Conventional-Realistic. **Career Cluster:** 04 Business, Management, and Administration. **Career Pathway:** 04.6 Administrative and Information Support. **Other Jobs in This Pathway:** Cargo and Freight Agents; Correspondence Clerks; Couriers and Messengers; Court Clerks; Customer Service Representatives; Data Entry Keyers; Dispatchers, Except Police, Fire, and Ambulance; Executive Secretaries and Executive Administrative Assistants; File Clerks; Freight Forwarders; Human Resources Assistants, Except Payroll and Timekeeping;

Information and Record Clerks, All Other; Insurance Claims Clerks; Insurance Policy Processing Clerks; Interviewers, Except Eligibility and Loan; License Clerks; Mail Clerks and Mail Machine Operators, Except Postal Service; Meter Readers, Utilities; Municipal Clerks; Office and Administrative Support Workers, All Other; Office Clerks, General; Office Machine Operators, Except Computer; Order Clerks; Patient Representatives; Postal Service Clerks; Postal Service Mail Sorters, Processors, and Processing Machine Operators; Procurement Clerks; Receptionists and Information Clerks; others.

Skills—Operation and Control: Controlling operations of equipment or systems.

Work Environment: More often outdoors than indoors; standing; walking and running; using hands; bending or twisting the body; repetitive motions; noise; very hot or cold; bright or inadequate lighting; contaminants; minor burns, cuts, bites, or stings.

Power Plant Operators

- ⊙ Annual Earnings: $65,280
- ⊙ Earnings Growth Potential: Medium (36.4%)
- ⊙ Growth: –2.5%
- ⊙ Annual Job Openings: 1,440
- ⊙ Self-Employed: 0.0%

Considerations for Job Outlook: Job prospects should be good for those with related training and good mechanical skills. As many power plant operators, distributors, and dispatchers near retirement age, companies will need workers to replace operators and dispatchers who retire. Many individuals may show interest in these high-paying jobs, and job prospects will be best for those with strong technical and mechanical skills.

Control, operate, or maintain machinery to generate electric power. Monitor and inspect power plant equipment and indicators to detect evidence of operating problems. Adjust controls to generate specified electrical power or to regulate the flow of power between generating stations and substations. Operate or control power generating equipment, including boilers, turbines, generators, and reactors, using control boards or semi-automatic equipment. Regulate equipment operations and conditions such as water levels, based on data from recording and indicating instruments or from computers. Take readings from charts, meters, and gauges at established intervals, and take corrective steps as necessary. Inspect records and log book entries, and communicate with other plant personnel, in order to assess equipment operating status. Start or stop generators, auxiliary pumping equipment, turbines, and other power plant equipment, and connect or disconnect equipment from circuits. Control and maintain auxiliary equipment, such as pumps, fans, compressors, condensers, feedwater heaters, filters, and chlorinators, to supply water, fuel, lubricants, air, and auxiliary power. Clean, lubricate, and maintain equipment such as generators, turbines, pumps, and compressors in order to prevent equipment failure or deterioration. Communicate with systems operators to regulate and coordinate transmission loads and frequencies and line voltages. Record and compile operational data, completing and maintaining forms, logs, and reports. Open and close valves and switches in sequence upon signals from other workers, in order to start or shut down auxiliary units. Collect oil, water, and electrolyte samples for laboratory analysis. Make adjustments or minor repairs, such as tightening leaking gland and pipe joints; report any needs for major repairs. Control generator output to match the phase, frequency, and voltage of electricity supplied to panels.

Education/Training Required: High school diploma or equivalent. **Education and Training Programs:** No related CIP programs; this job is learned through long-term on-the-job training. **Knowledge/Courses—Mechanical Devices:** Machines and tools, including their designs, uses, repair, and maintenance. **Physics:** Physical principles, laws, their interrelationships, and applications to understanding fluid, material, and atmospheric dynamics, and mechanical, electrical, atomic, and subatomic structures and processes. **Chemistry:** The chemical composition, structure, and properties of substances and of the chemical processes and transformations that they undergo. This includes uses of chemicals and their danger signs, production techniques, and disposal methods. **Engineering and Technology:** The practical application of engineering science and technology. This includes applying principles, techniques, procedures, and equipment to the design and production of various goods and services. **Public Safety and Security:** Relevant equipment, policies, procedures, and strategies to promote effective local, state, or national security operations for the protection of people, data, property, and institutions. **Computers and Electronics:** Circuit boards, processors, chips, electronic equipment, and

computer hardware and software, including applications and programming. **Work Experience Needed:** None. **On-the-Job Training Needed:** Long-term on-the-job training. **Certification/Licensure:** Licensure for some specializations in some states.

Personality Type: Realistic-Conventional. **Career Cluster:** 13 Manufacturing. **Career Pathway:** 13.1 Production. **Other Jobs in This Pathway:** Adhesive Bonding Machine Operators and Tenders; Assemblers and Fabricators, All Other; Avionics Technicians; Cabinetmakers and Bench Carpenters; Cleaning, Washing, and Metal Pickling Equipment Operators and Tenders; Coating, Painting, and Spraying Machine Setters, Operators, and Tenders; Computer-Controlled Machine Tool Operators, Metal and Plastic; Cooling and Freezing Equipment Operators and Tenders; Cost Estimators; Crushing, Grinding, and Polishing Machine Setters, Operators, and Tenders; Cutters and Trimmers, Hand; Cutting and Slicing Machine Setters, Operators, and Tenders; Cutting, Punching, and Press Machine Setters, Operators, and Tenders, Metal and Plastic; Drilling and Boring Machine Tool Setters, Operators, and Tenders, Metal and Plastic; Extruding and Drawing Machine Setters, Operators, and Tenders, Metal and Plastic; Extruding and Forming Machine Setters, Operators, and Tenders, Synthetic and Glass Fibers; others.

Skills—Equipment Maintenance: Performing routine maintenance on equipment and determining when and what kind of maintenance is needed. **Repairing:** Repairing machines or systems using the needed tools. **Troubleshooting:** Determining causes of operating errors and deciding what to do about them. **Operation and Control:** Controlling operations of equipment or systems. **Operation Monitoring:** Watching gauges, dials, or other indicators to make sure a machine is working properly. **Quality Control Analysis:** Conducting tests and inspections of products, services, or processes to evaluate quality or performance. **Equipment Selection:** Determining the kind of tools and equipment needed to do a job. **Installation:** Installing equipment, machines, wiring, or programs to meet specifications.

Work Environment: More often indoors than outdoors; sitting; using hands; noise; very hot or cold; contaminants; high places; hazardous conditions; hazardous equipment.

Preschool Teachers, Except Special Education

- Annual Earnings: $26,620
- Earnings Growth Potential: Low (33.3%)
- Growth: 24.9%
- Annual Job Openings: 23,240
- Self-Employed: 1.7%

Considerations for Job Outlook: Workers who have postsecondary education, particularly those with a bachelor's degree, should have better job prospects than those with less education. In addition, workers with the Child Development Associate (CDA) or Child Care Professional (CCP) credential should have better prospects than those without these certifications.

Instruct preschool-aged children in activities designed to promote social, physical, and intellectual growth needed for primary school in preschool, day care center, or other child development facility. Provide a variety of materials and resources for children to explore, manipulate, and use, both in learning activities and in imaginative play. Attend to children's basic needs by feeding them, dressing them, and changing their diapers. Establish and enforce rules for behavior and procedures for maintaining order. Read books to entire classes or to small groups. Teach basic skills such as color, shape, number, and letter recognition; personal hygiene; and social skills. Organize and lead activities designed to promote physical, mental, and social development, such as games, arts and crafts, music, storytelling, and field trips. Observe and evaluate children's performance, behavior, social development, and physical health. Meet with parents and guardians to discuss their children's progress and needs, determine their priorities for their children, and suggest ways that they can promote learning and development. Identify children showing signs of emotional, developmental, or health-related problems, and discuss them with supervisors, parents or guardians, and child development specialists. Enforce all administration policies and rules governing students. Prepare materials and classrooms for class activities. Serve meals and snacks in accordance with nutritional guidelines. Teach proper eating habits and personal hygiene. Assimilate arriving children to the school environment by greeting them, helping them remove outerwear, and selecting activities of interest to them.

Education/Training Required: Associate degree. **Education and Training Programs:** Child Care and Support Services Management; Early Childhood Education and Teaching. **Knowledge/Courses—Philosophy and Theology:** Different philosophical systems and religions. This includes their basic principles, values, ethics, ways of thinking, customs, practices, and their impact on human culture. **Therapy and Counseling:** Principles, methods, and procedures for diagnosis, treatment, and rehabilitation of physical and mental dysfunctions, and for career counseling and guidance. **Sociology and Anthropology:** Group behavior and dynamics, societal trends and influences, human migrations, ethnicity, and cultures and their history and origins. **Geography:** Principles and methods for describing the features of land, sea, and air masses, including their physical characteristics, locations, interrelationships, and distribution of plant, animal, and human life. **Customer and Personal Service:** Principles and processes for providing customer and personal services. This includes customer needs assessment, meeting quality standards for services, and evaluation of customer satisfaction. **Psychology:** Human behavior and performance; individual differences in ability, personality, and interests; learning and motivation; psychological research methods; and the assessment and treatment of behavioral and affective disorders. **Work Experience Needed:** None. **On-the-Job Training Needed:** None. **Certification/Licensure:** Licensure.

Personality Type: Social-Artistic. **Career Clusters:** 05 Education and Training; 10 Human Services. **Career Pathways:** 05.3 Teaching/Training; 10.1 Early Childhood Development and Services. **Other Jobs in These Pathways:** Adult Basic and Secondary Education and Literacy Teachers and Instructors; Agricultural Sciences Teachers, Postsecondary; Anthropology and Archeology Teachers, Postsecondary; Architecture Teachers, Postsecondary; Area, Ethnic, and Cultural Studies Teachers, Postsecondary; Art, Drama, and Music Teachers, Postsecondary; Athletes and Sports Competitors; Atmospheric, Earth, Marine, and Space Sciences Teachers, Postsecondary; Audio-Visual and Multimedia Collections Specialists; Biological Science Teachers, Postsecondary; Business Teachers, Postsecondary; Career/Technical Education Teachers, Middle School; Career/Technical Education Teachers, Secondary School; Chemists; Coaches and Scouts; Communications Teachers, Postsecondary; Computer Science Teachers, Postsecondary; Criminal Justice and Law Enforcement Teachers,

Postsecondary; Dietitians and Nutritionists; Education Teachers, Postsecondary; Elementary School Teachers, Except Special Education; Engineering Teachers, Postsecondary; others.

Skills—Learning Strategies: Selecting and using training/instructional methods and procedures appropriate for the situation when learning or teaching new things. **Social Perceptiveness:** Being aware of others' reactions and understanding why they react as they do. **Service Orientation:** Actively looking for ways to help people. **Coordination:** Adjusting actions in relation to others' actions. **Monitoring:** Monitoring or assessing your performance or that of other individuals or organizations to make improvements or take corrective action. **Time Management:** Managing one's own time and the time of others. **Negotiation:** Bringing others together and trying to reconcile differences. **Complex Problem Solving:** Identifying complex problems and reviewing related information to develop and evaluate options and implement solutions.

Work Environment: Indoors; standing; noise.

Printing Press Operators

- ⊙ Annual Earnings: $34,290
- ⊙ Earnings Growth Potential: High (40.4%)
- ⊙ Growth: –1.4%
- ⊙ Annual Job Openings: 3,920
- ⊙ Self-Employed: 4.9%

Considerations for Job Outlook: Newspapers and magazines have seen substantial declines in print volume in recent years, as these media have increasingly moved to online formats. With a declining volume of printed material in these areas, demand for print workers has decreased. This trend is expected to continue, which is expected to result in further employment declines in the printing industry. Employment declines for printing workers should be moderated by other segments of the industry that will likely experience steady demand, including print logistics (labels, wrappers, and packaging) and print marketing (catalogs and direct mail).

Set up and operate digital, letterpress, lithographic, flexographic, gravure, or other printing machines. Adjust digital files to alter print elements such as fonts, graphics, or color separations. Adjust ink fountain flow rates. Change press plates, blankets, or cylinders, as required. Clean ink fountains, plates, or printing unit cylinders when press runs are completed. Clean or oil presses or make minor repairs, using hand tools. Collect and inspect random samples during print runs to identify any necessary adjustments. Download or scan files to be printed, using printing production software. Examine job orders to determine quantities to be printed, stock specifications, colors, or special printing instructions. Feed paper through press cylinders and adjust feed and tension controls. Input production job settings into work station terminals that control automated printing systems. Load presses with paper and make necessary adjustments, according to paper size. Monitor automated press operation systems and respond to fault, error, or alert messages. Obtain or mix inks and fill ink fountains. Secure printing plates to printing units and adjust tolerances. Start presses and pull proofs to check for ink coverage and density, alignment, and registration. Verify that paper and ink meet the specifications for given jobs. Control workflow scheduling or job tracking, using computer database software. Direct or monitor work of press crews. Download completed jobs to archive media so that questions can be answered or jobs replicated. Maintain time or production records. Monitor environmental factors, such as humidity and temperature, that may impact equipment performance and make necessary adjustments. Monitor inventory levels on a regular basis, ordering or requesting additional supplies, as necessary. Set up or operate auxiliary equipment such as cutting, folding, plate-making, drilling, or laminating machines.

Education/Training Required: High school diploma or equivalent. **Education and Training Programs:** Graphic and Printing Equipment Operator Training, General Production; Printing Press Operator Training. **Knowledge/Courses—Mechanical Devices:** Machines and tools, including their designs, uses, repair, and maintenance. **Production and Processing:** Raw materials, production processes, quality control, costs, and other techniques for maximizing the effective manufacture and distribution of goods. **Chemistry:** The chemical composition, structure, and properties of substances and of the chemical processes and transformations that they undergo. This includes uses of chemicals and their danger signs, production techniques, and disposal methods. **Work Experience Needed:** None. **On-the-Job Training Needed:** Moderate-term on-the-job training. **Certification/Licensure:** None.

Personality Type: Realistic-Conventional. **Career Cluster:** 13 Manufacturing. **Career Pathway:** 03.2 Printing Technology. **Other Jobs in This Pathway:** Art, Drama, and Music Teachers, Postsecondary; Craft Artists; Data Entry Keyers; Desktop Publishers; Etchers and Engravers; Fine Artists, Including Painters, Sculptors, and Illustrators; Multimedia Artists and Animators; Proofreaders and Copy Markers.

Skills—Equipment Maintenance: Performing routine maintenance on equipment and determining when and what kind of maintenance is needed. **Repairing:** Repairing machines or systems using the needed tools. **Operation and Control:** Controlling operations of equipment or systems. **Equipment Selection:** Determining the kind of tools and equipment needed to do a job. **Troubleshooting:** Determining causes of operating errors and deciding what to do about them. **Operation Monitoring:** Watching gauges, dials, or other indicators to make sure a machine is working properly. **Quality Control Analysis:** Conducting tests and inspections of products, services, or processes to evaluate quality or performance. **Installation:** Installing equipment, machines, wiring, or programs to meet specifications.

Work Environment: Indoors; standing; walking and running; kneeling, crouching, stooping, or crawling; using hands; bending or twisting the body; repetitive motions; noise; contaminants; hazardous conditions; hazardous equipment.

Private Detectives and Investigators

- ⊙ Annual Earnings: $43,710
- ⊙ Earnings Growth Potential: High (40.7%)
- ⊙ Growth: 20.5%
- ⊙ Annual Job Openings: 1,490
- ⊙ Self-Employed: 18.7%

Considerations for Job Outlook: Competition is expected for most jobs, because private detective and investigator careers attract many qualified people, including relatively young retirees from law enforcement or military careers. The best opportunities for job seekers will be in entry-level jobs in detective agencies. People with related work experience, as well as those with interviewing and computer skills, may find more opportunities.

Gather, analyze, compile, and report information regarding individuals or organizations to clients, or detect occurrences of unlawful acts or infractions of rules in private establishment. Provide testimony as witnesses in court. Secure deceased bodies, and obtain evidence from them, preventing bystanders from tampering with bodies prior to medical examiners' arrival. Examine crime scenes to obtain clues and evidence such as loose hairs, fibers, clothing, or weapons. Obtain evidence from suspects. Record progress of investigations, maintain informational files on suspects, and submit reports to commanding officers or magistrates to authorize warrants. Check victims for signs of life such as breathing and pulse. Prepare charges or responses to charges, or information for court cases, according to formalized procedures. Obtain facts or statements from complainants, witnesses, and accused persons, and record interviews, using recording devices. Prepare and serve search and arrest warrants. Note, mark, and photograph locations of objects found, such as footprints, tire tracks, bullets, and bloodstains, and take measurements of each scene. Question individuals or observe persons and establishments to confirm information given to patrol officers. Preserve, process, and analyze items of evidence obtained from crime scenes and suspects, placing them in proper containers and destroying evidence no longer needed. Secure persons at scenes, keeping witnesses from conversing or leaving scenes before investigators arrive. Take photographs from all angles of relevant parts of crime scenes, including entrance and exit routes and streets and intersections.

Education/Training Required: Some college, no degree. **Education and Training Program:** Criminal Justice/Police Science. **Knowledge/Courses—Clerical Practices:** Administrative and clerical procedures and systems such as word processing, managing files and records, stenography and transcription, designing forms, and other office procedures and terminology. **Law and Government:** Laws, legal codes, court procedures, precedents, government regulations, executive orders, agency rules, and the democratic political process. **Customer and Personal Service:** Principles and processes for providing customer and personal services. This includes customer needs assessment, meeting quality standards for services, and evaluation of customer satisfaction. **Computers and Electronics:** Circuit boards, processors, chips, electronic equipment, and computer hardware and software, including applications and programming. **Sales and Marketing:** Principles and methods for showing, promoting, and selling products or services. This includes marketing strategy and tactics, product demonstration, sales techniques, and sales control systems. **Mathematics:** Arithmetic, algebra, geometry, calculus, statistics, and their applications. **Work Experience Needed:** 1 to 5 years. **On-the-Job Training Needed:** Moderate-term on-the-job training. **Certification/Licensure:** Licensure.

Personality Type: Enterprising-Conventional. **Career Cluster:** 12 Law, Public Safety, Corrections, and Security. **Career Pathway:** 12.3 Security and Protective Services. **Other Jobs in This Pathway:** Animal Control Workers; Criminal Justice and Law Enforcement Teachers, Postsecondary; Crossing Guards; First-Line Supervisors of Protective Service Workers, All Other; Forest Firefighters; Gaming Surveillance Officers and Gaming Investigators; Lifeguards, Ski Patrol, and Other Recreational Protective Service Workers; Parking Enforcement Workers; Police, Fire, and Ambulance Dispatchers; Retail Loss Prevention Specialists; Security Guards; Sheriffs and Deputy Sheriffs; Transit and Railroad Police.

Skills—Service Orientation: Actively looking for ways to help people. **Active Listening:** Giving full attention to what other people are saying, taking time to understand the points being made, asking questions as appropriate, and not interrupting at inappropriate times. **Negotiation:** Bringing others together and trying to reconcile differences. **Writing:** Communicating effectively in writing as appropriate for the needs of the audience. **Speaking:** Talking to others to convey information effectively. **Critical Thinking:** Using logic and reasoning to identify the strengths and weaknesses of alternative solutions, conclusions, or approaches to problems. **Persuasion:** Persuading others to change their minds or behavior. **Social Perceptiveness:** Being aware of others' reactions and understanding why they react as they do.

Work Environment: More often outdoors than indoors; sitting; using hands; repetitive motions; noise; very hot or cold; bright or inadequate lighting; contaminants.

Procurement Clerks

- ⊙ Annual Earnings: $37,640
- ⊙ Earnings Growth Potential: Medium (35.1%)
- ⊙ Growth: 5.7%
- ⊙ Annual Job Openings: 3,550
- ⊙ Self-Employed: 0.0%

Considerations for Job Outlook: Job prospects for financial clerks should be favorable, because many workers are expected to leave this occupation. Employers will need to hire new workers to replace those leaving the occupation.

Compile information and records to draw up purchase orders for procurement of materials and services. Prepare purchase orders and send copies to suppliers and to departments originating requests. Determine if inventory quantities are sufficient for needs, ordering more materials when necessary. Respond to customer and supplier inquiries about order status, changes, or cancellations. Perform buying duties when necessary. Contact suppliers to schedule or expedite deliveries and to resolve shortages, missed or late deliveries, and other problems. Review requisition orders to verify accuracy, terminology, and specifications. Prepare, maintain, and review purchasing files, reports, and price lists. Compare prices, specifications, and delivery dates to determine the best bid among potential suppliers. Track the status of requisitions, contracts, and orders. Calculate costs of orders, and charge or forward invoices to appropriate accounts. Check shipments when they arrive to ensure that orders have been filled correctly and that goods meet specifications. Compare suppliers' bills with bids and purchase orders to verify accuracy. Approve bills for payment. Locate suppliers, using sources such as catalogs and the Internet, and interview them to gather information about products to be ordered. Maintain knowledge of all organizational and governmental rules affecting purchases, and provide information about these rules to organization staff members and to vendors. Monitor in-house inventory movement and complete inventory transfer forms for bookkeeping purposes. Monitor contractor performance, recommending contract modifications when necessary. Prepare invitation-of-bid forms, and mail forms to supplier firms or distribute forms for public posting.

Education/Training Required: High school diploma or equivalent. **Education and Training Program:** General

Office Occupations and Clerical Services. **Knowledge/ Courses—Clerical Practices:** Administrative and clerical procedures and systems such as word processing, managing files and records, stenography and transcription, designing forms, and other office procedures and terminology. **Administration and Management:** Business and management principles involved in strategic planning, resource allocation, human resources modeling, leadership technique, production methods, and coordination of people and resources. **Mathematics:** Arithmetic, algebra, geometry, calculus, statistics, and their applications. **Communications and Media:** Media production, communication, and dissemination techniques and methods. This includes alternative ways to inform and entertain via written, oral, and visual media. **Economics and Accounting:** Economic and accounting principles and practices, the financial markets, banking, and the analysis and reporting of financial data. **Customer and Personal Service:** Principles and processes for providing customer and personal services. This includes customer needs assessment, meeting quality standards for services, and evaluation of customer satisfaction. **Work Experience Needed:** None. **On-the-Job Training Needed:** Moderate-term on-the-job training. **Certification/Licensure:** None.

Personality Type: Conventional-Enterprising. **Career Cluster:** 04 Business, Management, and Administration. **Career Pathway:** 04.6 Administrative and Information Support. **Other Jobs in This Pathway:** Cargo and Freight Agents; Correspondence Clerks; Couriers and Messengers; Court Clerks; Customer Service Representatives; Data Entry Keyers; Dispatchers, Except Police, Fire, and Ambulance; Executive Secretaries and Executive Administrative Assistants; File Clerks; Freight Forwarders; Human Resources Assistants, Except Payroll and Timekeeping; Information and Record Clerks, All Other; Insurance Claims Clerks; Insurance Policy Processing Clerks; Interviewers, Except Eligibility and Loan; License Clerks; Mail Clerks and Mail Machine Operators, Except Postal Service; Meter Readers, Utilities; Municipal Clerks; Office and Administrative Support Workers, All Other; Office Clerks, General; Office Machine Operators, Except Computer; Order Clerks; Patient Representatives; Postal Service Clerks; Postal Service Mail Carriers; Postal Service Mail Sorters, Processors, and Processing Machine Operators; Receptionists and Information Clerks; others.

Skills—Negotiation: Bringing others together and trying to reconcile differences. **Management of Financial Resources:** Determining how money will be spent to get the work done and accounting for these expenditures. **Active Learning:** Understanding the implications of new information for both current and future problem solving and decision making. **Management of Material Resources:** Obtaining and seeing to the appropriate use of equipment, facilities, and materials needed to do certain work. **Service Orientation:** Actively looking for ways to help people. **Reading Comprehension:** Understanding written sentences and paragraphs in work-related documents. **Active Listening:** Giving full attention to what other people are saying, taking time to understand the points being made, asking questions as appropriate, and not interrupting at inappropriate times. **Critical Thinking:** Using logic and reasoning to identify the strengths and weaknesses of alternative solutions, conclusions, or approaches to problems.

Work Environment: Indoors; sitting; repetitive motions; noise.

Production, Planning, and Expediting Clerks

- ⊙ Annual Earnings: $43,100
- ⊙ Earnings Growth Potential: High (40.6%)
- ⊙ Growth: 6.6%
- ⊙ Annual Job Openings: 8,880
- ⊙ Self-Employed: 1.2%

Considerations for Job Outlook: There should be favorable job opportunities for material recording clerks because of the need to replace workers who leave the occupation. The increase in RFID and other sensors will enable clerks who are more comfortable with computers to have better job prospects.

Coordinate and expedite the flow of work and materials within or between departments of an establishment according to production schedules. Examine documents, materials, and products, and monitor work processes to assess completeness, accuracy, and conformance to standards and specifications. Review documents such as production schedules, work orders, and staffing tables to determine personnel and materials requirements and material priorities. Revise production schedules when required due to design changes, labor or material shortages, backlogs, or other interruptions, collaborating with management, marketing, sales, production, and engineering. Confer with department supervisors and other personnel to assess progress and discuss needed changes. Confer with establishment personnel, vendors, and customers to coordinate production and shipping activities and to resolve complaints or eliminate delays. Record production data, including volume produced, consumption of raw materials, and quality control measures. Requisition and maintain inventories of materials and supplies necessary to meet production demands. Calculate figures such as required amounts of labor and materials, manufacturing costs, and wages, using pricing schedules, adding machines, calculators, or computers. Distribute production schedules and work orders to departments. Compile information such as production rates and progress, materials inventories, materials used, and customer information, so that status reports can be completed.

Education/Training Required: High school diploma or equivalent. **Education and Training Program:** Parts, Warehousing, and Inventory Management Operations. **Knowledge/Courses—Production and Processing:** Raw materials, production processes, quality control, costs, and other techniques for maximizing the effective manufacture and distribution of goods. **Clerical Practices:** Administrative and clerical procedures and systems such as word processing, managing files and records, stenography and transcription, designing forms, and other office procedures and terminology. **Computers and Electronics:** Circuit boards, processors, chips, electronic equipment, and computer hardware and software, including applications and programming. **Administration and Management:** Business and management principles involved in strategic planning, resource allocation, human resources modeling, leadership technique, production methods, and coordination of people and resources. **Mathematics:** Arithmetic, algebra, geometry, calculus, statistics, and their applications. **Customer and Personal Service:** Principles and processes for providing customer and personal services. This includes customer needs assessment, meeting quality standards for services, and evaluation of customer satisfaction. **Work Experience Needed:** None. **On-the-Job Training Needed:** Moderate-term on-the-job training. **Certification/Licensure:** None.

Personality Type: Conventional-Enterprising. **Career Cluster:** 16 Transportation, Distribution, and Logistics. **Career Pathway:** 16.3 Warehousing and Distribution Center Operations. **Other Jobs in This Pathway:** Logistics Analysts; Shipping, Receiving, and Traffic Clerks; Traffic Technicians.

Skills—Management of Material Resources: Obtaining and seeing to the appropriate use of equipment, facilities, and materials needed to do certain work. **Negotiation:** Bringing others together and trying to reconcile differences. **Management of Financial Resources:** Determining how money will be spent to get the work done and accounting for these expenditures. **Reading Comprehension:** Understanding written sentences and paragraphs in work-related documents. **Persuasion:** Persuading others to change their minds or behavior. **Time Management:** Managing one's own time and the time of others. **Speaking:** Talking to others to convey information effectively.

Work Environment: Indoors; sitting; noise; contaminants.

Property, Real Estate, and Community Association Managers

- Annual Earnings: $52,510
- Earnings Growth Potential: High (50.8%)
- Growth: 6.1%
- Annual Job Openings: 8,230
- Self-Employed: 50.5%

Considerations for Job Outlook: Job opportunities should be best for those with a college degree in business administration, real estate, or a related field and for those who get a professional certification. Because of the projected increase in the elderly population, particularly good job opportunities are expected for those with experience managing housing for older people and with experience managing health-care facilities.

Plan, direct, or coordinate the selling, buying, leasing, or governance activities of commercial, industrial, or residential real estate properties. Meet with prospective tenants to show properties, explain terms of occupancy, and provide information about local areas. Direct collection of monthly assessments; rental fees; and deposits and payment of insurance premiums, mortgage, taxes, and incurred operating expenses. Inspect grounds, facilities, and equipment routinely to determine necessity of repairs or maintenance. Investigate complaints, disturbances, and violations, and resolve problems, following management rules and regulations. Manage and oversee operations, maintenance, administration, and improvement of commercial, industrial, or residential properties. Plan, schedule, and coordinate general maintenance, major repairs, and remodeling or construction projects for commercial or residential properties. Negotiate the sale, lease, or development of property, and complete or review appropriate documents and forms. Maintain records of sales, rental or usage activity, special permits issued, maintenance and operating costs, or property availability. Determine and certify the eligibility of prospective tenants, following government regulations. Prepare detailed budgets and financial reports for properties. Direct and coordinate the activities of staff and contract personnel, and evaluate their performance. Maintain contact with insurance carriers, fire and police departments, and other agencies to ensure protection and compliance with codes and regulations.

Education/Training Required: High school diploma or equivalent. **Education and Training Program:** Real Estate. **Knowledge/Courses—Sales and Marketing:** Principles and methods for showing, promoting, and selling products or services. This includes marketing strategy and tactics, product demonstration, sales techniques, and sales control systems. **Clerical Practices:** Administrative and clerical procedures and systems such as word processing, managing files and records, stenography and transcription, designing forms, and other office procedures and terminology. **Economics and Accounting:** Economic and accounting principles and practices, the financial markets, banking, and the analysis and reporting of financial data. **Building and Construction:** Materials, methods, and the tools involved in the construction or repair of houses, buildings, or other structures such as highways and roads. **Administration and Management:** Business and management principles involved in strategic planning, resource allocation, human resources modeling, leadership technique, production methods, and coordination of people and resources. **Customer and Personal Service:** Principles and processes for providing customer and personal services. This includes customer needs assessment, meeting quality standards for services, and evaluation of customer satisfaction. **Work Experience Needed:** 1 to 5 years. **On-the-Job Training Needed:** None. **Certification/Licensure:**

Licensure for some specializations; voluntary certification by association.

Personality Type: Enterprising-Conventional. **Career Cluster:** 14 Marketing, Sales, and Service. **Career Pathway:** 14.2 Professional Sales and Marketing. **Other Jobs in This Pathway:** Appraisers, Real Estate; Assessors; Cashiers; Counter and Rental Clerks; Demonstrators and Product Promoters; Door-To-Door Sales Workers, News and Street Vendors, and Related Workers; Driver/Sales Workers; Energy Brokers; First-Line Supervisors of Non-Retail Sales Workers; First-Line Supervisors of Retail Sales Workers; Gaming Change Persons and Booth Cashiers; Hotel, Motel, and Resort Desk Clerks; Interior Designers; Lodging Managers; Marketing Managers; Marking Clerks; Meeting, Convention, and Event Planners; Merchandise Displayers and Window Trimmers; Models; Online Merchants; Order Fillers, Wholesale and Retail Sales; Parts Salespersons; Real Estate Brokers; Real Estate Sales Agents; Reservation and Transportation Ticket Agents and Travel Clerks; Retail Salespersons; Sales and Related Workers, All Other; Sales Engineers; Sales Representatives, Services, All Other; Sales Representatives, Wholesale and Manufacturing, Except Technical and Scientific Products; others.

Skills—Management of Financial Resources: Determining how money will be spent to get the work done and accounting for these expenditures. **Negotiation:** Bringing others together and trying to reconcile differences. **Management of Personnel Resources:** Motivating, developing, and directing people as they work, identifying the best people for the job. **Operations Analysis:** Analyzing needs and product requirements to create a design. **Persuasion:** Persuading others to change their minds or behavior. **Management of Material Resources:** Obtaining and seeing to the appropriate use of equipment, facilities, and materials needed to do certain work. **Service Orientation:** Actively looking for ways to help people. **Writing:** Communicating effectively in writing as appropriate for the needs of the audience.

Work Environment: More often indoors than outdoors; sitting.

Psychiatric Aides

- ⊙ Annual Earnings: $25,170
- ⊙ Earnings Growth Potential: Low (32.5%)
- ⊙ Growth: 15.1%
- ⊙ Annual Job Openings: 1,900
- ⊙ Self-Employed: 1.9%

Considerations for Job Outlook: As the nation's population ages and people live longer, there is likely to be an increase in the number of people with cognitive mental diseases such as Alzheimer's disease. Demand for psychiatric technicians and aides in residential facilities is expected to rise as a result. More psychiatric technicians and aides will also be needed in residential treatment facilities for people with developmental disabilities, mental illness, and substance abuse problems. There is a long-term trend toward treating psychiatric patients outside hospitals because it is more cost-effective and allows patients greater independence. Also, an increasing number of mentally disabled adults who were cared for by their parents will need help as their parents become too old to provide that care. In addition, an aging prison population has increased the need for psychiatric technicians and aides working in correctional facilities.

Assist mentally impaired or emotionally disturbed patients, working under the direction of nursing and medical staff. Provide mentally impaired or emotionally disturbed patients with routine physical, emotional, psychological, or rehabilitation care under the direction of nursing and medical staff. Work as part of a team that may include psychiatrists, psychologists, psychiatric nurses, and social workers. Aid patients in becoming accustomed to hospital routines. Organize, supervise, and encourage patient participation in social, educational, and recreational activities. Serve meals, and feed patients needing assistance or persuasion. Restrain or aid patients as necessary to prevent injury. Provide patients with assistance in bathing, dressing, and grooming, demonstrating these skills as necessary. Participate in recreational activities with patients, including card games, sports, or television viewing. Maintain patients' restrictions to assigned areas. Accompany patients to and from wards for medical and dental treatments, shopping trips, and religious and recreational events.

Education/Training Required: High school diploma or equivalent. **Education and Training Programs:** Health Aide Training; Psychiatric/Mental Health Services Technician Training. **Knowledge/Courses—Therapy and Counseling:** Principles, methods, and procedures for diagnosis, treatment, and rehabilitation of physical and mental dysfunctions, and for career counseling and guidance. **Psychology:** Human behavior and performance; individual differences in ability, personality, and interests; learning and motivation; psychological research methods; and the assessment and treatment of behavioral and affective disorders. **Sociology and Anthropology:** Group behavior and dynamics, societal trends and influences, human migrations, ethnicity, and cultures and their history and origins. **Medicine and Dentistry:** The information and techniques needed to diagnose and treat human injuries, diseases, and deformities. This includes symptoms, treatment alternatives, drug properties and interactions, and preventive health-care measures. **Public Safety and Security:** Relevant equipment, policies, procedures, and strategies to promote effective local, state, or national security operations for the protection of people, data, property, and institutions. **Transportation:** Principles and methods for moving people or goods by air, rail, sea, or road, including the relative costs and benefits. **Work Experience Needed:** None. **On-the-Job Training Needed:** Short-term on-the-job training. **Certification/Licensure:** Voluntary certification by association.

Personality Type: Social-Realistic-Conventional. **Career Cluster:** 08 Health Science. **Career Pathway:** 08.3 Health Informatics. **Other Jobs in This Pathway:** Clinical Psychologists; Communications Teachers, Postsecondary; Dental Laboratory Technicians; Editors; Engineers, All Other; Executive Secretaries and Executive Administrative Assistants; Fine Artists, Including Painters, Sculptors, and Illustrators; First-Line Supervisors of Office and Administrative Support Workers; Health Educators; Health Specialties Teachers, Postsecondary; Medical and Health Services Managers; Medical Appliance Technicians; Medical Assistants; Medical Records and Health Information Technicians; Medical Secretaries; Medical Transcriptionists; Mental Health Counselors; Occupational Health and Safety Specialists; Occupational Health and Safety Technicians; Orthotists and Prosthetists; Physical Therapists; Psychiatric Technicians; Public Relations Specialists; Receptionists and Information Clerks; Recreational Therapists; Rehabilitation Counselors; Substance Abuse and Behavioral Disorder Counselors; Therapists, All Other.

Skills—Social Perceptiveness: Being aware of others' reactions and understanding why they react as they do.

Service Orientation: Actively looking for ways to help people. **Coordination:** Adjusting actions in relation to others' actions. **Monitoring:** Monitoring or assessing your performance or that of other individuals or organizations to make improvements or take corrective action. **Learning Strategies:** Selecting and using training/instructional methods and procedures appropriate for the situation when learning or teaching new things. **Negotiation:** Bringing others together and trying to reconcile differences.

Work Environment: Indoors; more often sitting than standing; walking and running; noise; contaminants; exposed to disease or infections; minor burns, cuts, bites, or stings.

Psychiatric Technicians

- Annual Earnings: $28,470
- Earnings Growth Potential: High (44.9%)
- Growth: 15.5%
- Annual Job Openings: 2,460
- Self-Employed: 0.2%

Considerations for Job Outlook: As the nation's population ages and people live longer, there is likely to be an increase in the number of people with cognitive mental diseases such as Alzheimer's disease. Demand for psychiatric technicians and aides in residential facilities is expected to rise as a result. More psychiatric technicians and aides will also be needed in residential treatment facilities for people with developmental disabilities, mental illness, and substance abuse problems. There is a long-term trend toward treating psychiatric patients outside hospitals because it is more cost-effective and allows patients greater independence. Also, an increasing number of mentally disabled adults who were cared for by their parents will need help as their parents become too old to provide that care. In addition, an aging prison population has increased the need for psychiatric technicians and aides working in correctional facilities.

Care for individuals with mental or emotional conditions or disabilities, following the instructions of physicians or other health practitioners. Monitor patients' physical and emotional well-being and report unusual behavior or physical ailments to medical staff. Provide nursing, psychiatric, and personal care to mentally ill, emotionally disturbed, or mentally retarded patients. Observe and influence patients' behavior, communicating and interacting with them and teaching, counseling, and befriending them. Take and record measures of patients' physical condition, using devices such as thermometers and blood pressure gauges. Encourage patients to develop work skills and to participate in social, recreational, and other therapeutic activities that enhance interpersonal skills and develop social relationships. Collaborate with or assist doctors, psychologists, or rehabilitation therapists in working with mentally ill, emotionally disturbed, or developmentally disabled patients to treat, rehabilitate, and return patients to the community. Develop and teach strategies to promote client wellness and independence.

Education/Training Required: Postsecondary vocational training. **Education and Training Program:** Psychiatric/Mental Health Services Technician Training. **Knowledge/Courses—Therapy and Counseling:** Principles, methods, and procedures for diagnosis, treatment, and rehabilitation of physical and mental dysfunctions, and for career counseling and guidance. **Psychology:** Human behavior and performance; individual differences in ability, personality, and interests; learning and motivation; psychological research methods; and the assessment and treatment of behavioral and affective disorders. **Sociology and Anthropology:** Group behavior and dynamics, societal trends and influences, human migrations, ethnicity, and cultures and their history and origins. **Philosophy and Theology:** Different philosophical systems and religions. This includes their basic principles, values, ethics, ways of thinking, customs, practices, and their impact on human culture. **Medicine and Dentistry:** The information and techniques needed to diagnose and treat human injuries, diseases, and deformities. This includes symptoms, treatment alternatives, drug properties and interactions, and preventive health-care measures. **Customer and Personal Service:** Principles and processes for providing customer and personal services. This includes customer needs assessment, meeting quality standards for services, and evaluation of customer satisfaction. **Work Experience Needed:** None. **On-the-Job Training Needed:** Short-term on-the-job training. **Certification/Licensure:** Voluntary certification by association; licensure in a few states.

Personality Type: Social-Enterprising-Realistic. **Career Cluster:** 08 Health Science. **Career Pathway:** 08.3 Health Informatics. **Other Jobs in This Pathway:** Clinical Psychologists; Communications Teachers, Postsecondary; Dental

Laboratory Technicians; Editors; Engineers, All Other; Executive Secretaries and Executive Administrative Assistants; Fine Artists, Including Painters, Sculptors, and Illustrators; First-Line Supervisors of Office and Administrative Support Workers; Health Educators; Health Specialties Teachers, Postsecondary; Medical and Health Services Managers; Medical Appliance Technicians; Medical Assistants; Medical Records and Health Information Technicians; Medical Secretaries; Medical Transcriptionists; Mental Health Counselors; Occupational Health and Safety Specialists; Occupational Health and Safety Technicians; Orthotists and Prosthetists; Physical Therapists; Psychiatric Aides; Public Relations Specialists; Receptionists and Information Clerks; Recreational Therapists; Rehabilitation Counselors; Substance Abuse and Behavioral Disorder Counselors; Therapists, All Other.

Skills—Social Perceptiveness: Being aware of others' reactions and understanding why they react as they do. **Negotiation:** Bringing others together and trying to reconcile differences. **Service Orientation:** Actively looking for ways to help people. **Learning Strategies:** Selecting and using training/instructional methods and procedures appropriate for the situation when learning or teaching new things. **Persuasion:** Persuading others to change their minds or behavior. **Monitoring:** Monitoring or assessing your performance or that of other individuals or organizations to make improvements or take corrective action. **Reading Comprehension:** Understanding written sentences and paragraphs in work-related documents. **Active Learning:** Understanding the implications of new information for both current and future problem solving and decision making.

Work Environment: Indoors; standing; walking and running; using hands; repetitive motions; noise; exposed to disease or infections.

Purchasing Agents, Except Wholesale, Retail, and Farm Products

- Annual Earnings: $57,580
- Earnings Growth Potential: Medium (38.1%)
- Growth: 5.3%
- Annual Job Openings: 9,120
- Self-Employed: 1.3%

Considerations for Job Outlook: Growth will be driven largely by the performance of the wholesale and retail industries. Continued employment decreases in manufacturing, as well as decreases in the federal government, which includes defense purchasing, are expected. However, growth is expected for this occupation in firms that provide health-care and computer systems design and related services.

Purchase machinery, equipment, tools, parts, supplies, or services necessary for the operation of an establishment. Purchase the highest-quality merchandise at the lowest possible price and in correct amounts. Prepare purchase orders, solicit bid proposals, and review requisitions for goods and services. Research and evaluate suppliers based on price, quality, selection, service, support, availability, reliability, production and distribution capabilities, and the supplier's reputation and history. Analyze price proposals, financial reports, and other data and information to determine reasonable prices. Monitor and follow applicable laws and regulations. Negotiate, or renegotiate, and administer contracts with suppliers, vendors, and other representatives. Monitor shipments to ensure that goods come in on time, and trace shipments and follow up on undelivered goods in the event of problems. Confer with staff, users, and vendors to discuss defective or unacceptable goods or services and determine corrective action. Evaluate and monitor contract performance to ensure compliance with contractual obligations and to determine the need for changes. Maintain and review computerized or manual records of items purchased, costs, delivery, product performance, and inventories. Review catalogs, industry periodicals, directories, trade journals, and Internet sites and consult with other department personnel to locate necessary goods and services. Study sales records and inventory levels of current stock to develop strategic purchasing programs that facilitate employee access to supplies.

Education/Training Required: High school diploma or equivalent. **Education and Training Programs:** Insurance; Merchandising and Buying Operations; Sales, Distribution, and Marketing Operations, General. **Knowledge/Courses—Economics and Accounting:** Economic and accounting principles and practices, the financial markets, banking, and the analysis and reporting of financial data. **Transportation:** Principles and methods for moving people or goods by air, rail, sea, or road, including the relative costs and benefits. **Law and Government:** Laws, legal codes, court procedures, precedents, government regulations, executive orders, agency rules, and the democratic political process. **Production and Processing:** Raw materials, production processes, quality control, costs, and other techniques for maximizing the effective manufacture and distribution of goods. **Clerical Practices:** Administrative and clerical procedures and systems such as word processing, managing files and records, stenography and transcription, designing forms, and other office procedures and terminology. **Administration and Management:** Business and management principles involved in strategic planning, resource allocation, human resources modeling, leadership technique, production methods, and coordination of people and resources. **Work Experience Needed:** None. **On-the-Job Training Needed:** Long-term on-the-job training. **Certification/Licensure:** Voluntary certification by association.

Personality Type: Conventional-Enterprising. **Career Cluster:** 14 Marketing, Sales, and Service. **Career Pathway:** 14.3 Buying and Merchandising. **Other Jobs in This Pathway:** Retail Salespersons; Sales Representatives, Wholesale and Manufacturing, Except Technical and Scientific Products; Telemarketers; Wholesale and Retail Buyers, Except Farm Products.

Skills—Management of Financial Resources: Determining how money will be spent to get the work done and accounting for these expenditures. **Management of Material Resources:** Obtaining and seeing to the appropriate use of equipment, facilities, and materials needed to do certain work. **Negotiation:** Bringing others together and trying to reconcile differences. **Persuasion:** Persuading others to change their minds or behavior. **Active Learning:** Understanding the implications of new information for both current and future problem solving and decision making. **Operations Analysis:** Analyzing needs and product requirements to create a design. **Judgment and Decision Making:** Considering the relative costs and benefits of potential actions to choose the most appropriate one. **Complex Problem Solving:** Identifying complex problems and reviewing related information to develop and evaluate options and implement solutions.

Work Environment: Sitting.

Radiation Therapists

- Annual Earnings: $76,630
- Earnings Growth Potential: Low (33.2%)
- Growth: 20.1%
- Annual Job Openings: 670
- Self-Employed: 0.0%

Considerations for Job Outlook: The risk of cancer increases as people age, so an aging population will increase demand for radiation therapists. Early diagnosis and the development of more sophisticated treatment techniques will also increase employment.

Provide radiation therapy to patients as prescribed by a radiologist according to established practices and standards. Position patients for treatment with accuracy according to prescription. Administer prescribed doses of radiation to specific body parts, using radiation therapy equipment according to established practices and standards. Check radiation therapy equipment to ensure proper operation. Review prescriptions, diagnoses, patient charts, and identification. Follow principles of radiation protection for patients, radiation therapists, and others. Maintain records, reports, and files as required, including such information as radiation dosages, equipment settings, and patients' reactions. Conduct most treatment sessions independently, in accordance with long-term treatment plans and under general direction of patients' physicians. Enter data into computers, and set controls to operate and adjust equipment and regulate dosages. Observe and reassure patients during treatments, and report unusual reactions to physicians or turn equipment off if unexpected adverse reactions occur. Calculate actual treatment dosages delivered during each session. Check for side effects such as skin irritation, nausea, and hair loss to assess patients' reaction to treatment. Prepare and construct equipment such as immobilization, treatment, and protection devices. Educate, prepare, and reassure patients and their families by answering questions, providing physical assistance, and reinforcing physicians' advice regarding treatment reactions and post-treatment care.

Education/Training Required: Associate degree. **Education and Training Program:** Medical Radiologic Technology/Science—Radiation Therapist. **Knowledge/ Courses—Medicine and Dentistry:** The information and techniques needed to diagnose and treat human injuries, diseases, and deformities. This includes symptoms, treatment alternatives, drug properties and interactions, and preventive health-care measures. **Biology:** Plant and animal organisms and their tissues, cells, functions, interdependencies, and interactions with each other and the environment. **Physics:** Physical principles, laws, their interrelationships, and applications to understanding fluid, material, and atmospheric dynamics, and mechanical, electrical, atomic, and subatomic structures and processes. **Psychology:** Human behavior and performance; individual differences in ability, personality, and interests; learning and motivation; psychological research methods; and the assessment and treatment of behavioral and affective disorders. **Philosophy and Theology:** Different philosophical systems and religions. This includes their basic principles, values, ethics, ways of thinking, customs, practices, and their impact on human culture. **Therapy and Counseling:** Principles, methods, and procedures for diagnosis, treatment, and rehabilitation of physical and mental dysfunctions, and for career counseling and guidance. **Work Experience Needed:** None. **On-the-Job Training Needed:** None. **Certification/Licensure:** Licensure or certification.

Personality Type: Social-Realistic-Conventional. **Career Cluster:** 08 Health Science. **Career Pathway:** 08.2 Diagnostics Services. **Other Jobs in This Pathway:** Ambulance Drivers and Attendants, Except Emergency Medical Technicians; Anesthesiologist Assistants; Athletic Trainers; Cardiovascular Technologists and Technicians; Cytogenetic Technologists; Cytotechnologists; Diagnostic Medical Sonographers; Emergency Medical Technicians and Paramedics; Endoscopy Technicians; Health Diagnosing and Treating Practitioners, All Other; Health Specialties Teachers, Postsecondary; Health Technologists and Technicians, All Other; Healthcare Practitioners and Technical Workers, All Other; Histotechnologists and Histologic Technicians; Medical and Clinical Laboratory Technicians; Medical and Clinical Laboratory Technologists; Medical and Health Services Managers; Medical Assistants; Medical Equipment Preparers; Neurodiagnostic Technologists; Nuclear Equipment Operation Technicians; Nuclear Medicine Technologists; Ophthalmic Laboratory Technicians; Pathologists; Physical Scientists, All Other; Physician Assistants; Radiologic Technicians; others.

Skills—Operation and Control: Controlling operations of equipment or systems. **Equipment Selection:** Determining the kind of tools and equipment needed to do a job. **Equipment Maintenance:** Performing routine maintenance on equipment and determining when and what kind of maintenance is needed. **Science:** Using scientific rules and methods to solve problems. **Quality Control Analysis:** Conducting tests and inspections of products, services, or processes to evaluate quality or performance. **Operation Monitoring:** Watching gauges, dials, or other indicators to make sure a machine is working properly. **Troubleshooting:** Determining causes of operating errors and deciding what to do about them. **Operations Analysis:** Analyzing needs and product requirements to create a design.

Work Environment: Indoors; standing; walking and running; using hands; bending or twisting the body; repetitive motions; contaminants; exposed to radiation; exposed to disease or infections.

Radio, Cellular, and Tower Equipment Installers and Repairers

- ⊙ Annual Earnings: $42,160
- ⊙ Earnings Growth Potential: Medium (37.9%)
- ⊙ Growth: 29.3%
- ⊙ Annual Job Openings: 450
- ⊙ Self-Employed: 2.8%

Considerations for Job Outlook: Telecommunications companies providing many new services, such as faster Internet connections and video on demand, are expected to result in employment growth for these workers. But better equipment will require less maintenance work, slowing employment growth.

Repair, install, or maintain mobile or stationary radio transmitting, broadcasting, and receiving equipment, and two-way radio communications systems. Assemble or erect communications towers, using construction or rigging equipment. Bolt equipment into place, using hand or power tools. Check antenna positioning to ensure specified azimuths or mechanical tilts and adjust as necessary. Climb communication towers to install, replace, or repair antennas or auxiliary equipment used to transmit and receive radio waves. Inspect completed work to ensure all hardware is tight, antennas are level, hangers are properly fastened, proper support is in place, or adequate weather proofing has been installed. Install all necessary transmission equipment components, including antennas or antenna mounts, surge arrestors, transmission lines, connectors, or tower-mounted amplifiers (TMAs). Install or repair tower lighting components, including strobes, beacons, or lighting controllers. Install, connect, or test underground or aboveground grounding systems. Lift equipment into position, using cranes and rigging tools or equipment such as gin poles. Perform maintenance or repair work on existing tower equipment, using hand or power tools. Read work orders, blueprints, plans, datasheets or site drawings to determine work to be done. Replace existing antennas with new antennas as directed. Run appropriate power, ground, or coaxial cables. Test operation of tower transmission components, using sweep testing tools or software. Climb towers to access components, using safety equipment, such as full-body harnesses. Complete reports related to project status, progress, or other work details, using computer software. Locate tower sites where work is to be performed, using mapping software. Take site survey photos or photos of work performed, using digital cameras. Transport equipment to work sites, using utility trucks and equipment trailers.

Education/Training Required: Associate degree. **Work Experience Needed:** None. **On-the-Job Training Needed:** Moderate-term on-the-job training. **Certification/Licensure:** Voluntary certification by association.

Job Specialization: Radio Mechanics

Test or repair mobile or stationary radio transmitting and receiving equipment and two-way radio communications systems used in ship-to-shore communications and found in service and emergency vehicles. Repair circuits, wiring, and soldering, using soldering irons and hand tools to install parts and adjust connections. Test equipment functions such as signal strength and quality, transmission capacity, interference, and signal delay, using equipment such as oscilloscopes, circuit analyzers, frequency meters, and wattmeters. Install, adjust, and repair stationary and mobile radio transmitting and receiving equipment and two-way radio communication systems. Examine malfunctioning radio equipment to locate defects such as loose connections, broken wires, or burned-out components, using schematic diagrams and test equipment. Remove and replace defective components and parts

such as conductors, resistors, semiconductors, and integrated circuits, using soldering irons, wire cutters, and hand tools. Calibrate and align components, using scales, gauges, and other measuring instruments. Turn setscrews to adjust receivers for maximum sensitivity and transmitters for maximum output. Test emergency transmitters to ensure their readiness for immediate use. Mount equipment on transmission towers and in vehicles such as ships or ambulances. Insert plugs into receptacles, and bolt or screw leads to terminals in order to connect equipment to power sources, using hand tools. Test batteries, using hydrometers and ammeters, and charge batteries as necessary.

Education and Training Program: Communications Systems Installation and Repair Technology. **Knowledge/Courses—Telecommunications:** Transmission, broadcasting, switching, control, and operation of telecommunications systems. **Engineering and Technology:** The practical application of engineering science and technology. This includes applying principles, techniques, procedures, and equipment to the design and production of various goods and services. **Computers and Electronics:** Circuit boards, processors, chips, electronic equipment, and computer hardware and software, including applications and programming. **Design:** Design techniques, tools, and principles involved in production of precision technical plans, blueprints, drawings, and models. **Physics:** Physical principles, laws, their interrelationships, and applications to understanding fluid, material, and atmospheric dynamics, and mechanical, electrical, atomic, and subatomic structures and processes. **Mechanical Devices:** Machines and tools, including their designs, uses, repair, and maintenance.

Personality Type: Realistic-Investigative-Conventional. **Career Cluster:** 13 Manufacturing. **Career Pathway:** 03.6 Telecommunications. **Other Jobs in This Pathway:** Broadcast Technicians; Communications Equipment Operators, All Other; Electronic Home Entertainment Equipment Installers and Repairers; Film and Video Editors; Media and Communication Workers, All Other; Radio Operators; Sound Engineering Technicians; Telecommunications Equipment Installers and Repairers, Except Line Installers.

Skills—Repairing: Repairing machines or systems using the needed tools. **Equipment Maintenance:** Performing routine maintenance on equipment and determining when and what kind of maintenance is needed. **Installation:**

R

Installing equipment, machines, wiring, or programs to meet specifications. **Troubleshooting:** Determining causes of operating errors and deciding what to do about them. **Equipment Selection:** Determining the kind of tools and equipment needed to do a job. **Quality Control Analysis:** Conducting tests and inspections of products, services, or processes to evaluate quality or performance. **Operation and Control:** Controlling operations of equipment or systems. **Operation Monitoring:** Watching gauges, dials, or other indicators to make sure a machine is working properly.

Work Environment: Indoors; sitting; using hands; noise.

Radiologic Technologists and Technicians

- ⊙ Annual Earnings: $55,120
- ⊙ Earnings Growth Potential: Low (32.2%)
- ⊙ Growth: 27.7%
- ⊙ Annual Job Openings: 9,510
- ⊙ Self-Employed: 0.2%

Considerations for Job Outlook: Radiologic technologists with multiple certifications will have the best job prospects.

Take X-rays and CAT scans or administer nonradioactive materials into patient's blood stream for diagnostic purposes. Review and evaluate developed X-rays, or computer-generated information to determine whether images are satisfactory for diagnostic purposes. Use radiation safety measures and protection devices to comply with government regulations and to ensure safety of patients and staff. Explain procedures and observe patients to ensure safety and comfort during scans. Operate or oversee operation of radiologic and magnetic imaging equipment to produce images of the body for diagnostic purposes. Position and immobilize patients on examining tables. Position imaging equipment, and adjust controls to set exposure time and distance, according to specifications of examinations. Key commands and data into computers to document and specify scan sequences, adjust transmitters and receivers, or photograph certain images. Monitor video displays of areas being scanned, and adjust density or contrast to improve picture quality. Monitor patients' conditions and reactions, reporting abnormal signs to physicians. Set up examination rooms, ensuring that all necessary equipment is ready. Prepare and administer oral or injected contrast media to patients. Take thorough and accurate patient medical histories. Remove and process film. Record, process, and maintain patient data and treatment records, and prepare reports. Coordinate work with clerical personnel or other technologists. Demonstrate new equipment, procedures, and techniques to staff members, and provide technical assistance.

Education/Training Required: Associate degree. **Education and Training Programs:** Allied Health Diagnostic, Intervention, and Treatment Professions, Other; Medical Radiologic Technology/Science—Radiation Therapist; Radiologic Technology/Science—Radiographer. **Knowledge/Courses—Medicine and Dentistry:** The information and techniques needed to diagnose and treat human injuries, diseases, and deformities. This includes symptoms, treatment alternatives, drug properties and interactions, and preventive health-care measures. **Physics:** Physical principles, laws, their interrelationships, and applications to understanding fluid, material, and atmospheric dynamics, and mechanical, electrical, atomic, and subatomic structures and processes. **Customer and Personal Service:** Principles and processes for providing customer and personal services. This includes customer needs assessment, meeting quality standards for services, and evaluation of customer satisfaction. **Biology:** Plant and animal organisms and their tissues, cells, functions, interdependencies, and interactions with each other and the environment. **Psychology:** Human behavior and performance; individual differences in ability, personality, and interests; learning and motivation; psychological research methods; and the assessment and treatment of behavioral and affective disorders. **Chemistry:** The chemical composition, structure, and properties of substances and of the chemical processes and transformations that they undergo. This includes uses of chemicals and their danger signs, production techniques, and disposal methods. **Work Experience Needed:** None. **On-the-Job Training Needed:** None. **Certification/Licensure:** Voluntary certification by association; licensure in some states.

Personality Type: Realistic-Social. **Career Cluster:** 08 Health Science. **Career Pathways:** 08.2 Diagnostics Services; 08.1 Therapeutic Services. **Other Jobs in These Pathways:** Acupuncturists; Allergists and Immunologists; Ambulance Drivers and Attendants, Except Emergency

Medical Technicians; Anesthesiologist Assistants; Anesthesiologists; Art Therapists; Athletic Trainers; Cardiovascular Technologists and Technicians; Chiropractors; Clinical Psychologists; Community and Social Service Specialists, All Other; Counseling Psychologists; Counselors, All Other; Cytogenetic Technologists; Cytotechnologists; Dental Assistants; Dental Hygienists; Dentists, All Other Specialists; Dentists, General; Dermatologists; Diagnostic Medical Sonographers; Dietetic Technicians; Dietitians and Nutritionists; Emergency Medical Technicians and Paramedics; Endoscopy Technicians; Family and General Practitioners; Health Diagnosing and Treating Practitioners, All Other; Health Specialties Teachers, Postsecondary; Health Technologists and Technicians, All Other; Healthcare Practitioners and Technical Workers, All Other; Healthcare Support Workers, All Other; others.

Skills—Science: Using scientific rules and methods to solve problems. **Operation and Control:** Controlling operations of equipment or systems. **Service Orientation:** Actively looking for ways to help people. **Quality Control Analysis:** Conducting tests and inspections of products, services, or processes to evaluate quality or performance. **Operation Monitoring:** Watching gauges, dials, or other indicators to make sure a machine is working properly. **Programming:** Writing computer programs for various purposes. **Instructing:** Teaching others how to do something. **Social Perceptiveness:** Being aware of others' reactions and understanding why they react as they do.

Work Environment: Indoors; standing; walking and running; using hands; bending or twisting the body; repetitive motions; contaminants; exposed to radiation; exposed to disease or infections.

Rail Car Repairers

- ⊙ Annual Earnings: $47,740
- ⊙ Earnings Growth Potential: High (41.2%)
- ⊙ Growth: 17.1%
- ⊙ Annual Job Openings: 930
- ⊙ Self-Employed: 5.6%

Considerations for Job Outlook: Most job opportunities will come from the need to replace workers who retire or leave the occupation. Those with certificates from vocational schools or two-year degrees from community colleges should have very good job opportunities as employers strongly prefer these candidates. Those without formal training will have difficulty finding jobs. The majority of job openings are expected to be in sectors that sell, rent, or lease heavy vehicles and mobile equipment, where a large proportion of service technicians are employed. The construction and mining industries, which use large numbers of heavy equipment, are sensitive to fluctuations in the economy. As a result, job opportunities for service technicians in these sectors will vary with overall economic conditions. Job opportunities for farm equipment mechanics are seasonal and are generally best during warmer months.

Diagnose, adjust, repair, or overhaul railroad rolling stock, mine cars, or mass-transit rail cars. Repair or replace defective or worn parts such as bearings, pistons, and gears, using hand tools, torque wrenches, power tools, and welding equipment. Test units for operability before and after repairs. Record conditions of cars, and repair and maintenance work performed or to be performed. Remove locomotives, car mechanical units, or other components, using pneumatic hoists and jacks, pinch bars, hand tools, and cutting torches. Inspect components such as bearings, seals, gaskets, wheels, and coupler assemblies to determine if repairs are needed. Inspect the interior and exterior of rail cars coming into rail yards in order to identify defects and to determine the extent of wear and damage. Adjust repaired or replaced units as needed to ensure proper operation. Perform scheduled maintenance, and clean units and components. Repair, fabricate, and install steel or wood fittings, using blueprints, shop sketches, and instruction manuals. Repair and maintain electrical and electronic controls for propulsion and braking systems. Disassemble units such as water pumps, control valves, and compressors so that repairs can be made. Measure diameters of axle wheel seats, using micrometers, and mark dimensions on axles so that wheels can be bored to specified dimensions. Align car sides for installation of car ends and crossties, using width gauges, turnbuckles, and wrenches. Replace defective wiring and insulation, and tighten electrical connections, using hand tools. Test electrical systems of cars by operating systems and using testing equipment such as ammeters. Install and repair interior flooring, fixtures, walls, plumbing, steps, and platforms. Examine car roofs for wear and damage, and repair defective sections, using roofing material, cement, nails, and waterproof paint. Paint car exteriors, interiors, and fixtures. Repair car upholstery. Repair

R

window sash frames, attach weather stripping and channels to frames, and replace window glass, using hand tools.

Education/Training Required: High school diploma or equivalent. **Education and Training Program:** Heavy Equipment Maintenance Technology/Technician. **Knowledge/Courses—Mechanical Devices:** Machines and tools, including their designs, uses, repair, and maintenance. **Public Safety and Security:** Relevant equipment, policies, procedures, and strategies to promote effective local, state, or national security operations for the protection of people, data, property, and institutions. **Production and Processing:** Raw materials, production processes, quality control, costs, and other techniques for maximizing the effective manufacture and distribution of goods. **Work Experience Needed:** None. **On-the-Job Training Needed:** Long-term on-the-job training. **Certification/Licensure:** Voluntary certification by manufacturer.

Personality Type: Realistic-Conventional-Investigative. **Career Cluster:** 13 Manufacturing. **Career Pathway:** 13.3 Maintenance, Installation, and Repair. **Other Jobs in This Pathway:** Aircraft Mechanics and Service Technicians; Automotive Engineering Technicians; Automotive Specialty Technicians; Avionics Technicians; Biological Technicians; Camera and Photographic Equipment Repairers; Chemical Equipment Operators and Tenders; Civil Engineering Technicians; Coil Winders, Tapers, and Finishers; Computer, Automated Teller, and Office Machine Repairers; Construction and Related Workers, All Other; Control and Valve Installers and Repairers, Except Mechanical Door; Electric Motor, Power Tool, and Related Repairers; Electrical and Electronic Equipment Assemblers; Electrical and Electronics Repairers, Commercial and Industrial Equipment; Electrical and Electronics Repairers, Powerhouse, Substation, and Relay; Electrical Engineering Technicians; Electrical Engineering Technologists; Electromechanical Engineering Technologists; Electromechanical Equipment Assemblers; Electronics Engineering Technicians; Electronics Engineering Technologists; others.

Skills—Repairing: Repairing machines or systems using the needed tools. **Equipment Maintenance:** Performing routine maintenance on equipment and determining when and what kind of maintenance is needed. **Troubleshooting:** Determining causes of operating errors and deciding what to do about them. **Installation:** Installing equipment, machines, wiring, or programs to meet specifications. **Operation and Control:** Controlling operations of equipment or systems. **Equipment Selection:** Determining the kind of tools and equipment needed to do a job. **Quality Control Analysis:** Conducting tests and inspections of products, services, or processes to evaluate quality or performance. **Operation Monitoring:** Watching gauges, dials, or other indicators to make sure a machine is working properly.

Work Environment: Outdoors; standing; climbing; walking and running; kneeling, crouching, stooping, or crawling; using hands; bending or twisting the body; repetitive motions; noise; very hot or cold; bright or inadequate lighting; contaminants; cramped work space; high places; hazardous equipment; minor burns, cuts, bites, or stings.

Railroad Conductors and Yardmasters

- ⊙ Annual Earnings: $53,880
- ⊙ Earnings Growth Potential: Low (27.3%)
- ⊙ Growth: 4.7%
- ⊙ Annual Job Openings: 1,430
- ⊙ Self-Employed: 0.0%

Considerations for Job Outlook: Job opportunities should be favorable for this occupation. Although workers typically stay in railroad conductor and yardmaster jobs longer than workers in many other occupations, more conductors and yardmasters are nearing retirement than are workers in most occupations. When these workers begin to retire, many jobs should open up.

Coordinate activities of switch-engine crew within railroad yard, industrial plant, or similar location. Signal engineers to begin train runs, stop trains, or change speed, using telecommunications equipment or hand signals. Receive information regarding train or rail problems from dispatchers or from electronic monitoring devices. Direct and instruct workers engaged in yard activities, such as switching tracks, coupling and uncoupling cars, and routing inbound and outbound traffic. Keep records of the contents and destination of each train car, and make sure that cars are added or removed at proper points on routes. Operate controls to activate track switches and traffic signals. Instruct workers to set warning signals in front and at rear of trains during emergency stops. Direct engineers to move cars to fit planned train configurations, combining or separating cars to make up or break up trains. Receive instructions from dispatchers regarding trains' routes, timetables, and cargoes. Review schedules, switching orders, way bills, and shipping records to obtain cargo loading and unloading information and to plan work. Confer with engineers regarding train routes, timetables, and cargoes, and to discuss alternative routes when there are rail defects or obstructions. Arrange for the removal of defective cars from trains at stations or stops. Inspect each car periodically during runs. Observe yard traffic to determine tracks available to accommodate inbound and outbound traffic. Document and prepare reports of accidents, unscheduled stops, or delays. Confirm routes and destination information for freight cars. Supervise and coordinate crew activities to transport freight and passengers and to provide boarding, porter, maid, and meal services to passengers. Supervise workers in the inspection and maintenance of mechanical equipment in order to ensure efficient and safe train operation. Record departure and arrival times, messages, tickets and revenue collected, and passenger accommodations and destinations.

Education/Training Required: High school diploma or equivalent. **Education and Training Program:** Truck and Bus Driver Training/Commercial Vehicle Operator and Instructor Training. **Knowledge/Courses—Transportation:** Principles and methods for moving people or goods by air, rail, sea, or road, including the relative costs and benefits. **Public Safety and Security:** Relevant equipment, policies, procedures, and strategies to promote effective local, state, or national security operations for the protection of people, data, property, and institutions. **Mechanical Devices:** Machines and tools, including their designs, uses, repair, and maintenance. **Work Experience Needed:** None. **On-the-Job Training Needed:** Moderate-term on-the-job training. **Certification/Licensure:** Licensure.

Personality Type: Enterprising-Realistic-Conventional. **Career Cluster:** 16 Transportation, Distribution, and Logistics. **Career Pathway:** 16.1 Transportation Operations. **Other Jobs in This Pathway:** Aerospace Engineering and Operations Technicians; Air Traffic Controllers; Aircraft Cargo Handling Supervisors; Airfield Operations Specialists; Airline Pilots, Copilots, and Flight Engineers; Automotive and Watercraft Service Attendants; Automotive Master Mechanics; Aviation Inspectors; Bridge and Lock Tenders; Bus Drivers, School or Special Client; Bus Drivers, Transit and Intercity; Commercial Divers; Commercial Pilots; Crane and Tower Operators; First-Line Supervisors of Helpers, Laborers, and Material Movers, Hand; First-Line Supervisors of Transportation and Material-Moving Machine and Vehicle Operators; Freight and Cargo Inspectors; Heavy and Tractor-Trailer Truck Drivers; Hoist and Winch Operators; Laborers and Freight, Stock, and Material Movers, Hand; Light Truck or Delivery Services Drivers; Mates—Ship, Boat, and Barge; Motor Vehicle Operators, All Other; Motorboat Operators; Operating Engineers and Other Construction Equipment Operators; others.

Skills—Operation and Control: Controlling operations of equipment or systems. **Management of Personnel Resources:** Motivating, developing, and directing people as they work, identifying the best people for the job. **Operation Monitoring:** Watching gauges, dials, or other indicators to make sure a machine is working properly. **Quality Control Analysis:** Conducting tests and inspections of products, services, or processes to evaluate quality or performance. **Coordination:** Adjusting actions in relation to others' actions. **Monitoring:** Monitoring or assessing your performance or that of other individuals or organizations to make improvements or take corrective action. **Complex Problem Solving:** Identifying complex problems and reviewing related information to develop and evaluate options and implement solutions. **Time Management:** Managing one's own time and the time of others.

Work Environment: Outdoors; sitting; using hands; noise; very hot or cold; bright or inadequate lighting; contaminants; hazardous conditions; hazardous equipment.

Real Estate Brokers

- ⊙ Annual Earnings: $59,340
- ⊙ Earnings Growth Potential: Very high (55.9%)
- ⊙ Growth: 7.6%
- ⊙ Annual Job Openings: 2,970
- ⊙ Self-Employed: 57.3%

Considerations for Job Outlook: Although the real estate market depends on economic conditions, it is relatively easy to enter the occupation. In times of economic growth, brokers and sales agents will have good job opportunities. In an economic downturn, there tend to be fewer job opportunities, and brokers and agents often have a lower income due to fewer sales and purchases.

Operate real estate offices, or work for commercial real estate firms, overseeing real estate transactions. Sell, for a fee, real estate owned by others. Obtain agreements from property owners to place properties for sale with real estate firms. Monitor fulfillment of purchase contract terms to ensure that they are handled in a timely manner. Compare properties with similar properties that have recently sold, in order to determine their competitive market prices. Act as an intermediary in negotiations between buyers and sellers over property prices and settlement details, and during the closing of sales. Generate lists of properties for sale, their locations and descriptions, and available financing options, using computers. Maintain knowledge of real estate law; local economies; fair housing laws; and types of available mortgages, financing options, and government programs. Check work completed by loan officers, attorneys, and other professionals to ensure that it is performed properly. Arrange for financing of property purchases. Appraise property values, assessing income potential when relevant. Maintain awareness of current income tax regulations, local zoning, building and tax laws, and growth possibilities of the area where properties are located. Manage and operate real estate offices, handling associated business details. Supervise agents who handle real estate transactions. Rent properties or manage rental properties. Arrange for title searches of properties being sold. Give buyers virtual tours of properties in which they are interested, using computers. Review property details to ensure that environmental regulations are met. Develop, sell, or lease properties used for industry or manufacturing. Maintain working knowledge of various factors that determine farms' capacities to produce, including agricultural variables and proximity to market centers and transportation facilities.

Education/Training Required: High school diploma or equivalent. **Education and Training Program:** Real Estate. **Knowledge/Courses—Sales and Marketing:** Principles and methods for showing, promoting, and selling products or services. This includes marketing strategy and tactics, product demonstration, sales techniques, and sales control systems. **Building and Construction:** Materials, methods, and the tools involved in the construction or repair of houses, buildings, or other structures such as highways and roads. **Law and Government:** Laws, legal codes, court procedures, precedents, government

regulations, executive orders, agency rules, and the democratic political process. **Customer and Personal Service:** Principles and processes for providing customer and personal services. This includes customer needs assessment, meeting quality standards for services, and evaluation of customer satisfaction. **Personnel and Human Resources:** Principles and procedures for personnel recruitment, selection, training, compensation and benefits, labor relations and negotiation, and personnel information systems. **Economics and Accounting:** Economic and accounting principles and practices, the financial markets, banking, and the analysis and reporting of financial data. **Work Experience Needed:** 1 to 5 years. **On-the-Job Training Needed:** None. **Certification/Licensure:** Licensure.

Personality Type: Enterprising-Conventional. **Career Cluster:** 14 Marketing, Sales, and Service. **Career Pathway:** 14.2 Professional Sales and Marketing. **Other Jobs in This Pathway:** Appraisers, Real Estate; Assessors; Cashiers; Counter and Rental Clerks; Demonstrators and Product Promoters; Door-To-Door Sales Workers, News and Street Vendors, and Related Workers; Driver/Sales Workers; Energy Brokers; First-Line Supervisors of Non-Retail Sales Workers; First-Line Supervisors of Retail Sales Workers; Gaming Change Persons and Booth Cashiers; Hotel, Motel, and Resort Desk Clerks; Interior Designers; Lodging Managers; Marketing Managers; Marking Clerks; Meeting, Convention, and Event Planners; Merchandise Displayers and Window Trimmers; Models; Online Merchants; Order Fillers, Wholesale and Retail Sales; Parts Salespersons; Property, Real Estate, and Community Association Managers; Real Estate Sales Agents; Reservation and Transportation Ticket Agents and Travel Clerks; Retail Salespersons; Sales and Related Workers, All Other; Sales Engineers; Sales Representatives, Services, All Other; others.

Skills—Negotiation: Bringing others together and trying to reconcile differences. **Persuasion:** Persuading others to change their minds or behavior. **Judgment and Decision Making:** Considering the relative costs and benefits of potential actions to choose the most appropriate one. **Active Learning:** Understanding the implications of new information for both current and future problem solving and decision making. **Speaking:** Talking to others to convey information effectively. **Management of Financial Resources:** Determining how money will be spent to get the work done and accounting for these expenditures.

Service Orientation: Actively looking for ways to help people. **Reading Comprehension:** Understanding written sentences and paragraphs in work-related documents.

Work Environment: More often indoors than outdoors; sitting.

Real Estate Sales Agents

- ⊙ Annual Earnings: $39,070
- ⊙ Earnings Growth Potential: High (48.3%)
- ⊙ Growth: 12.2%
- ⊙ Annual Job Openings: 12,760
- ⊙ Self-Employed: 57.3%

Considerations for Job Outlook: Although the real estate market depends on economic conditions, it is relatively easy to enter the occupation. In times of economic growth, brokers and sales agents will have good job opportunities. In an economic downturn, there tend to be fewer job opportunities, and brokers and agents often have a lower income due to fewer sales and purchases.

Rent, buy, or sell property for clients. Present purchase offers to sellers for consideration. Confer with escrow companies, lenders, home inspectors, and pest control operators to ensure that terms and conditions of purchase agreements are met before closing dates. Interview clients to determine what kinds of properties they are seeking. Prepare documents such as representation contracts, purchase agreements, closing statements, deeds, and leases. Coordinate property closings, overseeing signing of documents and disbursement of funds. Act as an intermediary in negotiations between buyers and sellers, generally representing one or the other. Promote sales of properties through advertisements, open houses, and participation in multiple listing services. Compare properties with similar properties that have recently sold to determine competitive market prices. Coordinate appointments to show homes to prospective buyers. Generate lists of properties that are compatible with buyers' needs and financial resources. Display commercial, industrial, agricultural, and residential properties to clients, and explain their features. Arrange for title searches to determine whether clients have clear property titles. Review plans for new construction with clients, enumerating and recommending available options

and features. Answer clients' questions regarding construction work, financing, maintenance, repairs, and appraisals.

Education/Training Required: High school diploma or equivalent. **Education and Training Program:** Real Estate. **Knowledge/Courses—Sales and Marketing:** Principles and methods for showing, promoting, and selling products or services. This includes marketing strategy and tactics, product demonstration, sales techniques, and sales control systems. **Customer and Personal Service:** Principles and processes for providing customer and personal services. This includes customer needs assessment, meeting quality standards for services, and evaluation of customer satisfaction. **Law and Government:** Laws, legal codes, court procedures, precedents, government regulations, executive orders, agency rules, and the democratic political process. **Building and Construction:** Materials, methods, and the tools involved in the construction or repair of houses, buildings, or other structures such as highways and roads. **Economics and Accounting:** Economic and accounting principles and practices, the financial markets, banking, and the analysis and reporting of financial data. **Computers and Electronics:** Circuit boards, processors, chips, electronic equipment, and computer hardware and software, including applications and programming. **Work Experience Needed:** None. **On-the-Job Training Needed:** Long-term on-the-job training. **Certification/Licensure:** Licensure.

Personality Type: Enterprising-Conventional. **Career Cluster:** 14 Marketing, Sales, and Service. **Career Pathway:** 14.2 Professional Sales and Marketing. **Other Jobs in This Pathway:** Appraisers, Real Estate; Assessors; Cashiers; Counter and Rental Clerks; Demonstrators and Product Promoters; Door-To-Door Sales Workers, News and Street Vendors, and Related Workers; Driver/Sales Workers; Energy Brokers; First-Line Supervisors of Non-Retail Sales Workers; First-Line Supervisors of Retail Sales Workers; Gaming Change Persons and Booth Cashiers; Hotel, Motel, and Resort Desk Clerks; Interior Designers; Lodging Managers; Marketing Managers; Marking Clerks; Meeting, Convention, and Event Planners; Merchandise Displayers and Window Trimmers; Models; Online Merchants; Order Fillers, Wholesale and Retail Sales; Parts Salespersons; Property, Real Estate, and Community Association Managers; Real Estate Brokers; Reservation and Transportation Ticket Agents and Travel Clerks; Retail Salespersons; Sales and Related Workers, All

R

Other; Sales Engineers; Sales Representatives, Services, All Other; others.

Skills—Negotiation: Bringing others together and trying to reconcile differences. **Persuasion:** Persuading others to change their minds or behavior. **Service Orientation:** Actively looking for ways to help people. **Systems Evaluation:** Identifying measures or indicators of system performance and the actions needed to improve or correct performance relative to the goals of the system. **Judgment and Decision Making:** Considering the relative costs and benefits of potential actions to choose the most appropriate one. **Mathematics:** Using mathematics to solve problems. **Speaking:** Talking to others to convey information effectively. **Coordination:** Adjusting actions in relation to others' actions.

Work Environment: More often indoors than outdoors; sitting.

Receptionists and Information Clerks

- ⊙ Annual Earnings: $25,690
- ⊙ Earnings Growth Potential: Low (30.3%)
- ⊙ Growth: 23.7%
- ⊙ Annual Job Openings: 56,560
- ⊙ Self-Employed: 0.8%

Considerations for Job Outlook: Job opportunities are expected to be very good. Many job openings will arise from the need to replace those who transfer to other occupations. Those with related work experience and good computer skills should have the best job opportunities.

Answer inquiries and provide information to the general public, customers, visitors, and other interested parties. Operate telephone switchboards to answer, screen, and forward calls, providing information, taking messages, and scheduling appointments. Receive payments, and record receipts for services. Perform administrative support tasks such as proofreading, transcribing handwritten information, and operating calculators or computers to work with pay records, invoices, balance sheets, and other documents. Greet persons entering the establishment, determine nature and purpose of visits, and direct or escort visitors to specific destinations. Hear and resolve complaints from customers and public. File and maintain records. Transmit information or documents to customers, using computers, mail, or facsimile machines. Schedule appointments, and maintain and update appointment calendars. Analyze data to determine answers to questions from customers or members of the public. Provide information about the establishment, such as location of departments or offices, employees within the organization, or services provided. Keep a current record of staff members' whereabouts and availability. Collect, sort, distribute, and prepare mail, messages, and courier deliveries. Calculate and quote rates for tours, stocks, insurance policies, or other products and services. Take orders for merchandise or materials, and send them to the proper departments to be filled. Process and prepare memos, correspondence, travel vouchers, or other documents.

Education/Training Required: High school diploma or equivalent. **Education and Training Programs:** General Office Occupations and Clerical Services; Health Unit Coordinator/Ward Clerk Training; Medical Reception/Receptionist; Receptionist Training. **Knowledge/Courses—Clerical Practices:** Administrative and clerical procedures and systems such as word processing, managing files and records, stenography and transcription, designing forms, and other office procedures and terminology. **Customer and Personal Service:** Principles and processes for providing customer and personal services. This includes customer needs assessment, meeting quality standards for services, and evaluation of customer satisfaction. **Computers and Electronics:** Circuit boards, processors, chips, electronic equipment, and computer hardware and software, including applications and programming. **Communications and Media:** Media production, communication, and dissemination techniques and methods. This includes alternative ways to inform and entertain via written, oral, and visual media. **Work Experience Needed:** None. **On-the-Job Training Needed:** Short-term on-the-job training. **Certification/Licensure:** None.

Personality Type: Conventional-Enterprising-Social. **Career Clusters:** 04 Business, Management, and Administration; 08 Health Science. **Career Pathways:** 04.6 Administrative and Information Support; 08.3 Health Informatics. **Other Jobs in These Pathways:** Cargo and Freight Agents; Clinical Psychologists; Communications Teachers, Postsecondary; Correspondence Clerks; Couriers and Messengers; Court Clerks; Customer Service

Representatives; Data Entry Keyers; Dental Laboratory Technicians; Dispatchers, Except Police, Fire, and Ambulance; Editors; Engineers, All Other; Executive Secretaries and Executive Administrative Assistants; File Clerks; Fine Artists, Including Painters, Sculptors, and Illustrators; First-Line Supervisors of Office and Administrative Support Workers; Freight Forwarders; Health Educators; Health Specialties Teachers, Postsecondary; Human Resources Assistants, Except Payroll and Timekeeping; Information and Record Clerks, All Other; Insurance Claims Clerks; Insurance Policy Processing Clerks; Interviewers, Except Eligibility and Loan; License Clerks; Mail Clerks and Mail Machine Operators, Except Postal Service; Medical and Health Services Managers; Medical Appliance Technicians; Medical Assistants; others.

Skills—Service Orientation: Actively looking for ways to help people. **Speaking:** Talking to others to convey information effectively. **Active Listening:** Giving full attention to what other people are saying, taking time to understand the points being made, asking questions as appropriate, and not interrupting at inappropriate times.

Work Environment: Indoors; sitting; using hands; repetitive motions.

Recreational Vehicle Service Technicians

- ⊙ Annual Earnings: $34,000
- ⊙ Earnings Growth Potential: Medium (36.5%)
- ⊙ Growth: 22.2%
- ⊙ Annual Job Openings: 480
- ⊙ Self-Employed: 4.4%

Considerations for Job Outlook: Faster-than-average employment growth is projected.

Diagnose, inspect, adjust, repair, or overhaul recreational vehicles including travel trailers. Examine or test operation of parts or systems that have been repaired to ensure completeness of repairs. Repair plumbing and propane gas lines, using caulking compounds and plastic or copper pipe. Inspect recreational vehicles to diagnose problems; then perform necessary adjustment, repair, or overhaul. Locate and repair frayed wiring, broken connections, or incorrect wiring, using ohmmeters, soldering irons, tape,

and hand tools. Confer with customers, read work orders, and examine vehicles needing repair in order to determine the nature and extent of damage. List parts needed, estimate costs, and plan work procedures, using parts lists, technical manuals, and diagrams. Connect electrical systems to outside power sources, and activate switches to test the operation of appliances and light fixtures. Connect water hoses to inlet pipes of plumbing systems, and test operation of toilets and sinks. Remove damaged exterior panels, and repair and replace structural frame members. Open and close doors, windows, and drawers to test their operation, trimming edges to fit as necessary. Repair leaks with caulking compound, or replace pipes, using pipe wrenches. Refinish wood surfaces on cabinets, doors, moldings, and floors, using power sanders, putty, spray equipment, brushes, paints, or varnishes. Reset hardware, using chisels, mallets, and screwdrivers. Seal open sides of modular units to prepare them for shipment, using polyethylene sheets, nails, and hammers.

Education/Training Required: High school diploma or equivalent. **Education and Training Program:** Vehicle Maintenance and Repair Technologies, Other. **Knowledge/Courses—Mechanical Devices:** Machines and tools, including their designs, uses, repair, and maintenance. **Building and Construction:** Materials, methods, and the tools involved in the construction or repair of houses, buildings, or other structures such as highways and roads. **Chemistry:** The chemical composition, structure, and properties of substances and of the chemical processes and transformations that they undergo. This includes uses of chemicals and their danger signs, production techniques, and disposal methods. **Physics:** Physical principles, laws, their interrelationships, and applications to understanding fluid, material, and atmospheric dynamics, and mechanical, electrical, atomic, and subatomic structures and processes. **Design:** Design techniques, tools, and principles involved in production of precision technical plans, blueprints, drawings, and models. **Engineering and Technology:** The practical application of engineering science and technology. This includes applying principles, techniques, procedures, and equipment to the design and production of various goods and services. **Work Experience Needed:** None. **On-the-Job Training Needed:** Long-term on-the-job training. **Certification/Licensure:** Voluntary certification by association.

R

Personality Type: Realistic-Investigative-Conventional. **Career Cluster:** 13 Manufacturing. **Career Pathway:** 13.1 Production. **Other Jobs in This Pathway:** Adhesive Bonding Machine Operators and Tenders; Assemblers and Fabricators, All Other; Avionics Technicians; Cabinetmakers and Bench Carpenters; Cleaning, Washing, and Metal Pickling Equipment Operators and Tenders; Coating, Painting, and Spraying Machine Setters, Operators, and Tenders; Computer-Controlled Machine Tool Operators, Metal and Plastic; Cooling and Freezing Equipment Operators and Tenders; Cost Estimators; Crushing, Grinding, and Polishing Machine Setters, Operators, and Tenders; Cutters and Trimmers, Hand; Cutting and Slicing Machine Setters, Operators, and Tenders; Cutting, Punching, and Press Machine Setters, Operators, and Tenders, Metal and Plastic; Drilling and Boring Machine Tool Setters, Operators, and Tenders, Metal and Plastic; Extruding and Drawing Machine Setters, Operators, and Tenders, Metal and Plastic; Extruding and Forming Machine Setters, Operators, and Tenders, Synthetic and Glass Fibers; others.

Skills—Repairing: Repairing machines or systems using the needed tools. **Equipment Maintenance:** Performing routine maintenance on equipment and determining when and what kind of maintenance is needed. **Troubleshooting:** Determining causes of operating errors and deciding what to do about them. **Equipment Selection:** Determining the kind of tools and equipment needed to do a job. **Operation and Control:** Controlling operations of equipment or systems. **Quality Control Analysis:** Conducting tests and inspections of products, services, or processes to evaluate quality or performance. **Operation Monitoring:** Watching gauges, dials, or other indicators to make sure a machine is working properly. **Negotiation:** Bringing others together and trying to reconcile differences.

Work Environment: Outdoors; standing; walking and running; using hands; bending or twisting the body; noise; very hot or cold; bright or inadequate lighting; contaminants; cramped work space; high places; hazardous conditions; hazardous equipment; minor burns, cuts, bites, or stings.

Refractory Materials Repairers, Except Brickmasons

- ⊙ Annual Earnings: $42,700
- ⊙ Earnings Growth Potential: Medium (35.0%)
- ⊙ Growth: 9.5%
- ⊙ Annual Job Openings: 60
- ⊙ Self-Employed: 0.0%

Considerations for Job Outlook: No data available.

Build or repair equipment such as furnaces, kilns, cupolas, boilers, converters, ladles, soaking pits, and ovens, using refractory materials. Chip slag from linings of ladles or remove linings when beyond repair, using hammers and chisels. Bolt sections of wooden molds together, using wrenches, and line molds with paper to prevent clay from sticking to molds. Transfer clay structures to curing ovens, melting tanks, and drawing kilns, using forklifts. Install clay structures in melting tanks and drawing kilns to control the flow and temperature of molten glass, using hoists and hand tools. Measure furnace walls to determine dimensions; then cut required number of sheets from plastic block, using saws. Mix specified amounts of sand, clay, mortar powder, and water to form refractory clay or mortar, using shovels or mixing machines. Reline or repair ladles and pouring spouts with refractory clay, using trowels. Remove worn or damaged plastic block refractory linings of furnaces, using hand tools. Spread mortar on stopper heads and rods, using trowels, and slide brick sleeves over rods to form refractory jackets. Tighten locknuts holding refractory stopper assemblies together, spread mortar on jackets to seal sleeve joints, and dry mortar in ovens. Install preformed metal scaffolding in interiors of cupolas, using hand tools. Disassemble molds, and cut, chip, and smooth clay structures such as floaters, drawbars, and L-blocks. Dry and bake new linings by placing inverted linings over burners, building fires in ladles, or by using blowtorches. Drill holes in furnace walls, bolt overlapping layers of plastic to walls, and hammer surfaces to compress layers into solid sheets. Dump and tamp clay in molds, using tamping tools. Fasten stopper heads to rods with metal pins to assemble refractory stoppers used to plug pouring nozzles of steel ladles. Climb scaffolding, carrying hoses, and spray surfaces of cupolas with refractory mixtures, using spray equipment.

Education/Training Required: Postsecondary vocational training. **Education and Training Program:** Industrial Mechanics and Maintenance Technology. **Knowledge/Courses—Mechanical Devices:** Machines and tools, including their designs, uses, repair, and maintenance. **Production and Processing:** Raw materials, production processes, quality control, costs, and other techniques for maximizing the effective manufacture and distribution of goods. **Design:** Design techniques, tools, and principles involved in production of precision technical plans, blueprints, drawings, and models. **Chemistry:** The chemical composition, structure, and properties of substances and of the chemical processes and transformations that they undergo. This includes uses of chemicals and their danger signs, production techniques, and disposal methods. **Work Experience Needed:** None. **On-the-Job Training Needed:** Moderate-term on-the-job training. **Certification/Licensure:** None.

Personality Type: Realistic-Conventional-Investigative. **Career Cluster:** 13 Manufacturing. **Career Pathway:** 13.3 Maintenance, Installation, and Repair. **Other Jobs in This Pathway:** Aircraft Mechanics and Service Technicians; Automotive Engineering Technicians; Automotive Specialty Technicians; Avionics Technicians; Biological Technicians; Camera and Photographic Equipment Repairers; Chemical Equipment Operators and Tenders; Civil Engineering Technicians; Coil Winders, Tapers, and Finishers; Computer, Automated Teller, and Office Machine Repairers; Construction and Related Workers, All Other; Control and Valve Installers and Repairers, Except Mechanical Door; Electric Motor, Power Tool, and Related Repairers; Electrical and Electronic Equipment Assemblers; Electrical and Electronics Repairers, Commercial and Industrial Equipment; Electrical and Electronics Repairers, Powerhouse, Substation, and Relay; Electrical Engineering Technicians; Electrical Engineering Technologists; Electromechanical Engineering Technologists; Electromechanical Equipment Assemblers; Electronics Engineering Technicians; Electronics Engineering Technologists; others.

Skills—Repairing: Repairing machines or systems using the needed tools. **Equipment Maintenance:** Performing routine maintenance on equipment and determining when and what kind of maintenance is needed. **Troubleshooting:** Determining causes of operating errors and deciding what to do about them. **Operation and Control:** Controlling operations of equipment or systems. **Operation**

Monitoring: Watching gauges, dials, or other indicators to make sure a machine is working properly. **Equipment Selection:** Determining the kind of tools and equipment needed to do a job. **Quality Control Analysis:** Conducting tests and inspections of products, services, or processes to evaluate quality or performance. **Installation:** Installing equipment, machines, wiring, or programs to meet specifications.

Work Environment: Standing; walking and running; using hands; bending or twisting the body; repetitive motions; noise; very hot or cold; bright or inadequate lighting; contaminants; cramped work space; whole-body vibration; high places; hazardous conditions; hazardous equipment; minor burns, cuts, bites, or stings.

Refuse and Recyclable Material Collectors

- ⊙ Annual Earnings: $32,280
- ⊙ Earnings Growth Potential: High (42.5%)
- ⊙ Growth: 20.2%
- ⊙ Annual Job Openings: 6,970
- ⊙ Self-Employed: 7.8%

Considerations for Job Outlook: Job prospects for hand laborers and material movers should be favorable. Despite slower growth in this occupation, the need to replace workers who leave the occupation should create a large number of job openings. As automation increases, the technology used by workers in this occupation will become more complex. Employers will likely prefer workers who are comfortable using technology such as tablet computers and handheld scanners.

Collect and dump refuse or recyclable materials from containers into trucks. Inspect trucks prior to beginning routes to ensure safe operating condition. Refuel trucks, and add other necessary fluids, such as oil. Fill out any needed reports for defective equipment. Drive to disposal sites to empty trucks that have been filled. Drive trucks along established routes through residential streets and alleys or through business and industrial areas. Operate equipment that compresses the collected refuse. Operate automated or semi-automated hoisting devices that raise refuse bins and dump contents into openings in truck bodies. Dismount garbage trucks to collect garbage, and

R

remount trucks to ride to the next collection point. Communicate with dispatchers concerning delays, unsafe sites, accidents, equipment breakdowns, and other maintenance problems. Keep informed of road and weather conditions to determine how routes will be affected. Tag garbage or recycling containers to inform customers of problems such as excess garbage or inclusion of items that are not permitted. Clean trucks and compactor bodies after routes have been completed. Sort items set out for recycling, and throw materials into designated truck compartments. Organize schedules for refuse collection. Provide quotations for refuse collection contracts.

Education/Training Required: Less than high school. **Education and Training Programs:** No related CIP programs; this job is learned through informal short-term on-the-job training. **Knowledge/Courses—Transportation:** Principles and methods for moving people or goods by air, rail, sea, or road, including the relative costs and benefits. **Customer and Personal Service:** Principles and processes for providing customer and personal services. This includes customer needs assessment, meeting quality standards for services, and evaluation of customer satisfaction. **Work Experience Needed:** None. **On-the-Job Training Needed:** Short-term on-the-job training. **Certification/Licensure:** Licensure in some states for some specializations.

Personality Type: Realistic-Conventional. **Career Cluster:** 01 Agriculture, Food, and Natural Resources. **Career Pathway:** 01.5 Natural Resources Systems. **Other Jobs in This Pathway:** Biological Science Teachers, Postsecondary; Climate Change Analysts; Conveyor Operators and Tenders; Derrick Operators, Oil and Gas; Engineering Technicians, Except Drafters, All Other; Environmental Economists; Environmental Restoration Planners; Environmental Science and Protection Technicians, Including Health; Environmental Science Teachers, Postsecondary; Environmental Scientists and Specialists, Including Health; Fallers; Fish and Game Wardens; Fishers and Related Fishing Workers; Forest and Conservation Technicians; Forest and Conservation Workers; Foresters; Forestry and Conservation Science Teachers, Postsecondary; Gas Compressor and Gas Pumping Station Operators; Geological Sample Test Technicians; Geophysical Data Technicians; Helpers—Extraction Workers; Industrial Ecologists; Industrial Truck and Tractor Operators; Loading Machine Operators, Underground Mining; Log

Graders and Scalers; Logging Equipment Operators; Logging Workers, All Other; others.

Skills—Equipment Maintenance: Performing routine maintenance on equipment and determining when and what kind of maintenance is needed. **Repairing:** Repairing machines or systems using the needed tools. **Operation and Control:** Controlling operations of equipment or systems. **Troubleshooting:** Determining causes of operating errors and deciding what to do about them. **Equipment Selection:** Determining the kind of tools and equipment needed to do a job. **Operation Monitoring:** Watching gauges, dials, or other indicators to make sure a machine is working properly. **Quality Control Analysis:** Conducting tests and inspections of products, services, or processes to evaluate quality or performance.

Work Environment: Outdoors; more often sitting than standing; walking and running; using hands; bending or twisting the body; repetitive motions; noise; very hot or cold; contaminants; exposed to disease or infections; hazardous equipment; minor burns, cuts, bites, or stings.

Registered Nurses

- Annual Earnings: $65,950
- Earnings Growth Potential: Low (31.8%)
- Growth: 26.0%
- Annual Job Openings: 120,740
- Self-Employed: 0.9%

Considerations for Job Outlook: Overall, job opportunities for registered nurses are expected to be excellent. Employers in some parts of the country and in some employment settings report difficulty in attracting and keeping enough registered nurses. Job opportunities should be excellent, even in hospitals, because of the relatively high turnover of hospital nurses. To attract and keep qualified nurses, hospitals may offer signing bonuses, family-friendly work schedules, or subsidized training. In physicians' offices and outpatient care centers, registered nurses may face greater competition for positions because these jobs generally offer regular working hours and provide more comfortable working conditions than hospitals. Generally, registered nurses with at least a bachelor's degree in nursing (BSN) will have better job prospects than those without one.

Assess patient health problems and needs, develop and implement nursing care plans, and maintain medical records. Maintain accurate, detailed reports and records. Monitor, record, and report symptoms and changes in patients' conditions. Record patients' medical information and vital signs. Modify patient treatment plans as indicated by patients' responses and conditions. Consult and coordinate with health-care team members to assess, plan, implement, and evaluate patient care plans. Order, interpret, and evaluate diagnostic tests to identify and assess patients' condition. Monitor all aspects of patient care, including diet and physical activity. Direct and supervise less-skilled nursing or health-care personnel, or supervise a particular unit. Prepare patients for, and assist with, examinations and treatments. Observe nurses and visit patients to ensure proper nursing care. Assess the needs of individuals, families, or communities, including assessment of individuals' home or work environments, to identify potential health or safety problems. Instruct individuals, families, and other groups on topics such as health education, disease prevention, and childbirth, and develop health improvement programs. Prepare rooms, sterile instruments, equipment, and supplies, and ensure that the stock of supplies is maintained. Inform physicians of patients' condition during anesthesia. Administer local, inhalation, intravenous, and other anesthetics. Provide health care, first aid, immunizations, and assistance in convalescence and rehabilitation in locations such as schools, hospitals, and industry.

Education/Training Required: Associate degree. **Education and Training Programs:** Adult Health Nurse/Nursing; Clinical Nurse Specialist Training; Critical Care Nursing; Family Practice Nurse/Nursing; Maternal/Child Health and Neonatal Nurse/Nursing; Nurse Anesthetist Training; Nurse Midwife/Nursing Midwifery; Nursing Science; Occupational and Environmental Health Nursing; Pediatric Nurse/Nursing; Perioperative/Operating Room and Surgical Nurse/Nursing; Psychiatric/Mental Health Nurse/Nursing; Public Health/Community Nurse/Nursing; Registered Nursing/Registered Nurse Training. **Knowledge/Courses—Psychology:** Human behavior and performance; individual differences in ability, personality, and interests; learning and motivation; psychological research methods; and the assessment and treatment of behavioral and affective disorders. **Medicine and Dentistry:** The information and techniques needed to diagnose and treat human injuries, diseases, and deformities. This includes symptoms, treatment alternatives, drug

properties and interactions, and preventive health-care measures. **Therapy and Counseling:** Principles, methods, and procedures for diagnosis, treatment, and rehabilitation of physical and mental dysfunctions, and for career counseling and guidance. **Biology:** Plant and animal organisms and their tissues, cells, functions, interdependencies, and interactions with each other and the environment. **Philosophy and Theology:** Different philosophical systems and religions. This includes their basic principles, values, ethics, ways of thinking, customs, practices, and their impact on human culture. **Sociology and Anthropology:** Group behavior and dynamics, societal trends and influences, human migrations, ethnicity, and cultures and their history and origins. **Work Experience Needed:** None. **On-the-Job Training Needed:** None. **Certification/Licensure:** Licensure.

Personality Type: Social-Investigative-Conventional. **Career Cluster:** 08 Health Science. **Career Pathway:** 08.1 Therapeutic Services. **Other Jobs in This Pathway:** Acupuncturists; Allergists and Immunologists; Anesthesiologists; Art Therapists; Chiropractors; Clinical Psychologists; Community and Social Service Specialists, All Other; Counseling Psychologists; Counselors, All Other; Dental Assistants; Dental Hygienists; Dentists, All Other Specialists; Dentists, General; Dermatologists; Diagnostic Medical Sonographers; Dietetic Technicians; Dietitians and Nutritionists; Family and General Practitioners; Health Diagnosing and Treating Practitioners, All Other; Health Specialties Teachers, Postsecondary; Health Technologists and Technicians, All Other; Healthcare Practitioners and Technical Workers, All Other; Healthcare Support Workers, All Other; Home Health Aides; Hospitalists; Industrial-Organizational Psychologists; Internists, General; Licensed Practical and Licensed Vocational Nurses; Life, Physical, and Social Science Technicians, All Other; Low Vision Therapists, Orientation and Mobility Specialists, and Vision Rehabilitation Therapists; others.

Skills—Science: Using scientific rules and methods to solve problems. **Social Perceptiveness:** Being aware of others' reactions and understanding why they react as they do. **Quality Control Analysis:** Conducting tests and inspections of products, services, or processes to evaluate quality or performance. **Service Orientation:** Actively looking for ways to help people. **Learning Strategies:** Selecting and using training/instructional methods and procedures appropriate for the situation when learning or teaching

R

new things. **Coordination:** Adjusting actions in relation to others' actions. **Management of Material Resources:** Obtaining and seeing to the appropriate use of equipment, facilities, and materials needed to do certain work. **Instructing:** Teaching others how to do something.

Work Environment: Indoors; standing; walking and running; using hands; exposed to disease or infections.

Job Specialization: Acute Care Nurses

Provide advanced nursing care for patients with acute conditions such as heart attacks, respiratory distress syndrome, or shock. May care for pre- and postoperative patients or perform advanced, invasive diagnostic or therapeutic procedures. Analyze the indications, contraindications, risk complications, and cost-benefit tradeoffs of therapeutic interventions. Diagnose acute or chronic conditions that could result in rapid physiological deterioration or life-threatening instability. Distinguish between normal and abnormal developmental and age-related physiological and behavioral changes in acute, critical, and chronic illness. Manage patients' pain relief and sedation by providing pharmacologic and nonpharmacologic interventions, monitoring patients' responses, and changing care plans accordingly. Interpret information obtained from electrocardiograms (EKGs) or radiographs (X-rays). Perform emergency medical procedures such as basic cardiac life support (BLS), advanced cardiac life support (ACLS), and other condition-stabilizing interventions. Assess urgent and emergent health conditions using both physiologically and technologically derived data. Adjust settings on patients' assistive devices such as temporary pacemakers. Assess the impact of illnesses or injuries on patients' health; function; growth; development; nutrition; sleep; rest; quality of life; and family, social, and educational relationships. Collaborate with members of multidisciplinary health-care teams to plan, manage, or assess patient treatments. Discuss illnesses and treatments with patients and family members.

Education and Training Program: Critical Care Nursing. **Knowledge/Courses—Therapy and Counseling:** Principles, methods, and procedures for diagnosis, treatment, and rehabilitation of physical and mental dysfunctions, and for career counseling and guidance. **Medicine and Dentistry:** The information and techniques needed to diagnose and treat human injuries, diseases, and deformities. This includes symptoms, treatment alternatives, drug properties and interactions, and preventive health-care measures. **Psychology:** Human behavior and performance; individual differences in ability, personality, and interests; learning and motivation; psychological research methods; and the assessment and treatment of behavioral and affective disorders. **Biology:** Plant and animal organisms and their tissues, cells, functions, interdependencies, and interactions with each other and the environment. **Sociology and Anthropology:** Group behavior and dynamics, societal trends and influences, human migrations, ethnicity, and cultures and their history and origins. **Philosophy and Theology:** Different philosophical systems and religions. This includes their basic principles, values, ethics, ways of thinking, customs, practices, and their impact on human culture.

Personality Type: Social-Investigative-Realistic. **Career Cluster:** 08 Health Science. **Career Pathway:** 08.1 Therapeutic Services. **Other Jobs in This Pathway:** Acupuncturists; Allergists and Immunologists; Anesthesiologists; Art Therapists; Chiropractors; Clinical Psychologists; Community and Social Service Specialists, All Other; Counseling Psychologists; Counselors, All Other; Dental Assistants; Dental Hygienists; Dentists, All Other Specialists; Dentists, General; Dermatologists; Diagnostic Medical Sonographers; Dietetic Technicians; Dietitians and Nutritionists; Family and General Practitioners; Health Diagnosing and Treating Practitioners, All Other; Health Specialties Teachers, Postsecondary; Health Technologists and Technicians, All Other; Healthcare Practitioners and Technical Workers, All Other; Healthcare Support Workers, All Other; Home Health Aides; Hospitalists; Industrial-Organizational Psychologists; Internists, General; Licensed Practical and Licensed Vocational Nurses; Life, Physical, and Social Science Technicians, All Other; Low Vision Therapists, Orientation and Mobility Specialists, and Vision Rehabilitation Therapists; others.

Skills—Science: Using scientific rules and methods to solve problems. **Social Perceptiveness:** Being aware of others' reactions and understanding why they react as they do. **Reading Comprehension:** Understanding written sentences and paragraphs in work-related documents. **Operation Monitoring:** Watching gauges, dials, or other indicators to make sure a machine is working properly. **Service Orientation:** Actively looking for ways to help people. **Systems Evaluation:** Identifying measures or indicators of system performance and the actions needed to improve or correct performance relative to the goals of the system. **Operation and Control:** Controlling operations of equipment or systems. **Active Learning:** Understanding the implications of new information for both current and future problem solving and decision making.

Work Environment: Indoors; standing; walking and running; using hands; noise; contaminants; cramped work space; exposed to radiation; exposed to disease or infections.

Job Specialization: Advanced Practice Psychiatric Nurses

Provide advanced nursing care for patients with psychiatric disorders. May provide psychotherapy under the direction of psychiatrists. Teach classes on mental health topics such as stress reduction. Participate in activities aimed at professional growth and development, including conferences or continuing education activities. Direct or provide home health services. Monitor the use and status of medical and pharmaceutical supplies. Develop practice protocols for mental health problems based on review and evaluation of published research. Develop, implement, or evaluate programs such as outreach activities, community mental health programs, and crisis situation response activities. Treat patients for routine physical health problems. Write prescriptions for psychotropic medications as allowed by state regulations and collaborative practice agreements. Refer patients requiring more specialized or complex treatment to psychiatrists, primary care physicians, or other medical specialists. Provide routine physical health screenings to detect or monitor problems such as heart disease and diabetes. Participate in treatment team conferences regarding diagnosis or treatment of difficult cases. Interpret diagnostic or laboratory tests such as electrocardiograms (EKGs) and renal functioning tests. Evaluate patients' behavior to formulate diagnoses or assess treatments. Develop and implement treatment plans. Monitor patients' medication usage and results. Educate patients and family members about mental health and medical conditions, preventive health measures, medications, or treatment plans.

Education and Training Program: Psychiatric/Mental Health Nurse Training/Nursing. **Knowledge/Courses—Therapy and Counseling:** Principles, methods, and procedures for diagnosis, treatment, and rehabilitation of physical and mental dysfunctions, and for career counseling and guidance. **Psychology:** Human behavior and performance; individual differences in ability, personality, and interests; learning and motivation; psychological research methods; and the assessment and treatment of behavioral and affective disorders. **Medicine and Dentistry:** The information and techniques needed to diagnose and treat human injuries, diseases, and deformities. This includes symptoms, treatment alternatives, drug properties and interactions, and preventive health-care measures. **Sociology and Anthropology:** Group behavior and dynamics, societal trends and influences, human migrations, ethnicity, and cultures and their history and origins. **Philosophy and Theology:** Different philosophical systems and religions. This includes their basic principles, values, ethics, ways of thinking, customs, practices, and their impact on human culture. **Biology:** Plant and animal organisms and their tissues, cells, functions, interdependencies, and interactions with each other and the environment.

Personality Type: Social-Investigative. **Career Cluster:** 08 Health Science. **Career Pathway:** 08.1 Therapeutic Services. **Other Jobs in This Pathway:** Acupuncturists; Allergists and Immunologists; Anesthesiologists; Art Therapists; Chiropractors; Clinical Psychologists; Community and Social Service Specialists, All Other; Counseling Psychologists; Counselors, All Other; Dental Assistants; Dental Hygienists; Dentists, All Other Specialists; Dentists, General; Dermatologists; Diagnostic Medical Sonographers; Dietetic Technicians; Dietitians and Nutritionists; Family and General Practitioners; Health Diagnosing and Treating Practitioners, All Other; Health Specialties Teachers, Postsecondary; Health Technologists and Technicians, All Other; Healthcare Practitioners and Technical Workers, All Other; Healthcare Support Workers, All Other; Home Health Aides; Hospitalists; Industrial-Organizational Psychologists; Internists, General; Licensed Practical and Licensed Vocational Nurses; Life, Physical, and Social Science Technicians, All Other; Low Vision Therapists, Orientation and Mobility Specialists, and Vision Rehabilitation Therapists; others.

Skills—Social Perceptiveness: Being aware of others' reactions and understanding why they react as they do. **Science:** Using scientific rules and methods to solve problems. **Negotiation:** Bringing others together and trying to reconcile differences. **Service Orientation:** Actively looking for ways to help people. **Systems Evaluation:** Identifying measures or indicators of system performance and the actions needed to improve or correct performance relative to the goals of the system. **Persuasion:** Persuading others to change their minds or behavior. **Learning Strategies:** Selecting and using training/instructional methods and procedures appropriate for the situation when learning or teaching new things. **Reading Comprehension:** Understanding written sentences and paragraphs in work-related documents.

Work Environment: Indoors; sitting; exposed to disease or infections.

Job Specialization: Clinical Nurse Specialists

Plan, direct, or coordinate daily patient care activities in a clinical practice. Ensure adherence to established clinical policies, protocols, regulations, and standards. Coordinate or conduct educational programs or in-service training sessions on topics such as clinical procedures. Observe, interview, and assess patients to identify care needs. Evaluate the quality and effectiveness of nursing practice or organizational systems. Provide direct care by performing comprehensive health assessments, developing differential diagnoses, conducting specialized tests, or prescribing medications or treatments. Provide specialized direct and indirect care to inpatients and outpatients within a designated specialty such as obstetrics, neurology, oncology, or neonatal care. Maintain departmental policies, procedures, objectives, or infection control standards. Collaborate with other health-care professionals and service providers to ensure optimal patient care. Develop nursing service philosophies, goals, policies, priorities, or procedures. Develop, implement, or evaluate standards of nursing practice in specialty areas such as pediatrics, acute care, and geriatrics. Develop or assist others in the development of care and treatment plans. Make clinical recommendations to physicians, other health-care providers, insurance companies, patients, or health-care organizations. Plan, evaluate, or modify treatment programs based on information gathered by observing and interviewing patients, or by analyzing patient records. Present clients with information required to make informed health-care and treatment decisions.

Education and Training Program: Clinical Nurse Specialist Training. **Knowledge/Courses—Medicine and**

Dentistry: The information and techniques needed to diagnose and treat human injuries, diseases, and deformities. This includes symptoms, treatment alternatives, drug properties and interactions, and preventive health-care measures. **Biology:** Plant and animal organisms and their tissues, cells, functions, interdependencies, and interactions with each other and the environment. **Therapy and Counseling:** Principles, methods, and procedures for diagnosis, treatment, and rehabilitation of physical and mental dysfunctions, and for career counseling and guidance. **Psychology:** Human behavior and performance; individual differences in ability, personality, and interests; learning and motivation; psychological research methods; and the assessment and treatment of behavioral and affective disorders. **Sociology and Anthropology:** Group behavior and dynamics, societal trends and influences, human migrations, ethnicity, and cultures and their history and origins. **Philosophy and Theology:** Different philosophical systems and religions. This includes their basic principles, values, ethics, ways of thinking, customs, practices, and their impact on human culture.

Personality Type: Enterprising-Social-Conventional. **Career Cluster:** 08 Health Science. **Career Pathways:** 08.3 Health Informatics; 08.1 Therapeutic Services. **Other Jobs in These Pathways:** Acupuncturists; Allergists and Immunologists; Anesthesiologists; Art Therapists; Chiropractors; Clinical Psychologists; Communications Teachers, Postsecondary; Community and Social Service Specialists, All Other; Counseling Psychologists; Counselors, All Other; Dental Assistants; Dental Hygienists; Dental Laboratory Technicians; Dentists, All Other Specialists; Dentists, General; Dermatologists; Diagnostic Medical Sonographers; Dietetic Technicians; Dietitians and Nutritionists; Editors; Engineers, All Other; Executive Secretaries and Executive Administrative Assistants; Family and General Practitioners; Fine Artists, Including Painters, Sculptors, and Illustrators; First-Line Supervisors of Office and Administrative Support Workers; Health Diagnosing and Treating Practitioners, All Other; Health Educators; Health Specialties Teachers, Postsecondary; Health Technologists and Technicians, All Other; Healthcare Practitioners and Technical Workers, All Other; others.

Skills—Science: Using scientific rules and methods to solve problems. **Operations Analysis:** Analyzing needs and product requirements to create a design. **Instructing:** Teaching others how to do something. **Service**

Orientation: Actively looking for ways to help people. **Negotiation:** Bringing others together and trying to reconcile differences. **Persuasion:** Persuading others to change their minds or behavior. **Judgment and Decision Making:** Considering the relative costs and benefits of potential actions to choose the most appropriate one. **Active Learning:** Understanding the implications of new information for both current and future problem solving and decision making.

Work Environment: Indoors; standing; using hands; noise; contaminants; exposed to radiation; exposed to disease or infections.

Job Specialization: Critical Care Nurses

Provide advanced nursing care for patients in critical or coronary care units. Identify patients' age-specific needs, and alter care plans as necessary to meet those needs. Provide postmortem care. Evaluate patients' vital signs and laboratory data to determine emergency intervention needs. Perform approved therapeutic or diagnostic procedures based upon patients' clinical status. Administer blood and blood products, monitoring patients for signs and symptoms related to transfusion reactions. Administer medications intravenously, by injection, orally, through gastric tubes, or by other methods. Advocate for patients' and families' needs, or provide emotional support for patients and their families. Set up and monitor medical equipment and devices such as cardiac monitors, mechanical ventilators and alarms, oxygen delivery devices, transducers, and pressure lines. Monitor patients' fluid intake and output to detect emerging problems such as fluid and electrolyte imbalances. Monitor patients for changes in status and indications of conditions such as sepsis or shock, and institute appropriate interventions. Assess patients' pain levels and sedation requirements. Assess patients' psychosocial status and needs including areas such as sleep patterns, anxiety, grief, anger, and support systems. Collaborate with other health-care professionals to develop and revise treatment plans based on identified needs and assessment data. Collect specimens for laboratory tests. Compile and analyze data obtained from monitoring or diagnostic tests.

Education and Training Program: Critical Care Nursing. **Knowledge/Courses—Medicine and Dentistry:** The information and techniques needed to diagnose and treat human injuries, diseases, and deformities. This includes symptoms, treatment alternatives, drug properties and interactions, and preventive health-care measures. **Biology:** Plant and animal organisms and their tissues, cells, functions, interdependencies, and interactions with each other and the environment. **Psychology:** Human behavior and performance; individual differences in ability, personality, and interests; learning and motivation; psychological research methods; and the assessment and treatment of behavioral and affective disorders. **Therapy and Counseling:** Principles, methods, and procedures for diagnosis, treatment, and rehabilitation of physical and mental dysfunctions, and for career counseling and guidance. **Sociology and Anthropology:** Group behavior and dynamics, societal trends and influences, human migrations, ethnicity, and cultures and their history and origins. **Philosophy and Theology:** Different philosophical systems and religions. This includes their basic principles, values, ethics, ways of thinking, customs, practices, and their impact on human culture.

Personality Type: Social-Investigative-Realistic. **Career Cluster:** 08 Health Science. **Career Pathway:** 08.1 Therapeutic Services. **Other Jobs in This Pathway:** Acupuncturists; Allergists and Immunologists; Anesthesiologists; Art Therapists; Chiropractors; Clinical Psychologists; Community and Social Service Specialists, All Other; Counseling Psychologists; Counselors, All Other; Dental Assistants; Dental Hygienists; Dentists, All Other Specialists; Dentists, General; Dermatologists; Diagnostic Medical Sonographers; Dietetic Technicians; Dietitians and Nutritionists; Family and General Practitioners; Health Diagnosing and Treating Practitioners, All Other; Health Specialties Teachers, Postsecondary; Health Technologists and Technicians, All Other; Healthcare Practitioners and Technical Workers, All Other; Healthcare Support Workers, All Other; Home Health Aides; Hospitalists; Industrial-Organizational Psychologists; Internists, General; Licensed Practical and Licensed Vocational Nurses; Life, Physical, and Social Science Technicians, All Other; Low Vision Therapists, Orientation and Mobility Specialists, and Vision Rehabilitation Therapists; others.

Skills—Science: Using scientific rules and methods to solve problems. **Social Perceptiveness:** Being aware of others' reactions and understanding why they react as they do. **Operation and Control:** Controlling operations of equipment or systems. **Quality Control Analysis:** Conducting tests and inspections of products, services, or processes to evaluate quality or performance. **Operation Monitoring:** Watching gauges, dials, or other indicators to make sure a machine is working properly. **Service Orientation:** Actively looking for ways to help people. **Monitoring:** Monitoring or assessing your performance or that of other individuals or organizations to make improvements or take corrective action. **Active Learning:** Understanding the implications of new information for both current and future problem solving and decision making.

Work Environment: Indoors; standing; walking and running; using hands; bending or twisting the body; noise; contaminants; cramped work space; exposed to radiation; exposed to disease or infections.

Reinforcing Iron and Rebar Workers

- ⊙ Annual Earnings: $37,990
- ⊙ Earnings Growth Potential: Medium (35.0%)
- ⊙ Growth: 48.7%
- ⊙ Annual Job Openings: 1,320
- ⊙ Self-Employed: 0.0%

Considerations for Job Outlook: Rapid employment growth should result in good job opportunities. Because employers prefer workers who can do a variety of tasks, reinforcing iron and rebar workers with additional skills, such as welding, should have the best job opportunities. Those with prior military service are also viewed favorably during initial hiring. Like employment of many other construction workers, employment of reinforcing iron and rebar workers is sensitive to fluctuations in the economy. Workers may experience periods of unemployment when the overall level of construction falls. However, shortages of workers may occur in some areas during peak periods of building activity. Employment opportunities should be greatest in metropolitan areas, where most large commercial and multifamily buildings are constructed.

Position and secure steel bars or mesh in concrete forms in order to reinforce concrete. Cut rods to required lengths, using metal shears, hacksaws, bar cutters, or acetylene torches. Determine quantities, sizes, shapes, and locations of reinforcing rods from blueprints, sketches, or oral instructions. Space and fasten together rods in forms according to blueprints, using wire and pliers. Place blocks under rebar to hold the bars off the deck when reinforcing floors. Bend steel rods with hand tools and rodbending machines, and weld them with arc-welding equipment. Cut and fit wire mesh or fabric, using hooked rods, and position fabric or mesh in concrete to reinforce concrete. Position and secure steel bars, rods, cables, or mesh in concrete forms, using fasteners, rod-bending machines, blowtorches, and hand tools.

Education/Training Required: High school diploma or equivalent. **Education and Training Program:** Construction Trades, Other. **Knowledge/Courses—Building and Construction:** Materials, methods, and the tools involved in the construction or repair of houses, buildings, or other structures such as highways and roads. **Mechanical Devices:** Machines and tools, including their designs, uses, repair, and maintenance. **Public Safety and Security:** Relevant equipment, policies, procedures, and strategies to promote effective local, state, or national security operations for the protection of people, data, property, and institutions. **Transportation:** Principles and methods for moving people or goods by air, rail, sea, or road, including the relative costs and benefits. **Work Experience Needed:** None. **On-the-Job Training Needed:** Apprenticeship. **Certification/Licensure:** None.

Personality Type: Realistic-Conventional-Investigative. **Career Cluster:** 02 Architecture and Construction. **Career Pathway:** 02.2 Construction. **Other Jobs in This Pathway:** Boilermakers; Brickmasons and Blockmasons; Carpet Installers; Cement Masons and Concrete Finishers; Construction and Building Inspectors; Construction and Related Workers, All Other; Construction Carpenters; Construction Laborers; Construction Managers; Continuous Mining Machine Operators; Cost Estimators; Crane and Tower Operators; Dredge Operators; Drywall and Ceiling Tile Installers; Earth Drillers, Except Oil and Gas; Electrical Power-Line Installers and Repairers; Electricians; Electromechanical Equipment Assemblers; Engineering Technicians, Except Drafters, All Other; Excavating and Loading Machine and Dragline Operators; Explosives Workers, Ordnance Handling Experts, and Blasters; Extraction Workers, All Other; First-Line Supervisors of Construction Trades and Extraction Workers; Floor Layers, Except Carpet, Wood, and Hard Tiles; Floor Sanders and Finishers; Glaziers; Heating and Air Conditioning Mechanics and Installers; Helpers, Construction Trades, All Other; others.

Skills—Equipment Selection: Determining the kind of tools and equipment needed to do a job. **Operation and Control:** Controlling operations of equipment or systems. **Repairing:** Repairing machines or systems using the needed tools. **Equipment Maintenance:** Performing routine maintenance on equipment and determining when and what kind of maintenance is needed. **Troubleshooting:** Determining causes of operating errors and deciding what to do about them. **Quality Control Analysis:** Conducting tests and inspections of products, services, or processes to evaluate quality or performance. **Operation Monitoring:** Watching gauges, dials, or other indicators to make sure a machine is working properly. **Technology Design:** Generating or adapting equipment and technology to serve user needs.

Work Environment: Outdoors; standing; climbing; walking and running; kneeling, crouching, stooping, or crawling; using hands; bending or twisting the body; repetitive motions; noise; very hot or cold; contaminants; high places; hazardous equipment; minor burns, cuts, bites, or stings.

Reservation and Transportation Ticket Agents and Travel Clerks

- Annual Earnings: $33,300
- Earnings Growth Potential: Medium (39.2%)
- Growth: 5.8%
- Annual Job Openings: 3,080
- Self-Employed: 0.3%

Considerations for Job Outlook: Employment growth will vary by specialty. Projected employment change is most rapid for interviewers and correspondence clerks.

Make and confirm reservations for transportation or lodging, or sell transportation tickets. Plan routes, itineraries, and accommodation details, and compute fares and fees, using schedules, rate books, and computers. Make and confirm reservations for transportation and accommodations, using telephones, faxes, mail, and computers. Prepare customer invoices, and accept payment. Answer inquiries regarding such information as schedules, accommodations, procedures, and policies. Assemble and issue required documentation such as tickets, travel insurance policies, and itineraries. Determine whether space is available on travel dates requested by customers, and assign requested spaces when available. Inform clients of essential travel information such as travel times, transportation connections, and medical and visa requirements. Maintain computerized inventories of available passenger space, and provide information on space reserved or available. Confer with customers to determine their service requirements and travel preferences. Examine passenger documentation to determine destinations and to assign boarding passes. Provide boarding or disembarking assistance to passengers needing special assistance. Check baggage and cargo, and direct passengers to designated locations for loading. Announce arrival and departure information, using public-address systems. Trace lost, delayed, or misdirected baggage for customers. Promote particular destinations, tour packages, and other travel services. Provide clients with assistance in preparing required travel documents and forms. Open and close information facilities, and keep them clean during operation. Provide customers with travel suggestions and information such as guides, directories, brochures, and maps. Contact customers or travel agents to advise them of travel conveyance changes or to confirm reservations. Contact motel, hotel, resort, and travel operators to obtain current advertising literature.

Education/Training Required: High school diploma or equivalent. **Education and Training Programs:** Selling Skills and Sales Operations; Tourism and Travel Services Marketing Operations; Tourism Promotion Operations. **Knowledge/Courses—Customer and Personal Service:** Principles and processes for providing customer and personal services. This includes customer needs assessment, meeting quality standards for services, and evaluation of customer satisfaction. **Transportation:** Principles and methods for moving people or goods by air, rail, sea, or road, including the relative costs and benefits. **Sales and Marketing:** Principles and methods for showing, promoting, and selling products or services. This includes marketing strategy and tactics, product demonstration, sales techniques, and sales control systems. **Clerical Practices:** Administrative and clerical procedures and systems such as word processing, managing files and records, stenography and transcription, designing forms, and other office procedures and terminology. **Work Experience Needed:** None. **On-the-Job Training Needed:** Short-term on-the-job training. **Certification/Licensure:** None.

Personality Type: Conventional-Enterprising-Social. **Career Clusters:** 09 Hospitality and Tourism; 14

R

Marketing, Sales, and Service. **Career Pathways:** 09.3 Travel and Tourism; 14.2 Professional Sales and Marketing. **Other Jobs in These Pathways:** Appraisers, Real Estate; Assessors; Cashiers; Counter and Rental Clerks; Demonstrators and Product Promoters; Door-To-Door Sales Workers, News and Street Vendors, and Related Workers; Driver/Sales Workers; Energy Brokers; First-Line Supervisors of Non-Retail Sales Workers; First-Line Supervisors of Retail Sales Workers; Food Service Managers; Gaming Change Persons and Booth Cashiers; Hotel, Motel, and Resort Desk Clerks; Interior Designers; Lodging Managers; Managers, All Other; Marketing Managers; Marking Clerks; Meeting, Convention, and Event Planners; Merchandise Displayers and Window Trimmers; Models; Online Merchants; Order Fillers, Wholesale and Retail Sales; Parts Salespersons; Property, Real Estate, and Community Association Managers; Real Estate Brokers; Real Estate Sales Agents; Retail Salespersons; Sales and Related Workers, All Other; Sales Engineers; Sales Representatives, Services, All Other; others.

Skills—Service Orientation: Actively looking for ways to help people. **Negotiation:** Bringing others together and trying to reconcile differences. **Active Listening:** Giving full attention to what other people are saying, taking time to understand the points being made, asking questions as appropriate, and not interrupting at inappropriate times. **Persuasion:** Persuading others to change their minds or behavior. **Programming:** Writing computer programs for various purposes. **Mathematics:** Using mathematics to solve problems. **Speaking:** Talking to others to convey information effectively.

Work Environment: Indoors; sitting; using hands; repetitive motions; noise.

Residential Advisors

- ⊙ Annual Earnings: $24,540
- ⊙ Earnings Growth Potential: Low (29.7%)
- ⊙ Growth: 24.9%
- ⊙ Annual Job Openings: 4,570
- ⊙ Self-Employed: 0.6%

Considerations for Job Outlook: Rapid employment growth is projected.

Coordinate activities in resident facilities in secondary and college dormitories, group homes, or similar establishments. Enforce rules and regulations to ensure the smooth and orderly operation of dormitory programs. Provide emergency first aid and summon medical assistance when necessary. Mediate interpersonal problems between residents. Administer, coordinate, or recommend disciplinary and corrective actions. Communicate with other staff to resolve problems with individual students. Counsel students in the handling of issues such as family, financial, and educational problems. Make regular rounds to ensure that residents and areas are safe and secure. Observe students to detect and report unusual behavior. Determine the need for facility maintenance and repair, and notify appropriate personnel. Collaborate with counselors to develop counseling programs that address the needs of individual students. Develop program plans for individuals or assist in plan development. Hold regular meetings with each assigned unit. Provide requested information on students' progress and the development of case plans. Confer with medical personnel to better understand the backgrounds and needs of individual residents. Answer telephones, and route calls or deliver messages. Supervise students' housekeeping work to ensure that it is done properly. Develop and coordinate educational programs for residents. Direct and participate in on- and off-campus recreational activities for residents of institutions, boarding schools, fraternities or sororities, children's homes, or similar establishments. Assign rooms to students. Process contract cancellations for students who are unable to follow residence hall policies and procedures. Sort and distribute mail. Supervise the activities of housekeeping personnel. Order supplies for facilities. Chaperone group-sponsored trips and social functions. Compile information such as residents' daily activities and the quantities of supplies used to prepare required reports. Accompany and supervise students during meals.

Education/Training Required: Some college, no degree. **Education and Training Program:** Hotel/Motel Administration/Management. **Knowledge/Courses—Therapy and Counseling:** Principles, methods, and procedures for diagnosis, treatment, and rehabilitation of physical and mental dysfunctions, and for career counseling and guidance. **Psychology:** Human behavior and performance; individual differences in ability, personality, and interests; learning and motivation; psychological research methods; and the assessment and treatment of behavioral and affective disorders. **Sociology and Anthropology:** Group behavior and dynamics, societal trends and influences, human migrations, ethnicity, and cultures and their history and origins. **Philosophy and Theology:** Different philosophical systems and religions. This includes their basic principles, values, ethics, ways of thinking, customs, practices, and their impact on human culture. **Customer and Personal Service:** Principles and processes for providing customer and personal services. This includes customer needs assessment, meeting quality standards for services, and evaluation of customer satisfaction. **Public Safety and Security:** Relevant equipment, policies, procedures, and strategies to promote effective local, state, or national security operations for the protection of people, data, property, and institutions. **Work Experience Needed:** Less than 1 year. **On-the-Job Training Needed:** Short-term on-the-job training. **Certification/Licensure:** None.

Personality Type: Social-Enterprising-Conventional. **Career Cluster:** 09 Hospitality and Tourism. **Career Pathway:** 09.2 Lodging. **Other Jobs in This Pathway:** Building Cleaning Workers, All Other; First-Line Supervisors of Housekeeping and Janitorial Workers; Food Service Managers; Janitors and Cleaners, Except Maids and Housekeeping Cleaners; Lodging Managers; Maids and Housekeeping Cleaners.

Skills—Management of Financial Resources: Determining how money will be spent to get the work done and accounting for these expenditures. **Management of Material Resources:** Obtaining and seeing to the appropriate use of equipment, facilities, and materials needed to do certain work. **Negotiation:** Bringing others together and trying to reconcile differences. **Active Listening:** Giving full attention to what other people are saying, taking time to understand the points being made, asking questions as appropriate, and not interrupting at inappropriate times. **Critical Thinking:** Using logic and reasoning to identify the strengths and weaknesses of alternative solutions, conclusions, or approaches to problems. **Systems Analysis:** Determining how a system should work and how changes in conditions, operations, and the environment will affect outcomes. **Persuasion:** Persuading others to change their minds or behavior. **Management of Personnel Resources:** Motivating, developing, and directing people as they work, identifying the best people for the job.

Work Environment: Indoors; noise.

Respiratory Therapists

- ⊙ Annual Earnings: $55,250
- ⊙ Earnings Growth Potential: Low (26.4%)
- ⊙ Growth: 27.7%
- ⊙ Annual Job Openings: 5,270
- ⊙ Self-Employed: 1.4%

Considerations for Job Outlook: Respiratory therapists with certification or a bachelor's degree will have the best job prospects.

Assess, treat, and care for patients with breathing disorders. Set up and operate devices such as mechanical ventilators, therapeutic gas-administration apparatus, environmental control systems, and aerosol generators, following specified parameters of treatment. Provide emergency care, including artificial respiration, external cardiac massage, and assistance with cardiopulmonary resuscitation. Determine requirements for treatment, such as type, method, and duration of therapy; precautions to be taken; and medication and dosages, compatible with physicians' orders. Monitor patients' physiological responses to therapy, such as vital signs, arterial blood gases, and blood chemistry changes, and consult with physicians if adverse reactions occur. Read prescription, measure arterial blood gases, and review patient information to assess patient condition. Work as part of a team of physicians, nurses, and other health-care professionals to manage patient care. Enforce safety rules, and ensure careful adherence to physicians' orders. Maintain charts that contain patients' pertinent identification and therapy information. Inspect, clean, test, and maintain respiratory therapy equipment to ensure equipment is functioning safely and efficiently, ordering repairs when necessary. Educate patients and their families about patients' conditions, and teach appropriate disease management techniques such as breathing exercises and the use of medications and respiratory equipment. Explain treatment procedures to patients to gain cooperation and allay fears.

Education/Training Required: Associate degree. **Education and Training Program:** Respiratory Care Therapy/Therapist. **Knowledge/Courses—Medicine and Dentistry:** The information and techniques needed to diagnose and treat human injuries, diseases, and deformities. This includes symptoms, treatment alternatives, drug properties and interactions, and preventive health-care measures. **Biology:** Plant and animal organisms and their tissues, cells, functions, interdependencies, and interactions with each other and the environment. **Customer and Personal Service:** Principles and processes for providing customer and personal services. This includes customer needs assessment, meeting quality standards for services, and evaluation of customer satisfaction. **Therapy and Counseling:** Principles, methods, and procedures for diagnosis, treatment, and rehabilitation of physical and mental dysfunctions, and for career counseling and guidance. **Psychology:** Human behavior and performance; individual differences in ability, personality, and interests; learning and motivation; psychological research methods; and the assessment and treatment of behavioral and affective disorders. **Chemistry:** The chemical composition, structure, and properties of substances and of the chemical processes and transformations that they undergo. This includes uses of chemicals and their danger signs, production techniques, and disposal methods. **Work Experience Needed:** None. **On-the-Job Training Needed:** None. **Certification/Licensure:** Licensure.

Personality Type: Social-Investigative-Realistic. **Career Cluster:** 08 Health Science. **Career Pathway:** 08.1 Therapeutic Services. **Other Jobs in This Pathway:** Acupuncturists; Allergists and Immunologists; Anesthesiologists; Art Therapists; Chiropractors; Clinical Psychologists; Community and Social Service Specialists, All Other; Counseling Psychologists; Counselors, All Other; Dental Assistants; Dental Hygienists; Dentists, All Other Specialists; Dentists, General; Dermatologists; Diagnostic Medical Sonographers; Dietetic Technicians; Dietitians and Nutritionists; Family and General Practitioners; Health Diagnosing and Treating Practitioners, All Other; Health Specialties Teachers, Postsecondary; Health Technologists and Technicians, All Other; Healthcare Practitioners and Technical Workers, All Other; Healthcare Support Workers, All Other; Home Health Aides; Hospitalists; Industrial-Organizational Psychologists; Internists, General; Licensed Practical and Licensed Vocational Nurses; Life, Physical, and Social Science Technicians, All Other; Low Vision Therapists, Orientation and Mobility Specialists, and Vision Rehabilitation Therapists; others.

Skills—Science: Using scientific rules and methods to solve problems. **Repairing:** Repairing machines or systems using the needed tools. **Equipment Maintenance:**

Performing routine maintenance on equipment and determining when and what kind of maintenance is needed. **Operation and Control:** Controlling operations of equipment or systems. **Equipment Selection:** Determining the kind of tools and equipment needed to do a job. **Quality Control Analysis:** Conducting tests and inspections of products, services, or processes to evaluate quality or performance. **Operation Monitoring:** Watching gauges, dials, or other indicators to make sure a machine is working properly. **Service Orientation:** Actively looking for ways to help people.

Work Environment: Indoors; standing; walking and running; using hands; repetitive motions; contaminants; exposed to radiation; exposed to disease or infections.

Riggers

- ⊙ Annual Earnings: $43,020
- ⊙ Earnings Growth Potential: Medium (38.9%)
- ⊙ Growth: 10.5%
- ⊙ Annual Job Openings: 440
- ⊙ Self-Employed: 7.9%

Considerations for Job Outlook: A small increase is expected as growth in oil and gas extraction increases the demand for rigging.

Set up or repair rigging for construction projects, manufacturing plants, logging yards, ships, and shipyards, or for the entertainment industry. Signal or verbally direct workers engaged in hoisting and moving loads, in order to ensure safety of workers and materials. Attach loads to rigging to provide support or prepare them for moving, using hand and power tools. Install ground rigging for yarding lines, attaching chokers to logs and then to the lines. Clean and dress machine surfaces and component parts. Tilt, dip, and turn suspended loads to maneuver over, under, and/or around obstacles, using multipoint suspension techniques. Test rigging to ensure safety and reliability. Manipulate rigging lines, hoists, and pulling gear to move or support materials such as heavy equipment, ships, or theatrical sets. Fabricate, set up, and repair rigging, supporting structures, hoists, and pulling gear, using hand and power tools. Dismantle and store rigging equipment after use. Attach pulleys and blocks to fixed overhead structures such as beams, ceilings, and gin pole booms, using bolts and clamps. Align, level, and anchor machinery. Select gear such as cables, pulleys, and winches, according to load weights and sizes, facilities, and work schedules. Control movement of heavy equipment through narrow openings or confined spaces, using chainfalls, gin poles, gallows frames, and other equipment.

Education/Training Required: High school diploma or equivalent. **Education and Training Program:** Construction/Heavy Equipment/Earthmoving Equipment Operation. **Knowledge/Courses—Mechanical Devices:** Machines and tools, including their designs, uses, repair, and maintenance. **Building and Construction:** Materials, methods, and the tools involved in the construction or repair of houses, buildings, or other structures such as highways and roads. **Design:** Design techniques, tools, and principles involved in production of precision technical plans, blueprints, drawings, and models. **Production and Processing:** Raw materials, production processes, quality control, costs, and other techniques for maximizing the effective manufacture and distribution of goods. **Transportation:** Principles and methods for moving people or goods by air, rail, sea, or road, including the relative costs and benefits. **Engineering and Technology:** The practical application of engineering science and technology. This includes applying principles, techniques, procedures, and equipment to the design and production of various goods and services. **Work Experience Needed:** None. **On-the-Job Training Needed:** Short-term on-the-job training. **Certification/Licensure:** None.

Personality Type: Realistic-Conventional-Investigative. **Career Cluster:** 02 Architecture and Construction. **Career Pathway:** 02.2 Construction. **Other Jobs in This Pathway:** Boilermakers; Brickmasons and Blockmasons; Carpet Installers; Cement Masons and Concrete Finishers; Construction and Building Inspectors; Construction and Related Workers, All Other; Construction Carpenters; Construction Laborers; Construction Managers; Continuous Mining Machine Operators; Cost Estimators; Crane and Tower Operators; Dredge Operators; Drywall and Ceiling Tile Installers; Earth Drillers, Except Oil and Gas; Electrical Power-Line Installers and Repairers; Electricians; Electromechanical Equipment Assemblers; Engineering Technicians, Except Drafters, All Other; Excavating and Loading Machine and Dragline Operators; Explosives Workers, Ordnance Handling Experts, and Blasters; Extraction Workers, All Other; First-Line Supervisors of Construction Trades and Extraction Workers; Floor Layers, Except Carpet, Wood, and Hard Tiles; Floor Sanders and Finishers; Glaziers; Heating and Air Conditioning Mechanics and Installers; Helpers, Construction Trades, All Other; others.

Skills—Equipment Selection: Determining the kind of tools and equipment needed to do a job. **Repairing:** Repairing machines or systems using the needed tools. **Installation:** Installing equipment, machines, wiring, or programs to meet specifications. **Equipment Maintenance:** Performing routine maintenance on equipment and determining when and what kind of maintenance is needed. **Operation and Control:** Controlling operations of equipment or systems. **Troubleshooting:** Determining causes of operating errors and deciding what to do about them. **Quality Control Analysis:** Conducting tests and inspections of products, services, or processes to evaluate quality or performance. **Operation Monitoring:** Watching gauges, dials, or other indicators to make sure a machine is working properly.

Work Environment: More often outdoors than indoors; standing; walking and running; using hands; bending or twisting the body; noise; very hot or cold; bright or inadequate lighting; contaminants; cramped work space; high places; hazardous equipment; minor burns, cuts, bites, or stings.

Rolling Machine Setters, Operators, and Tenders, Metal and Plastic

- ⊙ Annual Earnings: $36,920
- ⊙ Earnings Growth Potential: Medium (38.2%)
- ⊙ Growth: 8.1%
- ⊙ Annual Job Openings: 880
- ⊙ Self-Employed: 0.0%

Considerations for Job Outlook: Despite slower-than-average employment growth, a number of these jobs are expected to become available for highly skilled workers because of an expected increase in retirements, primarily of baby boomers, in the coming years. In addition, workers who have a thorough background in machine operations, certifications from industry associations, and a good working knowledge of the properties of metals and plastics should have the best job opportunities.

R

Set up, operate, or tend machines to roll steel or plastic forming bends, beads, knurls, rolls, or plate or to flatten, temper, or reduce gauge of material. Adjust and correct machine setups to reduce thicknesses, reshape products, and eliminate product defects. Monitor machine cycles and mill operation to detect jamming and to ensure that products conform to specifications. Examine, inspect, and measure raw materials and finished products to verify conformance to specifications. Read rolling orders, blueprints, and mill schedules to determine setup specifications, work sequences, product dimensions, and installation procedures. Manipulate controls and observe dial indicators in order to monitor, adjust, and regulate speeds of machine mechanisms. Start operation of rolling and milling machines to flatten, temper, form, and reduce sheet metal sections and to produce steel strips. Thread or feed sheets or rods through rolling mechanisms, or start and control mechanisms that automatically feed steel into rollers. Set distance points between rolls, guides, meters, and stops, according to specifications. Position, align, and secure arbors, spindles, coils, mandrels, dies, and slitting knives. Direct and train other workers to change rolls, operate mill equipment, remove coils and cobbles, and band and load material. Fill oil cups, adjust valves, and observe gauges to control flow of metal coolants and lubricants onto workpieces. Record mill production on schedule sheets. Install equipment such as guides, guards, gears, cooling equipment, and rolls, using hand tools. Signal and assist other workers to remove and position equipment, fill hoppers, and feed materials into machines. Calculate draft space and roll speed for each mill stand in order to plan rolling sequences and specified dimensions and tempers. Select rolls, dies, roll stands, and chucks from data charts in order to form specified contours and to fabricate products. Activate shears and grinders to trim workpieces. Remove scratches and polish roll surfaces, using polishing stones and electric buffers.

Education/Training Required: High school diploma or equivalent. **Education and Training Programs:** Machine Tool Technology/Machinist; Sheet Metal Technology/Sheetworking. **Knowledge/Courses—Mechanical Devices:** Machines and tools, including their designs, uses, repair, and maintenance. **Production and Processing:** Raw materials, production processes, quality control, costs, and other techniques for maximizing the effective manufacture and distribution of goods. **Education and Training:** Principles and methods for curriculum and training design, teaching and instruction for individuals and groups, and the measurement of training effects. **Work Experience Needed:** None. **On-the-Job Training Needed:** Moderate-term on-the-job training. **Certification/Licensure:** None.

Personality Type: Realistic-Conventional. **Career Cluster:** 13 Manufacturing. **Career Pathway:** 13.1 Production. **Other Jobs in This Pathway:** Adhesive Bonding Machine Operators and Tenders; Assemblers and Fabricators, All Other; Avionics Technicians; Cabinetmakers and Bench Carpenters; Cleaning, Washing, and Metal Pickling Equipment Operators and Tenders; Coating, Painting, and Spraying Machine Setters, Operators, and Tenders; Computer-Controlled Machine Tool Operators, Metal and Plastic; Cooling and Freezing Equipment Operators and Tenders; Cost Estimators; Crushing, Grinding, and Polishing Machine Setters, Operators, and Tenders; Cutters and Trimmers, Hand; Cutting and Slicing Machine Setters, Operators, and Tenders; Cutting, Punching, and Press Machine Setters, Operators, and Tenders, Metal and Plastic; Drilling and Boring Machine Tool Setters, Operators, and Tenders, Metal and Plastic; Extruding and Drawing Machine Setters, Operators, and Tenders, Metal and Plastic; Extruding and Forming Machine Setters, Operators, and Tenders, Synthetic and Glass Fibers; others.

Skills—Equipment Maintenance: Performing routine maintenance on equipment and determining when and what kind of maintenance is needed. **Operation and Control:** Controlling operations of equipment or systems. **Repairing:** Repairing machines or systems using the needed tools. **Operation Monitoring:** Watching gauges, dials, or other indicators to make sure a machine is working properly. **Quality Control Analysis:** Conducting tests and inspections of products, services, or processes to evaluate quality or performance. **Troubleshooting:** Determining causes of operating errors and deciding what to do about them. **Equipment Selection:** Determining the kind of tools and equipment needed to do a job. **Installation:** Installing equipment, machines, wiring, or programs to meet specifications.

Work Environment: Standing; walking and running; using hands; bending or twisting the body; repetitive motions; noise; very hot or cold; bright or inadequate lighting; contaminants; cramped work space; hazardous conditions; hazardous equipment; minor burns, cuts, bites, or stings.

Roofers

- ⊙ Annual Earnings: $35,280
- ⊙ Earnings Growth Potential: Medium (36.4%)
- ⊙ Growth: 17.8%
- ⊙ Annual Job Openings: 5,250
- ⊙ Self-Employed: 26.5%

Considerations for Job Outlook: Job opportunities for roofers will occur primarily because of the need to replace workers who leave the occupation. The proportion of roofers who leave the occupation each year is higher than in most construction trades—roofing work is hot, strenuous, and dirty, and a considerable number of workers treat roofing as a temporary job until they find other work. Some roofers leave the occupation to go into other construction trades. Jobs are generally easier to find during spring and summer. As in many other construction occupations, employment of roofers is somewhat sensitive to fluctuations in the economy. Demand for roofers is less vulnerable to downturns than demand for other construction trades because much roofing work consists of repair and reroofing, in addition to new construction.

Cover roofs of structures with shingles, slate, asphalt, aluminum, wood, or related materials. Install, repair, or replace single-ply roofing systems, using waterproof sheet materials such as modified plastics, elastomeric, or other asphaltic compositions. Apply alternate layers of hot asphalt or tar and roofing paper to roofs, according to specification. Apply gravel or pebbles over top layers of roofs, using rakes or stiff-bristled brooms. Cement or nail flashing strips of metal or shingle over joints to make them watertight. Punch holes in slate, tile, terra cotta, or wooden shingles, using punches and hammers. Hammer and chisel away rough spots or remove them with rubbing bricks to prepare surfaces for waterproofing. Align roofing materials with edges of roofs. Mop or pour hot asphalt or tar onto roof bases. Apply plastic coatings and membranes, fiberglass, or felt over sloped roofs before applying shingles. Install vapor barriers and layers of insulation on the roof decks of flat roofs, and seal the seams. Install partially overlapping layers of material over roof insulation surfaces, determining distance of roofing material overlap using chalk lines, gauges on shingling hatchets, or lines on shingles. Inspect problem roofs to determine the best procedures for repairing them. Glaze top layers to make a smooth finish, or

embed gravel in the bitumen for rough surfaces. Cut roofing paper to size using knives; and nail or staple roofing paper to roofs in overlapping strips to form bases for other materials. Cut felt, shingles, and strips of flashing; and fit them into angles formed by walls, vents, and intersecting roof surfaces. Cover roofs and exterior walls of structures with slate, asphalt, aluminum, wood, gravel, gypsum, and related materials, using brushes, knives, punches, hammers and other tools. Clean and maintain equipment. Cover exposed nailheads with roofing cement or caulking to prevent water leakage and rust.

Education/Training Required: Less than high school. **Education and Training Program:** Roofer Training. **Knowledge/Courses—Building and Construction:** Materials, methods, and the tools involved in the construction or repair of houses, buildings, or other structures such as highways and roads. **Design:** Design techniques, tools, and principles involved in production of precision technical plans, blueprints, drawings, and models. **Engineering and Technology:** The practical application of engineering science and technology. This includes applying principles, techniques, procedures, and equipment to the design and production of various goods and services. **Transportation:** Principles and methods for moving people or goods by air, rail, sea, or road, including the relative costs and benefits. **Work Experience Needed:** None. **On-the-Job Training Needed:** Moderate-term on-the-job training. **Certification/Licensure:** None.

Personality Type: Realistic-Conventional. **Career Cluster:** 02 Architecture and Construction. **Career Pathway:** 02.2 Construction. **Other Jobs in This Pathway:** Boilermakers; Brickmasons and Blockmasons; Carpet Installers; Cement Masons and Concrete Finishers; Construction and Building Inspectors; Construction and Related Workers, All Other; Construction Carpenters; Construction Laborers; Construction Managers; Continuous Mining Machine Operators; Cost Estimators; Crane and Tower Operators; Dredge Operators; Drywall and Ceiling Tile Installers; Earth Drillers, Except Oil and Gas; Electrical Power-Line Installers and Repairers; Electricians; Electromechanical Equipment Assemblers; Engineering Technicians, Except Drafters, All Other; Excavating and Loading Machine and Dragline Operators; Explosives Workers, Ordnance Handling Experts, and Blasters; Extraction Workers, All Other; First-Line Supervisors of Construction Trades and Extraction Workers; Floor Layers, Except Carpet, Wood,

R

and Hard Tiles; Floor Sanders and Finishers; Glaziers; Heating and Air Conditioning Mechanics and Installers; Helpers, Construction Trades, All Other; others.

Skills—Operation and Control: Controlling operations of equipment or systems. **Operation Monitoring:** Watching gauges, dials, or other indicators to make sure a machine is working properly. **Coordination:** Adjusting actions in relation to others' actions. **Installation:** Installing equipment, machines, wiring, or programs to meet specifications.

Work Environment: Outdoors; standing; climbing; walking and running; kneeling, crouching, stooping, or crawling; using hands; bending or twisting the body; repetitive motions; noise; very hot or cold; bright or inadequate lighting; contaminants; cramped work space; high places; hazardous conditions; hazardous equipment; minor burns, cuts, bites, or stings.

Rotary Drill Operators, Oil and Gas

- ⊙ Annual Earnings: $51,310
- ⊙ Earnings Growth Potential: Medium (38.8%)
- ⊙ Growth: 7.1%
- ⊙ Annual Job Openings: 640
- ⊙ Self-Employed: 2.2%

Considerations for Job Outlook: Demand for oil and gas workers will depend on the demand for the products and services of two industries in particular: oil and gas extraction and support for mining activities. Because of higher prices for resources, oil and gas companies are more likely to drill in deeper waters and harsher environments than in the past. These complex operations require more workers. Higher prices will also encourage oil and gas companies to return to existing wells to try new extraction methods, thereby increasing demand for oil and gas workers. Also, changes in policy could expand exploration and drilling for oil and natural gas in currently protected areas, potentially boosting employment. However, new production technologies are expected to dampen overall demand for oil and gas workers.

Set up or operate a variety of drills to remove underground oil and gas, or remove core samples for testing during oil and gas exploration. Train crews, and introduce procedures to make drill work more safe and effective.

Observe pressure gauge and move throttles and levers in order to control the speed of rotary tables, and to regulate pressure of tools at bottoms of boreholes. Count sections of drill rod in order to determine depths of boreholes. Push levers and brake pedals in order to control gasoline, diesel, electric, or steam draw works that lower and raise drill pipes and casings in and out of wells. Connect sections of drill pipe, using hand tools and powered wrenches and tongs. Maintain records of footage drilled, location and nature of strata penetrated, materials and tools used, services rendered, and time required. Maintain and adjust machinery to ensure proper performance. Start and examine operation of slush pumps in order to ensure circulation and consistency of drilling fluid or mud in well. Locate and recover lost or broken bits, casings, and drill pipes from wells, using special tools. Weigh clay, and mix with water and chemicals to make drilling mud. Direct rig crews in drilling and other activities, such as setting up rigs and completing or servicing wells. Monitor progress of drilling operations, and select and change drill bits according to the nature of strata, using hand tools. Repair or replace defective parts of machinery, such as rotary drill rigs, water trucks, air compressors, and pumps, using hand tools. Clean and oil pulleys, blocks, and cables. Bolt together pump and engine parts, and connect tanks and flow lines. Remove core samples during drilling in order to determine the nature of the strata being drilled. Cap wells with packers, or turn valves, in order to regulate outflow of oil from wells. Line drilled holes with pipes, and install all necessary hardware, in order to prepare new wells. Position and prepare truck-mounted derricks at drilling areas that are specified on field maps. Plug observation wells, and restore sites.

Education/Training Required: Less than high school. **Education and Training Program:** Well Drilling/Driller. **Knowledge/Courses—Mechanical Devices:** Machines and tools, including their designs, uses, repair, and maintenance. **Chemistry:** The chemical composition, structure, and properties of substances and of the chemical processes and transformations that they undergo. This includes uses of chemicals and their danger signs, production techniques, and disposal methods. **Personnel and Human Resources:** Principles and procedures for personnel recruitment, selection, training, compensation and benefits, labor relations and negotiation, and personnel information systems. **Transportation:** Principles and methods for moving people or goods by air, rail, sea, or road, including the relative costs and benefits. **Mathematics:** Arithmetic, algebra, geometry, calculus, statistics, and their applications. **Physics:** Physical principles, laws, their interrelationships, and applications to understanding fluid, material, and atmospheric dynamics, and mechanical, electrical, atomic, and subatomic structures and processes. **Work Experience Needed:** None. **On-the-Job Training Needed:** Moderate-term on-the-job training. **Certification/Licensure:** None.

Personality Type: Realistic-Enterprising-Conventional. **Career Cluster:** 01 Agriculture, Food, and Natural Resources. **Career Pathway:** 01.5 Natural Resources Systems. **Other Jobs in This Pathway:** Biological Science Teachers, Postsecondary; Climate Change Analysts; Conveyor Operators and Tenders; Derrick Operators, Oil and Gas; Engineering Technicians, Except Drafters, All Other; Environmental Economists; Environmental Restoration Planners; Environmental Science and Protection Technicians, Including Health; Environmental Science Teachers, Postsecondary; Environmental Scientists and Specialists, Including Health; Fallers; Fish and Game Wardens; Fishers and Related Fishing Workers; Forest and Conservation Technicians; Forest and Conservation Workers; Foresters; Forestry and Conservation Science Teachers, Postsecondary; Gas Compressor and Gas Pumping Station Operators; Geological Sample Test Technicians; Geophysical Data Technicians; Helpers—Extraction Workers; Industrial Ecologists; Industrial Truck and Tractor Operators; Loading Machine Operators, Underground Mining; Log Graders and Scalers; Logging Equipment Operators; Logging Workers, All Other; others.

Skills—Repairing: Repairing machines or systems using the needed tools. **Equipment Maintenance:** Performing routine maintenance on equipment and determining when and what kind of maintenance is needed. **Operation and Control:** Controlling operations of equipment or systems. **Troubleshooting:** Determining causes of operating errors and deciding what to do about them. **Operation Monitoring:** Watching gauges, dials, or other indicators to make sure a machine is working properly. **Equipment Selection:** Determining the kind of tools and equipment needed to do a job. **Quality Control Analysis:** Conducting tests and inspections of products, services, or processes to evaluate quality or performance. **Management of Personnel Resources:** Motivating, developing, and directing people as they work, identifying the best people for the job.

Work Environment: Outdoors; standing; using hands; bending or twisting the body; repetitive motions; noise;

very hot or cold; bright or inadequate lighting; contaminants; cramped work space; whole-body vibration; high places; hazardous conditions; hazardous equipment; minor burns, cuts, bites, or stings.

Roustabouts, Oil and Gas

- Annual Earnings: $32,980
- Earnings Growth Potential: Low (33.7%)
- Growth: 8.3%
- Annual Job Openings: 1,550
- Self-Employed: 0.0%

Considerations for Job Outlook: Demand for oil and gas workers will depend on the demand for the products and services of two industries in particular: oil and gas extraction and support for mining activities. Because of higher prices for resources, oil and gas companies are more likely to drill in deeper waters and harsher environments than in the past. These complex operations require more workers. Higher prices will also encourage oil and gas companies to return to existing wells to try new extraction methods, thereby increasing demand for oil and gas workers. Also, changes in policy could expand exploration and drilling for oil and natural gas in currently protected areas, potentially boosting employment. However, new production technologies are expected to dampen overall demand for oil and gas workers.

Assemble or repair oil field equipment using hand and power tools. Unscrew or tighten pipes, casing, tubing, and pump rods, using hand and power wrenches and tongs. Bolt together pump and engine parts. Move pipes to and from trucks, using truck winches and motorized lifts or by hand. Keep pipe deck and main deck areas clean and tidy. Walk flow lines to locate leaks, using electronic detectors and by making visual inspections, and repair the leaks. Clean up spilled oil by bailing it into barrels. Dismantle and repair oil field machinery, boilers, and steam engine parts, using hand tools and power tools. Dig drainage ditches around wells and storage tanks. Guide cranes to move loads about decks. Supply equipment to rig floors as requested, and provide assistance to roughnecks. Dig holes, set forms, and mix and pour concrete into forms to make foundations for wood or steel derricks. Cut down and remove trees and brush to clear drill sites, to reduce

473

fire hazards, and to make way for roads to sites. Bolt or nail together wood or steel frameworks to erect derricks.

Education/Training Required: Less than high school. **Education and Training Program:** Heavy/Industrial Equipment Maintenance Technologies, Other. **Knowledge/Courses—Building and Construction:** Materials, methods, and the tools involved in the construction or repair of houses, buildings, or other structures such as highways and roads. **Mechanical Devices:** Machines and tools, including their designs, uses, repair, and maintenance. **Foreign Language:** The structure and content of a foreign (non-English) language including the meaning and spelling of words, rules of composition and grammar, and pronunciation. **Physics:** Physical principles, laws, their interrelationships, and applications to understanding fluid, material, and atmospheric dynamics, and mechanical, electrical, atomic, and subatomic structures and processes. **Transportation:** Principles and methods for moving people or goods by air, rail, sea, or road, including the relative costs and benefits. **Chemistry:** The chemical composition, structure, and properties of substances and of the chemical processes and transformations that they undergo. This includes uses of chemicals and their danger signs, production techniques, and disposal methods. **Work Experience Needed:** None. **On-the-Job Training Needed:** Moderate-term on-the-job training. **Certification/Licensure:** None.

Personality Type: Realistic. **Career Cluster:** 13 Manufacturing. **Career Pathway:** 13.3 Maintenance, Installation, and Repair. **Other Jobs in This Pathway:** Aircraft Mechanics and Service Technicians; Automotive Engineering Technicians; Automotive Specialty Technicians; Avionics Technicians; Biological Technicians; Camera and Photographic Equipment Repairers; Chemical Equipment Operators and Tenders; Civil Engineering Technicians; Coil Winders, Tapers, and Finishers; Computer, Automated Teller, and Office Machine Repairers; Construction and Related Workers, All Other; Control and Valve Installers and Repairers, Except Mechanical Door; Electric Motor, Power Tool, and Related Repairers; Electrical and Electronic Equipment Assemblers; Electrical and Electronics Repairers, Commercial and Industrial Equipment; Electrical and Electronics Repairers, Powerhouse, Substation, and Relay; Electrical Engineering Technicians; Electrical Engineering Technologists; Electromechanical Engineering Technologists; Electromechanical Equipment Assemblers; Electronics Engineering Technicians; Electronics Engineering Technologists; others.

Skills—Repairing: Repairing machines or systems using the needed tools. **Equipment Maintenance:** Performing routine maintenance on equipment and determining when and what kind of maintenance is needed. **Troubleshooting:** Determining causes of operating errors and deciding what to do about them. **Equipment Selection:** Determining the kind of tools and equipment needed to do a job. **Operation and Control:** Controlling operations of equipment or systems. **Quality Control Analysis:** Conducting tests and inspections of products, services, or processes to evaluate quality or performance. **Operation Monitoring:** Watching gauges, dials, or other indicators to make sure a machine is working properly. **Installation:** Installing equipment, machines, wiring, or programs to meet specifications.

Work Environment: Outdoors; standing; walking and running; kneeling, crouching, stooping, or crawling; balancing; using hands; bending or twisting the body; repetitive motions; noise; very hot or cold; bright or inadequate lighting; contaminants; cramped work space; whole-body vibration; high places; hazardous conditions; hazardous equipment; minor burns, cuts, bites, or stings.

Sailors and Marine Oilers

- ⊙ Annual Earnings: $36,800
- ⊙ Earnings Growth Potential: High (40.4%)
- ⊙ Growth: 21.3%
- ⊙ Annual Job Openings: 2,150
- ⊙ Self-Employed: 0.6%

Considerations for Job Outlook: Job prospects should be favorable. Many workers leave water transportation occupations, especially sailors and marine oilers, because recently hired workers often decide they do not enjoy spending a lot of time away at sea. In addition, a number of officers and engineers are approaching retirement, creating job openings. The number of applicants for all types of jobs may be limited by high regulatory and security requirements.

Stand watch to look for obstructions in the paths of vessels, measure water depths, turn wheels on bridges, or use emergency equipment as directed by captains, mates, or pilots. Provide engineers with assistance in repairing and adjusting machinery. Attach hoses and operate pumps in order to transfer substances to and from liquid cargo tanks. Give directions to crew members engaged in cleaning wheelhouses and quarterdecks. Load or unload materials from vessels. Lower and man lifeboats when emergencies occur. Participate in shore patrols. Read pressure and temperature gauges or displays, and record data in engineering logs. Record in ships' logs data such as weather conditions and distances traveled. Stand by wheels when ships are on automatic pilot, and verify accuracy of courses, using magnetic compasses. Steer ships under the direction of commanders or navigating officers, or direct helmsmen to steer, following designated courses. Chip and clean rust spots on decks, superstructures, and sides of ships, using wire brushes and hand or air chipping machines. Relay specified signals to other ships, using visual signaling devices such as blinker lights and semaphores. Splice and repair ropes, wire cables, and cordage, using marlinespikes, wirecutters, twine, and hand tools. Paint or varnish decks, superstructures, lifeboats, or sides of ships. Overhaul lifeboats and lifeboat gear, and lower or raise lifeboats with winches or falls. Operate, maintain, and repair ship equipment such as winches, cranes, derricks, and weapons systems. Measure depths of water in shallow or unfamiliar waters, using leadlines, and telephone or shout depth information to vessel bridges. Maintain ships' engines under the direction of the ships' engineering officers. Lubricate machinery, equipment, and engine parts such as gears, shafts, and bearings. Handle lines to moor vessels to wharfs, to tie up vessels to other vessels, or to rig towing lines. Examine machinery to verify specified pressures and lubricant flows. Clean and polish wood trim, brass, and other metal parts. Break out, rig, and stow cargo-handling gear, stationary rigging, and running gear.

Education/Training Required: Less than high school. **Education and Training Program:** Marine Transportation Services, Other. **Knowledge/Courses—Mechanical Devices:** Machines and tools, including their designs, uses, repair, and maintenance. **Transportation:** Principles and methods for moving people or goods by air, rail, sea, or road, including the relative costs and benefits. **Public Safety and Security:** Relevant equipment, policies, procedures, and strategies to promote effective local, state, or national security operations for the protection of people, data, property, and institutions. **Engineering and Technology:** The practical application of engineering science and technology. This includes applying principles, techniques, procedures, and equipment to the design and production of various goods and services. **Geography:** Principles and methods for describing the features of land, sea, and air masses, including their physical characteristics, locations, interrelationships, and distribution of plant, animal, and human life. **Production and Processing:** Raw materials, production processes, quality control, costs, and other techniques for maximizing the effective manufacture and distribution of goods. **Work Experience Needed:** None. **On-the-Job Training Needed:** Short-term on-the-job training. **Certification/Licensure:** Licensure.

Personality Type: Realistic-Conventional. **Career Cluster:** 16 Transportation, Distribution, and Logistics. **Career Pathway:** 16.1 Transportation Operations. **Other Jobs in This Pathway:** Aerospace Engineering and Operations Technicians; Air Traffic Controllers; Aircraft Cargo Handling Supervisors; Airfield Operations Specialists; Airline Pilots, Copilots, and Flight Engineers; Automotive and Watercraft Service Attendants; Automotive Master Mechanics; Aviation Inspectors; Bridge and Lock Tenders; Bus Drivers, School or Special Client; Bus Drivers, Transit and Intercity; Commercial Divers; Commercial Pilots; Crane and Tower Operators; First-Line Supervisors of Helpers, Laborers, and Material Movers, Hand; First-Line Supervisors of Transportation and Material-Moving Machine and Vehicle Operators; Freight and Cargo Inspectors; Heavy and Tractor-Trailer Truck Drivers; Hoist and Winch Operators; Laborers and Freight, Stock, and Material Movers, Hand; Light Truck or Delivery Services Drivers; Mates—Ship, Boat, and Barge; Motor Vehicle Operators, All Other; Motorboat Operators; Operating Engineers and Other Construction Equipment Operators; others.

Skills—Repairing: Repairing machines or systems using the needed tools. **Equipment Maintenance:** Performing routine maintenance on equipment and determining when and what kind of maintenance is needed. **Operation and Control:** Controlling operations of equipment or systems. **Troubleshooting:** Determining causes of operating errors and deciding what to do about them. **Equipment Selection:** Determining the kind of tools and equipment needed to do a job. **Operation Monitoring:** Watching gauges, dials, or other indicators to make sure a machine is working properly. **Quality Control Analysis:** Conducting tests and inspections of products, services, or processes to evaluate quality or performance. **Technology Design:** Generating or adapting equipment and technology to serve user needs.

Work Environment: More often outdoors than indoors; standing; walking and running; balancing; using hands; bending or twisting the body; noise; very hot or cold; bright or inadequate lighting; contaminants; cramped work space; whole-body vibration; high places; hazardous conditions; hazardous equipment.

Sales Representatives, Wholesale and Manufacturing, Except Technical and Scientific Products

- ◉ Annual Earnings: $53,540
- ◉ Earnings Growth Potential: High (49.1%)
- ◉ Growth: 15.6%
- ◉ Annual Job Openings: 55,990
- ◉ Self-Employed: 3.8%

Considerations for Job Outlook: Job candidates should see very good opportunities. Because workers frequently leave this occupation, there are usually a relatively large number of openings.

Sell goods for wholesalers or manufacturers to businesses or groups of individuals. Work requires substantial knowledge of items sold. Answer customers' questions about products, prices, availability, product uses, and credit terms. Recommend products to customers based on customers' needs and interests. Contact regular and prospective customers to demonstrate products, explain product features, and solicit orders. Estimate or quote prices, credit or contract terms, warranties, and delivery dates. Consult with clients after sales or contract signings to resolve problems and to provide ongoing support. Prepare drawings, estimates, and bids that meet specific customer needs. Provide customers with product samples and catalogs. Identify prospective customers by using business directories, following leads from existing clients, participating in organizations and clubs, and attending trade shows and conferences. Arrange and direct delivery and installation of products and equipment. Monitor market conditions; product innovations; and competitors' products, prices, and sales. Negotiate details of contracts and payments, and prepare sales contracts and order forms. Perform administrative duties, such as preparing sales budgets and reports, keeping sales records, and filing expense account reports. Obtain credit information

about prospective customers. Forward orders to manufacturers. Check stock levels, and reorder merchandise as necessary. Plan, assemble, and stock product displays in retail stores, or make recommendations to retailers regarding product displays, promotional programs, and advertising.

Education/Training Required: High school diploma or equivalent. **Education and Training Programs:** Apparel and Accessories Marketing Operations; Business, Management, Marketing, and Related Support Services, Other; Fashion Merchandising; General Merchandising, Sales, and Related Marketing Operations, Other; Insurance; Sales, Distribution, and Marketing Operations, General; Special Products Marketing Operations; Specialized Merchandising, Sales, and Marketing Operations, Other. **Knowledge/Courses—Sales and Marketing:** Principles and methods for showing, promoting, and selling products or services. This includes marketing strategy and tactics, product demonstration, sales techniques, and sales control systems. **Economics and Accounting:** Economic and accounting principles and practices, the financial markets, banking, and the analysis and reporting of financial data. **Customer and Personal Service:** Principles and processes for providing customer and personal services. This includes customer needs assessment, meeting quality standards for services, and evaluation of customer satisfaction. **Transportation:** Principles and methods for moving people or goods by air, rail, sea, or road, including the relative costs and benefits. **Mathematics:** Arithmetic, algebra, geometry, calculus, statistics, and their applications. **Production and Processing:** Raw materials, production processes, quality control, costs, and other techniques for maximizing the effective manufacture and distribution of goods. **Work Experience Needed:** None. **On-the-Job Training Needed:** Moderate-term on-the-job training. **Certification/Licensure:** Licensure for some specializations; voluntary certification by association.

Personality Type: Conventional-Enterprising. **Career Cluster:** 14 Marketing, Sales, and Service. **Career Pathways:** 14.2 Professional Sales and Marketing; 14.3 Buying and Merchandising. **Other Jobs in These Pathways:** Appraisers, Real Estate; Assessors; Cashiers; Counter and Rental Clerks; Demonstrators and Product Promoters; Door-To-Door Sales Workers, News and Street Vendors, and Related Workers; Driver/Sales Workers; Energy Brokers; First-Line Supervisors of Non-Retail Sales Workers; First-Line Supervisors of Retail Sales Workers; Gaming

Change Persons and Booth Cashiers; Hotel, Motel, and Resort Desk Clerks; Interior Designers; Lodging Managers; Marketing Managers; Marking Clerks; Meeting, Convention, and Event Planners; Merchandise Displayers and Window Trimmers; Models; Online Merchants; Order Fillers, Wholesale and Retail Sales; Parts Salespersons; Property, Real Estate, and Community Association Managers; Purchasing Agents, Except Wholesale, Retail, and Farm Products; Real Estate Brokers; Real Estate Sales Agents; Reservation and Transportation Ticket Agents and Travel Clerks; Retail Salespersons; Sales and Related Workers, All Other; Sales Engineers; others.

Skills—Negotiation: Bringing others together and trying to reconcile differences. **Persuasion:** Persuading others to change their minds or behavior. **Service Orientation:** Actively looking for ways to help people. **Operations Analysis:** Analyzing needs and product requirements to create a design. **Critical Thinking:** Using logic and reasoning to identify the strengths and weaknesses of alternative solutions, conclusions, or approaches to problems. **Social Perceptiveness:** Being aware of others' reactions and understanding why they react as they do. **Active Listening:** Giving full attention to what other people are saying, taking time to understand the points being made, asking questions as appropriate, and not interrupting at inappropriate times. **Speaking:** Talking to others to convey information effectively.

Work Environment: Outdoors; more often sitting than standing; walking and running; noise; contaminants.

Sawing Machine Setters, Operators, and Tenders, Wood

- ⊙ Annual Earnings: $26,220
- ⊙ Earnings Growth Potential: Low (33.0%)
- ⊙ Growth: 24.6%
- ⊙ Annual Job Openings: 1,810
- ⊙ Self-Employed: 5.9%

Considerations for Job Outlook: Those with advanced skills, including advanced math and the ability to read blueprints, should have the best job opportunities in manufacturing industries. Woodworkers who know how to create and carry out custom designs on a computer will likely be in strong demand. Some job openings will result from

the need to replace those who retire or leave the occupation for other reasons. However, employment in all woodworking specialties is highly sensitive to economic cycles. During economic downturns, workers are subject to layoffs or reductions in hours.

Set up, operate, or tend wood sawing machines. Adjust saw blades, using wrenches and rulers or by turning handwheels or pressing pedals, levers, or panel buttons. Inspect and measure workpieces to mark for cuts and to verify the accuracy of cuts, using rulers, squares, or caliper rules. Examine logs or lumber to plan the best cuts. Set up, operate, or tend saws and machines that cut or trim wood to specified dimensions, such as circular saws, band saws, multiple-blade sawing machines, scroll saws, ripsaws, and crozer machines. Inspect stock for imperfections and to estimate grades or qualities of stock or workpieces. Operate panelboards of saw and conveyor systems to move stock through processes and to cut stock to specified dimensions. Mount and bolt sawing blades or attachments to machine shafts. Monitor sawing machines, adjusting speed and tension and clearing jams to ensure proper operation. Select saw blades, types and grades of stock, and cutting procedures to be used, according to work orders or supervisors' instructions. Guide workpieces against saws, saw over workpieces by hand, or operate automatic feeding devices to guide cuts. Adjust bolts, clamps, stops, guides, and table angles and heights, using hand tools. Sharpen blades or replace defective or worn blades and bands, using hand tools. Count, sort, and stack finished workpieces. Lubricate and clean machines, using wrenches, grease guns, and solvents. Clear machine jams, using hand tools. Dispose of waste material after completing work assignments. Measure and mark stock for cuts. Examine blueprints, drawings, work orders, or patterns to determine equipment setup and selection details, procedures to be used, and dimensions of final products. Pull tables back against stops, and depress pedals to advance cutterheads that shape stock ends. Trim lumber to straighten rough edges and remove defects, using circular saws. Position and clamp stock on tables, conveyors, or carriages, using hoists, guides, stops, dogs, wedges, and wrenches.

Education/Training Required: High school diploma or equivalent. **Education and Training Program:** Cabinetmaking and Millwork. **Knowledge/Courses— Mechanical Devices:** Machines and tools, including their designs, uses, repair, and maintenance. **Production and**

Processing: Raw materials, production processes, quality control, costs, and other techniques for maximizing the effective manufacture and distribution of goods. **Design:** Design techniques, tools, and principles involved in production of precision technical plans, blueprints, drawings, and models. **Work Experience Needed:** None. **On-the-Job Training Needed:** Short-term on-the-job training. **Certification/Licensure:** None.

Personality Type: Realistic-Conventional-Investigative. **Career Cluster:** 13 Manufacturing. **Career Pathway:** 13.1 Production. **Other Jobs in This Pathway:** Adhesive Bonding Machine Operators and Tenders; Assemblers and Fabricators, All Other; Avionics Technicians; Cabinetmakers and Bench Carpenters; Cleaning, Washing, and Metal Pickling Equipment Operators and Tenders; Coating, Painting, and Spraying Machine Setters, Operators, and Tenders; Computer-Controlled Machine Tool Operators, Metal and Plastic; Cooling and Freezing Equipment Operators and Tenders; Cost Estimators; Crushing, Grinding, and Polishing Machine Setters, Operators, and Tenders; Cutters and Trimmers, Hand; Cutting and Slicing Machine Setters, Operators, and Tenders; Cutting, Punching, and Press Machine Setters, Operators, and Tenders, Metal and Plastic; Drilling and Boring Machine Tool Setters, Operators, and Tenders, Metal and Plastic; Extruding and Drawing Machine Setters, Operators, and Tenders, Metal and Plastic; Extruding and Forming Machine Setters, Operators, and Tenders, Synthetic and Glass Fibers; others.

Skills—Equipment Maintenance: Performing routine maintenance on equipment and determining when and what kind of maintenance is needed. **Repairing:** Repairing machines or systems using the needed tools. **Operation and Control:** Controlling operations of equipment or systems. **Operation Monitoring:** Watching gauges, dials, or other indicators to make sure a machine is working properly. **Troubleshooting:** Determining causes of operating errors and deciding what to do about them. **Equipment Selection:** Determining the kind of tools and equipment needed to do a job. **Installation:** Installing equipment, machines, wiring, or programs to meet specifications. **Quality Control Analysis:** Conducting tests and inspections of products, services, or processes to evaluate quality or performance.

Work Environment: Standing; walking and running; using hands; bending or twisting the body; repetitive motions; noise; very hot or cold; contaminants; hazardous equipment; minor burns, cuts, bites, or stings.

Secretaries and Administrative Assistants, Except Legal, Medical, and Executive

- ⊙ Annual Earnings: $31,870
- ⊙ Earnings Growth Potential: Medium (37.1%)
- ⊙ Growth: 5.8%
- ⊙ Annual Job Openings: 39,100
- ⊙ Self-Employed: 1.1%

Considerations for Job Outlook: In addition to jobs coming from employment growth, numerous job openings will arise from the need to replace secretaries and administrative assistants who transfer to other occupations or retire. Job opportunities should be best for applicants with extensive knowledge of computer software applications. Applicants with a bachelor's degree are expected to be in great demand and will act as managerial assistants who perform more complex tasks.

Perform routine clerical and administrative functions. Operate office equipment such as fax machines, copiers, and phone systems, and use computers for spreadsheet, word processing, database management, and other applications. Answer telephones and give information to callers, take messages, or transfer calls to appropriate individuals. Greet visitors and callers, handle their inquiries, and direct them to the appropriate persons according to their needs. Set up and maintain paper and electronic filing systems for records, correspondence, and other material. Locate and attach appropriate files to incoming correspondence requiring replies. Open, read, route, and distribute incoming mail and other material, and prepare answers to routine letters. Complete forms in accordance with company procedures. Make copies of correspondence and other printed material. Review work done by others to check for correct spelling and grammar, ensure that company format policies are followed, and recommend revisions. Compose, type, and distribute meeting notes, routine correspondence, and reports. Learn to operate new office technologies as they are developed and implemented. Maintain scheduling and event calendars. Schedule and confirm appointments for clients, customers, or supervisors. Manage projects, and contribute to committee and team work. Mail newsletters, promotional material, and other information. Order and dispense supplies. Conduct searches to find needed information, using such sources as the Internet. Provide services to customers, such as order placement and account information. Collect and disburse funds from cash accounts, and keep records of collections and disbursements. Prepare and mail checks. Establish work procedures and schedules, and keep track of the daily work of clerical staff. Coordinate conferences and meetings. Take dictation in shorthand or by machine, and transcribe information. Arrange conferences, meetings, and travel reservations for office personnel.

Education/Training Required: High school diploma or equivalent. **Education and Training Programs:** Administrative Assistant and Secretarial Science, General; Executive Assistant/Executive Secretary Training. **Knowledge/Courses—Clerical Practices:** Administrative and clerical procedures and systems such as word processing, managing files and records, stenography and transcription, designing forms, and other office procedures and terminology. **Customer and Personal Service:** Principles and processes for providing customer and personal services. This includes customer needs assessment, meeting quality standards for services, and evaluation of customer satisfaction. **Economics and Accounting:** Economic and accounting principles and practices, the financial markets, banking, and the analysis and reporting of financial data. **Computers and Electronics:** Circuit boards, processors, chips, electronic equipment, and computer hardware and software, including applications and programming. **English Language:** The structure and content of the English language including the meaning and spelling of words, rules of composition, and grammar. **Personnel and Human Resources:** Principles and procedures for personnel recruitment, selection, training, compensation and benefits, labor relations and negotiation, and personnel information systems. **Work Experience Needed:** None. **On-the-Job Training Needed:** Short-term on-the-job training. **Certification/Licensure:** Voluntary certification by association.

Personality Type: Conventional-Enterprising. **Career Cluster:** 04 Business, Management, and Administration. **Career Pathway:** 04.6 Administrative and Information Support. **Other Jobs in This Pathway:** Cargo and Freight Agents; Correspondence Clerks; Couriers and Messengers; Court Clerks; Customer Service Representatives; Data Entry Keyers; Dispatchers, Except Police, Fire, and Ambulance; Executive Secretaries and Executive Administrative Assistants; File Clerks; Freight Forwarders; Human Resources Assistants, Except Payroll and Timekeeping; Information and Record Clerks, All Other; Insurance Claims Clerks; Insurance Policy Processing Clerks; Interviewers, Except Eligibility and Loan; License Clerks; Mail Clerks and Mail Machine Operators, Except Postal Service; Meter Readers, Utilities; Municipal Clerks; Office and Administrative Support Workers, All Other; Office Clerks, General; Office Machine Operators, Except Computer; Order Clerks; Patient Representatives; Postal Service Clerks; Postal Service Mail Carriers; Postal Service Mail Sorters, Processors, and Processing Machine Operators; Procurement Clerks; Receptionists and Information Clerks; others.

Skills—Service Orientation: Actively looking for ways to help people. **Management of Financial Resources:** Determining how money will be spent to get the work done and accounting for these expenditures. **Writing:** Communicating effectively in writing as appropriate for the needs of the audience. **Time Management:** Managing one's own time and the time of others. **Management of Material Resources:** Obtaining and seeing to the appropriate use of equipment, facilities, and materials needed to do certain work. **Active Listening:** Giving full attention to what other people are saying, taking time to understand the points being made, asking questions as appropriate, and not interrupting at inappropriate times. **Reading Comprehension:** Understanding written sentences and paragraphs in work-related documents. **Speaking:** Talking to others to convey information effectively.

Work Environment: Indoors; sitting; repetitive motions.

Security and Fire Alarm Systems Installers

- ⊙ Annual Earnings: $39,540
- ⊙ Earnings Growth Potential: Medium (35.9%)
- ⊙ Growth: 32.9%
- ⊙ Annual Job Openings: 3,670
- ⊙ Self-Employed: 8.9%

Considerations for Job Outlook: Rapid employment growth is projected.

Install, program, maintain, and repair security and fire alarm wiring and equipment. Ensure that work is in accordance with relevant codes. Examine systems to locate problems such as loose connections or broken insulation. Test backup batteries, keypad programming, sirens, and all security features to ensure proper functioning and to diagnose malfunctions. Mount and fasten control panels, door and window contacts, sensors, and video cameras, and attach electrical and telephone wiring to connect components. Install, maintain, or repair security systems, alarm devices, and related equipment, following blueprints of electrical layouts and building plans. Inspect installation sites and study work orders, building plans, and installation manuals to determine materials requirements and installation procedures. Feed cables through access holes, roof spaces, and cavity walls to reach fixture outlets, and then position and terminate cables, wires, and strapping. Adjust sensitivity of units based on room structures and manufacturers' recommendations, using programming keypads. Test and repair circuits and sensors, following wiring and system specifications. Drill holes for wiring in wall studs, joists, ceilings, and floors. Demonstrate systems for customers, and explain details such as the causes and consequences of false alarms. Consult with clients to assess risks and to determine security requirements. Keep informed of new products and developments. Mount raceways and conduits, and fasten wires to wood framing, using staplers. Prepare documents such as invoices and warranties.

Education/Training Required: High school diploma or equivalent. **Education and Training Programs:** Electrician; Security System Installation, Repair, and Inspection Technology/Technician. **Knowledge/Courses—Telecommunications:** Transmission, broadcasting, switching, control, and operation of telecommunications systems. **Building and Construction:** Materials, methods, and the tools involved in the construction or repair of houses, buildings, or other structures such as highways and roads. **Mechanical Devices:** Machines and tools, including their designs, uses, repair, and maintenance. **Computers and Electronics:** Circuit boards, processors, chips, electronic equipment, and computer hardware and software, including applications and programming. **Public Safety and Security:** Relevant equipment, policies, procedures, and strategies to promote effective local, state, or national security operations for the protection of people, data, property, and institutions. **Design:** Design techniques, tools, and principles involved in production of precision technical plans, blueprints,

drawings, and models. **Work Experience Needed:** None. **On-the-Job Training Needed:** Moderate-term on-the-job training. **Certification/Licensure:** Licensure.

Personality Type: Realistic-Conventional. **Career Cluster:** 02 Architecture and Construction. **Career Pathways:** 02.3 Maintenance/Operations; 02.2 Construction. **Other Jobs in These Pathways:** Boilermakers; Brickmasons and Blockmasons; Carpet Installers; Cement Masons and Concrete Finishers; Coin, Vending, and Amusement Machine Servicers and Repairers; Construction and Building Inspectors; Construction and Related Workers, All Other; Construction Carpenters; Construction Laborers; Construction Managers; Continuous Mining Machine Operators; Cost Estimators; Crane and Tower Operators; Dredge Operators; Drywall and Ceiling Tile Installers; Earth Drillers, Except Oil and Gas; Electrical Power-Line Installers and Repairers; Electricians; Electromechanical Equipment Assemblers; Engineering Technicians, Except Drafters, All Other; Excavating and Loading Machine and Dragline Operators; Explosives Workers, Ordnance Handling Experts, and Blasters; Extraction Workers, All Other; First-Line Supervisors of Construction Trades and Extraction Workers; Floor Layers, Except Carpet, Wood, and Hard Tiles; Floor Sanders and Finishers; Glaziers; others.

Skills—Installation: Installing equipment, machines, wiring, or programs to meet specifications. **Repairing:** Repairing machines or systems using the needed tools. **Equipment Maintenance:** Performing routine maintenance on equipment and determining when and what kind of maintenance is needed. **Troubleshooting:** Determining causes of operating errors and deciding what to do about them. **Operation and Control:** Controlling operations of equipment or systems. **Equipment Selection:** Determining the kind of tools and equipment needed to do a job. **Quality Control Analysis:** Conducting tests and inspections of products, services, or processes to evaluate quality or performance. **Operation Monitoring:** Watching gauges, dials, or other indicators to make sure a machine is working properly.

Work Environment: More often indoors than outdoors; standing; climbing; using hands; repetitive motions; noise; very hot or cold; bright or inadequate lighting; contaminants; cramped work space; high places.

Security Guards

- Annual Earnings: $23,900
- Earnings Growth Potential: Low (27.8%)
- Growth: 18.8%
- Annual Job Openings: 35,950
- Self-Employed: 1.1%

Considerations for Job Outlook: Job opportunities for security guards will stem from growing demand for various forms of security. Additional opportunities will be due to turnover. Although many people are attracted to part-time positions because of the limited training requirements, there will be more competition for higher-paying positions that require more training. Those with related work experience, such as a background in law enforcement, and those with computer and technology skills should find the best job prospects.

Guard, patrol, or monitor premises to prevent theft, violence, or infractions of rules. Patrol industrial or commercial premises to prevent and detect signs of intrusion and ensure security of doors, windows, and gates. Answer alarms and investigate disturbances. Monitor and authorize entrance and departure of employees, visitors, and other persons to guard against theft and maintain security of premises. Write reports of daily activities and irregularities such as equipment or property damage, theft, presence of unauthorized persons, or unusual occurrences. Call police or fire departments in cases of emergency, such as fire or presence of unauthorized persons. Circulate among visitors, patrons, or employees to preserve order and protect property. Answer telephone calls to take messages, answer questions, and provide information during nonbusiness hours or when switchboard is closed. Warn persons of rule infractions or violations, and apprehend or evict violators from premises, using force when necessary. Operate detecting devices to screen individuals and prevent passage of prohibited articles into restricted areas. Escort or drive motor vehicle to transport individuals to specified locations or to provide personal protection. Inspect and adjust security systems, equipment, or machinery to ensure operational use and to detect evidence of tampering. Drive or guard armored vehicle to transport money and valuables to prevent theft and ensure safe delivery. Monitor and adjust controls that regulate building systems, such as air conditioning, furnace, or boiler.

Education/Training Required: High school diploma or equivalent. **Education and Training Programs:** Securities Services Administration/Management; Security and Loss Prevention Services. **Knowledge/Courses—Public Safety and Security:** Relevant equipment, policies, procedures, and strategies to promote effective local, state, or national security operations for the protection of people, data, property, and institutions. **Work Experience Needed:** None. **On-the-Job Training Needed:** Short-term on-the-job training. **Certification/Licensure:** Licensure in most states; voluntary certification by association in others.

Personality Type: Realistic-Conventional-Enterprising. **Career Cluster:** 12 Law, Public Safety, Corrections, and Security. **Career Pathways:** 12.1 Correction Services; 12.3 Security and Protective Services. **Other Jobs in These Pathways:** Animal Control Workers; Child, Family, and School Social Workers; Criminal Justice and Law Enforcement Teachers, Postsecondary; Crossing Guards; First-Line Supervisors of Correctional Officers; First-Line Supervisors of Police and Detectives; First-Line Supervisors of Protective Service Workers, All Other; Forest Firefighters; Gaming Surveillance Officers and Gaming Investigators; Lifeguards, Ski Patrol, and Other Recreational Protective Service Workers; Parking Enforcement Workers; Police, Fire, and Ambulance Dispatchers; Private Detectives and Investigators; Protective Service Workers, All Other; Psychology Teachers, Postsecondary; Retail Loss Prevention Specialists; Sheriffs and Deputy Sheriffs; Transit and Railroad Police.

Skills—Operation and Control: Controlling operations of equipment or systems.

Work Environment: More often indoors than outdoors; standing; walking and running; using hands; noise; contaminants.

Segmental Pavers

- Annual Earnings: $32,340
- Earnings Growth Potential: Low (33.5%)
- Growth: 30.8%
- Annual Job Openings: 90
- Self-Employed: 7.9%

Considerations for Job Outlook: Expected employment growth should result from new construction projects and from the need to repair and renovate existing highways, bridges, and other structures. Entry-level opportunities should be good.

Lay out, cut, and place segmental paving units. Supply and place base materials, edge restraints, bedding sand, and jointing sand. Prepare bases for installation by removing unstable or unsuitable materials, compacting and grading the soil, draining or stabilizing weak or saturated soils and taking measures to prevent water penetration and migration of bedding sand. Sweep sand from surfaces prior to opening to traffic. Set pavers, aligning and spacing them correctly. Sweep sand into the joints and compact pavement until the joints are full. Compact bedding sand and pavers to finish paved areas, using plate compactors. Design paver installation layout patterns and create markings for directional references of joints and stringlines. Resurface outside areas with cobblestones, terracotta tiles, concrete, or other materials. Discuss designs with clients. Cut paving stones to size and for edges, using splitters and masonry saws. Screed sand levels to even thicknesses, and recheck sand exposed to elements, raking and rescreeding if necessary. Cement the edges of paved areas.

Education/Training Required: High school diploma or equivalent. **Education and Training Program:** Concrete Finishing/Concrete Finisher. **Knowledge/Courses— Building and Construction:** Materials, methods, and the tools involved in the construction or repair of houses, buildings, or other structures such as highways and roads. **Mechanical Devices:** Machines and tools, including their designs, uses, repair, and maintenance. **Transportation:** Principles and methods for moving people or goods by air, rail, sea, or road, including the relative costs and benefits. **Engineering and Technology:** The practical application of engineering science and technology. This includes applying principles, techniques, procedures, and equipment to the design and production of various goods and services. **Design:** Design techniques, tools, and principles involved in production of precision technical plans, blueprints, drawings, and models. **Work Experience Needed:** None. **On-the-Job Training Needed:** Moderate-term on-the-job training. **Certification/Licensure:** None.

Personality Type: Realistic-Conventional. **Career Cluster:** 02 Architecture and Construction. **Career Pathway:** 02.2 Construction. **Other Jobs in This Pathway:** Boilermakers; Brickmasons and Blockmasons; Carpet Installers; Cement Masons and Concrete Finishers; Construction and Building Inspectors; Construction and Related Workers, All Other; Construction Carpenters; Construction Laborers; Construction Managers; Continuous Mining Machine Operators; Cost Estimators; Crane and Tower Operators; Dredge Operators; Drywall and Ceiling Tile Installers; Earth Drillers, Except Oil and Gas; Electrical Power-Line Installers and Repairers; Electricians; Electromechanical Equipment Assemblers; Engineering Technicians, Except Drafters, All Other; Excavating and Loading Machine and Dragline Operators; Explosives Workers, Ordnance Handling Experts, and Blasters; Extraction Workers, All Other; First-Line Supervisors of Construction Trades and Extraction Workers; Floor Layers, Except Carpet, Wood, and Hard Tiles; Floor Sanders and Finishers; Glaziers; Heating and Air Conditioning Mechanics and Installers; Helpers, Construction Trades, All Other; others.

Skills—Equipment Maintenance: Performing routine maintenance on equipment and determining when and what kind of maintenance is needed. **Operation and Control:** Controlling operations of equipment or systems. **Repairing:** Repairing machines or systems using the needed tools. **Troubleshooting:** Determining causes of operating errors and deciding what to do about them. **Equipment Selection:** Determining the kind of tools and equipment needed to do a job. **Coordination:** Adjusting actions in relation to others' actions. **Quality Control Analysis:** Conducting tests and inspections of products, services, or processes to evaluate quality or performance. **Operation Monitoring:** Watching gauges, dials, or other indicators to make sure a machine is working properly.

Work Environment: More often outdoors than indoors; more often sitting than standing; walking and running; repetitive motions; noise; very hot or cold; contaminants; hazardous equipment.

Self-Enrichment Education Teachers

- Annual Earnings: $36,100
- Earnings Growth Potential: High (48.4%)
- Growth: 20.9%
- Annual Job Openings: 9,150
- Self-Employed: 14.2%

Considerations for Job Outlook: Growth is expected as more people want to learn new hobbies and gain marketable skills. From 2010 to 2020, adults and children are expected to continue seeking new hobbies and pastimes and will take classes to learn these skills. Self-enrichment teachers will be needed to teach these classes. In addition, more people will seek to gain skills to make themselves more attractive to prospective employers.

Teach or instruct courses other than those that normally lead to an occupational objective or degree. Adapt teaching methods and instructional materials to meet students' varying needs and interests. Conduct classes, workshops, and demonstrations, and provide individual instruction to teach topics and skills such as cooking, dancing, writing, physical fitness, photography, personal finance, and flying. Monitor students' performance to make suggestions for improvement and to ensure that they satisfy course standards, training requirements, and objectives. Observe students to determine qualifications, limitations, abilities, interests, and other individual characteristics. Instruct students individually and in groups, using various teaching methods such as lectures, discussions, and demonstrations. Establish clear objectives for all lessons, units, and projects, and communicate those objectives to students. Instruct and monitor students in use and care of equipment and materials to prevent injury and damage. Prepare students for further development by encouraging them to explore learning opportunities and to persevere with challenging tasks. Prepare materials and classrooms for class activities. Enforce policies and rules governing students. Plan and conduct activities for a balanced program of instruction, demonstration, and work time that provides students with opportunities to observe, question, and investigate. Prepare instructional program objectives, outlines, and lesson plans. Maintain accurate and complete student records as required by administrative policy.

Education/Training Required: High school diploma or equivalent. **Education and Training Program:** Adult and Continuing Education and Teaching. **Knowledge/Courses—Education and Training:** Principles and methods for curriculum and training design, teaching and instruction for individuals and groups, and the measurement of training effects. **Fine Arts:** The theory and techniques required to compose, produce, and perform works of music, dance, visual arts, drama, and sculpture. **Communications and Media:** Media production, communication, and dissemination techniques and methods. This includes alternative ways to inform and entertain via written, oral,

and visual media. **Customer and Personal Service:** Principles and processes for providing customer and personal services. This includes customer needs assessment, meeting quality standards for services, and evaluation of customer satisfaction. **Sales and Marketing:** Principles and methods for showing, promoting, and selling products or services. This includes marketing strategy and tactics, product demonstration, sales techniques, and sales control systems. **English Language:** The structure and content of the English language including the meaning and spelling of words, rules of composition, and grammar. **Work Experience Needed:** 1 to 5 years. **On-the-Job Training Needed:** None. **Certification/Licensure:** Voluntary certification for some specializations.

Personality Type: Social-Artistic-Enterprising. **Career Cluster:** 05 Education and Training. **Career Pathway:** 05.3 Teaching/Training. **Other Jobs in This Pathway:** Adult Basic and Secondary Education and Literacy Teachers and Instructors; Agricultural Sciences Teachers, Postsecondary; Anthropology and Archeology Teachers, Postsecondary; Architecture Teachers, Postsecondary; Area, Ethnic, and Cultural Studies Teachers, Postsecondary; Art, Drama, and Music Teachers, Postsecondary; Athletes and Sports Competitors; Atmospheric, Earth, Marine, and Space Sciences Teachers, Postsecondary; Audio-Visual and Multimedia Collections Specialists; Biological Science Teachers, Postsecondary; Business Teachers, Postsecondary; Career/Technical Education Teachers, Middle School; Career/Technical Education Teachers, Secondary School; Chemists; Coaches and Scouts; Communications Teachers, Postsecondary; Computer Science Teachers, Postsecondary; Criminal Justice and Law Enforcement Teachers, Postsecondary; Dietitians and Nutritionists; Education Teachers, Postsecondary; Elementary School Teachers, Except Special Education; Engineering Teachers, Postsecondary; others.

Skills—Learning Strategies: Selecting and using training/instructional methods and procedures appropriate for the situation when learning or teaching new things. **Operations Analysis:** Analyzing needs and product requirements to create a design. **Instructing:** Teaching others how to do something. **Writing:** Communicating effectively in writing as appropriate for the needs of the audience. **Speaking:** Talking to others to convey information effectively. **Service Orientation:** Actively looking for ways to help people. **Reading Comprehension:** Understanding written sentences and paragraphs in work-related documents. **Monitoring:** Monitoring or assessing your performance or that of other individuals or organizations to make improvements or take corrective action.

Work Environment: Indoors; standing; repetitive motions.

Septic Tank Servicers and Sewer Pipe Cleaners

- ⊙ Annual Earnings: $33,740
- ⊙ Earnings Growth Potential: Medium (36.5%)
- ⊙ Growth: 20.6%
- ⊙ Annual Job Openings: 1,190
- ⊙ Self-Employed: 3.4%

Considerations for Job Outlook: Faster-than-average employment growth is projected.

Clean and repair septic tanks, sewer lines, or drains. Drive trucks to transport crews, materials, and equipment. Communicate with supervisors and other workers, using equipment such as wireless phones, pagers, or radio telephones. Prepare and keep records of actions taken, including maintenance and repair work. Operate sewer cleaning equipment, including power rodders, high velocity water jets, sewer flushers, bucket machines, wayne balls, and vac-alls. Ensure that repaired sewer line joints are tightly sealed before backfilling begins. Withdraw cables from pipes and examine them for evidence of mud, roots, grease, and other deposits indicating broken or clogged sewer lines. Install rotary knives on flexible cables mounted on machine reels, according to the diameters of pipes to be cleaned. Measure excavation sites, using plumbers' snakes, tapelines, or lengths of cutting heads within sewers, and mark areas for digging. Locate problems, using specially designed equipment, and mark where digging must occur to reach damaged tanks or pipes. Start machines to feed revolving cables or rods into openings, stopping machines and changing knives to conform to pipe sizes. Clean and repair septic tanks; sewer lines; or related structures such as manholes, culverts, and catch basins. Service, adjust, and make minor repairs to equipment, machines, and attachments. Inspect manholes to locate sewer line stoppages. Dig out sewer lines manually, using shovels. Cut damaged sections of pipe with cutters, remove broken sections from ditches,

and replace pipe sections, using pipe sleeves. Break asphalt and other pavement so that pipes can be accessed, using airhammers, picks, and shovels. Cover repaired pipes with dirt, and pack backfilled excavations, using air and gasoline tampers. Requisition or order tools and equipment. Rotate cleaning rods manually, using turning pins. Clean and disinfect domestic basements and other areas flooded by sewer stoppages. Tap mainline sewers to install sewer saddles. Update sewer maps and manhole charts.

Education/Training Required: Less than high school. **Education and Training Program:** Plumbing Technology/Plumber. **Knowledge/Courses—Building and Construction:** Materials, methods, and the tools involved in the construction or repair of houses, buildings, or other structures such as highways and roads. **Mechanical Devices:** Machines and tools, including their designs, uses, repair, and maintenance. **Sales and Marketing:** Principles and methods for showing, promoting, and selling products or services. This includes marketing strategy and tactics, product demonstration, sales techniques, and sales control systems. **Transportation:** Principles and methods for moving people or goods by air, rail, sea, or road, including the relative costs and benefits. **Production and Processing:** Raw materials, production processes, quality control, costs, and other techniques for maximizing the effective manufacture and distribution of goods. **Customer and Personal Service:** Principles and processes for providing customer and personal services. This includes customer needs assessment, meeting quality standards for services, and evaluation of customer satisfaction. **Work Experience Needed:** None. **On-the-Job Training Needed:** Moderate-term on-the-job training. **Certification/Licensure:** Licensure.

Personality Type: Realistic. **Career Cluster:** 02 Architecture and Construction. **Career Pathway:** 02.2 Construction. **Other Jobs in This Pathway:** Boilermakers; Brickmasons and Blockmasons; Carpet Installers; Cement Masons and Concrete Finishers; Construction and Building Inspectors; Construction and Related Workers, All Other; Construction Carpenters; Construction Laborers; Construction Managers; Continuous Mining Machine Operators; Cost Estimators; Crane and Tower Operators; Dredge Operators; Drywall and Ceiling Tile Installers; Earth Drillers, Except Oil and Gas; Electrical Power-Line Installers and Repairers; Electricians; Electromechanical Equipment Assemblers; Engineering Technicians, Except Drafters, All Other; Excavating and Loading Machine

and Dragline Operators; Explosives Workers, Ordnance Handling Experts, and Blasters; Extraction Workers, All Other; First-Line Supervisors of Construction Trades and Extraction Workers; Floor Layers, Except Carpet, Wood, and Hard Tiles; Floor Sanders and Finishers; Glaziers; Heating and Air Conditioning Mechanics and Installers; Helpers, Construction Trades, All Other; others.

Skills—Repairing: Repairing machines or systems using the needed tools. **Equipment Maintenance:** Performing routine maintenance on equipment and determining when and what kind of maintenance is needed. **Troubleshooting:** Determining causes of operating errors and deciding what to do about them. **Operation and Control:** Controlling operations of equipment or systems. **Equipment Selection:** Determining the kind of tools and equipment needed to do a job. **Installation:** Installing equipment, machines, wiring, or programs to meet specifications. **Management of Material Resources:** Obtaining and seeing to the appropriate use of equipment, facilities, and materials needed to do certain work. **Operation Monitoring:** Watching gauges, dials, or other indicators to make sure a machine is working properly.

Work Environment: Outdoors; standing; walking and running; using hands; bending or twisting the body; repetitive motions; noise; very hot or cold; bright or inadequate lighting; contaminants; cramped work space; exposed to disease or infections; hazardous equipment; minor burns, cuts, bites, or stings.

Service Unit Operators, Oil, Gas, and Mining

- ⊙ Annual Earnings: $40,750
- ⊙ Earnings Growth Potential: Low (32.9%)
- ⊙ Growth: 8.6%
- ⊙ Annual Job Openings: 1,210
- ⊙ Self-Employed: 2.2%

Considerations for Job Outlook: Demand for oil and gas workers will depend on the demand for the products and services of two industries in particular: oil and gas extraction and support for mining activities. Because of higher prices for resources, oil and gas companies are more likely to drill in deeper waters and harsher environments than in the past. These complex operations require more workers.

Higher prices will also encourage oil and gas companies to return to existing wells to try new extraction methods, thereby increasing demand for oil and gas workers. Also, changes in policy could expand exploration and drilling for oil and natural gas in currently protected areas, potentially boosting employment. However, new production technologies are expected to dampen overall demand for oil and gas workers.

Operate equipment to increase oil flow from producing wells or to remove stuck pipe, casing, tools, or other obstructions from drilling wells. Observe load variations on strain gauges, mud pumps, and motor pressure indicators; and listen to engines, rotary chains, and other equipment to detect faulty operations or unusual well conditions. Confer with other personnel to gather information regarding pipe and tool sizes, and borehole conditions in wells. Drive truck-mounted units to well sites. Install pressure-control devices onto well heads. Thread cables through pulleys in derricks and connect hydraulic lines, using hand tools. Start pumps that circulate water, oil, or other fluids through wells to remove sand and other materials obstructing the free flow of oil. Close and seal wells no longer in use. Operate controls that raise derricks and level rigs. Direct drilling crews performing such activities as assembling and connecting pipe, applying weights to drill pipes, and drilling around lodged obstacles. Perforate well casings or sidewalls of boreholes with explosive charges. Quote prices to customers; and prepare reports of services rendered, tools used, and time required so that bills can be produced. Direct lowering of specialized equipment to point of obstruction, and push switches or pull levers to back-off or sever pipes by chemical or explosive action. Plan fishing methods and select tools for removing obstacles, such as liners, broken casing, screens, and drill pipe, from wells. Analyze conditions of unserviceable wells to determine actions to be taken to improve well conditions. Assemble and lower detection instruments into wells with obstructions. Interpret instrument readings to ascertain the depth of obstruction. Assemble and operate sound-wave generating and detecting mechanisms to determine well fluid levels.

Education/Training Required: Less than high school. **Education and Training Program:** Mining Technology/ Technician. **Knowledge/Courses—Mechanical Devices:** Machines and tools, including their designs, uses, repair, and maintenance. **Transportation:** Principles and methods for moving people or goods by air, rail, sea, or road, including the relative costs and benefits. **Physics:** Physical principles, laws, their interrelationships, and applications to understanding fluid, material, and atmospheric dynamics, and mechanical, electrical, atomic, and subatomic structures and processes. **Customer and Personal Service:** Principles and processes for providing customer and personal services. This includes customer needs assessment, meeting quality standards for services, and evaluation of customer satisfaction. **Engineering and Technology:** The practical application of engineering science and technology. This includes applying principles, techniques, procedures, and equipment to the design and production of various goods and services. **Public Safety and Security:** Relevant equipment, policies, procedures, and strategies to promote effective local, state, or national security operations for the protection of people, data, property, and institutions. **Work Experience Needed:** None. **On-the-Job Training Needed:** Moderate-term on-the-job training. **Certification/Licensure:** Voluntary certification for some specializations.

Personality Type: Realistic-Conventional-Investigative. **Career Cluster:** 01 Agriculture, Food, and Natural Resources. **Career Pathway:** 01.5 Natural Resources Systems. **Other Jobs in This Pathway:** Biological Science Teachers, Postsecondary; Climate Change Analysts; Conveyor Operators and Tenders; Derrick Operators, Oil and Gas; Engineering Technicians, Except Drafters, All Other; Environmental Economists; Environmental Restoration Planners; Environmental Science and Protection Technicians, Including Health; Environmental Science Teachers, Postsecondary; Environmental Scientists and Specialists, Including Health; Fallers; Fish and Game Wardens; Fishers and Related Fishing Workers; Forest and Conservation Technicians; Forest and Conservation Workers; Foresters; Forestry and Conservation Science Teachers, Postsecondary; Gas Compressor and Gas Pumping Station Operators; Geological Sample Test Technicians; Geophysical Data Technicians; Helpers—Extraction Workers; Industrial Ecologists; Industrial Truck and Tractor Operators; Loading Machine Operators, Underground Mining; Log Graders and Scalers; Logging Equipment Operators; Logging Workers, All Other; others.

Skills—Repairing: Repairing machines or systems using the needed tools. **Equipment Maintenance:** Performing routine maintenance on equipment and determining when

and what kind of maintenance is needed. **Operation and Control:** Controlling operations of equipment or systems. **Troubleshooting:** Determining causes of operating errors and deciding what to do about them. **Installation:** Installing equipment, machines, wiring, or programs to meet specifications. **Operation Monitoring:** Watching gauges, dials, or other indicators to make sure a machine is working properly. **Equipment Selection:** Determining the kind of tools and equipment needed to do a job. **Quality Control Analysis:** Conducting tests and inspections of products, services, or processes to evaluate quality or performance.

Work Environment: Outdoors; standing; using hands; bending or twisting the body; repetitive motions; noise; very hot or cold; bright or inadequate lighting; contaminants; high places; hazardous conditions; hazardous equipment; minor burns, cuts, bites, or stings.

Sheet Metal Workers

- ⊙ Annual Earnings: $42,730
- ⊙ Earnings Growth Potential: High (40.1%)
- ⊙ Growth: 17.6%
- ⊙ Annual Job Openings: 4,700
- ⊙ Self-Employed: 3.5%

Considerations for Job Outlook: Job opportunities should be particularly good for sheet metal workers who complete apprenticeship training or who are certified welders. Some manufacturing companies report having difficulty finding qualified applicants. Workers who have programming skills, possess multiple welding skills, and show commitment to their work will have the best job opportunities. Employment of sheet metal workers, like that of many other construction workers, is sensitive to fluctuations in the economy.

Fabricate, assemble, install, and repair sheet metal products and equipment, such as ducts, control boxes, drainpipes, and furnace casings. Determine project requirements, including scope, assembly sequences, and required methods and materials, according to blueprints, drawings, and written or verbal instructions. Lay out, measure, and mark dimensions and reference lines on material, such as roofing panels, according to drawings or templates, using calculators, scribes, dividers, squares, and rulers. Maneuver completed units into position for installation, and anchor the units. Convert blueprints into shop drawings to be followed in the construction and assembly of sheet metal products. Install assemblies, such as flashing, pipes, tubes, heating and air conditioning ducts, furnace casings, rain gutters, and down spouts, in supportive frameworks. Select gauges and types of sheet metal or non-metallic material, according to product specifications. Drill and punch holes in metal for screws, bolts, and rivets.

Education/Training Required: High school diploma or equivalent. **Education and Training Program:** Sheet Metal Technology/Sheetworking. **Knowledge/Courses—Building and Construction:** Materials, methods, and the tools involved in the construction or repair of houses, buildings, or other structures such as highways and roads. **Mechanical Devices:** Machines and tools, including their designs, uses, repair, and maintenance. **Design:** Design techniques, tools, and principles involved in production of precision technical plans, blueprints, drawings, and models. **Engineering and Technology:** The practical application of engineering science and technology. This includes applying principles, techniques, procedures, and equipment to the design and production of various goods and services. **Production and Processing:** Raw materials, production processes, quality control, costs, and other techniques for maximizing the effective manufacture and distribution of goods. **Mathematics:** Arithmetic, algebra, geometry, calculus, statistics, and their applications. **Work Experience Needed:** None. **On-the-Job Training Needed:** Apprenticeship. **Certification/Licensure:** Voluntary certification for some specializations.

Personality Type: Realistic. **Career Cluster:** 13 Manufacturing. **Career Pathway:** 13.1 Production. **Other Jobs in This Pathway:** Adhesive Bonding Machine Operators and Tenders; Assemblers and Fabricators, All Other; Avionics Technicians; Cabinetmakers and Bench Carpenters; Cleaning, Washing, and Metal Pickling Equipment Operators and Tenders; Coating, Painting, and Spraying Machine Setters, Operators, and Tenders; Computer-Controlled Machine Tool Operators, Metal and Plastic; Cooling and Freezing Equipment Operators and Tenders; Cost Estimators; Crushing, Grinding, and Polishing Machine Setters, Operators, and Tenders; Cutters and Trimmers, Hand; Cutting and Slicing Machine Setters, Operators, and Tenders; Cutting, Punching, and Press Machine Setters, Operators, and Tenders, Metal and Plastic; Drilling and Boring Machine Tool Setters, Operators, and Tenders, Metal and Plastic; Extruding and Drawing Machine Setters, Operators, and Tenders, Metal and Plastic; Extruding and Forming Machine Setters, Operators, and Tenders, Synthetic and Glass Fibers; others.

Skills—Repairing: Repairing machines or systems using the needed tools. **Equipment Maintenance:** Performing routine maintenance on equipment and determining when and what kind of maintenance is needed. **Installation:** Installing equipment, machines, wiring, or programs to meet specifications. **Equipment Selection:** Determining the kind of tools and equipment needed to do a job. **Quality Control Analysis:** Conducting tests and inspections of products, services, or processes to evaluate quality or performance. **Technology Design:** Generating or adapting equipment and technology to serve user needs. **Mathematics:** Using mathematics to solve problems. **Troubleshooting:** Determining causes of operating errors and deciding what to do about them.

Work Environment: Outdoors; standing; walking and running; using hands; bending or twisting the body; repetitive motions; noise; very hot or cold; bright or inadequate lighting; contaminants; cramped work space; high places; hazardous equipment; minor burns, cuts, bites, or stings.

Shipping, Receiving, and Traffic Clerks

- ⊙ Annual Earnings: $28,790
- ⊙ Earnings Growth Potential: Low (33.2%)
- ⊙ Growth: 0.3%
- ⊙ Annual Job Openings: 17,740
- ⊙ Self-Employed: 0.1%

Considerations for Job Outlook: There should be favorable job opportunities for material recording clerks because of the need to replace workers who leave the occupation. The increase in RFID and other sensors will enable clerks who are more comfortable with computers to have better job prospects.

Verify and maintain records on incoming and outgoing shipments. Examine contents and compare with records, such as manifests, invoices, or orders, to verify accuracy of incoming or outgoing shipments. Prepare documents, such as work orders, bills of lading, and shipping orders, to route materials. Record shipment data, such as weight, charges, space availability, and damages and discrepancies, for reporting, accounting, and recordkeeping purposes. Determine shipping method for materials, using knowledge of shipping procedures, routes, and rates. Deliver or route materials to departments, using work devices such as handtrucks, conveyors, or sorting bins. Pack, seal, label, and affix postage to prepare materials for shipping, using work devices such as hand tools, power tools, and postage meters. Confer and correspond with establishment representatives to rectify problems such as damages, shortages, and nonconformance to specifications. Requisition and store shipping materials and supplies to maintain inventory of stock. Contact carrier representatives to make arrangements and to issue instructions for shipping and delivery of materials. Compute amounts, such as space available and shipping, storage, and demurrage charges, using calculator or price list.

Education/Training Required: High school diploma or equivalent. **Education and Training Programs:** General Office Occupations and Clerical Services; Traffic, Customs, and Transportation Clerk/Technician Training. **Knowledge/Courses—Transportation:** Principles and methods for moving people or goods by air, rail, sea, or road, including the relative costs and benefits. **Production and Processing:** Raw materials, production processes, quality control, costs, and other techniques for maximizing the effective manufacture and distribution of goods. **Work Experience Needed:** None. **On-the-Job Training Needed:** Short-term on-the-job training. **Certification/Licensure:** None.

Personality Type: Conventional-Realistic-Enterprising. **Career Clusters:** 04 Business, Management, and Administration; 16 Transportation, Distribution, and Logistics. **Career Pathways:** 04.6 Administrative and Information Support; 16.3 Warehousing and Distribution Center Operations. **Other Jobs in These Pathways:** Cargo and Freight Agents; Correspondence Clerks; Couriers and Messengers; Court Clerks; Customer Service Representatives; Data Entry Keyers; Dispatchers, Except Police, Fire, and Ambulance; Executive Secretaries and Executive Administrative Assistants; File Clerks; Freight Forwarders; Human Resources Assistants, Except Payroll and Timekeeping; Information and Record Clerks, All Other; Insurance Claims Clerks; Insurance Policy Processing Clerks; Interviewers, Except Eligibility and Loan;

License Clerks; Logistics Analysts; Mail Clerks and Mail Machine Operators, Except Postal Service; Meter Readers, Utilities; Municipal Clerks; Office and Administrative Support Workers, All Other; Office Clerks, General; Office Machine Operators, Except Computer; Order Clerks; Patient Representatives; Postal Service Clerks; Postal Service Mail Carriers; Postal Service Mail Sorters, Processors, and Processing Machine Operators; Procurement Clerks; Production, Planning, and Expediting Clerks; others.

Skills—Operation and Control: Controlling operations of equipment or systems. **Quality Control Analysis:** Conducting tests and inspections of products, services, or processes to evaluate quality or performance. **Programming:** Writing computer programs for various purposes. **Management of Financial Resources:** Determining how money will be spent to get the work done and accounting for these expenditures. **Management of Material Resources:** Obtaining and seeing to the appropriate use of equipment, facilities, and materials needed to do certain work. **Operation Monitoring:** Watching gauges, dials, or other indicators to make sure a machine is working properly. **Service Orientation:** Actively looking for ways to help people.

Work Environment: More often indoors than outdoors; standing; walking and running; using hands; repetitive motions; contaminants.

Skincare Specialists

- Annual Earnings: $29,190
- Earnings Growth Potential: Medium (39.6%)
- Growth: 24.6%
- Annual Job Openings: 2,040
- Self-Employed: 36.7%

Considerations for Job Outlook: The increase in employment reflects demand for new services being offered, such as mini sessions (quick facials at a lower cost) and mobile facials (making house calls). In addition, the desire among women and a growing number of men to reduce the effects of aging and to lead a healthier lifestyle through better grooming should result in employment growth, including skin treatments for relaxation and well-being.

Provide skincare treatments to face and body to enhance individuals' appearance. Sterilize equipment, and clean work areas. Keep records of client needs and preferences, and the services provided. Demonstrate how to clean and care for skin properly, and recommend skin-care regimens. Examine clients' skin, using magnifying lamps or visors when necessary, in order to evaluate skin condition and appearance. Select and apply cosmetic products such as creams, lotions, and tonics. Cleanse clients' skin with water, creams, or lotions. Treat the facial skin to maintain and improve its appearance, using specialized techniques and products such as peels and masks. Refer clients to medical personnel for treatment of serious skin problems. Determine which products or colors will improve clients' skin quality and appearance. Provide facial and body massages. Perform simple extractions to remove blackheads. Remove body and facial hair by applying wax. Apply chemical peels in order to reduce fine lines and age spots. Advise clients about colors and types of makeup, and instruct them in makeup application techniques. Sell makeup to clients. Collaborate with plastic surgeons and dermatologists in order to provide patients with preoperative and postoperative skin care. Give manicures and pedicures, and apply artificial nails. Tint eyelashes and eyebrows.

Education/Training Required: Postsecondary vocational training. **Education and Training Programs:** Cosmetology/Cosmetologist Training, General; Facial Treatment Specialist/Facialist Training. **Knowledge/Courses—Sales and Marketing:** Principles and methods for showing, promoting, and selling products or services. This includes marketing strategy and tactics, product demonstration, sales techniques, and sales control systems. **Chemistry:** The chemical composition, structure, and properties of substances and of the chemical processes and transformations that they undergo. This includes uses of chemicals and their danger signs, production techniques, and disposal methods. **Customer and Personal Service:** Principles and processes for providing customer and personal services. This includes customer needs assessment, meeting quality standards for services, and evaluation of customer satisfaction. **Work Experience Needed:** None. **On-the-Job Training Needed:** None. **Certification/Licensure:** Licensure.

Personality Type: Enterprising-Social-Realistic. **Career Cluster:** 10 Human Services. **Career Pathway:** 10.4 Personal Care Services. **Other Jobs in This Pathway:** Barbers; Embalmers; Funeral Attendants; Funeral Service Managers; Hairdressers, Hairstylists, and Cosmetologists; Laundry and Dry-Cleaning Workers; Makeup Artists, Theatrical and Performance; Manicurists and Pedicurists; Pressers, Textile, Garment, and Related Materials; Sewers, Hand; Sewing Machine Operators; Shampooers; Tailors, Dressmakers, and Custom Sewers; Textile Bleaching and Dyeing Machine Operators and Tenders.

Skills—Service Orientation: Actively looking for ways to help people.

Work Environment: Indoors; standing; using hands; bending or twisting the body; repetitive motions.

Social and Human Service Assistants

- ⊙ Annual Earnings: $28,740
- ⊙ Earnings Growth Potential: Low (33.3%)
- ⊙ Growth: 27.6%
- ⊙ Annual Job Openings: 18,910
- ⊙ Self-Employed: 0.1%

Considerations for Job Outlook: Low pay and heavy workloads cause many workers to leave this occupation, which creates good opportunities for new workers entering the field.

Assist in providing client services in a wide variety of fields, such as psychology, rehabilitation, or social work, including support for families. Keep records and prepare reports for owners or management concerning visits with clients. Submit reports, and review reports or problems with superiors. Interview individuals and family members to compile information on social, educational, criminal, institutional, or drug histories. Provide information and refer individuals to public or private agencies or community services for assistance. Consult with supervisors concerning programs for individual families. Advise clients regarding food stamps, child care, food, money management, sanitation, or housekeeping. Oversee day-to-day group activities of residents in institution. Visit individuals in homes or attend group meetings to provide information on agency services, requirements, and procedures. Monitor free, supplementary meal programs to ensure cleanliness of facilities and that eligibility guidelines are met for persons receiving meals. Meet with youth groups to acquaint them with consequences of delinquent acts. Assist in planning of food budgets, using charts and sample budgets. Transport and accompany clients to shopping areas or to appointments, using automobiles. Assist in locating housing for displaced individuals. Observe and discuss meal preparation, and suggest alternative methods of food preparation. Observe clients' food selections, and recommend alternative economical and nutritional food choices. Explain rules established by owners or management, such as sanitation and maintenance requirements or parking regulations.

Education/Training Required: High school diploma or equivalent. **Education and Training Program:** Mental and Social Health Services and Allied Professions, Other. **Knowledge/Courses—Therapy and Counseling:** Principles, methods, and procedures for diagnosis, treatment, and rehabilitation of physical and mental dysfunctions, and for career counseling and guidance. **Philosophy and Theology:** Different philosophical systems and religions. This includes their basic principles, values, ethics, ways of thinking, customs, practices, and their impact on human culture. **Psychology:** Human behavior and performance; individual differences in ability, personality, and interests; learning and motivation; psychological research methods; and the assessment and treatment of behavioral and affective disorders. **Customer and Personal Service:** Principles and processes for providing customer and personal services. This includes customer needs assessment, meeting quality standards for services, and evaluation of customer satisfaction. **Sociology and Anthropology:** Group behavior and dynamics, societal trends and influences, human migrations, ethnicity, and cultures and their history and origins. **Clerical Practices:** Administrative and clerical procedures and systems such as word processing, managing files and records, stenography and transcription, designing forms, and other office procedures and terminology. **Work Experience Needed:** None. **On-the-Job Training Needed:** Short-term on-the-job training. **Certification/Licensure:** None.

Personality Type: Conventional-Social-Enterprising. **Career Cluster:** 08 Health Science. **Career Pathway:** 08.1 Therapeutic Services. **Other Jobs in This Pathway:** Acupuncturists; Allergists and Immunologists; Anesthesiologists; Art Therapists; Chiropractors; Clinical Psychologists; Community and Social Service Specialists, All Other; Counseling Psychologists; Counselors, All Other; Dental Assistants; Dental Hygienists; Dentists, All Other Specialists; Dentists, General; Dermatologists; Diagnostic Medical Sonographers; Dietetic Technicians; Dietitians and Nutritionists; Family and General Practitioners; Health Diagnosing and Treating Practitioners, All Other; Health Specialties Teachers, Postsecondary; Health Technologists and Technicians, All Other; Healthcare Practitioners and Technical Workers, All Other; Healthcare Support Workers, All Other; Home Health Aides; Hospitalists; Industrial-Organizational Psychologists; Internists, General; Licensed Practical and Licensed Vocational Nurses; Life, Physical, and Social Science Technicians, All Other; Low Vision Therapists, Orientation and Mobility Specialists, and Vision Rehabilitation Therapists; others.

Skills—Social Perceptiveness: Being aware of others' reactions and understanding why they react as they do. **Service Orientation:** Actively looking for ways to help people. **Active Listening:** Giving full attention to what other people are saying, taking time to understand the points being made, asking questions as appropriate, and not interrupting at inappropriate times. **Science:** Using scientific rules and methods to solve problems. **Speaking:** Talking to others to convey information effectively. **Learning Strategies:** Selecting and using training/instructional methods and procedures appropriate for the situation when learning or teaching new things. **Systems Analysis:** Determining how a system should work and how changes in conditions, operations, and the environment will affect outcomes. **Persuasion:** Persuading others to change their minds or behavior.

Work Environment: Indoors; sitting.

Social Science Research Assistants

- Annual Earnings: $38,800
- Earnings Growth Potential: High (40.3%)
- Growth: 14.8%
- Annual Job Openings: 1,700
- Self-Employed: 0.4%

Considerations for Job Outlook: About-average employment growth is projected.

Assist social scientists in laboratory, survey, and other social science research. Code data in preparation for computer entry. Provide assistance in the design of survey instruments such as questionnaires. Prepare, manipulate, and manage extensive databases. Prepare tables, graphs, fact sheets, and written reports summarizing research results. Obtain informed consent of research subjects or their guardians. Edit and submit protocols and other required research documentation. Screen potential subjects in order to determine their suitability as study participants. Conduct Internet-based and library research. Supervise the work of survey interviewers. Perform descriptive and multivariate statistical analyses of data, using computer software. Recruit and schedule research participants. Develop and implement research quality control procedures. Track research participants, and perform any necessary follow-up tasks. Verify the accuracy and validity of data entered in databases; correct any errors. Track laboratory supplies and expenses such as participant reimbursement. Provide assistance with the preparation of project-related reports, manuscripts, and presentations. Present research findings to groups of people. Perform needs assessments and/or consult with clients in order to determine the types of research and information that are required. Allocate and manage laboratory space and resources. Design and create special programs for tasks such as statistical analysis and data entry and cleaning.

Education/Training Required: Associate degree. **Education and Training Program:** Social Sciences, General. **Knowledge/Courses—Psychology:** Human behavior and performance; individual differences in ability, personality, and interests; learning and motivation; psychological research methods; and the assessment and treatment of behavioral and affective disorders. **Sociology and Anthropology:** Group behavior and dynamics, societal trends and influences, human migrations, ethnicity, and cultures and their history and origins. **Clerical Practices:** Administrative and clerical procedures and systems such as word processing, managing files and records, stenography and transcription, designing forms, and other office procedures and terminology. **Computers and Electronics:** Circuit boards, processors, chips, electronic equipment, and computer hardware and software, including applications and programming. **English Language:** The structure and content of the English language including the meaning and spelling of words, rules of composition, and grammar. **Communications and Media:** Media production, communication, and dissemination techniques and methods. This includes alternative ways to inform and entertain via

written, oral, and visual media. **Work Experience Needed:** None. **On-the-Job Training Needed:** None. **Certification/Licensure:** None.

Personality Type: Conventional-Investigative. **Career Cluster:** 10 Human Services. **Career Pathway:** 10.3 Family and Community Services. **Other Jobs in This Pathway:** Chief Executives; Child, Family, and School Social Workers; Childcare Workers; City and Regional Planning Aides; Counselors, All Other; Eligibility Interviewers, Government Programs; Farm and Home Management Advisors; Home Economics Teachers, Postsecondary; Legislators; Managers, All Other; Marriage and Family Therapists; Nannies; Personal Care Aides; Probation Officers and Correctional Treatment Specialists; Protective Service Workers, All Other; Social and Community Service Managers; Social Scientists and Related Workers, All Other; Social Work Teachers, Postsecondary; Social Workers, All Other; Sociologists; Supply Chain Managers.

Skills—Programming: Writing computer programs for various purposes. **Science:** Using scientific rules and methods to solve problems. **Mathematics:** Using mathematics to solve problems. **Reading Comprehension:** Understanding written sentences and paragraphs in work-related documents. **Quality Control Analysis:** Conducting tests and inspections of products, services, or processes to evaluate quality or performance. **Management of Financial Resources:** Determining how money will be spent to get the work done and accounting for these expenditures. **Operations Analysis:** Analyzing needs and product requirements to create a design. **Technology Design:** Generating or adapting equipment and technology to serve user needs.

Work Environment: Indoors; sitting.

Job Specialization: City and Regional Planning Aides

Compile data from various sources, such as maps, reports, and field and file investigations, for use by city planners in making planning studies. Participate in and support team planning efforts. Prepare reports, using statistics, charts, and graphs, to illustrate planning studies in areas such as population, land use, or zoning. Research, compile, analyze, and organize information from maps, reports, investigations, and books for use in reports and special projects. Provide and process zoning and project permits and applications. Respond to public inquiries and complaints. Serve as liaison between planning department and other departments and agencies. Inspect sites, and review plans for minor development permit applications. Conduct interviews, surveys, and site inspections concerning factors that affect land usage, such as zoning, traffic flow, and housing. Prepare, maintain, and update files and records, including land use data and statistics. Prepare, develop, and maintain maps and databases. Perform clerical duties such as composing, typing, and proofreading documents; scheduling appointments and meetings; handling mail; and posting public notices. Perform code enforcement tasks.

Education and Training Program: Social Sciences, General. **Knowledge/Courses—Geography:** Principles and methods for describing the features of land, sea, and air masses, including their physical characteristics, locations, interrelationships, and distribution of plant, animal, and human life. **History and Archeology:** Historical events and their causes, indicators, and effects on civilizations and cultures. **Design:** Design techniques, tools, and principles involved in production of precision technical plans, blueprints, drawings, and models. **Law and Government:** Laws, legal codes, court procedures, precedents, government regulations, executive orders, agency rules, and the democratic political process. **Building and Construction:** Materials, methods, and the tools involved in the construction or repair of houses, buildings, or other structures such as highways and roads. **Sociology and Anthropology:** Group behavior and dynamics, societal trends and influences, human migrations, ethnicity, and cultures and their history and origins.

Personality Type: Conventional-Realistic. **Career Cluster:** 10 Human Services. **Career Pathway:** 10.3 Family and Community Services. **Other Jobs in This Pathway:** Chief Executives; Child, Family, and School Social Workers; Childcare Workers; Counselors, All Other; Eligibility Interviewers, Government Programs; Farm and Home Management Advisors; Home Economics Teachers, Postsecondary; Legislators; Managers, All Other; Marriage and Family Therapists; Nannies; Personal Care Aides; Probation Officers and Correctional Treatment Specialists; Protective Service Workers, All Other; Social and Community Service Managers; Social Science Research Assistants; Social Scientists and Related Workers, All Other; Social

Work Teachers, Postsecondary; Social Workers, All Other; Sociologists; Supply Chain Managers.

Skills—Science: Using scientific rules and methods to solve problems. **Systems Analysis:** Determining how a system should work and how changes in conditions, operations, and the environment will affect outcomes. **Negotiation:** Bringing others together and trying to reconcile differences. **Mathematics:** Using mathematics to solve problems. **Writing:** Communicating effectively in writing as appropriate for the needs of the audience. **Systems Evaluation:** Identifying measures or indicators of system performance and the actions needed to improve or correct performance relative to the goals of the system. **Speaking:** Talking to others to convey information effectively. **Operations Analysis:** Analyzing needs and product requirements to create a design.

Work Environment: Indoors; sitting.

Stationary Engineers and Boiler Operators

- ⊙ Annual Earnings: $53,070
- ⊙ Earnings Growth Potential: Medium (37.7%)
- ⊙ Growth: 6.1%
- ⊙ Annual Job Openings: 1,060
- ⊙ Self-Employed: 0.4%

Considerations for Job Outlook: Job opportunities should be best for those with apprenticeship training. Stationary engineer and boiler operator positions are relatively high paying, and engineering staffs are typically small. Although apprenticeship programs have a competitive application process, they are the most reliable path into the occupation. In addition, workers who are licensed before they look for work will have better job opportunities.

Operate or maintain stationary engines, boilers, or other mechanical equipment to provide utilities for buildings or industrial processes. Operate or tend stationary engines, boilers, and auxiliary equipment such as pumps, compressors and air-conditioning equipment, in order to supply and maintain steam or heat for buildings, marine vessels, or pneumatic tools. Observe and interpret readings on gauges, meters, and charts registering various aspects of boiler operation, in order to ensure that boilers are operating properly. Test boiler water quality or arrange for testing; and take any necessary corrective action, such as adding chemicals to prevent corrosion and harmful deposits. Monitor boiler water, chemical, and fuel levels, and make adjustments to maintain required levels. Activate valves to maintain required amounts of water in boilers, to adjust supplies of combustion air, and to control the flow of fuel into burners. Fire coal furnaces by hand or with stokers and gas- or oil-fed boilers, using automatic gas feeds or oil pumps. Monitor and inspect equipment, computer terminals, switches, valves, gauges, alarms, safety devices, and meters to detect leaks or malfunctions, and to ensure that equipment is operating efficiently and safely. Analyze problems and take appropriate action to ensure continuous and reliable operation of equipment and systems. Maintain daily logs of operation, maintenance, and safety activities, including test results, instrument readings, and details of equipment malfunctions and maintenance work. Adjust controls and/or valves on equipment to provide power, and to regulate and set operations of system and/or industrial processes. Switch from automatic controls to manual controls, and isolate equipment mechanically and electrically, in order to allow for safe inspection and repair work. Clean and lubricate boilers and auxiliary equipment and make minor adjustments as needed, using hand tools. Check the air quality of ventilation systems and make adjustments to ensure compliance with mandated safety codes.

Education/Training Required: High school diploma or equivalent. **Education and Training Program:** Building/Property Maintenance. **Knowledge/Courses—Mechanical Devices:** Machines and tools, including their designs, uses, repair, and maintenance. **Building and Construction:** Materials, methods, and the tools involved in the construction or repair of houses, buildings, or other structures such as highways and roads. **Chemistry:** The chemical composition, structure, and properties of substances and of the chemical processes and transformations that they undergo. This includes uses of chemicals and their danger signs, production techniques, and disposal methods. **Physics:** Physical principles, laws, their interrelationships, and applications to understanding fluid, material, and atmospheric dynamics, and mechanical, electrical, atomic, and subatomic structures and processes. **Design:** Design techniques, tools, and principles involved in production of precision technical plans, blueprints, drawings, and models. **Engineering and Technology:** The practical application of engineering science and technology. This

includes applying principles, techniques, procedures, and equipment to the design and production of various goods and services. **Work Experience Needed:** None. **On-the-Job Training Needed:** Long-term on-the-job training. **Certification/Licensure:** Licensure.

Personality Type: Realistic-Investigative-Conventional. **Career Cluster:** 13 Manufacturing. **Career Pathway:** 13.3 Maintenance, Installation, and Repair. **Other Jobs in This Pathway:** Aircraft Mechanics and Service Technicians; Automotive Engineering Technicians; Automotive Specialty Technicians; Avionics Technicians; Biological Technicians; Camera and Photographic Equipment Repairers; Chemical Equipment Operators and Tenders; Civil Engineering Technicians; Coil Winders, Tapers, and Finishers; Computer, Automated Teller, and Office Machine Repairers; Construction and Related Workers, All Other; Control and Valve Installers and Repairers, Except Mechanical Door; Electric Motor, Power Tool, and Related Repairers; Electrical and Electronic Equipment Assemblers; Electrical and Electronics Repairers, Commercial and Industrial Equipment; Electrical and Electronics Repairers, Powerhouse, Substation, and Relay; Electrical Engineering Technicians; Electrical Engineering Technologists; Electromechanical Engineering Technologists; Electromechanical Equipment Assemblers; Electronics Engineering Technicians; Electronics Engineering Technologists; others.

Skills—Repairing: Repairing machines or systems using the needed tools. **Equipment Maintenance:** Performing routine maintenance on equipment and determining when and what kind of maintenance is needed. **Troubleshooting:** Determining causes of operating errors and deciding what to do about them. **Operation and Control:** Controlling operations of equipment or systems. **Equipment Selection:** Determining the kind of tools and equipment needed to do a job. **Operation Monitoring:** Watching gauges, dials, or other indicators to make sure a machine is working properly. **Science:** Using scientific rules and methods to solve problems. **Installation:** Installing equipment, machines, wiring, or programs to meet specifications.

Work Environment: More often indoors than outdoors; standing; using hands; noise; very hot or cold; bright or inadequate lighting; contaminants; cramped work space; high places; hazardous conditions; hazardous equipment; minor burns, cuts, bites, or stings.

Stonemasons

- Annual Earnings: $36,640
- Earnings Growth Potential: Medium (38.7%)
- Growth: 36.5%
- Annual Job Openings: 890
- Self-Employed: 28.4%

Considerations for Job Outlook: Overall job prospects should improve over the coming decade as construction activity rebounds from the recent recession. As with many other construction workers, employment is sensitive to the fluctuations of the economy. On the one hand, workers may experience periods of unemployment when the overall level of construction falls. On the other hand, shortages of workers may occur in some areas during peak periods of building activity. The masonry workforce is growing older, and a large number of masons are expected to retire over the next decade, which will create many job openings. Highly skilled masons with a good job history and work experience in construction should have the best job opportunities.

Build stone structures, such as piers, walls, and abutments. Lay walks, curbstones, or special types of masonry for vats, tanks, and floors. Lay out wall patterns or foundations, using straight edges, rules, or staked lines. Shape, trim, face, and cut marble or stone preparatory to setting, using power saws, cutting equipment, and hand tools. Set vertical and horizontal alignment of structures, using plumb bobs, gauge lines, and levels. Mix mortar or grout and pour or spread mortar or grout on marble slabs, stone, or foundations. Remove wedges, fill joints between stones, and finish joints between stones, using trowels, and smooth mortar to attractive finishs, using tuck pointers. Clean excess mortar or grout from the surface of marble, stone, or monuments, using sponges, brushes, water, or acid. Set stone or marble in place, according to layouts or patterns. Lay brick to build shells of chimneys and smokestacks or to line or reline industrial furnaces, kilns, boilers, and similar installations. Replace broken or missing masonry units in walls or floors. Smooth, polish, and bevel surfaces, using hand tools and power tools. Drill holes in marble or ornamental stone and anchor brackets in holes. Repair cracked or chipped areas of stone or marble, using blowtorches and mastic, and remove rough or defective spots from concrete, using power grinders or chisels and

hammers. Remove sections of monuments from truck beds, and guide stone onto foundations, using skids, hoists, or truck cranes. Construct and install prefabricated masonry units. Dig trenches for foundations of monuments, using picks and shovels. Position molds along guidelines of walls, press molds in place, and remove molds and paper from walls. Line interiors of molds with treated paper and fill molds with composition-stone mixture.

Education/Training Required: High school diploma or equivalent. **Education and Training Program:** Masonry/Mason Training. **Knowledge/Courses—Building and Construction:** Materials, methods, and the tools involved in the construction or repair of houses, buildings, or other structures such as highways and roads. **Mechanical Devices:** Machines and tools, including their designs, uses, repair, and maintenance. **Design:** Design techniques, tools, and principles involved in production of precision technical plans, blueprints, drawings, and models. **Mathematics:** Arithmetic, algebra, geometry, calculus, statistics, and their applications. **Public Safety and Security:** Relevant equipment, policies, procedures, and strategies to promote effective local, state, or national security operations for the protection of people, data, property, and institutions. **Education and Training:** Principles and methods for curriculum and training design, teaching and instruction for individuals and groups, and the measurement of training effects. **Work Experience Needed:** None. **On-the-Job Training Needed:** Apprenticeship. **Certification/Licensure:** None.

Personality Type: Realistic. **Career Cluster:** 02 Architecture and Construction. **Career Pathway:** 02.2 Construction. **Other Jobs in This Pathway:** Boilermakers; Brickmasons and Blockmasons; Carpet Installers; Cement Masons and Concrete Finishers; Construction and Building Inspectors; Construction and Related Workers, All Other; Construction Carpenters; Construction Laborers; Construction Managers; Continuous Mining Machine Operators; Cost Estimators; Crane and Tower Operators; Dredge Operators; Drywall and Ceiling Tile Installers; Earth Drillers, Except Oil and Gas; Electrical Power-Line Installers and Repairers; Electricians; Electromechanical Equipment Assemblers; Engineering Technicians, Except Drafters, All Other; Excavating and Loading Machine and Dragline Operators; Explosives Workers, Ordnance Handling Experts, and Blasters; Extraction Workers, All Other; First-Line Supervisors of Construction Trades and

Extraction Workers; Floor Layers, Except Carpet, Wood, and Hard Tiles; Floor Sanders and Finishers; Glaziers; Heating and Air Conditioning Mechanics and Installers; Helpers, Construction Trades, All Other; others.

Skills—Repairing: Repairing machines or systems using the needed tools. **Equipment Selection:** Determining the kind of tools and equipment needed to do a job. **Equipment Maintenance:** Performing routine maintenance on equipment and determining when and what kind of maintenance is needed. **Operation and Control:** Controlling operations of equipment or systems. **Quality Control Analysis:** Conducting tests and inspections of products, services, or processes to evaluate quality or performance. **Management of Material Resources:** Obtaining and seeing to the appropriate use of equipment, facilities, and materials needed to do certain work. **Troubleshooting:** Determining causes of operating errors and deciding what to do about them. **Coordination:** Adjusting actions in relation to others' actions.

Work Environment: Outdoors; standing; walking and running; kneeling, crouching, stooping, or crawling; using hands; bending or twisting the body; repetitive motions; noise; very hot or cold; hazardous equipment; minor burns, cuts, bites, or stings.

Structural Iron and Steel Workers

- ⊙ Annual Earnings: $45,690
- ⊙ Earnings Growth Potential: High (42.0%)
- ⊙ Growth: 21.9%
- ⊙ Annual Job Openings: 2,540
- ⊙ Self-Employed: 4.3%

Considerations for Job Outlook: Those who are certified in welding and rigging should have the best job opportunities. Those with prior military service are also viewed favorably during initial hiring. As with many other construction workers, employment of iron workers is sensitive to the fluctuations of the economy.

Raise, place, and unite iron or steel girders, columns, and other structural members to form completed structures or structural frameworks. Read specifications and blueprints to determine the locations, quantities, and sizes of materials required. Verify vertical and horizontal alignment of structural-steel members, using plumb bobs, laser equipment, transits, and levels. Connect columns, beams, and girders with bolts, following blueprints and instructions from supervisors. Hoist steel beams, girders, and columns into place, using cranes, or signal hoisting equipment operators to lift and position structural-steel members. Bolt aligned structural-steel members in position for permanent riveting, bolting, or welding into place. Ride on girders or other structural-steel members to position them, or use ropes to guide them into position. Fabricate metal parts such as steel frames, columns, beams, and girders, according to blueprints or instructions from supervisors. Pull, push, or pry structural-steel members into approximate positions for bolting into place. Cut, bend, and weld steel pieces, using metal shears, torches, and welding equipment. Fasten structural-steel members to hoist cables, using chains, cables, or ropes. Assemble hoisting equipment and rigging, such as cables, pulleys, and hooks, to move heavy equipment and materials. Force structural-steel members into final positions, using turnbuckles, crowbars, jacks, and hand tools. Erect metal and precast concrete components for structures such as buildings, bridges, dams, towers, storage tanks, fences, and highway guard rails. Unload and position prefabricated steel units for hoisting as needed. Drive drift pins through rivet holes to align rivet holes in structural-steel members with corresponding holes in previously placed members. Dismantle structures and equipment. Insert sealing strips, wiring, insulating material, ladders, flanges, gauges, and valves, depending on types of structures being assembled. Catch hot rivets in buckets, and insert rivets in holes, using tongs. Place blocks under reinforcing bars used to reinforce floors.

Education/Training Required: High school diploma or equivalent. **Education and Training Programs:** Construction Trades, Other; Metal Building Assembly/Assembler. **Knowledge/Courses—Building and Construction:** Materials, methods, and the tools involved in the construction or repair of houses, buildings, or other structures such as highways and roads. **Engineering and Technology:** The practical application of engineering science and technology. This includes applying principles, techniques, procedures, and equipment to the design and production of various goods and services. **Mechanical Devices:** Machines and tools, including their designs, uses, repair, and maintenance. **Production and Processing:** Raw materials, production processes, quality control, costs, and other techniques for maximizing the effective manufacture and distribution of goods. **Design:** Design techniques, tools, and principles involved in production of precision technical plans, blueprints, drawings, and models. **Physics:** Physical principles, laws, their interrelationships, and applications to understanding fluid, material, and atmospheric dynamics, and mechanical, electrical, atomic, and subatomic structures and processes. **Work Experience Needed:** None. **On-the-Job Training Needed:** Apprenticeship. **Certification/Licensure:** Voluntary certification by association.

Personality Type: Realistic-Investigative-Conventional. **Career Cluster:** 02 Architecture and Construction. **Career Pathway:** 02.2 Construction. **Other Jobs in This Pathway:** Boilermakers; Brickmasons and Blockmasons; Carpet Installers; Cement Masons and Concrete Finishers; Construction and Building Inspectors; Construction and Related Workers, All Other; Construction Carpenters; Construction Laborers; Construction Managers; Continuous Mining Machine Operators; Cost Estimators; Crane and Tower Operators; Dredge Operators; Drywall and Ceiling Tile Installers; Earth Drillers, Except Oil and Gas; Electrical Power-Line Installers and Repairers; Electricians; Electromechanical Equipment Assemblers; Engineering Technicians, Except Drafters, All Other; Excavating and Loading Machine and Dragline Operators; Explosives Workers, Ordnance Handling Experts, and Blasters; Extraction Workers, All Other; First-Line Supervisors of Construction Trades and Extraction Workers; Floor Layers, Except Carpet, Wood, and Hard Tiles; Floor Sanders and Finishers; Glaziers; Heating and Air Conditioning Mechanics and Installers; Helpers, Construction Trades, All Other; others.

Skills—Equipment Selection: Determining the kind of tools and equipment needed to do a job. **Operation and Control:** Controlling operations of equipment or systems. **Repairing:** Repairing machines or systems using the needed tools. **Equipment Maintenance:** Performing routine maintenance on equipment and determining when and what kind of maintenance is needed. **Quality Control Analysis:** Conducting tests and inspections of products, services, or processes to evaluate quality or performance. **Installation:** Installing equipment, machines, wiring, or programs to meet specifications. **Troubleshooting:** Determining causes of operating errors and deciding what to do about them. **Operation Monitoring:** Watching gauges, dials, or other indicators to make sure a machine is working properly.

Work Environment: Outdoors; standing; climbing; walking and running; balancing; using hands; bending or twisting the body; repetitive motions; noise; very hot or cold; bright or inadequate lighting; contaminants; cramped work space; whole-body vibration; high places; hazardous conditions; hazardous equipment; minor burns, cuts, bites, or stings.

Structural Metal Fabricators and Fitters

- ⊙ Annual Earnings: $35,170
- ⊙ Earnings Growth Potential: Low (31.2%)
- ⊙ Growth: 15.7%
- ⊙ Annual Job Openings: 2,830
- ⊙ Self-Employed: 1.8%

Considerations for Job Outlook: Qualified applicants, including those with technical vocational training and certification, should have the best job opportunities in the manufacturing sector, particularly in growing, high-technology industries such as aerospace and electromedical devices. Some employers report difficulty finding qualified applicants looking for manufacturing employment. Many job openings should result from the need to replace workers leaving or retiring from this large occupation.

Fabricate, position, align, and fit parts of structural metal products. Position, align, fit, and weld parts to form complete units or subunits, following blueprints and layout specifications, and using jigs, welding torches, and hand tools. Verify conformance of workpieces to specifications, using squares, rulers, and measuring tapes. Tack-weld fitted parts together. Lay out and examine metal stock or workpieces to be processed in order to ensure that specifications are met. Align and fit parts according to specifications, using jacks, turnbuckles, wedges, drift pins, pry bars, and hammers. Locate and mark workpiece bending and cutting lines, allowing for stock thickness, machine and welding shrinkage, and other component specifications. Position or tighten braces, jacks, clamps, ropes, and bolt straps, or bolt parts in position for welding or riveting. Study engineering drawings and blueprints to determine materials requirements and task sequences. Move parts into position, manually or by using hoists or cranes. Set up and operate fabricating machines such as brakes, rolls, shears, flame cutters, grinders, and drill presses to bend, cut, form, punch, drill, or otherwise form and assemble metal components. Hammer, chip, and grind workpieces in order to cut, bend, and straighten metal. Smooth workpiece edges, and fix taps, tubes, and valves. Design and construct templates and fixtures, using hand tools. Straighten warped or bent parts, using sledges, hand torches, straightening presses, or bulldozers. Mark reference points onto floors or face blocks and transpose them to workpieces, using measuring devices, squares, chalk, and soapstone. Set up face blocks, jigs, and fixtures. Remove high spots and cut bevels, using hand files, portable grinders, and cutting torches. Direct welders to build up low spots or short pieces with weld. Lift or move materials and finished products, using large cranes. Heat-treat parts, using acetylene torches. Preheat workpieces to make them malleable, using hand torches or furnaces.

Education/Training Required: High school diploma or equivalent. **Education and Training Program:** Machine Shop Technology/Assistant. **Knowledge/Courses—Design:** Design techniques, tools, and principles involved in production of precision technical plans, blueprints, drawings, and models. **Building and Construction:** Materials, methods, and the tools involved in the construction or repair of houses, buildings, or other structures such as highways and roads. **Mechanical Devices:** Machines and tools, including their designs, uses, repair, and maintenance. **Production and Processing:** Raw materials, production processes, quality control, costs, and other techniques for maximizing the effective manufacture and distribution of goods. **Work Experience Needed:** None. **On-the-Job Training Needed:** Moderate-term on-the-job training. **Certification/Licensure:** Voluntary certification by association.

Personality Type: Realistic-Conventional. **Career Cluster:** 13 Manufacturing. **Career Pathway:** 13.1 Production. **Other Jobs in This Pathway:** Adhesive Bonding Machine Operators and Tenders; Assemblers and Fabricators, All Other; Avionics Technicians; Cabinetmakers and Bench Carpenters; Cleaning, Washing, and Metal Pickling Equipment Operators and Tenders; Coating, Painting, and Spraying Machine Setters, Operators, and Tenders; Computer-Controlled Machine Tool Operators, Metal and Plastic; Cooling and Freezing Equipment Operators and Tenders; Cost Estimators; Crushing, Grinding, and Polishing Machine Setters, Operators, and Tenders; Cutters and Trimmers, Hand; Cutting and Slicing Machine

Setters, Operators, and Tenders; Cutting, Punching, and Press Machine Setters, Operators, and Tenders, Metal and Plastic; Drilling and Boring Machine Tool Setters, Operators, and Tenders, Metal and Plastic; Extruding and Drawing Machine Setters, Operators, and Tenders, Metal and Plastic; Extruding and Forming Machine Setters, Operators, and Tenders, Synthetic and Glass Fibers; others.

Skills—Quality Control Analysis: Conducting tests and inspections of products, services, or processes to evaluate quality or performance. **Operation and Control:** Controlling operations of equipment or systems. **Installation:** Installing equipment, machines, wiring, or programs to meet specifications. **Troubleshooting:** Determining causes of operating errors and deciding what to do about them. **Operation Monitoring:** Watching gauges, dials, or other indicators to make sure a machine is working properly.

Work Environment: Standing; walking and running; using hands; bending or twisting the body; repetitive motions; noise; very hot or cold; contaminants; hazardous equipment; minor burns, cuts, bites, or stings.

Substance Abuse and Behavioral Disorder Counselors

- ⊙ Annual Earnings: $38,560
- ⊙ Earnings Growth Potential: Low (34.4%)
- ⊙ Growth: 27.4%
- ⊙ Annual Job Openings: 4,170
- ⊙ Self-Employed: 6.6%

Considerations for Job Outlook: Job prospects are excellent for substance abuse and behavioral disorder counselors, particularly for those with specialized training or education. Employers often have difficulty recruiting workers with the proper educational requirements and experience in working with addiction. In addition, many workers leave the field after a few years and need to be replaced. As result, those interested in entering this field should find favorable prospects.

Counsel and advise individuals with alcohol, tobacco, drug, gambling, eating disorder, or other problems. Counsel clients and patients individually and in group sessions to assist in overcoming dependencies, adjusting to life, and making changes. Complete and maintain accurate records and reports regarding the patients' histories and progress, services provided, and other required information. Develop client treatment plans based on research, clinical experience, and client histories. Review and evaluate clients' progress in relation to measurable goals described in treatment and care plans. Interview clients, review records, and confer with other professionals to evaluate individuals' mental and physical conditions and to determine individuals' suitability for participation in specific programs. Intervene as advocates for clients or patients to resolve emergency problems in crisis situations. Provide clients or family members with information about addiction issues and about available services and programs, making appropriate referrals when necessary. Modify treatment plans to comply with changes in client status. Coordinate counseling efforts with mental health professionals and other health professionals such as doctors, nurses, and social workers. Attend training sessions to increase knowledge and skills. Plan and implement follow-up and aftercare programs for clients to be discharged from treatment programs. Conduct chemical-dependency program orientation sessions. Counsel family members to assist them in understanding, dealing with, and supporting clients or patients.

Education/Training Required: High school diploma or equivalent. **Education and Training Programs:** Clinical/Medical Social Work; Mental and Social Health Services and Allied Professions, Other; Substance Abuse/Addiction Counseling. **Knowledge/Courses—Therapy and Counseling:** Principles, methods, and procedures for diagnosis, treatment, and rehabilitation of physical and mental dysfunctions, and for career counseling and guidance. **Psychology:** Human behavior and performance; individual differences in ability, personality, and interests; learning and motivation; psychological research methods; and the assessment and treatment of behavioral and affective disorders. **Sociology and Anthropology:** Group behavior and dynamics, societal trends and influences, human migrations, ethnicity, and cultures and their history and origins. **Philosophy and Theology:** Different philosophical systems and religions. This includes their basic principles, values, ethics, ways of thinking, customs, practices, and their impact on human culture. **Education and Training:** Principles and methods for curriculum and training design, teaching and instruction for individuals and groups, and the measurement of training effects. **Clerical Practices:** Administrative and clerical procedures and systems such as word processing, managing files and records, stenography

and transcription, designing forms, and other office procedures and terminology. **Work Experience Needed:** None. **On-the-Job Training Needed:** Moderate-term on-the-job training. **Certification/Licensure:** Licensure in many states; voluntary certification by association in others.

Personality Type: Social-Artistic-Investigative. **Career Clusters:** 08 Health Science; 10 Human Services. **Career Pathways:** 08.1 Therapeutic Services; 08.3 Health Informatics; 10.2 Counseling and Mental Health Services. **Other Jobs in These Pathways:** Acupuncturists; Allergists and Immunologists; Anesthesiologists; Area, Ethnic, and Cultural Studies Teachers, Postsecondary; Art Therapists; Chiropractors; Clergy; Clinical Psychologists; Communications Teachers, Postsecondary; Community and Social Service Specialists, All Other; Counseling Psychologists; Counselors, All Other; Dental Assistants; Dental Hygienists; Dental Laboratory Technicians; Dentists, All Other Specialists; Dentists, General; Dermatologists; Diagnostic Medical Sonographers; Dietetic Technicians; Dietitians and Nutritionists; Directors, Religious Activities and Education; Editors; Engineers, All Other; Epidemiologists; Executive Secretaries and Executive Administrative Assistants; Family and General Practitioners; Fine Artists, Including Painters, Sculptors, and Illustrators; First-Line Supervisors of Office and Administrative Support Workers; Health Diagnosing and Treating Practitioners, All Other; Health Educators; Health Specialties Teachers, Postsecondary; others.

Skills—Social Perceptiveness: Being aware of others' reactions and understanding why they react as they do. **Service Orientation:** Actively looking for ways to help people. **Persuasion:** Persuading others to change their minds or behavior. **Learning Strategies:** Selecting and using training/instructional methods and procedures appropriate for the situation when learning or teaching new things. **Active Listening:** Giving full attention to what other people are saying, taking time to understand the points being made, asking questions as appropriate, and not interrupting at inappropriate times. **Negotiation:** Bringing others together and trying to reconcile differences. **Monitoring:** Monitoring or assessing your performance or that of other individuals or organizations to make improvements or take corrective action. **Systems Analysis:** Determining how a system should work and how changes in conditions, operations, and the environment will affect outcomes.

Work Environment: Indoors; sitting.

Subway and Streetcar Operators

- ⊙ Annual Earnings: $63,820
- ⊙ Earnings Growth Potential: Medium (36.0%)
- ⊙ Growth: 9.2%
- ⊙ Annual Job Openings: 280
- ⊙ Self-Employed: 0.0%

Considerations for Job Outlook: Job opportunities for subway and streetcar operators should be good in cities where new rail systems are being built. There is likely to be more competition for jobs in cities with existing systems. Opportunities should be best for applicants with experience driving public transportation vehicles such as buses.

Operate subway or elevated suburban trains with no separate locomotive, or electric-powered streetcar, to transport passengers. Operate controls to open and close transit vehicle doors. Drive and control rail-guided public transportation, such as subways, elevated trains, and electric-powered streetcars, trams, or trolleys, in order to transport passengers. Monitor lights indicating obstructions or other trains ahead and watch for car and truck traffic at crossings to stay alert to potential hazards. Direct emergency evacuation procedures. Regulate vehicle speed and the time spent at each stop, in order to maintain schedules. Report delays, mechanical problems, and emergencies to supervisors or dispatchers, using radios. Make announcements to passengers, such as notifications of upcoming stops or schedule delays. Complete reports, including shift summaries and incident or accident reports. Greet passengers, provide information, and answer questions concerning fares, schedules, transfers, and routings. Attend meetings on driver and passenger safety to learn ways in which job performance might be affected. Collect fares from passengers, and issue change and transfers. Record transactions and coin receptor readings to verify the amount of money collected.

Education/Training Required: High school diploma or equivalent. **Education and Training Program:** Truck and Bus Driver Training/Commercial Vehicle Operator and Instructor Training. **Knowledge/Courses—Transportation:** Principles and methods for moving people or goods by air, rail, sea, or road, including the relative costs and benefits. **Public Safety and Security:** Relevant equipment, policies, procedures, and strategies to promote effective

local, state, or national security operations for the protection of people, data, property, and institutions. **Customer and Personal Service:** Principles and processes for providing customer and personal services. This includes customer needs assessment, meeting quality standards for services, and evaluation of customer satisfaction. **Telecommunications:** Transmission, broadcasting, switching, control, and operation of telecommunications systems. **Mechanical Devices:** Machines and tools, including their designs, uses, repair, and maintenance. **Communications and Media:** Media production, communication, and dissemination techniques and methods. This includes alternative ways to inform and entertain via written, oral, and visual media. **Work Experience Needed:** None. **On-the-Job Training Needed:** Moderate-term on-the-job training. **Certification/Licensure:** No data available.

Personality Type: Realistic-Conventional. **Career Cluster:** 16 Transportation, Distribution, and Logistics. **Career Pathway:** 16.1 Transportation Operations. **Other Jobs in This Pathway:** Aerospace Engineering and Operations Technicians; Air Traffic Controllers; Aircraft Cargo Handling Supervisors; Airfield Operations Specialists; Airline Pilots, Copilots, and Flight Engineers; Automotive and Watercraft Service Attendants; Automotive Master Mechanics; Aviation Inspectors; Bridge and Lock Tenders; Bus Drivers, School or Special Client; Bus Drivers, Transit and Intercity; Commercial Divers; Commercial Pilots; Crane and Tower Operators; First-Line Supervisors of Helpers, Laborers, and Material Movers, Hand; First-Line Supervisors of Transportation and Material-Moving Machine and Vehicle Operators; Freight and Cargo Inspectors; Heavy and Tractor-Trailer Truck Drivers; Hoist and Winch Operators; Laborers and Freight, Stock, and Material Movers, Hand; Light Truck or Delivery Services Drivers; Mates—Ship, Boat, and Barge; Motor Vehicle Operators, All Other; Motorboat Operators; Operating Engineers and Other Construction Equipment Operators; others.

Skills—Operation and Control: Controlling operations of equipment or systems. **Operation Monitoring:** Watching gauges, dials, or other indicators to make sure a machine is working properly. **Equipment Maintenance:** Performing routine maintenance on equipment and determining when and what kind of maintenance is needed. **Repairing:** Repairing machines or systems using the needed tools. **Troubleshooting:** Determining causes of operating errors and deciding what to do about them. **Equipment Selection:** Determining the kind of tools and equipment needed to do a job. **Management of Financial Resources:** Determining how money will be spent to get the work done and accounting for these expenditures. **Quality Control Analysis:** Conducting tests and inspections of products, services, or processes to evaluate quality or performance.

Work Environment: Outdoors; sitting; using hands; repetitive motions; noise; very hot or cold; bright or inadequate lighting; contaminants; hazardous conditions.

Supervisors of Construction and Extraction Workers

- ⊙ Annual Earnings: $59,150
- ⊙ Earnings Growth Potential: Medium (37.7%)
- ⊙ Growth: 23.5%
- ⊙ Annual Job Openings: 25,970
- ⊙ Self-Employed: 15.9%

Considerations for Job Outlook: A faster-than-average increase is expected as the streamlining of employment, such as reducing administrative staff, will reduce noncraft workers relative to supervisors.

Directly supervise and coordinate activities of construction or extraction workers. Examine and inspect work progress, equipment, and construction sites to verify safety and to ensure that specifications are met. Read specifications such as blueprints to determine construction requirements and to plan procedures. Estimate material and worker requirements to complete jobs. Supervise, coordinate, and schedule the activities of construction or extractive workers. Confer with managerial and technical personnel, other departments, and contractors to resolve problems and to coordinate activities. Coordinate work activities with other construction project activities. Locate, measure, and mark site locations and placement of structures and equipment, using measuring and marking equipment. Order or requisition materials and supplies. Record information such as personnel, production, and operational data on specified forms and reports. Assign work to employees based on material and worker requirements of specific jobs. Provide assistance to workers engaged in construction or extraction activities, using hand tools

and equipment. Train workers in construction methods, operation of equipment, safety procedures, and company policies. Analyze worker and production problems, and recommend solutions such as improving production methods or implementing motivational plans. Arrange for repairs of equipment and machinery. Suggest or initiate personnel actions such as promotions, transfers, and hires.

Education/Training Required: High school diploma or equivalent. **Education and Training Programs:** Blasting/Blaster; Building/Construction Finishing, Management, and Inspection, Other; Building/Construction Site Management/Manager; Building/Home/Construction Inspection/Inspector; Building/Property Maintenance; Carpentry/Carpenter; Concrete Finishing/Concrete Finisher; Construction Trades, Other; Drywall Installation/Drywaller; Electrical and Power Transmission Installation/Installer, General; Electrical and Power Transmission Installers, Other; Electrician; Glazier Training; Lineworker; Masonry/Mason Training; Painting/Painter and Wall Coverer Training; Plumbing Technology/Plumber; Roofer Training; Well Drilling/Driller. **Knowledge/Courses—Building and Construction:** Materials, methods, and the tools involved in the construction or repair of houses, buildings, or other structures such as highways and roads. **Mechanical Devices:** Machines and tools, including their designs, uses, repair, and maintenance. **Design:** Design techniques, tools, and principles involved in production of precision technical plans, blueprints, drawings, and models. **Engineering and Technology:** The practical application of engineering science and technology. This includes applying principles, techniques, procedures, and equipment to the design and production of various goods and services. **Production and Processing:** Raw materials, production processes, quality control, costs, and other techniques for maximizing the effective manufacture and distribution of goods. **Public Safety and Security:** Relevant equipment, policies, procedures, and strategies to promote effective local, state, or national security operations for the protection of people, data, property, and institutions. **Work Experience Needed:** More than 5 years. **On-the-Job Training Needed:** None. **Certification/Licensure:** None.

Personality Type: Enterprising-Realistic-Conventional. **Career Cluster:** 02 Architecture and Construction. **Career Pathway:** 02.2 Construction. **Other Jobs in This Pathway:** Boilermakers; Brickmasons and Blockmasons; Carpet Installers; Cement Masons and Concrete Finishers;

Construction and Building Inspectors; Construction and Related Workers, All Other; Construction Carpenters; Construction Laborers; Construction Managers; Continuous Mining Machine Operators; Cost Estimators; Crane and Tower Operators; Dredge Operators; Drywall and Ceiling Tile Installers; Earth Drillers, Except Oil and Gas; Electrical Power-Line Installers and Repairers; Electricians; Electromechanical Equipment Assemblers; Engineering Technicians, Except Drafters, All Other; Excavating and Loading Machine and Dragline Operators; Explosives Workers, Ordnance Handling Experts, and Blasters; Extraction Workers, All Other; Floor Layers, Except Carpet, Wood, and Hard Tiles; Floor Sanders and Finishers; Glaziers; Heating and Air Conditioning Mechanics and Installers; Helpers, Construction Trades, All Other; Helpers—Brickmasons, Blockmasons, Stonemasons, and Tile and Marble Setters; others.

Skills—Equipment Selection: Determining the kind of tools and equipment needed to do a job. **Management of Personnel Resources:** Motivating, developing, and directing people as they work, identifying the best people for the job. **Equipment Maintenance:** Performing routine maintenance on equipment and determining when and what kind of maintenance is needed. **Operation and Control:** Controlling operations of equipment or systems. **Quality Control Analysis:** Conducting tests and inspections of products, services, or processes to evaluate quality or performance. **Operations Analysis:** Analyzing needs and product requirements to create a design. **Management of Material Resources:** Obtaining and seeing to the appropriate use of equipment, facilities, and materials needed to do certain work. **Troubleshooting:** Determining causes of operating errors and deciding what to do about them.

Work Environment: Outdoors; standing; using hands; noise; very hot or cold; bright or inadequate lighting; contaminants; hazardous equipment.

Job Specialization: Solar Energy Installation Managers

Direct work crews installing residential or commercial solar photovoltaic or thermal systems. Plan and coordinate installations of photovoltaic (PV) solar and solar thermal systems to ensure conformance to codes. Supervise solar installers, technicians, and subcontractors for solar installation projects to ensure compliance with safety standards. Assess potential solar installation sites to determine feasibility and design requirements. Assess system performance or functionality at the system, subsystem, and component levels. Coordinate or schedule building inspections for solar installation projects. Monitor work of contractors and subcontractors to ensure projects conform to plans, specifications, schedules, or budgets. Perform start-up of systems for testing or customer implementation. Provide technical assistance to installers, technicians, or other solar professionals in areas such as solar electric systems, solar thermal systems, electrical systems, and mechanical systems. Visit customer sites to determine solar system needs, requirements, or specifications. Develop and maintain system architecture, including all piping, instrumentation, or process flow diagrams. Estimate materials, equipment, and personnel needed for residential or commercial solar installation projects. Evaluate subcontractors or subcontractor bids for quality, cost, and reliability. Identify means to reduce costs, minimize risks, or increase efficiency of solar installation projects. Prepare solar installation project proposals, quotes, budgets, or schedules.

Education and Training Programs: Blasting/Blaster; Building/Construction Finishing, Management, and Inspection, Other; Building/Construction Site Management/Manager; Building/Home/Construction Inspection/Inspector; Building/Property Maintenance; Carpentry/Carpenter; Concrete Finishing/Concrete Finisher; Construction Trades, Other; Drywall Installation/Drywaller; Electrical and Power Transmission Installation/Installer, General; Electrical and Power Transmission Installers, Other; Electrician; Glazier Training; Lineworker; Masonry/Mason Training; Painting/Painter and Wall Coverer Training; Plumbing Technology/Plumber; Roofer Training; Well Drilling/Driller.

Personality Type: No data available. **Career Cluster:** 02 Architecture and Construction. **Career Pathway:** 02.2 Construction. **Other Jobs in This Pathway:** Boilermakers; Brickmasons and Blockmasons; Carpet Installers; Cement Masons and Concrete Finishers; Construction and Building Inspectors; Construction and Related Workers, All Other; Construction Carpenters; Construction Laborers; Construction Managers; Continuous Mining Machine Operators; Cost Estimators; Crane and Tower Operators; Dredge Operators; Drywall and Ceiling Tile Installers; Earth Drillers, Except Oil and Gas; Electrical Power-Line Installers and Repairers; Electricians; Electromechanical

Equipment Assemblers; Engineering Technicians, Except Drafters, All Other; Excavating and Loading Machine and Dragline Operators; Explosives Workers, Ordnance Handling Experts, and Blasters; Extraction Workers, All Other; First-Line Supervisors of Construction Trades and Extraction Workers; Floor Layers, Except Carpet, Wood, and Hard Tiles; Floor Sanders and Finishers; Glaziers; Heating and Air Conditioning Mechanics and Installers; Helpers, Construction Trades, All Other; others.

Work Environment: No data available.

Surgical Technologists

- ☉ Annual Earnings: $40,950
- ☉ Earnings Growth Potential: Low (29.5%)
- ☉ Growth: 18.9%
- ☉ Annual Job Openings: 3,390
- ☉ Self-Employed: 0.2%

Considerations for Job Outlook: Job prospects should be best for surgical technologists who have completed an accredited education program and who maintain their professional certification.

Assist in operations, under the supervision of surgeons, registered nurses, or other surgical personnel. Count sponges, needles, and instruments before and after operations. Maintain proper sterile fields during surgical procedures. Hand instruments and supplies to surgeons and surgeons' assistants, hold retractors, cut sutures, and perform other tasks as directed by surgeons during operations. Prepare patients for surgery, including positioning patients on operating tables and covering them with sterile surgical drapes to prevent exposure. Scrub arms and hands, and assist surgical teams to scrub and put on gloves, masks, and surgical clothing. Wash and sterilize equipment, using germicides and sterilizers. Monitor and continually assess operating room conditions, including needs of the patient and the surgical team. Prepare dressings or bandages, and apply or assist with their application following surgeries. Clean and restock operating rooms, gathering and placing equipment and supplies and arranging instruments according to instructions such as those found on a preference card. Operate, assemble, adjust, or monitor sterilizers, lights, suction machines, and diagnostic equipment to ensure proper operation. Prepare, care for, and dispose of tissue specimens taken for laboratory analysis. Provide technical assistance to surgeons, surgical nurses, and anesthesiologists. Maintain supply of fluids such as plasma, saline, blood, and glucose for use during operations. Maintain files and records of surgical procedures. Observe patients' vital signs to assess physical condition.

Education/Training Required: Postsecondary vocational training. **Education and Training Programs:** Pathology/Pathologist Assistant Training; Surgical Technology/Technologist. **Knowledge/Courses—Medicine and Dentistry:** The information and techniques needed to diagnose and treat human injuries, diseases, and deformities. This includes symptoms, treatment alternatives, drug properties and interactions, and preventive health-care measures. **Biology:** Plant and animal organisms and their tissues, cells, functions, interdependencies, and interactions with each other and the environment. **Psychology:** Human behavior and performance; individual differences in ability, personality, and interests; learning and motivation; psychological research methods; and the assessment and treatment of behavioral and affective disorders. **Chemistry:** The chemical composition, structure, and properties of substances and of the chemical processes and transformations that they undergo. This includes uses of chemicals and their danger signs, production techniques, and disposal methods. **Therapy and Counseling:** Principles, methods, and procedures for diagnosis, treatment, and rehabilitation of physical and mental dysfunctions, and for career counseling and guidance. **Customer and Personal Service:** Principles and processes for providing customer and personal services. This includes customer needs assessment, meeting quality standards for services, and evaluation of customer satisfaction. **Work Experience Needed:** None. **On-the-Job Training Needed:** None. **Certification/Licensure:** Voluntary certification by association.

Personality Type: Realistic-Social-Conventional. **Career Cluster:** 08 Health Science. **Career Pathway:** 08.2 Diagnostics Services. **Other Jobs in This Pathway:** Ambulance Drivers and Attendants, Except Emergency Medical Technicians; Anesthesiologist Assistants; Athletic Trainers; Cardiovascular Technologists and Technicians; Cytogenetic Technologists; Cytotechnologists; Diagnostic Medical Sonographers; Emergency Medical Technicians and Paramedics; Endoscopy Technicians; Health Diagnosing and Treating Practitioners, All Other; Health Specialties Teachers, Postsecondary; Health Technologists and Technicians,

All Other; Healthcare Practitioners and Technical Workers, All Other; Histotechnologists and Histologic Technicians; Medical and Clinical Laboratory Technicians; Medical and Clinical Laboratory Technologists; Medical and Health Services Managers; Medical Assistants; Medical Equipment Preparers; Neurodiagnostic Technologists; Nuclear Equipment Operation Technicians; Nuclear Medicine Technologists; Ophthalmic Laboratory Technicians; Pathologists; Physical Scientists, All Other; Physician Assistants; Radiation Therapists; others.

Skills—Equipment Maintenance: Performing routine maintenance on equipment and determining when and what kind of maintenance is needed. **Equipment Selection:** Determining the kind of tools and equipment needed to do a job. **Operation Monitoring:** Watching gauges, dials, or other indicators to make sure a machine is working properly. **Repairing:** Repairing machines or systems using the needed tools. **Quality Control Analysis:** Conducting tests and inspections of products, services, or processes to evaluate quality or performance. **Operation and Control:** Controlling operations of equipment or systems. **Management of Material Resources:** Obtaining and seeing to the appropriate use of equipment, facilities, and materials needed to do certain work. **Coordination:** Adjusting actions in relation to others' actions.

Work Environment: Indoors; standing; using hands; bending or twisting the body; repetitive motions; contaminants; exposed to radiation; exposed to disease or infections; hazardous conditions; hazardous equipment; minor burns, cuts, bites, or stings.

Surveying and Mapping Technicians

- ⊙ Annual Earnings: $39,350
- ⊙ Earnings Growth Potential: Medium (37.9%)
- ⊙ Growth: 15.8%
- ⊙ Annual Job Openings: 2,000
- ⊙ Self-Employed: 4.7%

Considerations for Job Outlook: Recent advancements in mapping technology have led to new uses for maps and a need for more of the data used to build maps. As a result, surveying and mapping technicians should have more work.

Perform surveying and mapping duties, usually under the direction of engineers, surveyors, cartographers, or photogrammetrists. For task data, see Job Specializations.

Education/Training Required: High school diploma or equivalent. **Work Experience Needed:** None. **On-the-Job Training Needed:** Moderate-term on-the-job training. **Certification/Licensure:** Voluntary certification by association.

Job Specialization: Mapping Technicians

Calculate mapmaking information from field notes and draw and verify accuracy of topographical maps. Check all layers of maps to ensure accuracy, identifying and marking errors and making corrections. Determine scales, line sizes, and colors to be used for hard copies of computerized maps, using plotters. Monitor mapping work and the updating of maps to ensure accuracy, the inclusion of new or changed information, and compliance with rules and regulations. Identify and compile database information to create maps in response to requests. Produce and update overlay maps to show information boundaries, water locations, and topographic features on various base maps and at different scales. Trace contours and topographic details to generate maps that denote specific land and property locations and geographic attributes. Lay out and match aerial photographs in sequences in which they were taken, and identify any areas missing from photographs. Compare topographical features and contour lines with images from aerial photographs, old maps, and other reference materials to verify the accuracy of their identification. Compute and measure scaled distances between reference points to establish relative positions of adjoining prints and enable the creation of photographic mosaics. Research resources such as survey maps and legal descriptions to verify property lines and to obtain information needed for mapping. Form three-dimensional images of aerial photographs taken from different locations, using mathematical techniques and plotting instruments.

Education and Training Programs: Geographic Information Science and Cartography; Surveying Technology/Surveying. **Knowledge/Courses—Geography:** Principles and methods for describing the features of land, sea, and air masses, including their physical characteristics, locations, interrelationships, and distribution of plant, animal, and human life. **Design:** Design techniques, tools, and principles involved in production of precision technical plans, blueprints, drawings, and models. **Computers and Electronics:** Circuit boards, processors, chips, electronic equipment, and computer hardware and software, including applications and programming. **Engineering and Technology:** The practical application of engineering science and technology. This includes applying principles, techniques, procedures, and equipment to the design and production of various goods and services. **Mathematics:** Arithmetic, algebra, geometry, calculus, statistics, and their applications. **Clerical Practices:** Administrative and clerical procedures and systems such as word processing, managing files and records, stenography and transcription, designing forms, and other office procedures and terminology.

Personality Type: Conventional-Realistic. **Career Clusters:** 07 Government and Public Administration; 13 Manufacturing. **Career Pathways:** 07.1 Governance; 13.3 Maintenance, Installation, and Repair. **Other Jobs in These Pathways:** Administrative Services Managers; Aircraft Mechanics and Service Technicians; Automotive Engineering Technicians; Automotive Specialty Technicians; Avionics Technicians; Biological Technicians; Camera and Photographic Equipment Repairers; Chemical Equipment Operators and Tenders; Chief Executives; Chief Sustainability Officers; Civil Engineering Technicians; Coil Winders, Tapers, and Finishers; Compliance Managers; Computer, Automated Teller, and Office Machine Repairers; Construction and Related Workers, All Other; Control and Valve Installers and Repairers, Except Mechanical Door; Electric Motor, Power Tool, and Related Repairers; Electrical and Electronic Equipment Assemblers; Electrical and Electronics Repairers, Commercial and Industrial Equipment; Electrical and Electronics Repairers, Powerhouse, Substation, and Relay; Electrical Engineering Technicians; Electrical Engineering Technologists; Electromechanical Engineering Technologists; Electromechanical Equipment Assemblers; others.

Skills—Programming: Writing computer programs for various purposes. **Mathematics:** Using mathematics to solve problems. **Quality Control Analysis:** Conducting tests and inspections of products, services, or processes to evaluate quality or performance. **Management of Personnel Resources:** Motivating, developing, and directing people as they work, identifying the best people for the job. **Learning Strategies:** Selecting and using training/

instructional methods and procedures appropriate for the situation when learning or teaching new things. **Instructing:** Teaching others how to do something. **Operation and Control:** Controlling operations of equipment or systems. **Writing:** Communicating effectively in writing as appropriate for the needs of the audience.

Work Environment: Indoors; sitting; using hands; repetitive motions.

Job Specialization: Surveying Technicians

Adjust and operate surveying instruments such as theodolite and electronic distance-measuring equipment and compile notes, make sketches, and enter data into computers. Perform calculations to determine Earth curvature corrections, atmospheric impacts on measurements, traverse closures and adjustments, azimuths, level runs, and placement of markers. Record survey measurements and descriptive data using notes, drawings, sketches, and inked tracings. Search for section corners, property irons, and survey points. Position and hold the vertical rods, or targets, that theodolite operators use for sighting to measure angles, distances, and elevations. Lay out grids, and determine horizontal and vertical controls. Compare survey computations with applicable standards to determine adequacy of data. Set out and recover stakes, marks, and other monumentation. Conduct surveys to ascertain the locations of natural features and man-made structures on Earth's surface, underground, and underwater, using electronic distance-measuring equipment and other surveying instruments. Direct and supervise work of subordinate members of surveying parties. Compile information necessary to stake projects for construction, using engineering plans. Prepare topographic and contour maps of land surveyed, including site features and other relevant information, such as charts, drawings, and survey notes. Place and hold measuring tapes when electronic distance-measuring equipment is not used. Collect information needed to carry out new surveys using source maps, previous survey data, photographs, computer records, and other relevant information.

Education and Training Programs: Geographic Information Science and Cartography; Surveying Technology/Surveying. **Knowledge/Courses—Geography:** Principles and methods for describing the features of land, sea, and air masses, including their physical characteristics, locations, interrelationships, and distribution of plant, animal, and human life. **Design:** Design techniques, tools, and principles involved in production of precision technical plans, blueprints, drawings, and models. **Building and Construction:** Materials, methods, and the tools involved in the construction or repair of houses, buildings, or other structures such as highways and roads. **Mathematics:** Arithmetic, algebra, geometry, calculus, statistics, and their applications. **Law and Government:** Laws, legal codes, court procedures, precedents, government regulations, executive orders, agency rules, and the democratic political process. **Engineering and Technology:** The practical application of engineering science and technology. This includes applying principles, techniques, procedures, and equipment to the design and production of various goods and services.

Personality Type: Realistic-Conventional. **Career Clusters:** 02 Architecture and Construction; 07 Government and Public Administration. **Career Pathways:** 02.1 Design/Pre-Construction; 07.1 Governance. **Other Jobs in These Pathways:** Administrative Services Managers; Architects, Except Landscape and Naval; Architectural and Engineering Managers; Architectural Drafters; Architecture Teachers, Postsecondary; Cartographers and Photogrammetrists; Chief Executives; Chief Sustainability Officers; Civil Drafters; Civil Engineering Technicians; Compliance Managers; Drafters, All Other; Electrical Drafters; Electronic Drafters; Engineering Teachers, Postsecondary; Engineering Technicians, Except Drafters, All Other; Engineers, All Other; General and Operations Managers; Geodetic Surveyors; Interior Designers; Landscape Architects; Legislators; Managers, All Other; Mapping Technicians; Mechanical Drafters; Political Science Teachers, Postsecondary; Political Scientists; Postmasters and Mail Superintendents; Regulatory Affairs Managers; Reporters and Correspondents; Social and Community Service Managers; Storage and Distribution Managers; Surveyors; Transportation Managers.

Skills—Equipment Maintenance: Performing routine maintenance on equipment and determining when and what kind of maintenance is needed. **Operation and Control:** Controlling operations of equipment or systems. **Repairing:** Repairing machines or systems using the needed tools. **Science:** Using scientific rules and methods to solve problems. **Equipment Selection:** Determining the kind of tools and equipment needed to do a job. **Mathematics:** Using mathematics to solve problems. **Troubleshooting:** Determining causes of operating errors and deciding what to do about them. **Operation Monitoring:** Watching gauges, dials, or other indicators to make sure a machine is working properly.

Work Environment: More often outdoors than indoors; standing; walking and running; using hands; noise; very hot or cold; contaminants; hazardous equipment; minor burns, cuts, bites, or stings.

Tapers

- Annual Earnings: $44,910
- Earnings Growth Potential: Medium (38.9%)
- Growth: 34.9%
- Annual Job Openings: 1,430
- Self-Employed: 27.2%

Considerations for Job Outlook: Job prospects for drywall and ceiling tile installers and tapers should improve over the coming decade as construction activity rebounds from the recent recession. As with many other construction workers, employment of these workers is sensitive to the fluctuations of the economy. On the one hand, they may experience periods of unemployment when the overall level of construction falls. On the other hand, shortages of workers may occur in some areas during peak periods of building activity. Skilled drywall and ceiling tile installers and tapers with good work history and experience in the construction industry should have the best job opportunities.

Seal joints between plasterboard or other wallboard to prepare wall surface for painting or papering. Sand rough spots of dried cement between applications of compounds. Remove extra compound after surfaces have been covered sufficiently. Press paper tape over joints to embed tape into sealing compound and to seal joints. Mix sealing compounds by hand or with portable electric mixers. Install metal molding at wall corners to secure wallboard. Seal joints between plasterboard or other wallboard to prepare wall surfaces for painting or papering. Check adhesives to ensure that they will work and will remain durable. Apply texturizing compounds and primers to walls and ceilings before final finishing, using trowels, brushes, rollers, or spray guns. Sand or patch nicks or cracks in plasterboard or wallboard. Apply additional coats to fill in holes and make surfaces smooth. Use mechanical applicators that spread compounds and embed tape in one operation. Spread sealing compound between boards or panels and over cracks, holes, and nail and screw heads, using trowels, broadknives, or spatulas. Spread and smooth cementing material over tape, using trowels or floating machines to blend joints with wall surfaces. Select the correct sealing compound or tape. Countersink nails or screws below surfaces of walls before applying sealing compounds, using hammers or screwdrivers.

Education/Training Required: Less than high school. **Education and Training Program:** Construction Trades, Other. **Knowledge/Courses—Building and Construction:** Materials, methods, and the tools involved in the construction or repair of houses, buildings, or other structures such as highways and roads. **Design:** Design techniques, tools, and principles involved in production of precision technical plans, blueprints, drawings, and models. **Public Safety and Security:** Relevant equipment, policies, procedures, and strategies to promote effective local, state, or national security operations for the protection of people, data, property, and institutions. **Work Experience Needed:** None. **On-the-Job Training Needed:** Moderate-term on-the-job training. **Certification/Licensure:** None.

Personality Type: Realistic. **Career Cluster:** 02 Architecture and Construction. **Career Pathway:** 02.2 Construction. **Other Jobs in This Pathway:** Boilermakers; Brickmasons and Blockmasons; Carpet Installers; Cement Masons and Concrete Finishers; Construction and Building Inspectors; Construction and Related Workers, All Other; Construction Carpenters; Construction Laborers; Construction Managers; Continuous Mining Machine Operators; Cost Estimators; Crane and Tower Operators; Dredge Operators; Drywall and Ceiling Tile Installers; Earth Drillers, Except Oil and Gas; Electrical Power-Line Installers and Repairers; Electricians; Electromechanical Equipment Assemblers; Engineering Technicians, Except Drafters, All Other; Excavating and Loading Machine and Dragline Operators; Explosives Workers, Ordnance Handling Experts, and Blasters; Extraction Workers, All Other; First-Line Supervisors of Construction Trades and Extraction Workers; Floor Layers, Except Carpet, Wood, and Hard Tiles; Floor Sanders and Finishers; Glaziers; Heating and Air Conditioning Mechanics and Installers; Helpers, Construction Trades, All Other; others.

Skills—Repairing: Repairing machines or systems using the needed tools. **Equipment Selection:** Determining the kind of tools and equipment needed to do a job. **Installation:** Installing equipment, machines, wiring, or programs to meet specifications. **Equipment Maintenance:** Performing routine maintenance on equipment and determining when and what kind of maintenance is needed.

Work Environment: Standing; climbing; walking and running; kneeling, crouching, stooping, or crawling; balancing; using hands; bending or twisting the body; repetitive motions; noise; contaminants; cramped work space; high places.

Tax Preparers

- ⊙ Annual Earnings: $32,320
- ⊙ Earnings Growth Potential: High (42.6%)
- ⊙ Growth: 9.8%
- ⊙ Annual Job Openings: 2,630
- ⊙ Self-Employed: 26.0%

Considerations for Job Outlook: Slower-than-average job growth is projected.

Prepare tax returns for individuals or small businesses. Compute taxes owed or overpaid, using adding machines or personal computers, and complete entries on forms, following tax form instructions and tax tables. Prepare or assist in preparing simple to complex tax returns for individuals or small businesses. Use all appropriate adjustments, deductions, and credits to keep clients' taxes to a minimum. Interview clients to obtain additional information on taxable income and deductible expenses and allowances. Review financial records such as income statements and documentation of expenditures in order to determine forms needed to prepare tax returns. Furnish taxpayers with sufficient information and advice in order to ensure correct tax form completion. Consult tax law handbooks or bulletins in order to determine procedures for preparation of atypical returns. Calculate form preparation fees according to return complexity and processing time required. Check data input or verify totals on forms prepared by others to detect errors in arithmetic, data entry, or procedures.

Education/Training Required: High school diploma or equivalent. **Education and Training Programs:** Accounting Technology/Technician and Bookkeeping; Taxation.

Knowledge/Courses—Economics and Accounting: Economic and accounting principles and practices, the financial markets, banking, and the analysis and reporting of financial data. **Clerical Practices:** Administrative and clerical procedures and systems such as word processing, managing files and records, stenography and transcription, designing forms, and other office procedures and terminology. **Mathematics:** Arithmetic, algebra, geometry, calculus, statistics, and their applications. **Law and Government:** Laws, legal codes, court procedures, precedents, government regulations, executive orders, agency rules, and the democratic political process. **Computers and Electronics:** Circuit boards, processors, chips, electronic equipment, and computer hardware and software, including applications and programming. **Customer and Personal Service:** Principles and processes for providing customer and personal services. This includes customer needs assessment, meeting quality standards for services, and evaluation of customer satisfaction. **Work Experience Needed:** None. **On-the-Job Training Needed:** Moderate-term on-the-job training. **Certification/Licensure:** Voluntary certification by association.

Personality Type: Conventional-Enterprising. **Career Clusters:** 04 Business, Management, and Administration; 07 Government and Public Administration. **Career Pathways:** 04.2 Business, Financial Management, and Accounting; 07.5 Revenue and Taxation. **Other Jobs in These Pathways:** Accountants; Auditors; Billing, Cost, and Rate Clerks; Bioinformatics Technicians; Bookkeeping, Accounting, and Auditing Clerks; Brokerage Clerks; Brownfield Redevelopment Specialists and Site Managers; Budget Analysts; Business Teachers, Postsecondary; Compliance Managers; Credit Analysts; Financial Analysts; Financial Examiners; Financial Managers, Branch or Department; Gaming Cage Workers; Investment Fund Managers; Logistics Managers; Loss Prevention Managers; Managers, All Other; Natural Sciences Managers; Payroll and Timekeeping Clerks; Regulatory Affairs Managers; Security Managers; Statement Clerks; Statistical Assistants; Statisticians; Supply Chain Managers; Tax Examiners and Collectors, and Revenue Agents; Treasurers and Controllers; Wind Energy Operations Managers; Wind Energy Project Managers.

Skills—Mathematics: Using mathematics to solve problems. **Service Orientation:** Actively looking for ways to help people. **Reading Comprehension:** Understanding written sentences and paragraphs in work-related documents. **Active Listening:** Giving full attention to what other people are saying, taking time to understand the points being made, asking questions as appropriate, and not interrupting at inappropriate times. **Programming:** Writing computer programs for various purposes. **Speaking:** Talking to others to convey information effectively. **Critical Thinking:** Using logic and reasoning to identify the strengths and weaknesses of alternative solutions, conclusions, or approaches to problems. **Complex Problem Solving:** Identifying complex problems and reviewing related information to develop and evaluate options and implement solutions.

Work Environment: Indoors; sitting.

Taxi Drivers and Chauffeurs

- ⊙ Annual Earnings: $22,760
- ⊙ Earnings Growth Potential: Low (25.8%)
- ⊙ Growth: 19.6%
- ⊙ Annual Job Openings: 7,670
- ⊙ Self-Employed: 30.7%

Considerations for Job Outlook: Job prospects for taxi drivers and chauffeurs should be excellent. The occupation has low barriers to entry and a lot of turnover. Applicants with a clean driving record and flexible schedules should have the best chance of being hired. Most taxi drivers and chauffeurs work in metropolitan areas, and those areas that are experiencing fast economic growth should offer the most job opportunities.

Drive automobiles, vans, or limousines to transport passengers. Test vehicle equipment, such as lights, brakes, horns, and windshield wipers, to ensure proper operation. Notify dispatchers or company mechanics of vehicle problems. Drive taxicabs, limousines, company cars, or privately owned vehicles to transport passengers. Pick up passengers at prearranged locations, at taxi stands, or by cruising streets in high traffic areas. Perform routine vehicle maintenance such as regulating tire pressure and adding gasoline, oil, and water. Communicate with dispatchers by radio, telephone, or computer to exchange information and receive requests for passenger service. Record name, date, and taxi identification information on trip sheets, along with trip information such as time and place of pickup and drop-off, and total fee. Complete accident reports when necessary. Provide passengers with assistance entering and exiting vehicles, and help them with any luggage. Arrange to pick up particular customers or groups on a regular schedule.

Education/Training Required: Less than high school. **Education and Training Program:** Truck and Bus Driver Training/Commercial Vehicle Operator and Instructor Training. **Knowledge/Courses—Transportation:** Principles and methods for moving people or goods by air, rail, sea, or road, including the relative costs and benefits. **Psychology:** Human behavior and performance; individual differences in ability, personality, and interests; learning and motivation; psychological research methods; and the assessment and treatment of behavioral and affective disorders. **Work Experience Needed:** None. **On-the-Job Training Needed:** Short-term on-the-job training. **Certification/Licensure:** Licensure.

Personality Type: Realistic-Enterprising. **Career Cluster:** 16 Transportation, Distribution, and Logistics. **Career Pathway:** 16.1 Transportation Operations. **Other Jobs in This Pathway:** Aerospace Engineering and Operations Technicians; Air Traffic Controllers; Aircraft Cargo Handling Supervisors; Airfield Operations Specialists; Airline Pilots, Copilots, and Flight Engineers; Automotive and Watercraft Service Attendants; Automotive Master Mechanics; Aviation Inspectors; Bridge and Lock Tenders; Bus Drivers, School or Special Client; Bus Drivers, Transit and Intercity; Commercial Divers; Commercial Pilots; Crane and Tower Operators; First-Line Supervisors of Helpers, Laborers, and Material Movers, Hand; First-Line Supervisors of Transportation and Material-Moving Machine and Vehicle Operators; Freight and Cargo Inspectors; Heavy and Tractor-Trailer Truck Drivers; Hoist and Winch Operators; Laborers and Freight, Stock, and Material Movers, Hand; Light Truck or Delivery Services Drivers; Mates—Ship, Boat, and Barge; Motor Vehicle Operators, All Other; Motorboat Operators; Operating Engineers and Other Construction Equipment Operators; others.

Skills—Operation and Control: Controlling operations of equipment or systems. **Operation Monitoring:** Watching gauges, dials, or other indicators to make sure a machine is working properly. **Service Orientation:** Actively looking for ways to help people.

Work Environment: Outdoors; sitting; noise; very hot or cold; contaminants.

Teacher Assistants

- ⊙ Annual Earnings: $23,580
- ⊙ Earnings Growth Potential: Low (27.5%)
- ⊙ Growth: 14.8%
- ⊙ Annual Job Openings: 48,160
- ⊙ Self-Employed: 0.0%

Considerations for Job Outlook: In addition to job openings from employment growth, numerous openings will arise as assistants leave the job and must be replaced. Because this occupation requires limited formal education and has low pay, many workers transfer to other occupations or leave the labor force because of family responsibilities, to return to school, or for other reasons. Job opportunities for teacher assistants vary significantly by geography. Opportunities should be better in the South and West, which are expected to have rapid increases in enrollment, and in urban schools, which often have difficulty recruiting and keeping teacher assistants.

Perform duties that are instructional in nature or deliver direct services to students or parents. Provide extra assistance to students with special needs, such as non-English-speaking students or those with physical and mental disabilities. Tutor and assist children individually or in small groups to help them master assignments and to reinforce learning concepts presented by teachers. Supervise students in classrooms, halls, cafeterias, school yards, and gymnasiums, or on field trips. Enforce administration policies and rules governing students. Observe students' performance, and record relevant data to assess progress. Discuss assigned duties with classroom teachers to coordinate instructional efforts. Instruct and monitor students in the use and care of equipment and materials to prevent injuries and damage. Present subject matter to students under the direction and guidance of teachers, using lectures, discussions, or supervised role-playing methods. Organize and label materials and display students' work in a manner appropriate for their eye levels and perceptual skills. Type, file, and duplicate materials. Distribute teaching materials such as textbooks, workbooks, papers, and pencils to students. Use computers, audio-visual aids, and other equipment and materials to supplement presentations. Attend staff meetings and serve on committees, as required. Prepare lesson materials, bulletin board displays, exhibits, equipment, and demonstrations. Organize and supervise games and other recreational activities to promote physical, mental, and social development. Laminate teaching materials to increase their durability under repeated use. Distribute tests and homework assignments and collect them when they are completed. Carry out therapeutic regimens such as behavior modification and personal development programs, under the supervision of special education instructors, psychologists, or speech-language pathologists. Provide disabled students with assistive devices, supportive technology, and assistance accessing facilities such as restrooms.

Education/Training Required: High school diploma or equivalent. **Education and Training Programs:** Teacher Assistant/Aide Training; Teaching Assistant/Aide Training, Other. **Knowledge/Courses—Therapy and Counseling:** Principles, methods, and procedures for diagnosis, treatment, and rehabilitation of physical and mental dysfunctions, and for career counseling and guidance. **Psychology:** Human behavior and performance; individual differences in ability, personality, and interests; learning and motivation; psychological research methods; and the assessment and treatment of behavioral and affective disorders. **Sociology and Anthropology:** Group behavior and dynamics, societal trends and influences, human migrations, ethnicity, and cultures and their history and origins. **Work Experience Needed:** None. **On-the-Job Training Needed:** Short-term on-the-job training. **Certification/Licensure:** Licensure in some states.

Personality Type: Social-Conventional. **Career Cluster:** 05 Education and Training. **Career Pathway:** 05.3 Teaching/Training. **Other Jobs in This Pathway:** Adult Basic and Secondary Education and Literacy Teachers and Instructors; Agricultural Sciences Teachers, Postsecondary; Anthropology and Archeology Teachers, Postsecondary; Architecture Teachers, Postsecondary; Area, Ethnic, and Cultural Studies Teachers, Postsecondary; Art, Drama, and Music Teachers, Postsecondary; Athletes and Sports Competitors; Atmospheric, Earth, Marine, and Space Sciences Teachers, Postsecondary; Audio-Visual and Multimedia Collections Specialists; Biological Science Teachers, Postsecondary; Business Teachers, Postsecondary; Career/Technical Education Teachers, Middle School; Career/Technical Education Teachers, Secondary School; Chemists; Coaches and Scouts; Communications Teachers, Postsecondary;

Computer Science Teachers, Postsecondary; Criminal Justice and Law Enforcement Teachers, Postsecondary; Dietitians and Nutritionists; Education Teachers, Postsecondary; Elementary School Teachers, Except Special Education; Engineering Teachers, Postsecondary; others.

Skills—Learning Strategies: Selecting and using training/instructional methods and procedures appropriate for the situation when learning or teaching new things. **Instructing:** Teaching others how to do something. **Technology Design:** Generating or adapting equipment and technology to serve user needs. **Service Orientation:** Actively looking for ways to help people. **Social Perceptiveness:** Being aware of others' reactions and understanding why they react as they do.

Work Environment: Indoors; standing.

Team Assemblers

- Annual Earnings: $27,490
- Earnings Growth Potential: Low (34.4%)
- Growth: 5.5%
- Annual Job Openings: 24,100
- Self-Employed: 1.7%

Considerations for Job Outlook: Qualified applicants, including those with technical vocational training and certification, should have the best job opportunities in the manufacturing sector, particularly in growing, high-technology industries such as aerospace and electromedical devices. Some employers report difficulty finding qualified applicants looking for manufacturing employment. Many job openings should result from the need to replace workers leaving or retiring from this large occupation.

Work as part of a team having responsibility for assembling an entire product or component of a product. Rotate through all the tasks required in a particular production process. Perform quality checks on products and parts. Package finished products and prepare them for shipment. Shovel, sweep, or otherwise clean work areas. Determine work assignments and procedures. Provide assistance in the production of wiring assemblies. Review work orders and blueprints to ensure work is performed according to specifications. Complete production reports to communicate team production levels to management. Maintain production equipment and machinery. Supervise assemblers and train employees on job procedures. Operate machinery and heavy equipment, such as forklifts.

Education/Training Required: High school diploma or equivalent. **Education and Training Program:** Precision Production, Other. **Knowledge/Courses—Production and Processing:** Raw materials, production processes, quality control, costs, and other techniques for maximizing the effective manufacture and distribution of goods. **Work Experience Needed:** None. **On-the-Job Training Needed:** Moderate-term on-the-job training. **Certification/Licensure:** Voluntary certification by association.

Personality Type: Realistic-Conventional-Enterprising. **Career Cluster:** 13 Manufacturing. **Career Pathway:** 13.1 Production. **Other Jobs in This Pathway:** Adhesive Bonding Machine Operators and Tenders; Assemblers and Fabricators, All Other; Avionics Technicians; Cabinetmakers and Bench Carpenters; Cleaning, Washing, and Metal Pickling Equipment Operators and Tenders; Coating, Painting, and Spraying Machine Setters, Operators, and Tenders; Computer-Controlled Machine Tool Operators, Metal and Plastic; Cooling and Freezing Equipment Operators and Tenders; Cost Estimators; Crushing, Grinding, and Polishing Machine Setters, Operators, and Tenders; Cutters and Trimmers, Hand; Cutting and Slicing Machine Setters, Operators, and Tenders; Cutting, Punching, and Press Machine Setters, Operators, and Tenders, Metal and Plastic; Drilling and Boring Machine Tool Setters, Operators, and Tenders, Metal and Plastic; Extruding and Drawing Machine Setters, Operators, and Tenders, Metal and Plastic; Extruding and Forming Machine Setters, Operators, and Tenders, Synthetic and Glass Fibers; others.

Skills—Operation and Control: Controlling operations of equipment or systems. **Equipment Maintenance:** Performing routine maintenance on equipment and determining when and what kind of maintenance is needed. **Quality Control Analysis:** Conducting tests and inspections of products, services, or processes to evaluate quality or performance. **Operation Monitoring:** Watching gauges, dials, or other indicators to make sure a machine is working properly. **Repairing:** Repairing machines or systems using the needed tools. **Troubleshooting:** Determining causes of operating errors and deciding what to do about them. **Coordination:** Adjusting actions in relation to others' actions. **Equipment Selection:** Determining the kind of tools and equipment needed to do a job.

Work Environment: Indoors; standing; walking and running; using hands; bending or twisting the body; repetitive motions; noise; contaminants.

Telecommunications Equipment Installers and Repairers, Except Line Installers

- ⊙ Annual Earnings: $53,960
- ⊙ Earnings Growth Potential: High (43.0%)
- ⊙ Growth: 14.6%
- ⊙ Annual Job Openings: 5,930
- ⊙ Self-Employed: 2.8%

Considerations for Job Outlook: Although job opportunities will vary by specialty, those with postsecondary electronics training and strong computer skills should have the best job prospects. Popular technologies, such as video on demand and broadband Internet connections, require high data transfer rates in telecommunications systems. Central office, PBX installers, and headend technicians will be needed to service and upgrade switches and routers to handle increased traffic, resulting in very good job opportunities. By contrast, station installers and repairers can expect strong competition for most positions. Prewired buildings, the reliability of existing telephone lines, and increasing wireless technology usage may reduce the need for general installation and maintenance work.

Install, set up, rearrange, or remove switching, distribution, routing, and dialing equipment used in central offices or headends. Note differences in wire and cable colors so that work can be performed correctly. Test circuits and components of malfunctioning telecommunications equipment to isolate sources of malfunctions, using test meters, circuit diagrams, polarity probes, and other hand tools. Test repaired, newly installed, or updated equipment to ensure that it functions properly and conforms to specifications, using test equipment and observation. Drive crew trucks to and from work areas. Inspect equipment on a regular basis in order to ensure proper functioning. Repair or replace faulty equipment such as defective and damaged telephones, wires, switching system components, and associated equipment. Remove and remake connections in order to change circuit layouts, following work orders or diagrams. Demonstrate equipment to customers and explain how it is to be used, and respond to any inquiries or complaints. Analyze test readings, computer printouts, and trouble reports to determine equipment repair needs and required repair methods. Adjust or modify equipment to enhance equipment performance or to respond to customer requests. Request support from technical service centers when on-site procedures fail to solve installation or maintenance problems. Remove loose wires and other debris after work is completed. Communicate with bases, using telephones or two-way radios to receive instructions or technical advice, or to report equipment status. Assemble and install communication equipment such as data and telephone communication lines, wiring, switching equipment, wiring frames, power apparatus, computer systems, and networks. Collaborate with other workers to locate and correct malfunctions. Review manufacturer's instructions, manuals, technical specifications, building permits, and ordinances to determine communication equipment requirements and procedures. Test connections to ensure that power supplies are adequate and that communications links function.

Education/Training Required: Postsecondary vocational training. **Education and Training Program:** Communications Systems Installation and Repair Technology. **Knowledge/ Courses—Telecommunications:** Transmission, broadcasting, switching, control, and operation of telecommunications systems. **Mechanical Devices:** Machines and tools, including their designs, uses, repair, and maintenance. **Computers and Electronics:** Circuit boards, processors, chips, electronic equipment, and computer hardware and software, including applications and programming. **Engineering and Technology:** The practical application of engineering science and technology. This includes applying principles, techniques, procedures, and equipment to the design and production of various goods and services. **Design:** Design techniques, tools, and principles involved in production of precision technical plans, blueprints, drawings, and models. **Public Safety and Security:** Relevant equipment, policies, procedures, and strategies to promote effective local, state, or national security operations for the protection of people, data, property, and institutions. **Work Experience Needed:** None. **On-the-Job Training Needed:** Moderate-term on-the-job training. **Certification/Licensure:** Voluntary certification by association.

Personality Type: Realistic-Investigative-Conventional. **Career Cluster:** 03 Arts and Communications. **Career Pathway:** 03.6 Telecommunications. **Other Jobs in**

This Pathway: Broadcast Technicians; Communications Equipment Operators, All Other; Electronic Home Entertainment Equipment Installers and Repairers; Film and Video Editors; Media and Communication Workers, All Other; Radio Mechanics; Radio Operators; Sound Engineering Technicians.

Skills—Installation: Installing equipment, machines, wiring, or programs to meet specifications. **Repairing:** Repairing machines or systems using the needed tools. **Equipment Maintenance:** Performing routine maintenance on equipment and determining when and what kind of maintenance is needed. **Troubleshooting:** Determining causes of operating errors and deciding what to do about them. **Equipment Selection:** Determining the kind of tools and equipment needed to do a job. **Quality Control Analysis:** Conducting tests and inspections of products, services, or processes to evaluate quality or performance. **Operation and Control:** Controlling operations of equipment or systems. **Programming:** Writing computer programs for various purposes.

Work Environment: More often outdoors than indoors; standing; using hands; bending or twisting the body; repetitive motions; noise; very hot or cold; bright or inadequate lighting; contaminants; cramped work space; high places; hazardous conditions; hazardous equipment; minor burns, cuts, bites, or stings.

Telecommunications Line Installers and Repairers

- ⊙ Annual Earnings: $51,720
- ⊙ Earnings Growth Potential: High (46.9%)
- ⊙ Growth: 13.6%
- ⊙ Annual Job Openings: 5,140
- ⊙ Self-Employed: 2.8%

Considerations for Job Outlook: Good job opportunities are expected overall. Highly skilled workers with apprenticeship training or a two-year associate degree in telecommunications, electronics, or electricity should have the best job opportunities.

Install and repair telecommunications cable, including fiber optics. Travel to customers' premises to install, maintain, and repair audio and visual electronic reception equipment and accessories. Inspect and test lines and cables, recording and analyzing test results, to assess transmission characteristics and locate faults and malfunctions. Splice cables, using hand tools, epoxy, or mechanical equipment. Set up service for customers, installing, connecting, testing, and adjusting equipment. Measure signal strength at utility poles, using electronic test equipment. Place insulation over conductors, and seal splices with moisture-proof covering. Access specific areas to string lines and install terminal boxes, auxiliary equipment, and appliances, using bucket trucks, or by climbing poles and ladders or entering tunnels, trenches, or crawl spaces. String cables between structures and lines from poles, towers, or trenches and pull lines to proper tension. Install equipment such as amplifiers and repeaters in order to maintain the strength of communications transmissions. Lay underground cable directly in trenches, or string it through conduits running through trenches. Pull up cable by hand from large reels mounted on trucks, and then pull lines through ducts by hand or with winches. Clean and maintain tools and test equipment. Explain cable service to subscribers after installation, and collect any installation fees that are due. Compute impedance of wires from poles to houses in order to determine additional resistance needed for reducing signals to desired levels. Use a variety of construction equipment to complete installations, including digger derricks, trenchers, and cable plows. Dig trenches for underground wires and cables. Dig holes for power poles, using power augers or shovels; set poles in place with cranes; and hoist poles upright, using winches. Fill and tamp holes, using cement, earth, and tamping devices. Participate in the construction and removal of telecommunication towers and associated support structures.

Education/Training Required: High school diploma or equivalent. **Education and Training Program:** Communications Systems Installation and Repair Technology. **Knowledge/Courses—Telecommunications:** Transmission, broadcasting, switching, control, and operation of telecommunications systems. **Building and Construction:** Materials, methods, and the tools involved in the construction or repair of houses, buildings, or other structures such as highways and roads. **Engineering and Technology:** The practical application of engineering science and technology. This includes applying principles, techniques, procedures, and equipment to the design and production of various goods and services. **Customer and Personal Service:** Principles and processes for providing customer and personal services. This includes customer needs assessment, meeting quality standards for services, and evaluation of customer satisfaction. **Design:** Design techniques, tools, and principles involved in production of precision technical plans, blueprints, drawings, and models. **Mechanical Devices:** Machines and tools, including their designs, uses, repair, and maintenance. **Work Experience Needed:** None. **On-the-Job Training Needed:** Long-term on-the-job training. **Certification/Licensure:** Voluntary certification by association.

Personality Type: Realistic-Enterprising. **Career Cluster:** 13 Manufacturing. **Career Pathway:** 13.3 Maintenance, Installation, and Repair. **Other Jobs in This Pathway:** Aircraft Mechanics and Service Technicians; Automotive Engineering Technicians; Automotive Specialty Technicians; Avionics Technicians; Biological Technicians; Camera and Photographic Equipment Repairers; Chemical Equipment Operators and Tenders; Civil Engineering Technicians; Coil Winders, Tapers, and Finishers; Computer, Automated Teller, and Office Machine Repairers; Construction and Related Workers, All Other; Control and Valve Installers and Repairers, Except Mechanical Door; Electric Motor, Power Tool, and Related Repairers; Electrical and Electronic Equipment Assemblers; Electrical and Electronics Repairers, Commercial and Industrial Equipment; Electrical and Electronics Repairers, Powerhouse, Substation, and Relay; Electrical Engineering Technicians; Electrical Engineering Technologists; Electromechanical Engineering Technologists; Electromechanical Equipment Assemblers; Electronics Engineering Technicians; Electronics Engineering Technologists; others.

Skills—Troubleshooting: Determining causes of operating errors and deciding what to do about them. **Equipment Maintenance:** Performing routine maintenance on equipment and determining when and what kind of maintenance is needed. **Repairing:** Repairing machines or systems using the needed tools. **Operation and Control:** Controlling operations of equipment or systems. **Equipment Selection:** Determining the kind of tools and equipment needed to do a job. **Quality Control Analysis:** Conducting tests and inspections of products, services, or processes to evaluate quality or performance. **Operation Monitoring:** Watching gauges, dials, or other indicators to make sure a machine is working properly. **Installation:** Installing equipment, machines, wiring, or programs to meet specifications.

Work Environment: Outdoors; standing; walking and running; kneeling, crouching, stooping, or crawling; using hands; bending or twisting the body; repetitive motions; noise; very hot or cold; bright or inadequate lighting; contaminants; cramped work space; high places; hazardous conditions; hazardous equipment; minor burns, cuts, bites, or stings.

Telemarketers

- ⊚ Annual Earnings: $22,520
- ⊚ Earnings Growth Potential: Low (25.2%)
- ⊚ Growth: 7.4%
- ⊚ Annual Job Openings: 8,350
- ⊚ Self-Employed: 1.6%

Considerations for Job Outlook: Slower-than-average job growth is expected as these workers continue to be offshored.

Solicit donations or orders for goods or services over the telephone. Contact businesses or private individuals by telephone in order to solicit sales for goods or services, or to request donations for charitable causes. Deliver prepared sales talks, reading from scripts that describe products or services, in order to persuade potential customers to purchase a product or service or to make a donation. Explain products or services and prices, and answer questions from customers. Obtain customer information such as name, address, and payment method, and enter orders into computers. Record names, addresses, purchases, and reactions of prospects contacted. Adjust sales scripts to better target the needs and interests of specific individuals. Obtain names and telephone numbers of potential customers from sources such as telephone directories, magazine reply cards, and lists purchased from other organizations. Answer telephone calls from potential customers who have been solicited through advertisements. Telephone or write letters to respond to correspondence from customers or to follow up initial sales contacts. Maintain records of contacts, accounts, and orders. Schedule appointments for sales representatives to meet with prospective customers or for customers to attend sales presentations. Conduct client or market surveys in order to obtain information about potential customers.

Education/Training Required: Less than high school. **Education and Training Programs:** Insurance; Sales, Distribution, and Marketing Operations, General; Selling Skills and Sales Operations. **Knowledge/Courses—Sales and Marketing:** Principles and methods for showing, promoting, and selling products or services. This includes marketing strategy and tactics, product demonstration, sales techniques, and sales control systems. **Communications and Media:** Media production, communication, and dissemination techniques and methods. This includes alternative ways to inform and entertain via written, oral, and visual media. **Work Experience Needed:** None. **On-the-Job Training Needed:** Short-term on-the-job training. **Certification/Licensure:** None.

Personality Type: Enterprising-Conventional. **Career Clusters:** 06 Finance; 14 Marketing, Sales, and Service. **Career Pathways:** 14.3 Buying and Merchandising; 06.4 Insurance Services; 14.2 Professional Sales and Marketing. **Other Jobs in These Pathways:** Actuaries; Appraisers, Real Estate; Assessors; Business Teachers, Postsecondary; Cashiers; Claims Examiners, Property and Casualty Insurance; Counter and Rental Clerks; Demonstrators and Product Promoters; Door-To-Door Sales Workers, News and Street Vendors, and Related Workers; Driver/Sales Workers; Energy Brokers; First-Line Supervisors of Non-Retail Sales Workers; First-Line Supervisors of Retail Sales Workers; Gaming Change Persons and Booth Cashiers; Hotel, Motel, and Resort Desk Clerks; Insurance Adjusters, Examiners, and Investigators; Insurance Appraisers, Auto Damage; Insurance Sales Agents; Insurance Underwriters; Interior Designers; Lodging Managers; Marketing Managers; Marking Clerks; Meeting, Convention, and Event Planners; Merchandise Displayers and Window Trimmers; Models; Online Merchants; Order Fillers, Wholesale and Retail Sales; Parts Salespersons; Property, Real Estate, and Community Association Managers; others.

Skills—Persuasion: Persuading others to change their minds or behavior. **Service Orientation:** Actively looking for ways to help people. **Speaking:** Talking to others to convey information effectively. **Active Listening:** Giving full attention to what other people are saying, taking time to understand the points being made, asking questions as appropriate, and not interrupting at inappropriate times. **Negotiation:** Bringing others together and trying to reconcile differences.

Work Environment: Indoors; sitting; using hands; repetitive motions; noise.

Tellers

- ⊙ Annual Earnings: $24,590
- ⊙ Earnings Growth Potential: Very low (21.3%)
- ⊙ Growth: 1.3%
- ⊙ Annual Job Openings: 23,750
- ⊙ Self-Employed: 0.0%

Considerations for Job Outlook: Job prospects for tellers should be excellent because many workers leave this occupation.

Receive and pay out money. Keep records of money and negotiable instruments involved in a financial institution's various transactions. Cash checks and pay out money after verifying that signatures are correct, that written and numerical amounts agree, and that accounts have sufficient funds. Receive checks and cash for deposit, verify amounts, and check accuracy of deposit slips. Enter customers' transactions into computers to record transactions and issue computer-generated receipts. Balance currency, coin, and checks in cash drawers at ends of shifts, and calculate daily transactions using computers, calculators, or adding machines. Examine checks for endorsements and to verify other information such as dates, bank names, identification of the persons receiving payments, and the legality of the documents. Count currency, coins, and checks received, by hand or using currency-counting machines, to prepare them for deposit or shipment to branch banks or the Federal Reserve Bank. Order supplies of cash to meet daily needs. Receive and count daily inventories of cash, drafts, and travelers' checks. Prepare and verify cashier's checks. Sort and file deposit slips and checks. Process transactions such as term deposits, retirement savings plan contributions, automated teller transactions, night deposits, and mail deposits. Carry out special services for customers, such as ordering bank cards and checks. Identify transaction mistakes when debits and credits do not balance. Arrange monies received in cash boxes and coin dispensers according to denomination. Resolve problems or discrepancies concerning customers' accounts. Receive mortgage, loan, or public utility bill payments, verifying payment dates and amounts due. Explain, promote, or sell products or services such as travelers' checks, savings bonds, money orders, and cashier's checks, using computerized information

about customers to tailor recommendations. Obtain and process information required for the provision of services such as opening accounts, savings plans, and purchasing bonds. Process and maintain records of customer loans.

Education/Training Required: High school diploma or equivalent. **Education and Training Program:** Banking and Financial Support Services. **Knowledge/Courses—Sales and Marketing:** Principles and methods for showing, promoting, and selling products or services. This includes marketing strategy and tactics, product demonstration, sales techniques, and sales control systems. **Customer and Personal Service:** Principles and processes for providing customer and personal services. This includes customer needs assessment, meeting quality standards for services, and evaluation of customer satisfaction. **Economics and Accounting:** Economic and accounting principles and practices, the financial markets, banking, and the analysis and reporting of financial data. **Clerical Practices:** Administrative and clerical procedures and systems such as word processing, managing files and records, stenography and transcription, designing forms, and other office procedures and terminology. **Public Safety and Security:** Relevant equipment, policies, procedures, and strategies to promote effective local, state, or national security operations for the protection of people, data, property, and institutions. **Computers and Electronics:** Circuit boards, processors, chips, electronic equipment, and computer hardware and software, including applications and programming. **Work Experience Needed:** None. **On-the-Job Training Needed:** Short-term on-the-job training. **Certification/Licensure:** None.

Personality Type: Conventional-Enterprising. **Career Cluster:** 06 Finance. **Career Pathway:** 06.3 Banking and Related Services. **Other Jobs in This Pathway:** Bill and Account Collectors; Credit Analysts; Credit Authorizers; Credit Checkers; Loan Counselors; Loan Interviewers and Clerks; Loan Officers; New Accounts Clerks; Title Examiners, Abstractors, and Searchers.

Skills—Service Orientation: Actively looking for ways to help people. **Mathematics:** Using mathematics to solve problems. **Active Listening:** Giving full attention to what other people are saying, taking time to understand the points being made, asking questions as appropriate, and not interrupting at inappropriate times.

Work Environment: Indoors; more often sitting than standing; using hands; repetitive motions.

Terrazzo Workers and Finishers

- ⊙ Annual Earnings: $41,240
- ⊙ Earnings Growth Potential: Medium (39.0%)
- ⊙ Growth: 16.2%
- ⊙ Annual Job Openings: 110
- ⊙ Self-Employed: 6.1%

Considerations for Job Outlook: Job opportunities for cement masons and terrazzo workers are expected to be good, particularly for those with more experience and skills. During peak construction periods, employers report difficulty in finding workers with the right skills, because many qualified job seekers often prefer work that is less strenuous and has more comfortable working conditions. Applicants who take masonry-related courses at technical schools will have the best job opportunities. As with many other construction workers, employment of cement masons and terrazzo workers is sensitive to the fluctuations of the economy. On the one hand, workers may experience periods of unemployment when the overall level of construction falls. On the other hand, shortages of workers may occur in some areas during peak periods of building activity.

Apply a mixture of cement, sand, pigment, or marble chips to floors, stairways, and cabinet fixtures to fashion durable and decorative surfaces. Cut metal division strips and press them into the terrazzo base wherever there is to be a joint or change of color, to form desired designs or patterns, and to help prevent cracks. Blend marble chip mixtures and place into panels, then push a roller over the surface to embed the chips. Measure designated amounts of ingredients for terrazzo or grout according to standard formulas and specifications, using graduated containers and scale, and load ingredients into portable mixer. Mold expansion joints and edges, using edging tools, jointers, and straightedges. Spread, level, and smooth concrete and terrazzo mixtures to form bases and finished surfaces, using rakes, shovels, hand or power trowels, hand or power screeds, and floats. Grind curved surfaces and areas inaccessible to surfacing machines, such as stairways and cabinet tops, with portable hand grinders. Grind surfaces with power grinders and polish surfaces with polishing or surfacing machines. Position and secure moisture membrane and wire mesh prior to pouring base materials for terrazzo installation. Modify mixing, grouting, grinding, and cleaning procedures according to type of installation or material used. Wash polished terrazzo surface, using cleaner and water, and apply sealer and curing agent according to manufacturer's specifications, using brushes or sprayers. Mix cement, sand, and water to produce concrete, grout, or slurry, using hoes, trowels, tampers, scrapers, or concrete-mixing machines. Sprinkle colored marble or stone chips, powdered steel, or coloring powder over surfaces to produce prescribed finishes. Wet surfaces to prepare for bonding, fill holes and cracks with grout or slurry, and smooth, using trowel. Cut out damaged areas, drill holes for reinforcing rods, and position reinforcing rods to repair concrete, using power saws and drills. Clean installation sites, mixing and storage areas, tools, machines, and equipment, and store materials and equipment.

Education/Training Required: High school diploma or equivalent. **Education and Training Program:** Building/Construction Finishing, Management, and Inspection, Other. **Knowledge/Courses—Building and Construction:** Materials, methods, and the tools involved in the construction or repair of houses, buildings, or other structures such as highways and roads. **Mechanical Devices:** Machines and tools, including their designs, uses, repair, and maintenance. **Production and Processing:** Raw materials, production processes, quality control, costs, and other techniques for maximizing the effective manufacture and distribution of goods. **Design:** Design techniques, tools, and principles involved in production of precision technical plans, blueprints, drawings, and models. **Engineering and Technology:** The practical application of engineering science and technology. This includes applying principles, techniques, procedures, and equipment to the design and production of various goods and services. **Work Experience Needed:** None. **On-the-Job Training Needed:** Apprenticeship. **Certification/Licensure:** None.

Personality Type: Realistic. **Career Cluster:** 02 Architecture and Construction. **Career Pathway:** 02.2 Construction. **Other Jobs in This Pathway:** Boilermakers; Brickmasons and Blockmasons; Carpet Installers; Cement Masons and Concrete Finishers; Construction and Building Inspectors; Construction and Related Workers, All Other; Construction Carpenters; Construction Laborers; Construction Managers; Continuous Mining Machine Operators; Cost Estimators; Crane and Tower Operators; Dredge Operators; Drywall and Ceiling Tile Installers; Earth Drillers, Except Oil and Gas; Electrical Power-Line

Installers and Repairers; Electricians; Electromechanical Equipment Assemblers; Engineering Technicians, Except Drafters, All Other; Excavating and Loading Machine and Dragline Operators; Explosives Workers, Ordnance Handling Experts, and Blasters; Extraction Workers, All Other; First-Line Supervisors of Construction Trades and Extraction Workers; Floor Layers, Except Carpet, Wood, and Hard Tiles; Floor Sanders and Finishers; Glaziers; Heating and Air Conditioning Mechanics and Installers; Helpers, Construction Trades, All Other; others.

Skills—Equipment Selection: Determining the kind of tools and equipment needed to do a job. **Equipment Maintenance:** Performing routine maintenance on equipment and determining when and what kind of maintenance is needed. **Operation and Control:** Controlling operations of equipment or systems. **Repairing:** Repairing machines or systems using the needed tools. **Installation:** Installing equipment, machines, wiring, or programs to meet specifications. **Coordination:** Adjusting actions in relation to others' actions. **Quality Control Analysis:** Conducting tests and inspections of products, services, or processes to evaluate quality or performance. **Troubleshooting:** Determining causes of operating errors and deciding what to do about them.

Work Environment: Indoors; standing; walking and running; kneeling, crouching, stooping, or crawling; using hands; bending or twisting the body; repetitive motions; noise; bright or inadequate lighting; contaminants; cramped work space; hazardous conditions; hazardous equipment.

Tile and Marble Setters

- Annual Earnings: $37,080
- Earnings Growth Potential: High (42.7%)
- Growth: 25.4%
- Annual Job Openings: 2,770
- Self-Employed: 47.9%

Considerations for Job Outlook: Overall job prospects should improve over the coming decade as construction activity rebounds from the recent recession. As with many other construction workers, employment of tile and marble setters is sensitive to the fluctuations of the economy. On the one hand, workers may experience periods of unemployment when the overall level of construction falls. On the other hand, shortages of workers may occur in some areas during peak periods of building activity. Highly skilled workers with a good job history and work experience in construction will have the best opportunities.

Apply hard tiles, marble, and wood tiles to walls, floors, ceilings, and roof decks. Align and straighten tiles, using levels, squares, and straightedges. Determine and implement the best layouts to achieve desired patterns. Cut and shape tiles to fit around obstacles and into odd spaces and corners, using hand- and power-cutting tools. Finish and dress the joints and wipe excess grout from between tiles, using damp sponges. Apply mortar to tile backs, position the tiles, and press or tap with trowel handles to affix tiles to base. Mix, apply, and spread plaster, concrete, mortar, cement, mastic, glue, or other adhesives to form a bed for the tiles, using brushes, trowels, and screeds. Prepare cost and labor estimates based on calculations of time and materials needed for projects. Measure and mark surfaces to be tiled, following blueprints. Level concrete, and allow to dry. Build underbeds, and install anchor bolts, wires, and brackets. Prepare surfaces for tiling by attaching lath or waterproof paper or by applying a cement mortar coat onto a metal screen. Study blueprints and examine surfaces to be covered to determine amounts of materials needed. Cut, surface, polish, and install marble and granite or install precast terrazzo, granite, or marble units. Install and anchor fixtures in designated positions, using hand tools. Cut tile backing to required sizes, using shears. Remove any old tiles, grout, and adhesive, using chisels and scrapers, and clean surfaces carefully. Lay and set mosaic tiles to create decorative wall, mural, and floor designs.

Education/Training Required: Less than high school. **Education and Training Program:** Masonry/Mason Training. **Knowledge/Courses—Building and Construction:** Materials, methods, and the tools involved in the construction or repair of houses, buildings, or other structures such as highways and roads. **Design:** Design techniques, tools, and principles involved in production of precision technical plans, blueprints, drawings, and models. **Mechanical Devices:** Machines and tools, including their designs, uses, repair, and maintenance. **Work Experience Needed:** None. **On-the-Job Training Needed:** Long-term on-the-job training. **Certification/Licensure:** None.

Personality Type: Realistic-Conventional-Artistic. **Career Cluster:** 02 Architecture and Construction. **Career Pathway:** 02.2 Construction. **Other Jobs in This Pathway:** Boilermakers; Brickmasons and Blockmasons; Carpet Installers; Cement Masons and Concrete Finishers; Construction and Building Inspectors; Construction and Related Workers, All Other; Construction Carpenters; Construction Laborers; Construction Managers; Continuous Mining Machine Operators; Cost Estimators; Crane and Tower Operators; Dredge Operators; Drywall and Ceiling Tile Installers; Earth Drillers, Except Oil and Gas; Electrical Power-Line Installers and Repairers; Electricians; Electromechanical Equipment Assemblers; Engineering Technicians, Except Drafters, All Other; Excavating and Loading Machine and Dragline Operators; Explosives Workers, Ordnance Handling Experts, and Blasters; Extraction Workers, All Other; First-Line Supervisors of Construction Trades and Extraction Workers; Floor Layers, Except Carpet, Wood, and Hard Tiles; Floor Sanders and Finishers; Glaziers; Heating and Air Conditioning Mechanics and Installers; Helpers, Construction Trades, All Other; others.

Skills—Equipment Maintenance: Performing routine maintenance on equipment and determining when and what kind of maintenance is needed. **Equipment Selection:** Determining the kind of tools and equipment needed to do a job. **Repairing:** Repairing machines or systems using the needed tools. **Troubleshooting:** Determining causes of operating errors and deciding what to do about them. **Operation and Control:** Controlling operations of equipment or systems. **Mathematics:** Using mathematics to solve problems. **Operation Monitoring:** Watching gauges, dials, or other indicators to make sure a machine is working properly. **Quality Control Analysis:** Conducting tests and inspections of products, services, or processes to evaluate quality or performance.

Work Environment: Standing; kneeling, crouching, stooping, or crawling; using hands; bending or twisting the body; repetitive motions; noise; very hot or cold; bright or inadequate lighting; contaminants; cramped work space; hazardous equipment; minor burns, cuts, bites, or stings.

Tire Repairers and Changers

- Annual Earnings: $23,440
- Earnings Growth Potential: Low (26.6%)
- Growth: 18.5%
- Annual Job Openings: 4,390
- Self-Employed: 4.4%

Considerations for Job Outlook: About-average growth is projected.

Repair and replace tires. Identify and inflate tires correctly for the size and ply. Place wheels on balancing machines to determine counterweights required to balance wheels. Raise vehicles using hydraulic jacks. Remount wheels onto vehicles. Locate punctures in tubeless tires by visual inspection or by immersing inflated tires in water baths and observing air bubbles. Unbolt wheels from vehicles and remove them, using lug wrenches and other hand and power tools. Reassemble tires onto wheels. Replace valve stems and remove puncturing objects. Hammer required counterweights onto rims of wheels. Rotate tires to different positions on vehicles, using hand tools. Inspect tire casings for defects, such as holes and tears. Seal punctures in tubeless tires by inserting adhesive material and expanding rubber plugs into punctures, using hand tools. Glue boots (tire patches) over ruptures in tire casings, using rubber cement. Assist mechanics and perform other duties as directed. Separate tubed tires from wheels, using rubber mallets and metal bars, or mechanical tire changers. Patch tubes with adhesive rubber patches, or seal rubber patches to tubes using hot vulcanizing plates. Inflate inner tubes and immerse them in water to locate leaks. Clean sides of whitewall tires. Apply rubber cement to buffed tire casings prior to vulcanization process. Drive automobile or service trucks to industrial sites in order to provide services, and respond to emergency calls. Prepare rims and wheel drums for reassembly by scraping, grinding, or sandblasting. Order replacements for tires and tubes. Roll new rubber treads, known as camelbacks, over tire casings, and mold the semi-raw rubber treads onto the buffed casings. Buff defective areas of inner tubes, using scrapers. Place casing-camelback assemblies in tire molds for the vulcanization process, and exert pressure on the camelbacks to ensure good adhesion.

Education/Training Required: High school diploma or equivalent. **Education and Training Programs:** No related CIP programs; this job is learned through informal short-term on-the-job training. **Knowledge/Courses— Mechanical Devices:** Machines and tools, including their designs, uses, repair, and maintenance. **Transportation:** Principles and methods for moving people or goods by air, rail, sea, or road, including the relative costs and benefits. **Engineering and Technology:** The practical application of engineering science and technology. This includes applying principles, techniques, procedures, and equipment to the design and production of various goods and services. **Sales and Marketing:** Principles and methods for showing, promoting, and selling products or services. This includes marketing strategy and tactics, product demonstration, sales techniques, and sales control systems. **Work Experience Needed:** None. **On-the-Job Training Needed:** Moderate-term on-the-job training. **Certification/Licensure:** None.

Personality Type: Realistic-Conventional. **Career Cluster:** 13 Manufacturing. **Career Pathway:** 13.3 Maintenance, Installation, and Repair. **Other Jobs in This Pathway:** Aircraft Mechanics and Service Technicians; Automotive Engineering Technicians; Automotive Specialty Technicians; Avionics Technicians; Biological Technicians; Camera and Photographic Equipment Repairers; Chemical Equipment Operators and Tenders; Civil Engineering Technicians; Coil Winders, Tapers, and Finishers; Computer, Automated Teller, and Office Machine Repairers; Construction and Related Workers, All Other; Control and Valve Installers and Repairers, Except Mechanical Door; Electric Motor, Power Tool, and Related Repairers; Electrical and Electronic Equipment Assemblers; Electrical and Electronics Repairers, Commercial and Industrial Equipment; Electrical and Electronics Repairers, Powerhouse, Substation, and Relay; Electrical Engineering Technicians; Electrical Engineering Technologists; Electromechanical Engineering Technologists; Electromechanical Equipment Assemblers; Electronics Engineering Technicians; Electronics Engineering Technologists; others.

Skills—Repairing: Repairing machines or systems using the needed tools. **Equipment Maintenance:** Performing routine maintenance on equipment and determining when and what kind of maintenance is needed. **Operation and Control:** Controlling operations of equipment or systems. **Troubleshooting:** Determining causes of operating errors

and deciding what to do about them. **Equipment Selection:** Determining the kind of tools and equipment needed to do a job. **Quality Control Analysis:** Conducting tests and inspections of products, services, or processes to evaluate quality or performance. **Installation:** Installing equipment, machines, wiring, or programs to meet specifications. **Operation Monitoring:** Watching gauges, dials, or other indicators to make sure a machine is working properly.

Work Environment: Outdoors; standing; walking and running; kneeling, crouching, stooping, or crawling; using hands; bending or twisting the body; repetitive motions; noise; very hot or cold; contaminants; cramped work space; hazardous equipment; minor burns, cuts, bites, or stings.

Tour Guides and Escorts

- Annual Earnings: $23,620
- Earnings Growth Potential: Low (28.1%)
- Growth: 18.1%
- Annual Job Openings: 1,960
- Self-Employed: 11.7%

Considerations for Job Outlook: About-average employment growth is projected.

Escort individuals or groups on sightseeing tours or through places of interest. Conduct educational activities for school children. Escort individuals or groups on cruises, sightseeing tours, or through places of interest such as industrial establishments, public buildings, and art galleries. Describe tour points of interest to group members, and respond to questions. Monitor visitors' activities to ensure compliance with establishment or tour regulations and safety practices. Greet and register visitors, and issue any required identification badges or safety devices. Distribute brochures, show audiovisual presentations, and explain establishment processes and operations at tour sites. Provide directions and other pertinent information to visitors. Select travel routes and sites to be visited based on knowledge of specific areas. Research various topics, including site history, environmental conditions, and clients' skills and abilities to plan appropriate expeditions, instruction, and commentary. Provide for physical safety of groups, performing such activities as providing first aid and directing emergency evacuations. Provide information about wildlife varieties and habitats, as well as any relevant regulations such as those pertaining to hunting and fishing. Collect fees and tickets from group members. Teach skills, such as proper climbing methods, and demonstrate and advise on the use of equipment. Solicit tour patronage and sell souvenirs. Speak foreign languages to communicate with foreign visitors. Assemble and check the required supplies and equipment prior to departure. Drive motor vehicles to transport visitors to establishments and tour site locations. Perform clerical duties such as filing, typing, operating switchboards, and routing mail and messages. Train other guides and volunteers.

Education/Training Required: High school diploma or equivalent. **Education and Training Programs:** No related CIP programs; this job is learned through informal moderate-term on-the-job training. **Knowledge/Courses—History and Archeology:** Historical events and their causes, indicators, and effects on civilizations and cultures. **Geography:** Principles and methods for describing the features of land, sea, and air masses, including their physical characteristics, locations, interrelationships, and distribution of plant, animal, and human life. **Customer and Personal Service:** Principles and processes for providing customer and personal services. This includes customer needs assessment, meeting quality standards for services, and evaluation of customer satisfaction. **Sociology and Anthropology:** Group behavior and dynamics, societal trends and influences, human migrations, ethnicity, and cultures and their history and origins. **Psychology:** Human behavior and performance; individual differences in ability, personality, and interests; learning and motivation; psychological research methods; and the assessment and treatment of behavioral and affective disorders. **Transportation:** Principles and methods for moving people or goods by air, rail, sea, or road, including the relative costs and benefits. **Work Experience Needed:** None. **On-the-Job Training Needed:** Moderate-term on-the-job training. **Certification/Licensure:** Licensure for some specializations.

Personality Type: Social-Enterprising. **Career Cluster:** 09 Hospitality and Tourism. **Career Pathway:** 09.3 Travel and Tourism. **Other Jobs in This Pathway:** Food Service Managers; Lodging Managers; Managers, All Other; Reservation and Transportation Ticket Agents and Travel Clerks; Supply Chain Managers; Travel Agents.

Skills—Service Orientation: Actively looking for ways to help people.

Work Environment: Indoors; standing.

Traffic Technicians

- ⊙ Annual Earnings: $42,300
- ⊙ Earnings Growth Potential: Medium (39.2%)
- ⊙ Growth: 11.6%
- ⊙ Annual Job Openings: 280
- ⊙ Self-Employed: 0.0%

Considerations for Job Outlook: Slower-than-average employment growth is projected.

Conduct field studies to determine traffic volume, speed, effectiveness of signals, adequacy of lighting, and other factors influencing traffic conditions, under the direction of traffic engineers. Interact with the public in order to answer traffic-related questions; to respond to complaints and requests; or to discuss traffic control ordinances, plans, policies, and procedures. Prepare drawings of proposed signal installations or other control devices, using drafting instruments or computer automated drafting equipment. Plan, design, and improve components of traffic control systems to accommodate current and projected traffic and to increase usability and efficiency. Analyze data related to traffic flow, accident rate data, and proposed development to determine the most efficient methods to expedite traffic flow. Prepare work orders for repair, maintenance, and changes in traffic systems. Study factors affecting traffic conditions, such as lighting, and sign and marking visibility, in order to assess their effectiveness. Visit development and work sites to determine projects' effect on traffic and the adequacy of plans to control traffic and maintain safety, and to suggest traffic control measures. Lay out pavement markings for striping crews. Operate counters and record data to assess the volume, type, and movement of vehicular and pedestrian traffic at specified times. Provide technical supervision regarding traffic control devices to other traffic technicians and laborers. Gather and compile data from hand count sheets, machine count tapes, and radar speed checks, and code data for computer input. Place and secure automatic counters, using power tools, and retrieve counters after counting periods end. Measure and record the speed of vehicular traffic, using electrical timing devices or radar equipment. Study traffic delays by noting times of delays, the numbers of vehicles affected, and vehicle speed through the delay area.

Education/Training Required: Less than high school. **Education and Training Program:** Traffic, Customs, and Transportation Clerk/Technician Training. **Knowledge/Courses—Design:** Design techniques, tools, and principles involved in production of precision technical plans, blueprints, drawings, and models. **Engineering and Technology:** The practical application of engineering science and technology. This includes applying principles, techniques, procedures, and equipment to the design and production of various goods and services. **Building and Construction:** Materials, methods, and the tools involved in the construction or repair of houses, buildings, or other structures such as highways and roads. **Transportation:** Principles and methods for moving people or goods by air, rail, sea, or road, including the relative costs and benefits. **Public Safety and Security:** Relevant equipment, policies, procedures, and strategies to promote effective local, state, or national security operations for the protection of people, data, property, and institutions. **Law and Government:** Laws, legal codes, court procedures, precedents, government regulations, executive orders, agency rules, and the democratic political process. **Work Experience Needed:** None. **On-the-Job Training Needed:** Short-term on-the-job training. **Certification/Licensure:** None.

Personality Type: Realistic-Investigative-Enterprising. **Career Cluster:** 16 Transportation, Distribution, and Logistics. **Career Pathways:** 16.5 Transportation Systems/Infrastructure Planning, Management, and Regulation; 16.3 Warehousing and Distribution Center Operations. **Other Jobs in These Pathways:** Aviation Inspectors; Freight and Cargo Inspectors; Logistics Analysts; Production, Planning, and Expediting Clerks; Shipping, Receiving, and Traffic Clerks; Transportation Vehicle, Equipment and Systems Inspectors, Except Aviation.

Skills—Operations Analysis: Analyzing needs and product requirements to create a design. **Science:** Using scientific rules and methods to solve problems. **Systems Analysis:** Determining how a system should work and how changes in conditions, operations, and the environment will affect outcomes. **Operation and Control:** Controlling operations of equipment or systems. **Systems Evaluation:** Identifying measures or indicators of system performance and the actions needed to improve or correct performance relative to the goals of the system. **Troubleshooting:** Determining causes of operating errors and deciding what to do about them. **Operation Monitoring:** Watching gauges, dials, or other indicators to make sure a machine is working properly. **Mathematics:** Using mathematics to solve problems.

Work Environment: More often indoors than outdoors; sitting; noise; very hot or cold.

Transit and Railroad Police

- ⊙ Annual Earnings: $56,390
- ⊙ Earnings Growth Potential: Low (32.4%)
- ⊙ Growth: 5.6%
- ⊙ Annual Job Openings: 110
- ⊙ Self-Employed: 0.0%

Considerations for Job Outlook: Continued demand for public safety will lead to new openings for officers in local departments; however, both state and federal jobs may be more competitive. Because they typically offer low salaries, many local departments face high turnover rates, making opportunities more plentiful for qualified applicants. However, some smaller departments may have fewer opportunities as budgets limit the ability to hire additional officers. Jobs in state and federal agencies will remain more competitive as they often offer high pay and more opportunities for both promotions and interagency transfers. Bilingual applicants with a bachelor's degree and law enforcement or military experience, especially investigative experience, should have the best opportunities in federal agencies.

Protect and police railroad and transit property, employees, or passengers. Patrol railroad yards, cars, stations, and other facilities to protect company property and shipments and to maintain order. Examine credentials of unauthorized persons attempting to enter secured areas. Apprehend or remove trespassers or thieves from railroad property, or coordinate with law enforcement agencies in apprehensions and removals. Prepare reports documenting investigation activities and results. Investigate or direct investigations of freight theft, suspicious damage or loss of passengers' valuables, and other crimes on railroad property. Direct security activities at derailments, fires, floods, and strikes involving railroad property. Direct and coordinate the daily activities and training of security staff. Interview neighbors, associates, and former employers of job applicants to verify personal references and to obtain work history data. Record and verify seal numbers from boxcars containing frequently pilfered items, such as cigarettes and liquor, in order to detect tampering. Plan and implement special safety and preventive programs, such as fire and accident prevention. Seal empty boxcars by twisting nails in door hasps, using nail twisters.

Education/Training Required: High school diploma or equivalent. **Education and Training Programs:** Homeland Security, Law Enforcement, Firefighting, and Related Protective Services, Other; Security and Loss Prevention Services. **Knowledge/Courses—Public Safety and Security:** Relevant equipment, policies, procedures, and strategies to promote effective local, state, or national security operations for the protection of people, data, property, and institutions. **Transportation:** Principles and methods for moving people or goods by air, rail, sea, or road, including the relative costs and benefits. **Telecommunications:** Transmission, broadcasting, switching, control, and operation of telecommunications systems. **Law and Government:** Laws, legal codes, court procedures, precedents, government regulations, executive orders, agency rules, and the democratic political process. **English Language:** The structure and content of the English language including the meaning and spelling of words, rules of composition, and grammar. **Geography:** Principles and methods for describing the features of land, sea, and air masses, including their physical characteristics, locations, interrelationships, and distribution of plant, animal, and human life. **Work Experience Needed:** None. **On-the-Job Training Needed:** Short-term on-the-job training. **Certification/Licensure:** No data available.

Personality Type: Realistic-Enterprising-Conventional. **Career Cluster:** 12 Law, Public Safety, Corrections, and Security. **Career Pathway:** 12.3 Security and Protective Services. **Other Jobs in This Pathway:** Animal Control Workers; Criminal Justice and Law Enforcement Teachers, Postsecondary; Crossing Guards; First-Line Supervisors of Protective Service Workers, All Other; Forest Firefighters; Gaming Surveillance Officers and Gaming Investigators; Lifeguards, Ski Patrol, and Other Recreational Protective Service Workers; Parking Enforcement Workers; Police, Fire, and Ambulance Dispatchers; Private Detectives and Investigators; Retail Loss Prevention Specialists; Security Guards; Sheriffs and Deputy Sheriffs.

Skills—Persuasion: Persuading others to change their minds or behavior. **Negotiation:** Bringing others together and trying to reconcile differences. **Speaking:** Talking to others to convey information effectively. **Operation and Control:** Controlling operations of equipment or systems. **Programming:** Writing computer programs for various purposes. **Learning Strategies:** Selecting and using training/instructional methods and procedures appropriate for the situation when learning or teaching new things. **Systems Analysis:** Determining how a system should work and how changes in conditions, operations, and the environment will affect outcomes. **Social Perceptiveness:** Being aware of others' reactions and understanding why they react as they do.

Work Environment: More often indoors than outdoors; standing; noise; very hot or cold; bright or inadequate lighting; contaminants; hazardous conditions; minor burns, cuts, bites, or stings.

Transportation Inspectors

- Annual Earnings: $62,230
- Earnings Growth Potential: High (47.1%)
- Growth: 14.6%
- Annual Job Openings: 1,070
- Self-Employed: 9.1%

Considerations for Job Outlook: About-average employment growth is projected.

Inspect equipment or goods in connection with the safe transport of cargo or people. For task data, see Job Specializations.

Education/Training Required: Some college, no degree. **Work Experience Needed:** None. **On-the-Job Training Needed:** Short-term on-the-job training. **Certification/Licensure:** Voluntary certification for some specializations.

Job Specialization: Aviation Inspectors

Inspect aircraft, maintenance procedures, air navigational aids, air traffic controls, and communications equipment to ensure conformance with federal safety regulations. Inspect work of aircraft mechanics performing maintenance, modification, or repair and overhaul of aircraft and aircraft mechanical systems to ensure adherence to standards and procedures. Start aircraft and observe gauges, meters, and other instruments to detect evidence of malfunctions. Examine aircraft access plates and doors for security. Examine landing gear, tires, and exteriors of fuselage, wings, and engines for evidence of damage or corrosion and to determine whether repairs are needed. Prepare and maintain detailed repair, inspection, investigation, and certification records and reports. Inspect new, repaired, or modified aircraft to identify damage or defects and to assess airworthiness and conformance to standards, using checklists, hand tools, and test instruments. Examine maintenance records and flight logs to determine if service and maintenance checks and overhauls were performed at prescribed intervals. Recommend replacement, repair, or modification of aircraft equipment. Recommend changes in rules, policies, standards, and regulations based on knowledge of operating conditions, aircraft improvements, and other factors. Issue pilots' licenses to individuals meeting standards. Investigate air accidents and complaints to determine causes. Observe flight activities of pilots to assess flying skills and to ensure conformance to flight and safety regulations.

Education and Training Program: Aircraft Powerplant Technology/Technician. **Knowledge/Courses—Mechanical Devices:** Machines and tools, including their designs, uses, repair, and maintenance. **Physics:** Physical principles, laws, their interrelationships, and applications to understanding fluid, material, and atmospheric dynamics, and mechanical, electrical, atomic, and subatomic structures and processes. **Transportation:** Principles and methods for moving people or goods by air, rail, sea, or road, including the relative costs and benefits. **Chemistry:** The chemical composition, structure, and properties of substances and of the chemical processes and transformations that they undergo. This includes uses of chemicals and their danger signs, production techniques, and disposal methods. **Design:** Design techniques, tools, and principles involved in production of precision technical plans, blueprints, drawings, and models. **Law and Government:** Laws, legal codes, court procedures, precedents, government regulations, executive orders, agency rules, and the democratic political process.

Personality Type: Realistic-Conventional-Investigative. **Career Cluster:** 16 Transportation, Distribution, and Logistics. **Career Pathways:** 16.1 Transportation Operations; 16.5 Transportation Systems/Infrastructure Planning, Management, and Regulation. **Other Jobs in These Pathways:** Aerospace Engineering and Operations Technicians; Air Traffic Controllers; Aircraft Cargo Handling Supervisors; Airfield Operations Specialists; Airline Pilots, Copilots, and Flight Engineers; Automotive and Watercraft Service Attendants; Automotive Master Mechanics; Bridge and Lock Tenders; Bus Drivers, School or Special Client; Bus Drivers, Transit and Intercity; Commercial Divers; Commercial Pilots; Crane and Tower Operators; First-Line Supervisors of Helpers, Laborers, and Material Movers, Hand; First-Line Supervisors of Transportation and Material-Moving Machine and Vehicle Operators; Freight and Cargo Inspectors; Heavy and Tractor-Trailer Truck Drivers; Hoist and Winch Operators; Laborers and Freight, Stock, and Material Movers, Hand; Light Truck or Delivery Services Drivers; Mates—Ship, Boat, and Barge; Motor Vehicle Operators, All Other; Motorboat Operators; Operating Engineers and Other Construction Equipment Operators; Parking Lot Attendants; others.

Skills—Science: Using scientific rules and methods to solve problems. **Equipment Maintenance:** Performing routine maintenance on equipment and determining when and what kind of maintenance is needed. **Troubleshooting:** Determining causes of operating errors and deciding what to do about them. **Repairing:** Repairing machines or systems using the needed tools. **Operation and Control:** Controlling operations of equipment or systems. **Equipment Selection:** Determining the kind of tools and equipment needed to do a job. **Quality Control Analysis:** Conducting tests and inspections of products, services, or processes to evaluate quality or performance. **Operation Monitoring:** Watching gauges, dials, or other indicators to make sure a machine is working properly.

Work Environment: More often indoors than outdoors; sitting; noise.

Job Specialization: Freight and Cargo Inspectors

Inspect the handling, storage, and stowing of freight and cargoes. Prepare and submit reports after completion of freight shipments. Inspect shipments to ensure that freight is securely braced and blocked. Record details about freight conditions, handling of freight, and any problems encountered. Advise crews in techniques of stowing dangerous and heavy cargo. Observe loading of freight to ensure that crews comply with procedures. Recommend remedial procedures to correct any violations found during inspections. Inspect loaded cargo, cargo lashed to decks or in storage facilities, and cargo-handling devices to determine compliance with health and safety regulations and need for maintenance. Measure ships' holds and depths of fuel and water in tanks, using sounding lines and tape measures. Notify workers of any special treatment required for shipments. Direct crews to reload freight or to insert additional bracing or packing as necessary. Check temperatures and humidities of shipping and storage areas to ensure that they are at appropriate levels to protect cargo. Determine cargo transportation capabilities by reading documents that set forth cargo-loading and securing procedures, capacities, and stability factors. Read draft markings to determine depths of vessels in water. Issue certificates of compliance for vessels without violations. Write certificates of admeasurement that list details such as designs, lengths, depths, and breadths of vessels, and methods of propulsion.

Education and Training Programs: No related CIP programs; this job is learned through work experience in a related occupation. **Knowledge/Courses—Transportation:** Principles and methods for moving people or goods by air, rail, sea, or road, including the relative costs and benefits. **Engineering and Technology:** The practical application of engineering science and technology. This includes applying principles, techniques, procedures, and equipment to the design and production of various goods and services. **Public Safety and Security:** Relevant equipment, policies, procedures, and strategies to promote effective local, state, or national security operations for the protection of people, data, property, and institutions. **Physics:** Physical principles, laws, their interrelationships, and applications to understanding fluid, material, and atmospheric dynamics, and mechanical, electrical, atomic, and subatomic structures and processes. **Geography:** Principles and methods for describing the features of land, sea, and air masses, including their physical characteristics, locations, interrelationships, and distribution of plant, animal, and human life. **Mechanical Devices:** Machines and tools, including their designs, uses, repair, and maintenance.

Personality Type: Realistic-Conventional. **Career Cluster:** 16 Transportation, Distribution, and Logistics. **Career Pathways:** 16.5 Transportation Systems/Infrastructure Planning, Management, and Regulation; 16.1 Transportation Operations. **Other Jobs in These Pathways:** Aerospace Engineering and Operations Technicians; Air Traffic Controllers; Aircraft Cargo Handling Supervisors; Airfield Operations Specialists; Airline Pilots, Copilots, and Flight Engineers; Automotive and Watercraft Service Attendants; Automotive Master Mechanics; Aviation Inspectors; Bridge and Lock Tenders; Bus Drivers, School or Special Client; Bus Drivers, Transit and Intercity; Commercial Divers; Commercial Pilots; Crane and Tower Operators; First-Line Supervisors of Helpers, Laborers, and Material Movers, Hand; First-Line Supervisors of Transportation and Material-Moving Machine and Vehicle Operators; Heavy and Tractor-Trailer Truck Drivers; Hoist and Winch Operators; Laborers and Freight, Stock, and Material Movers, Hand; Light Truck or Delivery Services Drivers; Mates—Ship, Boat, and Barge; Motor Vehicle Operators, All Other; Motorboat Operators; Operating Engineers and Other Construction Equipment Operators; Parking Lot Attendants; Pilots, Ship; others.

Skills—Operation and Control: Controlling operations of equipment or systems. **Quality Control Analysis:** Conducting tests and inspections of products, services, or processes to evaluate quality or performance. **Operation Monitoring:** Watching gauges, dials, or other indicators to make sure a machine is working properly. **Science:** Using scientific rules and methods to solve problems. **Management of Personnel Resources:** Motivating, developing, and directing people as they work, identifying the best people for the job. **Troubleshooting:** Determining causes of operating errors and deciding what to do about them. **Writing:** Communicating effectively in writing as appropriate for the needs of the audience. **Judgment and Decision Making:** Considering the relative costs and benefits of potential actions to choose the most appropriate one.

Work Environment: More often outdoors than indoors; standing; noise; very hot or cold; bright or inadequate lighting; contaminants; cramped work space; high places; hazardous equipment.

Job Specialization: Transportation Vehicle, Equipment and Systems Inspectors, Except Aviation

Inspect and monitor transportation equipment, vehicles, or systems to ensure compliance with regulations and safety standards. Conduct vehicle or transportation equipment tests, using diagnostic equipment. Investigate and make recommendations on carrier requests for waiver of federal standards. Prepare reports on investigations or inspections and actions taken. Issue notices and recommend corrective actions when infractions or problems are found. Investigate incidents or violations such as delays, accidents, and equipment failures. Investigate complaints regarding safety violations. Inspect repairs to transportation vehicles and equipment to ensure that repair work was performed properly. Examine transportation vehicles, equipment, or systems to detect damage, wear, or malfunction. Inspect vehicles and other equipment for evidence of abuse, damage, or mechanical malfunction. Examine carrier operating rules, employee qualification guidelines, and carrier training and testing programs for compliance with regulations or safety standards. Inspect vehicles or equipment to ensure compliance with rules, standards, or regulations.

Education and Training Programs: No related CIP programs; this job is learned through work experience in a related occupation. **Knowledge/Courses—Mechanical Devices:** Machines and tools, including their designs, uses, repair, and maintenance. **Transportation:** Principles and methods for moving people or goods by air, rail, sea, or road, including the relative costs and benefits. **Public Safety and Security:** Relevant equipment, policies, procedures, and strategies to promote effective local, state, or national security operations for the protection of people, data, property, and institutions. **Engineering and Technology:** The practical application of engineering science and technology. This includes applying principles, techniques, procedures, and equipment to the design and production of various goods and services. **Administration and Management:** Business and management principles involved in strategic planning, resource allocation, human resources modeling, leadership technique, production methods, and coordination of people and resources. **Physics:** Physical principles, laws, their interrelationships, and applications to understanding fluid, material, and atmospheric dynamics, and mechanical, electrical, atomic, and subatomic structures and processes.

Personality Type: Realistic-Conventional-Investigative. **Career Cluster:** 16 Transportation, Distribution, and Logistics. **Career Pathways:** 16.1 Transportation Operations; 16.5 Transportation Systems/Infrastructure Planning, Management, and Regulation. **Other Jobs in These Pathways:** Aerospace Engineering and Operations Technicians; Air Traffic Controllers; Aircraft Cargo Handling Supervisors; Airfield Operations Specialists; Airline Pilots, Copilots, and Flight Engineers; Automotive and Watercraft Service Attendants; Automotive Master Mechanics; Aviation Inspectors;

Bridge and Lock Tenders; Bus Drivers, School or Special Client; Bus Drivers, Transit and Intercity; Commercial Divers; Commercial Pilots; Crane and Tower Operators; First-Line Supervisors of Helpers, Laborers, and Material Movers, Hand; First-Line Supervisors of Transportation and Material-Moving Machine and Vehicle Operators; Freight and Cargo Inspectors; Heavy and Tractor-Trailer Truck Drivers; Hoist and Winch Operators; Laborers and Freight, Stock, and Material Movers, Hand; Light Truck or Delivery Services Drivers; Mates—Ship, Boat, and Barge; Motor Vehicle Operators, All Other; Motorboat Operators; Operating Engineers and Other Construction Equipment Operators; others.

Skills—Equipment Maintenance: Performing routine maintenance on equipment and determining when and what kind of maintenance is needed. **Repairing:** Repairing machines or systems using the needed tools. **Troubleshooting:** Determining causes of operating errors and deciding what to do about them. **Science:** Using scientific rules and methods to solve problems. **Operation and Control:** Controlling operations of equipment or systems. **Quality Control Analysis:** Conducting tests and inspections of products, services, or processes to evaluate quality or performance. **Operation Monitoring:** Watching gauges, dials, or other indicators to make sure a machine is working properly. **Equipment Selection:** Determining the kind of tools and equipment needed to do a job.

Work Environment: Outdoors; standing; walking and running; using hands; bending or twisting the body; repetitive motions; noise; very hot or cold; bright or inadequate lighting; contaminants; cramped work space; hazardous equipment; minor burns, cuts, bites, or stings.

Transportation Security Screeners

- ⊙ Annual Earnings: $36,910
- ⊙ Earnings Growth Potential: Very low (15.8%)
- ⊙ Growth: 9.6%
- ⊙ Annual Job Openings: 1,040
- ⊙ Self-Employed: 0.0%

Considerations for Job Outlook: Job opportunities for security guards will stem from growing demand for various forms of security. Additional opportunities will be due to turnover. Although many people are attracted to part-time positions because of the limited training requirements, there will be more competition for higher-paying positions that require more training. Those with related work experience, such as a background in law enforcement, and those with computer and technology skills should find the best job prospects.

Conduct screening of passengers, baggage, or cargo to ensure compliance with Transportation Security Administration (TSA) regulations. Ask passengers to remove shoes and divest themselves of metal objects prior to walking through metal detectors. Check passengers' tickets to ensure that they are valid and to determine whether passengers have designations that require special handling such as providing photo identification. Close entry areas following security breaches or reopen areas after receiving notification that the airport is secure. Confiscate dangerous items and hazardous materials found in opened bags and turn them over to airlines for disposal. Contact leads or supervisors to discuss objects of concern that are not on prohibited object lists. Contact police directly in cases of urgent security issues, using phones or two-way radios. Decide whether baggage that triggers alarms should be searched or should be allowed to pass through. Direct passengers to areas where they can pick up their baggage after screening is complete. Inform other screeners when baggage should not be opened because it might contain explosives. Inform passengers of how to mail prohibited items to themselves, or confiscate these items. Inspect carry-on items, using X-ray viewing equipment, to determine whether items contain objects that warrant further investigation. Inspect checked baggage for signs of tampering. Locate suspicious bags pictured in printouts sent from remote monitoring areas, and set these bags aside for inspection. Monitor passenger flow through screening checkpoints to ensure order and efficiency. Notify supervisors or other appropriate personnel when security breaches occur. Perform pat-down or handheld wand searches of passengers who have triggered machine alarms, who are unable to pass through metal detectors, or who have been randomly identified for such searches. Record information about any baggage that sets off alarms in monitoring equipment. Send checked baggage through automated screening machines, and set bags aside for searching or rescreening as indicated by equipment.

Education/Training Required: High school diploma or equivalent. **Education and Training Program:** Homeland Security, Law Enforcement, Firefighting, and Related Protective Services, Other. **Knowledge/Courses—Public Safety and Security:** Relevant equipment, policies, procedures, and strategies to promote effective local, state, or national security operations for the protection of people, data, property, and institutions. **Law and Government:** Laws, legal codes, court procedures, precedents, government regulations, executive orders, agency rules, and the democratic political process. **Transportation:** Principles and methods for moving people or goods by air, rail, sea, or road, including the relative costs and benefits. **Customer and Personal Service:** Principles and processes for providing customer and personal services. This includes customer needs assessment, meeting quality standards for services, and evaluation of customer satisfaction. **Work Experience Needed:** None. **On-the-Job Training Needed:** Moderate-term on-the-job training. **Certification/Licensure:** None.

Personality Type: Realistic-Enterprising-Conventional. **Career Cluster:** 12 Law, Public Safety, Corrections, and Security. **Career Pathway:** 12.3 Security and Protective Services. **Other Jobs in This Pathway:** Animal Control Workers; Criminal Justice and Law Enforcement Teachers, Postsecondary; Crossing Guards; First-Line Supervisors of Protective Service Workers, All Other; Forest Firefighters; Gaming Surveillance Officers and Gaming Investigators; Lifeguards, Ski Patrol, and Other Recreational Protective Service Workers; Parking Enforcement Workers; Police, Fire, and Ambulance Dispatchers; Private Detectives and Investigators; Retail Loss Prevention Specialists; Security Guards; Sheriffs and Deputy Sheriffs; Transit and Railroad Police.

Skills—Operation and Control: Controlling operations of equipment or systems. **Operation Monitoring:** Watching gauges, dials, or other indicators to make sure a machine is working properly. **Equipment Selection:** Determining the kind of tools and equipment needed to do a job. **Equipment Maintenance:** Performing routine maintenance on equipment and determining when and what kind of maintenance is needed. **Quality Control Analysis:** Conducting tests and inspections of products, services, or processes to evaluate quality or performance. **Troubleshooting:** Determining causes of operating errors and deciding what to do about them. **Repairing:** Repairing machines or systems using the needed tools. **Persuasion:** Persuading others to change their minds or behavior.

Work Environment: Indoors; standing; walking and running; using hands; bending or twisting the body; repetitive motions; noise; bright or inadequate lighting; contaminants; exposed to radiation; exposed to disease or infections.

Transportation, Storage, and Distribution Managers

- ⊙ Annual Earnings: $80,860
- ⊙ Earnings Growth Potential: High (40.9%)
- ⊙ Growth: 10.0%
- ⊙ Annual Job Openings: 3,370
- ⊙ Self-Employed: 6.2%

Considerations for Job Outlook: In courier services, a small decrease is expected as better technology and routing increase efficiency and decrease the demand for transportation workers and managers in this industry.

Plan, direct, or coordinate transportation, storage, or distribution activities in accordance with organizational policies and applicable government laws or regulations. For task data, see Job Specializations.

Education/Training Required: High school diploma or equivalent. **Work Experience Needed:** More than 5 years. **On-the-Job Training Needed:** None. **Certification/Licensure:** None.

Job Specialization: Logistics Managers

Plan, direct, or coordinate purchasing, warehousing, distribution, forecasting, customer service, or planning services. Manage logistics personnel and logistics systems and direct daily operations. Train shipping department personnel in roles or responsibilities regarding global logistics strategies. Maintain metrics, reports, process documentation, customer service logs, or training or safety records. Implement specific customer requirements such as internal reporting or customized transportation metrics. Resolve problems concerning transportation, logistics systems, imports or exports, or customer issues. Develop risk management programs to ensure continuity of supply in emergency scenarios. Plan or implement improvements to internal or external logistics systems or processes. Recommend optimal transportation modes, routing, equipment, or frequency. Participate in carrier management processes such as selection, qualification, or performance evaluation. Negotiate transportation rates or services. Monitor product import or export processes to ensure compliance with regulatory or legal requirements. Establish or monitor specific supply chain–based performance measurement systems. Ensure carrier compliance with company policies or procedures for product transit or delivery. Direct distribution center operation to ensure achievement of cost, productivity, accuracy, or timeliness objectives. Create policies or procedures for logistics activities. Collaborate with other departments to integrate logistics with business systems or processes, such as customer sales, order management, accounting, or shipping. Analyze the financial impact of proposed logistics changes such as routing, shipping modes, product volumes or mixes, or carriers. Supervise the work of logistics specialists, planners, or schedulers. Plan or implement material flow management systems to meet production requirements. Direct inbound or outbound logistics operations, such as transportation or warehouse activities, safety performance, or logistics quality management.

Education and Training Program: Logistics, Materials, and Supply Chain Management. **Knowledge/Courses— Transportation:** Principles and methods for moving people or goods by air, rail, sea, or road, including the relative costs and benefits. **Production and Processing:** Raw materials, production processes, quality control, costs, and other techniques for maximizing the effective manufacture and distribution of goods. **Geography:** Principles and methods for describing the features of land, sea, and air masses, including their physical characteristics, locations, interrelationships, and distribution of plant, animal, and human life. **Administration and Management:** Business and management principles involved in strategic planning, resource allocation, human resources modeling, leadership technique, production methods, and coordination of people and resources. **Economics and Accounting:** Economic and accounting principles and practices, the financial markets, banking, and the analysis and reporting of financial data. **Personnel and Human Resources:** Principles and procedures for personnel recruitment, selection, training, compensation and benefits, labor relations and negotiation, and personnel information systems.

Personality Type: Enterprising-Conventional. **Career Clusters:** 04 Business, Management, and Administration;

16 Transportation, Distribution, and Logistics. **Career Pathways:** 16.2 Logistics, Planning, and Management Services; 04.2 Business, Financial Management, and Accounting; 04.1 Management. **Other Jobs in These Pathways:** Accountants; Administrative Services Managers; Agents and Business Managers of Artists, Performers, and Athletes; Auditors; Billing, Cost, and Rate Clerks; Biofuels Production Managers; Bioinformatics Technicians; Biomass Power Plant Managers; Bookkeeping, Accounting, and Auditing Clerks; Brokerage Clerks; Brownfield Redevelopment Specialists and Site Managers; Budget Analysts; Business Continuity Planners; Business Operations Specialists, All Other; Business Teachers, Postsecondary; Chief Executives; Chief Sustainability Officers; Communications Teachers, Postsecondary; Compliance Managers; Computer and Information Systems Managers; Construction Managers; Cost Estimators; Credit Analysts; Customs Brokers; Economics Teachers, Postsecondary; Economists; Energy Auditors; Environmental Economists; Financial Analysts; Financial Examiners; Financial Managers, Branch or Department; First-Line Supervisors of Office and Administrative Support Workers; others.

Skills—Management of Financial Resources: Determining how money will be spent to get the work done and accounting for these expenditures. **Management of Material Resources:** Obtaining and seeing to the appropriate use of equipment, facilities, and materials needed to do certain work. **Management of Personnel Resources:** Motivating, developing, and directing people as they work, identifying the best people for the job. **Negotiation:** Bringing others together and trying to reconcile differences. **Systems Evaluation:** Identifying measures or indicators of system performance and the actions needed to improve or correct performance relative to the goals of the system. **Time Management:** Managing one's own time and the time of others. **Monitoring:** Monitoring or assessing your performance or that of other individuals or organizations to make improvements or take corrective action. **Active Learning:** Understanding the implications of new information for both current and future problem solving and decision making.

Work Environment: Indoors; sitting.

Job Specialization: Storage and Distribution Managers

Plan, direct, and coordinate the storage and distribution operations within organizations or the activities of organizations that are engaged in storing and distributing materials and products. Supervise the activities of workers engaged in receiving, storing, testing, and shipping products or materials. Plan, develop, and implement warehouse safety and security programs and activities. Review invoices, work orders, consumption reports, and demand forecasts to estimate peak delivery periods and to issue work assignments. Schedule and monitor air or surface pickup, delivery, or distribution of products or materials. Interview, select, and train warehouse and supervisory personnel. Confer with department heads to coordinate warehouse activities, such as production, sales, records control, and purchasing. Respond to customers' or shippers' questions and complaints regarding storage and distribution services. Inspect physical conditions of warehouses, vehicle fleets, and equipment, and order testing, maintenance, repair, or replacement as necessary. Develop and document standard and emergency operating procedures for receiving, handling, storing, shipping, or salvaging products or materials. Examine products or materials to estimate quantities or weight and types of containers required for storage or transport. Issue shipping instructions and provide routing information to ensure that delivery times and locations are coordinated. Negotiate with carriers, warehouse operators, and insurance company representatives for services and preferential rates. Examine invoices and shipping manifests for conformity to tariff and customs regulations. Prepare and manage departmental budgets. Prepare or direct preparation of correspondence; reports; and operations, maintenance, and safety manuals. Arrange for necessary shipping documentation, and contact customs officials to effect release of shipments. Advise sales and billing departments of transportation charges for customers' accounts. Evaluate freight costs and the inventory costs associated with transit times to ensure that costs are appropriate. Participate in setting transportation and service rates.

Education and Training Programs: Aeronautics/Aviation/Aerospace Science and Technology, General; Aviation/Airway Management and Operations; Business Administration and Management, General; Business/Commerce, General; Logistics, Materials, and Supply Chain Management; Public Administration; Transportation/Mobility

Management. **Knowledge/Courses—Transportation:** Principles and methods for moving people or goods by air, rail, sea, or road, including the relative costs and benefits. **Personnel and Human Resources:** Principles and procedures for personnel recruitment, selection, training, compensation and benefits, labor relations and negotiation, and personnel information systems. **Production and Processing:** Raw materials, production processes, quality control, costs, and other techniques for maximizing the effective manufacture and distribution of goods. **Administration and Management:** Business and management principles involved in strategic planning, resource allocation, human resources modeling, leadership technique, production methods, and coordination of people and resources. **Economics and Accounting:** Economic and accounting principles and practices, the financial markets, banking, and the analysis and reporting of financial data. **Psychology:** Human behavior and performance; individual differences in ability, personality, and interests; learning and motivation; psychological research methods; and the assessment and treatment of behavioral and affective disorders.

Personality Type: Enterprising-Conventional. **Career Clusters:** 04 Business, Management, and Administration; 07 Government and Public Administration; 16 Transportation, Distribution, and Logistics. **Career Pathways:** 07.1 Governance; 04.1 Management; 16.2 Logistics, Planning, and Management Services; 16.1 Transportation Operations. **Other Jobs in These Pathways:** Administrative Services Managers; Aerospace Engineering and Operations Technicians; Agents and Business Managers of Artists, Performers, and Athletes; Air Traffic Controllers; Aircraft Cargo Handling Supervisors; Airfield Operations Specialists; Airline Pilots, Copilots, and Flight Engineers; Automotive and Watercraft Service Attendants; Automotive Master Mechanics; Aviation Inspectors; Biofuels Production Managers; Biomass Power Plant Managers; Bridge and Lock Tenders; Brownfield Redevelopment Specialists and Site Managers; Bus Drivers, School or Special Client; Bus Drivers, Transit and Intercity; Business Continuity Planners; Business Operations Specialists, All Other; Business Teachers, Postsecondary; Chief Executives; Chief Sustainability Officers; Commercial Divers; Commercial Pilots; Communications Teachers, Postsecondary; Compliance Managers; Computer and Information Systems Managers; Construction Managers; Cost Estimators; Crane and Tower Operators; Customs Brokers; others.

Skills—Management of Financial Resources: Determining how money will be spent to get the work done and accounting for these expenditures. **Management of Material Resources:** Obtaining and seeing to the appropriate use of equipment, facilities, and materials needed to do certain work. **Operations Analysis:** Analyzing needs and product requirements to create a design. **Management of Personnel Resources:** Motivating, developing, and directing people as they work, identifying the best people for the job. **Negotiation:** Bringing others together and trying to reconcile differences. **Coordination:** Adjusting actions in relation to others' actions. **Operation and Control:** Controlling operations of equipment or systems. **Systems Evaluation:** Identifying measures or indicators of system performance and the actions needed to improve or correct performance relative to the goals of the system.

Work Environment: Indoors; standing.

Job Specialization: Transportation Managers

Plan, direct, and coordinate the transportation operations within an organization or the activities of organizations that provide transportation services. Analyze expenditures and other financial information to develop plans, policies, and budgets for increasing profits and improving services. Set operations policies and standards, including determination of safety procedures for the handling of dangerous goods. Plan, organize, and manage the work of subordinate staff to ensure that the work is accomplished in a manner consistent with organizational requirements. Negotiate and authorize contracts with equipment and materials suppliers, and monitor contract fulfillment. Collaborate with other managers and staff members to formulate and implement policies, procedures, goals, and objectives. Monitor spending to ensure that expenses are consistent with approved budgets. Supervise workers assigning tariff classifications and preparing billing. Promote safe work activities by conducting safety audits, attending company safety meetings, and meeting with individual staff members. Direct investigations to verify and resolve customer or shipper complaints. Direct procurement processes including equipment research and testing, vendor contracts, and requisitions approval. Recommend or authorize capital expenditures for acquisition of new equipment or property to increase efficiency and services of operations department. Monitor operations to ensure that staff members comply with administrative policies and procedures, safety rules, union contracts, and government regulations. Direct activities related to dispatching, routing, and tracking transportation vehicles such as aircraft and railroad cars. Direct and coordinate, through subordinates, activities of operations department to obtain use of equipment, facilities, and human resources. Conduct employee training sessions on subjects such as hazardous material handling, employee orientation, quality improvement, and computer use. Prepare management recommendations, such as proposed fee and tariff increases, or schedule changes. Implement schedule and policy changes.

Education and Training Programs: Aeronautics/Aviation/Aerospace Science and Technology, General; Aviation/Airway Management and Operations; Business Administration and Management, General; Business/Commerce, General; Logistics, Materials, and Supply Chain Management; Public Administration; Transportation/Mobility Management. **Knowledge/Courses—Transportation:** Principles and methods for moving people or goods by air, rail, sea, or road, including the relative costs and benefits. **Geography:** Principles and methods for describing the features of land, sea, and air masses, including their physical characteristics, locations, interrelationships, and distribution of plant, animal, and human life. **Production and Processing:** Raw materials, production processes, quality control, costs, and other techniques for maximizing the effective manufacture and distribution of goods. **Personnel and Human Resources:** Principles and procedures for personnel recruitment, selection, training, compensation and benefits, labor relations and negotiation, and personnel information systems. **Administration and Management:** Business and management principles involved in strategic planning, resource allocation, human resources modeling, leadership technique, production methods, and coordination of people and resources. **Economics and Accounting:** Economic and accounting principles and practices, the financial markets, banking, and the analysis and reporting of financial data.

Personality Type: Enterprising-Conventional. **Career Clusters:** 04 Business, Management, and Administration; 07 Government and Public Administration; 16 Transportation, Distribution, and Logistics. **Career Pathways:** 16.1 Transportation Operations; 04.1 Management; 07.1 Governance; 16.2 Logistics, Planning, and Management Services. **Other Jobs in These Pathways:** Administrative Services Managers; Aerospace Engineering and Operations

Technicians; Agents and Business Managers of Artists, Performers, and Athletes; Air Traffic Controllers; Aircraft Cargo Handling Supervisors; Airfield Operations Specialists; Airline Pilots, Copilots, and Flight Engineers; Automotive and Watercraft Service Attendants; Automotive Master Mechanics; Aviation Inspectors; Biofuels Production Managers; Biomass Power Plant Managers; Bridge and Lock Tenders; Brownfield Redevelopment Specialists and Site Managers; Bus Drivers, School or Special Client; Bus Drivers, Transit and Intercity; Business Continuity Planners; Business Operations Specialists, All Other; Business Teachers, Postsecondary; Chief Executives; Chief Sustainability Officers; Commercial Divers; Commercial Pilots; Communications Teachers, Postsecondary; Compliance Managers; Computer and Information Systems Managers; Construction Managers; Cost Estimators; Crane and Tower Operators; Customs Brokers; others.

Skills—Management of Financial Resources: Determining how money will be spent to get the work done and accounting for these expenditures. **Systems Evaluation:** Identifying measures or indicators of system performance and the actions needed to improve or correct performance relative to the goals of the system. **Negotiation:** Bringing others together and trying to reconcile differences. **Systems Analysis:** Determining how a system should work and how changes in conditions, operations, and the environment will affect outcomes. **Social Perceptiveness:** Being aware of others' reactions and understanding why they react as they do. **Management of Material Resources:** Obtaining and seeing to the appropriate use of equipment, facilities, and materials needed to do certain work. **Management of Personnel Resources:** Motivating, developing, and directing people as they work, identifying the best people for the job. **Operations Analysis:** Analyzing needs and product requirements to create a design.

Work Environment: Indoors; sitting.

Travel Agents

- ◉ Annual Earnings: $33,930
- ◉ Earnings Growth Potential: High (42.2%)
- ◉ Growth: 10.0%
- ◉ Annual Job Openings: 1,720
- ◉ Self-Employed: 14.2%

Considerations for Job Outlook: Job prospects should be best for travel agents who specialize in specific destinations or particular types of travelers, such as groups with a special interest or corporate travelers.

Plan and sell transportation and accommodations for travel agency customers. Collect payment for transportation and accommodations from customers. Converse with customers to determine destinations, modes of transportation, travel dates, financial considerations, and accommodations required. Compute cost of travel and accommodations, using calculators, computers, carrier tariff books, and hotel rate books, or quote package tour's costs. Book transportation and hotel reservations, using computer terminals or telephones. Plan, describe, arrange, and sell itinerary tour packages and promotional travel incentives offered by various travel carriers. Provide customers with brochures and publications containing travel information such as local customs, points of interest, or foreign country regulations. Print or request transportation carrier tickets, using computer printer systems or system links to travel carriers.

Education/Training Required: High school diploma or equivalent. **Education and Training Programs:** Selling Skills and Sales Operations; Tourism and Travel Services Marketing Operations. **Knowledge/Courses—Geography:** Principles and methods for describing the features of land, sea, and air masses, including their physical characteristics, locations, interrelationships, and distribution of plant, animal, and human life. **Sales and Marketing:** Principles and methods for showing, promoting, and selling products or services. This includes marketing strategy and tactics, product demonstration, sales techniques, and sales control systems. **Transportation:** Principles and methods for moving people or goods by air, rail, sea, or road, including the relative costs and benefits. **Clerical Practices:** Administrative and clerical procedures and systems such as word processing, managing files and records, stenography and transcription, designing forms, and other office procedures and terminology. **Economics and Accounting:** Economic and accounting principles and practices, the financial markets, banking, and the analysis and reporting of financial data. **Customer and Personal Service:** Principles and processes for providing customer and personal services. This includes customer needs assessment, meeting quality standards for services, and evaluation of customer satisfaction. **Work Experience Needed:**

None. **On-the-Job Training Needed:** Moderate-term on-the-job training. **Certification/Licensure:** Voluntary certification by association.

Personality Type: Enterprising-Conventional. **Career Clusters:** 09 Hospitality and Tourism; 14 Marketing, Sales, and Service. **Career Pathways:** 14.2 Professional Sales and Marketing; 09.3 Travel and Tourism. **Other Jobs in These Pathways:** Appraisers, Real Estate; Assessors; Cashiers; Counter and Rental Clerks; Demonstrators and Product Promoters; Door-To-Door Sales Workers, News and Street Vendors, and Related Workers; Driver/Sales Workers; Energy Brokers; First-Line Supervisors of Non-Retail Sales Workers; First-Line Supervisors of Retail Sales Workers; Food Service Managers; Gaming Change Persons and Booth Cashiers; Hotel, Motel, and Resort Desk Clerks; Interior Designers; Lodging Managers; Managers, All Other; Marketing Managers; Marking Clerks; Meeting, Convention, and Event Planners; Merchandise Displayers and Window Trimmers; Models; Online Merchants; Order Fillers, Wholesale and Retail Sales; Parts Salespersons; Property, Real Estate, and Community Association Managers; Real Estate Brokers; Real Estate Sales Agents; Reservation and Transportation Ticket Agents and Travel Clerks; Retail Salespersons; Sales and Related Workers, All Other; Sales Engineers; Sales Representatives, Services, All Other; others.

Skills—Service Orientation: Actively looking for ways to help people. **Negotiation:** Bringing others together and trying to reconcile differences. **Persuasion:** Persuading others to change their minds or behavior. **Management of Financial Resources:** Determining how money will be spent to get the work done and accounting for these expenditures. **Active Listening:** Giving full attention to what other people are saying, taking time to understand the points being made, asking questions as appropriate, and not interrupting at inappropriate times. **Critical Thinking:** Using logic and reasoning to identify the strengths and weaknesses of alternative solutions, conclusions, or approaches to problems. **Social Perceptiveness:** Being aware of others' reactions and understanding why they react as they do.

Work Environment: Indoors; sitting.

Travel Guides

- ⊙ Annual Earnings: $30,670
- ⊙ Earnings Growth Potential: High (41.7%)
- ⊙ Growth: 23.8%
- ⊙ Annual Job Openings: 260
- ⊙ Self-Employed: 11.7%

Considerations for Job Outlook: Rapid employment growth is projected.

Plan, organize, and conduct long-distance travel, tours, and expeditions for individuals and groups. Verify amounts and quality of equipment prior to expeditions or tours. Arrange for tour or expedition details such as accommodations, transportation, equipment, and the availability of medical personnel. Attend to special needs of tour participants. Give advice on sightseeing and shopping. Lead individuals or groups to tour site locations and describe points of interest. Plan tour itineraries, applying knowledge of travel routes and destination sites. Administer first aid to injured group participants. Pilot airplanes or drive land and water vehicles to transport tourists to activity/tour sites. Explain hunting and fishing laws to groups to ensure compliance. Instruct novices in climbing techniques, mountaineering, and wilderness survival, and demonstrate the use of hunting, fishing, and climbing equipment. Evaluate services received on tours, and report findings to tour organizers. Pay bills and record checks issued. Provide tourists with assistance in obtaining permits and documents such as visas, passports, and health certificates, and in converting currency. Set up camps, and prepare meals for tour group members. Sell or rent equipment, clothing, and supplies related to expeditions. Resolve any problems with itineraries, service, or accommodations. Sell travel packages.

Education/Training Required: High school diploma or equivalent. **Education and Training Programs:** No related CIP programs; this job is learned through informal moderate-term on-the-job training. **Sales and Marketing:** Principles and methods for showing, promoting, and selling products or services. This includes marketing strategy and tactics, product demonstration, sales techniques, and sales control systems. **Geography:** Principles and methods for describing the features of land, sea, and air masses, including their physical characteristics,

locations, interrelationships, and distribution of plant, animal, and human life. **History and Archeology:** Historical events and their causes, indicators, and effects on civilizations and cultures. **Clerical Practices:** Administrative and clerical procedures and systems such as word processing, managing files and records, stenography and transcription, designing forms, and other office procedures and terminology. **Administration and Management:** Business and management principles involved in strategic planning, resource allocation, human resources modeling, leadership technique, production methods, and coordination of people and resources. **Transportation:** Principles and methods for moving people or goods by air, rail, sea, or road, including the relative costs and benefits. **Work Experience Needed:** None. **On-the-Job Training Needed:** Moderate-term on-the-job training. **Certification/Licensure:** Licensure in some locations.

Personality Type: Enterprising-Conventional. **Career Cluster:** 09 Hospitality and Tourism. **Career Pathway:** 09.3 Travel and Tourism. **Other Jobs in This Pathway:** Appraisers, Real Estate; Assessors; Cashiers; Counter and Rental Clerks; Demonstrators and Product Promoters; Door-To-Door Sales Workers, News and Street Vendors, and Related Workers; Driver/Sales Workers; Energy Brokers; First-Line Supervisors of Non-Retail Sales Workers; First-Line Supervisors of Retail Sales Workers; Gaming Change Persons and Booth Cashiers; Hotel, Motel, and Resort Desk Clerks; Interior Designers; Lodging Managers; Marketing Managers; Marking Clerks; Meeting, Convention, and Event Planners; Merchandise Displayers and Window Trimmers; Models; Online Merchants; Order Fillers, Wholesale and Retail Sales; Parts Salespersons; Property, Real Estate, and Community Association Managers; Real Estate Brokers; Real Estate Sales Agents; Reservation and Transportation Ticket Agents and Travel Clerks; Retail Salespersons; Sales and Related Workers, All Other; Sales Engineers; others.

Skills—Management of Financial Resources: Determining how money will be spent to get the work done and accounting for these expenditures. **Management of Material Resources:** Obtaining and seeing to the appropriate use of equipment, facilities, and materials needed to do certain work. **Negotiation:** Bringing others together and trying to reconcile differences. **Service Orientation:** Actively looking for ways to help people. **Persuasion:** Persuading others to change their minds or behavior. **Operation and**

Control: Controlling operations of equipment or systems. **Active Listening:** Giving full attention to what other people are saying, taking time to understand the points being made, asking questions as appropriate, and not interrupting at inappropriate times. **Learning Strategies:** Selecting and using training/instructional methods and procedures appropriate for the situation when learning or teaching new things.

Work Environment: Indoors; sitting.

Tree Trimmers and Pruners

- ⊙ Annual Earnings: $31,320
- ⊙ Earnings Growth Potential: Medium (36.5%)
- ⊙ Growth: 18.0%
- ⊙ Annual Job Openings: 1,800
- ⊙ Self-Employed: 25.9%

Considerations for Job Outlook: Job prospects are expected to be favorable. Those with experience should have the best job opportunities. Most job openings will come from the need to replace many workers who leave or retire from this very large occupation.

Cut away dead or excess branches from trees or shrubs to maintain right-of-way for roads, sidewalks, or utilities, or to improve appearance, health, and value of trees. Supervise others engaged in tree trimming work and train lower-level employees. Transplant and remove trees and shrubs, and prepare trees for moving. Operate shredding and chipping equipment, and feed limbs and brush into the machines. Remove broken limbs from wires, using hooked extension poles. Prune, cut down, fertilize, and spray trees as directed by tree surgeons. Spray trees to treat diseased or unhealthy trees, including mixing chemicals and calibrating spray equipment. Clean, sharpen, and lubricate tools and equipment. Clear sites, streets, and grounds of woody and herbaceous materials, such as tree stumps and fallen trees and limbs. Load debris and refuse onto trucks and haul them away for disposal. Inspect trees to determine if they have diseases or pest problems. Cut away dead and excess branches from trees, or clear branches around power lines, using climbing equipment or buckets of extended truck booms, and chainsaws, hooks, handsaws, shears, or clippers. Collect debris and refuse from tree trimming and removal operations into piles, using shovels, rakes, or other tools. Operate boom trucks, loaders, stump chippers, brush chippers, tractors, power saws, trucks, sprayers, and other equipment and tools. Apply tar or other protective substances to cut surfaces to seal surfaces, and to protect them from fungi and insects. Climb trees, using climbing hooks and belts, or climb ladders to gain access to work areas. Split logs or wooden blocks into bolts, pickets, posts, or stakes, using hand tools such as ax wedges, sledgehammers, and mallets. Cable, brace, tie, bolt, stake, and guy trees and branches to provide support. Trim jagged stumps, using saws or pruning shears. Trim, top, and reshape trees to achieve attractive shapes or to remove low-hanging branches. Water, root-feed, and fertilize trees. Harvest tanbark by cutting rings and slits in bark and stripping bark from trees, using spuds or axes. Install lightning protection on trees.

Education/Training Required: High school diploma or equivalent. **Education and Training Program:** Applied Horticulture/Horticultural Business Services, Other. **Knowledge/Courses—Biology:** Plant and animal organisms and their tissues, cells, functions, interdependencies, and interactions with each other and the environment. **Mechanical Devices:** Machines and tools, including their designs, uses, repair, and maintenance. **Transportation:** Principles and methods for moving people or goods by air, rail, sea, or road, including the relative costs and benefits. **Physics:** Physical principles, laws, their interrelationships, and applications to understanding fluid, material, and atmospheric dynamics, and mechanical, electrical, atomic, and subatomic structures and processes. **Public Safety and Security:** Relevant equipment, policies, procedures, and strategies to promote effective local, state, or national security operations for the protection of people, data, property, and institutions. **Sales and Marketing:** Principles and methods for showing, promoting, and selling products or services. This includes marketing strategy and tactics, product demonstration, sales techniques, and sales control systems. **Work Experience Needed:** None. **On-the-Job Training Needed:** Short-term on-the-job training. **Certification/Licensure:** Licensure in some states.

Personality Type: Realistic. **Career Cluster:** 01 Agriculture, Food, and Natural Resources. **Career Pathway:** 01.2 Plant Systems. **Other Jobs in This Pathway:** Agricultural Sciences Teachers, Postsecondary; Agricultural Technicians; Animal Scientists; Biochemists and Biophysicists; Biologists; Economists; Environmental Economists; Farm and Home Management Advisors; First-Line Supervisors of Landscaping, Lawn Service, and Groundskeeping Workers; First-Line Supervisors of Retail Sales Workers; Floral Designers; Food Science Technicians; Food Scientists and Technologists; Geneticists; Grounds Maintenance Workers, All Other; Landscaping and Groundskeeping Workers; Pesticide Handlers, Sprayers, and Applicators, Vegetation; Precision Agriculture Technicians; Retail Salespersons; Soil and Plant Scientists.

Skills—Operation and Control: Controlling operations of equipment or systems. **Equipment Maintenance:** Performing routine maintenance on equipment and determining when and what kind of maintenance is needed. **Repairing:** Repairing machines or systems using the needed tools. **Troubleshooting:** Determining causes of operating errors and deciding what to do about them. **Operation Monitoring:** Watching gauges, dials, or other indicators to make sure a machine is working properly. **Equipment Selection:** Determining the kind of tools and equipment needed to do a job. **Quality Control Analysis:** Conducting tests and inspections of products, services, or processes to evaluate quality or performance. **Management of Personnel Resources:** Motivating, developing, and directing people as they work, identifying the best people for the job.

Work Environment: Outdoors; standing; climbing; walking and running; balancing; using hands; bending or twisting the body; repetitive motions; noise; very hot or cold; bright or inadequate lighting; contaminants; cramped work space; whole-body vibration; high places; hazardous conditions; hazardous equipment; minor burns, cuts, bites, or stings.

Veterinary Assistants and Laboratory Animal Caretakers

- ☉ Annual Earnings: $22,830
- ☉ Earnings Growth Potential: Low (25.7%)
- ☉ Growth: 14.2%
- ☉ Annual Job Openings: 2,160
- ☉ Self-Employed: 2.3%

Considerations for Job Outlook: Overall job opportunities for veterinary assistants and laboratory animal caretakers are expected to be excellent. Although some establishments are replacing veterinary assistant positions with higher-skilled veterinary technicians and technologists, growth of the pet care industry means that the number of veterinary assistant positions should continue to increase. Furthermore, veterinary assistants experience a high rate of turnover, so many positions will be available through workers leaving the occupation.

Feed, water, and examine pets and other nonfarm animals for signs of illness, disease, or injury in laboratories and animal hospitals and clinics. Monitor animals' recovering from surgery and notify veterinarians of any unusual changes or symptoms. Hold or restrain animals during veterinary procedures. Clean and maintain kennels, animal holding areas, examination and operating rooms, and animal loading/unloading facilities to control the spread of disease. Administer medications, immunizations, and blood plasma to animals as prescribed by veterinarians. Provide emergency first aid to sick or injured animals. Assist veterinarians in examining animals to determine the nature of illnesses or injuries. Clean, maintain, and sterilize instruments and equipment. Perform routine laboratory tests or diagnostic tests, such as taking and developing X-rays. Administer anesthetics during surgery and monitor the effects on animals. Prepare surgical equipment, and pass instruments and materials to veterinarians during surgical procedures. Examine animals to detect behavioral changes or clinical symptoms that could indicate illness or injury. Fill medication prescriptions. Collect laboratory specimens such as blood, urine, and feces for testing. Provide assistance with euthanasia of animals and disposal of corpses. Record information relating to animal genealogy, feeding schedules, appearance, behavior, and breeding. Prepare feed for animals according to specific instructions such as diet lists and schedules. Educate and advise clients on animal health care, nutrition, and behavior problems. Prepare examination or treatment rooms by stocking them with appropriate supplies. Perform enemas, catheterizations, ear flushes, intravenous feedings, and gavages. Perform office reception duties such as scheduling appointments and helping customers. Perform hygiene-related duties such as clipping animals' claws and cleaning and polishing teeth. Exercise animals, and provide them with companionship. Dust, spray, or bathe animals to control insect pests. Groom, trim, or clip animals' coats. Sell pet food and supplies to customers.

Education/Training Required: High school diploma or equivalent. **Education and Training Program:** Veterinary/Animal Health Technology/Technician and Veterinary Assistant. **Knowledge/Courses—Biology:** Plant and animal organisms and their tissues, cells, functions, interdependencies, and interactions with each other and the environment. **Medicine and Dentistry:** The information and techniques needed to diagnose and treat human injuries, diseases, and deformities. This includes symptoms, treatment alternatives, drug properties and interactions, and preventive health-care measures. **Chemistry:** The chemical composition, structure, and properties of substances and of the chemical processes and transformations that they undergo. This includes uses of chemicals and their danger signs, production techniques, and disposal methods. **Sales and Marketing:** Principles and methods for showing, promoting, and selling products or services. This includes marketing strategy and tactics, product demonstration, sales techniques, and sales control systems. **Clerical Practices:** Administrative and clerical procedures and systems such as word processing, managing files and records, stenography and transcription, designing forms, and other office procedures and terminology. **Customer and Personal Service:** Principles and processes for providing customer and personal services. This includes customer needs assessment, meeting quality standards for services, and evaluation of customer satisfaction. **Work Experience Needed:** None. **On-the-Job Training Needed:** Short-term on-the-job training. **Certification/Licensure:** Voluntary certification by association.

Personality Type: Realistic-Social-Investigative. **Career Cluster:** 08 Health Science. **Career Pathway:** 08.2 Diagnostics Services. **Other Jobs in This Pathway:** Ambulance Drivers and Attendants, Except Emergency Medical Technicians; Anesthesiologist Assistants; Athletic Trainers; Cardiovascular Technologists and Technicians; Cytogenetic Technologists; Cytotechnologists; Diagnostic Medical Sonographers; Emergency Medical Technicians and Paramedics; Endoscopy Technicians; Health Diagnosing and Treating Practitioners, All Other; Health Specialties Teachers, Postsecondary; Health Technologists and Technicians, All Other; Healthcare Practitioners and Technical Workers, All Other; Histotechnologists and Histologic Technicians; Medical and Clinical Laboratory Technicians; Medical and Clinical Laboratory Technologists; Medical and Health Services Managers; Medical Assistants; Medical Equipment Preparers; Neurodiagnostic Technologists; Nuclear Equipment Operation Technicians; Nuclear Medicine Technologists; Ophthalmic Laboratory Technicians; Pathologists; Physical Scientists, All Other; Physician Assistants; Radiation Therapists; others.

Skills—Science: Using scientific rules and methods to solve problems. **Management of Financial Resources:** Determining how money will be spent to get the work done and accounting for these expenditures. **Management of Material Resources:** Obtaining and seeing to the appropriate use of equipment, facilities, and materials needed to do certain work. **Service Orientation:** Actively looking for ways to help people. **Operations Analysis:** Analyzing needs and product requirements to create a design. **Operation and Control:** Controlling operations of equipment or systems. **Mathematics:** Using mathematics to solve problems.

Work Environment: Indoors; standing; walking and running; kneeling, crouching, stooping, or crawling; using hands; bending or twisting the body; repetitive motions; noise; contaminants; exposed to radiation; exposed to disease or infections; minor burns, cuts, bites, or stings.

Veterinary Technologists and Technicians

- ☉ Annual Earnings: $30,140
- ☉ Earnings Growth Potential: Low (30.7%)
- ☉ Growth: 52.0%
- ☉ Annual Job Openings: 5,570
- ☉ Self-Employed: 0.2%

Considerations for Job Outlook: Overall job opportunities for veterinary technologists and technicians are expected to be excellent, particularly in rural areas. The number of veterinary technology programs has been growing, but rapid employment growth means that the number of positions available will continue to outpace the number of new graduates. Workers leaving the occupation will also result in job openings.

Perform medical tests in a laboratory environment for use in the treatment and diagnosis of diseases in animals. Observe the behavior and condition of animals, and monitor their clinical symptoms. Maintain controlled drug inventory and related log books. Administer anesthesia to animals, under the direction of veterinarians, and monitor animals' responses to anesthetics so that dosages can be adjusted. Care for and monitor the condition of animals recovering from surgery. Perform laboratory tests on blood, urine, and feces, such as urinalyses and blood counts, to assist in the diagnosis and treatment of animal health problems. Administer emergency first aid, such as performing emergency resuscitation or other life-saving procedures. Prepare and administer medications, vaccines, serums, and treatments, as prescribed by veterinarians. Fill prescriptions, measuring medications and labeling containers. Collect, prepare, and label samples for laboratory testing, culture, or microscopic examination. Prepare treatment rooms for surgery. Take and develop diagnostic radiographs, using X-ray equipment. Clean kennels, animal holding areas, surgery suites, examination rooms, and animal loading/unloading facilities to control the spread of disease. Take animals into treatment areas, and assist with physical examinations by performing such duties as obtaining temperature, pulse, and respiration data. Provide veterinarians with the correct equipment and instruments, as needed. Clean and sterilize instruments, equipment, and materials. Maintain laboratory, research, and treatment records, as well as inventories of pharmaceuticals, equipment, and supplies. Prepare animals for surgery, performing such tasks as shaving surgical areas. Give enemas and perform catheterizations, ear flushes, intravenous feedings, and gavages. Maintain instruments, equipment, and machinery to ensure proper working condition. Provide assistance with animal euthanasia and the disposal of remains. Supervise and train veterinary students and other staff members.

Education/Training Required: Associate degree. **Education and Training Program:** Veterinary/Animal Health Technology/Technician and Veterinary Assistant. **Knowledge/Courses—Biology:** Plant and animal organisms and their tissues, cells, functions, interdependencies, and interactions with each other and the environment. **Medicine and Dentistry:** The information and techniques needed to diagnose and treat human injuries, diseases, and deformities. This includes symptoms, treatment alternatives, drug properties and interactions, and preventive health-care measures. **Chemistry:** The chemical composition, structure, and properties of substances and of the chemical processes and transformations that they undergo. This includes uses of chemicals and their danger signs, production techniques, and disposal methods. **Customer and Personal Service:** Principles and processes for providing customer and personal services. This includes customer needs assessment, meeting quality standards for services, and evaluation of customer satisfaction. **Mathematics:** Arithmetic, algebra, geometry, calculus, statistics, and their applications. **Psychology:** Human behavior and performance; individual differences in ability, personality, and interests; learning and motivation; psychological research methods; and the assessment and treatment of behavioral and affective disorders. **Work Experience Needed:** None. **On-the-Job Training Needed:** None. **Certification/Licensure:** Licensure, registration, or certification in most states.

Personality Type: Realistic-Investigative. **Career Cluster:** 08 Health Science. **Career Pathway:** 08.1 Therapeutic Services. **Other Jobs in This Pathway:** Acupuncturists; Allergists and Immunologists; Anesthesiologists; Art Therapists; Chiropractors; Clinical Psychologists; Community and Social Service Specialists, All Other; Counseling Psychologists; Counselors, All Other; Dental Assistants; Dental Hygienists; Dentists, All Other Specialists; Dentists, General; Dermatologists; Diagnostic Medical Sonographers; Dietetic Technicians; Dietitians and Nutritionists; Family and General Practitioners; Health Diagnosing and Treating Practitioners, All Other; Health Specialties Teachers, Postsecondary; Health Technologists and Technicians, All Other; Healthcare Practitioners and Technical Workers, All Other; Healthcare Support Workers, All Other; Home Health Aides; Hospitalists; Industrial-Organizational Psychologists; Internists, General; Licensed Practical and Licensed Vocational Nurses; Life, Physical, and Social Science Technicians, All Other; Low Vision Therapists, Orientation and Mobility Specialists, and Vision Rehabilitation Therapists; others.

Skills—Science: Using scientific rules and methods to solve problems. **Equipment Maintenance:** Performing routine maintenance on equipment and determining when and what kind of maintenance is needed. **Operation and Control:** Controlling operations of equipment or systems. **Equipment Selection:** Determining the kind of tools and equipment needed to do a job. **Quality Control Analysis:** Conducting tests and inspections of products, services, or processes to evaluate quality or performance. **Service Orientation:** Actively looking for ways to help people. **Troubleshooting:** Determining causes of operating errors and deciding what to do about them. **Critical Thinking:** Using logic and reasoning to identify the strengths and weaknesses of alternative solutions, conclusions, or approaches to problems.

Work Environment: Indoors; standing; walking and running; using hands; bending or twisting the body; repetitive motions; noise; contaminants; exposed to radiation; exposed to disease or infections; minor burns, cuts, bites, or stings.

Water and Wastewater Treatment Plant and System Operators

- ⊙ Annual Earnings: $41,780
- ⊙ Earnings Growth Potential: Medium (39.2%)
- ⊙ Growth: 11.7%
- ⊙ Annual Job Openings: 4,150
- ⊙ Self-Employed: 0.3%

Considerations for Job Outlook: Job prospects for water and wastewater treatment plant and system operators should be excellent. New jobs will be created when existing plants expand and new plants are built. Applicants will also have many job opportunities because many current operators are expected to retire. In addition, the number of applicants for these positions is normally low, primarily because of the physically demanding and unappealing nature of some of the work. Job prospects will be best for those with training or education in water or wastewater systems and good mechanical skills.

Operate or control an entire process or system of machines, often through the use of control boards, to transfer or treat water or wastewater. Add chemicals such as ammonia, chlorine, or lime to disinfect and deodorize water and other liquids. Operate and adjust controls on equipment to purify and clarify water, process or dispose of sewage, and generate power. Inspect equipment or monitor operating conditions, meters, and gauges to determine load requirements and detect malfunctions. Collect and test water and sewage samples, using test equipment and color-analysis standards. Record operational data, personnel attendance, or meter and gauge readings on specified forms. Maintain, repair, and lubricate equipment, using hand tools and power tools. Clean and maintain tanks and filter beds, using hand tools and power tools. Direct and coordinate plant workers engaged in routine operations and maintenance activities.

Education/Training Required: High school diploma or equivalent. **Education and Training Program:**

Water Quality and Wastewater Treatment Management and Recycling Technology/Technician. **Knowledge/Courses—Physics:** Physical principles, laws, their interrelationships, and applications to understanding fluid, material, and atmospheric dynamics, and mechanical, electrical, atomic, and subatomic structures and processes. **Building and Construction:** Materials, methods, and the tools involved in the construction or repair of houses, buildings, or other structures such as highways and roads. **Mechanical Devices:** Machines and tools, including their designs, uses, repair, and maintenance. **Biology:** Plant and animal organisms and their tissues, cells, functions, interdependencies, and interactions with each other and the environment. **Chemistry:** The chemical composition, structure, and properties of substances and of the chemical processes and transformations that they undergo. This includes uses of chemicals and their danger signs, production techniques, and disposal methods. **Engineering and Technology:** The practical application of engineering science and technology. This includes applying principles, techniques, procedures, and equipment to the design and production of various goods and services. **Work Experience Needed:** None. **On-the-Job Training Needed:** Long-term on-the-job training. **Certification/Licensure:** Licensure.

Personality Type: Realistic-Conventional. **Career Cluster:** 01 Agriculture, Food, and Natural Resources. **Career Pathway:** 01.6 Environmental Service Systems. **Other Jobs in This Pathway:** Environmental Engineering Technicians; Hazardous Materials Removal Workers; Occupational Health and Safety Specialists.

Skills—Repairing: Repairing machines or systems using the needed tools. **Equipment Maintenance:** Performing routine maintenance on equipment and determining when and what kind of maintenance is needed. **Operation and Control:** Controlling operations of equipment or systems. **Troubleshooting:** Determining causes of operating errors and deciding what to do about them. **Equipment Selection:** Determining the kind of tools and equipment needed to do a job. **Operation Monitoring:** Watching gauges, dials, or other indicators to make sure a machine is working properly. **Quality Control Analysis:** Conducting tests and inspections of products, services, or processes to evaluate quality or performance. **Systems Evaluation:** Identifying measures or indicators of system performance and the actions needed to improve or correct performance relative to the goals of the system.

Work Environment: Outdoors; standing; climbing; walking and running; kneeling, crouching, stooping, or crawling; using hands; bending or twisting the body; repetitive motions; noise; very hot or cold; bright or inadequate lighting; contaminants; cramped work space; exposed to disease or infections; hazardous conditions; hazardous equipment; minor burns, cuts, bites, or stings.

Weighers, Measurers, Checkers, and Samplers, Recordkeeping

- ◉ Annual Earnings: $27,390
- ◉ Earnings Growth Potential: Low (33.0%)
- ◉ Growth: 12.0%
- ◉ Annual Job Openings: 3,420
- ◉ Self-Employed: 0.4%

Considerations for Job Outlook: There should be favorable job opportunities for material recording clerks because of the need to replace workers who leave the occupation. The increase in RFID and other sensors will enable clerks who are more comfortable with computers to have better job prospects.

Weigh, measure, and check materials, supplies, and equipment for the purpose of keeping relevant records. Collect or prepare measurement, weight, or identification labels; and attach them to products. Document quantity, quality, type, weight, test result data, and value of materials or products, in order to maintain shipping, receiving, and production records and files. Compare product labels, tags, or tickets; shipping manifests; purchase orders; and bills of lading to verify accuracy of shipment contents, quality specifications, and weights. Count or estimate quantities of materials, parts, or products received or shipped. Weigh or measure materials, equipment, or products to maintain relevant records, using volume meters, scales, rules, and calipers. Communicate with customers and vendors to exchange information regarding products, materials, and services. Compute product totals and charges for shipments. Collect product samples and prepare them for laboratory analysis or testing. Unload or unpack incoming shipments. Operate scalehouse computers to obtain weight information about incoming shipments such as those from waste haulers. Fill orders for products and samples, following order tickets, and forward or mail items. Sort products or materials into predetermined sequences or groupings for display, packing, shipping, or storage. Signal or instruct other workers to weigh, move, or check products. Maintain financial records, such as accounts of daily collections and billings, and records of receipts issued. Store samples of finished products in labeled cartons and record their location. Remove from stock products or loads not meeting quality standards, and notify supervisors or appropriate departments of discrepancies or shortages. Maintain, monitor, and clean work areas such as recycling collection sites, drop boxes, counters and windows, and areas around scale houses. Inspect incoming loads of waste to identify contents and to screen for the presence of specific regulated or hazardous wastes.

Education/Training Required: High school diploma or equivalent. **Education and Training Program:** General Office Occupations and Clerical Services. **Knowledge/Courses—Clerical Practices:** Administrative and clerical procedures and systems such as word processing, managing files and records, stenography and transcription, designing forms, and other office procedures and terminology. **Production and Processing:** Raw materials, production processes, quality control, costs, and other techniques for maximizing the effective manufacture and distribution of goods. **Work Experience Needed:** None. **On-the-Job Training Needed:** Short-term on-the-job training. **Certification/Licensure:** Voluntary certification for some specializations.

Personality Type: Conventional-Realistic. **Career Cluster:** 04 Business, Management, and Administration. **Career Pathway:** 04.6 Administrative and Information Support. **Other Jobs in This Pathway:** Cargo and Freight Agents; Correspondence Clerks; Couriers and Messengers; Court Clerks; Customer Service Representatives; Data Entry Keyers; Dispatchers, Except Police, Fire, and Ambulance; Executive Secretaries and Executive Administrative Assistants; File Clerks; Freight Forwarders; Human Resources Assistants, Except Payroll and Timekeeping; Information and Record Clerks, All Other; Insurance Claims Clerks; Insurance Policy Processing Clerks; Interviewers, Except Eligibility and Loan; License Clerks; Mail Clerks and Mail Machine Operators, Except Postal Service; Meter Readers, Utilities; Municipal Clerks; Office and Administrative Support Workers, All Other; Office Clerks, General; Office Machine Operators, Except Computer; Order Clerks; Patient Representatives; Postal Service

M

Clerks; Postal Service Mail Carriers; Postal Service Mail Sorters, Processors, and Processing Machine Operators; Procurement Clerks; Receptionists and Information Clerks; others.

Skills—Programming: Writing computer programs for various purposes. **Quality Control Analysis:** Conducting tests and inspections of products, services, or processes to evaluate quality or performance. **Mathematics:** Using mathematics to solve problems.

Work Environment: Indoors; sitting; using hands; repetitive motions; noise; contaminants; hazardous equipment.

Welders, Cutters, Solderers, and Brazers

- ⊙ Annual Earnings: $35,920
- ⊙ Earnings Growth Potential: Low (31.8%)
- ⊙ Growth: 15.0%
- ⊙ Annual Job Openings: 14,070
- ⊙ Self-Employed: 5.9%

Considerations for Job Outlook: Overall job prospects will vary by skill level. Job prospects should be good for welders trained in the latest technologies. Welding schools report that graduates have little difficulty finding work, and many welding employers report difficulty finding properly skilled welders. However, welders who do not have up-to-date training may face competition for jobs. For all welders, job prospects should be better for those willing to relocate.

Use hand-welding, flame-cutting, hand-soldering, or brazing equipment to weld or join metal components or to fill holes, indentations, or seams of fabricated metal products. For task data, see Job Specializations.

Education/Training Required: High school diploma or equivalent. **Work Experience Needed:** Less than 1 year. **On-the-Job Training Needed:** Moderate-term on-the-job training. **Certification/Licensure:** Voluntary certification for some specializations.

Job Specialization: Solderers and Brazers

Braze or solder together components to assemble fabricated metal parts with soldering irons, torches, or welding machines and flux. Melt and apply solder along adjoining edges of workpieces to solder joints, using soldering irons, gas torches, or electric-ultrasonic equipment. Heat soldering irons or workpieces to specified temperatures for soldering, using gas flames or electric current. Examine seams for defects, and rework defective joints or broken parts. Melt and separate brazed or soldered joints to remove and straighten damaged or misaligned components, using hand torches, irons, or furnaces. Melt and apply solder to fill holes, indentations, and seams of fabricated metal products, using soldering equipment. Clean workpieces to remove dirt and excess acid, using chemical solutions, files, wire brushes, or grinders. Guide torches and rods along joints of workpieces to heat them to brazing temperature, melt braze alloys, and bond workpieces together. Adjust electric current and timing cycles of resistance welding machines to heat metals to bonding temperature. Turn valves to start flow of gases, and light flames and adjust valves to obtain desired colors and sizes of flames. Clean equipment parts, such as tips of soldering irons, using chemical solutions or cleaning compounds. Brush flux onto joints of workpieces or dip braze rods into flux, to prevent oxidation of metal. Remove workpieces from fixtures, using tongs, and cool workpieces, using air or water. Align and clamp workpieces together, using rules, squares, or hand tools, or position items in fixtures, jigs, or vises. Sweat together workpieces coated with solder. Smooth soldered areas with alternate strokes of paddles and torches, leaving soldered sections slightly higher than surrounding areas for later filing. Remove workpieces from molten solder and hold parts together until color indicates that solder has set. Select torch tips, flux, and brazing alloys from data charts or work orders. Turn dials to set intensity and duration of ultrasonic impulses, according to work order specifications.

Education and Training Program: Welding Technology/ Welder. **Knowledge/Courses—Production and Processing:** Raw materials, production processes, quality control, costs, and other techniques for maximizing the effective manufacture and distribution of goods. **Mechanical Devices:** Machines and tools, including their designs, uses, repair, and maintenance.

Personality Type: Realistic. **Career Cluster:** 13 Manufacturing. **Career Pathway:** 13.1 Production. **Other Jobs in This Pathway:** Adhesive Bonding Machine Operators and Tenders; Assemblers and Fabricators, All Other; Avionics Technicians; Cabinetmakers and Bench Carpenters;

Cleaning, Washing, and Metal Pickling Equipment Operators and Tenders; Coating, Painting, and Spraying Machine Setters, Operators, and Tenders; Computer-Controlled Machine Tool Operators, Metal and Plastic; Cooling and Freezing Equipment Operators and Tenders; Cost Estimators; Crushing, Grinding, and Polishing Machine Setters, Operators, and Tenders; Cutters and Trimmers, Hand; Cutting and Slicing Machine Setters, Operators, and Tenders; Cutting, Punching, and Press Machine Setters, Operators, and Tenders, Metal and Plastic; Drilling and Boring Machine Tool Setters, Operators, and Tenders, Metal and Plastic; Extruding and Drawing Machine Setters, Operators, and Tenders, Metal and Plastic; Extruding and Forming Machine Setters, Operators, and Tenders, Synthetic and Glass Fibers; others.

Skills—Equipment Maintenance: Performing routine maintenance on equipment and determining when and what kind of maintenance is needed. **Repairing:** Repairing machines or systems using the needed tools. **Equipment Selection:** Determining the kind of tools and equipment needed to do a job. **Troubleshooting:** Determining causes of operating errors and deciding what to do about them. **Quality Control Analysis:** Conducting tests and inspections of products, services, or processes to evaluate quality or performance. **Operation Monitoring:** Watching gauges, dials, or other indicators to make sure a machine is working properly.

Work Environment: Indoors; more often sitting than standing; using hands; repetitive motions; noise; contaminants; minor burns, cuts, bites, or stings.

Job Specialization: Welders, Cutters, and Welder Fitters

Use hand-welding or flame-cutting equipment to weld or join metal components or to fill holes, indentations, or seams of fabricated metal products. Operate safety equipment, and use safe work habits. Weld components in flat, vertical, or overhead positions. Ignite torches or start power supplies and strike arcs by touching electrodes to metals being welded, completing electrical circuits. Clamp, hold, tack-weld, heat-bend, grind, or bolt component parts to obtain required configurations and positions for welding. Detect faulty operation of equipment or defective materials, and notify supervisors. Operate manual or semi-automatic welding equipment to fuse

metal segments, using processes such as gas tungsten arc, gas metal arc, flux-cored arc, plasma arc, shielded metal arc, resistance welding, and submerged arc welding. Monitor the fitting, burning, and welding processes to avoid overheating of parts or warping, shrinking, distortion, or expansion of material. Examine workpieces for defects, and measure workpieces with straightedges or templates to ensure conformance with specifications. Recognize, set up, and operate hand and power tools common to the welding trade, such as shielded metal arc and gas metal arc welding equipment. Lay out, position, align, and secure parts and assemblies prior to assembly, using straightedges, combination squares, calipers, and rulers. Chip or grind off excess weld, slag, or spatter, using hand scrapers or power chippers, portable grinders, or arc-cutting equipment. Analyze engineering drawings, blueprints, specifications, sketches, work orders, and material safety data sheets to plan layout, assembly, and welding operations. Connect and turn regulator valves to activate and adjust gas flow and pressure so that desired flames are obtained. Weld separately or in combination, using aluminum, stainless steel, cast iron, and other alloys. Mark or tag materials with proper job numbers, piece marks, and other identifying marks as required. Determine required equipment and welding methods, applying knowledge of metallurgy, geometry, and welding techniques.

Education and Training Program: Welding Technology/Welder. **Knowledge/Courses—Building and Construction:** Materials, methods, and the tools involved in the construction or repair of houses, buildings, or other structures such as highways and roads. **Mechanical Devices:** Machines and tools, including their designs, uses, repair, and maintenance. **Design:** Design techniques, tools, and principles involved in production of precision technical plans, blueprints, drawings, and models. **Engineering and Technology:** The practical application of engineering science and technology. This includes applying principles, techniques, procedures, and equipment to the design and production of various goods and services.

Personality Type: Realistic-Conventional. **Career Cluster:** 13 Manufacturing. **Career Pathway:** 13.1 Production. **Other Jobs in This Pathway:** Adhesive Bonding Machine Operators and Tenders; Assemblers and Fabricators, All Other; Avionics Technicians; Cabinetmakers and Bench Carpenters; Cleaning, Washing, and Metal Pickling Equipment Operators and Tenders; Coating, Painting, and

M

Spraying Machine Setters, Operators, and Tenders; Computer-Controlled Machine Tool Operators, Metal and Plastic; Cooling and Freezing Equipment Operators and Tenders; Cost Estimators; Crushing, Grinding, and Polishing Machine Setters, Operators, and Tenders; Cutters and Trimmers, Hand; Cutting and Slicing Machine Setters, Operators, and Tenders; Cutting, Punching, and Press Machine Setters, Operators, and Tenders, Metal and Plastic; Drilling and Boring Machine Tool Setters, Operators, and Tenders, Metal and Plastic; Extruding and Drawing Machine Setters, Operators, and Tenders, Metal and Plastic; Extruding and Forming Machine Setters, Operators, and Tenders, Synthetic and Glass Fibers; others.

Skills—Repairing: Repairing machines or systems using the needed tools. **Operation and Control:** Controlling operations of equipment or systems. **Troubleshooting:** Determining causes of operating errors and deciding what to do about them. **Equipment Maintenance:** Performing routine maintenance on equipment and determining when and what kind of maintenance is needed. **Equipment Selection:** Determining the kind of tools and equipment needed to do a job. **Operation Monitoring:** Watching gauges, dials, or other indicators to make sure a machine is working properly. **Quality Control Analysis:** Conducting tests and inspections of products, services, or processes to evaluate quality or performance. **Installation:** Installing equipment, machines, wiring, or programs to meet specifications.

Work Environment: Standing; using hands; bending or twisting the body; repetitive motions; noise; very hot or cold; bright or inadequate lighting; contaminants; hazardous equipment; minor burns, cuts, bites, or stings.

Welding, Soldering, and Brazing Machine Setters, Operators, and Tenders

- ⊙ Annual Earnings: $34,770
- ⊙ Earnings Growth Potential: Low (33.9%)
- ⊙ Growth: 6.5%
- ⊙ Annual Job Openings: 1,380
- ⊙ Self-Employed: 5.8%

Considerations for Job Outlook: Despite slower-than-average employment growth, a number of these jobs are expected to become available for highly skilled workers because of an expected increase in retirements, primarily of baby boomers, in the coming years. In addition, workers who have a thorough background in machine operations, certifications from industry associations, and a good working knowledge of the properties of metals and plastics should have the best job opportunities.

Set up, operate, or tend welding, soldering, or brazing machines or robots that weld, braze, solder, or heat-treat metal products, components, or assemblies. Turn and press knobs and buttons, or enter operating instructions into computers to adjust and start welding machines. Set up, operate, and tend welding machines that join or bond components to fabricate metal products or assemblies. Load or feed workpieces into welding machines in order to join or bond components. Give directions to other workers regarding machine setup and use. Correct problems by adjusting controls, or by stopping machines and opening holding devices. Inspect, measure, or test completed metal workpieces to ensure conformance to specifications, using measuring and testing devices. Record operational information on specified production reports. Start, monitor, and adjust robotic welding production lines. Read blueprints, work orders, and production schedules to determine product or job instructions and specifications. Assemble, align, and clamp workpieces into holding fixtures to bond, heat-treat, or solder fabricated metal components. Lay out, fit, or connect parts to be bonded, calculating production measurements as necessary. Conduct trial runs before welding, soldering, or brazing; make necessary adjustments to equipment. Dress electrodes, using tip dressers, files, emery cloths, or dressing wheels. Remove workpieces and parts from machinery after work is complete, using hand tools. Observe meters, gauges, and machine operations to ensure that soldering or brazing processes meet specifications. Select, position, align, and bolt jigs, holding fixtures, guides, and stops onto machines, using measuring instruments and hand tools. Compute and record settings for new work, applying knowledge of metal properties, principles of welding, and shop mathematics. Select torch tips, alloys, flux, coil, tubing, and wire, according to metal types and thicknesses, data charts, and records. Clean, lubricate, maintain, and adjust equipment to maintain efficient operation, using air hoses, cleaning fluids, and hand tools.

Education/Training Required: High school diploma or equivalent. **Education and Training Program:** Welding

Technology/Welder. **Knowledge/Courses—Production and Processing:** Raw materials, production processes, quality control, costs, and other techniques for maximizing the effective manufacture and distribution of goods. **Mechanical Devices:** Machines and tools, including their designs, uses, repair, and maintenance. **Engineering and Technology:** The practical application of engineering science and technology. This includes applying principles, techniques, procedures, and equipment to the design and production of various goods and services. **Public Safety and Security:** Relevant equipment, policies, procedures, and strategies to promote effective local, state, or national security operations for the protection of people, data, property, and institutions. **Design:** Design techniques, tools, and principles involved in production of precision technical plans, blueprints, drawings, and models. **Personnel and Human Resources:** Principles and procedures for personnel recruitment, selection, training, compensation and benefits, labor relations and negotiation, and personnel information systems. **Work Experience Needed:** None. **On-the-Job Training Needed:** Moderate-term on-the-job training. **Certification/Licensure:** Voluntary certification for some specializations.

Personality Type: Realistic-Conventional. **Career Cluster:** 13 Manufacturing. **Career Pathway:** 13.1 Production. **Other Jobs in This Pathway:** Adhesive Bonding Machine Operators and Tenders; Assemblers and Fabricators, All Other; Avionics Technicians; Cabinetmakers and Bench Carpenters; Cleaning, Washing, and Metal Pickling Equipment Operators and Tenders; Coating, Painting, and Spraying Machine Setters, Operators, and Tenders; Computer-Controlled Machine Tool Operators, Metal and Plastic; Cooling and Freezing Equipment Operators and Tenders; Cost Estimators; Crushing, Grinding, and Polishing Machine Setters, Operators, and Tenders; Cutters and Trimmers, Hand; Cutting and Slicing Machine Setters, Operators, and Tenders; Cutting, Punching, and Press Machine Setters, Operators, and Tenders, Metal and Plastic; Drilling and Boring Machine Tool Setters, Operators, and Tenders, Metal and Plastic; Extruding and Drawing Machine Setters, Operators, and Tenders, Metal and Plastic; Extruding and Forming Machine Setters, Operators, and Tenders, Synthetic and Glass Fibers; others.

Skills—Operation and Control: Controlling operations of equipment or systems. **Equipment Maintenance:** Performing routine maintenance on equipment

and determining when and what kind of maintenance is needed. **Operation Monitoring:** Watching gauges, dials, or other indicators to make sure a machine is working properly. **Repairing:** Repairing machines or systems using the needed tools. **Equipment Selection:** Determining the kind of tools and equipment needed to do a job. **Troubleshooting:** Determining causes of operating errors and deciding what to do about them. **Installation:** Installing equipment, machines, wiring, or programs to meet specifications. **Quality Control Analysis:** Conducting tests and inspections of products, services, or processes to evaluate quality or performance.

Work Environment: Standing; using hands; bending or twisting the body; repetitive motions; noise; very hot or cold; contaminants; hazardous equipment; minor burns, cuts, bites, or stings.

Wholesale and Retail Buyers, Except Farm Products

- ⊙ Annual Earnings: $50,490
- ⊙ Earnings Growth Potential: High (41.4%)
- ⊙ Growth: 9.0%
- ⊙ Annual Job Openings: 4,170
- ⊙ Self-Employed: 11.8%

Considerations for Job Outlook: Growth will be driven largely by the performance of the wholesale and retail industries. Continued employment decreases in manufacturing, as well as decreases in federal government, which includes defense purchasing, are expected. However, growth is expected for this occupation in firms that provide health-care and computer systems design and related services.

Buy merchandise or commodities, other than farm products, for resale to consumers at the wholesale or retail level, including both durable and nondurable goods. Use computers to organize and locate inventory, and operate spreadsheet and word processing software. Negotiate prices, discount terms, and transportation arrangements for merchandise. Manage the department for which they buy. Confer with sales and purchasing personnel to obtain information about customer needs and preferences. Examine, select, order, and purchase at the most favorable price merchandise consistent with quality, quantity,

M

specification requirements, and other factors. Analyze and monitor sales records, trends, and economic conditions to anticipate consumer buying patterns and determine what the company will sell and how much inventory is needed. Set or recommend mark-up rates, mark-down rates, and selling prices for merchandise. Authorize payment of invoices or return of merchandise. Interview and work closely with vendors to obtain and develop desired products. Conduct staff meetings with sales personnel to introduce new merchandise. Inspect merchandise or products to determine value or yield. Monitor competitors' sales activities by following their advertisements in newspapers and other media. Train and supervise sales and clerical staff. Consult with store or merchandise managers about budget and goods to be purchased. Provide clerks with information to print on price tags, such as price, mark-ups or mark-downs, manufacturer number, season code, and style number. Determine which products should be featured in advertising, the advertising medium to be used, and when the ads should be run.

Education/Training Required: High school diploma or equivalent. **Education and Training Programs:** Apparel and Accessories Marketing Operations; Apparel and Textile Marketing Management; Fashion Merchandising; Insurance; Merchandising and Buying Operations; Sales, Distribution, and Marketing Operations, General. **Knowledge/Courses—Production and Processing:** Raw materials, production processes, quality control, costs, and other techniques for maximizing the effective manufacture and distribution of goods. **Sales and Marketing:** Principles and methods for showing, promoting, and selling products or services. This includes marketing strategy and tactics, product demonstration, sales techniques, and sales control systems. **Economics and Accounting:** Economic and accounting principles and practices, the financial markets, banking, and the analysis and reporting of financial data. **Administration and Management:** Business and management principles involved in strategic planning, resource allocation, human resources modeling, leadership technique, production methods, and coordination of people and resources. **Building and Construction:** Materials, methods, and the tools involved in the construction or repair of houses, buildings, or other structures such as highways and roads. **Customer and Personal Service:** Principles and processes for providing customer and personal services. This includes customer needs assessment, meeting quality standards for services, and evaluation of

customer satisfaction. **Work Experience Needed:** None. **On-the-Job Training Needed:** Long-term on-the-job training. **Certification/Licensure:** Licensure for some specializations.

Personality Type: Enterprising-Conventional. **Career Cluster:** 14 Marketing, Sales, and Service. **Career Pathways:** 14.3 Buying and Merchandising; 14.2 Professional Sales and Marketing. **Other Jobs in These Pathways:** Appraisers, Real Estate; Assessors; Cashiers; Counter and Rental Clerks; Demonstrators and Product Promoters; Door-To-Door Sales Workers, News and Street Vendors, and Related Workers; Driver/Sales Workers; Energy Brokers; First-Line Supervisors of Non-Retail Sales Workers; First-Line Supervisors of Retail Sales Workers; Gaming Change Persons and Booth Cashiers; Hotel, Motel, and Resort Desk Clerks; Interior Designers; Lodging Managers; Marketing Managers; Marking Clerks; Meeting, Convention, and Event Planners; Merchandise Displayers and Window Trimmers; Models; Online Merchants; Order Fillers, Wholesale and Retail Sales; Parts Salespersons; Property, Real Estate, and Community Association Managers; Purchasing Agents, Except Wholesale, Retail, and Farm Products; Real Estate Brokers; Real Estate Sales Agents; Reservation and Transportation Ticket Agents and Travel Clerks; Retail Salespersons; Sales and Related Workers, All Other; Sales Engineers; others.

Skills—Management of Financial Resources: Determining how money will be spent to get the work done and accounting for these expenditures. **Management of Material Resources:** Obtaining and seeing to the appropriate use of equipment, facilities, and materials needed to do certain work. **Negotiation:** Bringing others together and trying to reconcile differences. **Persuasion:** Persuading others to change their minds or behavior. **Systems Evaluation:** Identifying measures or indicators of system performance and the actions needed to improve or correct performance relative to the goals of the system. **Mathematics:** Using mathematics to solve problems. **Operations Analysis:** Analyzing needs and product requirements to create a design. **Monitoring:** Monitoring or assessing your performance or that of other individuals or organizations to make improvements or take corrective action.

Work Environment: Indoors; sitting.

Woodworking Machine Setters, Operators, and Tenders, Except Sawing

- Annual Earnings: $27,090
- Earnings Growth Potential: Low (32.2%)
- Growth: 20.1%
- Annual Job Openings: 1,740
- Self-Employed: 0.4%

Considerations for Job Outlook: Those with advanced skills, including advanced math and the ability to read blueprints, should have the best job opportunities in manufacturing industries. Woodworkers who know how to create and carry out custom designs on a computer will likely be in strong demand. Some job openings will result from the need to replace those who retire or leave the occupation for other reasons. However, employment in all woodworking specialties is highly sensitive to economic cycles. During economic downturns, workers are subject to layoffs or reductions in hours.

Set up, operate, or tend woodworking machines, such as drill presses, lathes, shapers, routers, sanders, planers, and wood-nailing machines. Start machines, adjust controls, and make trial cuts to ensure that machinery is operating properly. Determine product specifications and materials, work methods, and machine setup requirements, according to blueprints, oral or written instructions, drawings, or work orders. Feed stock through feed mechanisms or conveyors into planing, shaping, boring, mortising, or sanding machines to produce desired components. Adjust machine tables or cutting devices and set controls on machines to produce specified cuts or operations. Set up, program, operate, or tend computerized or manual woodworking machines, such as drill presses, lathes, shapers, routers, sanders, planers, and wood-nailing machines. Monitor operation of machines, and make adjustments to correct problems and ensure conformance to specifications. Select knives, saws, blades, cutter heads, cams, bits, or belts, according to workpiece, machine functions, and product specifications. Examine finished workpieces for smoothness, shape, angle, depth-of-cut, and conformity to specifications, and verify dimensions, visually and using hands, rules, calipers, templates, or gauges. Install and adjust blades, cutterheads, boring-bits, or sanding-belts, using hand tools and rules. Inspect and mark completed workpieces and stack them on pallets, in boxes, or on conveyors so that they can be moved to the next work station. Push or hold workpieces against, under, or through cutting, boring, or shaping mechanisms. Change alignment and adjustment of sanding, cutting, or boring machine guides to prevent defects in finished products, using hand tools. Inspect pulleys, drive belts, guards, and fences on machines to ensure that machines will operate safely. Remove and replace worn parts, bits, belts, sandpaper, and shaping tools. Secure woodstock against guides or in holding devices, place woodstock on conveyors, or dump woodstock in hoppers to feed woodstock into machines.

Education/Training Required: High school diploma or equivalent. **Education and Training Programs:** Cabinetmaking and Millwork; Woodworking, General. **Knowledge/Courses—Production and Processing:** Raw materials, production processes, quality control, costs, and other techniques for maximizing the effective manufacture and distribution of goods. **Mechanical Devices:** Machines and tools, including their designs, uses, repair, and maintenance. **Design:** Design techniques, tools, and principles involved in production of precision technical plans, blueprints, drawings, and models. **Mathematics:** Arithmetic, algebra, geometry, calculus, statistics, and their applications. **Work Experience Needed:** None. **On-the-Job Training Needed:** Short-term on-the-job training. **Certification/Licensure:** None.

Personality Type: Realistic-Conventional-Investigative. **Career Cluster:** 13 Manufacturing. **Career Pathway:** 13.1 Production. **Other Jobs in This Pathway:** Adhesive Bonding Machine Operators and Tenders; Assemblers and Fabricators, All Other; Avionics Technicians; Cabinetmakers and Bench Carpenters; Cleaning, Washing, and Metal Pickling Equipment Operators and Tenders; Coating, Painting, and Spraying Machine Setters, Operators, and Tenders; Computer-Controlled Machine Tool Operators, Metal and Plastic; Cooling and Freezing Equipment Operators and Tenders; Cost Estimators; Crushing, Grinding, and Polishing Machine Setters, Operators, and Tenders; Cutters and Trimmers, Hand; Cutting and Slicing Machine Setters, Operators, and Tenders; Cutting, Punching, and Press Machine Setters, Operators, and Tenders, Metal and Plastic; Drilling and Boring Machine Tool Setters, Operators, and Tenders, Metal and Plastic; Extruding and Drawing Machine Setters, Operators,

M

and Tenders, Metal and Plastic; Extruding and Forming Machine Setters, Operators, and Tenders, Synthetic and Glass Fibers; others.

Skills—Equipment Maintenance: Performing routine maintenance on equipment and determining when and what kind of maintenance is needed. **Repairing:** Repairing machines or systems using the needed tools. **Equipment Selection:** Determining the kind of tools and equipment needed to do a job. **Operation and Control:** Controlling operations of equipment or systems. **Operation Monitoring:** Watching gauges, dials, or other indicators to make sure a machine is working properly. **Troubleshooting:** Determining causes of operating errors and deciding what to do about them. **Installation:** Installing equipment, machines, wiring, or programs to meet specifications. **Programming:** Writing computer programs for various purposes.

Work Environment: Standing; using hands; bending or twisting the body; repetitive motions; noise; contaminants; hazardous equipment; minor burns, cuts, bites, or stings.

Index

D

E

F

G

H

I

J

O

P

S

U

V

W

Y

Notes

Notes

Notes